Contemporary Employment Law

ASPEN PUBLISHERS

C. Kerry Fields
Professor of Clinical Finance and Business Economics
Marshall School of Business
University of Southern California

Henry R. Cheeseman
Professor of Clinical Finance and Business Economics
Marshall School of Business
University of Southern California

Law & Business

AUSTIN BOSTON CHICAGO NEW YORK THE NETHERLANDS

Aspen Publishers
Attn: Permissions Department
76 Ninth Avenue, 7th Floor
New York, NY 10011-5201

To contact Customer Care, e-mail customer.service@aspenpublishers.com, call 1-800-234-1660, fax 1-800-901-9075, or mail correspondence to:

Aspen Publishers
Attn: Order Department
PO Box 990
Frederick, MD 21705

Printed in the United States of America.

1 2 3 4 5 6 7 8 9 0

ISBN 978-0-7355-9644-3

Library of Congress Cataloging-in-Publication Data

Fields, C. Kerry.
Contemporary employment law / C. Kerry Fields, Henry R. Cheeseman.
p. cm.
Includes bibliographical references and index.
ISBN 978-0-7355-9644-3
1. Labor laws and legislation — United States — Textbooks. 2. Discrimination in employment — Law and legislation — United States — Textbooks. 3. Employee rights — United States — Textbooks. I. Cheeseman, Henry R. II. Title.

KF3319.85.F54 2010
344.7301 — dc22 2010020789

About Wolters Kluwer Law & Business

Wolters Kluwer Law & Business is a leading provider of research information and workflow solutions in key specialty areas. The strengths of the individual brands of Aspen Publishers, CCH, Kluwer Law International and Loislaw are aligned within Wolters Kluwer Law & Business to provide comprehensive, in-depth solutions and expert-authored content for the legal, professional and education markets.

CCH was founded in 1913 and has served more than four generations of business professionals and their clients. The CCH products in the Wolters Kluwer Law & Business group are highly regarded electronic and print resources for legal, securities, antitrust and trade regulation, government contracting, banking, pension, payroll, employment and labor, and healthcare reimbursement and compliance professionals.

Aspen Publishers is a leading information provider for attorneys, business professionals and law students. Written by preeminent authorities, Aspen products offer analytical and practical information in a range of specialty practice areas from securities law and intellectual property to mergers and acquisitions and pension/benefits. Aspen's trusted legal education resources provide professors and students with high-quality, up-to-date and effective resources for successful instruction and study in all areas of the law.

Kluwer Law International supplies the global business community with comprehensive English-language international legal information. Legal practitioners, corporate counsel and business executives around the world rely on the Kluwer Law International journals, loose-leafs, books and electronic products for authoritative information in many areas of international legal practice.

Loislaw is a premier provider of digitized legal content to small law firm practitioners of various specializations. Loislaw provides attorneys with the ability to quickly and efficiently find the necessary legal information they need, when and where they need it, by facilitating access to primary law as well as state-specific law, records, forms and treatises.

Wolters Kluwer Law & Business, a unit of Wolters Kluwer, is headquartered in New York and Riverwoods, Illinois. Wolters Kluwer is a leading multinational publisher and information services company.

Summary of Contents

Contents

Chapter 2: Recruitment, Selection, Testing, and Termination 37

Chapter 3: Contract and Tort Liability of Employers 79

Part II: Equal Opportunity Laws

Chapter 5: Equal Employment and Affirmative Action 175

Chapter 6: Race, Color, and National Origin Discrimination 211

Chapter 7: Sex Discrimination, Sexual Harassment, and Sexual Orientation Protection 243

Chapter 8: Religious Discrimination 287

Chapter 9: Rights of the Disabled in the Workplace 317

Chapter 10: Age Discrimination 351

Chapter 11: Work-Family Issues and Other EEO Protections 391

Part III: Employee Protections and Benefits

Chapter 12: Privacy in the Workplace 431

Chapter 13: Federal Labor Law 471

Chapter 14: Wage and Hour Laws 519

Chapter 16: Retirement and Employee Benefits 605

Part IV: The Global Employment Environment

Chapter 17: Immigration and Nationality 645

Chapter 18: Employment Law for the Global Employer 685

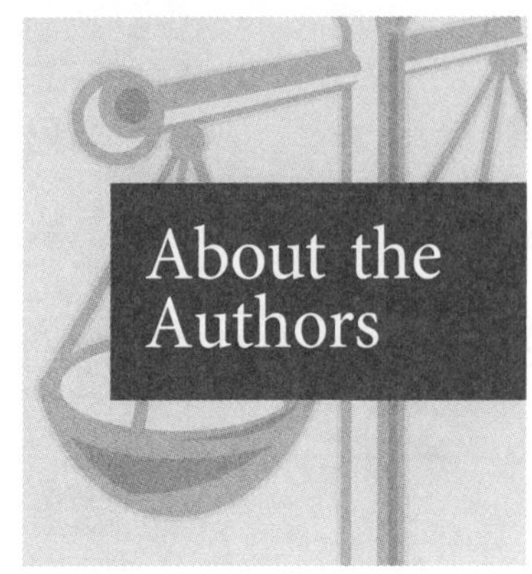

About the Authors

C. Kerry Fields

C. Kerry Fields is a professor at the University of Southern California Marshall School of Business, where he teaches courses in employment law and in business law. He is also a practicing attorney who has represented employers in administrative forums and federal and state courts with respect to employment and discrimination claims and has tried many cases to verdict in the state and federal courts. When he is not teaching, he spends his law practice time assisting business managers in identifying and solving business problems. He has received a number of teaching awards and is a frequent media commentator on issues in employment law and business ethics. Professor Fields received his bachelor's degree in business administration from the University of Southern California and his Juris Doctor from Santa Clara University School of Law.

Henry R. Cheeseman

Henry R. Cheeseman is a professor at the University of Southern California Marshall School of Business, where he teaches graduate courses on business law subjects, including employment law. He has practiced law and also taught business organizations and banking law courses at the Gould School of Law at the University of Southern California. Professor Cheeseman received a bachelor of science from Marquette University, a Juris Doctor from the UCLA School of Law, a Masters in Business Taxation from the University of Southern California, a Masters of Business Administration from the University of Chicago, and an LL.M. degree from Boston University. He has written more than 30 business law textbooks and has won numerous teaching awards at the University of Southern California.

Features of This Text

Comprehensive coverage of employment and labor compliance issues for businesses. Starting with an overview of the sources of employment law, including distinguishing workers from independent contractors, the text proceeds to review recruitment, selection, and testing guidelines, cases, and applicable laws. Employment contracts and common employment law torts are reviewed. Students will learn the procedures workers must follow to pursue discrimination and harassment claims. A global survey of applicable civil rights laws and regulations, including topics of recent interest, such as the 2010 Health Care Act, as amended, the Lilly Ledbetter Fair Pay Act of 2009, GINA, and the USERRA follow. Workplace privacy, federal labor law, wage and hour issues, health and safety, and retirement benefit issues are all presented. Two topics of special interest are immigration and employment law for the global employer.

Briefed cases in the language of the court appear in each chapter. Each case is followed by questions for student discussion, covering critical thinking, ethical issues, and contemporary applications.

Case-based examples are introduced throughout each chapter. Legal citations appear in notes at the ends of chapters to improve readability.

Workplace application features in each chapter challenge the business student to use the legal principles of that chapter to solve common business issues.

Ethical problems throughout the text focus on the practical but principled application of the law.

Concept summaries appear frequently in each chapter to review and reinforce student learning.

Key terms and concepts are listed at the end of each chapter.

Chapter summaries provide students with compact overviews of the chapters' main points.

End-of-chapter cases provide opportunity for additional review and assignments.

Human resource forms in each chapter extend student learning and improve comprehension. These forms, most of which were developed by the authors, provide real-world examples of applications of chapter concepts in the workplace and can form the basis of a toolkit of practical resources for business managers.

Full texts of relevant statutes are provided in the online resource.

Online Student Support Features

The companion website for *Contemporary Employment Law* by C. Kerry Fields and Henry R. Cheeseman at http://www.aspenlegalcollege.com/fields_employment includes additional resources for students, including the following:

- Additional practice questions, including sample true/false, multiple-choice, and short-answer questions to test student understanding of concepts.
- A Critical Legal Thinking Assignment for each chapter, in business memorandum form, to promote student writing and legal analysis skills. Each assignment is based on an actual court case.
- Additional human resource forms.
- Internet exercises in which students review pertinent websites and apply the information gained to issues presented.
- Blogs useful to students developing materials for their class presentations.
- Supplementary statutory and regulatory materials necessary to enable students to read and apply the legal authority required to solve the practical business problems presented in the Loislaw research, writing, and class presentations.
- Study aids to help students master the key concepts for this course. Visit the site to access interactive StudyMate exercises such as flash cards, matching, fill-in-the-blank, and crosswords. These activities are also available for download to an iPod or other hand-held device.

The text comes packaged with 4 months of prepaid access to Loislaw's online legal research database, available at http://www.loislawschool.com. Loislaw provides access to online research including up-to-date cases, statutes, rules, and regulations, and primary law for all 50 states and federal jurisdictions. The website to accompany this text includes Loislaw legal research and writing assignments, as well as Loislaw small-group projects and class presentations.

Blackboard and eCollege course materials are available to supplement this text. This online courseware is designed to streamline the teaching of the course, providing valuable resources from the book in an accessible electronic format.

Instructor's Manual

The Instructor's Manual provides lecture outlines, case synopses for each excerpted case, and references to Aspen Publishers' Casenote Series on Employment Law as well as answers to the case questions following each briefed case and to the end-of-chapter questions.

The Instructor's Manual is cross-referenced to materials available elsewhere for assignment to individual students and small groups. These include the vast Loislaw resources available to each student purchasing the text. Business students will be able to use Loislaw to conduct basic research and to help them identify the significant legal issues that will confront their organizations.

Statutory supplementary materials are presented in the online appendix.

PowerPoint Slides

Each chapter has classroom-ready PowerPoint slides to provide instructors with strong visual aids to highlight the important material in each chapter. All significant chapter material is presented in the slides. All briefed case slides begin with the issue and continue with a summary of the facts and the court's holding. In addition, each briefed case slide concludes with a related ethics issue to prompt further class discussion.

Test Bank

True/false, multiple-choice, fill-in, short-answer, and essay questions are included for each chapter.

Additional Materials

Relevant historical settings for some of the most important topics discussed in the text are presented for instructors' classroom use.

All of these materials are available on a CD-ROM or for download from our companion website.

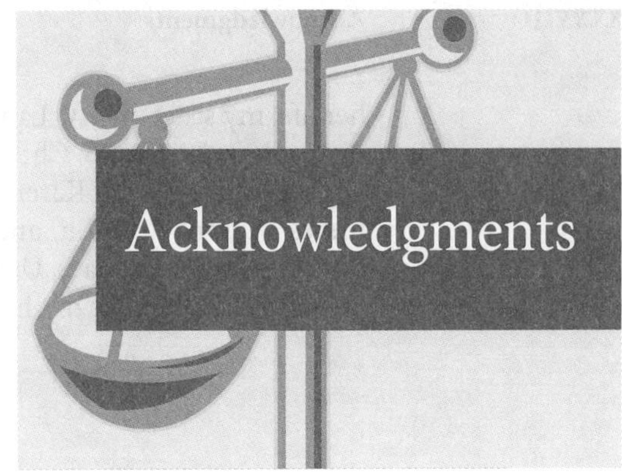

Acknowledgments

The authors thank all of the following persons without whose assistance this project would not have been realized: Carol McGeehan, Publisher; David Herzig, Associate Publisher; Lynn Churchill, Senior Acquisitions Editor; Christie Rears, Editor; all of Aspen Publishers. We also received the wonderful support of others within the Aspen family, including Betsy Kenny and Susan Boulanger.

We would also like to thank the numerous reviewers who contributed much time and direction to making this text a worthy reflection of their efforts: Adele Abrams, Catholic University of America; Kabrina Chang, Boston University; Sandra Defebaugh, Eastern Michigan University; Darlene Gerry, Idaho State University; Sharlene McEvoy, Fairfield University, and Beth Wolfson, Bentley University.

~

I would like to express my gratitude to Henry Cheeseman, my coauthor and fellow professor at the University of Southern California. Henry is an exceptionally gifted author of many business law textbooks that enjoy wide circulation. He has a quick wit, a rich sense of humor, and is a close friend. He exercised incredible patience and guidance as we persevered over the many years spent drafting this text.

I dedicate this book to my wife, Patricia, for her years of understanding, love, and support. I have been blessed with the support of our son and my law partner Kevin, our son and paralegal Brian, and the special love and support of our daughter Megan. I also thank Devon, Leigh, and Kaitlyn for allowing this project to take me away from family events. Thanks also to Marnell and Paul Blason, who helped me start this journey. I want to acknowledge the love and help my deceased parents, Cliff and Peggy Fields, offered to me over the years. Without the assistance of Kristi McBee this project would never have reached a conclusion. To the thousands of Trojans we have taught over the years at the Marshall School of Business at USC, thank you all. To those whom I have not mentioned by name, the error is mine and unintended.

— Kerry Fields

Through the years of one's life, certain people come along that affect you forever. One of those persons for me is my coauthor Kerry Fields. Kerry is my best friend, and I have been fortunate to have been able to work with Kerry in producing this book. We have met almost every Saturday for years to review the book's progress and to make decisions regarding its contents — but also to share time with a best friend.

I would like acknowledge Jin Du for bringing such great change to my life. I thank my twin brother, Gregory Cheeseman, for always being there for me, and Henry B. and Florence L. Cheeseman, my parents, now deceased, to whom I owe my ability and the temperament that allowed me to become a writer. I also thank other members of the Cheeseman family, including my sister Marcia, who regretfully was taken too early in her life; my sister-in-law Lana, who always selflessly devotes her time to helping others; my nephew Gregory S. Cheeseman, without whose help I would not be able to focus on writing, and his wife Karen; and my niece Nicky, her husband Jerry, and my grand-nieces Lauren, Addison, and Shelby. And I pay homage to the small town in which I grew up — Saint Ignace, Upper Michigan — where I learned the values of life. My house is in Los Angeles, but my home will always be in the Upper Peninsula of Michigan.

— **Henry Cheeseman**

Introduction

The workplace reflects the hopes and ideals of American society. When the electorate demands change, dramatic results follow. Progress began at the end of the nineteenth century with the adoption of laws protecting workers from harsh working conditions. It continued throughout the last century with the enactment of the 40-hour workweek and civil rights and worker safety laws. American politicians have readily responded to workers' demands. The last few decades show that this trend continues. Recently, workers' rights to equal opportunity in employment received additional protections from gender disparity in compensation as well as from discrimination based on genetic profiles. These laws have expanded the social safety net and afforded greater protection from workplace discrimination, and they have enhanced the enforcement rights of both government and private parties.

The idealized right of a business owner to exercise unfettered discretion in his or her operations has disappeared. Company management decision-making is now constrained by an expanding universe of federal and state legislation, regulation, and court decisions. Moreover, strong public support continues for employers to undertake more responsibility for the welfare of their workers. One recent example is mandated employer-sponsored health insurance benefits for employees. As a result of all these changes, the employment law landscape continually expands in scope and complexity.

As of 2010, with the United States in the midst of a deep recession, approximately 140 million workers were employed from a total population of approximately 237 million individuals. Another 8.9 million workers were unemployed or otherwise outside the labor force, representing a post–Depression era record national unemployment rate in excess of 10 percent. America's economic stability depends on job creation. That fact poses a serious challenge to our political and business leadership.

At the same time, U.S. companies are implementing global workforce strategies to meet the demands posed by international competition. Managers must recruit, train, and retain the "right" workers with the requisite backgrounds to respond to the challenging circumstances they face.

Managers must continually innovate within difficult business climates. Management teams must cultivate a supportive environment for their employees to assure their businesses remain competitive. Formerly, corporate litigation risks arising from noncompliance with employment laws were measured by the outcomes of single-party lawsuits. Today, the risks are much greater due to the proliferation of class-action lawsuits in which many parties join to seek damages.

These conditions make it clear that the study of employment law is important to the education of tomorrow's business leaders. Your course presents an interesting opportunity for you to learn about the legal environment of the workplace. Serving that purpose is the reason for this text, and we hope that you will enjoy the product of our labors.

Part I
The Employment Relationship

Chapter 1 Employment Law Overview

"If you have to support yourself, you had bloody well find some way that is going to be interesting." —Katharine Hepburn, actor and four-time Oscar winner

Learning Objectives

1. Recognize how governmental agencies and jurisdictions apply different tests to characterize the worker relationship.
2. State the factors suggesting that a worker is an employee.
3. Distinguish between an employee and an independent contractor.
4. Describe the advantages of using an independent contractor.
5. State the risks of misclassifying the status of workers.

Chapter Outline

- Introduction
- Sources of Employment Law
- Federal, State, and Local Laws and Ordinances
- Defining the Worker
- The Employment Relationship
- Employee Status Under Common Law
- Federal Law "Economic Realities" Test
- Employee Status Under Federal Labor Law
- Proposed Restatement Definition

Case 1.1 Lemmerman v. A.T. Williams Oil Co.

- The Worker as Independent Contractor
- Workplace Application: Independent Contractor Status

Case 1.2 CBS Corp. v. FCC

- The Worker as Leased Employee
- Outsourcing
- Section 530 Safe Harbor
- Human Resource Form: Independent Contractor Agreement

Chapter Opening scenario

Martin Farms was a grower in upstate New York. It retained migrant workers to help in its harvesting operations through Ramey Farms, a Texas-based labor contractor. Ramey recruited and supplied 42 farm workers from Arizona, who traveled to New York State to harvest cabbage and squash for Martin Farms. The workers did not receive written contracts. Representatives of Ramey Farms orally promised them \$6.00 per hour, ten hours or more of work per day, free housing, and transportation to and from New York. While Martin Farms exercised very little day-to-day control over Ramey's recruitment and management of the migrant workers, it did dictate when the recruitment would occur. Ramey arranged for most of the recruiting logistics and managed the workers once they arrived in New York. Martin Farms exercised power by giving Ramey instructions, and it expected that its instructions would be followed. Martin Farms instructed Ramey not to use a particular work crew the following year and dictated the maximum amount of hourly wage the workers were to be paid. Ramey controlled the workers' payroll, and Martin Farms paid Ramey a per-employee/per-hour fee to cover all of the workers' costs. The migrant farm workers sued Martin Farms because they claimed that while working in New York, Martin Farms provided substandard housing, did not pay all the wages due, and did not provide them with transportation back to Arizona when the work was completed. In considering the migrant workers' claims, the court had to determine whether Ramey Farms acted as both an independent contractor to Martin Farms and as an authorized agent of Martin Farms, subjecting Martin Farms to legal liability to the workers. What reasonable conclusion should the court reach?[1]

Introduction

Employers attempt to structure and apply their employment practices to comply with the nation's laws relating to the employment of workers. The law's broad scope reaches every aspect of the employer–worker relationship. Often, employers find it difficult to recognize when and how to apply a particular law or regulation to their business. Their compliance obligations are made more complex because of overlapping statutes, regulations, and ordinances. Tens of thousands of court decisions, regulatory agency interpretations of laws, public policies, as well as evolving societal standards continually challenge managers, compelling them to stay informed about employment and discrimination law. The failure to understand and properly apply the law can expose the employer to great financial risk. While a private employer may classify and treat its workers in one manner, governmental regulation and enforcement can require a contrary result. Legislatures, courts, and administrative agencies have long been involved in that relationship. Rooted in contract and agency law, employment law is the subject of considerable government regulation. Concerned over what rules should regulate businesses and their employees, government has aggressively intervened in the business–worker relationship.

In this chapter, we will study the sources of both the laws that govern the worker relationship of the laws that define differences among worker classifications. We will focus on the factors utilized by courts and administrative agencies to extend employment status protections to workers. By properly planning and administering the worker relationship, managers can avoid exposure to legal liabilities and can aid in protecting both worker and employer rights.

Sources of Employment Law

The Civil and Public Branches of the Law

Initially, the study of employment and labor law can appear daunting; however, classifying their parts makes them understandable. The employment relationship is governed by a complex set of **laws, rules**, and **regulations**. Collectively referred to as the **"law,"** these mandates govern the social and economic order among individuals and their relationship to society. What constitutes the **law** is selected by society to regulate personal and business conduct. The **law** acts as a common bond and promoter of civil behavior among societal members. There are two major categories of **law**; namely, **civil law**, which involves private disputes, and **public law**, which governs a person's personal rights and obligations in relation to government. Our studies of contract law (including its application to covenants not to compete and nondisclosure of trade secrets) and tort law (which addresses wrongful conduct within the employment relationship) involves the **civil law** branch. Other features of **civil law** include property law, inheritance, family law, and the law relating to business entities. The **public law** branch of our law tree includes criminal law, relating to offenses against society; constitutional law, relating to individuals' rights and relationships to their local, state, and federal governments; administrative law, which focuses on the powers of executive branch administrative agencies; and international law, which involves the legal relationships among nations. Employment and labor law involves many of these topics, and we shall address them in our course of this study.

Law
Mandates that govern the social and economic order among individuals and the individual's relationship to society.

This study will draw on many documents from the federal, state, and local government levels. These include federal and state **constitutions, statutes**, and **executive orders**; local **ordinances**; the **rules, regulations**, and **orders** of administrative agencies; and published decisions of federal and state courts. The **"law"** refers to statutory enactments by Congress and state legislatures as laws as well as those issued by counties and municipalities as **ordinances**.

Ordinance
A law enacted by a local jurisdiction such as a county, borough, or municipality.

The sources governing the work relationship include the following:

- **Constitutions.** Both federal and state governments operate through a legal system by which rights are granted to the government by the people to be governed. The people establish the rights and duties of the government and of the people and the relationships between government and governed.

- *Examples:* The United States Constitution, as amended and state constitutions.

- **Federal, state, and municipal statutes and ordinances.** Legislative branches issue written commands to promote or prohibit conduct.
  - *Examples:* **Title VII** of the **Civil Rights Act**; Occupational Safety and Health Act; N.Y. Civil Rights Law; and Austin, Texas, Code of Ordinances, Vols. I–IV.
- **Administrative rules and regulations.** Created by each branch of government under a grant of authority to provide services, administrative agencies issue directives and decisions in certain areas of interest.
  - *Examples:* Equal Employment Opportunity Commission, Department of Labor, Internal Revenue Service, and state workers' compensation agencies.
- **Judicial decisions.** Judicial decisions interpret the acts of the executive and legislative branches and litigants.
  - *Examples:* Published court decisions that have been made determining whether laws were constitutional, resolving a claim for wrongful termination of employment, or enjoining a party from disclosing trade secrets to a competitor.

Executive Order
Directives by the chief executive to executive branch departments to promote, prohibit, or inhibit conduct relating to the executive's policy decisions.

- **Executive orders.** Executive orders, issued by the president or a governor to executive branch agencies, promote or prohibit policy decisions.
- **Contractual agreements.** Contractual agreements exist between the employer and the employee.
  - *Examples:* Employment agreements, employment manuals, and practices, and collective bargaining agreements.

The Law Defines Rights and Duties

These sources of **law** recognize a **legal right** and **duty** as two fundamental aspects of the **law**. Each must coexist with the other. A **legal right** is the ability to have an individual interest respected by others and enforced through court process. A **legal right** is recognized in many settings. It can arise from a two party contract, or it might be a freedom recognized and enforced by the government or a private party. A **legal duty** is imposed on an individual either by contract or by applicable law as a requirement not to interfere with the legal interests of another. It is the standard of care that society expects every person to exercise with regard to others. Sometimes duties are imposed by statutes or local ordinances and at other times by judicial decisions.

Substantive and Procedural Law

Recognition of **legal rights** and **duties** occurs in the context of **substantive** and **procedural laws**. The **substantive law** establishes by statute and case precedents the principles and definitions of rights and legal relationships. We will spend most of our study of employment and labor law (i.e., the law governing management and a unionized workforce) reviewing their **substantive law** aspects. The **procedural law** addresses the means and methods of the legal process, by which private dispute resolution forums, administrative agencies, and courts handle the resolution of disputes over **substantive** legal rights.

Checks and Balances

Each branch of government created by the federal or state **constitution** is equal to the other branches. The legislative branch enacts laws that govern the rights and responsibilities of persons in the employment law context. The executive branch is charged with the enforcement of the laws. To assist the executive branch, many **administrative agencies** have been created to administer employment and labor law. Most agencies are within the executive branch of government; they possess the legal authority to affect the rights of private persons through their **rules, regulations**, and **orders.** Examples of such agencies include the U.S. Department of Labor and the Equal Employment Opportunity Commission. They are given their authority by Congress in recognition of the increasing complexity of our society.

Congress, and its state counterparts, may enact an **enabling statute** that creates an agency to which it can delegate the power to issue **rules, regulations**, and interpretative **orders** to put into effect its mandates. Recognized as having special expertise in an area of law, **administrative agency** decisions are afforded considerable weight by the courts in considering agency actions. The **judicial branch** is known as the court system, and its responsibility is to interpret and apply the **laws, rules**, and **regulations** created by the legislative and executive branches of government and to determine private disputes. The consequence of establishing separately instituted forces to exercise governmental power is known as the American system of **checks** and **balances.**

The Role of the Judicial Branch

American law traces its development to the laws of England. With their conquest of England in 1066, the Normans brought to England a King's court system by which the common application of uniform rules was sought. This became known as the **"common law."** Over time, English **common law** put the rights of the people ahead of those of the crown. As needs arose, the English courts developed various remedies to address changing damage claims. Courts of equity, wherein nonmonetary remedies were available if money damages were inadequate, soon joined law courts that gave only monetary remedies. Nonmonetary remedies were used to rescind contracts, issue orders of specific performance of contractual terms and conditions, and enjoin some action of a party. From the **precedent** of early English **common law** court decisions, American courts began to develop a body of law and procedures to adjust the duties and responsibilities of the employer and the employee.

The U.S. court system is a common law system that relies on the **adversary system** for the **adjudication** of matters. In this system, a party to a lawsuit files an appropriate court pleading to commence the proceedings in a proper court. The **trier of fact,** whether a judge or jury, determines the facts. The court applies the law to the dispute for a final determination between the parties to the suit. This process is known as **adjudication**. In contrast to this system, countries that adopt a **civil law** system employ judges who investigate the facts and conduct the presentation of evidence.

As the body of court decisions grew, the **common law** adopted a practice employed by American courts known as ***stare decisis***. Under this doctrine, lower courts, in considering similar cases, must apply the decision of the highest court in a jurisdiction on the subject at issue. Lower trial courts in both federal and state venues are required to follow ***stare decisis*** until the higher court reverses or amends its prior decision. Until then, the decision of the higher court is followed as binding **precedent** by all lower courts in that jurisdiction.

Article III of the U.S. Constitution established the federal court system. The federal courts have the power or **subject-matter jurisdiction** to decide those cases that Congress authorizes them to decide, except for matters relating to the constitutionality of an act of Congress or the executive branch. The federal court system is premised upon two types of **subject-matter jurisdiction**. The first is known as **federal-question jurisdiction**, in which the federal courts have the authority to decide a dispute arising under federal law. Disputes arising under the federal employment laws we will study may be decided by federal courts under federal-question jurisdiction. Other federally controlled disputes are resolved through the actions of a federal **administrative agency**, such as the National Labor Relations Board. Along with federal trial court decisions, the decisions of federal administrative agencies on matters affecting employment and labor law may be appealed to federal courts of appeal.

The second type of subject-matter jurisdiction is **diversity jurisdiction**, in which the amount in controversy exceeds $75,000 and all parties to the litigation are diverse in their citizenship. Generally, this means that the parties to the employment lawsuit are citizens of different U.S. states. Under the Class Action Fairness Act of 2005, a class-action lawsuit may be brought in federal court when there is even minimal diversity, which means that any plaintiff is a citizen of a different state from any defendant. Employment and labor law disputes are often heard in federal courts based on these two types of **subject-matter jurisdiction**.

The primary trial courts of the federal court system are the United States District Courts. There are 94 federal judicial districts throughout the United States and its territories. There is at least one district court in each state, the District of Columbia, and Puerto Rico. Three U.S. territories, the Virgin Islands, Guam, and the Northern Mariana Islands, have district courts that hear federal cases. Decisions of these courts may be appealed to the United States Courts of Appeals. There are thirteen federal courts of appeals. They are geographically defined for areas of the country. All the courts of appeals hear appeals from some administrative agency decisions and rulemaking; however, most of those are heard in the U.S. Court of Appeals for the Federal Circuit in Washington, D.C. The courts of appeals are considered powerful and influential in setting case precedents within the federal court system. The decisions of the federal courts of appeals serve as the final decision in most federal court litigation. Federal courts of appeals' decisions serve as binding precedent for all lower federal courts (i.e., federal district courts and bankruptcy courts) within that circuit. Lower federal courts must follow the binding precedent under the ***stare decisis*** doctrine in deciding future similar cases.

The U.S. Supreme Court accepts a little over one hundred cases each year for review. For most types of cases, there is no right of automatic appeal to the Supreme Court; rather, the Supreme Court selects the cases that it wishes to hear. When a party to a case desires the Supreme Court to hear it, where no appeal is available as a matter of right, the party formally petitions the Supreme Court to grant a writ of certiorari. A minimum of four of the nine justices must agree to grant a writ of certiorari. When a writ is issued, the Supreme Court is certifying to the lower federal court that the Supreme Court will review the case. Only matters of great legal significance or ones involving a split of opinion among the circuit courts of appeals are typically granted a writ. If a writ of *certiorari* is denied by the Supreme Court, the decision of the lower court remains unaffected.

Federal, State, and Local Laws and Ordinances

The Federal Constitution

The founding fathers ensured that the supreme law of the land would be the United States Constitution. Article VI sets forth the **Supremacy Clause**:

> *This Constitution, and the Laws of the United States which shall be made in Pursuance thereof; and all Treaties made, or which shall be made, under the Authority of the United States, shall be the supreme Law of the Land; and the Judges in every State shall be bound thereby, any Thing in the Constitution or Laws of any state to the Contrary notwithstanding.*

Federal law controls a significant portion of the law of employment. State legislatures, **administrative agencies**, and courts may provide for other rights and remedies in this context provided they do not conflict with applicable federal law. In the event of such a conflict, federal law prevails. Under the **Supremacy Clause** of the U.S. Constitution, the offending state law or local ordinance is unconstitutional. In an 1819 decision of the U.S. Supreme Court in *McCulloch v. Maryland*, 17 U.S. 316 (1819), Chief Justice John Marshall wrote, "In every such case, the act of Congress, or the treaty, is supreme; and the law of the State, though enacted in the exercise of powers not controverted, must yield to it."

Whenever Congress enacts laws within its power, the resulting legislation **preempts** or overrides any conflicting state law. Through federalism, the state laws defer to the national policy interests that underlie the federal law. Congressional power to enact legislation is broadly interpreted, and even its intention to preempt a given area of the law will preempt nonconflicting state and local law. When no such congressional action has occurred or been expressed, then nonconflicting state and local law is permissible. For example, Congress can enact a discrimination law that covers 15 or more employees, but a state may enact a similar law protecting other forms of discrimination covering fewer than 15 employees. In such a case, the employer would be required to conform to both the state and federal laws.

In a similar manner, when federal **administrative agencies** issue rules or regulations they have the same **preemptive** effect on those issued by their state or local agency counterparts. Careful human resource managers and employers must recognize the myriad sources of the legal principles governing the operation of their businesses.

Preempt
The legal doctrine by which the laws of a higher authority displace the application of laws issued by a lower jurisdiction when the lower jurisdiction's laws conflict with those of the higher jurisdiction.

The laws and regulations issued under federal and state **laws** and local **ordinances** may apply simultaneously to covered employers. They are to be read together to give the maximum protection to the employee. While they quite often address the same areas of conduct, they are to be reviewed as if they both applied to the same situation.

In the area of civil rights, Congress acknowledges that federal legislation will be read in concert with state and local laws. Thus, federal civil rights statutes, such as the Civil Rights Act of 1964, whose primary employment law section is referred to as Title VII, do not **preempt** state and local discrimination laws. Compliance with one applicable law, therefore, does not discharge the employer's responsibility to comply with the requirements of other applicable laws.

When a state law or local ordinance affords more protection than that offered by federal law, that law or ordinance is not preempted (i.e., displaced) by the federal law.

In such circumstances, the federal, state, and local law will be read together. Many state laws, for example, afford more protection to the worker than federal law allows. Examples of such laws include state wage and hour laws requiring employers to pay more than the federal minimum wage rate and more stringent state safety and health requirements than those required by federal health and safety laws and regulations. The responsibilities of human resource managers, compliance officers, and their legal counsel continue to expand as the **laws, rules**, and **regulations** change each year on the federal, state, and local levels.

The Equal Employment Opportunity Commission (EEOC) provides guidance for employment issues by creating guidelines for employers to follow. Unlike Congressional legislative mandates to the courts or when ***stare decisis*** applies, trial and appellate courts are *not* required to follow the EEOC guidelines. ***Stare decisis*** is a legal principle by which judges are required to follow prior legal precedents established by prior decisions. In all states except Louisiana, which follows a mixed system of common law and civil law, trial and intermediate appellate courts must follow and apply prior precedent that applies in a particular case. Courts, however, have looked to the EEOC for guidance in analyzing facts presented by litigants.

Defining the Worker

For most of the last century, the federal government has been increasingly involved in how an employer defines a worker as either an **employee** or an **independent contractor**. On its website, the Internal Revenue Service (IRS) states:

> It is critical that you, the business owner, correctly determine whether the individuals providing services are employees or independent contractors. Generally, you must withhold income taxes, withhold and pay Social Security and Medicare taxes, and pay unemployment tax on wages paid to an employee. You do not generally have to withhold or pay any taxes on payments to independent contractors. . . . In determining whether the person providing service is an employee or an independent contractor, all information that provides evidence of the degree of control and independence must be considered.[2]

Independent Contractor
A nonemployee worker who exercises independent judgment in the means and methods of performing work for and under contract with a principal.

A universal rule or formula does not exist to determine whether an individual worker is an **employee** or **independent contractor**. Depending on the situation, the term ***employee*** can have many different meanings. An **employee** is defined as a person who acts under a contract in the service of another who has the right to **direct and control** the person in the means and methods of how the services are performed. In contrast, an ***independent contractor*** is defined as a person who exercises independent judgment in the means and methods of performing work for the person with whom the independent contractor has contracted. Generally, the determination of whether a person is an **employee** or an **independent contractor** must be made upon the particular facts in each case. Multiple factor tests exist among federal, state, and local jurisdictions to aid in this determination. The lack of a common rule for defining a worker's status has been a troublesome issue for employers, **employees**, governmental agencies, and the courts.

Properly classifying someone as an **employee** or under some other status can present serious legal and economic consequences for the business owner. An employer's practice in classifying a worker under one statute may be found in violation of an

employee's rights relative to a different statute. The determination of employment status is very important in this field of the law. Compliance with complex tax laws and regulations and the legally compelled need to provide fringe benefits and absorb liability for employee torts and discriminatory actions are all duties imposed on an employer relative to a worker classified as an **employee**.

The Employment Relationship

A commonly used definition of an **employee** is "[a] person who works in the service of another person (the employer) under an express or implied contract of hire, under which the employer has the right to control the details of work performance."[3] That simple statement is subject to myriad interpretations and statutory constructions, most aimed at defining the status of the worker in light of the purposes for which the statute or doctrine was adopted. Courts rarely accept, without further inquiry, an employer's classification of its workers as controlling. The actual circumstances of the work relationship guide the courts, not the characterization given by the parties. This is especially true in cases involving the extension of worker protection laws that bar waiver of statutory rights. As an example, workers' compensation laws provide medical coverage and lost-wage protection to **employees** who are injured on the job but bar these workers' from suing the employer directly for those injuries and damages.

> ***Example:*** If a worker who has been under the direct control of a business owner and is injured operating equipment provided to the worker at the owner's place of business, the worker should be able to receive workers' compensation benefits for job-related injuries. Even if the business owner characterizes the worker as an independent contractor rather than an employee, the worker's entitlement to those benefits will remain.

Before we begin our review of the various "tests" courts apply to determine **employee** status, we must recognize one important exception to the basic principle under which **employees** are classified according to the purposes of the National Labor Relations Act. The National Labor Relations Act, a subject of a later chapter in our text, governs the employer-unionized workforce relationship. Under that act, Congress defined the worker as an **"employee"** under the common law, but it excepted from its protection those workers who were in **supervisorial** or **managerial** positions.

Perhaps most telling of the confusion regarding the law's classification of **employee** status is a comment from a 1999 U.S. Department of Labor fact-finding report:

> The Commission concludes that the ancient doctrine of master and servant provides a poor vehicle for delivering federal employment policy into the twenty-first century. The law in this area should be modernized and streamlined: there is no need for every federal employment and labor statute to have its own definition of employee. We recommend that Congress adopt a single, coherent concept of employee and apply it across the board in employment and labor law.[4]

The employment relationship can be manifested in a variety of circumstances. Most often, the law of agency governs it. The **Restatement (Second) of Agency** §220 defines the term *servant* as "a person employed to perform services in the affairs of another and who, with respect to the physical conduct in the performance of the services, is subject to the other's control or right to control." It lists ten factors to assist in distinguishing between workers as employees and as independent contractors:

- the extent of control which, by the agreement, the master may exercise over the details of the work;
- whether or not the one employed is engaged in a distinct occupation or business;
- the kind of occupation, with reference to whether, in the locality, the work is usually done under the direction of the employer or by a specialist without supervision;
- the skill required in the particular occupation;
- whether the employer or the workman supplies the instrumentalities, the tools, and the place of work for the person doing the work;
- the length of time for which the person is employed;
- the method of payment, whether by the time or by the job;
- whether or not the work is part of the regular business of the employer;
- whether or not the parties believe they are creating the relation of master and servant; and
- whether the principal is or is not in business.

These factors are considered by courts and administrative agencies in determining whether an employment relationship exists.

In its holding in *Community for Creative Non-Violence v. Reid*,[5] the Supreme Court interpreted the term ***employee*** under federal copyright law to determine if a work was prepared by an employee or an independent contractor. In *Reid*, the Supreme Court construed the term ***employee*** to incorporate the general common law of agency rather than the law of any particular state. In so doing, it set forth a test, incorporating the **Restatement** definition of **"employee,"** for determining who qualifies as an **"employee"** under the common law:

> In determining whether a hired party is an employee under the general common law of agency, we consider the hiring party's right to control the manner and means by which the product is accomplished. Among the other factors relevant to this inquiry are the skill required; the source of the instrumentalities and tools; the location of the work; the duration of the relationship between the parties; whether the hiring party has the right to assign additional projects to the hired party; the extent of the hired party's discretion over when and how long to work; the method of payment; the hired party's role in hiring and paying assistants; whether the work is part of the regular business of the hiring party; whether the hiring party is in business; and the tax treatment of the hired party. . . .
>
> While establishing that all of these factors are relevant and that "no one of these factors is determinative. . . .[6]

Employee Status Under Common Law

Respondeat Superior
The legal doctrine imposing liability on an employer for the acts and omissions of an employee.

In the employer–employee or employment relationship, the principal or employer has the right to control the physical conduct and activities of the **employee**. According to the long-standing common-law doctrine of *respondeat superior*, an employer is liable to third parties for the foreseeable negligent acts and omissions committed by an **employee** in the course and scope of employment.[7]

Common-Law Test

Under the federal retirement and benefits law known as the Employee Retirement Income Security Act (ERISA), the U.S. Supreme Court has endorsed the **common-law test**. That test requires courts to consider "the hiring party's right to control the manner and means by which the product is accomplished" (*Nationwide Mutual Ins. Co. v. Darden*, 503 U.S. 318, 323-24 (1992)). In that decision, the Supreme Court held that "traditional agency law criteria" to control the work should guide courts in determining who was an **employee** for purposes of applying federal pension law. However, Justice Souter's opinion for the unanimous Court stated "[w]e have often been asked to construe the meaning of 'employee' where the statute containing the term does not helpfully define it." He stated that the federal pension law definition of *employee* as "any individual employed by an employer" is completely circular. The Court summarized its **common-law** definition of **employee**, adopted in an earlier case, as follows:

Common-Law Test
A test to determine employment status that focuses on the hiring principal's right to control the manner and means by which the worker pursues the work result to be accomplished.

> In determining whether a hired party is an employee under the general common law of agency, we consider the hiring party's right to control the manner and means by which the product is accomplished. Among the other factors relevant to this inquiry are the skill required; the source of the instrumentalities and tools; the location of the work; the duration of the relationship between the parties; whether the hiring party has the right to assign additional projects to the hired party; the extent of the hired party's discretion over when and how long to work; the method of payment; the hired party's role in hiring and paying assistants; whether the work is part of the regular business of the hiring party; whether the hiring party is in business; the provision of employee benefits; and the tax treatment of the hired party.[8]

IRS 20-Factor Test

Interestingly, the Internal Revenue Code does not define **"employee."** The IRS has issued a set of guidelines generally referred to as the **20-Factor Test**. The IRS test is termed the **"right to control"** test, because each factor was designed to evaluate how work is performed. Under IRS rules and **common law** principles, **independent contractors** control the manner and means by which contracted services, goods, or results are achieved. The more control a business exercises over the manner and means of work performance, the more likely the workers will be classified as **employees**. A worker does not have to meet all **20 factors** to qualify as an **employee** or **independent contractor**, and no single factor is determinative of a worker's status. Issued as **Revenue Ruling 87-41**, the **20 factors** considered by the IRS are:

1. **Instructions.** Level of instruction given by company to the worker is a strong indicator of status.
2. **Training.** Amount of training requested or required of the worker by the company can indicate status. Independent contractors do not need additional training.
3. **Integration.** Degree of business integration of the worker's services into the company's operations is considered.

4. **Services personally performed.** Extent of personal services required by the company to be performed by particular workers is evaluated.
5. **Assistants.** Control by a company of assistants utilized by the worker with respect to their hiring, supervision, and compensation indicates an employment relationship.
6. **Continuing relationship.** Continuity of the relationship between the company and a worker will indicate the permanence as employment of the relationship.
7. **Hours of work.** The worker's ability to determine his or her work schedule will indicate status. Companies may require contractors to observe certain work hours for legitimate business reasons.
8. **Full-time status.** The company's demand of full-time work from a worker indicates an employment relationship.
9. **Job location.** Requiring a worker to provide services on-site at company premises suggests an employment relationship.
10. **Order of work.** The company's insistence that a worker follow a specific sequencing of work indicates his or her status as an employee.
11. **Reports.** Requirements that workers provide regular reports to the company suggest an employment rather than a contractor relationship.
12. **Method of payment.** Methods of payment indicate status when workers are paid for results obtained (as for contractors) or for time or effort expended (as for employees).
13. **Payment of expenses.** Independent contractors normally bear the costs of their business and travel expenses.
14. **Provision of tools and materials.** Workers who perform most of their work using company-provided equipment, tools, and materials are more likely to be considered employees.
15. **Investment in facilities.** Independent contractors typically invest in and maintain their own work facilities. In contrast, employees rely on their employers to provide the work facilities.
16. **Realization of profit or loss.** Workers who receive predetermined earnings and have little chance to realize significant profit or loss through their work generally are classified as employees.
17. **Work for multiple companies.** Workers who simultaneously provide services for several unrelated companies are likely to qualify as independent contractors.
18. **Availability to public.** Workers regularly making their services available to the general public are, for the most part, considered independent contractors.
19. **Control over discharge.** A company's unilateral right to discharge a worker suggests an employment relationship. A company's ability to terminate relationships with independent contractors generally depends on the contract terms.
20. **Right to quit.** Most employees can unilaterally terminate their work for a company without liability. Independent contractors cannot terminate services without liability, except as permitted by their contracts.

While the IRS has not formally repealed this test, it has recentered its analysis, beginning in 1997, with the issuance of the following guidelines for its field auditors' use in determining worker classifications. The IRS Training Manual identifies three primary categories of evidence and the facts most commonly evaluated.[9] When considering whether an individual is an **employee** or acts in the capacity of an

independent contractor, the IRS considers three categories of behavior. These guidelines also aid courts and administrative agencies in worker classification; they are:

- **Behavioral control**
- **Financial control**
- **Elements of the relationship**

With regard to **behavioral control**, the IRS will consider whether the business has the right to **direct and control** how the work is performed through instructions, training, or other means of direction. In addition, in a lawsuit the court will determine if the employer directs the person as to where, how, and when to perform the work. Requiring the wearing of common uniforms, mandating how the work is to be performed, and supplying the requirements to perform the work, including work spaces, tools, and supplies, are considerations examined by courts in determining whether the worker is an **employee** or **independent contractor**. Finally, the higher the degree of skill or the licensing or certification required for a position, the more likely it is that a worker in the position will be accorded **independent contractor** rather than **employee** status. In the area of **financial control**, the IRS reviews the facts showing the employer's **right to control** the business aspects of the worker's position. In its review, the court will consider whether business expenses are reimbursed, whether the worker has a significant personal investment in the business, and whether the worker supplies tools, licenses, and vehicles. More importantly, the extent to which the worker makes his or her services available to the general market is reviewed, including whether the worker is engaged by other persons, advertises services, and maintains business licenses and insurances. The manner and form of compensation are analyzed for commonality with typical employment terms. Finally, the extent to which the worker can realize a profit or loss is reviewed, since **employees** do not, and **independent contractors** do, bear such opportunity or risk. IRS auditors also consider the **elements of the worker–employer relationship**, and to do so they review the written contracts describing the relationship the parties intended to create. Fringe benefits, for example, are extended to **employees** but not to those considered to be **independent contractors**. Lastly, auditors consider the permanency of the relationship.

Cumulatively, these factors have become known as the **"direct and control"** test. This test advances a public policy of assuring that someone is responsible for the potential harm and damage workers might cause. the test satisfies that policy because employers can control the workplace environment. Employers can mitigate risk by procuring insurance and through risk-shifting indemnification agreements with third parties.

Even those workers who can be classified as **independent contractors** under the common-law rules may nevertheless be treated as **employees** by statute (i.e., a **statutory employee**) for certain employment tax purposes. They will be deemed statutory employees if they fall within one of four categories meeting the three conditions set forth under federal Social Security and Medicare tax law. These categories are (1) drivers who distribute produce or pick up laundry or dry cleaning, if the driver is an agent of the business or paid on commission; (2) full-time life insurance salespersons who work for one life insurance company; (3) work-at-home individuals who work on goods or materials supplied by another that must be returned to the supplier of those goods and who must follow furnished specifications; and (4) full-time traveling salespersons who turn in orders from wholesalers, retailers, and contractors.

Federal Law "Economic Realities" Test

Under the **"economic realities"** test, the issue is whether the worker is economically dependent on the business to which the services are rendered or is effectively in business for himself or herself. Generally, courts apply this test only when determining whether workers are **independent contractors** or **employees** under a statute designed to protect or benefit **employees** (such as a minimum wage or workers' compensation statute) and the statute does not require that the determination be made under only **common-law** factors. The Fair Labor Standards Act (FLSA) sets forth the federal wage and hour requirements imposed on employers. The act contains the same definition as that used in ERISA, namely, "any individual employed by an employer," which is vague, at best. However, the FLSA defines the term *employ* to mean "suffer or permit work." The Supreme Court in its *Nationwide* decision held that the employment relationship extends to those recognized under the **common-law test** under a test known as the **"economic realities"** test. For purposes of wage and hour laws, an individual's status is determined using six factors:

1. which party has the right to control the means and manner of production;
2. the worker's opportunity for realizing profit or loss based on his or her own performance and management;
3. which party supplies the equipment or materials used to accomplish the task;
4. the degree of skill required;
5. the permanence of the relationship; and
6. whether the job being performed is integral to the company's business.

Many state court decisions follow this multifactor analysis in difficult cases when determining **employee** status for purposes of employee protection laws, such as workers' compensation benefit laws. In each situation, the employer should determine the statutory purpose of the law at issue; for example, the definition of **employee** under workers' compensation statutes is different from that under other statutes. The workers' compensation statutes cover a broad spectrum of workers. One commentator has stated "[t]he modern tendency is to find employment when the work being done is an integral part of the regular business of the employer, and when the worker, relative to the employer, does not furnish an independent business or professional service."[10] The careful employer must consult the laws of each state. For example, in its *S.G. Borello & Sons v. Dept. of Industrial Relations* decision, the California Supreme Court held that the **"common law"** test is merely "useful" when determining **employee** status under that state's workers' compensation statute.[11] The court held that the **economic-realities** test was more meaningful and promoted the remedial purpose of the state's workers' compensation statute. The court further suggested that the **economic-realities** test should be utilized in determining **employee** status under California antidiscrimination and other employment-related statutes.

Economic-Realities Test
A test to determine a worker's status in which the worker's activities are viewed in the context of a statute designed to protect or benefit employees.

Employee Status Under Federal Labor Law

The National Labor Relations Act (NLRA) was enacted in 1935 to protect the rights of **employees** and employers, to promote collective bargaining, and to declare unlawful certain prior practices of both management and labor. Responding to an earlier decision of the Supreme Court, Congress amended the act to exclude **independent contractors, supervisors**, and **managers** from its coverage. In response to the amendment, the National Labor Relations Board (NLRB), the administrative agency responsible for enforcing the act, adopted the **"direct and control"** test to determine **employee** status.

Supervisors under the NLRA are defined as:

> [A]ny individual having authority, in the interest of the employer, to hire, transfer, suspend, lay off, recall, promote, discharge, assign, reward, or discipline other employees, or responsibility to direct them, or to adjust their grievances, or effectively to recommend such action, if in connection with the foregoing the exercise of such authority is not of a merely routine or clerical nature, but requires the use of independent judgment.[12]

Managerial Employee
A person who formulates and applies corporate polices to subordinate workers.

Managerial employees are defined under the NLRA as those who "formulate and effectuate management policies by expressing and making operative the decisions of the employer."[13] The law has created considerable debate with regard to a number of recent court decisions. With respect to the managerial exception from **employee** status under the NLRA, the Supreme Court has held that full-time faculty members at a large private university were "managerial" employees since the "faculty's professional interests — as applied to governance at a university — cannot be separated from those of the institution . . . The 'business' of a university is education."[14] In *NLRB v. Health Care & Retirement Corp.*,[15] the Court held that licensed practical nurses who directed lesser skilled **employees** were **supervisors** under the act. The Court concluded that the nurses' professional interests in caring for patients were not distinct from that of the nursing home as employer. In *NLRB v. Kentucky River Community Care, Inc.*[16] the Supreme Court found that the NLRB had improperly concluded that registered nurses were not within the statutory definition of supervisors. In response to that criticism, the NLRB articulated a new standard for supervisorial responsibility:

> Where an individual is engaged a part of the time as a supervisor and the rest of the time as a unit employee, the legal standard for a supervisory determination is whether the individual spends a regular and substantial portion of his/her work time performing supervisory functions. Under the Board's standard, "regular" means according to a pattern or schedule, as opposed to sporadic substitution. The Board has not adopted a strict numerical definition of substantiality and has found supervisory status where the individuals have served in a supervisory role for at least 10-15 percent of their total work time.[17]

Proposed Restatement Definition

A significant development has recently occurred relative to defining employment and distinguishing it from other types of relationships. The American Law Institute (ALI), composed of judges, law professors, and practicing lawyers, has issued a proposed **Restatement of the Law (Third) Employment Law**. It is the ALI's intention that its work, when completed, will provide the much-needed guidance, applicable nationwide, for legislatures and courts attempting to define the classes of individuals to be treated as employees, to identify workers protected from employment torts, and to state the duties imposed upon employers and employees. The ALI definition is as follows:

§1.01 of the Restatement of the Law Third Employment Law (proposed)
General Conditions for Existence of Employment Relationship

(1) Unless otherwise provided by law or by §1.02 [relating to volunteers] or §1.03 [relating to those individuals who through an ownership interest control all or a part of a business], an individual renders services as an employee of an employer if:

(a) the individual acts, at least in part, to serve the interests of the employer,

(b) the employer consents to receive the individual's services, and

(c) the employer precludes the individual from rendering the services as part of an independent business.

This definition is based upon the judicial decisions interpreting the tests discussed above. The ALI notes that:

> [t]he U.S. Supreme Court in a number of cases has ruled that where the statutory language does not provide meaningful guidance, Congress is presumed to have intended the "common-law" test to apply.
>
> The common-law right to control test was originally developed not to provide a comprehensive definition of employee status, but, rather, to address the distinct question of when it is appropriate to hold a principal liable in *respondeat superior* for the torts of its agent. Under the test, the principal normally was vicariously liable only for the actions of those agents whose work the principal retained the "right to control." A principal that retained the right to control the manner and means by which the work was performed was termed an "employer" and the agent in question an "employee." Absent such control, the imposition of vicarious liability is normally considered inappropriate.

In the following case, a court considered whether an eight-year-old boy was held to be an employee of an oil company because he was paid a few dollars an hour when he did odd jobs at a gas station. When he slipped and hurt his hand, he tried to sue the oil company for negligence.

CASE 1.1

COURT JURISDICTION CAN BE LACKING WHEN A STATUTE LIMITS A WORKER'S REMEDIES

LEMMERMAN V. A.T. WILLIAMS OIL CO.

350 S.E.2d 83 (1986)

Supreme Court of North Carolina

Facts. The mother of Shane Tucker, aged eight, brought him to work with her as a cashier at service station–convenience store because she lacked childcare.

While he was there, Shane would perform odd jobs, for which the store manager paid him. He slipped on the sidewalk on the property, fell, and cut his hand. He and his mother sued the oil company that operated the premises. They argued that Shane's injuries were caused by the company's negligence. Lemmerman was appointed *guardian ad litem* for purposes of bringing the lawsuit for Shane. In its defense, the company alleged that Shane was its employee and that his sole remedy was to file a claim under the state's workers' compensation act. In response to a motion, the trial court dismissed the lawsuit for lack of subject-matter jurisdiction. The court of appeals affirmed the trial court's ruling. Lemmerman appealed to the state supreme court.

Issue. Does a court have the power to hear a dispute when a statute specifically provides for a non-court remedy?

Language of the Court. Frye, J.: **Plaintiff Shane testified at his deposition that he routinely accompanied his mother to her job as part-time cashier at defendant's store and service station. . . . According to his description, he ordinarily did his homework, ate a snack, and performed odd jobs about the station. These jobs consisted of picking up trash in the store, taking out the garbage, and stocking cigarettes and drinks. He had been doing these jobs for almost a month at the time of the accident. The child said that the jobs generally took him between half an hour and one hour to complete. In return, the store manager . . . would pay him a dollar, and occasionally more depending on the amount of work he had done. A fair reading of the child's testimony discloses that he clearly expected to be paid for his efforts.**

We believe that this evidence amply supports the trial judge's findings that [the manager] who had the authority to hire and fire employees, hired the minor plaintiff to do odd jobs as needed in defendant's service station/convenience store business. Specifically, these tasks included stocking cigarettes and drinks and picking up trash. At the time of the accident, Shane was engaged in doing these tasks.

We also agree with the trial judge's conclusion that plaintiff Shane was defendant's employee at the time of the accident. . . . This Court has previously defined an employee as follows: "An employee is one who works for another for wages or salary, and the right to demand pay for his services from his employer would seem to be essential to his right to receive compensation under the Workmen's Compensation Act. . . ." (Citation omitted.)

The trial judge found that [the manager] had hired the child, that he had authority to hire and fire employees for defendant, and that the jobs Shane did were in the course of defendant's business and that he was engaged in doing them when he fell. We believe these facts, taken together, will support the conclusion that the plaintiff Shane was an employee of defendant at the time of the accident.

Decision. No. A court must refrain from exercising jurisdiction when a worker's status is that of an employee. On the job injury claims must be determined under the workers' compensation system and not by a lawsuit heard in court.

CASE QUESTIONS

Critical Legal Thinking. On appeal, it was argued that Shane was performing the services gratuitously. Did the fact that he was paid defeat that contention? Would Shane have a claim for the employer's failure to pay in accordance with wage and hour laws?

Business Ethics. Does this decision permit the company to profit from its own illegal act of employing a minor?

Contemporary Business. Should the court have considered the employer's violation of North Carolina child-labor statutes? Can you think of any other circumstances that should have caused the court to recognize jurisdiction to decide Shane's case?

The Worker as Independent Contractor

An **independent contractor** is *not* an **employee** of any employer. The individual is an independent businessperson who contracts with others to sell goods and services to them. He or she is retained to achieve a specific objective and exercises discretion to control the means and methods of performing the objective of the contract. Businesses report their payments to an **independent contractor** on IRS Form 1099 and do not withhold taxes from the payments or provide any benefits to the workers employed by the **independent contractor**.

Unlike the principal-agency relationship, which is the essence of an employer-employee relationship, the relationship of **independent contractor** to principal creates different liabilities for the parties. An **independent contractor** is any person or party who works for another under conditions that are not sufficient to create control by the principal. Except for the expected product or result, the **independent contractor** is free to exercise discretion in how the work is to be performed. As stated in the above section on defining **employee** status, there is no absolute rule or formula for determining whether a person is an **independent contractor** or an **employee**.

Distinguishing **employees** from **independent contractors** focuses on the principal's **right to control** the "physical conduct" of **employees** and readily applies to the context of imposing tort liability upon the doctrine of *respondeat superior*. Business liability is predicated upon the principal's ability to control the circumstances that might lead to tort liability. These circumstances are ones that the principal usually creates, manages, or insures against risk of harm. Since the principal retains the benefits of the workers' labor, it is only fair that such additional burdens be placed upon the employer. Case law establishes that the courts undertake a practical, fairness-based approach to determining worker status. If the principal lacks the **right to control** all the physical details of the work, an employment relationship may still exist if the other factors indicate that the worker is not operating an independent business. For example, unskilled workers who provide only their own labor ordinarily will not be held to be providing services as an **independent contractor**, regardless of whether an employer has abdicated a degree of control over the details of the work. The modern trend of American law requires that the worker have the entrepreneurial discretion to operate an independent business, including the substantial investment in property to operate the business and the ability to employ others.

Concept Summary
Independent Contractor Terminology

The following terms have these meanings within the law of independent contractor relationships:

- **Contractor** An individual (also known as an **independent contractor**) who contracts to perform work for a principal. Not required to follow instructions from the principal on how to perform services.
- **Company** A general term describing an entity for which the work is performed. By itself, the term does not determine whether its workers are employees or independent contractors.
- **Employee** A worker who is deemed by law to be in an employment relationship with a business employer.
- **Employer** A business that is deemed by law to be in an employment relationship with an employee.
- **Principal** A party or business that has contracted for the services of an independent contractor.
- **Worker** A person who performs services for another. By itself, the term does not determine whether the worker is an employee or an independent contractor.

The case law determining **independent contractor** status has continued its inquiry beyond merely the **right to control** the physical details of the work. Courts look to whether the worker's services were part of an independent business or were integrated into the principal's business. They also look to the nature of the work and the industry involved.

> ***Example:*** Victoria Lis Alberty-Velez sued a Puerto Rican television station for pregnancy and gender discrimination. She had worked for many years as a host of various programs. The show's producer set the location and hours of filming and established the basic content of the program. The station provided the lights, camera, and makeup. Alberty-Velez was responsible for providing her clothing and hair styling and was paid a flat sum per episode. No income taxes or social security taxes were deducted from her check, and she was not provided fringe benefits, such as health insurance. A federal court applied the common-law test of determining employee status. In concluding that Alberty-Velez was an independent contractor, the court considered, among other facts, the following: as a television actress Alberty-Velez occupied a skilled position requiring talent and training not available on the

job; she provided her clothing and image-related supplies necessary for her appearance; she was not assigned any work other than that of a particular program; and she was paid a flat fee per episode. She could not successfully argue that the station sufficiently controlled her work. The court held that the situation must be considered in light of the work performed and the industry involved.[18]

Workplace Application
Independent Contractor Status

Before deciding to retain a worker as an **employee** or an **independent contractor**, the employer should carefully consider the purpose and nature of the work relationship.

Independent Contractor Advantages

An employer does *not* pay the following on behalf of the **independent contractor**:

- federal unemployment tax (F.U.T.A. and I.R.C. §3301)
- Social Security tax (F.I.C.A. and I.R.C. §3111)
- state and local taxes
- workers' compensation costs
- fringe benefits, such as medical insurance, vacations, and retirement plans

The employer's legal exposure to the following is reduced in independent contractor arrangements:

- threats of unionization (NLRA)
- requirements to pay workers in accord with federal wage laws (FLSA)
- laws regulating discrimination against **employees**
- wrongful termination claims of workers
- contracts of the **independent contractor** relating to the work to be performed
- torts (harm caused by wrongful conduct) of the **independent contractor** (i.e., the employer is not vicariously liable for the acts of the **independent contractor**)

These administrative burdens on the employer are reduced or eliminated:

- costs of maintaining human resource and payroll functions eliminated
- record keeping obligations reduced
- direct supervision of workers' costs reduced

Independent Contractor Disadvantages

A business suffers the following when using an independent contractor:

- loss of control (the employer cannot dictate how the work is performed)
- the contract between the business and the worker controls the terms applicable to terminating the relationship
- loss/disruption of morale and continuity within the workforce

Business Liability for Reclassification of the Worker as an Employee

The burden is on the employer to establish that the worker is not an **employee**. Sympathetic courts and administrative agencies frequently reclassify workers as **employees**. If the employer misclassifies the worker as an **independent contractor**, ruinous financial consequences can occur. They can include the following for workers subsequently reclassified:

- The employer must pay both the employer's and the employee's portion of all payroll taxes for a retroactive three-year period.
- The taxing authorities will estimate income withholding should have been on all compensation paid to the reclassified workers for a retroactive three-year period.
- Penalties and interest will be due and payable for:
  - All federal and state payroll taxes that should have been paid;
  - The employer's failure to pay state and federal unemployment taxes;
  - Failure to file proper tax returns; and
  - Failure to pay, file, and deposit payroll tax payments due federal and state tax authorities.
- Personal liability will be imposed on corporate officers and other responsible persons for 100 percent of the total withholding taxes not paid.[19]

The IRS may assess payroll taxes until three years after the date of the tax return for the year in question. In cases of fraud in the classification of **employees**, if the employer failed to file a payroll tax return, the period in which the IRS can pursue the employer is unlimited. Other statutes will govern state tax authorities.

In addition to these tax matters, the reclassification of the worker to **employee** status will subject the employer to the following:

- workers may make retroactive claims that they were not paid in accordance minimum wage and overtime requirements under federal and state laws and local ordinances;
- the business will have to pay penalty assessments for its failure to obtain workers' compensation as required under state law;
- the employer's pension and other benefit plans may be disqualified if the reclassification of **independent contractors** to **employee** status reduces the number of participating **employees** below the requirements of federal pension and welfare benefit law;[20]
- penalties may be imposed on the employer for not properly classifying the worker for purposes of federal immigration law; and
- the employer may be exposed to liability for damages from failing to give proper notice when closing a worksite or plant as required under federal and state mass layoff laws.

One of the more interesting cases to consider, whether workers are **employees** or **independent contractors**, is provided by the Federal Communications Commission's imposition of a fine against the CBS television network relating to the broadcast of a Super Bowl halftime show.

CASE 1.2

DETERMINING EMPLOYEE STATUS REQUIRES A WEIGHING OF FACTORS

CBS CORPORATION, ET AL. V. F.C.C.

535 F.3d 167 (3rd Cir. 2008)

U.S. Court of Appeals for the Third Circuit

Facts. On February 1, 2004, CBS presented a live broadcast of the National Football League's Super Bowl XXXVIII. Nearly 90 million viewers watched the halftime show during which Janet Jackson and Justin Timberlake had an alleged "wardrobe malfunction." Janet Jackson was the announced headliner, and Justin Timberlake was a "surprise guest" for the final minutes of the show. He was unveiled on stage during the conclusion of the show. He and Jackson performed his popular song "Rock Your Body" as the show's finale.

Following the broadcast the Federal Communications Commission fined the network $550,000 because it contended the performance violated broadcast decency standards. The FCC objected to sexually suggestive choreography, which portrayed Timberlake seeking to dance with Jackson, and Jackson alternating between accepting and rejecting his advances. The performance ended with Timberlake singing, "gonna have you naked by the end of this song," and simultaneously tearing away part of Jackson's bustier. CBS had implemented a five-second audio delay to guard against the possibility of indecent language being transmitted on air, but it did not employ similar precautionary technology for video images. As a result, Jackson's bare right breast was exposed on camera for nine-sixteenths of one second.

CBS issued a public statement of apology for the incident. CBS stated Jackson and Timberlake's wardrobe stunt was unscripted and unauthorized, claiming it had no advance notice of any plan by the performers to deviate from the script. CBS appealed the fine to the federal court of appeals on many grounds. Among them was its contention that it was not liable for their actions because they were independent contractors and not network employees.

Issue. Whether or not Janet Jackson and Justin Timberlake were CBS employees at the time the network broadcast "indecent" material during the 2004 Super Bowl halftime show.

Language of the Court. Scirica, C.J. . . . **The parties dispute whether the conduct giving rise to liability was performed by CBS's employees. CBS asserts, and the FCC denies, that Jackson and Timberlake were independent contractors and therefore outside the scope of respondeat superior.**

. . . [The Supreme Court decision in] Reid did not provide guidance on the relative weight each factor should be assigned when performing a balancing analysis. But the Court has indicated that determining the appropriate balance is a case-specific endeavor: There are innumerable situations which arise in the common law where it is difficult to say whether a particular individual is an employee or an independent contractor. . . . In such a situation . . . there is no shorthand formula or magic phrase that can be applied to find the answer, but all of the incidents of the relationship must be assessed and weighed with no one factor being decisive. What is important is that the total factual context is assessed in light of the pertinent common-law agency principles . . . under the common law, respondeat superior is limited to the employer-employee relationship.

Accordingly, all of the Reid factors are relevant, and no one factor is decisive, but the weight each factor should be accorded depends on the context of the case. . . . [R]ather than balancing those factors it did consider, the Commission focused almost exclusively on CBS's right of control over the performers. . . . But it is undisputed that CBS's actual control over the Halftime Show performances did not extend to all aspects of the performers' work. The performers, not CBS, provided their own choreography and retained substantial latitude to develop the visual performances that would accompany their song. . . . [T]he performers retained discretion to make those choices in the first instance and provided some of their own materials.

It is undisputed that both Jackson and Timberlake were hired for brief, one-time performances; CBS could not assign more work to [them]. Second, Jackson and Timberlake selected and hired their own choreographers, backup dancers, and other assistants without any involvement on the part of CBS. Third, Jackson and Timberlake were compensated by onetime, lump-sum contractual payments and "promotional considerations" rather than by salaries or other similar forms of remittances, without the provision of employee benefits. Fourth, the skill required of a performer hired to sing and dance as the headlining act for the Halftime Show—a performance during a Super Bowl broadcast, as the FCC notes, that attracted nearly 90 million viewers and was the highest-rated show during the 2003-04 television season—is substantial even relative to the job of a general entertainer, which is itself a skilled occupation.

Also weighing heavily in favor of Jackson and Timberlake's status as independent contractors is CBS's assertion in its briefs, which the FCC does not refute, that it paid no employment tax. Had the performers been employees

rather than independent contractors, federal law would have required CBS to pay such taxes. . . . The FICA tax scheme . . . requires employers to share the FICA tax liabilities of their employees but not of their independent contractors. Finally, there is no evidence that Jackson, Timberlake, or CBS considered their contractual relationships to be those of employer-employee. . . . On balance, the relevant factors here weigh heavily in favor of a determination that Jackson and Timberlake were independent contractors rather than employees of CBS.

Decision. No. The performers were independent contractors who acted for a limited purpose for one isolated, brief program and *respondeat superior* does not apply.

CASE QUESTIONS

Critical Legal Thinking. If CBS had been more involved in the production of the performance would the decision have been different? What factors would be significant in holding Jackson and Timberlake to be employees of CBS?

Business Ethics. Does the court's holding make it easier for companies to escape liability for their workers' misbehavior?

Contemporary Business. Can you think of other circumstances where entertainers have created liability for injuries to third parties on the part of a production company or performing venue?

Concept Summary
Common Tests for Employee Status

Purpose	Test
Income taxes	IRS 20-Factor Test, common law
Fair Labor Standards Act (FLSA)	Economic realities
National Labor Relations Act (NLRA)	Common law
Employment discrimination	Common law and economic realities (federal court circuits are split)
Employee Retirement Income Security Act (ERISA)	Common law, IRS 20-Factor Test
Social Security/Medicare taxes	Common law
Other purposes	Use common law unless definition of employee in the statute is more expansive so as to include those who might not qualify as an employee under the common-law test (*Nationwide Mutual Ins. Co. v. Darden*, 503 U.S. 318 (1992)).

The IRS also recognizes two categories of **statutory nonemployees**. They are direct sellers and licensed real estate agents. They are treated as self-employed for all federal tax purposes if substantially all payments for their services as direct sellers or real estate agents are directly related to sales or other output, rather than to the number of hours worked; and if their services are performed under a written contract that they will not be treated as employees for federal tax purposes.

The Worker as Leased Employee

Leased Employee
A type of contingent worker lent to an employer by a third-party business. The third-party business is primarily responsible for the worker's legal compliance.

The **leased employee** relationship is slightly different from those previously discussed in this chapter. This person is a type of contingent worker. Employee leasing is a contractual arrangement in which a third-party business (also known as a **professional employer organization** (**PEO**)) "employs" the staff of the business and undertakes all of the administrative functions of the employer, including payroll reporting and providing fringe benefits. A fee plus cost reimbursement is paid to the leasing company. By aggregating the employees of several companies into one group, **PEOs** can offer better fringe benefits to the workers. The relationship between the **PEO** and its workers is an employment relationship.

A **leased employee** does not insulate the **PEO**'s client company from worker safety and employment discrimination laws. If the client company exhibits sufficient common law **"direct and control"** over the workers, then the **leased employees** will be considered **employees** for purposes of employment discrimination laws. In most cases, the client company will retain day-to-day supervision of the workers and will have some authority to hire and fire the workers of the **PEO** business. Another category of employee worker is the temporary worker, that is, someone assigned to work at a specific firm for a limited duration or for a specific project.

Some courts have applied the **"shared employee doctrine"** to **leased employee** relationships. In the event a worker is employed by two or more entities who may or may not have the **right to control** the specific activities of the shared employee, courts will often utilize the **economic-realities** test to determine if the employer–employee relationship exists. Some courts have found joint responsibility for the separate wrongful conduct or acts of the other employer. This can occur when the regular, dedicated staff already employed in a business is transferred to the **PEO**. The client company rather than the **PEO** has responsibility for the day-to-day supervision of the **leased employee.**

The **leased employee** may pose several additional problems for the business owner. **Leased employees** may qualify as participants under the pension, retirement, and health plans of the owner. The **common-law test** is applied for **leased employees** to qualify under those plans.[21] Under the federal FLSA the concept of **joint employment liability** is well recognized, and the leasing employer and the client company will have joint liability for compliance with federal and state wage and hour laws. Under the workers' compensation system of compensating injured workers, the worker may not directly sue the employer. If a court or administrative agency should hold that the worker is the employee of the leasing employer, then the leasing employer and the client company are not **joint employers**. That result would permit the injured **leased employee** to sue the client company for negligence. Moreover, under the NLRA, multiple business entities may constitute a "single employer" for various compliance purposes under federal labor law. Additionally, the client company may also face liability for unpaid payroll taxes and audits if it has not managed the relationship in accordance with the requirements of the law.

Outsourcing

Outsourcing is similar to **employee leasing**. **Outsourcing** occurs when a company subcontracts part of its business operations to another company. With **outsourcing**, an outside company manages an entire project or part of the business that the company formerly managed itself. The **outsourcing** company implements its own work procedures and manages and supervises the workforce for the third-party employer. Usually **outsourcing** does not result in establishing **joint-employer liability**. Examples of **outsourcing** include having another company manage the human resources or information technology (IT) departments. While the objective of outsourcing is cost reduction, customer service sometimes suffers. Most of us have encountered the frustrations of dealing with a telephone-based customer service function that has been outsourced to an overseas location.

Section 530 Safe Harbor

The Revenue Act of 1978[22] provides a defense to a challenge of an employer's classification of its workers. Under this defense, known as the **Section 530 safe harbor**, a worker may be classified as an **independent contractor** if certain criteria are met. An **independent contractor** may qualify under this section of the Revenue Act if the company:

1. filed IRS Form 1099s for the independent contractors in a timely manner;
2. has not treated workers in substantially similar situations as employees; and
3. had a reasonable basis for treating the workers as independent contractors.

In the area of income taxation, employers report wages of employees to taxing authorities on a W-2 form. The employer form shows the deductions taken from income for payment of federal and state taxes and social security and other taxes. The IRS 1099 forms are issued by principles to independent contractors. On a 1099 form, the income earned will be stated, but no deductions will be made for income or other taxes. The income reports to the taxing authorities track independent contractors' earned income.

The employer's good-faith compliance with the law is considered in determining whether this **safe-harbor** defense will apply. The employer may rely on prior private-letter rulings the IRS has issued to the employer relating to worker classifications, case precedent, published rulings, regulations, and memoranda issued by the IRS In addition, if the employer has been previously audited over the worker classification, and the audit did not result in assessments for payroll taxes for workers having similar positions with the employer, then the employer can rely on the prior audit results. Long-standing, recognized practices regarding worker classification within a significant segment (more than 25 percent) of the employers in its industry will also aid the employer in arguing good-faith compliance with the law.

If the employer-taxpayer can establish the reasonableness of the worker's classification as an **independent contractor**, the burden of proving that the worker was an **employee** falls upon the IRS. In arguing the **safe-harbor** defense, the employer must have cooperated fully with the reasonable requests of the IRS.

Human Resource Form
Independent Contractor Agreement

This Independent Contractor Agreement ("Agreement") is effective this _______ day of _______by and between Corporation (hereinafter "Corporation") and _______, an individual (hereinafter "Consultant").

RECITALS

A. Corporation is a software engineering company with a principal place of business in Richmond, Virginia;

B. Consultant represents that he/she has the requisite experience, means, and methods to perform the requirements of this Agreement independent of Corporation; and,

C. Corporation desires to appoint Consultant as its independent sales agent and Consultant desires to be appointed as an independent sales agent to Corporation.

NOW, THEREFORE, the parties agree as follows:

1. **Recitals.** The foregoing recitals are incorporated herein as if set forth in full.
2. **Scope of Services.** Consultant agrees to the best of his/her ability to provide an active and industrious sales effort in the solicitation of sales orders for Corporation's software products. In addition, Consultant agrees to perform such other services as may be agreed upon by the parties. Consultant shall render such reports and meet with Corporation representatives as may from time to time be reasonably required.
3. **Term.** This Agreement shall commence on the last day of _______, and continue for an initial term of two years, unless such term is terminated sooner pursuant to the provisions of this Agreement.
4. **Territory.** During the term of this Agreement, Consultant shall represent Corporation as an independent sales consultant for Corporation's software products in the states of Virginia, Maryland, and Delaware. Consultant shall devote such time, attention, and effort as he/she shall decide is necessary to perform the purposes of this Agreement. Consultant shall determine the method, details, and means of performing the services required of him/her. At his/her own expense, he/she may hire employees or other subcontractors to perform the sales efforts required of him/her.
5. **Compensation.** Corporation agrees to pay Consultant for the services and obligations set forth herein, the sums as are set forth in Corporation's sales commission schedule dated _______, which is incorporated herein as if set forth in full. Commissions shall be paid to Consultant thirty (30) days following Corporation's

receipt of payment in full for each customer order placed by Consultant with Corporation. Commissions payable shall be net of any customer discounts, rebates, allowances, refunds, or other credits granted to customer, shipping costs, returns received from prior Consultant orders, and sales taxes payable upon such transactions.

6. **Consultant's status.** Consultant is not and shall not be deemed an employee of Corporation. Consultant shall not be eligible for any employee benefits adopted by Corporation from time to time. Consultant shall be responsible for the payment of his/her own costs and expenses incurred in connection with his/her performance hereunder, which costs shall not be reimbursable by Corporation. Consultant shall timely file and pay all required self-employment tax, withholding reports and estimates and shall furnish Corporation with copies or other evidence of prompt and timely filing and payment upon request.

7. **Termination.** This Agreement shall terminate upon the earlier of: (a) the death or legal incapacity of Consultant; (b) the filing of any petition by Corporation under any chapter of the Bankruptcy Act, or other federal or state insolvency or bankruptcy act; (c) the filing of any petition against Corporation under any chapter of the Bankruptcy Act, or other federal or state insolvency or bankruptcy act if not dismissed within thirty (30) days; (d) the appointment of a receiver or trustee to take possession of all or substantially all of the assets of Corporation if not discharged within thirty (30) days; (e) a general assignment for the benefit of creditors of Corporation; or (f) the dissolution and winding up of the business of Corporation.

8. **Nondisclosure of Information Concerning Business.** Consultant agrees he/she will not, directly or indirectly, divulge, disclose or communicate information concerning matters affecting or relating to the business of Corporation to any person at any time unless disclosure is required for, or of aid or advantageous to, the successful operations of Corporation or the performance of Consultant's duties. Without limiting the generality of the foregoing, Consultant shall not disclose the names of any of Corporation's customers, the prices Corporation obtains or has obtained, or for which it may sell or has sold its products or services, its manner of operation, its plans, its processes, or any other information about or concerning the business of Corporation. Without regard to whether any of the matters in this Paragraph would otherwise be deemed confidential, material, or important, the parties stipulate that as between them, the above are confidential, material, and important and gravely affect the conduct of the business of Corporation and its goodwill and any breach of the terms of this Paragraph would be a material breach of this Agreement.

9. **Miscellaneous.** This Agreement shall not be amended, altered, or changed except by a written agreement signed by the parties hereto. If any provision of this Agreement is unenforceable or unlawful under any applicable law of any jurisdiction, in such jurisdiction the remainder of this Agreement's provisions shall be deemed fully enforceable in accordance with their terms. This Agreement contains the complete agreements or representations by, or between, the parties, written or oral, which may have related to the subject matter hereof in any way. The law of the State of Virginia shall govern all questions concerning the construction, validity, and interpretation of this Agreement, and performance of the obligations imposed by this Agreement. Should any litigation be commenced between the parties to this Agreement concerning any of the matters stated herein, the prevailing party shall be entitled to recover its reasonable attorney's fees and costs from the other party in such an action.

Corporation	Consultant
By: ________	By: ________
Its President	[Consultant's name]

Key Terms and Concepts

- Civil law
- Public law
- Statutes and ordinances
- Executive orders
- Substantive law
- Procedural law
- Administrative agencies
- Enabling statute
- Rules, regulations, and orders
- Common law
- Adversary system
- *Stare decisis*
- Precedent
- Adjudication
- Subject-matter jurisdiction
- Federal-question jurisdiction
- Diversity jurisdiction
- Preempt
- Employee
- Independent contractor
- Restatement (Second) of Agency
- Common-law test
- Direct and control
- 20-Factor Test
- Revenue Ruling 87-41
- Behavioral control
- Financial control
- Elements of the relationship
- Statutory employee
- Economic-realities test
- Supervisors
- Managerial employee
- *Respondeat superior*
- Statutory nonemployees
- Leased employee
- Professional Employer Organization
- Shared-employee doctrine
- Joint-employee liability
- Outsourcing
- Section 530 safe harbor

Chapter Summary

- The sources of employment law are varied. An employer must comply with federal and state laws and regulations, local ordinances, and its own policies and procedures. Employment is treated as an important opportunity to improve the individual and, consequently, bestow the benefits of work upon society. Our legal system, while complex, is intended to balance the benefits and burdens of the employment relationship.

- The federal Constitution requires that the laws of states and local municipal governments comply with the legal requirements issued by laws adopted by Congress, federal administrative agencies, and judicial decisions.

- The role of the judicial branch is to interpret the actions of the litigants relative to the applicable relevant legal principles involved in the dispute. In our system, only the judicial branch can declare whether some action is in accord with constitutional requirements, statutory requirements, or prior court decisions. Lower courts within a judicial system are required to follow the decisions on a subject of the highest court in that jurisdiction. This principle is known as *stare decisis*. It applies in all states except Louisiana, which follows both common law and civil law.

- Courts are divided into federal and state jurisdictional systems. Recourse to the courts may be sought only in a manner consistent with the requirements established for them by the legislative branch of government.

■ The classification of a worker as an employee or as an independent contractor has important legal and tax liability consequences for both the principal and the worker.

■ Depending on the nature of the relationship between the business and the worker, the courts will employ various tests to classify a worker as either an employee or an independent contractor.

■ Under the direct-and-control test, the hiring party has the right to control the manner and means by which the products of worker effort are achieved. The courts consider the degree of worker skill required to perform the work; who supplies the tools and equipment necessary to perform the work; the location of the work; the duration of the worker–employer relationship; and the worker's freedom to accept or decline work assignments. In addition, the courts consider the degree to which the worker appears to maintain an independent business and is exposed to the risk of financial loss.

■ Courts may also use three factors developed by the IRS to determine whether a worker is an employee: behavioral control, financial control, and the specific elements of the existing relationship. A former test (the 20-factor test) used by the IRS to determine employment status is not as well recognized today as it had been in the past.

■ Under the federal law, the "economic realities" test is used to determine employee status for federal wage and hour and pension and benefit purposes. Under this test, the court will consider (1) which party has the right to control the means and manner of production; (2) the worker's opportunity for realizing profit or loss based on his or her own performance and management; (3) which party supplies the equipment or materials used to accomplish the task; (4) the degree of skill required; (5) the permanence of the relationship; and (6) whether the job being performed is integral to the company's business.

■ The National Labor Relations Act (NLRA) excludes independent contractors, supervisors, and managers from its coverage. The National Labor Relations Board (NLRB) has adopted the common law direct-and-control test to determine employee status for purposes of federal union law.

■ According to a definition proposed under the Restatement of the Law (Third) Employment Law, a worker will be classified as an employee if (a) the worker acts to serve the interests of the employer, (b) the employer receives those services, and (c) the employer precludes the individual from rendering the services as part of an independent business. This definition is among the most liberal and encompassing.

■ Under the doctrine of *respondeat superior*, the employer is liable for the torts and contract liabilities of the worker. When working with independent contractors, the employer is not responsible for those torts and contracts. The independent contractor is liable for all taxes and fringe benefits that would otherwise be paid by an employer. The independent contractor is usually engaged in a separate business and assumes the risk of financial loss.

■ Under the law, the employer is responsible for assuring that all taxes and contributions are made on its and the employee's behalf. These include the payment of tax withholding, unemployment, social security taxes, and fringe benefit payments, such as health insurance premiums. The employer is responsible for any injuries suffered by the worker during the course and scope of his or her employment. The risk of reclassifying a worker from independent contractor to employee status can be expensive to the employer. The employer will be required to pay both the employer and employee portions of the outstanding payroll taxes, including any assessed penalties. In addition, the employer will be exposed to penalties related to pension and benefit plans.

■ The leased employee relationship involves the use of a contingent worker. A third-party business, known as a professional employer organization (PEO), employs the staff of the business and undertakes all administrative functions of the employer, including payroll reporting and provision of fringe benefits to the workers.

■ Using outsourcing, companies subcontract part of their business operations to another company. The outside company manages an entire project or part of the business that the company formerly performed itself.

■ The Internal Revenue Service (IRS) provides a safe-harbor provision excusing the misclassifying of workers as independent contractors when they should have been treated as employees. It requires that the employer file Form 1099s, that workers in substantially similar situations as the employees in question were not treated differently, and that the employer had a reasonable basis for treating the workers as independent contractors.

■ Many companies wish to employ independent contractors in lieu of employees because it shifts most legal responsibility for the acts and omissions of workers from the company to the independent contractor. However, the IRS will most often presume an employment relationship, leaving the company to shoulder more legal responsibility than it desires. To avoid the liabilities of an employment relationship, a company must follow strict, arm's-length treatment of contractors and deal with them much differently than they do employees.

Online Student Support

- Loislaw legal research and writing assignments.
- Loislaw group projects and class presentations.
- Loislaw access, providing online research including up-to-date cases, statutes, rules, and regulations. Primary law for all 50 states and federal jurisdictions. Registration required for access to this resource.
- Practice questions, including sample true/false, multiple choice, and short answer questions to test your understanding of concepts.
- Additional human resource forms.
- Internet exercises.
- Blogs.
- Supplementary statutory and regulatory materials.

Case Problems

1.1 Sherrie Ann Adcok sued Chrysler Corporation for employment discrimination alleging that the company's refusal to award her a dealership was the result of sex discrimination. Under the dealership appointment agreement, the dealer (not Chrysler) controls the dealership and the day-to-day vehicle-selling operations. The dealer maintains discretion over dealership employment decisions and over the means and manner of advertising. The dealer (not Chrysler) owns the dealership, premises, equipment, and vehicles sold by the dealership. Adcok argued that it was an employment relationship because Chrysler controlled the decisions about what cars could be purchased, retained approval of the appearance of the dealership, specified the dealer location, and required that certain financial requirements continued to be met. Chrysler had easy access to and use of the dealer's accounting information. In considering all of the factors that weigh both for and against an employment relationship, how should the court rule? (*Adcok v. Chrysler Corp.*, 166 F.3d 1290 (9th Cir. 1999))

1.2 John Weary served as a special agent to sell Northwestern Mutual life insurance products in Tennessee. A third party who had the authority to appoint sales agents to act on behalf of the life insurance company issued the agreement appointing Weary as an agent. The agreement stated that Weary was an independent contractor and was to be paid on a commission basis. After he failed to meet sales targets, Weary was terminated by the third party. Weary sued the life insurer for age discrimination in employment, arguing that he had been required to comply with rules and guidelines established by the insurer, although he admitted that he paid for his own equipment and worked out of his house. Which of the tests covered in this chapter should the court employ to determine whether Weary was an employee or an independent contractor to Northwestern Mutual? (*Weary v. Cochran*, 377 F.3d 522 (6th Cir. 2004))

1.3 A class-action lawsuit was filed by FedEx Ground Package System, suing FedEx for reimbursement for work-related expenses. The FedEx Ground Package System drivers contended they were employees and not independent contractors. When hired, they executed an agreement identifying themselves as independent contractors. Under that agreement, drivers provide their own trucks meeting the company's specifications, mark the truck with the FedEx logo, pay all costs of operating and maintaining the truck, and use the truck exclusively in the service of FedEx (or mask the logo if the truck is used for any other purpose). FedEx reserved the right to reassign the drivers or assign additional drivers in the driver's territory. The drivers agreed to have FedEx management employees travel with them four times each year to ensure they were meeting FedEx standards and to train with FedEx. The drivers could elect to have their truck operating costs paid by FedEx and deducted from their weekly "settlements." FedEx argued that the drivers enjoyed a "true entrepreneurial opportunity depending on how well the [drivers] perform[ed]." Who should prevail in this dispute? (*Estrada v. FedEx Ground Package Systems, Inc.*, 154 Cal. App. 4th 1 (2007))

1.4 Bridget O'Connor majored in social work at Marymount College in New York. As a component of her major, O'Connor was required during her senior year to perform volunteer fieldwork at one of several Marymount-approved social-service agencies. She was placed at a hospital for the mentally disabled. The internship was considered "work study" for financial aid purposes. It was an unpaid internship. While on assignment at the hospital, one of the licensed psychiatrists referred to O'Connor, in her presence, as "Miss Sexual Harassment"—a term he later explained was intended as a compliment, to convey the idea that she was physically attractive and, as such, was likely to be an object of sexual harassment. The doctor made other inappropriate sexual remarks, including suggesting that he and O'Connor should participate in an "orgy." O'Connor's complaints against the doctor were investigated, and O'Connor was reassigned to another facility, where she completed her internship hours. She filed suit against Marymount and the original facility, claiming sexual harassment. Marymount defended the suit on the grounds that O'Connor was not an employee. Which of the 20 common factors would you apply to determine whether Bridget O'Connor was entitled to relief? (*O'Connor v. Davis*, 126 F.3d 112 (2d Cir. 1997))

1.5 Twenty-six non-English-speaking adult garment workers who worked at a factory in New York's Chinatown sued their immediate employers and the Liberty Apparel Company. Liberty was a garment manufacturer that contracted out the last phase of its production process to the workers' employers. The workers contended that almost 75 percent of their time was spent working on Liberty jobs. Liberty employed people to monitor the assembly of its garments, but it disputed how much time it spent supervising the work. The workers sued under federal and state laws for the payment of the legally mandated minimum wage and the payment of overtime. How should the court analyze whether the defendants were joint employers of the workers? (*Zheng v. Liberty Apparel Co., Inc.*, 355 F.3d 61 (2d Cir. 2003))

End Notes

1. *Ochoa, et al. v. J.B. Martin and Sons Farms, Inc.*, 287 F.3d 1182 (9th Cir. 2002).
2. www.irs.gov/businesses/small/article/0,,id=99921,00.html.
3. *Black's Law Dictionary*, 8th ed. (Eagan, MN: Thomson West, 2004).
4. The Dunlop Commission on the Future of Worker-Management Relations — Final Report, pp. 65-66, issued to Secretary of Labor Robert B. Reich and Secretary of Commerce Ronald H. Brown (1994), http://digitalcommons.ilr.cornell.edu/key_workplace/2.
5. 490 U.S. 730 (1989).
6. 490 U.S. 730, 751-52.
7. Restatement (Third) of Agency §2.04.
8. 503 U.S. at 323-24 citing *Community for Creative Non-Violence v. Reid*, 490 U.S. 730, 750-51.
9. A copy of the manual may be downloaded at http://www.irs.gov/pub/irs-utl/emporind.pdf.
10. Larsen, The Law of Workers Compensation, §43.10 (1976).
11. 48 Cal. 3d 341 (1989).
12. 29 U.S.C. §152(11).
13. *NLRB v. Bell Aerospace Co. Div. of Textron, Inc.*, 416 U.S. 267, 288 (1974).
14. *NLRB v. Yeshiva University*, 444 U.S. 672 (1980).
15. 511 U.S. 571 (1994).
16. 532 U.S. 706 (2001).
17. *Oakwood Healthcare, Inc.*, 348 N.L.R.B. No. 37 (2006).
18. *Alberty-Velez v. Corporacion de Puerto Rico*, 361 F.3d 1 (1st Cir. 2004).
19. I.R.C. §6672.
20. I.R.C. §§401, 410.
21. *Burrey v. Pacific Gas & Elec. Co.*, 159 F.3d 388 (9th Cir. 1998).
22. Pub. L., 95-600, 92 Stat. 2885.

Chapter 2
Recruitment, Selection, Testing, and Termination

"Happiness lies not in the mere possession of money; it lies in the joy of achievement, in the thrill of creative effort. The joy and moral stimulation of work no longer must be forgotten in the mad chase of evanescent profits." —Franklin D. Roosevelt, thirty-second President of the United States, First Inaugural Address, March 4, 1933

Learning Objectives

1. Describe how job descriptions minimize employment disputes.
2. Define what criteria constitute a business necessity.
3. Determine what may be stated in applicant advertising.
4. Differentiate between lawful and unlawful recruiting practices.
5. Recognize lawful and unlawful hiring, testing, and selection criteria.
6. Understand what exceptions to at-will employment might arise.
7. State what procedures should be reviewed prior to terminating an employee.

Chapter Outline

- Introduction
- Recruiting

Case 2.1 Griggs v. Duke Power Co.

- Management Application: Employer Restraints in Hiring and Termination
- Employee Selection Criteria

Case 2.2 Dothard v. Rawlinson

- Management Application: Job References

Case 2.3 Bradley v. Pizzaco of Nebraska, Inc. dba Domino's Pizza

- Management Application: The Meaning of Business Necessity
- Focus on Ethics: Internet Job Postings
- Human Resource Form: Integration Clause

Case 2.4 EEOC v. Consolidated Service Systems

Case 2.5 Kotch v. Board of River Port Pilot Commissioners

- Management Application: Selecting Qualified Candidates

Case 2.6 Stutts v. Freeman

- Testing to Screen Employees

Case 2.7 Albemarle Paper Co. v. Moody

- EEOC Compliance Reporting
- Termination of Employment
- Human Resource Management: Exit Interview Questions
- Workplace Application: What Do Employees Have to Tolerate at Work?
- Human Resource Form: Moonlighting Policy

Chapter Opening scenario

The Village of Elmwood Park, Illinois, has a low percentage of African Americans living within its boundaries. The city does not have an African American among its more than 100 employees and has never employed one. The city adheres to a "philosophy" of granting a preference to residents over nonresidents in hiring for municipal positions. The mayor stated that the preference is a way of "giving something back" to the residents for their payment of real estate taxes to the city. The city relies primarily on "word of mouth" notice of vacancies as its source of job applicants. According to the mayor, there was no need to advertise for open positions. The city does not post vacancies for positions other than for police and firefighting positions. Does this hiring process constitute an unlawful barrier to black employment, or is it a lawful hiring process?[1]

Introduction

The law of employment consists of a complex set of federal and state common law doctrines, statutes, case precedents, and administrative agency rules. These affect the recruitment, hiring, compensation, and other terms and conditions of employment. These different sources do not provide an easy categorization of what laws apply in each context. The law seeks to balance the rights and duties of the employer and the employee, although most businesspersons and their attorneys would suggest that the balance tips in favor of employee rights. Conflicts erupt over whose interests should prevail in virtually every area of the work relationship. Our study will reflect that employment law seeks to constantly address the changing needs of workers in our society and the legal and ethical rules that govern the employment relationship.

For all businesses, the prospect of hiring and retaining workers holds both benefits and great risks. Employees present many unique employment issues that employers assume in exchange for the right to control and direct. Employment rights and duties often conflict within the employment context. If a business is found to have improperly treated its workers, it faces potential civil lawsuits for damages and criminal prosecution seeking the imposition of fines, penalties, and tax liability. Violations of discrimination, wage and hour, tax, and other regulatory compliance requirements impose substantial risks upon the employer. In previous years, the greatest source of concern was an individual plaintiff lawsuit or a governmental audit. The biggest risk today in terms of potential financial exposure is a class-action lawsuit brought on behalf of individual workers. We begin with the requirements imposed on employers in the hiring process. We will examine the most commonly encountered issues during the hiring process and the laws relating to them. We will consider how employers can test workers and what should happen upon the termination of an employee.

Recruiting

Complying with a myriad of federal and state laws and regulations to fill an open job position is a daunting task for any employer. In this chapter, we will review the procedures the employer should utilize in hiring personnel. Obtaining employment is an emotionally charged atmosphere. The employer is confronted with considerable risk in this stage of the employment relationship. The applicant begins the job search with excited anticipation that a new opportunity will lead to a better quality of life. The employer is looking for a "good fit" between the requirements of the position and the applicant's qualifications. If not properly managed, the hiring process can expose employers to serious legal risks.

Good employment practices recognize as well the value of the human resource function within the organization and of having a reliable process for filling open employment positions. During the hiring process, employers must exercise good judgment while adhering to ever-changing legal requirements.

Business Planning: When Hiring Begins

Effective organizations develop concrete and measurable goals for their continuing success. By having an identifiable business plan, the owners and managers of a company can identify what it is they wish to accomplish. Every business has the goal of profitably selling a product and/or service to others. Often some invention or other business opportunity will underlie the business purpose. Successful business executives and managers recognize that they must rely on a well-trained, loyal, and enthusiastic workforce to fulfill the mandates of the business plan. They understand that the employees of an organization are one of its most important assets. Recognizing the value of human capital can help a company to compete more effectively in the marketplace. Identifying the employee required to accomplish a particular task is one critical component of a good business plan.

Management must identify the experience and skills needed for the positions to be filled within the organization. Once the job descriptions and functions are completed, the task of recruiting job applicants becomes easier. The strategic goals of the company can be better addressed when management has a clear understanding of how they can be reached through the hiring and retention of an excellent workforce.

There are many sources for locating the appropriate applicant pool. The employer can use a local office of the state employment agency. It can retain the services of a private employment agency that, for a fee, will screen applicants fitting the job description and the needs of the employer. Universities and colleges maintain career-service offices that will provide student interns and graduates with a variety of backgrounds and skill sets. The employers also advertise online or in the traditional classified advertising sections of newspapers, although use of print newspapers for this purpose is in rapid decline.

Applicants may also be sought through word-of-mouth referrals from the business's owners, managers, or current employees. Finally, professional and industry organizations often have publications or other places where job openings may be listed, or they may offer informal opportunities for encounters between potential employers and employees.

Other employee-recruiting options include meeting temporary shortages by hiring workers through a temporary personnel service agency. Finally, elsewhere in the text we will discuss the opportunities presented by hiring an independent contractor in lieu of hiring an employee.

Whatever approach a business takes to finding applicants, it must exercise care to develop procedures that respect the rights of applicants and employees throughout the hiring process. These processes become the first line of defense to any employment and discrimination claims that may arise.

In recent years, the human resources function has grown in importance and responsibility within the business organization. Decades ago, human resource managers were relegated to the status of "first to be hired" at the commencement of operations and "first to be fired" during business declines; they have now become key members of the management team. Talented candidates are available both domestically and internationally, and the modern employer can select from literally thousands of potential applicants using a variety of screening methods. Ensuring that the key legal issues are recognized and properly addressed throughout the hiring process is critically important to turning promising candidates into productive members of the employer's team. When the employer establishes a comprehensive hiring plan as part of its overall business plan, it can promote employee morale and minimize the risks of litigation.

The human resources manager works with senior management to understand the managers' underlying vision and technical needs within the context of core business operations. The human resource department can help the management team to identify the job descriptions, skills, and other attributes of the employees needed for the profitable operation of the business. When business managers work cooperatively with their peers in the human resource department, they build a better employee workforce. Achieving a smooth link between the two functions of production of goods and services and maintenance of human capital is a challenging task, but a worthwhile one: Integrating these functions well creates a more harmonious workforce capable of meeting the challenges presented by multinational competition and soaring raw material and fringe benefit costs.

Hiring employees involves several stages. In the pre-employment planning and interview phase, job-related information is sought from a pool of qualified candidates. Once a candidate is selected, a conditional offer of employment is made. During this time, the employer is able to learn more about the prospective employee. Testing and medical examinations may occur. Disability-related questions may be introduced during this phase to ensure that the individual can perform the essential functions of the position. Every applicant must be required, subject to reasonable accommodations for religion and disability, to take the same screening tests as all other applicants. The third phase is the employee's actual commencement of work with the employer. Now, the employer may pursue disability-related questioning or examinations only if they are job related and a **business necessity**.

Business Necessity Criteria that bear a substantial relationship to job requirements.

Concept Summary
Implementing the Plan

The recruitment process involves soliciting and receiving information regarding applicants and verification of that information. Employers must be careful that they do not elicit or use impermissible information. Access to that information may be prohibited by statute, result in discrimination in employment claims, or intrude into the protected privacy interests of the applicant. In all cases, the employer must not use discriminatory selection methods. The key areas of concern are:

- **Defining the job qualifications and selection criteria** This involves identifying the essential functions of the job so that the employer complies with applicable employment laws relating to disability. In addition, the bona fide **occupational qualifications** for the position must be identified. These qualifications represent the qualities or attributes employers are allowed to consider in their hiring, promotion, and retention decisions about specific applicants or employees (e.g., level of experience or education, ability to speak a foreign language, or familiarity with a particular industry).
- **Recruiting**
- **Interviewing applicants**
- **References, background checks, testing, and post-offer medical examinations**

Defining the Job Qualifications

Just as employees may not be subjected to unlawful discrimination, applicants within protected classes are equally protected from discriminatory selection processes. Proving discrimination in the hiring process can be difficult. Courts and government agencies enforcing discrimination laws and regulations look to the qualifications of the rejected applicants from protected classes and statistical evidence establishing the exclusion of protected class members.

Hiring standards that set unjustifiable standards for minority, female, or other groups protected by federal, state, or local discrimination laws and regulations are illegal. As we shall study within the law of equal opportunity, the source of much of this protection for these individuals springs from Title VII of the Civil Rights Act of 1964.[2] However, an employer will be justified and legally excused from adhering to these employee rights if the employer can establish that the hiring criteria used bear a substantial relationship to the job requirements. This defense is known as the **business-necessity** test.

As enacted in 1964, Title VII held employers liable only for **disparate treatment**. The act makes it unlawful for an employer "to fail or refuse to hire or to discharge any individual, or otherwise discriminate against any individual with respect to his compensation, terms, conditions, or privileges of employment, because of such individual's race, color, religion, sex, or national origin."[3] A **disparate treatment** plaintiff must show that the defendant has a discriminatory intent or motive for taking a job-related action. These terms will be studied in Chapter 4, but at this point, we consider them as part of the employee selection process. In the following case, the Court interpreted Title VII to prohibit, in some cases, employers' neutral practices that are

Title VII
Section of the Civil Rights Act of 1964 that pertains to discrimination in employment on the basis of race, color, national origin, sex, and religion. This federal law prohibits most workplace discrimination and harassment. It covers employers, state and local governments, and educational institutions with 15 or more employees. Later amendments have been enacted to protect against discrimination because of pregnancy, sex stereotyping, and sexual harassment of employees.

Disparate Treatment
Discrimination that occurs when an individual is intentionally treated less favorably than are others because of his or her race, color, sex, religion, national origin, age, or disability.

"discriminatory in operation." The *Griggs* court held that the "touchstone" for **disparate impact** liability is the lack of **"business necessity"** for those practices.

Disparate Impact
Discrimination that occurs when a facially neutral selection standard disqualifies particular races or groups at a significantly higher rate than it does other races or groups and that is not justified by a business necessity.

CASE 2.1

THE BUSINESS NECESSITY OF HIRING CRITERIA IS NARROWLY CONSTRUED

GRIGGS V. DUKE POWER CO.

401 U.S. 424 (1971)

Supreme Court of the United States

Facts. Willie Griggs filed a class action lawsuit against his employer, Duke Power Company, on behalf of himself and similarly situated African American employees. He challenged the "inside" transfer policy that required employees who wanted to work in all but the lowest paying jobs to obtain a minimum score on two separate aptitude tests as well to have a high school diploma. He contended that Duke's practices unlawfully discriminated against black employees in violation of Title VII. His employer defended the practice as being a business necessity for the safety of employees and the public, since the work was conducted at a power plant. Duke Power maintained a practice of not requiring the high school education for white employees in departments that had been previously populated only by whites. The district court dismissed Griggs's claim, and the federal court of appeals affirmed that decision. The Supreme Court granted *certiorari.*

Issue. Did Duke Power Company's internal transfer policy requiring a high school education and certain minimum aptitude test scores violate Title VII of the 1964 Civil Rights Act when neither standard is related to job performance?

Language of the Court. C.J. Burger: **We granted the writ in this case to resolve the question whether an employer is prohibited by the Civil Rights Act of 1964, Title VII, from requiring a high school education or passing of a standardized general intelligence test as a condition of employment in or transfer to jobs when (a) neither standard is shown to be significantly related to successful job performance, (b) both requirements operate to disqualify Negroes at a substantially higher rate than white applicants, and (c) the jobs in question formerly had been filled only by white employees as part of a longstanding practice of giving preference to whites.**

Congress did not intend by Title VII, however, to guarantee a job to every person regardless of qualifications. In short, the Act does not command that any person

be hired simply because he was formerly the subject of discrimination, or because he is a member of a minority group. Discriminatory preference for any group, minority or majority, is precisely and only what Congress has proscribed. What is required by Congress is the removal of artificial, arbitrary, and unnecessary barriers to employment when the barriers operate invidiously to discriminate on the basis of racial or other impermissible classification.

The Act proscribes not only overt discrimination but also practices that are fair in form, but discriminatory in operation. The touchstone is business necessity. If an employment practice which operates to exclude Negroes cannot be shown to be related to job performance, the practice is prohibited.

The evidence, however, shows that employees who have not completed high school or taken the tests have continued to perform satisfactorily and make progress in departments for which the high school and test criteria are now used. The promotion record of present employees who would not be able to meet the new criteria thus suggests the possibility that the requirements may not be needed even for the limited purpose of preserving the avowed policy of advancement within the Company. In the context of this case, it is unnecessary to reach the question whether testing requirements that take into account capability for the next succeeding position or related future promotion might be utilized upon a showing that such long-range requirements fulfill a genuine business need. In the present case the Company has made no such showing.

The Company's lack of discriminatory intent is suggested by special efforts to help the undereducated employees through Company financing of two-thirds the cost of tuition for high school training. But Congress directed the thrust of the Act to the consequences of employment practices, not simply the motivation. More than that, Congress has placed on the employer the burden of showing that any given requirement must have a manifest relationship to the employment in question.

The facts of this case demonstrate the inadequacy of broad and general testing devices as well as the infirmity of using diplomas or degrees as fixed measures of capability. History is filled with examples of men and women who rendered highly effective performance without the conventional badges of accomplishment in terms of certificates, diplomas, or degrees. Diplomas and tests are useful servants, but Congress has mandated the commonsense proposition that they are not to become masters of reality.

Decision. Yes. The employer could not establish that its discriminatory hiring criteria was necessary to job performance.

CASE QUESTIONS

Critical Legal Thinking. The Supreme Court held that the effect of the employer's actions and not its intent was controlling. Do you agree with that result and why?

Business Ethics. What should be required of a business to demonstrate that such tests are "reasonably related" to the position for which the test is required?

Contemporary Business. Should the same business necessity standards be applied to the small business enterprise as they would to large, publicly traded companies?

Nothing in the Civil Rights Act precludes the use of testing or measuring procedures; obviously, they are useful. What Congress has forbidden is giving these devices and mechanisms controlling force unless they are demonstrably a reasonable measure of job performance. Congress has not commanded that the less qualified be preferred over the better qualified simply because of minority origins. Far from disparaging job qualifications as such, Congress has made such qualifications the controlling factor so that race, religion, nationality, and sex become irrelevant. What Congress has commanded is that all selection procedures must measure the person for the job and not the person in the abstract.

Under the **business-necessity** test, once a worker initially proves that he or she has been discriminated against in violation of a discrimination statute, the employer may then show that the job qualification is a **business necessity**. Following that proof, the worker can try to show that the employer is using a pretextual reason for its actions against the worker. The employer may employ selection criteria that, although neutral in their application, exclude members of one or more protected classifications of persons at a higher rate than other groups because the employer can establish that the hiring standard is actually a **business necessity**.

Management Application
Employer Restraints in Hiring, Promotion, and Termination

The following is a short summary of the many federal and state statutes describing qualities, attributes, or circumstances that limit an employer's right to hire, promote, and terminate workers in a discriminatory fashion. Each of these will be discussed in detail in the next few chapters of our study:

- contractual provisions in an employment contract
- race, color, national origin, or ancestry
- sex (a.k.a. gender), including pregnancy, childbirth, and gender identity
- age over 40
- physical or mental disability
- religion
- union or other concerted activity
- antiretaliation and whistleblower statutes
- protection afforded under leave of absence statutes
- other important public policies which restrain such actions

To be effective, an employer's procedures for disciplining and terminating employees should incorporate the following:

- properly defined job descriptions specifying job-related requirements;

- clearly identified measurements of successful performance in the job position;
- management's reserved right to deviate from the guidelines in exceptional circumstances;
- notification of all employees of the rules that can lead to discipline or termination and the consequences of not following those rules;
- fair and complete performance evaluations on a periodic basis (evaluations should utilize objective, rather than subjective, standards and characteristics of the employee performance desired, and evaluators should be trained and should attend performance reviews as they occur);
- complete and confidential records relating to employees;
- means to protect the integrity of internal employee investigations;
- consistent actions taken with respect to employees (ensure all documentation is in place to justify an immediate decision, such as termination of employment);
- mechanisms to provide employees the opportunity to discuss performance reviews with managers or to appeal any adverse actions taken against them (ensure the employee's version of the facts has been taken into consideration); and
- agreement among all participating managers, supervisors, and human resource team members on any adverse action taken against an employee.

Employee Selection Criteria

As will be discussed more fully in the chapter on employment litigation and Equal Employment Opportunity Commission (EEOC) procedure, the law frequently targets two basic types of employment discrimination: discrimination related to **disparate treatment** (distinctions between two equally qualified individuals because of a legally protected characteristic, such as race or gender), and **disparate impact** (distinctions between two equally qualified individuals based on anything other than productivity). These principles dictate that employers must be aware of the consequences of making distinctions among applicants and employees regarding the following criteria.

Preferring Citizens over Noncitizens

An employer may not discriminate against a person because of their national origin; lack of United States' citizenship; status as an alien lawfully admitted to the United States; or status as a refugee. These rights are protected under federal law as part of the Immigration Reform and Control Act of 1986 (IRCA)[4] and various state statutes. It is illegal for an employer to knowingly recruit for employment or to hire applicants who are unauthorized aliens or to continue to employ them once that status is known. However, it is legal to prefer a citizen or national of the United States to another who is an alien if they are equally qualified.[5] However, the employer may not adopt a blanket policy of always selecting citizens over noncitizens. IRCA covers three subjects: employment verification and antidiscrimination provisions relating to noncitizenship status; legal recognition of certain alien classes; and agricultural worker reforms. For those in specialty occupations needed for the American economy, a temporary or permanent work authorization to remain in the United States can be obtained by applying for an H-1B visa.

Age as a Criterion

Absent a bona fide business purpose, use of age as a hiring criterion is unlawful under the Age Discrimination in Employment Act of 1967 (ADEA).[6] Employment selection practices with respect to physical fitness and other such qualifications must be justified by legitimate factors unrelated to age. In *EEOC v. Massachusetts*,[7] the Court of Appeals for the First Circuit held that a Massachusetts state law requiring state and local government employees over the age of 70 to pass annual physical examinations as a condition of continued employment violated the ADEA. The court held the state law was "not reconcilable with the plain purpose of [the ADEA], which prohibits employers from discrimination against any individual with respect to his compensation, terms, conditions, or privileges of employment, because of such individual's age." Massachusetts was unable to demonstrate that its law was based on "reasonable factors other than age."

Credit History

Selection of applicants based on their credit histories may have a **disparate impact** on minority applicants. The employer must establish a direct relationship to job performance, and the inquiry must be related to job performance. Credit and background investigative reports are governed by the **Fair Credit Reporting Act**.[8] Bankruptcy, once an absolute bar to securing certain employment positions, is now unlawful as a basis for disqualifying applicants who have sought bankruptcy protection.[9]

Fair Credit Reporting Act
A federal law regulating entities that collect and disseminate credit and background investigative reports, including those of job applicants and employees.

Grooming, Weight, and Height Standards

An employer may set reasonable grooming standards that promote a business purpose. Wide latitude is given to employers who establish nonoffensive standards. Courts are reluctant to interfere in the exercise of the employer's grooming standards as long as they are based on actual job requirements. A no-beard policy may be unlawful under Title VII as racial discrimination because a substantial percentage of African American men suffer from pseudofolliculitis barbae, which makes shaving painful and difficult. To enforce such a policy would potentially exclude from employment a significant portion of the male African American workforce. In *Barnes v. City of Cincinnati*,[10] the Sixth Circuit Court of Appeals ruled that it was actionable sex discrimination under Title VII to discriminate against someone for failing to conform to gender norms. Thus, appearance-standard requirements should not include stereotyping based on perceived gender norms.

Employers must also be careful to avoid the use of discriminate height and weight standards in selecting employees. Such criteria may have a **disparate impact** on certain protected classes. In the following case, the Supreme Court considered whether an employer must prove a **"business necessity"** for height and weight requirements that have a **disparate impact** on women.

CASE 2.2

HEIGHT AND WEIGHT REQUIREMENTS MUST BE A BUSINESS NECESSITY IF THEY RESULT IN DISPARATE IMPACT UPON PROTECTED CLASSES OF PERSONS

DOTHARD V. RAWLINSON

433 U.S. 321 (1977)

Supreme Court of the United States

Facts. Dianne Rawlinson sought employment with the Alabama Board of Corrections as a prison guard, referred to as a "correctional counselor." At the time she applied for a position as correctional counselor trainee, Rawlinson was a 22-year-old college graduate whose major course of study had been correctional psychology. The state refused to hire Rawlinson because she failed to meet the minimum 120-pound weight requirement established by an Alabama statute. The statute also established a height minimum of 5 feet 2 inches. Ultimately, Rawlinson sued, alleging that she had been denied employment because of her sex, in violation of federal law. A three-judge federal district court ruled in her favor. The Board of Corrections for the state of Alabama appealed to the U.S. Supreme Court, which granted *certiorari.*

Issue. Could an employer screen applicants based upon their height and weight as a business necessity for a job position, even though the requirement had a disparate impact upon women?

Language of the Court. Steward, J: **Like most correctional facilities in the United States, Alabama's prisons are segregated on the basis of sex. Currently the Alabama Board of Corrections operates four major all-male penitentiaries. The Board also operates the Julia Tutwiler Prison for Women, the Frank Lee Youth Center, the Number Four Honor Camp, the State Cattle Ranch, and nine Work Release Centers, one of which is for women. The Julia Tutwiler Prison for Women and the four male penitentiaries are maximum-security institutions. Their inmate living quarters are for the most part large dormitories, with communal showers and toilets that are open to the dormitories and hallways. The Draper and Fountain penitentiaries carry on extensive farming operations, making necessary a large number of strip searches for contraband when prisoners re-enter the prison buildings.**

A correctional counselor's primary duty within these institutions is to maintain security and control of the inmates by continually supervising and observing their activities. To be eligible for consideration as a correctional counselor, an applicant must possess a valid Alabama driver's license, have a high school education or its equivalent, be free from physical defects, be between the ages of 20 1/2 years and 45 years at the time of appointment, and fall between the minimum height and weight requirements of 5 feet 2 inches, and 120 pounds, and the maximum of 6 feet 10 inches, and 300 pounds. Appointment is by merit, with a grade assigned each applicant based on experience and education. No written examination is given.

The gist of the claim that the statutory height and weight requirements discriminate against women does not involve an assertion of purposeful discriminatory motive, rather, that these facially neutral qualification standards work in fact disproportionately to exclude women from eligibility for employment by the Alabama Board of Corrections. We dealt in *Griggs v. Duke Power Co.*, supra, and *Albemarle Paper Co. v. Moody*, 422 U.S. 405, with similar allegations that facially neutral employment standards disproportionately excluded Negroes from employment and those cases guide our approach here.

Those cases make clear that to establish a prima facie case of discrimination, a plaintiff need only show that the facially neutral standards in question select applicants for hire in a significantly discriminatory pattern. Once it is thus shown that the employment standards are discriminatory in effect, the employer must meet "the burden of showing that any given requirement [has] . . . a manifest relationship to the employment in question." (citing Griggs) If the employer proves that the challenged requirements are job related, the plaintiff may then show that other selection devices without a similar discriminatory effect would also "serve the employer's legitimate interest in 'efficient and trustworthy workmanship.'" (Citation omitted.)

Although women 14 years of age or older compose 52.75% of the Alabama population and 36.89% of its total labor force, they hold only 12.9% of its correctional counselor positions. In considering the effect of the minimum height and weight standards on this disparity in rate of hiring between the sexes, the District Court found that the 5'2" requirement would operate to exclude 33.29% of the women in the United States between the ages of 18-79, while excluding only 1.28% of men between the same ages. The 120-pound weight restriction would exclude 22.29% of the women and 2.35% of the men in this age group. When the height and weight restrictions are combined, Alabama's statutory standards would exclude 41.13% of the female population while excluding less than 1% of the male population. Accordingly, the District Court found that Rawlinson had made out a prima facie case of unlawful sex discrimination.

We turn, therefore, to the appellants' argument that they have rebutted the prima facie case of discrimination by showing that the height and weight requirements are job related. In the District Court, however, the appellants produced no evidence correlating the height and weight requirements with the requisite amount of strength thought essential to good job performance.

Indeed, they failed to offer evidence of any kind in specific justification of the statutory standards. If the job-related quality that the appellants identify is bona fide, their purpose could be achieved by adopting and validating a test for applicants that measures strength directly. Such a test, fairly administered, would fully satisfy the standards of Title VII because it would be one that "measure[s] the person for the job and not the person in the abstract." *Griggs v. Duke Power Co.*, 401 U.S., at 436. But nothing in the present record even approaches such a measurement.

Decision. Yes. Height and weight standards could be a business necessity, but the employer failed to establish this fact. If such standards are utilized, they must be job related and applied in an equal manner between the sexes.

CASE QUESTIONS

Critical Legal Thinking. Would the result have been different if the state would have been able to demonstrate the business necessity for the height and weight minima?

Business Ethics. Should we consider the effect on the prisoners' privacy rights when they are searched by guards of the opposite sex?

Contemporary Business. What would have been a better test for the state to employ in screening applicants? What criteria would you propose that the State of Alabama use in future selection procedures in light of this decision?

Management Application
Job References

Former employees or prospective new employers often request employment references. Job references often evoke defamation lawsuits. Companies should follow specific protocols with respect to employment references. This is particularly important when the employee was terminated for cause. Some companies now refuse to provide a reference; however, if a company elects to provide them, the following guidelines should be observed:

- Never respond to oral requests for information.
- Ensure that the subject of the inquiry has given written permission for your company to supply a reference and that the request for information is within the limits of that consent. The permission form should specifically state what information may be given to the outsider.
- Only verifiable facts should be provided, and opinions and conclusions as to employee performance should be avoided. Seemingly innocent responses to such questions as "Is

this person eligible for rehire?" can provoke litigation.

- Include favorable facts as much as possible to mitigate the probability of a lawsuit. The converse is also true, in that references describing only strengths but omitting any factually accurate negative assessments may expose the employer to liability.
- Permit only designated individuals within the company to respond to requests for references. Do not allow line supervisors to issue references. Direct the request to the human resources department.
- Ensure that personnel files are up-to-date and accurate.
- Finally, be accurate and truthful in the reference statements. Any misrepresentation that prevents the ex-employee from obtaining employment can subject the employer to compensatory and punitive damage claims from the ex-employee. In addition, courts recognize that an employer's negligent references for an ex-employee to a successor employer may subject the original employer to tort liability for harm created if the ex-employee commits a serious crime or wrongdoing at the new employer's location.

CASE 2.3

REQUIRING EMPLOYEES TO BE CLEAN-SHAVEN MAY BE DISCRIMINATORY

BRADLEY V. PIZZACO OF NEBRASKA, INC. DBA DOMINO'S PIZZA

7 F.3d 795 (8th Cir. 1993), *Cert. Denied* 502 U.S. 1057

U.S. Court of Appeals for the Eighth Circuit

Facts. Langston Bradley, a former Domino's Pizza deliveryman, alleged that the pizza chain discriminated against him because of race when it fired him for failure to appear clean-shaven in compliance with the franchisor's no-beard policy. He alleged that he suffered from *pseudofolliculitis barbae*, a skin condition affecting approximately 50 percent of African American males, half of whom cannot shave at all. He claimed that the no-beard policy deprived him and others similarly situated of equal employment opportunities in violation of Title VII of the Civil Rights Act of 1964.

Issue. Does the employer have the right to enforce a clean-shaven grooming policy if the enforcement of such policy has a disparate impact on a protected class?

Language of the Court. Bowman, J: The 1991 [Civil Rights] Act expressly reinstated the law of "business justification" . . . Under the Griggs standard, the burden is on the defendant employer to prove both a "compelling need" for the challenged policy, and the lack of an effective alternative policy that would not produce a similar disparate impact. (Citations omitted.)

The EEOC contends that the record conclusively demonstrates that Domino's has failed to show business justification under Griggs for its inflexible no-beard policy and that we need not remand to the District Court for a determination of that issue. We agree.

[T]he burden is on Domino's to show a substantial business justification for its strict no-beard policy. This burden is a heavy one. (Citation omitted.) Domino's must show "a manifest relationship to the employment in question." (Citations omitted.) Domino's must also show a "compelling need . . . to maintain that practice . . . and that there is no alternative to the challenged practice." (Citations omitted.)

Domino's offered the testimony of Paul D. Black, Domino's vice president for operations. Black said it was "common sense" that "the better our people look, the better our sales will be." Black also cited a public opinion survey indicating that up to twenty percent of customers would "have a negative reaction" to a delivery person wearing a beard. Further, Black speculated that Domino's would encounter difficulty enforcing any exceptions to their dress and grooming code. Black did not offer evidence of any particular exception that was tried without success; rather, he merely stated that monitoring the hair length and moustaches of employees at five thousand Domino's locations is difficult.

Black's testimony was largely speculative and conclusory. Such testimony, without more, does not prove the business necessity of maintaining the strict no-beard policy. See Hawkins, 697 F.2d at 815 ("An employer cannot rely on purely conclusory testimony by company personnel to prove that a [challenged practice] is job-related and required by business necessity.").

In addition to Black's testimony, Domino's offered the results of a public opinion survey it commissioned. The survey purported to measure public reaction to beards on pizza shop employees. The survey showed that up to twenty percent of those surveyed would react negatively to a deliveryman wearing a beard.

Although this Circuit has not directly addressed customer preference as a business justification for policies having a disparate impact on a protected class, cases from other circuits have not looked favorably on this kind of evidence. . . . (Customer preference may only be taken into account when it goes to a matter affecting the company's ability to perform the primary necessary function or service it offers, rather than a tangential aspect of that

service or function), cert. denied, (citations omitted) (holding that customer preference for slim female flight attendants did not justify a discriminatory policy where weight was unrelated to job performance), (citation omitted). The existence of a beard on the face of a deliveryman does not affect in any manner Domino's ability to make or deliver pizzas to their customers. Customer preference, which is at best weakly shown by Domino's survey, is clearly not a colorable business justification defense in this case. Significantly, the survey makes no showing that customers would order less pizza in the absence of a strictly enforced no-beard rule.

Domino's . . . has failed to prove a compelling need for the strict no-beard policy as applied to those afflicted with PFB and has failed to present any evidence suggesting that the current policy is without workable alternatives or that it has a manifest relationship to the employment in question. . . . Domino's is free to establish any grooming and dress standards it wishes; we hold only that reasonable accommodation must be made for members of the protected class who suffer from PFB. We note that the burden of a narrow medical exception for African American males who cannot shave because of PFB appears minimal. The employer, of course, should not be precluded from requiring that any beards permitted under this narrow medical exception be neatly trimmed, clean, and not in excess of a specified length.

Decision. No. An employer may not enforce a no-beard policy if it has a disparate impact on certain protected employees if the policy cannot be sustained as a business necessity.

CASE QUESTIONS

Critical Legal Thinking. In the absence of an adverse impact on a protected group of employees, to what degree should an employer's personal preferences control employment decisions?

Business Ethics. Do you think it is fair to hold an employer liable for damages when changing societal norms might find the activity not as offensive at a later point in time (e.g., the increasing use of profanity in the workplace)?

Contemporary Business. Can you think of any jobs that would require by their nature a clean-shaven appearance?

Management Application
The Meaning of Business Necessity

Employers often seek to utilize a BFOQ (bona fide occupational qualification) or a business necessity for the characteristics they seek in their employees. For these qualifications to be legal, they must:

- relate to the essence of the business operation (*Diaz v. Pan American World Airways, Inc.*, 442 F.2d 385 (5th Cir. 1971): requiring flight attendants to be female was not essential to the operation of the business or to the job of flight attendant);
- not be justified by mere cost savings (*Smallwood v. United Airlines, Inc.*, 661 F.2d 303 (4th Cir. 1981): held as illegal discrimination an airline's maximum hiring age of 35 for pilots because the "period of peak productivity" would be extended);
- not be based upon paternalistic motives (*Intl. Union, UAW v. Johnson Controls*, 499 U.S. 187 (1991): Court held as discriminatory a fetal protection policy that excluded fertile women, but not fertile men, from positions involving lead exposure);
- not be based solely upon customer preference (*Olsen v. Marriott International, Inc.*, 75 F. Supp. 1052 (D. Ariz. 1999): hotel chain could not prove that being female was a BFOQ for massage therapist positions; customer preferences will not support a BFOQ); and
- respect privacy considerations (*Hernandez v. Univ. of St. Thomas*, 793 F. Supp. 214 (D. Mn. 1992): 72-year-old male denied opportunity to be custodian in an all-women's dormitory; the scope of such privacy considerations is an open, undefined issue).

Recruiting and Interviewing

Job searches can begin with word-of-mouth referrals or with other traditional information sources, such as newspaper want ads, employment agencies, and union hiring halls. An employer is not required to use any particular method to attract applicants. In fact, using a variety of channels to attract a diverse workforce is the most appropriate method.

Advertising and Section 704(b) of Title VII of the Civil Rights Act of 1964

Section 704 of the CRA states in part:

> It shall be an unlawful employment practice for an employer, labor organization, employment agency, or joint labor-management committee controlling apprenticeship or other training or retraining including on-the-job training programs, to print or publish or cause to be printed or published any notice or advertisement relating to employment by such an employer or membership . . . indicating any preference, limitation, specification, or discrimination, based on race, color, religion, sex, or national origin, except that such a notice or advertisement may indicate a preference, limitation, specification or discrimination

based on religion, sex, or national origin when religion, sex, or national origin is a bona fide occupational qualification for employment.

With the enactment of the Civil Rights Act of 1964, discriminatory classified advertising was prohibited. Although those placing the ads, such as employers and unions, would clearly violate Title VII of that Act by placing discriminatory advertising, the offending newspaper publishers are not liable because Title VII does not apply to the disseminators of the discriminatory advertising. The discriminatory advertising of one employer can create liability for another if an applicant was discouraged from applying because the applicant was rejected from the first position.

In the 1972 case of *Hailes v. United Air Lines*,[11] a male applicant had been rejected from a "stewardess" position with the airline when he responded to a "help wanted—female" advertisement. When United Airlines ran a similar ad, he was successful in his Title VII suit against United because he was able to show that he was deterred from applying due to the improper advertising. Newspaper or online advertising must not include statements that apply to protected classes more often than to the general population or include wording that indicates age, gender, sex, or reference to another protected classification (under both federal and applicable state law).

An employer may require that applicants have certain educational attainments or licenses if those are needed for the position. In certain situations, employers may insist that job applicants be free of criminal records. The **business necessity** requirements of each position must be carefully evaluated before placing advertisements. The EEOC permits job applicants to be asked their race, sex, and national origin only if it is done pursuant to the employer's efforts toward affirmative action.

Advertisements should be phrased to avoid creating contractual liability for the employer. They should be worded as neutrally as possible. They should avoid using such phrases as "looking for long term position," "job security," and "best compensation package in the industry." Advertisements that specify sex, race, religion, age, national origin, disability, or information relating to these characteristics invite invasion of privacy and employment discrimination claims.

Internet-Applicant Rule
A requirement that federal contractors who accept employment applications submitted electronically retain records on any applicant meeting these four criteria: the applicant expresses interest in a position through the Internet; the contractor considers the person for employment; the person appears to be qualified for the position; and the individual does not withdraw from consideration for employment.

Internet Advertising

The Office of Federal Contract Compliance Programs (OFCCP) within the U.S. Department of Labor issued a rule in 2006 that that office will use to enhance its enforcement of nondiscrimination requirements in federal contracting. Under this rule, an Internet applicant is defined as any individual who satisfies the following criteria: the person submits an expression of interest in employment through the Internet or related electronic technology; the federal contractor considers the person for employment; the person's expression of interest indicates that the person is qualified for the position; and the individual at no point up to receiving an employment offer from the contractor withdraws from consideration of employment.

In general, the **Internet-applicant rule** states:

- a federal contractor must solicit demographic information about Internet applicants (race, gender, and ethnicity data) and retain records relating to hiring done through the use of the Internet; and
- a federal contractor may be compelled to produce adverse impact analyses it has done pursuant to the Uniform Guidelines on Employee Selection Procedures.

In light of the information that the OFCCP secures from federal contracting employers, the OFCCP compares the proportion of women and minorities in the contractor's Internet applicant pool with labor force statistics or other data on the percentages of women and minorities in the relevant labor force to evaluate the impact of required qualifications. If a significant difference is found, the OFCCP will investigate further as to whether the contractor's recruitment and hiring practices conform with E.O. 11246 standards.

> ***Example:*** A contractor initially searches an external job database with 50,000 job seekers for three basic qualifications for a bilingual emergency room nursing supervisor job (a four-year nursing degree, state certification as an RN, and fluency in English and Spanish). The initial screen for the first three basic qualifications narrows the pool to 10,000. The contractor then adds a fourth preestablished basic qualification — three years of emergency room nursing experience — which narrows the pool to 1,000. Finally, the contractor adds a fifth pre-established basic qualification — two years of supervisory experience — which results in a pool of 75 job seekers. Under the Internet applicant rule, only the 75 job seekers meeting all five basic qualifications would be Internet applicants, assuming the other three prongs of the "Internet applicant" definition were met.

Nothing in this process prevents the employer from using additional lawful testing in furtherance of the hiring process.[12]

The EEOC had a proposed rule on Internet applications but decided in 2008 not to finalize it. The agency was unable to agree with two other federal agencies on how to define an Internet applicant. As a result, employers would be well advised to adopt and consistently apply a procedure similar to that required by the OFCCP.

Focus on Ethics
Internet Job Postings

In all cases, an employer must not be lulled into a false sense of security that the ease of Internet advertising exempts the employer from complying with the law. Some Internet websites do not impose any requirements on employers posting job openings. Take a few moments to review advertising posting on Craigslist .org, for example, and determine how many listings would violate the laws covered so far, as they apply to employee recruitment. Do you recognize as discriminating against people with physical or mental disabilities those ads that use such phrases as "must operate 10-key by touch" or "typing skills minimum of 40 words per minute"?

Rehabilitated Drug and Alcohol Abusers

Embracing the rehabilitation of former drug and alcohol abusers, the Americans with Disabilities Act (ADA)[13] prohibits certain forms of discrimination. An employer may refuse to hire an applicant because of his or her current use of alcohol, illegal drugs, or illicitly used prescription medications. An employer may not discriminate against an individual under any of the following circumstances: the individual participates in a supervised rehabilitation program and no longer engages in drug or alcohol abuse; the individual has successfully rehabilitated from past drug abuse and no longer engages in such abuse; or the individual was erroneously regarded by the employer as someone who was or is engaged in illegal drug use.

The ADA provides that persons who are "currently engaged in the illegal use of drugs" are excluded from the definition of a "qualified individual with disability." Thus, an employer may conduct a drug test for the current use of illegal drugs before making an offer of employment.

Education

All educational requirements must be scrutinized for their **disparate impact** on minorities under the Supreme Court's holding in *Griggs*.

English Fluency

Level of oral communication skills must be reasonably related to job performance if it is considered during the hiring process. Rules requiring use in the workplace of English only do not necessarily violate Title VII, and reference should be made, as always, to state and local laws. Nevertheless, the EEOC has issued Guidelines on Discrimination Because of National Origin in which the Commission presumes that a blanket "English-only" rule violates Title VII, while a less restrictive practice may be justified by a legitimate **business necessity**. Many federal courts do not place much weight upon this particular EEOC policy.

Human Resource Form
Integration Clause

In extending an offer to an applicant, the employer should always confirm the offer in a written letter to the applicant and request that the applicant read, sign, and return the letter to the employer. The employer will include what lawyers call an integration clause to protect it from any potential misunderstandings with the applicant accepting the offer. A sample integration clause would read as follows:

This letter confirms our mutual agreement as to the complete terms and conditions of your employment. You acknowledge and agree no oral or written promise, term, or condition of employment has been made to you to induce you to accept this offer of employment except for those items stated in this letter.

Physical Requirements

The ADA, which applies to employers with 15 or more employees, prohibits using qualification standards, employment tests, or other selection criteria that tend to screen out disabled individuals, unless the standard, test, or criterion is related to the position in question and is consistent with business necessity.[14] Even if these criteria are job-related, the employer must consider whether the individual could meet the requirements with reasonable accommodation.

Employers may require as a qualification standard that an individual not pose a direct threat to health or safety in the workplace. Furthermore, an employer may not limit, segregate, or classify a job applicant or an employee in a way that adversely affects the status or opportunities of that applicant or employee because of his or her disability. For example, an employer cannot require that the only new employees who must pass a probationary period are those who are disabled.

> ***Example:*** An employer asks an applicant whether he can perform a particular job function, and, in answering the inquiry, the applicant states that he has multiple sclerosis. At this point, the employer has not made a prohibited pre-offer inquiry. However, while continuing the pre-offer process, the employer may not then ask the applicant questions about his multiple sclerosis, such as "How debilitating is your multiple sclerosis?" "Does it limit your ability to work?" or "Do you expect your condition to get worse?"[15]

Veterans or Military Status

Employers may use an applicant's status as a veteran or active duty service member as a factor in employee selection or may give special preference to veterans without recrimination. However, employers may not discriminate against those who received other than an honorable discharge when making hiring, firing, or other employment-related decisions.

Improper Interview Questions

Interview questions must be job related and must follow the same guidelines used in advertising for a position. The interview questions must be justified by the employer in view of the position to be filled. Questions should focus on whether the applicant has the right education, training, and skills for the position; whether he or she can satisfy the job's requirements or essential functions (after they are described to the applicant); how much time off the applicant took in a previous job (but not why); the reason the applicant left a previous position; and the nature of disciplinary episodes during previous employment. Requesting or using the following information while making hiring decisions is usually impermissible:

- Arrest history
- Credit rating history or history of garnishments
- Availability to work on Saturdays and Sundays
- Physical or mental impairments (or how the applicant became disabled)
- Use of medication
- Prior workers' compensation history
- Whether childcare will be a problem

Word-of-Mouth Advertising and Nepotism

Referring friends and acquaintances to a potential employer by word of mouth need not be a discriminatory practice. It is often the most effective and cheapest way of attracting prospective applicants who already know of the employer's expectations through their contact with the current employee. Despite its advantages, when minorities are significantly underrepresented in a workforce, the employer's undue reliance on word-of-mouth recruiting can be evidence of intentional discrimination. Several cases have held that when word-of-mouth hiring is the employer's primary means of recruiting and results in a predominately Caucasian workforce, discrimination can be presumed.

In *NAACP v. Corinth,*[16] a U.S. District Court held that a case of **disparate treatment** discrimination could be proved through statistical evidence coupled with the fact that job vacancies were announced only through word of mouth to potential applicants. The 1975 federal appellate decision in *Barnett v. W.T. Grant Co.*[17] involved the recruiting of over-the-road drivers for a trucking company. Despite the advantages of ensuring that good drivers would seek to attract equally qualified employees to the company, the appeals court rejected word-of-mouth recruiting as the primary means of filling open positions. The court condemned such hiring as discriminatory because it tended to perpetuate an all-white workforce.

These decisions show that employers must avoid heavy reliance on word-of-mouth advertising for new applicants. If it is only one of several means used to attract candidates, the courts are more lenient in permitting it. For example, when an employer uses a variety of means, including word of mouth, and a large number of African Americans apply and are hired, such methods are permissible.

CASE 2.4

WORD OF MOUTH ADVERTISING MAY BE PERMITTED WITHIN ETHNIC MINORITY COMMUNITIES

EEOC V. CONSOLIDATED SERVICE SYSTEMS

989 F.2d 233 (7th Cir. 1993)

U.S. Court of Appeals for the Seventh Circuit

Facts. The EEOC appealed the dismissal of its case against Consolidated Service Systems, a Chicago janitorial and cleaning service owned by a Korean immigrant. Mr. Hwang had purchased the company in 1983 from another Korean immigrant. The Commission charged that Hwang discriminated in favor of persons of Korean origin in violation of Title VII of the Civil Rights Act of 1964 by relying mainly on word of mouth to fill his open job positions. Because of his efforts, 81 percent of his new employees were Korean, even though only 1 percent of the Chicago area workforce was Korean.

Issue. Does an employer's reliance upon word-of-mouth referrals in its hiring practices constitute discrimination under Title VII?

Language of the Court. Posner, C.J.: . . . The Equal Employment Opportunity Commission brought this suit in 1985 against a small company, which provides janitorial and cleaning services at a number of buildings in the Chicago area. The owner of the company is a Korean immigrant, as are most of its employees. The suit charges that the company discriminated in favor of persons of Korean origin, in violation of Title VII of the Civil Rights Act of 1964, 42 U.S.C. §2000e et seq., by relying mainly on word of mouth to obtain new employees. After a bench trial, the district judge dismissed the suit on the ground that the Commission had failed to prove discrimination. . . . Between 1983, when Mr. Hwang, the company's owner, bought the company from its previous owner, also a Korean, and the first quarter of 1987, 73 percent of the applicants for jobs with Consolidated, and 81 percent of the hires, were Korean. Less than 1 percent of the work force in Cook County is Korean and at most 3 percent of the janitorial and cleaner work force. It doesn't take a statistician to tell you that the difference between the percentage of Koreans in Consolidated's work force and the percentage of Koreans in the relevant labor market, however exactly that market is defined, is not due to chance. But is it due to discrimination? The district judge found it was not, and we do not think his finding was clearly erroneous.

Consolidated is a small company. The EEOC's lawyer told us at argument that the company's annual sales are only $400,000. We mention this fact not to remind the reader of David and Goliath, or to suggest that Consolidated is exempt from Title VII (it is not) or to express wonderment that a firm of this size could litigate in federal court for seven years (and counting) with a federal agency, but to explain why Mr. Hwang relies on word of mouth to obtain employees rather than reaching out to a broader community less heavily Korean. It is the cheapest method of recruitment. Indeed, it is practically costless. Persons approach Hwang or his employees — most of whom are Korean too — at work or at social events, and once or twice Hwang has asked employees whether they know anyone who wants a job.

If an employer can obtain all the competent workers he wants, at wages no higher than the minimum that he expects to have to pay, without beating the bushes for workers — without in fact spending a cent on recruitment — he can reduce his costs of doing business by adopting just the stance of Mr. Hwang. No inference of intentional discrimination can be drawn from the pattern we have described, even if the employer would prefer to employ people drawn predominantly or even entirely from his own ethnic or, here, national-origin community.

The applicant referred by an existing employee is likely to get a franker, more accurate, more relevant picture of working conditions than if he learns about the job from an employment agency, a newspaper ad, or a hiring supervisor. The employee can give him the real low-down about the job. The result is a higher probability of a good match, and a lower probability that the new hire will be disappointed or disgruntled, perform badly, and quit. An employee who refers someone for employment may get in trouble with his employer if the person he refers is a dud; so word of mouth recruitment in effect enlists existing employees to help screen new applicants conscientiously.

In a nation of immigrants, this must be reckoned an ominous case despite its outcome. The United States has many recent immigrants, and today as historically they tend to cluster in their own communities, united by ties of language, culture, and background. Often they form small businesses composed largely of relatives, friends, and other members of their community, and they obtain new employees by word of mouth. These small business — grocery stores, furniture stores, clothing stores, cleaning services, restaurants, gas stations — have been for many immigrant groups, and continue to be, the first rung on the ladder of American success. Derided as clannish, resented for their ambition and hard work, hated, or despised for their otherness, recent immigrants are frequent targets of discrimination, some of it violent. It would be a bitter irony if the federal agency dedicated to enforcing the antidiscrimination laws succeeded in using those laws to kick these people off the ladder by compelling them to institute costly systems of hiring. There is equal danger to small black-run businesses in our central cities. Must such businesses undertake in the name of nondiscrimination costly measures to recruit non-black employees?

Decision. Despite an employer's preference for employees of a certain race or national origin, the employer is not liable for discrimination unless it acts upon that preference. Using word-of-mouth advertising does not give rise to an inference of discrimination on the part of the employer. The Court of Appeals affirmed the district court decision in favor of the employer.

CASE QUESTIONS

Critical Legal Thinking. To what extent do you believe the court's decision was influenced by the fact that an immigrant who, in turn, employed immigrants from his native country operated the company?

Business Ethics. What if Consolidated never hired anyone from any other nationality or race? Would this have been ethical? Would this have been legal?

Contemporary Business. To what extent should intent to discriminate be part of a court's analysis in word of mouth hiring cases?

Workers often complain that **nepotism** constitutes discrimination. **Nepotism** is the practice of bestowing favored treatment on one's relatives, especially in the areas of hiring and promotion. **Nepotism** is often the subject of legislation for public sector employees; only recently has the subject entered the policies of private sector employees. By itself, **nepotism** is not illegal or wrongful, but when it is not justified by a **business necessity**, the policy may evoke lawsuits by disgruntled former employees who feel they were discriminated against because they were marginalized in favor of a person related to the decision-maker.

Nepotism
The practice of bestowing favored treatment on one's relatives, especially in the areas of hiring and promotion.

CASE 2.5

NEPOTISM DOES NOT VIOLATE EQUAL PROTECTION CLAUSE

KOTCH V. BOARD OF RIVER PORT PILOT COMMISSIONERS

330 U.S. 552 (1947)

Supreme Court of the United States

Facts. Kotch and other plaintiffs had at least 15 years' experience in the river, the port, and elsewhere, and possessed all the statutory qualifications to be river pilots, except for serving a required six-month apprenticeship under a Louisiana officer pilot. The pilotage system operated under the authority of state law. The plaintiffs were denied appointment as state pilots. They alleged in state court that unfettered discretion of incumbent pilots to select only the relatives and friends of incumbent pilots violated the equal protection clause of the Fourteenth Amendment. The Supreme Court of Louisiana held that the pilotage law did not violate the Constitution. Kotch and the others appealed to the Supreme Court, which granted *certiorari*.

Issue. Does the practice of nepotism in appointing new state river pilots under applicable state statutes violate the Equal Protection Clause of the Fourteenth Amendment?

Language of the Court. Black, J.: **The history and practice of pilotage demonstrate that, although inextricably geared to a complex commercial economy, it is also a highly personalized calling. A pilot does not require a formalized technical education so much as a detailed and extremely intimate, almost intuitive, knowledge of the weather, waterways and conformation of the harbor or river which he serves. This seems to be particularly true of the approaches to New Orleans through the treacherous and shifting channel of the Mississippi River. Moreover, harbor entrances where pilots can most conveniently make their homes and still be close to places where they board incoming and leave outgoing ships are usually some distance from the port cities they serve. These "pilot towns" have begun, and generally exist today, as small communities of pilots, perhaps near but usually distinct from the port cities. In these communities, young men have an opportunity to acquire special knowledge of the weather and water hazards of the locality and seem to grow up with ambitions to become pilots in the traditions of their fathers, relatives, and neighbors. We are asked, in effect, to say that Louisiana is without constitutional authority to conclude that apprenticeship under persons specially interested in a pilot's future is the best way to fit him for duty as a pilot officer in the service of the State.**

The practice of nepotism in appointing public servants has been a subject of controversy in this country throughout our history. Some states have adopted constitutional amendments or statutes to prohibit it. These have reflected state policies to wipe out the practice. However, Louisiana and most other states have adopted no such general policy. We can only assume that the Louisiana legislature weighed the obvious possibility of evil against whatever useful function a closely knit pilotage system may serve. Thus the advantages of early experience under friendly supervision in the locality of the pilot's training, the benefits to morale and esprit de corps which family and neighborly tradition might contribute, the close association in which pilots must work and live in their pilot communities and on the water, and the discipline and regulation which is imposed to assure the State competent pilot service after appointment, might have prompted the legislature to permit Louisiana pilot officers to select those with whom they would serve.

The number of people, as a practical matter, who can be pilots is very limited. No matter what system of selection is adopted, all but the few occasionally selected must of necessity be excluded. . . . We are aware of no decision of this Court holding that the Constitution requires a state governor, or subordinates responsible to him and removable by him for cause, to select state public servants by competitive tests or by any other particular method of selection. The object of the entire pilotage law, as we have pointed out, is to secure for the State and others interested the safest and most efficiently operated pilotage system practicable. We cannot say that the method adopted in Louisiana for the selection of pilots is unrelated to this objective. . . . We do not need to consider hypothetical questions concerning any similar system of selection which might conceivably be practiced in other professions or businesses regulated or operated by state governments. It is enough here that considering the entirely unique institution of pilotage in the light of its history in Louisiana, we cannot say that the practice appellants attack is the kind of discrimination which violates the equal protection clause of the Fourteenth Amendment.

Decision. No. The close association in which pilots must work and live in their pilot communities assures the state will enjoy competent pilot service.

CASE QUESTIONS

Critical Legal Thinking. Is the application of this case limited to the unique work position involved?

Business Ethics. Is the Court condoning an unfair and unethical practice relative to governmental employment?

Contemporary Business. Can you think of any other situations in which nepotistic hiring practices could advance the needs of the organization?

Interviewing

Federal law requires that employers not use impermissible criteria in selecting employees. In particular, any characteristic as to which a person is protected from discrimination may not, by itself, be the basis for an adverse employment decision. As we will learn later with regard to discrimination, an employer may not use an applicant's race, color, sex, age, national origin, religion, or disability as a basis for a hiring decision. State and local laws and ordinances frequently extend protection to applicants with other characteristics as well.

Employers must carefully communicate during the interview process. The employer may be liable for statements made to applicants during the recruitment process on which applicants may rely to their detriment. Misrepresentations involving factual comparisons made between the company and its competition as to such factors as compensation, benefits, and career paths and opportunities are material statements that might induce an applicant to accept a position. If the implied promises are not realized, the hired person might later bring an action for damages for breach of contract or fraud against the employer. As we shall study in a later chapter, employees may file suit against the employer based on such express or implied promises that induced them to switch jobs and, quite often, to move across the country to take the new position.

Management Application
Selecting Qualified Candidates

To select the most qualified applicants, an employer should:

- determine the skills needed to fill an open position;
- identify the job's essential functions and performance metrics;
- write a thorough job description and explain how the employee's performance will be measured;
- determine suitable salary and benefits for the position that are comparable to other positions within and outside of the company;
- determine how to find the best-qualified applicants;
- select applications and interview the most qualified candidates based on the job's description and specifications;
- screen applicants in accordance with lawful procedures;
- provide a written offer to the employee that outlines the terms and conditions of the hiring; and
- follow through with proper orientation and training procedures.

Raiding Other Employers

Employers should be aware that a prospective employee might have executed a **non-competition contract** or a contract that contains a trade-secrets or proprietary information agreement. If a new hire violates such an agreement, not only is the employee liable for any damages caused to the former employer but so is the new employer who benefited from the misappropriated confidential information.

Even when the newly hired employee has not executed such a contract, the law has long recognized an implied obligation on the part of the new employee not to disclose information to the new employer. It is important for those charged with hiring new employees to be cognizant of applicants' legal obligations to former employers. Failing to maintain this awareness can expose both the new employer and the new employee to joint and several liability to the former employer for damages arising from appropriation of trade secrets. The rights of former employers to pursue damage claims and seek injunctive relief against the new employer may arise within the hiring context. The applicant or the newly hired may be in possession of confidential business information that will harm the business interests of the former employer. This topic will be discussed more fully in the next chapter.

The employer may be held liable for any discriminatory selection criteria used by its hiring agent, such as an employment agency or a union hiring hall. Under the EEOC Guidelines published in December 1997, an employer using a temporary employment agency or staffing firm may be jointly and several liable with that agency or firm for discriminatory hiring, assignments, wage payments, or harassment. In the following case from the Eleventh Circuit Court of Appeals, the employer's testing procedures were reviewed in light of the requirements to accommodate applicants with disabilities for federal jobs under the Rehabilitation Act of 1973. While reading the case, consider whether it is appropriate to hold an employer liable for the failures of a testing procedure designed for the employer by outside consultants.

CASE 2.6

EMPLOYER'S TEST MUST ACCURATELY REFLECT THE ABILITIES OF ALL APPLICANTS, INCLUDING THOSE WITH DYSLEXIA

STUTTS V. FREEMAN

694 F.2d 666 (11th Cir. 1983)

U.S. Court of Appeals for the Eleventh Circuit

Facts. Joseph Stutts applied to enter an apprenticeship program for the position of heavy equipment operator with the defendant Tennessee Valley Authority, a governmental entity. Stutts argued before the U.S. District Court that, due to his dyslexia, he was an "otherwise qualified handicapped individual" under The Rehabilitation Act of 1973. His application was denied because of a "low" score on the General Aptitude Test Battery, a test used by TVA to predict the probability of an applicant's success in the training program. At the trial court level the district court granted summary judgment in favor of the TVA, and Stutts appealed to the Eleventh Circuit Court of Appeals.

Issue. Must an employer make reasonable accommodations in the testing of handicapped applicants?

Language of the Court. Fay, J.: **While we do not decide the question whether Mr. Stutts was "an otherwise qualified handicapped individual," we agree that summary judgment should not have been granted in TVA's favor and reverse the holding of the trial court.**

Mr. Stutts has been diagnosed as having the condition of dyslexia, which impairs his ability to read. The record indicates that this disability renders Mr. Stutts incapable of reading beyond the most elementary level, and leads to an inability to perform well on written tests such as the GATB. There is evidence that Mr. Stutts was evaluated by doctors and tested with non-written tests after receiving results of his GATB test and was judged to have above average intelligence, coordination and aptitude for a position as a heavy equipment operator. TVA tried to obtain the results of these non-verbal tests in connection with Mr. Stutts' application for the apprenticeship training program, but was unable to do so. Attempts to persuade the testing service to give Mr. Stutts an oral GATB were unsuccessful because scoring on the written GATB is based on standardized and uniform testing conditions and cannot be accurately translated from an oral test. Despite TVA's knowledge of and unsuccessful efforts to obtain alternate forms of evaluation, Mr. Stutts' non-selection was based solely on his low score on the written GATB test.

The policy underlying the Rehabilitation Act of 1973 is clear—"to promote and expand employment opportunities in the public and private sectors for handicapped individuals." Both parties agree that Mr. Stutts is a handicapped individual and that the main hiring criteria—the GATB test—could not accurately reflect Mr. Stutts' abilities. There is considerable evidence supporting Mr. Stutts' contention that he is fully capable of performing well as a heavy equipment operator and we find a genuine issue as to whether or not he could successfully complete the training program, either with the help of a reader or by other means. Congress has clearly directed entities in its sphere of control to make efforts to expand employment opportunities for handicapped persons. TVA has not satisfied its obligation under the statute by merely asking for results of alternate testing methods and accepting a rejection.

We do not hold that Mr. Stutts must be given a position as a heavy equipment operator, nor do we hold that he must be admitted into the training program. We do hold that when TVA uses a test which cannot and does not accurately reflect the abilities of a handicapped person, as a matter of law they must do more to accommodate that individual than TVA has done in regard to Mr. Stutts. TVA argues that their efforts on behalf of Mr. Stutts showed that he received better treatment than a non-handicapped applicant. TVA sought to have a non-written GATB test given to Mr. Stutts. They tried to obtain the

results of other examinations and tests given Mr. Stutts after his dyslexic condition was discerned. But the fact remains that these efforts were not successful. In the final analysis TVA made its decision based on the GATB test. TVA's unsuccessful efforts do not amount to "reasonable accommodation" of the handicapped as required by 45 C.F.R. §84.12 (1981).

Decision. The court of appeals reversed the granting of the order for summary judgment by the trial court because the TVA had not made a reasonable accommodation in the testing of a dyslexic applicant.

CASE QUESTIONS

Critical Legal Thinking. Do you agree with the decision of this case? Why or why not?

Business Ethics. Under the ADA an employer is required to make a reasonable accommodation to the known physical and or mental limitations of an otherwise qualified applicant, unless doing so would impose an undue burden on the employer. What do you think are the reasonable limitations to the requirement to make a "reasonable accommodation" for an applicant or employee with a recognized disability?

Contemporary Business. Can you think of any positions for which a reasonable accommodation should not or cannot be made for a disability?

Testing to Screen Employees

Recruitment and promotion practices may often involve testing or background investigations that may reflect **disparate impact discrimination**. The employer's decision to hire, promote, or terminate an employee must be based on lawful employment criteria. Generally, unlawful criteria involve any information that would identify an individual as having protected characteristics. The right to seek or to act on such information is heavily disfavored under the law.

Pre-Employment Testing and Investigations

Questions, inquiries, testing, and verification of facts regarding an applicant during the recruitment process must be handled carefully. Any of these actions, which directly or indirectly constitute discrimination of the type protected by federal, state, or local law, can result in substantial risk to the employer. Employers cannot elicit information that they are not allowed to consider in selecting an employee. For example, questions regarding the person's childcare needs, year of graduation from high school, club memberships, personal interests, and so on are unlawful inquiries because they could constitute discrimination based on gender, marital status, age, national origin, or other protected consideration. Liability under state or local antidiscrimination statutes and ordinances can be far-reaching for the untrained interviewer.

The law of disability discrimination specifies when an employer may make "disability-related inquiries" (i.e., inquiries that are likely to elicit information about the person's disability). An employer may not ask questions about a disability or require medical examinations until after it makes a conditional job offer to the applicant.[18] An employer may require the successful passage of a medical examination as a condition to the offer of employment. In any case, the inquiries and examination have to be job related, consistent with the business necessities of the position, and applicable to all applicants entering the same position or status. Testing intended to screen for the illegal use of drugs is not considered a "medical examination" and does not violate the prohibition against preemployment medical exams or inquiries. Genetic testing of applicants is barred, and an employer is generally limited to monitoring employees for exposure to hazardous substances.

Employers may not indirectly intrude into the protected status of their employees. Protected status includes private information regarding the individual that is not publicly known. Employers may not inquire into the private, personal matters of their employees because the inquiry may reveal information about that protected status.

> ***Example:*** Employees successfully challenged the Lawrence Berkeley Labs' medical and genetic testing program because the testing would disclose protected status claims relating to sex- and race-linked traits and conditions.[19]

Unless the position involves a peculiar risk or activity, employers are not required to conduct **criminal background checks** of its applicants. The courts will review the totality of the circumstances to determine the lawfulness of any alleged invasion of the applicant's privacy rights. Employers should carefully review local and state laws as they may relate to prior employment inquires, credit checks, and prior arrest and/or conviction records with regard to making employment decisions. All information provided by the applicant is subject to employer verification. The employer's interest is to receive and evaluate only information that is relevant to the position.

There are numerous exceptions to the general rules in this area, and employers are well advised to tread carefully. If the applicant would expose others to danger or harm in a proposed position, it may be appropriate to conduct a criminal background check. State laws vary with regard to whether an employer is restricted from requesting or using arrest, conviction, or sealed or expunged criminal or juvenile records. Other states require a "compelling need" for the information. In those states, an employer must have a "compelling need" to conduct a background check for prior incidents involving sexual misconduct, controlled substances, or crimes involving weapons or violence. For example, the courts would endorse criminal background checks on potential employees who would be working with children, the disabled, or the elderly. Any information so disclosed to the employer must be treated with complete confidentiality so that the targeted individual's privacy rights are protected during the research and decision-making processes.

Drug testing of applicants is widespread among American employers. The key limitation to its use is the Fourth Amendment of the U.S. Constitution, which bars unreasonable searches and seizures. This provision of the Amendment is often applied to protect employees of public entities, less often to workers in the private sector. Random drug testing of employees not engaged in safety-related positions is almost universally held wrongful or illegal by the courts. State laws and local ordinances can restrict employers' rights in this area, as will be addressed in the chapter on employees' privacy rights.

Using **employment testing** that has a **disparate impact** on groups protected by Title VII is unlawful, as the following decision analyzed.

CASE 2.7

PRE-EMPLOYMENT TESTING THAT RACIALLY DISCRIMINATES MUST BE PROFESSIONALLY VALIDATED IN ACCORD WITH EEOC GUIDELINES

ALBEMARLE PAPER CO. V. MOODY

422 U.S. 405 (1975)

Supreme Court of the United States

Facts. Seeking an injunction to stop an employer's testing practices, African American employees and their union sued Albemarle Paper Co. The testing had a disproportionate adverse impact upon these employees, and the testing was not shown to have been related to job performance.

Issue. What must an employer show to establish that preemployment tests that are racially discriminatory in effect, though not in intent, are sufficiently "job related" to survive challenge under Title VII?

Language of the Court. Stewart, J.: . . . **In *Griggs v. Duke Power Co.*, (citation omitted) this Court unanimously held that Title VII forbids the use of employment tests that are discriminatory in effect unless the employer meets "the burden of showing that any given requirement [has] . . . a manifest relationship to the employment in question." In the present case . . . we are concerned only with the question whether Albemarle has shown its tests to be job related.**

The question of job relatedness must be viewed in the context of the plant's operation and the history of the testing program. The plant, which now employs about 650 persons, converts raw wood into paper products. It is organized into a number of functional departments, each with one or more distinct lines of progression, the theory being that workers can move up the line as they acquire the necessary skills. The number and structure of the lines have varied greatly over time. For many years, certain lines were themselves more skilled and paid higher wages than others, and until 1964 these skilled lines were expressly reserved for white workers. In 1968, many of the unskilled

"Negro" lines were "end-tailed" onto skilled "white" lines, but it apparently remains true that at least the top jobs in certain lines require greater skills than the top jobs in other lines. In this sense, at least, it is still possible to speak of relatively skilled and relatively unskilled lines.

Four months before this case went to trial, Albemarle engaged an expert in industrial psychology to "validate" the job relatedness of its testing program. He spent a half day at the plant and devised a "concurrent validation" study, which was conducted by plant officials, without his supervision. The expert then subjected the results to statistical analysis. The study dealt with 10 job groupings, selected from near the top of nine of the lines of progression. Jobs were grouped together solely by their proximity in the line of progression; no attempt was made to analyze jobs in terms of the particular skills they might require. All, or nearly all, employees in the selected groups participated in the study — 105 employees in all, but only four Negroes. Within each job grouping, the study compared the test scores of each employee with an independent "ranking" of the employee, relative to each of his coworkers, made by two of the employee's supervisors. The supervisors, who did not know the test scores, were asked [in the words of a plant official] to "determine which ones they felt irrespective of the job that they were actually doing, but in their respective jobs, did a better job than the person they were rating against. . . ."

On the basis of these results, the District Court found that "[t]he personnel tests administered at the plant have undergone validation studies and have been proven to be job related." Like the Court of Appeals, we are constrained to disagree. The EEOC has issued "Guidelines" for employers seeking to determine, through professional validation studies, whether their employment tests are job related. . . . These Guidelines draw upon and make reference to professional standards of test validation established by the American Psychological Association. The EEOC Guidelines are not administrative "regulations" promulgated pursuant to formal procedures established by the Congress. But, as this Court has heretofore noted, they do constitute "[t]he administrative interpretation of the Act by the enforcing agency," and consequently they are "entitled to great deference." (Citation omitted.) . . .

The message of these Guidelines is the same as that of the Griggs case — that discriminatory tests are impermissible unless shown, by professionally acceptable methods, to be "predictive of or significantly correlated with important elements of work behavior which comprise or are relevant to the job or jobs for which candidates are being evaluated."

Decision. An employer must prove the job relatedness of its testing program throughout the entire relationship between an employer and worker.

CASE QUESTIONS

Critical Legal Thinking. Did the subjective input of the supervisors' comparison of two paired employees doom the testing standards of Albemarle Paper Company?

Business Ethics. How would you inject the opinions of knowledgeable supervisors into the promotion policies in your own company?

Contemporary Business. Identify the types of jobs whereby applicant testing would be job related. What validated tests would you employ to screen applicants for those positions?

If testing is used, employers must be aware that the test results may tend to screen out workers due to their protected characteristics. Only permissible information may be sought from the testing process. An employer can avoid liability for discrimination under **Title VII** if it can prove that the tests utilized accurately predict successful performance on the job. No tests administered to applicants can result in **disparate impact** or **disparate treatment** of the individual or class of persons applying for a position. When tests and processing procedures have such an effect, the employer must defend its use of the test or selection procedure.

An employer should retain an expert who is familiar with the EEOC's Uniform Guidelines and applicable legal standards. These Guidelines were issued under the provisions of Section 703 of the Civil Rights Act of 1964 and cover three different categories of tests:

Criterion-Related Testing
An evaluative approach that substantiates the validity of a test by comparing the test outcomes with measures of job performance.

1. ***Criterion-related*** studies establish by statistical data that the test can predict or provide a significant correlation with successful work behaviors. The employer must have thoroughly analyzed the jobs assigned to its workers.
2. ***Content validation*** establishes that the content of the test is representative of the important aspects of job performance.
3. ***Construct studies*** demonstrate that the test measures the degree to which job candidates have the significant characteristics important for job performance.

Content Validation
Measures of how well a job applicant scores in performing tasks required for the job.

Construct Studies
Tests that measure job applicants' characteristics that are considered important to the performance of a particular job.

The test must relate to the position for which the test is administered. Employers must be sensitive to the fact that the test may act as a bar to many applicants and must administer the test or alternative screening device in a manner that is lawful and fair to all applicants. For example, a typing test can be discriminatory against applicants who have manual dexterity issues; in this circumstance, the employer would want to substitute another means of data entry, such as use of speech recognition software as a substitute standard for keyboarding. **Content validation** measures how well the applicant scores in tasks that are required for the job. For example, firefighters may be required to be able to carry a certain weight up several flights of stairs. This can be used to make sure that the applicant would be able to go up a flight of stairs wearing the heavy firefighter suits, tanks, and masks that are required for the job. On the other hand, criterion validation can be used once a company has demonstrated a positive correlation between success on a certain test and success in job performance.

Given the high costs of complying with the EEOC Guidelines, the courts take a practical approach to the problem. The Supreme Court has not ruled whether strict compliance with these guidelines is required. Lower courts have allowed practices to depart from the requirements of the EEOC regulations if they are based on common sense and practical approaches to addressing the issue. In a similar manner, the employer must review all alternative testing procedures to ensure that it implements the ***least discriminatory approach*** during applicant selection.

> ***Example:*** The Ford Motor Company settled a nationwide class-action suit brought by African Americans who were rejected for an apprenticeship program after taking a cognitive test. The written test measured verbal, numerical, and spatial reasoning to evaluate mechanical aptitude. Even though it had been validated in 1991, the test continued to have a statistically significant **disparate impact** by excluding African American applicants. Less discriminatory selection procedures were developed that would have served Ford's needs, but they were not adopted. In its settlement agreement, Ford agreed to replace the test with a selection procedure, to be designed by a jointly selected industrial psychologist, that would predict job success and reduce **adverse impact**. In addition, Ford paid more than $8 million in damages.[20]

Employers must balance their requirements for testing with the risks that they may face for invasion of privacy.

> ***Example:*** The Seventh Circuit Court of Appeals upheld the dismissal of a suit brought by a public employee who subjected to a mandatory psychological test to retain her job. The test did not constitute a search for purposes of the Fourth Amendment of the U.S. Constitution; however, the court suggested that the employee should pursue a lawsuit for invasion of privacy in state court.[21]

As long as employers act reasonably, they may select tiebreaking procedures in the selection process.

> ***Example:*** Raul Lopez, a firefighter for the City of San Antonio, Texas, sued the city claiming that he should have been ranked first on the promotion list. The Texas law regarding promotion of public employees provides "the [examination] grade . . . shall be computed by adding the applicant's points for seniority to the applicant's grade on the written examination . . . . If a tie score occurs, the commission shall determine a method to break the tie." The city promotional commission decided to use the written examination score as the first tiebreaker and seniority in rank as the second tiebreaker for equal total scores. The Texas Court of Appeals upheld the city's method as violating neither the applicable collective bargaining agreement nor law.[22]

Testing procedures that have an unlawful bias cannot be used even if they are part of an affirmative action program intended to overcome past discriminatory employment practices. Whenever a discriminatory effect results, overt discrimination in testing constitutes an unlawful employment practice.

> ***Example:*** In *Ricci v. DeStefano*, 557 U.S. ___ (2009),[23] the Supreme Court considered whether a public employer could disregard test results and make promotional decisions based in part on race, under its affirmative action program. The City of New Haven, Connecticut, had been sued many times in the past for alleged employment discrimination. Fearing the costs of litigation, city officials elected to disregard testing results in making promotional decisions within the fire department. This case appears later as part of our discussion of affirmative action. The exams at issue in the *Ricci* case were job related and consistent with **business necessity**. The Court found that the city ignored the evidence supporting the exam's validity and could not show that an equally valid, less discriminatory testing procedure was available. New Haven's fear of being sued by nonwhite firefighters

was not a valid defense for overt discrimination against the white employees. The Court found that the city's reliance on race was to the detriment of individuals who passed the examination and qualified for promotions. As such, it held that discarding the test results was impermissible employment discrimination.

EEOC Compliance Reporting

Employers with 1,000 or more employees must file an annual **EEO1 report** describing their workforce demographics. Employers with a government contract with a value of $50,000 per year or more who employ 50 or more employees must have an Affirmative Action Plan. The requirement also applies to employers who do not have a contract with the government but have 50 or more employees and provide goods or services worth $50,000 to an organization to fulfill a prime contract. An employer with 15 or more employees must differentiate qualified job applicants from job seekers and maintain records showing the differentiation process. Failure to comply with these requirements can result in fines and damage claims made in response to government audits of employer records and employee lawsuits for discrimination.

Termination of Employment

Terminating employees poses serious risks to the employer. The potential for a wrongful termination suit (i.e., a suit against a former employer for violating the rights of the former employee) may be the most obvious risk to management. In addition, the former employee could sue the ex-employer for fraud damages arising from the promises made by the employer during the recruitment and employment periods. The former employer faces the specter of compromised confidential information from the disgruntled former employee.

Employers should follow a specific termination protocol when terminating employees. In this manner, they can ensure that confidential data will be preserved and the potential for lawsuits minimized. Computer passwords, access keys, email accounts, and so on should be rendered inoperative when the termination is to occur. Many employers create a mirror image of the employee's hard drives before they can be altered or wiped clean. Following the termination, company-supplied computers (notebook/laptop, desktop, etc.), cell phones, and other electronic equipment should be screened to detect any incidents of any intentional harm to the company.

The law does not require severance packages. However, many employers offer them as a morale-boosting practice. A well-written severance package will include provisions ensuring that the individual understands that by accepting the package he or she becomes ineligible to file a lawsuit.

In the next chapter, we will study the characteristics of at-will employment and the exceptions to the right of employers to discharge employees without cause. In particular, while employment in most states is presumed to be terminable "at will," there are several exceptions to the presumption. Numerous statutory and common-law exceptions have been created to counteract the harsh and immediate effects of a discharge from employment occurring at the will of the employer. It should be noted that a worker may nonetheless resign from a company when faced by conditions so extraordinary and egregious that any reasonable person would do so. This situation is defined as a constructive discharge, and it is treated as if the employer unlawfully terminated the employee. These exceptions to the at-will rule, including any related tort claims, are known as "wrongful discharge" or "wrongful termination." If the employee fails to establish that an exception to at-will status exists based on a statute, public policy, or contract term, the employer can obtain a dismissal of the wrongful-termination claim, even when there is a good reason for the termination of employment.

Human Resource Management
Exit Interview Questions

A well-run human resource department within a company will have a standard set of questions to ask departing employees to ensure that the reason for the separation from the company is known and documented. A sample of those that might be posed follows:

- What were your expectations when you were hired?
- Did we meet your expectations? If not, where did we fall short?
- What do you view as the shortcomings of our organization?
- What can we do to improve our company?
- What frustrated you while you worked for us?
- Do you have any suggestions to make us a better firm?
- If you had a recommendation to make us a stronger company, what would it be?
- Do you believe that you were treated fairly while you worked here?
- Are there any concerns you would like to share with us?

When an employer is required to provide a good cause for termination, the decision can be made on any reasonable ground related to the successful performance of the position. For example, a tenured professor of engineering was discharged because he received three consecutive annual post-tenure findings of "does not meet expectations." When he challenged his firing in court, his discharge for lack of collegiality was upheld. His interactions with colleagues had been so disruptive that the effective and efficient operation of his department was impaired.[24]

Probationary employment status can bar the employee from contesting a discharge. The City of New Orleans police department employed Ashley Terry as a parking control officer. During that time she was accepted by the city as a "police recruit" and began training at the police academy. After completing training, she was promoted to a probationary status police officer. She was terminated from her job following a disciplinary hearing when it was determined she had improperly displayed her firearm in public while off duty. The city's civil service commission denied her appeal because under the civil service rules under which she was employed there was no provision for appeal by a probationary employee.[25] Public employment is often subject to such conditions not often encountered in the private employment sector.

Workplace Application
What Do Employees Have to Tolerate at Work?

You are a human resource manager for a regional telecommunications company located in Indiana. You now have an almost all-white office staff of four management employees and two nonmanagement employees. The staff claims that your company has discriminated against them by creating an unpleasant and racially hostile work environment. These white employees allege that the source of this hostility is a vulgar, loudmouthed co-worker, Bob Weymon, who is the only black employee. The staff claims that your company permits Weymon to perform his disruptive antics and that they can no longer tolerate his behavior.

Throughout the past several years, your company employed Weymon as a planning engineer in its South Bend, Indiana, office, where he was the only black engineer in his department. Weymon and the white employees worked in semiprivate cubicles, several to a large room, in reasonably close proximity to one another. By all accounts, Weymon is a very disagreeable person. The white employees explain to you that Weymon harassed everyone in sight. They claim that he often physically threatens his co-workers, engages in loud, angry tirades (typically directed at his computer terminal), yells obscenities, stands atop his desk, plays music on his computer at loud and disruptive levels, and uses foul and vulgar language, often directed at female employees. According to the white employees, nothing in Weymon's behavior indicated any sort of racial intent. He did not mistreat only whites; he mistreated everyone. Weymon was an equal-opportunity pain.

The white employees have made several prior complaints to senior management about Weymon. In response, your company had downgraded Weymon in his prior performance appraisals and reduced his salary opportunities. In addition, you are aware that one of the nonmanagement employees has filed a grievance with the union representing certain employees complaining of an incident in which Weymon subjected them to "a barrage of foul language, including words unacceptable in any office or public setting." Your manager responded to this grievance by admonishing Weymon to refrain from using foul language. When you question the complaining party regarding the grievance, he declines to cooperate. He fears that if Weymon is disciplined, he will file an EEOC complaint against the company and him.

The white employees have made other oral and informal complaints to management regarding Weymon's conduct. Your company has an equal employment opportunity policy addressing racial harassment, and it periodically publishes a booklet informing employees of their equal employment opportunity rights. While the white employees acknowledge that they are aware of the policy regarding harassment and received the published literature, they have not contacted the human resource coordinator regarding Weymon's behavior and have not filed an official complaint until now.[26]

Discussion Questions

1. Should Weymon's behavior be characterized as a personality conflict between employees that is not the business of either the employer or the federal courts?
2. Should it be considered an unethical and unlawful employment practice for an employer to refuse to discipline or terminate an employee because of the employer's fear of a discrimination charge?
3. If Weymon's behavior is directed at all employees regardless of their protected class, what action will you recommend the company take with regard to complaints about Weymon?

Human Resource Form
Moonlighting Policy

In order to control inappropriate off-duty conduct by its employees, the employer should have a written policy on outside work or moonlighting. A sample employee policy might read:

MOONLIGHTING POLICY

Our company requires that its employees give their best efforts in performing their work assignments. While the company has no objection to an employee holding another work position as long as the employee effectively meets the performance standards for his or her position with the company, the company requires that all outside employment not involve any competing business without first obtaining written company approval. The company will hold all employees to the same standards of performance and work shift schedules as if the employee did not hold the outside position.

Key Terms and Concepts

- Business necessity
- Bona Fide Occupational Qualification
- Disparate treatment
- Disparate impact
- Credit history, Fair Credit Reporting Act
- Internet-applicant rule
- Nepotism
- Non-competition contract
- Criminal background checks
- At-will employment
- Drug testing
- Preemployment testing
- Criterion-related testing
- Content validation
- Construct studies
- Least discriminatory approach
- EEO1 report

Chapter Summary

- Selection of employees should begin with properly defining the job qualifications and selection criteria. The recruiting and interviewing process should consistently seek to screen applicants in a nondiscriminatory manner. If investigations, testing, or other criteria are applied with regard to the selection, the process must be fair and must not result in a disparate impact on or treatment of those within groups recognized as protected in our society. The process should be as blind as possible to the characteristics of the individual applicant while not resulting in an adverse impact from a screening process unfair to all.

- Job qualifications for selection, promotion, training, or retention must be narrowly defined and must apply to the actual position.

- Disparate treatment discrimination involves distinctions between two equally qualified individuals because of a legally protected characteristic (i.e., race, gender, religion, national origin, age, or disability status).

- Disparate impact discrimination involves distinctions between two equally qualified individuals because of a basis other than productivity.

- Employers may refuse to hire an applicant because of current alcohol abuse, illicit drug use, or abuse of prescription medicines. However, if the individual is participating in a supervised rehabilitation program and is no longer abusing drugs or alcohol, the employer may not discriminate. This prohibition also applies if the applicant was rehabilitated and no longer engages in such use or was erroneously regarded by the employer as being such an abuser.

- All recruiting and interviewing of applicants must be as neutral as possible to avoid a selection process biased for or against applicants due to their individual characteristics. All applicants must be qualified for the position, subject to reasonable accommodations for religion and disability, and the screening must conform to the business necessities of the position.

Online Student Support

- Loislaw legal research and writing assignments.
- Loislaw group projects and class presentations.
- Loislaw access, providing online research including up-to-date cases, statutes, rules, and regulations. Primary law for all 50 states and federal jurisdictions. Registration required for access to this resource.
- Practice questions, including sample true/false, multiple choice, and short answer questions to test your understanding of concepts.
- Additional human resource forms.
- Internet exercises.
- Blogs.
- Supplementary statutory and regulatory materials.

Case Problems

2.1 A direct application to an employer is a common means of obtaining employment. If an employer places heavy reliance on such a form of recruitment, would this be subject to attack as an unlawful hiring practice? Make the arguments for and against whether such a practice should be so considered. Does an employer consider an online application to be different from a "walk-in" application? (*EEOC v. American National Bank*, 652 F.2d 1176 (4th Cir. 1981))

2.2 Employers argue that the civil rights laws protect persons from unlawful employment decisions and not information gathered in the application process. In this manner, an employer may gather information on how suitable a candidate may be for a particular position. The regulations of the EEOC and, therefore, plaintiffs' attorneys contend that even this conduct violates the law. If you were the manager of a human resource department, how would you gather information necessary to the hiring process but not comporting to the EEOC's point of view?

2.3 The Ninth Circuit Court of Appeals was required to review a four-month disciplinary suspension as constituting illegal retaliation. The case involved discipline imposed on several employees who publicly protested to the employer's personnel manager about an "affirmative action award" given by a local school board who was a major customer of their employer. How would the court rule as to the appropriateness of the discipline? When should the employer's economic interests prevail or control employee disciplinary matters? (*EEOC v. Crown Zellerbach Corp.*, 720 F.2d 1008 (9th Cir. 1983))

2.4 Robert Byrnie, with almost 22 years of teaching experience, was ranked least qualified of four second-round interview candidates for a teaching position with the Town of Cromwell [Connecticut] Public Schools. He alleged several civil rights violations based on disparate treatment and alleged that the reasons given for hiring another candidate were a pretext. He also alleged disparate impact claims because he alleged a specific employment practice of not hiring older and male teachers was inappropriate. Cromwell asserted that he lacked "familiarity with the basic competencies necessary for effective teaching," even though he had been the English Department's first choice for long-term substitute teaching assignments over the previous five years. Cromwell also asserted that Byrnie interviewed poorly with the board. After the case was filed, the school board did not keep the application materials and destroyed the interview notes and ballots completed by the screening committee. If you were the judge considering Mr. Byrnie's contention of entitlement to judgment based on the inferences that can be drawn from Cromwell's actions, how would you rule? (*Byrnie v. Town of Cromwell*, 243 F.3d 93 (2001))

2.5 Professor Clyde Summers wrote an article entitled "Employment At-Will in the United States: The Divine Right of Employers." It argues that American law has failed the employee except with regard to certain types of discrimination (3 U. Pa. J. Lab. & Empl. L., 65-84-86 (2002)). Professor Summers notes that even discrimination laws require only that all employees be treated equally. He asserts that the current trend in the law is to give more deference to employers' exercise of discretion. With the decline in the power of organized labor, he opines that the great majority of American workers are less protected than they would be in foreign jurisdictions. Based on your own experiences and reading, do you agree with Professor Summers's assessment on the status of employee protections?

End Notes

1. *U.S. v. Village of Elmwood Park*, 1987 U.S. Dist. Lexis 2077, 43 FEP 995 (1987).
2. 42 U.S.C. §§2000e-2000e-17.
3. 42 U.S.C. §2000-e(a)(1).
4. 8 U.S.C. §1324b.
5. 8 U.S.C. §1324b(a)(4).
6. 29 U.S.C. §§621-634.
7. 987 F2d 64, 70 (1st Cir 1993).
8. 15 U.S.C. §§1681 1681t.
9. 11 U.S.C. §525(b).
10. 401 F3d 729 (6th Cir 2005).
11. 464 F. 2d 1006 (5th Cir. 1972).
12. http://www.dol.gov/ofccp/regs/compliance/faqs/iappfaqs.htm#Q1GI.
13. 42 U.S.C. §12101.
14. 42 U.S.C. §12111.
15. http://www.eeoc.gov/facts/jobapplicant.html.
16. 83 F.R.D. 46 (1972).
17. 518 F. 2d 543 (4th Cir. 1975).
18. 42 U.S.C. §12112(d)(2).
19. *Norman-Bloodshaw v. Lawrence Berkeley Laboratories*, 135 F.3d 1260 (9th Cir. 1998).
20. EEOC, press release, June 1, 2005, http://www.eeoc.gov/eeoc/newsroom/release/archive/6-1-05.html.
21. *Greenawalt v. Indiana Dept. of Corrections*, 397 F.3d 587 (7th Cir. 2005).
22. *City of San Antonio v. Lopez*, _______ Texas Ct. App. _______ (2009).
23. 129 S.Ct. 2658 (2009).
24. *Bernold v. Bd. of Gov. of Univ. of North Carolina*, 683 S.E. 2d 428 (2009).
25. *Terry v. Department of Police*, 23 So.3d 974 (2009).
26. *Vore, Wray, Shanfelt et al. v. Indiana Bell Telephone*, 32 F.3d 1161 (7th Cir. 1994).

Chapter 3
Contract and Tort Liability of Employers

"Our characters are the result of our conduct." —Aristotle, Nicomachean Ethics, *c. 335 B.C.*

Learning Objectives

1. Define at-will employment.
2. Explain the contractual exceptions to employment at-will.
3. State the statutory and public policy exceptions to at-will.
4. Define the common workplace torts.
5. Understand the concept of vicarious liability for employers.
6. Identify the benefits of non-compete and trade-secret contracts.

Chapter Outline

- Introduction
- Employment "At-Will"
- Exceptions to the "At-Will" Rule

Case 3.1 Rooney v. Tyson
Case 3.2 Foley v. Interactive Data Corp.

- Management Application: Do Employee Handbooks Create Too Much Liability?

Case 3.3 Garcetti v. Ceballos

- Management Application: When Does "At-Will" Employment Commence?
- Human Resource Form: Documenting At-Will Status
- Business Torts: Companion Claims in Employment Litigation
- Management Application: Vicarious Tort Liability and *Respondeat Superior*

Case 3.4 Wagner v. Texas A&M

- Management Application: Emotional Distress and Workers' Compensation

Case 3.5 Raymond v. IBM
Case 3.6 Burlington Industries, Inc. v. Ellerth
Case 3.7 Hill v. Lockheed Martin Logistics Mgmt.

- Management Application: Employee's Scope of Employment
- Negligent Hiring, Retention, and Supervision
- Management Application: Is There Insurance Coverage?
- Restrictive Covenants and Trade Secrets

Case 3.8 Pepsico, Inc. v. Redmond and The Quaker Oats Company

- Human Resource Form: Trade Secrets Agreement

Chapter Opening scenario

Mr. Haass seeks to open his own accounting practice after making partner at a national public accounting firm. He has been in charge of client development for many years. His employer and his place of residence are located in a state in which the courts will enforce the covenant-not-to-compete agreement that Mr. Haass executed when he first joined the firm twenty years ago. Learning that he may be terminating his relationship with the firm, the other managers are distressed to learn that he might take the firm's most profitable clients and most talented accountants with him when he leaves. After several conversations with him, the firm's management has told him, "We introduced you to our clients, and while you were in our employ you developed your relationships with them. If you leave the firm you may not compete against us by taking those clients with you." Mr. Haass offers a very hostile response, and while still employed by the firm, he seemingly withdraws from the firm's day-to-day activities.

The firm's other partners become very suspicious of Mr. Haass's intentions. They begin to intercept his e-mail, open his business mail, and review his cell-phone billings, for which the firm reimburses him on a monthly basis. Over the next several months, Mr. Haass virtually abandons his responsibilities with the firm and does not actively work at the firm. After several rebukes by his partners, he is terminated at a partner meeting. What arguments can be made for and against his position that a court should interpret the covenant-not-to-compete agreement by focusing on whether the identities of the clients are "confidential" or not? If Mr. Haass cannot openly work with those clients, thus competing with his prior firm, is he effectively banned from pursuing his occupation? Has the accounting firm committed any wrongful conduct against him for which he might sue for damages?[1]

Introduction

Employment and labor law does not restrict its reach to discriminatory acts. The complexity of managing a modern workforce includes identifying risks within both contractual and tort contexts. In this chapter, we will study those duties and responsibilities that pertain to the employment relationship. Recognizing that the subjects studied in this chapter often accompany a claim for wrongful termination, we will cover those that managers most frequently encounter. A company's responsibility for the acts of its employees is distinct from the responsibilities imposed on it by independent contractors.

We begin our study with a review of the **at-will** concept. This doctrine is traceable to English law and was further developed when, before the Civil War, U.S. courts began to establish that employment often involved contracts of no definite length. As such, either the worker or the employer could terminate the relationship. In 1877, a legal commentator first stated the **at-will doctrine** as follows:

> With us the rule is inflexible that a general or indefinite hiring is . . . hiring at will, and if the servant seeks to make it out a yearly hiring, the burden is upon him to establish it by proof. A hiring at so much a day, week, month, or year, no time being specified, is an indefinite hiring, and no presumption attaches that it was for a day even, but only at the rate fixed for whatever time the party may serve.[2]

Since that time, almost every state has accepted this statement of **at-will** employment as part of the definition of the business–worker relationship. The concept advanced workers' right to work for whom they pleased, but at the same time, it facilitated employer behaviors that did not advance the workers' condition. In some circumstances, employers took unfair advantage of the workers with regard to their health, safety, and compensation. This vacuum caused both courts and legislatures to create the law and policies that we will now study.

At-Will Employment
Employment that is terminable by either party without liability to the other; the general condition of employment, with some exceptions.

Employment "At-Will"

The general rule of employment law is that employment can be terminated at the will of either the employer or the employee. The law does not require prior notice to the employee, except in limited circumstances, including those relating to mass layoffs, a situation falling under federal and state laws that we will review in a later chapter. Otherwise, federal law does not intrude into the **at-will** relationship and leaves the subject area to the province of the states. Unlike many other legal rules that can be complicated in their explanation, the **at-will doctrine** simply describes employment as terminable at the will of either party.

To overcome the presumption that his or her employment was at-will, the terminated employee must fit within one of the recognized exceptions to the general rule. If the employee falls within one of the exceptions to at-will status, the employer may be liable to the employee for **wrongful discharge** damages. An employer does not need to terminate an employee to incur liability for **wrongful discharge**. If the employee resigns because working conditions are so intolerable that any reasonable person in that employee's position would resign, the employer can be liable for **constructive discharge** of the employee. The conditions causing the employee to resign must be so extraordinary and egregious as to go beyond any that might ordinarily lead someone to quit a displeasing job. Single, isolated acts of misconduct or personal irritation are insufficient to constitute constructive discharge. Rather, as noted, qualifying conditions must be such that a reasonable employee would not be able to tolerate them. Further, the worker must have given the employer actual notice of those conditions. The law requires that the employer either must have created the intolerable working conditions triggering the

Constructive Discharge
Workplace conditions so intolerable, extraordinary, and egregious that they would cause a reasonable person to quit employment.

resignation or must have known about them and failed to remedy them. Actions short of termination may support retaliation or a discrimination claim by the employee against the employer. For example, sexually harassing working conditions might constitute basis for a constructive discharge.

Exceptions to the "At-Will" Rule

In modern times, it has been popular for politicians and courts to decry the employment at-will rule. They feared that the freedom of the employer to discharge an employee could create hardship for the employee and the employee's family, leaving taxpayers to bear the expense of unemployment benefits. Therefore, courts and legislatures have created a number of exceptions to the general **at-will** employment status. These exceptions generally fall into one or more of the following categories:

- Express or implied contracts requiring termination only for cause; and
- Violations of statutes or strong public policies.

Express and Implied Contracts of Employment

Express and Implied Employment Contracts
Binding promises of the employer that arise in the employment context from oral or written promises made directly to an applicant or employee or impliedly through employee handbooks or manuals.

Express and **implied employment contracts** requiring termination only for cause are often litigated. When an employee promises services for a definite duration, the employer can terminate the employee only under the terms of the contract. For example, if a contract provided that an employee could be terminated only for a material breach of the employment contract, the employer would be unable to terminate the employee in the absence of a breach. In other cases in which employees have served under agreements for "lifetime" employment courts have expressed some willingness to enforce these agreements if the employee has provided substantial consideration in addition to the services rendered. For example, if the employee incurred substantial relocation expenses or had foregone other lucrative opportunities in exchange for such a promise, the employer may have a difficult time arguing that such an individual served in an **at-will** capacity.

> ***Example:*** Employees who have begun working should be entitled to a fair opportunity to perform satisfactorily before being terminated. Failure to allow the employee that opportunity supports the employee's claim that the employee detrimentally relied upon the employer's implied promise. An employee who left a prior employment, even after being offered a raise to stay, was awarded damages in a suit brought against the new employer because the employee was fired on the first day of employment.[3]

In the following case, the court had to determine whether the length of the contract was sufficiently definite that the contract could be considered other than **at-will**. The question in the case was whether the promise was express and not indefinite.

CASE 3.1

MIKE TYSON GETS K.O.'D BY HIS FORMER TRAINER

ROONEY V. TYSON

697 N.E. 2d 571 (1998)

New York Court of Appeals

Facts. In 1980, at 14 years of age, Tyson was placed under the supervision of Cus D'Amato, a renowned boxing figure and manager. When Tyson's mother died in 1983, D'Amato also became Tyson's legal guardian. At the beginning of the young man's boxing career, Kevin Rooney and D'Amato agreed that Rooney would train Tyson without compensation until the fighter became a professional athlete. The two further agreed that when Tyson advanced to professional ranks, Rooney would be Tyson's trainer "for as long as [Tyson] fought professionally."

Rooney trained Tyson for 28 months without compensation. In March 1985, Tyson turned professional and began enjoying meteoric success. D'Amato died that same year. James Jacobs became Tyson's manager in 1986. When rumors started in some sports media that Rooney would be replaced as Tyson's trainer, Rooney queried Jacobs. To quell the speculation, Tyson allegedly authorized Jacobs to state publicly "Kevin Rooney will be Mike Tyson's trainer as long as Mike Tyson is a professional fighter." Jacobs sent Rooney a copy of a press release to that effect. Thereafter, Rooney continued to train Tyson and was compensated for each of Tyson's professional fights until 1988.

In 1988, apparently in connection with Rooney's alleged comments regarding Tyson's divorce and other business-related litigation, Rooney allegedly read a newspaper article stating that Tyson would no longer train with Rooney. Tyson formally terminated his boxer–trainer relationship with Rooney later that year.

Issue. Does an oral contract between a fight trainer and a professional boxer to train the boxer "for as long as the boxer fights professionally" establish a definite duration, or does it constitute employment for an indefinite duration within the scope of the at-will rule?

Language of the Court. Bellacosa, J.: **The case was tried in the Federal District Court for the Northern District of New York; a jury rendered a $ 4,415,651 verdict for Rooney. The Trial Judge granted Tyson's post-trial motion for judgment as a matter of law; the verdict was set aside and the lawsuit dismissed. Rooney appealed to the Second Circuit Court of Appeals. It certified the question to this Court in order to decide its appeal in accordance with governing New York substantive law. We narrowly answer the core question as posed, that this durational clause satisfies New York's standard with sufficient definitiveness. The jury in Federal court in Albany returned its verdict in favor of Rooney in 1996. Tyson countered after the trial that the agreement was for an indefinite duration and was terminable at will under New York law and therefore unenforceable as a matter of law, regardless of the jury's verdict. The District Court agreed with Tyson's legal position and granted him the post-trial victory. The trial judge reasoned that "under New York law, terms such as 'permanent employment,' 'until retirement' or 'long term' do not state a definite term of employment as a matter of law." The court concluded that "the alleged term of the employment contract, 'for as long as Tyson boxes professionally,' does not state a term of definite duration as a matter of law." It finally declared that "the nature of the proof offered at trial cannot sustain a finding that the employment relationship was anything other than one at-will."**

The range of the employment relationship, concededly created and actualized for several years in the framework of this Federal dispute, is established by the definable commencement and conclusion of Tyson's professional boxing career. Though the times are not precisely predictable and calculable to dates certain, they are legally and experientially limited and ascertainable by objective benchmarks. That is what makes this case distinctive within the myriad of arrangements people may undertake.

Decision. Yes. The oral contractual language is capable of being determined and is sufficient to satisfy an employment term of definite duration.

CASE QUESTIONS

Critical Legal Thinking. Do you agree with the New York Court of Appeals that the court should apply a standard for the term of the contract outside of the precise terms of the agreement?

Business Ethics. Do you think this is a fair decision? What advice would you give other employers considering the term of employment?

Contemporary Business. In the dissenting opinion, it is argued that the majority opinion endorses a concept of indefinite employment. What are your personal views relative to those expressed by the dissent?

Express contracts of employment include executive contracts of employment, offer letters, employment applications, fringe-benefit agreements, and collective-bargaining agreements. When a contract contains all of the terms and conditions of the relationship and expressly states whether the contract length is for a definite term or is at-will, it is difficult for either party to argue that the terms of agreement differ from those stated in the contract.

Implied contractual liability may also arise within statements made in employment manuals and handbooks that the employer creates and distributes to the employees. The law will recognize an implied employment contract when the parties do not explicitly agree to terms but their words or conduct reasonably imply that they have agreed to certain terms. If the language is specific enough to give assurances to the employees that termination will only occur upon certain conditions, then the presumption of **at-will** status will be overcome. For example, if an employment manual stated that an employee would only be discharged after a series of progressive disciplinary procedures, then discharging an employee without following the procedures can result in a **wrongful discharge** claim. Oral assurances of continued job security can also create a contract to terminate only for cause. Disclaimers of termination only for cause must be conspicuous and clear to a reasonable person to avoid liability for an implied contract to terminate only for cause. Of course, narrowly defining "for cause" is equally important, as any ambiguity will be resolved in favor of the employee.

> ***Example:*** Mr. Pugh was employed by See's Candies for 32 years, starting as a dishwasher and eventually earning promotion to vice-president and a place on the board of directors. Despite record sales and a conspicuous role accompanying the See's president to visit overseas candy manufacturers, Pugh was terminated without any reason being expressed. He sued for wrongful termination. In part, Pugh relied on the frequent statements by his superiors, such as, "If you are loyal to [See's] and do a good job, your future is secure." During his employment, the company had a practice of not terminating employees except for good cause. Pugh never received any criticisms of his work or notices that he needed to improve his performance. The California Supreme Court held that an employer's right to terminate is not absolute and is subject to public policy and express and implied contract exceptions. It held that Pugh had been arbitrarily fired in violation of the implied contract between him and the company.[4]

Students should be wary of applying the implied contract liability theory too broadly. An employment contract that is implied from the circumstances can strain the application of the facts of *Pugh*. This case might serve as a precedent for an implied contract for lifetime employment; however, it is best viewed as a general theory of employer liability that is subject to the facts of each case.

Concept Summary
Employer's Implied Contractual Liability

In the absence of an express written or oral contract, an employee may be able to establish that there exists an implied promise by the employer not to terminate the employment relationship except for good cause. Circumstances supporting such a contractual promise include:

- the employer's handbook, past personnel policies and practices;
- the employee's longevity with the employer;
- communications and actions of the employer assuring the employee of long-term employment (such as bonuses, advancements, promotional track assignments, etc.); and
- the customs and practices of the employer's industry.

Implied Covenant of Good Faith and Fair Dealing
A "catch-all" basis on which to award damages to a discharged employee for a firing that occurred without good cause under the circumstances. A minority of states allow this exception to the at-will doctrine.

The **implied covenant of good faith and fair dealing** has been recognized by some states as a "catch-all" ground for awarding contractual damages to a discharged employee. The employee in *Foley v. Interactive Data* alleged he was fired for reporting to upper management that the Federal Bureau of Investigation was investigating his new supervisor for embezzlement at his last job. In determining whether such conduct affected public, rather than private, interests, the court suggested it is helpful to consider whether the employer and employee could have entered into an enforceable agreement *prohibiting* the employee from engaging in the conduct. Applying that test, the court determined *Foley* could not state a claim.

CASE 3.2

DEPENDING ON STATE LAW, A BAD-FAITH DISCHARGE LAWSUIT CAN RESULT FROM A TERMINATION OF EMPLOYMENT

FOLEY V. INTERACTIVE DATA CORP.

47 Cal.3d 654 (1988)

Supreme Court of California

Facts. Foley was employed by a subsidiary of Chase Manhattan Bank that marketed computer-based decision-support services. Foley received a steady series of salary increases, promotions, bonuses, awards, and superior performance evaluations. He was named consultant manager of the year and was promoted to branch manager of the bank's Los Angeles office. His annual salary rose dramatically, and he received a merit bonus two days before his discharge in March 1983. He alleged in his lawsuit that the company's officers made repeated oral assurances of job security so long as his performance remained adequate. During his tenure, he also signed various trade-secret agreements that did not indicate that his performance was at-will.

Foley learned that Kuhne, his immediate supervisor, was under investigation by the Federal Bureau of Investigation for embezzling from his former employer. Foley reported what he knew about Kuhne to a senior manager, because he was "worried about working for Kuhne and having him in a supervisory position, in view of Kuhne's suspected criminal conduct." Foley asserted he "made this disclosure in the interest and for the benefit of his employer," allegedly because he believed that because defendant and its parent do business with the financial community on a confidential basis, the company would have a legitimate interest in knowing about a high executive's alleged prior criminal conduct. In September 1983, after Foley's discharge, Kuhne pleaded guilty in federal court to a felony count of embezzlement.

In response to Foley's communication, the senior manager allegedly told Foley not to discuss "rumors" and to "forget what he heard" about Kuhne's past. Foley was told the bank had decided to replace him for "performance reasons" and that he could transfer to a position in another division in Waltham, Massachusetts. Foley was told that if he did not accept a transfer, he might be demoted; he was not told he might be fired. One week later, in Waltham, Foley was told he was not doing a good job; six days later, he was told he could continue as branch manager if he "agreed to go on a 'performance plan.'" However, Foley's boss informed Foley that he had the choice of resigning or being fired. The manager offered Foley neither a performance plan nor an option to transfer to another position.

The trial court dismissed Foley's complaint based on his at-will status. The court of appeal affirmed the dismissal. Foley appealed to the state supreme court.

Issue. If state law does not recognize a cause of action for wrongful discharge, can the employee assert an implied contractual covenant of good faith and fair dealing between the employer and employee that entitles the employee to be terminated only for good cause?

Language of the Court. Lucas, C.J.: **Even where employment is at will, numerous federal and state statutes already impose express limitations on the right of an employer to discharge at will. . . . Plaintiff here alleged repeated oral assurances of job security and consistent promotions, salary increases and bonuses during the term of his employment contributing to his reasonable expectation that he would not be discharged except for good cause.**

Permitting proof of and reliance on implied-in-fact contract terms does not nullify the at-will rule, it merely treats such contracts in a manner in keeping with general contract law. . . . Plaintiff alleges that he supplied the company valuable and separate consideration by signing an agreement whereby he promised not to compete or conceal any computer-related information from

defendant for one year after termination. The noncompetition agreement and its attendant "Disclosure and Assignment of Proprietary Information, Inventions, etc." may be probative evidence that "it is more probable that the parties intended a continuing relationship, with limitations upon the employer's dismissal authority [because the] employee has provided some benefit to the employer, or suffers some detriment, beyond the usual rendition of service."

Decision. Yes. An implied-in-fact contract to not discharge except for good cause may exist within an employment context.

CASE QUESTIONS

Critical Legal Thinking. An employer's decision to terminate an employee can be arbitrary and unwise and still not be actionable. In this decision, the Supreme Court of California held that a separate emotional distress claim for wrongful termination from employment did not exist. The contractual nature of the employment relationship was preserved by this court and did not extend tort remedy for bad faith discharge to the employment arena. Do you think that this is a wise policy decision by this court?

Business Ethics. In a subsequent decision of that court, the court held that if the employer emphasized the at-will nature of employment, then the implied covenant of good faith and fair dealing would not transform the at-will relationship into something other than that condition (*Guz v. Bechtel National, Inc.*, 24 Cal. 4th 317 (2000)). What could you do to ensure that your company retained the unfettered right to discharge at-will?

Contemporary Business. Foley lost his case for wrongful discharge in violation of public policy because this exception to the "at-will" status applies only where the interests at issue involve public policy and not the private interests of the employer. Does this limit the potential for individuals, who report corporate improprieties, to serve as whistleblowers?

Management Application
Do Employee Handbooks Create Too Much Liability?

The need for uniformity in the treatment of employees becomes apparent as a company grows larger. Policies need to be consolidated for the benefit of employees as well as their managers. The advantages of having a consolidated policy is clear in that consistency will reduce the risk of discrimination claims made by individuals within a protected class. In addition, the clarity of a stated, written policy will promote morale and lessen miscommunication within the organization. Termination often invites a lawsuit on the basis that the former employee was treated unfairly or inconsistently. Written protocols relating to promotion eligibility, fringe benefits, disciplinary procedures, and terminations must be administered fairly and consistently to reduce the risk of lawsuits.

The major disadvantage of employee handbooks or manuals is that they limit employer discretion. In addition, because laws and circumstances change, they need to be periodically updated and revised to conform to current business needs. Many companies distribute loose-leaf manuals to employees; others favor publishing the handbook or policies on the employer's intranet. While a company intranet allows policies to be updated promptly, some type of acknowledgement process should be used to ensure that employees are aware of changes.

Statutory or Public Policy Exceptions

Both legislative enacted laws and regulations and judicially created public policies provide certain exceptions for terminations violating strong **statutory** or **public policies**. Generally, these exceptions fall within these categories:

- Numerous federal and state **statutes** limit the employer's right to terminate and discipline employees.

  Example: **Antidiscrimination Statutes:** Refusing to hire, promote, or train or unfairly discharging or disciplining employees based on their race, color, national origin or ancestry, sex (including pregnancy, childbirth, and gender identity), age, physical or mental disability, religion, and genetic information.

  Example: **Leave of Absence Statutes:** Covered employers may not discipline or discharge eligible employees for exercising a statutory right to leave, including those for pregnancy, disability, work-related leaves, the "serious health condition" of the employee or of a family member, jury duty and voting (under some state laws), and military service.

  Example: **Whistleblowing Statutes:** These protect employees from being discharged, disciplined, or retaliated against by their employer for reporting such things as discrimination against an employee following the employee's report to superiors regarding the employer's violation of a statute, the employer's submission to the government of a false or fraudulent claim for payment or some other fraudulent record, and unsafe work conditions.

- **Public policy** considerations prohibit an employer from coercing employees to commit or conceal some unlawful activity. For a **public policy** limitation to at-will employment to be recognized, a fundamental public policy expressed in a statute or a constitutional provision must support the claim that the termination violated law. The **public policy** on which the exception to the rule is based must be one that benefits the public at large, not just the individual employee or employer. This exception does not protect private party disputes. The interests involved must affect the widespread public interests.

  Example: Some state laws expressly prohibit an employer from requiring nonowner employees to execute a covenant-not-to-compete agreement with the employer following termination of employment. Terminating an employee for refusing to execute such a non-compete covenant would violate public policy and would provide the basis for a wrongful termination action against the employer.

Retaliatory terminations that are deemed to violate public policy are usually based on terminations made because the employee refused to violate the law (such as by refusing to commit perjury); the employee was performing a statutory obligation (such as when subpoenaed to testify, testifying in court); the employee exercised a legal right (such as refusing an employer's order to stop associating with certain people after work); and the employee opposed or reported the employer's unlawful conduct (such as by reporting the employer's discriminatory acts).

Montana is the only state that has adopted the Model Employment Termination Act. This model piece of legislation states "an employer may not terminate the employment of an employee without good cause." The act limits the application of at-will termination for employees who have been employed by an employer for at least one year. The act provides that parties may substitute a severance pay agreement for the good-cause requirement. The good-cause requirement also applies when the parties have an oral or written contract for a fixed duration. The act suggests that disputes arising under it be resolved by arbitration and not court action.[5]

Protection for Whistleblowers

Who is a **whistleblower**? According to *Black's Law Dictionary* (8th ed. 2004), a whistleblower is "[a]n employee who reports employer wrongdoing to a governmental or law enforcement agency." Typically, the person is an insider who reports the misconduct within the agency to senior managers. Sometimes someone outside the organization may equally be considered a **whistleblower**. In exchange for furthering the public good by making the disclosure, the **whistleblower** is often protected from retaliation on the job.

Whistleblower
An employee who reports the wrongdoings of employers to authorities.

Example: After a girl's basketball coach at a public high school complained unsuccessfully to his supervisor that the team was not receiving equal funding and equal access to athletic equipment and facilities, the coach began to receive poor performance evaluations and was replaced as coach. He sued for discriminatory retaliation following his complaint about sex discrimination in violation of Title IX. The U.S. Supreme Court agreed with him.[6]

Much controversy and differences exist in the myriad of state statutes that grant limited to full legal protection to **whistleblowers** for making their disclosures. The laws are complex and inconsistent among state and local jurisdictions. Most states recognize this protection as either a common law or a statutory exception to the at-will doctrine of employment. The majority of states provide for such protection. However, about a dozen states have enacted statutory protection for **whistleblowers**. In addition, the majority of states offer additional special protections for governmental employees who act as **whistleblowers**.

In the following 5-4 decision, the Supreme Court scaled back the protections for governmental workers who become **whistleblowers**. While it pertains to a public employee speech case, it serves as an important precedent for both the public and private work sectors.

CASE 3.3

WHISTLEBLOWERS DO NOT ENJOY ABSOLUTE FREE SPEECH

GARCETTI V. CEBALLOS

547 U.S. 410 (2006)

Supreme Court of the United States

Facts. The Los Angeles County District Attorney's Office had employed Richard Ceballos since 1989 as a deputy district attorney. He exercised certain supervisory responsibilities over other lawyers. In February 2000, a defense attorney contacted Ceballos about a pending criminal case. In response, Ceballos determined that an affidavit used to obtain a critical search warrant contained serous misrepresentations. He submitted a memo to his supervisors that summarized his findings. Ceballos continued to intervene with regard to the prosecution's continued use of the affidavit at trial, but eventually the trial court rejected the challenge to the warrant. Ceballos claimed that in the aftermath of his objections he was subjected to a series of retaliatory employment actions. The actions included a demotion, transfer to another courthouse, and denial of a promotion. He filed suit for a violation of his civil rights and his First and Fourteenth Amendment rights. The district court ruled that he was not entitled to First Amendment protection for the contents of his memo. The Ninth Circuit Court of Appeals reversed, holding that his allegations of wrongdoing in the memo were protected free speech. The Supreme Court granted *certiorari.*

Issue. Whether a memorandum prepared by a district attorney in the scope of his official job duties was protected speech under the First Amendment.

Language of the Court. Kennedy, J.: . . . **The Court's [prior] decisions . . . have sought both to promote the individual and societal interests that are served when employees speak as citizens on matters of public concern and to respect the needs of government employers attempting to perform their important public functions. See, e.g., Rankin, 483 U.S., at 384 (recognizing "the dual role of the public employer as a provider of public services and as a government entity operating under the constraints of the First Amendment"). Underlying our cases has been the premise that while the First Amendment invests public employees with certain rights, it does not empower them to "constitutionalize the employee grievance." (Citations omitted.)**

Exposing governmental inefficiency and misconduct is a matter of considerable significance. As the Court noted in Connick, public employers should, "as a matter of good judgment," be "receptive to constructive criticism offered by their employees." . . . The dictates of sound judgment are reinforced by the powerful network of legislative enactments — such as whistleblower protection laws and labor codes — available to those who seek to expose wrongdoing. . . . Cases involving government attorneys implicate additional safeguards in the form of, for example, rules of conduct and constitutional obligations apart from the First Amendment. See, e.g., Cal. Rule Prof. Conduct 5-110 (2005) ("A member in government service shall not institute or cause to be instituted criminal charges when the member knows or should know that the charges are not supported by probable cause"); . . . These imperatives, as well as obligations arising from any other applicable constitutional provisions and mandates of the criminal and civil laws, protect employees and provide checks on supervisors who would order unlawful or otherwise inappropriate actions.

We reject, however, the notion that the First Amendment shields from discipline the expressions employees make pursuant to their professional duties. Our precedents do not support the existence of a constitutional cause of action behind every statement a public employee makes in the course of doing his or her job.

Decision. No. When public employees make statements as part of their official duties, they are not speaking as citizens for First Amendment purposes. The Constitution does not insulate their statements from employer discipline.

CASE QUESTIONS

Critical Legal Thinking. Does this ruling free a government manager to make necessary personnel decisions without fear of lawsuits?

Business Ethics. One critic, Stephen Kohn, chairman of the National Whistleblower Center, said that "[t]he ruling is a victory for every crooked politician in the United States." What is the proper balance between addressing official wrongdoing and maintaining efficient administration of public offices?

Contemporary Business. Can you think of any other examples when governmental whistleblowers should be able to speak without fear of losing their jobs?

A federal statute protects all federal employees and federal job applicants who are **whistleblowers**.[7] Unless the law prohibits disclosure, the statute protects those who disclose evidence that the employee or applicant reasonably believes shows:

- A violation of any law, rule, or regulation, or
- Gross management, a gross waste of funds, an abuse of authority, or a substantial and specific danger to public health or safety.

Two powerful **whistleblower** statutes with supporting federal regulations supplement the general federal **whistleblower** statute. The most widely used of these two federal statutes is the antiretaliation provision of the **False Claims Act**. Originally enacted during the Civil War to prosecute those defrauding the federal government, the act was amended in 1986 to state:

> *Any employee who is discharged, demoted, suspended, threatened, harassed, or in any other manner discriminated against in the terms and conditions of employment by his or her employer because of lawful acts done by the employee on behalf of his employer or others in furtherance of an action under this section, including investigation for, initiation of, testimony for, or assistance in an action filed or to be filed under this section, shall be entitled to all relief necessary to make the employee whole.*[8]

The statute has far-reaching implications. It extends to any activity funded by the federal government for which the money sought from the government is not lawfully due the proposed recipient of that funding. False-claim proceedings can arise in such diverse industries as defense contracting, federally funded public works construction projects, educational institutions, government vendors, health-care providers and facilities, and companies using governmental facilities or property. In exchange for the information, the government can either bring a lawsuit or one may be brought in the name of the government to collect the value of the misdeed, and the claimant may recover a generous contingency fee for his or her efforts (known as a **qui tam** provision). Thus, a broad base of potential private sector employees could report misdeeds to federal authorities and be protected from retaliation in their private sector employment.

The second leading federal statute is the **Sarbanes-Oxley Act (SOX)**, enacted by Congress in 2002 to encourage corporate fraud reporting following the Enron, World-Com, and other corporate scandals of that time. Federal courts will refer to the general body of employment discrimination law for guidance in some areas, but where the **SOX** statue provides a specific framework, the court follows the statute. **SOX** created new protections for **whistleblowers**. Specifically, employees of public companies who disclose adverse information to a regulatory body or a work supervisor or who assist in investigations are protected from retaliation. In addition, **SOX** requires an inside corporate counsel to report to the president of the company evidence of a material violation of securities law or a breach of fiduciary duty or similar violation by the company; if there is no appropriate response to the company's audit committee, the violation must be reported to another committee of independent directors or to the full board of directors.[9] The act applies to public reporting companies and requires, among other things, that senior executives take individual responsibility for the accuracy and completeness of corporate financial reports. Section 1107 of **SOX** states:

> *Whoever knowingly, with the intent to retaliate, takes any action harmful to any person, including interference with the lawful employment or livelihood of any person, for providing to a law enforcement officer any truthful information relating to the commission or possible commission of any federal offence, shall be fined under this title, imprisoned not more than 10 years, or both.*

Under §1514A of **SOX** it is stated:

> *No [publicly registered] company or any officer, employee, or agent of such company, may discharge, demote, suspend, threaten, harass, or in any other manner discriminate against an*

employee in the terms and conditions of employment because of any lawful act done by the employee — (1) to provide information . . . which the employee reasonably believes constitutes [mail, wire, bank, or securities fraud; or (2) to file . . . testify . . . or . . . assist in [any legal proceeding relating to that fraud], any rule or regulation of the Securities and Exchange Commission, or any provision of Federal law relating to fraud against shareholders.

Many recent federal court decisions make clear that the complaining person must be engaged in a protected activity sufficient to satisfy the first element of the prima facie whistleblower claim under **SOX**. Under §1514A the proof required of a **whistleblower** claimant can be high.

Concept Summary
Whistleblower Protection Under Sarbanes-Oxley

Unlike the proof used in employment discrimination cases, the **SOX** whistleblower must prove:

- engagement in a protected activity;
- employer knowledge of the protected activity;
- commencement of an unfavorable personnel action; and
- the existence of circumstances suggesting that the protected activity was a contributing factor in the unfavorable action.

Even if the plaintiff proves his or her **SOX** case, "[t]he defendant employer may avoid liability if it can demonstrate by clear and convincing evidence that it 'would have taken the same unfavorable personnel action in the absence of [protected] behavior.'"[10]

Few cases define what constitutes a protected activity. In one Fifth Circuit Court of Appeals case, the Court held that to constitute protected activity, "[a]n employee's complaint must 'definitively and specifically relate' to one of the six enumerated categories found in §1514A: mail fraud; wire fraud; bank fraud; securities fraud; any rule or regulation of the SEC; or (6) any provision of federal law relating to fraud against shareholders."[11]

Example: Judy Collins served as a director of marketing for a Florida homebuilder. She was terminated within an initial 90-day assessment review period during which either party could terminate the employment without giving a reason. Shortly after starting her employment, she began having conflicts with her manager stemming from the use of an advertising agency that Collins thought was being overpaid. She suspected kickbacks were occurring from outside vendors to company managers. Collins did not specifically tell her superiors that illegal activity was taking place in the company when she was terminated for personality conflicts with her superiors. Collins's claim was protected under the whistleblower protections of SOX as Beazer Homes, her employer, was a publicly traded company. Her allegations supported a claim that the company violated its internal accounting controls under the Securities Act of 1934. Summary judgment for the employer was denied and the case was allowed to proceed to trial.[12]

A number of other federal acts also protect **whistleblowers**. A partial list includes the Water Pollution Control Act;[13] the Clean Air Act;[14] the Comprehensive Environmental Response, Compensation & Liability Act;[15] the Davis-Bacon Act;[16] Section 11(c) of the Occupational Safety & Health Act;[17] and the Fair Labor Standards Act.[18]

Example: While the Occupational Safety and Health Administration is responsible for protecting workers' safety and health, it cannot possibly inspect every workplace in the country or identify every potential health and safety hazard that might exist. It is critical that workers feel free to raise these concerns without fear of retaliation by their employers. Section 11(c) of the Occupational Safety & Health Act prohibits retaliation by employers against workers who "blow the whistle" by exposing workplace health and safety hazards.

Section 105(c) of the Federal Mine Safety and Health Act of 1977, The Mine Act, protects the rights of miners, their representatives, and applicants for employment against discriminatory acts. This federal safety act relates to the safety of underground and surface mines. It protects persons working in these facilities from acts of discrimination, such as retaliation, that they might incur after reporting a health or safety concern to the federal regulators. This act also allows the individual to sue for damages suffered because of protected activities, such as **whistleblowing**.

Employers must be cognizant of the employee's First Amendment rights. An employer may not terminate an employee in retaliation for exercising free speech right protected by the First Amendment. That Amendment protects the right of employees to speak out on matters of public interest and concern. Such statements may also be interpreted as protected under an applicable **whistleblower** statute.

Each state has developed certain public policies with which employers must comply. For example, virtually all states have a prohibition against terminating an employee for filing a workers' compensation claim. Employers must replace injured workers with healthy ones so production does not suffer; but allowing termination of injured employees would lead to dismal, unsafe working environments. Moreover, most state laws prohibit the termination of **at-will** employees who report unsafe or illegal activities permitted by the employer. Employers must be aware that courts will readily entertain an employee's claim that the discharge violated **public policy**. An employer can violate **public policy** when terminating an employee who persists in pursuing an unwarranted claim.

Example: Manuel Barbosa told his payroll department and his supervisor that he and two co-workers were not paid overtime. The employer made the payments and then discovered it was not possible that they had worked overtime. Barbosa offer to repay the employer, but the employer discharged him claiming he lied about the overtime. Such a discharge can violate public policy because Barbosa should be allowed to prove that he had a reasonable good-faith belief that he was entitled to overtime and, if proved, that he had not lied to the employer. Discharge would then be without justification.[19]

Management Application
When Does "At-Will" Employment Commence?

Karon Comeaux filed suit against Brown & Williamson Tobacco Corporation alleging that B & W had reneged on its promise to him of employment. In 1987, Comeaux applied for a sales representative position and alleged that, after several interviews with B & W, the company's hiring manager told him orally that he was hired. Comeaux claims that his offer of employment was contingent on his moving to live within five minutes of his first sales stop in Fremont, California. He passed a physical examination, gave notice to his then-current employer, and moved with his new wife from San Jose, California, to Fremont. After moving to be near his new job, Comeaux was then told by B & W that, while there were no problems with his employment, his start date with B & W would be delayed. B & W ran a credit check without Comeaux's consent and on discovering a poor credit history decided to revoke its prior offer of employment. The district court granted a motion for summary judgment in favor of B & W on many theories, including the integration clause in its application and that, in any event, Comeaux would have been an at-will employee of the company. In his appeal, Comeaux argued two theories: that he was entitled to be hired because he relied on the employer's representations and so quit his job and moved to the new employer's location; and he was told that he could be fired only for cause, despite contrary wording in his application.

At the time Comeaux applied for his position with B & W, he signed an employment application that included the following integration clause language:

> *It is agreed and understood that by assigning me work with such salary as may be incident thereto that this application shall constitute the terms of the contract of employment and that the relation between me and the Corporation shall be a hiring at-will, terminable at any time by either of the parties thereto.*

B & W contended that, because of the above clause, its employment relationship with Comeaux was "at-will" and that it could terminate Comeaux at any time, for any reason, without liability. It asserted that its decision to "terminate" Comeaux even before he was assigned work and a salary is governed by the at-will language in the employment application. Comeaux, in response, contended that his employment relationship with B & W could be terminated for just cause only. Relying on two alternative theories, he contends that B & W personnel made oral assurances to him at the time he signed the employment application, indicating that employment would be terminated only for violations of company policy and that his relocation and resignation from his prior job constitute independent consideration sufficient to create a "for cause" employment relationship.[20]

Discussion Questions

1. Did the B & W contract come into effect at the time of Comeaux's application or when B & W assigned Comeaux work and a salary? The contract read: "[B]y assigning me work [and] salary this application shall constitute the terms of the contract of employment [which] shall be a hiring at-will, terminable at any time."
2. How would you characterize the ethical conduct of B & W when it violated its own internal policy by failing to inform Comeaux that his future employment was contingent on the results of a credit check?
3. What would you recommend the company do to minimize its exposure to similar claims in the future?

Human Resource Form
Documenting At-Will Status

Employers should adopt the following language in employment applications and manuals:

IN APPLICATIONS

If I am hired, I agree to conform to all rules, practices, and standards of the ________ ("Corporation"). I further agree that my employment and all benefits can be terminated at will, with or without cause, and with or without notice to me, at any time, either at my election or that of the Corporation. I understand that no employee or agent of the Corporation, except for the President or the Vice President of Human Resources, has the authority to enter into any agreement for employment for any specified period of time. If an agreement is made that my employment is to be other than at-will, a written agreement specifying the intent to do so must be signed by me and the President of the Corporation for it to be enforceable.

IN WRITTEN ACKNOWLEDGEMENTS EXECUTED BY NEW EMPLOYEES

I have received and read a copy of the Corporation Employee Handbook. I understand that the policies, rules, and benefits described in it are subject to change at the sole discretion of management at any time. I further understand that my employment is terminable at will, by either myself or the Firm, regardless of the length of my employment or the granting of benefits of any kind.

I understand that no contract of employment other than "at will" has been expressed or implied, and that no circumstances arising out of my employment will alter my "at will" employment relationship unless expressed in writing, with the understanding specifically set forth and signed by the President of the Corporation and myself. I understand that my signature below indicates that I have read and understand the above statements and have read and received a copy of the Corporation Employee Handbook.

IN THE EMPLOYMENT MANUAL

<u>At-Will Employment at Our Company</u>. You are free to terminate your employment with the Corporation at any time, with or without a reason, and the Corporation has the right to terminate your employment at any time, with or without a reason. Although the Corporation may choose to terminate employment for cause, cause is not required. This is called "at-will" employment. No one other than the President or the Vice President of Human Resources can enter into an agreement for employment for a specified period or make any agreement or representations contrary to this policy. If an agreement is made that your employment is to be other than at-will, a written agreement specifying the intent to do so must be signed by the President of the Corporation and by you for it to be enforceable.

Business Torts: Companion Claims in Employment Litigation

Employment disputes often erupt into legal proceedings that involve a variety of legal theories. Besides claims of discrimination against protected classes of persons, both protected and unprotected employees may assert other types of legal claims that have developed from **common law** or **nonstatutory theories**. The types of damages that the claimant seeks to recover may involve not only those relating to the employment, such as for lost wages, but also those arising in **tort**. A **tort** is a civil wrong, whether intentional or accidental, for which a claim for damages may be brought. A **tort** addresses *wrongful conduct* committed between private parties.

We will review the most commonly encountered **torts** within the employment context. These **tort causes of action** include:

- infliction of emotional distress
- defamation
- interference with contractual relations
- invasion of privacy claims
- misrepresentation and fraud
- false imprisonment or false arrest
- negligent evaluation and termination
- negligent hiring, retention, supervision, and retaliation

Defamation
A factually false statement communicated to a third person regarding a person or business that causes injury to reputation or character. It can also expose the target to public hatred, contempt, or ridicule. The communication can be made orally, in writing, or through images.

Many of these torts accompany the typical wrongful termination claim that a plaintiff pursues against an employer. They often involve compensatory as well as punitive damages. For example, if an employer falsely accused an employee of theft, the employee could sue the employer for damages for **defamation** of character. In the **defamation** case, the employee might recover **compensatory damages** for the harm caused to the employee's reputation.

In contrast, a crime declares conduct as *illegal* if it is considered so serious that it offends society and should result in *criminal punishment*. Certain conduct might be *both* a tort and a crime. For example, an individual might be sued in civil court for the **tort** of battery, that is, the unconsented, unwelcome contact with the person of another; but he may also be charged with criminal assault by law enforcement and face criminal charges for the same conduct. When we identify a situation as wrongful, we are addressing tortious behavior; but when we state that conduct is illegal, we are classifying the conduct as criminal. Do not misuse the terms.

Management Application
Vicarious Tort Liability and *Respondeat Superior*

Restatements are model definitions created by legal experts, professors, and judges for adoption by legislatures and courts. Restatement (Second) of Agency §219(1) provides that "a master is subject to liability for the torts of his servants committed while acting in the scope of their employment." This legal principle, known as the doctrine of ***respondeat superior***, traces its roots to Roman law.

As a matter of **public policy,** the courts have imposed liability on an employer for the acts of the employee. When working within the scope of his or her employment, the employee's acts are deemed the act of the employer. The employee is as an agent working on behalf of the employer as principal. In apportioning liability between the employee and the employer to pay for the harm suffered by the injured third party, the employer is viewed as having the financial resources to pay for the resulting harm and carries insurance to cover damages created by the employee.

The imposition of derivative liability on the employer is termed **vicarious tort liability**. This is liability imposed on the employer without the direct fault of the employer. Arguments that the employee acted outside the scope of employment are difficult to win. Juries are sympathetic to the injured person. In contrast to vicarious liability, the employer is always liable for the direct harm it causes an injured person.

In the workers' compensation branch of the law, liability is imposed because the injury "arises out of and in the course of employment." In contrast, **vicarious tort liability** imposed on an employer arising from the doctrine of ***respondeat superior*** is narrower. In a ***respondeat superior*** case, the harm suffered by the third person from an act or omission of the employee imposes liability only when it is a foreseeable risk arising from the employment. Remember that defining whether an employee was acting within the "scope of employment" for third-party tort claims is entirely different from those rules applied in the workers' compensation system because the public policies underlying ***respondeat superior*** and workers' compensation are entirely different.

The company that retains through contract the services of an independent contractor is not liable for the torts of the independent contractor. For example, if a company retains a contractor and the contractor wrongfully mistreats the contractor's own workers, the company is not liable for the resulting harm. Subject to some exceptions, the doctrine of ***respondeat superior*** does not apply to the acts of the independent contractor. However, the employer is always liable to workers for the harm caused by the employer's own negligent acts. Other exceptions include work involving hazardous activities and the employer's failure to supervise the independent contractor's work to the extent that such failure contributed to the physical injuries suffered by the independent contractor's workers. Further consideration of these liability issues will be discussed in the chapter on occupational safety and workers' compensation.

Infliction of Emotional Distress

This tort involves conduct by an employer conduct so extreme and outrageous that it was certain or substantially certain to result in emotional distress. This tort may occur independently of any physical injury or contact between the parties and involves distress that a reasonable person would view as severe. Ordinary emotions related to

Cause of Action
A legally recognized claim based on a set of facts that gives a person the right to petition a court or arbitrator for damages or relief against another person.

Compensatory Damages
Damages awarded to replace the actual loss or harm suffered, such as personal property loss or for pain and suffering.

losing one's job do not constitute grounds for this tort; the conduct has to be *extreme and outrageous* enough to offend any reasonable person. State laws vary as to the elements of this **cause of action**. Most state law appellate decisions hold that termination of employment alone does not support **punitive damages**. However, juries evaluating an employee's tort claim for intentional or negligent infliction of emotional distress often award such damages. For example, if an employer knowingly allowed supervisors to directly or indirectly allow others to be harassed and humiliated at work by such base conduct as would offend the reasonable person, the employer may be liable under the doctrine of ***respondeat superior*** to a third-party plaintiff and be required to pay **compensatory damages** as well as **punitive damages**.

The issue of this tort most often occurs with regard to the manner in which the employer handles the termination of the employee. Merely discharging an **at-will** employee does not constitute **intentional infliction of emotional distress**; however, if the employer mishandled the situation, it could very well lead to such a claim.

CASE 3.4

CONDUCT MUST BE SO VILE AS TO SURPASS ALL POSSIBLE BOUNDS OF DECENCY

WAGNER V. TEXAS A&M ET AL.

939 F.Supp. 1297 (S.D. Tex. 1996)

U.S. District Court for the So. District of Texas

Facts. Professor Wagner was a tenured member of the medical school faculty at Texas A&M. He was a department chair when he alleged that another professor in the Department, Dr. Michael Trulson ("Trulson"), had engaged in scientific fraud. In response to Wagner's allegations, Trulson allegedly accused Wagner of homosexuality and improprieties such as drug abuse, theft, fraud, and improper use of prescription medicine. Due to Wagner's persistence in pursuing the fraud allegations against Trulson, Trulson was eventually discharged from his position. Wagner contends that when he returned from a sabbatical, he was prohibited from teaching or attending his neuroanatomy class. . . . In response to his complaints that he was being retaliated against for being a whistleblower, an independent committee found that Wagner's claims about Trulson were well founded and that his reputation had been damaged by the university's handling of the Trulson matter. However, Wagner's class schedule and appointment were constantly adjusted upon his return from a medical leave. The school also asserted that it had no further duty to negotiate with Wagner for his reintegration into the faculty as required by the committee. Wagner filed a complaint alleging many causes of action including intentional infliction of emotional distress and defamation. The Company moved for summary judgment.

Issue. On the facts presented, could Wagner sue for infliction of emotional distress?

Language of the Court. Crone, J.: . . . **To intentional infliction of emotional distress, Wagner must establish: (1) the Defendants acted intentionally or recklessly; (2) the Defendants' conduct was extreme and outrageous; (3) the Defendants' actions caused him emotional distress; and (4) the emotional distress he suffered was severe. (Citations omitted.) While "extreme and outrageous," as used in the second element of this standard is an amorphous phrase that escapes precise definition, there appears to be a consensus that conduct is "outrageous" if it is "atrocious" and surpasses "all possible bounds of decency," such that it is "utterly intolerable in a civilized community." . . . Generally, the case is one in which a recitation of the facts to an average member of the community would lead him to exclaim, "Outrageous." . . . Liability does not extend to mere insults, indignities, threats, annoyances, petty oppressions, or other trivialities. . . . There is no occasion for the law to intervene in every case where someone's feelings are hurt.**

Although Wagner may be suffering from emotional distress, he has not shown any extreme and outrageous conduct by the Defendants during the relevant time period. As noted above, only events that occurred after November 30, 1993, fall within the applicable statute of limitations. . . . The conduct alleged by Wagner after November 30, 1993, is far less egregious than other actions found not to constitute intentional infliction of emotional distress as matter of law in a number of cases. . . . Only in the most unusual of situations does conduct move out of the "realm of an ordinary employment dispute," into the classification of "extreme and outrageous," as required for the tort of intentional infliction of emotional distress. . . . While the Defendants' actions may have been thoughtless and perhaps unlawful under other theories, their conduct was not so vile and reprehensible that it surpassed "all possible bounds of decency" or can be viewed as "utterly intolerable in a civilized community." Under these circumstances, summary judgment is proper as to Wagner's claim for intentional infliction of emotional distress.

Decision. No. The conduct complained about was not extreme and outrageous. The conduct involved ordinary employment issues with which the courts will not become involved.

CASE QUESTIONS

Critical Legal Thinking. Do you think this is a fair application of the law by the court? Did the medical school act ethically?

Business Ethics. If the medical school deliberately rescheduled Wagner's teaching load so that he would teach a class on material with which he had no familiarity, removed resources for his use, and denied the existence of agreements for the terms of his retirement, what further arguments could you make on his behalf that these actions constituted infliction of emotional distress?

Contemporary Business. Does this decision encourage employers to create unpleasant environments compelling the employee to quit? Does this invite constructive discharge claims?

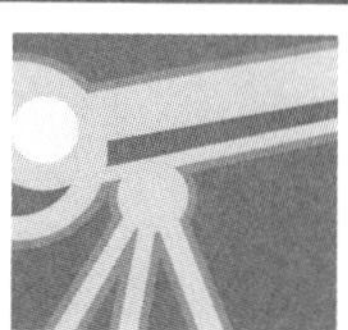

Management Application
Emotional Distress and Workers' Compensation

Some state laws bar recovery arising from the tort of intentional infliction of emotional distress if it relates to an employment-related claim. They mandate that the employee recover monies under the workers' compensation system of that state. Workers' compensation is a system under which employees with workplace injuries are paid monies for their injuries; they may not then sue their employer in court for damages. In response to a speedier resolution and usually a finding of employer liability, the system prevents the employer from having to defend itself in court. Normally, the claimant would not receive the full value of the injuries suffered through a workers' compensation award. However, the majority of states do not restrict the emotional distress damages to the workers' compensation forum. They view the tortious conduct as outside the scope of employment or otherwise not recoverable as a workers' compensation claim. The appellate courts in these states have often held that the physical and mental effect of the employee's termination is outside the employment relationship and that the distress often occurs after the employment relationship ceased.

Defamation

Courts have defined **defamation** in a number of ways. It can involve a claim of a false communication causing injury to a person's reputation or exposing the person to public hatred, contempt, or ridicule. Another **defamation** plaintiff might contend is that the publication tended to prevent third parties from dealing or associating with that person. The **defamatory** statement does not include a mere opinion: It is an unprivileged publication of a false statement to a third person injuring the plaintiff. **Defamatory** statements arise in two forms: **libel**, which is **defamation** arising from a written publication, and **slander**, which arises from an oral utterance. Whether the statement is written or oral, the **defamation** must be published. **Defamatory** remarks made through an Internet communication are treated as libelous. For example, **defamatory** material, which is published and disseminated to company employees through a company intranet, wiki, or even an e-mailed cartoon, can result in the author being sued for **defamation**. An employer may be held liable as a publisher of **defamatory** statements if the company knew or reasonably should have known the publication was untrue.

Defenses to the tort of **defamation** rest on either statements that are absolutely privileged or on others that are qualifiedly privileged. An absolute privilege is one that insulates the employer from liability. A qualified privilege is one that protects someone from being liable for defamation if it can be proved that the statements were made without malice. These defenses include the following:

1. **Truth.** A communication must be *completely* true for the absolute privilege or defense of truth to apply.
2. **Opinion.** A communication based on opinion and not an assertion of a fact is another absolute privilege.
3. **References.** Most jurisdictions recognize a qualified privilege of a former employer to respond to a job reference inquiry from a subsequent prospective employer if the communication was limited to factual, truthful statements about performance, where the reasons for termination made to employees within the company were communicated on a "need to know" basis.

Defamation is a serious risk to employers who are unaware of the many situations in which it may arise. Every sequence of contact between an individual and an employer can give rise to a defamation claim. The most common instances include:

- references and recommendations for former employees and acquaintances to prospective employers (unless state law provides a qualified privilege from defamation);
- employee performance reviews;
- internal employee investigations; and
- self-compelled defamation.

A reference relative to past or current employees is an area of special concern for many employers. Before making a recommendation to a third party, an employer must consider whether the employee has given permission to make the recommendation. If permission was not granted, the employer may become liable for any misstatements, errors, or omissions in the comments made. Moreover, the grant of permission does not shield the recommender from a libel claim. In response to libel claims made against prior and current employers by unhappy workers, many companies have adopted a "no comment" reference policy. In such circumstances, only minimum information, such as dates of employment and positions held, will be provided. If an employer shares information beyond this, the employer may become a party to a **defamation** suit; in addition, the employer could be sued for a failure to provide any qualifying language in the information provided. A good practice for employers to adopt is to require the employer and the employee to agree at the time of hiring what information can be shared with third parties. While that arrangement may not insulate the employer from a **defamation** suit, it can provide suitable information about the employee to a prospective employer.

Some courts have considered whether a corporation is communicating within itself when its supervisors make **defamatory** statements about fellow employees. Such a rule endorses the concept that a corporation should be able to conduct privileged internal discussion of such matters. Other courts have rejected that interpretation, as the following example illustrates.

> ***Example:*** Avery Caldwell, a department manager, was the target of criticism in memos to Caldwell's supervisors written by Staples, one of his subordinates. The relationship between Caldwell and Staples quickly deteriorated, and Staples received a demotion. Caldwell became convinced that computer files had been erased and that Staples was responsible for the erasure. Caldwell told the personnel office and other people within his department that Staples had sabotaged the computers. Staples's lawsuit for defamation was upheld even though the allegedly defamatory statements were made only to persons in the company.[21]

In certain cases, the former employee makes the **defamatory** statement because he or she feels compelled to do so because of defamatory communications made by the former employer. These cases are based on the theory of **"self-compelled publication"** of a **defamatory** statement. In a growing number of states, courts have held a former employer liable for **defamation** if the former employee is given false and **defamatory** grounds for his or her discharge from employment. The former employee would then be compelled to reveal the alleged reasons for the discharge to potential employers. Some courts have held that the former employer coerces the former employee to publicize the defamatory statement. However, other state decisions hold a contrary view, indicating that former employees should not be able to create unilaterally their own causes of action by publishing a **defamatory** statement to a prospective employer. However, this was not the holding of the court in the following case.

CASE 3.5

COMPELLED SELF-PUBLICATION OF REASONS FOR TERMINATION OF PRIOR EMPLOYMENT MAY BE DEFAMATORY

RAYMOND V. IBM

954 F. Supp. 744 (D.Vt. 1997)

U.S. District Court for Dist. of Vermont

Facts. David Raymond worked for IBM when he became concerned over several issues with his manager, including concerns about safety. He took these concerns to a senior manager, in accordance with IBM's "Open Door" policy. Through this policy, an employee may request a review by higher management of his or her manager's actions. During that same time Bob Howard, a co-worker, had reported to Raymond's manager that he and Raymond had broken into an

IBM office and read confidential personnel files. Following an investigation, Raymond was fired.

Raymond filed suit against IBM, alleging, among other things, that IBM was liable for defamation under the doctrine of compelled self-publication. IBM moved for summary judgment on all counts.

Issue. Under the facts presented, should the court adopt the theory of self-compelled defamation?

Language of the Court. Sessions, J.: **Raymond alleges that IBM defamed him under the doctrine of compelled self-publication, because he was forced to repeat the allegedly unfounded reason he was fired in the course of applying for other employment. IBM argues that it is entitled to summary judgment because this doctrine is not and should not be recognized in Vermont, and because Raymond was not forced to disclose the reason he was fired.**

In order to make out a case of defamation, the statement in question must have been communicated to someone other than the plaintiff. If the plaintiff is responsible for the publication to a third party, ordinarily this requirement of publication is not satisfied. (Citation omitted.) . . . However, publication may be established if the Company knows that of necessity the plaintiff must disclose the statement. . . .

In *Lewis v. Equitable Life Assurance Society*, 389 N.W.2d 876 (Minn. 1986), a leading case on the doctrine of compelled self-publication, the Supreme Court of Minnesota adopted a narrow exception to the rule that publication by the plaintiff will not permit recovery. The Court held that when the originator of the defamatory statement "knows, or should know, of circumstances whereby the defamed person has no reasonable means of avoiding publication of the statement," the resultant damages "are fairly viewed as the direct result of the originator's actions." To succeed on his claim, therefore, a plaintiff must show both foreseeability and necessity. . . . Courts in eleven jurisdictions have recognized the doctrine of compelled self-publication. Courts in seven jurisdictions have rejected the doctrine. It seems likely, given Vermont's longstanding recognition of a Company's liability for a plaintiff's publication-by-necessity, that Vermont would join Minnesota and the other jurisdictions which recognize the doctrine . . .

Raymond may satisfy the publication element of his defamation claim by presenting evidence that IBM knew, or should have known, that Raymond had no reasonable means of avoiding publication, or, in other words, that he was under strong compulsion to publish the statement. . . . Whether Raymond was compelled to disclose the reason he was fired will be an issue for the finder of fact.

Of course, IBM's affirmative defenses are not abrogated. If, for example, the company can demonstrate that its qualified privilege for the protection of legitimate business interests applied to these circumstances, then, to defeat the privilege, Raymond must show that IBM acted with malice.

Decision. Yes. The U.S. District Court held that if presented with the question, Vermont would adopt the tort cause of action for self-compelled defamation.

CASE QUESTIONS

Critical Legal Thinking. What do you think the jury will decide when it hears Raymond's case?

Business Ethics. Do you think IBM acted with malice so that its defense of terminating Raymond for legitimate business reasons would be unavailable?

Contemporary Business. How would you as a juror decide the amount of any damages Raymond may have suffered or in the future will suffer because of these allegedly defamatory statements?

Interference with Contractual Relations

Interference with Contractual Relations
Tortious conduct involving actions that intentionally and without excuse interfere with the contractual benefits of another person.

"Contractual Relations" constitutes a catch-all **tort** that can impose liability on an employer. The Restatement (Second) of Torts, §766 defines the **tort** as when:

> *One who intentionally and improperly interferes with the performance of a contract (except a contract to marry) between another and a third person by inducing or otherwise causing the third person not to perform the contract, is subject to liability to the other for the pecuniary loss resulting to the other from the failure of the third person to perform the contract.*

Some state courts require that an existing contractual relationship or business expectancy must exist. Many state court decisions permit recovery of such damages even in the context of **at-will** employment contracts. An employer must avoid inducing a breach of an employment contract existing between a competitor employer and an applicant for employment. A competitor may sue the prospective employer for damages suffered for interference with contractual relations between the applicant and the competitor-employer. The facts and circumstances are unique to each case, but acts beyond those of mere competition may give rise to a cause of action. Hiring the key employees of a competitor to cripple the third-party employer may be actionable. In reaching its decision, the trier of fact weighs the actions and interests of each party involved in the litigation.

Invasion of Privacy Claims

As we will study in a later chapter, most states recognize invasion of privacy claims committed against an employee. The most common form is the **tort** of "public disclosure of private facts," which involves disclosure of true but embarrassing facts about a person. Disclosure of criminal records from youth or some other embarrassing episode in one's life constitutes such a **tort**. Another version of the tort consists of overly invasive surveillance or investigation into one's private affairs. The third type involves intrusion into seclusion, where the employee's expectation of privacy is breached by the employer. The last type is publication in a false light, whereby the employer is responsible for publishing views or positions ostensibly but not truly held by the employee.

Misrepresentation and Fraud

Lawsuits for misrepresentation and fraud causes of action may arise from the interview process. Usually, they arise when the employer makes material misstatements of fact relating to the terms and conditions of the proposed employment. The applicant relies on these misstatements in deciding to leave his or her current job to accept employment with the new company. An employer who knowingly made false representations about the duration of the position, the character of the work, or the resources and support available might mislead an applicant into relocating and accepting an unsuitable position. Sympathetic juries would likely award punitive damages to the employee. Related to this **tort** theory are claims founded upon **misrepresentations made by third parties**. Section 311 of the Restatement (Second) of Torts provides that:

> *(1) One who negligently gives false information to another is subject to liability for physical harm caused by action taken by the other in reasonable reliance upon such information, where such harm results (a) to the other, or (b) to such third persons as the actor should expect to be put in peril by the action taken. (2) Such negligence may consist of failure to exercise reasonable care (a) in ascertaining the accuracy of the information, or (b) in the manner in which it is communicated.*

Successor employers who have relied upon an inaccurate or untrue letter of recommendation given by a former employer have utilized this tort theory. For example, if the employee posed a substantial, foreseeable risk of physical injury to a prospective employer or third parties and that risk was not disclosed in the recommendation, that omission could impose liability on the former employer.

False Imprisonment

The employer's conduct of an interview with an employee suspected of improper behavior can lead to tort liability for the employer. The elements of **false imprisonment** are direct restraint for some appreciable period, compelling the employee to stay or go against the employee's will. For example, if through the threat of force or force itself an employee confesses to conduct the employee did not commit, this **tort** cause of action would permit this innocent person to sue for damages. When conducting interviews, employers should make it very clear that the employee is under no compulsion to stay. Employers investigating a workplace incident must exercise restraint in the conduct of their interviews. Otherwise, they may be liable in damages for the tort of intentional infliction of emotional distress. The more difficult the circumstances imposed upon the employee, the more likely a trier of fact will find for the plaintiff.

False Imprisonment Direct restraint of a person for an appreciable period against his or her will.

Example: A fired employee was allowed to proceed to trial because of an abusive interrogation. An inventory manager at a Vermont grocery store food distribution center was discharged for taking damaged goods home, even though employees were permitted to do so. The basis for his claim for intentional infliction of emotional distress was the nature of the meeting and the manner in which he was fired. The meeting was called without prior notice to him. The meeting lasted for three hours without an opportunity for him to have lunch at his normal time or to allow him to have a rest break. He was repeatedly badgered to amend and sign a statement he had previously signed and to sign an additional statement. Throughout this meeting, the employee did not feel free to leave. Immediately after the meeting, the store's representative directed him to clean out his desk; the employee, who had served the business loyally for 18 years, did not expect this dismissal. The court held that mere termination of employment would not support a case for intentional inflection of emotional distress, but if the manner of termination is oppressive and an abuse of a position of authority over the plaintiff existed, the employee could sue.[22]

False Arrest

Liability for false arrest may attach to an employer when it knowingly gives false information to law enforcement and insists on an arrest. Only the employer's good-faith belief in the information based upon probable cause that the employee has committed a crime will relieve the employer from liability. Employers should be wary about accusing an employee of theft or other crimes because **tort** liability will usually attach if the accusation does not result in a criminal conviction. Most employers will quietly dismiss the employee rather than become involved with an unsuccessful prosecution for the crime and then possibly defending a civil lawsuit for **false arrest, defamation, intentional infliction of emotional distress**, and **wrongful termination of employment**. Since these are intentional torts, the law does not permit the employer's insurance policies to afford coverage for them.

Liability for an Employee's Actions

As we have discussed, an employer may become liable for an employee's tortious conduct under some circumstances. Employers are vicariously liable, under the *respondeat superior* doctrine, for the negligent acts or omissions committed by their employee within the course and scope of their employment. The act or omission must be either authorized or be so related to the authorized act that it can be considered part of the employer's authority to perform the act. Generally, an employer will not be held liable for the intentional, nonauthorized acts and omissions of employees; however, the facts often dictate the result in a case. The more egregious the conduct, the more likely it is that the trier of fact will find the employer liable for some or all of the harm caused to the victim.

The next decision considers the holding of the U.S. Supreme Court as to when an employer should be liable for an employee's wrongful actions toward another employee. In this case, the employer claimed that while a supervisor committed the wrongful acts, the employer was completely unaware of them and should not be held liable to the plaintiff.

CASE 3.6

EMPLOYERS MAY BE HELD VICARIOUSLY LIABLE FOR SUPERVISORS' ACTIONS

BURLINGTON INDUSTRIES, INC. V. ELLERTH

524 U.S. 742 (1998)

Supreme Court of the United States

Facts. After fifteen months as a salesperson for Burlington Industries, Kimberly Ellerth quit her job because she claimed that her supervisor, Ted Slowik, who was a vice president, had subjected her to constant sexual harassment. She claimed that she was constructively discharged. In her suit she emphasized three alleged incidents in which Slowik's comments could be construed as threats to deny her tangible job benefits. In the summer of 1993, while on a business trip, Slowik invited Ellerth to the hotel lounge, an invitation Ellerth felt compelled to accept because Slowik was her boss. When Ellerth gave no encouragement to remarks Slowik made about her breasts, he told her to "loosen up" and warned, "You know, Kim, I could make your life very hard or very easy at Burlington." In March 1994, when Ellerth was being considered for a promotion, Slowik expressed reservations during the promotion interview because she was not "loose enough." The comment was followed by his reaching over and rubbing her knee. Ellerth did receive the promotion; but when Slowik called to announce it, he told Ellerth, "You're gonna be out there with men who work in factories, and they certainly like women with pretty butts and legs." In May 1994, Ellerth telephoned Slowik, and he responded, "I don't have time for you right now, Kim — unless you want to tell me what you're wearing." Ellerth told Slowik she had to go and ended the call. A day or two later, in another telephone conversation, Slowik added something along the lines of, "Are you wearing shorter skirts yet, Kim, because it would make your job a whole heck of a lot easier." A short time later, she quit and explained she quit because of Slowik's behavior.

During her tenure at Burlington, Ellerth did not inform anyone in authority about Slowik's conduct, despite knowing Burlington had a policy against sexual harassment. In fact, she chose not to inform her immediate supervisor (not Slowik) because "it would be his duty as my supervisor to report any incidents of sexual harassment." On one occasion, she told Slowik that a comment he made was inappropriate.

Ellerth sued Burlington for sexual harassment and constructive discharge in violation of Title VII. The district court granted summary judgment to

Burlington. The court found Slowik's behavior, as described by Ellerth, severe and pervasive enough to create a hostile work environment, but it found Burlington neither knew nor should have known about the conduct. The federal court of appeals reversed in a decision that produced eight separate opinions and no consensus for a controlling rationale. Burlington appealed to the Supreme Court, which granted *certiorari.*

Issue. Can an employee sue for damages even though the employee did not suffer adverse tangible job consequences without showing the employer is negligent or otherwise at fault for a supervisor's actions towards the employee?

Language of the Court. Kennedy, J.: **Although a supervisor's sexual harassment is outside the scope of employment because the conduct was for personal motives, an employer can be liable, nonetheless, where its own negligence is a cause of the harassment. An employer is negligent with respect to sexual harassment if it knew or should have known about the conduct and failed to stop it. Negligence sets a minimum standard for employer liability under Title VII; but Ellerth seeks to invoke the more stringent standard of vicarious liability. . . . R-elying on existing case law which held out the promise of vicarious liability for all quid pro quo claims, Ellerth focused all her attention in the Court of Appeals on proving her claim fit within that category. Given our explanation that the labels quid pro quo and hostile work environment are not controlling for purposes of establishing employer liability, Ellerth should have an adequate opportunity to prove she has a claim for which Burlington is liable. Although Ellerth has not alleged she suffered a tangible employment action at the hands of Slowik, which would deprive Burlington of the availability of the affirmative defense, this is not dispositive. In light of our decision, Burlington is still subject to vicarious liability for Slowik's activity, but Burlington should have an opportunity to assert and prove the affirmative defense to liability.**

Decision. Yes. An employee who refused the unwelcome and threatening sexual advances of her supervisor but did not suffer adverse and tangible damages could recover against an employer without showing that the employer was negligent or at fault for the subject conduct. An employer may be held vicariously liable to an employee for a hostile work environment created by the supervisor immediately over the employee, but the employer could also assert an affirmative defense to liability or damages if the employee did not suffer any adverse consequences from the behavior. The Court held that the affirmative defense could be raised if the employee exercised reasonable care to prevent and correct any sexually harassing behavior and the victim unreasonably failed to take advantage of any preventive or corrective procedures provided by the employer or to avoid harm. In this particular case, the Court held the company was liable for the vice president's actions but that the company could assert the affirmative defense on remand to the district court for further proceedings.

CASE QUESTIONS

Critical Legal Thinking. Review the court decision in *Hill v. Lockheed* below and discuss whether that court's decision is reasonable in light of the *Ellerth* holding.

Business Ethics. Should bias be imputed to the employer when a subordinate lacking decision-making authority substantially influences an employment decision?

Contemporary Business. Is this decision fair to employers? Should it make a difference if the supervisor acted with wrongful intent in making an adverse employment decision against a subordinate?

In the following case, the federal court of appeals explains the proof necessary to establish a discrimination claim and clarifies who is a supervisory employee for purposes of establishing employer liability.

CASE 3.7

ONLY SUPERVISORIAL EMPLOYEES WHO POSSESS DECISION-MAKING AUTHORITY CREATE EMPLOYER LIABILITY

HILL V. LOCKHEED MARTIN LOGISTICS MGMT.

354 F.3d 277 (4th Cir. 2004) *Cert. Denied*, 543 U.S. 1132

U.S. Fourth Circuit Court of Appeals

Facts. Ethel Hill worked as a sheet-metal mechanic for Lockheed Martin. During her last eight months of employment with Lockheed, Hill received three written reprimands according to Lockheed's standard operating procedure. Following company procedures, she was discharged after receiving too many reprimands within a given time period. In June 1998, Hill filed a charge of discrimination and retaliation with the EEOC alleging that she had been discharged because of her sex and age. She claimed Ed Fultz, a safety inspector and her supervisor, was a discriminatory animus against her as evidenced by his calling her a "useless old lady" who needed to be retired, a "troubled old lady," and a "damn woman," on several occasions while they were working together. The U.S. District Court concluded that Hill failed to establish that the decision-makers at Lockheed who terminated her employment did not have the intent to discriminate against her on the basis of her sex and age. She appealed to the U.S. Court of Appeals for the Fourth Circuit.

Issue. Can an employer be liable for the actions of an employee who lacks decision-making authority?

Language of the Court. Traxler, J.: . . . **The discrimination statutes, however, do not make employers vicariously liable for the discriminatory acts and motivations of everyone in their employ, even when such acts or motivations lead to or influence a tangible employment action. On the contrary, by defining employer to include "any agent" of the employer, Congress "evinced an intent to place some limits on the acts of employees for which employers are to be held responsible." (Citations omitted.)**

In Ellerth, the Court defined the limits of such agency as encompassing employer liability for the acts of its employees holding supervisory or other actual power to make tangible employment decisions . . . (holding that "as a general proposition, only a supervisor, or other person acting with the authority of the company," can undertake a tangible employment action).

Tangible employment actions are the means by which the supervisor brings the official power of the enterprise to bear on subordinates. A tangible employment decision requires an official act of the enterprise, a company act. The decision in most cases is documented in official company records, and may be subject to review by higher level supervisors.

For these reasons, a tangible employment action taken by the supervisor becomes for Title VII purposes the act of the employer. Whatever the exact contours of the aided in the agency relation standard, its requirements will always be met when a supervisor takes a tangible employment action against a subordinate. In that instance, it would be implausible to interpret agency principles to allow an employer to escape liability.

In sum . . . an aggrieved employee who rests a discrimination claim under Title VII or the ADEA upon the discriminatory motivations of a subordinate employee must come forward with sufficient evidence that the subordinate employee possessed such authority as to be viewed as the one principally responsible for the decision or the actual decision maker for the employer.

Decision. No. Upon consideration of the facts, the Court found that the employee did not present sufficient evidence of intentional discrimination by the safety inspector's action. The safety inspector was not an actual decision-maker of the employer and, as a result, the employer was not liable to the plaintiff.

CASE QUESTIONS

Critical Legal Thinking. Does this decision insulate employers from liability if they establish a review committee to work independently of the immediate supervisor who makes the adverse employment decision?

Business Ethics. Is the rationale for this decision fair to employees?

Contemporary Business. State and apply your definition of the type of management authority required to impose liability upon the employer.

Management Application
Employee's Scope of Employment

Employers are liable for employee's torts if they occur while the employee is acting within the scope of his or her employment. The issue of whether the tort was committed while the employee was acting within the scope of employment is addressed in the following case.

Lapp Roofing and Sheet Metal Company, Inc. (Lapp Roofing), an Ohio corporation headquartered in Dayton, Ohio, provides construction services in several states. Lapp Roofing sent James Goldick and other Lapp Roofing employees to work on a roofing project in Wilmington, Delaware. Lapp Roofing's company policy prohibited employees from driving company vehicles for personal purposes. Lapp Roofing entrusted Goldick, as job foreman, with a white Ford van to transport the workers to the job site and to provide transportation to meals and other necessities.

While in Wilmington, Goldick and another Lapp Roofing employee, James McNees, went to Gators Bar and Restaurant. Goldick, after eating and drinking for several hours, was ejected from the bar. Shortly thereafter, Goldick drove the company van onto the curb in front of the bar, striking two people in the parking lot and seven individuals on the curb outside the bar. Subsequently, the police stopped the van and apprehended Goldick. Goldick was arrested and pleaded guilty to criminal assault charges.

Christopher M. Keating and the other injured individuals filed a personal injury lawsuit against Goldick and Lapp Roofing. Lapp Roofing defended, alleging that it was not liable because Goldick's negligent conduct was committed outside the scope of his employment. Was Goldick's negligent conduct committed within the scope of his employment for Lapp Roofing? The court said no. The court stated:

> *There comes a point in every litigation where common sense will make some conclusions obvious. No reasonable person could conclude this limitation on available transportation would provide the mechanism to expand the coverage to a drunken brawl that occurred after hours and was unassociated with the employee's work or associated with his stay. Such conduct is so adverse to the employer that no conceivable benefit could be derived. It is completely unrelated to the employer's business and does not advance the work for which the employees were sent to this location. Here, Goldick used the van to go drinking with another employee and drove the van in the parking lot and on the curb injuring various individuals. No jury could reasonably conclude that Goldick's conduct was actuated, even in part, by a purpose to serve his employer. This incident did not occur during working hours and Goldick decided to go to Gators and become intoxicated for purely personal reasons and not to serve Lapp Roofing's interests whatsoever.*

The superior court of Delaware held that Goldick was not acting within the course and scope of his employment when his negligent conduct occurred. The superior court granted summary judgment to Lapp Roofing on this issue.[23]

Discussion Questions

1. Define scope of employment. Why is this concept important?
2. Did Lapp Roofing act ethically in denying liability for the negligent conduct of one of its employees?
3. If the negligent conduct had occurred when Goldick was driving to a restaurant for a meal, would Lapp Roofing have been liable?

Negligent Hiring, Retention, and Supervision

Many states recognize by case law or statute claims of negligent hiring, supervision, and retention when an employee harms an innocent party. Generally, to prove such a case, the plaintiff must establish that:

1. the employer should have discovered by reasonable investigation the known or probable propensities of an employee;
2. the employer failed to exercise reasonable care with regard to the placement of the person in an employment position;
3. it was foreseeable to the employer that the employee posed a threat of injury to others; and
4. harm was caused to a third party by the employee.

The employer should carefully consider the fitness of an employee for a position and will be held liable for negligently failing to take further action such as investigating, discharging, or reassigning the employee. Courts look to the foreseeability of a potential claim for **negligent hiring, training**, or **supervision**. If an employer has not been put on notice of the necessity to exercise a greater degree of control or supervision over a particular employee, then it is less likely that a trier of fact would hold the employer liable for the harm caused. The facts of each case often dictate the result. In each of the following cases, see if you agree with the court's decision on whether the employer was liable:

- In a 1994 Georgia case, the plaintiff who had been struck with a stick by a parking lot employee failed to prevail against the employer. In this case, the Court found that "*the record contains the affidavit of Gary Worstell, the company's owner and manager. Worstell stated that he had no knowledge that the parking attendant was a violent person and that he was not aware of any prior violent acts or violent propensities of the attendant. Worstell also stated that he had never received any complaints about the attendant. Plaintiff alleges that the company had constructive notice of the attendant's violent propensity because the attendant checked 'yes' in response to a question on his employment application regarding whether he had been arrested for any criminal charges, excluding minor offenses. Although the record reflects that the attendant had been convicted of several violations of the Georgia Controlled Substances Act, the record is devoid of any evidence that the parking attendant had a propensity towards violence or that the Company knew of that propensity. Furthermore, plaintiff's argument that the Company had a duty to conduct a background investigation before they employed the attendant is without merit.*"[24]
- In the 1976 Louisiana decision of *Mays v. Pico Finance Company, Inc.*[25] the plaintiff was a rape victim who argued two theories of employer liability. One argument was the manager who had committed the crime was acting in the course and scope of his employment. The second argument was that the employer was negligent in hiring the manager because it conducted only a cursory background check at the time of hiring.
    - The court first considered whether a manager was acting in the course of employment so as to make the employer liable to the victim when the manager committed the crime. In this regard the court stated: "*The determinative question is whether the tortious conduct of the employee 'was so*

closely connected in time, place, and causation to his employment-duties as to be regarded a risk of harm fairly attributable to the employer's business, as compared with conduct motivated by purely personal considerations entirely extraneous to the employer's interests.' . . . The tortious conduct in the instant case was certainly not closely connected in time, place or causation with Pico Finance of Ruston, Inc. Shockley was not working on the Saturday in question. His duties did not include hiring employees or any other activity in connection with the Monroe office. His trip to Monroe with plaintiff was purely for his own personal considerations. Shockley was not acting for Pico on the day of the tortious conduct. Shockley may have given plaintiff the impression he was acting for Pico, but he was not actually doing so. He was not performing any duty which he was employed to perform. The motive of the employee in performing the act is of paramount importance. Shockley's motives were strictly personal. Shockley was not acting in the course and scope of his employment at the time of the wrongful conduct and his employer is not responsible for his intentional tort."

- □ The court then considered the negligent hiring claim. The court stated, "*[p]laintiff also contends Pico Finance was negligent in hiring Shockley and that such negligence was a legal cause of the harm to plaintiff. Pico did not make more than a cursory check of Shockley's background. A thorough investigation would have revealed that Shockley had pled guilty to theft, was an alcoholic, and had personality problems. However, there was no evidence of past sex offenses. The jury found that Shockley's history could not reasonably lead Pico to anticipate that Shockley might commit rape. We agree with that finding. Even if Pico had a duty to protect plaintiff from the actions of an off-duty employee she originally met at the office, which is highly questionable, the harm plaintiff suffered could not have been foreseen.*"

- ■ When an Arkansas employer hired two ex-convicts, it created a great potential liability for itself, as the Arkansas Supreme Court determined in its 1987 decision in *American Automobile Auction, Inc. v. Titsworth.*[26] In that decision, the Court's opinion highlights the employer's disregard for the safety of its business invitees: "*On the night of the auction, McPeek went to Moak's office and asked if he was invited to or barred from the auction. Moak asked him to leave and come back some other time and discuss it. Moak then watched McPeek go into the auction. McPeek caused a disturbance. [Moak's] employees, Doster and Ball, commenced to forcibly eject McPeek. Titsworth, a large man, attempted, without fighting, to protect McPeek and, at the same time, get him out of the auction area. Employee Doster told Titsworth: 'Turn him loose, we're going to teach him a lesson. This is the reason I pay this boy [Ball] $100.00 a week is to take care of punks like him.' Employees Doster and Ball then viciously attacked McPeek in the auction area. McPeek drew a knife and started to fight back. Titsworth pleaded with them to stop before someone was killed. Titsworth then got McPeek away from the auction and led him across the street to Titsworth's truck. The employees, Doster and Ball, got a shovel and a bumper jack, went across the street to Titsworth's truck, and severely beat both Titsworth and McPeek. The beatings were so tumultuously administered that a crowd of 50 people gathered before it ended. Even so, [Moak] the president of the [defendant] corporation remained in his office. These facts and the reasonable inferences therefore establish that [the] corporation hired Ball, an ex-convict, for the purpose of forcefully ejecting people*

> *from the auction and teaching 'punks' a lesson. Ball was paid $100.00 per week but only worked one day a week. Ball normally drank at work and had a bottle of beer in his hand when the intentional torts occurred. Doster, another ex-convict, knew that McPeek and his partner owed the defendant corporation's president, Moak, a debt and he had repossessed a truck from the partner. On the night at issue, Moak told McPeek to leave the premises, but saw him walk into the auction area. At this point, [Moak] as the president of [the] corporation knew, or by the exercise of reasonable diligence should have known, that McPeek might be forcibly ejected by his employees, Doster and Ball. Still he did not exercise any supervisory care on behalf of the Corporation. Clearly, an employer who hires two ex-convicts, one of whom is normally drinking, and entrusts to them the job of forcibly ejecting patrons, has a duty to exercise reasonable care to avoid harm to those patrons by exercising supervisory care when the employer knows, or by the exercising of reasonable diligence ought to know, that such employees are about to forcibly eject a patron."*

As these cases reflect, even in those circumstances in which an employer cannot be held **vicariously liable** for its employee's misdeeds the employer may still be held liable under the **negligent hiring, retention, and supervision theory**. In order to prevail, the injured party must prove that the employer could have foreseen that the employee would cause harm to the victim and yet failed to properly supervise the employee.

Management Application
Is There Insurance Coverage?

Employers often find employment litigation very expensive to defend and any damages assessed quite costly. One reason is that the typical jury pool contains many more employees than it does executives or owners. Jurors' empathetic responses to fact patterns that place employers in particularly unfavorable light may subject a company to substantial risk. The typical general liability policy a company maintains covers "personal injury" and "advertising injury." While almost all such policies exclude employment-related claims, some extended coverage may be available if the claims involve injury arising out of defamation, privacy violations, false imprisonment, or discrimination. Another source for coverage is the liability portion of a manager's homeowner's insurance policy, which often mimics the coverage afforded under a business liability policy. A homeowner's policy may afford defense and indemnification when the wrongful activity occurred outside the scope of employment. In all cases, an employer should consult with employment legal counsel and with its insurance broker to obtain sufficient employment practices coverage.

Restrictive Covenants and Trade Secrets

Covenants Not to Compete

Employers expend considerable resources to train and employ workers who then often gain complete access to sensitive business information, including business opportunities, customers, and the trends and strategies followed and pursued by the employer. The information to which employees have access is often thought to be so valuable that the employer would not want employees to quit and begin working for a competitor or start their own competing businesses. The temptation is to restrict the employees' ability to transport the employer's business information and goodwill to a competitor. Conversely, the employer wants to attract the most suitable candidates in the job market, without worrying that they may be encumbered with restrictions from their previous employers.

A restrictive **covenant not to compete** is a written contract executed by an employee with an employer. The agreement provides that, for a certain time period, the employee will not compete with the employer within a specified geographic area or with particular customers. In the majority of states, such agreements are lawful; however, in many states they are void as against **public policy**. The law of states supporting employees' freedom to contract will often restrict the enforceability of such agreements to circumstances involving the purchase and sale of all or substantially all of the stock an employee who is also a shareholder owns in the company. For example, if Hector Gonzales was a ten-year employee of a privately held company in which he owned 25 percent of the outstanding stock, then on his termination of employment the company could repurchase his stock and enforce a valid **covenant not to compete**. If Hector was **wrongfully terminated,** he could sue for damages and seek to prevent the enforcement of the covenant; but if he leaves of his own accord, he should seek to avoid triggering the enforcement provisions of the **covenant not to compete**.

Covenant Not to Compete
A written contract executed by an employee with an employer in which the employee agrees that for a certain number of years the employee will not compete with the employer within a geographic area or as to particular customers.

Rulings among state courts diverge substantially with respect to the enforceability of **covenants not to compete**. In an employment survey text such as this, only generalizations can be offered. An enforceable restrictive covenant must protect the legitimate business interests of the employer without restraining competition. One court defined a legitimate business interest as "a business interest, not fictitious, which, when weighed against the public's interest in a free economic arena, is worthy of protection in order to encourage and stimulate business efforts and innovations."[27] Protectable interests include:

- the protection of corporate goodwill following the sale of a meaningful percentage of the employer's business or assets; and
- the protection of goodwill following the dissolution of a partnership and buy-out of a partnership interest.

Whatever form it may take, the courts require that the terms of the agreement be reasonable. The term "reasonable" reaches to the extent of the covenant's application (e.g., in the geographic area in which the employer is located); how long the non-competition constraint will last; and the scope of the barred competitive activity. The covenant can bar actual competition, solicitation of the former employer's customers, and notification to others that were once employed by the former employer. Usually, the more sophisticated and skilled the worker, the more likely the covenant will be upheld for a reasonable period. The less skilled the worker (such as an entry-level clerk), the more likely the covenant will not be enforced. Without a protectable interest, even a narrowly drawn agreement will not be enforced. In all enforceable cases, a legitimate employer's business interest can be reasonably protected as the covenant is written. Courts consider a number of questions when confronted with a request to enforce a covenant not to compete. Among them are:

- Is there a state statute governing the enforceability of the covenant?
- What employer interest is at stake, and how is it defined?
- Was the agreement executed properly and without duress?
- What factors will the court consider in determining the reasonableness of its reach and geographic scope?
- What duty does a prospective employee have to disclose that he or she is bound by a prior covenant?
- Are there related prohibitions against solicitation of the former employer's customers?

Employers and employees must both be cautious with respect to deciding whether a covenant not to compete will be enforced. When an employer is located in one state that may enforce the covenant against a mere employee, but the employee resides and performs his or her work in a state that would bar enforcement, complex litigation issues are presented to the courts. An employee can be enjoined by one court in one jurisdiction while litigating in another jurisdiction to declare the covenant was unenforceable.

Confidential Information Nonpublic information, data, compilations, techniques, know-how, algorithms, software, and formulas as well as research and planning that are not generally known to the public, are of economic benefit to the holder, and are the subject of reasonable efforts to maintain their secrecy.

> ***Example:*** At the commencement of his employment, Shashi Batra (a resident of California) executed an employment agreement with The Estee Lauder Company (with a principal place of business in New York). The agreement contained confidentiality and non-competition provisions. Following his decision to set up a competing company in California, he sued in California state court to declare the covenant not to compete unenforceable under state law. The company sought an injunction in federal court in New York against him. It asserted he breached his non-compete agreement and stole company trade secrets. The employee had been in charge of developing brand strategies and worked out of California. The federal district court in New York held that New York law applied to the employer's claim. California's interest in the dispute (i.e., the place of residence of the defendant) was not materially greater than the interest of New York in deciding the dispute (where such covenants were enforceable against former employees).[28]

Trade Secrets and Confidentiality Agreements

Protectable Trade Secret Information, including a formula, pattern, compilation, program device, method or technique, or process from which a company derives independent economic value.

All but a handful of states have adopted laws to protect proprietary and confidential information generated by an employer. The protection is afforded to the company because the **confidential information** is a business asset not known to others outside the company and the employer derives economic benefit from the confidential information. Under a model act entitled the **Uniform Trade Secrets Act (UTSA)**, information is defined as a **protectable trade secret**. The act defines a **trade secret** as:

> Information, including a formula, pattern, compilation, program device, method, technique, or process, that:

1. derives independent economic value, actual or potential, from not being generally known to, and not being readily ascertainable by proper means by, other persons who obtain economic value from its disclosure or use, and,
2. is the subject of efforts that are reasonable under the circumstances to maintain its secrecy.

Misappropriation of a trade secret occurs when the **trade secret** is disclosed without authorization or is used by someone who acquired it by improper means or who reasonably should have known the information was a **trade secret** and yet acquired it by improper means from a third party. Merely possessing another's **trade secret** information is not actionable. It is the improper use of **trade secret** information that creates the liability for **misappropriation**. Under the UTSA and the laws of many states, a court may issue an injunction to stop the actual or threatened disclosure and/or use of the **trade secret**. Courts will carefully review the facts, sometimes *in camera* (i.e., in chambers rather than in an open courtroom), to evaluate the conflicting claims. The parties dispute the existence of a **trade secret** and what relief, if any, should be afforded the injured party. Damages may be awarded for the unfair competition created by the wrongdoer. The damages may include lost profits and unjust enrichment damages that the company will suffer because the **trade secret** information was in the hands of a competitor. Punitive damages may also be awarded in cases of willful or intentional theft of **trade secrets**.

Companies may also invoke the theory of **inevitable disclosure of trade secrets** when the employee did not execute an enforceable **covenant not to compete** or a confidential **trade-secrets** agreement. Under this theory, employers rely on the assumption that a court will act to protect their **trade secrets**. Courts have made various responses to this theory because it can act as an after-the-fact **covenant not to compete**.

Finally, the **Economic Espionage Act of 1996**[29] makes the theft or misappropriation of a **trade secret** a federal crime. The law criminalizes any **trade secret** theft that benefits a foreign power and any theft that is for commercial or economic purposes. The statute provides two different types of penalties depending on the use made of the information. Under this act, the federal courts have jurisdiction for acts committed outside of the United States when the perpetrator was a U.S. citizen, the victim was a U.S. citizen, and the offense had a direct substantial effect within the United States. The U.S. law is unique in that many other nations actively support and finance business espionage using their government spy services as well as bribery and corruption to obtain the information.

Courts will not protect information of an employer that merely involves general knowledge or methods known in a particular industry. The protection of **trade secrets** often presents a difficult problem for the employer who has not utilized a written trade-secrets agreement with a new employee. Some courts, like the one in the *Pepsico* decision below, have used the theory of the **inevitable disclosure doctrine** to protect those employers. The theory is used to prove a claim of **trade secret misappropriation** by showing that the former employee's new employment will result in the inevitable reliance upon the former employer's trade secrets. The courts generally require a degree of similarity in the two jobs and a degree of competition between the old and new employer.

CASE 3.8

INEVITABLE DISCLOSURES OF TRADE SECRETS IN THE SPORTS DRINK WARS

PEPSICO, INC. V. WILLIAM E. REDMOND AND THE QUAKER OATS COMPANY

54 F.3d 1262 (7th Cir. 1995)

U.S. Court of Appeals for the Seventh Circuit

Facts. William Redmond Jr. worked for Pepsico in its Pepsicola North America division ("PCNA") from 1984 to 1994. Eventually Redmond was promoted to General Manager of the business unit covering all of California, a unit having annual revenues of more than $500 million and representing 20 percent of PCNA's profit for all of the United States. Redmond's relatively high-level position at PCNA gave him access to inside information and trade secrets. Redmond, like other Pepsico management employees, had signed a confidentiality agreement with Pepsico. That agreement stated in relevant part that he would not disclose at any time, to anyone other than officers or employees of [Pepsico], or make use of, confidential information relating to the business of [Pepsico] obtained while in the employ of [Pepsico], which shall not be generally known or available to the public or recognized as standard practices. In the early 1990s, there was fierce competition among the beverage companies for sports drinks, and both Pepsi's All Sport and Quaker Oats' Gatorade were fighting for store shelf space.

After Redmond accepted an offer with Gatorade, Pepsico filed a federal court diversity suit a week later, seeking a temporary restraining order to enjoin Redmond from assuming his duties at Quaker and to prevent him from disclosing trade secrets or confidential information to his new employer. After an extended hearing, the federal district court issued an injunction against Redmond barring him from divulging Pepsico trade secrets and confidential information in his new job with Quaker and from assuming any duties with Quaker relating to beverage pricing, marketing, and distribution. Redmond and Quaker Oats appealed the district court decision to the federal Court of Appeals for the Seventh Circuit.

Issue. Should an employee be enjoined from working for a competitor when it is reasonable to assume that, inevitably, confidential trade secrets of a former employer will be disclosed to the new employer?

Language of the Court. Flaum, J.: **At the [district court's preliminary injunction hearing] Pepsico offered evidence of a number of trade secrets and** confidential information it desired protected and to which Redmond was privy. First, it identified PCNA's "Strategic Plan," an annually revised document that contains PCNA's plans to compete, its financial goals, and its strategies for manufacturing, production, marketing, packaging, and distribution for the coming three years. Strategic Plans are considered highly confidential. . . . PCNA managers [including Redmond] received the most recent Strategic Plan at a meeting in July, 1994. . . . Second, Pepsico pointed to PCNA's Annual Operating Plan ("AOP") as a trade secret. The AOP is a national plan for a given year and guides PCNA's financial goals, marketing plans, promotional event calendars, growth expectations, and operational changes in that year. The AOP [is implemented by PCNA unit General Managers, including Redmond], contains specific information regarding all PCNA initiatives for the forthcoming year. The AOP bears a label that reads "Private and Confidential — Do Not Reproduce" and is considered highly confidential by PCNA managers. . . . Pepsico also showed that Redmond had intimate knowledge of PCNA "attack plans" for specific markets. . . . Finally, Pepsico offered evidence of PCNA trade secrets regarding innovations in its selling and delivery systems. . . . Redmond has knowledge of this secret. . . .

Having shown Redmond's intimate knowledge of PCNA's plans for 1995, Pepsico argued that Redmond would inevitably disclose that information to Quaker in his new position, at which he would have substantial input as to Gatorade and Snapple pricing, costs, margins, distribution systems, products, packaging and marketing, and could give Quaker an unfair advantage in its upcoming skirmishes with Pepsico. Redmond argued that the information to which he had been exposed was irrelevant. This irrelevance would derive not only from the fact that Redmond would be implementing pre-existing plans but also from the fact that PCNA and Quaker distribute their products in entirely different ways. . . . The Companies also pointed out that Redmond had signed a confidentiality agreement with Quaker preventing him from disclosing "any confidential information belonging to others," as well as the Quaker Code of Ethics, which prohibits employees from engaging in "illegal or improper acts to acquire a competitor's trade secrets." Redmond additionally promised at the hearing that should he be faced with a situation at Quaker that might involve the use or disclosure of PCNA information, he would seek advice from Quaker's in-house counsel and would refrain from making the decision. . . .

The question of threatened or inevitable misappropriation in this case lies at the heart of a basic tension in trade secret law. Trade secret law serves to protect "standards of commercial morality" and "encourage invention and innovation" while maintaining "the public interest in having free and open competition in the manufacture and sale of unpatented goods." (Citations omitted.) Yet that same law should not prevent workers from pursuing their livelihoods when they leave their current positions. (Citations omitted.) . . . This tension is particularly exacerbated when a plaintiff sues to prevent not the actual misappropriation of trade secrets but the mere threat that it will occur. While the ITSA [Illinois Trade Secrets Act] plainly permits a court to enjoin the threat of misappropriation of trade secrets, there is little law in Illinois or in this circuit establishing what constitutes threatened or inevitable misappropriation.

Pepsico finds itself in the position of a coach, one of whose players has left, playbook in hand, to join the opposing team before the big game. Quaker and Redmond's protestations that their distribution systems and plans are entirely different from PCNA's are thus not really responsive. . . . Pepsico has asserted that Redmond cannot help but rely on PCNA trade secrets as he helps plot Gatorade and Snapple's new course, and that these secrets will enable Quaker to achieve a substantial advantage by knowing exactly how PCNA will price, distribute, and market its sports drinks and new age drinks and being able to respond strategically.

Decision. We affirm the district court's order enjoining Redmond from assuming his responsibilities at Quaker through May 1995, and preventing him forever from disclosing PCNA trade secrets and confidential information.

CASE QUESTIONS

Critical Legal Thinking. Is this decision fair to employees? If a jurisdiction has adopted the inevitable disclosure rule, could its application lead to barring an individual from ever working for a competitor? What kinds of information do you think are entitled to such protection?

Business Ethics. What do you think of the relative ethics exhibited by both sides to this dispute? Does it make a difference knowing that Pepsico merged with Quaker Oats in 2001?

Contemporary Business. If trade secrets tend to grow stale with the lapse of time, what is a reasonable period to enforce them? Can you think of any examples when technological changes rapidly eclipse the value of proprietary information?

Despite the decision in *Pepsico*, many state courts have rejected the application of the **inevitable disclosure doctrine** because it unfairly bars the employment of a former employee without a showing of actual harm to the first employer. It prevents a former employee from working for a competitor despite the failure of the **trade secret** owner to show that the former employee has taken or threatens to use the **trade secrets**.

Example: EarthWeb, Inc. sought an injunction against Mark Schlack, a former EarthWeb vice president responsible for website content. It sought to bar him from being employed by IDG, a competitor. EarthWeb showed that Schlack reviewed and/or created a substantial number of documents containing sensitive information and had responsibility for a wide range of proprietary matters. EarthWeb argued that under its non-compete agreement with Schlack he should be barred from new employment because the new company competed with it and the enforcement of the agreement was necessary to prevent disclosure of EarthWeb's trade secrets. A federal court sitting in New York stated, "In its purest form, the inevitable disclosure doctrine treads an exceedingly narrow path through judicially disfavored territory. Absent evidence of actual misappropriation by an employee, the doctrine should be applied in only the rarest of cases." The court noted that a drawback to the doctrine is that courts are left without a frame of reference because there is no express non-compete agreement to test for reasonableness. Enforcing such a rule in the context of an Internet business would stifle new ideas and commerce.[30]

Human Resource Form
Trade Secrets Agreement

An employer should always have employees execute a confidentiality and trade-secrets agreement even if a covenant-not-to-compete agreement is available to the employer. The following is a sample of such an agreement:

TRADE SECRET AGREEMENT

The Company ("COMPANY") has disclosed or may disclose to George Washington ("EMPLOYEE") business information, technical information, and/or proprietary and confidential information COMPANY wishes to protect from public disclosure ("Proprietary Information") in connection with a proposed employment of EMPLOYEE.

Confidential Proprietary Information, as used in this Agreement, is all information or material that gives COMPANY some competitive business advantage, or the opportunity to obtain that advantage, or the disclosure of which could be detrimental to COMPANY's interests, is owned by COMPANY or in which COMPANY has an interest, and is marked either "Confidential Information" or "Proprietary Information."

Proprietary Information includes, but is not limited to: inventions; drawings; file data; documentation; diagrams; specifications; know-how; processes; formulas; models; flow charts; research and development procedures and test results; marketing techniques, materials, and plans; price lists; pricing policies; business plans; information relating to the identities, characteristics, and agreements of customers and/or suppliers; financial information and projections; and employee files. Proprietary Information also includes any information described above that COMPANY obtains from another party and treats as Proprietary Information and designates as confidential. Notwithstanding the above, no information is Proprietary Information if it is generic information or general knowledge that any person could have learned in the ordinary course of business or is otherwise publicly known and in the public domain.

In consideration of any disclosure of Proprietary Information and any negotiations concerning the proposed employment EMPLOYEE agrees that:

1. He will hold in confidence and not detrimentally possess or use or disclose any Proprietary Information except information he can document (a) is in the public domain through no fault of EMPLOYEE, (b) was properly known to EMPLOYEE, without restriction, before disclosure by COMPANY, or (c) was properly disclosed by EMPLOYEE to another person without restriction, and will not reverse engineer or attempt to derive the composition or underlying information, structure, or ideas of any Proprietary Information. The foregoing does not grant EMPLOYEE a license in or to any of the Proprietary Information.
2. During and after the term of this Agreement, EMPLOYEE will not intentionally disclose, and will use his best efforts to prohibit the unintentional disclosure, to any third party of any Proprietary Information concerning COMPANY, unless COMPANY expressly agrees in advance in writing to such disclosure. This obligation applies

not only to technical information, but also to any business information that COMPANY treats as confidential. Any information of COMPANY that is not readily, publicly available will be considered Proprietary Information unless COMPANY advises to the contrary.

3. EMPLOYEE will not make any unauthorized copy of any Proprietary Information disclosed or otherwise reduced to written form, including without limitation any sales literature, business forms, policy directives, commission schedules, and customer lists.

4. EMPLOYEE will immediately notify COMPANY if Proprietary Information is disclosed.

5. If EMPLOYEE breaches, or threatens to commit a breach of, his duty to maintain the confidentiality of the Proprietary Information, COMPANY will have the following rights and remedies, each of which will be in addition to, and not in lieu of, any other rights and remedies available to COMPANY at law or in equity:

a. Specific Performance: The right and remedy to have the duty of confidentiality specifically enforced by any court having equity jurisdiction, all without the need to post a bond or any other security, or to prove any amount of actual damage, or that money damages would not provide an adequate remedy, it being acknowledged and agreed that any such breach or threatened breach will cause irreparable injury to COMPANY and that monetary damages will not provide an adequate remedy.

b. Accounting and Indemnification: The right and remedy to require (i) to account for and pay over to COMPANY all compensation, profits, monies, accruals, increments, or other benefits derived or received by EMPLOYEE or by any associated party deriving such benefits as a result of any breach of the duty of confidentiality; and (ii) to indemnify COMPANY against any other losses, damages (including special and consequential damages), costs and expenses, including actual attorney's fees and court costs, which may be incurred by COMPANY and which result from, or arise out of, any breach or threatened breach of the duty of confidentiality.

6. The terms of this Agreement remain in effect with respect to any Proprietary Information until COMPANY can document that the information has become generic information or general knowledge that any person could have learned in the ordinary course of business or is otherwise publicly known and in the public domain.

7. This Agreement is governed by the laws of the State of Xanadu and may be modified or waived only in writing. If any provision is found to be unenforceable, such provision will be limited or deleted to the minimum extent necessary so that the remaining terms remain in full force and effect. The prevailing party in any dispute or legal action regarding the subject matter of this agreement shall be entitled to recover attorney's fees and costs.

Dated: ____________

Company:

By: ______________________

Title: Director of Human Resources

____

George Washington, Employee

Key Terms and Concepts

- Express or implied employment contracts
- Implied contractual liability
- Wrongful discharge or wrongful termination
- Constructive discharge
- Terminations violating strong public policies
- Implied covenant of good faith and fair dealing
- Whistleblowers
- Retaliation
- Intentional or negligent infliction of emotional distress
- Defamation, libel, and slander
- Interference with contractual relations

- Invasion of privacy claims
- Misrepresentation and fraud
- False imprisonment
- False arrest
- Negligent evaluation and termination
- Negligent hiring, retention, and supervision
- Tort
- Compensatory damages
- Punitive damages
- Vicarious tort liability
- Self-compelled publication
- Covenant not to compete
- Protectable trade secret
- Uniform Trade Secrets Act
- Economic Espionage Act
- Misappropriation
- Confidential information
- Inevitable disclosure of trade secrets
- Confidentiality agreement

Chapter Summary

- Generally, all employment is "at will," which allows the employer to terminate employment at any time without a reason for doing so; at the same time, the employee may terminate his or her employment without any reason and without prior notice.

- There are several exceptions to the "at-will" doctrine. These include contractual terms under which either party has agreed that termination will occur on a basis other than "at will." For example, the employer may agree that the employee may be terminated only for cause, such as the material failure to perform after repeated warnings from the employer. Other exceptions are public policies such as the employer's interference with lawfully protected rights such as jury duty service or the employer's failure to act in a good-faith and fair-dealing manner with employees.

- Many tort causes of action are recognized within the employment law field. These can result in the assessment of compensatory damages and, occasionally, punitive damages. They arise from intentional conduct on the part of the employer or the employee. Damages can be assessed if injuries were suffered even though harm was not intended. Sometimes duties are owed to third parties, such as the liability that can result from negligent references, retention, and supervision.

- Whistleblowers are protected under the public policy exception to the at-will doctrine. However, they are not protected from discharge or retaliation if the interests involve only private corporate policies. Whistleblowers include applicants or employees who report employer wrongdoing to a governmental or law-enforcement agency. The misconduct must affect a public policy for the individual to be protected from retaliation or other adverse employment actions. Whistleblowers should be aware that SOX is not a general whistleblower statute and does not offer general protection against retaliatory acts. The protected activity must satisfy the first element of a whistleblower claim. Second, simply because an employee voices complaints about an employer's accounting practices or financial controls does not mean that the employee is automatically entitled to protection under SOX. The law offers protection only to allegations of actual unlawful conduct relating to the securities laws, not merely conduct that violates internal accounting procedures.

- The majority of states recognize employers' rights to restrict the future employment opportunities of employees who have acquired significant information that might harm the former employer if the employee sought to compete against it. A parallel restriction relating to trade-secret contracts limits former employees' from taking actual trade secrets to the detriment of the former employer.

Online Student Support

- Loislaw legal research and writing assignments.
- Loislaw group projects and class presentations.
- Loislaw access, providing online research including up-to-date cases, statutes, rules, and regulations. Primary law for all 50 states and federal jurisdictions. Registration required for access to this resource.
- Practice questions, including sample true/false, multiple choice, and short answer questions to test your understanding of concepts.
- Additional human resource forms.
- Internet exercises.
- Blogs.
- Supplementary statutory and regulatory materials.

Case Problems

3.1 James Eales, a physician's assistant at a medical group, was fired from his job after six years of employment. He sued the clinic for wrongful discharge. During litigation, the clinic conceded that Eales had been offered a job that would last until he reached retirement age and that he was fired without cause. In addition, Eales testified that he would not have given up his previous job if the clinic's offer had not been for permanent employment. The trial court held that the contract created was for an indefinite term, terminable at the will of either party. On appeal, how should the court rule? Should the employee be terminated only for good cause, even if the contract was at will because it was for an indefinite period? (*Eales v. Tanana Valley Medical-Surgical Group, Inc.*, 663 P.3d 985 (Alaska. 1983))

3.2 Anthony Nicosia was hired by Wakefern Food Corporation and terminated after 18 years of service. Wakefern claimed that Nicosia had stolen merchandise from the company. Nicosia contends that he was terminated without receiving the benefit of the progressive discipline steps outlined in an 11-page section of the employee manual distributed to all employees. The 11-page section did not contain a disclaimer that immediate termination could occur in the event of serious offenses. Nicosia claimed that the manual created an implied employment contract and that Wakefern breached it by terminating him without following the manual's procedural protections. How should the court rule on Nicosia's claim? (*Nicosia v. Wakefern Food Corporation*, 643 A.2d 554 (N.J. Sup. Ct. 1994))

3.3 The employer's supervisors personally delivered a notice of termination and a final paycheck to the 22-year company employee while he lay in bed recuperating from a heart condition. The supervisors barged into the employee's home and fired him for alleged misconduct while he lay in his mother-in-law's home. Archer was on indefinite sick leave because of his heart condition when he was terminated. What tort theories of recovery should Archer pursue? What damages, if any, would you award in such a case? (*Archer v. Farmer Bros. Co.*, 70 P.23d 495 (Colo. App. 2002))

3.4 William Urban was terminated from his position with a subsidiary company when the parent company sought to enforce against him a covenant not to compete. He was prohibited from engaging in competition with his former employer or from soliciting its clients in any of the U.S. counties in which they conducted business. Urban had executed an agreement enforceable between an employer and employee. What factors do you think the court should employ to judge the reasonableness of the covenant not to complete? What rights and remedies should the employer and employee have upon the employee's termination? (*Century Business Services, Inc. v. Urban*, 2008 Ohio 5744, 2008 Ohio App. LEXIS 4829 (2008))

3.5 Irving Slifkin accepted an oral offer of employment from Condec Corporation to serve as the general counsel of the corporation. At that time, he was nearing retirement age. Later, he prepared a memorandum that set forth the terms of his employment, including that he would remain employed until he became fully vested in the former employer's pension benefits. Both parties executed the agreement. Shortly thereafter, Slifkin's employment was terminated, and Slifkin sued for wrongful termination of employment. Should the court determine that what was implied in the agreement for employment was definite enough for enforcement? (*Slifkin v. Condec Corp.*, 538 A.2d 231 (Conn. App. Ct. 1988))

End Notes

1. *Peat Marwick Main v. Haass,* 818 S.W.2d 381 (Tex. Sup. Ct. 1991).
2. H. Wood, Master and Servant, §134 (3d ed. 1886).
3. *Gorham v. Benson Optical,* 539 NW2d 798 (Minn. Ct. App. 1995).
4. *Pugh v. See's Candies, Inc.*, 203 Cal. App. 3d 743 (1988).
5. Mont. Code Ann. Sections 39-2-901 to 39-2-915.
6. *Jackson v. Birmingham Bd. of Educ.*, 544 U.S. 167 (2005).
7. 5 U.S.C. §2302.
8. 31 U.S.C. §3730(h).
9. 15 U.S.C. §7245.
10. *Collins v. Beazer Homes USA, Inc.*, 334 F. Supp. 2d 1365, 1375 (N.D. Ga. 2004).
11. *Allen v. Administrative Review Board,* 514 F.3d 468, 476-77 (5th Cir. 2008).
12. *Collins v. Beazer Homes USA, Inc., supra.*
13. 33 U.S.C. §2623(b).
14. 42 U.S.C. §7622.
15. 42 U.S.C. §9610.
16. 40 U.S.C. §276(a).
17. 29 U.S.C. §660.
18. 29 U.S.C. §215(a)(3).
19. *Barbosa v. Impco Technologies,* 179 Cal. App. 4th 1116 (2009).
20. *Comeaux v. Brown & Williamson Tobacco Co.*, 915 F.2d 1264 (9th Cir. 1990).
21. *Staples v. Bangor Hydro-Electric Co.*, 629 A.2d 601 (1993).
22. *Crump v. P & C Food Markets, Inc.*, 576 A.2d 441 (Vt. 1990).
23. *Keating v. Goldick and Lapp Roofing,* 2004 Del. Super. Lexis 102.
24. *Worstell Parking, Inc. v. Aisida,* 442 S. E. 2d 469 (1994).
25. 339 So. 2d 382 (1976).
26. 730 S.W. 2d 499.
27. *United Laboratories, Inc. v. Kuykendall,* 361 S.E.2d 292, *aff'd in part,* 370 S.E.2d 375 (1988).
28. *The Estee Lauder Companies, Inc. v. Shashi Batra,* 450 F. Supp. 2d 158 (S.D.N.Y. 2006).
29. 18 U.S.C. §1831 *et seq.*
30. *Earthweb, Inc. v. Schlack,* 71 F.Supp.2d 299 (S.D.N.Y. 1999).

Chapter 4
Employment Litigation and EEOC Procedure

"We win justice quickest by rendering justice to the other party." —*Mahatma Gandhi*

Learning Objectives

1. Identify the major federal laws regulating equal employment opportunities.
2. Define classes protected from discrimination in employment.
3. Distinguish among the various types of discrimination claims.
4. Explain how a claimant would prove a case of discrimination.
5. Know employer defenses to discrimination claims.
6. Recognize the forums for resolving discrimination claims.

Chapter Outline

Chapter Opening scenario

Carolyn Evans always wanted to be an airline attendant. She was hired by United Airlines but was forced to resign because of the airline's "no marriage" rule for female flight attendants. Even though that rule was found to violate Title VII in an unrelated lawsuit, when she was rehired she was given no credit for her prior service, as was required by United's seniority system. She did not file an Equal Employment Opportunity Commission (EEOC) charge regarding her initial termination, but she did so when she was rehired and did not receive her seniority. She argued that while any lawsuit based on the original discrimination might have been barred by the elapse of too much time, United's refusal to give her credit for her prior service gave present effect to past illegal acts and thereby perpetuated the consequences of discrimination. She complains that the airline's seniority system had a continuing impact on her pay and fringe benefits. The airline retorts that there was no present violation of law occurring and that what occurred in the past is time barred. It also states that, in any event, the seniority system reflects the requirements of United's collective bargaining agreement with the union for the flight attendants. Who do you think is right?[1]

Introduction

Every year employment discrimination caseloads overwhelm the dockets of the federal courts. The Administrative Office of the U.S. Courts reports that about one in every eight cases pending in the U.S. district courts relates to an alleged civil rights violation.[2] That caseload does not include disputes resolved through other means, such as private-party mediations and arbitrations. This chapter will review who is protected under the most significant federal employment laws and how a claim is resolved within our judicial system and through alternative dispute resolution procedures. Disputes arising in a unionized workplace involve different approaches to labor-management conflicts and will be considered in the labor law chapter.

Definitions of Discrimination

The term ***employment discrimination*** is subtle. A coarse definition of the term would state that it occurs when an employer distinguishes between two individuals relative to a term or condition of employment because they belong to different groups. Within employment law, distinguishing among employees because of differences in productivity are lawful; however, making other distinctions based on group or individual characteristics invites scrutiny. In our effort to provide fundamental fairness to all workers, American discrimination laws seek to eliminate workplace injustice due to characteristics over which the individual has no control. These are immutable characteristics and include, among others, race, color, sex, age, sexual orientation, and disability. These characteristics provide protection from employment discrimination. The law seeks to eliminate those inherently arbitrary distinctions while preserving those that are deemed meritorious. Legislatures and courts have struggled to distinguish the invidious from the meritorious characteristics.

Protected Classes of Individuals

Certain distinctions among people have historically resulted in discrimination in employment. Legislatures and courts act to ensure that employment decisions are free from wrongful influences and biases. Past discriminatory practices can perpetuate unfairness and the law seeks to eliminate them in the workplace.

Table 4.1 lists possible discrimination claims and the federal law, if any, that protects each claim.

TABLE 4.1. Federal Laws Protecting Discrimination Claimants

Discrimination Claim	Protections Afforded under Federal Law
Age	ADEA (Age Discrimination in Employment Act of 1967); Age Discrimination Employment Act of 1975; E.O. (Executive Order) 11141
Race	Title VI; Title VII; E.O. 11246; 42 U.S.C. §§1981, 1983, and 1985; Article I §8
Color	Title VI; Title VII; 42 U.S.C. §1981; E.O. 11246; Article I §8
Ancestry and/or National Origin	Title VI; Title VII; 42 U.S.C. §1981; E.O. 11246; Article I §8; IRCA
Sex	Title VII; E.O. 11246; Article I §8; Equal Pay Act
Pregnancy	Title VII; Family and Medical Leave Act
Marital Status	None at this time
Religion	Title VII; E.O. 11246; Article I, §8
Medical Condition and Mental Disability	Rehabilitation Act; Americans with Disabilities Act (as amended by the Americans with Disabilities Amendments Act of 2008); Family and Medical Leave Act
Sexual Orientation	None at this time
Equal Pay	Equal Pay Act; Fair Labor Standards Act; Lilly Ledbetter Fair Pay Act (amended Title VII, ADA, Rehabilitation Act of 1973, and ADEA to include discrimination claims possible each time wages, benefits, or other compensation is paid)
Citizenship	IRCA
Armed Forces Service	USERRA (Uniformed Services Employment and Reemployment Rights Act)
Genetic Information	GINA (Genetic Information Nondiscrimination Act of 2008)

In addition to the protections afforded individuals under federal law, many more are offered under state law and local ordinances. Protected characteristics include the following: marital status, sexual orientation (including transgender identity), tobacco and alcohol use, pregnancy, childbirth or related medical condition, mental disability, HIV/AIDS, arrest and criminal history records, and weight and personal appearance. For example, as an equal-opportunity employer, the District of Columbia does not discriminate in its hiring of qualified candidates with regard to their race, color, religion, national origin, sex, age, marital status, personal appearance, sexual orientation, family responsibilities, matriculation, physical handicap, or political affiliation.[3]

Size of Employer

Congress has fashioned the law to conform to the size of the employer. Courts have interpreted who is a covered employee for purposes of applying a discrimination law to a particular employer. Usually, the law applies to the number of employees paid on a payroll system maintained by the business. In *Walters v. Metro. Educational Enterprises,*[4] the Supreme Court ruled that each employee should be counted for each full week between the commencement and the termination of employment. Thus, part-time and temporary employees can make an unsuspecting employer subject to discrimination laws; however, the law applies differently with regard to the Fair Labor Standards Act, which we study in a later chapter.

Table 4.2 lists major federal antidiscrimination laws and the number of employees an employer must have for each law to apply.

TABLE 4.2. Size of Employer Requirement

Federal Antidiscrimination Law	Number of Employees or Other Conditions Required for Law to Apply
The Civil Rights Act of 1866 ("§1981")	15 or more (Following a §1983 lawsuit against a government employee acting "under color of state law" for civil rights, the governmental unit and or employee must be named as defendant.)
Title VII (including Pregnancy Discrimination Act of 1978)	15 or more (excludes bona fide private membership organizations)
Equal Pay Act (Fair Labor Standards Act) and Lilly Ledbetter Fair Pay Act	2 or more employees of different genders who are subject to minimum wage provisions Gross sales of at least $500,000 Employees engaged in interstate commerce
Age Discrimination in Employment Act	20 or more on each working day for 20 or more weeks during a measuring calendar year Applies to all state and local government employers
Americans with Disabilities Act	15 or more

Federal Antidiscrimination Law	Number of Employees or Other Conditions Required for Law to Apply
Rehabilitation Act of 1973	Employers with contracts of $10,000 or more Employers with at least 50 employees and a federal government contract required to maintain written affirmative action plans
Executive Order No. 11246	Employers with contracts of $10,000 or more
Family and Medical Leave Act	50 or more employees (within a 75-mile radius, if there are multiple worksites)
IRCA	Different applications depending on size of employer (generally, applies to employers with 15 or more employees, but exemptions available for employers with fewer than 4 employees)
USERRA	Applies to all public and private employers
GINA	15 or more

Title VII covers private employers, nonfederal public employees, and educational institutions with 15 or more employees. All federal government agencies, private and public employment agencies, labor unions, and other labor groups must comply with it as well.

Title VII covers employees of Congress and the federal executive branch, as do the Age Discrimination in Employment Act and the Americans with Disabilities Act; but each branch of government has its own specific enforcement procedures and available remedies. Because of the political context of many positions in Congress and the executive branch, it is not illegal for an employer to consider applicants' political party affiliation and state of residency. State government political appointments follow a similar approach to filling open positions.

Under state statutes, the threshold for the application of nonfederal discrimination statutes and regulations may be much lower than the 15 employees required under federal law. These statutes range in application from just one person to groups of fewer than five persons.

Types of Discrimination Claims

Only unlawful acts of discrimination and not mere acts of unfairness are legally actionable. For example, employment decisions are not discriminatory if they are based on the individual's personal initiative or advanced education. To demonstrate unlawful discrimination, a claimant must establish a nexus between the employment condition or decision and a prohibited act or practice of discrimination under which they suffered damages. Federal and state laws prohibit three types of discrimination. The first type is a claim of **"disparate treatment,"** which is premised on intentional discrimination against an individual. The second type is based on a **"disparate impact"** theory, also known as **adverse impact discrimination**. The third type is known as **unlawful retaliation. Retaliation** claims arise from an employer's acts against a worker who protests wrongful conduct towards that worker or another individual.

The first type of discrimination claim, **disparate treatment**, focuses on the employer's **discriminatory intent** with respect to the adverse employment action undertaken against the employee. A **disparate treatment** discrimination claim lies when due to considerations of race, color, national origin, or religion an individual is treated less favorably than are others. A **disparate treatment** discrimination claim requires proof of **discriminatory intent**. One way parties provide evidence of **discriminatory intent** is to employ **statistical proof** demonstrating decision-making bias involving racial or ethnic considerations. Plaintiffs may pursue the proof of discriminatory treatment in cases involving hiring, discharge, promotion, and demotion. **Disparate treatment** proof also applies to §1981, the Rehabilitation Act of 1973, and other federal benefit statutes.

To make a **disparate impact** discrimination claim, the complaining party does not need to establish proof of **discriminatory intent. Disparate impact** claims involve a **facially neutral** employment practice that adversely affects a **protected class**. A **facially neutral** employment practice does not appear to be discriminatory on its face, but is discriminatory in its application or effect on the worker. In cases of **disparate impact**, the trier of fact examines the effects of the facially neutral employment practice and *not* the intent of the employer. Evidence must show an adverse effect on a **protected class**, while the employer must be unable to show that the challenged employment practice is necessary for the operation of its business.

The proof required to prevail in a **retaliation** claim has been significantly reduced with the Supreme Court's decision in *Burlington Northern & Santa Fe Railway Co. v. White*, discussed later in this chapter. By its decision, instead of requiring a showing that the employer engaged in conduct that adversely affected the individual worker, the court adopted a much lower threshold of harm in that the worker must establish that he or she was subject to **retaliation**.

Proving a Discrimination Claim

An employment discrimination claimant may establish a case of discrimination by employing one of three alternative methods of proving the case:

- Meeting the four-pronged test set forth in the decisions discussed below, *McDonnell Douglas Corporation v. Green* and *Texas Department of Community Affairs v. Burdine*;
- Producing "statistical evidence" of unlawful discrimination as set forth in the *Hazelwood* case discussed below; or
- Presenting **direct or circumstantial evidence** of the employer's discriminatory intent in a **mixed-motives** case, as discussed below in relation to the *Desert Palace v. Costa* decision discussed below.

The plaintiff must prove a **prima facie** case of discrimination under a civil rights statute. **Prima facie** means that when a plaintiff proves certain facts by a **preponderance of evidence**, the plaintiff is entitled to damages or other relief against the employer, subject to the employer's proof of a defense to the plaintiff's allegations. The standard of **preponderance of evidence** means the plaintiff's evidence established that the claim of employment discrimination is more likely to be true than not.

The plaintiff may use **direct evidence** (i.e., proof that establishes a fact by itself, such as an employer's statement that it discriminated against an employee). The plaintiff may also employ **circumstantial evidence** in proving the case (i.e., by showing facts from which a reasonable inference or presumption can be made that discrimination occurred).

Direct Evidence
Proof that establishes a fact by itself, without the need to infer the fact, such as an admission by wrongdoer.

In its *McDonnell Douglas* decision, the Supreme Court devised a test in the context of **summary judgment motion** practice. In response to a litigant's **motion for summary judgment**, the court can decide a case because no dispute exists between the parties as to the material facts of the case or where the court is of the opinion that a party is entitled to judgment as a matter of law. The test was adopted to determine if a plaintiff had enough **circumstantial evidence** to raise a **triable issue of fact**. Determination of a **triable issue of fact** requires the judge to determine prior to trial whether what happened is so clear that no trial is required. If the evidence creates a clear dispute in the facts, the case must be tried. If not, either the plaintiff or the defendant employer may win because the court grants a **motion for summary judgment**. The purpose of this procedure is to determine whether the plaintiff has made out a **prima facie** case. Most discrimination cases brought in federal court are subject to motions for summary judgment. This procedure reduces the number of cases tried in court.

Circumstantial Evidence
Admissible evidence that proves facts from which a reasonable inference or presumption can be made.

Once a plaintiff has offered enough evidence to establish a **prima facie** case of discrimination, and the defendant employer has articulated a legitimate, nondiscriminatory reason for its action, the plaintiff employee may still move for summary judgment on the ground that the reason proffered by the employer was a **"pretext."** If the court grants the motion, then one side receives judgment in its favor. The trial court's decision may be appealed to a federal court of appeals. If the court denies the **motion for summary judgment** (or the motion is never made), the issue of whether the plaintiff was the victim of unlawful discrimination is disputed and must be decided at trial by a court or jury trial.

A victim of discrimination must first pursue a claim through the administrative forums discussed below or by filing a lawsuit in court. A **prima facie** case must be proven based on allegations of **disparate treatment** or **disparate impact**. As the Supreme Court stated in its decision in *Teamsters v. United States,*[5] "disparate treatment is the most easily understood type of discrimination. The employer simply rates some people less favorably than others rate because of their race, color, religion, sex, or national origin. Proof of discriminatory motive is critical, although it can in some situations be inferred from the mere fact of differences in treatment. Undoubtedly disparate treatment was the most obvious evil Congress had in mind when it enacted Tile VII." Additional grounds for **disparate treatment** discrimination claims include disability and age discrimination. Usually, this means that the victim of the disparate treatment has been treated less favorably, but it can also mean that the victim has been treated differently. For example, if **protected class** members are given deliberately favorable performance evaluations, unequal treatment by itself can also constitute **disparate treatment** discrimination.

The key to a successful plaintiff's case for **disparate treatment** is to prove the defendant's **discriminatory intent**. This proof is made through the introduction of **evidence** of the employer's motivation or intent in making the unfavorable or adverse employment decision. Since plaintiffs rarely have **direct evidence** of the defendant's intent to discriminate against them, they must rely on **circumstantial evidence**. The process of proving discrimination by **disparate treatment** involves a multi-step process presented in *McDonnell Douglas Corporation v. Green.*

CASE 4.1

THE ELEMENTS FOR A PRIMA FACIE CASE OF DISPARATE TREATMENT

MCDONNELL DOUGLAS CORP. V. GREEN

411 U.S. 792 (1973)

Supreme Court of the United States

Facts. Mr. Green was described by the trial court as a "long-time activist in the civil rights movement." He alleged that his former employer was discriminatory in its employment practices and led a protest in the company parking lot in which cars were stalled on the main roads leading to the lots for the purpose of blocking access to the lots by other employees. As a result, he was arrested, convicted, and fined for obstructing traffic. Following his conviction, his employer advertised for mechanics, Mr. Green's occupation. When he applied for reemployment, he was rejected.

Mr. Green sued his employer on the basis that he was denied employment because of his involvement in the civil rights protests in the parking lots. The district court dismissed his suit as an unprotected exercise of his civil rights due to his illegal "stall-in" of traffic. The federal court of appeals affirmed the dismissal of one claim but held that the EEOC had made a favorable determination that his employer had discriminated against him for his lawsuit to proceed in federal court. The Supreme Court granted *certiorari.*

Issue. If the defendant employer presents a nondiscriminatory reason for the discrimination, must the plaintiff then show that the reason for the employer's decision was a pretext for discrimination?

Language of the Court. Powell, J.: **Congress did not intend by Title VII, however, to guarantee a job to every person regardless of qualifications. In short, the Act does not command that any person be hired simply because he was formerly the subject of discrimination, or because he is a member of a minority group. Discriminatory preference for any group, minority or majority, is precisely and only what Congress has proscribed. What is required by Congress is the removal of artificial, arbitrary, and unnecessary barriers to employment when the barriers operate invidiously to discriminate on the basis of racial or other impermissible classification.**

The complainant in a Title VII trial must carry the initial burden under the statute of establishing a prima facie case of racial discrimination. This may be

done by showing (i) that he belongs to a racial minority; (ii) that he applied and was qualified for a job for which the employer was seeking applicants; (iii) that, despite his qualifications, he was rejected; and (iv) that, after his rejection, the position remained open and the employer continued to seek applicants from persons of complainant's qualifications. In the instant case, we agree with the Court of Appeals that respondent proved a prima facie case. . . . Petitioner sought mechanics, respondent's trade, and continued to do so after respondent's rejection. Petitioner, moreover, does not dispute respondent's qualifications and acknowledges that his past work performance in petitioner's employ was "satisfactory." The burden then must shift to the employer to articulate some legitimate, nondiscriminatory reason for the employee's rejection . . . . Here petitioner has assigned respondent's participation in unlawful conduct against it as the cause for his rejection. We think that this suffices to discharge petitioner's burden of proof at this stage and to meet respondent's prima facie case of discrimination.

In view of the seriousness and harmful potential of an African American former employee's participation in a "stall-in" whereby cars were stopped along roads leading to an employer's plant so as to block access to the plant during the morning rush hour, and in view of the accompanying inconvenience to other employees, the employer's subsequent refusal to rehire the former employee cannot be said to have lacked a rational and neutral business justification.

Decision. Yes. Once a discrimination action is rebutted by the employer by showing it had a nondiscriminatory, legitimate business reason for its decision, the plaintiff must show that the reason for the adverse employment action was a pretext. McDonnell Douglas had a legitimate reason not to rehire Green.

CASE QUESTIONS

Critical Legal Thinking. What should a court do at the time of trial to prevent injustice to either party if the case is based largely upon circumstantial evidence?

Business Ethics. The Supreme Court held that the effect of the employer's actions and not its intent was controlling. Do you agree with that result and why?

Contemporary Business. What arguments can be marshaled to extend this analysis to the concept of **constructive discharge**, by which a victim of discrimination alleges intolerable and discriminatory working decisions that caused the victim to resign?

Later court decisions stress that the *McDonnell Douglas* test for **disparate treatment** should be applied liberally and flexibly to promote the purposes of equal employment opportunity. In some cases, a plaintiff may prevail without establishing that the position applied for remained available after the plaintiff's rejection.

A recent federal appellate court opinion clarified what a district court should consider when requested to rule upon a pre-trial **motion for summary judgment** in a **disparate treatment** discrimination lawsuit. In reviewing a plaintiff's appeal from the granting of a **motion for summary judgment** against an African American involving his termination for sexually harassing a female co-worker, the court stated follows:

> Much ink has been spilled regarding the proper contours of the prima-facie-case aspect of *McDonnell Douglas* . . . . It has not benefited employees or employers; nor has it simplified or expedited court proceedings. In fact, it has done exactly the opposite, spawning enormous confusion, and wasting litigant and judicial resources.
>
> Lest there be any lingering uncertainty, we state the rule clearly: In a Title VII disparate-treatment suit where an employee has suffered an adverse employment action and an employer has asserted a legitimate, non-discriminatory reason for the decision, the district court need not — *and should not* — decide whether the plaintiff actually made out a prima facie case under *McDonnell Douglas.* Rather, in considering an employer's motion for summary judgment or judgment as a matter of law in those circumstances, the district court must resolve one central question: Has the employee produced sufficient evidence for a reasonable jury to find that the employer's asserted non-discriminatory reason was not the actual reason and that the employer intentionally discriminated against the employee on the basis of race, color, religion, sex, or national origin?[6]

Concept Summary
Proving Discrimination Claims

A plaintiff must prove:

1. membership in a protected class;
2. application and qualification for a position for which the employer was seeking applicants (i.e., qualification for the position or satisfactory performance of job requirements);
3. rejection despite being qualified (or the sufferance of an adverse employment action at the hands of the employer); and
4. continued availability of the position after the rejection, with employer continuing to seek applicants with plaintiff's qualifications.

In other words, other facts point to a discriminatory effect or intent surrounding the adverse action taken. The employer's reasons were a pretext or an artifice to mask actual discrimination.

Statistical Proof in Discrimination Cases

Another way to prove **discriminatory intent** is by citing statistics demonstrating a racial or ethnic imbalance in the workforce due to the employer's conduct. A **disparate treatment** claim may be brought as a pattern and practice case by which a lawsuit is brought on behalf of a class of affected employees. Both sides of such a dispute may use statistical proof to meet their respective burdens of proving or disproving the prima facie case. Quite often, statistical proof is used in the **disparate treatment** type of case to show intentional discrimination against a class of persons or to show that the employer's rationale for its decision was **pretextual**. In a **disparate impact** case, the most commonly invoked comparisons involve the relative selection rates from one group and from a larger group, also known as the potential selection group. The comparison demonstrates the effect of the alleged discriminatory practice on the **protected class** of claimants. For example, if the job position required a master's degree, those applicants from a **protected class** possessing this degree would be compared with the majority group class also meeting those requirements. Under the **Civil Rights Act (CRA) of 1991, statistical proof** must be related to an identifiable, specific act within the hiring process unless the claimant "demonstrates to the court that the elements of the [employer's] decision making process are not capable of separation for analysis."[7] Parties to cases involving the use of statistics must employ statisticians as experts to interpret the data, clarify the degree of disparity, and discuss the validity of the sample size. In the following case, the Supreme Court stated what guidelines should be used when employing statistics to prove a claim of employment discrimination.

CASE 4.2

STATISTICS MAY PROVE PATTERN OR PRACTICE (DISPARATE TREATMENT) DISCRIMINATION

HAZELWOOD SCHOOL DISTRICT V. UNITED STATES

433 U.S. 299 (1977)

Supreme Court of the United States

Facts. Hazelwood School District followed relatively unstructured procedures in hiring its teachers. As a buyer's market began to develop for public school teachers, Hazelwood curtailed its recruiting efforts. A number of African American applicants were not hired. By comparison, according to 1970 census figures, of more than 19,000 teachers employed in that year in the St. Louis area, 15.4 percent were African American. That percentage figure included the St. Louis City School District, which in recent years has followed a policy of attempting to maintain a 50 percent African American teaching staff. Apart from that school district, 5.7 percent of the teachers in the county were African American in 1970. The United States sued the school district because statistics showed a "pattern or practice" of unlawful discrimination. The district court ruled for the school district; however, the federal court of appeals reversed the decision. The Supreme Court granted *certiorari.*

Issue. Whether a court may disregard evidence that an employer has treated actual job applicants in a nondiscriminatory manner and rely on undifferentiated workforce statistics to employment discrimination.

Language of the Court. Stewart, J.: **The [question] petitioners raise, in short, is whether a basic component in the Court of Appeals' finding of a pattern or practice of discrimination — the comparatively small percentage of African American employees on Hazelwood's teaching staff — was lacking in probative force.**

Evidence of long lasting and gross disparity between the composition of a work force and that of the general population thus may be significant even though 703 (j) makes clear that Title VII imposes no requirement that a work force mirror the general population." . . . Where gross statistical disparities can be shown, they alone may in a proper case constitute prima facie proof of a pattern or practice of discrimination. . . . There can be no doubt, in light of the Teamsters case, that the District Court's comparison of Hazelwood's teacher work force to its student population fundamentally misconceived the role of statistics in employment discrimination cases.

It is thus clear that a determination of the appropriate comparative figures in this case will depend upon further evaluation by the trial court. As this Court admonished in Teamsters: "[S]tatistics . . . come in infinite variety . . . [T]heir usefulness depends on all of the surrounding facts and circumstances." (Citation omitted.) Only the trial court is in a position to make the appropriate determination after further findings. And only after such a determination is made can a foundation be established for deciding whether or not Hazelwood engaged in a pattern or practice of racial discrimination in its employment practices in violation of the law. . . . Accordingly, the judgment is vacated, and the case is remanded to the District Court for further proceedings consistent with this opinion. It is so ordered.

Decision. No. Where gross statistical disparities can be shown, they alone in a proper case may constitute proof of a pattern or practice of Title VII discrimination.

CASE QUESTIONS

Critical Legal Thinking. The Supreme Court ordered the case remanded to the district court to make further findings. Do you think that judges have the ability to fairly deal with complex statistical analyses?

Business Ethics. Recent Supreme Court decisions decry the use of statistics in proving discrimination cases because of the tendency to develop set-asides or *de facto* quota arrangements for protected classes. What place do you think the use of statistics has in the modern employment environment?

Contemporary Business. Can you think of another circumstance in which standard deviations between 2 and 3 would constitute acceptable proof of discrimination?

Class-Action Lawsuits

In **class-action** lawsuits, one or more persons sue or are sued as representatives of a large group of persons similarly situated and interested in the outcome of the lawsuit. The court in the jurisdiction in which such a suit is brought has wide discretion to decide if it can be brought. Certain procedural minimums must be met:

- the class must be so large or dispersed that actual participation of the individual members of the class would be impractical;
- questions of law and fact must be common to all members of the class;
- these common questions must outweigh the particular interests of the individual members; and
- the named parties must adequately represent the interests of their class.

Notification to actual and potential class members is required; unless a member of the class opts out of the action at the beginning of the case, all persons electing to be in the class will thus be bound by the decision reached. **Class-action** lawsuits have been the basis of many prominent employment discrimination decisions.

Four-Fifths Rule
An EEOC guideline that holds that a selection rate for any race, sex, or ethnic group that is less than four-fifths the selection rate of the most frequently selected group will generally be regarded as evidence of adverse impact.

Workplace Application
The Four-Fifths Rule or 80-Percent Rule

In 1978, the EEOC and other federal agencies adopted a set of guidelines entitled the Uniform Guidelines on Employee Selection Procedures. The purpose of the guidelines was to provide information to employers in the area of employee testing; however, the guidelines apply to all aspects of the employment relationship. Their primary focus is the effects that selection standards have on **disparate impact** cases. The Guidelines define the **"four-fifths** or **80-percent rule"** as "a selection rate for any race, sex, or ethnic group which is less than four-fifths (or eighty percent) of the rate for the group with the highest rate will generally be regarded by the Federal enforcement agencies as evidence of **adverse impact,** while a greater than four-fifths rate will generally not be regarded by Federal enforcement agencies as evidence of **adverse impact**." For example, if 100 Mexican Americans were applicants for positions as firefighters and 30 were hired, then the selection rate would be .30 or 30 percent. If 200 Caucasians were applicants for the same position and 100 were hired, then the selection rate for Caucasians would be .50 or 50 percent. A 30 percent hiring rate for Mexican Americans is less than 80 percent of the Caucasian selection rate; therefore the selection process has a presumptive **disparate impact** (30 percent is less than the product of .8 times .50).

The **80-percent rule** is more of a rule of thumb for the convenience of the parties. It has been subject to criticism by the courts. Courts more often prefer that the plaintiff establish that the difference between the number of members of the protected class selected and the number that would be anticipated in a random selection system is more than two or three standard deviations.[8] The defendant can then rebut the plaintiff's prima facie case by showing that the selection method is job related and consistent with a business necessity by showing that the method (usually, a test) is "validated."

What the Employer Must Prove

Burden of Proof
The requirement that a plaintiff convince a judge or jury that the plaintiff is entitled to the relief sought.

The *McDonnell Douglas* principle concerning the **prima facie** case of **disparate treatment** and the employer's **burden of proof** of overcoming it once a **prima facie** case has been made has been applied in promotion, discipline, discharge, and other employment decision contexts. Once plaintiff's **prima facie** case has been proven, the burden shifts to the employer to show that it had a legally justifiable defense to the action. If the employer fails to establish, for example, that its action was **job-related** and a **business necessity**, the plaintiff wins the case. The employer's explanation must be easily understood so that it is not too vague, inconsistent, or lacking in credibility. For example, in one case a federal court of appeals observed that:

> [W]here the bank did attempt to offer specific nondiscriminatory reasons, the explanations were often inconsistent and contradictory. If a black person had more education than the white person receiving a promotion, the bank claimed that it made its selection on the basis of experience. Conversely, if an African American employee had more experience than the white promoted, the bank claimed that education was the key to performing that job. And if the African American employee had more experience and a better education, the bank often simply stated that the white employee was better qualified without giving a reason for the decision.[9]

As a result, the federal court held that the employer failed to rebut (or defeat) the **prima facie** case with its "limited attempt at an alternative explanation."

This appellate decision followed the holding made the year before by the U.S. Supreme Court in its unanimous *Burdine* decision. The *Burdine* holding stated that the employer would rebut a plaintiff's **prima facie** case of discrimination by producing evidence of a legitimate reason for its adverse employment decision as to the plaintiff. In the following case, the Supreme Court stated the kind of evidence required for the employer to defend itself in a case of **disparate treatment**.

CASE 4.3

AFTER A PRIMA FACIE SHOWING BY PLAINTIFF, THE EMPLOYER MUST PROVE A NONDISCRIMINATORY BASIS FOR ITS ACTIONS

TEXAS DEPT. OF COMMUNITY AFFAIRS V. BURDINE

450 U.S. 248 (1981)

Supreme Court of the United States

Facts. Joyce Burdine, a 40-year-old employee, was terminated, and she sued her employer for gender discrimination in violation of Title VII of the Civil Rights

Act of 1964. The district court found that the employer had sufficiently rebutted the allegation that Burdine was terminated due to gender discrimination. The Court of Appeals reversed this decision. It held that the defendant in a Title VII case bears the burden of proving by a preponderance of the evidence the existence of legitimate, nondiscriminatory reasons for the employment action and also must prove by objective evidence that those hired were better qualified than the plaintiff, and that the testimony for petitioner did not carry either of these burdens. Due to a conflict among the circuit courts of appeal, the Supreme Court granted *certiorari.*

Issue. [W]hether, after the plaintiff has proved a prima facie case of discriminatory treatment, the employer must prove more than a legitimate, nondiscriminatory reason for its decision.

Language of the Court. Powell, J.: **This case requires us to address again the nature of the evidentiary burden placed upon the defendant in an employment discrimination. The narrow question presented is whether, after the plaintiff has proved a prima facie case of discriminatory treatment, the burden shifts to the defendant to persuade the court by a preponderance of the evidence that legitimate, nondiscriminatory reasons for the challenged employment action existed.**

Petitioner, the Texas Department of Community Affairs (TDCA), hired respondent, a female, in January 1972, for the position of accounting clerk in the Public Service Careers Division (PSC). [After turnover in her department and threatened funding for her agency, her position was eliminated.] [Burdine] filed this suit . . . [and] alleged that the failure to promote and the subsequent decision to terminate her had been predicated on gender discrimination in violation of Title VII. After a bench trial, the District Court held that the decisions not to promote and to terminate respondent were [not] prompted by gender discrimination.

The burden of establishing a prima facie case of disparate treatment is not onerous. The plaintiff must prove by a preponderance of the evidence that she applied for an available position for which she was qualified, but was rejected under circumstances which give rise to an inference of unlawful discrimination. The prima facie case serves an important function in the litigation: it eliminates the most common nondiscriminatory reasons for the plaintiff's rejection. Establishment of the prima facie case in effect creates a presumption that the employer unlawfully discriminated against the employee. If the trier of fact believes the plaintiff's evidence, and if the employer is silent in the face of the presumption, the court must enter judgment for the plaintiff because no issue of fact remains in the case. The burden that shifts to the defendant, therefore, is to rebut the presumption of discrimination by producing evidence that the plaintiff was rejected, or someone else was preferred, for a legitimate, nondiscriminatory reason. The defendant need not persuade the court that it was actually motivated by the proffered reasons. . . . It is sufficient if the defendant's evidence raises a genuine issue of fact as to whether it discriminated against the plaintiff.

To accomplish this, the defendant must clearly set forth, through the introduction of admissible evidence, the reasons for the plaintiff's rejection. The explanation provided must be legally sufficient to justify a judgment for the defendant. If the defendant carries this burden of production, the presumption raised by the prima facie case is rebutted, and the factual inquiry proceeds to a new level of specificity. Placing this burden of production on the defendant thus serves simultaneously to meet the plaintiff's prima facie case by presenting a legitimate reason for the action and to frame the factual issue with sufficient clarity so that the plaintiff will have a full and fair opportunity to demonstrate pretext. The sufficiency of the defendant's evidence should be evaluated by the extent to which it fulfills these functions. The plaintiff retains the burden of persuasion. She now must have the opportunity to demonstrate that the proffered reason was not the true reason for the employment decision. She may succeed in this either directly by persuading the court that a discriminatory reason more likely motivated the employer or indirectly by showing that the employer's proffered explanation is unworthy of credence.

Decision. No. When the plaintiff has proved a case of discrimination, the employer only has to prove the nondiscriminatory reasons for its actions. The plaintiff then has the opportunity to prove that the reason was a pretext for discrimination.

CASE QUESTIONS

Critical Legal Thinking. What rebuttal evidence do you think an employer could present to the trier of fact that would show the adverse decision was made for lawful reasons?

Business Ethics. What types of records would you recommend human resource managers maintain to defend the employer from future employment discrimination claims?

Contemporary Business. Identify the types of information you would advise supervisors to maintain with regard to the performance of employees for whom they are responsible.

A plaintiff's **prima facie** case, combined with sufficient evidence to show that the employer's defenses and justifications are false, may permit the trier of fact to conclude that unlawful discrimination has occurred. In *St. Mary's Honor Center v. Hicks,*[10] the Supreme Court stated, "it is not enough to . . . disbelieve the employer; the fact finder must believe the plaintiff's explanation of intentional discrimination." As in other civil cases, the trier of fact, whether it is a judge or jury, will weigh the evidence presented and consider a number of factors relating to the evidence.

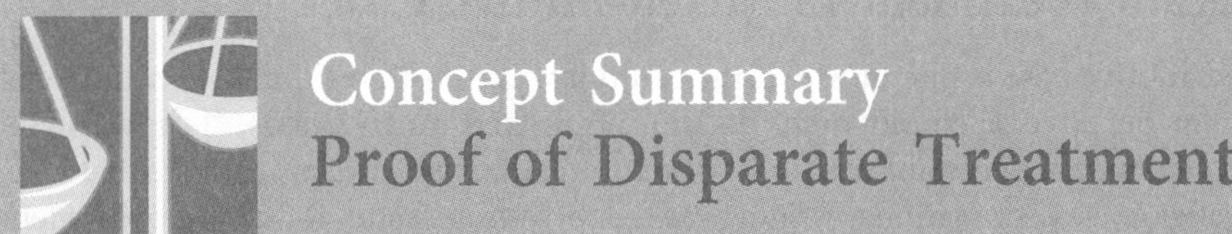

Concept Summary
Proof of Disparate Treatment

In disparate treatment case under either Title VII or §1981, the plaintiff must prove:

- an intentional discriminatory move, by presenting direct evidence of discrimination, circumstantial evidence, or racial animus (i.e., evil intent); and
- intentional discrimination, without direct evidence, under the burden-shifting scheme of the decisions in *McDonnell Douglas v. Green* and *Texas Dept. of Community Affairs v. Burdine* (i.e., the plaintiff proves discrimination, and the employer offers a legitimate reason for the adverse employment action, but the plaintiff proves that the reason was a pretext or cover story for actual discrimination).

Disparate Impact Discrimination Cases

Disparate impact discrimination occurs when an employer does not intend to discriminate but a company practice or policy has the effect of producing discrimination among members of a **protected class**. Such policies or practices are applied in a **facially neutral** manner without making any adverse reference to race, color, national origin, or religion, and they are not based on a business necessity. Nevertheless, the policy or practice has a significant negative impact upon those in a **protected class**.

The **CRA of 1991** allows a plaintiff to prove a case of **disparate impact** by producing evidence showing that a **facially neutral** employment practice had a discriminatory effect on the plaintiff as a member of a **protected class** and that the employer refused to adopt a less discriminatory practice. This proof may be made by **direct evidence** or **circumstantial evidence**. An intent or motivation to discriminate is *not* required for **disparate impact** to occur; thus, innocent employers can be held liable for damages when they used inappropriate means and methods in their employment procedures. The **disparate impact** claim can arise at any time in the relationship between an individual and the employer (i.e., from application to termination). The **CRA of 1991**, which codified the **disparate impact** discrimination claim, specifically recognized the employer's defenses of **"business necessity"** and **"job-relatedness."**

In its 1976 decision in *Washington v. Davis,*[11] the Supreme Court held that the **disparate impact** theory of discrimination would apply *primarily* in Title VII cases. Congress later expanded its application to cases brought under the Americans with Disabilities Act. That means that plaintiffs seeking damages for civil rights violations other than under Title VII and ADA claims may *not* rely on **disparate impact** evidence to prove their cases.

Disparate Treatment in Mixed-Motive Cases

A **mixed-motive** case is one in which the claim involves both legitimate *and* unlawful reasons for the adverse employment decision. In **mixed-motive** cases, "[a]n unlawful employment practice is established when the complaining party demonstrates that race, color, religion, sex, or national origin was a motivating factor for any employment practice, even though other factors also motivated the practice."[12]

Mixed-Motive Evidence
An employer's evidence showing that the same adverse decision would have been made even in the absence of the impermissible motivating factor.

The evidence of the **mixed motives** of an employer's adverse employment decision was first considered by the Supreme Court in its 1989 decision in *Price Waterhouse v. Hopkins.*[13] In that case, the Supreme Court held that if a plaintiff's **direct evidence** tended to show that a discriminatory act had occurred, then the employer must prove a legitimate reason for its decision (i.e., provide a convincing argument that it would have made the same business decision in the absence of discrimination). *Hopkins* is a fascinating case involving the decision not to promote a capable female C.P.A. to partnership in an international accounting firm because she was not "feminine" enough. The **CRA of 1991** clarified, affirmed, and partly overruled the *Hopkins* decision. The **CRA of 1991** stated the following guidelines for **mixed-motive** employment cases:

- A plaintiff need only show by a **preponderance of evidence** that race, color, religion, sex, or national origin was a *motivating factor* in the employer's decision.
- If the employer can show that it had a **mixed motive** for its employment decision, it bears the burden of proof to show that a **legitimate business reason** was the reason for its decision.

Legitimate Business Reason
A business requirement that justifies treating one or more applicants or employees differently from others.

After enactment of the **CRA of 1991**, plaintiffs may not recover money damages (including **back pay and compensatory** and **punitive damages**) for **mixed-motive** verdicts. The employer is still subject to **equitable orders**, including injunctions against the employer from continuing the past practices and declaratory relief (i.e., a legal determination that what the employer has done in the past was unlawful), and the award of attorney fees to the plaintiff. The attentive student will recognize that in material part the **CRA of 1991** reduced the risk posed to employers by the **mixed-motive** scenario. Able defense lawyers will always direct their efforts to recharacterize a hiring decision as a **mixed-motive** case. By doing so, the defendant employer can avoid liability for money damages. The plaintiff is then entitled to only injunctive relief, attorney's fees, and costs. Orders of reinstatement, as well as money damages, are not available to the plaintiff who has been met with a successful **mixed-motive** defense.

In its decision in *Desert Palace v. Costa,*[14] the court considered the claim of Catharina Costa, who was fired from her job as a heavy equipment operator at one of the company's properties, Caesars Palace, a casino and hotel in Las Vegas, Nevada. The U.S. District Court had instructed the jury to determine that sex was a motivating factor in the firing, even if other lawful reasons for her termination existed. The jury ruled in her favor and the casino appealed, arguing that the jury instructions improperly shifted the burden of proof to the defendant employer. The question before the Supreme Court was whether a plaintiff need show direct evidence of discrimination obtain a **mixed-motive** jury instruction under Title VII as amended by the **CRA of 1991**.

CASE 4.4

CIRCUMSTANTIAL EVIDENCE MAY BE USED IN MIXED-MOTIVE BIAS CASES

DESERT PALACE V. COSTA

539 U.S. 90 (2003)

Supreme Court of the United States

Facts. Desert Palace, Inc. operates Caesars Palace Hotel & Casino in Las Vegas. It employed Catharina Costa as a casino warehouse worker and heavy equipment operator. Costa experienced a number of problems with the Caesars management and with her co-workers. Following a series of disciplinary incidents, including a suspension, Costa was terminated after she was involved in a physical altercation with a co-worker in a warehouse elevator. While both employees were disciplined, Costa was terminated and the male employee involved in the altercation received only a 5-day suspension. Costa filed suit in the U.S. District Court asserting claims of sex discrimination and sexual harassment under Title VII. The District Court dismissed the sexual harassment claim, but allowed the claim for sex discrimination to be heard by a jury.

At trial, Costa presented evidence that she was singled out for "intense stalking" by one of her supervisors, she received harsher discipline than men for the same conduct, she was treated less favorably than men in the assignment of overtime, and supervisors repeatedly falsified her disciplinary record and that they "frequently used or tolerated" sex-based slurs against her. The trial court instructed the jury with a mixed-motive instruction:

> *You have heard evidence that the defendant's treatment of the plaintiff was motivated by the plaintiff's sex and also by other lawful reasons. If you find that the plaintiff's sex was a motivating factor in the defendant's treatment of the plaintiff, the plaintiff is entitled to your verdict, even if you find that the defendant's conduct was also motivated by a lawful reason. However, if you find that the defendant's treatment of the plaintiff was motivated by both gender and lawful reasons, you must decide whether the plaintiff is entitled to damages. The plaintiff is entitled to damages unless the defendant proves by a preponderance of the evidence that the defendant would have treated plaintiff similarly even if the plaintiff's gender had played no role in the employment decision.*

Attorneys for Caesars Palace unsuccessfully objected to the jury instruction and argued that direct, not just circumstantial, evidence was required to prove Costa's claim of discrimination. The jury rendered a verdict in Costa's favor, awarding back pay, compensatory damages, and punitive damages, and the Court of Appeals for the Ninth Circuit affirmed. The U.S. Supreme Court granted *certiorari.*

Issue. Can a worker use circumstantial evidence to prove the case in a mixed-motives discrimination lawsuit?

Language of the Court. Thomas, J.: **The question before us in this case is whether a plaintiff must present direct evidence of discrimination in order to obtain a mixed-motive instruction under Title VII of the Civil Right Act of 1964, as amended by the Civil Rights Act of 1991. We hold that direct evidence is not required.**

Title VII's silence with respect to the type of evidence required in mixed-motive cases also suggests that we should not depart from the "[c]onventional rul[e] of civil litigation [that] generally appl[ies] in Title VII cases. That rule requires a plaintiff to prove his case "by a preponderance of the evidence using direct or circumstantial evidence." . . . We have often acknowledged the utility of circumstantial evidence in discrimination cases. . . . The reason for treating circumstantial and direct evidence alike is both clear and deep-rooted: "Circumstantial evidence is not only sufficient, but may also be more certain, satisfying and persuasive than direct evidence."

The adequacy of circumstantial evidence also extends beyond civil cases; we have never questioned the sufficiency of circumstantial evidence in support of a criminal conviction, even though proof beyond a reasonable doubt is required. . . . It is not surprising, therefore, that neither petitioner nor its amici curiae can point to any other circumstance in which we have restricted a litigant to the presentation of direct evidence absent some affirmative directive in a statute. In order to obtain a [mixed-motive] instruction . . . , a plaintiff need only present sufficient evidence for a reasonable jury to conclude by a preponderance of the evidence, that [a protected characteristic] was a motivating factor for any employment practice.

Decision. Yes. Direct evidence of discrimination is not required in mixed-motive cases. Plaintiffs may use circumstantial evidence in proving discrimination in a mixed-motive case.

CASE QUESTIONS

Critical Legal Thinking. Does this decision make it easier to win a lawsuit for discrimination in the workplace?

Business Ethics. What actions should you undertake as a senior executive to eliminate hidden biases existing within the ranks of managers who report to you?

Contemporary Business. What other types of civil disputes lend themselves to the admission of circumstantial evidence?

The *Costa* Court unanimously held that **direct evidence** of discrimination is not required; **circumstantial evidence** is sufficient proof. A plaintiff need only present sufficient evidence for a jury to conclude by a **preponderance of the evidence** that "race, color, religion, sex, or national origin was a *motivating factor* for any employment practice."

In the 2006 U.S. Supreme Court decision in *Burlington Northern & Santa Fe,* described below, the Court broadened the legal standard of what constitutes a retaliatory action by an employer that would entitle an employee to pursue a Title VII discrimination or harassment claim. Section 704 of the Title VII prohibits employers from retaliating against employees who pursue discrimination and harassment claims. The case was a significant victory for employees and civil rights organizations because the business community had argued for a narrower standard for Title VII liability.

Concept Summary
Proving Unlawful Retaliation

In order to prove discrimination based upon retaliation, a plaintiff must prove:

- the retaliatory action occurred but it does not necessarily cause financial loss;
- the retaliatory action occurred but it need not occur at the workplace;
- the action suffered was "materially adverse"—"harmful to the point that it could well dissuade a reasonable worker from making or supporting a charge of discrimination"; and
- the retaliatory action would be recognized as occurring by any reasonable employee.

CASE 4.5

THE ANTIRETALIATION PROVISIONS OF TITLE VII ARE TO BE BROADLY INTERPRETED TO PREVENT EMPLOYMENT DISCRIMINATION

BURLINGTON NORTHERN & SANTA FE RY. CO. V. WHITE

548 U.S. 53 (2006)

Supreme Court of the United States

Facts. Sheila White, the only female maintenance employee in the Burlington Northern Santa Fe Railway yard in Memphis, Tennessee, sued for sexual harassment. In response, the employer suspended White's supervisor but at the same time told White that she would be assigned to track labor, a position that involved dirtier and more physically demanding effort on her part. White filed a complaint with the EEOC claiming unlawful gender discrimination and retaliation for her complaint. She was suspended without pay for insubordination; after Burlington found that White had not been insubordinate she was reinstated and given her back pay for the days she had been suspended. The district court and Sixth Circuit Court of Appeals held that since White had not suffered any "adverse employment action," then she had not suffered any damages. Given the conflicting opinions of the federal courts of appeal, the Supreme Court granted *certiorari.*

Issue. Whether Title VII's antiretaliation provision forbids only those employer actions and resulting harms that are related to employment or the workplace.

Language of the Court. Breyer, J.: **A separate section of the [Civil Rights] Act—its antiretaliation provision—forbids an employer from "discriminat[ing] against" an employee or job applicant because that individual "opposed any practice" made unlawful by Title VII or "made a charge, testified, assisted, or participated in" a Title VII proceeding or investigation. §2000e–3(a).**

We conclude that the antiretaliation provision does not confine the actions and harms it forbids to those that are related to employment or occur at the workplace. We also conclude that the provision covers those (and only those) employer actions that would have been materially adverse to a reasonable employee or job applicant. In the present context that means that the employer's actions must be harmful to the point that they could well dissuade a reasonable worker from making or supporting a charge of discrimination.

The antiretaliation provision [of Title VII] protects an individual not from all retaliation, but from retaliation that produces an injury or harm. . . . In our view, a plaintiff must show that a reasonable employee would have found the challenged action materially adverse, "which in this context means it well might have 'dissuaded a reasonable worker from making or supporting a charge of discrimination.'" (Citation omitted.)

Applying this standard to the facts of this case, we believe that there was a sufficient evidentiary basis to support the jury's verdict on White's retaliation claim. (Citation omitted.) The jury found that two of Burlington's actions amounted to retaliation: the reassignment of White from forklift duty to standard track laborer tasks and the 37-day suspension without pay.

Burlington does not question the jury's determination that the motivation for these acts was retaliatory. But it does question the statutory significance of the harm these acts caused. . . . First, Burlington argues that a reassignment of duties cannot constitute retaliatory discrimination where, as here, both the former and present duties fall within the same job description. . . . We do not see why that is so. Almost every job category involves some responsibilities and duties that are less desirable than others. Common sense suggests that one good way to discourage an employee such as White from bringing discrimination charges would be to insist that she spend more time performing the more arduous duties and less time performing those that are easier or more

agreeable. That is presumably why the EEOC has consistently found "[r]etaliatory work assignments" to be a classic and "widely recognized" example of "forbidden retaliation." To be sure, reassignment of job duties is not automatically actionable. Whether a particular reassignment is materially adverse depends upon the circumstances of the particular case, and "should be judged from the perspective of a reasonable person in the plaintiff's position, considering 'all the circumstances.'" . . . Second, Burlington argues that the 37-day suspension without pay lacked statutory significance because Burlington ultimately reinstated White with backpay. Burlington says that "it defies reason to believe that Congress would have considered a rescinded investigatory suspension with full back pay" to be unlawful, particularly because Title VII, throughout much of its history, provided no relief in an equitable action for victims in White's position . . . .

Neither do we find convincing any claim of insufficient evidence. White did receive backpay. But White and her family had to live for 37 days without income. They did not know during that time whether or when White could return to work. Many reasonable employees would find a month without a paycheck to be a serious hardship. And White described to the jury the physical and emotional hardship that 37 days of having "no income, no money" in fact caused. Brief for Respondent 4, n. 13 ("That was the worst Christmas I had out of my life. No income, no money, and that made all of us feel bad. . . . I got very depressed"). Indeed, she obtained medical treatment for her emotional distress. A reasonable employee facing the choice between retaining her job (and paycheck) and filing a discrimination complaint might well choose the former. That is to say, an indefinite suspension without pay could well act as a deterrent, even if the suspended employee eventually received backpay . . . . The jury's conclusion that the 37-day suspension without pay was materially adverse was a reasonable one.

Decision. No. Retaliation claims are not limited to discriminatory actions that affect the terms and conditions of the employment; the employee can show retaliation by showing that a reasonable person would find the challenged action adverse. The retaliatory action need not cause financial loss, and the action need not occur at the workplace.

CASE QUESTIONS

Critical Legal Thinking. Analyze the strength of the employer's claim that a retroactive payment of wages to White defeated her claim for damages.

Business Ethics. Do you think it was ethical for the employer to claim that a retroactive payment of wages to White defeated her claim for damages?

Contemporary Business. If you were the director of human resources for the company, what lessons learned would you glean from this decision?

Retaliation Claims

In 2009, The Supreme Court held in *Crawford v. Nashville and Davidson County, Tennessee [Metro]*[15] that the **antiretaliation** provisions of Title VII apply to employees who participate in an employer's internal investigation of sexual harassment. In that decision, the Court considered the claims of a female employee, Crawford, who had been terminated because she had described sexually harassing conduct by another employee. The employer asserted that the termination was because of Crawford's alleged embezzlement. The federal court of appeals held that opposition in the context of a **retaliation claim** "demands active, consistent 'opposing' activities to warrant . . . protection against retaliation." The Court reversed the federal court of appeals' finding that Crawford's participation in the investigation did not constitute protected "opposition" to an unlawful employment.

In its opinion, the Supreme Court recited the reasons why protection from **retaliation** is a cornerstone right recognized under Title VII:

> *Metro [as it sees] it, if retaliation is an easy charge when things go bad for an employee who responded to enquiries, employers will avoid the headache by refusing to raise questions about possible discrimination.*
>
> *The argument is unconvincing, for we think it underestimates the incentive to enquire that follows from our decisions in Burlington Industries, Inc. v. Ellerth, . . . and Faragher v. City of Boca Raton . . . . Ellerth and Faragher hold "[a]n employer . . . subject to vicarious liability to a victimized employee for an actionable hostile environment created by a supervisor with . . . authority over the employee." (Citation omitted.) Although there is no affirmative defense if the hostile environment "culminates in a tangible employment action" against the employee (citation omitted) . . . an employer does have a defense "[w]hen no tangible employment action is taken" if it "exercised reasonable care to prevent and correct promptly any" discriminatory conduct and "the plaintiff employee unreasonably failed to take advantage of any preventive or corrective opportunities provided by the employer or to avoid harm otherwise," ibid. Employers are thus subject to a strong inducement to ferret out and put a stop to any discriminatory activity in their operations as a way to break the circuit of imputed liability . . . (citing studies demonstrating that Ellerth and Faragher have prompted many employers to adopt or strengthen procedures for investigating, preventing, and correcting discriminatory conduct). The possibility that an employer might someday want to fire someone who might charge discrimination traceable to an internal investigation does not strike us as likely to diminish the attraction of an Ellerth-Faragher affirmative defense.*
>
> *If it were clear law that an employee who reported discrimination in answering an employer's questions could be penalized with no remedy, prudent employees would have a good reason to keep quiet about Title VII offenses against themselves or against others. This is no imaginary horrible given the documented indications that "[f]ear of retaliation is the leading reason why people stay silent instead of voicing their concerns about bias and discrimination." . . . The appeals court's rule would thus create a real dilemma for any knowledgeable employee in a hostile work environment if the boss took steps to assure a defense under our cases. If the employee reported discrimination in response to the enquiries, the employer might well be free to penalize her for speaking up. But if she kept quiet about the discrimination and later filed a Title VII claim, the employer might well escape liability, arguing that it "exercised reasonable care to prevent and correct [any discrimination] promptly" but "the plaintiff employee unreasonably failed to take advantage of . . . preventive or corrective opportunities provided by the employer." (Citation omitted.) Nothing in the statute's text or our precedent supports this catch-22.*

Management's Defenses

An employer may seek to defend a discrimination claim by presenting evidence that the claimant was not treated any differently than were other similarly situated employees. Federal and state laws provide for several affirmative defenses in employment discrimination cases. An affirmative defense is a legal principle that limits or excuses a defendant's liability, even if a plaintiff's claim is proved, because of superseding facts or public policies. Among the defenses providing full or partial protection from a plaintiff's claims are the following:

- Statute of limitations
- Bona Fide Occupational Qualification (BFOQ)
- Business necessity
- Job relatedness
- After-acquired evidence
- Laches (as an equitable defense to back-pay and front-pay awards)
- Mixed motives
- Tolling
- Plaintiff's failure to mitigate his or her damages

Statute of Limitations

State-court private tort and contract actions and lawsuits filed under Sections 1981 and 1983 are not subject to exhaustion of administrative remedies required under Title VII. In such actions, the remedy sought is one of damages, and they often lend themselves to class-action status for violation of regulatory laws.

For claims brought under Title VII, ADEA, and the ADA, the claimant must first file charges with the EEOC or a state **706 agency** (discussed below). The purpose of this requirement is to take advantage of these agencies' investigatory powers and conciliation services. The EEOC may now file lawsuits on behalf of individuals. The U.S. Justice Department prosecutes civil rights violations perpetrated by state or local agencies. Claims brought under state civil rights laws and regulations often afford the claimant the election of a private party lawsuit or an administrative adjudication before a state civil rights agency.

At the time of publication, the Supreme Court had granted *certiorari* to review a Seventh Circuit Court of Appeals decision involving the **statute of limitations**. In *Lewis v. City of Chicago,* 528 F.3d 488 (2008), *cert granted* __________ U.S. __________, 130 S. Ct. 497 (2009), the Court will determine if, in a **disparate impact** case, the Title VII statute of limitations is measured from announcement, or use, of an unlawful practice. In this case, the City of Chicago in 1995 administered a written test to applicants for firefighter jobs. It notified applicants of the results in January 1996; plaintiffs waited until March 21, 1997, to file an EEOC charge that the test had a **disparate impact** on black applicants. The charge was filed more than 400 days after the plaintiffs were notified of the test results, but within 300 days of when the city hired applicants. The Seventh Circuit reversed the trial court's ruling that each hiring revitalized the statute and that the plaintiffs' suit was timely filed. It rejected the plaintiffs' argument that the city's violation was a "continuing violation" and tolled the running of the statute of limitations. Students should consult the online student resource for an update.

BFOQ

An employer seeking to establish a bona fide occupational qualification must prove that a practice on its face that excludes an entire **protected class** is justified because all or substantially all of the members are unable to perform the job requirements safely and efficiently. The EEOC's policy is to interpret a **BFOQ** narrowly. It is extraordinarily difficult to establish a **BFOQ**. Note that race may *never* be a **BFOQ**.

Business Necessity

An employer seeks to justify a **disparate impact** practice by proving an overriding legitimate business purpose, such as that the practice advances the public health, safety, or morals for which purpose the business serves. Once this defense is established, the plaintiff may still prevail on a **disparate impact** claim if the plaintiff can show that an alternative and effective business practice with a less discriminatory effect might have been used and the employer refused to adopt it. This is also known as **business justification**.

Job Related
The specific skills, education, and training needed to perform a task.

Job Relatedness

Job relatedness or security regulations promulgated under federal or state law may serve as affirmative defense.

After-Acquired Evidence

This legal doctrine allows the employer to use information gathered after termination, providing it had additional factual grounds for the termination. After making the adverse employment decision, if the employer is able to discover evidence that would constitute reasonable ground for refusing to hire or for discharging the plaintiff, the employer can assert that, had it known of the wrongdoing, it would have undertaken the same action based on that after-acquired knowledge. The use of this defense is fairly circumscribed.

Laches

This defense permits the employer to argue that it is entitled to a reduction for pay awarded when the plaintiff engaged in unreasonable, inexcusable, and prejudicial delay in the prosecution of the claim against the employer. This defense may operate to bar suits entirely or to impose a duty on a charging party to monitor the EEOC's progress in the sense that the plaintiff's back-pay award may be reduced if the court determines the charging party waited too long to request a right-to-sue letter from the EEOC or 706 agency. The defense requires two elements: *unreasonable delay* (usually the courts require this to be a very substantial period in which the plaintiff did not monitor the EEOC investigation of the charge) and *prejudice* to the defendant employer (such as unavailability of witnesses or lost evidence). The defendant can argue that the delay adversely affected its ability to defend itself on the merits.

Mixed Motives

A defendant employer can utilize a **mixed-motive** defense to a discrimination claim. If the plaintiff cannot prove that a prohibited discriminatory ground was a *motivating factor,* then the employer could prevail by showing that it would have taken the same adverse employment action even absent discriminatory intent.[16]

Employers may also utilize other defenses that have been recognized by courts within other specific employment discrimination claims. For example, a religious organization hiring for a position related to the practice or support of its faith need not make reasonable accommodations to broaden the applicant pool beyond adherents of that faith. There are other examples, including specific defenses available in disability cases; these include undue hardship on the employer to comply with the requirements of the Americans with Disabilities Act and contagious disease cases.

These defenses spring from the provisions of Section 703(h) of Title VII, which provides, in part: "Notwithstanding any other provision of this title, it shall not be an unlawful employment practice for an employer to apply different standards of compensation, or different terms, conditions, or privileges of employment pursuant to a bona fide seniority or merit system . . . provided that such differences are not the result of an intention to discriminate because of race, color, religion, sex, or national origin. . . ."

> ***Example:*** If an employer had maintained a nondiscriminatory seniority system in concert with its obligations under a collective bargaining agreement with a union representing the employees, the seniority system might pass scrutiny under Section 703(h).

Tolling and Mitigation

The last two concepts employers may use as defenses within the employment dispute resolution process are **tolling** and **mitigation**. Under the principle of **tolling**, the employer may suspend the accrual of potential front-pay and back-pay liability by extending an unconditional job offer identical or substantially equivalent to the offer that originally discriminated. The claimant remains free to pursue a lawsuit prior to the effective date of the offer. Like **tolling, mitigation** occurs within the realities of litigation. Under **mitigation**, plaintiffs have an affirmative duty to reduce the potential damages they may suffer because of the harm they have suffered. They must act with reasonable diligence to find and accept substantially equivalent employment, which affords them promotional opportunities, compensation, responsibilities, and status virtually identical to those in the position from which they were terminated. The employer must show that the plaintiff has failed to act reasonably to reduce back-pay awards. A plaintiff's **failure to mitigate** damages results in a reduction of the amount of damages awarded to the plaintiff, if any.

Front Pay
Damages awarded for lost earnings during the period between judgment and reinstatement or, if reinstatement does not occur, payment in place of reinstatement.

In the following U.S. Supreme Court case, *McKennon v. Nashville Banner Publishing*, the court addressed the issue of whether an employee discharged in violation of the Age Discrimination in Employment Act of 1967 is barred from all relief when, after the discharge, the employer discovers evidence of wrongdoing that, in any event, would have led to the employee's termination on lawful and legitimate grounds. The **after-acquired evidence** rule had been a matter of conflicting opinions among the federal courts of appeal prior to this decision.

CASE 4.6

AFTER-ACQUIRED EVIDENCE WILL NOT DEFEAT DISCRIMINATION CLAIMS

McKENNON V. NASHVILLE BANNER PUBLISHING

513 U.S. 352 (1995)

Supreme Court of the United States

Facts. Alleging that her discharge by respondent Nashville Banner Publishing Company violated the Age Discrimination in Employment Act of 1967 (ADEA), Christine McKennon filed suit seeking a variety of legal and equitable remedies available under the ADEA, including back pay. After she admitted in her deposition that she had copied several of the Banner's confidential documents during her final year of employment, the District Court granted summary judgment for the company, holding that McKennon's misconduct was grounds for her termination and that neither back pay nor any other remedy was available to her under the ADEA. The Court of Appeals affirmed on the same rationale. The Supreme Court granted a *writ of certiorari.*

Issue. Whether an employee discharged in violation of the Age Discrimination in Employment Act of 1967 is barred from all relief when, after discharge, the employer discovers evidence of wrongdoing that, in any event, would have led to the employee's termination on lawful and legitimate grounds.

Language of the Court. Kennedy, J.: **The ADEA makes it unlawful for any employer: "to discharge any individual or otherwise discriminate against any individual with respect to his compensation, terms, conditions, or privileges of employment, because of such individual's age." (Citation omitted.)**

In preparation of the case, the Banner took McKennon's deposition. She testified that, during her final year of employment, she had copied several confidential documents bearing upon the company's financial condition. . . . Her motivation, she averred, was an apprehension she was about to be fired because of her age. When she became concerned about her job, she removed and copied the documents for "insurance" and "protection." A few days after these deposition disclosures, the Banner sent McKennon a letter declaring that removal and copying of the records was in violation of her job responsibilities and advising her (again) that she was terminated. The Banner's letter also recited

that had it known of McKennon's misconduct it would have discharged her at once for that reason.

The ADEA and Title VII share common substantive features and also a common purpose: "the elimination of discrimination in the workplace." (Citation omitted.) Congress designed the remedial measures in these statutes to serve as a "spur or catalyst" to cause employers "to self-examine and to self-evaluate their employment practices and to endeavor to eliminate, so far as possible, the last vestiges" of discrimination. (Citation omitted.) Deterrence is one object of these statutes. . . . It would not accord with this scheme if after-acquired evidence of wrongdoing that would have resulted in termination operates, in every instance, to bar all relief for an earlier violation of the Act.

Once an employer learns about employee wrongdoing that would lead to a legitimate discharge, we cannot require the employer to ignore the information, even if it is acquired during the course of discovery in a suit against the employer and even if the information might have gone undiscovered absent the suit.

Where an employer seeks to rely upon after-acquired evidence of wrongdoing, it must first establish that the wrongdoing was of such severity that the employee in fact has been terminated on those grounds alone if the employer had known of it at the time of the discharge. The concern that employers might as a routine matter undertake extensive discovery into an employee's background or performance on the job to resist claims under the Act is not an insubstantial one, but we think the authority of the courts to award attorney's fees, mandated under the statute . . . and to invoke the appropriate provisions of the Federal Rules of Civil Procedure will deter most abuses.

Decision. No. An employee discharged in violation of the ADEA is not barred from all relief when, after discharge, the employer discovers evidence of wrongdoing that, in any event, would have led to termination on lawful and legitimate grounds had the employer known of it.

CASE QUESTIONS

Critical Legal Thinking. Who really was the prevailing party in this litigation? Discuss the conflicting interests of both parties given the circumstances relating to McKennon's firing.

Business Ethics. What do you think of the ethics exhibited by both sides in this dispute? Does this invite employers to "dig up dirt" on terminated employees?

Contemporary Business. Following this decision, what instructions would you issue human resource managers in your company relative to the after-acquired evidence doctrine?

EEOC Charges, Litigation, and Arbitration

The EEOC is a federal agency created by the Civil Rights Act of 1964. Any person claiming to be the victim of unlawful employment practices may file a charge with the EEOC under Title VII. Additionally, any person, agency, or organization may file a charge with the Commission on behalf of such a person. In the case of the third-party filing, a party may withhold his or her name from the charge and remain anonymous to the employer during the filing stages; however, the third party will be required to provide the claimant's information to the Commission.

Timely Filing the Charge of Discrimination

The charge of discrimination may be filed by mail or in person at the EEOC office nearest to the claimant. All laws enforced by the EEOC, except for the Equal Pay Act, require that a charge be filed with the EEOC before the claimant may file a lawsuit. There are strict time limits within which a charge must be filed:

- To protect the charging party's rights, a written charge must be filed with the EEOC within 180 days from the date of the alleged violation..
- The 180-day filing deadline is extended to 300 days if a state or local antidiscrimination law also covers the charge. For age discrimination charges covered by the Age Discrimination in Employment Act, only state laws extend the filing limit to 300 days.
- These filing time limits do not apply to claims under the Equal Pay Act, because under that act persons filing a court case do not need to file a charge with EEOC first. However, since many EPA claims also involve Title VII sex discrimination issues, claimants should file charges under both laws within the stated time limits.
- Federal employees or applicants for employment are covered differently.

Most states created their own state and local enforcement agencies for employment discrimination claims. These agencies, which contract with the EEOC, are called **"706 agencies"** after section 706 of the Civil Rights Act of 1964. One of the purposes of **706 agencies** is to help filter and screen the more serious cases requiring EEOC investigation. Those cases that do not require EEOC investigation are handled at the state level through a state-specific **706 agency**. This is a work-sharing arrangement between the EEOC and the state **706 agencies**. This process is known as "exhausting administrative remedies."

If a charge is filed with the state **706 agency** and is covered by federal law, the **706 agency** "dual files" the charge with the EEOC to protect federal rights. The charge is usually retained by the **706 agency** from investigation to disposition. Once the charge has been filed, the employer is notified. There are a number of ways the charge may then be handled:

- If the initial facts support a finding of a violation of the law, the charge may be assigned a priority investigation; otherwise, it may be assigned for a follow-up investigation to determine the likelihood that a violation has occurred. The

Commission may act on the charge the day a charge is filed, if it is received within 180 days after the occurrence of the alleged violation. In a state with a **706 agency**, the Commission may act on a charge within 60 days either after proceedings have been commenced in the local **706 agency** or, if proceeding were terminated earlier, anytime within 30 days after the termination. In all cases within a jurisdiction with a **706 agency** the charge must be filed within 300 days of the alleged violation.

- When a state has a **706 agency**, the EEOC requires that the state agency investigate the claim for 60 days before the EEOC will review the complaint. There are some benefits to filing a claim through a **706 agency** as opposed to the EEOC. When a party files a claim through a **706 agency**, the party has 300 days rather than 180 days under the EEOC jurisdiction within which to file a claim of unlawful discrimination.
- Claimants in states with **706 agencies** must timely file with the EEOC within 240 days from the time of the violation to the time of the state filing; otherwise, the charge is not timely filed. If the claimant waits 241 days or more before filing with a state or local **706 agency** or indirectly through the Commission, assuming the state agency investigates the claim for the entire 60-day period, the claimant's filing with the EEOC is untimely. It is untimely because it will be filed on the three hundred and first day after the alleged violation. Such circumstances jeopardize the claimant's right to proceed with an employment discrimination case as a federal court will dismiss the case because the administrative charge was untimely.
- The EEOC may seek to settle a charge at any stage of the investigation if the employer and the claimant are interested in doing so. If settlement is unsuccessful, the investigation continues.
- In its investigation, the EEOC may make written requests for information, take witness statements, and make employer facility visits. When the investigation concludes, the EEOC will discuss the evidence with the claimant or the employer, as appropriate.
- The EEOC may select the charge for inclusion in its mediation program if the employer and the claimant are interested. If the matter settles, the charge is withdrawn. If mediation is unsuccessful, the investigation continues to a fact-finding conference.
- At the fact-finding conference, both the claimant and the employer present evidence to an employee of the EEOC. If the EEOC finds there is reasonable cause to believe that discrimination has occurred, a letter of determination is issued explaining the agency's determination that discrimination has occurred. The EEOC then attempts conciliation with the employer to develop a remedy for the discrimination. If the case is successfully conciliated, the charge is withdrawn.
- If the EEOC cannot reach a conciliation between the parties, the agency will decide whether the EEOC will bring suit in federal court against the employer. Given the high volume of claims the EEOC processes and its limited resources, it prosecutes few cases.
- If the EEOC decides not to file suit, a **right-to-sue** letter is issued to the claimant. That letter permits the employee to file a private lawsuit against the employer in federal court.
- The EEOC may dismiss a pending charge at any time if it decides in its best judgment to do so.

It is not uncommon for an employee to file a charge with the EEOC or **706 agency** and then withdraw it almost immediately, obtain a right-to sue-letter, and file a lawsuit. This will prevent the EEOC from having the chance to investigate. Sometimes the employee will do this because he or she wishes to join a pending class-action lawsuit. Surprisingly, the Supreme Court has permitted the EEOC to continue its investigation of the charge even after issuing the claimant a right-to-sue letter.[17]

Timely Filing a Lawsuit Following the Filing of the Charge of Discrimination

LITIGATION. A charging party may file a lawsuit within 90 days after a **right-to-sue** letter is issued by the EEOC. Under Title VII, the Americans with Disabilities Act, and GINA, a charging party can request a **right-to-sue** from the EEOC 180 days after the charge is filed with the Commission. The claimant may then sue within 90 days after receiving the **right-to-sue** letter. Under the Age in Discrimination Act, a lawsuit may be filed at any time 60 days after filing a charge with the EEOC but not later than 90 days after the EEOC gives notice that it has completed action on the charge. Under the Equal Pay Act, a lawsuit must be filed within two years (three years for willful violations) of the alleged discriminatory employer pay practice. The filing with the EEOC is a prerequisite to filing suit; otherwise, the federal court lacks subject-matter jurisdiction, and the case must be dismissed. The findings in the administrative proceeding before the EEOC or the **706 agency** may be introduced into evidence in the federal discrimination lawsuit with the discretion of the district court.

Workplace Application
Lilly Ledbetter Fair Pay Act of 2009

In response to a 2007 decision by the Supreme Court, Congress passed the **Lilly Ledbetter Fair Pay Act of 2009**. The decision in *Ledbetter v. Goodyear Tire & Rubber Co., Inc.*[18] considered the plight of Lilly Ledbetter.

For nineteen years of her employment at Goodyear Tire's Gadsden, Alabama, plant, Lilly Ledbetter was consistently given lower rankings in her annual performance and salary reviews and low pay raises relative to her male peers. Although her salary originally kept pace with that of the men, by the end of 1997 her salary was significantly less than her male counterparts' salaries. Ledbetter earned $3,727 per month, and the lowest-paid males received $4,286 per month. In her suit, Ledbetter alleged that Goodyear had subjected her to **disparate treatment** as an area manager, a position held largely by men. In March 1998, she submitted an EEOC questionnaire, and in July 1998 she formally filed a discrimination charge with the EEOC.

After taking early retirement in November 1998, Ledbetter filed her civil rights suit. Goodyear had not made any decisions relating to her pay during the 180-day period for gender discrimination in violation of Title VII of the Civil Rights Act of 1964. The jury awarded her over $3.5 million, which the district judge later reduced to $360,000.

Goodyear appealed to the U.S. Court of Appeals for the Eleventh Circuit, which reversed the lower court. It ruled that the jury could only examine

Ledbetter's evidence of discrimination as far back as the last annual salary review before the start of the 180-day limitations period. The court found no evidence of discrimination in the reviews done in that period, so it reversed the district court judgment and dismissed the complaint. Ledbetter appealed to the Supreme Court.

In its 5-4 decision, the Supreme Court held that Ledbetter's complaints were time barred and affirmed the decision of the federal court of appeals. The elapse of each pay period for which she had a claim for a violation of the Equal Pay Act was its own separate violation of Title VII, and Ledbetter could not sue for those periods for which the 180-day administrative claim-filing period required by Title VII had elapsed.

The Lilly Ledbetter Fair Pay Act of 2009 overturned the Supreme Court's decision. Under the act, employees could sue at any time after alleged discrimination occurred, as long as they have received any compensation affected by it in the preceding 180 days. However, while this act allows the filing of a lawsuit to recover the amount of wage disparity, it must be read in conjunction with the Equal Pay Act. That act permits a plaintiff to sue for wage disparity for the two prior years. Willful violations of the Equal Pay Act permit a three-year recovery period. Claims beyond these two- or three-year periods are barred by the statute of limitations.

Discussion Questions

1. What would you have done in these circumstances? Would you have taken the case "all the way" to the Supreme Court?
2. In response to her EEOC charge, Goodyear moved Ledbetter, then age 60, to a strenuous job at the plant. She had to lift 80-pound tires in a dimly lit room with no mechanical assistance. Her orthopedist told her two years of such work would cripple her. She quit after ten months and sued. Comment on the ethics of such action by Goodyear. What legal theories of discrimination could Ledbetter assert because of the job reassignment?
3. What are the implications of the Lilly Ledbetter Fair Pay Act? What will it mean for business in the future?

In a 2009 decision, the federal Court of Appeals for the Third Circuit held that the Lilly Ledbetter Fair Pay Act applied to a request for a raise. In *Mikul v. Allegheny County,*[19] the court held that when Mary Lou Mikul requested a pay raise in 2004 and 2005 and did not receive a response, her pay claim was timely and held that the employer's investigative report and the unanswered request for a raise were not compensation decisions that triggered the running of the statute of limitations. Mikul filed her charge with the EEOC within 300 days of receiving a discriminatory paycheck, and the court held her Title VII claim was timely filed. A recent case in the Ninth Circuit Court of Appeals underscores the necessity for claimants and their counsel to ensure that a particular **706 agency** actually has jurisdiction over the claim. In *MacDonald v. Grace Church Seattle,* 457 F.3d 1079 (9th Cir. 2006), the Ninth Circuit Court of Appeals held that Suzanne MacDonald's claim of gender discrimination by her former employer was filed beyond the 180-day EEOC filing period. Ms. MacDonald had filed a gender discrimination and **retaliation** charge under Title VII of the Civil Rights Act of 1964 with the Washington State Human Rights Commission and the EEOC. The target of her charge was her former employer, Grace Church Seattle. MacDonald had served as an office administrator for the church, and she claimed that her immediate supervisor, who was also the church's pastor, sexually harassed her. She alleged that the last discriminatory act occurred on April 30, 2002, when she was allegedly terminated from her employment by the church in **retaliation** for reporting the pastor's harassment. MacDonald filed her charges with the EEOC and the Washington Commission, a **706 agency**, more than 180 days but less than 300 days after the last act of discrimination. On July 2, 2003, the EEOC dismissed MacDonald's administrative claim. She then filed a federal district court action alleging gender discrimination and retaliation under Title VII, wrongful discharge in violation of Washington state public policy, and a state cause of action for invasion of privacy. The court of appeals noted that, generally, Title VII establishes two potential time limitation periods requiring a plaintiff to file an administrative charge with the EEOC within 180 days of the last act of discrimination. However, the limitations period is extended to 300 days if the plaintiff first institutes proceedings with a "state or local agency with authority to grant or seek relief from such practice." Where the **706 agency** lacks jurisdiction, the EEOC exercises its jurisdiction and the 180-day filing period must be observed. This was the holding in the *MacDonald* case because the Washington state agency does not regulate sex discrimination and does not have jurisdiction over nonprofit organizations. The court of appeals affirmed the district court's dismissal of MacDonald's claim.

Alternative Dispute Resolution
A nonjudicial process that seeks to resolve disputes between parties, including through mediation and arbitration.

Mediation
A form of alternative dispute resolution in which a neutral third party assists the parties in a dispute to reach a settlement.

Arbitration
A legal proceeding in which disputes are resolved by a neutral third party appointed by the parties to make a binding and final determination.

ALTERNATIVE DISPUTE RESOLUTION. Pursuing claims in a judicial setting can be a lengthy and time-consuming process for both the employee and employer. Each party may also be embarrassed if unfavorable facts about the employment relationship are disclosed in the public forum of a courtroom. To avoid these circumstances, employers often choose to adopt one or more elements of a process known as **alternative dispute resolution**, the procedures of which include **mediation** and **arbitration**. If this choice is made, however, employers must be careful to ensure that employees retain rights equivalent to those they would be afforded in a court proceeding. For example, if the employer's procedures are deemed inherently unfair or materially fail to preserve the due process rights of the employee to seek redress, the employee can successfully challenge an unfavorable result obtained in arbitration.

Mediation. This process occurs when a neutral person meets with the parties to facilitate their mutual resolution of a dispute. Unlike arbitration, the **mediation** process usually relies on a single neutral person to serve as intermediary between the parties. Although they are not required to be attorneys, most mediators are lawyers who exclusively mediate disputes. The **mediation** process is voluntary, although most state and federal trial judges now mandate that parties engage in **mediation** at an early stage in court proceedings as a condition to proceeding with their lawsuit. In a **mediation**, the parties' positions are solicited, their emotional points of view and legal claims explored, and, if requested by the parties, an evaluation of the risks of proceeding further can be offered by an experienced mediator. The issues addressed in **mediation** may be defined as broadly or as narrowly as the parties decide. To encourage free discussion, most jurisdictions enforce a rule against disclosure of what is discussed during **mediation** and bar the use of statements made in **mediation** in later proceedings. If **mediation** does not resolve the conflict, the parties may proceed with litigation or arbitration.

Arbitration. Although often described as an informal process, **arbitration** is not informal. It should be undertaken with the same seriousness and financial commitment as if the controversy were pending before a trial court. It is informal in that it takes place in an office as opposed to a courtroom. Generally, the trier of fact is one or more persons experienced in the resolution of employment disputes. Depending on what procedures have been agreed to in advance, **arbitration** proceedings may be more relaxed; they need not follow courtroom procedures regarding procedural and evidentiary rules. Parties to **arbitration** must appreciate the adversarial nature of the proceedings, even though these may appear similar to an informal bench (or judge) trial. The arbitrator will normally require the parties to submit legal briefs on the issues to be decided in advance of the hearing. Opening and closing statements will be made and oral and documentary evidence will be taken; the proceedings are often recorded so that a transcript of the proceedings can be prepared.

One of the disadvantages of **arbitration** in the employment context is that the parties may not know all of the evidence they will confront in the hearing. Since the parties are generally free to set an appropriate discovery procedure, a party may not have received or appreciated all the evidence they will face in the hearing. In the absence of such an agreement, the rules of the governing **arbitration** agency, if any, will control. As a default, the arbitrator(s) will decide what is appropriate in the circumstances. In addition, the parties are rarely permitted to file dispositive motions, such as a **motion for summary judgment**, as they would be able to do in court. For example, the employee's claim may be barred for reasons of a technical defect, such as the **statute of limitations**, because the claim is deemed too stale to be heard by a trier of fact. In the absence of such motion practice, an employer will need to prepare for the **arbitration** and request a ruling at the time of the **arbitration**. The courts rarely disturb the parties' election to arbitrate their disputes since keeping disputes out of the courthouse improves judicial efficiencies.

Considerable legal authority supports an individual's advance agreement to use alternative dispute resolution, including arbitration. For example, §118 of the **Civil Rights Act of 1991** provides that "where appropriate and to the extent authorized by law, the use of alternative dispute resolution, including arbitration is encouraged to resolve disputes arising under [Title VI and the ADEA]." A Title VII plaintiff may only be forced to forego statutory remedies and arbitrate claims if the plaintiff has knowingly agreed to submit such disputes to arbitration.[20]

Workplace Application
Employment Contracts Subject to Arbitration

Many employment contracts contain arbitration clauses. Thus, if a dispute arises regarding such an employment contract, the parties have agreed to submit the dispute to arbitration. This means the dispute is not heard in court but is instead heard and decided by a private arbitrator. The arbitrator, a neutral third party, is designated in the employment contract. Arbitrators are usually members of the American Arbitration Association (AAA) or another arbitration association. After the hearing is complete, the arbitrator reaches a decision and issues an award. The parties often agree in advance to be bound by an arbitrator's decision and remedy, which is called **binding arbitration**. Congress enacted the **Federal Arbitration Act** (FAA) in 1925, which provides that arbitration agreements involving commerce are valid, irrevocable, and enforceable contracts, unless some grounds exist at law or equity (e.g., fraud, duress) to revoke them.

Consider the following case of arbitration of an employment contract dispute. Circuit City Stores, Inc., a national retailer of consumer electronics, hired Saint Clair Adams as a sales counselor. Adams signed an employment contract that included the following arbitration clause:

> I agree that I will settle any and all previously unasserted claims, disputes, or controversies

arising out of or relating to my application or candidacy for employment, employment, and/or cessation of employment with Circuit City, exclusively by final and binding arbitration before a neutral Arbitrator. By way of example only, such claims include claims under federal, state, and local statutory or common law, such as the Age Discrimination in Employment Act, Title VII of the Civil Rights Act of 1964, the Americans with Disabilities Act, the law of contract and the law of tort.

Two years later Adams filed an employment discrimination lawsuit against Circuit City in court. Circuit City sought to enjoin the court proceeding and to compel arbitration. The U.S. District Court granted Circuit City's request. The U.S. Court of Appeals reversed, holding that employment contracts are not subject to arbitration. Adams appealed to the U.S. Supreme Court. The issue the U.S. Supreme agreed to address was whether the parties had to resolve their difference in arbitration because they had agreed to it. The U.S. Supreme Court held that employment contracts are subject to arbitration. The Supreme Court stated:

> Congress enacted the Federal Arbitration Act (FAA) in 1925. The FAA was a response to hostility of American courts to the enforcement of arbitration agreements. To give effect to this purpose, the FAA compels judicial enforcement of a wide range of written arbitration agreements. The FAA's coverage provision, Section 2, provides that "a written provision in any contract evidencing a transaction involving commerce to settle by arbitration a controversy thereafter arising out of such contract or transaction, or the refusal to perform the whole or any part thereof, shall be valid, irrevocable, and enforceable, save upon such grounds as exist at law or in equity for the revocation of any contract."

The U.S. Supreme Court held that employment contracts, including the one in this case between Circuit City and Adams, are subject to arbitration if a valid arbitration agreement has been executed. The Supreme Court reversed the decision of the Court of Appeals and remanded the case for further proceedings.[21]

Discussion Questions

1. What is arbitration? How does it differ from litigation using the court system?
2. Whom do you think benefits most from arbitration clauses in employment contracts: employers or employees? Why?
3. Is it ethical for employers to include arbitration clauses in employment contracts?

Federal Arbitration Act (FAA)
A federal law upholding arbitration agreements as valid, irrevocable, and enforceable contracts, unless an exception applies.

In *Gilmer v. Interstate/Johnson Lane,*[22] the Supreme Court held that an employee could be compelled to **arbitrate** his age discrimination claim. The Court broadly interpreted the requirements of the **FAA** to permit the arbitration of such claims. In its *Circuit City Stores, Inc. v. Adams*[23] decision, the Supreme Court made clear that it intended the **FAA** to apply broadly to all employment disputes, except for those involved in the transportation industry. With the *Circuit City* decision, an employer may compel an employee to submit all forms of employment claims, including discrimination claims, to binding arbitration. Subsequent federal appellate decisions and state Supreme Court decisions have clarified the need for a well-balanced arbitration provision to allow the breadth of the *Circuit City* decision to be enforced by courts. However, under the Court's decision in *EEOC v. Waffle House, Inc.,*[24] the court made clear that the EEOC is not precluded from suing by an arbitration agreement between the employer and employee. EEOC may sue in court on behalf of an individual or a class of individuals without restraint from the provisions of an arbitration clause that might bind the individual employee. These claims are those brought by the EEOC under Title VII and the ADA.

At the time of publication, the Supreme Court had granted *certiorari* to review a decision of the U.S. Court of Appeals for the Second Circuit. The Court will consider whether imposing class arbitration on parties whose arbitration clauses are silent on the issue is consistent with the **FAA**.[25] The litigants in that case are parties to international contracts containing arbitration clauses. The contracts are silent as to whether arbitration is permissible on behalf of a class of contracting parties. Students should consult the online student resource for an update.

Management Application
Drafting Arbitration Provisions

Drafting one universal arbitration clause for use in all types of employment disputes is problematic. At best, the language chosen will be a compromise among conflicting interests and strategies. In all cases, the state laws for the locations in which employers are engaged should be consulted through local legal counsel to ensure that the proposed alternative dispute mechanisms are compliant. Failure to follow state law can lead to catastrophic results because the clause may be set aside by courts, thus allowing hundreds if not thousands of employees to file suit in court, by class action or otherwise, against the employer. Some states have held that overreaching arbitration clauses are tantamount to unfair business practices and, in consequence, the employers have been subject to punitive damage awards. The key points in an arbitration clause in an employment agreement include the following:

- Selection of the arbitration forum (e.g., AAA);
- Establishing the number and qualifications of neutral arbitrators;
- Providing for pre-trial discovery substantially equivalent to that afforded courtroom adversaries;
- The taking of live testimony and the receipt of written evidence by both parties;
- The issuance of a written award within a reasonable time frame after submission of the dispute;
- A statement of whether the law to be followed is the substantive law of the state in which the employment dispute arises;
- A careful description as whether and how the arbitration proceeding may limit the rights and remedies of the employee to pursue judicial relief, including the waiver of a trial by jury;
- A provision that the employer will pay the fees and expenses of the forum (in full or at least those in excess of the filing fee for a court-filed complaint);
- An opportunity for the prospective employee to review and acknowledge the full and binding effect of the arbitration process on his or her prospective rights; and
- A mechanism to confirm the arbitration award into a legally enforceable court judgment following completion of the arbitration proceeding.

It is also unclear whether claims arising under FMLA, discussed in a later chapter, are subject to arbitration procedures. The law is developing with regard to the scope of the enforceability of compelling arbitration with regard to all aspects of the employment relationship. Some federal courts have held that Congress did not intend to exempt FMLA disputes from the reach of the FAA.

Remedies

Statutes

Remedies vary depending on the statutory basis on which the claimant seeks relief. The available remedies must be tailored to the facts and circumstances of each case. The remedies available under federal discrimination statutes are set forth in Table 4.3.

TABLE 4.3. Remedies Available under Federal Antidiscrimination Statutes

Federal Statutes	Remedies
Title VII (as amended, the CRA of 1991), the ADA, and §501 of the Rehabilitation Act	i. Reinstatement of position, back pay, and, in appropriate cases, injunctive relief when the defendant was engaged in intentional unlawful discrimination. Back pay is limited to two years from the filing of a charge with the EEOC. ii. Damages may include compensatory and punitive damages for intentional discrimination based on disparate treatment (but not disparate impact). iii. Compensatory damages may address injuries for future monetary losses expected to be incurred and emotional pain and suffering. However, they may not include back pay or interest on back pay or recovery of front-pay damages. iv. With a Title VII claim, the plaintiff is entitled to a jury trial on the issue of damages. v. Section 501 of the Rehabilitation Act requires affirmative action by federal government agencies. vi. Failure to make a reasonable accommodation as required by the ADA and the Rehabilitation Act may result in an award of compensatory and/or punitive damages.
Civil Rights Acts of 1866 (42 U.S.C. §§1981, 1982)	i. Under these acts, the complaining party is entitled to reinstatement of their position (if terminated), back pay and/or front pay, and, where appropriate, injunctive relief. ii. Damages: nominal, compensatory (for the injuries proven to have been caused by the deprivation of constitutional rights), special (for mental and/or emotional distress), and, where appropriate, punitive (to punish the offending party if the conduct involved "reckless or callous indifference to plaintiff's federally protected rights" or if the defendant was motivated by "evil motive or intent").
Equal Pay Act (EPA), and Age Discrimination in Employment Act (ADEA)	i. Employers are liable for unpaid wages or overtime and compensation and such equitable relief as may be appropriate, including reinstatement and promotion. Front pay must be awarded if reinstatement is not ordered. ii. Possible liability under criminal law: any employer who willfully violates the EPA is subject to a $10,000 fine, and up to six months in jail (for second and subsequent convictions) or both. iii. Under the ADEA, remedies include equitable relief, including judgments compelling employment, reinstatement, or promotion. However, the ADEA has been construed as not permitting the recovery of compensatory or punitive damages. Private employers, but not the federal government, may be liable for amounts of lost wages or unpaid overtime compensation. Double damages may be awarded against private employers for disregarding knowingly and recklessly the law's requirements. iv. Attorney's fees are recoverable along with court costs.

Recovery of Court Costs and Attorney's Fees

Costs are the out-of-pocket expenses incurred by a party during the course of a legal proceeding. They include the following types of costs typically incurred in preparation for or during a proceeding: filing fees, photocopying costs, court reporter fees for videotaping and stenographic costs, docket costs on appeal, jury fees, postage, long distance telephone costs, travel expenses, and fees and expenses of any experts required.

Attorney's fees may be assessed only against parties, not their attorneys, in the absence of a finding that the attorneys have acted in bad faith. A prevailing party in a discrimination case is entitled to recover attorney's fees. The determination of a prevailing party is normally determined by whether a particular party obtains a judgment against the other party. However, a party who fails to obtain some actual relief on the merits of their claim is not entitled to recover attorney's fees. Under Title VII and the Americans with Disabilities Act a prevailing defendant may recover attorney's fees where the plaintiff's suit was "frivolous, unreasonable or groundless or [if the plaintiff] continued to litigate after it clearly became so or was brought in bad faith."[26]

Management Application
How a Court Calculates Attorney's Fee Awards

The prevailing party submits written records supporting the hours spent and the billing rates of the attorneys, paralegals, and other members of the law firm team working on the case. Excessive hours are excluded. In cases involving multiple defendants, the court will allocate the payment of fees among the responsible parties.

The prevailing market rate is that which lawyers of similar ability and experience in the community normally charge their clients for the type of work in question. In litigation, this is known as calculating the lodestar. In its decision in *Hensley v. Eckerhart,*[27] the U.S. Supreme Court considered the following factors in determining what would be a reasonable amount to award a successful litigant:

- The time and labor required;
- The novelty and difficulty of the questions presented;
- The skill requisite to perform the legal service properly;
- The preclusion of employment by the attorney due to the acceptance of the case;
- The customary fee;
- Whether the fee was fixed or contingent;
- The time limitations imposed by the client or the circumstances;
- The amount involved and the results obtained;
- The experience, reputation, and ability of the attorney;
- The relative desirability of the case;
- The nature and length of the relationship between the attorney and client; and
- Awards in similar cases.

In appropriate cases, the lodestar may be increased or reduced depending upon the circumstances.

Outcomes

According to the Bureau of Justice Statistics for the U.S. Department of Justice, plaintiffs do not fare well in trials conducted before the U.S. District Courts. In a 2008 press release, the Department of Justice identified the following trends in federal court civil rights litigation:

- The number of civil rights cases filed in federal courts declined 20 percent between 2003 and 2006.
- Civil rights cases concluded by trial dropped from 8 percent to 3 percent from 1990 to 2006, while dismissals increased from 66 percent to 72 percent.
- Plaintiffs won a third of civil rights trials on average from 1990 to 2006. The percentage awarded damages declined during the period, from 83 percent to 79 percent.
- Plaintiffs' median damage awards ranged from $114,000 in 2001 to $154,000 in 2005. In 2006, the median damage amount awarded to prevailing plaintiffs averaged $150,000.
- During this period, jury trials resulted in median damage awards ($146,125) that were about two times higher than awards ($71,500) from bench trials (i.e., those in which a judge decides a case without a jury). The rate at which plaintiffs won at trial did not differ appreciably between jury and bench trials.[28]

Key Terms and Concepts

- Protected classes
- Disparate treatment
- Disparate impact
- Unlawful retaliation
- Discriminatory intent
- Statistical proof of discrimination
- Pattern and practice case
- Facially neutral
- Motion for summary judgment
- Triable issue of material fact
- Pretext
- Prima facie case
- Preponderance of the evidence
- Direct evidence
- Circumstantial evidence
- Burden of proof
- Business necessity or justification defense
- Constructive discharge
- CRA of 1991
- Mixed-motive evidence
- Four-fifths rule
- 80-percent rule
- Section 703(h)
- Statute of limitations
- BFOQ
- Job relatedness
- After-acquired evidence
- Laches
- Tolling
- Mitigation
- Back pay
- Front pay

- Emotional distress damages
- Punitive damages
- Equitable orders
- 706 agencies
- Lilly Ledbetter Fair Pay Act of 2009
- Right-to-sue letter
- Injunctive relief
- Alternative dispute resolution
- Mediation
- Arbitration
- Federal Arbitration Act

Chapter Summary

- Certain groups of individuals receive protection from discrimination in employment. As protected classes of persons, they are able to invoke the protections of federal, state, and local laws if they are discriminated against by an employer, whether in the form of disparate treatment or of disparate impact. A disparate treatment claim requires proof that the employer intentionally discriminated against the claimant; a disparate impact claim does not require such proof. Most often, a claimant will prove their disparate impact claim with statistical evidence.

- As a plaintiff, the claimant will present evidence of the alleged discrimination. This evidence can take the form of direct or, most often, circumstantial evidence by which the prima facie case of discrimination is made. The plaintiff can prove a discrimination claim under Title VII and in age discrimination cases using the *McDonnell Douglas* test. This so-called test reflects the principle that direct evidence of intentional discrimination is rare, and that such claims must be proved by circumstantial evidence. By successive steps of increasingly narrow focus, the test allows inference of discrimination based on facts that create a reasonable likelihood of bias and that cannot be satisfactorily explained. The specific elements of a prima facie case may vary depending on the particular facts. Generally, the plaintiff must provide evidence of:
  - membership in a protected class;
  - qualification for the position sought or satisfactory job performance in the position currently held;
  - sufferance of an adverse employment action (such as termination, demotion, or denial of an available job); and
  - another circumstance suggesting discriminatory motive.

If, at trial, the plaintiff establishes a prima facie case, a presumption of discrimination arises. This presumption, though "rebuttable," will require the court to enter judgment for the plaintiff because no issue of fact remains in the case. At this point in the trial, the burden shifts to the employer to rebut the presumption by producing admissible evidence sufficient to "raise a genuine issue of material fact" and to "justify a judgment for the [employer]" that its adverse employment action was taken for a legitimate, nondiscriminatory reason.

If the employer sustains this burden of proof, the presumption of discrimination disappears.[29] The employee then has the duty of showing that the employer's explanation is a mere pretext or subterfuge to hide its true intentions. The plaintiff attacks the employer's proffered reasons as pretexts for discrimination or may offer other evidence of the employer's discriminatory motive. In an appropriate case, evidence of dishonest reasons, considered together with the elements of the prima facie case, may permit a finding of prohibited bias. Throughout the process of proving a discrimination case, the burden of proof (i.e., the burden of persuading the trier of fact that the plaintiff was a victim of unlawful discrimination) remains with the plaintiff.

■ When the employer has a mixed motive or a combined reason for the adverse employment decision, part of which is discriminatory, the claimant need only show that the discrimination was simply a motivating factor in the employer's decision-making.

■ The term *motivating factor* means that if the employer was asked at the moment of the decision what its reasons were and it gave a truthful response, one of those reasons would be the employee's characteristic (e.g., race or ethnicity) or circumstances.[30]

■ Another characterization of a disparate impact claim is one of unintentional discrimination.

■ The discrimination dispute normally begins with the timely filing of a claim for discrimination under a federal statute with the EEOC. The claimant has only 180 days from the last act of discrimination to file such a claim. If the claimant is located in a state with a 706 agency with jurisdiction over the claim, the claimant may invoke a longer 300-day (in reality, 240-day) period to pursue a remedy for the alleged violation. If a resolution is not achieved following the claim filing, the claimant will receive a right-to-sue letter from the agency. At that point, the claimant may file suit in the federal district court.

■ There are several types of damages that may be awarded to claimants filing discrimination claims; the statutes under which the claims arise govern the remedies available.

■ Frequently, employers seek to remove themselves from the risk of facing juries sympathetic to the plight of plaintiffs. Since the enactment of the CRA of 1991, civil rights claims may be tried before juries. Seeking to avoid a jury, employers will require that all employment disputes be resolved by alternative dispute resolution procedures, including mediation and binding arbitration. Agreements to arbitrate employment disputes are not binding upon the EEOC if it wishes to pursue a claim against an employer on behalf of one or more similarly situated employees.

Online Student Support

- Loislaw legal research and writing assignments.
- Loislaw group projects and class presentations.
- Loislaw access, providing online research including up-to-date cases, statutes, rules, and regulations. Primary law for all 50 states and federal jurisdictions. Registration required for access to this resource.
- Practice questions, including sample true/false, multiple choice, and short answer questions to test your understanding of concepts.
- Additional human resource forms.
- Internet exercises.
- Blogs.
- Supplementary statutory and regulatory materials.

Case Problems

4.1 An individual lawsuit will have much less effect on an employer than if that same claim were part of a group of claims presented in a class action against the employer. Class-action waivers were inserted in the dispute resolution packet that Mr. Gentry received when he worked for Circuit City stores. The arbitration agreement in the packet contained a class-action waiver and a form that gave the employee a month to opt out of the arbitration agreement, which Gentry did not do. Will the fact that the employees were given an opportunity to opt out of the arbitration agreement prevent the employees from filing a class action for overtime pay they claim they are due? (*Gentry v. Superior Court*, 135 Cal. App. 4th 944 (2006))

4.2 If Title VII claims must be timely brought and the Civil Rights Acts of 1866 and 1871 (i.e., §§1981 and 1983 claims) contain no federal statute of limitations, federal courts look to state law for the limitations period applicable to such actions. However, which state limitations actions should apply to discrimination claims? What kind of state law lawsuit claim would be most analogous to a federal discrimination claim? (*Wilson v. Garcia*, 471 U.S. 261, 265 (1985))

4.3 The Supreme Court has held that punitive damages may be recovered in a §1983 lawsuit. However, how far up the chain of command should they be assessed against a city police department in which an individual was sexually harassed? Should it extend all the way to the police commissioner, who was unaware of the conduct but was responsible for the acts of his subordinates? (*Keenan v. City of Philadelphia*, 983 F. 2d 459 (1992))

4.4 Determine whether an applicant may sue for discrimination based on the assertion that the preferences or prejudices of staff members are a BFOQ. (See *Parson v. Kaiser Aluminum & Chemical Corporation*, 727 F.2d 473 (5th Cir. 1984))

4.5 If courts are to construe the terms *job related* and *business necessity*, what standards should a court employ to define these defenses? Should the standard be stringent or adaptive to the circumstances? (But would the latter make the standard too arbitrary?) Compare *Kirby v. Colony Furniture*, 613 F.2d 696 (8th Cir. 1980) (an employer must show a "compelling need" to maintain a practice for which there is no substitute) with *New York City Transit Authority v. Beazer*, 440 U.S. 568 (1970) (focuses on job relatedness as "a manifest relationship to the employment in question"). What language would you employ to guide the trial court?

End Notes

1. *United Airlines, Inc. v. Evans*, 431 U.S. 553 (1977).
2. *http://www.uscourts.gov/judbus2007/appendices/C02Sep07.pdf.*
3. D.C. Human Rights Act of 1977.
4. 519 U.S. 202 (1997).
5. 431 U.S. 324 (1977).
6. *Brady v. Office of the Sergeant at Arms*, 520 F.3d 490, 493 (D.C. 2008).
7. 42 U.S.C. §2000e-2(k) (1) (A) (i), (B) (i).
8. 1 Lindemann and Grossman, *Employment Discrimination Law*, 105-06 (4th ed. 2007).
9. *Paxton v. United National Bank*, 688 F.2d 552, 566 (8th Cir. 1982).
10. 509 U.S. 502 (1993).
11. 426 U.S. 229 (1976).
12. 42 U.S.C. §2002e-2(m).
13. 490 U.S. 228 (1989).
14. 539 U.S. 90 (2003).
15. 555 U.S. ________ (2009).
16. *Harris v. City of Santa Monica*, ________ Cal. App. 4th ________ (2009).
17. *EEOC v. Federal Express Corp.*, ________ F.3d ________ (9th Cir. 2008).
18. 550 U.S. 618 (2007).
19. ________F.3d ________ (3d Cir. 2009).
20. *Prudential Ins. Co. of America v. Lai*, 42 F.3d 1299 (9th Cir. 1994).
21. *Circuit City Stores, Inc. v. Adams*, 532 U.S. 105 (2001).
22. 500 U.S. 20 (1991).
23. 532 U.S. 105 (2001).
24. 534 U.S. 279 (2002).
25. *Stolt-Nielsen S.A. v. AnimalFeeds International Corp.*, 548 F.3d 85 (2d Cir. 2008), *cert. granted*, ________ U.S.________, 129 S.Ct. 2793 (2009).
26. *Christiansburg Garment Co. v. EEOC*, 434 U.S. 412 (1978).
27. 461 U.S. 424 (1983).
28. *http://www.ojp.usdoj.gov/bjs/abstract/crcusdc06.htm.*
29. *St. Mary's Honor Center v. Hicks*, 509 U.S. 502 (1993).
30. *Price Waterhouse v. Hopkins*, 490 U.S. 228 (1989).

Part II
Equal Opportunity Laws

Chapter 5
Equal Employment and Affirmative Action

"The promise of America is a simple promise: Every person shall share in the blessings of this land. And they shall share on the basis of their merits as a person. They shall not be judged by their color or by their beliefs, or by their religion, or by where they were born, or the neighborhood in which they live." —Lyndon B. Johnson, thirty-sixth President of the United States

Learning Objectives

1. Explain the scope and application of §§1981 and 1983.
2. Know the scope of the Civil Rights Act of 1964 and identify areas of employment discrimination left to state regulation.
3. Understand how the Civil Rights Act of 1991 changed the law.
4. Define lawful affirmative action.
5. State the difference between lawful affirmative action and quotas.
6. Recognize the legal limits of voluntary affirmative action plans.

Chapter Outline

- Introduction
- Reconstruction Era (or Civil War) Amendments
- The Civil Rights Act of 1964

Case 5.1 Heart of Atlanta Motel v. U.S.

- The Civil Rights Act of 1991
- Management Application: Employer Liability for Discrimination
- Overview of the Coverage Afforded by Other Federal Equal Opportunity Laws
- Executive Order 11246: Federally Funded Affirmative Action
- Public Sector Affirmative Action Race-Based Plans

Case 5.2 Wygant v. Jackson Board of Education

Case 5.3 U.S. Steelworkers v. Weber

- The Limitations of Voluntary Affirmative Action

Case 5.4 Johnson v. Transportation Agency, Santa Clara County

- Reverse Discrimination

Case 5.5 Ricci v. DeStefano

- Focus on Ethics: Affirmative Action in Major League Baseball
- Preferential Treatment of Native Americans
- Human Resource Form: Acknowledgment of Policies

Chapter Opening scenario

Bryant is a light-skinned African American woman who wears business suits and business attire to work even on days when casual dress is permitted. At the time of the dispute she had short, curly hair dyed blond from its natural brown color. Other co-workers, including her supervisor, wore what Bryant describes as "Afrocentric" attire to work. Her supervisor told her there was no need to dress formally and that she should dress like her supervisor. Her supervisor began to snicker about her dyed hair and once referred to Bryant and her blond hair as a "wannabe," which Bryant claims is a common phrase within the black community meaning that someone wants to be white. Eventually, she was excluded from staff meetings and received critical performance evaluations.[1] As you read this chapter, answer the following questions:

Does the supervisor's conduct violate Title VII of the Civil Rights Act of 1964?
Does the supervisor's conduct violate Section 1981 of the Civil Rights Act of 1866?
To counsel Bryant effectively, what further facts would you want to know about her treatment at work?

Introduction

The 1960s brought rapid and profound social change to America. The remedies afforded by common law we studied in the earlier chapters of this book became increasingly inadequate to protect the interests of all American workers. The right to terminate an employee at any time with no reason given unfairly screened employers from liability for discriminatory practices. With increasing social unrest and demands for change, Congress began to legislate civil rights acts to provide widespread relief from these prior practices. Their constitutionality resting on congressional power to legislate pursuant to the Commerce Clause, these acts, beginning with the landmark Civil Rights of Act of 1964, provided broad relief to many working Americans. This act built on earlier efforts made after the Civil War to enact civil rights legislation. These acts commonly known as Sections 1981 and 1983 provide unique forms of relief to plaintiffs. Pursuant to the Civil Rights Act of 1991, Congress expanded the reach of §1981 to address all discriminatory practices based on race and national origin at any point within the entire employment relationship. In a 2008 decision, the Supreme Court extended its application to include retaliation claims.

Affirmative Action Public policies that take into account an individual's protected characteristic in employment, public contracting, and other public programs.

A private or public employer may adopt or agree to a consent order for the adoption and implementation of an affirmative action plan without violating Title VII or §1981 if it is intended to address the effects of prior discrimination. Nothing prohibits the adoption by an employer of a voluntary affirmative action plan; however, the courts and the Equal Employment Opportunity Commission (EEOC) impose certain criteria on such plans. If the plan is ruled unlawful, the employer will be held liable for employment discrimination.

In this chapter we will study the coverage of the major civil rights laws through which employees and occasionally those related to them may receive the protection of equal opportunity in employment. In addition, we will address affirmative action programs, including the required plans in the arenas of federal contracting and funding and public employment and the voluntary affirmative action plans of private employers.

Reconstruction Era (or Civil War) Amendments

Until 1864, many in Congress doubted that the express language of the Constitution afforded them the opportunity to abolish slavery through legislation. They felt that a constitutional amendment would be required. As a result, seven months following the end of the Civil War, the Thirteenth Amendment to the Constitution was proposed by Congress by which slavery was abolished everywhere in the United States. This Amendment rendered inoperative the three-fifths compromise. It was ratified by 27 of the 36 states on December 18, 1865. The Fourteenth Amendment to the Constitution granted citizenship to the former slaves, and any other person born in the United States or naturalized, and required that all citizens be granted equal protection under the law. It was ratified in 1868 by 28 of the 37 states. The Fifteenth Amendment to the Constitution, adopted in 1879, made it unlawful to deny any citizen the right to vote because of race or color or because of former slavery. It was ratified in 1870 by 29 of the 37 states. These amendments are collectively known as the Civil War Amendments or the Reconstruction Era Amendments. The Civil Rights Acts of 1866 and 1871, 42 U.S.C. §§1981, 1983, were adopted to effectuate the purposes of the Thirteenth Amendment to the Constitution. As history would soon make clear, these enactments were only a first step on the long odyssey of the American civil rights movement.

Following are the texts of the Civil War Amendments:

Thirteenth Amendment:
Section 1. Neither slavery nor involuntary servitude, except as a punishment for crime whereof the party shall have been duly convicted, shall exist within the United States, or any place subject to their jurisdiction.
Section 2. Congress shall have power to enforce this article by appropriate legislation.

Fourteenth Amendment:
Section 1. All persons born or naturalized in the United States, and subject to the jurisdiction thereof, are citizens of the United States and of the State wherein they reside. No State shall make or enforce any law which shall abridge the privileges or immunities of citizens of the United States; nor shall any State deprive any person of life, liberty, or property, without due process of law; nor deny to any person within its jurisdiction the equal protection of the laws.
[*Note:* This Section is known as the **Equal Protection Clause.**]

Equal Protection Clause
Part of the Fourteenth Amendment that affords persons equal protection of the law from state action, including public contracting.

Section 2. Representatives shall be apportioned among the several States according to their respective numbers, counting the whole number of persons in each State, excluding Indians not taxed. But when the right to vote at any election for the choice of electors for President and Vice President of the United States, Representatives in Congress, the Executive and Judicial officers of a State, or the members of the Legislature thereof, is denied to any of the male inhabitants of such State, being twenty-one years of age and citizens of the United States, or in any way abridged, except for participation in rebellion, or other crime, the basis of representation therein shall be reduced in the proportion which the number of such male citizens shall bear to the whole number of male citizens twenty-one years of age in such State.

. . .

Section 4. The validity of the public debt of the United States, authorized by law, including debts incurred for payment of pensions and bounties for services in suppressing insurrection or rebellion, shall not be questioned. But neither the United States nor any State shall assume or pay any debt or obligation incurred in aid of insurrection or rebellion against the United States, or any claim for the loss or emancipation of any slave; but all such debts, obligations and claims shall be held illegal and void.

Section 5. The Congress shall have power to enforce, by appropriate legislation, the provisions of this article.

Fifteenth Amendment:

Section 1. The right of citizens of the United States to vote shall not be denied or abridged by the United States or by any State on account of race, color, or previous condition of servitude.

Section 2. The Congress shall have power to enforce this article by appropriate legislation.

As the nation struggled to adapt to the new landscape shaped by these amendments, various challenges to the application of these amendments were filed in state and federal courts. In connection therewith, Congress enacted The Civil Rights Acts of 1866 and 1871 (more commonly referred to as **Sections 1981** and **1983**) to give effect to the purposes of the Thirteenth Amendment.

The provisions of **42 U.S.C. §1981** are:

All persons within the jurisdiction of the United States shall have the same right in every State and Territory to make and enforce contracts, to sue, be parties, give evidence, and to the full and equal benefit of all laws and proceedings for the security of persons and property as is enjoyed by white citizens, and shall be subject to like punishment, pains, penalties, taxes, licenses, and exactions of every kind, and to no other.

Section 1981
Federal law protecting individuals from intentional racial or national origin discrimination in employment and housing.

Section 1981 granted to "all persons" the same rights to "make and enforce contracts" as were enjoyed by "white citizens." The main purpose of this statute is to prohibit race discrimination in contracts. In 1975, in *Johnson v. Railway Express Agency, Inc.*,[2] the Supreme Court held that **§1981** prohibits only private discrimination in contracts, including those involving employment. **Section 1981** is relied on by plaintiffs in employment litigation because the relationship between an individual and an employer is a contractual one. Federal courts have ruled that at-will employment relationships (i.e., employment relationships based on an implied or express contract between the employer and employee) are subject to **§1981.** The statute provides that individuals who deprive others of their civil rights may be sued and held *personally* liable in damages for the harm caused by such deprivation. Courts have extended the acts to prohibit

national origin discrimination, but they do *not* apply to discrimination based on religion or gender.

Section 1983 provides a cause of action for deprivation of civil rights through state action (such as when a police officer acting on behalf of the state targets persons based on their race or color). **Section 1983** applies only to the actions of governmental employees or agencies, not to private individuals or employers. The related §1985 prohibits conspiracies (i.e., agreements) to violate the civil rights of others.

Section 1983
Federal law that protects individuals from violations of their constitutional rights by persons acting under state or federal authority.

Lawsuits for violation of civil rights under **§§1981-1985** may be filed in federal or state court. An employer is covered regardless of the number of its employees. State statutes of limitations apply to these claims. Both compensatory and punitive damages are available remedies for plaintiffs.

Civil Rights Act of 1964

Changing Social Conditions

The **Civil Rights Act of 1964** was passed in response to the dramatic transformation of American society by the civil rights movement. Evening television news broadcasts in May 1963 awakened the conscience of the American people to the issues of racial discrimination. Americans throughout the nation watched in their living rooms the acts of hatred and senseless brutality inflicted on peaceful civil rights demonstrators in Birmingham, Alabama. After weeks of bombings, riots, and extreme pronouncements by local public officials, order was restored after federal troops arrived. The incidents in Birmingham made clear to the American people that it was time to address the wrongs that had been suffered for centuries by the poor, the oppressed, and the disadvantaged classes of society. They also well knew the exemplary service rendered by minority community members in the armed forces. A vocal majority of churches and legislatures favored civil rights legislation. President John F. Kennedy sensed the country would, for the first time in its history, embrace a major civil rights bill, which he proposed in June of 1963 — over 100 years after President Lincoln's Emancipation Proclamation.

Civil Rights Act of 1964
The federal law protecting individuals against the outlawed unequal application of voter registration requirements, racial segregation in public schools, and discrimination in employment or facilities serving the general public based on race, color, religion, sex, and national origin. Amendments have extended coverage to pregnancy discrimination.

The **Civil Rights Act of 1964** was submitted to Congress in the summer of 1963, a time of continuing civil unrest. The headlines were full of accounts of conflicts over **public accommodations**. This issue gave rise to the "sit-ins" in the South at commercial establishments and on public campuses. Throughout the South, landowners denied African Americans the right to use and occupy public places. African Americans were denied access to restaurants, restrooms, parks, motels, and all other public places simply because of their race. The drafters of the **Civil Rights Act of 1964** rested its constitutional underpinnings on the congressional power to regulate **interstate commerce** under the **Commerce Clause** as well as on the implementation powers afforded Congress under the **Fourteenth Amendment**. The issue was an explosive one because leaders of both political parties saw the bill as an unconstitutional invasion of rights reserved to the states under the **Tenth Amendment**.

As originally proposed, the Act had many components. One part was a voting rights proposal; another addressed the **public accommodation** rights of all Americans with respect to public areas. **Title VII** of the **Civil Rights Act of 1964** dealt with discrimination in employment. Vice-President Lyndon Johnson helped persuade the administration to broaden the bill's scope and to present the bill to the southern voices of opposition in Congress as one based on morality; namely, his argument was that it was time to address the racial inequalities imposed on African Americans. It is interesting to note that two legislators amended the bill during deliberations to extend its reach to **sex discrimination** in an effort to thwart the bill's passage.

In November 1963, President Kennedy was assassinated while the bill was under congressional consideration. Following his death, strong public support for the bill emerged, leading to its eventual passage, which many considered part of his epitaph. In the decades following its enactment, the breadth of the law's coverage has created lasting and universal change within American society and, particularly, with respect to its employment laws. **Title VII** has become the most well-known federal civil rights law.

Major Features of the Civil Rights Act of 1964

Titles I-VI: These titles prohibited unequal treatment in voter registration and ended discrimination in places of public accommodation. They supported desegregation of state public schools. They continued the Civil Rights Commission established under the **Civil Rights Act of 1957**. In addition, this part of the act prohibited discrimination based on race, color, or national origin by state or local governmental agencies in all programs and activities receiving federal funding.

Title VII: The provisions of the act are straightforward. The law made it unlawful for any business to discriminate in employment on the basis of race, color, religion, sex, or national origin.[3] **Title VII** also prohibits retaliation against employees who oppose such unlawful discrimination in the workplace or who testify, assist, or participate in workplace investigations. The act applies to hiring, terms or conditions of employment, union membership and representation of union members, and employment referral services. It also established the EEOC to enforce its provisions. It applied only to employers who employ or employed 15 or more employees for more than 19 weeks in the current or preceding calendar year.

The Constitutionality of the Civil Rights Act of 1964

The United States Supreme Court began to align itself with the civil rights movement in the 1950s and provided the basis on which Congress could enact the **Civil Rights Act of 1964**. As the climate of public opinion changed, so too did the Court's commitment to equal rights. In the following decision, the Court upheld the constitutionality of the Act.

CASE 5.1

THE CIVIL RIGHTS ACT OF 1964 IS AUTHORIZED BY THE COMMERCE CLAUSE

HEART OF ATLANTA MOTEL V. U.S.

379 U.S. 241 (1964)

Supreme Court of the United States

Facts. The Heart of Atlanta Motel operated 216 motel rooms available to members of the public and was located two blocks from downtown Atlanta. It was in close proximity to a federally funded highway. The motel solicited patronage from outside the state of Georgia through various national advertising media, including magazines of national circulation, billboards, and signs throughout Georgia. It accepted convention trade from outside Georgia and approximately 75 percent of its registered guests were from outside the state. The motel refused to accept African Americans as guests in direct violation of the Civil Rights Act of 1964. The federal district court sustained the constitutionality of the act and issued a permanent injunction restraining the motel owner from "refusing to accept Negroes as guests in the motel by reason of their race or color" and from "(m)aking distinction whatever upon the basis of race or color in the availability of the goods, services, facilities, privileges, advantages or accommodations offered or made available to the guests of the motel, or to the general public, within or upon any of the premises of the Heart of Atlanta Motel, Inc." The motel owners and the government cooperated with each other to ensure a prompt review of the issue before the Supreme Court. In its action the motel owner sought a court declaration that the Civil Rights Act of 1964 was unconstitutional.

Issue. Did Congress exceed its powers under the Commerce Clause by enacting the provisions of the Civil Rights Act of 1964?

Language of the Court. Clark, J.: **. . . While the Act as adopted carried no congressional findings the record of its passage through each house is replete with evidence of the burdens that discrimination by race or color places upon interstate commerce. . . . This testimony included the fact that our people have become increasingly mobile with millions of people of all races traveling from State to State; that Negroes in particular have been the subject of discrimination in transient accommodations, having to travel great distances to**

secure the same; that often they have been unable to obtain accommodations and have had to call upon friends to put them up overnight . . . and that these conditions had become so acute as to require the listing of available lodging for Negroes in a special guidebook which was itself "dramatic testimony to the difficulties" Negroes encounter in travel. . . . These exclusionary practices were found to be nationwide . . . This testimony indicated a qualitative as well as quantitative effect on interstate travel by Negroes. We shall not burden this opinion with further details since the voluminous testimony presents overwhelming evidence that discrimination by hotels and motels impedes interstate travel.

It is doubtful if in the long run appellant will suffer economic loss as a result of the Act. . . . Neither do we find any merit in the claim that the Act is a taking of property without just compensation. The cases are to the contrary. . . . We find no merit in the remainder of appellant's contentions, including that of "involuntary servitude." As we have seen, 32 States prohibit racial discrimination in public accommodations. These laws but codify the common-law innkeeper rule which long predated the Thirteenth Amendment.

Decision. No. When adopting the Act, it had the power to do so granted by the Commerce Clause of the Constitution.

CASE QUESTIONS

Critical Legal Thinking. If the operations of a business are facilitated through a local municipality's receipt of federal funds (such as for public road construction and maintenance), could it be argued that the Commerce Clause will always provide a sound basis to argue in favor of federal preemption?

Business Ethics. How would you have answered the question the Court raised "To what commerce does this power extend . . . what is this power?"

Contemporary Business. Would it have made a material difference to the Court's analysis if the motel's clientele were mostly from the state of Georgia and rarely involved interstate travelers?

Coverage of Title VII

Title VII prohibits discrimination in all aspects of employment. The most important provision of Title VII is §703:

> (a) It shall be an unlawful employment practice for an employer —
> (1) to fail or refuse to hire or to discharge any individual, or otherwise to discriminate against any individual with respect to his compensation, terms, conditions, or privileges of employment, because of such individual's race, color, religion, sex, or national origin; or
> (2) to limit, segregate, or classify his employees or applicants for employment in any way which would deprive or tend to deprive any individual of employment opportunities or otherwise adversely affect his status as an employee, because of such individual's race, color, religion, sex, or national origin.

Section 703(b) prohibits discrimination by employment agencies on the same grounds, and §703(c) prohibits such discrimination by labor organizations.

Section 703 provides certain exception to Title VII's anti-discrimination provisions:

- Religion, sex, or national origin, but not race, is a bona fide occupational qualification (BFOQ) reasonably necessary to the normal operation of the business.
- The employer acts pursuant to a bona fide seniority or merit system, or measures earnings by quantity or quality of production.
- The employer acts on the results of a professionally developed ability test that is "not designed, intended, or used to discriminate because of race, color, religion, sex, or national origin."
- Differences in pay based on sex are authorized by the Equal Pay Act of 1963.

Amendments to Title VII

Title VII has been amended three times. The first expanded the act's coverage (including extending its application to governmental employees and extending its application to U.S. citizens working abroad for American-owned or controlled companies) and increased EEOC powers. The Pregnancy Discrimination Act of 1978 included discrimination on the basis of "pregnancy, childbirth, and related medical conditions." The Civil Rights Act of 1991 legislatively reversed several Supreme Courts cases related to the burden of proof, granted the right to a jury trial and permitted compensatory and punitive damages to the plaintiff's remedies.

Title VII is very different in application and purpose than a **§1981** claim. Under **Title VII**, a worker must first timely file a complaint with the EEOC or a state discrimination agency having jurisdiction over the claim of discrimination. The worker does not have to file a **§1981** claim with the EEOC. The worker may immediately file suit in federal court.

Pairing of Remedies

The **Civil Rights Act of 1964** addresses employment discrimination based on race, ethnicity, and other federally guaranteed rights. These laws allow a plaintiff to sue under *both* **Title VII** and **§§1981 and 1983**, if both are applicable. Plaintiffs subject to **racial or national origin discrimination** may concurrently pursue alternative remedies under the statutes. The Supreme Court has held that **§1981** applies to both public and private employers and to unions. Unlike **Title VII, §1981** requires no statutory minimum number of employees for its application. In addition, **§1981** allows plaintiffs to seek **compensatory and punitive damages** *without* any statutory limitation, while **Title VII** places caps on compensatory and punitive damage awards. However, for a plaintiff to succeed with a **§1981** claim, the plaintiff must prove intentional discrimination. An advantage to concurrently pursuing a **Title VII** claim, unlike a claim under **§1981** alone, is that a **Title VII** claimant may pursue a claim based upon disparate treatment.

Concept Summary
Differences between §1981 and Title VII

- Section 1981 applies to all employers regardless of size, unlike Title VII, which applies to employers with 15 or more employees.
- Section 1981 claims are filed directly in federal court, not with the EEOC or any other state or federal agency.
- Section 1981 applies to disparate treatment discrimination and not disparate impact cases.
- Section 1981 plaintiffs can potentially recover unlimited damages, unlike claimants under Title VII, which has caps on the amount of damages that can be recovered.
- Section 1981 enjoys a longer statute of limitations, which is borrowed from the state statute of limitations for personal injury actions. Title VII has limited periods of time to file a charge with either the EEOC or a 706 agency.

Dimensions of Equal Employment Opportunity

In the last chapter the classifications of persons protected by Title VII were stated. These classifications specifically extend to the following individuals and circumstances:

Race or color: Included within this category are: persons of all races. American case law has defined this term to include African Americans, Caucasians, persons of Latino or Asian origin or descent, and indigenous Americans (including Eskimos, Native Hawaiians, and Native Americans). The prohibition on discrimination based on "color" also has been interpreted by some courts to mean that a light-skinned African American worker could pursue a discrimination case based on the actions of her darker-skinned supervisor.[4]

National origin: The Supreme Court has interpreted national origin as referring to "the country where a person was born, or, more broadly, the country from which his or her ancestors came."[5] It does not include discrimination based solely on citizenship.[6]

English-only rules in workplaces: Generally, these rules are upheld by courts.[7]

Sex: Title VII prohibits discrimination based on gender and applies to both men and women.

Separate work rules: Employer rules or policies that apply only to one gender violate Title VII.[8]

Separate benefits: Employers may not maintain different fringe benefits for women than for men.[9]

Pregnancy: The 1978 amendment to Title VII extended protection from discrimination to women who are pregnant or have pregnancy-related disabilities. They must be treated in the same manner as the employer would treat similarly situated temporarily disabled employees.

Sexual harassment: Although racial, religious, ethnic, or sexual harassment are all forms of disparate treatment, sexual harassment is treated to a different legal analysis. Two types are recognized. *Quid pro quo* harassment (i.e., unwelcome sexual advances, requests for sexual favors, and other verbal or physical conduct of a sexual nature) constitutes sexual harassment when (1) submission to such conduct is made either explicitly or implicitly a term or condition of employment; or (2) submission to or rejection of such conduct by an individual is used as a basis for employment decisions affecting such individual.[10] The second form, *hostile work environment* i.e., unwelcome sexual advances, requests for sexual favors, and other verbal or physical conduct of a sexual nature), constitutes sexual harassment having the purpose or effect of unreasonably interfering with an individual's work performance or creating an intimidating, hostile, or offensive working environment.

Equal pay: A later chapter on gender discrimination will address the protections afforded each gender for differences relating to disparity in pay.

Religion: The term "religion" includes "all aspects of religious observance and practice, as well as belief." EEOC guidelines state that protected religious practices "include moral or ethical beliefs as to what is right and wrong which are sincerely held with the strength of traditional religious views."

Exemptions: Title VII exempts from coverage a "religious corporation, association, educational institution, or society with respect to the employment of individuals of a particular religion to perform work connected with the carrying on by such corporation, association, educational institution, or society of its activities." Religious discrimination is also not unlawful under Title VII where religion is a BFOQ.

Other statutes afford parallel protections to individuals under other civil rights statutes. Two of these protected classifications relate to disability and age:

Disability: Recent legislation has greatly expanded the reach of the Americans with Disabilities Act (ADA). The law now defines a disability as (1) a physical or mental impairment that substantially limits a major life activity; or (2) a record of a physical or mental impairment that substantially limited a major life activity; or (3) when an entity (e.g., an employer) takes an action prohibited by the ADA based on an actual or perceived impairment.

Age: All persons 40 years of age and older are protected from discrimination on the basis of age in hiring, promotion, discharge, compensation or terms, conditions or privileges of employment (The Age Discrimination Act of 1975).[11]

Issues Unaddressed by the Civil Rights Act of 1964

Despite the simplicity of its statements and the laudable goals that underlay its enactment, the scope of the Civil Rights Act of 1964 was imperfect. Among the issues it failed to address were the following:

- Title I did not abolish literacy tests, which were used to disqualify those who sought to register to vote.
- Title II, which barred discrimination in places of public accommodation, excepted private clubs from the reach of the act without defining them.
- Title III's provisions regarding school desegregation did not authorize busing of students as a means to overcome segregation due to place of residence.
- Title IV authorized, but did not require, the withdrawal of federal funds from local and state agencies practicing discrimination.
- Title V did not give the EEOC meaningful enforcement powers.

In addition to these coverage issues, three major exemptions to the application of the Civil Rights Act of 1964 also persisted after its passage. The following types of employers were exempted from the application of the Act:

- Federal government agencies (later included through a 1972 amendment to the act known as the Equal Employment Opportunity Act of 1972);
- Indian tribes;
- Religious institutions, insofar as their activities related to their institutional practices, including the operation of educational facilities; and
- Bona fide nonprofit private membership organizations.

Students should recognize that **Title VII** does not apply in nonemployment contexts. However, in interpreting discrimination claims in those other situations, courts will refer to **Title VII** case precedent for guidance. Unless protected by state law or local ordinance, the following characteristics are *not* protected from employment discrimination by private-sector employers under federal law:

- non–U.S. citizenship
- sexual orientation (including effeminacy in men)

- marital status
- welfare benefit status

Executive orders and not legislation affords protection with regard to sexual orientation for federal employees.

Several statutory exceptions permit discrimination against otherwise protected individuals. These include the following:

- discrimination on the basis of religion, sex, or national origin if based on a BFOQ; and
- discrimination on the basis of national security requirements.

An employer may apply different standards of compensation or provide different terms, conditions, or privileges of employment pursuant to:

- a bona fide seniority or merit pay system;
- differences in cost of living due to employees who work in different locations;
- authorizations provided in the Equal Pay Act;
- special benefits afforded veterans; and
- provisions of foreign treaties which exempt foreign-owned corporations from compliance with equal opportunity law.

Civil Rights Act of 1991

Twenty years after *Griggs*, the **Civil Rights Act of 1991** was enacted. The act included a provision codifying the prohibition on **disparate impact** discrimination. It was passed to legislatively overrule five U.S. Supreme Court decisions issued following the enactment of the **Civil Rights Act of 1964**. These cases were issued by the Court in its 1989 term.[12] This act amended **Title VII, §1981, the Rehabilitation Act**, the **ADA**, and the **Age Discrimination in Employment Act (ADEA)**. The legislation also addressed the expansion of remedies available in workplace discrimination and harassment.

This act provided for the following:

- **Jury trials** and **compensatory and punitive damages** would be available now for claims of alleged discrimination under **Title VII** and the **ADA**. This extended compensatory damages to religious, gender, and disability claims. Formerly, such relief was available only to claimants alleging discrimination based on race and national origin.
- When a plaintiff can adduce evidence that an employment practice has a **disparate impact** on a protected class, the employer must demonstrate that the challenged practice is "job related for the position in question and consistent with business necessity."
    - This requirement codified the concepts of "business necessity" and "job relatedness" as discussed by the Court in its *Griggs* decision.
    - This statute expanded the potential for employer liability under **Title VII** in **disparate impact** discrimination cases; but, as we shall learn about age

discrimination, Congress did not do the same for claims made under **ADEA**, which follows almost verbatim **Title VII.**

- Plaintiffs may receive a declaratory judgment (i.e., a judgment of a court in a civil case that declares the rights, duties, or obligations of the parties to the lawsuit) or receive injunctive relief and recover attorney's fees and court costs if the plaintiff proves that race, color, religion, sex, or national origin was a **"motivating factor"** for the employment practice. However, a plaintiff is not entitled to reinstatement, back pay, or compensatory or punitive damages if the defendant establishes that it would have taken the same action absent that motivation.
- Restriction of the right to challenge a consent decree the **affirmative action** provisions of which adversely affect the challenger when notice and reasonable opportunity to object was previously given to the challenger.
- Extension of the application of **Title VII** and the **ADA** to American citizens working in a foreign country for an American employer or a foreign company controlled by an American employer.
- Prohibition of **race-norming** by which employment test scores are adjusted on the basis of classifications protected under **Title VII**.
- Recovery of expert fees as part of attorney's fees in all cases under **Title VII**, the **ADA**, and **§1981** in which attorney's fees are recoverable.
- Amendment of **§1981** to extend its application to private discrimination as well as governmental discrimination.
- Setting the statute of limitations period for challenging discriminatory seniority systems under **Title VII** to begin when the plaintiff suffered an injury due to the seniority system.
- Establishment of a Glass Ceiling Commission to study the "opportunities for, and artificial barriers to the advancement of women and minorities to management and decision-making positions in business."

Race-norming
The employment practice of adjusting scores on a standardized test by using different curves for different racial groups.

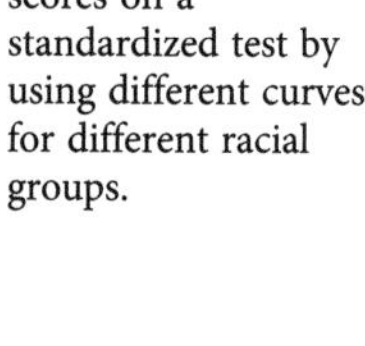

Management Application
Employer Liability for Discrimination

As will be developed in later chapters, employer liability is dependent on the circumstances:

- **Hostile environment.** Harassment by a supervisor in a hostile environment case does not automatically make the employer liable.[13] Imputed liability to the employer can result if the supervisor was acting within the scope of his or her employment or the harassment can be imputed to the employer.
- **Negligent harassment by a co-worker.** Employer negligence can be proved by showing the employer knew or in the exercise of reasonable care should have known of the harassment and failed to take corrective action.[14] The related legal concept is known as estoppel. This legal doctrine creates liability for the employer when the employer causes an employee to mistakenly believe the supervisor is acting for the employer or knows of the harassment and fails to correct it.
- **Harassment by a supervisor.** The Supreme Court has held that an employer is liable for actionable

hostile environment sexual harassment by a supervisor with immediate (or higher) authority over the harassed employee.[15] This concept, known as **apparent authority** — the authority implied when a principal by words or conduct suggests to third person that the supervisor is authorized to act on behalf of the principal — can thus create liability for the employer.

Overview of the Coverage Afforded by Other Federal Equal Opportunity Laws

Title VII has been amended to increase its scope. The Equal Employment Opportunity Act of 1972 expanded its coverage to include government employees and to strengthen the enforcement powers of the EEOC. The Pregnancy Discrimination Act of 1978 extended the reach of the Title VII's sex discrimination provisions. This act declared unlawful discrimination against women because of pregnancy, childbirth, or a related medical condition. In addition, the Family and Medical Leave Act of 1993 offers job protections to employees based on a medical condition of the employee or employee's family.

Other obligations imposed on employers emanate from the **ADA**, the **Equal Pay Act of 1963**, and the **ADEA**. The EEOC was established pursuant to the **Civil Rights Act of 1964** to administer the laws and monitor compliance. Specific laws also apply to those who contract with the federal government; receive federal financial assistance, such as colleges and universities; and government employers. The employment of disabled and Vietnam-era veterans is promoted by the **Rehabilitation Act of 1973**, enacted by Congress to advance that purpose. Under 38 U.S.C. §4212, federal contractors and subcontractors are to undertake affirmative action to employ and promote those veterans.

The antidiscrimination provisions of the **Immigration Reform and Control Act of 1986 (IRCA)** apply to all employers with four or more employees. It prohibits discrimination against applicants and employees based on their citizenship or national origin. The act also addresses hiring, retention, and documentation.

Executive Order 11246: Federally Funded Affirmative Action

President Lyndon Johnson issued Executive Order 11246, which prohibits every federal contractor and subcontractor from discriminating based on race, color, religion, sex, or national origin. It also required them to take **affirmative action**. This order has wide application and includes workers engaged in rendering services to the federal government, including those who supply goods, use federal property, or are engaged in federal construction contracts or federally funded construction contracts.

Executive Order 11246
An order issued by President Lyndon Johnson prohibiting every federal contractor and subcontractor from discriminating based on race, color, religion, sex, or national origin.

The secretary of labor is responsible for enforcing this Executive Order, and this responsibility has been delegated to the Office of Federal Contract Compliance Programs (OFCCP). This agency has issued a vast body of federal regulations on the subjects of antidiscrimination and **affirmative action**. These regulations require all written personnel policies to state that sex discrimination against employees is prohibited. Moreover, any union labor agreement applying to work to be performed under federal contracts must be consistent with the OFCCP's guidelines.[16] Any state statute or local ordinance in conflict with **Executive Order 11246** is preempted by federal law.[17]

State governments and local jurisdictions that contract with the federal government (either directly or as a recipient of funding) are subject to **Executive Order 11246**. In addition, they are subject to the **Rehabilitation Act of 1973**[18] for contracts of $10,000 or more and to the **Vietnam Era Veterans Readjustment Assistance Act**[19] for contracts of $50,000 or more for those employing 50 or more persons. All facilities of a government contractor, even those not involved directly in work performed under the government contract, are subject to the federal government's **affirmative action** rules.[20] Under these laws, a federal contractor would have to implement **affirmative action** plans consistent even if it is not working exclusively under federal contract.

In addition to the express directive of **Executive Order 11246**, a requirement within **Title VI** of the Civil Rights Act of 1964 requires **affirmative action. Title VI of the Civil Rights Act of 1964** prohibits discrimination on the basis of race, color, or national origin in programs and activities receiving federal financing.[21] Under this title, each federal department and agency providing such financing must issue rules, regulations, or orders to achieve the objectives of the statute. This task was delegated to the attorney general of the United States by a 1980 executive order. That department has issued equal employment opportunity regulations for all federally assisted programs, and it coordinates the enforcement of **Title VI** by all federal departments and agencies.[22] Under this act, colleges and universities receiving federal grants or accepting federally insured student loans must undertake **affirmative action** programs.

Affirmative action *does not require* preferences. In fact, **Title VII** prohibits such preferential treatment. §703(j) of Title VII states in part:

> *Nothing contained in this [subsection (j)] shall be interpreted to require any employer . . . to grant preferential treatment to any individual or to any group because of the race, color, religion, sex, or national origin of such individual or group on account of an imbalance which may exist with respect to the total number or percentage of persons of any race, color, religion, sex, or national origin employed by any employer . . . in comparison with the total number or percentage of persons of such race, color, religion, sex, or national origin in any . . . area, or in the available work force in any . . . area.*[23]

The Supreme Court has interpreted this provision of Title VII as not requiring **affirmative action**. In *Teamsters v. U.S.* 431 U.S. 324 (1977) the Court observed that:

> *[e]vidence of longlasting and gross disparity between the composition of a work force and that of the general population . . . may be significant even though §703(j) makes clear that Title VII imposes no requirement that a work force mirror to the general population.*[24]

In its 1971 decision in *Griggs v. Duke Power* the Supreme Court noted that Title VII does not require preferences:

> *[T]he [Civil Rights Act of 1964] does not command that any person be hired simply because he was formerly the subject of discrimination, or because he is a member of a minority group. Discriminatory preference for any group, minority or majority, is precisely and only what Congress has proscribed.*[25]

Consistent with its holding in *Griggs*, the Supreme Court decided in *McDonald v. Santa Fe Trail Transportation Co.*[26] that discrimination against whites was prohibited by **Title VII**.

Public Sector Affirmative Action Race-Based Plans

Analyzing the Supreme Court's treatment of **affirmative action plans** can be challenging, but some guidelines may be derived from their study. In *Adarand Constructors, Inc. v. Pena*,[27] the Court considered a claim of a nonminority contractor who was not awarded a federally funded highway construction contract because of bidding preferences awarded to the prevailing contractor. Under the terms of the federal contract, Mountain Gravel, the prime contractor, would receive additional compensation if it hired small businesses controlled by "socially and economically disadvantaged individuals." Another bidder, Gonzales Construction Company, was awarded the subcontract because it was certified as a minority business, a designation that Adarand did not possess. Mountain Gravel awarded the subcontract to Gonzales, despite Adarand's low bid. Mountain Gravel's chief estimator submitted an affidavit stating that Mountain Gravel would have accepted Adarand's bid had it not been for the additional payment it received by hiring Gonzales. The Court held that all racial classifications, regardless of governmental directive, are subject to **strict scrutiny** review under the Equal Protection Clause. For the racial preferences to pass constitutional muster they "must serve a **compelling governmental interest**, and must be narrowly tailored to further that interest." The Court added that compensation programs that are truly based on disadvantage, rather than race, would be evaluated under lower equal protection standards. However, because race is not a sufficient condition for a presumption of disadvantage and the award of favored treatment, all race-based classifications must be judged under the **strict scrutiny** standard of review for determining constitutionality. Moreover, even proof of past injury does not in itself establish the suffering of present or future damages. This case marked a departure from the Court's past practice of giving great deference to congressionally sanctioned affirmative action programs.

Strict Scrutiny Most stringent standard of judicial review of equal protection issues. Any government activity or regulation that classifies persons based on a suspect class (i.e., race) is reviewed for lawfulness using a strict scrutiny test. Approach must be justified by compelling governmental interest, narrowly tailored, and involve the least restrictive means to achieve that result.

It is worth noting the comments of Justice Sandra Day O'Connor in writing for the majority:

> *[f]inally, we wish to dispel the notion that **strict scrutiny** is "strict in theory, but fatal in fact" (citation omitted). The unhappy persistence of both the practice and the lingering effects of racial discrimination against minority groups in this country is an unfortunate reality, and government is not disqualified from acting in response to it. . . . When race-based action is necessary to further a **compelling interest**, such action is within constitutional constraints if it satisfies the "narrow tailoring" test this Court has set out in previous cases.*[28]

Affirmative Action and Equal Protection

The Supreme Court first considered the constitutionality of **affirmative action** under the Equal Protection Clause of the Fourteenth Amendment in *University of California v. Baake*.[29] In that decision, the Court struck down a medical school's preferential admissions policy that set aside a specific number of admits to minority members. The purpose of the admissions plan was to advance a public purpose of remedying societal discrimination and not the past practices of the medical school. The sharply divided Court created a legacy of conflicting decisions in courts of appeals before two later Supreme Court decisions refined their position. The Court considered the constitutionality of two University of Michigan admissions policies with **affirmative action** components. In *Grutter v. Bollinger*,[30] the law school gave applicants no "mechanical, predetermined diversity 'bonuses' based on [their] race or ethnicity." Each law school applicant was given individualized consideration as a part of a "holistic" review of the candidate. The Court observed that "[t]he Law School asserts only one justification for their use of race in the admission process: obtaining 'the educational benefits that flow from a diverse student body.' " The Court agreed with that argument and held a compelling governmental interest can be served through narrowly tailored use of race in admissions. However, during that same term the Court held as unconstitutional a numerical qualification system of admission to the Michigan undergraduate program that arbitrarily awarded extra points to every single applicant from an "underrepresented minority" group.[31] Equal protection was respected in the law school program because it provided individual consideration of each applicant and their contribution to a diverse student body. In contrast, the undergraduate program used a formula whereby the effect was to make "the factor of race . . . decisive."

As federal courts struggle to weigh the arguments of future **affirmative action** programs, they should be guided by the Court's comments regarding diversity. In *Grutter*, the Court stated:

> *Truly individualized consideration demands that race be used in a flexible, nonmechanical way. It follows from this mandate that universities cannot establish quotas for members of certain racial groups or put members of those groups on separate admissions tracks (citing* Baake*) nor can universities insulate applicants who belong to certain racial or ethnic groups from the competition for admission. . . . Universities can, however, consider race or ethnicity more flexibly as a "plus" factor in the context of individualized consideration of each and every applicant.*
>
> *We are satisfied that the Law School's admissions program . . . does not operate as a quota.*

The Supreme Court has spent considerable effort in defining what constitutes a quota in several of its decisions. In *Richmond v. J.A. Croson*, the Court defined a "quota" as a program in which certain fixed number or proportion of opportunities is "reserved exclusively for certain minority groups." In another decision the Court commented that quotas "impose a fixed number or percentage which must be attained, or which cannot be exceeded"[32] and "insulate the individual from comparison with all other candidates for the available seats."[33] In contrast, the Court endorses a hiring goal. It has held that "a permissible goal . . . require[s] only a good-faith effort . . . to come within a range demarcated by the goal itself,"[34] and permits consideration of race as a "plus" factor in any given case while still ensuring that each candidate "compete[s] with all other qualified applicants."[35]

Outside the arena of undergraduate and graduate school admissions, the Supreme Court first considered a challenge to an **affirmative action plan** under the **Equal Protection Clause** in a 1986 decision. In *Wygant v. Jackson Board of Education*,[36] the Court declared a preferential layoff and termination policy favoring nonwhites as unconstitutional.

CASE 5.2

RACE-BASED LAYOFF PRACTICES MAY FAIL STRICT SCRUTINY TEST

WYGANT V. JACKSON BOARD OF EDUCATION

476 U.S. 267 (1986)

Supreme Court of the United States

Facts. Under the collective bargaining agreement between a union and the Jackson (Michigan) Board of Education, it was agreed that if it became necessary to lay off teachers, those with the most seniority would be retained, except that at no time would there be a greater percentage of minority personnel laid off than the current percentage of minority employed at the time of the layoff. As a result of this provision, nonminority teachers were laid off, while minority teachers with less seniority retained their positions. The school board defended the plan not on the need to remedy past discrimination practices but rather on the benefits of promoting minority role models in education. The displaced nonminority teachers sued on the grounds that the action violated the Equal Protection Clause and various state and federal statutes. The district court upheld the layoff provision, and the court of appeals affirmed. The Supreme Court granted *certiorari.*

Issue. Can a school board adopt preferential protection against layoffs based on the race or national origin of its employees?

Language of the Court. Powell, J.: **"Any preference based on racial or ethnic criteria must necessarily receive a most searching examination to make sure that it does not conflict with constitutional guarantees." (Citation omitted.) There are two prongs to this examination. First, any racial classification "must be justified by a compelling governmental interest." (Citations omitted.) Second, the means chosen by the State to effectuate its purpose must be "narrowly tailored to the achievement of that goal." (Citation omitted.) We must decide whether the layoff provision is supported by a compelling state purpose and whether the means chosen to accomplish that purpose are narrowly tailored.**

This Court never has held that societal discrimination alone is sufficient to justify a racial classification. Rather, the Court has insisted upon some showing

of prior discrimination by the governmental unit involved before allowing limited use of racial classifications in order to remedy such discrimination. This Court's reasoning in *Hazelwood School District v. United States*, (citation omitted), illustrates that the relevant analysis in cases involving proof of discrimination by statistical disparity focuses on those disparities that demonstrate such prior governmental discrimination. In Hazelwood the Court concluded that, absent employment discrimination by the school board, "nondiscriminatory hiring practices will in time result in a work force more or less representative of the racial and ethnic composition of the population in the community from which employees are hired." (Citation omitted), quoting *Teamsters v. United States*, (citation omitted) . . . . Based on that reasoning, the Court in Hazelwood held that the proper comparison for determining the existence of actual discrimination by the school board was "between the racial composition of [the school's] teaching staff and the racial composition of the qualified public school teacher population in the relevant labor market." (Citation omitted.) Hazelwood demonstrates this Court's focus on prior discrimination as the justification for, and the limitation on, a State's adoption of race-based remedies. . . . Unlike the analysis in Hazelwood, the role model theory employed by the District Court has no logical stopping point. The role model theory allows the Board to engage in discriminatory hiring and layoff practices long past the point required by any legitimate remedial purpose. Indeed, by tying the required percentage of minority teachers to the percentage of minority students, it requires just the sort of year-to-year calibration the Court [has] stated was unnecessary.

Decision. No. Although unable to agree on an opinion, five members of the Court agreed in a plurality opinion that the layoffs were in violation of the Equal Protection Clause.

DISCUSSION QUESTIONS

Critical Legal Thinking. In this case, the plurality of judges agreed that the plan failed because it related to layoffs of existing employees and that hiring preferences do not burden innocent individuals to the same degree that layoffs impose. Do you agree with this assessment? Why or why not?

Business Ethics. How would you have "narrowly tailored" the plan to accomplish the societal goals promoted by the school board?

Contemporary Business. Do you think that the Court would reach the same decision today in light of different membership on the Court and its holdings in *Grutter*? What place, if any, does the promotion of "role modeling" for others within our society have within the employment context?

The Supreme Court continued to apply its **strict scrutiny** equal protection standard of review in *City of Richmond v. J.A. Croson Co.*[37] In the *City of Richmond* decision, Justice O'Connor authored the plurality decision striking down a Richmond, Virginia, ordinance requiring that 30 percent of all city construction contracts be awarded to minority-owned subcontractors. The Court found that the city could not justify the ordinance with any "direct evidence of race discrimination on the part of the city in letting contracts or any evidence that the city's prime contractors had discriminated against minority-owned subcontractors."[38] Among the reasons the Court held the ordinance unconstitutional was that the city had failed to consider race neutral alternatives and that the percentage used was not "tied to any injury suffered by anyone."[39]

The following case recognizes that the employer undertook the affirmative action plan at issue without a prior history of racial discrimination as well as in conjunction with a collective bargaining agreement. The plan modified an existing seniority system to reduce or eliminate the system's adverse impact upon minorities and women.

CASE 5.3

EMPLOYERS' VOLUNTARY AFFIRMATIVE ACTION PLANS MAY BE LAWFUL UNDER TITLE VII

U.S. STEELWORKERS V. WEBER

443 U.S. 193 (1979)

Supreme Court of the United States

Facts. This case arose from the operation of the affirmative action plan at Kaiser's plant in Gramercy, Louisiana. Until 1974, this Kaiser plant had hired only persons with prior experience as craft workers. Because blacks had long been excluded from craft unions, few were able to present these credentials for employment in this field. As a consequence, before 1974 only 1.83 percent (5 out of 273) of the skilled craft workers at the Gramercy plant were black, even though the work force in the Gramercy area was approximately 39 percent black. Kaiser and USWA (i.e., the union) agreed to an affirmative action plan. The plan did not require the termination of white workers and was to last only until the percentage of black skilled workers approximated that of blacks in the local workforce. When the program was initiated, 7 black workers and 6 white workers were selected for the training program. The most senior black selected into the program had less seniority than several white production workers whose bids for admission were rejected. Thereafter, one of those white production workers, Brian Weber, filed a class-action complaint alleging discrimination in violation of 703(a) and (d) of Title VII. The district court held that the plan violated Title VII and the court of appeals affirmed the decision. The Supreme Court granted *certiorari.*

Issue. May a private employer and a union implement an affirmative action training plan designed to eliminate conspicuous racial imbalance in the employer's almost exclusively white craftwork force?

Language of the Court. Brennan, J.: **Challenged here is the legality of an affirmative action plan — collectively bargained by an employer and a union — that reserves for black employees 50% of the openings in an in-plant craft-training program until the percentage of black craft workers in the plant is commensurate with the percentage of blacks in the local labor force.**

Since the Kaiser-USWA plan does not involve state action, this case does not present an alleged violation of the Equal Protection Clause of the Fourteenth Amendment. Further, since the Kaiser-USWA plan was adopted voluntarily, we are not concerned with what Title VII requires or with what a court might order to remedy a past proved violation of the Act. The only question before us is the narrow statutory issue of whether Title VII forbids private employers and unions from voluntarily agreeing upon bona fide affirmative action plans that accord racial preferences in the manner and for the purpose provided in the Kaiser-USWA plan. That question was expressly left open in McDonald v. Santa Fe Trail Transp. Co., (citation omitted), which held, in a case not involving affirmative action, that Title VII protects whites as well as blacks from certain forms of racial discrimination.

Had Congress meant to prohibit all race-conscious affirmative action; as [Weber] urges, it easily could have answered both objections by providing that Title VII would not require or permit racially preferential integration efforts. But Congress did not choose such a course. Rather, Congress added 703 (j) which . . . does not state that "nothing in Title VII shall be interpreted to permit" voluntary affirmative efforts to correct racial imbalances. The natural inference is that Congress chose not to forbid all voluntary race-conscious affirmative action.

We need not today define in detail the line of demarcation between permissible and impermissible affirmative action plans. It suffices to hold that the challenged Kaiser-USWA affirmative action plan falls on the permissible side of the line. The purposes of the plan mirror those of the statute. Both were designed to break down old patterns of racial segregation and hierarchy. Both were structured to "open employment opportunities for Negroes in occupations which have been traditionally closed to them."

At the same time, the plan does not unnecessarily trammel the interests of the white employees. The plan does not require the discharge of white workers and their replacement with new black hires. . . . Nor does the plan create an absolute bar to the advancement of white employees; half of those trained in the program will be white. Moreover, the plan is a temporary measure; it is not intended to maintain racial balance, but simply to eliminate a manifest racial imbalance. Preferential selection of craft trainees at the Gramercy plant will end as soon as the percentage of black skilled craftworkers in

the Gramercy plant approximates the percentage of blacks in the local labor force.

Decision. Yes. In a 5-2 decision, the Court held that Title VII's prohibition in §703 against racial discrimination does not condemn all private, voluntary, race-conscious affirmative action plans.

DISCUSSION QUESTIONS

Critical Legal Thinking. Does this decision insulate employers from giving special job preferences to blacks without being harassed by reverse discrimination lawsuits?

Business Ethics. The Court relied upon the "spirit" of Title VII for its interpretation of what Title VII meant; is this case one of judicial legislation?

Contemporary Business. Does this decision put more pressure on companies to adopt voluntary action programs for definable groups? Are there limits to whom such preferences should be extended?

The Limitations of Voluntary Affirmative Action

In *Weber*, the Supreme Court emphasized that a requirement that compelled the discharge of white employees and their replacement by African Americans would be unlawful. That decision also suggested that a voluntary **affirmative action plan** may not prevent white employees from advancing within the organization. In *McLaughlin v. Great Lakes Dredge & Dock Co.*,[40] the court held that a white employee cannot be discharged for the purpose of promoting or improving the position of a minority employee; it further recognized that even if a workplace does not require the discharge of whites or absolutely bar white employment, a court may still find that the rights of white employees have been "trammeled," as the holding in *Weber* offers. The more difficult question of when an absolute "bar" occurs is raised when a single position has only one white and one African American applicant. Under the Supreme Court's decision in *Johnson v. Santa Clara Transportation Agency*,[41] an employer could apply a properly constructed voluntary **affirmative action plan** and hire the minority employee over the white employee for a single opening. It is important for students to note that *Johnson* recited the fact that the plan did not necessarily require the discharge of a white employee or present an absolute bar to the advancement of a white employee within the organization. The subject of an applicant's race or gender with respect to a **voluntary affirmative action plan** may be taken into account along with many other factors when considering eligible candidates.

Concept Summary
Voluntary Affirmative Action Plans

All of the following conditions must be met for an affirmative action plan to be constitutional:

1. There must be statistical evidence of disparity in the employment of members of minority communities; some courts have described a permissible affirmative action plan as a response to a manifest imbalance in its workforce.[42]
2. The plan must be temporary and not permanent.
3. The rights of minority employees must not "unnecessarily trammel the interests of the white employees" by requiring their termination or permanent impediment to advancement.[43]

CASE 5.4

PROPERLY DRAFTED VAPS ARE CONSTITUTIONALLY PERMISSIBLE

JOHNSON V. TRANSPORTATION AGENCY, SANTA CLARA COUNTY

480 U.S. 616 (1987)

Supreme Court of the United States

Facts. The Supreme Court relied on its earlier decision in the *Weber* case to uphold a California county transportation agency's voluntary affirmative action plan. As a result of this plan, the county agency promoted Diane Joyce, a female applicant, to the position of road dispatcher. A male, Paul Johnson, also applied for the position and had scored slightly higher than Joyce on the interview for the job opening. Additionally, three supervisors had recommended Johnson for the promotion. Johnson asserted a claim in which he alleged that the public employer, a county mass transportation agency, violated Title VII by denying him the promotion. This promotion was within the context of the agency's unilateral promulgation of an affirmative action plan, which, among other things, governs the promotion of employees.

Issue. Whether in making the promotion the public employer impermissibly took into account the sex of the applicants in violation of Title VII of the Civil Rights of 1964.

Language of the Court. Brennan, J.: **In December 1978, the Santa Clara County Transit Board District Board of Supervisors adopted an Affirmative Action Plan ("Plan") for the County Transportation Agency. The Plan implemented a County Affirmative Action Plan, which had been adopted, declared the County, because "mere prohibition of discriminatory practices is not enough to remedy the effects of past practices and to permit attainment of an equitable representation of minorities, women and handicapped persons." Relevant to this case, the Agency Plan provides that, in making promotions to positions within a traditionally segregated job classification in which women have been significantly underrepresented, the Agency is authorized to consider as one factor the sex of the qualified applicant. . . . Specifically, while women constituted 36.4% of the area labor market, they composed only 22.4% of the Agency employees. Furthermore, women working at the Agency were concentrated largely in the EEOC job categories traditionally held by women: Women made up 76% of Office and Clerical Workers, but only 7.1% of Agency Officials and Administrators, 5.6% of Professionals, 9.7% of Technicians and 22% of Service and Maintenance Workers. As for the job classification relevant to this case, none of the 238 Skilled Craft Worker positions were held by a woman. . . .**

As an initial matter, the Agency adopted as a benchmark for measuring progress in eliminating underrepresentation the long-term goal of a workforce that mirrored in its major job classifications the percentage of women in the area labor market. . . . The Plan therefore directed that annual short-term goals be formulated that would provide a more realistic indication of the degree to which sex should be taken into account in filling positions . . . the Plan stressed that such goals "should not be construed as 'quotas' 'that must be met,'" but as reasonable aspirations in correcting the imbalance in the Agency's workforce . . . [I]n evaluating the compliance of an Affirmative Action Plan with Title VII's, . . . continued prohibition on discrimination, we must be mindful of "This Court's and Congress' consistent emphasis on 'the value of voluntary efforts to further the objective of the law.'" (Wygant, 476 U.S., at 290). . . . The Agency has identified a conspicuous imbalance in job categories traditionally segregated by race and sex. It is made clear from the outset, however, that employment decisions may not be justified solely by reference to this imbalance, but must rest on a multitude of practical, realistic factors. It has therefore committed itself to annual adjustment of goals so as to provide a reasonable guide for actual hiring and promotion decisions. The Agency earmarks no positions for anyone; sex is but one of several factors that may be taken into account in evaluating qualified applications for a position. As both the Plan's language and its manner of operation attest, the Agency has no intention of establishing a workforce whose permanent composition is dictated by rigid numerical standards . . .

Decision. A public agency can appropriately consider gender within an affirmative action program. That program must represent a moderate, flexible, case-by-case approach to effecting a gradual improvement in the representation of minorities and women in the employer's workforce.

CASE QUESTIONS

Critical Legal Thinking. In this 6-3 decision, the three dissenting justices pointed out that the low female representation in the Agency's workforce may have been due to the unpleasant nature of the jobs. Do you think that this fact should have been taken into consideration by the Court? In part the dissent stated: "It is absurd to think that the nationwide failure of road maintenance crews, for example, to achieve the Agency's ambition of 36.4% female representation is attributable primarily, if even substantially, to systematic exclusion of women eager to shoulder pick and shovel. It is a 'traditionally segregated job category' not in the Weber sense, but in the sense that, because of longstanding social attitudes, it has not been regarded by women themselves as desirable work."

Business Ethics. To what degree do you think that the Court was influenced by the fact the plaintiff was not the only eligible candidate and that while retaining his position in the organization he would be eligible for future promotions? Is this a satisfactory explanation for the Court's decision?

Contemporary Business. Can you cite any recent examples of affirmative action plans discussed in the news?

The Future of Voluntary Affirmative Action Plans

Under the *Gruter* decision, the Supreme Curt reaffirmed *Baake.* In *Gruter* it ruled that a university has a **compelling governmental interest** in seeking a racially diverse student body with respect to its law school. However, such **affirmative action** programs must provide individualized review of each applicant. Moreover, the program must be narrowly tailored to effect its purpose. In the *Gratz* decision, the court struck down a crude method of **affirmative action** that added points to the scores of applicants from minority or underrepresented communities. In *Parents Involved in Community Schools v. Seattle School District No. 1,*[44] the Court held the openly race-conscious public school assignment policies of the Seattle School District were unconstitutional. However, the Court left open to school boards other indirect means to achieve diversity in the schools, such as recruiting students in a targeted fashion or redrawing attendance zones based on demographics. Might such education-based cases might be extended to the employment context? That is a difficult question, which the Court has yet to answer. These cases appear to suggest future extension to the public employment context. Eventually, they will likely apply to the private sector. The logical extension of these cases would suggest that for a **voluntary affirmative action plan** to meet the narrowly tailored requirement of *Gruter*, it must provide individual consideration for each applicant.

Reverse Discrimination

Claims of **reverse discrimination** may be made on the basis of gender or race. In such claims, a male or white employee alleges having been made the victim of discrimination.[45] The claim is premised on the argument that any preferential discrimination is unlawful under Title VII and §1981 unless undertaken pursuant to a lawful **affirmative action plan**.

> ***Example:*** Two white employees were discharged for stealing cargo, but a black employee who did the same thing was not discharged. The Supreme Court held that Title VII protects all persons regardless of race from discrimination in private employment. Culpable unions and employers are equally liable for **reverse discrimination**.[46]

Proving a Reverse Discrimination Claim

The male or white plaintiff must show a causal relationship between the alleged historical or current favoritism shown the other gender or race and the adverse action of which plaintiff complains.

> ***Example:*** When a white IRS agent complained that he had been passed over for promotions in favor of blacks and women, an appellate court noted, "[a]ssuming, without granting, that Carter has demonstrated both the existence of an institutionalized system of **affirmative action** and its negative cumulative effect on white male revenue agents by placing beyond their reach the necessary work experience, awards, and relative fitness ratings, Carter has not causally connected his own individual work experiences with his failure to obtain the particular promotion here at issue."[47]

This case example demonstrates that courts will not review the lawfulness of an **affirmative action plan** until after the plaintiff proves that he or she suffered an adverse employment action due to the **disparate treatment** resulting from the **affirmative action plan**.

In the following 2009 decision the Supreme Court held that a city's decision to ignore test results for city firefighting positions violated Title VII. This decision was decided by a 5-4 vote of the Court members. The case teaches that the administration of an examination, as part of a hiring process, must be fair to all persons, regardless of race.

CASE 5.5

WITHOUT A VALID DEFENSE, PUBLIC JOB PROMOTIONAL DECISIONS BASED ON RACE VIOLATE TITLE VII

RICCI V. DESTEFANO

557 U.S. ______, 129 S. Ct. 2658 (2009)

Supreme Court of the United States

Facts. In 2003, 118 New Haven, Connecticut, firefighters took examinations to qualify for a lieutenant or captain promotion. Promotion examinations in New Haven were infrequent, so the stakes were high. The written and oral promotional examinations had been professionally developed and validated. The results would determine which firefighters would be considered for promotions during the next two years, and the order in which they would be considered. Many firefighters studied for months, at considerable personal and financial cost..

When the examination results showed that white candidates had outperformed minority candidates, the mayor and other local politicians opened a public debate that turned rancorous. Some firefighters argued the tests should be discarded because the results showed the tests to be discriminatory. They threatened a discrimination lawsuit if the city made promotions based on the tests. Other firefighters said the exams were neutral and fair. And they, in turn, threatened a discrimination lawsuit if the city, relying on the statistical racial disparity, ignored the test results and denied promotions to the candidates who had performed well. Ultimately, the city sided with those who protested the test results. It threw out the examinations, believing that the examination process reflected significant unlawful disparate impact discrimination. Certain white and Hispanic firefighters who likely would have been promoted based on their good test performance sued the City and some of its officials. The federal district court granted summary judgment in favor of the city, and the court of appeals affirmed that judgment. The Supreme Court granted *certiorari.*

Issue. Can an employer intentionally discriminate against white employees by rigidly applying an affirmative action plan in favor of minorities?

Language of the Court. Kennedy, J.: . . . **Our analysis begins with this premise: The City's actions would violate the disparate-treatment prohibition of Title VII absent some valid defense. . . . As the District Court put it, the City rejected the test results because "too many whites and not enough minorities would be promoted were the lists to be certified." (Citation omitted.) . . . Without some** other justification, this express, race-based decisionmaking violates Title VII's command that employers cannot take adverse employment actions because of an individual's race.

. . . The City rejected the test results solely because the higher scoring candidates were white. The question is not whether that conduct was discriminatory but whether the City had a lawful justification for its race-based action.

Title VII does not prohibit an employer from considering, before administering a test or practice, how to design that test or practice in order to provide a fair opportunity for all individuals, regardless of their race. . . . We hold only that, under Title VII, before an employer can engage in intentional discrimination for the asserted purpose of avoiding or remedying an unintentional disparate impact, the employer must have a strong basis in evidence to believe it will be subject to disparate-impact liability if it fails to take the race-conscious, discriminatory action.

Respondents also lacked a strong basis in evidence of an equally valid, less-discriminatory testing alternative that the City, by certifying the examination results, would necessarily have refused to adopt. . . . The record in this litigation documents a process that, at the outset, had the potential to produce a testing procedure that was true to the promise of Title VII: No individual should face workplace discrimination based on race. Respondents thought about promotion qualifications and relevant experience in neutral ways. They were careful to ensure broad racial participation in the design of the test itself and its administration. As we have discussed at length, the process was open and fair.

The problem, of course, is that after the tests were completed, the raw racial results became the predominant rationale for the City's refusal to certify the results. The injury arises in part from the high, and justified, expectations of the candidates who had participated in the testing process on the terms the City had established for the promotional process. Many of the candidates had studied for months, at considerable personal and financial expense, and thus the injury caused by the City's reliance on raw racial statistics at the end of the process was all the more severe. Confronted with arguments both for and against certifying the test results — and threats of a lawsuit either way — the City was required to make a difficult inquiry. But its hearings produced no strong evidence of a disparate-impact violation, and the City was not entitled to disregard the tests based solely on the racial disparity in the results.

Decision. No. An employer must demonstrate a strong basis in evidence that, had it not taken the action, it would have been liable for disparate impact discrimination.

CASE QUESTIONS

Critical Legal Thinking. In a concurring opinion, Justice Scalia stated: "I join the Court's opinion in full, but write separately to observe that its resolution of this dispute merely postpones the evil day on which the Court will have to confront the question: Whether, or to what extent, are the disparate-impact provisions of Title VII of the Civil Rights Act of 1964 consistent with the Constitution's guarantee of equal protection? The question is not an easy one." How would you address Justice Scalia's concerns? Has he begun the public discussion of whether this part of the employment discrimination laws is unconstitutional?

Business Ethics. The Court found that the city committed disparate treatment discrimination, which the city argued it had not. What if the city had been repeatedly sued for employment discrimination practices in the past and could not afford more litigation? How would you describe the ethics of city managers in making the decision to ignore the test results?

Contemporary Business. What is your view as to how long affirmative action programs should remain part of the American workplace?

Focus on Ethics
Affirmative Action in Major League Baseball

Prior to 1947, Major League Baseball (MLB) and its franchise baseball teams refused to employ African American players. Because African Americans could not play in Major League Baseball, they formed the Negro Leagues in which African Americans could play baseball. In 1947, Jackie Robinson broke the color barrier and became the first African American to play in major league baseball in modern history when he joined the Brooklyn Dodgers.

With the coming of integration in major league baseball, many African American baseball players became members of MLB teams. However, the integration of major league baseball caused the demise of the Negro Leagues. The Negro League teams went out of business and were not able to offer any pension or medical benefits to their former players.

In 1993, MLB created a plan that provided medical coverage and an annual payment of $10,000 to African Americans who had played for the Negro Leagues before 1948. A player only had to have played one year in the Negro Leagues to qualify for these benefits.

Caucasian players who had played for MLB teams had to have four years of employment before qualifying for MLB medical and pension benefits. Several Caucasian MLB players who did not meet this requirement brought a lawsuit in U.S. district court alleging that the MLB affirmative action plan that provided medical and pension benefits to players of Negro Leagues after only one year of service but not for Caucasian players until after four years of service violated Title VII of the Civil Rights Act of 1964. The U.S. district court granted summary judgment to MLB. The plaintiffs appealed the decision. The U.S. court of appeals upheld the district court's decision. It affirmed the lower court's finding that the MLB affirmative action plan granting Negro League players medical and pension benefits under qualifications that were less than those applying to Caucasian players was lawful and not a violation of Title VII. The court of appeals stated:

The decision to provide benefits under the Negro League Plans only to individuals, all African-Americans, who were injured by MLB's policy of excluding members of their race from playing MLB baseball does not discriminate against Caucasians. Although the players who qualify under the Negro League Plans are all African-American, it was African-Americans and not Caucasians who were discriminated against on the basis of their race. It is true that only players who played in the Negro Leagues are eligible to receive benefits under the plans. It is also true, however, that the Negro Leagues were formed to provide the opportunity to play professional baseball to those who were otherwise excluded because of their race.

In short, the plans were adopted for the specific purpose of providing benefits to those who had been discriminated against by being denied the opportunity to play MLB baseball and to qualify for MLB benefits. To the extent that MLB sought to remedy in part its past discriminatory conduct, it acted honorably and decently and not out of an improper or invidious motive. MLB has thus shown a legitimate, non-discriminatory reason for its decision to provide benefits to former Negro League Players.

The court of appeals upheld the district court's grant of summary judgment to MLB.[48]

Ethics Questions

1. Assume you owned an MLB team before 1947 and believed that your business would fail if you integrated your team. Was your decision to exclude African American baseball players ethical? Define the ethical standards you would employ to reach your decision.
2. Did Major League Baseball act "honorably and decently" in adopting the preferential medical and pension benefits programs for African American players of the Negro Leagues? Argue the case for and against your position.
3. Was the affirmative action plan justified under the circumstances of this case?

Preferential Treatment of Native Americans

Section 703(b) language excludes "an Indian tribe" from the definition of employer. This exclusion reflects the historical legal treatment of Indian nations as sovereign, political entities. An identical exclusion appears in the **ADA**. Tribal employers are exempt from **Title VII** requirements under §701(b) of the **Civil Rights Act of 1964**. Thus, an employee of a tribal employer cannot sue for what would otherwise be a clear violation of **Title VII**.

Although **Title VII** prohibits discrimination on the basis of national origin, the **Native American Preference Exemption** allows employers on or near Indian reservations to prefer Indians to non-Indians. **Section 703(i)** authorizes preferential treatment in the hiring of Native Americans by Indian reservation businesses. A section of **Title VII** exempts its application to Native Americans:

Nothing contained in this subchapter shall apply to any business or enterprise on or near an Indian reservation with respect to any publicly announced employment practice of such business or enterprise under which a preferential treatment is given to any individual because he is an Indian living on or near a reservation.[49]

To invoke this exception, the employer must make a public announcement, and the employment must be located on or near an Indian reservation. In *Malabed v. North Slope Borough*,[50] the federal court held unconstitutional a local ordinance that gave employment preference to Native Americans, because the Inupiat Eskimo land in question was not a reservation and the ordinance violated the equal protection clause. Moreover, the preference is for Native Americans, in general, and may not be used for the exclusive benefit of one tribe to the exclusion of members of another tribe. When an otherwise qualified Hopi Indian was not hired by a power plant operator owned and operated by the Navajo nation, he could sue for employment discrimination under **Title VII.**[51] The courts use a subjective standard in deciding the proximity of the employer to a reservation in defining "near Indian reservations."

A state policy permitting only Native Americans to display and sell their handicrafts on state-owned property is not **reverse discrimination**, as no apparent discrimination against the white majority exists and the activity promotes Indian educational and cultural objectives.[52] Such preferences do not excuse acts of **reverse discrimination** by Native Americans, as was found to have occurred in *Garret v. Hodel.*[53] In that case, a Caucasian female employee who was the only non–American Indian senior manager within the Bureau of Indian Affairs received unfair performance evaluations, which made unfair and discriminatory remarks about her based on her race.

Related tribal activities, such as health care businesses, housing authorities, or gaming casinos or any other entity that furthers the economic interests of a tribe, are clearly exempt from the reach of **Title VII.** Recent case law suggests that a commercial activity owned by both a tribe and a nontribal entity will not receive exemption from **Title VII.** A few courts have held that Native Americans are also protected from race discrimination under both **Title VII** and **§1981.**

Federal courts of appeals have also held that age discrimination in employment coverage under the **ADEA**, when applied to Indian tribes, is contrary to the principle of tribal sovereign immunity.[54]

Human Resource Form
Acknowledgment of Policies

I acknowledge receipt of the following company policies as part of my hiring and orientation:

- Policy on Anti-Discrimination and Equal Opportunity
- Policy Against Harassment of Employees

I acknowledge that I have read and agree to comply with each of these policies, including any amendments to them. I promise I will refrain from any behavior that may be considered discriminatory or harassing with respect to others. I will do my best to promote a workplace that is free of hostile and discriminatory conduct. I will report any violation of company policies to my supervisor and, as required, to the human resources department.

Dated: ________________ ________________

Employee's signature

Key Terms and Concepts

- Civil War Amendments
- §1981
- §1983
- Equal Protection Clause
- Title VI of the Civil Rights Act of 1964
- Title VII of the Civil Rights Act of 1964
- Interstate Commerce Clause
- Executive Order 11246
- Civil Rights Act of 1991
- Compensatory damages
- Punitive damages
- Age Discrimination in Employment Act
- Americans with Disabilities Act
- Rehabilitation Act of 1973
- Immigration Reform and Control Act of 1986
- Motivating factor
- Race-norming
- Affirmative action
- Strict scrutiny review of Equal Protection
- Compelling governmental interest test
- Narrowly tailored plans
- Voluntary affirmative action plan
- Reverse discrimination
- Indian preferences exemption

Chapter Summary

- The history of civil rights in America was affected by compromises made at the time of the adoption of the Constitution, the imbalance in economic opportunities between northern and southern states, political power held by proponents of segregation for many decades, and U.S. Supreme Court decisions that narrowly interpreted the Constitution so as to deny Congress the opportunity to enact effective civil rights laws.

- Claimants alleging race or national origin discrimination may pursue claims for discrimination relating to employment contracts (i.e., essentially, they cover all employment claims) under §§1981 and 1983 of the U.S. Code, since these types do not have a limitation on recovery as do Title VII claims.

- The Civil Rights Act of 1964 prohibits employment discrimination based on race, color, religion, sex, or national origin; as amended, it applies to private employers of more than 15 employees and to the federal government as an employer and extends protection for pregnancy discrimination. Some applications of Title VII can be negated by conflicting federal statutes, including those relating to arbitration agreements, pension and retirement law, and labor law.

- The Civil Rights Act of 1991 expanded the remedies afforded Title VII claimants, although it eliminated race-norming in testing applicants and employees with regard to employment opportunities.

- Several other federal laws relate to equal employment opportunities, including Fair Employment and Housing Act, the Equal Pay Act, the Family and Medical Leave Act, the Rehabilitation Act, ADEA, and the ADA.

- An affirmative action plan is intended to assist disadvantaged persons who have suffered past discrimination with regard to employment, educational, or other vocational opportunities. It is also known as reverse discrimination when it favors members of race- or gender-defined minority communities over those from the historically favored community with respect to such programs.

■ Since affirmative action plans are a form of intentional discrimination, the courts require that the discrimination be as limited as possible to advance the objectives sought (i.e., "narrowly tailored") and that a compelling reason for the plan or program should be identified. Moreover, the plan may not "*unnecessarily trammel*" the interests of others and may not foreclose the employment or promotional opportunities of others.

■ For an affirmative action program to be lawful it must not impose undue burdens on nonminorities. The Supreme Court has articulated a compelling governmental interest test for racial preference programs, which must be narrowly tailored to address the issue.

■ Programs reserving positions for minorities solely on the basis of race are unconstitutional. This includes university admissions programs based on a racial quota system. However, programs that consider racial minority membership as one of many factors in granting admission may be lawful.

■ Although an employer may engage in a voluntary affirmative action plan when the appropriate preconditions exist, absent a court order as a remedy for the employer's past discrimination, neither a private nor a public employer is required by Title VII to adopt such a plan. An unresolved question for employers is whether a voluntary affirmative action plan must be "remedial" to be lawful under Title VII. Most affirmative action plans are remedial and thus are more defensible under an equal protection analysis. Absent a prior history of discrimination, such plans would likely be unlawful.

■ With respect to employment decisions, certain preferences exist favoring Native Americans working on or near Indian reservations; these are lawful due to the Indian preferences exemption within Title VII.

Online Student Support

- Loislaw legal research and writing assignments.
- Loislaw group projects and class presentations.
- Loislaw access, providing online research including up-to-date cases, statutes, rules, and regulations. Primary law for all 50 states and federal jurisdictions. Registration required for access to this resource.
- Practice questions, including sample true/false, multiple choice, and short answer questions to test your understanding of concepts.
- Additional human resource forms.
- Internet exercises.
- Blogs.
- Supplementary statutory and regulatory materials.

Case Problems

5.1 The Ninth Circuit Court of appeals was required to review a four-month disciplinary suspension as constituting illegal retaliation. The case involved discipline imposed on several employees who publicly protested an "affirmative action award" given by a local school board that was a major customer of their employer. How would the court rule as to the appropriateness of the discipline? When should the employer's economic interests prevail or control employee disciplinary matters? (*EEOC v. Crown Zellerbach Corp.*, 720 F.2d 1008 (9th Cir. 1983))

5.2 Would an employee of an employment agency state a constructive discharge claim under §1981 by alleging that she was compelled to quit because she was required by her employer to classify applicant callers by their accents and speech patterns?

5.3 Would a court find state action (which means that the state government is involved in the discrimination) where a restaurant (which discriminated) was leased to a private organization by a public authority that owned and operated an off-street parking and retail store building? (*Burton v. Wilmington Parking Authority*, 365 U.S. 715 (1961)) Do you think this would affect how you as a landlord would draft leases with prospective tenants? What duty, if any, should be imposed on a private landlord to ensure that the lessee is not violating discrimination laws?

5.4 If an affirmative action plan was justified due to a "manifest racial imbalance" could it still unnecessarily trammel the rights of non-African American employees? Rather than using race as one factor as in the Johnson decision, a Birmingham, Alabama, fire department made race the only factor for 50 percent of the promotions from its list of eligible candidates. How do you think the court should rule with regard to the quota for hiring within the fire department? Do you think such a quota would be more acceptable in an entry level position, as opposed to midlevel positions? How does a city utilize a percentage approach in its decision-making without appearing arbitrary to the court? (*In Re: Birmingham Reverse Discrimination Employment Litigation*, 20 F.3d 1525 (11th Cir. 1994))

5.5 Favoring members of one racial group over another is unlawful under Title VII and the Civil Rights Acts. Does the prohibition extend to discrimination involving equally qualified candidates of different races? (*Butta v. Anne Arundel County*, 473 F. Supp. 83 (D. Md. 1979))

End Notes

1. *Bryant v. Begin Manage Program*, 281 F.Supp.2d 561 (E.D. N.Y. 2003).
2. 421 U.S. 454 (1975).
3. 42 U.S.C. §2000e-2.
4. *Walker v. Sec. of Treasury*, 742 F. Supp.670 (N.D. Ga. 1990), *aff'd*, 953 F.2d 650 (11th Cir.), *cert. denied*, 506 U.S. 853 (1992).
5. *Espinoza v. Farah Manufacturing Co.*, 414 U.S. 86, 88 (1973).
6. *Fortino v. Quasar Co.*, 950 F.2d 389 (7th Cir. 1991).
7. *Garcia v. Spun Steak Co.*, 998 F.2d 1480 (9th Cir. 1993); *Garcia v. Gloor*, 618 F.2d 264 (5th Cir. 1980), *cert. denied*, 449 U.S. 1113 (1981).
8. *Phillips v. Martin Marietta Corp.*, 400 U.S. 542 (1971) (Court held employer rule forbidding employment of women with preschool age children as discriminatory).
9. *City of Los Angeles Department of Water and Power v. Manhart*, 435 U.S. 702 (1978).
10. See, generally, *EEOC Guidelines on Discrimination Because of Sex*, 29 C.F.R. §1604.11(a)(1)-(2).
11. 42 U.S.C. §§6101-107.
12. *Wards Cove Packing v. Atonio*, 490 U.S. 642 (1989); *Patterson v. McLean Credit Union*, 491 U.S. 164 (1989); *Martin v. Wilks*, 490 U.S. 755 (1989); *Price Waterhouse v. Hopkins*, 490 U.S. 228 (1989); and *Lorance v. AT & T Technologies, Inc.*, 490 U.S. 900 (1989).
13. *Meritor Savings Bank v. Vinson*, 477 U.S. 57, 70-73.
14. *Hunter v. Allis Chalmers Corp.*, 797 F.3d 1417 (7th Cir. 1986); EEOC, *Policy Guidance on Sexual Harassment*, 29 C.F.R. §1604.11(d).
15. *Burlington Industries, Inc. v. Ellerth*, 524 U.S. 742 (1998) and *Faragher v. Boca Raton*, 524 U.S. 775 (1998).
16. 41 C.F.R. 60-20.1.
17. 41 C.F.R. §60-2.33.
18. 20 U.S.C. §793(a).
19. 38 U.S.C. §4212(a).
20. 29 U.S.C. §793(c)(c)(2)(A).
21. 42 U.S.C. §2000d.
22. 28 C.F.R. §§42.101-112.
23. 42 U.S.C. §2000e-2(j).
24. Id. at 339-40 n20.
25. 401 U.S. 424, 430-01.
26. 427 U.S. 273 (1976).
27. 515 U.S. 200 (1995).
28. 515 U.S. at 237.
29. 438 U.S. 265 (1978).
30. 539 U.S. 306 (2003).
31. *Gratz v. Bollinger*, 539 US. 244 (2003).
32. *Sheet Metal Workers v. EEOC*, 478 U.S. 421, 495 (1986) (O'Connor, J., concurring in part and dissenting in part).
33. *Bakke*, supra, at 317 (opinion of Powell, J.).
34. *Sheet Metal Workers v. EEOC, supra*, at 495.

35. *Johnson v. Transportation Agency, Santa Clara* 480 U.S. 616, 638 (1987).
36. 476 U.S. 267 (1986).
37. 488 U.S. 469 (1989).
38. Id. at 480.
39. Id. at 499.
40. 495 F. Supp. 857 (N.D. of Ohio, 1980).
41. 480 U.S. 616 (1987).
42. *Doe v. Kamehameha Schools et al.*, 416 F.3d 1025 (9th Cir. 2005), *rehearing ordered* 441 F.3d 1029 (9th Cir. 2006).
43. *Weber*, 443 U.S. at 208.
44. 551 U.S. 701 (2007).
45. *Bass v. Board of County Commissioners, Orange County, Florida*, 256 F.3d 1095 (11th Cir. 2001).
46. *McDonald v. Santa Fe Trail Transportation Co.*, 427 U.S., 273 (1976).
47. *Carter v. O'Neill*, 78 Fed Appx. 978 (5th Cir. 2003).
48. *Moran v. Selig, as Commissioner of Major League Baseball*, 447 F.3d 748 (9th Cir. 2006).
49. 42 U.S.C. §2000e-2(i).
50. 42 F. Supp. 2d 927 (D. Alaska 1999), *aff'd* 335 F.3d 864 (9th Cir. 2003).
51. *Dawavendewa v. Salt River Project Agric. Improvements & Power Dist.*, 154 F.3d 1117 (9th Cir. 1998).
52. *Livingston v. Ewing*, 601 F.2d 1110 (10th Cir. 1979).
53. 717 F.Supp. 4 (D.D.C. 1989).
54. *EEOC v. Fond du Lac Heavy Equip. & Constr. Co.*, 986 F.2d 246 (8th Cir. 1993).

Chapter 6
Race, Color, and National Origin Discrimination

"I have a dream this afternoon that my four little children will not come up in the same young days that I came up within, but they will be judged on the basis of the content of their character, and not the color of their skin." —*Martin Luther King Jr., speech at Detroit civil rights rally, June 1963*

Learning Objectives

1. Define "race."
2. Distinguish between racial and color-based discrimination claims.
3. State the differences between racial and national origin discrimination.
4. Describe the employer defenses to race and color discrimination.
5. Identify the relief available under §1981 not available under Title VII.

Chapter Outline

- Introduction
- The Meaning of "Race" Under §1981
- Racial Discrimination Under Title VII

Case 6.1 McCullough v. Real Foods, Inc.
Case 6.2 Ash v. Tyson Foods, Inc.

- Management Application: Walgreen Settlement
- Culture as Racial Identification

Case 6.3 Hollins v. Atlantic Co.

- Other Forms of Race-Based Disparate Treatment Claims
- Management Application: Race Discrimination
- Racial Harassment
- Management Application: Advantages of §1981 Claims
- Color Discrimination
- Employer Defenses to Race and Color Discrimination

Case 6.4 CBOCS West, Inc. v. Humphries

- National Origin Discrimination
- Management Application: National Origin Discrimination
- Facility with English
- National Origin Harassment

Case 6.5 EEOC v. WC&M Enterprises, Inc. dba Streater-Smith Honda

- Human Resource Form: Manager's Receipt of Harassment Policy

Chapter Opening scenario

Mamdouh El-Hakem, a person of Arabic ancestry, sued his former employer BJY, Inc. and Gregg Young, the company's CEO, for employment racial discrimination under Title VII and §1981. His claims stemmed from Young's repeated references to El-Hakem as "Manny." Despite El-Hakem's strenuous objections, Young insisted on using the non-Arabic name rather than "Mamdouh," El-Hakem's given name. Young has openly expressed the opinion that a "Western" name would increase El-Hakem's chances for success and would be more acceptable to BJY's clientele. Is this behavior sufficient to create a racially hostile work environment? Are Young's actions sufficient to establish a discrimination claim?[1]

Introduction

Race
A term not defined in Title VII, but usually interpreted, in the context of discrimination, in terms of ancestry or the physical or cultural characteristics associated with a certain race.

Color Discrimination
Discrimination based on skin color, complexion, shade, or tone. May occur between persons of different races or between persons of the same race or ethnicity.

National Origin
Country or place from which an individual or at least some of his or her ancestors originated.

Title VII of the Civil Rights Act of 1964 is the best known of the federal laws that protect individuals from discrimination in employment based on, among other grounds, **race**, **color**, and **national origin**. It is important to note that the law is prohibitory in nature and does not require or compel employers to hire individuals with specific characteristics. As noted in our introduction of employment discrimination statutes, earlier civil rights statutes provide remedies against discrimination by private employers based on race and against conspiracies to discriminate on the basis of race. The first of these statutes is **§1981(a)**, which was the first section of the Civil Rights Act of 1866, and the second, formerly Section 2 of the Ku Klux Klan Act, is now codified as 42 U.S.C. **§1983**. Under **§1983**, private litigants have the right to sue for deprivation of constitutional and federal statutory rights by persons acting under "color of law" (i.e., acting under governmental authority). The two statutes are better known by their code sections than by their formal names. In addition, **Executive Order No. 11246** prohibits race and color discrimination by federal contractors or subcontractors.

In fiscal year 2009, the EEOC received almost 34,000 charges of **racial discrimination**. This reflected statistic reflected a recent surge in **race** and **color-based discrimination** filings. The EEOC received more than 11,100 filings in that same period for charges involving **national origin discrimination**, an increase of over 5 percent from the prior year.

The Meaning of "Race" Under §1981

Section 1981 was originally enacted as the **Civil Rights Act of 1866**. Congress passed it during the Reconstruction Era following the end of the Civil War. The act was passed to eliminate the effects of the Black Codes enacted by southern state legislatures. In relevant part, **§1981** states:

> *All persons within the jurisdiction of the United States shall have the same right . . . to make and enforce contracts . . . and to the full and equal benefit of all laws and proceedings . . . as is enjoyed by white citizens.*

In its 1976 decision in *Runyon v. McCrary*, the Supreme Court held that although **§1981** does not itself use the word "race," the statute forbids all "racial" discrimination in the making of private as well as public contracts.[2] A conspiracy to discriminate based on race or national origin is known as a §1985 claim.

Section 1985
A federal law protecting individuals from racial and gender-based discrimination in employment and from interference with contractual, property, and other rights. Often involves conspiracies to harm or injure others based on race or gender.

Racial Discrimination Claims Under Title VII

Causes of action for violations under both **Title VII** and **§1981** are most often encountered in lawsuits brought by minority group members. However, the question sometimes arises whether these laws protect Caucasians, as well, from racial discrimination. Yes, these laws are color blind. Members of the white or Caucasian race are protected under both **Title VII** and **§1981**. They enjoy the same protection from **racial discrimination** as do members of other racial groups.

The following decision in *McCullough v. Real Foods, Inc.* clarifies the three phases of evidentiary proof employed by the courts in deciding a **race discrimination** case. During the first phase, the plaintiff proves the elements of its case. In the second, the employer is entitled to present proof of nondiscriminatory reasons for the employment decision. In the third phase, the plaintiff presents proof that the employer's reasons for making its adverse decision are pretextual. With the introduction of the pretextual proof, the plaintiff requests the trier of fact to make the reasonable inference of intentional discrimination against plaintiff.

Comparative Qualifications
Comparison of the particular skills, education, experience, or abilities possessed by qualified applicants or employees.

CASE 6.1

RACIAL DISCRIMINATION INFERRED IN PROMOTION OF UNQUALIFIED CAUCASIAN OVER A QUALIFIED AFRICAN AMERICAN EMPLOYEE

MCCULLOUGH V. REAL FOODS, INC.

140 F.3d 1123 (8th Cir. 1998)

U.S. Court of Appeals for the Eighth Circuit

Facts. Cynthia McCullough was a college-educated black woman who had worked at a deli counter in a grocery store owned by relatives until the store was sold. After the sale, McCullough continued working at the deli, where the store's owner, Ron Meredith, supervised her. Kathy Craven, a white woman, was hired to work part-time in the deli. She had prior experience as a checker and as a baker. However, she had no prior experience as a deli worker, and she had only a sixth-grade education. Her reading, writing, and mathematical skills were poor, and she required the assistance of McCullough in performing several deli functions. She could not, for example, calculate prices by herself, and she had difficulty reading recipes, according to McCullough.

Three months after Craven's arrival, Ron Meredith decided to appoint one of his deli employees "deli manager." At this time, McCullough and Craven were the only two deli employees. Meredith did not set up formal criteria for this employment decision, but rather relied on subjective criteria such as his perception of each of the two employees' abilities, work ethic, and dedication to the job.

McCullough believes that the decision to promote Craven over McCullough was an act of intentional racial discrimination. In support, she points to her superior education and more extensive deli experience. Additionally, she points to an incident in which Meredith greeted a white employee while ignoring her. The federal district court granted the employer a motion for summary judgment in its favor, and McCullough appealed to the court of appeals.

Issue. Was McCullough subjected to racial discrimination in employment?

Language of the Court. Hansen, C.J.: **We analyze the facts under the burden-shifting framework set out in McDonnell Douglas and its progeny. Under this framework, McCullough must first present evidence that will establish a prima facie case. In this failure to promote case, McCullough must demonstrate the following four elements: (1) that she belonged to a protected class, (2) that she met the minimum qualifications and applied for the position, (3) that despite her qualifications she was denied the position, and (4) that her employer promoted a person of similar qualifications who was not a member of the protected group.**

She satisfied all four elements: she is black, she was qualified for the job of deli manager, she was not given the job, and the job was in fact given to a minimally qualified white woman. A rebuttable presumption of discrimination is thus established. Real Foods has articulated several nondiscriminatory reasons for passing over McCullough as a candidate for deli manager. These reasons include the following: she planned to quit soon, she refused to work past 3:00 P.M., she wanted a large amount of time off, and she refused to accept the job for less than nine dollars an hour. We need not examine the evidentiary basis for these articulated reasons. We need only determine whether they constitute one or more facially nondiscriminatory reasons for the employment decision. We hold that they do.

When, as here, the prima facie case has been successfully rebutted, the presumption of discrimination "drops out of the picture." The burden then shifts back to the plaintiff to present evidence sufficient to support two findings — the plaintiff must present evidence which creates a fact issue as to whether the employer's proffered reasons are mere pretext. Second, she must present

evidence which creates a reasonable inference that the adverse employment decision was an act of intentional racial discrimination.

We first address the question of whether McCullough met her burden of creating an issue of fact as to whether Real Foods' proffered nondiscriminatory reasons are pretextual. The district court held that she met this burden, and we agree. Real Foods' proffered reasons centered on statements McCullough herself allegedly made. McCullough claims that she never made such statements, and that Real Foods' proffered reasons are predicated on bald-faced lies. These allegations of falsity, if proved, would certainly support an inference in a reasonable jury that the proffered reasons were mere pretext rather than the actual impetus behind the decision.

We next address the question of whether McCullough has met her burden of creating a reasonable inference that Real Foods' proffered nondiscriminatory reasons were in reality a pretext for discrimination. Both this court and the Supreme Court have made clear that a plaintiff in a pretext case must establish "both that the reason was false, and that discrimination was the real reason." (Citation omitted.)

We know from our experience that more often than not people do not act in a totally arbitrary manner, without any underlying reasons, especially in a business setting. Thus, when all legitimate reasons for rejecting an applicant have been eliminated as possible reasons for the employer's actions, it is more likely than not the employer, who we generally assume acts only with some reason, based his decision on an impermissible consideration such as race.

Decision. Yes. McCullough presented evidence sufficient to support a reasonable inference that Real Foods' failure to promote her to the position of deli manager was motivated by racial animus. That inference is enough to prevent summary judgment for the employer.

CASE QUESTIONS

Critical Legal Thinking. The court criticized the use of subjective criteria because employers could easily mask intentions to discriminate. In light of this decision, what place do managers' subjective impressions have in managing employees?

Business Ethics. To rebut the plaintiff's prima facie case, what nondiscriminatory reasons did the employer assert in its defense in the *McCullough* case? If you were the judge, would you have found a reasonable inference of intentional discrimination?

Contemporary Business. Courts are increasingly involved in contested racial discrimination cases. Do you think society imposes on them the role of "second-guessing" personnel decisions?

In the *Ash v. Tyson Foods* decision, the Supreme Court considered the issue of the use of a racial epithet and its impact on a decision not to provide two African American employees the opportunity to be promoted. The Supreme Court held that the evidence that the person making the promotional decisions used the term "boy" could be evidence of evil racial bias. The speaker's meaning may depend on various factors, including context, inflection, tone of voice, local custom, and historical usage. Another part of the decision appears to relax the proof plaintiffs' must show to prove pretextual racial discrimination.

CASE 6.2

COURTS MUST LOOK FOR EVIDENCE BEYOND THE USE OF PEJORATIVE TERMS TO DETERMINE AN INTENT TO RACIALLY DISCRIMINATE

ASH V. TYSON FOODS, INC.

546 U.S. 454 (2006)

Supreme Court of the United States

Facts. Anthony Ash and John Hithon were two African American superintendents at a poultry plant operated by Tyson Foods. They had sought promotions to fill two open shift manager positions. Instead, two Caucasian male employees were selected. The rejected employees filed suit in federal court alleging that they had been discriminated against on the basis of their race in violation of **§1981** and **Title VII** of the Civil Rights Act of 1964. At the time of trial they offered evidence that Hatley, the Tyson's manager who made the promotional decisions, had referred to each of them in the past as "boy." They argued that this name-calling was evidence of intent to racially discriminate against them.

Following a jury award to plaintiffs, the court granted employer's motion for a judgment in its favor. The Court of Appeals for the Eleventh Circuit affirmed the judgment in favor of the defendant. Ash and Hithon appealed to the Supreme Court, which granted *certiorari* to clarify the standard of determining pretext in employment decision-making.

Issue. Is use of the term "boy" by an employer's manager sufficient to establish evidence of intent to racially discriminate?

Language of the Court. Per Curiam: **First, there was evidence that Tyson's plant manager, who made the disputed hiring decisions, had referred on some occasions to each of the petitioners as "boy." Petitioners argued this was evidence**

of discriminatory animus. The Court of Appeals disagreed, holding that "while the use of 'boy' when modified by a racial classification like 'black' or 'white' is evidence of discriminatory intent, the use of 'boy' alone is not evidence of discrimination."

Second, the Court of Appeals, in finding petitioners' evidence insufficient, cited one of its earlier precedents and stated: "Pretext can be established through comparing qualifications only when 'the disparity in qualifications is so apparent as virtually to jump off the page and slap you in the face."(Citation omitted.) . . . Under this Court's decisions, qualifications evidence may suffice, at least in some circumstances, to show pretext.

[The court of appeals when it utilized] the visual image of words jumping off the page to slap you (presumably a court) in the face is unhelpful and imprecise as an elaboration of the standard for inferring pretext from superior qualifications. Federal courts have articulated various other standards, and in this case the Court of Appeals qualified its statement by suggesting that superior qualifications may be probative of pretext when combined with other evidence. . . . This is not the occasion to define more precisely what standard should govern pretext claims based on superior qualifications. Today's decision, furthermore, should not be read to hold that petitioners' evidence necessarily showed pretext. The District Court concluded otherwise. It suffices to say here that some formulation other than the test the Court of Appeals articulated in this case would better ensure that trial courts reach consistent results.

Decision. Yes. The usage of a racially offensive epithet can be proof of discriminatory intent. Also, the Court recognized that a plaintiff can prove discrimination by comparing his or her qualifications to those of others who were more favorably treated.

On Remand to the Court of Appeals for the Eleventh Circuit. The Court of Appeals concluded again that the use of "boy" by the supervisor was not sufficient, either alone or with the other evidence, to allow a jury reasonably to find that Tyson's stated reasons for not promoting the plaintiffs were due to racial discrimination. It found the usages were conversational and as found by the district court were nonracial in context. But even if somehow construed as racial, the court concluded that the comments were ambiguous stray remarks and insufficient circumstantial evidence of bias to provide a reasonable basis for a finding of racial discrimination in the denial of the promotions. The court found it significant that the statements were remote in time to the employment decision, totally unrelated to the promotions at issue, and showed no indication of general racial bias in the decision-making process at the plant or by Hatley.

CASE QUESTIONS

Critical Legal Thinking. Is the Court's definition of pretext understandable and concrete enough to be enforced? Consider, for example, the statement that "disparities in qualifications must be of such weight and significance that no reasonable person, in the exercise of impartial judgment, could have chosen the candidate selected over the plaintiff for the job in question."

Business Ethics. If you were sitting on a jury considering the facts in *Ash*, how relevant is the elapse of time between the occurrence of the insults against him and the employer's adverse actions against him?

Contemporary Business. The courts require fairly specific causal connections between words or actions experienced in the workplace and adverse hiring decisions. What advice would you give to a personnel manager who must investigate claims such as the ones presented in this case?

Management Application
Walgreen Settlement

Racial discrimination in employment was outlawed by **Title VII** of the Civil Rights Act of 1964. However, even today vestiges of race and color discrimination appear in employment decisions. The Equal Employment Opportunity Commission (EEOC) adopted the "Eradicating Racism & Colorism from Employment" (E-RACE) initiative to bring actions against employers who engage in race and color discrimination. Following its adoption of the E-RACE Initiative, the EEOC has pursued many high-profile race- and color-discrimination cases. Consider the following case.

The EEOC sued the Walgreen Company, which operates more than 6,000 stores throughout the country, for engaging in race and color discrimination. The charge asserted was that Walgreen systematically discriminated against African Americans for promotion to retail managers and discriminated against pharmacy employees in promotions, compensation, and assignments because of race and color. In addition to the EEOC action, several African American employees of Walgreen brought civil lawsuits against the company.

The EEOC filed its complaint against Walgreen. The case was brought in the U.S. district court. After investigation of the charges, Walgreen Company agreed to settle all charges — the EEOC action and the private lawsuits — by agreeing to pay $24 million to a class of African American employees and former employees nationwide. The federal court overseeing the case ruled that the consent decree is fair, reasonable, and adequate. The award is one of the largest awards obtained by the EEOC in a race- and color-discrimination lawsuit.

The court also issued an injunction prohibiting the Walgreen Company from engaging in similar conduct in the future. The consent decree requires Walgreen to employ outside consultants to develop standardized, nondiscriminatory store assignment and promotion standards and to review Walgreen's employment practices. The EEOC retained jurisdiction over the consent decree for five years.

An EEOC spokesperson said, "The EEOC's case is a good example of the Commission's renewed emphasis on class and systemic litigation and furthers the agency's E-RACE Initiative, which is designed to address major issues of race and color discrimination."[3]

Discussion Questions

1. In reforming its corporate policies, what would be the content of a new Corporate Ethics Compliance Policy for Walgreen?
2. Does systematic race and color discrimination by an employer constitute a particularly harmful form of discrimination?
3. Was the injunction issued in this case necessary? Why or why not?

Concept Summary
Proving a §1981 Race Discrimination

A plaintiff must prove:

- intentional discrimination proved by direct or circumstantial evidence; or,
- if lacking direct evidence, the plaintiff may invoke the inference of unlawful discrimination through the *McDonnell Douglas* analysis, including sufficient evidence of pretext.

While many remarks can fall into the "stray remark" category, some statements clearly reflect the employer's discriminatory animus (or intent) toward the plaintiff. Apparently, some courts require that quite a bit of proof be adduced by the plaintiff to defeat an employer's motion for summary judgment in a **§1981** case.

> ***Example:*** Within three days of beginning employment as a public school teacher, Mary King claimed, Hardesty, a school administrator, had (1) asked King if she had white in her blood because she was light-skinned; (2) told King that his family had been slaveholders; (3) told King that "white people teach black kids, African American students, better than someone from their own race"; (4) asked King how she felt about the word "nigger" and used the word in King's presence; (5) asked King if she dated white males and said "once you go black, you never go back"; (6) told racial jokes in the office; (7) referred to African American male employees as "big black bucks" and "my boys"; (8) referred to African American students as "slaves," "crack babies," and "ghetto kids"; (9) used the words "ho" and "whore" to refer to female African American students; and (10) made racially derogatory statements about the parents of African American students. King was offended by Hardesty's comments and asked him, on multiple occasions, to refrain from making such comments, but Hardesty would respond: "I can run this school any way I want to"; "No one questions my actions because I am the administrator"; or "I can run [the school] any damn way I please." While admitting that the administrator made offensive racial remarks to King, the school district argued that they did not lead to an inference of racial animus toward King. While concluding that many of the foregoing remarks fell into the "stray remark" category not supporting a **§1981** claim, the court found that Hardesty's statement "white people teach black kids . . . better than someone from their own race," was evidence that directly reflected a discriminatory attitude.[4]

Other courts have held that use of racially inflammatory epithets is far more indicative of discriminatory intent. In one case, the employer unsuccessfully argued that its supervisor did not contribute to a hostile work environment when it used the word "*n*_____." In commenting on the word, the court stated, "perhaps no single act can more quickly alter the conditions of employment and create an abusive working environment . . . than the use of an unambiguously racial epithet . . . by a supervisor in the presence of his subordinates . . . [T]he fact that black employees also may have spoken the term . . . does not mitigate the harm caused by [the supervisor's] use of that epithet; a supervisor's use of the term impacts the work environment far more severely than use by co-equals."[5]

Culture as Racial Identification

Employers are permitted to insist that employees conform to reasonable grooming standards. But what is the legal effect of grooming standards that intrude into areas of cultural identification? Specifically, in the following case, an employer's grooming standards sought to eliminate employee use of a hairstyle identified with members of a particular race. The following case is instructive because few cases involve direct evidence of intent to discriminate based on enforcement of grooming standards. In these cases, plaintiffs must rely on circumstantial rather than direct evidence to prove employment discrimination.

CASE 6.3

DISCIPLINING EMPLOYEES FOR HAIRSTYLES MAY SUGGEST INTENT TO DISCRIMINATE

HOLLINS V. ATLANTIC CO.

188 F.3d 652 (6th Cir. 1999)

U.S. Court of Appeals for the Sixth Circuit

Facts. Atlantic Company, Inc. was a manufacturing company in Willoughby Hills, Ohio, where Eunice Hollins, an African American woman, had worked as a machine operator since July 25, 1994. Atlantic's grooming policy states in relevant part: "Women should have a neat and well groomed hair style. Rollers and other hair setting aids are not permitted. For safety, women may be required to have their hair tied back." Another section of Atlantic's policy manual describes Atlantic's personal appearance policies more generally: "When it comes to your appearance as part of our Company, there are certain standards important to our operation which you must follow. We don't ask just some of our people to follow these standards, but that everyone follow them."

On August 17, 1994, Hollins arrived at work with her hair styled in a fashion known as "finger waves." The foreman informed Hollins that her style was unacceptable to the company because it was "too different" and did not meet company policy. Nevertheless, he later testified that by his standards and those of the company, the employee's hairstyle was neat and well groomed, and safe, but that it was also "eye catching." The next day Hollins appeared at work with the same hairstyle. Another plant supervisor informed her that the style was unacceptable and did not meet company guidelines or policy. He told Hollins that if she did not like the policy, she should not work at Atlantic. A plant manager also thought the hairstyle was again "eye catching" and, therefore, inappropriate. Hollins subsequently changed her hair to a plain style that she did not prefer. The company's antagonistic attitude toward her hairstyle continued until Hollins filed discrimination complaints, alleging that she had been subject to racial discrimination in the application of the appearance and grooming standards.

Issue. Can a disparate treatment case of racial discrimination arise from an employer's grooming standards?

Language of the Court. Ryan, C.J.: **This is a case in which an employer's supervisors undertook to evaluate the suitability of a female employee's hairstyle and, not surprisingly, got in over their heads. Eunice Hollins, an African-American, sued her employer, and its associated companies, collectively hereinafter "Atlantic," alleging unlawful disparate treatment on the basis of race under [§1981, Title VII and a state statute] in application of Atlantic's personal grooming standards to Hollins' hairstyle preferences. The district court held that Hollins failed to make out a prima facie case on either theory and entered summary judgment for Atlantic. We reverse the district court's decision as to the disparate treatment claim, affirm as to the retaliation claim, and remand the case for further proceedings.**

There is no dispute that the plaintiff belongs to a protected class. The district court [granted summary judgment in favor of the employer because] she "presented no evidence that any supervisor . . . determined that a non-protected employee wore a comparable hairstyle and was not notified of being in violation of the . . . policy." . . . Here, however, [Hollins'] affidavit [submitted to the court regarding the employer's motion for summary judgment] assert[s] that white women wore identical hairstyles — i.e., engaged in the identical, not just comparable, conduct — but received different treatment. Moreover, the affidavits establish that the relevant employees all dealt with the same supervisors and Atlantic's policy manual.

Taking the [plaintiff's] affidavits as true [upon appeal], we conclude that Hollins has raised a question of fact whether Atlantic's grooming policy — which she claims was not applied to the white women — was a pretext for its treatment of Hollins. Indeed, [the supervisors] both testified that Hollins' hairstyles fit within the express language of Atlantic's policy as "neat and well groomed," but still violated a separate unwritten expression of policy, apparently developed specifically for Hollins, related to whether the styles were "eye catching" or otherwise called attention to her. Under these circumstances, a jury could reasonably infer that Atlantic applied its grooming policy to Hollins in an unlawfully discriminatory manner when it singled her out for different treatment.

Decision. Yes. Hollins's evidence of disparate treatment is sufficient to rebut Atlantic's defense of safety standards and permit a fact finder to infer unlawful discrimination.

CASE QUESTIONS

Critical Legal Thinking. Why did the plaintiff pursue both Title VII and §1981 remedies in her action against her employer? Does this decision address an employee's personal privacy?

Business Ethics. What boundaries of personal grooming may the employer can enforce? Must the offending grooming standard be identified with cultural characteristics to be discriminatory?

Contemporary Business. If not so related to culture standards or a medical condition, could an employer enforce, for example, personal hygiene standards?

Note: This case is one in which courts have begun to recognize a subset of **racial discrimination**; namely, **personal appearance discrimination**. For an employee to prevail in a **racial discrimination** case based on dress and grooming preferences that reflect cultural identity, he or she will have to establish a clear relationship between the grooming issue and the adverse action taken. For example, an African American employee who regularly came to work dressed in an African style of clothing and wearing his or her hair in dreadlocks or cornrows would have to cite an employer's comments and actions regarding those choices to establish a **Title VII** case based on racial and race-related personal appearance discrimination. If the employee failed to do so, the employer would prevail.[6]

Personal Appearance Discrimination
Unfavorable treatment due to a person's outward appearance, irrespective of sex, with regard to bodily condition or characteristics, manner or style of dress, or manner or style of personal grooming, including hair style and facial hair. Not protected under federal law, but subject to a few state laws (relative to height and weight) and municipal ordinances.

Other Forms of Race-Based Disparate Treatment Claims

Racial discrimination takes many forms. Courts have held it illegal for employers to adversely treat employees who maintained intimate associations with minorities.[7] To eradicate the vestiges of race discrimination, courts have interpreted Title VII broadly. For example, it has been found offensive for employers to prevent their hiring managers from recruiting and hiring minority members.[8] Making adverse employment decisions by relying on assumptions based on racial stereotypes about how people behave creates substantial legal risk for an employer. Such practices expose employers to the risk of both individual and class-action lawsuits.

Discriminatory practices persisted in some workplaces for quite some time. In court decisions issued as long as twenty years after the Civil Rights Act of 1964 was enacted, courts had to deal with the employers' segregation of lockers, recreation areas, and even restrooms.[9] Regardless of the reason, an employer may not intentionally assign members of minority groups to sales territories composed of minorities.[10]

The State of California as recently as 2005 routinely segregated prisoners by **race** when they first entered or reentered prison. The U.S. Supreme Court held the practice as unconstitutional, and the state entered into a consent decree to change its practices. Reviewed in *Johnson v. State of California*,[11] this segregation was defended on the grounds that it reduced the violence perpetrated by race-based gangs within the prison population. The Supreme Court rejected the claim that the policy was "neutral" because all prisoners were "equally" segregated. The Court held that racial classifications must receive strict scrutiny review, even when they may be said to affect the races equally. The case was remanded to the Ninth Circuit Court of Appeals. Upon remand, the State of California desegregated its prison housing.

Strict scrutiny involves thorough judicial review to determine if a classification of a group of persons (such as by race) interferes with a fundamental right (such as the right to a public education) or violates due process or equal protection under the U.S. Constitution. A compelling governmental need must be shown for the disputed issue to survive the constitutional challenge.

Management Application
Race Discrimination

Race discrimination sometimes results from what looks like a race-neutral rule that has, in practice, a discriminatory effect. Consider the following case. The town of Harrison, New Jersey, is a small, primarily white community located in Hudson County, New Jersey. Harrison adopted Ordinance 747, stipulating that "all officers and employees of the Town shall, as a condition of employment, be bona fide residents of the Town." The implementation of this ordinance over a number of years resulted in a town workforce in which none of the 51 police officers, 55 firefighters, or 80 nonuniformed employees was black.

Although only 0.2 percent of Harrison's population is black, the town is clearly aligned with Essex County to the west and is considered an extension of the adjacent city of Newark. Adjacent counties are within an easy commute of Harrison. By reason of its geographic location and the flow of transportation facilities, Harrison could reasonably be viewed as a functional component of Newark and as part of Essex County. Newark's population is approximately 60 percent black. Essex County's civilian labor force totals 391,612, of which 130,397 (or 33.3 percent) are black.

Several blacks from the Newark area applied for employment with the town of Harrison, but they were rejected because they did not meet the residency requirement. The National Association for the Advancement of Colored People (NAACP), Newark branch, sued the town for race discrimination in violation of Title VII. The U.S. district court dismissed the plaintiff's complaint. The NAACP appealed. The U.S. court of appeals held that the residency requirement of the town of Harrison was a neutral rule that caused a racially discriminatory effect and therefore violated Title VII of the Civil Rights Act of 1964. The court stated:

> *For all practical purposes, Harrison has no black residents. Thus, to limit employment or applications for employment to residents effectively excludes black persons from employment by the municipality. There is strong evidence that, if the residency requirement were removed, qualified black persons would seek positions with Harrison's municipal government. Thus, Harrison's facially neutral residency requirements have been shown to have a disproportionate impact upon black persons.*

The U.S. court of appeals held that the plaintiffs had established that Harrison's residency ordinance constituted disparate-impact race discrimination in violation of Title VII of the Civil Rights Act of 1964. The court issued an injunction against enforcement of the ordinance.[12]

Discussion Questions

1. What is the rationale behind town ordinances requiring that all town employees be residents? What are the advantages of having town employees who are also residents? What are the disadvantages? Was the Harrison residency requirement ethical?
2. What problems might arise with the concept of equal employment opportunity if city employees must be city residents?
3. Would a residency requirement rule cause disparate impact discrimination if it were adopted by New York City or Los Angeles?

Racial Harassment

Courts have determined that **racial harassment**, like **racial discrimination,** violates **Title VII**. For facts to be actionable, the harassment must be so **severe and pervasive** as to be distinguishable from a normal employment relationship and create a **racially hostile work environment**. Thus, an employer's careless or intentional tolerance of an ongoing pattern of racially offensive or derogatory comments can lead to the filing of a **Title VII** lawsuit.

What is a **hostile work environment**? As in other forms of legally prohibited discrimination, employer liability attaches when the employer fails to take reasonable steps to investigate or prevent **harassment.** Isolated incidents will not be sufficient grounds for a harassment case to proceed to trial. Many courts have generally recognized repeated demeaning racial statements as constituting sufficient proof to hold the employer liable for **racial harassment.** Simple rudeness is insufficient to prove a hostile workplace. To be actionable, the misconduct must be based on **race** considerations.

Courts have generally held that circumstances could be deemed **severe and pervasive** enough to support a **racial harassment** claim when:

- racial insults continued on a near-daily basis;[13]
- supervisors referred to African American subordinates in a racially inflammatory manner;[14] and
- the plaintiff was subjected to daily racial slurs, offensive jokes, and concerted isolation by co-workers.[15]

The facts in the following circumstances did not support a racial harassment claim:

- the racist statements or behavior occurred on only one occasion and were not deemed pervasive or severe;[16] and
- two racially offensive comments were made over a two-year period. The two comments, alone without other evidence, did not create a racially offensive environment.[17]

Finally, a federal court held that an objective standard, and not the plaintiff's perception, determined whether a racially **hostile work environment** existed.[18] The incidents must affect the employee's work performance.[19]

Applying the Law Developed Under Sexual Harassment

As we will study in the chapter on sex discrimination, the Supreme Court in 1998 issued two landmark sexual harassment decisions: *Burlington Industries, Inc. v. Ellerth*[20] and *Faragher v. City of Boca Raton.*[21] Lower courts quickly adopted these two decisions for use in the context of **racial harassment**. Also in the 1998 term, the Court decided that same-sex harassment was actionable under **Title VII**.

The federal Court of Appeals for the Eighth Circuit has extended the application in that case to include **racial harassment** of a subordinate African American employee by his African American supervisor.[22] Thus, same-race racial harassment can be actionable. **Hostile work environments** are often established through the testimony of fellow employees. The trier of fact will heavily weigh their perceptions for reliability.

Management Application
Advantages of §1981 Claims

- Before the Civil Rights Act of 1991 amended it, **§1981** addressed race-based contract claims. The amendment did not change in that it applies only to racial discrimination. It does not apply to discrimination based on gender, religion, or national origin, as would a **Title VII** claim.
- In its current form, **§1981** allows employees who allege intentional discrimination (e.g., disparate treatment) to seek remedies under both **§1981** and **Title VII**.
- Victims of race discrimination may prefer to pursue a **§1981** claim to one under **Title VII** because **§1981** involves fewer administrative procedures than **Title VII**, enjoys a longer statute of limitations, and does not cap damages. In addition, parties may be added to a **§1981** lawsuit who were not named in the original EEOC charge (e.g., an employee's union can be added as a co-defendant in the litigation after the process has begun).
- Subject to caps, **§1981** presents another advantage over **Title VII** in that the period for which back pay may be awarded is not limited. **Title VII** limits back pay to a period beginning two years before the charge was filed.[23]

Color Discrimination

One court has defined the term *"color"* as referring to skin hue "such as in the case where a dark-color African-American individual is discriminated against in favor of a light-colored African-American individual." The EEOC describes **color discrimination** as follows:

> Even though race and color clearly overlap, they are not synonymous. Thus, color discrimination can occur between persons of different races or ethnicities, or between persons of the same race or ethnicity. Although Title VII does not define "color," the courts and the Commission read "color" to have its commonly understood meaning—pigmentation, complexion, or skin shade or tone. Thus, color discrimination occurs when a person is discriminated against based on the lightness, darkness, or other color characteristic of the person.

Concept Summary
Proving Color Discrimination

A plaintiff must prove that the claimant:

- is a member of a protected group;
- was subject to an adverse employment action;
- was qualified for the position; and
- was replaced by an individual outside the protected class or was treated less favorably than a similarly situated employee outside of the protected class.[24]

Although such claims are very rare, a complaint based solely on discrimination due to the pigmentation of one's skin has been recognized in **Title VII** litigation. Thus, when Tracy Walker, a light-skinned African American, was terminated for poor performance by her dark-skinned African American supervisor at the IRS, her **color discrimination** claim was recognized as a claim distinct from a racial discrimination claim.[25]

Employer Defenses to Race and Color Discrimination

Courts have rejected the employer's invocation of a **bona fide occupational qualification (BFOQ)** as an affirmative defense to **race** and **color discrimination** claims. *Race and color may never be BFOQs.*

Section 1981 does not provide a cause of action against state (i.e., governmental) actors; instead, claims against them or allegations of **§1981** violations must be brought pursuant to **§1983**. State **statutes of limitation** often provide longer periods in which to sue under **§1981** (suits against private parties) than under **§1983** (suits against governmental agencies). To avoid the bar of an elapsed statute under **§1983**, a plaintiff may not sue a governmental entity for a violation under **§1981**. The Supreme Court decision in *Jett v. Dallas Independent School District*[26] held that **§1981** does not provide a remedy against governmental actors. Many, but not all, federal courts of appeals have held that the Civil Rights Act of 1991 did not disturb the holding in the *Jett* decision. Whether this undecided issue among the circuits will be ultimately resolved by the U.S. Supreme Court remains an open question.

> ***Example:*** In September 2003, McGovern, a Caucasian male, filed a complaint of race discrimination with the EEOC against his employer, the City of Philadelphia, but did not sue within 90 days after receiving his right-to-sue letter from the EEOC. Terminated in December 2004, McGovern did not file his civil rights violation lawsuit until almost three years later. The Pennsylvania statute for actions under **§1981** is four years and under **§1983** two years. Having lost the opportunity to sue under Title VII or **§1983**, McGovern tried to avail himself of the longer four-year statute under **§1981**. He lost because the federal court of appeals held that his misguided attempt could not revive an elapsed statute against a governmental agency.[27]

In the following decision, the Supreme Court considered whether **§1981** of the **Civil Rights Act of 1866** extends its reach to **retaliation** claims as well as to claims of **race discrimination**.

CASE 6.4

SECTION 1981 CLAIMS ENCOMPASS RETALIATION AS WELL AS RACE CLAIMS

CBOCS WEST, INC. V. HUMPHRIES

553 U.S. 442 (2008)

Supreme Court of the United States

Facts. Hedrick Humphries, an African American male, was an associate manager at a Cracker Barrel restaurant. The federal court of appeals decision on which the Supreme Court granted *certiorari* provided the factual context for the question presented to the Court. Humphries's reviews during his first two years of employment were "generally excellent," and his immediate supervisor characterized his performance as "his best associate manager." Upon a change in supervisors, he began to receive negative performance reviews. He alleged that his supervisor regularly made racially insulting remarks including "all African Americans are drunk or high on drugs" and that "all Mexicans have a bunch of kids" and that the supervisor who was a Caucasian was "there for the white people" and that he was "going to take care of the white people."

Despite Humphries's complaints to upper management, the restaurant chain never launched an investigation. After he complained to his manager that other associate managers were treating other African American employees unfairly, he claimed he was berated for "going outside the management group." Following his dismissal, Humphries claimed he was terminated not only because of his race but also for his prior complaints to managers that another black co-worker had been dismissed for race-based reasons. He was issued a right-to-sue letter by the EEOC and then filed a complaint based on race discrimination and retaliation under **Title VII** and **§1981**. After several procedural missteps, his case was dismissed, and he appealed to the Court of Appeals for the Seventh Circuit, which held that retaliation was a basis for bringing suit under **§1981**. Cracker Barrel appealed to the U.S. Supreme Court, and the Court granted *certiorari*.

Issue. Does **§1981** forbid retaliation against an individual who complains of discrimination against others?

Language of the Court. Breyer, J.: **CBOCS points to the plain text of §1981 and . . . concludes [it] "does not provide for a cause of action based on retaliation." But that fact alone is not sufficient to carry the day. After all, this Court has long held that the statutory text of §1981's sister statute, §1982, provides protection from retaliation for reasons related to the enforcement of the express statutory right.**

Second, CBOCS argues that Congress, in 1991 when it reenacted §1981 with amendments, intended the reenacted statute not to cover retaliation. CBOCS rests this conclusion primarily upon the fact that Congress did not include an explicit anti-retaliation provision or the word "retaliation" in the new statutory language — although Congress has included explicit anti-retaliation language in other civil rights statutes. We believe, however . . . there was no need for Congress to include explicit language about retaliation.

Third, CBOCS points out that §1981, if applied to employment-related retaliation actions, would overlap with Title VII. It adds that Title VII requires that those who invoke its remedial powers satisfy certain procedural and administrative requirements that §1981 does not contain . . . [a]nd CBOCS says that permitting a §1981 retaliation action would allow a retaliation plaintiff to circumvent Title VII's . . . mechanisms, thereby undermining their effectiveness. This argument, however, proves too much. Precisely the same kind of Title VII §1981 "overlap" and potential circumvention exists in respect to employment-related direct discrimination. Yet, Congress explicitly created the overlap. . . . Nor is it obvious how we can interpret §1981 to avoid employment-related overlap without eviscerating §1981 to non-employment contracts where no such overlap exists.

Decision. Yes. **§1981** encompasses claims of retaliation.

CASE QUESTIONS

Critical Legal Thinking. If federal courts have recognized retaliation remedies within race discrimination suits since 1991 (pursuant to the Civil Rights Act of 1991), why do you believe that the Court accepted this case for consideration?

Business Ethics. Humphries handled his case without a lawyer and jeopardized his lawsuit at various points by not properly prosecuting his case in accordance with procedural requirements. Is this a situation where the Court is legislating? Should the Court have helped the plaintiff in this manner?

Contemporary Business. Dissenting Justices Thomas and Scalia argued that §1981 should not be read as affirmatively guaranteeing rights to engage in particular conduct (i.e., what someone does) rather than preventing injury to individuals based on their race (i.e., §1981 should be limited to discrimination against individuals based on their race). They argued "[r]etaliation is not discrimination based on race. When an individual is subjected to reprisal because he has complained about racial discrimination, the injury he suffers is not on account of his race; rather, it is the result of his conduct. . . . This distinction is sound, and it reflects the fact that a claim of retaliation is both logically and factually distinct from a claim of discrimination — logically because retaliation based on conduct and discrimination based on status are mutually exclusive categories, and factually because a claim of retaliation does not depend on proof that any status-based discrimination actually occurred. Consider, for example, an employer who fires any employee who complains of race discrimination, regardless of the employee's race. Such an employer is undoubtedly guilty of retaliation, but he has not discriminated on the basis of anyone's race. Because the employer treats all employees — black and white — the same, he does not deny any employee 'the same right . . . to make and enforce contracts . . . as is enjoyed by white citizens.'" What is your opinion of this interpretation?

National Origin Discrimination

Title VII specifically prohibits **national origin discrimination** within the employment context. **National origin** pertains to the place of an individual's birth. This concept is distinct from citizenship. Citizenship relates to an individual's governmental allegiance. As will be discussed in more detail in a later chapter, the Immigration Reform and Control Act of 1986 (IRCA) makes it unlawful for employers to discriminate against any individual based on **national origin,** other than regarding employment of unauthorized aliens. Employers with four or more employees are liable under IRCA. This statutory liability exists only if a **Title VII** claim for **national origin discrimination** cannot be filed.

Proof of and remedies for **national origin discrimination** follow the same rules as apply to other types of **Title VII** discrimination. Thus, a plaintiff could pursue remedies due to **national origin discrimination** based on disparate treatment *or* disparate impact *or under both* theories. These claims arise in the same contexts as other similar types of discrimination. They have been recognized to arise within **hostile work environments** as well.

The Supreme Court has defined the term ***"national origin"*** within the context of **Title VII** to mean "the country where a person was born, or from which his or her ancestors came."[28] The EEOC has defined the term more broadly. In its "Guidelines on Discrimination Because of National Origin" the Commission states: "The Commission defines **national origin discrimination** broadly as including, but not limited to, the denial of equal employment opportunity because of an individual's, or his or her ancestor's place of origin; or because an individual has the physical, cultural or linguistic characteristics of a **national origin** group."[29]

With extreme rarity, a claim of **business necessity** might be used as a defense to an otherwise neutral national origin policy having an adverse impact on members of a protected class. The **necessity** must relate to the normal operation of a particular business. For example, a person who ran a French or Italian restaurant would be allowed to advertise for and hire exclusively French- or Italian-born chefs.

Concept Summary
Permitted Acts of National Origin Discrimination

Despite the prohibition of discrimination on the basis of national origin, the EEOC Guidelines do provide for a few exceptions:

- It is not unlawful to deny employment opportunities to an individual who does not fulfill job-related national security requirements.
- A BFOQ exception is permitted but must be strictly construed.

Title VII addresses national origin discrimination, *not* discrimination against aliens. In those circumstances in which citizenship requirements have the purpose or effect of discriminating against an individual on the basis of national origin, they are prohibited; however, citizenship requirements exist for certain federal employment positions. Note that national origin discrimination is often accompanied by claims of religious discrimination; as explained in the chapter on religious discrimination, membership in a particular religion may be required by certain types of employers.

Determining **national origin discrimination** can involve some unusual interpretations. For example, in *Bennun v. Rutgers State University*,[30] the court was presented with a plaintiff who claimed he was of "Hispanic" nationality. The defendant argued that although he was not born Hispanic—his mother was Romanian and his father a Sephardic Jew who was born in Palestine—he was Hispanic, despite his parentage, because he was born in Argentina. The court agreed, relying on the predominance of Hispanic culture in his country of birth. He spoke Spanish at home, and the court noted that the Census Bureau relies on language to determine its classifications when taking the decennial census. Furthermore, the court considered it important that the plaintiff's father's heritage was traceable to those Jews who were expelled from Spain during the Inquisition. Notably, the federal court of appeals gave deference to the district court's ability to observe the plaintiff's appearance, speech, and mannerisms.

In *Hassan v. Auburn University*,[31] the court held that a protected **national origin** classification can rest on the subgroups of other nationalities. In *Hassan*, the plaintiff was born in Egypt, and the position he sought was given to a Canadian of Turkish descent. Although the two candidates could be considered as falling within the same broadly protected group—people of Arabic descent—the court decided that an employer might exercise a bias against certain subgroups of foreign-born persons while not exhibiting any bias toward others.

Concept Summary
Associational Protections for National Origin

In its definition of "national origin," the EEOC expands broadly the protections from **national origin discrimination** that it offers individuals. The parameters include associations that would be protected against discrimination because of:

- marriage or association with a person of a specific national origin;
- membership in, or association with, an organization identified with or seeking to promote the interests of national groups;
- attendance at, or participation in, schools, churches, temples, or mosques generally used by persons of a particular national origin; and
- use of an individual's or spouse's name that is associated with a particular national origin.[32]

Management Application
National Origin Discrimination

Title VII of the Civil Rights Act of 1964 prohibits employers from engaging in national origin discrimination. National origin discrimination occurs if an employer discriminates against a job applicant or employee because of national heritage, country of origin, or culture. Employers are sometimes found to have discriminated against employees because of national origin. Consider the following case.

Irma Rivera is a Hispanic woman who was born in Puerto Rico. She was employed by Baccarat, Inc., a distributor of fine crystal, as a sales representative in its retail store in Manhattan, New York City. Rivera was the store's top sales representative for two years in a row. The store's sales manager at the time stated that Rivera was "one of the best salespeople I have encountered in my 15 years in quality tabletop and gift retailing."

Jean Luc Negre became the new president of Baccarat, assuming ultimate authority for personnel decisions. Soon thereafter, Negre angrily told Rivera that he did not like her attitude and that he did not want her to speak Spanish on the job. Nine months later, a manager of Baccarat notified Rivera that Negre had made a decision to terminate her. Rivera pressed the manager to tell her why she was being fired. According to Rivera, the manager replied, "Irma, he doesn't want Hispanics." Negre also terminated Ivette Brigantty, another Hispanic sales representative. The non-Hispanic salesperson was retained by the store.

Rivera sued Baccarat for national origin discrimination in violation of Title VII. The U.S. district court found Baccarat liable for national origin discrimination. The court stated:

> *Under Equal Employment Opportunity Commission (EEOC) regulations, national origin discrimination includes the denial of employment opportunity because an individual has the linguistic characteristics of a national origin group. Accent and national origin are obviously inextricably intertwined in many cases. Thus, unless an employee's accent materially interferes with her job performance, it cannot legally be the basis for an adverse employment action.*
>
> *In this case, Ms. Rivera testified that during her one face-to-face meeting with Mr. Negre, he specifically stated that he did not like her accent. Mr. Negre's criticism of Ms. Rivera's accent, his statement that he did not want Hispanic sales employees and the fact that the two Hispanic sales employees were discharged while the non-Hispanic salesperson was retained all buttress the jury's finding of liability.*

The district court awarded Ms. Rivera $104,000 in damages, prejudgment interest, and $102,000 in attorney's fees.[33]

Discussion Questions

1. How does race discrimination differ from national origin discrimination?
2. Could Negre's actions ever be justified by concerns over Rivera's alleged Puerto Rican accent? Can individuals be stereotyped according to their accent? Were there any business justifications for Negre's actions?
3. Can you think of any occasions when you have perceived the existence of national origin discrimination in business?

Differences Between EEOC Charges and Court Allegations

The Supreme Court allowed an Arab-American to pursue a **§1981** race claim in *St. Francis College v. Al-Khazraji.*[34] In that case, a U.S. citizen born in Iraq alleged he was of "Arabian ancestry." The Court held he was protected from **racial discrimination** under **§1981** if the bias against him in denying tenure was due to his ancestry, rather than to his **national origin** or his religion. In its decision, the Supreme Court observed that the modern concept of racial identity is much different than that understood at the time of the enactment of **§1981**. The Court noted:

> *There is a common popular understanding that there are three major human races — Caucasoid, Mongoloid, and Negroid. Many modern biologists and anthropologists, however, criticize racial classifications as arbitrary and of little use in understanding the variability of human beings. It is said that genetically homogeneous populations do not exist and traits are not discontinuous between populations; therefore, a population can only be described in terms of relative frequencies of various traits. Clear-cut categories do not exist. The particular traits which have generally been chosen to characterize races have been criticized as having little biological significance. It has been found that differences between individuals of the same race are often greater than the differences between the "average" individuals of different races. These observations and others have led some, but not all, scientists to conclude that racial classifications are for the most part sociopolitical, rather than biological, in nature.*

The Court has adopted a vague boundary in defining the term ***"race,"*** seemingly equating it with ***national origin***. As a result, we can expect cases to be brought by individuals today that prior generations would not have anticipated.

Under some circumstances, courts will construe these terms as having the same meaning. Generally, claims arising from a "wholly different type of discrimination," rather than as originally stated in the EEOC or 706 agency charges, will bar a subsequent lawsuit in federal court on other grounds.[35] Some courts have recognized that a claim of racial bias is conceptually distinct from a claim of **national origin discrimination**.[36] Despite this theoretical difference, the majority of court decisions take a practical approach, holding that employers should not use some procedural fault within an EEOC charge to shield illegal discrimination. Employers' motions for summary judgment made between the charge and the lawsuit most often arise over whether certain individual characteristics indicate discrimination based on **race** or **national origin.** Courts do not countenance such technical dismissals of discrimination claims. Using fairness as their guideline, courts made the following observations:

- "The crucial element of a charge of discrimination [with the EEOC] is the factual statement contained therein. . . . The selection of the type of discrimination alleged, i.e., the selection of which box to check, is in reality nothing more than the attachment of a legal conclusion to the facts alleged."[37]
- "The remedial purpose of Title VII and the paucity of legal training among those whom it is designed to protect require charges filed before the EEOC be construed liberally."[38]
- "Khan's allegation in the complaint of race discrimination can be viewed as merely a refinement of the charge of national origin discrimination. Certainly it is not at all clear that the discrimination suffered by persons from particular countries, for example Trinidad, results from their national origin rather than

the circumstance that they are usually not Caucasians. Thus, Kahn may include a claim of race discrimination in his complaint."[39]

- "The EEOC can reasonably be expected to investigate both racial and national origin bias when a complainant claims to have been discriminated [against] because he is an Asian Indian."[40]
- "Whether being Hispanic constitutes a race or a national origin category is a semantic distinction with historical implications not worthy of consideration here. . . . [G]iven the uncertainty among courts as to whether 'Hispanic' is better characterized as a race or a national origin, Alonzo's claims of racial discrimination are reasonably related to his claims of a national origin discrimination as they fall within the reasonable scope of [an] EEOC investigation."[41]

In summary, federal case law recognizes that a claimant may sue on grounds not alleged in the EEOC charge if the EEOC or 706 agency investigation should have reasonably included that charge.

Hispanic Preferences

Basing employment decisions on the **racial** or **national origin** preferences of clients, customers, or co-workers constitutes intentional **race** and or **national origin discrimination**. Employment decisions that are based on the discriminatory preferences of customers or co-workers are just as unlawful as decisions based on an employer's own discriminatory preferences.

Recently, the EEOC has sued a number of employers who have unlawfully discharged or otherwise discriminated against employees because of their race (African American) and replaced them with Hispanic workers. For example, a North Carolina condominium housekeeping company discharged six African American housekeepers because of their race and national origin (non-Hispanic) and immediately replaced them with Hispanic workers. The settlement with the EEOC included an award of damages and significant remedial relief. In another case, the EEOC filed suit against a supermarket chain alleging that the employer fired or forced long-term Caucasian and African American employees to resign and replaced them with Hispanic workers after it assumed control of a particular facility. The employer was required to pay damages to settle the case; distribute a formal, written antidiscrimination policy; provide periodic training to all its employees on the policy and Title VII's prohibition against such discrimination; send periodic reports to the EEOC; and post a "Notice to Employees" concerning the lawsuit.[42]

Facility with English

An employee's difficulty with the English language can be the basis for three separate employer violations of law. The EEOC reported that in the year 2000, 45 million Americans (17.5 percent of the population) spoke a language other than English in the home. Of those individuals, approximately 10.3 million individuals (4.1 percent of the population) spoke little or no English. The EEOC has issued regulations that prohibit an employer from basing an employment decision on an employee's foreign accent unless the accent materially interferes with job performance.

A second type of discrimination involves an employer's requirement that an employee be fluent in English. This requirement is permitted only when fluency is required for effective job performance. The third type of language-related **national origin discrimination** can arise in the workplace when the employer mandates that employees use only English during the workday.

Accented English

An employer can make adverse employment decisions based on accent only if the accent materially interferes with the employee's ability to perform essential job functions. The burden of proof of the business necessity for the decision rests with the employer. Within the employment context, an inability to clearly and effectively communicate in English may be taken into account in hiring and retention decisions. When a position involves constant oral communication — as, for example, in teaching, customer service, sales, or telemarketing — an employer may require that an accent not materially interfere with the ability to communicate. For example, a person with a noticeable Filipino accent was unlawfully demoted from his position as supervisor when a court found that his accent would not interfere with the duties required for his position.[43]

In another case, a different federal circuit court of appeals found that the employer could lawfully refuse to hire an individual with a pronounced Filipino accent that made it difficult to understand him over the telephone, a constant activity involved in the position. Moreover, the applicant was unable to show that the employer acted with any discriminatory motive or intent.[44] However, in the right circumstance, the plaintiff will prevail. **National origin discrimination** cases involving accented English suggest that "accent and national origin are inextricably intertwined."[45] Discrimination based on the manner of one's speech can be **national origin discrimination.**[46]

English-Only Workplaces

Employers must clearly demonstrate a business necessity for requiring bilingual employees to speak only English in the workplace. The EEOC guidelines on this subject state:

> **§1606.7 Speak-English-Only rules**
> (a) *When applied at all times.* A rule requiring employees to speak only English at all times in the workplace is a burdensome term and condition of employment. The primary language of an individual is often an essential national origin characteristic. Prohibiting employees at all times, in the workplace, from speaking their primary language or the language they speak most comfortably, disadvantages an individual's employment opportunities on the basis of national origin. It may also create an atmosphere of inferiority, isolation and intimidation based on national origin which could result in a discriminatory working environment. Therefore, the Commission will presume that such a rule violates Title VII and will closely scrutinize it.
>
> (b) *When applied only at certain times.* An employer may have a rule requiring that employees speak only in English at certain times where the employer can show that the rule is justified by business necessity.
>
> (c) *Notice of the rule.* It is common for individuals whose primary language is not English to inadvertently change from speaking English to speaking their primary language. Therefore, if an employer believes it has a business necessity for a speak-English-only rule at certain times, the employer should inform its employees of both the general circumstances when speaking

> only in English is required, and the consequences of violating the rule. If an employer fails to effectively notify its employees of the rule and makes an adverse employment decision against an individual based on a violation of the rule, the Commission will consider the employer's application of the rule as evidence of discrimination on the basis of national origin.[47]

Not all courts are sympathetic to the EEOC's guidelines on the subject of English-only rules. For example, in one case a meat supply company did not require applicants to speak or understand English but once employed, required all employees to speak only English at work. The majority of the affected employees could speak varying degrees of English, but several of them spoke no English at all. After the employer learned that some of the bilingual workers were hurling derogatory insults in Spanish at the other monolingual Spanish-speaking workers and impeding safety at the plant, it issued the following rule:

> *Is hereafter the policy of this Company that only English will be spoken in connection with work. During lunch, breaks, and employees' own time, they are obviously free to speak Spanish if they wish. However, we urge all of you not to use your fluency in Spanish in a fashion which may lead other employees to suffer humiliation. [The company also adopted a rule that prohibited offensive racial, sexual, or personal remarks of any kind.]*

Following its adoption, the company made a few exceptions to the policy for certain job functions. When two employees sued for national origin discrimination based on the English-only rule, the Ninth Circuit Court of Appeals rejected the English-only EEOC Guidelines. It rejected the EEOC's position that English-only rules were *per se* illegal. Instead, it held that such a rule is not presumed discriminatory in the absence of proof to the contrary. The Court offered that an employer might be able to justify such a rule for specific safety reasons based on a business necessity defense.[48]

Bilingualism does not receive special protection from the courts. In one case, *Prado v. Luria & Son, Inc.*,[49] an employer prevailed with the **business necessity** defense when sued by a Hispanic customer service manager who preferred to speak Spanish at work. In this action, the plaintiff sued under **Title VII** and **§1981** and claimed that she was forced to leave her employment because of a discriminatory and **hostile work environment**. The federal district court granted judgment in favor of the employer on the basis that a court has no authority to require employers to promote bilingual persons to supervisory positions as an alternative to an English-only workplace rule. In its decision the court stated:

> *Nonetheless, bilingualism as criteria for employment may survive a challenge for discrimination as furthering a legitimate employer interest — accommodating customers who cannot speak English.*
>
> *The policy is suspect, however, as discriminatory against persons who speak only English where it is geared primarily to benefit employees, rather than customers, who are not proficient in English. The second part of the plaintiff's argument, that the employer should hire only bilingual supervisors, underscores how such a criteria, if misapplied, could swallow the policy behind the employment requirement for bilingualism and give constitutional ammunition to English speaking employees who find it threatening to their occupational interests.*

Persuasive facts often dictate the result, as is so often the case in employment discrimination litigation. In the *Prado* case, the court rejected the EEOC Guidelines as not binding on the court and found no indicia of disparate impact discrimination against Prado.

To rebut the presumption used by the EEOC, employers must notify employees of the general circumstances when English must be used and the consequences of violating the employer's rule. An employer's failure to make such disclosures will lead the EEOC to consider the application of an English-only rule to be national origin discrimination.

National Origin Harassment

Discrimination based on national origin, like other protected classifications, can create a **hostile work environment**. Victims of such situations can find protection under the law even if the wrongdoer did not specifically refer to their national origin during the subject incidents. The court will review the context and pattern of harassment experienced by the claimant. Courts look to "[t]he real social impact of workplace behavior," noting that it "often depends on a constellation of surrounding circumstances, expectations, and relationships which are not fully captured by a simple recitation of the words used or the physical acts performed."[50]

In the following case, the usually conservative federal Court of Appeals for the Fifth Circuit reversed a dismissal of a **national origin** and religious **harassment** claim brought by the EEOC for alleged discrimination against a South Asian who was a practicing Muslim. The decision highlights the need for employers to recognize and confront continuing misconduct and harassment by some of their employees against others on the basis of national origin. A defendant's mistaken belief that the victim's characteristics are of a different nationality still establishes a cause of action for national origin discrimination and harassment.

National Origin Harassment
Treating applicants or employees unfavorably due to their national origin (or presumed national origin); may involve responses to the ethnicity, accent, or appearance of or other perceptions regarding the individual.

CASE 6.5

NATIONAL ORIGIN HARASSERS DO NOT NEED TO KNOW VICTIM'S ACTUAL NATIONAL ORIGIN

EEOC V. WC&M ENTERPRISES, INC. DBA STREATER-SMITH HONDA

496 F.3d 393 (5th Cir. 2007)

U.S. Court of Appeals for the Fifth Circuit

Facts. Mohammed Rafiq was hired as a car salesman by Streater-Smith Honda in Conroe, Texas. He was born in India and was a practicing Muslim. Following September 11, 2001, he began to have problems with harassment at work. When the United States undertook military action against Afghanistan later in 2001, his co-workers began to call him "Taliban." His complaints to the managers met with no success. Other salespeople mocked him and asked Rafiz, "Why don't you just go back where you came from since you believe what you believe?" In October 2002, Rafiq got into a dispute with his manager when the manager told him that it was mandatory for all employees to attend a United Way meeting. When Rafiq questioned what, if any, connection there was between the United Way and his job, the manager said, "This is America. That's the way things work over here. This is not the Islamic country where you come from." After the confrontation, Rafiq received a written warning from the manager, stating that Rafiq "was acting like a Muslim extremist" and that he could not work with Rafiq because of his "militant stance." After another episode a week later, Rafiq was fired. After filing a charge of discrimination with the EEOC, the agency filed a lawsuit against the dealership alleging it had subjected Rafiq to a hostile work environment on the basis of religion and national origin. The dealership was granted summary judgment by the district court, and the EEOC appealed to the Fifth Circuit Court of Appeals.

Issue. To bring a harassment claim based on national origin, must the harasser specifically refer to the victim's actual place of origin?

Language of the Court. Dennis, J.: . . . **Nothing in the [EEOC Guidelines on Discrimination Because of National Origin] requires that the discrimination be based on the victim's actual national origin. The EEOC's final guidelines make this point clear: In order to have a claim of national origin discrimination under Title VII, it is not necessary to show that the alleged discriminator knew the particular national origin group to which the complainant belonged. . . . [I]t is enough to show that the complainant was treated differently because of his or her foreign accent, appearance, or physical characteristics.**

Guidelines on Discrimination Because of National Origin, 45 Fed.Reg. 85,632, 85,633 (Dec. 29, 1980); see also *Langadinos v. Appalachian Sch. of Law,* No. (citation omitted) ("The plaintiff may still establish a cause of action under the Civil Rights Act despite the defendant's mistaken belief that his ethnic characteristics are those of a person of Italian, rather than Greek, descent."); *Kanaji v. Children's Hosp. of Philadelphia* (citation omitted) ("Defendant fails to cite a single case where a court has held that a plaintiff alleging 'national origin' discrimination must specify a 'country' or 'nation' of origin."); *LaRocca v. Precision Motorcars, Inc.* (citation omitted) ("The fact that [coworker] ignorantly used the wrong derogatory ethnic remark toward the plaintiff is inconsequential.").

In this case, the evidence that the EEOC presented supports its claim that Rafiq was harassed based on his national origin. Indeed, several of the challenged statements refer to national origin generally (even though they do not accurately describe Rafiq's actual country of origin): (1) Kiene's comment to Rafiq, "Why don't you just go back where you came from since you believe what you believe?"; (2) Swigart's statement, "This is America. That's the way things work over here. This is not the Islamic country where you come from"; and (3) Kiene's and Argabrite's practice of referring to Rafiq as "Taliban" and calling him an "Arab."

Decision. No. Knowledge of a plaintiff's actual national origin is not necessary to sue for national origin discrimination.

CASE QUESTIONS

Critical Legal Thinking. Did it make a difference in this case that the victim resented the remarks of his co-workers? Would the case have been decided differently if a co-worker, rather than the victim, objected to the remarks?

Business Ethics. If it can be assumed that Rafiq was not physically injured or emotionally distressed by the remarks, why does the law define the offending behavior as harassment?

Contemporary Business. Can you cite any other examples of harassment of Muslim employees in the workplace? What should employers do to halt this type of harassment?

Human Resource Form
Manager's Receipt of Harassment Policy

Our company does not tolerate harassment of its employees. Our company is an equal opportunity employer and does not discriminate against employees or job applicants on the basis of any status or condition protected by federal, state, and local law. As a manager within our company, I acknowledge receipt of the company's "Policy against Harassment of Employees." I understand that the company can be held responsible for acts of unlawful harassment because of acts and situations I commit, tolerate, encourage, or fail to investigate and report to senior management. I also acknowledge that should I become aware at any time during my employment of any unlawful harassment or a work environment that is hostile intimidation or offensive to a reasonable person I must immediately report it to company senior managers. Furthermore, I will immediately report any rumors of unlawful harassment to those managers. I agree to cooperate fully in the investigation of any employment harassment or discrimination claim. I will not retaliate against anyone who makes such a claim or against those who cooperate in such an investigation.

I understand and acknowledge that if I participate in any violation of this policy, I will be subject to disciplinary action, including termination of employment. I recognize that I can be personally sued for violating this policy.

Dated: ____________________ ____________________

Manager's signature

Key Terms and Concepts

- Race
- Color
- National origin
- Sections 1981, 1985
- Executive Order No. 11246
- Title VII
- Personal appearance discrimination
- Racial harassment
- Racially hostile work environment
- Associational protections
- Comparative qualifications
- Color discrimination
- BFOQ defense
- Business necessity defense
- National origin discrimination
- English-only workplaces
- Retaliation claims
- National origin harassment

Chapter Summary

- Racial discrimination gives rise to a cause of action under Title VII and §1981 claims. If the actor is working on behalf of a state or local governmental employer, a §1983 claim may be brought. A conspiracy to discriminate based on race is known as a §1985 claim.

- A §1981 claim prohibits only discrimination based on race or color, whereas Title VII is much broader in application. Title VII also prohibits discrimination on the basis of sex (now deemed to mean gender), religion, national origin, and pregnancy.

- Color discrimination is a separate and distinct claim for discrimination under Title VII.

- Race and color claims of discrimination may be brought even if the perpetrator and the victim are of the same race or color.

- When a misleading or false reason is given for an adverse employment action, the reason is deemed a pretext. To establish that the reason for the action was pretextual, a plaintiff will need to show other facts from which a reasonable inference can be made that the action was done intentionally and with race-based motivations.

- Employers should weigh the relative qualifications of each candidate using the same criteria before making an employment decision.

- When race is used in a selection process, it is subject to the strict scrutiny review of the courts for violations of due process or equal protection.

- Race may never be used as a BFOQ in employment decision-making.

- Severe and pervasive hostile work environments are determined not only by the victim's reaction but also by the reactions of fellow co-workers.

- The courts determine national origin circumstantially.

- The courts are split in their application of the EEOC Guidelines relating to national origin discrimination.

- An employer's requirement that employees speak English only at the workplace will be reviewed very carefully and must rest on a business necessity rationale.

Online Student Support

- Loislaw legal research and writing assignments.
- Loislaw group projects and class presentations.
- Loislaw access, providing online research including up-to-date cases, statutes, rules, and regulations. Primary law for all 50 states and federal jurisdictions. Registration required for access to this resource.
- Practice questions, including sample true/false, multiple choice, and short answer questions to test your understanding of concepts.
- Additional human resource forms.
- Internet exercises.
- Blogs.
- Supplementary statutory and regulatory materials.

Case Problems

6.1 A lawsuit was filed by an African American employee who claimed he was subjected to the following statements made with reference to him by a female African American supervisor: he was called "little black sheep" on one occasion; compared to another employee as being as different as "night and day"; referred to as "Princess Diana" in reference to his sexual orientation; told "look how nice and wavy and straight Dominic's hair is" and then "oh, Jerry, your hair is nice too"; and was informed that "another store in the chain has requested a manager who is fair skinned" [which the employee was not]. Are these statements discriminatory in meaning? How should the court rule on this as a color discrimination claim? Does the sexual orientation comment factor into establishing a claim? (*Brack v. Shoney's, Inc.*, 249 F.Supp.2d 938 (W.D. Tenn. 2003))

6.2 Does an employer violate Title VII when it enforces a no beard policy against an African American male suffering from pseudofollicultis barbae, a skin disorder resulting from ingrown hair that is aggravated by shaving and affects 50 percent of African American males but less than 1 percent of white males? Is the employer required to make an exception if the employee requests that he be allowed to grow a beard? (See *Bradley, EEOC v. Pizzaco of Nebraska*, 7 F.3d 795 (8th Cir. 1993))

6.3 Could a television station assign a black anchorman to the weekend news shift because of its perception that weekend news is "black news"? If this was more profitable for the station but denied its African American weekend anchor the more prestigious and lucrative weekday shift, would a claim for racial discrimination exist? (*Lowery v. WMC-TV*, 658 F.Supp. 1240, *vacated on other grounds*, 661 F.Supp. 65 (W.D. Tenn. 1987))

6.4 Would grounds exist for an African American supervisor to protest his firing because of his complaints that a white woman co-worker had been discriminated against by management? If so, why? (*Rucker v. Higher Education Aids Board*, 669 F.2d 1179 (7th Cir. 1982))

6.5 Would a black woman who worked for a telephone-marketing firm have a strong case for race discrimination if she had been assigned to call households in black neighborhoods using a "black" script? (*Ferrill v. Parker Group*, 168 F.3d 468 (11th Cir. 1990))

End Notes

1. *Mamdouh El-Hakem v. BJY, Inc.*, 415 F.3d 1068 (9th Cir. 2005).
2. 427 U.S. 160, 168 (1976).
3. *EEOC v. Walgreen Company*, 07-CV-172-GPM, and *Tucker v. Walgreen Company*, 05-CV-440-GPM (S.D. Ill. (2008)), as reported in press release available at *http://www.eeoc.gov/eeoc/newsroom/release/3-25-08.cfm*.
4. *King v. Hardesty*, 517 F.3d 1049 (8th Cir. 2008).
5. *Rodgees v. Western-Southern Life Ins. Co.*, 12 F.3d 668 (7th Cir. 1993).
6. *McManus v. MCI Communications*, 748 A.2d 949 (D.C. Cir. 2000).
7. *Tetro v. Elliot Popham Pontiac, etc.*, 173 F.3d 988 (6th Cir. 1999) (terminating a white employee for fathering an interracial child); and *LaRocca v. Precision Motorcars, Inc.*, 45 F.Supp. 2d 762 (D. Neb. 1999) (termination for maintaining friendships with members of a minority group).
8. *Chandler v. Fast Lane, Inc.*, 868 F.Supp. 1138 (E.D. Ark. 1994).
9. *Perry v. Manocherian*, 675 F. Supp. 1417 (S.D.N.Y. 1987).
10. *U.S. v. Real Estate One, Inc.*, 433 F.Supp. 1140 (E.D. Mich. 1977), wherein the court held that a realtor's practice of assigning sales territories to salespeople based on their race was illegal under Title VII.
11. 543 U.S. 499 (2005).
12. *National Association for the Advancement of Colored People, Newark Branch v. Town of Harrison, New Jersey*, 907 F.2d 1408 (3d Cir. 1990).
13. *Pavon v. Swift Transp. Co.*, 192 F.3d 902 (9th Cir. 1999).
14. *Richardson v. State Dept. of Correctional Services*, 180 F.3d 426 (2d Cir. 1999).
15. *Moore v. Kuka Welding Systems & Robot Corp.*, 171 F.3d 1073 (6th Cir. 1999).
16. *Brown v. Coach Stores, Inc.*, 163 F.3d 706 (2d Cir. 1998).
17. *Witt v. Roadway Express*, 136 F.3d 1424 (10th Cir. 1998).
18. *Shabat v. Blue Cross Blue Shield*, 925 F.Supp. 977 (W.D. N.Y. 1996).
19. *Harrison v. Metro Govt. of Nashville & Davidson County*, 80 F.3d 1107 (6th Cir. 1996).
20. 524 U.S. 742 (1998).
21. 524 U.S. 775 (1998).
22. *Ross v. Douglas County*, 234 F.3d 391 (8th Cir. 2000).
23. 42 U.S.C. §2000e-5(g).
24. *Clayton v. Meijer, Inc.*, 281 F.3d 605, 610 (6th Cir. 2002).
25. *Walker v. Sec. of Treasury*, 713 F. Supp. 403 (N.D. Ga.1989).
26. 491 U.S. 701 (1989).
27. *McGovern v. City of Philadelphia*, 544 F.3d 114 (3d Cir. 2009).
28. *Espinoza v. Farah Manufacturing Co.*, 414 U.S 86 (1973).
29. 29 C.F.R. §1606.1 (2005).
30. 941 F.2d 154 (3d Cir. 1991).
31. 833 F. Supp. 866 M.D. Ala. 1993, *aff'd* 15 F.3d 1097 (11th Cir. 1994).
32. 29 C.F.R. §1606.1 (a-d) (2005).
33. *Rivera v. Baccarat, Inc.*, 10 F.Supp.2d 318 (S.D.N.Y. 1998).
34. 481 U.S. 604 (1987).
35. *Peterson v. Ins. Co. of N.A.*, 884 F.Supp.107 (S.D.N.Y. 1995).
36. *Dixit v. City of New York Dept. of Gen. Srvs*, 972 F. Supp. 730,734 (S.D.N.Y. 1997).
37. *Sanchez v. Standard Brands, Inc.*, 431 F.2d 455, 462 (5th Cir. 1970).
38. *Green v. Los Angeles County Supt. of Schools*, 883 F.2d 1472, 1476 (9th Cir. 1989).
39. *Kahn v. Pepsi Cola Bottling Group*, 526 F.Supp. 1268, 1270 (E.D.N.Y. 1981).
40. *Dixit*, supra.
41. *Alonzo v. Chase Manhattan Bank, N.A.*, 25 F.Supp. 2d 455 (S.D.N.Y. 1998).
42. *http://www.eeoc.gov/eeoc/initiatives/e-race/caselist.cfm#hispanic*.
43. *Carino v. Univ. of Oklahoma Board of Regents*, 750 F.2d 815 (10th Cir. 1984).
44. *Fragante v. City & County of Honolulu*, 888 F.2d 591 (9th Cir. 1989).
45. *Ang v. Procter & Gamble Co.*, 932 F.2d 540 (6th Cir. 1991).
46. *Berke v. Ohio Dept. of Public Welfare*, 628 F.2d 980 (6th Cir. 1980).
47. 29 C.F.R. §1607.
48. *Garcia v. Spun Steak Co.*, 998 F.2d 1480 (9th Cir. 1993), *cert. denied* 512 U.S. 1228 (1994).
49. 975 F. Supp. 1349 (S.D. Fla. 1997).
50. *Oncale v. Sundowner Offshore Services, Inc.*, 523 U.S. 75, 81-82 (1998).

Chapter 7
Sex Discrimination, Sexual Harassment, and Sexual Orientation Protection

"Where there are no distinctions there can be no superiority; perfect equality affords no temptation." —Thomas Paine, founding father of the United States, author of Common Sense

Learning Objectives

1. Understand the application of the Equal Pay Act of 1963.
2. Identify the advantages of suing under Title VII rather than the Equal Pay Act.
3. Define the differences between sexual discrimination and sexual harassment.
4. List various forms of sexual harassment.
5. Define the meaning of a sexual BFOQ and the exceptions to its application.
6. Distinguish permissible gender differences with regard to an employer's dress and grooming standards.
7. State the differences between sexual orientation and sexual identity discrimination.

Chapter Outline

Chapter Opening scenario

Cynthia Taylor was a U.S. Postal Service superintendent when she was demoted during a massive reorganization. She had received the second highest performance evaluations in her group and had not been disciplined before the reorganization. According to her, a supervisor told her that he had to pick between a man and a woman. Because the man was married and had children and needed the money more than Taylor, he chose the man. Can a decision to hire or promote a male worker over a female worker based on such income considerations constitute unlawful gender discrimination?[1]

Introduction

Today virtually all corporate mission or vision statements take stands against workplace **sex discrimination, sexual harassment**, and **harassment due to sexual orientation** as being incompatible with the corporation's culture. Advances in communication and focused efforts to abolish institutional discrimination have made people more aware of how harmful past practices have been to both women and minorities. However, such sensitivity did not always prevail. Before the Civil Rights Act of 1964, which provided some protection for women against discrimination based on sex (or gender), many women were often prohibited from working in certain industries or fields "for their protection." The courts use the terms ***"sex"*** and **"gender"** interchangeably.

Gender
Characteristics distinguishing males and females, including social roles and behaviors.

Gender Discrimination
The unfair treatment in employment of a person because of his or her gender.

As World War II started, nearly 15 million men and a little over 200,000 women were employed in combat duties. The United States exempted certain job categories from the draft in an effort to prevent the collapse of domestic industrial and agricultural industries. However, the draft and the war left many of the nation's farms and factories with a dearth of employees. Women soon began to fill this employment void. About half of the women who joined the workforce had never before worked for wages. After the war ended, a majority of women left the workforce and returned home, either by their own choice or unwillingly, because they were displaced by returning servicemen who resumed their positions. This forced unemployment — a form of harassment — was quietly ignored for a very long time in our history. It took the tumultuous times of the 1970s to bring the issue to the attention of the American public. The feminist movement of that era and key court decisions compelled American society to recognize and attempt to redress past discriminatory practices.

The Bureau of Labor Statistics, part of the United States Department of Labor, monitors and tracks employment statistics. The information they can provide is helpful in understanding how far American society has advanced and how much more effort is required to create equality in the workforce. As of 2004, a little over 46 percent of the workforce was composed of women. Although women make up 50 percent of management, professional, and related occupations, they are clustered in professions sometimes referred to as "pink collar." Teaching and administrative support are examples of "pink collar" occupations. One of the downsides to working in a "pink collar" job is that they tend to correlate with lower pay. As an example, women comprise almost 99 percent of all dental hygienists, but only 22 percent of dentists.

Recent trends, however, suggest that this situation may be changing, although at a very slow pace. According to the 2004 Bureau of Labor Statistics, 52 percent of high school graduates and 56 percent of college graduates are women. As women become the more-educated gender, their numbers in higher paying employment fields should increase as well. In addition, in 1987 approximately 18 percent of wives earned more than their husbands, but in 2003 this percentage increased to approximately 25 percent. Despite these advances, pay disparity continues to be a serious problem within American business. Sexism, sexual harassment, and gender favoritism toward males continue to be workplace problems.

Typically, women still feel the challenges presented by the **glass ceiling**: a perceived barrier that keeps women from the highest rungs of corporate leadership. As recent case law demonstrates, this form of discrimination is not selective. Incidents of **sex discrimination** and **sexual Harassment** occur without regard to ethnicity, **sexual orientation**, race, or color. Employers can reduce their exposure to such claims by instituting dedicated anti-harassment training and by continuously auditing their workforce. Gender discrimination continues to be a problem. In the fiscal year 2009, more than 28,000 charges were filed with the EEOC alleging sex-based discrimination. The level of discrimination charge filings with the agency is expected to continue its increasing trend.

Glass Ceiling
A perceived barrier preventing certain classes of individuals from climbing the highest rungs of corporate leadership.

Sexual Harassment
Unwelcome sexual conduct that is a term or condition of employment; may include intimidation, bullying, or coercion of a sexual nature.

We will address the gender-related Pregnancy Discrimination Act amendment to **Title VII** in a later chapter.

Gender Pay Discrimination

The **Equal Pay Act** of 1963 requires that male and female employees performing the same work for the same employer receive the same pay. It specifically prohibits wage differentials based on sex for positions requiring equal skill, effort, and responsibility and performed under similar working conditions.[2] The law, an amendment to the **Fair Labor Standards Act**, regulates wage and hour laws for employees, in response to Congress's finding that pay disparity depressed wages and living standards, promoted labor disputes, disrupted commerce, and constituted an unfair method of competition.

Equal Pay Act
A1963 federal law prohibiting wage differentials based on gender for positions requiring equal skill, effort, and responsibility and that are performed under similar working conditions.

The **Equal Pay Act** does not require equal pay for work of comparable worth. That concept, which represents an attempt to restructure wage scales to overcome past inequities, has been promoted by advocates of women's rights as a strong tool for bringing the standard of living achievable by women up to that of men.

The **Equal Pay Act** compels employers to maintain equal wage scales only for equal, or substantially equivalent, work involving equal skill, effort, and responsibility and work performed under similar working conditions.

The **Equal Pay Act** permits differences in pay if they are based on *bona fide* systems respecting seniority, merit, and incentives or on other factors besides sex. A seniority system that provides increasing pay scales according to length of service would provide a defense to the employer. The system must be consistently applied to all employees, with no arbitrary exceptions permitted. A merit system that rewards employees for exceptional performance is permitted under the act. The act also permits employees to receive differential compensation for the quality or quantity of their production. Employers who cannot prove that a pay difference is based on a *bona fide* system must be able to show that it relates to job requirements, is beneficial to the employer's business, furthers the employer's business, is applied to both genders, was fully known to both employer and employees, and is applied only for the stated business reasons. Examples of factors other than sex that have been used to justify pay differences include differences in education, participation in bona fide training programs, experience, training and ability, assignment to evening or night shifts, and differences in job classifications.

While not often the basis for individual lawsuits, the statute is frequently invoked by the U.S. Department of Labor when conducting payroll audits of employers. In the usual case, an individual plaintiff would pursue relief for compensation disparity through a **Title VII** action, which has the advantage that the employee does not have to establish the element of equal work under similar working conditions required under the Equal Pay Act.

> ***Example:*** Marianne Stanley was hired as head coach of the women's basketball team for the University of Southern California (U.S.C.) in 1989, and the program had a winning record under her coaching. When her contract was to be renewed, she requested that her salary be made equivalent to that of the men's basketball coach, but her request was refused. Her contract was not renewed, and she sued under the **Equal Pay Act**. She lost her suit because the court determined that George Raveling, the men's basketball coach, had more coaching experience, had coached the men's Olympic basketball team, had been twice named national coach of the year and twice named PAC-10 coach of the year, possessed nine years of marketing and promotional experience, and had written several books on basketball. Stanley did not have the same qualifications, and the court held that U.S.C. exercised a nondiscriminatory reason for the pay differential based on disparate levels of experience and qualifications.[3]

An employer may not reduce the wages of higher-paid employees to equalize pay disparities to comply with the **Equal Pay Act**. One of the advantages of pursuing a claim under the **Equal Pay Act** is a two-year statute of limitations. For willful violations, the statute is extended to three years. Recall that under **Title VII** discrimination claims to the EEOC have to be made within 180 days.

The existence of wage differentials compelled by a collective bargaining agreement does not excuse employers from liability under the **Equal Pay Act**, as the next case established.

CASE 7.1

PAY DIFFERENTIALS FOR DIFFERENCES IN WORKING CONDITIONS MUST INVOLVE DIFFERENT SURROUNDINGS OR HAZARDS

CORNING GLASS WORKS V. BRENNAN, SECRETARY OF LABOR

417 U.S. 188 (1974)

Supreme Court of the United States

Facts. Male employees at the Corning Glass Works (Corning) had previously performed night-shift inspections and were paid more than were females who performed the day-shift inspections. A plant-wide pay differential according to shift, a result of the unionization of the plant, was superimposed on the existing base-wage differentials between the two shifts. Thereafter, Corning opened up the night-shift jobs to women who had equal seniority with the men on the shift, allowing them to bid for the higher-paid night inspection jobs as vacancies opened up. The Secretary of Labor filed two lawsuits, in two different district courts, to enjoin Corning from violating the Equal Pay Act of 1963. At the district court level, two conflicting decisions were issued; upon appeal to the respective federal courts of appeals, the district courts' decisions were affirmed. The Supreme Court granted *certiorari*.

Issue. Does the practice of pay differentials for day and night shifts required by a union agreement violate the Equal Pay Act of 1963?

Language of the Court. Marshall, J.: . . . **The [Equal Pay] Act's basic structure and operation are similarly straightforward. In order to make out a case under the Act, the Secretary must show that an employer pays different wages to employees of opposite sexes "for equal work on jobs the performance of which requires equal skill, effort, and responsibility, and which are performed under similar working conditions."**

[T]he most telling evidence of congressional intent is the fact that the Act's amended definition of equal work incorporated the specific language of the job evaluation plan described at the hearings by Corning's own representative — that is, the concepts of "skill," "effort," "responsibility," and "working conditions."

Nowhere in any of these definitions is time of day worked mentioned as a relevant criterion. The fact of the matter is that the concept of "working

conditions," as used in the specialized language of job evaluation systems, simply does not encompass shift differentials. Indeed, while Corning now argues that night inspection work is not equal to day inspection work, all of its own job evaluation plans, including the one now in effect, have consistently treated them as equal in all respects, including working conditions. And Corning's Manager of Job Evaluation testified . . . that time of day worked was not considered to be a "working condition." Significantly, it is not the Secretary in this case who is trying to look behind Corning's bona fide job evaluation system to require equal pay for jobs which Corning has historically viewed as unequal work. Rather, it is Corning which asks us to differentiate between jobs which the company itself has always equated. We agree with the Second Circuit that the inspection work at issue in this case, whether performed during the day or night, is "equal work" as that term is defined in the Act.

We agree that the record amply supports the District Court's conclusion that Corning had not sustained its burden of proof. As its history revealed, "the higher night rate was in large part the product of the generally higher wage level of male workers and the need to compensate them for performing what were regarded as demeaning tasks" (citation omitted). The differential in base wages originated at a time when no other night employees received higher pay than corresponding day workers, and it was maintained long after the company instituted a separate plant-wide shift differential which was thought to compensate adequately for the additional burdens of night work. The differential arose simply because men would not work at the low rates paid women inspectors, and it reflected a job market in which Corning could pay women less than men for the same work. That the company took advantage of such a situation may be understandable as a matter of economics, but its differential nevertheless became illegal once Congress enacted into law the principle of equal pay for equal work.

Decision. Yes. The Equal Pay Act is to be broadly construed and applied so that both sexes are paid the same base wage. Continuing wage differentials between shifts due to historical sex discrimination will be prohibited by an injunction.

CASE QUESTIONS

Critical Legal Thinking. Can you envision circumstances in which wage differentials between the sexes would be sustainable?

Business Ethics. How can historical gender discrimination in pay be eliminated?

Contemporary Business. Can you think of any reasons for which unequal pay between the sexes should be permitted? What impact do you believe the EPA has had in fostering equality between the sexes?

Concept Summary
Proving a Violation Under the Equal Pay Act

A plaintiff must prove that:

- Higher wages were paid to an opposite-sex employee;
- These wages were paid for equal work requiring substantially similar skill, effort, and responsibilities; and
- The work was performed under similar working conditions.

No proof of discriminatory intent is required.[4]

Focus on Ethics
Violation of the Equal Pay Act

Employers are not supposed to pay employees different wages for doing the same work, with a number of exceptions. They sometimes do, however, and sometimes they are caught. Consider the following case.

Sheila Ann Glenn, Patricia Johns, and Robbie Nugent are three female employees who work for the General Motors Corporation (GM). The three females work in the position known as "Follow-Up" in the tools stores department of GM. A Follow-Up basically ensures that adequate tools are on hand in GM plants to keep the plants running. For ten years these female employees were paid less than all of the male employees in the same position, and the highest-paid of three female workers earned less than the lowest paid man. When hired, all three women received lower starting salaries than men hired at the same time for the same job. The three women sued GM for violating the Equal Pay Act.

GM defended, arguing that the exception "(4) a differential based on any factor other than sex" justified the lower salaries paid to women than to men for the same work. GM argued that under the economic theory of supply and demand, many women were willing to work for less than men, and this permitted GM to pay lower wages to women than to men for the same job. The U.S. district court rejected GM's theory, found that GM had violated the Equal Pay Act, and awarded the three women damages. GM appealed this decision.

The U.S. court of appeals upheld the decision of the district court that GM violated the Equal Pay Act. The court of appeals rejected GM's attempt to justify the differential in pay as being based on the exception "factors other than sex." The appeals court held that GM's supply and demand argument could not be used to justify the pay differential between the three woman and the men who performed the same job. The court noted that even if some women were willing to work for less pay than men doing the same job, this did not permit employers to pay women less than men for the same work. The court of appeal stated:

> *The argument that supply and demand dictates that women may be paid less is exactly the kind of*

evil that the Equal Pay Act was designed to eliminate and has been rejected. The market force theory that a woman will work for less than a man is not a valid consideration under the Equal Pay Act.

The court of appeals rejected the market force theory as a "factor other than sex" and affirmed the decision of the district court in favor of the plaintiff women.[5]

Ethics Questions

1. Is it ethical to apply the market force "supply and demand" theory to wage discrimination cases?
2. Was it ethical for GM to assert the market force theory as a defense for the pay differential between female and male workers?
3. What are the ethical considerations underlying the Equal Pay Act?

Sex Discrimination

Congress protected against **sex** or **gender discrimination** and **harassment** through **Title VII** of the Civil Rights Act of 1964. **Title VII** states:

> *It shall be unlawful employment practice for an employer to (1) fail or refuse to hire or to discharge any individual, or otherwise to discriminate against any individual with respect to his compensation, terms, conditions, or privileges or employment, because of such individual's . . . sex [gender]. (Citation omitted.)*

Congress drafted **Title VII** to combat racial and ethnic inequalities in employment as discussed in previous chapters. However, Virginia Democratic Representative and civil rights foe Howard Smith inserted "sex" as a protected class in the proposed Civil Rights bill in an attempt to defeat it. His belief that **gender protection** would be controversial and would derail the bill's passage backfired when the bill passed by a vote of 168-133. As it turns out, what he thought would act as a "poison pill" killing the bill resulted in protections for women against gender-based **sexual harassment** and **discrimination**.

> ***Example:*** Karyn Risch was a 17-year veteran of the Royal Oak, Michigan, police department. Though qualified to apply for promotion, she was passed over six times by the police chief in favor of male candidates who had received lower scores under the department's promotional system. Only one female officer had ever served as a manager in the department. Her experience dissuaded many other female officers from applying for promotion. Following her receipt of a right-to-sue letter, Risch sued the city for sex discrimination due to its failure to promote her. The department argued that while she was subjected to **sex discrimination**, it was because other better qualified applicants were selected. In reviewing a summary judgment order dismissing her lawsuit, a federal court of appeals reviewed all of the facts and found that her case should proceed to trial. The facts included the lack of women in command positions, the evidence of promotion of male officers with lesser qualifications, and the repeated degrading remarks about women made by male officers and department managers.[6]

The law does not prohibit all differences between the sexes in pay or other terms and conditions of employment. **Sex discrimination** involves treating someone unfavorably because of that person's sex. The basis for the discrimination is illegal if it has a negative impact on the employment of people of a certain sex and is not job related or necessary to the operation of the business. Courts have been presented with a variety of allegations of **sex discrimination**. One court held that it was lawful to fire a female employee because of her consensual and sexually provocative behavior towards her boss, which caused the boss's wife to have her fired.[7] In the following case involving sexual favoritism, the court concluded that "[a] male executive's romantically motivated favoritism toward a female subordinate is not sex discrimination even when it disadvantages a male competitor of the woman." In reading the case, consider if the at-will nature of Preston's employment outweighed any consideration of a finding of **sex discrimination**.

CASE 7.2

TITLE VII DOES NOT PROTECT EMPLOYEES FROM ALL UNFAIR GENDER-RELATED DECISIONS

PRESTON V. WISCONSIN HEALTH FUND

397 F.3d 539 (2005)

U.S. Court of Appeals for the Seventh Circuit

Facts. Jay Preston, a dentist, charged that the Wisconsin Health Fund, his former employer, discriminated against him based on gender in violation of Title VII. He claimed that his employer replaced him as director of the Fund's dental clinic with Linda Hamilton. The Fund is a health and welfare fund operated by the Teamsters union. The dental clinic under Preston had been hemorrhaging money for many years. Preston presented ideas for stemming the flow to the fund's CEO, Trojak, in a well-written business plan, despite which Preston was fired. Preston had an M.B.A. as well as a dental degree. He was replaced by Hamilton, a much younger dentist, who had no apparent credentials for the job except eagerness. There were unsubstantiated rumors that the CEO and Hamilton were having an affair. The trial court granted summary judgment for the Fund, and he appealed to the Seventh Circuit Court of Appeals.

Issue. To sue for sex discrimination, must a plaintiff show evidence of discrimination beyond the fact that someone of the opposite sex was awarded the job that the plaintiff wanted to retain?

Language of the Court. Posner, J.: **A male executive's romantically motivated favoritism toward a female subordinate is not sex discrimination even when it disadvantages a male competitor of the woman. Such favoritism is not based on a belief that women are better workers, or otherwise deserve to be treated better, than men; indeed, it is entirely consistent with the opposite opinion.**

The effect on the composition of the workplace is likely to be nil, especially since the disadvantaged competitor is as likely to be another woman as a man — were Preston a woman, Trojak would still have fired him to make way for Hamilton unless Trojak was romantically entangled with both of them. Neither in purpose nor in consequence can favoritism resulting from a personal relationship be equated to sex discrimination. (Citations omitted.)

Preston tries to bolster his case by pointing to the fact that Trojak gave large raises to several women and by noting that there was even talk in the workplace of "Bruce and his harem." But he provides no details that would enable a trier of fact to infer that the raises were motivated by the recipients' sex. All we know is the amount of the raises, the number of recipients, and the sex ratio of the recipients — five women to two men. To infer discrimination we would need to know more. We would need to know the sex composition of the Fund's workforce, whether there were men who had jobs comparable to those of the five women but didn't get similar raises, and whether the raises were due to the women's being promoted to new jobs and if so whether men had a fair opportunity to compete for those promotions. There are some answers in the record but Preston makes nothing of them. He insists that the bare fact that more women than men got large raises, together with the favoritism shown Linda Hamilton, is enough to get him to a jury. . . . But when as in this case no reason is given why men might be expected to discriminate against men, the plaintiff, to raise a triable issue of discrimination, must present some evidence beyond the bare fact that a woman got a job that a man wanted to get or keep. A gross disparity in qualifications might be such evidence — but for the fact in this case that the plaintiff himself is insisting that the reason the less-qualified Hamilton was given the job of the more-qualified Preston was personal and, as we have explained, unrelated to sex discrimination. All that is left is the undeveloped evidence of the raises given to the other women.

Decision. Yes. Replacement of a male employee by female employee with whom supervisor was rumored to be having an affair because of favoritism due to romantic involvement is not sex discrimination. Summary judgment for the employer was affirmed.

CASE QUESTIONS

Critical Legal Thinking. What evidence should have been presented by Preston for him to prevail in his sex discrimination lawsuit?

Business Ethics. If the romantic involvement of Trojak and Hamilton had been established, would that have made a difference in the case? It is unethical to make a decision based, in part, on such personal considerations?

Contemporary Business. Can you think of any situation from recent news accounts in which romantic involvement played a role in an employment decision?

Management Application
Sex Discrimination

Title VII of the Civil Rights Act of 1964 prohibits employers from discriminating against an employment applicant or employee based on gender. Employers, however, sometimes do discriminate because of gender. Most gender discrimination lawsuits are brought by women who have been discriminated against by an employer. Consider the following case.

The position of director of the Madison County Veterans Service Agency became vacant. The Madison County Board of Supervisors (Board) appointed a committee of five men to hold interviews. Maureen E. Barbano applied for the position and was interviewed by the committee. Upon entering the interview, Barbano heard someone say, "Oh, another woman." When the interview began, Donald Greene, a committee member, said he would not consider "some woman" for the position. He then asked Barbano personal questions about her plans for having a family and whether her husband would mind if she had to "run around the country with men" and transport male veterans. Barbano alleged that the questions were irrelevant and discriminatory. No committee member asked Barbano any substantive questions. Ultimately, the Board acted on the committee's recommendation and hired a male candidate. Barbano sued Madison County for gender discrimination in violation of Title VII. The U.S. district court held that the defendant engaged in gender discrimination in violation of Title VII. The court awarded Barbano damages. Madison County appealed.

The U.S. court of appeals affirmed the judgment of the district court. The court of appeals found that there was little doubt that Greene's statements during the interview were discriminatory. Greene said he would not consider "some woman" for the position. His questioning Barbano about whether she would get pregnant and quit was also discriminatory, since it was unrelated to a bona fide occupational qualification. Similarly, Greene's question about whether Barbano's husband would mind if she had to "run around the country with men" and his statement that he would not want his wife to do it were discriminatory. The court of appeals stated:

> *Given the discriminatory tenor of the interview, and the acquiescence of the other Committee members to Greene's line of questioning, it follows that the trial court judge could find that those present at the interview, and not merely Greene, discriminated against Barbano. The record before us supports the district court's finding that the Board discriminated in making the hiring decision.*

The court of appeals held that the defendant, Madison County, had engaged in gender discrimination in violation of Title VII and affirmed the district court's decision that awarded damages to plaintiff Barbano.[8]

Discussion Questions

1. Why are questions concerning family obligations made illegal by Title VII?
2. Was Greene's conduct unethical and morally reprehensible?
3. What actions should employers take to ensure their interviewers and other personnel understand Title VII and other antidiscrimination laws?

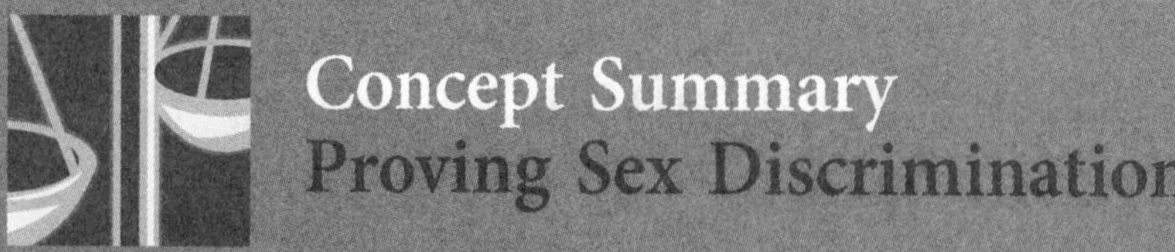

Concept Summary
Proving Sex Discrimination

A plaintiff must prove:

- membership of a protected class;
- qualification and application for the position/promotion/training;
- rejection of application despite these qualifications; and
- that equally or less qualified employees who were not members of the protected class received the position, promotion, or training.

As part of the **Civil Rights Act of 1991**, President George H. Bush established a 21-member bipartisan **Glass Ceiling Commission** to investigate the artificial barrier faced by women and minorities seeking advancement and promotions in employment situations. The Commission's report demonstrated the existence of an apparent **glass ceiling** limiting opportunities for women and minorities. According to the report, 97 percent of Fortune 500 senior managers were white, and approximately 95 percent of those senior managers were male.

Gender as a BFOQ

One exception to the general rule that an employer is not allowed to discriminate based on gender arise when there is a **bona fide occupational qualification** (**BFOQ**) involving gender. The **BFOQ** exception appears in Section 703 of the Civil Rights Act of 1964. A **BFOQ** exists when it is reasonably necessary to discrimination in the normal operation of a particular business. Without the **BFOQ,** the essence of the business operation would be undermined. Since a **BFOQ** is a form of allowable discrimination, courts very narrowly construe its application.

An employer always has the burden of proving a **BFOQ** is necessary. Courts consider a few factors when reviewing whether a **BFOQ** defense is valid: (1) The relationship between the classification and job performance; (2) the necessity of the classification for successful performance of the job; and (3) the job performance affected is the essence of the employer's business operation. A **BFOQ** cannot be used to cater to customer preferences, and it cannot be used to justify racial discrimination. One of the first cases to address the issue involved an airline that claimed customer preference for female flight attendants justified its discriminatory policy of not hiring males as flight attendants. The court rejected the **BFOQ** argument except where "the essence of the business operation would be undermined by not hiring members of one sex exclusively."[9] A **BFOQ** is traditionally used film or theatrical production, for example, where it is considered a **BFOQ** to have a female actor play a female role. Other court decisions have allowed gender-based **BFOQ**s in other limited circumstances; for example, gender-based staffing can be justified as a **BFOQ** when it meets the medical care or privacy concerns of patients.[10]

The 1977 Supreme Court decision *Dothard v. Rawlinson,*[11] which we studied earlier in the text, provides an example of how the courts first dealt with a gender-based **BFOQ**. In that decision, the Court considered whether a state correctional system could exclude female applicants for the position of prison guard under the belief that a female prison guard is more likely than a male guard to be assaulted, thus directly undermining her ability to provide security, the essence of a guard's responsibility. In *Dothard*, the Court decided that **gender discrimination** had occurred with respect to Dianne Rawlinson and all other female applicants for the position of prison guard with the Alabama prison system. They had been denied the position because of the application of statutory height and weight requirements and because only men were selected for positions requiring close physical proximity to inmates. The state employer failed to show that the requirements were essential to good performance of the job.

In the following case, the Court rejected an employer's asserted **BFOQ** defense. When reading this case, consider whether an employer could select employees on the basis of their relative beauty and physical attractiveness. If an employer hired only attractive members of both sexes, without regard to any other protected classification, would that hiring practice be unlawful under **Title VII**? Would it be ethical?

CASE 7.3

SEX APPEAL IS NOT A BFOQ

WILSON V. SOUTHWEST AIRLINES COMPANY

517 F. Supp 292 (N.D. Tex. 1981)

U.S. District Court for the Northern District of Texas

Facts. Gregory Wilson and more than 100 male applicants filed suit against Southwest Airlines claiming Southwest's open refusal to hire males for the flight attendant position was a violation of Title VII of the Civil Rights Act of 1964. In addition, the plaintiffs claimed that the published height-weight requirement for flight attendants functioned to exclude more males than females.

Southwest began its operations at Dallas's Love Field, and in its early history exuded an image of feminine spirit, fun, and sex appeal. Unabashed allusions to love and sex pervaded all aspects of Southwest's public image. They had television commercials with attractive attendants in fitted outfits (skirts were optional), "love bites" (toasted almonds), "love potions" (cocktails), and a ticketing system featuring a "quickie machine" for instant gratification. Southwest used this spirit to enjoy tremendous success. From 1979 through 1980, the company's earnings grew from $17 million to $28 million while most other major airlines were suffering heavy losses. Southwest had one of the highest returns on investments in the airline industry.

Southwest admitted that its refusal to hire males was intentional, but it claimed that it was a protected employment practice under a BFOQ defense. It reasoned that its attractive female flight attendants and ticket agents personified the airline's sexy image and fulfilled its public promise to take passengers skyward with "love." It claimed that its attractive flight attendants were the largest single component of its success, and the maintenance of female-only hiring was, therefore, crucial to the airline's continued financial success.

Issue. Is female sex appeal a bona fide occupational qualification for the jobs of flight attendant and ticket agent with Southwest Airlines?

Language of the Court. **This circuit follows a two-step BFOQ test: (1) does the particular job under consideration require that the worker be of one sex only; (2) is that requirement reasonably necessary to the "essence" of the employer's business. Applying the first level test results in the conclusion that being female is not a qualification required to perform successfully the jobs of flight attendant and ticket agent with Southwest. The functions which Southwest claims the female sex appeal serves of attracting and entertaining male passengers and fulfilling customer expectations for female service are tangential to the essence of the occupations and business involved. Accordingly, the ability of the airline to perform its primary business function, the transportation of passengers, would not be jeopardized by hiring males.**

There is not enough competent proof that the customer preference for females is so strong that Defendant's male passengers would cease doing business with Southwest. The test is one of business necessity, not business convenience. The fact that the vibrant marketing campaign was necessary to distinguish Southwest in its early years does not lead to the conclusion that sex discrimination was then, or is now, a business necessity. Southwest has therefore failed to establish competent proof that revenue loss would result directly from hiring males.

In order not to undermine Congress' purpose to prevent employers from "refusing to hire an individual based on stereotyped characterizations of the sexes" a BFOQ for sex must be denied where sex is merely useful for attracting customers of the opposite sex, and where hiring both sexes will not alter or undermine the essential function of the employer's business.

Decision. No. The court held for the plaintiff that female sex appeal is not a bona fide occupational qualification for the jobs of flight attendant and ticket agent with Southwest Airlines.

CASE QUESTIONS

Critical Legal Thinking. Should the airline prevail if it could have proved it was suffering a loss of revenue because it could no longer market itself as a sexy airline?

Business Ethics. Should the BFOQ consequences of gender preferences by customers be considered a business necessity? What limits should be placed on the business necessity exception?

Contemporary Business. Is the court inhibiting the judgment of business managers as to how to compete in the marketplace?

Management Application
Gender Preferences in Hiring

Your company operates a number of pirate-themed restaurants. Historically, with rare exceptions, Caribbean pirates were male. Your cast of actors who entertain guests during dinner are all male. The few female employees are characterized as "wenches," and they serve meals wearing suggestive costumes. The company is very profitable and seems to enjoy a high repeat customer business. Surveys undertaken by an independent consumer research firm confirm that customers have a preference for your restaurants' predominately male crew and for the costuming of the female employees. Your executives are aware of the several cases that have been brought by the EEOC against other themed restaurants. Your management team reviews the case of *EEOC v. Joe's Stone Crab, Inc.*[12] In that case, women did not apply for the well-paid waiter positions because of the company's history of hiring only male waiters. The court made an analysis similar to that in the *Hazelwood* case discussed in an earlier chapter and concluded that the workforce statistics and the imbalance between male and female employees demonstrated that the company's reputation for hiring only male waiters could be used as evidence of discrimination.

Your company has also read newspaper accounts of the $1 million settlement made by the EEOC with Lawry's, a famous prime rib restaurant chain, which has historically hired only women as waitresses. You have to make the decision whether the company will change its gender staffing policies. At present, the well-paid actor positions are filled entirely by men and some of the wait staff is composed of attractive women. The women on your team think that times have changed and that it is sexist for the company to continue its policies. You are worried about the publicity of a lawsuit.

Discussion Questions

1. Is your company's practice the result of a gender stereotype or a BFOQ?
2. How could you prove that gender was crucial to the performance of the pirate job and that it relates to the core function of the business?
3. Do customer preferences as to the composition of the workforce have much influence upon your decision-making?
4. What will you do if your decision to integrate males and females throughout all staffing positions results in an immediate drastic decrease in sales?

Gender Stereotyping: Dress Codes and Grooming Standards

Gender Stereotyping Requiring or expecting a person to act, behave, or dress a certain way based on his or her gender.

"Immutable Characteristics" Unalterable physical traits, including skin color, hair texture, or certain facial features associated with persons of a particular race, color, sex, or national origin, even though not all members of that group necessarily share the trait.

Dress codes, or a lack thereof, can often create problems within a company. Problems arise due to the absence of specific laws or regulations governing employee dress and appearance. As a result, some employees may desire to express themselves in a manner that others find offensive. Some employees may want to test the limits to the free expression of personal taste, and these experiments can have disruptive effects on employee morale. Students should note that grooming and dress standards by themselves are entirely outside the purview of **Title VII**, because Congress intended the act to prohibit only discrimination based on **"immutable characteristics"** associated with a worker's sex. An **immutable characteristic** includes skin color, hair texture, or certain facial features, even if not all members of the same race, color, sex, or national origin share the characteristic. Without a federal law to provide guidance, some states have created laws that apply as long as the standards do not discriminate on the basis of gender, race, religion, sex, or any other federally protected status. Other recent claimants, such as the one in the *Jesperson* decision reviewed below, have unsuccessfully tried to convince federal courts that opposition to their grooming preferences constituted **sex discrimination** within the purview of **Title VII**.

Employers are given great leeway in setting dress codes and grooming standards. As the *Kelley* decision demonstrates, when an employer's grooming and appearance policy is rationally related to a **business necessity**, the policy will not violate **Title VII**. *Kelley* and *Jesperson* examine issues involving grooming and work attire standards.

CASE 7.4

POLICE FORCE GROOMING STANDARDS DO NOT INTRUDE ON FREE EXPRESSION RIGHTS

KELLEY V. JOHNSON

425 U.S. 238 (1976)

Supreme Court of the United States

Facts. Plaintiff Eugene R. Kelley, a policeman, sued Edward Johnson, Commissioner of the Suffolk County, New York, Police Department. Kelley sought to challenge the validity of the county's male hair grooming regulation for its police force as violating his right to free expression under the First Amendment and his guarantees of due process and equal protection under the Fourteenth Amendment. The regulation was directed at the style and length of hair, sideburns, and mustaches. Beards and goatees were prohibited, except for medical reasons; and wigs conforming to the regulation could be worn for cosmetic reasons. Kelley won in the district court and the court of appeals. The Supreme Court granted *certiorari.*

Issue. Do an employer's hair and grooming standards violate a person's constitutional rights of free expression?

Language of the Court. Rehnquist, C.J.: **Section 1 of the Fourteenth Amendment to the United States Constitution provides in pertinent part: "No State shall . . . deprive any person of life, liberty, or property, without due process of law." This section affords not only a procedural guarantee against the deprivation of "liberty," but likewise protects substantive aspects of liberty against unconstitutional restrictions by the State. . . . Each of those cases involved a substantial claim of infringement on the individual's freedom of choice with respect to certain basic matters of procreation, marriage, and family life. But whether the citizenry at large has some sort of "liberty" interest within the Fourteenth Amendment in matters of personal appearance is a question on which this Court's cases offer little, if any, guidance.**

Respondent has sought the protection of the Fourteenth Amendment not as a member of the citizenry at large, but, on the contrary, as an employee of the police department of Suffolk County, a subdivision of the State of New York. While the Court of Appeals made passing reference to this distinction, it was thereafter apparently ignored. We think, however, it is highly significant.

The Police Department in accordance with its well-established duty to keep the peace placed myriad demands upon the members of the police force, duties which have no counterpart with respect to the public at large. Kelley must wear a standard uniform, specific in each detail. When in uniform he must salute the flag. He may not take an active role in local political affairs by way of being a party delegate or contributing or soliciting political contributions. He may not smoke in public. All of these regulations infringe on Kelley's freedom of choice in personal matters.

We believe that the hair length regulation cannot be viewed in isolation, but must be rather considered in the context of the county's chosen mode of organization for its police force.

The promotion of safety of persons and property is unquestionably at the core of the State's police power, and virtually all state and local governments employ a uniform police force to aid in the accomplishment of that purpose. Choice of organization, dress, and equipment for law enforcement personnel is a decision entitled to the same sort of presumption of legislative validity as are state choices designed to promote other aims within the cognizance of the State's police power. We think Suffolk County's police regulations involved here are entitled to similar weight. The question is not as the Court of Appeals conceived whether the State can establish a genuine public need for the specific regulation. It is whether respondent can demonstrate that there is no rational connection

between the regulations, based as it is on the county's method of organizing its police force, and the promotion of safety of persons and property.

The overwhelming majority of state and local police of the present day are uniformed. This choice may be based on a desire to make police officers readily recognizable to the members of the public, or a desire for the esprit de corps which such similarity is felt to inculcate within the police force itself. Either one is sufficiently rational justification for regulations as to defeat respondent's claim based on the liberty guarantee of the Fourteenth Amendment.

Decision. No. The court reversed the appeals court's judgment and held that the regulation did not violate any constitutional right guaranteed the police officer.

CASE QUESTIONS

Critical Legal Thinking. Was the fact that Kelley was a public safety employee a distinguishing factor in the Court's decision? Would it have made a difference if Kelley worked as a night watchman for a private security firm?

Business Ethics. What effect, if any, do external fashion trends and influences have on grooming standards?

Contemporary Business. Is an employer permitted to establish limits on an employee's appearance? Can you think of any workplace restrictions you or your friends have encountered with respect to personal appearance?

CASE 7.5

GROOMING STANDARDS ARE PERMISSIBLE IF THEY ARE NOT MOTIVATED BY SEX STEREOTYPING

JESPERSEN V. HARRAH'S OPERATING COMPANY, INC.

444 F.3d 1104 (9th Cir. 2006)

U.S. Court of Appeals for the Ninth Circuit

Facts. Plaintiff, Darlene Jespersen, was a bartender at the sports bar in Harrah's Casino in Reno, Nevada, for more than 20 years. She was commended throughout her 20 years by both guests and management as highly effective and as providing excellent service. In February 2000, Harrah's implemented its "Beverage Department Image Transformation" policy to create a "brand standard of excellence" throughout its casinos. Female beverage servers were required to wear stockings and colored nail polish and to wear their hair "teased, curled or styled." Harrah's new appearance standards were referred to as the "Personal Best" program. The program was later amended to require all female beverage servers to wear makeup.

Ms. Jespersen refused to wear the makeup. Harrah's gave Ms. Jespersen 30 days to apply for a position with the company that did not require makeup. After 30 days, Ms. Jespersen had not applied for another job, and she was terminated. Ms. Jespersen sued Harrah's alleging the makeup requirement for female beverage servers constituted disparate-treatment sex discrimination. The district court granted Harrah's motion for summary judgment, and Jespersen appealed to the Ninth Circuit Court of Appeals.

Issue. Does the requirement to wear makeup constitute disparate-treatment sex discrimination in violation of Title VII?

Language of the Court. Schroeder, C.J.: **We have previously held that grooming and appearance standards that apply differently to women and men do not constitute discrimination on the basis of sex. We concluded that grooming and dress standards were entirely outside the purview of Title VII because Congress intended that Title VII only prohibit discrimination based on "immutable characteristics" associated with a worker's sex.**

In later cases, we recognized, however, that an employer's imposition of more stringent appearance standards on one sex than the other constitutes sex discrimination even where the appearance standards regulate only "mutable" characteristics such as weight. We have previously held, a sex-differentiated appearance standard that imposes unequal burdens on men and women is disparate treatment that must be justified as a BFOQ.

Harrah's contends that the burden of the makeup requirement must be evaluated with reference to all of the requirements of the policy, including those that burden men only. We agree with Harrah's approach. Jespersen contends that the makeup requirement imposes "innumerable" tangible burdens on women that men do not share because cosmetics can cost hundreds of dollars per year and putting on makeup requires a significant investment in time. As the non-moving party that bore the ultimate burden of proof at trial, Jespersen had the burden of producing admissible evidence that the "Personal Best" appearance standard imposes a greater burden on female beverage servers than it does on male beverage servers. There is, however, no evidence in the record in support of this contention. Because there is no evidence in the record from which we can assess the burdens that the "Personal Best" policy imposes on male bartenders either, Jespersen's claim fails for that reason alone.

We hold that under the "unequal burdens" test, which is this Circuit's test for evaluating whether an employer's sex-differentiated appearance standards

constitute sex discrimination in violation of Title VII, Jespersen failed to introduce evidence raising a triable issue of fact as to whether Harrah's "Personal Best" policy imposes unequal burdens on male and female employees.

Decision. No. The Court affirmed the District Court's grant of Harrah's motion for summary judgment.

CASE QUESTIONS

Critical Legal Thinking. Would the decision be the same if Harrah's required that female beverage servers have blond hair? If it is more costly to wear makeup than not, should that constitute an "unequal burden"?

Business Ethics. Was this a fair decision to both parties? What if Jespersen's sexual orientation was such that she found wearing makeup inappropriate to her image?

Contemporary Business. Should employers place limits on employees' hair and grooming choices? If so, how would you appropriately define grooming standards for the employees of your company, and how would the standards be enforced?

Sexual Harassment

Although the Civil Rights Act of 1964 offered women some protection, they were still subject to harassment and discriminatory behavior by their peers, supervisors, or management. It was not until its decision in *Meritor Savings Bank, FSB v. Vinson* that the United States Supreme Court held that sexual harassment violated **Title VII** of the Civil Rights Act of 1964. The Court in *Meritor* held that the scope of **Title VII** should not be restricted to economic damages arising from such discrimination but that it also prohibited the creation of a "hostile work environment." The court held that it was the intention of Congress to balance "the entire spectrum of treatment of men and women" in the workplace. Such protection included sexual harassment actions that can lead to noneconomic damages. The Supreme Court also stated in the following decision that the guidelines issued by the EEOC are entitled to great weight by the courts.

CASE 7.6

A HOSTILE WORK ENVIRONMENT IS A FORM OF SEX DISCRIMINATION

MERITOR SAVINGS BANK, FSB V. VINSON

477 U.S. 57 (1986)

Supreme Court of the United States

Facts. Plaintiff Michelle Vinson was an employee at Meritor Savings Bank. Vinson sued Meritor alleging that her supervisor, Sidney Taylor, had sexually harassed her at work. She claimed that Taylor had sexual relations with her approximately 40 to 50 times to which she had only consented for fear of losing her job. Vinson testified that she was fondled in front of other employees, followed into the restroom where Taylor exposed himself to her, and forcibly raped on several occasions. She claimed that other employees at the Bank were also touched and fondled by Taylor. Claiming she was afraid of Taylor she never reported his harassment and never used or followed the bank's complaint procedures. She was fired for taking excessive time off, and she sued for sexual harassment, but the district court held the bank was without notice of Taylor's behaviors and could not be held liable for his actions.

The Court of Appeals for the District of Columbia Circuit reversed. It held that a violation of Title VII may be found by a violation of either a quid pro quo relationship between employment and sexual favors or when a hostile or offensive working environment is created. It also held that an employer is absolutely liable for sexual harassment practiced by a supervisor even if the employer was not aware of the conduct. The Supreme Court granted *certiorari*.

Issue. Is a hostile working environment a form of sexual harassment for which a person can sue under Title VII?

Language of the Court. Rehnquist, C.J.: **Without question, when a supervisor sexually harasses a subordinate because of the subordinate's sex, the supervisor "discriminated[s]" on the basis of sex. [The court then addressed the bank's contention that Title VII only protects tangible "economic" losses and not psychological aspects of the workplace environment. The Court stated the language of Title VII is not limited to "economic" or "tangible" discrimination.] The phrase "terms, conditions, or privileges of employment" evinces a congressional intent "to strike at the entire spectrum of disparate treatment of**

men and women" in employment. In 1980 the EEOC issued Guidelines specifying that "sexual harassment," as there defined, is a form of sex discrimination prohibited by Title VII. As an "administrative interpretation of the Act by the enforcing agency," ***Griggs v. Duke Power Co.*** **(citation omitted), these Guidelines, " 'while not controlling upon the courts by reason of their authority, do constitute a body of experience and informed judgment to which courts and litigants may properly resort for guidance.' "**

The EEOC Guidelines fully support the view that harassment leading to non-economic injury can violate Title VII. Nothing in Title VII suggests that a hostile environment based on discriminatory sexual harassment should not be likewise prohibited. The Guidelines thus appropriately drew from, and were fully consistent with, the existing case law.

As the Court of Appeals for the Eleventh Circuit wrote in ***Henson v. Dundee*** **(citation omitted): "Sexual harassment which creates a hostile or offensive environment for members of one sex is every bit the arbitrary barrier to sexual equality at the workplace that racial harassment is to racial equality. Surely, a requirement that a man or woman run a gauntlet of sexual abuse in return for the privilege of being allowed to work and make a living can be as demeaning and disconcerting as the harshest of racial epithets."**

Decision. Yes. A violation of Title VII may occur with either a quid pro quo relationship between employment and sexual favors or when a hostile or offensive working environment is created. It also held that an employer is absolutely liable for sexual harassment practiced by a supervisor even if the employer was not aware of the conduct.

CASE QUESTIONS

Critical Legal Thinking. Although the Supreme Court affirmed the decision of the court of appeals, it also held that it was a mistake to exclude evidence regarding Vinson's provocative dress and publicly expressed fantasies. Is this evidence relevant to determining if sexual harassment occurred?

Business Ethics. Why does the law impose liability on a corporate employer whose management is unaware of the harassment occurring at lower management tiers in the organization?

Contemporary Business. If liability can be imposed on an employer for the harassing behavior of a supervisor, what training and monitoring programs would you institute in your company to reduce your company's exposure to such risk?

Types of Sexual Harassment

As the *Meritor* case makes clear, two classes of persons have a potential claim for **sex discrimination**: first, those who have been exposed to ***quid pro quo*** situations, where the exchange of sexual conduct for employment benefits was propositioned; and second, employees or others who have been subjected to a **hostile work environment**. The EEOC defines **sexual harassment** as unwelcome sexual conduct that is a term or condition of employment:

> *Harassment based on sex is a violation of Section 703 of Title VII of the 1964 Civil Rights Act as amended in 1972. Unwelcome sexual advances, requests for sex favors and other verbal or physical conduct of a sexual nature constitute sex harassment when:*
>
> *The conduct is made either exclusively or implicitly a term or condition of employment (**quid pro quo**). The conduct unreasonably interferes with work performance or creates a hostile or offensive working environment.*

Quid Pro Quo Sexual Harassment Unlawful conduct in which the harasser uses submission to or rejection of sexual requests as a basis for employment decisions, such as hiring, firing, compensation, and promotions.

Quid pro quo sexual harassment involves a workplace benefit promised in exchange for sexual activity by the harassed worker. A **hostile work environment** is one in which unwanted sexual activity takes place, thus creating a hostile or abusive work environment that interferes with the victim's ability to perform the work. It is also so severe and/or pervasive that it affects a term or condition of the victim's employment.

Sexual harassment need not exist over a long period of time for it to be considered pervasive. Courts consider the frequency and/or intensity of the offensive conduct. Courts do not recognize **sexual harassment** for "every sexual innuendo or flirtation,"[13] every crude joke or sexually explicit remark made on the job,[14] and "trivial and merely annoying vulgarity."[15] Isolated incidents do not state a claim for **hostile environment sexual harassment.**

> ***Example:*** Rachel Stacy worked for Shoney's but quit because she claimed sexual harassment on the basis of the following statements made by her direct male supervisor: (1) daily comments to Stacy that her tan looked good and that he wished that he could see more of it; (2) a comment to Stacy that he liked it better when she wore her hair down; (3) in response to Stacy's request for a cigarette, the statement that she could have anything she wanted from him and asking if there was anything else that she wanted; (4) after asking if it would cause a problem with her husband if she stayed after work to go over her training manuals, the comment that if he had someone that looked like Stacy he would not let her leave the house; (5) daily comments regarding Stacy's appearance, which plaintiff never identified with specificity; (6) the statement that he would move in with Stacy and take care of her in response to Stacy's statement that it was awkward sharing an apartment with another couple; (7) the comment that all Stacy had to do was stand there and look pretty in response to Stacy's question about the duties of a dining room manager; (8) statements made several times over the phone to Stacy at work indicating that he missed her; (9) in response to the dishwasher's question of whether or not Stacy was his sister, the comment that he never had a sister that looked like that; (10) the daily "ssshh" sounds made as Stacy walked away from him; and (11) the comment that Stacy and he could work the night shift together. While the court found her supervisor's conduct immature and inappropriate, it did not constitute sexual harassment.[16]

A finding of **sexual harassment** requires an intensive fact finding effort by the trier of fact. The decisions finding **hostile-environment sexual harassment** in the workplace typically find that a female (or male) employee was subjected to individual acts of harassment combined with evidence of sexual graffiti (or an equivalent) throughout the workplace or that continued for a sustained period.

> ***Example:*** The following is an extreme case of a sexually harassing, hostile work environment to which some female employees have been exposed. The case could have been established with a far less hostile work environment. Ms. Waltman claimed she was subjected to sexual harassment and sexual discrimination when she worked at a paper plant. She claimed that it began when an employee several times broadcast obscenities directed toward Waltman over the public address system. In response, other employees began making suggestive comments to Waltman. A supervisor did not discipline the offending employee. Waltman received over 30 pornographic notes in her locker. Sexually explicit pictures and graffiti were drawn on the building walls and in the elevator. Some of these were directed toward her. Employees had sexually oriented calendars on the walls and in their lockers, which were kept open. They also hung used tampons from their lockers. Several workers propositioned Waltman. Waltman complained to her manager, who told her she should expect this type of behavior working with men. Six months later one employee told another that Waltman was a whore and that she would get hurt if she did not keep her mouth shut. She was threatened with sexual assault and pinched in inappropriate places. The company did not conduct an independent, internal investigation of the incidents Waltman alleged nor did it take any concerted steps to remove the pornographic graffiti around the mill. It also did not take any disciplinary action against any of its employees. Waltman never invoked the established grievance procedure at the plant. In a split decision, with a female justice dissenting, a federal court of appeals upheld Waltman's claim.[17]

Keep in mind that **sexual harassment** is not limited to egregious acts. To list a few examples, **sexual harassment** can occur through jokes, touching (both physical and imitative), staring, and making comments. Typically, however, the milder the conduct, the more responsibility the complainant has to express objection.

A **hostile work environment** claim of **sexual harassment** is more difficult for the plaintiff to demonstrate than a ***quid pro quo*** **sexual harassment** claim because the plaintiff has the burden of proving that the action was **severe** or **pervasive** enough to create a **hostile work environment**. As the U.S. Supreme Court stated in its *Meritor Savings* decision, for a **sexual harassment** claim to be actionable, it must be sufficiently **severe or pervasive** enough to alter the conditions of the victim's employment and create an **abusive working environment**. Therefore, actions that were consensual cannot be used as a basis for a **hostile work environment** claim of **sexual harassment**. A victim can claim a **hostile work environment** when consensual actions change into unwanted actions by one party.

> ***Example:*** The California Supreme Court held that raunchy talk can sometimes be a necessary part of the job. It upheld the dismissal of a sexual harassment suit brought by a former writers' assistant on the NBC television show *Friends*. The sexually coarse and vulgar language used regularly in the writers' room did not create a hostile work environment. The language was not directed toward the plaintiff, and the vast majority of the comments were not about her or any of her co-workers. The court held that the female plaintiff failed to establish that the alleged conduct was engaged in because of her gender. With regard to the comments about the female cast members, the Court found they were not sufficiently severe or pervasive enough to create a hostile or offensive work environment.[18]

Employer Liability for Harassment

In 1998, the Supreme Court issued two opinions that defined the liability of employers for **sexual harassment by supervisors**. In *Faragher v. City of Boca Raton*[19] and *Burlington Industries, Inc. v. Ellerth,*[20] the Court held employers are subject to **vicarious liability** for **unlawful harassment by supervisors**. The basis for this holding is that the law has long held an employer liable for the acts of its supervisors, and the rule encourages employers to eliminate harassment from the workplace. The Court held that if the **supervisor's harassment** culminates in a tangible employment action (e.g., an employee is fired or passed over for promotion), the employer is held liable; if it does not, the employer may be able to avoid liability or limit damages by establishing an affirmative defense that includes two necessary elements: (a) the employer exercised reasonable care to prevent and promptly correct any harassing behavior, and (b) the employee unreasonably failed to take advantage of any preventive or corrective opportunities provided by the employer or to avoid harm otherwise.

Since these decisions were issued, both courts and the EEOC have applied this standard to all other forms of **harassment** arising from other protected classifications such as race. **Harassment** does not violate federal law unless it involves discriminatory treatment on the basis of a protected classification. These decisions impose an affirmative obligation on the employer to remedy sexually hostile conduct in the workplace. This duty requires employers to:

- prepare and disseminate a policy prohibiting **sexual harassment**;
- provide a procedure for lodging complaints; and
- provide a thorough and complete investigation of all complaints regardless of the gender of the claimant.

The *Ellerth* and *Faragher* decisions describe a **supervisor** as a person with immediate or successively higher authority over another employee. The Supreme Court reached this conclusion because the misconduct is facilitated by the **supervisor**, who is empowered to act by the authority delegated by the employer. Courts do not apply a mechanical test to define a supervisor. Instead, they consider the person's authority as exercised on the job. For example, a court would look to see if the person had the authority to undertake or recommend employment decisions affecting the employee or could direct the worker's daily work activities.

When the alleged harasser is not a supervisor (this also includes nonemployees, such as customers and vendors), the employer is responsible only if it knew or should have known of the harassment and took no steps to prevent it. Additionally, people who are not the target of **harassment** but who work in environments in which **sexual harassment** is occurring can file "third party" and "bystander" harassment suits. The contours of harassment's definition are changing. It must occur in other than an isolated context. Under a **sexual harassment** standard, simple teasing, offhand comments, and isolated nonegregious incidents will not amount to actionable harassment.

An employer is strictly liable under **Title VII** if ***quid pro quo*** **harassment** or **discrimination** is found to have taken place. There is no affirmative defense to this form of harm under federal law. The plaintiff must introduce proof other than vague comments and unsupported allegations insufficient to cause a reasonable person to believe that retaining the job was conditioned on having a sexual relationship with the supervisor. Moreover, if the victim has received reassurances from other managers about the relative security of the position, the employer can rely on that evidence in defending a ***quid pro quo*** claim of **sexual harassment**.[21]

Sometimes employers can become liable for **sexual harassment** against women because they specifically define the type of employee they do not want. They hire women possessing only certain characteristics, such as not being pregnant, falling under a certain height, or without children not yet in school. Although the employer may have good reasons for these preferences based upon prior experience, such hiring restrictions constitute gender discrimination because women are entitled as a matter of right to equal opportunity in employment. In the absence of an exception to the general prohibition of **sex discrimination**, since the employer used gender to distinguish among applicants, a discrimination charge based on gender is likely to occur.

The *Ellerth* and *Faragher* decisions state that the plaintiff's own behavior is relevant in determining whether **unlawful harassment** has occurred. Some courts have held that they must consider the plaintiff's provocative speech or attire in a **sexual harassment** case. That consideration is not necessary when the facts dictate that **sexual harassment** has occurred.

> ***Example:*** Judith Ann Jones was employed by Wesco Investments, Inc. From the start of her employment with Wesco, she was barraged with repeated sexual advances, requests for sexual favors, and other verbal or physical contact of a sexual nature. Ben Rose, the president of the company, would come up behind her and rub his hands up and down the sides of her body, touching her breasts. He would pinch Jones, pat her on the bottom, and kiss her on the top of the head. At one point, Rose even put his hand on her outside thigh. His oral comments included a statement that someday her breasts would be his. On one occasion, Rose entered the kitchen area in the Wesco suite and informed Ms. Jones that he thought it was a good idea that Ms. Jones spend more time in the kitchen area where it was cool because he could see her nipples much better in the cool temperature. On at least three occasions, Rose requested her to accompany him to unoccupied apartment buildings, ostensibly for advice involving the building or redecoration of the apartments. Each time, Rose put his arm around Jones before she could get away. On one of these occasions, Rose also kissed her on the lips before she could pull away. On each of the above occasions, Jones would push Rose away, leave the room, or inform Rose that she was only interested in a business relationship. Doing so halted Rose's advances, but only temporarily. His uninvited attentions recommenced with the next available opportunity. Surprisingly, Rose unsuccessfully argued that his behavior did not constitute a **hostile working environment** involving **sexual harassment**. In his losing appellate brief, Rose argued that liability should not be imposed on employers because the workplace is a traditional place for men and women to meet marriage partners.[22]

Under such case law, the behavior of the claimant relative to the **sexual harassment** claim is relevant to making a harassment finding. As the following case shows, sometimes the claimant's own provocative style can result in a termination without employer liability for a **hostile work environment.** The behavior of the plaintiff in the following case is the antithesis of the law's protection from ***quid pro quo*** **harassment**.

CASE 7.7

WORK ATTIRE CAN DEFEAT A HOSTILE WORK ENVIRONMENT CLAIM

SCHMITZ V. ING SECURITIES, FUTURES & OPTIONS, INC.

191 F.3d 456 (7th Cir. 1999)

U.S. Court of Appeals for the Seventh Circuit

Facts. In January 1995, Laura Schmitz joined the Chicago offices of ING Securities, Futures & Options, Inc. (ING) as a receptionist. Her direct supervisor was Anna Melinauskas, whose supervisor was the Chief Financial Officer (CFO), William Pauly. Schmitz's job entailed greeting guests, answering the phones, sorting the mail, and aiding in various office tasks. Although ING had no formal written dress code policy, Pauly commented frequently about Schmitz's inappropriate clothing as well as the clothing of three other ING female employees. Pauly criticized Schmitz saying her skirts and blouses were too tight, too short, or too revealing, and he called her an exhibitionist.

Schmitz admitted that the length of her skirts reached five or six inches above her knee and that she wore leggings or stretch pants at least once a week. Some of her outfits included miniskirts worn with thigh-high stockings, a low-cut blouse revealing her cleavage, and a tight blue acetate dress that Pauly observed "left nothing to the imagination."

Pauly told Schmitz that he would never let his wife leave the house dressed as Schmitz was dressed. Although Schmitz confronted Pauly about his comments, Pauly responded that they were made to cultivate an image that would further her career. An incident did occur, however, where Pauly had entered the reception area and proceeded to stick out his chest and strut in front of the desk where Schmitz was sitting; while strutting on his tiptoes, he stated, "Schmitz, why do you always parade through the office like this?" Nevertheless, Pauly never asked Schmitz for a date, never expressed any sexual interest in her, and never touched her. Following her termination for poor work performance, she sued for termination due to a hostile work environment. The district court granted summary judgment for ING, finding that Schmitz failed to establish that anyone at ING had sexually harassed her or that ING had retaliated against her when she was terminated. She appealed to the Court of Appeals for the Seventh Circuit.

Issue. Did Pauly's remarks regarding Schmitz's attire constitute a hostile work environment sexual harassment claim?

Language of the Court. Schmitz fails to satisfy the first prong because she cannot show that she was subjected to sexual advances or requests for sexual favors. Title VII is directed against conditions in employment, not "against unpleasantness per se." Workplace harassment is not automatically discrimination "merely because the words used have sexual content or connotations." Distasteful or inappropriate remarks do not rise to the level of being deeply offensive, intimidating, and sexually harassing. Moreover, Pauly's behavior towards Schmitz lacks the requisite severity required of sexual harassment. Schmitz must show that her work environment was hostile or abusive and that a reasonable person would think so too.

Pauly criticized her clothing and remarked on the provocativeness of her attire with the expressed aim of bettering her professional image and her career prospects. The record also shows that Pauly criticized the attire of at least three other women at the office, and one of them responded by correcting her outfit.

Finally, we note that Pauly was not the only one critical of Schmitz's inappropriate attire. Two of Schmitz's female superiors — her direct supervisor Melinauskas and ING's human resources director Riley — stated that on several occasions they had informally commented to Schmitz that some of her outfits were not appropriate for a business environment. Further, Melinauskas also stated that some of Schmitz's clothing spurred office guests to comment. In one incident, a vendor visiting the ING office commented to Schmitz that she should not slouch at the reception desk because her cleavage was visible when she did so.

Schmitz also contends that ING retaliated against her by firing her after she complained about Pauly's behavior. To establish a prima facie case for retaliation, Schmitz must show that: 1) she engaged in a statutorily protected activity; 2) she suffered an adverse action by her employer; and 3) there is a causal link between the protected expression and the adverse action.

Schmitz fails to establish the third prong of the test. Although Schmitz asserts that her termination occurred "fairly soon" after she made her harassment complaint, ING maintains that it terminated her based on her inadequate work performance. In order to succeed in her retaliation claim, she must discredit ING's explanation. This she does not do. ING's termination memorandum contains references to at least twenty different specific problems in Schmitz's performance, among them her unprofessional dress and work product. The record supports these criticisms, primarily because Schmitz points to nothing in the record that refutes the flaws in her work performance listed in ING's termination memorandum.

Decision. No. The work environment was not hostile. In addition, because Schmitz could not rebut ING's claims that her work performance was unsatisfactory, she did not establish that ING fired her in retaliation for her complaints regarding her claimed discrimination.

CASE QUESTIONS

Critical Legal Thinking. Would the decision have been the same if Pauly's criticism of Schmitz's attire arose out of Pauly's desire to bring back professional and formal attire to the office?

Business Ethics. What is considered appropriate attire for men and women to wear to the office? Should the employer make an accommodation if Schmitz could not afford more professional-looking clothes?

Contemporary Business. Take a survey among class members as to what constitutes appropriate business attire; have them describe "business casual" attire for an office.

Determining what standard a court should employ in determining if **sexual harassment** has occurred is a matter of significance to both parties to a **sexual harassment** claim. Moreover, the courts must consider the perspective from which the behavior should be viewed and interpreted. Sexual harassment disputes have posed several questions for the courts that have heard them. Among these are the following: (i) Whose perspective will control the analysis — that of the victim, the alleged harasser, or a reasonable person? (ii) Does the gender or sexual orientation of the victim affect the decision? (iii) Should the trier of fact consider any special sensitivities of the alleged harassment victim?

The U.S. Supreme Court in *Harris v. Forklift Systems, Inc.*[23] noted that the standard of whether conduct is abusive should be that of a "reasonable person" in the plaintiff's position, considering "all of the circumstances." *Harris* is also an important case for another reason. The Court held that a claimant need *not* prove serious adverse psychological injury to establish a **hostile work environment**. The reasonable person standard used in the *Harris* decision was widely criticized for being male-biased. Over time, courts began to adopt a **reasonable victim's** perspective, and this seems to be the current trend among courts facing such cases. By adopting a **"reasonable victim"** standard, federal circuit courts of appeals require that both a subjective and an objective element demonstrate **sexual harassment**. Thus, **sexual harassment** against a woman is judged on the basis of whether the **"reasonable woman"** would find the conduct or environment sexually harassing. A "reasonable man" standard would apply to harassment of a male worker. Not constrained by the limits of federal decisional law, some state legislatures have enacted clarifying legislation. Some of these states have adopted a **"reasonable woman"** standard in cases involving a female victim.

Concept Summary
Proving Sexual Harassment and Hostile Work Environment

Sexual harassment consists of unwelcome advances or other verbal or physical conduct of a sexual nature if:

- submission is a condition of employment;
- submission affects employment decisions;
- the purpose or effect of the conduct is to unreasonably interfere with the employee's work performance; or
- the conduct creates an intimidating, hostile, or offensive environment.

For an employee to prevail in a **sexual harassment claim** based on a **"hostile work environment"** the plaintiff must prove an additional element: that the employer knew or should have known of the harassment and failed to take proper remedial action.

Management Application
Hostile Work Environment

Sexual harassment in the workplace violates Title VII of the Civil Rights Act of 1964 when it creates a hostile work environment. Consider the following case. The Pennsylvania State Police (PSP) hired Nancy Drew Suders as a police communications operator for the McConnellsburg barracks. Suders's supervisors were Sergeant Eric D. Easton, station commander at the McConnellsburg barracks, Patrol Corporal William D. Baker, and Corporal Eric B. Prendergast. Those three supervisors subjected Suders to a continuous barrage of gender harassment that ceased only when she resigned from the force.

Easton would bring up the subject of people having sex with animals each time Suders entered his office. He told Prendergast, in front of Suders, that young girls should be given instruction in how to gratify men with oral sex. Easton also would sit down near Suders, wearing spandex shorts, and spread his legs apart. Baker repeatedly made obscene gestures in Suders's presence by grabbing his genitals and shouting out a vulgar comment inviting oral sex. Baker made this gesture as many as five to ten times per night throughout Suders's employment at the barracks. Further, Baker would rub his rear end in front of her and remark, "I have a nice ass, don't I?"

Five months after being hired, Suders contacted Virginia Smith-Elliot, PSP's equal opportunity officer, stating that she was being harassed at work and was afraid. Smith-Elliot's response appeared to Suders to be insensitive and unhelpful. Two days later, Suders resigned from the force. Suders sued PSP in U.S. district court alleging that she had been subject to gender harassment and constructively discharged and forced to resign. The district court held that although the evidence was sufficient for a jury to conclude that Suders's supervisors had engaged in sexual harassment, PSP was not vicariously liable for the supervisors' conduct. The U.S. district court granted PSP's motion for summary judgment. On appeal, the U.S. court of appeals reversed and remanded the case for trial on the merits against PSP. PSP appealed to the U.S. Supreme Court.

The issue before the U.S. Supreme Court was whether an employer can be held vicariously liable when the sexual harassment conduct of its employees is so severe that the victim of the harassment resigns. In its opinion, the U.S. Supreme Court stated:

> *To establish hostile work environment, plaintiffs like Suders must show harassing behavior sufficiently severe or pervasive to alter the conditions of their employment. The very fact that the discriminatory conduct was so severe or pervasive that it created a work environment abusive to employees because of their gender offends Title VII's broad rule of workplace equality. Beyond that, we hold, to establish "constructive discharge," the plaintiff must make a further showing: She must show that the abusive working environment became so intolerable that her resignation qualified as a fitting response. Essentially, Suders presents a "worse case" harassment scenario, harassment ratcheted up to the breaking point. Harassment so intolerable as to cause a resignation may be effected through co-worker conduct, unofficial supervisory conduct, or official company acts. Unlike an actual termination, which is always effected through an official act of the company, a constructive discharge need not be. A constructive discharge involves both an employee's decision to leave and precipitating conduct.*

The Supreme Court agreed with the U.S. court of appeals that Suders's case presented genuine issues of material fact concerning her hostile work environment and constructive discharge claims. The Supreme Court remanded the case for further proceedings consistent with its opinion.[24]

Discussion Questions

1. What is vicarious liability? What is constructive discharge?
2. Could Suders's supervisors be disciplined for failing to prevent her resignation? How did they fail to act ethically?
3. Can you think of any examples of sexual harassment in the workplace?

Sexual Orientation Discrimination

Because of the circumstances in which "sex" was added to the Civil Rights Act, Congress provided little discussion or guidance on what **sex-based discrimination** and **harassment** entails. No record indicates what Congress intended the "sex" class to encompass, leaving courts to interpret the scope of this language. Many decisions in federal circuit courts of appeals, including the First, Fourth, and Eighth, have concluded that **Title VII** should be interpreted narrowly as relating to gender only. Therefore, **sexual orientation** in these circuits under **Title VII** has effectively been excluded from protection. However, some states, even within the jurisdiction of these federal circuits, have expanded the definition of what "sex" encompasses in this context. Decisions from other federal circuit courts of appeals, including the Sixth and Ninth, have expanded the protections afforded under the specific language of the Civil Rights Act to include limited protection for **sexual orientation**, including **transgender** individuals. As will be discussed later in this chapter, these federal appellate decisions are based on the concept of sex stereotyping and *not* on **sexual orientation** itself as a protected characteristic.

Sexual Orientation
The choice of an adult sexual partner according to gender.

Initially, it should be noted that there is a distinct difference between **sexual orientation harassment** involving an actor and victim of the same or opposite sex and employment discrimination based on **sexual orientation**. The first type is protected under federal discrimination law, but the second type is not. **Same-sex harassment** is unlawful under **Title VII**. The Supreme Court has considered one case involving sexual harassment of a male employee by other male employees on an oil drilling platform in *Oncale v. Sundowner Offshore Services, Inc.*[25] In that decision, the Supreme Court rejected a *per se* rule that same-sex harassment was not entitled to protection under **Title VII**. The harassing conduct need not be motivated by sexual intent. In its *Oncale* decision, the Court held that **harassment** is a type of discrimination based on a protected characteristic, such as sex.

In *Oncale*, the Supreme Court gave three examples of ways a victim can prove discrimination because of gender: (1) establishing that the harassers were motivated by sexual desire, which generally requires "credible evidence" that the harasser was a homosexual; (2) establishing that the harassment demonstrates that "the harasser [was] motivated by general hostility to the presence of [men] in the workplace"; or (3) establishing that the harasser treated men differently in a mixed-sex workplace.

Sexual harassment is a form of **sex discrimination** because it adversely affects the work environment and is based on the victim's protected characteristic (e.g., gender). While the Court recognized **sexual harassment** in its decision, it limited **sexual harassment** lawsuits with regard to those who wish to present claims relating to sexual orientation.

Concept Summary
Proving Sexual Orientation Harassment

In order to prevail, the plaintiff must show:

- The motivation of the actor must be attributable to sexual desire or general hostility to the plaintiff's gender; and
- The conduct must be severe or pervasive unwelcome sexual conduct.

If the motive is a general loathing to the employee's gender (male or female) or to a specific gender performing a particular job, the motivation is clearly gender based. Under the *Oncale* decision, the motivation of the actor must be carefully examined. If the motivation is based on the attire or actions of the victim, then "gay-bashing" is more difficult to determine. The difficulty is in determining whether the hostility is toward the victim's sexual orientation, which is not protected by **Title VII**, or is due to to improper gender stereotyping, which is covered by **Title VII** and prohibited by the decision in *Price Waterhouse v. Hopkins*[26] (female CPA was not "feminine" enough to be made a partner in accounting firm).

Several federal circuit courts of appeals have held that discrimination or harassment because of a person's nonconformity with a gender stereotype, including effeminacy in men and masculinity in women, is a form of **sex discrimination**; however, **Title VII** has never been held to apply directly to **sexual orientation discrimination**. Several courts have attempted to distinguish **sex discrimination** from **sexual orientation discrimination** following the *Oncale* decision. The federal appellate decisions continue to refine the law in this area. Among them are:

- In *Nichols v. Azteca Restaurant Enterprises, Inc.*,[27] Antonio Sanchez was subjected to a relentless campaign of harassment. Male co-workers repeatedly referred to him in Spanish and English as "she" and "her." They mocked him for walking and carrying his serving tray "like a woman," and taunted him by calling him a "faggot." The abuse occurred daily over several years. Sanchez complained, but his employer did little to stop the harassment. After Sanchez was fired, he sued for sexual harassment and retaliation. The Ninth Circuit rejected the restaurant's argument that the harassment was based on sexual orientation. It ruled that the sexual harassment arose because Sanchez did not conform to gender stereotypes.

- *Bibby v. Coca-Cola*[28] involved the harassment of a male employee. The harassment included pushing him against a wall and blocking his path with a forklift. He was denounced with statements such as "everyone knows you're gay as a three dollar bill," and "everybody knows you're a faggot." While recognizing that failing to conform to a gender stereotype can constitute harassment, the court held Bibby's claims did not fit within same-sex harassment. Bibby did not allege that he was harassed because he was a man, his harasser were motivated by sexual desire, the harassers were hostile to the presence of men in the workplace, or he was harassed because he failed to comply with societal stereotypes of how men should appear or behave. Would the result have been different if Bibby had alleged the last type of discrimination?

In the following case, the court had to consider if **sexual orientation protection** falls within the **Title VII** definition of **sexual discrimination.**

CASE 7.8

TITLE VII DOES NOT PROHIBIT SEXUAL ORIENTATION HARASSMENT

SIMONTON V. RUNYON

225 F.3d 122 (2d Cir. 2000)

U.S. Court of Appeals for the Second Circuit

Facts. Dwayne Simonton sued the Postmaster General and the U.S.P.S. under Title VII of the Civil Rights Act for abuse and harassment he suffered by reason of his sexual orientation. The U.S. district court dismissed his complaint on the basis that Title VII does not prohibit discrimination based on sexual orientation.

Issue. Does Title VII afford protection from discrimination based on sexual orientation?

Language of the Court. Walker, J.: **Simonton was employed as a postal worker in Farmingdale, New York, for approximately twelve years. He repeatedly received satisfactory to excellent performance evaluations. He was, however, subjected to an abusive and hostile work environment by reason of his sexual orientation. The abuse he allegedly endured was so severe that he ultimately suffered a heart attack.**

For the sake of decency and judicial propriety, we hesitate before reciting in detail the incidents of Simonton's abuse. Nevertheless, we think it is important both to acknowledge the appalling persecution Simonton allegedly endured and to identify the precise nature of the abuse so as to distinguish this case from future cases as they arise. We therefore relate some, but not all, of the alleged harassment that forms the basis for this suit.

Simonton's sexual orientation was known to his co-workers who repeatedly assaulted him with such comments as "go f*** yourself, f*g," "suck my d***," and "so you like it up the a**?" Notes were placed on the wall in the employees' bathroom with Simonton's name and the name of celebrities who had died of AIDS. Pornographic photographs were taped to his work area, male dolls were placed in his vehicle, and copies of Playgirl magazine were sent to his home. Pictures of an erect penis were posted in his work place, as were posters stating that Simonton suffered from mental illness as a result of "bu*g h*le disorder." There were repeated statements that Simonton was a "f***ing f*gg*t."

There can be no doubt that the conduct allegedly engaged in by Simonton's co-workers is morally reprehensible whenever and in whatever context it occurs, particularly in the modern workplace. Nevertheless, as the First Circuit recently explained in a similar context, "we are called upon here to construe a statute as glossed by the Supreme Court, not to make a moral judgment." . . . When interpreting a statute, the role of a court is limited to discerning and adhering to legislative meaning. The law is well-settled in this circuit and in all others to have reached the question that Simonton has no cause of action under Title VII because Title VII does not prohibit harassment or discrimination because of sexual orientation.

In Oncale, the Supreme Court rejected a per se rule that same-sex sexual harassment was non-cognizable under Title VII. The Court reasoned that "nothing in Title VII necessarily bars a claim of discrimination 'because of . . . sex' merely because the plaintiff and the defendant (or person charged with acting on behalf of the defendant) are of the same sex." Oncale did not suggest, however, that male harassment of other males always violates Title VII. Oncale emphasized that every victim of such harassment must show that he was harassed because he was male.

We likewise do not see how Oncale changes our well-settled precedent that "sex" refers to membership in a class delineated by gender. The critical issue, as stated in Oncale, "is whether members of one sex are exposed to disadvantageous terms or conditions of employment to which members of the other sex are not exposed." Simonton has alleged that he was discriminated against not because he was a man, but because of his sexual orientation. Such a claim remains non-cognizable under Title VII.

Decision. No. Title VII does not protect individuals from sexual orientation discrimination.

CASE QUESTIONS

Critical Legal Thinking. Is this case distinguishable from the Supreme Court's *Oncale* decision referenced in the court's opinion? If so, how?

Business Ethics. Does the application of *stare decisis* result in an unfair application of the law?

Contemporary Business. What consequences would follow if employers granted same-sex civil rights to employees within their organizations?

If a terminated employee claims **sexual discrimination**, an unethical employer could claim that the individual was fired not because of **sexual discrimination**, but because of the individual's **sexual orientation**. Under federal law, **sexual orientation discrimination** is not prohibited; however, many states and local jurisdictions have enacted laws that protect individuals from this form of discrimination. Some of those courts have held that **transgender** employees are protected under state sex discrimination laws. In addition, those afflicted with HIV are protected from discrimination under the Americans with Disabilities Act.

While no federal law prohibits this type of discrimination, **Executive Order 13087**, issued in 1998, specifically prohibits discrimination based on **sexual orientation** in federal government employment. Federal government employees are also protected from discrimination under the Civil Service Reform Act of 1978 that prohibits **sexual orientation discrimination**. In addition, 20 states and the District of Columbia have laws that prohibit **sexual orientation discrimination and/or gender identity/ expression discrimination in employment**. These states are California, Colorado, Connecticut, Hawaii, Illinois, Iowa, Maine, Maryland, Massachusetts, Minnesota, Nevada, New Hampshire, New Jersey, New Mexico, New York, Oregon, Rhode Island, Vermont, Washington, and Wisconsin. Hundreds of local governments prohibit discrimination in their workplaces as well.

Executive Order 13087
A presidential order issued by President Clinton in 1998 prohibiting discrimination based on sexual orientation in federal civilian employment. Certain positions and executive agencies are excepted from its coverage.

Maryland's Code of Fair Employment Practices Executive Order 01.1.2007.16 and statute Annotated Code Article 49B prohibit discrimination on the basis of **sexual orientation**. They prohibit discrimination in employment, housing, public accommodation, state services, institutional health care, and the conduct of businesses. The statute covers employers with 15 or more employees. The law defines **sexual orientation** as the identification of an individual as to male or female homosexuality, heterosexuality, or bisexuality.[29]

Under its statute, Maryland defines the following types of **sexual orientation discrimination**:

- intentionally giving preferential treatment to candidates or employees with respect to promotions due to their sexual orientation;
- unjustifiably rating some employees lower than other employees in work performance evaluations because of their sexual orientation;
- intentionally discriminating against an employee or applicant who is perceived as having a particular sexual orientation, even if she or he is not of that orientation;

- threatening or bullying a co-worker simply because of his or her sexual orientation; and/or
- making disparaging remarks about a co-worker's sexual orientation to the extent that a hostile and intimidating work environment results.

Sexual/Gender Identity A person's various individual attributes, as they are understood to be masculine and/or feminine.

Sexual Identity Discrimination Wrongful treatment of a worker due to the person's self-identification with a gender, whether it is the same as or opposite to the person's birth gender.

Transgendered Individual A person who identifies with and adopts the gender identity of a member of the opposite biological sex.

Sexual identity discrimination is not the same as **sexual orientation discrimination**. Gender identity involves a person's self-identification with a gender, whether it is the same or the opposite of the one with which he or she was born. **Sexual orientation** involves attraction to others. A **transgendered** individual identifies with and adopts the gender identity of a member of the biological sex opposite from his or her birth gender. A homosexual is attracted sexually to persons of the same sex. The American Psychiatric Association's *Diagnostic and Statistical Manual of Mental Disorders* defines transgender status as a diagnosable mental disorder, but not homosexuality. Sometimes other persons claim that they have been discriminated against due to arrangements made on behalf of a **transgendered individual**.

> ***Example:*** Carla Cruzan, a female teacher at a Minneapolis school district, sued the district for sex discrimination because it allowed a transgendered co-worker to use the women's faculty restroom. The individual, formerly known as David Nielsen, had worked in the district for 30 years as a male, but had recently transitioned from male to female and was now known as Debra Davis. He was afforded accommodations by the school district pursuant to the provisions of state law protecting transgendered individuals. Ms. Cruzan claimed she was discriminated against, but the court held that she had not suffered any adverse employment action. She could not establish that she suffered from a sexually harassing hostile work environment. The school environment was not permeated with discriminatory intimidation, ridicule, and insult. The court dismissed her claim.[30]

The law in this area is slowly developing. Among the questions presented to both employers and courts is whether a **BFOQ** defense could be asserted if the presence of a **transgendered** individual offended prevailing social norms against having a person of the opposite sex present in a given situation. Customer preferences would *not* be available if state or local law protects the **transgendered** worker.

A few federal courts have held that a **transsexual** individual had established membership in a protected class by alleging discrimination on the basis of a failure to conform to a **sexual stereotype. Title VII** is violated when an employer discriminates against any employee, transsexual or not, because he or she has failed to act or appear sufficiently masculine or feminine to satisfy the employer's prejudices.

> ***Example:*** Izza Lopez, also known as Raul Lopez, suffered from **gender identity disorder**. While she is biologically male, she had lived her life as a woman. Lopez planned to undergo sex reassignment surgery when she was financially able to do so. She applied for a job with a medical clinic. After being offered a position, the HR director informed her that a background check revealed that she was male, and the clinic withdrew its offer of employment based on Lopez having "misrepresented" himself as a woman during the interview process. Lopez filed a sex discrimination lawsuit. The court relied on the Supreme Court's decision in *Price Waterhouse v. Hopkins* to hold that while **transgender discrimination** is not itself unlawful, it is when it is based on failure to conform to traditional sexual stereotypes.[31]

San Francisco was the first city to enact an ordinance protecting **sexual orientation**. Its administrative code prevented the city from entering into contracts with companies that discriminated against employees based on **sexual orientation**. Section 12.B.1 of the ordinance provides:

> *All contracting agencies of the City, or any department thereof, acting for or on behalf of the City and County, shall include in all contracts and property contracts hereinafter executed or amended in any manner or as to any portion thereof, a provision obligating the contractor not to discriminate on the basis of the fact or perception of a person's race, color, creed, religion, national origin, ancestry, age, sex, sexual orientation, gender identity, domestic partner status, marital status, disability or Acquired Immune Deficiency Syndrome, HIV status (AIDS/HIV status), weight, height, association with members of classes protected under this chapter or in retaliation for opposition to any practices forbidden under this chapter against any employee of, any City employee working with, or applicant for employment with such contractor and shall require such contractor to include a similar provision in all subcontracts executed or amended thereunder.*

In 1996 and 1997, the city code was amended to require companies with city contracts to offer benefits to employees with domestic partners equal to those they provided to married employees. In particular, the ordinance defines **sexual orientation** as the choice of human adult sexual partner according to gender. It states that **sexual** or **gender identity** is a person's various individual attributes, as they are understood to be masculine and/or feminine.

When there is no applicable federal law protecting the employee from **sexual orientation discrimination**, the employee may rely on those contractual and tort remedies reviewed. Those most often employed in such litigation include intentional or negligent infliction of emotional distress, harassment, invasion of privacy, and defamation. If the adverse employment action related to a discriminatory action affecting the person's protected classification, that ground would be invoked to protect the rights of the victim.

> ***Example:*** An employer harasses a bisexual employee solely on the grounds that the employee's orientation is "offensive to God." The personal religious beliefs of the employer would be a legitimate basis for discriminatory conduct against the employee. The employee would be protected from the harassment only if the discrimination were premised on some other protected characteristic.

As is discussed in the chapter on privacy rights, the Supreme Court has considered decisions involving gay rights. In 1996, the Supreme Court held in *Romer v. Evans*[32] that a provision of the Colorado Constitution that prohibited the state or any of its subdivisions from adopting any laws that gave privileged status to homosexuals was unconstitutional. In *Lawrence v. Texas*,[33] the Court held in a 5-4 decision that the State of Texas lacked a legitimate interest in regulating private sexual conduct of consenting adults.

Human Resource Form
Sample Sexual Harassment Policy

Our company will not tolerate any type of unlawful harassment of its employees. Our policy is one of zero tolerance of such behavior. You are required to follow the policy prohibiting unlawful harassment. Harassment violates federal law if it involves discriminatory treatment based on race, color, sex (with or without sexual conduct), religion, national origin, age, disability, genetic information, or because the employee opposed job discrimination or participated in an investigation or complaint proceeding under the EEO statutes. Federal law does not prohibit simple teasing, offhand comments, or isolated incidents that are not extremely serious. The conduct must be sufficiently frequent or severe enough to create a hostile work environment or result in a "tangible employment action," such as hiring, firing, promotion, or demotion.

The following are examples of unlawful conduct that are prohibited by this policy:

1. unwanted sexual advances toward any person;
2. offering employment benefits in exchange for sexual favor;
3. making or threatening reprisals after receiving a negative response to a sexual advance;
4. visual conduct, such as leering, making sexual gestures, or displaying sexually suggestive objects, pictures, or drawings;
5. any verbal abuse or communication of a sexual nature about an individual's body, using sexually degrading words or using obscene words; and
6. physical touching or impeding or blocking movement of a victim.

If you have a complaint that another person (including a company vendor) is in violation of this policy or a policy against other types of harassment, please follow the steps set forth in the company's Employee Manual. You may begin your reporting with your immediate supervisor or the Human Resources Department.

We will conduct a prompt and thorough investigation. All those with information will be reviewed. After a determination is made, the results will be communicated to the complainant and to the person who allegedly violated our policy. If wrongdoing is determined to have occurred, immediate remedial action will be taken. Discipline, including possible termination of employment, will be imposed on the responsible parties.

Please execute a copy of this policy to indicate that you have read and understand our policy regarding sexual harassment.

Dated: ____________ Employee: ____________

Reverse Discrimination Against Males

Analysis of **reverse discrimination** in employment begins with the Supreme Court's decision in *McDonnell Douglas Corporation v. Green.*[34] Under this decision, a plaintiff can prove discrimination under **Title VII**, the Family and Medical Leave Act, and other federal statutes addressing reverse sex or gender discrimination either by direct evidence of discrimination or through a series of shifting burdens of proof. The plaintiff alleging indirect evidence of **reverse sex discrimination** bears the initial burden of proving a prima facie case of discrimination by a preponderance of the evidence. In its *McDonnell Douglas* decision, the Supreme Court announced that in future cases an employment discrimination plaintiff must be a member of a minority against whom discrimination has traditionally been practiced.

Federal circuit courts of appeals have not been ready to make findings in favor of alleged **reverse discrimination** plaintiffs. Frequently, they require that a plaintiff must also establish background circumstances that support an inference that the employer is "one of those unusual employers who discriminate[s]against the majority." Thus, such a plaintiff has a heightened standard with respect to the burden of proof. Generally, plaintiffs cannot meet that burden.

Outcomes

Sex-based discrimination class-action lawsuit settlements have made employers and their lawyers increasingly cautious. Most class-action lawsuits are not tried to a verdict or decision; rather, they are settled during the pre-trial or pre-arbitration process. Among those of recent note are the following:

- In 2010, Wal-Mart was defending a 3,000 person sex discrimination class-action lawsuit by women claiming the company discriminated against them in pay and promotions. The case exposed the company to the largest civil rights suit in the U.S. legal history.
- Costco is defending a similar class-action lawsuit brought by female employees. It is charged that the company maintains a "glass ceiling" at the store-management level that prevents women from being promoted to higher-level positions. The settlement of that suit will depend on procedural rulings made in the Wal-Mart class-action suit.
- The owner of the Outback Steakhouse chain agreed in 2009 to pay $19 million for glass-ceiling violations affecting its female employees.[35]
- In 2009, Dell settled a sexual discrimination class-action suit for $9.9 million and agreed to fund base-pay adjustments for its current female employees. The plaintiffs claimed that the company practiced "systemic company-wide" gender discrimination involving salaries, career opportunities, and promotions.
- In 2004, the EEOC and Morgan Stanley reached a $54 million settlement of a sex discrimination lawsuit concerning compensation and promotional disparities brought by a class of female officers and women eligible for positions as company officers.
- In 2000, $531 million was awarded to a class of 1,100 women who worked for the U.S. Information Agency.
- Also in 2000, $192.5 million was awarded to a class of female workers employed by the Coca Cola Company.

Key Terms and Concepts

- Equal Pay Act of 1963
- Glass ceiling and Glass Ceiling Commission
- Sexual harassment
- *Quid pro quo* sexual harassment
- Hostile or offensive working environment
- Gender discrimination
- BFOQ
- Immutable characteristic
- Business necessity
- Sexual orientation discrimination
- Executive Order 13087
- Sexual identity discrimination
- Reverse gender discrimination
- Transgendered individual

Chapter Summary

- Discrimination based on the sex of a job applicant or employee is unlawful under many state and federal laws. Among the most well known of these laws are Title VII, the Equal Pay Act of 1963, Executive Order 11246, and the federal Constitution.

- Sex discrimination is unlawful in all the many forms it has taken in the workplace. The Equal Pay Act prohibits discrimination that involves paying lower wages to workers of one sex than to workers of the other for equal work on jobs requiring equal skill, effort, and responsibility performed under similar working conditions.

- An exception to the Equal Pay Act allows differences in pay that are based on bona fide seniority, merit, or incentive systems or on factors other than sex.

- The advantage of pursuing a Title VII action is that the employee need not establish the element of equal work under similar working conditions as required under the Equal Pay Act.

- Sex discrimination involves treating an individual unfavorably because of his or her gender. Such discrimination is illegal if it has a negative impact on the employment experience of people of a certain gender and is not job related or necessary to the operation of the business.

- Grooming standards and dress codes can constitute sexual discrimination only if they are applied in a sexually discriminatory manner. If they are not motivated by sexual stereotyping, they are legal.

- Title VII prohibits discrimination based on immutable characteristics associated with a worker's sex. Those characteristics include skin color, hair texture, or certain facial features, even if not all members of the protected group have them.

- Sexual harassment can constitute a form of sex discrimination. There are two types of sexual harassment: quid pro quo and hostile work environment. *Quid pro quo* sexual harassment involves a workplace benefit promised in exchange for sexual activity by the harassed worker. A hostile work environment involves unwanted activity based on the victim's gender that creates a hostile or abusive work environment and interferes with the person's ability to perform his or her work. Such harassment must also be so severe and/or pervasive that it affects a term or condition of the victim's employment.

- Courts apply a "reasonable victim" standard when considering the effect of the alleged harassment or discrimination in the workplace.

- The Supreme Court decisions in *Ellerth* and *Faragher* imposed vicarious liability for unlawful harassment by supervisors. These decisions impose the employer's affirmative obligation to remedy sexually hostile conduct in the workplace. This duty requires employers to prepare and disseminate a policy prohibiting sexual harassment, provide a procedure for lodging complaints, and provide a thorough and complete investigation of all complaints regardless of the claimant's gender.

■ The *Ellerth* and *Faragher* decisions describe a supervisor as a person with immediate or successively higher authority over an employee. The Supreme Court reached this conclusion because discriminatory misconduct is aided by the supervisor's apparent authority as delegated by the employer.

■ The plaintiff's own behavior is examined by courts to determine if it provoked the hostile work environment.

■ In *Oncale,* the Supreme Court gave three examples of ways a victim can prove same-sex gender discrimination: (1) by establishing that the harasser was motivated by sexual desire, which generally requires "credible evidence" that the harasser was a homosexual; (2) by establishing that the harassment demonstrates that "the harasser [was] motivated by general hostility to the presence of [men] in the workplace"; or (3) by establishing that the harasser treated men differently in a mixed-sex workplace.

■ Courts closely scrutinize asserted BFOQ and business necessity defenses in sex discrimination and harassment cases. They apply an even more heightened scrutiny standard in cases of alleged reverse gender discrimination.

Online Student Support

- Loislaw legal research and writing assignments.
- Loislaw group projects and class presentations.
- Loislaw access, providing online research including up-to-date cases, statutes, rules, and regulations. Primary law for all 50 states and federal jurisdictions. Registration required for access to this resource.
- Practice questions, including sample true/false, multiple choice, and short answer questions to test your understanding of concepts.
- Additional human resource forms.
- Internet exercises.
- Blogs.
- Supplementary statutory and regulatory materials.

Case Problems

7.1 Lisa Ann Burns posed for nude centerfold pictures outside of work hours. She did not pose in a provocative or suggestive manner at work. At work, she was subjected to sexual comments by her female manager-trainer. She testified that other employees showed her advertisements for pornographic films, talked about sex, requested her to watch pornographic movies, and directed lewd gestures at her. She gave excuses rather than direct refusals because she feared the loss of her job. She sued her employer for sexual harassment for permitting a hostile and offensive work environment. If the employer raised the defense that her outside conduct was such that the uninvited sexual advances were not offensive to her, how should the court rule? (*Burns v. McGregor Electronic Industries, Inc.*, 989 F.2d 959 (8th Cir. 1993))

7.2 Sandra Ortiz-Del Valle sued the national Basketball Association (NBA) for violating Title VII for intentional discrimination due to her gender. She argued that the NBA had a continuous policy of barring women from employment as NBA referees based on the fact that no woman had ever been hired as a referee or invited to referee training camp until 1994. Despite praise from league officials regarding her skills, she was not hired. If she could not prove that she suffered any loss of earnings because she could not prove she would have been hired as a referee, how should the court rule on her claim? (*Ortiz-Del Valle v. NBA,* 42 F. Supp. 2d 334 (S.D.N.Y. 1999))

7.3 Rodney Barekman worked for the city of Republic, Missouri, as a policeman. Theresa Sweet was one of his supervisors, and he objected to her jokes about male and female genitalia, talk about having to urinate, and descriptions of her underwear, her sex life, and various sexual acts in his presence. Nearly all of the other male and female police officers and employees engaged in such behavior. Barekman eventually became Sweet's supervisor, but Sweet's actions continued to include kissing him on the cheek and giving him cards signed "Love" and "Love Ya." Barekman did not report the behavior or "write up" Sweet for her actions. He gave her gifts, rubbed her neck, and gave her a birthday card in November 2001 signed, "Love, Rodney." Sweet sued for a hostile work environment and claimed Barekman harassed her. Barekman resigned under protest and then sued the city because he had been exposed to a sexually hostile work environment. How should the court rule with respect to his claims? (*Barekman v. City of Republic,* 232 S.W. 3d 675 (Mo. App. 2007))

7.4 Dena Swackhammer sued her former employer, Sprint, for gender discrimination. As a former company vice president, she claimed that Sprint's explanation for her termination was a pretext to mask intentional discrimination. Sprint argued that Swackhammer violated the company's ethical policies by failing to supervise one of her employees properly. Swackhammer claimed that Sprint's reason was a pretext because the company should have considered her prior favorable work history with the company. Sprint argued that whether or not it was mistaken or used poor business judgment, it still honestly believed in its reason for the termination and that it had acted in good faith on its belief that Swackhammer violated company policy. Swackhammer claimed she would not have been terminated if she were a male. How should the court rule in response to Sprint's motion for summary judgment on her claims? (*Swackhammer v. Sprint/United Management Co.*, 493 F.3d 1160 (10th Cir. 2007))

7.5 David Krasner sued his former employer for sexual discrimination based on a sexually hostile work environment and retaliation in violation of Title VII. He claimed he had encountered an atmosphere infected with overt sexism in which career advancement based on sexual favoritism was accepted, male supervisors promoted a sexist and demeaning image of women in the workplace, and advancement was governed by a "casting couch." Krasner tried to dissuade his supervisor from engaging in a sexual relationship with a subordinate. Following his complaints about favoritism and his supervisor's improper management of the department, Krasner complained to the human resources department. The company investigated and found no violation of law or its internal ethics policy. A month later Krasner was terminated. The reasons given for his termination were a reduction of work following a reorganization, his failure to work well with his supervisor, insubordination, and failure to perform his job. According to the company's code of ethics, it was improper to fire an employ in retaliation for making any good faith ethical complaint. State the reasons for and against Krasner's case of sexual discrimination. Should the court dismiss his lawsuit? (*Krasner v. HSH Nordbank AG,* _____ F. Supp. 2d. _____ (S.D.N.Y. 2010))

End Notes

1. *Taylor v. Runyon,* 175 F.3d 861 (11th Cir. 1999).
2. 29 U.S.C. §206(d)(1).
3. *Stanley v. University of Southern California,* 178 F.3d 1069 (9th Cir. 1999).
4. *Warren v. Solo Cup Company,* 516 F.3d 627 (7th Cir. 2008).
5. *Glenn v. General Motors Corporation,* 841 F.2d 567 (11th Cir. 1988), *cert denied,* 488 U.S. 948 (1988).
6. *Risch v. Royal Oak Police Department,* 581 F.3d 383 (6th Cir. 2009).
7. *Tenge v. Phillips Modern AG Co, et al.*, 446 F.3d 903 (8th Cir. 2006).
8. *Barbano v. Madison County,* 922 F.2d 139 (2d Cir. 1990).
9. *Diaz v. Pan American World Airways, Inc.*, 442 F.2d 385 (5th Cir. 1971),
10. *Healey v. Southwood Psychiatric Hospital,* 78 F.3d 128 (3d Cir. 1996).
11. 433 U.S. 321 (1977).
12. 220 F.3d 1263 (11th Cir. 2000) and 296 F.3d 1265 (11th Cir. 2002), *cert. denied.*
13. *Ferguson v. E.I. du Pont de Nemours,* 560 F. Supp. 1172, 1197 (D. Del. 1983).
14. *Downes v. FAA,* 775 F.2d 288, 293 (Fed. Cir. 1985).
15. *Rabidue v. Osceola Refining Co.*, 584 F. Supp. 419, 433 (E.D.Mich. 1984).
16. *Stacy v. Shoney's, Inc.*, 755 F. Supp. 751 (E.D.Ky. 1997).
17. *Waltman v. Intl. Paper Co.*, 875 F.2d 468 (5th Cir. 1989).
18. *Lyle v. Warner Brothers Television Productions,* 38 Cal. 4th 264, 132 P.2d 211 (2006).
19. 524 U.S. 775 (1998).
20. 524 U.S. 951 (1998).
21. *Craig v. M&O Agencies, Inc.*, 496 F.3d 1047 (9th Cir. 2007).
22. *Jones v. Wesco,* 846 F.2d 1154 (8th Cir. 1988).
23. 510 U.S. 17 (1993).
24. *Pennsylvania State Police v. Suders,* 542 U.S. 129 (2004).
25. *Oncale v. Sundowner Offshore Services, Inc.*, 523 U.S. 75 (1988).
26. 490 U.S. 228 (1989).
27. 256 F. 3d 864 (9th Cir. 2001).
28. 260 F.3d 257 (3d Cir. 2001).
29. Article 49B §15 (j).
30. *Cruzan v. Special School Dist. #1,* 294 F.3d 981 (8th Cir. 2002).
31. *Lopez v. River Oaks Imaging & Diagnostic Group,* 542 F.Supp.2d 653 (S.D. Texas 2008).
32. 517 U.S. 620 (1996).
33. 539 U.S. 558 (2003).
34. 411 U.S. 792 (1973).
35. *http://www.eeoc.gov/eeoc/newsroom/release/12-29-09a.cfm.*

Chapter 8
Religious Discrimination

"Ultimately, America's answer to the intolerant man is diversity, the very diversity which our heritage of religious freedom has inspired." —Robert F. Kennedy, U.S. Senator, Attorney General

Learning Objectives

1. Define protected religious practices and beliefs.
2. Recognize the limits of judicial inquiry into religious beliefs.
3. State the definition of a sincerely held belief.
4. Consider what actions are required for a reasonable accommodation for religious observance.
5. Identify the defenses available to an employer when confronted with a religious discrimination claim.

Chapter Outline

- Introduction
- Statutory Protection Against Religious Discrimination
- Management Application: The Surge in Religion-Based Discrimination Claims
- What Is a Religious Practice or Observance?

Case 8.1 *Thomas v. Review Board of Indiana Employment Security Division*

- Management Application: Changing Landscape of Religious Affiliation

Case 8.2 *Young v. Southwestern Savings & Loan Association*

Case 8.3 *EEOC v. IBP, Inc.*

- Management Application: What Is a Religion?
- The Duties to Inform and of Reasonable Accommodation

Case 8.4 *Ansonia Board of Education v. Philbrook*

Case 8.5 *Trans World Airlines, Inc. v. Hardison*

- Focus on Ethics: Sincerely Held Beliefs
- What Is the Duty of a Union?
- Religious Harassment

Case 8.6 *Venters v. City of Delphi*

- Focus on Ethics: Company Affinity Groups
- Neutral, Generally Applicable Standards

Case 8.7 *Kalsi v. New York City Transit Authority*

- Exemptions and Exceptions
- Management Application: The Case of the Evangelizing Supervisor
- Human Resource Form: Religious Accommodation Request

Chapter Opening scenario

Up until 2002, Lynette Petruska had been a university chaplain for five years at Gannon University, a private Catholic diocesan college. Petruska was the first female to serve in the position of chaplain at Gannon. When she was promoted to the position, she was aware that the position was available because Father Rouch had left for three years to pursue further graduate studies. She sought assurances that she would not simply be replaced when Rouch returned or another qualified male became available. She was told by the university president that future employment decisions would be based solely on her performance, not her gender.

When a sex scandal erupted involving the university president, she strenuously objected to Gannon's campaign to cover up the scandal. When a new president was appointed, some of Petruska's responsibilities were reassigned, and she was instructed to limit her comments at university events. During a restructuring in 2001, the university demoted her. In response, she filed a Title VII sex discrimination and retaliation claim as well as claims under state law for constructive discharge.

Will the university's position as a religious educational institution insulate it from all of Petruska's claims? Would allowing Petruska's claims to proceed against the university result in an unconstitutional entanglement of religion and employment?[1]

Introduction

Statistics maintained by the Equal Employment Opportunity Commission (EEOC) for the 2009 fiscal year show that the number of religion-based claims of discrimination rose 17 percent over the prior two-year period. Employment discrimination claims involving religion typically arise when an employer fails or refuses to provide a reasonable accommodation for an employee's religious practices. The three most frequent conflicts involve these issues: observance of religious practices (such as weekly Sabbath, church attendance, and holy days); wearing distinctive religious clothing (for example, Sikh turbans); and grooming requirements related to religious observance (such as beards and dreadlocks). Infrequently, claims will arise from a conflict between a job assignment and a tenet of a practitioner's religious faith.

Religious Discrimination
An employer's failure to ensure that the conditions of employment allow for an applicant's or worker's sincerely held religious beliefs and practices, unless doing so creates undue hardship.

Statutory Protection Against Religious Discrimination

Title VII of the Civil Rights Act of 1964 provides statutory protections against **religious discrimination**. Title VII states: "It shall be unlawful employment practice for an employer to (1) fail or refuse to hire or to discharge any individual, or otherwise to discriminate against any individual with respect to his compensation, terms, conditions, or privileges or employment, because of such individual's . . . religion."[2]

The term ***"religion"*** was not defined by Title VII. In 1972, Title VII was amended to add a definition of religion as provided in Section 701(j): "The term '***religion***' includes all aspects of religious observance and practice, as well as belief, unless an employer demonstrates the inability to **reasonably accommodate** an employee's or prospective employee's religious observance or practice without **undue hardship** on the conduct of the employer's business."[3] Title VII therefore covers not only what faith belief an individual may hold but also religion as expressed through words and deeds. Title VII offers broad protection to employees regarding their personal religious practices and beliefs. Expressions of religious beliefs are typically what require **reasonable accommodation** from an employer. The majority of religious accommodation cases relate to conflicts arising from employers' refusals to adjust work schedules to accommodate the religious observances of their employees.

Sincerely Held
A fact-specific finding determination as to an employee's fidelity to religious beliefs and practices.

Undue Hardship
Circumstance excusing an employer from accommodating an employee's religious practices if doing so involves more than ordinary administrative costs, diminished efficiency of other workers, infringement on other employees' rights, impairment of workplace safety, or increased work responsibilities for others.

Management Application
The Surge in Religion-Based Discrimination Claims

The uptick in claims based on religious discrimination reflects the demands of modern society. With modern communications creating a 24-7 operational environment, employers expect employees to be available to meet customer needs well beyond the traditional workweek. Many relish tales of the "workaholic" executive who brings a laptop on vacation or skips vacations altogether. Furthermore, the high tech economy of the United States has promoted immigration from all parts of the world, with the diverse religious practices that entails. For several decades, Americans have focused on material aspirations rather than religious ones. As a result, conflicts have arisen between the observant believer and the demands of an increasingly complex workplace.

What Is a Religious Practice or Observance?

Title VII protects employees from **religious discrimination**. It is important to understand what constitutes a **religious practice or observance**. The EEOC recognizes all "moral and ethical beliefs as to what is right and wrong which are sincerely held with the strength of religious views."[4] Under this definition, courts have treated such things as opposition to abortion as a religious belief.[5] Keep in mind that a religious belief need not be popular or well known to be protected under the laws against religious discrimination.

Religious Practice or Observance
Beliefs, prayers, worship, and outwardly expressed rituals and ceremonies of a religious nature.

However, to fall within the protections of the statute, the belief must be **"sincerely held."** It may extend beyond formal doctrinal teaching and religious traditions. Potentially, many aspects of religious belief and practice continue to require **employer accommodation**.

CASE 8.1

A TERMINATION MOTIVATED BY RELIGION IS NOT FOR "GOOD CAUSE"

THOMAS V. REVIEW BOARD OF INDIANA EMPLOYMENT SECURITY DIVISION

450 U.S. 707 (1981)

Supreme Court of the United States

Facts. On his application form for employment at Blaw-Knox, Thomas listed his membership in the Jehovah's Witnesses and noted that his hobbies were Bible study and Bible reading. However, he placed no conditions on his employment, and he did not describe his religious tenets in any detail on the form. When transferred to a department that fabricated turrets for military tanks, he realized his work was weapons related. No other positions were available that were not directly involved in the production of weapons.

Because no transfer to another department would resolve his problem, Thomas asked for a layoff. The company denied his request. He then quit, asserting that he could not work on weapons without violating the principles of his religion. The Indiana unemployment compensation review board denied him unemployment compensation benefits by applying disqualifying provisions of Indiana state law finding that he did not have good cause to quit. When the case reached the Indiana Supreme Court, the Court denied Thomas benefits, holding that he had voluntarily quit his position. The Supreme Court granted *certiorari.*

Issue. Did a state violate a worker's First Amendment rights when it denied him unemployment compensation benefits even though he quit his job because it violated the tenets of his religion?

Language of the Court. Burger, C.J.: **The narrow function of a reviewing court in this context is to determine whether there was an appropriate finding that petitioner terminated his work because of an honest conviction that such work was forbidden by his religion.**

In a variety of ways we have said that "[a] regulation neutral on its face may, in its application, nonetheless offend the constitutional requirement for

governmental neutrality if it unduly burdens the free exercise of religion." (Citation omitted.) Here, as in Sherbert, the employee was put to a choice between fidelity to religious belief or cessation of work; the coercive impact on Thomas is indistinguishable from Sherbert, where the Court held: "[N]ot only is it apparent that appellant's declared ineligibility for benefits derives solely from the practice of her religion, but the pressure upon her to forego that practice is unmistakable. . . . While the compulsion may be indirect, the infringement upon free exercise is nonetheless substantial."

When the focus of the inquiry is properly narrowed, however, we must conclude that the interests advanced by the State do not justify the burden placed on free exercise of religion. The respondents contend that to compel benefit payments to Thomas involves the State in fostering a religious faith.

There is no evidence in the record to indicate that the number of people who find themselves in the predicament of choosing between benefits and religious beliefs is large enough to create "widespread unemployment," or even to seriously affect unemployment — and no such claim was advanced by the Review Board. Similarly, although detailed inquiry by employers into applicants' religious beliefs is undesirable, there is no evidence in the record to indicate that such inquiries will occur in Indiana, or that they have occurred in any of the states that extend benefits to people in the petitioner's position. Nor is there any reason to believe that the number of people terminating employment for religious reasons will be so great as to motivate employers to make such inquiries.

There is, in a sense, a "benefit" to Thomas deriving from his religious beliefs, but this manifests no more than the tension between the two Religious Clauses which the Court resolved in Sherbert: "In holding as we do, plainly we are not fostering the 'establishment' of the Seventh-day Adventist religion in South Carolina, for the extension of unemployment benefits to Sabbatarians in common with Sunday worshippers reflects nothing more than the governmental obligation of neutrality in the face of religious differences, and does not represent that involvement of religious with secular institutions which it is the object of the Establishment Clause to forestall."

Decision. Yes. Thomas is entitled to unemployment benefits if he quit his job because his work violated his religious convictions.

CASE QUESTIONS

Critical Legal Thinking. Should a religious adherent embracing the use of a controlled substance such as peyote be treated in the same manner?

Business Ethics. Does this case open the door to arbitrary and fanciful claims of religious beliefs when a conflict develops between an employer and employee over work assignments?

Contemporary Business. How do you think the court would decide a conflict between conscience and criminal codes?[6]

Management Application
Changing Landscape of Religious Affiliation

For many decades, bringing personal religious views into the workplace was unthinkable. That is not the case in the modern workplace. Many workers infuse their workplaces with evidence of their religious faith. Employees demand that their employers respect the employees' right to practice their faith at work. As a result, employers struggle to balance their right to operate their businesses with the employee's rights of religious freedom.

The definition of religion is exceptionally broad. In 2008, the Pew Forum on Religion and Public Life published a long-awaited comprehensive statistical survey on religious beliefs in the United States. Based on interviews with more than 35,000 Americans, the survey reports on the diverse spectrum of American religious beliefs. The country's religious traditions are undergoing dramatic change. The survey revealed the following:

> More than one-quarter of American adults (28%) have left the faith in which they were raised in favor of another or no religion at all. . . . About one in six Americans state they are unaffiliated with any particular religion. . . . The predominant Protestant population of the country is now characterized by diverse and fragmentized denominations loosely affiliated with three different traditions. . . . The number of foreign-born Catholics immigrating to the U.S. is sustaining growth within the Catholic tradition which would otherwise be experiencing the greatest net loss of adherents. . . . Finally, about 12% of Americans define themselves as unaffiliated with any particular religion, half of which describe their religious beliefs as "nothing in particular."[7]

Review this survey to determine what effects the changes in demographics and religious affiliation of adult workers portend for the American workplace. In the future, will employers be confronted with increasing numbers of requests for reasonable accommodation of sincerely held religious beliefs?

Concept Summary
Proving Religious Discrimination

The plaintiff must prove that:

- The plaintiff had a sincere religious belief that conflicted with a requirement of the employer;
- The plaintiff informed the employer of the conflict; and
- The employer failed to accommodate the sincerely held belief or took an adverse employment action based on that belief.

The employee does not have to explain religious beliefs or make any effort to compromise beliefs or practices before seeking the accommodation.

CASE 8.2

ATHEISTS MAY ASSERT RELIGIOUS DISCRIMINATION CLAIMS

YOUNG V. SOUTHWESTERN SAVINGS & LOAN ASSOCIATION

509 F.2d 140 (5th Cir. 1975)

U.S. Court of Appeals for the Fifth Circuit

Facts. At the time Mrs. Young accepted employment as a teller at Southwestern's Bellaire, Texas, branch, she knew that all of Southwestern's employees were required to attend a monthly staff meeting at the downtown Houston office. Employees are paid for attending these 45-minute meetings regarding various business matters, such as organization policy, current economic conditions, and future plans. The employees at one far-flung financial outpost in Houston were exempted from this requirement. On arriving at her first such meeting, Mrs. Young discovered that the meeting began with a short religious talk and a prayer, both delivered by a local Baptist minister.

This theological appetizer, although nondenominational, was somewhat uncongenial to plaintiff, who was an atheist. There was no question of the sincerity of Mrs. Young's religious beliefs. Mrs. Young decided that although she did not object to the business portion of the meetings, she felt that her freedom of conscience was being violated by forced attendance at "prayer meetings." Without registering a protest, plaintiff resolved not to attend any further meetings. When Mrs. Young told her supervisor she would not attend any more such meetings, the supervisor told her that attendance was mandatory and that she could "close [her] ears" during the prayer. She refused and quit. When she was asked to submit a letter of resignation, she refused and said, "No, I am being fired." Her supervisor assured her she was not being fired, but Mrs. Young left without further discussion. The U.S. district court dismissed her Title VII case, finding she had voluntarily resigned and had failed to show any discriminatory act arising out of the meetings. She appealed to the Fifth Circuit Court of Appeals.

Issue. May an atheist assert protection from religious discrimination?

Language of the Court. Goldberg, J.: **In this case, Mrs. Young enjoyed her work and Southwestern valued her services. The only possible reason for her resignation was her resolution not to attend religious services which were**

repugnant to her conscience, coupled with the certain knowledge from Bostain, her supervisor, that attendance at the staff meetings — in their entirety — was mandatory and the reasonable inference that if she would not perform this condition of her employment, she would be discharged. In these circumstances, when she could hope no longer that her absence at the meetings would not be noticed, she could reasonably infer that in one week, one month or two months, she would be discharged because of the conflict between her religious beliefs and company policy. Surely it would be too nice a distinction to say that Mrs. Young should have borne the considerable emotional discomfort of waiting to be fired instead of immediately terminating her association with Southwestern. This is precisely the situation in which the doctrine of constructive discharge applies, a case in which an employee involuntarily resigns in order to escape intolerable and illegal employment requirements.

Title VII was designed to restrain discrimination in employment because of religion. The subtle and unrealistic distinction drawn by Southwestern here between resignation and discharge does not deter us from enforcing the statutory mandate. Accommodation as a defense must be unsubtle, direct, undelayed and communicated without equivocation. The statutory defense of accommodation is not met by some post hoc hypothesis. Reversed and remanded.

Decision. Yes. The plaintiff employee had established a case of religious discrimination. She resigned only because the defendant employer had required her attendance at meetings that opened with prayer.

CASE QUESTIONS

Critical Legal Thinking. Was Young constructively discharged? If employees met before the work portion of the meeting to pray nondenominationally, would the court have rendered a different opinion?

Business Ethics. The dissent argued that Young would need to show her employer required or tolerated practices so inconsistent with her religious beliefs that she could not continue working while remaining true to those beliefs. Should religious discrimination extend to nonbeliefs as well?

Contemporary Business. Southwestern actually had a nonpublicized policy of excusing employees from the prayer portions of these meetings. Would the appellate court have reached a different result if Southwestern had made every employee fully aware of the policy?

CASE 8.3

THE SINCERITY OF RELIGIOUS BELIEFS SHOULD BE MEASURED WHEN A WORK CONFLICT ARISES

EEOC v. IBP, Inc.

824 F. Supp. 147 (C.D. Ill, 1993)

U.S. District Court for the Central District of Illinois

Facts. IBP hired Richard Boyer to work at its Joslin, Illinois, beef processing plant. The company promoted him after he had worked for several months on various scheduled Saturday shifts. Subsequently, Boyer converted to Seventh Day Adventism and notified IBP that he no longer could work Saturdays due to his religious tenets. Following this notification, Boyer's supervisors met with him to discuss ways to accommodate his religious beliefs. IBP offered as an accommodation allowing Boyer to trade shifts, and they offered to accompany him to the production floor to solicit a swap. However, Boyer informed IBP that he considered it a sin to ask someone to work for him on the Sabbath, although he agreed to allow IBP to arrange a shift swap for him. Such efforts were unsuccessful.

Boyer was terminated following absences from assigned Saturday work shifts. He then held a series of jobs, including one for which he was terminated in 1989 after his refusal to work on Saturdays. Sometime in July or August of 1990, however, Boyer began attending classes at a truck driving school on Friday evenings, and in 1991, he agreed to drive a truck for his employer on a Saturday. When asked why he broke the Sabbath, Boyer replied he had "lost faith" in 1990. In May 1992, the EEOC filed suit on Boyer's behalf claiming religious discrimination. IBP asserted Boyer's beliefs were insincere and that it had fulfilled its duty to accommodate by offering a shift trade. The employer moved for summary judgment against the EEOC.

Issue. What is a sincerely held religious belief?

Language of the Court. McDade, J.. **A prima facie case is established when an employee shows that he or she: (1) holds a sincere religious belief that conflicts with an employment requirement; (2) has informed the employer about the conflict; and (3) was discharged or disciplined for failing to comply with the conflicting employment requirement.**

IBP's challenge to the sincerity of Plaintiff's belief can be disposed of quickly. The Supreme Court defines a religious belief as "not merely a matter of personal preference, but one of deep religious conviction, shared by an

organized group, and intimately related to daily living." (Citation omitted.) IBP claims that although society recognizes the Seventh Day Adventist Church as an organized religious group, Plaintiff cannot prove that his belief in the sanctity of the Sabbath, as taught by that religion, was sincere and intimately related to his daily living for two reasons.

First, IBP argues that Plaintiff's abandonment of his faith sixteen (16) months after acquiring it is "irrefutable evidence" . . . that his religious beliefs were not sincere at the time IBP discharged him. Second, IBP contends that Plaintiff's beliefs were insincere because he acted in a manner inconsistent with these beliefs by attending Friday evening classes in 1990 and agreeing to work on Saturdays in 1991 and 1992. These arguments are meritless.

Plaintiff's absence of faith prior to December 1988 and his loss of faith in 1990 do not prove that his beliefs were insincere in April 1989. The Court has not found, and IBP has not cited, any case in which a court found that the length of time a person held a belief was relevant to determine the question of sincerity, and this Court will not be the first to do so. Instead, the Court finds that sincerity should be measured by the employee's words and conduct at the time the conflict arose between the belief and the employment requirement.

Decision. The analysis of the sincerity of plaintiff's belief "should be measured by the employee's words and conduct at the time the conflict arose between the belief and the employment requirement."

CASE QUESTIONS

Critical Legal Thinking. How should a court determine the sincerity of religious beliefs?

Business Ethics. Does the court ruling in *EEOC v. IBP, Inc.* suggest that conversions of faith may be more likely to occur when employees object to unpopular work shifts?

Contemporary Business. Does this case suggest that employees can take advantage of employers who cannot inquire into the strength of the employee's beliefs?

Reasonable Accommodation (Religion)
An employer must make reasonable adjustments to the work environment to permit an applicant or employee to practice his or her religious beliefs.

Religion
Sincerely held, religious, ethical, or moral beliefs as to what is right and wrong; need not include a belief in a supreme being.

Employers find assessing the sincerity of an employee's religious beliefs is difficult to do. In the 2006 decision in *Baker v. The Home Depot,*[8] the Second Circuit Court of Appeals rejected the employer's contention that, because the plaintiff had worked on the Sabbath in the past, he could not establish that his **sincere religious belief** precluded him from working on the Sabbath at the time in question. The court held that the **sincerity of an individual's religious beliefs** is inherently within that individual's unique purview. A worker's conversion to Judaism and increasing attention to the details of observing religious traditions does not excuse an employer from offering a **reasonable accommodation.**[9]

Management Application
What Is a Religion?

The courts have been presented with a number of diverse challenges to defining and recognizing a sincere religious belief. A sampling of the curious rulings reflects scope of the issue:

- **Ku Klux Klan (KKK)** — is *not* a religion.
  - ☐ *Slater v. King Soopers, Inc.*, 809 F. Supp. 809 (D. Colo, 1992). The U.S. District Court judge held "I conclude that the KKK is not a religion for purposes of Title VII. Rather the KKK is political and social in nature."
- **Espousing white supremacy** — *is* a religion.
  - ☐ *Peterson v. Wilmur Communications, Inc.*, 205 F. Supp.2d 1014 (E.D. Wis. 2002). The EEOC regulation means that "religion" under Title VII includes belief systems that espouse notions of morality and ethics and supply a means of distinguishing "right from wrong." In this case, a racist organization qualified as a "religion" subject to Title VII protection. The district court awarded damages against a company in favor of a demoted supervisor. The owner of the small company saw one of his supervisors in the newspaper. The supervisor held a t-shirt with a picture of a man who in the previous year had killed two people and wounded nine others in a two-state shooting spree targeting African Americans, Jews, and Asians. He was identified as the pastor of the World Wide Church of the Creator. This "church" espouses "Creativity," which provides that all persons of color are savages who intend to mongrelize the white race. It also promotes the view that African Americans are subhuman and should be "ship[ped] back to Africa," and that the Holocaust never occurred, but, if it did, Nazi Germany "would have done us a tremendous favor." The owner feared that it would be difficult for his minority employees to work for this supervisor and complained about unfair discipline from him. The court held that the World Church of the Creator, albeit a racist one, qualified as a religion and the supervisor was entitled to damages.
  - ☐ *See also Augustine v. Anti-Defamation League of B'nai-B'rith*, 75 Wis.2d 207 (1977).
- **Wicca** — *is* a religion.
  - ☐ *Benz v. Rogers Memorial Hospital*, 2006 U.S. Dist. LEXIS 8451 (2006 E.D. Wis. 2006).
- **Veganism** — is *not* a religion.
  - ☐ *Friedman v. Southern California Permanente Medical Group*, 102 Cal. App. 4th 29 (2002).
- **A person's legal conclusion** — is *not* a religion.
  - ☐ *EEOC v. Allendale Nursing Centre*, 996 F. Supp. 712 (W.D. Mich. 1998). Claim that Social Security is unbiblical and obtaining a Social Security card violates religion was rejected. (Surprisingly, the EEOC supported the view that it would be permissible to not furnish a Social Security card for tax purposes.)
- **Belief in cold fusion** — *is* a religion.
  - ☐ *LaViolette v. Department of Commerce, www.eooc.gov/decisions/A0101748.txt.*
- **Belief in Kozy Kitten People/Cat Food** — is *not* a religion.
  - ☐ *Brown v. Pena*, 441 F. Supp. 1382 (D.C. Fl. 1977). "Plaintiff's "personal religious creed" concerning Kozy Kitten Cat Food can only be described as such a mere personal preference, and, therefore, is beyond the parameters of the concept of religion as protected by the constitution, or be a logical extension of [Title VII]."

Courts find beliefs to be a religion if they "occupy the same place in the life of the worker as an orthodox belief in God holds in the life of one clearly qualified." The worker must show that the belief is "sincerely held" and "religious" in his or her own view of behavior. Courts must give "great weight" to the plaintiff's own characterization of his or her beliefs as a religion. Thus, a belief system need not have a concept of a God, Supreme Being, or an afterlife. The beliefs at issue must be more than "secular" ones.

> ***Example:*** Ruby Edwards was first employed by the School Board of the City of Norton, Virginia, as a teacher's aide. While employed she became a member of the Worldwide Church of God, and her affiliation became known to her employer. As a member of this church, Edwards felt church doctrine required her to abstain from secular work on seven annual holy days, six of which occurred during the school year. That required her to be absent from her job if the days did not fall on weekends. She requested and obtained permission to be absent from work to observe these holy days; however, after three years of granting these requests, the school board refused her request. In analyzing her claim, the federal court held that "a religious belief excludes mere personal preference grounded upon a non-theological basis, such as personal choice deduced from economic or social ideology. Rather, it must consider man's nature or the scheme of his existence as it relates in a theological framework. Furthermore, the belief must have an institutional quality about it and must be sincerely held by plaintiff." The court held that it would not determine what was a required religious observance and that the school board failed to prove undue hardship because the school board offered only mere opinion and speculation about the plaintiff's need for an accommodation.[10]

What are the commonsense limitations of a court's recognition of what defines a religion? If employers received so many requests for accommodations that it created problems for them, should our legislature change the law?

The Duties to Inform and of Reasonable Accommodation

Employees have the duty to timely inform employers of religious beliefs and what **accommodation** the belief requires. Employers may not require employees to provide detailed explanations of their beliefs or of why an **accommodation** is needed. If the employee does not provide the employer with notice of a need for an accommodation, the employee cannot claim the employer did not provide the accommodation. The decision-maker regarding an adverse employment action must be aware of the individual's need for an **accommodation**.

> ***Example:*** An interviewer who, like the job candidate, was Jewish made a conditional offer of employment. When the interviewer communicated her decision to her manager, the conditional offer was rescinded at the direction of her manager. He recalled negative impressions of the applicant from an earlier encounter at a job fair. The manager who made this decision was unaware of the applicant's religion. The U.S. district court held that the applicant failed to establish a case of religious discrimination because there was no evidence the manager knew of the applicant's faith when he ordered the withdrawal of the conditional offer of employment.[11]

One of the most common **reasonable accommodations** requested for religious reasons is arrangement of an employee's work schedule to avoid working on religious days (holy days, Sabbath days, and so on). Employers can avoid this liability by allowing employees to take a certain number of flexible days off each year. This allows employers to provide days off to **accommodate** various religious traditions and beliefs.

The employee and the employer have a mutual obligation to attempt a **reasonable accommodation** (see *Ansonia*, below). In *Brener v. Diagnostic Center Hospital,*[12] the Fifth Circuit Court of Appeals considered the suit of a Jewish pharmacist claiming religious discrimination because the pharmacy's scheduling system was rendered inflexible by the reluctance of other employees to trade schedules with him. The court held that the employee made no consistent attempt to exchange shifts, choosing instead not to report for work. The court opined:

> ... bilateral cooperation is appropriate in the search for an acceptable reconciliation of the needs of the employee's religion and the exigencies of the employer's business. Although the statutory burden to accommodate rests with the employer, the employee has a correlative duty to make a good faith attempt to satisfy his needs through means offered by the employer. A reasonable accommodation need not be on the employee's terms only.[13]

By making a **reasonable accommodation**, employers can reduce their litigation expense. Employers should seriously consider an employee's stated religious beliefs and practices. Note, however, that for employers to establish a **reasonable accommodation defense**, the court does not require that the employee agree to the **accommodation**, just that the employer provides a **reasonable accommodation** to the employee. "The reasonableness of an employer's attempt to accommodate is determined on a case-by-case basis."[14]

CASE 8.4

LATITUDE IS AFFORDED TO EMPLOYERS IN MAKING A REASONABLE ACCOMMODATION

ANSONIA BOARD OF EDUCATION V. PHILBROOK

476 U.S. 60 (1986)

Supreme Court of the United States

Facts. Ronald Philbrook was a teacher employed by Ansonia Board of Education in Arizona. He was a member of a church whose tenets required members to refrain from secular employment during designated holy days, a practice that caused him to miss approximately six school days each year. Under the teachers' union contract, Philbrook was entitled to only three days annual leave for religious holidays. He could not use sick leave for religious observances. Philbrook used his three religious holidays and took three unpaid days of leave. Despite his request, the board of education repeatedly rejected Philbrook's proposal that he be allowed to use three paid days of personal leave or be allowed to pay for the cost of a substitute teacher while receiving regular pay for those three days. Ultimately,

Philbrook sued in the federal district court for religious discrimination; but he lost in the trial court because he had not violated his religious convictions or risked losing his job. The Court of Appeals reversed and remanded. The Board appealed to the U.S. Supreme Court, which granted *certiorari.*

Issue. Must an employer accept the employee's preferred accommodation absent proof of undue hardship?

Language of the Court. Rehnquist, C.J.: **As we noted in our only previous consideration of 701(j), its language was added to the 1972 amendments on the floor of the Senate with little discussion. Trans World Airlines, Inc. v. Hardison (citations omitted). In Hardison, . . . we determined that an accommodation causes "undue hardship" whenever that accommodation results in "more than a de minimis cost" to the employer. Hardison had been discharged because his religious beliefs would not allow him to work on Saturdays and claimed that this action violated the employer's duty to effect a reasonable accommodation of his beliefs. Because we concluded that each of the suggested accommodations would impose on the employer an undue hardship, we had no occasion to consider the bounds of a prima facie case in the religious accommodation context or whether an employer is required to choose from available accommodations the alternative preferred by the employee. The employer in Hardison simply argued that all conceivable accommodations would result in undue hardship, and we agreed.**

We find no basis in either the statute or its legislative history for requiring an employer to choose any particular reasonable accommodation. By its very terms the statute directs that any reasonable accommodation by the employer is sufficient to meet its accommodation obligation. The employer violates the statute unless it "demonstrates that [it] is unable to reasonably accommodate . . . an employee's . . . religious observance or practice without undue hardship on the conduct of the employer's business." (Citation omitted.) Thus, where the employer has already reasonably accommodated the employee's religious needs, the statutory inquiry is at an end. The employer need not further show that each of the employee's alternative accommodations would result in undue hardship. As Hardison illustrates, the extent of undue hardship on the employer's business is at issue only where the employer claims that it is unable to offer any reasonable accommodation without such hardship.

The legislative history of 701(j), as we noted in Hardison . . . is of little help in defining the employer's accommodation obligation. . . . [C]ourts have noted that "bilateral cooperation is appropriate in the search for an acceptable reconciliation of the needs of the employee's religion and the exigencies of the employer's business." . . . Under the approach articulated by the Court of Appeals, however, the employee is given every incentive to hold out for the most beneficial accommodation, despite the fact that an employer offers a reasonable resolution of the conflict. This approach, we think, conflicts with both the language of the statute and the views that led to its enactment.

Decision. No. An employer has met its obligation under 701(j) by demonstrating a reasonable accommodation offer was made to the employee.

DISCUSSION QUESTIONS

Critical Legal Thinking. This decision approaches the issue from the practical standpoint of an employer. Is this a logical extension of prior case law or is it more reflective of the composition of the Court?

Business Ethics. Is the cost to employers of the requirement to offer employees religious accommodation too high? ?

Contemporary Business. Note that the Court does not invite courts to weigh "reasonableness" in meeting this standard. Does this mean that employers may now be creative in responding to requests for reasonable accommodation based on religion?

Undue Hardship on the Employer

Courts use a different approach in reviewing **religious discrimination** claims than other types of claims filed under Title VII of the Civil Rights Act. Discrimination against an employee is permitted if making an accommodation would cause the employer an **"undue hardship."** Title VII does not define **"undue hardship,"** and courts have determined that employers along with the courts must determine what it means on a case-by-case basis. A few cases do provide guidance on its general meaning, however. The Supreme Court defines when an accommodation becomes an **"undue hardship"** in the following decision.

CASE 8.5

REASONABLE ACCOMMODATION DOES NOT REQUIRE VIOLATION OF SENIORITY POLICIES

TRANS WORLD AIRLINES, INC. V. HARDISON

432 U.S. 63 (1977)

Supreme Court of the United States

Facts. Larry Hardison was a member of the Worldwide Church of God and believed it was his religious duty to rest from secular work on Saturdays, his Sabbath. Hardison's employer, Trans World Airlines (TWA), terminated

Hardison because he refused to work on Saturdays. His position, that of clerk, required 24-hour staffing, every day of the year. Hardison was subject to a seniority system in a collective bargaining agreement between TWA and the machinist union. Under this agreement, the most senior employees have first choice for job and shift assignments, and the most junior employees work the remaining jobs and shifts. Initially TWA transferred Hardison to another position, but conflicts arose with his work assignments. Hardison suggested that he work only four days per week, but TWA rejected the proposal and discharged him when he refused to work on Saturdays. Hardison sued TWA and union IAM under Title VII. The District ruled in favor of both TWA and the union. The court of appeals affirmed the judgment for the union but reversed the judgment for TWA holding that TWA had not accommodated Hardison. The Supreme Court granted *certiorari*.

Issue. Does Title VII require an employer to accommodate the religious needs of its employees if doing so violates the terms of seniority rights pursuant to a labor agreement?

Language of the Court. White, J.: . . . **Whenever there are not enough employees who choose to work a particular shift, however, some employees must be assigned to that shift even though it is not their first choice. Such was evidently the case with regard to Saturday work; even though TWA cut back its weekend workforce to a skeleton crew, not enough employees chose those days off to staff the Stores Department through voluntary scheduling. In these circumstances, TWA and IAM agreed to give first preference to employees who had worked in a particular department the longest.**

Had TWA nevertheless circumvented the seniority system by relieving Hardison of Saturday work and ordering a senior employee to replace him, it would have denied the latter his shift preference so that Hardison could be given his. The senior employee would also have been deprived of his contractual rights under the collective-bargaining agreement.

It was essential to TWA's business to require Saturday and Sunday work from at least a few employees even though most employees preferred those days off. Allocating the burdens of weekend work was a matter for collective bargaining. In considering criteria to govern this allocation, TWA and the union had two alternatives: adopt a neutral system, such as seniority, a lottery, or rotating shifts; or allocate days off in accordance with the religious needs of its employees. TWA would have had to adopt the latter in order to assure Hardison and others like him of getting the days off necessary for strict observance of their religion, but it could have done so only at the expense of others who had strong, but perhaps nonreligious, reasons for not working on weekends. There were no volunteers to relieve Hardison on Saturdays, and to give Hardison Saturdays off, TWA would have had to deprive another employee of his shift preference at least in part because he did not adhere to a religion that observed the Saturday Sabbath.

Title VII does not contemplate such unequal treatment. . . . It would be anomalous to conclude that by "reasonable accommodation" Congress meant that an employer must deny the shift and job preference of some employees, as well as deprive them of their contractual rights, in order to accommodate or prefer the religious needs of others, and we conclude that Title VII does not require an employer to go that far.

Our conclusion is supported by the fact that seniority systems are afforded special treatment under Title VII itself. Section 703 (h) provides in pertinent part:

> **Notwithstanding any other provision of this subchapter, it shall not be an unlawful employment practice for an employer to apply different standards of compensation, or different terms, conditions, or privileges of employment pursuant to a bona fide seniority or merit system . . . provided that such differences are not the result of an intention to discriminate because of race, color, religion, sex, or national origin. . . . (Citation omitted.)**

Decision. No. The Court determined that anything more than a *de minimis* cost to an employer constituted an "undue hardship" for purposes of section 701(j) and found that the accommodations proposed by Hardison would have constituted an undue hardship. These costs included lost efficiency in other positions or the payment of higher wages to other employees. Furthermore, the Court found that the employer had made a reasonable effort at making the accommodation.

CASE QUESTIONS

Critical Legal Thinking. Two dissenting justices argued that the Court's reading of section 701(j) reflected a gutting of the reasonable accommodation requirement. They argued that the *de minimis* interpretation of what constitutes an "undue burden" nullified any obligation to make such an accommodation. What do you think about the *de minimis* argument advanced by the dissent?

Business Ethics. Starting with the *Hardison* case, the use of seniority provisions in a collective bargaining agreement have been used to invoke the employers' undue hardship defense. Do seniority rights of some employees defeat the rights of other employees to pursue their religious observances? Does this undermine the protection afforded by Title VII?

Contemporary Business. Do you think employees would become creative in defining their religious beliefs if the *Hardison* rule were not in effect? Can you think of a viable alternative to the approach taken by the majority in *Hardison*?

De minimus Cost for Accommodation
Insubstantial expense to the employer to provide a religious accommodation to an applicant or employee.

Focus on Ethics
Sincerely Held Beliefs

Bradley Baker worked for The Home Depot, a company that operates stores nationwide selling wood, building equipment, home supplies, and other items. When Home Depot first employed Baker, he worked regular shifts that included Sundays. After sixth months of employment, Baker notified Home Depot that he was a member of the Gospel Fellowship Church and that his church beliefs prevented him from working on Sundays.

At first Home Depot made accommodations and did not schedule Baker for Sunday work. One year later, however, Home Depot began scheduling Baker for Sunday work. Each time Home Depot scheduled Baker for Sunday work, he did not show, citing his need to have Sunday off to practice his religion. Home Depot then offered an accommodation that allowed Baker, when scheduled for Sunday work, to take the morning off to attend church services and then work the rest of the day. Baker rejected this accommodation. When Baker did not show up on his scheduled Sundays, Home Depot terminated his employment.

Baker sued Home Depot for religious discrimination in violation of Title VII. Home Depot countered that it had made an appropriate accommodation by offering Baker Sunday mornings off. The accommodation would require Baker to work later on Sundays because it would otherwise cause undue hardship to Home Depot related to rescheduling and overtime expenses. In addition, Home Depot asserted that Baker's request, if granted, would have a negative effect on employee morale.

The federal district court entered judgment in favor of Home Depot. Upon appeal, the federal appellate court held that excusing Baker from Sunday morning shifts but not from working the rest of the day was not a reasonable accommodation. The court held that granting the request would not cause undue hardship to Home Depot. The court of appeals remanded the case to the district court to determine whether offering Baker a part-time position that did not require Sunday work or offering him the ability to swap shifts with employees who were willing to work his Sunday schedule would constitute a reasonable accommodation for his religious beliefs and practices.[15]

Ethics Questions

1. Does this case suggest that unscrupulous employees may "get religion" to have weekends off?
2. Would this case be different if Baker worked for a small company? Suppose that company was open daily, employed only 15 workers, and required all of them to work an equal number of Sundays throughout the year?
3. Review the cases in the online support section for this chapter. Have the courts pursued an undisciplined approach to defining religion? What are your thoughts on whether the duties of accommodation of religion at work are promoting or hindering ethical conduct?

Concept Summary Religious Accommodation

The EEOC's guidelines regarding reasonable accommodations were disapproved in the *Ansonia Board of Education v. Philbrook* case. What follows are suggestions based on existing case law and some suggestions from the EEOC of what might constitute reasonable religious accommodation.

- Voluntary swaps among employees to avoid the religious conflict. The employer may assist in this regard by providing a favorable atmosphere for shift swapping, promoting communication about the needs of particular employees, and making resources available for the accommodation.
- Flexible work scheduling.
- Lateral transfers and job changes.
- Rescheduling the events causing the conflict.
- Flexibility in dress and grooming standards.

The case of *Reed v. The Great Lakes Cos., Inc.*[16] exposes the tensions that can arise regarding requests for religious accommodation and an employee's right to disobey a supervisor's directive. Reed sued his employer for **religious discrimination**. As part of the opening of a new hotel, the Gideons provided a free Bible for each room. At a meeting, besides delivering Bibles, the Gideons did some Bible reading and praying. Reed was offended by the religious character of the meeting and left in the middle of it. Later in the day the manager informed Reed of his displeasure and embarrassment because Reed had left the meeting abruptly. Reed told the manager that he was not required to attend a religious event. The manager told him, "Don't do that again. You embarrassed me." Reed replied, "You can't compel me to attend a religious event," to which the manager replied that Reed would do what he was told to do. Reed responded, "Oh, hell no, you won't, not when it comes to my spirituality," whereupon the manager fired him for insubordination. During the litigation, Reed refused to indicate what if any religious affiliation or beliefs (or nonbeliefs) he had and what type of accommodation would be necessary. Lacking that evidence, the court held that Reed had not presented a viable case for **religious discrimination**.

What Is the Duty of a Union?

While Title VII refers only to the obligation of an "employer" to **reasonably accommodate**, the courts have held that the duty to make such an accommodation also extends to unions. In *EEOC v. Union Independiente de la Autoridad de Acueducto y Alcantarillados de Puerto Rico,*[17] the First Circuit Court of Appeals stated "[r]ead literally, Title VII addresses only the obligation of an 'employer' to accommodate an employee's religious beliefs and observances. However, courts have uniformly imposed upon labor organizations the same duty to provide **reasonable accommodations**."

Religious Harassment

Employers must allow time for critical analysis and reflection when confronted with a claim of **religious discrimination** or **harassment**. What should an employer do when an employee is advocating for a certain religious belief or practice to another individual and the other individual does not want to listen? An employer will need to make accommodations to the advocate but also to the individual who feels harassed by the advocator.

When an employee harasses another employee about his or her religious beliefs, or advocates for a religious practice, and in turn creates a hostile working environment for that individual, the employer may be held liable for **religious discrimination**. Such was the holding in the following case.

CASE 8.6

EMPLOYERS MAY BE LIABLE FOR CREATING A RELIGIOUSLY HOSTILE ENVIRONMENT

VENTERS V. CITY OF DELPHI, ET AL.

123 F.3d 956 (7th Cir. 1997)

U.S. Court of Appeals for the Seventh Circuit

Facts. The City of Delphi, Indiana, employed Jennifer Venters as a radio dispatcher. Larry Ives was the Police Chief. From the time Ives began his tenure, he made it clear that he was a born-again Christian who believed that his personal principles of faith should guide him in performing his duties as the city police chief. Ives also believed that God had sent him to Delphi to save as many souls from damnation as he could. Ives spoke to Venters repeatedly about her salvation in a manner intended to lead Venters to the belief her mode of living was immoral. Ives continuously criticized Venters for living with another single woman, asserting she had set a bad moral example for the other woman's teenaged son. He also told Venters that because she was single it was inappropriate for her to receive visits from married police officers. He also confronted Venters about rumors that she had entertained police officers at her home with sexually explicit videos and other pornographic materials.

In an effort to save her soul, Ives provided Venters with a Bible and other religious materials, including a videotape entitled *Hell's Fire and Heaven's Gate.* Although Venters felt that this behavior was unwelcome, she never expressed her own religious beliefs and even tried to appear interested in Ives's conversations to placate him. After a conflict with her boss, Venters was demoted from her position, received a pay cut, and was reassigned to the night shift. Ives urged Venters to consider spiritual counseling with a group that offered "cult deprogramming."

Later, Ives told Venters that after having observed her behavior, he had become convinced that she had sexual relations with family members and perhaps even with animals and that she was sacrificing animals in Satan's name. Ives told Venters that suicide was preferable to continuing her life of sin. It was during this conversation that Venters told Ives he had crossed the line. Ives did not stop, and he informed Venters that she was being fired. The district court granted summary judgment to Ives after determining that Venters's Title VII claim was foreclosed because she never informed Ives of her religious beliefs and did not request that those beliefs be accommodated. She appealed to the Seventh Circuit Court of Appeals.

Issue. Is an employee always required to inform an employer of religious views in order to sue for religious discrimination arising from a hostile work environment?

Language of the Court. Rovner, J.: **Where an employee alleges religious discrimination on the ground that she was unable to fulfill a job requirement due to her religious beliefs or observances, we have held that a prima facie case requires the employee to demonstrate that the belief or observance was religious in nature, that she called it to the attention of her employer, and that the religious belief or observance was the basis of her discharge or other discriminatory treatment.**

[P]roperly understood, Venters' claim is not that the city refused to accommodate her religious practices in some way, but that she was discharged because she did not measure up to Ives' religious expectations. What matters in this context is not so much what Venters' own religious beliefs were, but Ives' asserted perception that she did not share his own. . . . She need not put a label on her own religious beliefs, therefore, or demonstrate that she communicated her religious status and needs as she would if she were complaining that the city had failed to accommodate a particular religious practice. Venters need only show that her perceived religious shortcomings (her unwillingness to strive for salvation as Ives understood it, for example) played a motivating role in her discharge. . . . Simply put, "the question . . . is whether the plaintiff has established a logical reason to believe that the decision [to terminate her] rests on a legally forbidden ground." (Citation omitted.)

The reach of Title VII is not limited solely to discrimination that can be described as "economic" or "tangible." It extends to workplace harassment that is attributable to the plaintiff's sex as well as to her religion. From the evidence before us, a jury could reasonably characterize Venters' work environment at the Delphi police station as hostile and abusive. Venters has made clear that she found Ives' words to her offensive; she has also made clear that in view of his threats to terminate her if she did not "save" herself, she found it difficult to tell Ives that she did not wish to engage in these discussions. Accepting Venters' recounting of the facts, we also think that a reasonable person in Venters' position would have found her work environment hostile.

Decision. No. Venters's evidence supported a claim of discriminatory discharge and workplace harassment on religious discrimination. The district court order was reversed.

CASE QUESTIONS

Critical Legal Thinking. Should Venters be able to recover damages from the city if the city managers and council members were unaware of the circumstances and so failed to act?

Business Ethics. If religious evangelization can create a hostile work environment, could political party affiliation create a hostile work environment? Would an employee be lawfully protected from harassment for not subscribing to the views of a particular political party espoused by a supervisor?

Contemporary Business. Does religious discrimination occur when the manager is pleasant and cooperative toward those who share his faith beliefs but rude and cold to those who do not?

Focus on Ethics
Company Affinity Groups

General Motors developed its Affinity Group program. The program, which makes company resources available to recognized groups, began as an outgrowth of the company's efforts to support employees from diverse backgrounds and improve company performance. Affinity Groups were eligible to receive resources, including the use of company facilities and equipment, for group activities as well as funds to support the group's mission. The program guidelines prohibited the conferral of Affinity Group status on any group promoting or advocating a religious position. Citing these guidelines, GM declined to grant Affinity Group status to a proposed Christian Employee Network.

Other companies, such as Intel, recognize groups such as the Intel Baha'i Group, Intel Bible-Based Christian Network, Intel Jewish Community, and Intel Muslim Employee Group. Texas Instruments recognizes similar groups organized on the basis of a religious affinity.[18]

Ethics Questions

1. What effect might such religious affinity programs have on employee morale — for members and for nonmembers?
2. Is it probable that these corporate programs might offend employees? Can you foresee any effect of such groups on corporate ethics policies?
3. Do such programs constitute impermissible "discrimination"?

Neutral, Generally Applicable Standards

Occasionally, employees wishing to wear religious attire or to follow grooming standards inconsistent with their positions will confront their employers on the issue. When the standards apply to all employees and were implemented to promote health and safety goals, they will not be deemed a constitutional intrusion into the religious beliefs of the employees. No **reasonable accommodation** can be made in those circumstances, and one public policy must supersede another in that situation. Employers also are not required to make an **accommodation** when it would create an **undue hardship** on the conduct of the business. **Undue hardship** is evaluated on a case-by-case basis. For example, the Ninth Circuit Court of Appeals affirmed the granting of summary judgment for Chevron when it refused to exempt a Sikh employee from the requirement that all machinists be clean-shaven, the policy being based on the necessity of wearing a respirator with a gas-tight face seal because of potential exposure to toxins.[19] The requirements of health and safety regulations will usually control in conflicts between a neutral, generally applicable safety standard and a claim involving **religious discrimination**, as the following decision in *Kalsi* reflects.

CASE 8.7

SAFETY REGULATIONS MAY LAWFULLY INTERFERE WITH RELIGIOUS BELIEFS

KALSI V. NEW YORK CITY TRANSIT AUTHORITY

62 F. Supp. 2d 745 (S.D.N.Y. 1998)

U.S. District Court for the So. District of New York

Facts. Charan Singh Kalsi was a member of the Sikh religion, which requires him to wear a turban on his head at all times, other than when he is sleeping or bathing. The transit authority (TA) operates the subway system in New York City. Kalsi was hired by TA from a civil service list and began a one-week training period for a position as a car inspector. The policy in effect at the time Kalsi began his training required car inspectors to wear TA-provided hard hats in many areas of the maintenance shops, including the pits, alongside and inside subway cars, and near overhead hoists and cranes, areas in which most car inspectors worked. While in training, plaintiff refused to wear the hard hat. TA terminated Kalsi because he refused to wear a hard hat. He sued TA for religious discrimination under Title VII and for other damages. TA filed a motion for summary judgment claiming that the circumstances allowed no reasonable accommodation for Kalsi and that his termination was justified.

Issue. Can an employee complain of religious discrimination if equipment required for a job and mandated by federal safety regulations interferes with the employee's religion?

Language of the Court. Gleeson, J.: . . . **Plaintiff has earned a job that indisputably has safety hazards. The TA had evaluated those hazards and concluded that they warranted the hard hat policy. . . . Plaintiff has failed to establish his discharge occurred in circumstances giving rise to an inference of discrimination. Plaintiff cannot simply rely on the fact that he was terminated as evidence of disparate treatment. Rather, he must point to facts that suggest the termination was motivated, at least in part, by religious animus.**

. . . Title VII's obligation to make a reasonable accommodation of religious practices should not be confused with the obligation imposed by the Americans with Disabilities Act ("ADA") to make reasonable accommodation of disabilities. Perhaps because the accommodation of religious beliefs and practices raises constitutional questions under the Establishment Clause, the Supreme Court has interpreted narrowly Title VII's duty to make reasonable accommodations, holding that any accommodation imposing "more than a de minimis cost" amounts to an undue hardship. *Trans World Airlines, Inc. v. Hardison* (citation omitted).

Whether accommodation of an employee's religious practice would cause an employer undue hardship "must be determined based on the particular factual context of each case." (Citation omitted.) . . . Title VII does not require employers to absorb the cost of all less than catastrophic physical injuries to their employees in order to accommodate religious practices.

The potential costs to the TA of permitting plaintiff to perform Car Inspectors' work without a hard hat of course include the cost of injury to plaintiff himself. Those costs are potentially substantial, particularly if he suffers catastrophic injury. The TA, which has been authorized by New York State to "self-insure" for Workers Compensation purposes, would bear them, and plaintiff concedes that he cannot waive that protection.

Moreover, the potential for injury goes beyond the plaintiff. Car Inspectors do not work alone. If plaintiff's turban catches fire in a pit, for example, he may not be the only one burned, especially if conditions exist that will accelerate the fire. If he is electrocuted while performing a task with another employee, that employee may suffer injury too, either from the electric shock or the sudden incapacitation of plaintiff. Others might well suffer injury in rescuing plaintiff from accidents caused by his decision not to wear the hard hat. An accommodation that requires the TA to bear these risks would impose an undue hardship on it. . . . Because all of the plaintiff's proposed accommodations, even the belatedly-proposed ones, would impose an undue hardship on the TA, his Title VII reasonable accommodation claim is dismissed.

Decision. No. The court properly granted the employer's summary judgment motion as to Kalsi's claims of religious discrimination.

CASE QUESTIONS

Critical Legal Thinking. An employer cannot discriminate against any employee's religious practices unless the employer can show it cannot reasonably accommodate the practice without undue hardship on the conduct of the employer's business. Should this be considered on a case-by-case basis?

Business Ethics. How should employers of a small workforce deal with this issue? Would adopting a legitimate seniority system without discriminatory intent be of avail to the employer?

Contemporary Business. Why do you think courts make only narrow inquiries into the right to religious accommodations under Title VII?

Exemptions and Exceptions

The statutory prohibition against **religious discrimination** does not apply to certain religious entities. Under certain conditions, active participation or faithful adherence to a particular religion can be a **BFOQ**, a bona fide occupational qualification. Title VII contains a **religious organization exemption**. As currently codified, the religious exemption in Section 702(a) reads as follows:

> This subchapter shall not apply . . . to a religious corporation, association, educational institution, or society with respect to the employment of individuals of a particular religion to perform work connected with carrying on by such corporation, association, educational institution, or society of its activities.[20]

This provision of Title VII exempts from its coverage those hiring decisions made by religious employers based on religion. Thus, this term would allow a church to discriminate by hiring only those people who are active adherents of the church's tenets. However, the religious organization would still be required to comply with the other elements of Title VII. For example, a Baptist summer camp might require that camp counselors be active members of a Baptist church, but the camp would not be able to discriminate against applicants based on their race, sex, or national origin.

In enacting Title VII, Congress emphasized the applicability of the exemption to parochial schools operated by religious institutions in §703(e)(2), which states:

> Notwithstanding any other provision of this subchapter . . . it shall not be an unlawful employment practice for a school, college, university, or other education institution of learning to hire and employ employees of a particular religion if such school, college, university, or other education institution of learning is, in whole or in substantial part, owned, supported, controlled, or managed by a particular religion or by a particular religious corporation, association, or society, or if the curriculum of such school, college, university, or other education institution of learning is directed toward the propagation of a particular religion.

The effect of these two sections is to allow church-affiliated schools to use religious preferences in employment decision-making.

"Ministerial Exemption" An exemption that prevents the application to clergy members of Title VII, including the provisions relating to race, sex, national origin, and religion.

In addition to the congressional exemption for religious employers, the courts have created an additional exemption known as the **"ministerial exemption."** This exemption prevents the application to clergy members of Title VII, including the provisions relating to race, sex, national origin, and religion.[21]

> ***Example:*** Billie B. McClure was an ordained minister of the Salvation Army. She claimed that the Army discriminated against her because of her sex. The U.S. Court of Appeals for the Fifth Circuit held that Title VII could not constitutionally interfere with the church's decision involving church administration.[22]

The definition of religious minister appears to enjoy a capacious judicial reading. This status has included youth ministers, ordained Episcopal priests, pastoral workers, diocesan press secretaries, music teachers, and choir directors. The **ministerial exception** applies to "religious institutions," not merely churches, "whenever that entity's mission is marked by clear or obvious religious characteristics."[23] Title VII does not prohibit "a religious corporation, association, educational institution, or society" from discriminating in favor of employees "of a particular religion." In the event that a *religious organization exemption* might apply, a claimant would be well advised to bring a claim under other theories of discrimination. For example, an employee of a religious organization would still be entitled to pursue claims based on contract, tort, or state discrimination laws or claims arising under a federal statute other than Title VII, such as the Equal Pay Act.

Management Application
The Case of the Evangelizing Supervisor

IKON Office solutions employed Charles Massie as an account executive whose duties entailed cold calling of business establishments and trying to interest them in IKON's products. He was obliged to achieve a minimal acceptable level for sales of the company's products and services. Massie received several written and oral warnings regarding his inadequate performance throughout the term of his employment. Massie has acknowledged, in writing, the level of his performance, but explained that part of the reason for his production problems was his lack of training for the position. At considerable expense to IKON, Massie was subsequently sent to sales training school.

When Massie began his employment, IKON gave him a copy of the employee handbook, for which he signed a receipt. The handbook contained specific policies against the use of its e-mail facilities for sending or receiving nonbusiness-related materials, such as personal messages and jokes. All violations of this policy were to be reported to the employee's manager.

About six months after his hire, Massie sent nonwork-related e-mails to his co-workers. A certain e-mail referred to "New Barbies," with specific citations to "exoticbarbie," "sororitybarbie," and "transbarbie." In another e-mail, Massie asked a female coworker whether she was a fan of the music group Def Leppard or a specified pornographic star. His supervisor instructed Massie to cease sending e-mails of that character. Nevertheless, several months later Massie was continuing to send inappropriate e-mails to others, some of which included foul and disrespectful content. When warned again that further use of the e-mail system in this manner would constitute insubordination, Massie sent an e-mail to his supervisor's boss complaining about office morale and asserting, without support, that the supervisor liked to proselytize in the workplace.

Massie asserted that in the month prior to his termination, his supervisor compelled him to read the Bible in the supervisor's office on at least five occasions. He says that he received a "visual bible" attachment from his supervisor that required him to read a Bible passage on his computer before he could access his regular files. He did not report to IKON the purported conflict between his religion and what he alleges was his supervisor's proselytizing.[24] As the Human Resource Manager, you must decide what action, if any, the company should take with regard to Massie.

Discussion Questions

1. What further facts would you require regarding the supervisor's penchant for evangelizing subordinate employees?
2. Massie tells you that he will sue for religious harassment if you elect to terminate his employment. Will you fire him?
3. What decisions should the company make toward Massie and the supervisor?

Human Resource Form
Religious Accommodation Request

Name:
Employee I.D. #:
Contact information:
Home Phone:
Work Phone:
E-mail Address:
Department and Job Title:
Immediate Manager:

Name of religion, if any (*note:* a religious accommodation does not require that you belong to an organized religion):

Please state the specific religious practices and/or requirements that you feel need reasonable accommodation:

Describe what working conditions (e.g., tasks, responsibilities, work schedules) are affecting or limiting your religious beliefs and require religious accommodation:

Accommodation requested:
Name of religious holiday:
Day(s), date(s), and time(s) of religious holiday (e.g., "sundown [date] to sundown [date]"):

Describe work shift/schedule affected:

Describe all clothing accommodations requested:

What other information can you provide us so that we can evaluate your request?

We may need to contact a recognized religious representative who is familiar with your needs and who could substantiate your request. You do not need to have such a relationship for your request to be granted, but, if you do, please provide the contact information:

Authorization

I authorize my employer to discuss my request for a religious accommodation with the above-listed contact person.

____
Employee signature and date

Key Terms and Concepts

- Religion
- Religious discrimination
- Religious practice or observance
- Reasonable accommodation
- Sincerely held belief
- Undue hardship
- *De minimis* cost for accommodation
- Religion as a BFOQ
- Discrimination as workplace religious harassment
- Ministerial exemption

Chapter Summary

- Title VII provides protection against an employee's religious observance or practice. An employee, though, is not obligated to automatically accept a religious practice and make accommodations for those practices. The law requires the employee to establish that the belief is sincerely held before an employer has a duty to accommodate on religious grounds.

- Beliefs based on mere personal preferences, convenience, and expediency do not constitute a religious belief.

- For a claimant to establish a prima facie case of failure to make a reasonable accommodation of religious beliefs or practices, the claimant must show the existence of a sincere religious belief or practice that conflicts with an employment requirement, *and* that the claimant provided notice to the employer regarding the conflicting belief or practice, *and* that the claimant was subjected to an adverse employment action due to adherence to the religious belief or practice.

- A claimant need not make any effort to compromise religious belief before seeking a religious accommodation from the employer.

- For the employer to avoid liability after a claimant has established a prima facie case of failure to make a reasonable accommodation, the employer must demonstrate that a reasonable accommodation was offered but was not accepted *or* that an undue hardship exists, making a reasonable accommodation impossible.

- In certain limited situations, religion may act as a BFOQ.

Online Student Support

- Loislaw legal research and writing assignments.
- Loislaw group projects and class presentations.
- Loislaw access, providing online research including up-to-date cases, statutes, rules, and regulations. Primary law for all 50 states and federal jurisdictions. Registration required for access to this resource.
- Practice questions, including sample true/false, multiple choice, and short answer questions to test your understanding of concepts.
- Additional human resource forms.
- Internet exercises.
- Blogs.
- Supplementary statutory and regulatory materials.

Case Problems

7.1 David Kelly was a bailiff for the municipal courts of Marion County, Indiana, when he was terminated for poor job performance and improper conduct. He persisted after his supervisor's warning not to proselytize and read the Bible to prisoners and in public areas of the courthouse. He brought suit claiming that he was harassed and ultimately fired due to his religious beliefs. Is the employer's discharge of Kelly appropriate? (*Kelly v. Municipal Courts,* 97 F.3d 902 (11th Cir. 1996))

7.2. Mr. Shpargel was employed at a deli in West Bloomfield, Michigan, when he was terminated for failing to plan for and prepare deli trays for customers observing Yom Kippur, as he had been directed by his boss, Steve Goldberg. When he sued for religious discrimination, asserting that the directive would have required him to miss Yom Kippur services, the restaurant argued Shpargel failed to demonstrate a sincere belief in Judaism and in attending services for Yom Kippur, he did not recognize all of the Jewish holidays, and he had previously worked overtime to prepare deli trays for Yom Kippur in 1993. What is the relevancy of his prior attendance at Yom Kippur services in the past? To what degree will the court review the depth of Mr. Shpargel's faith? (*Shpargel v. Stage & Co.*, 914 F. Supp. 1468 (E.D. Mich. 1996))

7.3 Glynda Hall has sued Baptist Memorial College of Health Sciences for religious discrimination because of a conflict between her own religious beliefs and those of her church-affiliated employer. Hall was terminated after she became an ordained minister of a nondenominational church with a large congregation of gays and lesbians. What tests should the court employ to determine if the medical college is sufficiently religious in purpose to be exempt from Title VII? (*Hall v. Baptist Memorial Health Care Corp.*, 27 F. Supp. 2d 1029 (W.D. Tenn. 1998))

7.4 Aaron Kreilkamp, a grocery bagger, sued his employer, Copps's Food Store in Madison, Wisconsin. As Christmas approached, front-end employees such as Kreilkamp were directed to wear holiday-themed necklaces that were sold in the store. Kreilkamp was given a gingerbread man necklace to wear, but he refused to do so because one of his birth parents was Jewish. Does he have a case of religious discrimination? (*Kreilkamp v. Roundy's, Inc.*, 428 F. Supp. 3d 903 (W.D. Wis. 2006))

7.5. Mr. Cary, as a union employee of Anheuser-Busch, Inc., objected to some routine employee obligations, such as signing a consent form for drug testing mandated by the collective bargaining agreement, on the basis that as a Baptist minister he could not do so. He claimed that he had counseled others as to substance abuse and that such drug testing would reveal substance abuse problems in others, a practice he could not condone. Is Mr. Cary obligated to explain in detail his religious beliefs, or is his statement sufficient to support a claim for religious discrimination when he is terminated for refusing to execute the form? (*Cary v. Carmichael,* 908 F. Supp. 1334 (E. D. Va. 1995)).

End Notes

1. *Petruska v. Gannon University, et al.*, 462 F. 3d. 294 (3d Cir. 2006), *cert. denied* 127 S. Ct. 2098 (2006).
2. 42 U.S.C. 2000e-2(a).
3. 42 U.S.C. 2000(j).
4. 29 C.F.R §1605.1 (2001).
5. *Wilson v. U.S. West Communications,* 58 F.3d 1337 (8th Cir. 1995).
6. *Employment Division v. Smith,* 458 U.S. 660 (1988).
7. The Pew Forum on Religion and Public Life, U.S. Religious Landscape Survey, available at *http://religions.pewforum .org/reports.*
8. 445 F.3d 541 (2d Cir. 2006).
9. *Vetter v. Farmland Industries, Inc.*, 884 F.Supp. 1287 (N.D. Iowa, 1995).
10. *Edwards v. School Board,* 483 F. Supp. 620 (W.D. Va. 1980), *vacated in part on other grounds,* 658 F. 2d 951 (4th Cir. 1981).
11. *Lubetsky v. Applied Card Systems, Inc.*, 296 F.3d 1301 (11th Cir. 2002).
12. 671 F.2d 141 (5th Cir. 1982).
13. Id. at 145-46.
14. *Cooper v. Oak Rubber Co.*, 15 F.3d 1375 (6th Cir. 1994).
15. *Baker v. The Home Depot,* 445 F.3d 541 (2d Cir. 2006).
16. 330 F.3d 931 (7th Cir. 2003).
17. 279 F.3d 49 (1st Cir. 2002).
18. *Moranski v. General Motors Corp.*, 433 F.3d 537 (7th Cir. 2005).
19. *Bhatia v. Chevron U.S.A., Inc.*, 734 F. 2d 1382 (9th Cir. 1984).
20. §702(a), 42 U.S.C. §2000e-1(a).
21. §703(e)(2), 42 U.S.C. §2000e-2(e)(2).
22. *McClure v. Salvation Army,* 460 F.2d 553 (1972).
23. *Shalieshsabou v. Hebrew Home of Greater Washington,* 363 F.3d 299, 309-10 (4th Cir. 2004).
24. *Massie v. IKON Office Solutions, Inc.*, 381 F. Supp. 2d 91 (N.D.N.Y. 2005).

Chapter 9 Rights of the Disabled in the Workplace

"The moral test of government is how it treats those who are in the dawn of life . . . the children; those who are in the twilight of life . . . the elderly; and those who are in the shadow of life . . . the sick . . . the needy . . . and the disabled." —Hubert H. Humphrey, U.S. Senator and thirty-eighth Vice President of the United States

Learning Objectives

1. State the ADA definition of a disability.
2. Identify employers subject to the ADA.
3. Explain who qualifies as an individual with a disability.
4. Define an ADA covered physical or mental impairment.
5. State the rights of a person who is "regarded as" being disabled.
6. Distinguish the ADA from the Rehabilitation Act.

Chapter Outline

- Introduction
- Overview of Disability Discrimination
- Management Application: Disability and Medical Exams

Case 9.1 *Chevron USA, Inc. v. Echazabal*

- Reasonable Accommodation
- Focus on Ethics: Reasonable Accommodation and Undue Hardship
- Impact of the ADA on Hiring
- Remedies

Case 9.2 EEOC v. Wal-Mart Stores, Inc.

- Relationship to SSDI

Case 9.3 Cleveland v. Policy Management Systems Corp.

- Rehabilitation Act of 1973
- Focus on Ethics: Was There Disability Discrimination?
- Human Resource Form: Drug and Alcohol Policy

Chapter Opening scenario

Bill Harold applies for a position as the sales manager at a used car lot. He is not disabled, but in his job interview he discloses to the owner of the lot that his spouse has a disability. The owner thereupon declines to hire Bill because the employer believes that he would have to miss work or frequently leave work early to care for his spouse. Is the employer's action a violation of the Americans with Disabilities Act?[1]

Introduction

Several important federal statutes govern discrimination directed toward workers with disabilities. Of these, two quite similar laws — the **Rehabilitation Act of 1973** and the **Americans with Disabilities Act of 1990 (ADA)**, as amended by the **Americans with Disabilities Act Amendments Act of 2008 (ADAAA)** — are the most significant for our study. A number of other statutes extend protections to government employees. Employers should be aware that almost all states have laws and regulations that prohibit disability-based discrimination and impose additional affirmative action duties on employers with as few as one employee.

Protecting people with disabilities from workplace discrimination poses many challenges for employers. The threshold question is how to define who is **"disabled"** for purposes of **disability discrimination** law. In this chapter, we review the balance struck between providing employment opportunities for the **disabled** and the employer's right to select the most qualified persons for roles in its workforce.

Disability
A recognized physical or mental impairment that substantially limits one or more of the major life activities of the affected individual.

Americans with Disabilities Act Amendments Act of 2008 (ADAAA)
The federal law intended to overturn a series of Supreme Court decisions that interpreted the ADA so narrowly as to make it difficult to prove an impairment was a covered disability.

Before the enactment of the **ADAAA**, the law on **disability discrimination** focused on determining whether a worker was **disabled.** The new law focuses on the discrimination experienced by the individual. The **ADAAA** requires that the term ***"disabled"*** be defined expansively so as to provide "broad coverage" for individuals.[2] The **ADAAA** restored a congressional intent in the application of the law to provide "a clear and comprehensive national mandate for the elimination of discrimination" with respect to disability. It rejected several Supreme Court decisions that had the effect of severely limiting the protections promised by the original **ADA**. Congress also ordered the Equal Employment Opportunity Commission (EEOC), which enforces the **ADA**, to issue new regulations to conform to Congress's restated intent. The **ADAAA** states that courts had been defining *disability* too restrictively.

In fiscal year 2008, the EEOC received 19,453 charges of **disability discrimination**, which represented an almost 10 percent increase from the prior year. Most frequent among these charges were claims of disability based on depression (6.7 percent), orthopedic impairments (nonparalytic and paralytic; 18.8 percent), and being "regarded as having a disability" (12.6 percent). The agency resolved 16,705 of pending charges, with monetary benefits to the claimants of more than $57 million. Of the resolved charges, almost 60 percent were resolved in favor of the employer: no reasonable cause was found for the claim of **disability discrimination**. Claims resolved in favor of claimants most often involved disability due to depression (5.7 percent), diabetes (4.2 percent), orthopedic impairments (18.8 percent), and "regarded as having a disability" (14.3 percent).

Overview of Disability Discrimination

Disability Discrimination
The less favorable treatment by a covered employer or entity of an applicant or employee because the person has a history of a disability or is believed to have a physical or mental impairment expected to last six months or longer.

The **Americans with Disabilities Act of 1990** (**ADA**) is one of the most significant labor and employment laws enacted since the Civil Rights Act of 1964. As amended, it provides:

- a broad definition of the term *disability;*
- that private sector employers must justify job requirements and selection criteria for every employee. Unlike other employment disputes, in questions of disability discrimination the burden is on the employer to justify a rational basis for the way the work was organized, assigned, and evaluated among employees;
- protection for those employees and applicants who are qualified for the essential job functions;
- that employers must make **reasonable accommodations** up to the point of undue hardship;
- protection from discrimination in public services and an accommodation requirement for state and local government providers of services. **ADA** prohibits discrimination in places of public accommodation and commercial facilities. Operators of such accommodations and facilities must remove physical barriers from existing facilities and design new facilities that allow their use by the **disabled**;
- protection from retaliation following protests against practices unlawful under **ADA** or participation in investigations or proceedings relating to them;
- protection for rehabilitated alcoholics and illicit drug abusers; and
- that any federal, state, or local law providing greater protection to the **disabled** is not preempted by the act.

Americans with Disabilities Act of 1990 (ADA)
The federal law making it illegal to discriminate against a qualified person with a disability in private-sector and state and local government employment and outlawing retaliation in response to discrimination claims. Employers must reasonably accommodate known physical or mental limitations of an otherwise qualified disabled individual, unless doing so would impose undue hardship on the employer's business.

Our discussion will focus on **disability discrimination** arising in the workplace. Students should be aware that the scope of the **ADA** also extends to discrimination with respect to public accommodations. This part of the act applies to owners and operators of public accommodations and commercial facilities. Examples of these would include airlines, airports, hotels, buses, and retail establishments. A review of such matters is outside the scope of this text.

Qualified Individual with a Disability
A person with a disability who meets the required level of skills, experience, education, or other requirements for a position and who can perform the essential functions of the job.

An equal employment opportunity is an opportunity to secure the same level of performance or to enjoy the same benefits and privileges of employment that are available to the average, similarly situated employee without a **disability**. In summary,

Reasonable Accommodation (Disability)
A modification or adjustment to a job or work environment enabling a qualified applicant or employee with a recognized disability to pursue employment or perform the essential job functions. There are three categories of reasonable accommodation: job application changes (accommodation in the form or method of applying for the job); changes to the work environment or the manner of performing the work; and changes that enable an employee with a disability to enjoy equal benefits and privileges of employment (such as access to training).

the **ADA** requires **reasonable accommodation** to qualified individuals with a disability in three aspects of employment:

- equal opportunity in the application process;
- equal opportunity to perform the essential functions of a job; and
- equal benefits and privileges of employment.

The laws and regulations relating to the **ADA** set out many examples of prohibited **disability discrimination.**[3] A partial list includes the following:

- limiting, segregating, or classifying a job applicant or an employee in a manner that adversely affects the individual's status or opportunities because of a disability;
- the use of standards, criteria, or methods of administration that either have a discriminatory effect against **disabled** individuals or perpetuate the discrimination of others who are subject to common administrative control;
- excluding or denying equal jobs or benefits to a qualified applicant or employee because of the known disability of another individual with whom he or she has a relationship or an association; this provision is intended to protect any qualified individual, whether or not the individual has a disability, from discrimination. It provides protection from discrimination due to association with someone who has a disability.
- the use of qualification standards, tests, or other selection criteria that tend to screen out or that do screen out one or more individuals with disabilities, unless the standards are shown to be related to the position and are justified by business necessity; and
- failing to select and administer employment tests in the most effective manner to ensure that the results accurately reflect the skills, aptitude, or other factors that the test purports to measure.

Congressional Findings Concerning Disabilities in the Workplace

In the congressional hearings leading to the passage of the **ADA**, Congress made the following findings:

1. some 43,000,000 Americans have one or more physical or mental disabilities, and this number is increasing as the population as a whole grows older;
2. historically, society has tended to isolate and segregate individuals with disabilities, and, despite some improvements, such forms of discrimination against individuals with disabilities continue to be a serious and pervasive social problem;
3. discrimination against individuals with disabilities persists in such critical areas as employment, housing, public accommodations, education, transportation, communication, recreation, institutionalization, health services, voting, and access to public services;
4. unlike individuals who have experienced discrimination on the basis of race, color, sex, national origin, religion, or age, individuals who have experienced discrimination on the basis of disability have often had no legal recourse to redress such discrimination;

5. individuals with disabilities continually encounter various forms of discrimination, including outright intentional exclusion, the discriminatory effects of architectural, transportation, and communication barriers, overprotective rules and policies, failure to make modifications to existing facilities and practices, exclusionary qualification standards and criteria, segregation, and relegation to lesser services, programs, activities, benefits, jobs, or other opportunities;
6. census data, national polls, and other studies have documented that people with disabilities, as a group, occupy an inferior status in our society, and are severely disadvantaged socially, vocationally, economically, and educationally;
7. individuals with disabilities are a discrete and insular minority who have been faced with restrictions and limitations, subjected to a history of purposeful unequal treatment, and relegated to a position of political powerlessness in our society, based on characteristics that are beyond the control of such individuals and resulting from stereotypic assumptions not truly indicative of the individual ability of such individuals to participate in, and contribute to, society;
8. the nation's proper goals regarding individuals with disabilities are to assure equality of opportunity, full participation, independent living, and economic self-sufficiency for such individuals; and
9. the continuing existence of unfair and unnecessary discrimination and prejudice denies people with disabilities the opportunity to compete on an equal basis and to pursue those opportunities for which our free society is justifiably famous, and costs the United States billions of dollars in unnecessary expenses resulting from dependency and nonproductivity.

Since 1990, these reasons continue to underlie the need for the **ADA** to protect those with disabilities from employment discrimination.

Definition of Disability

The **ADAAA** retained the **ADA**'s basic definition of **"disability."** Under the **ADA** and its regulations, the definition of **"disability"** was borrowed from one used in the **Rehabilitation Act of 1973** with regard to an **"individual with handicaps."** As such, and taking into account the **ADAAA**, the term ***disability*** means a ***qualified individual*** who meets any *one* of the following criteria:

- having a physical or mental impairment that substantially limits one or more of the major life activities of the individual; and/or
- having a **record of such an impairment** that substantially limited a **major life activity** (such as cancer that is in remission); and/or
- being regarding as having such an impairment (as when an entity, such as employer, takes an action prohibited by the **ADA** based on an actual or perceived impairment).[1]

These elements are referred to as the "three prongs" of the definition. The intended effect of the **ADAAA** is to cause courts to focus more on whether employment **disability discrimination** has occurred and less on whether a **disability** exists, the focus of the courts under prior law. Before the change in the law, many in the disabled community could not avail themselves of the protections offered under the statute because court decisions had narrowly defined the circumstances under which a person could qualify for **ADA** protection.

Impairment
A condition that substantially limits a person in the performance of one or more life activities when compared to an average person in the general population. The determination is made without regard to the use of mitigating measures, such as medication. If the person's condition would qualify without such aids, the person has a protected disability. Impairments do not include conditions requiring eyeglasses and contact lenses.

Major Life Activity
An expansive definition used in disability cases for the variety of tasks important in most people's daily lives.

Congress Rejected the Supreme Court's Narrow Application of the ADA

For many years, congressional expectations in enacting the **ADA** were frustrated because of Supreme Court decisions, collectively known as the *Sutton trilogy*, that narrowed the application of the **ADA**. These decisions strictly interpreted the act. Under them, the Court ruled that individuals with successfully treated disabilities were not protected as persons with disabilities under the **ADA**. Thus, those persons who could function well due to mitigating measures such as medications or prosthetic devices were not protected. These cases also required that the disability must limit *more than one* **major life activity**. Because of these cases, federal courts set a high bar for plaintiffs to prove that they were entitled to protection under the **ADA**. These cases created a paradox for disability plaintiffs because mitigating measures such as medications and other aids had to be considered in determining whether an individual's impairment substantially limited a **major life activity**.

Congress was further frustrated following the Court's decision in *Toyota Motor Manufacturing, Kentucky, Inc. v. Williams*, 534 U.S. 184 (2002). Under that decision, the Court required that **disabled** persons would have to prove that their impairment prevented or severely restricted them from performing a range of tasks central to those most people carried out in the course of daily living. The standard was not whether the individual was unable to perform her specific job tasks, but rather any manual tasks in life in general. This interpretation made proof of a qualifying disability almost impossible to prove. Many plaintiffs were unable to take their cases to trial because employers frequently prevailed in motions for summary judgment.

Employers

The **ADA** covers employers with *15 or more employees* who are engaged in an industry affecting interstate commerce for each working day in each of 20 or more calendar weeks in the current or preceding calendar year, and agents of such persons.[5] Its coverage extends to employment agencies, labor organizations, and joint labor-management committees. It exempts from its coverage the U.S. government, Indian tribes, and bona fide private membership clubs that are tax exempt under the Internal Revenue Code. The act prohibits discrimination against a **qualified individual with a disability**.

Essential Functions of a Job
The functions that an individual must be able to perform unaided or with the assistance of a reasonable accommodation; this determination is made based on the functions to be performed, the skills required to perform them, and the time necessary for and criticality of the tasks.

Qualified Individual

The act, as amended, extends its protections to **"qualified individuals with a disability."** That term encompasses individuals with disabilities who, *with or without* **reasonable accommodation**, *can perform the* **essential functions** of the employment position the individuals hold or desire. The employer's judgment is given consideration as to what functions of a job are essential, and when an employer has prepared a written description before advertising for or interviewing job applicants, that description will be considered evidence of the essential functions of the job.[6]

An individual must be able to perform the **essential functions of a job** unaided or with the assistance of a **reasonable accommodation**. The following questions help define the **essential functions of a job**.

- Does the position exist to perform a particular function?
- Are only a few employees available to perform the job function, as compared to the overall volume of work to be done?
- Does the work require specialized tasks?
- How much time is spent performing the particular function?
- What is the criticality of performing the function?

> ***Example:*** If an employee spends the vast majority of his or her time working at a cash register, this would be evidence that operating the cash register is an essential job function. In another case, although a firefighter may not regularly have to carry an unconscious adult out of a burning building, the consequences of failing to require the firefighter to be able to perform this function would be serious.[7]

One area of continuing concern for employers is whether a worker with a disability can perform the **essential functions of a job** but cannot match the speed or quality standards the employer demands. The EEOC's Interpretive Guidance on this subject states the following:

> [T]he inquiry into essential functions is not intended to second guess an employer's business judgment with regard to production standards, whether qualitative or quantitative, nor to require employers to lower such standards. . . . If an employer requires its typists to be able to accurately type 75 words per minute, it will not be called upon to explain why an inaccurate work product, or a typing speed of 65 words per minute would not be adequate. Similarly, if a hotel requires its service workers to clean thoroughly 16 rooms per day, it will not have to explain why it requires thorough cleaning, or why it chose a 16 room rather than a 10 room requirement. However, if an employer does require accurate 75 words per minute typing or the thorough cleaning of 16 rooms, it will have to show that it actually imposes such requirements on its employees in fact, and not simply on paper. It should also be noted that, if it is alleged that the employer intentionally selected the particular level of production to exclude individuals with disabilities, the employer might have to offer a legitimate, nondiscriminatory reason for its selection.[8]

An employer is prohibited from using discriminatory selection standards or selection criteria in the hiring of employees, including the following:

> utilizing standards, criteria, or methods of administration . . . that have the effect of discrimination on the basis of disability, . . . using employment tests or other selection criteria that screen out or tend to screen out an individual with a disability or a class of individuals with disabilities unless the standard, test or other selection criteria, as used by the covered entity, is shown to be job-related for the position in question and is consistent with business necessity.

Reasonable Accommodation

The **ADA** states that **reasonable accommodation** involves:

- making existing facilities used by employees readily accessible to and usable by individuals with disabilities; and

- job restructuring, part-time, or modified work schedules; reassignment to a vacant position; acquisition or modification of equipment or devices; appropriate adjustment or modifications of examinations, training materials, or policies; the provision of qualified readers or interpreters; and other similar accommodations for individuals with disabilities.

If an applicant or employee is unable to perform a job as required or is unable to do so without endangering themselves or the health or safety of others, the employer need not hire or retain the employee. However, employers should first consider the duty to make a **reasonable accommodation** before making any adverse employment decision. The employer should carefully consult with disability organizations and other individuals with the same or a similar disability to analyze whether the **essential functions of the job** may be performed with a **reasonable accommodation**.

Actual Physical or Mental Impairment

Given the broad scope of the term ***actual physical or mental impairment***, the **ADA** does not define it. The regulations of the **ADA** and court opinions require that assessments be made on a case-by-case basis to determine the presence and consequence of such impairments. While the legislation and regulations cannot include a complete list of all of the specific conditions that constitute impairments, the legislation does include the following definition of the term ***physical or mental impairment***:

- any physiological disorder or condition, cosmetic disfigurement, or anatomical loss affecting one or more of the following body systems: neurological; musculoskeletal; special sense organs; respiratory; including speech organs; cardiovascular; reproductive; digestive; genitourinary; hemic and lymphatic; skin; and endocrine.
- any mental or psychological disorder such as mental retardation, organic brain syndrome, emotional or mental illness, and specific learning disabilities. The phrase **"physical or mental impairment"** includes, but is not limited to, such contagious and noncontagious diseases and conditions as: orthopedic, visual, speech, and hearing impairments, cerebral palsy, epilepsy, muscular dystrophy, multiple sclerosis, cancer, heart disease, diabetes, mental retardation, emotional illness, specific learning disabilities, HIV (whether symptomatic or asymptomatic), tuberculosis, drug addiction, and alcoholism. However, homosexuality and bisexuality are not considered impairments under the **ADA** and implementing regulations.[9]

Physical or Mental Impairment
Any disorder, condition, disfigurement, or anatomical loss that affects a major body system or mental or psychological state. The ADAAA requires expansive interpretation and application of the term in favor of individuals.

For the first time, the EEOC, in its proposed regulations implementing the **ADAAA**, lists examples of impairments that will consistently meet the definition of a **disability**. Such impairments include but are not limited to the following:

Blindness
Deafness
Intellectual disabilities
Partially or completely missing limbs
Mobility impairments requiring the use of a wheelchair

Autism
Cancer
Cerebral palsy
Diabetes
Epilepsy
HIV/AIDS
Multiple sclerosis
Muscular dystrophy

Major depression
Bipolar disorder
Post-traumatic stress disorder
Obsessive-compulsive disorder
Schizophrenia

Substantially Limits a Major Life Activity

The **ADAAA** requires that the term ***"substantially limits"*** must be interpreted consistently with the findings and purposes of the act. The findings of the act state that the EEOC and the Supreme Court have incorrectly interpreted the term **"substantially limits"** to require a greater degree of limitation in performing a **major life activity** than had been intended by Congress.

Substantially Limits a Major Life Activity
A factual finding regarding an impairment's nature and severity, duration or expectation of duration, and permanence or long-term impact or expected impact on a person.

The EEOC's proposed regulations make it clear that an impairment does need to prevent, or significantly or severely restrict, the individual from performing a **major life activity** for it to be considered **"substantially limiting."** Instead, the determination of whether an individual is substantially limited in performing a **major life activity** should be subject to a commonsense test of comparing an individual's ability to perform a specific **major life activity** with that of most people within the population. Due to the enactment of the **ADDAA**, inquiry no longer focuses on whether the worker is unable to perform the tasks associated with a specific job. Instead, the question is whether the worker is unable to perform the variety of tasks that are important in most people's daily lives.

These regulations expand the definition of **"major life activities"** through two nonexhaustive lists of what constitutes **"major life activities."** Frustrated by the EEOC definition, Congress defined **"major life activities"** in the **ADAAA** to include, but not be limited to, the following:

Caring for oneself
Performing manual tasks
Seeing
Hearing
Eating
Sleeping
Walking
Standing
Lifting
Bending
Speaking
Breathing
Learning
Reading
Concentrating
Thinking
Communicating
Working

The **ADAAA** added a *new* **major life activity** category: **major bodily functions**, which includes the operation of a major bodily organ, function, or system, including, but not limited to, the following:

Functions of the immune system
Normal cell growth
Digestive
Bowel
Bladder
Neurological
Brain
Respiratory
Circulatory
Endocrine
Reproductive functions

In addition to these, the EEOC added the following additional **major bodily functions** pursuant to its regulations: special sense organs, and skin, hemic, lymphatic, and musculoskeletal systems.

These regulations also provide that an impairment that is episodic or in remission is a **disability** if it would **substantially limit a major life activity** when active. However, temporary nonchronic impairments of short duration that result in little or no residual effect will usually not meet the definition of a covered **disability**.

The EEOC emphasizes the physiological origin of impairment. The EEOC has ruled that pregnancy is not an **ADA** disability because although pregnancy is a **physical impairment**, it is not a disorder. The temporary nature of pregnancy is an additional reason why it is excluded from **ADA** coverage.

Certain illnesses have dormant stages and periods of flare-ups. Sufferers of many of these illnesses are afflicted with chronic, nonlife-threatening conditions; examples include chronic fatigue, fibromyalgia, interstitial cystitis, herpes, and psoriasis. These conditions can support a claim of **disability**. The current law should give hope to those whose impairments are episodic or in remission.

> ***Example:*** The employer of nurse Katherine Cehrs argued that she was **disabled** only when her chronic psoriasis flared up. Due to its transitory nature, the employer argued, psoriasis could not be considered a **physical impairment**. The federal court of appeals held that it was not necessary for an individual to experience flare-ups on a daily basis for her condition to be characterized as a covered **physical impairment**. Due to the nature of the disease and its physiological impact, even during its dormancy, the condition was sufficient to support a claim of **disability discrimination**.[10]

Employers may also claim that the diminished capacity of a worker during a flare-up period precludes the worker from being qualified for the position.

> ***Example:*** Connie Haschmann suffered from lupus. After Time Warner fired her from her position as vice president of finance, she alleged the termination violated the **ADA**. She had worked at other divisions of the company and received superior evaluations every year. She was fired from a position to which she had been promoted for excellent performance. The course of her disease was unpredictable. It had periods of inactivity and periods of flare. During a temporary flare, lupus causes joint pain, inflammations, and extreme fatigue. It can affect a person's ability to process information. During a flare-up, Haschmann requested leave under the Family and Medical Leave Act, but she was terminated. A doctor reported that, given her condition, it would be difficult for Haschmann to perform her job duties during a flare period; other testimony indicated that she was capable of performing her job during periods of remission. A jury awarded her damages. On appeal, Time Warner claimed that Haschmann could not invoke the protections of the **ADA** because she was not able to perform the essential functions of her position; she was unqualified for the position, the company contended. The court held that the plaintiff was qualified for the position until the flare-ups occurred and that she could be granted a short medical leave of absence to accommodate her condition. The court did note that the reasonableness of the length of the leave was a question for the jury.[11]

The Supreme Court has observed that individualized assessment of an impairment is necessary when the impairment is one in which symptoms vary widely from person to person.[12] By directing courts to consider whether an **impairment** would **substantially limit a major life activity** if it were active, the **ADAAA** allows courts to consider individual situations more carefully.

Concept Summary
Proving Disability Discrimination Under the ADA, as Amended

A plaintiff must prove:

- that the person was a **"qualified individual,"**
- with a **disability** (i.e., the plaintiff was in the protected class of physically and mentally disabled protected persons because of circumstances within the definition of disability), and
- the plaintiff was excluded from the position sought because of the recognized **disability**.

Mitigating Measures

The **ADAAA** expands the definition of what it means to be **disabled**, emphasizing that the definition should be broadly interpreted and without extensive analysis and providing that employers can no longer take into account **mitigating measures** such as medication in determining if a person is considered **disabled** under the **ADA**. An exception is made for "ordinary eyeglasses or contact lenses," which may be taken into account in determining an individual's **disabled** status. That provision means that if an employer uses a qualification standard based on a person's uncorrected vision, the employer must show that the standard is **job related** and consistent with **business necessity**.

This legislation will increase the overall number of workers classified as **disabled** and requiring a **reasonable accommodation** from employers. As a result, employers will need to spend more time analyzing the existence of disabilities.

Management Application
Disability and Medical Exams

The EEOC has issued guidelines regarding pre-employment disability-related inquiries and medical testing. The guidelines provide that employers may ask disability-related questions and may require job applicants take qualification examinations only after extending a conditional job offer — that is, the offer becomes official following a successful medical examination or is subject to the employer's **reasonable accommodation** of a disclosed or reported **disability**. However, an employer may ask job applicants whether they can perform the essential functions of the job and how they would perform the job, with or without a reasonable accommodation.

After an offer is extended to an applicant, the law allows an employer to condition the job offer on the applicant's answers to certain medical questions or successfully passing an employer-paid medical exam. However, the employer may set these conditions only if all new employees in the same job classification must answer those questions or take such an exam.

Once the person is hired and has started work, an employer generally can ask medical questions or require a medical exam only if the employer needs documentation to support an employee's request for an accommodation. The employer may also make such a request if the employer reasonably believes the employee is not able to perform a job successfully or safely because of a medical condition.

All medical records and information concerning the medical and disability condition of applicants and employees must be maintained confidentially and in an area separate from other personnel files.[13]

What Is Not a Disability

Individuals with one or more of the following physical or mental characteristics but none of the conditions discussed above would not be considered disabled under the **ADA**:

- transvestism, transsexualism, pedophilia, exhibitionism, voyeurism, gender identity disorders not resulting from **physical impairment**, or other sexual behavior disorders;
- compulsive gambling, kleptomania, or pyromania;
- psychoactive substance use disorders resulting from current illegal use of drugs.

Moreover, for purposes of the definition of **disability**, homosexuality and bisexuality are not impairments and therefore are not disabilities under the **ADA**.

Not all differences between and among individuals are considered **physical or mental impairments**. For example, the **ADA** specifically provides that the following are not covered by the act:

- hair or eye color;
- left-handedness;
- height, weight, or muscle tone that is within "normal" range and is not the result of a physiological disorder;
- characteristic predisposition to illness or disease;
- pregnancy;
- conditions that are not the result of a physiological disorder;
- personality traits, such as poor judgment or a quick temper, where such traits are not symptoms of a mental or psychological disorder; and
- poverty, lack of education, or a prison record.

Example: While advanced age is *not* a disability (but might constitute a basis for employment protection under age discrimination), the impairments common to the elderly (such as weakened eyesight or hearing loss) *are* considered disabilities.

Record of Impairment

Under the second prong for the definition of disability under the **ADA**, an individual must have a record of a **physical or mental impairment** that **substantially limits** the individual in the performance of one or more of the **major life activities**. Under **ADA** regulations, the term *record* means an individual "has a **record of such an impairment**," that is, has a history of, or has been misclassified as having, a **mental or physical impairment** that **substantially limits one or more major life activities**.

Record of Such Impairment
Having a history of a disability or perceived disability.

Regarded as Having an Impairment

The third element or prong of the definition includes the term **"regarded as having an impairment."** This term was not defined in the **ADA**, but the **ADAAA** made significant changes to the definition of disability. The term ***"regarded as having an impairment"*** is the essence of the protections intended by the original act. The **ADAAA** approves the approach of the Supreme Court in its *School Board of Nassau County v. Arline,* 480 U.S. 273 (1987). In that case, the Court considered the situation of an elementary school teacher who had contracted and recovered from tuberculosis 20 years earlier but had suffered a series of relapses. After the third relapse, she was terminated. The Supreme Court observed, "Congress acknowledged that society's accumulated myths and fears about disability and disease are as handicapping as are the physical limitations that flow from actual impairment."[14] Since the school district received federal funding, the teacher was covered by the provisions of **§504** of the **Rehabilitation Act**. Having a contagious disease would make her a handicapped person within that code section, and her record of **impairment** limited her **"major life activities."** The Supreme Court remanded the case to the district court to determine whether the risk of transmission of the disease to others was such that it rendered her not "otherwise qualified." A new characterization appears in the **ADAAA**:

> An individual meets the requirement of **"being regarded as having such an impairment"** if the individual establishes that he or she has been subjected to an action prohibited under this Act because of an actual or perceived physical or mental impairment whether or not the impairment limits or is perceived to limit a **major life activity**.

"Regarded as Having Such Impairment— with Regard to Substantially Limited Impairment"
A situation in which an applicant or employee is subject to an action prohibited by the ADA (e.g., failure to hire or termination) because the employer perceives the person to have a nontransitory and nonminor impairment.

Now an individual need only prove that he or she was subjected to prohibited conduct because of an **actual or perceived physical or mental impairment**, regardless of whether the impairment actually limits a major life activity or is only perceived as doing so. The focus is on the employer's perception of the person's condition. The plaintiff is covered under the "regarded as" prong, no matter how limiting the employer believes the impairment to be. In this way, the employee only has to prove that he or she was perceived as being impaired, not whether the impairment actually reaches the level of a protected disability. Under the **ADAAA**, employers need not provide **reasonable accommodations** to employees who are **"regarded as" disabled**, unless those persons satisfy another prong of the disability definition.

> ***Example:*** Suppose an employee has controlled high blood pressure that cannot be classified as a disability. If an employer reassigns the individual to less strenuous work because of unsubstantiated fears that the individual will suffer a heart attack if he or she continues to perform strenuous work, the employer would be regarding the individual as **disabled**.[15]

An individual satisfies the *second prong* of the **"regarded as"** definition if the individual is impaired in his or her effectiveness by the attitudes of others toward the condition. For example, an individual may have a prominent facial scar or disfigurement or a condition that periodically causes an involuntary jerk of the head but does not limit the individual's **major life activities**. If an employer discriminates against such an individual because of the negative reactions of customers, the employer would be regarding the individual as **disabled** and acting on the basis of that perceived disability.[16]

> ***Example:*** Clark Howell was a math teacher for the New Haven public school system. He suffered with depression. He was transferred to a lower paying position when he returned from an administrative leave for a psychiatric review. After Howell told his principal about his medication, the principal told him, "I know all about your problems with your medication," and "I don't know what side effects those pills you take might be having on your behavior, but I can't trust you anymore." The principal also told a student that Howell was an employee who "went psycho." According to Howell, the principal told the football coach that Howell's "health problems" were a source of "concern." The court found that these circumstances were sufficient to allow Howell to proceed with a case of disability discrimination under the **"regarded as"** disabled definition.[17]

An individual satisfies the *third prong* of the **"regarded as"** definition of **"disability"** if the employer or other covered entity erroneously believes the individual has an impairment that the individual actually does not have. This situation could occur, for example, if an employer discharged an employee in response to a rumor that the employee was infected with human immunodeficiency virus (HIV). Even though the rumor is totally unfounded and the individual has no impairment at all, the individual is considered as having a **disability** because the employer perceived of the individual as **disabled**. Thus, in this example, the employer, by discharging this employee, is discriminating based on **disability**.

A **qualified individual with a disability** may be disqualified from the protection of the **ADA**. Individuals with conditions that cause them to be a **"direct threat"** to their own health and safety or to that of others around them are *not* qualified, unless the threat can be eliminated by a **reasonable accommodation**.

CASE 9.1

ADA COVERAGE EXCLUDES PROTECTION FOR THOSE WHO ARE A DIRECT THREAT TO THEMSELVES

CHEVRON USA, INC. V. ECHAZABAL

536 U.S. 73 (2002)

Supreme Court of the United States

Facts. Mario Echazabal worked for an independent contractor at one of Chevron's oil refineries until Chevron refused to hire him because he suffered from hepatitis C, a liver condition. Chevron's doctors would not approve his application because the position would expose him to toxic chemicals that would increase the risk of harm to his liver. The district court granted Chevron a summary judgment in response to Echazabal's ADA lawsuit. The Ninth Circuit Court of Appeals reversed the trial court because it found that the ADA only provided for a "threat to others" defense to hiring and did not include a "threat to self" defense. The circuit court so held despite an EEOC regulation authorizing the refusal to hire an individual because his performance on the job would endanger his own health, owing to a disability. The Supreme Court granted *certiorari* to resolve conflicting opinions between the Ninth, Eleventh, and Seventh Circuit Courts of Appeal.

Issue. Does the ADA permit discrimination against those persons whose health would be threatened by the conditions of the workplace?

Language of the Court. **Souter, J.: . . . [The] ADA creates an affirmative defense for action under a qualification standard "shown to be job-related for the position in question and . . . consistent with business necessity." Such a standard may include "a requirement that an individual shall not pose a direct threat to the health or safety of other individuals in the workplace," . . . if the individual cannot perform the job safely with reasonable accommodation. . . . By regulation, the EEOC carries the defense one step further, in allowing an employer to screen out a potential worker with a disability not only for risks that he would pose to others in the workplace but for risks on the job to his own health or safety as well: "The term 'qualification standard' may include a requirement that an individual shall not pose a direct threat to the health or safety of the individual or others in the workplace." . . . Chevron relies on the regulation here, since it says a job in the refinery would pose a "direct threat" to Echazabal's health.**

When Congress specified threats to others in the workplace, for example, could it possibly have meant that an employer could not defend a refusal to hire when a worker's disability would threaten others outside the workplace? If Typhoid Mary had come under the ADA, would a meat packer have been defenseless if Mary had sued after being turned away?

Chevron's reasons for calling the regulation reasonable are unsurprising: moral concerns aside, it wishes to avoid time lost to sickness, excessive turnover from medical retirement or death, litigation under state tort law, and the risk of violating the national Occupational Safety and Health Act of 1970. . . .

Echazabal points out that there is no known instance of OSHA enforcement, or even threatened enforcement, against an employer who relied on the ADA to hire a worker willing to accept a risk to himself from his disability on the job. In Echazabal's mind, this shows that invoking OSHA policy and possible OSHA liability is just a red herring to excuse covert discrimination. But there is another side to this. The text of OSHA itself says its point is "to assure so far as possible every working man and woman in the Nation safe and healthful working conditions," . . . and Congress specifically obligated an employer to "furnish to each of his employees employment and a place of employment which are free from recognized hazards that are causing or are likely to

cause death or serious physical harm to his employees," . . . Although there may be an open question whether an employer would actually be liable under OSHA for hiring an individual who knowingly consented to the particular dangers the job would pose to him, . . . there is no denying that the employer would be asking for trouble: his decision to hire would put Congress's policy in the ADA, a disabled individual's right to operate on equal terms within the workplace, at loggerheads with the competing policy of OSHA, to ensure the safety of "each" and "every" worker.

Decision. Yes. The Court held the text of the ADA suggests threat to an employer's hiring standards "may include," but not be limited to, harm to others. Threat to self should be a permissible ground for refusal to hire.

CASE QUESTIONS

Critical Legal Thinking. Do you think it is fair to the disabled for an employer to make the decision regarding the suitability of the position for an individual instead of allowing the disabled person to make the decision?

Business Ethics. Describe an employment policy and practice that would strike a balance between the goals of preserving workplace safety and of avoiding invasion of employees' personal privacy.

Contemporary Business. To what extent should co-workers be asked to bear the burden of reducing the risks from a disabled employee? For example, what if co-workers could be safeguarded through vaccination or by wearing additional protective safety attire?

To prove a person poses a direct threat, the employer must show that the employee currently poses a specific risk of significant harm. This judgment must be based on objective medical evidence.

> ***Example:*** A hospital terminated a doctor because he was HIV-positive. The doctor was a neurosurgical resident still in training and had been stuck with a needle while treating an individual with the disease. The hospital's panel of experts recommended that the doctor be allowed to return to surgical practice, with the exception of certain procedures, and that he rigorously follow infection control procedures. The hospital's administration rejected the recommendations and terminated the doctor from the residency program. The federal court considering his disability discrimination case held that the risk he presented could not be eliminated by a reasonable accommodation.[18]

Disability Harassment Unwelcome behavior toward a person with a disability or perceived disability, including frequent or severe behavior that creates a hostile or offensive work environment or results in an adverse employment action.

Limited Protection for Drug Abusers and Alcoholics

The definition of a covered **disability** does *not* include any person who is currently engaged in the illegal use of drugs the possession or distribution of which is unlawful.

In addition, a **disability** cannot be defined by the mere consumption of a drug prescribed by a licensed health care professional or by other drug use authorized by law.[19] However, in some situations, prior illegal use of controlled substances may not be used as a basis for discrimination. The **ADA** provides that:

- an employer may prohibit all employees in the workplace from illegal use of drugs and alcohol or from being under the influence of illegal drugs or alcohol;
- an employer may require that employees conform to the requirements set forth in the Drug-Free Workplace Act of 1988; and
- an employer may hold all persons to the same standards of performance and behavior, even those whose performance is adversely affected by drug use or alcoholism.

These standards protect the integrity of the workforce and public safety without fostering discrimination against employees with drug or alcohol problems.

Reasonable Accommodation

The **ADA** requires that the applicant or employee be able to perform the **essential functions** of the position. If the individual's impairment impedes performance to the employer's standards and requirements for nondisabled persons, the employer may be required to make a **reasonable accommodation**. An employer is not required to make an accommodation if it can show that compliance would impose an **undue hardship** on the operation of the business.[20] This standard is a flexible one that is resolved on a case-by-case basis. The law does not mandate that an **accommodation** must be made or in what form. The circumstances of each individual and the particular position are unique.

Undue Hardship (Disability) The determination that accommodation of a person's disability would be too difficult or too expensive to provide, in light of the employer's size, financial resources, and the needs of the business. An employer may not refuse an accommodation simply on the basis of cost. An employer need not provide the exact accommodation desired by the disabled individual, but may choose among satisfactory alternates.

An individual, or someone acting on their behalf, must let the employer know that an **accommodation** is needed for a covered physical or medical condition. The employee may use "plain English" and does not need to mention the **ADA** or the phrase **"reasonable accommodation."** When an applicant is applying for a position, the employer may explain the hiring process and inquire if a **reasonable accommodation** is needed. The employer must provide a **reasonable accommodation** to a qualified applicant with a **disability** that will enable the individual to have an equal opportunity to participate in the application process and be considered for a position (unless the employer can show undue hardship).

> ***Example:*** An employer is impressed with an applicant's resume and contacts the individual to come in for an interview. The applicant, who is deaf, requests a sign language interpreter for the interview. The employer cancels the interview and refuses to consider the applicant further because it believes it would have to hire a full-time interpreter if the person were hired. The employer has violated the **ADA**. The employer should have proceeded with the interview, using a sign language interpreter (absent undue hardship), and at the interview inquired to what extent the individual would need a sign language interpreter to perform any essential functions requiring communication with other people.[21]

An employer may be required to make reasonable accommodations related to job performance to eliminate obstacles. An employer never has to reallocate the **essential**

functions of the job to others as a **reasonable accommodation**. It can do so if it wishes as to marginal functions of the position.

In addition, the employer may permit the use of accrued paid leave, or unpaid leave, as a form of **reasonable accommodation** when necessitated by an employee's **disability**. An employer need not provide paid leave beyond that provided to similarly situated employees. Employers should allow an employee with a **disability** to exhaust accrued paid leave first and then provide unpaid leave.[22] An employer may not apply a "no fault" termination policy to employees with disabilities. Such a policy requires an automatic termination after the employee has been on leave for a period of time. The employer may use such a policy with a disabled employee only if it can show that another effective accommodation would allow the person to perform the **essential functions of the job** or that granting the additional leave would create an **undue hardship**.

In deciding what constitutes a **reasonable accommodation**, the following are considered:

- the nature and cost of the accommodation needed;
- the overall financial resources of the facility or facilities involved in providing the **reasonable accommodation**; the number of persons employed at such facility; the effect on expenses and resources or the impact otherwise of such accommodation on the operation of the facility;
- the overall financial resources of the business; its overall size with respect to the number of its employees; the number, type, and location of its facilities; and
- the type of business operation(s), including the number of workers, structure, and functions of the workforce of the business and the geographic separateness, and administrative or fiscal relationship prevailing overall in the workplace.

Example: A small employer may not be required to provide a **reasonable accommodation** for a **disabled** job applicant, whereas a large, multistate employer in the same industry may be required to do so.

Example: The employer's size and resources affect the application of the **"undue hardship"** qualification. The EEOC successfully prosecuted a case against Wal-Mart on behalf of a job applicant who had cerebral palsy. It showed that the applicant was qualified to perform the essential functions of the greeter and cashier positions for which he applied. This showing established the prima facie case that Wal-Mart's failure to hire the applicant violated the **ADA**. Once that showing was established, the burden of proof shifted to Wal-Mart to offer a nondiscriminatory reason for its adverse employment action. The Wal-Mart job descriptions for greeter and cashier stated no experience or qualification was required, and an EEOC retained vocational rehabilitation consultant offered specific **reasonable accommodations** that would enable the rejected applicant to enjoy the required mobility and periods of standing required for both jobs. These included the use of a sit-to-stand wheelchair, drafting-type high stool with armrests for additional balance, a narrow wheelchair, and an electronic scooter.[23]

The **reasonable accommodation** of religious beliefs under **Title VII** must be made as long as the accommodation does *not* require more than a *de minimis* cost. If it does involve more than that amount, then the employer is not required to offer a **reasonable accommodation**. However, a disability under **Title VII** must be accommodated *unless* compliance involves significant expense or difficulty for that employer.

The **ADA** does not require a **reasonable accommodation** that would result in the violation of the nondiscriminatory seniority rights of other employees. The nature and cost of the accommodation are case specific, and the decision will be made in response to the employer's resources and operations.

Keeping the foregoing in mind, the actual cost to the average employer may not be as financially devastating as one might initially assume. In its proposed regulations implementing the **ADAAA**, the EEOC stated that three studies showed a large variance in costs for making a reasonable accommodation. The agency reported that the cost studies varied from a high of $1,434 to a low of $462.00.[24]

Focus on Ethics
Reasonable Accommodation and Undue Hardship

Title I of the **ADA** provides rights to the **disabled** in the workplace. Title I requires an employer to make reasonable accommodations to individuals with disabilities that do not cause undue hardship to the employer. The terms "reasonable accommodation" and "undue hardship" are often difficult to apply in **ADA** cases. Consider the following case.

Lorie Vande Zande, age 35, is paralyzed from the waist down because of a tumor of the spinal cord. Vande Zande worked for the housing division of the state of Wisconsin's Department of Administration for three years. Her job tasks were typing, mailing, filing, copying, planning meetings, and preparing public information materials.

For Vande Zande to do her work, her employer made accommodations relating to her disability. These included paying to have bathrooms modified, installing a ramp, purchasing special adjustable furniture, purchasing a cot that Vande Zande needed for personal care, adjusting her work schedule to accommodate her medical appointments, and making changes to the locker room.

Vande Zande complained that the employer's accommodations did not go far enough. Vande Zande's paralysis makes her prone to develop pressure ulcers, treatment for which requires her to stay home for several weeks. Vande Zande requested that her employer provide her with a computer and let her work from home during these periods. When her employer refused, Vande Zande sued her employer, alleging that her employer did not make a reasonable accommodation for this symptom of her disability.

The U.S. district court granted summary judgment to the state of Wisconsin. Vande Zande appealed. The U.S. court of appeals also sided with the employer, finding that the employer had made reasonable accommodations for Vande Zande's disability but was not required to accommodate her request to work from home. The court of appeals stated:

> *No jury, however, could in our view be permitted to stretch the concept of "reasonable accommodation" so far. Most jobs in organizations public or private involve teamwork under supervision rather than solitary unsupervised work, and teamwork under supervision generally cannot be performed at home without a substantial reduction in the quality of the employee's performance. Generally, therefore, an employer is not required to accommodate a disability by allowing the disabled worker to work, by himself, without supervision, at home. It would take a very extraordinary case for the employee to be able to create a triable issue of the employer's failure to allow the employee to work at home.*

Vande Zande argues that the defendant displayed a "pattern of insensitivity or discrimination." In this case, all we have in the way of a pattern is that the employer made a number of reasonable and some more than reasonable accommodations and turned down only requests for unreasonable accommodations. From such a pattern no inference of unlawful discrimination can be drawn.

The U.S. court of appeals affirmed the district court's grant of summary judgment to the state of Wisconsin.[25]

Ethics Questions

1. Did the state of Wisconsin make reasonable accommodations for Vande Zande's disability prior to her request to work at home?
2. Would permitting Vande Zande to perform her job from home have caused an undue burden on her employer?
3. Do you think employers would voluntarily accommodate employees with disabilities if the ADA had not been enacted?

Impact of the ADA on Hiring

Title I of the **ADA** limits an employer's opportunity to inquire during the hiring process about an applicant's physical and mental conditions or workers' compensation claim history.

Because a disability may continue after an employee returns to work following a workers' compensation leave of absence, the employer must make a **reasonable accommodation** for the employee. The employer may not require that the employee return to the position with the same capabilities as they enjoyed prior to the incident leading to the workers' compensation claim.

The **ADA** states that "a test to determine the illegal use of drugs shall not be considered a medical examination. . . . Nothing in this subchapter shall be construed to encourage, prohibit, or authorize the conducting of drug testing for the illegal use of drugs by job applicants or employees or making employment decisions based on such test results."[26] For positions involving transportation, applicants and employees may be tested for illegal drug use or on-duty alcohol impairment to ensure safety. Employers can remove persons from safety-sensitive positions if they test positive for illegal drug use or on-duty alcohol impairment.

Remedies

Each federal agency to which the **ADA** applies is required to issue regulations implementing its enforcement. Under the terms of the statute, the **ADA** recognizes that proof of disability discrimination can be made on both the disparate treatment and disparate impact theories. The **ADA** generally prohibits discrimination against those with disabilities; but it also provides broadly available defenses to a **disability discrimination** claim. Disparate treatment against persons with disabilities is permissible if the employee cannot perform the **essential functions of the job**. By adopting **job function criteria**, the employer can lawfully screen candidates who cannot perform those functions, even if the disabled bear a proportionately higher rejection rate.

While the federal courts struggle to interpret the meaning of these amendments to the **ADA**, the **ADAAA** has led to some interesting potential applications. For example, reading is now a **major life activity**. If reading were not **an essential function of a job**, the application process would have to be revised.

"**Perceived as** disabled" plaintiffs need no longer show that their employers thought they were substantially limited in a **major life activity**.

"**Regarded as** disabled" plaintiffs must have a **disability** that is expected to last more than six months. Moreover, employers are relieved from providing **reasonable accommodations** to them. In this new disability law environment, supervisors and managers must recognize that a larger pool exists of people who may qualify for reasonable accommodations in the workplace.

The new focal point of post-**ADAAA** disability discrimination claims will be whether the individual is qualified for the position — i.e., whether the individual can perform the **essential functions of the job**. Employers must redouble their efforts to review the definitions of job functions in detail. If they do so with the help of occupational therapists and consultants, they should be able to minimize their litigation risks. Additionally, the **ADAAA** expressly prohibits a **reverse discrimination claim** by an individual asserting that he or she was discriminated against for not having a **disability**.

With the **ADAAA**, more cases should be successfully resolved in favor of plaintiffs. However, awards will not be substantial because back-pay or front-pay awards are often small because plaintiffs have the duty to mitigate damages by accepting other employment. Section 1981 provides for compensatory and punitive damages under the **ADA**. These damages can provide a more complete award for the emotional harm caused by **disability discrimination**.

The problem that **disability discrimination** claimants face with a §1981 claim is that it generally requires a showing of intentional conduct on the part of employers. Thus, disparate impact theories of discrimination will be unavailable to such claimants. The entitlement to punitive damages is the same for **Title VII** and the **ADA**.[27] Despite the obstacles to the award of punitive damages in **disability discrimination** cases, a few decisions have recognized the appropriateness of such awards, as the following case considered.

CASE 9.2

EMPLOYER CONDUCT WITH THE KNOWLEDGE THAT IT MAY BE ACTING IN VIOLATION OF FEDERAL LAW GIVES RISE TO A CLAIM FOR PUNITIVE DAMAGES

EEOC V. WAL-MART STORES, INC.

187 F.3d 1241 (10th Cir. 1999)

U.S. Court of Appeals for the Tenth Circuit

Facts. In 1991, Wal-Mart hired Eduardo Amaro, with the knowledge that he was hearing impaired and would need an interpreter in certain circumstances, including training sessions and meetings. In 1993, Amaro left a mandatory training session requiring viewing of a videotape because there was neither closed-captioning nor an interpreter, and he consequently could not understand the presentation. Amaro's supervisor, Kim Wiggins, ordered him to return to the session, explaining that a co-worker who could finger-spell, but was not a certified American Sign Language interpreter, would interpret for him. When Amaro rejected this suggestion, Wiggins reported the matter to the store manager, Robert Dunn.

The next day, January 20, 1993, Amaro, who had worked in the receiving department, where his responsibilities included scanning and marking labels, was transferred to the maintenance department to perform janitorial duties. Amaro questioned the transfer and again requested an interpreter, but Wiggins responded with a note accusing him of refusing to perform his job. On the following day, January 21, 1993, Wiggins and Amaro, without an interpreter, met with Dunn, who, in a written note, informed Amaro that the transfer was necessary for two reasons: because payroll reductions had affected the staffing in the receiving department, while creating an opening in the maintenance department, and because the maintenance position would "involve less communications and be more simple for you." To no avail, Amaro requested an interpreter to explain the transfer, which he viewed as a demotion, and threatened to file a complaint with the EEOC. Dunn thereupon suspended Amaro.

Claiming that he was being assigned a dead-end job because he had refused to attend the video training session, Amaro refused the transfer. Dunn immediately terminated Amaro, who then filed a discrimination claim with the EEOC. Although Wal-Mart rehired Amaro in June 1993, the EEOC filed suit on his behalf in October 1993. Amaro intervened, also asserting ADA claims. The jury returned a verdict for the plaintiffs, awarding Amaro compensatory damages and punitive damages. On appeal to the Eleventh Circuit Court of Appeals, Wal-Mart argued against the award of punitive damages.

Issue. What is the evidentiary showing required to recover punitive damages under a vicarious liability theory against an employer accused of violating the ADA?

Language of the Court. Lucero, J.: **Wal-Mart appeals the punitive damage award. . . . The evidence shows that Wal-Mart knew Amaro was hearing impaired and employed him with the knowledge that in certain circumstances, including meetings and training sessions, he would need an interpreter. . . . The store manager, who ultimately approved Amaro's suspension, testified that he was familiar with the accommodation requirements of the ADA and its prohibition against discrimination and retaliation in the workplace. From this evidence, a reasonable jury could have concluded that Wal-Mart intentionally discriminated against Amaro in the face of a perceived risk that its action would violate federal law.**

Wal-Mart argues that vicarious liability for punitive damages in this case is improper because the employees who discriminated against Amaro did not occupy positions of managerial control.

We have concluded that, while occupying managerial positions and acting within the scope of their employment for Wal-Mart, Wiggins and Dunn engaged in recklessly indifferent intentional discrimination against Amaro so as to

warrant an award of punitive damages. . . . However, "holding employers liable for punitive damages when they engage in good faith efforts to comply with Title VII" and other antidiscrimination statutes like the ADA may violate the basic principle that it is "improper ordinarily to award punitive damages against one who himself is personally innocent and therefore liable only vicariously."

We therefore consider whether Wiggins and Dunn's conduct ran contrary to Wal-Mart's good-faith efforts to comply with the ADA. . . . It is clear . . . Congress intended to encourage "employers to adopt antidiscrimination policies and to educate their personnel on [federal] prohibitions" against workplace discrimination. . . . Thus, the extent to which an employer has adopted antidiscrimination policies and educated its employees about the requirements of the ADA is important in deciding whether it is insulated from vicarious punitive liability. Wal-Mart certainly had a written policy against discrimination, but that alone is not enough. Our review of the record leaves us unconvinced that Wal-Mart made a good faith effort to educate its employees about the ADA's prohibitions.

Decision. Managers who possess hiring and firing authority and responsibility to ensure compliance with discrimination laws may make the employer liable for punitive damages when they engage with reckless indifference in intentional discrimination against disabled individuals.

CASE QUESTIONS

Critical Legal Thinking. Is the doctrine of vicarious liability an appropriate one to apply against an employer?

Business Ethics. If you were a Wal-Mart official, what facts would you have identified that suggest the advisability of settling this case before trial?

Critical Legal Thinking. Can you think of other situations in which a jury should assess punitive damages?

Private-party litigants pursue the procedures established by Title VII. These procedures require that the parties exhaust mediation before the EEOC or a similar state agency before proceeding to file a lawsuit.

Due to the comprehensive nature of the procedures and remedies available under the **ADA**, the majority of federal courts do not allow claims to be prosecuted against public entities under §§1983 and 1985 (i.e., claims arising when someone is deprived of rights secured by federal law by a person acting under the color of state law). The **ADA** is the exclusive remedy for violations of its terms and may not be bypassed by bringing suit under these civil rights statutes.

The extraterritorial reach of the **ADA** is impressive. In one case, the Supreme Court held that the **ADA** applied to foreign-flag cruise ships operating in U.S. waters. As a result, cruise ship operators using U.S. ports are required to conform to the requirements of the **ADA** and must remove architectural and other structural barriers to movement and communication from their ships.[28]

Relationship to SSDI

As we shall explore in a later chapter, an injured employee may be entitled to disability benefits under Social Security. To collect them, the applicant must prove that he or she cannot perform any "substantial gainful activity." The disability must have lasted, or be expected to last, for at least 12 continuous months. In the following case, the Supreme Court considered whether a person could claim an SSDI benefit and later state a claim under the **ADA** for the employer's failure to make a **reasonable accommodation**.

CASE 9.3

PURSUIT AND RECEIPT OF SSDI BENEFITS DOES NOT PRECLUDE AN ADA CLAIM

CLEVELAND V. POLICY MANAGEMENT SYSTEMS CORP.

526 U.S. 795 (1998)

Supreme Court of the United States

Facts. Carolyn Cleveland suffered a disabling stroke and lost her job at Policy Management Systems Corporation (PPMC). She sought and obtained Social Security Disability Insurance (SSDI) benefits from the Social Security Administration (SSA). About that same time, Cleveland also brought suit in the federal district court under the ADA, claiming her former employer discriminated against her on account of her disability. She claimed that PPMC had "terminated" her employment without reasonably "accommodating her disability." She alleged that she requested, but was denied, accommodations such as training and additional time to complete her work. She submitted a supporting affidavit from her treating physician. The district court did not evaluate her reasonable accommodation claim on the merits but granted summary judgment to the defendant because, in that court's view, Cleveland, by applying for and receiving SSDI benefits, had conceded that she was totally disabled. That fact, the court concluded, now estopped Cleveland from proving an essential element of her ADA claim, namely that she could "perform the essential functions" of her job, at least with "reasonable accommodation." The Fifth Circuit Court of Appeals affirmed the district court's grant of summary judgment. The Supreme Court granted *certiorari* in light of disagreements among the circuit courts of appeals in such cases.

Issue. Does pursuit and receipt of SSDI benefits preclude an ADA claim?

Language of the Court. Breyer, J.: The case before us concerns an ADA plaintiff who both applied for, and received, SSDI benefits. It requires us to review a Court of Appeals decision upholding the grant of summary judgment on the ground that an ADA plaintiff's "representation to the SSA that she was totally disabled" created a "rebuttable presumption" sufficient to "judicially estop" her later representation that, "for the time in question," with reasonable accommodation, she could perform the essential functions of her job. . . . The Court of Appeals thought, in essence, that claims under both Acts would incorporate two directly conflicting propositions, namely "I am too disabled to work," and "I am not too disabled to work." In our view, however, despite the appearance of conflict, . . . there are too many situations in which an SSDI claim and an ADA claim can comfortably exist side by side.

For one thing, as we have noted, the ADA defines a "qualified individual" to include a disabled person "who . . . can perform the essential functions" of her job "with reasonable accommodation."

By way of contrast, when the SSA determines whether an individual is disabled for SSDI purposes, it does not take the possibility of "reasonable accommodation" into account, nor need an applicant refer to the possibility of reasonable accommodation when she applies for SSDI. . . . The omission reflects the facts that the SSA receives more than 2.5 million claims for disability benefits each year; its administrative resources are limited; the matter of "reasonable accommodation" may turn on highly disputed workplace-specific matters; and an SSA misjudgment about that detailed, and often fact-specific matter would deprive a seriously disabled person of the critical financial support the statute seeks to provide. . . . The result is that an ADA suit claiming that the plaintiff can perform her job with reasonable accommodation may well prove consistent with an SSDI claim that the plaintiff could not perform her own job (or other jobs) without it.

For another thing, in order to process the large number of SSDI claims, the SSA administers SSDI with the help of a five-step procedure that embodies a set of presumptions about disabilities, job availability, and their interrelation. The SSA asks:

Step One: Are you presently working? (If so, you are ineligible.)

Step Two: Do you have a "severe impairment," i.e., one that "significantly limits" your ability to do basic work activities? (If not, you are ineligible.)

Step Three: Does your impairment "meet or equal" an impairment on a specific (and fairly lengthy) SSA list? (If so, you are eligible without more.)

Step Four: If your impairment does not meet or equal a listed impairment, can you perform your "past relevant work"? (If so, you are ineligible.)

Step Five: If your impairment does not meet or equal a listed impairment and you cannot perform your "past relevant work," then can you perform other jobs that exist in significant numbers in the national economy? (If not, you are eligible.)

Hence, an individual might qualify for SSDI under the SSA's administrative rules and yet, due to special individual circumstances, remain capable of "performing the essential functions" of her job.

We hold that an ADA plaintiff cannot simply ignore the apparent contradiction that arises out of the earlier SSDI total disability claim. Rather, she must proffer a sufficient explanation. When faced with a plaintiff's previous sworn statement asserting "total disability" or the like, the court should require an explanation of any apparent inconsistency with the necessary elements of an ADA claim. To defeat summary judgment, that explanation must be sufficient to warrant a reasonable juror's concluding that, assuming the truth of, or the plaintiff's good faith belief in, the earlier statement, the plaintiff could nonetheless "perform the essential functions" of her job, with or without "reasonable accommodation."

Decision. No. Under some circumstances, a disabled individual might receive both SSDI benefits and a reasonable accommodation under the ADA from the employer. The individual must be allowed to explain the conflicting positions.

CASE QUESTIONS

Critical Legal Thinking. Does the Court's decision reach a just and fair result? Did the Court force a reconciliation of seemingly incompatible terms? How would Ms. Cleveland explain the conflicting positions she has taken?

Business Ethics. How should this decision be applied to the circumstances of a small employer?

Contemporary Business. Would a small employer be able to rely on a defense to the application of the ADA? If so, which one(s)? How would you communicate such a defense to the affected employee?

Concept Summary
Differences Between the Rehabilitation Act and the ADA

Generally, the substantive standard for determining liability under the two statutes is the same. The differences between them are as follows:

- **Coverage:** The **Rehabilitation Act** imposes duties only on those programs or activities receiving federal financial assistance. The **ADA** imposes duties on all private sector employers covered by **Title VII** and on all state and local entities. However, §504 of the **Rehabilitation Act** (employers who are not federal contractors but receive or participate in federal financing) applies to employers with 15 employees or less.

- **Liability: Rehabilitation Act** claimants must prove that a plaintiff's disability was the sole reason for the adverse employment action. Under the **ADA**, the plaintiff has more flexibility in proving a discrimination case (e.g., discrimination because the plaintiff is regarded as having a disability).
- **Exhaustion requirement: Rehabilitation Act** claimants in employment cases need not exhaust any administrative requirements before filing suit. The **ADA** requires that an EEOC or 706 agency claim be filed.
- **Exclusions:** The **Rehabilitation Act** does not exclude religious and religiously affiliated organizations. However, that same organization might be excluded from **ADA** coverage.
- **Remedies:** The **Rehabilitation Act** offers broader remedies than does the **ADA**. The **ADA** provides only injunctive relief, not compensatory or punitive damages. Compensatory damages may be available to **Rehabilitation Act** plaintiffs depending on the holding of their respective federal circuit courts of appeals. Individuals may be subject to suit under the **Rehabilitation Act** even though they are not subject to suit under the **ADA**.
- **Longer statute of limitations:** State personal injury statutes govern **Rehabilitation Act** statutes of limitations. Those statutes often provide that a claim may be brought several years after an injury has been sustained. An **ADA** plaintiff must timely proceed with a claim before filing suit in court within 90 days of receipt of the right-to-sue letter.

Rehabilitation Act of 1973

This act prohibits covered employers from discriminating against qualified individuals with physical or mental disabilities. Sections **504** and **794** of the **Rehabilitation Act of 1973** provide:

> *No otherwise qualified individual with a disability . . . shall, solely by reason of her or his disability, be excluded from the participation in, be denied the benefits of, or be subject to discrimination under any program or activity receiving Federal financial assistance or under any program or activity conducted by an Executive agency.*
>
> *This Act provides an additional source of protection for the qualified worker with a mental or physical disability. Its reach is limited to: federal employers, employers with federal contractors or subcontracts, and those which receive financial assistance from a federally funded program.*

The Department of Labor administers this act. It has three key categories of employers:

- **Section 501 of the Rehabilitation Act** governs federal employers who are prohibited from discriminating against workers with disabilities and requires the federal employer to make a **reasonable accommodation** for such employees. Covered employers must also develop and implement affirmative action plans for individuals with disabilities.
- **Section 503 of the Rehabilitation Act** governs employers with covered contracts or subcontracts with the federal government in excess of $10,000. If the employer has at least 50 employees and a covered contract of $50,000 or more, it must maintain a written affirmative action program. It provides that government contractors and subcontractors must undertake affirmative action to employ, and to advance in employment, **qualified individuals with**

disabilities.[29] The regulations under this Act prohibit contractors from discriminating against individuals because of disability.[30]

- **Section 504 of the Rehabilitation Act** covers employers that are not federal contractors but receive or participate in several forms of federal financing. If one program or activity within an organization receives federal financing assistance, then, under a 1988 amendment to the act, the entire organization is covered. All employers that receive federal funds will be subject to **§504**. It does *not* require an affirmative action plan, as required under the preceding section of the act. It does require employers to make **reasonable accommodations** to **qualified individuals** with **known physical or mental disabilities**.

Rehabilitation Act of 1973
The federal law prohibiting discrimination on the basis of disability in federal employment, in the employment practices of federal contractors, or in programs operated by federal agencies or receiving federal funding and requiring affirmative action to prevent or reverse such discrimination.

Employers are not required to hire disabled persons who cannot perform the **"essential functions of the position,"** even with a **reasonable accommodation**.

> ***Example:*** Dunbar Prewitt sued the U.S. Postal Service under **§501** for denying him employment. He was a disabled Vietnam War veteran, and due to gunshot wounds, had limited mobility of his left arm and shoulder. He was hired as a clerk at a Jackson, Mississippi, Post Office and, despite his handicap, performed his duties, which included arduous work, satisfactorily. He left the Post Office, returned to school, and reapplied for employment as a clerk/carrier, a position with requirements similar to those of the job he had left before returning to school. In reviewing his **§501** claim the Fifth Circuit Court of Appeals stated: "To summarize: (1) Prewitt, the disabled claimant, may establish a prima facie of unlawful discrimination by proving that: (a) except for his physical handicap, he is qualified to fill the position; (b) he has a handicap that prevents him from meeting the physical criteria for employment; and (c) the challenged physical standards have a disproportionate impact on persons having the same handicap from which he suffers. To sustain this prima facie case, there should also be a facial showing or at least plausible reasons to believe that the handicap can be accommodated or that the physical criteria are not "job related."[31]

Disabled federal applicants and employees may bring a private lawsuit against the federal government under **§501**. The federal employee will first exhaust administrative remedies before filing suit. The majority of federal courts of appeals have held that there is no private right to sue under **§503**. However, there is a private right of action under **§504**, prohibiting discrimination based on handicaps in programs or activities that receive federal financial assistance. The substantive provisions of the **Rehabilitation Act** were modeled on Title VI of the Civil Rights Act of 1964 and on Title IX. Title IX prohibits sex discrimination in any education program or activity receiving federal financial assistance. Students may be familiar with this law with regard to the gender equity in college sports programs and educational opportunities. Title VI had the single purpose "to make sure that the funds of the United States are not used to support racial discrimination."[32] It is intended to prevent service providers receiving federal funds from discriminating in programs available to individuals. In interpreting the act, a court will look to the judicial interpretation of those two major civil rights statutes.

> ***Example:*** The U.S. government sued Baylor University Hospital to permit access for the Department of Health and Human Services so that the agency could investigate a disability discrimination complaint made by a patient under **§504**. Baylor stipulated that it received Medicare and Medicaid funds (which are federal health care funding sources for the aged, disabled, and poor). It argued that these were insurance programs and were exempt from the Rehabilitation Act's coverage. In deciding the dispute, a federal court of appeals stated,

"The language and legislative history of the **Rehabilitation Act** make it abundantly clear that Congress intended the scope and effect of that statute's prohibition of discrimination on the basis of handicap to be exactly equivalent to Title VI's prohibition on the basis of race." A federal court of appeals upheld the decision of the district court that the hospital, as a recipient of Medicare and Medicaid payments, was required to comply with the Rehabilitation Act.[33]

Sections 503 and **504** extend protection from disability discrimination only to **"qualified individuals with a disability."** This definition is one basis of the **ADA**. The act defines such a person as one who:

1. has a **physical or mental impairment** that **substantially limits one or more major life activities**; and
2. has a record of such an impairment; or
3. is **regarded as** having such an impairment.[34]

Under the **ADAAA**, the definition of disability under the **Rehabilitation Act** is the same as that under the **ADA**.[35] Under the **Rehabilitation Act**, *individual* means a disabled person who, with or without **reasonable accommodation**, can perform the **essential functions of the job.** The law under the **ADA** applies to claims made under the **Rehabilitation Act**, as the **ADA** is based upon this act.

Finally, a significant development has recently occurred with regard to the coverage of **§504**. In *Fleming v. Yuma Regional Med. Center*,[36] the Ninth Circuit Court of Appeals held that **§504** applies to independent contractors just as it does to employees. Section 504(d) refers to "the standards applied under Title I of the Americans with Disabilities Act . . . as such sections relate to employment." The appellate court extended its application so that an independent contractor may assert a disability claim against an employer under the **Rehabilitation Act**. In *Fleming*, an anesthesiologist who worked as an independent contractor sued the medical center at which he worked alleging a discriminatory constructive discharge. The court held that the **Rehabilitation Act** provides a cause of action to any individual subjected to **disability discrimination** by any program or activity receiving financial assistance.

Focus on Ethics
Was There Disability Discrimination?

Sally Harrison-Pepper, a university professor, sued Miami University in Ohio for violations of **Title VII**, the Equal Pay Act, and the **Rehabilitation Act of 1973**. Harrison-Pepper had been hired as a tenure-track professor in 1988. While working at the university, she contracted lupus, and the university agreed to reduce her involvement in university service activities and her workload. Harrison-Pepper was promoted to full professor in 1995. She claimed that, while she was away from campus for six of seven semesters (all but one of the absences were unrelated to her medical condition), the university retaliated against her for complaints to the university provost over perceived pay disparities. She claimed that the university engaged in sex discrimination in employment by paying her a lower salary than it paid her male colleagues. In addition, because she received smaller salary increases than she deserved, she claimed that she was retaliated against following her protests to the provost.[37]

Ethics Questions

1. Did the university have any obligation to grant Harrison-Pepper large merit-based raises while she was on leaves of absence?
2. What is required for Harrison-Pepper to succeed with her retaliation claim that after voicing complaints about pay disparities her raise percentages decreased?

Human Resource Form
Drug and Alcohol Policy

Our company forbids the use, possession, distribution, or sale of nonprescribed controlled substances (illegal drugs) and alcohol by anyone while on company business or its premises. No employees under the influence of such drugs or alcohol may be on company premises. This prohibition applies not only to all company employees but also to its vendors and independent contractors.

Our company reserves the right to conduct blood and urine testing or other appropriate medical tests, to be screened by a licensed medical laboratory at our expense, whenever the company has the reasonable suspicion that a person subject to this policy is under the influence of drugs or alcohol. Any employee involved in an accident while on company business will be subject to immediate drug and alcohol testing for the presence of such substances. Refusal to cooperate timely with a request to submit to and complete such testing will result in disciplinary action, including termination of employment.

Dated: ___________________________

Key Terms and Concepts

- ADA
- ADAAA
- Disability
- Qualified individual with a disability
- Essential functions of the job
- Three prongs of the definition of disability
- Physical or mental impairment
- Substantially limits a major life activity
- Major bodily functions
- Record of impairment
- Regarded as having an impairment
- Mitigating measures
- Direct threat
- Reasonable accommodation
- Undue hardship
- Rehabilitation Act of 1973, §§501, 503, and 504

Chapter Summary

■ A disability under the **ADA** is defined under one of three criteria. Disability discrimination occurs when an employer or other entity covered by the ADA, as amended, or the Rehabilitation Act, as amended, treats a qualified individual with a disability who is an applicant or employee unfavorably because of his or her disability. Disability discrimination also occurs when a covered employer or other entity treats an applicant or employee less favorably because he or she has a history of disability or because he or she is believed to have a physical or mental impairment that is not transitory (lasting or expected to last six months or less) and minor (even if he or she does not have such an impairment).

■ Under the **ADAAA**, the term ***disability*** means a *qualified individual* who meets any *one* of the following: having a physical or mental impairment that substantially limits one or more of the major life activities of the individual; and/or, having a record of such an impairment that substantially limits a major life activity (such as cancer that is in remission); and/or being regarding as having such an impairment (as when an entity, such as employer, takes an action prohibited by the ADA based on an actual or perceived impairment).

■ Employers must treat the nondisabled and disabled equally if they are equally qualified and the disabled person does not require accommodation. If the disabled person can be reasonably accommodated without undue hardship, then covered employers must treat them specially so that the person will have an equal employment opportunity. Employers of 15 or more employees, employment agencies, labor organizations, and joint labor-management committees are covered by the act.

■ If an employer is considering an adverse action with regard to a qualified individual with a disability, the employer must establish that whatever has prompted the dispute (e.g., the requirement to wear a respirator, for example) was job related and a business necessity. Any test that the employer seeks to use in its screening procedures must relate to the essential functions of a job.

■ Disabilities include physical and mental impairments that substantially limit an individual in the performance of one or more major life activities. Title I of the ADA protects "qualified employees with disabilities" from employment discrimination. A "qualified employee with disabilities" means the individual satisfies the skill, experience, education, and other job-related requirements of the position sought or held and can perform the primary job tasks of the position, with or without reasonable accommodation.

■ The qualified disabled individual must meet the job-related qualifications and may not be a direct threat to anyone, including him- or herself.

■ A reasonable accommodation must be offered as long as it does not impose an undue hardship on the employer.

■ Under the ADAAA, the federal disability law will allow more people to qualify as disabled. It also provides that "an impairment that is episodic or in remission is a disability if it would substantially limit a major life activity when active."

■ Following the ADAAA, the *Sutton trilogy* decisions of the Supreme Court will define a condition to be a disability if it materially limits just one major life activity or major bodily function.

■ Following *Toyota Manufacturing, Kentucky, Inc. v. Williams*, post-ADAAA, a disabled person's impairment must substantially limit his or her ability to perform *one or more* major life activities.

■ In a post-ADAAA environment, companies should review job descriptions to ensure that they include all elements of the tasks actually required to be performed.

- Section 501 of the Rehabilitation Act governs federal employers, prohibiting them from discriminating against workers with disabilities and requiring them to make a reasonable accommodation. Such employers must also develop and implement affirmative action plans for individuals with disabilities.

- Section 503 of the Rehabilitation Act covers employers with covered contracts or subcontracts with the federal government in excess of $10,000. If the employer has at least 50 employees and a covered contact of $50,000 or more, it must maintain a written affirmative action program. Section 503 provides that government contractors and subcontractors must undertake affirmative action to employ and to advance in employment qualified individuals with disabilities. The regulations under this act prohibit contractors from discriminating against individuals because of disability.

- Section 504 of the Rehabilitation Act cover employers that are not federal contractors but that receive or participate in several forms of federal financing. If one program or activity within an organization receives federal financing assistance, then the entire organization is covered. All employers who receive federal funds will be subject to §504. Section 504 requires employers to make reasonable accommodations to qualified individuals with known physical or mental disabilities.

Online Student Support

- Loislaw legal research and writing assignments.
- Loislaw group projects and class presentations.
- Loislaw access, providing online research including up-to-date cases, statutes, rules, and regulations. Primary law for all 50 states and federal jurisdictions. Registration required for access to this resource.
- Practice questions, including sample true/false, multiple choice, and short answer questions to test your understanding of concepts.
- Additional human resource forms.
- Internet exercises.
- Blogs.
- Supplementary statutory and regulatory materials.

Case Problems

9.1 Sidney Sanders sued his employer, Arneson Products, under the ADA for his termination while he was on leave for a cancer-related psychological disorder. While on leave, other employees assumed his duties. He had a single episode of psychological impairment that lasted from December 19, 1992, to April 5, 1993, and it had no permanent residual effect on him. Is Sanders a "qualified individual with a disability" who is entitled to protection under the ADA? (*Sanders v. Arneson Products, Inc.*, 91 F.3d 1351 (9th Cir. 1996), *cert. denied*, 520 U.S. 1116)

9.2 John Reeves was employed as an airport operations supervisor for a contractor who operated the Westchester County, New York, airport. He was afflicted with severe anxiety symptoms that were diagnosed as a panic disorder with agoraphobia. Reeves did not claim that his impairment substantially limited him in the exercise of any of the major life activities listed in the EEOC regulations, but rather that his "everyday mobility" was impaired. Was his condition a "mental impairment" for purposes of protection under the ADA? Does impairment of "everyday mobility" constitute an impairment of a major life activity? (*Reeves v. Johnson Control World Services, Inc.*, 140 F.3d 144 (2d Cir. 1991))

9.3 Craig Wallin was twice discharged from his position as a corrections officer at the Minnesota

Correctional Facility at Stillwater and was twice reinstated after union grievance proceedings. After his second discharge and subsequent reinstatement, Wallin sued his employer claiming that he was discriminated against (and harassed) because of his disabilities of alcoholism and depression, in violation of the ADA. If you were representing Wallin, what evidence would you seek to establish an inference of discrimination? To what extent would you seek to apply the harassment standard established by the Supreme Court in *Faragher v. City of Boca Raton* of harassment so "severe or pervasive" as to "alter the conditions of [the victim's] employment and create an abusive working environment"? (*Wallin v. Minnesota Dept. of Corrections,* 153 F.3d 6121 (8th Cir. 1999))

9.4 Deciding what activities constitute a "major life activity" for purposes of complying with the ADA can be a challenging task for employers. Glacier Northwest, Inc. terminated Matthew Head after he negligently caused a piece of heavy construction equipment to become stuck in the mud. In terminating him, Glacier cited damage to the loader in violation of an equipment abuse policy. Before his termination, Head was diagnosed with bipolar disorder, a severe form of depression. Head had informed Glacier of this diagnosis. Sleeping, interacting with others, reading, and thinking were deemed major life activities by the court. If you were representing Head, how would you argue that the employer's employment decision was motivated by factors protected within the ADA context? (*Head v. Glacier Northwest, Inc.,* 413 F.3d 1053 (9th Cir. 2005))

9.5 Two workers worked for Scrivner's grocery warehouse, where both had previously sustained various on-the-job injuries. After they occurred, Scrivner established new performance standards that required its warehouse workers to accomplish their jobs in a shorter amount of time. When the two workers were unable to meet the pace of the new standards, they were discharged. They argued that they were disabled, had records of disability, and were regarded by Scrivner as being disabled. Review the ADA analysis that the federal district court should undertake and make a determination of whether the workers are entitled to protection under the ADA. (*Milton v. Scrivner, Inc.*, 53 F.3d 1118 (10th Cir. 1995))

End Notes

1. 29 C.F.R. Part 1630, Appendix §1630.8; *Prewitt v. U.S.P.S.,* 662 F.2d 292 (5th Cir. 1981).
2. 42 USC §1225(a).
3. 42 U.S.C. §12112(b)(1)-(7); 29 C.F.R. §§1630.5-13.
4. 42 U.S.C. §12205 §3(1).
5. 42 U.S.C. §12111-12117.
6. 42 U.S.C. §12111(8).
7. 29 C.F.R. Part 1630, Appendix, §1630.2(n).
8. *Id.*
9. 42 U.S.C. §12211(a); 28 C.F.R. §§35.104, 36.104; 49 C.F.R. §37.3(1)(iv).
10. *Cehrs v. Northeast Ohio Alzheimer's Research Center et al.,* 155 F.3d 755 (6th Cir. 1998).
11. *Haschmann v. Time Warner Entertainment Co.,* 151 F.3d 591 (7th Cir. 1998).
12. *Toyota Motor Mfg., Ky., Inc. v. Williams,* 534 U.S. 184 (2002).
13. *http://www.eeoc.gov/laws/types/disability.cfm.*
14. 480 U.S. 273, 284 (1987).
15. 29 C.F.R. §1630.2.
16. See Senate Report at 24; House Labor Report at 53; House Judiciary Report at 30–31.
17. *Howell v. New Haven Board of Educ.,* 309 F.Supp.2d 286 (D. Conn. 2004).
18. *Doe v. Univ. of Maryland Med. System Corp.,* 50 F.3d 1261 (4th Cir. 1995).
19. 42 U.S.C. §12111(6), §12114 (a).
20. 42 U.S.C. §123112(b)(5)(A), 29 C.F.R. §1630.9.
21. *http://www.eeoc.gov/policy/docs/accommodation.html#reasonable.*
22. *Id.*
23. *EEOC v. Wal-Mart Stores, Inc.,* 477 F.3d 561 (8th Cir. 2007).
24. *http://edocket.access.gpo.gov/2009/E9-22840.htm.*
25. *Vande Zande v. State of Wisconsin Department of Administration,* 44 F.3d 538 (7th Cir. 1995).
26. 42 U.S.C. §12114 (d).
27. 42 U.S.C. §1981(a)(2).
28. *Spector v. Norwegian Cruise Line, Ltd.,* 545 U.S. 119 (2005).

29. 29 U.S.C. §793.
30. 41 C.F.R., Part 60-741.1.
31. *Prewitt v. U.S. Postal Service,* 754 F.2d 641 (5th Cir. 1981).
32. 110 Cong. Rec. 6544 (comments of Senator Humphrey).
33. *U.S. v. Baylor Univ. Med. Ctr.,* 736 F.2d 1039, 147 (5th Cir. 1984).
34. 29 U.S.C. §706(8); 45 C.F.R. §84.3(j)(2)(i).
35. 42 U.S.C. §12205(7).
36. 587 F.3d 938 (9th Cir. 2009).
37. *Harrison-Pepper v. Miami University,* 246 F. Supp. 2d 854 (S.D. Ohio 2003).

Chapter 10
Age Discrimination

Men, like peaches and pears, grow sweet a little while before they begin to decay. —Oliver Wendell Holmes, Supreme Court Justice

Learning Objectives

1. Identify those employers covered by the ADEA.
2. Describe the employees protected by the ADEA.
3. Understand which actions are prohibited by the act.
4. Explain how to prove an age discrimination claim.
5. Recognize the defenses to an age discrimination claim.
6. Know the requirements for an effective waiver of ADEA rights.

Chapter Outline

- Introduction
- Coverage of the Act
- Prohibited Acts

Case 10.1 Gomez-Perez v. Potter

- Enforcement and Filing

Case 10.2 O'Connor v. Consolidated Coin Caterers Corp.
Case 10.3 General Dynamics Land Systems, Inc. v. Cline

- Management Application: EEOC Regulations

Case 10.4 Gross v. FBL Financial Services, Inc.

- Defenses and Exceptions

Case 10.5 Western Air Lines v. Criswell
Case 10.6 EEOC v. Insurance Co. of North America

- Focus on Ethics: Age Discrimination

Case 10.7 Kentucky Retirement Systems v. EEOC

- Reduction in Force
- Remedies
- Older Workers Benefit Protection Act

Case 10.8 EEOC v. Cosmair

- Management Application: Targeting Workers by Age

Chapter Opening scenario

Baxter Healthcare Corporation had employed Peter Luks for more than 20 years when he was discharged. A new supervisor gave Luks a negative evaluation in a performance review. The supervisor found that Luks did not provide sufficient leadership, direction, and managerial support to the team of technical employees under him. When reassigned, another supervisor found at the following annual review that Luks needed to make more of an effort to submit his business reports in a timely manner, to be open to new ideas and suggestions, to follow through on implementing new ideas, and to prioritize his work effectively. A year later, Luks received an evaluation that stated he was not meeting expectations. Failing to reach the goals in a performance improvement plan the company established for him, the company terminated him. Luks was 52 years old at the time of his termination. The company did not fill Luks's position, but rather redistributed his work to others. He filed suit for age discrimination based on his own subjective assessments that his performance was adequate. He claimed that his supervisor was heard to state that "he wanted to get rid of the 'good old boys'" and that he was looking for "higher energy" employees. Do these facts support the inference that Luks was discharged because of his age?[1]

Introduction

Federal law provides two sources for protection against discrimination based on an employee's age: the **Age Discrimination in Employment Act of 1967 (ADEA)** and the **Older Workers' Benefit Protection Act of 1990 (OWBPA)**, amending **ADEA**. In passing the CRA of 1964, Congress directed the secretary of labor to provide a study relating to age discrimination so that it could later consider remedial legislation. Two events prompted the enactment of the **ADEA**. The report of the secretary of labor identified that half of all private job openings were barred to applicants over the age of 55, and a quarter were closed to applicants over the age of 45. The second was President Johnson's 1967 message to Congress on older Americans, in which he noted that a persistent average of 850,000 unemployed Americans were over the age of 45 — 27 percent of all unemployed persons, and 40 percent of the country's long-term unemployed. Congress had not had the time to study age protection as part of its earlier Civil Rights Act legislation; instead, it enacted age-related discrimination protection three years later.

The **ADEA** was enacted "to promote employment of older persons based on their ability rather than age; to prohibit arbitrary age discrimination in employment; [and] to help employers and workers find ways of meeting problems arising from the impact of age on employment." The **ADEA** applies to employers with 20 or more employees engaged in interstate commerce, employment agencies, labor organizations, and the federal government. The **ADEA** does not apply to Indian tribal employers.

The **ADEA** makes it unlawful for an employer "to fail or refuse to hire or to discharge any individual or otherwise discriminate against any individual with respect to his compensation, terms, conditions, or privileges of employment, because of such individual's age." The statute applies to hiring, promotions, and advancement; termination of employment; hostile work environments; retirement programs; and **Reductions in Force (RIF)**. The Equal Employment Opportunity Commission (EEOC) has approved a rule that allows employers to coordinate the health benefits they offer employees and retirees with Medicare (or comparable state health benefits) without violating the **ADEA**.

The EEOC has recently seen a surge in **age discrimination** filings. In fiscal year 2009, the EEOC received almost 23,000 charges of age discrimination, reflecting a continuing upward trend over the last several years. The EEOC resolved more than 20,000 age discrimination charges in that year and recovered more than $72.0 million in monetary benefits for charging parties and other aggrieved individuals (not including monetary benefits obtained through litigation).[2] This increase in claims for age discrimination probably is attributable to corporate downsizing.

ADEA
A federal law known as the Age Discrimination in Employment Act of 1967; applies to employers having 20 or more employees.

Age Discrimination
Employment discrimination against persons age 40 or older. The act does not protect workers under the age of 40, although some states have laws that protect younger workers from age discrimination.

Coverage of the Act

The **ADEA** protects only employees who are at least 40 years of age. When originally enacted, it protected only those between the ages of 40 and 65. Congress later raised the upper limitation to 70 years, and completely abandoned an age cap in 1986. Currently, the **ADEA** has no age ceiling. The EEOC has the enforcement authority for the act.

Employers

The **ADEA** applies to employers with at least 20 employees in an industry affecting interstate commerce.[3] It applies to those who employ "twenty or more employees for each working day in each of twenty or more calendar weeks in the current or preceding calendar year." Companies incorporated in a foreign country but controlled by a U.S. employer are subject to the **ADEA**. U.S. citizens employed by a U.S. employer to work in a foreign country are covered, unless compliance with the **ADEA** would violate the laws of that foreign country. The act covers foreign employers with a U.S. office, and the 20-person threshold can be achieved by counting employees on a worldwide basis. Independent contractors are not afforded protection by the **ADEA**.

Labor organizations and employment agencies are subject to the **ADEA**. A covered labor organization is one which "exists for the purpose [of] . . . dealing with employers concerning grievances, labor disputes, wages, rates of pay, hours, or other terms or conditions of employment." A labor organization is also an entity that has a hiring hall or is a certified employee representative, or if not certified, holds itself out as the employee's bargaining representative. An employment agency is one which "regularly undertakes with or without compensation" to provide employees for an employer.

Even though the **ADEA** specifically applies to state governments, the Supreme Court has held that state employees may not sue states for damages under the **ADEA**. In a 1996 decision, the Supreme Court held that state employees could not sue their state employers in federal court under the Americans with Disabilities Act if the state had not waived its right to sovereign immunity under the Eleventh

Amendment. This doctrine is one that traces its history to English kings and prevents persons from suing a government without the government's permission. Without a waiver of that doctrine, a court will dismiss a lawsuit against a federal, state, or local government. That earlier decision provided the basis for a 2000 Supreme Court decision in *Kimel v. Board of Regents*[4] that state employers are not subject to the **ADEA**. In *Kimel*, the Supreme Court held that in enacting the **ADEA** Congress did not have the power to eliminate sovereign immunity for state employers. Moreover, the Court held that treating state employees differently than private sector employees with respect to age discrimination protection did not violate Equal Protection principles under the Fourteenth Amendment.

Employees

All individuals over the age of 40 are protected from age discrimination in public and private employment. The recent *Kimel* decision makes clear that for state employers to be subject to the **ADEA**, the states must waive their sovereign immunity. With this qualification, it can be asserted that any person over the age of 40 is protected from employment discrimination based solely on age. The reach of the statute's protections extends not only to employees but also to applicants and discharged former employees. The **ADEA** applies to most federal employees, and the Congressional Accountability Act of 1995 extended the **ADEA** to congressional employees. State elected officials and their personal staff, political appointees, and legal advisers are excluded from the definition of a covered employee, although state employees covered by civil service laws are considered employees.

Exceptions

The **ADEA** provides for several important exceptions. While mandatory retirement policies generally constitute a violation of the **ADEA**, the act permits employers to establish compulsory retirement for a **bona fide executive** or **high policy-making employee** who has reached the age of 65 and is entitled to a pension benefit of at least $44,000.[5] This provision also allows not only forced retirement but also forced demotion of executives who reach retirement age. Courts will also support demotions in lieu of terminations to promote the business needs of a company.

Bona Fide Executive
Mandatory retirement of an executive at age 65 if person is in high policy-making position and entitled to a pension above a stipulated minimum yearly amount.

> ***Example:*** At over 40 years of age, Dr. Koprowski was removed as the director of a medical research institute. Deemed a bona fide executive, the doctor sued for age discrimination because he claimed that, to be demoted from his position, a compulsory retirement program had to be in place under the language of the **ADEA**. The district court concluded "[t]he fact that Congress has carved out a narrow exception for bona fide executives should not alter the overall intent of Congress to effectuate a system by which employees are treated based on ability rather than age. To allow employers to 'demote' or transfer bona fide executives from positions of high policy-making to position with less responsibility is certainly more consistent with promoting the continued employment of 'older person' than is requiring that employers completely retire such individuals. Under that scenario the employee loses out, if he is not ready to retire, as does the employer, who loses a resource that may no longer be equipped for some tasks but can certainly perform a host of others."[6]

The **ADEA** does not extend to members of the Armed Forces, active or reserve units, but does apply to civilian employees working within the military departments of government (such as the Department of Defense). In 1996, Congress amended the **ADEA** to permit state and local governments the option of requiring mandatory retirement ages for certain public safety employees. For example, a community may wish to have most members of its police, firefighting, and rescue workforces younger than near-retirement age.

An exception for tenured faculty at institutions of higher learning has expired. The **ADEA** does allow universities to offer "supplemental benefits" to tenured employees who become eligible to retire to encourage them to retire voluntarily. These benefits are in addition to those normally offered to employees. If certain requirements are met, the supplemental benefits may be reduced or eliminated because of age without violating the **ADEA**. However, the **ADEA** continues to prohibit universities from reducing or ceasing nonsupplemental benefits based on age.

Prohibited Acts

The **ADEA** applies to employer practices throughout the employment cycle, from application through termination. Discrimination regarding salary, leave, and other benefits may also violate the act. Some of the more prominent issues encountered with respect to **age discrimination** claims involve the following:

- **Job advertisements:** It is generally unlawful to refer to age preferences, limitations, or specifications in job notices or advertisements. The advertisement may specify an age limit only in the rare circumstance in which age is a **BFOQ** reasonably necessary to the normal operations of a business.
- **Pre-hiring inquiries:** The **ADEA** does not specifically prohibit an employer from asking an applicant's age or date of birth; however, doing so exposes the employer to an age discrimination charge. Such requests are scrutinized to ensure they are made for a lawful purpose, rather than with intent to discriminate.
- **Promotions and demotions:** An employer may not refuse to select a candidate for promotion because the individual is over the age of 40. An employer might select a younger candidate because it can obtain a longer relationship with the employee, as opposed to someone who might be retiring in the near term. As long as age is not the basis for the decision, an employer may also demote an older employer. For example, one court upheld the demotion of a drug store manager to a cashier's position because the older employee was unable to adapt to new technologies.[7]
- **Benefits:** The **OWBPA** amended the **ADEA** to prohibit employers from denying benefits to older employees. This act is discussed later in this chapter.

Age as a BFOQ
An employer may enforce age limits where age is a BFOQ reasonably necessary to the normal operation of the particular business, such as hiring young actors to play young characters or imposing retirement on pilots for medical fitness reasons.

In addition to federal protections, most employees also enjoy protection under *state law.* Almost all states have enacted statutory protection against age discrimination in employment. Typically, a state fair-employment practices statute or separate antidiscrimination age protection statute will afford those protections. Where both federal and state statutes are violated, the employee can elect to pursue one or both of these available remedies.

Retaliation as a Prohibited Act

In *Gomez-Perez v. Potter*, presented below, the Supreme Court resolved a conflict between the circuit courts of appeals. It held that **retaliation** is an implied form of discrimination "on the basis of sex" and that under **ADEA** retaliation was a form of discrimination "based on age." A section of the **ADEA** provided:

> It shall be unlawful for any employer to discriminate against employees or applicants for employment, for an employment agency to discriminate against any individual, or for a labor organization to discriminate against any member thereof or applicant for membership, because such individual member, or applicant for membership, has opposed any practice made unlawful by this section, or because such individual, member, or applicant for membership has made a charge, testified, assisted, or participated in any manner in an investigation, proceeding, or litigation under this Act.

As originally enacted, the **ADEA** applied only to private employers and, as stated, prohibited **retaliation** by employers. In 1974, Congress amended the statute to cover federal employees as well. Rather than just incorporating the above language as to federal employees, Congress enacted an entirely separate section respecting their **ADEA** rights. Congress did not include a provision prohibiting **retaliation**. The question presented was the same as arose in the *CBOCS* case; that is, did the prohibition against **age discrimination** impliedly include protection from **retaliation**? Court observers were interested in knowing how a court split in political ideology would construe a civil rights statute in the 2008 *Gomez-Perez v. Potter* decision.

CASE 10.1

RETALIATION CLAIMS MAY BE BROUGHT BY FEDERAL WORKERS UNDER THE ADEA

GOMEZ-PEREZ V. POTTER

553 U.S. 474 (2008)

Supreme Court of the United States

Facts. Myrna Gomez-Perez, 45 years old, worked as a clerk for the U.S. Postal Service (USPS) in Puerto Rico. She sued for retaliation on the ground that she had been subject to retaliatory treatment after she filed an age discrimination complaint against her supervisors. The federal district court granted summary judgment to the USPS on the ground that the USPS had not waived sovereign immunity as to retaliation claims under the ADEA. Gomez appealed to the U.S. Court of Appeals for the First Circuit. It held that the USPS had waived sovereign immunity but upheld the summary judgment because the ADEA did not recognize a cause of action for retaliation by federal employers. The Supreme Court granted *certiorari.*

Issue. Does the ADEA protect federal sector employees from retaliation when that protection is not stated in the act?

Language of the Court. Alito, J: . . . **The federal-sector provision of the ADEA provides that "[a]ll personnel actions affecting employees or applicants for employment who are at least 40 years of age . . . shall be made free from any discrimination based on age." The key question in this case is whether the statutory phrase "discrimination based on age" includes retaliation based on the filing of an age discrimination complaint. We hold that it does.**

In reaching this conclusion, we are guided by our prior decisions interpreting similar language in other antidiscrimination statutes. In *Sullivan v. Little Hunting Park, Inc.*, (citation omitted), a white man (Sullivan) held membership shares in a non-stock corporation that operated a park and playground for residents of the area in which he owned a home. . . . But when Sullivan rented his house and attempted to assign a membership share to an African-American (Freeman), the corporation disallowed the assignment because of Freeman's race and subsequently expelled Sullivan from the corporation for protesting that decision. Sullivan sued the corporation, and we held that his claim that he had been expelled "for the advocacy of Freeman's cause" was cognizable under §1982. . . . A contrary holding, we reasoned, would have allowed Sullivan to be "punished for trying to vindicate the rights of minorities" and would have given "impetus to the perpetuation of racial restrictions on property."

More recently, in *Jackson v. Birmingham Bd. of Ed.*, . . . Jackson, a public school teacher, sued his school board under Title IX, "alleging that the Board retaliated against him because he had complained about sex discrimination in the high school's athletic program." (Citation omitted.) Title IX provides in relevant part that "[n]o person in the United States shall, on the basis of sex, . . . be subjected to discrimination under any education program or activity receiving Federal financial assistance." . . . Holding that this provision prohibits retaliation, we wrote: "Retaliation against a person because that person has complained of sex discrimination is another form of intentional sex discrimination. . . . Retaliation is, by definition, an intentional act. It is a form of 'discrimination' because the complainant is being subjected to differential treatment. Moreover, retaliation is discrimination 'on the basis of sex' because it is an intentional response to the nature of the complaint: an allegation of sex discrimination. We conclude that when a funding recipient retaliates against a person because he complains of sex discrimination, this constitutes intentional 'discrimination' 'on the basis of sex,' in violation of Title IX."

Congress was presumably familiar with Sullivan and had reason to expect that this ban would be interpreted "in conformity" with that precedent. Under the reasoning of Sullivan, retaliation for complaining about age discrimination, is "discrimination based on age," "just as retaliation for advocacy on behalf

of [the] black lessee in Sullivan was discrimination on the basis of race." . . . Thus, . . . the absence of a federal-sector provision . . . does not provide a sufficient reason to depart from the reasoning of Sullivan and Jackson.

Decision. Yes. The ADEA prohibits retaliation against federal employees who complain of age discrimination.

CASE QUESTIONS

Critical Legal Thinking. The dissenting justices argued that Congress intended to cover only discrimination based on age and that the Court should not divine new remedies when they are not stated in the legislation. What does this case say about *stare decisis* and construing what the Court thinks Congress knew at the time it amended the ADEA to include federal employee coverage?

Business Ethics. Many legal commentators were surprised that the government would take the position that it did in this case. On what ethical grounds could the government argue that it is permissible to retaliate against an individual who seeks to enforce federal civil rights?

Contemporary Business. Why did the Court find a remedy in this instance when it strictly construed the reach of the ADEA in its *Kimel* decision? Can you think of ways to distinguish the two cases?

Enforcement and Filing

The EEOC is responsible for enforcing the provisions of the **ADEA**. To encourage informal resolution of age discrimination claims, the **ADEA** *requires* claimants to file complaints with the EEOC before they can sue in federal court. Private litigants must first file charges with the EEOC or with a state 706 agency that has jurisdiction. The administrative charges must be filed within the time limits provided for claims brought under Title VII. After receiving the charge, the EEOC or the 706 agency conducts an investigation. If the claim has merit, the agency may seek compliance through a number of informal means.

Courts hold that the **ADEA** authorizes a different filing period for a lawsuit after the agency charge is filed. The **ADEA** explicitly contemplates early termination of an EEOC investigation. Once 60 days have elapsed after the filing of a discrimination charge, an **ADEA** plaintiff may file suit in federal court. If the claimant wishes to wait until a final determination is made by the EEOC, then the claimant must file suit in federal court within 90 days of receiving notice of the agency's final action. As with other types of civil rights claims, the federal courts have been permissive in allowing an improper or incomplete age discrimination charge to be the eventual basis for a lawsuit in federal courts. The federal courts have generously construed procedural defects between the charge and the formal court pleadings in favor of the **ADEA** claimant.[8]

Effect of Arbitration Clauses

The Supreme Court has held that the **ADEA** does not preclude the enforcement of an individual agreement to arbitrate **ADEA** claims.

> ***Example:*** Gilmer was required by his employer to sign a registration application with the New York Stock Exchange (NYSE). The application contained an agreement to arbitrate any controversy arising out of his employment or termination of employment. He was terminated at age 62. He filed a charge with the EEOC and sued in federal court. The employer filed a motion to compel arbitration on the application and the Federal Arbitration Act. The Supreme Court held that an **ADEA** claim may be subject to compulsory arbitration.[9]

If a collective bargaining agreement clearly and unmistakably requires employees to arbitrate claims under the **ADEA**, courts will enforce the agreement to arbitrate. Such a provision does not defeat rights normally resolved pursuant to the procedures protected under the National Labor Relations Act.

> ***Example:*** Members of a New York union challenged a job reassignment to less desirable jobs leading to a loss of income. Their union contract stated that claims arising under the **ADEA** were to be resolved by arbitration. While the arbitration was proceeding, the workers filed an age discrimination claim with the EEOC. The Supreme Court held that as in any contractual negotiation, a union may agree to the inclusion of an arbitration provision in the labor agreement in return for other concessions from the employer. Courts generally may not interfere in this bargained for exchange. In a heavily divided opinion, the Supreme Court distinguished prior precedent because the earlier cases did not involve, as this case did, an express waiver of the right to litigate discrimination claims.[10]

Class-action **age discrimination** litigation has a unique aspect as compared to other types of Title VII class-action lawsuits. Class certification procedures normally require a procedure to determine numerosity, common and typical claims, and fair and adequate representatives. Under the **ADEA**, the only criterion for a class action is that the plaintiffs be similarly situated. Unlike participants in other types of class actions, who are automatically bound to the judgment in the class-action suit unless they opt out of the class, a person in an age discrimination class action must opt into the lawsuit before filing a written consent with the federal court.

The nature of aging and the truth that everyone encounters it creates unique problems in **age discrimination** litigation not found in other types of employment discrimination cases. First, issues often arise of decreasing levels of performance with increasing age. Second, older workers, who have more seniority, normally enjoy higher compensation than do younger employees. Both of these facts present interesting issues within **ADEA** litigation.

> ***Example:*** The EEOC brought an **ADEA** enforcement proceeding against Clay Printing Company. A management consultant recommended that the company eliminate overstaffing and efficiencies and restructure its management and sales compensation structures. He also recommended that Clay undertake employee evaluations to identify good employees and those "who was hurting the company, and [were] dead wood." The consultant observed,

"Too many people have been around here too long and make too much money," and "If employees had been there 10 years or more, they needed to move on." The court granted summary judgment for the employer because the decisions to terminate employees over age 40 were in line with reducing costs and overhead, not with an attempt to discriminate based on age.[11]

When the older workers can prove that the employer deliberately retained younger workers and offered untrue reasons for discharging older workers, the older workers can prevail in their **age discrimination** claims.

Example: Douglass Duffy sued Wheeling-Pittsburgh for age discrimination. He had been employed as a salesperson for more than 25 years when he was terminated as part of a 15 percent reduction in workforce necessitated by weak economic conditions in the steel industry. The company terminated the oldest and most highly paid salespersons, including Duffy. The company defended against his claim of age discrimination by arguing that it decided on his discharge for financial reasons. A federal court of appeals affirmed the district court's finding that the company's rationale was a pretext. Duffy's performance was superior to that of the younger men retained, and the court relied upon a vice president's statement that the company was "anxious to get younger and more aggressive people in the field."[12]

The Supreme Court ruled in the following employment termination case that a plaintiff need not establish that he or she was replaced by someone younger than 40. Instead, the plaintiff must merely show that the replacement was younger.

CASE 10.2

SUBSTANTIALLY YOUNGER REPLACEMENTS MAY BE EVIDENCE OF ADEA VIOLATIONS

O'CONNOR V. CONSOLIDATED COIN CATERERS CORP.

517 U.S. 308 (1996)

Supreme Court of the United States

Facts. Consolidated Coin Caterers Corp. (Consolidated) fired James O'Connor, who was 56 years old, and replaced him with a 40-year-old. O'Connor sued Consolidated on the basis that his termination violated the ADEA. The district court granted summary judgment in favor of Consolidated. The Court of Appeals for the Fourth Circuit affirmed the judgment, holding that O'Connor had not proved his case because he failed to show that someone younger than 40 years of age had replaced him. The Supreme Court granted *certiorari*.

Issue. Can an employee file an age discrimination suit under the ADEA if the replacement employee is 40 years old or older?

Language of the Court. Scalia, J.: This case presents the question whether a plaintiff alleging that he was discharged in violation of the Age Discrimination in Employment Act of 1967 (ADEA) . . . must show that he was replaced by someone outside the age group protected by the ADEA to make out a prima facie case under the framework established by *McDonnell Douglas Corp. v. Green* (citation omitted).

We have never had occasion to decide whether that application of the Title VII rule to the ADEA context is correct, but since the parties do not contest that point, we shall assume it. (Citation omitted.) On that assumption, the question presented for our determination is what elements must be shown in an ADEA case to establish the prima facie case that triggers the employer's burden of [showing a legitimate business reason for its decision].

As the very name "prima facie case" suggests, there must be at least a logical connection between each element of the prima facie case and the illegal discrimination for which it establishes a "legally mandatory, rebuttable presumption" (citation omitted). The element of replacement by someone under 40 fails this requirement. The discrimination prohibited by the ADEA is discrimination "because of [an] individual's age," . . . though the prohibition is "limited to individuals who are at least 40 years of age." This language does not ban discrimination against employees because they are aged 40 or older; it bans discrimination against employees because of their age, but limits the protected class to those who are 40 or older. The fact that one person in the protected class has lost out to another person in the protected class is thus irrelevant, so long as he has lost out because of his age. Or to put the point more concretely, there can be no greater inference of age discrimination (as opposed to "40 or over" discrimination) when a 40-year-old is replaced by a 39-year-old than when a 56-year-old is replaced by a 40-year-old. Because it lacks probative value, the fact that an ADEA plaintiff was replaced by someone outside the protected class is not a proper element of the McDonnell Douglas prima facie case.

Perhaps some courts have been induced to adopt the principle urged by respondent in order to avoid creating a prima facie case on the basis of very thin evidence — for example, the replacement of a 68-year-old by a 65-year-old. While the respondent's principle theoretically permits such thin evidence (consider the example above of a 40-year-old replaced by a 39-year-old), as a practical matter, it will rarely do so, since the vast majority of age-discrimination claims come from older employees. . . . Because the ADEA prohibits discrimination on the basis of age and not class membership, the fact that a replacement is substantially younger than the plaintiff is a far more reliable indicator of age discrimination than is the fact that the plaintiff was replaced by someone outside the protected class. The judgment of the Fourth Circuit is reversed, and the case is remanded for proceedings consistent with this opinion.

Decision. Yes. In this 9-0 decision, the Court held that although the ADEA limits its protection to those who are 40 or older, it prohibits discrimination against those protected employees because of age, not membership in the protected class of those over 40 years of age.

CASE QUESTIONS

Critical Legal Thinking. In this case the Supreme Court modified the proof requirements for a prima facie case for an ADEA plaintiff by eliminating the requirement of being outside the protected class. Can a person who is younger than 40 be subjected to age discrimination?

Business Ethics. If you were interviewing an age discrimination claimant, what facts would you find significant to your investigation?

Contemporary Business. How large an age gap is necessary for you to infer age discrimination has occurred?

In its 1993 **ADEA** decision in *Hazen Paper Co. v. Biggins,*[13] the Supreme Court required plaintiffs to prove that an employer took adverse action "because of" age and that age was the "reason" the employer acted. The Court held that Congress did not amend the **ADEA** when it permitted disparate impact claims to Title VII coverage. The *Hazen* Court held that proof of intentional discrimination is required for disparate treatment age-related discrimination claims. In its *Hazen* decision, the Court stated:

> *The disparate treatment theory is of course available under the* **ADEA***, as the language of that statute makes clear. . . .*
>
> *In a disparate treatment case, liability depends on whether the protected trait (under the* **ADEA***, age) actually motivated the employer's decision. . . . Disparate treatment, thus defined, captures the essence of what Congress sought to prohibit in the* **ADEA***. It is the very essence of age discrimination for an older employee to be fired because the employer believes that productivity and competence decline with old age. As we explained in EEOC v. Wyoming (citation omitted), Congress' promulgation of the* **ADEA** *was prompted by its concern that older workers were being deprived of employment on the basis of inaccurate and stigmatizing stereotypes. "Although age discrimination rarely was based on the sort of animus motivating some other forms of discrimination, it was based in large part on stereotypes unsupported by objective fact. . . . Moreover, the available empirical evidence demonstrated that arbitrary age lines were in fact generally unfounded and that, as an overall matter, the performance of older workers was at least as good as that of younger workers."*

As a result of the *Hazen* decision, many employers implemented productivity- and skill-based job descriptions. Thus, an older employee must keep his or her skills current or face lawful adverse action by the employer (such as a demotion).

In 2004, the Supreme Court considered in its *General Dynamics Land Systems, Inc. v. Cline* decision whether an employer could favor one class of over-age-40 employees over another such class.

CASE 10.3

THE RELATIVELY YOUNG CANNOT CLAIM THE AGE DISCRIMINATION PROTECTIONS DUE TO THE RELATIVELY OLD

GENERAL DYNAMICS LAND SYSTEMS, INC. V. CLINE

540 U.S. 581 (2004)

Supreme Court of the United States

Facts. General Dynamics renegotiated its union contract with the United Auto Workers to provide full health care benefits only to retirees who were more than 50 years old on July 1, 1997. Dennis Cline and others aged 40 to 49 years of age sued for age discrimination because of differences in compensation. The district called the federal claim one of "reverse age discrimination," and held that the law did not recognize a cause of action for suit under the ADEA. The Sixth Circuit Court of Appeals reversed, and the Supreme Court granted *certiorari.*

Issue. Does the ADEA prohibit "reverse age discrimination" against workers over age 40 by providing benefits that are more favorable to a class of older workers?

Language of the Court. Souter, J.: **The common ground in this case is the generalization that the ADEA's prohibition covers "discriminat[ion] . . . because of [an] individual's age," . . . that helps the younger by hurting the older.**

Congress . . . called for a study of the issue by the Secretary of Labor, ibid., who concluded that age discrimination was a serious problem, but one different in kind from discrimination on account of race. . . . When the Secretary ultimately took the position that arbitrary discrimination against older workers was widespread and persistent enough to call for a federal legislative remedy, . . . he placed his recommendation against the background of common experience that the potential cost of employing someone rises with age, so that the older an employee is, the greater the inducement to prefer a younger substitute. The report contains no suggestion that reactions to age level off at some point, and it was devoid of any indication that the Secretary had noticed unfair advantages accruing to older employees at the expense of their juniors.

The testimony at both [Congressional] hearings dwelled on unjustified assumptions about the effect of age on ability to work. See, e.g., House Hearings 151 (statement of Rep. Joshua Eilberg) ("At age 40, a worker may find that age

restrictions become common. . . . By age 45, his employment opportunities are likely to contract sharply; they shrink more severely at age 55 and virtually vanish by age 65"); id., at 422 (statement of Rep. Claude Pepper) ("We must provide meaningful opportunities for employment to the thousands of workers 45 and over who are well qualified but nevertheless denied jobs which they may desperately need because someone has arbitrarily decided that they are too old"); Senate Hearings 34 (statement of Sen. George Murphy) ("[A]n older worker often faces an attitude on the part of some employers that prevents him from receiving serious consideration or even an interview in his search for employment"). The hearings specifically addressed higher pension and benefit costs as heavier drags on hiring workers the older they got. See, e.g., House Hearings 45 (statement of Norman Sprague) (Apart from stereotypes, "labor market conditions, seniority and promotion-from-within policies, job training costs, pension and insurance costs, and mandatory retirement policies often make employers reluctant to hire older workers"). The record thus reflects the common facts that an individual's chances to find and keep a job get worse over time; as between any two people, the younger is in the stronger position, the older more apt to be tagged with [a] demeaning stereotype. Not surprisingly, from the voluminous records of the hearings, we have found (and Cline has cited) nothing suggesting that any workers were registering complaints about discrimination in favor of their seniors.

The federal reports are as replete with cases taking this position as they are nearly devoid of decisions like the one reviewed here. To start closest to home, the best example is *Hazen Paper Co. v. Biggins* (citation omitted), in which we held there is no violation of the ADEA in firing an employee because his pension is about to vest, a basis for action that we took to be analytically distinct from age, even though it would never occur without advanced years. . . . We said that "the very essence of age discrimination [is] for an older employee to be fired because the employer believes that productivity and competence decline with old age," whereas discrimination on the basis of pension status "would not constitute discriminatory treatment on the basis of age [because t]he prohibited stereotype [of the faltering worker] would not have figured in this decision, and the attendant stigma would not ensue . . ." (citation omitted). And we have relied on this same reading of the statute in other cases. . . . While none of these cases directly addresses the question presented here, all of them show our consistent understanding that the text, structure, and history point to the ADEA as a remedy for unfair preference based on relative youth, leaving complaints of the relatively young outside the statutory concern.

Decision. No. In a 6-3 decision the court held that the ADEA does not stop an employer from favoring an older employee over a younger one.

CASE QUESTIONS

Critical Legal Thinking. Would a contrary decision have harmed the global competitiveness of an international employer? Does this case substantially reduce the prospect of making a reverse age discrimination claim? May employers favor an older employee over a younger employee without fear of incurring liability under the ADEA?

Business Ethics. Was this an ethical decision for the company to have made?

Contemporary Business. If you were a decision-maker at General Dynamics, what alternatives would you consider before reducing health coverage benefits?

Management Application
EEOC Regulations

The EEOC has revised its regulations regarding the interpretation of what is "age" under the ADEA following the Supreme Court's in its *General Dynamics Land Systems* decision. As a result, employers can make age-based employment decisions that favor employees over age 40. Revised in 2007, the regulation now reads:

§1625.2 Discrimination prohibited by the Act. It is unlawful for an employer to discriminate against an individual in any aspect of employment because that individual is 40 years old or older, unless one of the statutory exceptions applies. Favoring an older individual over a younger individual because of age is not unlawful discrimination under the ADEA, even if the younger individual is at least 40 years old. However, the ADEA does not require employers to prefer older individuals and does not affect applicable state, municipal, or local laws that prohibit such preferences.

§1625.4 Help wanted notices or advertisements.

(a) Help wanted notices or advertisements may not contain terms and phrases that limit or deter the employment of older individuals. Notices or advertisements that contain terms such as 25 to 35, young, college student, recent college graduate, boy, girl, or others of a similar nature, violate the Act, unless one of the statutory exceptions applies. Employers may post help wanted notices or advertisements expressing a preference for older individuals with terms such as over age 60, retirees, or supplement your pension.

(b) Help wanted notices or advertisements that ask applicants to disclose or state their age do not, in themselves, violate the Act. Because asking applicants to state their age may tend to deter older individuals from applying, or otherwise indicate discrimination against older individuals, employment notices or advertisements that include such requests will be closely scrutinized to assure that the requests were made for a lawful purpose.

The procedures and requirements of an **ADEA** suit are the same as those of Title VII. As the *O'Connor* decision provides, proof of prima facie showing **age discrimination** does not require that the plaintiff's replacement be a person younger than 40 years of age. Since the Court's decision in *O'Connor,* federal courts of appeals require that the replacement employee must be "significantly younger" than the discharged employee for the **ADEA** plaintiff to establish a prima facie case of **age discrimination**. Because this term is subjective, courts have issued divergent opinions as to what "significantly younger" means. Examples of such conflicting interpretations include holdings that a six-year difference is not significantly younger;[14] a prima facie case was established when a 49-year-old plaintiff was replaced by a 46-year-old;[15] but a ten-year difference in age between employees was deemed substantial enough.[16] Courts have endorsed a **hostile work environment claim** under the ADEA.

Disparate Treatment Proof

Age Harassment Offensive remarks, behaviors, and conduct with reference to a person's age; requires frequent or severe conduct creating a hostile or offensive work environment.

Under this theory, a successful plaintiff must prove that age "actually played a role in [the employer's decision-making] process and had a determinative influence on the outcome.[17] To succeed on an **ADEA** claim, it must be established that the plaintiff would not have been terminated "but for" the employer's intentional age-based discrimination.[18]

A plaintiff in an age discrimination case may prove discrimination by presenting either direct or circumstantial evidence.[19] **Direct evidence** usually requires an admission that the decision-maker's actions were based on age.[20] Where **circumstantial evidence** of discriminatory intent is relied on, generally the burden-shifting method of proof set forth in *McDonnell Douglas Corp. v. Green*[21] is applied. The Supreme Court in *Reeves* observed that the *McDonnell Douglas* Title VII proof approach applies in **ADEA** cases when parties do not dispute it. The plaintiff must first establish a prima facie case of discrimination, then the defendant may state one or more legitimate, nondiscriminatory reasons for its actions, after which the plaintiff has an opportunity to show that the defendant's reasons are **pretextual**.

Disparate Impact Proof

In a 2005 decision, the Supreme Court ruled that a plaintiff may assert an **adverse (disparate) impact** claim under the **ADEA**. In *Smith v. City of Jackson*,[22] the Court settled conflicting decisions among the federal courts of appeals. In an 8-0 decision written by Justice Stevens, the Court held that the **ADEA** does permit such suits. The Court held that the **ADEA** was narrower than Title VII and allowed otherwise prohibited action where the discrimination was based on reasonable factors other than age. In *Smith*, the Court reaffirmed that, as for Title VII cases, a **disparate impact** case under **ADEA** should focus on the effects of the employer's facially neutral employment practice on the employee rather than on the employer's motivation (or intent).

Concept Summary
Proving Age Discrimination

An age discrimination plaintiff must prove that:

- the plaintiff was over the age of 40;
- the plaintiff suffered an adverse employment action;
- the plaintiff was qualified for the position but was rejected despite being qualified; and
- the position remained open after the adverse action was taken and the employer continued to seek applications from other people with similar qualifications to those of the plaintiff or hired someone younger than plaintiff.

In a mixed motives case (i.e., one involving both discriminatory and nondiscriminatory reasons for the adverse action), a plaintiff must prove age was the determining factor in the employer's action. After the decision in *Gross*, proving age discrimination became more difficult. A plaintiff must prove that age was the *deciding factor* in the employer's adverse decision. Proving that age was a motivating factor is no longer enough to prevail.

Mixed-Motives Proof

The more frequent case presented for decision involves a mixed-motives case of employment age discrimination. The Supreme Court has made it much more difficult for plaintiffs to succeed in such cases. In a bitterly divided 5-4 decision in *Gross v. FBL Financial Services*, the Supreme Court defined the standard of proof required for an age discrimination claim. Notably, the court held that the **ADEA** does not authorize a mixed-motives age discrimination claim (i.e., that the employer discriminated against the employee because of age, but also had a nondiscriminatory basis for its decision). The Supreme Court specifically held that courts are not to apply the shifting burdens of proof as is done in Title VII decisions such as *Price Waterhouse* and *Desert Palace, Inc. v. Costa*; namely, upon proving discrimination, the burden then falls on the employer to show a legitimate business reason for its action, after which the plaintiff can show that the reason was merely pretextual for the discrimination. Under this 2009 decision, the Supreme Court maintains claimants must show a direct connection between age and the discriminatory act of the employer. Even when a worker produces evidence that age a motivating factor in an adverse decision, the burden of proof *does not shift* to the employer to show that it would have taken the action regardless of age.

An interesting comment made by the Court in *Gross* is one that students can appreciate. The Court criticized the way its prior decisions led to discussions of shifting burdens of proof in proving Title VII cases. It noted that jury verdicts in age discrimination cases were frequently overturned by trial and appellate courts. The Court cited such cases, referring to them as "the murky water of shifting burdens in discrimination cases."

CASE 10.4

ADEA PLAINTIFF MUST PROVE AGE WAS THE "BUT FOR" CAUSE OF THE EMPLOYER'S ACTION AND CANNOT RELY ON THE BURDEN-SHIFTING "MIXED MOTIVES" PROOF AVAILABLE UNDER TITLE VII

GROSS V. FBL FINANCIAL SERVICES, INC.

__________ U.S. __________, 129 S. Ct. 2343 (2009)

Supreme Court of the United States

Facts. Jack Gross worked for FBL Financial Group for 30 years and held the position of claims administration director. He was reassigned to a position he considered a demotion, and his prior responsibilities were reassigned to another employee. He sued for age discrimination under the ADEA. The district court gave the jury a mixed-motive instruction that it must return a verdict for Gross if he proved that age played a motivating factor in his demotion. The jury returned a verdict for him. FBL appealed to the Eighth Circuit Court of Appeals, which reversed the district court's decision. The court of appeals held that decisions issued under Title VII controlled the proof of an ADEA violation. Due to conflicts among the circuit courts regarding proof in age discrimination cases, the Supreme Court granted *certiorari.*

Issue. Must a plaintiff present direct evidence of age discrimination in a mixed-motives case under the ADEA?

Language of the Court. Thomas, J.: . . . **Our inquiry . . . must focus on the text of the ADEA to decide whether it authorizes a mixed-motives age discrimination claim. It does not . . . A plaintiff must prove by a preponderance of the evidence (which may be direct or circumstantial), that age was the "but-for" cause of the challenged employer decision [citing its *Reeves v. Sanderson Plumbing, Inc.* decision].**

We reject [the] contention that our interpretation of the ADEA is controlled by Price Waterhouse. . . . In any event, it is far from clear that the Court would have the same approach were it to consider the question today in the first instance. . . . Whatever the deficiencies of Price Waterhouse in retrospect, it has become evident in the years since that case was decided that its burden-shifting framework is difficult to apply. For example, in cases tried to a jury, courts have found it particularly difficult to craft an instruction to explain its burden-shifting framework. See, e.g., *Tyler v. Bethlehem Steel Corp.* (citation omitted) (referring to "the murky water of shifting burdens in discrimination cases"); *Visser v. Packer Engineering Associates, Inc.* (citation omitted) ("The difficulty judges have in formulating [burden-shifting] instructions and jurors have in applying them can be seen in the fact that jury verdicts in ADEA cases are supplanted by judgments notwithstanding the verdict or reversed on appeal more frequently than jury verdicts generally"). Thus, even if Price Waterhouse was doctrinally sound, the problems associated with its application have eliminated any perceivable benefit to extending its framework to ADEA claims.

We hold that a plaintiff bringing a disparate-treatment claim pursuant to the ADEA must prove, by a preponderance of the evidence, that age was the "but-for" cause of the challenged adverse employment action. The burden of persuasion does not shift to the employer to show that it would have taken the action regardless of age, even when a plaintiff has produced some evidence that age was one motivating factor in that decision. Accordingly, we vacate the judgment of the Court of Appeals and remand the case for further proceedings consistent with this opinion.

Decision. Yes. A plaintiff who brings a disparate treatment ADEA claim must prove that age was the cause for the employer's action. The employer does not have to show that it would have taken the same action regardless of age, even when the plaintiff has shown that age was a motivating factor.

CASE QUESTIONS

Critical Legal Thinking. The conservative justices on the Court who held that workers must prove that age bias was the determining factor in making the adverse decision voted in the majority. How does this standard of proof compare to workers' claims for race or sex discrimination under Title VII?

Business Ethics. Is it obvious to you how you would prove a "but for" standard in age discrimination? Was the Court trying to clear up the less than perfect-after-the-fact sorting out process of a mixed-motive case? What is the more ethical standard to apply, the "but for" or "solely because of" standard or the burden-shifting standard involving a "motivating factor"?

Contemporary Business. If you were to rewrite the law on proving employment discrimination, would you embrace the approach taken by the majority in *Gross*?

The decision in *Gross* has been unpopular with members of Congress. Before the *Gross* ruling, an employee had to prove that age was a *motivating factor* in an adverse employment decision, and the employer would then have to prove the decision was based on a legitimate reason other than age. The *Gross* decision changed this. Now the employer must prove the adverse action would not have been taken "but for" the employee's age. The Court ruled that employers did not have to show that they would have taken the same action regardless of the claimant's age. Congress has been considering legislation that would reverse the decision. It would align the standard of proof in **age discrimination** cases with the standard of proof used in Title VII cases. Under the proposed legislation, after an employee proves that age was a *motivating factor*, the employer will then have to prove it otherwise complied with the age discrimination law.

Reverse Age Discrimination

The **ADEA** does not prohibit reverse **age discrimination.** In such cases, an employer favors employees over the age of 40 to the detriment of those younger than 40.

> ***Example:*** Caterpillar began negotiating with the union representing workers at two Iowa plants when it determined that it needed to close them. The company created a supplemental retirement benefit plan for workers 50 or older with 10 years of service. The plants were closed, and two employees between the ages of 40 and 50 sued Caterpillar for age discrimination on the basis that the supplemental plan discriminated against them because they were

> too young to qualify. The federal court of appeals upheld the district court's dismissal of their case. It held that the **ADEA** "does not protect the young as well as the old, or even, we think, the *younger* against the older." The **ADEA** does not provide a remedy for reverse age discrimination.[23]

Individuals under the age of 40 are protected from age-based **retaliation** for engaging in protected activity. As an example, a person under age 40 who testified or presented evidence as part of an internal investigation pertaining to an alleged EEO violation involving age discrimination against other workers would be protected under Title VII. **Retaliation** is a separate basis for worker protection under Title VII.

Defenses and Exceptions

In its 1985 decision in *TWA v. Thurston,*[24] the Supreme Court considered the lawfulness of an airline's policy of forcing pilots, in violation of the **ADEA**, to retire at age 60. The Supreme Court held that the policy discriminated against a protected class of individuals and violated the **ADEA**. The Court held that TWA's transfer policy did violate the **ADEA** because it denied the privilege of employment to 60-year-old captains on the basis of age. Although the **ADEA** did not require the airline to grant transfer privileges to disqualified captains, if TWA had a policy giving disqualified captains the right to become flight engineers, it could not deny that opportunity to some captains because of their age. The pilots had challenged that part of the policy that forbade them from transferring to the lower-level position of flight engineer, for which other individuals were eligible, and the Court held that the policy did not implement a **BFOQ** or a **bona fide seniority system**. The Court held that the policy as it existed, constituted **age discrimination**. These two grounds join others recognized under **ADEA** statutory language and by the courts as affirmative defenses for employers facing **ADEA** claims:

- Bona fide occupational qualification (**BFOQ**)
- Bona fide seniority system
- Existence of a valid arbitration compulsory agreement that requires the dispute to be brought in arbitration and not federal court. In this instance, the plaintiff's case may not proceed and must be filed in an arbitration forum.[25]
- Good cause to discharge or take adverse action against the employee
- Voluntary early retirement incentives
- Reasonable factors other than age (**RFOA**)
- Voluntary and knowing waiver of rights (**OWBPA**)
- Executive exemption and high policy-maker exemption
- State and local public safety employees

Reasonable Factor Other Than Age (RFOA)
Employers may take an adverse action against an applicant or employee over age 40 if the basis of the decision is reasonable and other than the person's age.

Bona Fide Occupational Qualification

With regard to **BFOQ** defenses asserted in **ADEA** cases, the Supreme Court has adopted a practical approach. In its *Criswell* decision, the Supreme Court held that the **BFOQ** exception was an extremely narrow exception to the general prohibition of **age discrimination**.

CASE 10.5

BFOQ IN AGE CASES IS APPLIED NARROWLY

WESTERN AIR LINES V. CRISWELL

472 U.S. 400 (1985)

Supreme Court of the United States

Facts. The plaintiffs were airline flight engineers who were compelled to retire at age 60. At the time of their forced retirement, they still possessed the pilot licenses and medical examination qualifications required by the Federal Aviation Administration. They sued the airline for age discrimination. The airline defended its work rule on the ground that it was "reasonably necessary" for the safe operation of the airline. Expert witnesses offered conflicting testimony on that issue at the time of trial.

Issue. What must an employer show to support a BFOQ based on safety considerations?

Language of the Court. Stevens, J.: **Criswell, Starley, and Ron brought this action against Western contending that the under-age-60 qualification for the position of flight engineer violated the ADEA. . . . [At the time of trial] the actual capabilities of persons over age 60, and the ability to detect disease or a precipitous decline in their faculties, were the subject of conflicting medical testimony.**

Throughout the legislative history of the ADEA, one empirical fact is repeatedly emphasized: the process of psychological and physiological degeneration caused by aging varies with each individual. "The basic research in the field of aging has established that there is a wide range of individual physical ability regardless of age." As a result, many older American workers perform at levels equal or superior to their younger colleagues.

The restrictive language of the statute and the consistent interpretation of the administrative agencies charged with enforcing the statute convince us that, like its Title VII counterpart, the BFOQ exception "was in fact meant to be an extremely narrow exception to the general prohibition" of age discrimination contained in the ADEA.

[T]he ADEA requires that "age qualifications be something more than convenient" or "reasonable"; they must be "reasonably necessary . . . to the particular

business," and this is only so when the employer is compelled to rely on age as a proxy for the safety-related job qualifications validated in the first inquiry. This showing could be made in two ways. The employer could establish that it " 'had reasonable cause to believe, that is, a factual basis for believing, that all or substantially all [persons over the age qualifications] would be unable to perform safely and efficiently the duties of the job involved.' " Alternatively, the employer could establish that age was a legitimate proxy for the safety-related job qualifications by proving that it is " 'impossible or highly impractical' " to deal with the older employees on an individualized basis.

Decision. Employers must conduct individual evaluations of employees over age 40 based on merit alone and not age.

CASE QUESTIONS

Critical Legal Thinking. In the wake of this decision, how receptive will courts be to an employer's contention that certain qualifications are BFOQs for a position? What does this decision compel employers to do to justify qualifications for a position?

Business Ethics. Does this decision unfairly intrude into the rights of an airline to determine what requirements it may demand of its cockpit employees? If individual evaluations periodically administered to employees were too expensive, what ethical action would you suggest to airline management to persuade older employees to retire?

Contemporary Business. Can you think of any instances in which managers might want to assert job qualifications that conflict with age considerations?

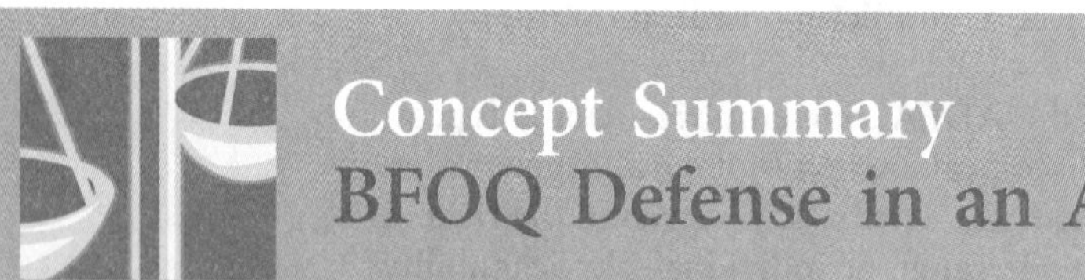

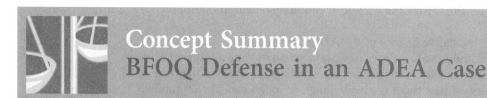

Concept Summary
BFOQ Defense in an ADEA Case

The employer must establish the following:

- The policy at issue is "reasonably necessary to the essence of [the employer's] business."
- It is compelled to rely on age as the determinative factor of its employment policy or practice because:
  - it has a factual basis for believing that all or nearly all employees above an age lack the qualifications required for the position, or
  - it is highly impractical for the employer to screen or test employees for the necessary qualifications required by the policy or practice.

Reasonable Factors Other Than Age

In *Smith v. City of Jackson*,[26] the Supreme Court distinguished the **ADEA** from Title VII, as amended by the CRA of 1991:

1. The **RFOA** provision available under the **ADEA** *is not an available defense* to a Title VII claim.
2. A successful **ADEA disparate impact** claimant would have to allege and prove specific employment practices are responsible for the discrimination.
3. An **RFOA** defense is different from a **business necessity defense** under Title VII. As the *Smith* Court stated: "Unlike the **business necessity** test, which asks whether there are other ways for the employer to achieve its goals that do not result in a **disparate impact** on a **protected class**, the reasonableness inquiry [**RFOA**] includes no such requirement."

Proposed EEOC Regulations **Defining Reasonable Factors Other Than Age**

The EEOC is in the process of issuing regulations defining the meaning of "reasonable factors other than age" (RFOA) under the ADEA.[27] The Supreme Court decisions in *Smith v. City of Jackson* and *Meacham v. Knolls Atomic Power Laboratory* suggested to the Commission that it needed to revise its regulations clarifying the scope of the RFOA defense. Consistent with the *Smith* and *Meacham* decisions, the proposed revision explains that whether a particular employment practice is based on RFOA turns on the facts and circumstances of each situation and on whether the employer acted prudently in light of those facts. The Commission states that this standard is lower than Title VII's business-necessity test, but higher than the Equal Pay Act's "any other fact" test. In particular, the Commission is proposing that its regulations be amended to read as follows:

Sec. 1625.7 Differentiations based on reasonable factors other than age.

* * * * *

(b) Whether a differentiation is based on reasonable factors other than age ("RFOA") must be decided on the basis of all the particular facts and circumstances surrounding each individual situation.

(1) **Reasonable.** A reasonable factor is one that is objectively reasonable when viewed from the position of a reasonable employer (i.e., a prudent employer mindful of its responsibilities under the ADEA) under like circumstances. To establish the RFOA defense, an employer must show that the employment practice was both reasonably designed to further or achieve a legitimate business purpose and administered in a way that reasonably achieves that purpose in light of the particular facts and circumstances that were known, or should have been known, to the employer. Factors relevant to determining whether an employment practice is reasonable include, but are not limited to, the following:

(i) Whether the employment practice and the manner of its implementation are common business practices;

(ii) The extent to which the factor is related to the employer's stated business goal;

(iii) The extent to which the employer took steps to define the factor accurately and to apply the factor fairly and accurately (e.g., training, guidance, instruction of managers);

(iv) The extent to which the employer took steps to assess the adverse impact of its employment practice on older workers;

(v) The severity of the harm to individuals within the protected age group, in terms of both the degree of injury and the numbers of persons adversely affected, and the extent to which the employer took preventive or corrective steps to minimize the severity of the harm, in light of the burden of undertaking such steps; and

(vi) Whether other options were available and the reasons the employer selected the option it did.

(2) **Factors Other Than Age.** When an employment practice has a significant disparate impact on older individuals, the RFOA defense applies only if the practice is not based on age. In the typical disparate impact case, the practice is based on an objective non-age factor and the only question is whether the practice is reasonable. When disparate impact results from giving supervisors unchecked discretion to engage in subjective decision making, however, the impact may, in fact, be based on age because the supervisors to whom decision making was delegated may have acted on the basis of conscious or unconscious age-based stereotypes. Factors relevant to determining whether a factor is "other than age" include, but are not limited to, the following:

(i) The extent to which the employer gave supervisors unchecked discretion to assess employees subjectively;

(ii) The extent to which supervisors were asked to evaluate employees based on factors known to be subject to age-based stereotypes; and

(iii) The extent to which supervisors were given guidance or training about how to apply the factors and avoid discrimination.

As the Commission explains in its notice of rulemaking, an employer need not adopt an employment practice that has the least severe impact on members of the protected age group. Quoting from the *Smith v. Jackson* decision, the EEOC stated: "Unlike the business necessity test, which asks whether there are other ways for the employer to achieve its goals that do not result in a disparate impact on a protected class, the reasonableness inquiry includes no such requirement." This means that the availability of other options is one of the factors relevant to deciding whether the employer's practice was a reasonable one.

Experience as a Selection Factor

Several appellate decisions have considered whether "overqualified" was used as a pretext for **age discrimination**. In the following case, the Ninth Circuit Court of Appeals held that age was not a pretext as long as the employer based its decision on at least one objectively defined job criterion. This decision, like many other federal court opinions on the issue, raises the bar for plaintiffs bringing age-based discrimination claims.

Some employers utilize a limitation on years of experience, stating in advertisements the maximum number of years of prior relevant work experience they desire job applicants to possess. This limitation may be used to eliminate more highly compensated candidates, align new hire compensation to existing pay scales within the organization, facilitate mutual expectations relative to job performance, or otherwise eliminate potential morale issues within a unit. As long as the employer adheres to that cap, the age limitation may be enforced. If it does not, trouble and litigation will follow.

> ***Example:*** An employer was allowed to rely on an "experience cap," stating the maximum number of prior years of work experience it wished an applicant to possess. Stephen Kolslow was a 53-year-old attorney, 25 years out of law school, who sought an associate attorney position from a firm advertising for attorneys with between two and six years of experience. Denied an interview, Kolslow sued for age discrimination but lost. The court held that the employer's decision was motivated by factors other than age, even if the motivating factor correlated with age. There was no **ADEA** violation because the employer was motivated by experience, not age. The court held that the employer could ignore the age of the applicant because it was analytically distinct from his years of experience.[28]

The *EEOC v. Insurance Co. of North America* decision follows the line of cases in which the employer may be free to set objective experience limitations for particular positions.

CASE 10.6

"OVERQUALIFIED" CANNOT BE A PRETEXT FOR "TOO OLD"

EEOC V. INSURANCE CO. OF NORTH AMERICA

49 F.3d 1418 (9th Cir. 1995)

U.S. Court of Appeals for the Ninth Circuit

Facts. In June 1988, the insurance company placed an ad in a Phoenix newspaper for a "loss control representative." The advertisement stated that the "ideal candidate" would have a B.S. degree or equivalent experience, possess two years of property/casualty loss control experience, demonstrate verbal and written communication skills, be able to travel, and would be a self-motivated professional. Pugh, who had more than 30 years of experience in loss control and engineering, submitted a resume in response to the advertisement. Pugh was not selected for an interview. Eventually, the company hired a 28-year-old woman with no loss control experience from outside the pool of applicants who responded to the advertisement. Pugh filed a charge with the EEOC alleging age discrimination. On several occasions during the EEOC's investigation of Pugh's charge, the insurance company told the EEOC that it had not considered Pugh for the position because he was overqualified. The district court found that Pugh had established a case of age discrimination but the company had offered legitimate, nondiscriminatory reasons for failing to hire him. The reasons were that his application was unprofessional in appearance and his background was too technical and engineering-oriented for the position. The court found that the reasons were not pretextual.

Issue. Is an employer using a pretext when it hires a much younger, inexperienced candidate over an age-protected experienced candidate?

Language of the Court. Canby, J.: **Although the ADEA does not prohibit rejection of overqualified job applicants per se, courts have expressed concern that such a practice can function as a proxy for age discrimination if "overqualification" is not defined in terms of objective criteria.**

In this case, ICNA's rejection of Pugh due to his overqualification for the position at issue was based on at least one defined concern. [A supervisor] explained that he feared that someone with Pugh's extensive background in the loss control field would delve too deeply into the accounts to which he would be assigned. He explained that if Pugh became too involved in uncomplicated risks, he would impose upon insureds' time to an inappropriate degree. [His] reason for rejecting Pugh was objective and non-age-related. This uncontradicted evidence supports the conclusion that the decision that Pugh was "overqualified" for the position was not a mask for age discrimination. The EEOC did not produce evidence that this neutral reason was pretextual. Accordingly, we agree with the district court's determination that Pugh did not present enough evidence [of discrimination].

Decision. No. An employer may base its decision not to hire an age-protected candidate on legitimate business grounds and not violate the ADEA.

CASE QUESTIONS

Critical Legal Thinking. If "overqualification" is a barrier to workers, how should an employer define the job requirements so that it does not forego hiring workers who will work for lower wages but have rich work experience?

Business Ethics. Does the "overqualified" tag mostly discriminate against workers in a poor economy? Is there an injustice operating against all but the most junior skilled applicant?

Contemporary Business. At some point in a person's career does experience serve as a disadvantage to securing other employment opportunities? How should older, more experienced applicants position themselves for employment in a competitive environment?

Despite the holding in cases such as the preceding one, a number of courts have also held that an employer's articulated reason that the applicant was "overqualified" may be pretextual and, thus, unlawful. Some courts have held that the phrase "overqualified" "may often be simply a code word for too old." Such was the holding of the court in the following case involving Time, Inc., an international publisher of magazines, books, and prerecorded media products.

Focus on Ethics
Age Discrimination

The Age Discrimination in Employment Act (ADEA) and amendments thereto prohibit employers from engaging in age discrimination when making employment decisions. Sometimes employers are caught engaging in unlawful age discrimination. Consider the following case.

Preview Subscription Television, Inc. (Preview) was a subsidiary of Time Incorporated. Preview hired Thomas Taggart as a print production manager for Preview's magazine *Guide*. Taggart was 58 years old at the time and had more than 30 years' experience in the printing industry. Six months later Time notified Preview employees that Preview would be dissolved and, although not guaranteed a job, Preview employees would receive special consideration for other positions at Time and its subsidiaries. Time sent weekly job bulletins to former Preview employees, including Taggart.

Taggart applied for 32 positions in various divisions at Time and its subsidiaries, including *Sports Illustrated, People Magazine, Life, Money*, and *Discover* magazines. Although Taggart interviewed for many of these openings, he was not offered employment. Time explained this by saying that Taggart was "overqualified" for many of the positions. Taggart contends that Time used this as an excuse not to hire him because of his age and that Time hired less qualified, younger applicants for many of the positions for which he was rejected.

Taggart sued Time for age discrimination in violation of the ADEA. The U.S. district court granted Time's motion for summary judgment. Taggart appealed. The U.S. court of appeals held that an employer's stated reason for not hiring an applicant for a position because he was "overqualified" is a fact situation from which a reasonable juror could infer age discrimination.

The court of appeals noted that Taggart was over 40 and belonged to the protected age group. The fact that Taggart was found overqualified for some of the positions at Time supported his allegation that he was capable of performing those jobs. Further, Time hired persons younger than Taggart for those jobs. Thus, Taggart established a prima facie case of age discrimination. The court of appeals reversed the district court's decision and remanded the case for trial.[29]

Ethics Questions

1. Do you think older job applicants and workers need protection from age discrimination? Why or why not?
2. Was it ethical for Time to use "overqualified" as a reason for not hiring Mr. Taggart?
3. Do you think age discrimination is encountered often in the workplace? Should older workers make room in the workplace for younger ones?

Reasonable Factors Other Than Age in Pension Plan Cases

Age discrimination claims often arise with regard to employees' eligibility for normal retirement benefits. In the following case, the Kentucky state pension plan applied to employees who received disability retirement. Under the state plan, individuals who were disabled before they were eligible for retirement received greater benefits than individuals who were eligible for retirement at the point they became disabled.

Under the **ADEA**, where an employer adopts a pension plan that includes age as a factor and then treats employees differently based on pension status, the plaintiff must show that the **disparate treatment** was "actually motivated" by **age discrimination**.

CASE 10.7

RETIREMENT PLANS CAN TREAT WORKERS DIFFERENTLY IF THE DIFFERENCES ARE NOT ACTUALLY MOTIVATED BY AGE DISCRIMINATION

KENTUCKY RETIREMENT SYSTEMS V. EEOC

554 U.S.____________, 128 S. Ct. 2361 (2008)

Supreme Court of the United States

Facts. The state of Kentucky established a disability retirement benefits plan for employees. It disqualified employees from receiving disability benefits on reaching normal retirement benefits age. It also calculated benefits so that younger employees received greater benefits than older employees with age the only differing factor. The EEOC sued to declare the program discriminatory against older workers. The federal district court granted Kentucky summary judgment, holding that the EEOC could not establish age discrimination; but the Sixth Circuit Court of Appeals held that the Plan did violate the ADEA. The Supreme Court granted *certiorari*.

Issue. Can retirement plans provide different levels of benefits based on age?

Language of the Court. Breyer, J.: . . . **In *Hazen Paper Co. v. Biggins* (citation omitted), the Court explained that where, as here, a plaintiff claims age-related "disparate treatment" (i.e., intentional discrimination "because of . . . age") the plaintiff must prove that age "actually motivated the employer's decision." . . . The Court noted that "[t]he employer may have relied upon a formal, facially discriminatory policy requiring adverse treatment" because of age, or "the employer may have been motivated by [age] on an ad hoc, informal basis." . . . But "[w]hatever the employer's decision-making process," a plaintiff alleging disparate treatment cannot succeed unless the employee's age "actually played a role in that process and had a determinative influence on the outcome." . . . (Citation omitted) . . . (describing "disparate-impact" theory, not here at issue, which focuses upon unjustified discriminatory results).**

Hazen Paper indicated that discrimination on the basis of pension status could sometimes be unlawful under the ADEA, in particular where pension status

served as a "proxy for age. . . . Hazen Paper also left open "the special case where an employee is about to vest in pension benefits as a result of his age, rather than years of service." . . . We here consider a variation on this "special case" theme.

. . . [W]e must decide whether a plan that (1) lawfully makes age in part a condition of pension eligibility, and (2) treats workers differently in light of their pension status, (3) automatically discriminates because of age. The Government argues "yes." But, following Hazen Paper's approach, we come to a different conclusion. In particular, the following circumstances, taken together, convince us that, in this particular instance, differences in treatment were not "actually motivated" by age.

First, as a matter of pure logic, age and pension status remain "analytically distinct" concepts. . . . That is to say, one can easily conceive of decisions that are actually made "because of" pension status and not age, even where pension status is itself based on age. Suppose, for example that an employer pays all retired workers a pension, retirement eligibility turns on age, say 65, and a 70-year-old worker retires. Nothing in language or in logic prevents one from concluding that the employer has begun to pay the worker a pension, not because the worker is over 65, but simply because the worker has retired.

Second, . . . Congress has otherwise approved of programs that calculate permanent disability benefits using a formula that expressly takes account of age. For example, the Social Security Administration now uses such a formula in calculating Social Security Disability Insurance benefits.

Third, there is a clear non-age-related rationale for the disparity here at issue. . . . [T]the whole purpose of the disability rules is, as Kentucky claims, to treat a disabled worker as though he had become disabled after, rather than before, he had become eligible for normal retirement benefits. Fourth, although Kentucky's Plan placed an older worker at a disadvantage in this case, in other cases, it can work to the advantage of older workers. Consider, for example, two disabled workers, one of whom is aged 45 with 10 years of service, one of whom is aged 40 with 15 years of service. Under Kentucky's scheme, the older worker would actually get a bigger boost of imputed years than the younger worker (10 years would be imputed to the former, while only 5 years would be imputed to the latter). And that fact helps to confirm that the underlying motive is not an effort to discriminate "because of . . . age."

Fifth, Kentucky's system does not rely on any of the sorts of stereotypical assumptions that the ADEA sought to eradicate. It does not rest on any stereotype about the work capacity of "older" workers relative to "younger" workers. . . . The Plan does assume that all disabled workers would have worked to the point at which they would have become eligible for a pension. It also assumes that no disabled worker would have continued working beyond the point at which he was both (1) disabled; and (2) pension eligible. But these "assumptions" do not involve age-related stereotypes, and they apply equally to all workers, regardless of age.

The rule we adopt today for dealing with this sort of case is clear: Where an employer adopts a pension plan that includes age as a factor, and that employer then treats employees differently based on pension status, a plaintiff, to state a disparate treatment claim under the ADEA, must adduce sufficient evidence to show that the differential treatment was "actually motivated" by age, not pension status. And our discussion of the factors that lead us to conclude that the Government has failed to make the requisite showing in this case provides an indication of what a plaintiff might show in other cases to meet his burden of proving that differential treatment based on pension status is in fact discrimination "because of" age. . . .

Given the reasons set forth [above], we conclude that evidence of that motivation was lacking here.

Decision. No, in a 5-4 decision, the Court held that Kentucky's retirement system for employees in hazardous duty positions did not violate the ADEA. The Court found that Kentucky's retirement system was not motivated by age discrimination, but by a desire to allow the disabled to receive retirement compensation. Since the state's rules were based on pension eligibility, not on age, the Court found the retirement system to be lawful.

CASE QUESTIONS

Critical Legal Thinking. The dissent argued the ADEA prohibits disparate treatment unless some specific exemption or defense in the Act applies. Furthermore, they found that the language of the OWBPA clearly prohibited any age-based disparities in pension plans. Who has the better argument — the majority opinion, or the dissent?

Business Ethics. The majority relied heavily on the Court's earlier decision in *Hazen Paper* and held a "clear non age-related rationale" for the disparities in the Kentucky plan. Is it fair to treat pension benefits under "the ADEA . . . somewhat more flexibly and leniently in respect to age" than other circumstances?

Contemporary Business. Can you think of any examples wherein fringe benefit plans may treat workers differently based on a neutral classification such as date of hire?

Noncapability
An employer may lawfully use an employee's nonfitness for continued employment, advancement, or training to defend an age discrimination claim.

Noncapability (or *Business Necessity*) Is a Defense to an ADEA Lawsuit

Example: Charles Pottenger sued Potlatch Corporation for age discrimination following his discharge after 32 years of service. He had received a performance review rating of "meeting requirements" for the job. Unfortunately, the CEO viewed Pottenger as not having the commitment to make the hard decisions necessary to make the company successful.

While holding that Pottenger had proved a prima facie case, the court found that Potlatch had articulated a legitimate, nondiscriminatory reason for terminating him — lack of confidence in his management decision-making. Potlatch was entitled to terminate Pottenger because he was incapable of providing desperately needed strong management skills.[30]

Neutral/Objective Criteria to Be Used

If an employer utilizes neutral criteria in making its decision to terminate selected employees, it will have a strong defense against an **age discrimination** claim. Many employers use a scoring procedure whereby certain desirable traits are weighted more heavily than are other factors and that give additional credit to employees with greater seniority. Such criteria should be as objective as possible to avoid misunderstandings and potential litigation. They should include the ability to perform multiple tasks, exposure to more of the business' activities, and seniority or salary, but they may not be used to circumvent the **ADEA**.

Reduction in Force

The most often encountered problem relating to **age discrimination** occurs not in hiring but in reductions in the workforce **(RIF)**. The federal appellate courts disagree on whether distributing work to younger retained employees is tantamount to "replacement" for purposes of establishing **age discrimination**. In these types of cases the proof is the same as stated for hiring, except the fourth factor is modified because "[t]he employer must then produce evidence that, having decided in good faith that he should reduce the size of his workforce, [the employer] included the plaintiff within the class of workers to be laid off for reasons unrelated to any discriminatory considerations."[31]

Reduction in Force (RIF)
An employer has the right to reduce its workforce in a nondiscriminatory manner and to select which employees to retain based on their possession of the requisite skills, experience, and training.

In a 7-1 decision in the 2008 *Meacham v. Knolls Atomic Power Laboratory*[32] case, the Supreme Court answered the question left open in the *Smith v. City of Jackson* case as to whether it is the burden of plaintiff or the defendant employer to prove the elements of **RFOA**. In *Meacham,* a private company servicing U.S. Navy warships was ordered by the government to reduce its workforce. The company had its managers score their subordinates on "performance," "flexibility," and "critical skills." Based on these scores, along with points awarded for years of service, employees were selected for retention or termination. Of the 31 who were fired, 30 were 40 years or older. In response to their termination, Meacham and others filed suit alleging a disparate-impact claim under the **ADEA**. They relied on a statistical expert's testimony that results so skewed by age could rarely occur by chance, and that the subjective evaluations of "flexibility" and "critical skills" had direct relationships to the outcomes of who would be terminated. The Court ruled that when an employer's business practices place a disproportionate burden on older workers, the employer has the burden of showing that the decision was based on **RFOA**. The Supreme Court noted that the **RFOA** focuses on whether the factor relied on to make the decision was "reasonable." The Court flatly rejected the use of a business necessity defense in **ADEA** disparate impact cases, stating that the **RFOA** defense applies.

Remedies

More frequently, private **ADEA** litigants pursue violations on their own behalf rather than relying on the EEOC to prosecute a case on their behalf. The **ADEA** provides for jury trials for private sector employees and employees of local governments, but it does not provide for that right as to federal employees. Remedies under the **ADEA** may include reinstatement, affirmative injunctions (i.e., compelling the employer to take some action), back pay, front pay, recovery of attorneys' fees, and double damages as liquidated damages where the defendant has committed a willful violation of the **ADEA**. The **ADEA** does not provide for recovery of damages for pain and suffering.

In *Trans World Airlines v. Thurston,*[33] the Supreme Court held that a willful violation is one in which the employer "knew or showed reckless disregard for the matter of whether its conduct was prohibited by the **ADEA**." Proof of a "willful" violation requires evidence of more than mere negligent or unreasonable conduct. If a decision-maker wrongly, but in good faith and nonrecklessly, believes that the **ADEA** permits a particular age-based decision, the violation of the **ADEA** is not "willful." Once the determination of willfulness is made, an award of **liquidated damages** is mandatory, and the court must double the amount of back-pay damages. They cannot be assessed in an action against the federal government but may be recovered in actions against nonfederal public agencies. The Supreme Court has not recognized punitive damages as appropriate in **ADEA** cases. If presented with the issues, the Court would probably hold that the **liquidated damages** are in lieu of punitive damage awards for age discrimination claimants.

Liquidated Damages
A fixed amount of damages, usually twice the amount of unpaid back pay due a claimant.

Despite these protections, **age discrimination** does continue. Some critics claim that the **ADEA** merely camouflages the incidences of **age discrimination**. They argue that other practices have replaced blatant **age discrimination**, including early retirement incentives, RIFs, and **RFOA** initiatives. They maintain that when employers undertake layoffs they should ensure that employees over age 40 are not laid off in greater numbers than are employees age 40 or younger.

Older Workers Benefit Protection Act

Either within the settlement of an **ADEA** administrative or court action or in connection with a severance program or other employment termination, an employer may ask an employee to waive rights or pending claims under the **ADEA**. However, the **ADEA**, as amended by the 1991 **OWBPA**, sets out specific minimum standards that must be followed for a waiver to be considered "*knowing and voluntary*" and enforceable. The following **OWBPA** requirements govern the form of a waiver, which must:

1. Be in writing and be in an understandable form;
2. Specifically refer to the **ADEA** rights or claims;
3. Not waive rights or claims that may arise in the future;
4. Not bar an employee from filing a claim with the EEOC or cooperating in an EEOC investigation;

5. Be in exchange for valuable consideration (i.e., the employee must receive something of value to which he or she was not already entitled);
6. Advise the individual in writing to consult an attorney before signing the waiver;
7. Provide the employee with at least 21 days to consider the agreement and at least 7 days to revoke the agreement after signing it; or, if an employer requests an **ADEA** waiver in connection with an exit incentive program or other employment termination program offered to a group or class of employees, the individual is given a period of at least 45 days within which to consider the agreement; and
8. Provide that for a period of at least 7 days following the execution of the agreement, the individual employee may revoke the waiver agreement and that the agreement will not become effective or enforceable until the revocation period has expired.[34]

The **OWBPA** requirements to waive **ADEA** claims do not apply to any dispute involving the employee and his or her claims under the Employee Retirement Income Security Act (ERISA) claims. Occasionally, employers may fail to comply with the **OWBPA** release language requirements. Courts are sympathetic to the positions asserted by employees who later wish to sue for age discrimination when they have signed a defective waiver and release agreement.

Older Workers Benefit Protection Act of 1990 (OWBPA)
The federal law that amended the ADEA to prohibit employers from denying benefits to older employees. Waivers of age discrimination claims must be knowing or voluntary.

> ***Example:*** Delores Oubre worked as a scheduler at a power plant run by Entergy Operations, Inc. After receiving a poor performance rating, her supervisor told her to either improve her performance or accept a voluntary severance package. After consulting with attorneys, she signed a release in which she agreed to "waive, settle, release and discharge any and all claims, demands, damages, actions, or causes of action . . . that I may have against Entergy. . . ." In return, she was paid $6,258 in severance. The release violated the requirements of the OWBPA. On that basis, the Supreme Court permitted Oubre to sue for age discrimination. The Court held that an employee may not waive an **ADEA** claim unless the waiver or release satisfies the act.[35]

Contract law defenses to the enforcement of an **OWBPA** release may be asserted even if the employer followed the requirements of the law. If an employer misled an employee as to the meaning of the release or used undue influence or pressure with regard to the execution of the agreement, then the former employer could assert these defenses to set the release aside.

> ***Example:*** When criminal charges against a teacher were dismissed, he sought to set aside his resignation to the district. He claimed that his resignation was invalid because, when he signed it, he was under severe mental and emotional strain and was unable to think clearly due to having just completed his police questioning, arrest, and booking. He executed the resignation in response to a visit to his apartment by the school district superintendent and the principal of his school. They told him that they had his best interests at heart and that he should execute the immediate resignation form. If similar circumstances occurred in reference to the execution of an **OWBPA** release, the courts would set it aside as the California court did for the teacher in *Odorizzi v. Bloomfield School District.*[36]

CASE 10.8

AN OWBPA-COMPLIANT RELEASE DOES NOT EXTEND TO WAIVERS OF ADMINISTRATIVE RIGHTS

EEOC V. COSMAIR

821 F.2d 1085 (5th Cir. 1987)

U.S. Court of Appeals for the Fifth Circuit

Facts. Robert Lee Terry was fired at age 53 as a sales representative for the L'Oreal Hair Care Division of Cosmair. He was offered a continuation of his salary and medical benefits for 37 weeks following his discharge in exchange for a release. Terry signed the release without consulting his attorney. If Terry had not signed the release he would not have been offered any severance benefits. He filed age discrimination charges against his employer. When he did so, his former employer discontinued his severance benefits. Terry then filed a second EEOC charge for retaliation for filing a charge with the EEOC. The EEOC filed suit on Terry's behalf and obtained a preliminary injunction requiring it to continue the benefits in exchange for the release of the ADEA claims. The former employer appealed to the Court of Appeals for the Fifth Circuit.

Issue. Does a release under OWBPA bind the EEOC?

Language of the Court. Clark, C.J.: **According to the Commission, Cosmair could not suspend payments in response to Terry's filing a charge; doing so was retaliation. Cosmair can only rely on the release as a defense to Terry's ADEA cause of action. The district court agreed with the EEOC, holding that a release is at most a defense to an ADEA claim and cannot be used to impede EEOC enforcement of the civil rights laws.**

As the Supreme Court stated in *EEOC v. Shell Oil Co.* (citation omitted): "[A] charge of employment discrimination is not the equivalent of a complaint initiating a lawsuit. The function of the [ADEA] charge, rather, is to place the EEOC on notice that someone . . . believes that an employer has violated the [Act]." Indeed, charges can be filed by persons other than the employee who allegedly suffered from the discrimination.

Cosmair represented at oral argument, however, that the parties intended that the release waive Terry's right to file a charge. To the extent we accept this representation, and some testimony at the preliminary injunction hearing and language in Terry's charge supports it, we hold, alternatively, that a waiver of the right to file a charge is void as against public policy. Therefore, any attempt by Terry to waive his right to file a charge is void.

The EEOC depends on the filing of charges to notify it of possible discrimination (citations omitted). . . . A charge not only informs the EEOC of discrimination against the employee who files the charge or on whose behalf it is filed, but also may identify other unlawful company actions. For example, in his charge Terry named two co-workers who allegedly had been fired or forced into early retirement because of age discrimination. When the EEOC acts on this information, "albeit at the behest of and for the benefit of specific individuals, it acts also to vindicate the public interest in preventing employment discrimination." (Citations omitted.) . . . We hold that an employer and an employee cannot agree to deny to the EEOC the information it needs to advance this public interest. A waiver of the right to file a charge is void as against public policy.

Since Terry could not waive his right to file a charge, he did not breach the release when he filed a charge. The district court found, and its finding is not clearly erroneous, that Cosmair terminated Terry's severance payments solely because he filed a charge. Since Cosmair had no legal excuse for suspending payments, this constitutes retaliation. Thus, the EEOC established a substantial likelihood that it would succeed on the merits of its claim that Cosmair retaliated against Terry in violation of the ADEA.

Decision. No. The EEOC may pursue its own claims in response to the filing of the charge and is not bound by the waiver.

CASE QUESTIONS

Critical Legal Thinking. Why did the court of appeals wish to keep the EEOC charge filing open to claimants who had executed OWBPA releases? What public interests are served by the holding in this case?

Business Ethics. Was this decision an overly technical interpretation of the release language? Do you agree with the court? Why or why not?

Contemporary Business. How should employers protect themselves from a retrospective interpretation of the parties' intentions at the time of termination of employment?

Management Application
Targeting Workers by Age

Sean Bahri and others working for the Home Depot chain in Tigard, Oregon, claimed they had been subjected to age discrimination under the **ADEA** and an Oregon state law prohibiting discrimination. As part of its defense to the **ADEA** lawsuit, Home Depot argued that an **ADEA** plaintiff should be required to show that the plaintiffs rendered satisfactory job performance at all times to prevail. In this case, the plaintiffs established that when a certain individual was assigned as store manager, a disproportionate number of older workers were terminated and replaced by younger, less experienced workers. In addition, the manager referred to female employees as his "girls." He repeatedly made unwelcome comments about people's style of dress, hair, shoes, and personal relationships. He also commented to Bahri that Home Depot could hire two employees for what it was paying Bahri, who testified that it was clear that Home Depot wished to terminate older workers and replace them with less expensive, younger ones. Home Depot claimed that Bahri suffered no adverse employment action because he was not discharged but instead abandoned his job, while Bahri countered that he was constructively discharged.[37] What information in the personnel records or the discovery in the lawsuit would you seek to infer that the manager was targeting older workers?

Key Terms and Concepts

- ADEA
- Bona fide executive or high policy-making employee
- BFOQ
- Older Workers Benefit Protection Act (OWBPA)
- Pretext
- Prima facie
- Protected class
- Reverse age discrimination
- Disparate treatment
- Direct evidence
- Circumstantial evidence
- Reasonable Factor Other Than Age (RFOA)
- Noncapability
- Reduction in Force (RIF)
- Hostile work environment
- Liquidated damages

Chapter Summary

- The ADEA makes it wrongful for an employer to take any adverse employment action against any person age 40 or over or otherwise to discriminate in compensation, terms, conditions, or privileges of employment because of that individual's age.

- The ADEA applies to employers with 20 or more employees. Like Title VII, the ADEA is enforced by the EEOC.

- The ADEA permits employers to impose mandatory retirement with respect to certain categories of employees, such as executives, high policy-makers, and public safety employees.

■ As for other forms of discrimination claims, a plaintiff can pursue two types of claims in an ADEA case: disparate treatment and disparate impact. Disparate treatment occurs when the employer intentionally discriminates. Such claims require proof of the employer's intention when it took the adverse action. Disparate impact occurs when the employer's acts or policies are facially neutral but adversely impact a class of employees and are not otherwise reasonable. These types of claims do not require proof of intent to discriminate. In a mixed-motives case, the plaintiff must prove that age was the deciding factor in the adverse action affecting the employee. Retaliation is also prohibited in ADEA cases.

■ A terminated employee age 40 or older who is replaced by an individual also age 40 or older can claim discrimination under the ADEA if the age difference is "substantial." The ADEA prohibits discrimination against protected individuals because of age, not class membership (i.e., individuals over age 40).

■ The ADEA prohibits employers from discriminating because of age between two individuals who are both over age 40.

■ The language of the ADEA is identical to the language used in Title VII except for substitution of the word "age" for the words "race, color, religion, sex, or national origin."

■ The employer may use several strong defenses against an ADEA claim. In particular, the ADEA itself recognizes the BFOQ and RFOA defenses.

■ The Supreme Court has established a two-part test of the BFOQ defense in an ADEA context. The employer must establish a reasonable necessity for the practice, and it must be compelled to rely on age as the determinative factor.

■ Under the Supreme Court's Title VII decision in *Wards Cove Packing Co. v. Antonio,* 490 U.S. 642 (1989), a plaintiff must identify the specific employment practice under which he or she has been adversely affected. If the plaintiff does so, the employer can assert a business necessity defense. The employer need only establish the existence (and not prove by a preponderance of evidence) that it had a "legitimate business justification" for its business practice. If the employer does reach this low threshold, then the plaintiff may still prevail by proving by a preponderance of evidence that another practice would satisfy the business justification without having a disparate impact upon the plaintiff. This decision was made inapplicable to Title VII cases by Congressional enactment of the Civil Rights Act of 1991, but it still applies in cases brought under the ADEA. When Congress amended Title VII to overrule the *Wards Cove* decision to expand employer liability for disparate impact under Title VII, it did not amend the ADEA. Thus, ADEA plaintiffs must overcome any RFOA asserted by the employer.

■ Age discrimination claims may be waived under OWBPA if the requirements for the waiver are followed. Such waivers do not bar the filing of age discrimination charges with the EEOC; they only bar the right to personal recovery from a personal lawsuit or proceeds obtained by the EEOC in response to investigation or litigation.

Online Student Support

■ Loislaw legal research and writing assignments.

■ Loislaw group projects and class presentations.

■ Loislaw access, providing online research including up-to-date cases, statutes, rules, and regulations. Primary law for all 50 states and federal jurisdictions. Registration required for access to this resource.

■ Practice questions, including sample true/false, multiple choice, and short answer questions to test your understanding of concepts.

- Additional human resource forms.
- Internet exercises.
- Blogs.
- Supplementary statutory and regulatory materials.

Case Problems

10.1 If a school district issues a teacher retention plan with new options for protected class teachers who elect to retire, is it also required to extend those same options in subsequent plans for those teachers continuing to work when the plan is amended at a later time? (*Abrahamson v. Bd. of Educ. of the Wappingers Falls Cent. Sch. Dist.*, 374 F.3d 66 (2d Cir.), *cert denied*, 543 U.S. 984 (2004))

10.2 Does it make any difference if younger employees are subject to the same adverse employment policies and practices as those over age 40? (*Mechnig v. Sears, Roebuck & Co.*, 864 F.2d 1359 (7th Cir. 1988))

10.3 A difficulty confronting American business owners is how to deal with an older workforce that enjoys a costly wage and benefit package without violating the provisions of the ADEA. Quite often, older workers earn more compensation than the younger members in the company. If termination of older workers for financial reasons would violate the ADEA, how would you deal with reducing the cost of labor within such a business? When would salary and seniority act as a "proxy" for age in an organization? What business decision would you make and what employer defenses could you rely on to justify your decision? (*Metz v. Transit Mix, Inc.*, 828 F.2d 1202 (7th Cir. 1987))

10.4 Courts allow an EEOC charge to serve as the basis for a subsequently filed lawsuit under the ADEA only if the subject of the lawsuit is reasonably related to the matters claimed in the EEOC administrative complaint. Provide a definition of whether an age discrimination claim filed in federal court that is not stated in the earlier EEOC charge could be found to have been reasonably related to the discrimination complained of in the EEOC charge. (*Bonham v. Regions Mortgage, Inc.*, 129 F. Supp. 2d 1315 (M.D. Ala. 2001); and *Caldwell v. Federal Express Corp.*, 1308 F. Supp 29 (D. Me. 1995))

10.5 What evidence other than statistical evidence should be offered by age discrimination plaintiffs? Will statistics alone support or defeat such a claim in the courts? If you were a judge deciding whether to allow the introduction of statistical evidence into the trial proceedings, what characteristics of that evidence would you want to verify before admitting it? (*Evers v. Alliant Techsystems, Inc.*, 241 F.3d 948 (8th Cir. 2001))

End Notes

1. *Luks v. Baxter Healthcare Corp.*, 467 F3d 1049 (7th Cir. 2006).
2. *http://archive.eeoc.gov/stats/adea.html.*
3. 20 U.S.C. §630(b).
4. 528 U.S. 62 (2000).
5. 29 U.S.C. §631(a).
6. *Koprowski v. Wistar Inst. of Anatomy and Biology*, 819 F. Supp. 410 (E.D. Pa. 1992).
7. *Shorett v. Rite Aid of Maine, Inc.*, 155 F.3d 8 (1st Cir. 1998).
8. *Federal Express Corp. v. Holowecki*, _______ U.S. _______, 128 S.Ct. 1147 (2008).
9. *Gilmer v. Interstate/Johnson Lane Corp.*, 500 U.S. 20 (1990).
10. *14 Penn Plaza LLC v. Pyett et al.*, _______ U.S. _______, 129 S.Ct. 1456 (2009).
11. *EEOC v. Clay Printing Co.*, 955 F.2d 936 (4th Cir. 1992).
12. *Duffy v. Wheeling Pittsburgh Steel Corp.*, 738 F.2d 1393 (3d Cir. 1984).
13. 507 U.S. 604 (1993).

14. *Grosjean v. First Energy Corp.*, 349 F. 3d 332,340 (6th Cir. 2003).
15. *Carter v. City of Miami,* 870 F.2d 578 (11th Cir. 1989).
16. *Hartley v. Wisconsin Bell, Incorporated,* 124 F.3d 887 (7th Cir. 1997).
17. *Reeves v. Sanderson Plumbing Prod., Inc.*, 530 U.S. 133, 141 (2000).
18. *Chiaramonte v. Fashion Bed Group, Inc.*, 129 F.3d 391, 396 (7th Cir. 1997).
19. *Adreani v. First Colonial Bankshares Corp.*, 154 F.3d 389, 393 (7th Cir. 1998).
20. *Troupe v. May Dep't Stores Co.*, 20 F.3d 734, 736 (7th Cir. 1994).
21. 411 U.S. 792 (1973).
22. 544 U.S. 228 (2005).
23. *Hamilton v. Caterpillar, Inc.*, 966 F.2d 1226 (7th Cir. 1992).
24. 469 U.S. 111 (1985).
25. *Gilmer v. Interstate/Johnson Lane Corp.*, 500 U.S. 20 (1991).
26. 544 U.S. 228 (2005).
27. *http://edocket.access.gpo.gov/2010/2010-3126.htm.*
28. *Koslow v. Epstein, Becker & Green,* 77 F.E.P. Cases (BNA) 250 (D.D.C. 1998).
29. *Taggart v. Time Inc.*, 924 F.2d 43 (2d Cir. 1991).
30. *Pottenger v. Potlatch Corp.*, 329 F.3d 740 (9th Cir. 2003).
31. *Thorn v. Sundstrand Aerospace Corp.*, 207 F.3d 383, 387 (7th Cir. 2000).
32. ____________ U.S. ____________, 128 S.Ct. 2395 (2008).
33. 469 U.S. 111 (1985).
34. 29 U.S.C. §626(f)(1).
35. *Oubre v. Entergy Operations, Inc.*, 522 U.S. 422 (1998).
36. 246 Cal.App.2d 123 (1996).
37. *Bahri v. Home Depot USA, Inc.*, 242 F. Supp. 2d 922 (D. Or. 2002).

Chapter 11
Work–Family Issues and Other EEO Protections

"This legislation . . . [is] the first civil rights bill of the new century of the life sciences. With its passage, we take a quantum leap forward in preserving the value of new genetic technology and protecting the basic rights of every American." —Edward M. "Ted" Kennedy, U.S. Senator, upon enactment of GINA

Learning Objectives

1. Discuss the scope of the Family and Medical Leave Act.
2. Describe the workplace rights of pregnant women and their partners.
3. Recognize common examples of pregnancy discrimination.
4. Identify the rights of persons associated with protected individuals.
5. Explain the job protection rights of service personnel.
6. Understand the application of federal and state genetic discrimination laws.

Chapter Outline

- Introduction
- Family and Medical Leave Act

Case 11.1 Erdman v. Nationwide Ins. Company

- Management Application: Women in the Labor Force
- The Pregnancy Discrimination Act

Case 11.2 Stout v. Baxter Healthcare Corp.

- Focus on Ethics: Limited Effect of the Pregnancy Discrimination Act

Case 11.3 Spivey v. Beverly Enterprises, Inc.

- Focus on Ethics: Pregnancy Discrimination Act
- Sex-Plus Discrimination

Case 11.4 Phillips v. Martin Marietta Corp.
Case 11.5 Automobile Workers v. Johnson Controls, Inc.

- Focus on Ethics: Sexual Favoritism
- Management Application: EEOC Policy Guidance for Workplace Discrimination Against Caregivers
- Management Application: Sex-Plus Discrimination
- Family Responsibility Discrimination
- Appearance-Based Discrimination
- Rights of Service Members and Their Families
- Genetic Discrimination Laws
- Genetic Information Nondiscrimination Act of 2008
- Human Resource Form: Unpaid FMLA Leave Request

Chapter Opening scenario

Charmaine, a mother of two preschool-age children, files an EEOC charge alleging sex discrimination after her application for a position in her employer's executive training program was rejected. The employer asserts that it rejected Charmaine because candidates who were selected had better performance appraisals or more managerial experience and because she is not "executive material." The employer also contends that half of the selectees were women, thereby showing that her rejection could not have been because of gender. However, the investigation reveals that Charmaine had more managerial experience and/or better performance appraisals than several selectees had. As to some selectees, she was better qualified, including both men and women, as weighted pursuant to the employer's written selection policy. In addition, while the employer selected both men and women for the program, the only selectees with preschool-age children were men. Under the circumstances, has Charmaine suffered wrongful discrimination? If so, on what grounds could she pursue her case?[1]

Introduction

This chapter, which concludes our discussion of equal opportunity laws, will address several important issues frequently encountered in employment involving the balance between personal and workplace demands on individuals, especially caregivers. The workplace population increasingly includes both single parents and middle-aged workers coping with the needs of elderly family members. These conditions suggest that employer policies on personal and family leave are becoming increasingly important to the individual worker. The chapter covers "sex-plus" discrimination relating to the effects of stereotyping on individuals; the rights of persons associated with members of a protected class, who may enjoy protection from "associational" discrimination; the law affording protection from pregnancy discrimination; and the workplace rights of service members and their families. Our study concludes with a review of the recent law designed to protect persons from genetic discrimination in the workplace.

Family and Medical Leave Act

The **Family and Medical Leave Act (FMLA)**[2] became effective in August 1993. The **FMLA** entitles employees, both male and female, to take up to 12 weeks of unpaid, job-protected leave in a 12-month period for any of the following situations or needs:

- the birth and care of the newborn child of the employee;
- the placement with the employee of a son or daughter for adoption or foster care;

- to care for an immediate family member (spouse, child, or parent) with a serious health condition;
- to take medical leave when the employee is unable to work because of the employee's own serious health condition;
- to care for a service member who has experienced a serious injury or illness while on active duty; and
- any "qualifying exigency" arising because the employee is in the National Guard or Reserves and is or soon will be placed on active duty.

The "family" part of the act relates to those stated situations. Federal law does not provide time off for parent-teacher conferences or personal counseling. However, many state laws do provide such protections, and employers must comply with more than federal law in operating their businesses. The parental leave ends 12 months from the date of the birth, adoption, or foster care placement. If an expectant mother's medical condition requires **FMLA** leave before the birth of the child, that leave is a qualifying event. Although we discuss workplace protections afforded pregnant women later in this chapter, note that under the **FMLA**, an absence by an employee for a **pregnancy-related condition** could constitute a serious health condition.

FMLA
Family and Medical Leave Act; a 1993 federal act requiring covered employers to provide eligible employees job protections for unpaid leave due to the serious health conditions of the employee or a family member or to care for a new child.

Serious Health Condition
An illness, injury, impairment, or physical or mental condition requiring hospitalization or continuing treatment by a health care provider.

General notices of the **FMLA** must be set forth in employee handbooks and other written material concerning benefits or leave or must be provided upon hire. The **FMLA** protects employees from being penalized by employers for taking time off as allowed under the act. The employee does not need to specify that they desire an **FMLA** leave to invoke its protections. The employee need only notify the employer of a desire to take time off for a situation that falls within the act. The employer must recognize that the request falls within the protections of the act. Failure to do so can subject the employer to liability under the **FMLA**. Under the act an employer cannot discipline an employee for leaves granted and protected under **FMLA**. It is important that employers align all parental and medical leave polices with the provisions of the **FMLA**, even though employers are allowed to provide a more generous leave policy.

FMLA Coverage

The **FMLA** applies to:

- employees who work for a public employer of any size, including state, local, and federal governments;
- employees of a private company with 50 or more employees; and
- employees who work for a company with fewer than 50 employees at one worksite may be covered if the employer has at least 50 employees within 75 miles of that worksite.

The **FMLA** covers employees who:

- worked for that employer for at least 12 months before taking leave;
- worked at least 1,250 hours within the 12 months prior to taking the leave; and
- experience a qualifying event and give timely notice to the employer of the need for the leave.

The time in service and hours requirements must be met as of the leave commencement date and not at the earlier time when the leave is requested. Employers must carefully review employee timesheets to verify eligibility. Failure to give proper credit for hours worked or credit to the hour threshold can result in a violation of the act. For workers who are exempt from time-keeping requirements, including executives, administrators, and professional employees, the employer has the burden of showing that the employee has not worked the minimum number of hours. Time spent in fulfilling an employee's military service obligations (National Guard or Reserve duty) is counted toward the employee's time requirement of 1,250 hours and 12 months.

The employer has the option in counting the 12-month period as a calendar year, a fixed 12-month leave, or a rolling 12-month calendar based on when the employee last took a family medical leave. The employer must grant a family or medical leave request to "eligible" employees, but it may require the employee to use any accrued paid vacation or sick leave toward any part of the 12-week leave provided by the act.

Notice to the Employer

An employee must give at least 30 days' notice of his or her desire for **FMLA** leave, if the need for the leave is foreseeable. An employee's failure to comply with the employer's leave procedures can be the basis for delaying or denying an employee's request for **FMLA**-qualifying leave. Only under extenuating circumstances may the employee delay in giving notice of the need for leave.

Under current federal regulations, the employee must comply with the notice provisions:

> [T]he employee must specifically reference either the qualifying reason for leave or the need for **FMLA** leave. Calling in "sick" without providing more information will not be considered sufficient notice to trigger an employer's obligations under the Act. The employer will be expected to obtain any additional required information through informal means. An employee has an obligation to respond to an employer's questions designed to determine whether an absence is potentially **FMLA**-qualifying.[3]

Serious Health Conditions

Defining a **serious health condition** can be complex. It includes more than mere disability, yet the term does not include all medical issues suffered by an employee or immediate family member. Moreover, leaves need not be granted for the care of grandparents, aunts or uncles, in-laws, or adult children unless they are disabled and incapable of caring for themselves. However, the definition of family members for qualifying events related to military service includes children of any age as well as "next of kin" (i.e., the nearest blood relative to the service member). Department of Labor regulations provide that such a condition entitles an employee to leave because of an illness, injury, impairment, or physical or mental condition that involves either (1) inpatient care, or (2) continuing treatment by a health care provider. The complex regulations address what those terms mean and specifically provide for definitions of frequency of treatment; the employer's right to request recertification of medical conditions; what constitutes a chronic, permanent, or long-term condition; periods of incapacity due to pregnancy; or parental care constituting continuing treatment.[4] Examples of illness that generally *do not qualify* as serious health conditions include the common cold, earaches, routine headaches, routine dental and medical visits, plastic surgery for cosmetic purposes, the flu, upset stomachs, sore throats, minor ulcers, and treatments for acne.

The **FMLA** regulations do not require employees to use their leave in a single, continuous 12-week block. When medically necessary, leave may be taken intermittently or on a reduced leave schedule. Employers usually choose to require the employee to provide medical certification in support of the need for leave. However, to determine if the employee's circumstances have changed, intermittent or reduced schedule leaves for serious medical conditions may require the employee to obtain recertification of the need for leave.

Employer's Response

Within five business days of learning that an employee's leave may qualify under the **FMLA**, an employer is required to provide notice of potential eligibility for leave, which must be accompanied by a rights and responsibilities notice. Within five business days of obtaining enough information to determine whether the leave qualifies for **FMLA**, the employer must notify the employee of its determination. If an employer fails to provide timely notice, employers may retroactively designate the leave as **FMLA** leave absent a showing of harm to the employee. If an employee suffers individual harm because the employer fails to follow the notification rules, the employer may be liable to the employee for his or her out-of-pocket costs. During this five day period, the employer may also request that the employee provide a medical certification supporting the leave request. The employer's health care provider, human resource professionals, leave administrators, or managers, but not the employee's direct supervisor, may contact the employee's health care provider for the medical certification. The employer can request additional information if the certification is incomplete or insufficient. Generally, employers may not deny or delay the start of a qualified **FMLA** leave. They are entitled to verify the veracity of the claim and should do so promptly and carefully to comply with the act and to avoid violating the employee's privacy rights.

Consequences of FMLA Leave

The employer is required to restore the employee to the same position he or she held before the leave began or to an equivalent position with equivalent benefits, pay, and other terms and conditions of employment. During a **FMLA** leave, the leave must be treated as continued service for purposes of vesting and eligibility to participate in pensions and other retirement plans. Changes to benefit plans, including improvements to fringe benefit plans, are to be extended to the employee on such leave. Moreover, if an employer's bonus program is tied to job performance, the employer is required to extend a bonus on a pro-rata basis to the employee. The employer is to consider the employee as otherwise eligible for a bonus and must pay a percentage of it based on the period of attendance during the bonus period.

Leave for Care of Service Members

In 2008, President Bush signed the National Defense Authorization Act,[5] which amended the **FMLA** to provide expanded leave rights to employees to care for service members injured during active duty and for qualifying exigencies. The amended **FMLA** provides:

- eligible employees may take up to 26 weeks of unpaid leave in a single 12-month period to care for a spouse, son, daughter, parent, or "next of kin" who is a "covered service member" with a serious injury or illness incurred in the line of duty. This caregiver leave may be combined with other **FMLA** leave, up to a total of 26 weeks during the single 12-month period.
- specific characterizations of "qualifying exigencies" include:
  - issues arising from a family member's short notice (7 days or less) of deployment;
  - military events and related activities (e.g., ceremonies, etc.) related to the active duty or call to active duty status of a family member;
  - certain child care and related activities;
  - making or updating financial or legal arrangements to address a family member's absence due to the call to active duty;
  - attending counseling for the employee, the active duty family member, or a child of the active duty member when the need for counseling arises from the call to active duty or the active duty status of the family member;
  - taking up to five days of leave to spend time with a family member who is on short-term temporary rest and recuperation leave during deployment;
  - attending certain post-deployment activities (e.g., arrival ceremonies); and
  - "any other event that the employer and employee agree is a qualifying exigency."

Remedies

Federal law expressly prohibits employers from discriminating against or discharging any employee who exercises or attempts to exercise any rights provided by the **FMLA**. Employees who are denied rights under the act may sue their employer in a private lawsuit in state or federal court or may file a claim with the U.S. Department of Labor. A private lawsuit must be filed within two years after the violation or within three years if the employer acted willfully. Employers found violating the act are responsible for the lost or denied wages. If the employee did not suffer a wage loss, the employer is responsible for out-of-pocket costs such as the cost of providing care to family members. The employee may also seek equitable relief, including reinstatement, promotion, attorney's fees, and costs. The **FMLA** provides that the employer will be liable for damages and liquidated damages and the district courts "may" reduce the amount of liquidated damages if the employer's good faith is established. Thus, employers face a doubling of plaintiff's damages.[6] Trial courts are likely to impose liquidated damages (an amount equal to the amount of damages awarded for lost compensation plus interest) unless the defendant employer can prove that it acted "in good faith" in believing that the "act or omission was not a violation of the FMLA."

Example: Melissa Brown had worked as a food service director since 2002. In August 2004, the nursing home employer contracted with Nutrition Management Services Company to provide food services for the nursing home. Nutrition Management hired Brown to continue as a food service director. In October 2004, Brown was terminated when Nutrition Management learned she was pregnant. She sued on the ground that her termination was an unlawful interference with her **FMLA** rights. The company argued that Brown was not eligible for **FMLA** leave, having only worked a few months for the company. The jury found that Nutrition Management was a successor in interest to Brown's prior employer (the nursing home, which was an **FMLA**-covered employer), and, the length of time worked and hours worked made her eligible for **FMLA** leave. In finding that company did not act in good faith, the court was particularly critical of the human resource director, an attorney by training who had general knowledge of employment law. He made no effort to investigate the facts or to become aware of the factors that might qualify Brown for the leave. As a result, the court awarded Brown liquidated damages in addition to her back pay.[7]

In the following case, the court recognized that hours worked "off the clock" count toward **FMLA** leave eligibility if the employer was aware of those hours. In the *Erdman* case, the employer knew about them because it regularly gave the employee compensatory time off for the extra hours she worked to care for a child. There was an informal agreement that the employee could work from home in exchange for extra vacation time instead of pay. The court had to consider of this agreement comported with the requirements of the **FMLA**.

CASE 11.1

ALL HOURS WORKED COUNT FOR FMLA LEAVE, AND EMPLOYERS MAY BE SUED FOR RETALIATION

ERDMAN V. NATIONWIDE INS. COMPANY

582 F.3d 500 (2009)

U.S. Court of Appeals for the Third Circuit

Facts. Nationwide Insurance Company hired Brenda Erdman in 1980. She held full-time positions until 1998 when she requested part-time work that would allow her to care for her daughter, Amber, who was born with Down syndrome. Nationwide granted this request, as well as a later request to switch to a four-day week. As a part-time employee, Erdman accrued unofficial "comp time," working overtime outside the office in exchange for extra vacation time. She was evaluated as an efficient, productive employee. In 2002, her supervisor told her not to work extra hours. However, her new supervisor never discussed her flexible schedule and practice of working extra hours for comp time. In 2003, her supervisor told her that the part-time position would be eliminated, and that Erdman would have to take a full-time job again. She accepted the new position, but the company claimed she became angry, erratic, and insubordinate.

In April 2003, Erdman requested FMLA leave for July through August instead of taking vacation time. Less than a month later, before the leave was officially approved, Nationwide terminated her. The company stated that she was fired for behavioral problems. Erdman sued for retaliation under the FMLA and for violations of the Americans with Disabilities Act (ADA). The district court granted Nationwide summary judgment, and Erdman appealed to the court of appeals.

Issue. Does the FMLA cover all hours worked, and can a plaintiff sue for retaliation under the act?

Language of the Court. Hardiman, J.: **The first question is whether a reasonable jury could have concluded that Nationwide had actual or constructive notice that Erdman worked at least 1,250 hours, making her eligible under the FMLA. For FMLA purposes, all work that "the employer knows or has reason to believe . . . is being performed" counts toward the threshold requirement. . . . The parties agree that hours worked off-site or beyond an employee's regular schedule count if "[the employer] knows or has reason to believe that an employee is continuing to work extra hours." . . . "[A]n employer need not have actual knowledge of such off-site work; constructive knowledge will suffice." (Citation omitted.) Nationwide does not dispute that Erdman regularly worked outside of the office for many years, and that [the company] consistently authorized payment for these hours or allowed Erdman to use them as "comp" time.**

Nationwide argues that if Erdman is eligible for FMLA leave, she cannot recover on a retaliation theory because she did not actually take leave. We begin by noting that it would be patently absurd if an employer who wished to punish an employee for taking FMLA leave could avoid liability simply by firing the employee before the leave begins. However, the question is not whether an employer may escape liability altogether; the question is whether such action constitutes interference with the employee's FMLA rights, retaliation against the employee, or both.

We hold that firing an employee for a valid request for FMLA leave may constitute interference with the employee's FMLA rights as well as retaliation against the employee.

Decision. Yes, the company must count all hours worked and is responsible for recordkeeping errors. A plaintiff could claim retaliation even if the leave had not yet been officially denied.

CASE QUESTIONS

Critical Legal Thinking. What if the person was ineligible for FMLA leave at the commencement of the leave period? Does this case grant the right to sue for interference?

Business Ethics. How would you have dealt with Erdman's request for FMLA leave if the company actually did have grounds to terminate her for unprofessional conduct?

Contemporary Business. What does this case suggest with regard to the importance of tracking hours worked away from the office? How should employers record that time?

COBRA Benefits While on FMLA Leave

One of the most significant consequences of the **FMLA** relates to extended health care benefits during the leave period. The act requires an employer to maintain coverage under any group health plan for an employee on **FMLA** leave under the same conditions the coverage would have been provided if the employee had continued working. The premiums are paid in the same contribution ratio as before the leave. For example, if the employer had paid 80 percent of the premiums, then the employer must continue to pay that percent of the insurance premium during the leave, up to the maximum of 12 workweeks during a 12-month leave period.

COBRA
The Consolidated Omnibus Budget Reconciliation Act of 1985 is a federal law providing some employees with the ability to continue health insurance coverage for a limited time after leaving employment.

Coverage provided under **FMLA** is not COBRA coverage, and **FMLA** leave is not a qualifying event under COBRA. COBRA coverage is discussed in a later chapter. A COBRA qualifying event may occur when the employer's obligation to maintain health benefits under **FMLA** ceases, such as when an employee notifies an employer of the employee's intention not to return to work. However, if an employee chooses not to retain health coverage during the **FMLA** leave, benefits must be restored to the same level as was provided when the leave began. When the benefits are restored upon the employee's return to work, they must be restored without any qualifying period, physical examination, or exclusions for preexisting conditions.

Management Application
Women in the Labor Force

During the past several decades, the participation of women in the labor force has steadily increased. One result of this change in demographics has been a transformation of the workplace. Because women provide most of the caregiving required in most families, women workers and their employers have been challenged to find a balance between the demands of home and family and of the workplace. The U.S. Bureau of Labor Statistics 2009 Databook[8] shows the following trends:

- In 2008, 59.5 percent of women were in the labor force.
- From 1975 to March 2000, the participation in the workforce of mothers with children under age 18 rose from 47 percent to a peak of 73 percent. As of 2008, the participation rate for mothers was 71 percent.
- In general, mothers with older children (6 to 17 years of age, none younger) are more likely to work than are mothers with children under 6 years of age.
- In 2008, women accounted for more than half of all workers in several industry sectors, including financial activities, education and health services, leisure and hospitality, and other service sectors.
- In 2008, 25 percent of employed women usually worked part time (fewer than 35 hours per week). In comparison, 11 percent of employed men usually worked part time.
- In 2007, more dual income couples were in married-couple families. In comparison, only 18 percent of households relied solely on a husband's earnings.
- In 2007, working wives contributed 36 percent of their families' incomes, up 9 percent from 1970. The proportion of working women who earned more than their spouses was 26 percent.

These trends show that the workforce is about half female, including a large number of mothers with young children. Dual-earner families have become the norm in the American workplace. Examine the Databook and determine what other trends in the labor force, if any, you believe are transforming the workplace. Share your conclusions with your fellow students.

The Pregnancy Discrimination Act

PDA
The Pregnancy Discrimination Act is a federal act passed in 1978, amending Title VII, prohibiting employment discrimination on the basis of pregnancy, childbirth, or related medical conditions.

Approximately 14 years after Congress enacted the Civil Rights Act of 1964, the act was amended to include section (k), commonly referred to as the **Pregnancy Discrimination Act (PDA).**[9] Under the terms of the **PDA**, Title VII's prohibition of discrimination "because of sex" was expanded to include pregnancy, childbirth, or related medical conditions. The amendment requires that women affected by pregnancy, childbirth, or related medical conditions be treated the same as other applicants or employees for all employment-related purposes, including hiring, pregnancy and maternity leave, health insurance, and fringe benefits. The protections provided by the **PDA** are only applicable to companies with 15 or more employees; however, states may amend or add to the protections provided by the Civil Rights Act of 1964 to extend this protection to employees of companies and organizations with fewer than 15 employees.

In Fiscal Year 2009, the Equal Employment Opportunity Commission (EEOC) received more than 6,100 charges of **pregnancy-based discrimination**. The agency resolved more than 5,500 pregnancy-related discrimination charges that year and recovered $16 million in monetary benefits for charging parties and other aggrieved individuals (not including monetary benefits obtained through litigation).

Title VII, as amended, does *not* require the employer to make special concessions to pregnant employees; but the employer must treat persons with **pregnancy-related conditions** in the same manner as persons with other medical conditions who are similar in their ability to perform work. If an employee becomes pregnant and unable to perform her work functions, the employer is required to provide job modifications, flexible scheduling, reconfigured job assignments, alternative assignments, disability leave, or leave without pay in the same manner as would be provided other employees who were not pregnant but were unable to perform their job functions.

> ***Example:*** Patricia is a pregnant machine operator at the Clark Bottling Company. She is told by her doctor to refrain temporarily from lifting more than 20 pounds. As part of her job as a machine operator, Patricia is required to carry materials that weigh more than 20 pounds several times a day. She requests to be relieved of this function, but her request is refused. The supervisor, Tom, informs her that he cannot reassign her job duties, but he can transfer her to another, lower-paying position that does not require any lifting for the duration of her pregnancy. She accepts the transfer. If the employer had reassigned the lifting duties for other employees, including those who had been injured or were recovering from surgery, Patricia would have a sex discrimination claim to pursue.

Employers may not exclude prescription contraceptives from prescription drug plan coverage. The **PDA** does not require an employer to pay for health insurance benefits for abortion, except where the life of the mother would be endangered if the fetus were carried to term, or where medical complications have arisen from an abortion. An employer may elect to provide abortion benefit rights. As a related matter, an employer may not discriminate against women employees who have had an abortion. Courts have held that the term "related medical condition" in the **PDA** included an abortion.[10]

The **PDA** does not require affirmative action or directed action with respect to pregnancy, childbirth, or related medical conditions in any particular way. It instructs employers to treat those conditions neutrally — that is, to treat such persons the same as other persons who are not affected by pregnancy but have the same inability to work.

Example: Desiree Calabro was a salesperson for a BMW dealership. She was required to have a driver's license for her position, but her license was suspended. She was also newly pregnant. The day before confirmation of her license suspension, the CEO of the dealership, upon learning she was pregnant, "threw his hands up in the air and said, 'Oh, great, Desiree is pregnant. Is she staying, is she going, and what is she doing?' " A witness described the CEO as being "very unhappy with the situation," while two other managers at the meeting also "groaned" in dismay. The trial record contained evidence that when a male employee had a suspended license, the dealership moved him over to a position not requiring a license and later transferred him back to his original position. Desiree was not offered a similar position to which to transfer during her license suspension. She was terminated for lacking a license. She sued for pregnancy discrimination. The court held that the circumstances of Calabro's termination could lead to a reasonable inference that her pregnancy played at least some role in the dealership's decision to fire her.[11]

CASE 11.2

ENFORCING ATTENDANCE REQUIREMENTS DURING PREGNANCY WILL NOT BE DISCRIMINATORY IF OTHER EMPLOYEES ARE SIMILARLY TREATED

STOUT V. BAXTER HEALTHCARE CORP.

282 F.3d 856 (2002)

U.S. Court of Appeals for the Fifth Circuit

Facts. Wilma Stout filed a complaint for sex discrimination against her employer, Baxter Healthcare. Stout, who was pregnant at the time, was hired as a probationary employee for the first 90 days of her employment. As a probationary employee, Stout was subject to a strict attendance policy that dictated that anyone who missed more than three days of work during the probationary period would be terminated. Stout received positive performance reviews and maintained perfect attendance during the first two months. However, in the last month Stout experienced early labor and suffered a miscarriage, rendering her unable to work for two weeks. Baxter terminated her because of her absenteeism, which was in excess of her probationary allowance.

After receiving a right-to-sue letter from the EEOC, Stout sued Baxter claiming pregnancy discrimination under the PDA. The district court granted a motion for summary judgment in favor of the employer. Stout appealed to the court of appeals.

Issue. Does the PDA require preferential treatment of pregnant employees?

Language of the Court. Garwood, C.J.: **Stout's claim of disparate treatment has no merit. She argues that she was fired "because of" her pregnancy. But, to the contrary, all of the evidence in the record indicated that she "was fired because of her absenteeism, not because of her pregnancy." There is no evidence she would have been treated differently if her absences had been due to some reason unrelated to pregnancy or if she had been absent the same amount but not pregnant. Baxter's policy does not in any way mention or focus on pregnancy, childbirth or any related medical condition. Although Baxter's policy results in the dismissal of any pregnant or post-partum employee who misses more than three days of work during the probationary period, it equally requires the termination of any non-pregnant employee who misses more than three days. Such a policy does not violate the PDA.**

There is no evidence that Stout (or any other pregnant probationary employee) was treated any differently than any other probationary employee who missed work. Stout claims that the policy affects all pregnant women and that therefore she has provided sufficient evidence to prove a prima facie disparate impact case.

This is not the law—the PDA does not require preferential treatment of pregnant employees and does not require employers to treat pregnancy related absences more leniently than other absences. To hold otherwise would be to transform the PDA into a guarantee of medical leave for pregnant employees, something we have specifically held that the PDA does not do.

Decision. No. Absenteeism policies are to be applied fairly to all employees.

CASE QUESTIONS

Critical Legal Thinking. Would the court's decision have been the same if Stout had missed the final four days of her 90-day probationary period?

Business Ethics. What if the employer allowed time off for prearranged vacations, but did not allow time off for premature childbirth or pregnancy complications?

Contemporary Business. Can you think of any other circumstances in which an employee's individual characteristics would require preferential treatment?

Focus on Ethics
Limited Effect of the Pregnancy Discrimination Act

While the purposes of the **PDA** are noble, its ability to address the reality that follows childbirth is limited. Many women argue that the **PDA** does not address the demands of balancing work and a busy home life. In the United States, the burdens imposed by child rearing fall disproportionately on women. As we will review in the last chapter of our text, many European countries, including Sweden, financially support and encourage children's development by providing for a comprehensive child care program along with parental insurance and child benefit systems. Sweden's Ministry of Education, Research, and Culture manages the responsibility for public child care.

Ethics Questions

1. If single-parent, child-rearing, and two-income families have become commonplace in the United States, is it time for government to reevaluate the models used in other countries with respect to family welfare policies?
2. Should child support orders in family court include provision for child-care costs to allow the custodial parent the opportunity to work?
3. Has the congressional response to the enactment of the FMLA been adequate, if the act provides for unpaid leave?

CASE 11.3

PREGNANCY DOES NOT ENTITLE EMPLOYEES TO PREFERENTIAL WORK RESTRICTIONS

SPIVEY V. BEVERLY ENTERPRISES, INC.

196 F.3d 1309 (11TH CIR. (1999))

U.S. Court of Appeals for the Eleventh Circuit

Facts. Michelle Spivey was employed as a certified nurse's assistant at the Boaz Health and Rehabilitation Center owned and operated by Beverly Enterprises, Inc., d.b.a. Boaz Health and Rehabilitation Center. Her primary responsibilities at the Boaz facility were to lift and reposition patients, assist with patient baths and meals, and provide general patient care. After Spivey became pregnant, she developed concerns that lifting a 250-pound patient could cause harm to her unborn child and requested assistance. Complying with Beverly Enterprises' request, Spivey obtained certification from her obstetrician imposing a 25-pound lifting restriction.

Beverly told Spivey that she would not be provided with an accommodation due to the company's modified duty policy. The policy stated that employees were excused from meeting their job responsibilities only if they qualified for modified duty as the result of a work-related injury. Spivey consequently attempted to have the lifting restriction removed by her obstetrician. The doctor, however, refused this request. Because of the medical restriction that precluded Spivey from lifting more than 25 pounds, Beverly Enterprises terminated her employment.

Spivey sued Beverly for discriminating against pregnant employees by granting modified duty only to those injured on the job and not to pregnant employees.

Issue. Is the PDA violated when an employer provides an accommodation of modified duty to those injured on the job but not to workers who become pregnant?

Language of the Court. Black, C.J.: **Spivey has not offered direct evidence that Beverly Enterprises intended to discriminate against pregnant employees. Spivey must therefore present circumstantial evidence from which an inference of intentional discrimination can be drawn.**

There is no dispute that Spivey was no longer qualified to work as a nurse's assistant. The lifting restriction on Spivey clearly prevented her from performing the responsibilities required of this position. Beverly Enterprises, however, was under no obligation to extend an accommodation to pregnant employees. The PDA does not require that employers give preferential treatment to pregnant employees. Spivey also has failed to establish that she suffered from a differential application of work rules.

Under the PDA, the employer must ignore an employee's pregnancy and treat her "as well as it would if she were not pregnant." Ignoring Spivey's pregnancy would still leave Beverly Enterprises with an employee who suffered from a non-occupational injury. Beverly Enterprises, as per its policy, was therefore entitled to deny Spivey a modified assignment as long as it denied modified duty to assignments to all employees who were not injured on the job.

In addition to her disparate treatment claim, Spivey alleges that Beverly Enterprises' policy of providing modified duty only to employees who are injured on the job has a disparate impact on pregnant employees. Spivey has failed to present any statistical evidence to demonstrate that Beverly Enterprises' policy in practice has a disproportionate impact on pregnant employees.

Spivey must produce competent evidence showing that termination because of Beverly Enterprises' modified duty policy falls disproportionately on pregnant employees. Spivey has failed to offer any evidence at all that Beverly Enterprises' modified duty policy results in a disproportionate termination of

pregnant employees. The District court was therefore correct to conclude that Spivey had failed to establish a claim of disparate impact discrimination.

Decision. As long as an employer treats similarly temporarily disabled employees equally, pregnancy does not require special accommodations. The district court's grant of summary judgment for defendant on all of plaintiff's claims was affirmed.

CASE QUESTIONS

Critical Legal Thinking. Should the employer have been required to provide an accommodation to Spivey?

Business Ethics. Was the court's decision fair and just in your opinion?

Contemporary Business. Should pregnant employees be given preferential treatment? If so, how much preferential treatment should they be given?

Focus on Ethics
Pregnancy Discrimination Act

The **PDA** amended Title VII to provide that discrimination because of sex includes discrimination "because of or on the basis of pregnancy, childbirth, or related medical conditions." The question in many cases concerns what rights the PDA protects. Consider the following case.

Cheryl Hall worked for Nalco Company for six years as a sales secretary in the company's Chicago-area office. Hall requested a leave of absence to undergo in vitro fertilization (IVF). IVF is an assisted reproduction technology that involves administration of fertility drugs to the woman, surgical extraction of her eggs, fertilization of the eggs in a laboratory, and surgical implantation of the resulting embryos into the woman's womb. Each IVF treatment takes weeks to complete and multiple treatments are sometimes needed to achieve a successful pregnancy.

The company approved Hall's leave from March 24 to April 21 for IVF treatment. After Hall returned to work, she informed the company that the first procedure had been unsuccessful and that she intended to undergo IVF again. She filed for another leave of absence to begin August 18. Nalco began a reorganization that led to the consolidation of two Chicago offices. Hall's manager told her that only one sales secretary would be retained and that Hall was being dismissed and the other sales secretary was being retained. The manager told Hall that her termination "was in her best interest due to her health condition." Nalco's employee-relations manager had noted in Hall's file "Absenteeism — infertility treatment."

Hall filed a discrimination charge with the EEOC and then filed a lawsuit in U.S. district court against Nalco alleging sex discrimination in violation of Title VII. Hall specifically alleged that her termination violated the Pregnancy Discrimination Act. The U.S. district court granted summary judgment for Nalco on the ground that infertile women are not a protected class under the PDA because infertility is a gender-neutral condition. Hall appealed. The U.S. court of appeals reversed, stating:

> *Employees terminated for taking time off to undergo IVF — just like those terminated for taking time off to give birth or receive other pregnancy-related care — will always be women. This is necessarily so; IVF is one of several assisted reproductive technologies that involve a surgical impregnation procedure. Thus, contrary to the district court's conclusion, Hall was terminated not for the gender-neutral condition of infertility, but rather for the gender-specific quality of childbearing capacity. The court of appeals held that Hall had stated a cognizable sex-discrimination claim under the PDA, reversed the district court's grant of summary judgment for Nalco, and remanded the case for a jury to decide.*[12]

Ethics Questions

1. What effect do you think the PDA has had on the number of claims filed for pregnancy discrimination in employment?
2. Based on the facts of this case, do you think Nalco acted ethically in this case? If not, prepare a written employment policy on the subject.
3. If you were a juror, how would you decide this case?

Sex-Plus Discrimination

The following U.S. Supreme Court decision was one of the first sex discrimination decisions issued by the Court. The Supreme Court considered whether an employer could refuse to hire women who were parents of preschool-age children.

CASE 11.4

GENDER DISCRIMINATION INCLUDES RELIANCE ON STEREOTYPES BASED ON FAMILY RESPONSIBILITIES

PHILLIPS V. MARTIN MARIETTA CORP.

400 U.S. 352 (1971)

Supreme Court of the United States

Facts. Martin Marietta Corporation denied employment to Mrs. Ida Phillips because the company did not accept applications from women with preschool-age children. The company did employ men with preschool-age children. Phillips sued the company for sex discrimination. The federal district court granted summary judgment against her. The Fifth Circuit Court of Appeals affirmed the judgment. The Supreme Court granted *certiorari.*

Issue. Does gender discrimination include employers' stereotypical presumptions about the work habits of mothers with preschool-age children?

Language of the Court. Per Curiam opinion. **Section 703 (a) of the Civil Rights Act of 1964 requires that persons of like qualifications be given employment opportunities irrespective of their sex. The Court of Appeals therefore erred in reading this section as permitting one hiring policy for women and another for men — each having pre-school-age children. The existence of such conflicting family obligations, if demonstrably more relevant to job performance for a woman than for a man, could arguably be a basis for distinction under §703 (e) of the Act. But that is a matter of evidence tending to show that the condition in question "is a bona fide occupational qualification reasonably necessary to the normal operation of that particular business or enterprise." The record before us, however, is not adequate for resolution of these important issues. . . . Summary judgment was therefore improper and we remand for fuller development of the record and for further consideration.**

Decision. Yes. Individual applicants must be viewed on their own merits and not through stereotypes.

CASE QUESTIONS

Critical Legal Thinking. The purpose of Title VII is to ensure equality in employment opportunities. Even if Martin Marietta was factually correct that absenteeism is higher among women with preschool-age children, such discrimination is against the law. It is difficult to balance the demands of the workplace with the personal needs of mothers of young children. Do you agree with this decision?

Business Ethics. Do you think that the employer in this case could establish its defense under a bona fide occupational qualification (BFOQ)?

Contemporary Business. If you do not agree with this decision, what do you suggest would be a better approach for our society to take on this issue?

Other federal courts have recognized this theory of liability under **Title VII** as **"gender-plus"** or **"sex-plus" discrimination.** After the *Phillips* decision, federal courts have decided that **sex-plus discrimination** occurs when a person is subjected to employment discrimination based on gender and some other protected characteristic.[13] For example, a male employee who alleged that his employer discriminated against him because his spouse was pregnant was held to have standing to sue for discrimination because of sex. He contended that when the employer terminated him and his wife the same day, he was discriminated against because of sex due to his wife's **pregnancy.**[14]

Sex-Plus Discrimination
Employer policies or practices by which the employer treats employees unfairly on the basis of gender plus another characteristic, such as marital status, race, or age.

"Benevolent" discrimination stereotyping is a prohibited practice as the following case, *Automobile Workers v. Johnson Controls, Inc.*, holds. Adverse employment decisions based on **gender stereotypes** are sometimes well intentioned and may be perceived by the employer as being in the employee's best interest. For example, an employer might assume that a working mother would not want to relocate to another city, even if it would mean a promotion. Of course, adverse actions that are based on **sex stereotyping** violate Title VII, even if the employer is not acting out of hostility.

CASE 11.5

BENEVOLENT SEX DISCRIMINATION (FETAL PROTECTION) IS FORBIDDEN BY TITLE VII

AUTOMOBILE WORKERS V. JOHNSON CONTROLS, INC.

499 U.S. 187 (1991)

Supreme Court of the United States

Facts. Johnson Controls, Inc. manufactures batteries in which lead is a primary ingredient. Occupational exposure to lead includes the risk of fetal harm. In 1982, Johnson excluded women from jobs that exposed them to lead after testing showed their blood levels contained excessive amounts of lead. In 1984, a class action was filed challenging the fetal protection policy as sex discrimination. Mary Craig was among these women and chose to be sterilized to avoid losing her job. The federal district court granted summary judgment in favor of the employer on the business necessity defense, which the Seventh Circuit affirmed. Due to a conflict in rulings among the federal circuit courts of appeal, the Supreme Court granted *certiorari.*

Issue. In an attempt to protect fetuses from potential harm, may an employer discriminate against women solely because of their ability to become pregnant?

Language of the Court. Blackmun, J.: . . . **"The Pregnancy Discrimination Act has now made clear that, for all Title VII purposes, discrimination based on a woman's pregnancy is, on its face, discrimination because of her sex." (Citation omitted.) In its use of the words "capable of bearing children" . . . Johnson Controls explicitly classifies on the basis of potential for pregnancy. Under the PDA, such a classification must be regarded, for Title VII purposes, in the same light as explicit sex discrimination. Respondent has chosen to treat all its female employees as potentially pregnant; that choice evinces discrimination on the basis of sex.**

We hold that Johnson Controls' fetal-protection policy is sex discrimination forbidden under Title VII unless respondent can establish that sex is a "bona fide occupational qualification." . . . The wording of the BFOQ defense contains several terms of restriction that indicate that the exception reaches only special situations. The statute thus limits the situations in which discrimination is permissible to "certain instances" where sex discrimination is "reasonably necessary" to the "normal operation" of the "particular" business. Each one of these terms — certain, normal, particular — prevents the use of general subjective standards and favors an objective, verifiable requirement. But the most telling term is "occupational"; this indicates that these objective, verifiable requirements must concern job-related skills and aptitudes.

Johnson Controls argues that its fetal-protection policy falls within the so-called safety exception to the BFOQ. Our cases have stressed that discrimination on the basis of sex because of safety concerns is allowed only in narrow circumstances.

Our case law . . . makes clear that the safety exception is limited to instances in which sex or pregnancy actually interferes with the employee's ability to perform the job. This approach is consistent with the language of the BFOQ provision itself, for it suggests that permissible distinctions based on sex must relate to ability to perform the duties of the job. Johnson Controls suggests, however, that we expand the exception to allow fetal-protection policies that mandate particular standards for pregnant or fertile women. We decline to do so. Such an expansion contradicts not only the language of the BFOQ and the narrowness of its exception, but the plain language and history of the Pregnancy Discrimination Act.

The PDA's amendment to Title VII contains a BFOQ standard of its own: unless pregnant employees differ from others "in their ability or inability to work," they must be "treated the same" as other employees "for all employment-related purposes." This language clearly sets forth Congress' remedy for discrimination based on pregnancy and potential pregnancy. Women who are either pregnant or potentially pregnant must be treated like others "similar in their ability . . . to work." . . . In other words, women as capable of doing their jobs as their male counterparts may not be forced to choose between having a child and having a job.

We conclude that the language of both the BFOQ provision and the PDA which amended it, as well as the legislative history and the case law, prohibit an employer from discriminating against a woman because of her capacity to become pregnant unless her reproductive potential prevents her from performing the duties of her job.

It is no more appropriate for the courts than it is for individual employers to decide whether a woman's reproductive role is more important to herself and her family than her economic role. Congress has left this choice to the woman as hers to make.

The judgment of the Court of Appeals is reversed, and the case is remanded for further proceedings consistent with this opinion.

Decision. No. The PDA prohibits sex-specific fetal-protection policies.

CASE QUESTIONS

Critical Legal Thinking. If you were on the Supreme Court, how would you have decided this case? How much scientific evidence regarding the risk of harm to fetuses should have been presented in the record before the Court issued its decision?

Business Ethics. What is the role of an employer in protecting the health of its workers?

Contemporary Business. If the law of more than 40 states allows a child to sue for prenatal injuries from exposure to dangerous levels of lead, what steps should an employer take regarding its efforts to protect employees' reproductive health?

Sexual Favoritism
Title VII does not prohibit isolated instances of preferential treatment based on consensual romantic relationships. If an employee is coerced into sexual conduct, however, the situation can become quid pro quo harassment or constitute a sexually hostile work environment.

Focus on Ethics
Sexual Favoritism

As we learned in the chapter on sex discrimination, most *quid pro quo* sexual harassment cases involve conduct that is tantamount to extortion — i.e., an employee must choose between employment and sexual conduct with a supervisor. Can individuals lawfully use sex appeal to advance their employment prospects? Life experience suggests that the answer is "yes," as do some court opinions.

> ***Example:*** Seven male respiratory therapists employed by the Westchester County Medical Center sued their employer alleging that they had been discriminated against based on sex in violation of Title VII and the Equal Pay Act. They claimed that their department head adopted promotion standards designed to disqualify them and favor a female applicant with whom he was in an intimate relationship. Finding that both men and women would be equally disfavored in that process, the court found Title VII protects individuals from discrimination based on their gender, "not on his or her sexual affiliations."[15]

The distinction between *quid pro quo* and favoring a paramour is "the coercive nature of the employer's acts, rather than the fact of the relationship itself."[16]

Ethics Questions

1. What stereotypes of behavior and ability emerge in sexual favoritism cases? What should be the courts' approach to these issues?
2. Is the better test in sexual favoritism situations the one articulated in *Philips v. Martin Marietta Corp.*? That is, an employer's preferences for specific persons because of personal relationships with them may engender stereotyping and possible claims of sexual harassment.
3. To what extent should federal courts be involved in measuring the consensual nature of sexual relationships that seems to lead to favoritism?

Management Application
EEOC Policy Guidance for Workplace Discrimination Against Caregivers

In May 2007, the EEOC issued its federal policy to provide guidance with respect to employers' disparate treatment discrimination against caregivers.[17] The agency supplemented its policy statement two years later with a best-practices document to assist employers.[18] In part, the policy states:

- Women continue to be the primary caregiver in most families. Of course, workers' caregiving responsibilities are not limited to child care, and include many other forms of caregiving. An increasing proportion of caregiving goes to the elderly, and this trend will likely continue as the Baby Boomer population ages. As with child care, women are primarily responsible for caring for society's elderly, including care of parents, in-laws, and spouses. Unlike child care, however, elder-care responsibilities generally increase over time as the disabled ages, and elder care can be much less predictable than child care because of health crises that typically arise. As eldercare becomes more common, workers in the "sandwich generation," those between the ages of 30 and 60, are more likely to face work responsibilities alongside child-care and elder-care responsibilities.
- According to the most recent U.S. census, nearly a third of families have at least one family member with a disability, and about one in ten families with children under 18 includes a child with a disability. Of the men and women who provide care to relatives or other individuals with a disability, most are employed.
- While caregiving responsibilities disproportionately affect working women, their effects may be even more pronounced among some women of color, particularly African American women, who have a long history of working outside the home. African American mothers with young children are more likely to be employed, and both African American and Hispanic women are more likely to be raising children in a single-parent household than are white or Asian American women. Women of color also may devote more time to caring for members of the extended family, including both grandchildren and elderly relatives, than do their white counterparts.
- Although women are still responsible for a disproportionate share of family caregiving, men's role has increased. Between 1965 and 2003, the amount of time that men spent on child care nearly tripled, and men spent more than twice as long performing household chores in 2003 as they did in 1965. Working mothers are also increasingly relying on fathers as primary child-care providers.

As more mothers have entered the labor force, families have increasingly faced conflicts between work and family responsibilities, sometimes resulting in a "maternal wall" that limits the employment opportunities of workers with caregiving responsibilities. Lower-paid workers, who are disproportionately people of color, perhaps feel these conflicts most profoundly. Discipline or even discharge can occur when a worker violates an employer policy to address caregiving responsibilities and/or family crises.

The impact of work-family conflicts also extends to professional workers, contributing to the maternal wall or "glass ceiling" that prevents many women from advancing in their careers. As a recent EEOC report reflects, even though women constitute about half of the labor force, they are a much smaller proportion of managers and officials. The disparity is greatest at the highest levels in the business world, with women accounting for only 1.4 percent of Fortune 500 CEOs. Thus, one of the recommendations made by the federal Glass Ceiling Commission in 1995 was for organizations to adopt policies that allow workers to balance work and family responsibilities throughout their careers.

Employment decisions based on caregiver stereotypes violate the federal antidiscrimination statutes, even when an employer acts upon such stereotypes unconsciously or reflexively. As the Supreme Court has explained, "[W]e are beyond the day when an employer could evaluate employees by assuming or insisting that they match the stereotype associated with their group." Thus, for example, employment decisions based on stereotypes about working mothers are unlawful because "the antidiscrimination laws entitle individuals to be evaluated as individuals rather than as members of groups having certain average characteristics."

The EEOC policy has many illustrations of various circumstances under which discrimination against a worker with caregiving responsibilities constitutes unlawful disparate treatment under Title VII or the ADA. The EEOC stated that investigators would review the evidence of sex-based disparate treatment of female caregivers in reviewing evidence such as the following: the employer subjected women employees to less favorable treatment after they became pregnant or assumed caregiving responsibilities; and employers, based only on stereotypes of mothers or other female caregivers, treated female workers without children or other caregiving responsibilities more favorably than they did females who were caregivers.

In mixed-motive cases, the EEOC notes that an employer violates Title VII if the charging party's gender was a *motivating factor* in the challenged employment decision, regardless of whether the employer was also motivated by legitimate business reasons. However, when an employer proves it would have taken the same action even absent the discriminatory motive, the complaining employee will not be entitled to reinstatement, back pay, or damages.

Discussion Questions

1. What stereotypes come to mind when considering the situation of caregivers who must take time off from work to attend to others?
2. How difficult would it be for a caregiver to prove that the caregiver's gender was a motivating factor for an employment decision?
3. Does providing caregivers with flexible scheduling adequately address the issues presented by the need for frequent absences from work? What suggestions can you make for a "best practices" approach to the workplace trend of increasing numbers of workers with caregiver responsibilities?

Management Application
Sex-Plus Discrimination

Suzanne Guglietta sued her former employer Meredith Corporation for sex, pregnancy, and age discrimination in violation of Title VII. She alleged that while employed as a TV station producer, she took a maternity leave. On returning to work, she asked that she be assigned to a different shift to accommodate her child-care needs. Her employer refused to do so, and she was terminated. Guglietta claimed that the failure to provide the child-care accommodation was tantamount to "sex-plus" discrimination. The court held that the need for child care was not a "sex-plus" characteristic that could be considered along with her gender discrimination claim.[19]

Discussion Questions

1. How could Guglietta reply on the EEOC Guidelines in her court case? What would she have to prove to prevail?
2. Should sex-plus discrimination be formally recognized by courts as an ancillary form of discrimination based on a protected classification?
3. To address this commonly encountered issue, should Congress consider a more generous child-care tax credit?

Family Responsibility Discrimination

Despite its evolution as a theory of discrimination, the courts require that a race or gender-neutral claim of **family responsibility discrimination** would not state a claim under Title VII. In *Adamson v. Multi Community Diversified Services, Inc.*,[20] the district court dismissed a father's age discrimination claim. The decision was affirmed on appeal, including a claim of "familial status" discrimination. In so holding, the Tenth Circuit Court of Appeals stated "Title VII protects neither the family unit nor individual family members from discrimination based on their 'familial status' alone. . . . 'Familial status' is not a classification based on sex any more than is being a sibling' or 'relative' generally. It is, by definition, gender neutral. The use of gender to parse those classifications into subcategories of 'husbands, wives, and daughters' is a social and linguistic convention that neither alters this fact nor elevates those subcategories to protected status."[21] Unless there is a **Title VII** protected classification at issue or a "serious" health issue under the **FMLA** is involved, **family responsibilities discrimination** will not lie. As noted in the EEOC Guidance stated above, the federal EEO laws do not prohibit discrimination against caregivers *per se*. Only Alaska and the District of Columbia have outlawed family responsibility discrimination.

Caregivers
Federal EEO statutes do not prohibit discrimination based solely on parental or other caregiver status. If discrimination is based on a related characteristic, such as sex or race, protection may be afforded the employee.

Family Responsibility Discrimination
Disparate treatment against employees based on their responsibilities to care for family members, such as children or aging parents. Not prohibited under Title VII.

Marital Status Discrimination

The EEOC has found unlawful any employment practice that forbids or restricts the employment of married women if that rule is not also applicable to married men.[22] For example, if marital status is relevant to a position, then it must be evenly applied when making employment decisions. The EEOC will not permit enforcement of a rule requiring all females to resign upon marriage where no such rule is imposed on male employees.[23] Many states protect persons from marital status discrimination regardless of gender. It is important for the employer to be familiar with state law as well as federal law relating to employment discrimination.

ADA-Associational Discrimination

Some employees have suffered discrimination due to their association or relationship with a family member with an ADA-recognized disability. The ADA expressly prohibits discrimination against employees based on their known association or relationship with a disabled person, including a child or family member.[24]

Associational Discrimination
Discrimination or retaliation against employees based on their association with members of classes protected under Title VII, such as the caregiver for a disabled person.

> ***Example:*** An employer is interviewing applicants for a computer programmer position. The employer determines that one of the applicants, Arnold, is the best qualified, but the employer is reluctant to hire him because he disclosed during the interview that he is a divorced father and has sole custody of his disabled son. Because the employer concludes that Arnold's caregiving responsibilities for a disabled son may have a negative effect on his attendance and work performance, it decides to offer the position to the second-best qualified candidate and encourages Arnold to apply for any future openings if his caregiving responsibilities change. Under the circumstances, the employer has violated the ADA by refusing to hire Arnold because of his association with a disabled individual.[25]

Appearance-Based Discrimination

Appearance-Based Discrimination
Image-based discrimination relating to preferences or rules regulating an employee's personal appearance.

Few jurisdictions within the United States have addressed **appearance-based discrimination**. With the exception of these few circumstances, employers are free to discriminate against the unattractive person. While France protects discrimination based on physical appearance,[26] only two U.S. jurisdictions prohibit the practice. A District of Columbia ordinance prohibits employment discrimination based on "personal appearance." The ordinance defines the term *personal appearance* as "the outward appearance of any person, irrespective of sex, with regard to bodily condition or characteristics, manner or style of dress, and manner or style of personal grooming, including but not limited to, hair style and beards."[27] A Santa Cruz, California, municipal ordinance prohibits discrimination based on "physical characteristics," defined as "a bodily condition or characteristic of any person which is from birth, accident, or disease, or from any natural physical development, or any event outside the control of that person including individual physical mannerisms."[28] While other statutes address discrimination based on height or weight, these two ordinances appear unique among jurisdictions in addressing appearance more generally. The few cases that have considered these ordinances pose interesting problems for employers and courts.

> ***Example:*** The D.C. Commission on Human Rights found Atlantic Richfield (ARCO) had constructively discharged Elisa Janitis because of her personal appearance. The Commission awarded Janitis damages for back pay, compensatory damages, and court costs. Janitis wore her low-cut blouses very tight, causing buttons to pop open and show cleavage. She was criticized by her female superior for wearing the low-cut blouses, for sitting with her legs open, and for other suggestive office conduct. ARCO appealed and a federal court affirmed that Janitis had been the victim of **personal appearance discrimination.**[29] If the holding in this case were uniformly adopted by other courts across the nation, it would be very difficult for an employer to enforce a dress code at work or avoid hostile work environment sexual harassment claims.

Mere unattractiveness is not a protected characteristic as a "disability" within the meaning of the ADA. However, severe obesity has been qualified by the EEOC as a disability under that act. Physical and mental conditions related to the obese condition would be covered under the ADA. Deciding whether an employee's physical appearance is related to "impairment" within the protection of the ADA is a fact-based analysis.

Rights of Service Members and Their Families

The year 1994 ushered in the policy of maintaining the all-volunteer armed forces. No longer relying on involuntary conscription of men, the U.S. adopted a human resource policy consisting of three groups: (1) career uniformed service people, (2) noncareer full-time enlisted and officer personnel, and (3) the Reserves. The Reserve service includes active and inactive duty for training, full-time National Guard duty, and duty performed by intermittent disaster response personnel for the Public Health Service. The uniformed services consist of the Army, Navy, Marine Corps, Air Force, and Coast Guard and their respective reserve units, the Army National Guard or Air National Guard and the commissioned corps of the Public Health Service. In 1994, Congress enacted the **Uniform Services Employment and Reemployment Rights Act of 1994 (USERRA).**[30] It expands on the Vietnam Era Veterans' Readjustment Assistance Acts of 1972 and 1974 to include post–Vietnam War veterans. It requires federal contractors to undertake affirmative action to employ qualified special disabled veterans. The scope of the obligation requires that such contractors and their subcontractors not discriminate against disabled veterans applying for positions for which they are qualified.

The purpose of the **USERRA** is to protect the civilian jobs of members of the uniformed services following the completion of their service commitment. The law prohibits discrimination by employers with regard to employment or reemployment based on military service. The ban is broad and extends to most areas of employment, including hiring, promotion, reemployment, termination, and benefits. It is unlawful for an employer to deny a military leave of absence. The act states that:

1. *all employees of all employers are covered* by the **USERRA**;
2. in the absence of military necessity, the employee gives the employer oral or written notice of the need to serve;
3. employees are entitled to reemployment following up to five years of cumulative absence (with exceptions relating to special operational programs and missions);
4. the employee separation from the service must be under honorable conditions;
5. service members must report more or less immediately following service of less than 31 days and within 90 days of discharge when the service period exceeds 180 days; and
6. service members injured or disabled during service are allowed up to two years to return to their jobs.

Example: A court broadly read the **USERRA** to protect an employee who claimed he was not hired because his military service precluded him from starting work as a police patrol officer on the date required by the City of Somerville, Massachusetts. Before receiving a job offer, he enlisted in the U.S. Army for a term that would last until after his start date. The City refused to hire him because he would not be finished with his service commitment in time to attend the police academy.[31]

USERRA
This 1994 federal law applies to U.S. employers, requiring them to reemploy returning service members in the jobs they would have attained had they not been on active duty, including the same seniority, status, pay, and benefits.

The employer may require documentation relating to the period of service. The returning employee must be treated as if military leave was not taken. The individual must be returned to the same job he or she would have held but for the military service. The returning employee must be credited with seniority and extended other rights and benefits held on the date of the military leave departure. A potential problem confronting employers is providing veterans with timely reemployment when their former positions have been filled. Congress attempted to provide some guidance about when the employer's obligation to rehire may be excused or modified. The exceptions are:

1. if the employer's circumstances have so changed as to make such rehiring impossible or unreasonable; however, the employer must undertake reasonable efforts to train or otherwise qualify a returning veteran within the organization or otherwise place the veteran within the organization at the best available position;

2. when accommodating former employees who have been disabled (or whose disabilities have been aggravated) while in the service would create an undue hardship upon the employer; however, the employer has the obligation to assign the position to a nearly equivalent position if one is available with the same compensation, status, and seniority; and
3. such former employees need not be rehired if they were temporary employees.

Employers are advised to check state statutes that may provide more expansive or additional relief to returning veterans. State service is often related to service in National Guard units related to disaster relief efforts, including fires, earthquakes, hurricanes, and floods.

> ***Example:*** While courts broadly construe the **USERRA** in favor of its military beneficiaries, a Naval Reserve officer lost her case for discrimination and retaliation when the company had reasonable grounds for its actions. The officer claimed the employer violated the act by changing her work schedule and ultimately terminating her. Both before her deployment and after her return to work at a management consulting firm, the officer had had a history of professional misbehavior. She could not rely on the act to protect her from adverse action for an indefinite period. A federal court of appeals affirmed the district court's summary judgment order in favor of the employer because the officer had not been treated differently from other employees and the company had reinstated her properly.[32]

USERRA created an administrative procedure to enforce its provisions. A worker will claim a denial of **USERRA** rights by filing a complaint with the secretary of labor, who is charged with the duty to investigate, although exhausting this remedy is not a requirement for a private sector employee. The employee may file suit without filing the claim. A federal employee's claims are adjudicated before the Merit Systems Protection Board and appeal from such a determination is made to the U.S. Court of Appeals for the Federal Circuit. Regardless of the type of employer, a court may order the employer to comply with the act and award back pay and front pay as well as an additional amount for liquidated damages for willful employer violations of the act. The statute prohibits the award of fees or court costs against a plaintiff, but it authorizes an award of attorneys' fees, expert witness fees, and litigation costs if the plaintiff wins his or her case.[33]

Concept Summary
Proving USERRA Discrimination

A USERRA discrimination case is handled differently than cases under Title VII. The claimant must prove:

- military service was a "substantial or motivating factor" in an adverse employment action (the burden then shifts to the employer); and
- the employer must prove it would have taken the adverse action against the employee regardless of the plaintiff's protected military status.

In a USERRA case, the claimant need not prove that the employer's stated reason was a pretext. This makes a USERRA more likely to survive a motion for summary judgment, leading to trial before a jury.

Genetic Discrimination Laws

Until 2008, when Congress enacted a specific antidiscrimination law protecting an individual from misuse of genetic information, only a handful of federal protections applied to genetics. **Genetic discrimination** occurs when an employer or an insurance company treats an individual differently because of a gene mutation that causes or increases the risk of an inherited disorder. Employers and insurance carriers may routinely maintain in a person's medical records results of genetic testing the public disclosure of which could result in discrimination against the individual.

Constitutional Protection

It may be argued that the federal Constitution protects against **genetic discrimination** under the Equal Protection clause and under the right to privacy. Personal medical and/ or genetic information may be so protected. The argument would be based on the Supreme Court decision in *Griswold v. Connecticut*,[34] in which the Court recognized a fundamental right to privacy. At least one court has held that an employee has a protected privacy right interest with respect to personal information concerning a medical condition. A medical doctor claimed his current employer improperly disclosed to his prospective employer the presence of sickle-cell anemia, which resulted in the loss of a job offer.[35]

Americans with Disabilities Act

The **ADA** prohibits discrimination against a person who is regarded as having a disability. Employees with symptomatic genetic disabilities or unexpressed genetic conditions are protected under this act. The **ADA** does not protect potential workers from employers' requests for **genetic information** after a conditional offer of employment has been made. Moreover, the **ADA** does not protect workers from requirements to protect job-related medical information, consistent with business necessity.

Health Insurance Portability and Accountability Act

In 1996, Congress enacted the Health Insurance Portability and Accountability Act (HIPAA) to protect insurance coverage for workers and their families with regard to job changes, to establish a national set of standards for electronic health care transactions, and to ensure patient privacy regarding information in medical records. The **HIPAA** regulations prohibit group health plans from using any factor related to health status, including genetic information, as a basis for determining insurance eligibility or for increasing premiums. For preexisting conditions, the act limits exclusions in employee group health plans to 12 months and prohibits such exclusions if the individual has been covered previously for that condition for 12 months or more. However, **HIPAA** does not prohibit employers from refusing to offer health coverage to employees.

Title VII

Employees suffering from a genetic disorder "racially or ethnically linked to race or ethnicity" may claim protections from discrimination based on race or national origin.

Examples would include sickle cell disease, occurring predominately among African Americans; breast or prostate cancer, afflicting women and men, respectively; and Tay-Sachs disease, occurring predominately among Ashkenazi Jews. Taken as a whole, relatively few genetic conditions or disorders have a strong connection with a racial or ethnic group. As such, Title VII offers only limited scope of potential coverage for such conditions.

Title VII offers limited legal authority protection from genetic testing. One federal court of appeals has considered the claims of a group of Lawrence Laboratory employees working for the University of California, Berkeley. The plaintiffs sued under Title VII for medical examinations administered to nonwhites and women but not to whites or men. At various times, the tests included tests for genetic markers for sickle cell anemia and for nongenetic conditions such as venereal disease and pregnancy. The Ninth Circuit held in *Norman-Bloodshaw v. Lawrence Berkeley Laboratories*[36] that the lab had violated Title VII because of the conditions under which the tests had been administered.

Genetic Information Nondiscrimination Act of 2008

GINA
The Genetic Information Nondiscrimination Act of 2008 (GINA) is a federal law making it illegal for health insurers to deny an individual coverage or to charge him or her a higher rate or premium based solely on the individual's genetic predisposition to develop a disease in the future.

In 2000, President Clinton issued an executive order that prohibited discrimination in federal executive branch employment because of protected genetic information. Federal applicants and employees in the executive branch who believed that a department or agency had violated the executive order could make a claim under §503 of the Rehabilitation Act. However, since the act extended only to federal executive branch employment, it did not address the majority of the nation's employees.

Previously, a multiagency federal report identified the need for a federal law protecting individuals from genetic discrimination in the private sector. The report noted that individuals might be denied jobs or benefits because they possess particular genetic traits—even if that trait had no bearing on the applicants' ability to do the job. In addition, since some genetic traits are found more frequently in specific racial or ethnic groups, such discrimination could disproportionately affect those groups. Surveys showed that individuals and health professionals were increasingly concerned about the misuse of genetic information. The report indicated that, unless prohibited by law, two types of genetic testing could occur in the workplace: genetic screening and genetic monitoring. Genetic screening examines the genetic makeup of employees or applicants for specific inherited traits (e.g., screening for sickle cell anemia among African Americans). Genetic monitoring determines if a change has occurred over time in an individual's genetic material due to workplace exposure to hazardous substances. The report concluded that the effort to restrict the use of genetic information in the workplace promotes the larger ethical, legal, and social foundations upon which earlier civil rights legislation rests.[37]

These concerns caused Congress to enact the **Genetic Information Nondiscrimination Act of 2008 (GINA)**.[38] Congress made several findings, among them the following:

> Federal law addressing genetic discrimination in health insurance and employment is incomplete in both the scope and depth of its protections. Moreover, while many states

> have enacted some type of genetic non-discrimination law, these laws vary widely with respect to their approach, application, and level of protection. Congress has collected substantial evidence that the American public and the medical community find the existing patchwork of State and Federal laws to be confusing and inadequate to protect them from discrimination. Therefore, federal legislation establishing a national and uniform basic standard is necessary to fully protect the public from discrimination and allay their concerns about the potential for discrimination, thereby allowing individuals to take advantage of genetic testing, technologies, research, and new therapies.

HIPAA was an incomplete solution to these concerns. That law guarantees the privacy of an individual's bona fide medical information. **GINA**'s passage meant that employers and health insurers could not use **genetic information** obtained through screening tests to discriminate against an employee or insurance applicant. Prior to its passage, the main opponents to **GINA** were members of the insurance industry.

"Genetic testing" is broadly defined under the act and includes an analysis of human DNA, RNA, chromosomes, proteins, or metabolites that detect genotypes, mutations, or chromosomal changes. Routine medical procedures such as blood counts, cholesterol tests, and liver function tests are permitted and are not protected under **GINA**. Also excluded from the act are analyses of infectious agents such as bacteria, viruses, and fungi.

> ***Example:*** An employer may not use **genetic information** to make decisions regarding hiring, firing, promoting, or placing an individual within the organization. However, GINA would not cover an HIV test because HIV is not DNA and testing for its presence does not constitute a genetic test under the **GINA** definition.

"Genetic information" includes information about:

- a person's "genetic tests";
- **"genetic tests"** of a person's family members (up to and including fourth-degree relatives);
- any manifestation of a disease or disorder in a family member; and
- participation of a person or family member in research that includes **genetic testing**, counseling, or education.

"Genetic information" does not include information about sex or age, both of which constitute independently protected statuses.

This act makes it unlawful for employers, labor organizations and training programs, and employment agencies to:

> [F]ail or refuse to hire, or to discharge, any employee, or otherwise to discriminate against any employee with respect to the compensation, terms, conditions of employment of the employee because of genetic information with respect to the employee; or,
>
> Limit, segregate, or classify the employees of an employer in any way that would deprive or tend to deprive any employee of employment opportunities or otherwise adversely affect the status of the employee as an employee because of **genetic information** with respect to the employee.

GINA also prohibits retaliation against an individual for opposing an unlawful genetic discrimination practice or for testifying, assisting, or participating in a related investigation.[39] The act bans discrimination by a group health plan and the health insurer against individuals based on **genetic information.** It also prohibits employers and insurers from requiring **genetic tests** from an individual or his or her family.

The act includes certain exceptions that allow an employer to possess otherwise prohibited information:

- where the request was inadvertent;
- where health or genetic services are offered by the employer under a bona fide employee wellness program and: (a) the employee provides voluntary written consent, (b) only the employee and the licensed health care professional receive the information, and (c) information is not disclosed to the employer in a way that would identify any specific employee;
- where required by the certification provision of **FMLA** or corresponding state medical leave laws;
- where the employee's family medical history is available through commercially and publicly available documents, such as magazines and newspapers; or
- where information is to be used to monitor the effect of hazardous substances in the workplace, but only if: (a) the employer provides advance written notice to the employee, (b) the employee consents, (c) the monitoring is required by law, (d) the employee is informed of the specific results, and (e) the employer receives the information in any way that does not disclose the identity of the specific employee.

GINA mandates that if, through inadvertent disclosure to it, the employer possesses genetic information on an employee or applicant through no fault of its own, then the employer must:

- maintain the information in files separate and apart from other files;
- treat the information as a confidential medical record; and
- prohibit disclosure, unless made:
  - to the employee on his or her request,
  - to an occupational or other health researcher,
  - upon court order,
  - to a government official investigating compliance with **GINA**, or
  - in connection with the employee's compliance with the certification provisions of the **FMLA.**

The law is enforced by the EEOC in the same manner as a **Title VII** violation. However, unlike **Title VII, GINA** specifically states that "disparate impact" claims are not cognizable under **GINA.**[40]

As of the date of publication, no genetic-employment discrimination decisions have been issued by U.S. or state courts. However, in 2001 the EEOC settled a lawsuit against Burlington Northern Santa Fe Railroad for secretly testing its employees for a rare genetic condition that causes carpal tunnel syndrome as one of its many symptoms. The EEOC argued that the employer's testing protocols were unlawful under the ADA because they were not job related.

Concept Summary GINA

GINA:

- applies to all employers covered under Title VII;
- prohibits the use of genetic information to deny employment or insurance coverage;
- ensures that genetic test results are kept private; and
- prevents an insurer from basing eligibility or premiums on genetic information.

What GINA Does Not Cover

While many specific areas of workplace genetic discrimination are addressed in **GINA**, the act does not cover all relevant practices or concerns. For example, Gina does not

- prevent health care providers from recommending genetic tests to their patients;
- mandate coverage for particular tests or treatments;
- prohibit medical underwriting (i.e., issuance and pricing of health insurance policies) based on current health status;
- cover life, disability, or long-term care insurance;
- apply to members of the military; or
- preempt state laws.

Three federal agencies — the Internal Revenue Service, Department of Labor, and Department of Health and Human Services — have issued joint **GINA** regulations that became effective in December 2009. In general, these regulations prohibit health plans from discriminating against covered individuals based on genetic information. Health insurance companies may not use genetic information to make eligibility, coverage, underwriting, or premium-setting decisions. They may not request or require individuals or their family members to undergo genetic testing or to provide genetic information. However, health insurers may request genetic information where coverage of a particular claim would only be appropriate in the presence of a known genetic risk. Insurers may also request (but not require) a voluntary genetic test in the context of the carrier's collaboration in medical research. The EEOC is expected to issue final regulations as well.

Protection Afforded Under State and Local Laws

Wisconsin was the first state to ban genetic testing and discrimination in the workplace in 1991. Laws against **genetic discrimination** in the workplace are now in effect in 34 states and the District of Columbia. According to the National Conference of State Legislatures, "all of them prohibit discrimination based on the results of genetic tests; many extend the protections to inherited characteristics, and some include test results of family members, family history, and information about genetic testing. . . . Most states also restrict employer access to genetic information. . . . Some states may also make exceptions to statutory requirements, if, for example, genetic information may identify individuals who may be a safety risk in the workplace."[41]

GINA does not preempt state and local laws that offer more extensive genetic information discrimination protection. The typical state law targets health insurance plans by making it illegal to use genetic information to determine eligibility or to set premiums, require applicant testing, or make unauthorized disclosures. Some states allow consensual genetic testing, but the exception is limited in that the consent must be "informed" and must relate to a BFOQ. Some states have comprehensive prohibitions against genetic testing, including Oregon,[42] New Hampshire,[43] and New York.[44]

Minnesota offers the broadest form of state protection for genetic information in employment. Its statute, Minn. Rev. Statute 181.974, states:

181.974 Genetic Testing in Employment

Subdivision 1. **Definitions.**

For the purposes of this section, the following terms have the meanings given them in this subdivision.

(a) "Genetic test" means the analysis of human DNA, RNA, chromosomes, proteins, or certain metabolites in order to detect disease-related genotypes or mutations. Tests for metabolites fall within the definition of genetic test when an excess or deficiency of the metabolites indicates the presence of a mutation or mutations. Administration of metabolic tests by an employer or employment agency that are not intended to reveal the presence of a mutation does not violate this section, regardless of the results of the tests. Test results revealing a mutation are, however, subject to this section.

(b) "Employer" means any person having one or more employees in Minnesota, and includes the state and any political subdivisions of the state.

(c) "Employee" means a person who performs services for hire in Minnesota for an employer, but does not include independent contractors.

(d) "Protected genetic information" means:

(1) information about a person's genetic test; or

(2) information about a genetic test of a blood relative of a person.

Subd. 2. **Use of protected genetic information prohibited.**

(a) No employer or employment agency shall directly or indirectly:

(1) administer a genetic test or request, require, or collect protected genetic information regarding a person as a condition of employment; or

(2) affect the terms or conditions of employment or terminate the employment of any person based on protected genetic information.

(b) No person shall provide or interpret for any employer or employment agency protected genetic information on a current or prospective employee.

Subd. 3. **Penalties.**

Any person aggrieved by a violation of this section may bring a civil action, in which the court may award:

(1) up to three times the actual damages suffered due to the violation;

(2) punitive damages;

(3) reasonable costs and attorney fees; and

(4) injunctive or other equitable relief as the court may deem appropriate.

Minnesota's neighbor state, South Dakota, provides for a cause of action against an employer who engages in a wrongful use of genetic information with respect to an employee or applicant. South Dakota law states:

> 60-2-20. Use of genetic information in employment practices prohibited—Exceptions—Action for damages. It is an unlawful employment practice for an employer to seek to obtain, to obtain, or to use genetic information, as defined in §60-2-21, of an employee or a prospective employee to distinguish between or discriminate against employees or prospective employees or restrict any right or benefit otherwise due or available to an employee or a prospective employee. However, it is not an unlawful employment practice for an employer to seek to obtain, to obtain, or to use genetic information if:
>
> (1) The employer is a law enforcement agency conducting a criminal investigation; or
>
> (2) The employer relies on the test results from genetic information obtained by law enforcement through a criminal investigation, the employer legally acquires the test results, the employer keeps the test results confidential except as otherwise required by law, and the employer uses the test results for the limited purpose of taking disciplinary action against the employee based only on the alleged misconduct.
>
> Any employee or prospective employee claiming to be aggrieved by this unlawful employment practice may bring a civil suit for damages in circuit court. The court may award reasonable attorney fees and costs in addition to any judgment awarded to the employee or prospective employee.
>
> 60-2-21. "Genetic information" defined. For the purposes of §60-2-20, genetic information is information about genes, gene products, and inherited characteristics that may derive from the individual or a family member. This includes information regarding carrier status and information derived from laboratory tests that identify mutations in specific genes or chromosomes, physical medical examinations, family histories, and direct analysis of genes or chromosomes.

Human Resource Form
Unpaid FMLA Leave Request

Employee's Name: ______________

Date of Request: ______________

The undersigned employee requests a leave of absence to begin on ______________ and to end on ______________ for the following reason[s]:

1. ______________ the birth of my child, ______________ the placement of a child with me for adoption or foster care;

2. ______________ a serious health condition affecting my ______________ spouse, ______________ child, ______________ parent for which I am required to provide care; or,

3. ____________ a serious health condition that makes me unable to perform one of more of the essential functions of my job.

A "serious health condition" means an illness, injury, impairment, or mental condition that in the case of family leaves requires that you are needed to care for your family member or in the case of medical leave makes you unable to perform the essential functions of the job and which in all situations involves:

(1) a period of incapacity or treatment in connection with, or consequent to, inpatient care (i.e., an overnight stay) in a hospital, hospice, or residential medical care facility;

(2) a period of incapacity requiring absence from work, school, or other regular daily activities of more than 3 calendar days, which also involves continuing treatment by (or under the supervision of) a health care provider; or

(3) the continuing treatment by a health care provider for:

- **(a)** a period of incapacity due to pregnancy or prenatal care;
- **(b)** a period of incapacity or treatment for such incapacity due to a chronic serious health condition;
- **(c)** a period of incapacity that is permanent or long term due to a condition for which treatment may not be effective; or
- **(d)** a period of absence to receive multiple treatments by a health care provider either for restorative surgery after an accident or for a condition that would likely result in a period of incapacity of more than three consecutive calendar days.

The following is only a summary of your rights to take a leave of absence. You are required to consult with the company human resources department who will provide you with a complete oral and written explanation of your benefit. You are eligible for family or medical leave only if you have been employed by the company for at least 12 months and have completed at least 1,250 hours of service in the 12-month period immediately prior to your request for the leave of absence. You are entitled to up to 12 weeks of family and medical leave, in total, in the 12-month period measured backward from the date you previously used either family leave or medical leave. For any type of family or medical leave, if you have any unused vacation, sick, or personal days when you begin your unpaid leave, the company requires you to substitute all of this paid time off for all or part of your unpaid leave of absence. However, the unpaid leave (both medical and family leave) and the paid time-off (vacation, sick, and personal days) used during the leave of absence, in total, may not exceed the maximum 12 weeks in the 12-month period.

We will request certification of the need for this request and may request recertification of your right to continue your leave during your absence from work. You may be available to take intermittent or reduced-schedule leave, and you may receive further information from the human resources department. Upon your return from your approved leave, you are entitled to the same position you held when your leave commenced, or an equivalent position with equivalent pay, benefits, and other terms and conditions of employment. If you fail to return to work following your leave, this failure to return will be treated as a voluntary termination of employment by you. The human resources department will provide you with further information on personal leaves of absence, notification requirements, and certifications.

If you are covered by the company's insurance plans, you must pay your share of insurance premiums during your unpaid family and medical leave. If you are on FMLA leave and your premium is more than 30 days late, your health insurance will be terminated. We will notify you in writing 15 days or more before your coverage will end.

Dated: ____________ ____________________

Employee's signature

Key Terms and Concepts

- Family and Medical Leave Act (FMLA)
- Serious health condition
- Pregnancy Discrimination Act (PDA)
- Pregnancy-related condition
- Benevolent discrimination
- Family-responsibilities discrimination
- Gender-plus or sex-plus discrimination
- Discrimination against caregivers
- ADA-associational discrimination
- Appearance-based discrimination
- Uniform Services Employment and Reemployment Rights Act of 1994 (USERRA)
- Health Insurance Portability and Accountability Act (HIPPA)
- Genetic discrimination
- Genetic information
- Genetic testing
- Genetic Information Nondiscrimination Act of 2008 (GINA)

Chapter Summary

- As the workforce is increasingly presented with divergent personal responsibilities that must be balanced with those of the workplace, employers must be sensitive to a new level of discrimination claims. If an employee is subjected to disparate treatment because of protected status (e.g., those within Title VII, as amended, the ADA, ADEA, USERRA, or otherwise) then that status combined with caregiving responsibilities may give rise to a civil rights violation and/or employment litigation claim.

- The PDA prohibits discrimination based on sex. The employer must treat persons with pregnancy-related conditions in the same manner as it treats persons with other medical conditions who have a similar ability to perform work.

- Sex discrimination can arise when the employer seeks to address operational disruptions caused by parents with preschool-age children who must be absent from work more frequently than other employees who do not have such caregiving responsibilities. In each case, the employer must treat such employees in the same manner as they would treat other employees and not take exception for or against those with caregiving responsibilities.

- The EEOC has issued new guidelines with respect to caregivers and notes that an employer can defend disparate treatment claims only if its adverse employment decision was founded on legitimate business reasons. If the decision is motivated by an improper factor, the employer has violated Title VII. The EEOC Guidelines on Discrimination against Caretakers provide that:
  - Treating female caregivers less favorably than male caregivers is unlawful sex discrimination under Title VII, even if the employer does not discriminate against women without caregiving responsibilities.
  - Females may not be treated less favorably based on the assumption that they will become caregivers.
  - Employment opportunities may not be denied to individuals based on assumptions that they will not be able to balance their work and family responsibilities or that they will not be committed to their jobs.
  - Employers should be careful to avoid mixed-motive decisions whereby gender-based stereotypes are combined with legitimate business reasons.
  - Sex stereotyping is forbidden even if it is done for benevolent reasons.

- Under the ADA, an employer may not discriminate against a qualified person because of that person's relationship with someone who has a disability.

- The FMLA entitles both male and female employees to take up to 12 weeks of unpaid leave in a 12-month period for any of the following: birth or adoption or foster care of a child or a serious health condition of the employee or his or her spouse, child, or parent. The employer must grant the family or medical leave to eligible employees, but it may require the use of any accrued vacation or sick leave towards the 12 weeks of leave. Twenty-six weeks of leave are extended to those who are caring for members of the armed services, National Guard, and Reserves who have been injured during active duty.

- USERRA prohibits discrimination against persons because of their service in the Armed Forces Reserve, the National Guard, or other uniformed services. USERRA prohibits an employer from denying any benefit of employment based on an individual's membership, application for membership, performance of service, application for service, or obligation for service in the uniformed services. USERRA also protects the right of veterans, reservists, National Guard members, and certain other members of the uniformed services to reclaim their civilian employment after military service or training.

- GINA prohibits employers from discharging, refusing to hire, or otherwise discriminating against employees based on genetic information. It also applies to labor unions and employment agencies. The act prohibits discrimination by group health plans and health insurers against individuals based on genetic information and prohibits insurers from requiring genetic tests. The law is enforced by the EEOC.

Online Student Support

- Loislaw legal research and writing assignments.
- Loislaw group projects and class presentations.
- Loislaw access, providing online research including up-to-date cases, statutes, rules, and regulations. Primary law for all 50 states and federal jurisdictions. Registration required for access to this resource.
- Practice questions, including sample true/false, multiple choice, and short answer questions to test your understanding of concepts.
- Additional human resource forms.
- Internet exercises.
- Blogs.
- Supplementary statutory and regulatory materials.

Case Problems

11.1 Phyllis Torbeck was an executive secretary at AHM, an Oklahoma City advertising agency. She was told the position would require some overtime. After becoming pregnant, Torbeck began to receive negative performance reviews and was unable to work the required overtime. AHM terminated her for insubordination because she refused to work overtime. After filing her claim with the agency, the EEOC sued AHM under the PDA. Who should win the case and why? (*EEOC v. Ackerman, Hood & McQueen, Inc.*, 956 F.2d 944 (10th Cir. 1992))

11.2 Does a person have to be pregnant to sue for pregnancy discrimination? Suzanne Kocak resigned as an obstetric nurse at a community hospital due to pregnancy complications. After delivering her child, she applied for a part-time position and was not hired. She claimed that the personnel manager at the time of her part-time application asked whether she was pregnant or intended to have more children. Kocak asserted that the manager later told her the decision was based on the complications caused by her past pregnancy. The defendant produced evidence that Kocak was not rehired because she was an unreliable employee and was avidly disliked by her peers. How should the federal district court rule on the defendant's motion for summary judgment on Kocak's PDA claim? (*Kocak v. Community Health Partners of Ohio, Inc.*, 400 F.3d 466 (2005))

11.3 General Dynamics terminated John Hodgens because he took what it viewed was unnecessary medical leave that was unprotected under the Family and Medical Leave Act. He took leave due to a heart problem that did not constitute a "serious health condition" disability under the ADA. Hodgens contended that his FMLA-protected absences were medically necessary and rendered him "unable to perform" his job. Does the FMLA protect an employee whose illness is not yet diagnosed and/or defined as a "serious health condition"? (*Hodgens v. General Dynamics Corporation*, 144 F.3d 151 (1st Cir. 1998))

11.4 Can the Baltimore Police Department enforce its policy of restricting the number of police officers, other than new recruits, who could join the reserves of the armed forces? The officer was not a member of a military reserve unit at the time of his hiring. He applied for permission from the department to join an active reserve unit but was placed on a waiting list because the department had set a limit on the number of officers able to join the reserves. He joined a Marine Corps reserve unit anyway. The department ordered him to remove himself from active military reserve status. If faced with dismissal for not doing so, what are the officer's legal rights, if any, under USERRA to join the reserves? (*Kolkhorst v. Tilghman*, 897 F.2d 1282 (4th Cir. 1990))

11.5 Clinton Robinson sued Morris Moore Chevrolet-Buick under USERRA claiming that he was improperly fired as a used car sales representative in retaliation for his absences from work due to fulfilling his obligations in the U.S. Army Reserves. Robinson claims that he "was selling well and had never been disciplined or counseled" prior to requesting time off for a mandatory Army physical. He alleged a chronology of events from which his military obligations may have been a motivating factor for his discharge. Morris Moore argued that Robinson would have been fired because he was frequently late to work, often left work without permission, and violated many other company rules. Morris Moore alleges it is entitled to judgment based on the "mixed-motive" rule of proof (i.e., that it had a legitimate business reason for the termination and did not rely on unlawful motivations for its decision). Under USERRA, should the court grant summary judgment (i.e., there is no conflict in the evidence such that the court can decide the case without a trial) or let the case go to trial? (*Robinson v. Morris Moore Chevrolet-Buick, Inc.*, 974 F.Supp. 571 (E.D. Tex. 1997))

End Notes

1. *http://www.eeoc.gov/policy/docs/caregiving.html.*
2. 29 U.S.C. 2601 *et seq.*, 29 C.F.R. Part 825, Subparts A-H.
3. 29 C.F.R. §825.303(b) (2009).
4. 29 C.F.R. 825.114.
5. Pub. Law 110-181 (2008).
6. 29 U.S.C. §216(b).
7. *Brown v. Nutrition Mgmt Srvcs Co.*, ________ F.Supp. 2d ______ (E.D. Pa. 2009).
8. *http://www.bls.gov/cps/wlf-databook2009.htm.*
9. Pub. Law 95-555 (1978).
10. *Doe v. C.A.R.S. Protection Plus, Inc.*, 527 F.3d 358 (3d Cir. 2008).
11. *Calabro v. Westchester BMW, Inc.*, 398 F.Supp. 2d 281 (S.D. N.Y. 2005).
12. *Hall v. Nalco Company*, 534 F.3d 644 (7th Cir. 2008).
13. *Derungs v. Wal-Mart Stores, Inc.*, 374 F.3d 428 (6th Cir. 2004).
14. *Nicol v. Imagematrix, Inc.*, 773 F.Supp. 802 (E.D. Va. 1991).
15. *DeCintio v. Westchester County Medical Center*, 807 F. 2d 304 (2d Cir. 1986).
16. Id. at 307.
17. *http://www.eeoc.gov/policy/docs/caregiving.html.*

18. *http://www.eeoc.gov/policy/docs/caregiver-best-practices.html.*
19. 301 F. Supp. 2d 209 (D. Conn. 2004).
20. 514 F.3d 1136 (10th Cir. 2008).
21. 514 F.3d at 1148.
22. 29 C.F.R. §1604.4.
23. *Sprogis v. United Air Lines, Inc.*, 444 F.2d 1194 (7th Cir. 1971).
24. 42 U.S.C. §12101.
25. *http://www.eeoc.gov/policy/docs/caregiving.html#ada.*
26. French Labor Code, Article L. 122-45 (1982).
27. D.C. Code Ann. §2-1402.11(a).
28. Santa Cruz, Ca. Mun. Code 9.83.01-13 (1992).
29. *Atlantic Richfield Co. v. D.C. Comm. on Human Rights*, 515 A.2d 1095 (D.C. App. 1986).
30. 38 U.S.C. §4301 *et seq.*
31. *McLain v. City of Somerville*, 424 F.Supp. 2d 329 (D. Mass. 2006).
32. *Francis v. Booz Allen & Hamilton*, 452 F.3d 299 (4th Cir. 2005).
33. 38 U.S.C. 4323(h)(2).
34. 381 U.S. 479 (1965).
35. *Fleming v. St. Univ. of N.Y.*, 502 F.Supp. 2d 324 (E.D.N.Y. 2007).
36. 135 F.3d 1260 (9th Cir. 1998).
37. National Institutes of Health, National Human Genome Research Institute, *http://www.genome.gov.*
38. Pub. L. No. 110-233, 122 Stat. 881 (2008).
39. Pub. L. No. 110-233, §207(f), 122 Stat. at 917.
40. §208, 122 Stat. at 917.
41. *http://www.ncsl.org/default.aspx?tabid=14279.*
42. Or. Rev. Stat. §659A.300(5).
43. N.H. Rev. Stat. Ann. 141:H-1.IV.
44. N.Y. Exec. Law §296 (McKinney 2005).

Part III
Employee Protections and Benefits

Chapter 12
Privacy in the Workplace

"Privacy is no longer a social norm." —Mark Zuckerberg, Facebook founder

Learning Objectives

1. Distinguish between constitutionally protected and common law expectations of privacy.
2. Identify the privacy rights of federal employees in the workplace.
3. Recognize the privacy rights of employees in the private sector.
4. State the most common forms of tortious invasions of privacy.
5. Identify and define what limitations on employers exist regarding specific information-gathering practices.
6. Understand the kinds of surveillance and monitoring an employer may conduct in the workplace.

Chapter Outline

- Introduction
- Overview of Employee Privacy Rights
- Workplace Application: Federal Right to Privacy Laws
- Collecting and Handling Employee Information
- Post-Hiring Medical and Physical Exams

Case 12.1 Borse v. Piece Goods Shop, Inc.

- Management Application: Employee Polygraphs
- Employee Searches and Investigations

Case 12.2 O'Connor v. Ortega

- Surveillance and Monitoring

Case 12.3 Smyth v. Pillsbury Company

Case 12.4 Vega-Rodriguez v. Puerto Rico Telephone Co.

- Eavesdropping as an Invasion of Privacy
- Focus on Ethics: Offensive E-Mails in the Workplace
- Protecting Private Information from Disclosure
- Employees' Rights to Privacy Inside and Outside the Workplace

Case 12.5 Grusendorf v. City of Oklahoma City

Case 12.6 Quon et al. v. Arch Wireless Operating Company, Inc.

- Privacy Rights of Union Members
- Local Ordinances and Regulations
- Focus on Ethics: The Inadvertent E-Mail
- Human Resource Form: Privacy Waivers

Chapter Opening scenario

John O'Brien was hired by Papa Gino's, a Boston area pizza chain, and promoted to area supervisor after nine years of employment. O'Brien then had a falling out with higher management. He contends that he was fired for failing to promote an employee under his supervision who was the son of one of his supervisors and godson to the president of Papa Gino's. The company contended that O'Brien was dismissed for poor performance and for illegal drug use, while he claimed he was forced to take a polygraph test under the threat of losing his job over the drug use rumors. The examiner's report from the polygraph test indicated that he believed O'Brien lied about using drugs. O'Brien was fired, and he sued for wrongful termination and invasion of privacy. As to the privacy claim, the company contends that O'Brien impliedly gave permission in his employment contract for the company to make whatever investigations it deemed necessary, including the polygraph examination. How should the court rule on O'Brien's claim against Papa Gino's?[1]

Introduction

We discussed pre-employment privacy issues in an earlier chapter. This chapter addresses the privacy practices and issues *after* the worker has been hired. We begin our examination of the right of privacy for current employees by reviewing what the term means within the workplace. We will then discuss how this right affects the collection and handling of employee information and what medical and physical examinations may take place. Employer searches and investigations, as well as surveillance and monitoring of employees on the job, will be reviewed. Finally, we will review what rights employers have to monitor and affect employee conduct outside the workplace. These are important issues to employees as they concern protecting the confidentiality of information in their personnel files, medical examination results, and their employer's ongoing surveillance and security practices. Also, employees have specific ideas of how far an employer may intrude on their non-workplace personal behaviors.

Individuals have the right to keep others from learning information about them. This interest must be balanced against the right of the employer to safely and legally manage its business. Federal legislation offers limited protection to federal employees. However, the law of privacy has remained confused and uneven in the private sector. The explosion of changes within the areas of technology and communication has created new legal issues surrounding expectations of privacy in the workplace.

Overview of Employee Privacy Rights

What Is Privacy?

The word ***"privacy"*** is often used without common agreement as to what it encompasses. At its heart, it is a personal and subjective condition touching on personal information and behavior. We highly value the notion of possessing information about ourselves that few, if any, other persons share. Many have sought to define **privacy**, but its interpretation must ultimately rest on legal rules defining individual rights.

The **Restatement (Second) of Torts, §205A** provides:

Restatement
A treatise by legal scholars addressing uncertainties as to the state of the law and indicating the common trend in understanding or the legal interpretation of an issue.

> *One who invades the right to privacy of another is subject to liability for the resulting harm to the interest of the other. The right to privacy is invaded by the unreasonable intrusion upon the seclusion of another.*

Social networking, microblogging, voicemail, e-mail, blogs, office intranets, text messaging, databases, and computer networks have become staples of our personal and business lives. Because of the pervasiveness of these technologies, claims of invasion of individual **privacy** are arising ever more frequently. The law is struggling to state how the employer's need to know about employee behavior should be balanced with the right of the individual to be left alone. Furthermore, organizations must collect and retain increasing amounts of information to comply with the demands for regulatory compliance. The government is interested in ensuring that such compliance occurs within parameters that safeguard national security interests.

Constitutional and Common Law Rights

Although the right to **privacy** is not expressly stated in the U.S. Constitution, the Supreme Court has determined a federal constitutional right to **privacy** in several individual rights cases. Beginning with its 1965 decision in *Griswold v. Connecticut*, 381 U.S. 479 (1965), the Supreme Court held that various guarantees of liberty stated in the Bill of Rights create zones of **privacy**. These constitutional guarantees prohibit intrusion into areas that must be the preserve of personal freedom. In his concurring opinion in the *Griswold* case, Justice Goldberg stated:

> *The protection guaranteed by the [Fourth and Fifth] Amendments is much broader in scope. The makers of our Constitution undertook to secure conditions favorable to the pursuit of happiness. They recognized the significance of man's spiritual nature, of his feelings and of his intellect. They knew that only a part of the pain, pleasure and satisfactions of life are to be found in material things. They sought to protect Americans in their beliefs, their thoughts, their emotions and their sensations. They conferred, as against the Government, the right to be let alone — the most comprehensive of rights and the right most valued by civilized men.*

Fundamental Rights
Court recognition of individual freedoms so essential to liberty that government may not intrude on them.

With this decision, federal courts recognized personal **privacy rights** in a variety of contexts, including reproductive rights, sexual histories, the right to be free of unreasonable testing and examination procedures, and unreasonable searches and seizures. These rights are among those which the law protects as **fundamental rights** guaranteed to each person even if not expressly stated in the U.S. Constitution.

The Supreme Court infers a federal constitutional **right to privacy** from various Bill of Rights protections and from the protections of the **Fourth** and **Fourteenth Amendments** of the Constitution. These two amendments provide, in part, that persons are to be free from unreasonable searches and seizures and from the taking of life, liberty, or property without due process and that they are to be accorded equal protection of the law. Under the **Fourth Amendment, privacy** rights apply only to the federal government and its employees and contractors. Any federally recognized **privacy protections** apply *only* when government action affects an individual's rights to **privacy**. Known as **"state action,"** the federal **privacy** laws *do not apply* to nongovernmental intrusions. They do not apply to intrusions by private employers. However, federal and state constitutional law applies in the context of private-sector workplace searches decided under **Fourth Amendment** principles.

State Action
Action by or on behalf of a governmental body that violates the civil rights or legal interests of a person.

Fourth Amendment
Relative to employment, this amendment protects a person's "reasonable expectation of privacy," including the right to be free from unreasonable searches and seizures by the government.

Equal Protection Clause
Part of the Fourteenth Amendment that affords persons equal protection of the law from state action.

By virtue of the **Due Process** and **Equal Protection clauses** of the U.S. Constitution, federal and state governments are prohibited from unreasonable governmental intrusion into personal rights. Prompted by its *Griswold* decision, the U.S. Supreme Court has expanded the scope of **privacy rights**, particularly in areas recognized in other portions of the Constitution, including freedom of speech and association.

The distinction between **state action** and private action is not always sharp. For example, drug and alcohol tests conducted by private employers to comply with government requirements have been found to be subject to the constitutional prohibition against undue searches and seizures. In one case, the federal government required railroads to ensure that blood and urine tests of certain employees were conducted following major train accidents. The railroads were private-sector employers. The Supreme Court held that the **Fourth Amendment** is applicable to those tests, which were mandated or authorized by federal regulations, especially because the results were shared with governmental regulators.[2] In another decision, a federal court of appeals held that employees working for a government contractor were protected by the **Fourth Amendment** with respect to drug testing.[3]

Federal and state employers must be aware that these constitutional protections afford the public employee expansive **privacy rights**. What is reasonable in one context may be found unreasonable and an **invasion of privacy** in another context. **Privacy rights** protected by the U.S. Constitution differ from **privacy** rights protected under state tort law. More than two dozen states have adopted constitutional provisions or enacted statutes that protect a person's right to **privacy**. Some state laws provide for a private cause of action for invasion of an individual's **privacy** interests.

Lacking specific state **privacy** laws to apply, state courts developed a tort theory of recovery for **invasion of privacy**. An employer held liable for committing a tort against an employee will be liable to that person for damages. Four distinct causes of action are recognized under the common heading of a tortious **invasion of privacy**. They have in common their basis in the individual's right to be left alone. Businesses encounter these theories in the employment context as well as in their relationships with third parties. They are:

- **Appropriating the name or likeness of another for one's own commercial use or benefit.**
  - *Example* Advertising copy, which requires waivers and releases for the commercial use of photographs or images of a person. An employer may use

an employee's likeness in its advertising only if it is incidental and not essential to the content.

- **Unreasonable intrusion into a person's private affairs or right to be left alone.**
  - ☐ ***Example*** Surveillance of a person in private places, nonconsensual examination of personal property or files, or eavesdropping. Lawsuits are frequently filed by employees against their employers for emotional distress damages arising from disclosure of personnel file information and medical histories and treatments.
  - ☐ In the typical case, the circumstances are viewed as an affront to one's dignity.[4]
- **Public disclosure of private facts about an individual.** This invasion involves publication of information that would be highly offensive to a reasonable person and is not of legitimate public interest.
  - ☐ ***Example*** A former employee could sue a former employer who posted an interoffice memo about the plaintiff's termination on a bulletin board visible to dozens of employees.[5]
- **Placing a person in a "false light" by unreasonable and highly objectionable publicity.** This tort requires that the wrongdoer had prior knowledge of its falsity or acted in reckless disregard as to the falsity of the matter and the false light in which the victim would be placed. This form of the tort is closely related to defamation. The usual case involves an invasion of **privacy** claim, which is defended by asserting the privilege of newsworthy publication.
  - ☐ ***Example*** A newspaper editorial alleging certain facts as true regarding a candidate for city council office, where the candidate is deemed a public figure. "If the publication does not proceed widely beyond the bounds of propriety and reason in disclosing facts about those closely related to an aspirant for public office, the compelling public interest in the unfettered dissemination of information will outweigh society's interest in preserving such individuals' right to privacy."[6]

Privacy rights as recognized by the U.S. Constitution differ from those **privacy rights** protected by tort law in two important ways. First, the privacy rights are based on very different theories of liability. Second, the constitutional approach protects individuals from governmental intrusions, while tort law primarily protects against **invasions of privacy** by private parties. The law was slow to recognize an individual's **right of privacy**. However, advances in science and technology and changing societal attitudes have compelled the law to recognize and protect it.

An **invasion of privacy** situation might arise within a contractual context. Employee handbooks and manuals become either express or implied contracts between the employer and the employee. Representations made that certain information respecting an employee will be held in confidence may result in a breach of contract action against the employer if that information is improperly disclosed. As will be discussed in the chapter on labor law, an employee represented by a union might not have an expectation of **privacy** in the workplace if such rights were waived in the collective bargaining agreement between the employer and the union. Those agreements may permit limited inspections and searches of the employee's property or provide for random drug testing to which, in a nonunion context, the employee might otherwise be entitled to object.

State Protection of Privacy

Several states have adopted **privacy** right protections through either constitutional or legislative enactments. More than 30 states have adopted laws prohibiting or restricting employers from testing employees and prospective employees for genetic traits. Other states restrict employers' inquiries into an individual's HIV status. The following states have enacted broad **privacy** protection statutes:

Alaska	Alaska Const. art. I, §22
Arizona	Ariz. Const. art. II, §8
California	Calif. Const. art. I, §1
Connecticut	Conn. Gen. Stat. §31-48B (2006) (freedom from communications and electronic surveillance); Conn. Gen. Stat. §31-51x (requiring nexus to safety for drug testing)
Florida	Fla. Const. art. I, §§12, 23
Hawaii	Haw. Const. art. I, §§6, 7
Illinois	Ill. Const. art. I, §6
Louisiana	La. Const. art. I §5
Montana	Mont. Const. art. II, §10
South Carolina	S.C. Const. art. I, §10
Washington	Wash. Const. art. I, §7

In general, these statutes apply to state governmental action against an individual, and it is uncertain whether courts would apply the **privacy** statutes in the private employment context. However, in California a private individual's **privacy** right is expressly recognized in Article I, Section I, of its Constitution:

> *All people are by nature free and independent and have inalienable rights. Among these are enjoying and defending life and liberty, acquiring, possessing, and protecting property, and pursuing and obtaining safety, happiness, and privacy.*

Although California recognizes the right to **privacy**, it is not an absolute right. Some intrusion into **privacy** will be permitted if a compelling governmental interest is justified. The California Supreme Court provided guidance in a case of national interest, *Hill v. National Collegiate Athletic Assn.*, 7 Cal.4th 1 (1994). In this decision, the state supreme court established a balancing test to determine whether an employer has violated an individual's right to **privacy**. Hill was a student athlete enrolled at Stanford University who objected to NCAA-imposed random drug testing conducted by the university. In resolving the conflict between the athlete's right to **privacy** and the NCAA's interests in ensuring fair and healthy competition, the court stated how the state **privacy** right applies in an **invasion of privacy** case. Although the case does not involve the workplace, the *Hill* case established that an employee can sue for **invasion of privacy** if the employee can prove that the means used by the employer was not the least intrusive alternative.

Concept Summary
Proving a Privacy Invasion

The plaintiff must prove:

- a legally protected **privacy** interest is involved such that society would recognize the information or activity as private;
- there was an objectively reasonable expectation of **privacy** under the circumstances (circumstances may include whether the employer gave advance notice of the intrusion, the opportunity for the employee to voluntarily consent to the invasion, and the occupation of the plaintiff and the surrounding circumstances); and
- a serious invasion of **privacy** is involved.

Once the claimant meets the burden of proof on the issue, the defendant employer can establish that its actions were justified by some competing, legally authorized or socially beneficial interest. If the employer can show that its conduct was reasonably calculated to further that interest, the plaintiff is given the opportunity to show that a less-intrusive alternative was available to further the employer's interest.

In evaluating the alternatives, the California Supreme Court held in the *Hill* case that courts must consider whether the intrusion was limited, whether confidential information was carefully shielded and disseminated on a need-to-know basis, and whether the employer's objectives could be readily and effectively accomplished by other means with little or no impact on the **privacy** interests.

Workplace Application
Federal Right-to-Privacy Laws

Law	Coverage
Drivers Privacy Protection Act of 1994 18 U.S.C. §2721	Confidential driver's license information may not be disclosed to an employer except in limited circumstances.
Fair Credit Reporting Act 14 U.S.C. §§1681 *et seq.*	Job applicants and employees are permitted to know of the existence and content of any personal credit files on them maintained by the employer. If the employer compiles an investigative consumer report, the employee must be informed and given the right to inspect it.

Law	Coverage
Family Education Rights and Privacy Act — the Buckley Amendment 20 U.S.C. §1232 *et seq.*	Student records and personal information are protected from disclosure.
Federal Privacy Act of 1974 5 U.S.C. §552a	Federal agencies and those contracting with the federal government must provide employees with the opportunity to determine the scope of the information being kept on them by their employers, to review that information, to correct erroneous information, and to prevent the information from being used for a purpose other than that for which it was collected. The act covers public sector employees only and allows them to sue for violations.
Safe Streets Act 18 U.S.C. §§2510 *et seq.*	It is a crime to intentionally intercept any wire, oral, or electronic communication, including electronic mail or video teleconference. This includes recording conversations when there is a reasonable expectation of **privacy**, which may be waived by one party's consent. Employers may potentially listen in on an employee's conversation on an extension telephone used in the ordinary course of business if there is a legitimate business reason to do so.
Electronic Communications Privacy Act of 1986 (**Electronic Communications Privacy Act or Wiretap Act**)	Enacted to address the inadequacies of the federal wiretap law to protect computer transmission technologies. This act prohibits the interception, recording, or disclosure of wire, electronic, and audio communications, including e-mail and voice mail. Employers may monitor these communications for legitimate business reasons, but they must immediately stop monitoring them if they prove to be or become personal. Interception is permissible if conducted by law enforcement personnel with a warrant in the conduct of a criminal investigation.
Stored Communications Act (part of the Electronic Communications Privacy Act)	Providers of communications services may not divulge private communications. The act covers ECS and RCS entities. An ECS is any service that provides users with the ability to send or receive wire or electronic communications. An ECS may *not* divulge communications without the consent of the addressee or intended recipient of such communication. An RCS provides computer storage or processing services for an electronic communications system. An RCS *may* divulge the contents of a communication with the consent of the customer-subscriber.
Privacy for Consumers and Workers Act of 1993	Employer monitoring of an employee's communications is not proscribed, but the act requires the employer to give notice to employees when their workplace communications are being monitored or recorded electronically.

Collecting and Handling Employee Information

The federal Privacy Act regulates how federal government agencies maintain personnel records. Records are defined under that act to include "any item, collection, or grouping of information about an individual that is maintained by an agency."[7] Employees of federal agencies must be given copies of their personnel records and are allowed to make copies of them. They are entitled to contest the accuracy of the records by making a written statement to be included in the official record and in disclosures of those records to other parties. Moreover, the federal agencies must obtain the employees' consent before disclosing any information from their personnel records to outside persons. The act limits the types of information that may be kept about employees and requires agencies to keep accurate personnel records on their employees.

In the private sector, a number of federal statutes regulate the record-keeping requirements facing employers. While a complete listing of all of them here would be impractical, the Guide to Record Retention Requirements in the Code of Federal Regulations, an annual publication issued by the Office of the Federal Register, National Archives and Records Administration, provides a useful resource for gathering more information on federal requirements. Some employee records are required to be kept apart from personnel files. Applicable federal and state laws require that the following be kept specially protected because of **privacy** requirements:

ADA
Americans with Disabilities Act; the federal law, as amended, prohibiting employers from discriminating against qualified job applicants and employees. Applies to programs and activities of state and local governments with respect to discrimination against persons with a disability. Prohibits private entities providing public accommodations from denying goods, services, and programs to persons with a disability. Requires that new construction and modifications be accessible to persons with a disability.

- Verification of the right to work in the United States (Form I-9).
- EEOC charges of discrimination and investigation reports.
- "Medical condition" or medical history information obtained under the Americans with Disabilities Act (ADA),[8] which must be kept on forms in files separate from personnel files and treated as confidential:
  - The ADA requires that any information relating to the medical condition or history of an applicant or employee must be kept on separate forms, in medical files separate from general personnel information, and treated as confidential. Disclosure of an employee's medical records or information is permitted only (1) when supervisors and managers require information about work restrictions and necessary accommodations, (2) when first-aid and safety personnel require information about a disability that might require emergency treatment, and (3) when government officials are investigating compliance with the act.[9]
  - As with the ADA, §504 of the Rehabilitation Act[10] and its accompanying regulations require that confidentiality of medical records and information be maintained. However, an employer may inform supervisors or managers about work restrictions and provide information to others when emergency treatment is required.[11] The Rehabilitation Act applies to federal contractors and grantees.
- Employee medical records received by the employer under The Family and Medical Leave Act of 1993.[12] These must be kept separate from personnel files and treated as confidential.[13]
- Medical and hazardous material exposure records created in compliance with the Occupational Safety and Health Act. Employees and their unions have a right of access to them. Records of medical monitoring of employees and their

workplaces for exposure to toxic substances and related conditions are to be maintained.

- Regulations under the Occupational Safety and Health Act[14] require government investigators to obtain a written order signed by the assistant secretary of labor before they can have access to personally identifiable employee medical information. The employer must prominently post a copy of the order and its accompanying cover letter for at least 15 working days before allowing access to the records.[15]

- Workplace investigation reports that may contain sensitive, potentially embarrassing or humiliating personal information.
- Workers' compensation and disability claims.

The Health Insurance Portability and Accountability Act (HIPAA) does not cover employers, but parties with access to protected health information (possibly including an employer) must limit the uses and disclosure of that information, train staff on the **privacy** of medical information, designate a **privacy** officer with responsibility for compliance, and notify employees of their rights.

State and local laws may have more specific requirements for the appropriate handling of sensitive personal information maintained about employees to ensure its confidentiality. Under such laws, "medical information" is defined very broadly and can include medical history, mental or physical condition, and treatment. **Privacy** litigation claims are usually brought by former employees. They often include employer inquiries about or disclosure of protected medical information about the employee. These inquires can arise on an employee's return to work after an injury, in the course of determining whether a reasonable accommodation can or should be made for a disability, or when determining fitness for return to duty.

Post-Hiring Medical and Physical Exams

An employee may require a medical examination or undertake reasonable medical inquires if they are job related and consistent with a business necessity. Fitness-for-duty medical examinations are allowed if an employee's job performance has seriously declined or if there is a risk that the worker may harm himself or others. All persons in similar circumstances should be treated in the same manner.

Occasionally, an employer may be required to establish whether a person can perform the essential functions of the job. Usually, this situation arises when an employer is dealing with a worker with a disability recognized by the ADA. The employer must engage in a good-faith, lawful process with the employee to provide a reasonable accommodation for the disability if the accommodation would not impose undue hardship on the employer. To determine if such an accommodation is possible and what hardship it might impose on the employer can necessitate gathering personal information about the employee's needs. Employers would usually provide the employee and the employee's doctor a complete description of the essential functions of the job.

Drug Testing

Drug testing after hiring usually falls into one of four categories: (1) random testing, (2) testing based on a reasonable suspicion of intoxication, (3) testing related to off-duty activities, and (4) fitness for duty. Mandatory testing of employees, without other circumstances being present, has been held a violation of an employee's right to **privacy**. Current employees may be subject to random drug testing if they hold safety-sensitive or security-sensitive positions. Employees in workplaces where toxic or other hazardous materials or conditions are found may be compelled to undergo periodic drug testing.

A current user of illegal drugs is not protected by federal or state law. Individuals with past addictions or who are "regarded as" addicts are protected by the ADA. Alcoholics may be considered to have a disability and may be protected by the ADA if they are qualified to perform the essential functions of the job. An employer may discipline an addict or alcoholic if the use of the substances or alcohol affects job performance or conduct. The employer can prohibit the use of alcohol or drugs in the workplace and can require that employees not be under the influence of alcohol or drugs in the workplace.[16]

Under the Omnibus Transportation Employee Testing Act of 1991, a private employer can conduct testing in each of four categories: pre-hiring, reasonable suspicion, random, and post-accident. Under the act, the collection of specimen samples and collection procedures must promote the subject individual's **privacy** interests. The federal government has issued extensive regulations covering safety-related or security sensitive positions, for example in the railroad, trucking, and airline industries.

The Drug-Free Workplace Act of 1988[17] governs the behaviors of federal contractors and federal grant recipients. These parties must prohibit the use and possession of any controlled substance in the workplace and must post a notice of the prohibition. They must also establish a "drug-free awareness program."

STATE LAW TORT REMEDIES. Seven states have enacted legislation governing testing employees for alcohol or drug abuse. The coverage of these statutes varies greatly. California recognizes a right to **privacy** in private-sector workplaces. Montana, Iowa, Vermont, and Rhode Island have banned random or blanket drug testing without probable cause or suspicion of substance abuse (such testing would be permitted immediately following an on-the-job accident involving serious injury or death). Minnesota, Maine, and Connecticut permit random testing only for those in "safety sensitive" positions. These states also have specific requirements regarding confirmatory testing, the use of certified laboratories, the confidentiality of test results, and other **privacy** safeguards. In other states without specific law on the subject, court challenges to private employer drug testing programs often occur. Generally, these suits are based on state law rather than federal constitutional law. They are also based on common law actions that allege specific intentional tort injuries and, occasionally, breach of contract claims. In the majority of states, private-sector employers have been given broad discretion to test their employees provided the invasion of **privacy** is not too intrusive.

In the following case, the plaintiff brought suit against her former employer for wrongful termination. She claimed that the company dismissed her when she refused to submit to post-hiring urinalysis screening and personal property searches. She was allowed to pursue her claim of wrongful discharge under Pennsylvania's public policy exception to the at-will employment doctrine.

CASE 12.1

EMPLOYEES CAN SUE FOR NON-SAFETY-RELATED, MANDATORY DRUG TESTING OF EMPLOYEES OR PENALTIES FOR REFUSING A DRUG TEST

BORSE V. PIECE GOODS SHOP, INC.

963 F.2d 611 (3d Cir. 1992)

U.S. Court of Appeals for the Third Circuit

Facts. Sarah Borse was employed as a salesclerk for 15 years before her employer adopted a drug and alcohol policy that required its employees to sign a form giving their consent to urinalysis screening for drug use and to searches of their personal property located on the employer's premises. Borse refused on the grounds that the policy violated her right to privacy and her rights under the Fourth Amendment, and she was eventually discharged. Borse sued for retaliation while asserting she could not be terminated as an at-will employee because of the violation of public policy. The federal district court granted a motion to dismiss the complaint in favor of Borse's employer, from which she appealed to the Third Circuit Court of Appeals.

Issue. Is an employer justified in discharging an employee because she refused to submit to drug testing and private property searches at the workplace?

Language of the Court. Becker, J.: . . . **Although we have rejected Borse's reliance upon constitutional provisions as evidence of a public policy allegedly violated by the Piece Goods Shop's drug and alcohol program, our review of Pennsylvania law reveals other evidence of a public policy that may, under certain circumstances, give rise to a wrongful discharge action related to urinalysis or to personal property searches. Specifically, we refer to the Pennsylvania common law regarding tortious invasion of privacy.**

We can envision at least two ways in which an employer's urinalysis program might intrude upon an employee's seclusion. First, the particular manner in which the program is conducted might constitute an intrusion upon seclusion as defined by Pennsylvania law. The process of collecting the urine sample to be tested clearly implicates "expectations of privacy" that society has long recognized as reasonable.

As the United States Supreme Court has observed: There are few activities in our society more personal or private than the passing of urine. Most people

describe it by euphemisms if they talk about it at all. It is a function traditionally performed without public observation; indeed, its performance in public is generally prohibited by law as well as social custom.

Second, urinalysis "can reveal a host of private medical facts about an employee, including whether she is epileptic, pregnant, or diabetic." (Citation omitted.) A reasonable person might well conclude that submitting urine samples to tests designed to ascertain these types of information constitutes a substantial and highly offensive intrusion upon seclusion.

The same principles apply to an employer's search of an employee's personal property. If the search is not conducted in a discreet manner or if it is done in such a way as to reveal personal matters unrelated to the workplace, the search might well constitute a tortious invasion of the employee's privacy.

In sum, based on our prediction of Pennsylvania law, we hold that dismissing an employee who refused to consent to urinalysis testing and to personal property searches would violate public policy if the testing tortiously invaded the employee's privacy.

Decision. No. While the court did not extend Fourth Amendment protections to the context of private sector employment, it did hold that mandatory drug testing can be a violation of an employee's right to privacy.

CASE QUESTIONS

Critical Legal Thinking. Should courts consider an invasion of privacy by an employer as a breach of public policy?

Business Ethics. Should the courts be more concerned with what the test results may show as to the employee's fitness for duty rather than with the nature of the test itself?

Contemporary Business. Can you recall any examples of post-hiring drug testing and searches that you or your friends experienced in the workplace? Do you believe legislation is necessary to address these conflicting interests?

Not all courts have taken the approach adopted by the *Borse* court. Several courts have upheld the drug testing of employees. Some courts, for example, have held that employee testing and other searches based on a reasonable, individual, and particularized reason for the search are constitutional.

Example: Brenda Jennings was denied an injunction from a Texas court of appeals to restrain her employer from testing its employees by urinalysis to determine if they had recently consumed illegal drugs. Because Jennings was an at-will employee working for a private employer "concerned" about illegal drug use among its employees and the consequent threats to the company's business and employees, the court upheld the testing program. The court approved random drug testing to detect illegal drug consumption. If the testing revealed evidence of such use, the employee would be asked to participate in a rehabilitation program at company expense. The company would terminate any employee who either declined to give a urine sample or tested positive and refused to participate in a rehab program. In so holding, the court applied a decision of the Texas supreme court that narrowly construed exceptions to the freedom of an employer to terminate at-will employees.[18]

Management Application
Employee Polygraphs

The **Employee Polygraph Protection Act of 1998 (EPPA)** is a federal statute that greatly limits an employer's right to polygraph employees. Use of polygraphs as a screening device for job applicants is generally banned for private employers in all but a few industries.[19] This act does not apply to federal, state, or local government employees or to employees of federal government contractors that deal with defense and intelligence agencies.[20] In addition, private security firms and drug companies that manufacture or distribute controlled substances have a limited exemption that allows polygraph testing of prospective and current employees under certain conditions.[21] Under the **EPPA**, polygraphs may be used by private-sector employers on current employees only, pursuant to a "specific incident exception," which has four requirements:

1. There must be an ongoing investigation of economic loss or injury (construed restrictively, such as theft, embezzlement, misappropriation, espionage, or sabotage);
2. The particular employee must have had access to the property that is the subject of the investigation;
3. The employer must have a reasonable suspicion based on facts in addition to access that the particular employee is involved; and
4. The employer must provide the employee with written notification before the administration of the test, which must state the following:
   - **a.** the specific loss or injury; the fact that the employee had access to what was lost or injured; the reason why the employee is under suspicion;
   - **b.** the time and place of the examination; the nature of instruments to be used; the fact that the examination will be conducted by a licensed examiner (the **EPPA** requires that the polygraph examiner be licensed, maintain a minimum bond of $50,000, and administer no more than five exams in one day); the duration of the examination; the employee's right to consult with counsel; the employee's right to tape the proceedings; the employee's right to terminate the examination at any time;
   - **c.** the fact that no degrading or intrusive questions or questions regarding religion, politics, race, sex, or attitudes toward labor unions will be asked;
   - **d.** the fact that the examination is not required as a condition of employment; and
   - **e.** the fact that statements made may be used against the employee.

The employee has the right before the test to review all test questions in writing. The examination may not occur if written evidence shows that the employee suffers from conditions that could cause positive results (i.e., that the conditions could make responses appear to be untruthful even if they were not). The employer must discuss the test results with the employee before taking any adverse employment action. No adverse action may be taken solely on the basis of polygraph test results. The employer is permitted to disclose the results of the test only to the examinee, in litigation proceedings, or to a governmental agency for criminal prosecution.

Violations of the act are punishable by fines of up to $10,000. An employee or prospective employee whose rights have been violated may file a civil action in federal or state court within three years and seek reinstatement, promotion, and back pay. The court in its discretion may also grant the prevailing party its costs and attorney fees. Any waivers by an employee of the act's protections are invalid unless they are part of a signed settlement agreement regarding a pending action or complaint. Lastly, this law does not preempt any provision of state or local law or of any negotiated collective bargaining agreement that prohibits polygraph tests or is more restrictive about polygraph tests than this act.

A voice stress analysis by an employer is governed by the **EPPA** as well.

Employee Searches and Investigations

In its precedent-setting holding in the *O'Connor v. Ortega* decision below, the Supreme Court held: (1) employees do not lose their protections under the **Fourth Amendment** because they work for a public employer; (2) the reasonableness of an employee's expectation of **privacy** must be considered within the specific facts presented in a case; (3) requiring a public employer to secure a warrant whenever it wished to enter an employee's workspace would be unreasonable and unduly burdensome; and (4) a public employer's intrusion into a workspace for noninvestigatory, work-related purposes as well as for work-related misconduct investigations must be judged by the reasonableness of the employer's actions in the circumstances — both the employer's intrusion and the scope of the intrusion must be reasonable.

EPPA
Employee Polygraph Protection Act of 1998; a federal law generally preventing employers from requiring lie detector tests from applicants or employees.

CASE 12.2

PUBLIC EMPLOYEES ENJOY A REASONABLE EXPECTATION OF PRIVACY

O'CONNOR V. ORTEGA

480 U.S. 709 (1987)

Supreme Court of the United States

Facts. A doctor employed in a state psychiatric hospital attracted the attention of his supervisors. Concerned that he was engaged in a number of improprieties, including possibly acquiring a computer by coercing contributions from the resident patients, the doctor was placed on administrative leave. As part of an ensuing investigation of his conduct, hospital officials searched his office, including his desk and file cabinets, several times and seized both personal and state-owned items. When his employment was terminated, the doctor sued his employer, alleging the hospital's search of his desk violated his Fourth Amendment rights. The Ninth Circuit Court of Appeals ruled that the searches violated the doctor's privacy rights under the Fourth Amendment, and the hospital appealed to the Supreme Court.

Issue. Does a state employee have an expectation of privacy as to his office desk?

Language of the Court. O'Connor, J.: . . . **Our cases establish that Dr. Ortega's Fourth Amendment rights are implicated only if the conduct of the Hospital officials . . . infringed "an expectation of privacy that society is prepared to consider reasonable." . . . We have no talisman that determines in all cases those privacy expectations that society is prepared to accept as reasonable. . . . - Because the reasonableness of an expectation of privacy, as well as the appropriate standard for a search is understood to differ according to context, it is essential first to delineate the boundaries of the workplace context. The workplace includes those areas and items that are related to work and are generally within the employer's control. At a hospital, for example, the hallways, cafeteria, offices, desks, and file cabinets, among other areas are all part of the workplace. These areas remain part of the workplace context even if the employee has placed personal items in them, such as a photograph placed in a desk or a letter posted on an employee bulletin board. Not everything that passes through the confines of the business address can be considered part of the workplace context, however. An employee may bring closed luggage to the office prior to leaving on a trip, or a handbag or briefcase each workday. While whatever expectation of privacy the employee has in the existence and the outward appearance of the luggage is affected by its presence in the workplace, the employee's expectation of privacy in the contents of the luggage is not affected in the same way. The appropriate standard for a workplace search does not necessarily apply to a piece of closed personal luggage, a handbag, or a briefcase that happens to be [at the business].**

Decision. No. The Court concluded that public employers must be given wide latitude to conduct reasonable searches. They are not required to meet the probable cause requirements imposed on law enforcement in conducting searches. The standard of reasonableness is the same one that applies to private-sector employers as well. However, the Court found that the doctor had a reasonable expectation of privacy, including in his desk and cabinets. The Court reversed the appellate court and remanded it to the trial court for further findings on the issue of the reasonableness of the search in light of the doctor's expectation of privacy. A case-by-case analysis of the reasonableness of the search is required.

CASE QUESTIONS

Critical Legal Thinking. Does the holding in *Ortega* imply that private employees are not afforded protection from unreasonable searches?

Business Ethics. Define the arguments you would make in favor of an employee's protected expectation of privacy in workspace areas such as a locker, purse, or locked desk drawer.

Contemporary Business. What other examples can you cite in which the employer's interest outweighs the employees' privacy interests?

Private Employer Property Searches

Very little statutory or case authority exists for private-sector employers seeking to search the work areas and property of employees. Quite often, court decisions turn on whether the conduct was inadvertent or intentional with respect to the alleged invasion of **privacy**.

UNAUTHORIZED CREDIT CHECKING. A disgruntled employee may not obtain, without the targeted employee's consent, the credit card records of a fellow employee suspected of taking unauthorized sick days, nor may such ill-obtained information be shared with management. The employer had no legitimate interest in receiving confidential credit information.[22]

OPENING MAIL MARKED "PERSONAL" AND SEARCHING PERSONAL DOCUMENTS LEFT ON A DESK. A jury was allowed to decide whether the mail opening procedures at a law firm violated the **privacy** rights of an employee when the employer opened employee mail that had been marked as "personal." The jury was also to decide whether the search of personal documents left on a desk was a substantial and highly offensive intrusion if the person who conducted the search had the right to do so under the law.[23]

Privacy
The desire or right to be left alone or the right to restrict public access to personal information, history, and affairs.

EMPLOYEE BAGS, LUNCH BOXES, AND PURSES. If an employer has announced a policy of random inspections of bags leaving the premises in the possession of employees, as long as the search is conducted in a reasonable manner, disciplinary action is sustained if taken against an employee who refused to open his lunch box.[24]

PHYSICAL SEARCHES. A K-Mart manager exhibited a total lack of judgment when he ordered a strip search of an employee in front of a customer who suspected the employee had stolen money from a customer. Upon hearing a customer's complaint that the checker had taken $20 the customer had left on the counter while looking for an item on sale, the manager pulled out the checker's jacket pockets, looked inside and found nothing. Then, two searches of the checker's work area ensued in the presence of store customers, along with a register balance check, neither of which turned up the missing money. The 32-year-old male store manager then told the young female checker to go to the women's public restroom for the purpose of disrobing while a female assistant manager and the female customer watched. When no missing money was found, the customer left in a loud protest. The following day, the young checker returned to work but felt she was under continued surveillance. She quit and sued. The court ruled that the personal search was abusive because compelling an employee to disrobe in front of a customer was embarrassing, humiliating, and the source of great emotional distress.[25]

False Imprisonment

Employers who use coercive conduct to physically restrain an employee may commit the tort of false imprisonment. Generally, conducting a prolonged interview of an employee suspected of wrongful activity, without force or threat of physical restraint but under the threat of termination of employment only does not constitute false imprisonment.

Employee Misconduct Investigations

Under federal law, an employer may hire a third party to investigate alleged employee misconduct without prior consent of the employee. However, if the employer takes an adverse employment action because of the results of the investigation, the employer must give the employee a summary of the investigation report that resulted in the adverse action.[26]

Surveillance and Monitoring

Due to the costs of developing proprietary information and systems, employers will routinely monitor the information on an employee's computer. This can be accomplished in a number of ways, including the use of software that allows the employer to capture what is on the employees' screens as well as what Internet sites employees have visited and their e-mail communications. Other software can enable the employer to monitor the number of keystrokes typed and the amount of idle time on the computer. Both e-mail and voice mail cases arising from workplace invasion of **privacy** claims have been resolved in the employer's favor, particularly if prior authorization has been obtained from or notifications given to the employees.

It is fairly settled law that an employer has the right to intercept employee e-mail and telephone communications. Neither case law decisions nor state statutes provide **privacy** protection for e-mail within the workplace. In general, office e-mail is no more deserving of **privacy** protection than is a conversation among employees held in an open office area. What remains to be understood is the reaction of courts and juries to continued monitoring of e-mail and online activity during off hours. As employees use company-issued computers and cell phones both during and after work hours, the parameters of employer interceptions of employee communications will change. Employees may easily recognize that a business telephone at work may be monitored but bristle at the suggestion that the employer may intercept what an employee posts on social networking websites. The **Electronic Communications Privacy Act of 1986 (ECPA)** permits employers to intercept the employees' electronic communications when the employee consents in writing to allow the employer to do so, if during the ordinary course of business the employer intercepts such communications because it fits within the business-related exception to the **ECPA**, and when the business entity itself provides the e-mail service for use by employees.

The federal district court in the case below decided whether the right to **privacy** was invaded by an "intrusion upon seclusion." In *Smyth*, the court distinguished between the invasion of **privacy** resulting from a urine-based drug test and that resulting from a search of an employee's e-mail located on a company e-mail system.

CASE 12.3

AN EMPLOYER MAY TERMINATE EMPLOYMENT OVER THE CONTENTS OF AN EMAIL

SMYTH V. PILLSBURY COMPANY

914 F. Supp. 97 (E.D. Pa. 1996)

U.S. District Court for the Eastern Dist. of Pennsylvania

Facts. Michael Smyth was an at-will employee of The Pillsbury Company. The company maintained an e-mail system to promote internal corporate communications among employees. In his complaint, Smyth alleged the company repeatedly assured its employees, including Mr. Smyth, that all e-mail communications would remain confidential and privileged and that they could not be intercepted and used by the company against its employees as grounds for termination or reprimand. Smyth contended that e-mail he exchanged with his supervisor was confidential and not subject to disciplinary action. The company contended differently and terminated his employment over the content of the e-mails. Mr. Smyth filed suit for wrongful termination of his employment as a violation of public policy.

Issue. Does the interception of e-mail by an employer violate public policy so as to constitute the basis for a wrongful discharge?

Language of the Court. Weiner, J.: **Defendant alleges in its motion to dismiss that the e-mails concerned sales management and contained threats to "kill the backstabbing bastards" and referred to the planned Holiday party as the "Jim Jones Kool-Aid affair." Pennsylvania is an employment at-will jurisdiction and an employer "may discharge an employee with or without cause, at pleasure, unless restrained by some contract. However, in the most limited of circumstances, exceptions have been recognized where discharge of an at-will employee threatens or violates a clear mandate of public policy. . . . A "clear mandate" of public policy must be of a type that "strikes at the heart of a citizen's social right, duties and responsibilities." . . . Plaintiff claims that his**

termination was in violation of "public policy" which precludes an employer from terminating an employee in violation of the employee's right to privacy as embodied in Pennsylvania common law. . . . We do not find a reasonable expectation of privacy in e-mail communications voluntarily made by an employee to his supervisor over the company e-mail system notwithstanding any assurances that such communications would not be intercepted by management. Once plaintiff communicated the alleged unprofessional comments to a second person (his supervisor) over an e-mail system which was apparently utilized by the entire company, any reasonable expectation of privacy was lost. . . . We find no privacy interests in such communications.

Even if we found that an employee had a reasonable expectation of privacy in the contents of his e-mail communications over the company e-mail system, we do not find that a reasonable person would consider the defendant's interception of these communications to be a substantial and highly offensive invasion of his privacy. . . . [T]he company's interest in preventing inappropriate and unprofessional comments or even illegal activity over its e-mail system outweighs any privacy interest the employee may have in those comments.

Decision. No. The employer's interest in maintaining the integrity of its corporate communications system outweighed any personal privacy interests.

CASE QUESTIONS

Critical Legal Thinking. Does the employer have the right to review all Internet activity of employees who use company computers to surf the Internet during work?

Business Ethics. Should employees be permitted a limited period of time during the day to be able to check personal e-mails on company computers? Should an employee be disciplined for using a company computer to e-mail inappropriate content to a third party, even if the employee was using a non-business personal e-mail account?

Contemporary Business. What other examples of workplace privacy interest conflicts can you cite?

Surveillance Rights

Employers may photograph, surveil, or closely observe employees within their work areas for a legitimate business reason without risk of invading their **privacy**. When observations are made from public places, employees are unlikely to have any expectation of **privacy**. Trespassing into private areas will almost surely result in an invasion of **privacy** claim. A constitutional challenge to the use of video surveillance cameras is discussed in the following case.

CASE 12.4

PRIVACY EXPECTATIONS RELATING TO VIDEO SURVEILLANCE WILL DEPEND ON THE CIRCUMSTANCES

VEGA-RODRIGUEZ V. PUERTO RICO TELEPHONE CO.

110 F.3d 174 (1st Cir. 1997)

U.S. Court of Appeals for the First Circuit

Facts. The Puerto Rico Telephone Company continuously monitored its employees' work areas by means of video surveillance. The company's work center contained a large L-shaped work area that was completely open; no individual employee had an assigned office, cubicle, work station, or desk there. Three cameras surveyed the work space, and a fourth traced all traffic passing through the main entrance to the company's offices. After the surveillance system was installed, two employees protested that the surveillance constituted an unreasonable search prohibited by the Fourth Amendment and their privacy rights and abridged their rights under the First and Fourteenth Amendments. They also sought protection under the Fourth Amendment from unreasonable searches. The district court dismissed the employees' lawsuit, and the employees appealed.

Issue. Does continuous video surveillance contravene the "right of the people to be secure in their persons . . . against unreasonable searches"?

Language of the Court. Selya, J.: **Intrusions upon personal privacy do not invariably implicate the Fourth Amendment. Rather, such intrusions cross the constitutional line only if the challenged conduct infringes upon some reasonable expectation of privacy. . . .**

Generally speaking, business premises invite lesser privacy expectations than do residences. . . . The watershed case is *O'Connor v. Ortega*, 480 U.S. 709, 107 S. Ct. 1492 (1987). O'Connor's central thesis is that a public employee sometimes may enjoy a reasonable expectation of privacy in his or her workplace vis-à-vis searches by a supervisor or other representative of a public employer.

It is simply implausible to suggest that society would recognize as reasonable an employee's expectation of privacy against being viewed while toiling in the

Center's open and undifferentiated work area. PRTC did not provide the work station for the appellants' exclusive use, and its physical layout belies any expectation of privacy. Security operators do not occupy private offices or cubicles. They toil instead in a vast, undivided work space — work areas so patulous as to render a broadcast expectation of privacy unreasonable. The precise extent of an employee's expectation of privacy often turns on the nature of an intended intrusion. In this case the nature of the intrusion strengthens the conclusion that no reasonable expectation of privacy attends the work area. Employers possess a legitimate interest in the efficient operation of the workplace and one attribute of this interest is that supervisors may monitor at will that which is in plain view within an open work area. Here, moreover, this attribute has a greater claim on our allegiance because the employer acted overtly in establishing the video surveillance: PRTC notified its work force in advance that video cameras would be installed and disclosed the cameras' field of invasion. Hence, the affected workers were on clear notice from the outset that any movements they might make and any objects they might display within the work area would be exposed to the employer's sight.

Decision. No. Employees do not have an objectively reasonable expectation of privacy in the open areas of their workplace.

CASE QUESTIONS

Critical Legal Thinking. Would the court have ruled differently if the employees had worked in their own assigned, lockable offices or work cubicles?

Business Ethics. Would it have made a difference if the employer had installed the surveillance equipment covertly?

Contemporary Business. What should an employer do if it suspects wrongful conduct is occurring in nonpublic areas such as dressing rooms or restrooms?

The lawful boundary of employer surveillance of employees is uncharted and constantly changing. Much of a trier of fact's task in applying an **"objectively reasonable expectation of privacy"** relates to whether the policy or practice was previously disclosed to the employee and how intrusive it is considered to be. Legal precedents, common experience, and the specific circumstances are reviewed. For example, employees would recognize the appropriateness of an employer's surveillance and observation of their performance in open work areas. However, no one would seriously argue that the same right extends to workplace dressing room or restroom areas. Relationships recognized as confidential, such as that between doctor and patient, must be respected by the employer, even when the employer may suspect fraud. Employers have a valid interest in monitoring employee activities and communications in certain areas of the workplace. Balancing the interests of the employer and the employee's rights to **privacy** will be a continuing challenge for employers.

State Law

Videotaping of private spaces in the workplaces has been the subject of state legislation, as the following excerpts from state law demonstrate:

CALIFORNIA. "No employer may cause an audio or video recording to be made of an employee in a restroom, locker room, or room designated by an employer for changing clothes."[27]

MICHIGAN. "A person shall not do either of the following: (a) Install, place, or use in any private place, without the consent of the person or persons entitled to **privacy** in that place, any device for observing, recording, transmitting, photographing, or eavesdropping upon the sounds or events in that place. (b) Distribute, disseminate, or transmit for access by any other person a recording, photograph, or visual image the person knows or has reason to know was obtained in violation of this section."[28]

NEW YORK. "A person is guilty of unlawfully installing or maintaining a two-way mirror or other viewing device when, being the owner or manager of any premises, he knowingly permits or allows such a device to be installed or maintained in or upon such premises, for the purpose of surreptitiously observing the interior of any fitting room, restroom, toilet, bathroom, washroom, shower, or any room assigned to guests or patrons in a motel, hotel or inn."[29]

Eavesdropping as an Invasion of Privacy

The overhearing of another's private words, either by ear or through some artificial assistance, such as a mechanical or electronic device, is deemed eavesdropping. Eavesdropping includes the recording of words as well. An eavesdropping episode can involve both criminal and civil proceedings. State laws vary in the degree of protection afforded to claimants. The interception of wire or radio communications — wiretapping — is regulated by the federal Crime Control Act enacted in 1968.

Eavesdropping does not include listening to a conversation on a telephone extension[30] or to conversations that take place over telephone lines that "beep" when taping takes place.[31] When the communications take place in a public place, occur in the presence of members of the public, and no steps are taken to preserve the **privacy** of communications, interception by the placement of electronic surveillance microphones has been held not to constitute eavesdropping.[32] Placing eavesdropping devices in a residence is almost universally seen as an invasion of **privacy**.

It is the behavior of the defendants that invites the claim. When detectives hired by a legal team defending an employer followed a plaintiff's automobile, looked through the hedge adjoining her home, peeped through her windows, skulked around her home, and overheard her conversations without a mechanical device, the plaintiff's claim was allowed to proceed to trial.[33] Eavesdropping does include a monitored wiretap on the plaintiff's telephone[34] and listening devices planted in rooms.[35]

Focus on Ethics
Offensive E-Mails in the Workplace

One major issue facing employers is the sending of sexually offensive and harassing e-mails by employees in the workplace. An employer has the legal right to monitor e-mails sent and received by employees at work and to obtain and review e-mails that have been stored by employees on their office computers. Often, employees are terminated for sending sexually offensive and harassing e-mails at work. Consider the following case.

Dow Chemical Company operates a manufacturing facility in Midland, Michigan. Dow had widely disseminated its policies regarding e-mail usage at work and had specifically and clearly informed its employees that it was inappropriate to send sexually explicit e-mail at work. Dow's Internet Usage Policy stated:

> *Users will not knowingly send or download mail or other communications, files or programs containing potentially offensive, or* harassing *material, particularly relative to sex. Violations of the Internet Usage Policy may result in disciplinary action, up to and including termination of employment.*

Dow's Corporate Policy on Computer Systems and Telecommunications Security warned employees that they could be terminated for using computer files that contained "obscene, offensive, and harassing material." Dow reiterated these warnings in publications posted on Dow's Intranet and in its "Newslines" periodically published to its Midland employees.

Gene Husen worked at the Dow facility and was employed as a head operator alternative in the ion exchange copolymer department. Dow conducted a search of e-mail messages sent and received by its employees on a certain day and reviewed stored e-mails. Husen was found to have sent e-mails to fellow employees depicting the following images:

1. A cartoon of Popeye and Olive Oyl engaged in sexual intercourse;
2. A cartoon Mickey Mouse with his nose in a woman's anus;
3. Tweety Bird with a nude woman;
4. A man whose genitalia were exposed;
5. A woman's breasts;
6. A cartoon of male genitalia dressed up; and
7. A nude woman with her legs spread open.

Dow deemed Husen to be a serious offender and terminated him for his conduct. Husen, who belonged to a labor union, brought a lawsuit in U.S. district court against Dow Chemical, alleging that its termination of him violated a collective bargaining agreement between Dow and the labor union.

The U.S. district court found that Dow's actions in monitoring Husen's e-mails and reviewing Husen's stored e-mails were lawful, and that its termination of Husen was also lawful. The court granted Dow's motion for summary judgment and dismissed the case.[36]

Ethics Questions

1. What legal risks for Dow did Husen create by sending sexually explicit and offensive e-mails to fellow workers?
2. Were Dow's e-mail policies and its notice of these policies adequate to convey its rules regarding the unacceptable content of e-mail to Husen and other employees?
3. Is the law that permits employers to monitor and recover employees' e-mails a good law? Should employees be required to share personal e-mail account information with their employers?

Protecting Private Information from Disclosure

In order to ensure employer compliance with statutes having widespread public policy implications, many laws and regulations exist on the federal, state, and local level requiring employers to maintain business records substantiating compliance with those laws and regulations. Like medical records, these **required disclosure** records should be maintained separate from employees' individual personnel files. Such record keeping includes the following:

- information on the profiles of applicants and employees regarding applications, hires, promotions and demotions, layoffs, and dismissals;
- payroll records to ensure proper tax reporting compliance;
- "I-9" work authorization records for immigration status; and
- workplace safety and health records for reportable personal injuries and deaths.

Employees' Rights to Privacy Inside and Outside the Workplace

What should an employer do with respect to retaining an employee if the employer reads in the newspaper that the employee has been released pending trial following the employee's arrest for a crime? The prevailing legal view is that the off-duty behavior of employees is not subject to the disciplinary action of an employer. For the employer to take action against the employee, the employer must establish a clear relationship between the alleged misconduct and the negative effect on the business or on others in the company. The best approach is to place the employee on leave of absence pending the disposition of the case.

The use of a private investigator to surveil an employee outside of the workplace can lead to employer liability. No matter how inviting the opportunity may be for an employer to do so, the employer should proceed with extreme caution. Investigation of employees who have presented suspect workers' compensation or medical claims may lead to employer liability for invasion of **privacy** under the principal-agency theory. The trier of fact is asked to determine whether in the particular circumstances the investigator and, eventually, the employer had a legitimate interest in the surveillance and whether the subject conduct was unreasonably intrusive or offensive to a reasonable person.

Monitoring Employees' After-Hours Internet Activity

Increasing demands to service customers and clients at all hours of the day begin to erode the former wall between the employee's work time and private time. Key employees must react to those demands during their private time. As they attempt to service them through employer-supplied computers and cell phones, former distinctions erode between what constitutes private as compared to business communications.

Moreover, each advance in communication technology will ultimately be adapted for use by employees during their nonworking hours. Within this context, employers now face the prospect that employees now are more likely than past generations of employees to post personal and sensitive business information on blogs, shared personal Web sites, and recruiting and industry Web sites. The employer's interest in preserving its reputation and protecting trade secrets must be balanced against the likely invasion of the employee's right to **privacy**, a violation of public policy, or infringement of free speech. In these circumstances, both parties will refer to state law as well as the federal **ECPA**.

The **ECPA** was enacted to safeguard the **privacy** of "wire communications." The act prohibits the intentional "interception" of "any wire, oral, or electronic communication" and the disclosure of the contents of such communications "knowing or having reason to know the information was obtained" through an interception in violation of the act. Each of these terms has precise definitions under the act. Violations of the **ECPA** entitle the injured party whose communication was wrongfully intercepted or used to injunctive relief, actual damages suffered, punitive damages "in appropriate cases," and attorney's fees and litigation costs.

There are two exemptions to the **ECPA**. The first is the "prior consent" exemption, which permits interception when one of the parties to the communication has given their "prior consent" to it. This first exemption does not apply if the purpose of the interception is to commit a tort or a criminal act. Access to stored electronic data is also permitted when it is given by a user of a service. This can be accomplished by the employee's acknowledgment of the employer's right to search such services at the commencement of employment. The second exemption refers to the "system provider" exemption. In this second instance, employers who provide their own internal e-mail service have access to their own stored communications. In both of these cases, the employer's best practice would include obtaining the employee's prior consent to such interceptions and routinely monitoring the communications of its employees in the ordinary course of business.

Current Trends

The courts have begun to address the issue of the expectation of **privacy** with regard to Internet communications. Civil court judges must often rely on prior appellate decisions in criminal court proceedings. Typically, the issue arises as a result of the employee's challenge that the interception of e-mail or reading of e-mail is an invasion of his or her **privacy**. While the law is still developing in this area, the current trend is that courts have found no **reasonable expectation of privacy** in e-mail messages or the e-mail storage systems in which they are placed. In addition, Internet "chat room" conversations have not been subject to **privacy** protections. However, some state **privacy** statutes protect real-time discussion software such as Internet messaging systems, absent an implied consent to a recording of the message traffic. At least one court has considered what types of Internet communications are not private. In a Washington state appellate case, Mr. Townsend, a criminal defendant in a criminal prosecution for attempted second-degree rape of a minor child, sought to dismiss the charges on the basis that the interception of e-mail and ICQ, which was a real time client-to-client communications software, between him and a police detective posing as a minor female violated the Washington Privacy Act. That act had been described as one of the most restrictive in the nation and made inadmissible evidence obtained in violation of its provisions. The court observed that:

> *The subjective intentions of the parties to the communication are among the factors to be considered, as well as other factors bearing on the reasonableness of the participants' expectations, such as the duration and subject matter; the location of the communication and the presence of potential third parties; and the role of the non-consenting party and his or her relationship to the consenting party. . . . The mere possibility that interception is technologically feasible does not render public a communication that is otherwise private. . . . Here, Mr. Townsend's messages to "Amber" [a fictitious person created by the police detective] certainly were intended only for her. His subjective expectations are clear; he specifically asked "Amber" not to "tell anyone about us." . . . Moreover, the subject matter itself clearly suggests the communications were private. The possibility of interception alone does not refute this suggestion. The communications were private.*

The court found that the e-mail and ICQ messages were private communications, but that consent had been implied from the use of the technology. The court stated:

> *[a] person sends an e-mail message with the expectation that it will be read and perhaps printed by another person. To be available for reading or printing, the message first must be recorded on another computer's memory. Like a person who leaves a message on a telephone answering machine, a person who sends an e-mail message anticipates that it will be recorded. That person thus implicitly consents to having the message recorded on the addressee's computer. Because Mr. Townsend understood that his e-mail messages would be recorded on a device that would make the messages available for "Amber" to read, he consented to the recording [which is an exception to the state's privacy statute].*

The court further held that the ICQ **privacy** policy expressly warned users of "[un]authorized exposure of information and material you listed or sent, on or through the ICQ system, to other users, the general public or other specific entities for which the information and material was not intended by you." The court held that the criminal defendant had consented to the recording of his e-mail and his messaging communications.[37]

The court in *U.S. v. Charbonneau*[38] found that no reasonable expectation **of privacy** existed with regard to private electronic chat rooms. An FBI agent who posed as a pedophile and operated in private chat rooms received pornographic pictures from Mr. Charbonneau. After the FBI searched Charbonneau's house and obtained further evidence and a confession, Charbonneau moved to suppress the admissibility of the e-mail communications. He argued the federal government had violated his **Fourth Amendment** rights relative to the expectation of **privacy** of chat-room communications. The federal district court rejected this argument, holding that an e-mail message, like a letter, cannot be afforded a reasonable expectation of **privacy** once that message is received. The court also held that a sender of an e-mail runs the risk of the message being sent to an unintended recipient, such as an FBI agent, and that chat rooms provided no semblance of **privacy**.

Controlling the Employee's Lifestyle

In a number of areas, an employer may seek to control an employee's "lifestyle" choices. Regulation at the workplace may take the following forms:

- off-hours use of tobacco and alcohol;
- mandated dress and grooming standards;
- prohibiting outside employment; and
- interfering with social relationships, such as dating or sexual relationships, which are perceived by the employer to conflict with its business.

The employees' private activities, both inside and outside the workplace, are subject to employer monitoring only when they are directly related to the employer's business activities and only to the extent reasonably necessary to advance those interests. The constitutionally and common-law protected rights of the employee relating to free speech, association, equal protection, and **privacy** often collide with the interests of the employer to operate its business in a reasonable manner.

These issues are resolved by legislatures and courts in the same manner as other **privacy rights** issues are resolved: namely, by balancing the conflicting interests of the employee with the legitimate business interests of the employer. With evolving social standards, the courts deliberately do not follow a fixed set of rules. Instead, the courts look to the circumstances of the purported conflict and weigh them against the business interests of the employer.

> ***Example:*** Ms. Rulon-Miller, an IBM employee, dated Matt Blum, an employee of an IBM competitor. Her position at IBM did not expose her to sensitive, confidential information. Rulon-Miller was terminated when she argued that her continued dating of Blum did not constitute a "conflict of interest." She sued for invasion of her **privacy**, and IBM defended on the ground that her employment was "at-will." Rulon-Miller prevailed in her lawsuit because there was no evidence of a conflict of interest that had helped or could help IBM's competitor. Her personal **privacy** interests prevailed when there was no showing of harm to the employer's business interests.[39]

Due Process Clause
A fundamental right and constitutional guarantee that all legal proceedings will be held on prior notice and will provide a fair opportunity for the party to rebut the charges confronting him or her. Guaranteed under the Fifth and Fourteenth Amendments.

In 2003, the U.S. Supreme Court struck down a Texas statute prohibiting private, consensual homosexual activity. In its 6-3 decision in *Lawrence and Garner v. Texas*,[40] the Supreme Court held that the state law was an unconstitutional invasion of the Equal Protection rights afforded the arrestees under the Fourteenth Amendment. Texas criminalized sexual intimacy between same-sex couples but not the identical behavior by heterosexual couples. "Their right to liberty under the Due Process Clause gives them the full right to engage in their conduct without intervention of the government," wrote Justice Kennedy. He continued:

> *The Texas statute furthers no legitimate state interest which can justify its intrusion into the personal and private life of the individual, . . . Had those who drew and ratified the Due Process Clauses of the Fifth Amendment or the Fourteenth Amendment known the components of liberty in its manifold possibilities, they might have been more specific. They did not presume to have this insight. They knew times can blind us to certain truths and later generations can see that laws once thought necessary and proper in fact serve only to oppress. As the Constitution endures, persons in every generation can invoke its principles in their own search for greater freedom.*

As a result of this decision, the law provides legal protection for workplace romances and the lawful sexual practices of adult employees. A relationship with co-workers involving such private activity could be constitutionally protected. A cautionary note must be stated. Since constitutional claims are generally recognized only when there is state (i.e., governmental) action, employees of governmental agencies would be so protected. Private-sector employees would be protected when state laws protected state residents from such intrusions. Employers must be aware of the scope of state and local laws with respect to personal conduct rights and practices.

CASE 12.5

EMPLOYERS MAY IMPOSE LIFESTYLE RESTRICTIONS RATIONALLY RELATED TO JOB REQUIREMENTS

GRUSENDORF V. CITY OF OKLAHOMA CITY

816 F.2d 539 (10th Cir. 1987)

U.S. Court of Appeals for the Tenth Circuit

Facts. A firefighter trainee violated the city fire department's nonsmoking rule, which prohibited firefighter trainees from smoking on or off duty for one year. Greg Grusendorf, one such trainee, took three puffs from a cigarette while on a lunch break from his job as a firefighter trainee with the Oklahoma City Fire Department. He was fired that afternoon by his supervisor on the ground he had violated the terms of an agreement he signed as a precondition of employment that he would not smoke a cigarette, either on or off duty, for a period of one year from the time he began work. He sued under 42 U.S.C. §1983, which provides a person with a constitutionally recognized right to sue for damages if such a right has been violated by a governmental agency. He lost in the district court and appealed to the Court of Appeals for the Tenth Circuit.

Issue. Does a nonsmoking condition imposed by a governmental employer require the employee to surrender his constitutional rights of liberty and privacy guaranteed by the Bill of Rights?

Language of the Court. Barrett, J.: **The rights of liberty and privacy that Grusendorf relies upon are not clearly spelled out in the constitution.... Grusendorf argues that although there is no specific constitutional right to smoke, it is implicit in the Fourteenth Amendment that he has a right of liberty**

or privacy in the conduct of his private life, a right to be let alone, which includes the right to smoke. . . .

Grusendorf contends that the government may not unreasonably infringe upon its employees' freedom of choice in personal matters that are unrelated to the performance of any duties. It can hardly be disputed that the Oklahoma City Fire Department's non-smoking regulation infringes upon the liberty and privacy of the firefighter trainees. The regulation reaches well beyond the work place and well beyond the hours for which they receive pay. It burdens them after their shift has ended, restricts them on weekends and vacations, in their automobiles and backyards and even, with the doors closed and the shades drawn, in the private sanctuary of their own homes.

To resolve the issue of whether or not Grusendorf's rights of liberty or privacy were violated by the non-smoking regulation, it is instructive to study the Supreme Court's approach in *Kelley v. Johnson*. . . . In Kelley, the Court explained that the issue was not whether there existed a genuine public need for the regulation but "whether respondent can demonstrate that there is no rational connection between the regulation . . . and the promotion of safety of persons and property."

In applying the Kelley approach to our case, we begin by assuming that there is a liberty interest within the Fourteenth Amendment that protects the right of firefighter trainees to smoke cigarettes when off duty. At the same time, however, we take into account the heightened interest the state government has in regulating the firefighters by virtue of being their employer. Thus, we extend to the non-smoking regulation a presumption of validity.

Decision. No. The court of appeals held that while Grusendorf's liberty and privacy interests were affected by the rule, the interests involved did not reach the status of a constitutionally guaranteed fundamental right.

CASE QUESTIONS

Critical Legal Thinking. Do you think the Supreme Court should reassess the view it articulated in *Bowers v. Hardwick*, 478 U.S. 186 (1986), that federal courts should not take an expansive view of their authority to discover new fundamental rights?

Business Ethics. How should courts weigh personal rights of liberty and privacy in a world where privacy is becoming increasingly difficult to find and protect? What tests would you use to define those rights?

Contemporary Business. What policies would you enact as an employer with regard to the nonwork time behaviors of your employees?

Hearts and Flowers in the Workplace

Romantic relationships pose special problems and risks for employers. Employers should be alert to potential charges of sexual harassment even in the context of consensual relationships. Circumstances change and misunderstandings frequently arise so that what was formerly welcomed behavior becomes harassing. Employers should also be alert to morale issues that might arise if other employees perceive favoritism shown by a supervisor toward a subordinate because of a personal relationship.

The Ninth Circuit Court of Appeals held that the City of El Segundo, California, had infringed on a job applicant's rights of **privacy** and free association when she was forced to disclose personal sexual matters in a polygraph examination. She was denied a position as a police officer because she admitted having had an affair with a married police officer. The court concluded that the rejection of the applicant was wrongful because:

- The applicant's private, off-duty sexual activities were constitutionally protected;
- The police department could demonstrate no impact on on-the-job performance;
- The police department had no specific, narrow policies as to such conduct;
- There was no indication of any sexual deviance; and
- The affair was not a matter of public knowledge; as such, it could not adversely affect the employer's reputation in the community.[41]

Other federal cases have held that city police departments do have the right to discharge an employee if the above standards are not met. In *Fugate v. Phoenix Civil Service Board*,[42] city police officers did not to have a constitutionally protected right of **privacy** to engage in sexual relations with prostitutes while on duty. The court found that the officers' job performance was threatened by obvious conflicts of interest and the possibility of blackmail, and the activities were widely known and threatened to undermine the department's reputation in the community.

Apparently, morals standards can be enforced against public employees and employees from whom a high degree of moral rectitude is expected. When Lewell Marcum was discharged from his job as a deputy sheriff because of his intimate relationship with a married woman, he sued the county sheriff for a violation of his right to free association as guaranteed by the First and Fourteenth Amendments. A federal court of appeals upheld the grant of summary judgment in favor of his employer. It concluded "the adulterous nature of the relationship does not portray a relationship of the most intimate variety afforded protection under the Constitution."[43]

In a recent case the Ninth Circuit Court of Appeals expanded its analysis of **privacy** rights within the digital era of communications in the following case. In *Quon*, the court found that a police department violated the **Fourth Amendment** and state constitutional rights of employees by reviewing "personal" text messages on city-owned pagers. The wireless provider violated the Stored Communications Act (SCA) by providing transcripts to the city.

CASE 12.6

EMPLOYERS' CONDUCT CAN IMPLY REASONABLE EXPECTATION OF PRIVACY

QUON ET AL. V. ARCH WIRELESS OPERATING COMPANY, INC.

529 F.3d 892 (9th Cir. 2008), *cert. granted* _______ U.S. _______ (2009)

U.S. Court of Appeals for the Ninth Circuit

Facts. Jeff Quon and other police officer employees of the city of Ontario, California, sued the city, city officials, its police department, and a wireless company alleging, among other things, a violation of the Fourth Amendment. The wireless company provided text messaging-capable pagers to city employees. The city's informal policy was that text messages would not be audited if an employee paid the overages. The officers' supervisors and police chief requested and received copies of pager transcripts. When department officials learned of the explicit sexual content of the communications, Quon and others were subject to discipline. Quon sued. The district court held that the paging service was a computer storage system and thus not liable under the SCA for the release of the transcripts to the employer. Quon and others appealed to the Ninth Circuit Court of Appeals.

Issues. Does a SWAT team member have a reasonable expectation of privacy in text messages transmitted on his SWAT pager, where the police department has an official privacy policy but lieutenant not charged with policy-making announced an informal policy of allowing some personal use of the pagers?

Language of the Court. Wardlaw, J.: ... **The extent to which the Fourth Amendment provides protection for the contents of electronic communications in the Internet age is an open question. The recently minted standard of electronic communication via e-mails, text messages, and other means opens a new frontier in Fourth Amendment jurisprudence that has been little explored. Here, we must first answer the threshold question: Do users of text messaging services such as those provided by Arch Wireless have a reasonable expectation of privacy in their text messages stored on the service provider's network? We hold that they do.**

Appellants did not expect that Arch Wireless would monitor their text messages, much less turn over the messages to third parties without Appellants'

consent. . . . Given that Appellants had a reasonable expectation of privacy in their text messages, we now consider whether the search was reasonable. We hold that it was not.

A search is reasonable "at its inception" if there are "reasonable grounds for suspecting . . . that the search is necessary for a noninvestigatory work-related purpose such as to retrieve a needed file." O'Connor, 480 U.S. at 726. Here, the purpose was to ensure that officers were not being required to pay for work-related expenses. This is a legitimate work-related rationale, as the district court acknowledged.

However, the search was not reasonable in scope. As O'Connor makes clear, a search is reasonable in scope "when the measures adopted are reasonably related to the objectives of the search and not excessively intrusive in light of . . . the nature of the [misconduct]." . . . Thus, "if less intrusive methods were feasible, or if the depth of the inquiry or extent of the seizure exceeded that necessary for the government's legitimate purposes . . . the search would be unreasonable. . . ." (Citations omitted.) . . .

. . . . Instead, the Department opted to review the contents of all the messages, work-related and personal, without the consent of Quon or the remaining Appellants. This was excessively intrusive in light of the noninvestigatory object of the search, and because Appellants had a reasonable expectation of privacy in those messages, the search violated their Fourth Amendment rights.

Decision. Yes. An individual does not lose Fourth Amendment rights merely because they work for the government. The city's informal policy rendered the employee's expectation of privacy reasonable. The city's review of those messages without the consent of the employees was excessively intrusive.

CASE QUESTIONS

Critical Legal Thinking. In this case, the employer had issued an unequivocal policy that such equipment was not to be used for personal communications and that the pagers were covered by the employer's policy with respect to monitoring and auditing. Why did such policies not protect the employer in this case? What advice would you give employers in light of this decision?

Business Ethics. Did the informal policy of permitting personal use of the device increase the expectation of privacy? What are the ethical limits of personal use of company property?

Contemporary Business. How can we define incidental private use of company electronic equipment such as computers, cell phones, PDAs, and the like?

Privacy Rights of Union Members

Since 1984, the National Labor Relations Board has held that, in the absence of a **reasonable expectation of privacy**, it is a violation of the federal National Labor Relations Act for an employer to videotape or photograph employees engaged in protected activity such as lawful picketing. Merely observing protected union activities in public areas is not wrongful, but the use of the video- or film-recording equipment has a tendency to intimidate employees and make them believe they will be subject to retaliation by the employer. The District Court of Appeals for the District of Columbia summarized the law under the National Labor Relations Act as follows:

> *Section 8(a)(1) of the NLRA makes it "an unfair labor practice for an employer to interfere with, restrain, or coerce employees in the exercise of their right . . . " to self-organize . . . The courts have held that an employer's conduct violates Section 8(a)(1) if it creates the impression among employees that they are subject to surveillance. . . . This prohibition against surveillance does not prevent employers from "observing public union activity, particularly where such activity occurs on company premises" so long as the employer does not engage in conduct that is so "'out of the ordinary' that it creates the impression of surveillance." . . . Even during the course of an organizing campaign, an employer has the right to maintain a security force at the level "necessary to the furtherance of legitimate business interest."*[44]

Local Ordinances and Regulations

By enacting **privacy** ordinances, municipalities are often at the forefront of personal **privacy** legislation. A local law or ordinance is as binding on an employer operating within a local jurisdiction as are federal or state laws. Every employer must be aware of and comply with local ordinances that offer more expansive protection than state or federal laws do. For example, the City and County of San Francisco has enacted a worker **privacy** ordinance stating: "It is the purpose of this Article to protect employees against unreasonable inquiry and investigation into off-the-job conduct, associations, and activities not directly related to the actual performance of job responsibilities." It contains certain prohibitions on employer control of employees' outside activities such as the following: "No employer may make, adopt, or enforce any rule or policy forbidding or preventing employees from engaging or participating in personal relationships, organizations, activities, or otherwise restricting their freedom of association, unless said relationships, activities, or associations have a direct and actual impact on the employees' ability to perform their assigned responsibilities."[45] However, claimants must be certain of the application of these local statutes as they often are restricted to limited classes of individuals.

> ***Example:*** Robert Landon, an African American male, sued his employer Northwest Airlines for terminating him for damaging an airplane. After the accident, he tested positive for marijuana metabolites and was fired. He sued Northwest Airlines in Minnesota, its principal place of business, for violation of his rights under federal law, the California Constitutional

provision guaranteeing **privacy**, and the San Francisco Worker Privacy Ordinance. He claimed that the employer's directive to submit to a urine test was unreasonable under the ordinance. Unfortunately for Mr. Landon, San Francisco's airport is located in San Mateo County and not within the city and county of San Francisco. For this and a myriad of other reasons, his claims were dismissed by the federal district court in Minnesota.[46]

Focus on Ethics
The Inadvertent E-Mail

Assume that you are the supervisor of several employees, one of whom asks your assistant to retrieve a file that has been left behind in the employee's office. The employee needs your assistant to bring the file to a meeting at which the information in the file will be used. While retrieving the file, your assistant looks at the employee's computer screen and quickly notes personal e-mails are being sent and received from the company computer through a private personal e-mail account accessed from the company's computers during the workday. Your company has no policy or practice with regard to limiting employees' access to their personal e-mail accounts during the workday. The subject line on many of the e-mail messages indicate to your assistant that this employee is contemplating leaving the company and working for a competitor. Your assistant calls you into the employee's office, and you are informed of the content of the e-mails. You are alarmed about the prospect of losing this key employee to a competitor to and from whom many of the messages appear to be sent. You open a few of the e-mails and determine that, as of today, the employee apparently has not disclosed confidential information to the competitor soliciting her for employment. The subject employee is a team leader for an important project and has access to both confidential and nonproprietary information on your company. The premature disclosure of the company's current projects could prove to be strategically harmful to your company. The employee's continued involvement on the current project is critical to the financial success of the company, and if the employee were to quit at an inopportune time the company would incur substantial losses. This employee has already voiced feelings that the company invades her privacy and expressed beliefs that male managers in the company do not view female managers as equals.

Ethics Questions

1. Should you disclose the information about the employee's e-mails to anyone?
2. On confronting the employee, what should be the company's response to charges that the company has been snooping and invading personal private e-mail that was not sent on the company e-mail system?
3. Was the employee's inadvertent disclosure of future career plans enough to allow you to terminate the employee's at-will status without fear of a lawsuit for wrongful termination based on public policy for invading her **privacy**?
4. What is your recommendation to the senior management about this situation?

Human Resource Form
Privacy Waivers

There is a direct relationship between the strength of an employee's expectation of **privacy** in the workplace and the outcome of a trial. The greater the expectation of **privacy**, the greater the likelihood the employee will prevail in litigation. When hiring and promoting employees, the employer would be well advised to obtain written authorization and ratifications from the employee that permit the employer to conduct searches of the workplace. A generic authorization to be executed by the employee might read as follows:

Consent to Work Area Inspection

I agree that my work area, including my desk and/or locker and computer equipment, is the exclusive property of my employer. My employer has the right, with or without prior notice to me, to open and inspect my desk, locker, file cabinets, computer, company vehicle, packages, purse, briefcase, and food and beverage containers, as well as any contents found in or on the foregoing. I authorize my supervisors or an authorized company representative to inspect these areas at any time of day. I understand and agree to this consent and understand that I may refuse an offer of employment, if one is made to me, and that my continued employment is subject to this consent.

Date: ____________ ____________________________

Print name: ____________

Key Terms and Concepts

- The Restatement (Second) of Torts, §205A definition of privacy
- Fundamental rights
- Fourth Amendment privacy protections
- Fourteenth Amendment privacy protections
- State action
- Invasion of privacy
- Appropriating another's likeness
- Intrusion into seclusion
- Public disclosure of private facts
- Placing a person in a false light
- Objectively reasonable expectation of privacy
- Tort law
- Reasonable expectation of privacy
- Ordinances and privacy rights
- EPPA

Chapter Summary

- The right of privacy is not subject to an exact definition. It is generally defined as an expectation that confidential information about a person will not be disclosed to a third person, such as an employer.

- Public-sector employees and government contractors are protected by the federal Constitution from invasions of privacy if they are intrusive or unreasonable, depending upon the nature of the employment and the purpose and scope of the search or invasion.

■ The Fourth and Fourteenth Amendments to the Constitution apply to curb wrongful intrusions by government into the lives of its citizens. Known as state action, the government must be directly or indirectly involved in the invasion of privacy to invoke these constitutional protections.

■ Private-sector employment does not typically involve state action. Invasions of privacy in the private sector are tested under state constitutions, statutes, and tort law remedies.

■ Privacy rights are respected only in areas in which a person would reasonably expect to be private.

■ Employers may monitor employees' private outside activities in a circumscribed manner only when such activities directly affect the employers' business activities.

■ There are no privacy rights to information that is of public record or voluntarily disclosed by a person in a public forum.

■ An employee can waive his or her reasonable expectation of privacy explicitly or implicitly. The circumstances of each case will control whether a court will find that the employee had a reasonable expectation of privacy.

■ The EPPA limits the use of polygraphs in the private sector. The usual exception to its use by private employers is in the context of an "ongoing investigation." If an employer is to use the ongoing investigation exception, the polygraph may be required to be taken only when: (1) the employer is engaged in an ongoing investigation involving economic loss or injury to the employer's business, (2) the employee to be tested had access to the property in question, and (3) the employer has a reasonable suspicion that the employee was involved in the incident. No specific notices are required to be given and maintained. The applicant or employee who is subjected to the improper use of a polygraph test may sue the employer for damages.

■ Even if some personal use of employer-supplied communication devices is permitted, company policies should explicitly state that employees have no expectation of privacy. Employers should not allow supervisors to make informal exceptions to this policy.

■ Agreements between a union and an employer and federal labor law can control the determination of whether a union member enjoys a reasonable expectation of privacy.

Online Student Support

- Loislaw legal research and writing assignments.
- Loislaw group projects and class presentations.
- Loislaw access, providing online research including up-to-date cases, statutes, rules, and regulations. Primary law for all 50 states and federal jurisdictions. Registration required for access to this resource.
- Practice questions, including sample true/false, multiple choice, and short answer questions to test your understanding of concepts.
- Additional human resource forms.
- Internet exercises.
- Blogs.
- Supplementary statutory and regulatory materials.

Case Problems

12.1 A federal district court in Connecticut refused to issue an injunction regarding the imposition of discipline on a group of corrections officers for their membership in a motorcycle club (The Outlaws). The discipline was challenged as an infringement of the First Amendment's protection of freedom of association. Argue for and against the correctional officers' position. (*Piscottano v. Murphy*, 317 F. Supp. 2d 97 (D. Conn. 2004))

12.2 How extensive should the employer's power to restrict off-hours conduct be? The state of Alabama permits state employees who are paid less than $75,000 to engage in private-sector employment on their own time if no other legal prohibition or "conflict" exists (Ala. Code §36-1-11). Do you think an employer should have the right to control after-hours conduct? If so, what limitations if any should apply, and how would you concretely state and measure inappropriate conduct? Alabama has chosen a monetary threshold to permit such outside employment. What do you think would be an appropriate threshold?

12.3 Some states, including California, Minnesota, and Rhode Island, protect those of a particular gender identity or orientation from discrimination in employment (Cal. Civ. Code §51(5) (employer's perception of the employee's or applicant's "appearance"); Minn. Stat. §363.01 (41a) (protects others' perception of a self-image not associated with one's biological sex); R.I. Gen. Laws §28-5-6 (gender-related self-image and appearance)). You have been assigned to create two versions of a new employment policy for consideration by senior management. Assuming your business is not located in a state that affords protection from harassment for gender orientation, write a clear and concise human resource policy statement promoting and denying employment protection of applicants' and employees' sexual orientation. How would such a policy be enforced without invasion of others' privacy interests? Could an employer lawfully monitor suspected violations of such a policy?

12.4 If an employer's president came into possession of an employee's "journal" or diary (it had been taken by another employee from the employee's desk), would his reading and retention of it for some hours act as an invasion of privacy, even though he copied the pages in which derogatory references to him were made? (See *Ghassomians v. Ashland Indep. School District*, 55 F. Supp. 3d 675 (E.D. Ky. 1998)). Is reading a diary different from intercepting mail delivered to a business office or telephone calls on office telephones? Would it have made a difference to the employee's reasonable expectation of privacy if the journal had been open, closed, or locked when it was discovered by the fellow employee?

12.5 You are an employer who has received evidence of sexual harassment by one of your employees towards a nonemployee. If, due the nature of your firm's business, the public disclosure of the harassment would bring it embarrassment and financial ruin, do you have the right as an employer to conduct any investigation of your employee? What rights would entitle you to conduct an investigation, and to what degree could you conduct such an investigation? What rights does your employee have relative to your investigation of his or her off-hours conduct?

End Notes

1. *O'Brien v. Papa Gino's of America, Inc.*, 780 F.2d 1067 (1st Cir. 1986).
2. *Skinner v. Railway Labor Executives' Assn.*, 489 U.S. 602 (1989).
3. *Bluestein v. Skinner*, 908 F.2d 451 (9th Cir. 1990).
4. *Shulman v. Group W Productions, Inc.*, 18 Cal.4th 200 (1998) (California Supreme Court addressed the balance between privacy and press freedom. Plaintiffs, two members of a family who were not public figures, did not consent to the videotaping and recording of their extrication from a traffic accident. The videotape and soundtrack were broadcast on a documentary television show. The state supreme court held that the plaintiffs did not have a cause of action for publication of private facts but they could sue for unreasonable intrusion into seclusion. The court noted that intrusion into seclusion cases are fact specific and, as a result, no exact definition exists).
5. *Payton v. City of Santa Clara*, 132 Cal.App.3d 152 (1982).
6. *Kapellas v. Kofman*, 1 Cal.3d 20 (1969).
7. 5 U.S.C. §552(a)(4) (2009).
8. 42 U.S.C. §12101.
9. 42 U.S.C. §12112(d)(3)(B)(i)-(iii).
10. 29 U.S.C. §§701-796l.
11. See, 41 C.F.R. §60-741.6(c)(i)-(iii).
12. 29 U.S.C. §§2601-2654.
13. 29 C.F.R. §825.500(g).
14. 29 U.S.C. §§651-678.
15. 29 C.F.R. §1910.1020(e)(3)(ii).
16. 42 U.S.C. §12114(c).
17. 41 U.S.C. §701.
18. *Jennings v. Minco Tech Labs, Inc.*, 765 S.W.2d 497 (Tx. App. 1989).
19. 29 U.S.C. §2006(e)-(f).
20. 29 U.S.C. §2006(b).
21. 29 U.S.C. §2006(e), (f).
22. *Pulla v. Amoco Oil Co.*, 34 F. Supp. 2d 1299 (N.D. Okla. 1999).
23. *Doe v. Kohn Nast & Graft, P.C.*, 866 F. Supp. 190 (E.D. Pa. 1994).
24. *Simpson v. Unemployment Corp. Bd. of Review*, 450 A. 2d 305 (Pa. Com. Ct. 1982).
25. *Bodewig v. K-Mart*, 635 P. 2d 657 (Ore. Ct. of App.1981).
26. 415 U.S.C. §1681a(x)(2).
27. Labor Code §435.
28. Mich. Comp. Laws §750.593d.
29. N.Y. Gen. Bus. Law §395b.
30. *Rathbun v. U.S.*, 355 U.S. 107 (1957).
31. *PBA Local No. 38 v. Woodbridge Police Dept.*, 832 F. Supp. 808 (D.N.J. 1993).
32. *Kee v. City of Rowlett, Tex.*, 247 Fed. 3d 206 (5th Cir. 2001).
33. *Pinkerton National Detective Agency, Inc. v. Stevens*, 132 S.E. 119 (1963).
34. *Fowler v. Southern Bell*, 343 Fed 2d 150 (5th Cir. 1965).
35. *McDaniel v. Atlanta Coca-Cola Bottling*, 2 S.E. 810 (1939) (The bottler suspected the plaintiff was presenting a fake claim that she encountered a foreign substance in a bottle of Coke, secreted a listening device in her hospital room, and listened to her conversations from a room above).
36. *Husen v. Dow Chemical Company*, 2006 U.S. Dist. Lexis 14868 (E.D. Mich. 2006).
37. *State of Washington v. Townsend*, 20 P. 3d 1027 (2001).
38. 979 F. Supp. 1177 (S.D. Ohio 1997).
39. *Rulon-Miller v. Intl. Business Mach. Corp.*, 162 Cal. App. 3d 241 (1984), *overruled* in part *Guz v. Bechtel National Inc.*, 24 Cal. 4th 317 (2000) (overruled as to *Rulon-Miller* court's holding on covenant of good faith and fair dealing).
40. 539 U.S. 558 (2003).
41. *Thorne v. City of El Segundo*, 726 F2d 459 (9th Cir 1983).
42. 791 F2d 736, (9th Cir 1986).
43. *Marcum v. McWhorter* 308 F.3d 635 (6th Cir. 2002).
44. *Parsippany Hotel Management Co. v. N.L.R.B.*, 99 F.3d 413, 420 (D.C. Cir. (1996),
45. S.F. Police Code §3300A.2(1).
46. *Landon v. Northwest Airlines*, 72 F.3d 620 (8th Cir. 1995).

Chapter 13
Federal Labor Law

The labor movement was the principal force that transformed misery and despair into hope and progress. Out of its bold struggles, economic and social reform gave birth to unemployment insurance, old-age pensions, government relief for the destitute and, above all, new wage levels that meant not mere survival but a tolerable life. The captains of industry did not lead this transformation; they resisted it until they were overcome. When in the thirties the wave of union organization crested over the nation, it carried to secure shores not only itself but the whole society. —Martin Luther King Jr., speech to AFL-CIO, October 1965

Learning Objectives

1. Define the scope and application of the significant federal labor laws.
2. Distinguish between lawful and unfair labor practices.
3. Explain the rights and duties of an employer subject to a bargaining agreement.
4. Explain the rights and duties of a union subject to a bargaining agreement.
5. Identify the mandatory subjects of collective bargaining.
6. State the rights of a union to strike and employers' responses to strikes.
7. Explain what is meant by good-faith bargaining.
8. Recognize the rights of union members relative to their union.

Chapter Outline

Chapter Opening scenario

David Dugan had begun working at Rockaway Industries in Springdale, Arkansas, in 1997. In 2002, the United Food Commercial Workers Union began a union-organizing campaign at the facility. Dugan became a member of the organizing committee and participated in organizing the employees to join a union. Rockaway issued Dugan a disciplinary notice for interrupting a co-worker for ten minutes to discuss union-related activities. Allegedly threatened by another employee for his pro-union stance, Dugan's complaint did not result in any discipline to the other employee for lack of evidence. He was suspended for interrupting another employee's work to discuss union matters. Dugan was eventually terminated by Rockaway for ignoring repeated warnings that he needed a visitor's badge to come onto company property on his day off to distribute union literature, for bringing a tape recorder onto the premises to tape conversations with supervisors, and for keeping employees from performing their duties. The National Labor Relations Board agreed with the union's unfair labor practice charge that Rockaway had discriminated against Dugan because it discouraged membership in any labor organization. Dugan claims he was engaged in a lawful, protected organizing activity at Rockaway. Although Rockaway openly opposed the union, other than in its dealings with Dugan no evidence indicated it ever threatened or intimidated employees for engaging in union activity. Rockaway distributed information to its employees encouraging them to weigh the pros and cons of unionization, although it warned the employees not to discuss union issues during work time. Should Dugan be reinstated to his position or should the termination stand?[1]

Introduction

The desire of workers to organize and more fully enjoy the benefits of their labor has a storied past within American history. In this chapter, we will study one of the exceptions to the at-will rule of employment: the right of an employer to discharge an employee can be modified by a union-management labor agreement. We begin our review with a short history of some of the important episodes from the history of U.S. labor-management relations. We will then analyze the reach of the most important federal labor laws regulating union and protected activities in private-sector employment. Among them is the **National Labor Relations Act (NLRA)**. That statute and the regulations issued by the **National Labor Relations Board (NLRB)** substantially preempt the ability of states to enact legislation involving union activities. We conclude our study with a discussion of the impact and future of labor relations in this country.

According to the Annual Report of the National Labor Relations Board for fiscal year 2009, the agency dealt with approximately 23,000 charges alleging that employers or labor organizations committed unfair labor practices prohibited by federal law, adversely affecting covered employees. During this period, the **NLRB** received 2,912 requests to hold union elections, including 2,696 petitions to conduct secret-ballot elections in which workers in appropriate groups select or reject unions to represent them in collective bargaining with workers. The **NLRB** also obtained over $77 million in reimbursements to employees illegally discharged or otherwise discriminated against in violation of their organizational rights. The Board's administrative law judges issued 190 decisions during the year.[2] To understand the importance of the Board's role in the modern labor-management relationship, it is useful to understand some of the history of the labor movement before we review the current law of the rights and duties affecting employers and unions.

The Road to a Federal Labor Policy

Early American history reflects the lack of an individual's freedom of choice with regard to employment. That history is entangled with issues of slavery, indentured servitude, apprenticeships, and inequality among and between classes and genders. American workers' passion for independence from Britain was linked also to their desire to better their own condition. The involvement of the worker helped transform the country, as workers realized the promise of the benefits of political organization and action. However, the first few decades following our independence highlight largely unsuccessful efforts to organize workers. For example, in 1786, Philadelphia printers organized a union and conducted the first strike in the United States. A few years later, in 1794, Philadelphia shoemakers organized a union in an effort to secure better wages. For a decade, that union was successful in obtaining wage increases. However, in 1805 the shoemakers' union members went on strike. The strike collapsed when the union leaders were indicted and a jury found them guilty of conspiracy. The leaders were fined, and, as a result, the union went bankrupt. The law established in that case widely influenced judicial thought for many decades, namely, that labor unions were illegal conspiracies.

Labor Union
Organization or association of individuals formed for the purpose of negotiating with employers on behalf of employees with regard to rates of pay, wages, hours of employment, or other conditions of employment.

The period from 1830 through the Civil War saw significant developments in the American labor movement. Because of strong labor advocacy, the ten-hour workday was adopted throughout many states. However, employers often pressured or blacklisted employees into agreeing to waive that requirement. With increasing immigration, many workers would accept an employer's terms of employment. During this period, as much as one-third of the U.S. labor force was composed of children under age 16, who often worked in dangerous conditions and for low pay. While some unions were organized, including the first national union, the National Cooperative of Cordwainers (shoemakers), they could not effect large-scale changes for their members. The many financial panics, widespread conflicts over the effects of immigration in the workforce, and lack of a coherent labor policy retarded the growth of organized labor during this period. Moreover, tension was growing over the issue of slavery as it related to the workplace. Some Northern workers and manufacturers felt that Southern employers' use of such labor gave those employers an unfair competitive advantage. The period was marked by stridency in virtually all aspects of the labor landscape.

Between the end of the Civil War and the beginning of the twentieth century, the economic influence of organized workers gained respect and for that brief period political attention was increasingly paid to organized labor. In some states, factory workers were able to secure some moderate gains in wages and reductions in working hours. However, the Panic of 1873, which led to a severe financial depression, prompted bitter antagonism between workers and the wealthy classes who controlled the financial, transportation, and manufacturing industries. Fortunes of the rich collapsed along with many national unions, which were unable to secure any benefits for their workers. Nevertheless, by the early 1880s, the restoration of the nation's economic health began. Known as the Progressive Era, this period of reform extended to just before World War I. It was during this period that railroads expanded their coverage throughout the country, the demand for factory workers increased, and immigration into the United States soared. The increased availability of immigrant labor again shifted bargaining power to the employer at the expense of the working classes. Wages remained depressed, and issues of health, safety, and working conditions were often ignored because of the ready supply of replacement workers.

By the early 1900s, many national and regional unions had formed, including the AFL-CIO. Membership in unions increased as workers sought better pay and working conditions. Organized labor focused on industrialized plants in the northeast and often conducted strikes to improve working conditions. Many employers did not welcome the increasing power of organized labor. At the turn of the last century, employers responded to the chaotic conditions created by workers' strikes by turning to the federal courts. They used antitrust law to maintain the upper hand in response to workers' organizing efforts. During that period, employers argued successfully that labor organizing was an illegal conspiracy that restrained trade in violation of the Sherman Antitrust Act of 1890. Federal courts freely granted injunctions against union activities. The Supreme Court even ruled that employers could issue **yellow-dog contracts**, that is, a contract under which the employer and the employee agree as a condition of hiring that the employee will not join a labor union. The Court prevented unions from soliciting workers to join unions because they were illegally inducing workers to breach their **yellow-dog contracts** with employers.[3] These court injunctions were contrary to the great weight of public opinion. Congress inadequately responded to the workers' plight when it amended the Sherman Antitrust Act by enacting §6 of the **Clayton Antitrust Act** in 1914. That act provided:

Yellow-Dog Contract
An agreement between an employer and a potential employee that, as a condition of being hired or of continuing employment, the employee will not join a labor union.

> The labor of a human being is not a commodity or article of commerce. Nothing contained in the antitrust laws shall be construed to forbid the existence and operation of labor, agricultural, or horticultural organizations, instituted for the purposes of mutual help,

> and not having capital stock or conducted for profit, or to forbid or restrain individual members of such organizations from lawfully carrying out the legitimate objects thereof; nor shall such organizations, or the members thereof, be held or construed to be illegal combinations or conspiracies in restraint of trade, under the antitrust laws.[4]

That law declared only that unions could exist — it didn't bar the continued issuance of court injunctions against union strikes and boycotts. While workers had the right to organize, employers were not obligated to bargain fairly with them concerning the terms and conditions of their employment. When the United States entered World War I in 1917, the labor movement had three million workers. President Wilson established the War Labor Board to mediate between labor and management. However, it lacked enforcement powers and was disbanded after the war.

The decade of the 1920s was a period of great labor unrest. Except for the **Railway Labor Act (RLA)**, this period did not offer any significant redress for workers because the country was distracted by many serious events. Labor-management strife reached a high point during this period as America began a period of reindustrialization. However, by the end of that decade, the Depression, a period of immense economic and social upheaval, had begun. President Hoover and Congress held that the solution to the economic crisis was the restoration of public and business confidence in the economy. As history reflects, that philosophy failed. While the effects of the Depression were devastating for most Americans, organized labor experienced dramatic growth. Sit-down strikes at large auto plants led car manufacturers and others to recognize the unions. Mass migration from the rural South to the industrialized North caused other related labor problems. The first of the significant federal protections offered to employees that has had long-standing effect on organized labor was the **RLA**.

Railway Labor Act

The **RLA**, passed in 1926, required employers to bargain collectively and prohibited discrimination against unions. It was the beginning of a new era in labor-management relations. Originally, it applied to interstate railroads and their related companies. In 1936, it was amended to include interstate airlines. The importance of the **RLA** is that it guaranteed workers the right to bargain collectively and provided a means to resolve disputes. The national Railroad Adjustment Board, a federal agency, has exclusive jurisdiction over disputes arising out of **collective bargaining agreements (CBA)** between railway employers and unions. Now within the jurisdiction of the U.S. Department of Transportation, units within that department become involved in contract disputes at key points during a covered labor dispute.

Under the **RLA**, rail and air carriers and their employees may invoke the services of the **National Mediation Board** to facilitate the resolution of a labor dispute. Either side to the dispute may request the Board to interpret a **CBA** subject to the act. Union members must exhaust their remedies under the **CBA** before proceeding to court to enforce rights against their unions or employers. The **National Mediation Board** does not investigate and hold a union election unless a dispute has arisen among the employees. The **National Mediation Board** is intended to be an investigative agency and not an adjudicatory one, of the type we will study in the context of the **NLRB**.

Railway Labor Act
The 1926 federal act requiring that transportation industry employers bargain collectively and not discriminate against unions.

Collective Bargaining Agreement (CBA)
A negotiated agreement between a labor union and an employer.

National Mediation Board
The federal agency that facilitates the resolution of labor-management disputes in the transportation industry.

Sometimes a dispute between a transportation carrier and its employees cannot be resolved by means of the **RLA**. If the **National Mediation Board** believes that the dispute substantially threatens to interrupt interstate commerce, the Board notifies the president of the United States, who may create an emergency board to investigate and to report back within 30 days of its creation. This 30-day cooling-off period allows time to investigate the dispute and may be extended by an act of Congress.[5] Maintenance of the status quo by the parties to a covered dispute is the central purpose of the act's dispute resolution processes. The parties can then proceed to arbitrate or otherwise resolve their differences.

Notable Events in American Labor History

- ***Haymarket Affair, Chicago, Illinois, 1886.*** American labor unions prepared for a general strike in support of a then recent proposal by a labor federation that the eight-hour workday should become standard. Striking workers who had been locked out at the McCormick Harvesting Machine Co. plant met. Armed police officers guarded the replacement strikebreakers hired by the company. When the strikers surged toward the plant gates to harass the strikebreakers, the police fired on the nonviolent strikers, killing several of them. A peaceful rally was scheduled for the following day at Chicago's Haymarket Square; however, during the final speech of the day, when the police moved toward the speakers' stand to end the rally, a bomb was thrown, killing a police officer. That led the police to open fire and, shooting indiscriminately, they killed and wounded some of their own as well as some workers. At the rally organizers' trial for conspiracy, a jury convicted them for the deaths and injuries suffered that day. Some of the convicted were hanged, while others were sentenced to life imprisonment. Several years later, those who were still imprisoned were pardoned by the Illinois governor as victims of a travesty of justice, despite contrary public opinion.
- ***Cripple Creek Miners strike of 1894.*** Following the decision of Colorado mine owners to extend the workday from eight to ten hours with no change in the daily wage of $3.00, miners struck the mines. This strike is regarded by historians as one of the most unusual labor actions in American history. The strike included violent actions by both miners and local law enforcement, the ordering of martial law by the governor, the intervention of the state militia to protect miners, court decisions by biased judges, lynching mobs charging jails, and a local Colorado sheriff cooperating in the organization of a private army to guard the mines. The Colorado governor ordered the state militia to restore order, and it did so by capturing the mine owners' private army. The restoration of order and concessions by the owners empowered the union and altered the face of Colorado politics for decades.
- ***The "Bread and Roses" strike of 1912.*** The immigrant workers in Lawrence, Massachusetts, were led by the Industrial Workers of the World. The mostly immigrant, female, and ethnically diverse workforce struck for more than two months to protest abusive working conditions in the textile mills. Dangerous working conditions and the employment of children under the age of 14 were common. The state militia was called in to restore peace, but its actions resulted in assaults on children and their mothers. President Taft ordered a nationwide investigation into factory conditions.

Unfortunately for the workers, the gains they secured from the mill owners were lost over the next few years.

- ***The strikes of the 1920s through the 1950s.*** Throughout this period, workers' strikes against their employers in the auto, shipping, agriculture, newspaper, and textile fields were widespread. The reasons for the strikes varied. For example, coal miners often struck the operations of coal companies to protest the dangerous conditions to which they were exposed and the inadequate compensation they received for their work. For the most part, these strikes were unsuccessful. Union membership declined in the late 1950s as white-collar workers came to outnumber blue-collar workers for the first time, women entered the workforce in large numbers, and the country started its transition to a service-based economy.
- ***Public union strikes of the 1960s.*** Public-sector employees organized and joined unions in the early part of the 1960s. Bargaining and employee strikes resulted in increased wages and benefits and allowed unionization to achieve a permanent place in public-sector employment.
- ***Union action during the 1970s.*** In 1970, U.S. postal workers conducted the first nationwide strike of public employees to protest low wages, inadequate benefits, and unhealthy working conditions. In response, Congress reorganized the Postal Service, modernizing the department and providing for collective bargaining. Strikes at other high profile employers such as General Motors, the New York City Police Department, major league baseball, the *Washington Post,* and Coors Beer improved working conditions and compensation for most of the affected workers.
- ***The 1980s and the diminishing role of the unions.*** President Reagan, a former actor who had previously been elected six times as president of the Screen Actors Guild union in Hollywood, seriously diminished the effectiveness of the unions during this decade, beginning with the firing of federal air traffic controllers in 1981. Other notable strikes of that period include the major league baseball strike, also in 1981, strikes in the professional indoor soccer league and professional football, and boycotts of the Screen Actors and Emmy Awards ceremonies by members of the Screen Actors Guild and the American Federation of Television and Radio Artists.
- ***The 1990s and the twenty-first century.*** As U.S. employment shifted from industries employing organized labor, such as manufacturing, to high tech, professional service, and white-collar jobs, unions lost significant membership. Many unions struck to maintain jobs and fringe benefits. Among those creating headlines during the 1990s and early 2000s were the following: the southern California supermarket strike of 2003–04 (involving 70,000 strikers for over five months); the 2004–05 National Hockey League lockout (which has had lasting repercussions on the sport); transit strikes throughout the United States; auto workers' strikes; and strikes by the Actors and Writers Guild of America, which shut down movie and television production and resulted in the relocation of entertainment production overseas. Despite these events, at the end of 2009, union membership was 12.3 percent (15.3 million) of all U.S. workers.

The Norris-La Guardia Act (the Anti-Injunction Act)

The Norris-La Guardia Act took effect in 1932. It removed legal and judicial impediments to the organizing activities of unions. The act declared that union members would have the freedom of association guaranteed them under the First Amendment. The act barred courts from issuing injunctions to prevent strikes, picketing, or boycotts.

Before its enactment, a federal court could issue injunctions prohibiting a union's threatened or actual strike, picketing, or boycotting of a company. One federal court stated, "Congress passed the Act as a reaction to the widespread misuse by federal courts of issuing injunctions in labor-management controversies."[6] This federal law also made illegal the use of **yellow-dog contracts** in the United States.

The purpose of the law was to allow employees to establish unions and to withdraw from the jurisdiction of the federal courts the power to issue an injunction in nonviolent labor actions. Courts retained the power to issue injunctions to prevent fraudulent acts or acts of violence, including coercive or intimidating picketing. To pursue such an injunction, an employer must present at an evidentiary hearing before a federal court evidence that substantial and irreparable injury has been done to its property; if a finding of fact is made that the injury would continue without the injunction, one is issued.[7] This act does not apply to state courts; state judges are empowered to issue injunctions if any of the workers' activities can be considered violent or a threat to peaceful assembly under state law.

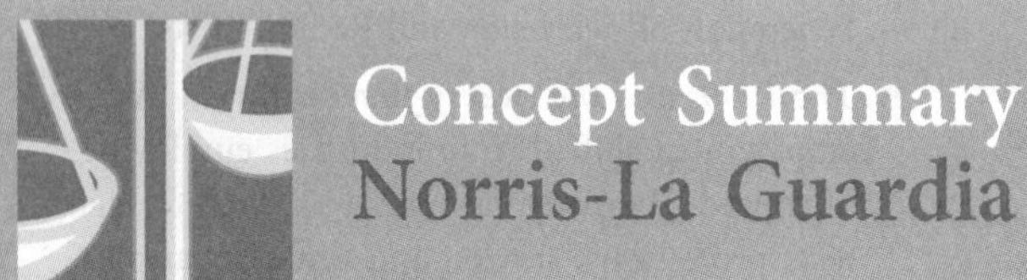

Concept Summary Norris-La Guardia

The Norris-La Guardia Act:

- protects union activities such as lawful strikes and picketing; and
- makes it difficult for employers to obtain injunctions against union activities.

Union Organizing

A **labor union** is an organization or association of individuals formed for the purpose of negotiating with employers on behalf of employees with regard to the terms and conditions of employment. The union may or may not be organized under the authority of federal law, such as the **RLA** or the **NLRA**. Unions permit the parties to bargain collectively on any lawful subject, but federal law requires bargaining on mandatory subjects. These include wages, hours, and other terms and conditions of employment. Over their history, unions have been successful in improving the working conditions of the American worker. Many things that we take for granted resulted from the efforts of unions and management to reach a common understanding about suitable terms and conditions in the workplace. For example, through the efforts of unions, the following have been adopted: the 8-hour workday and 40-hour workweek; paid overtime; and fringe benefits, such as employer-paid health care and retirement plans. In addition, the labor movement united with health and public interest groups to pass The Mine Act and the Occupational Health and Safety Act. Unions also help fund research into industrial accidents and diseases.

National Labor Relations Act (NLRA)
Also known as the Wagner Act; the 1935 federal law recognizing and protecting the rights of workers to organize and collectively bargain with employers. Requires employers to bargain with the exclusive representative of the workers.

Right to Join a Union

Meaningful federal protection of workers' rights to organize and collectively bargain began with the **NLRA**. Also known as the **Wagner Act** and enacted by Congress in 1935, the NLRA gives most private-sector employees the right to join a union and to have that union negotiate with employers on their behalf. The act provides another important right as well: the right to refuse to join and participate with a union. This right has been strengthened by right-to-work laws, discussed later in this chapter. The **Taft-Hartley Act**, more formally known as the **Labor-Management Relations Act (LMRA)**, amended the **NLRA** in 1947.

Labor-Management Relations Act (LMRA)
Also known as the Taft-Hartley Act; a federal law addressing unfair labor practices on the part of unions.

The cornerstone of individual rights relating to unions is set forth in §7 of the **NLRA**. As it now reads, it provides for the following:

> Employees shall have the right to self-organization, to form, join, or assist labor organizations, to bargain collectively through representatives of their own choosing, and to engage in other concerted activities for the purpose of collective bargaining or other mutual aid or protection and shall also have the right to refrain from any or all such activities except to the extent that such right may be affected by an agreement requiring membership in a labor organization as a condition of employment [as authorized by law].

Among the activities protected under this law are the following: forming or attempting to form a union among employees; joining a union; assisting a union in organizing the employees of an employer; and striking or picketing to secure better terms and conditions of employment.

Once the workers decide on union representation and the union is certified as their representative, then the union representative is the exclusive representative of all those employees. The employer must deal with the union on all matters concerning "wages, hours and other terms and conditions of employment." The employer may not act unilaterally in any matter within that category of bargaining. The employer may not deal directly with individual employees or groups of employees on such issues.

Covered Employers and Employees

For purposes of federal jurisdiction, any entity that has the right to control working conditions is an employer. The **NLRA** does not cover unions as employers or their nonemployee organizers, and it was not intended to apply to employees working temporarily outside the United States for American employers.

The **NLRA**, as amended, protects any worker whose work ceased as a result of a labor dispute or an **unfair labor practice** and who has not obtained any regular and substantially equivalent employment.[8] However, *it does not include any of the following categories of workers*:

Unfair Labor Practice
Conduct and practices by either employers or unions determined under the NLRA or by the NLRB to be unlawful.

- agricultural laborers;
- domestic workers in homes;
- workers employed by a parent or spouse;
- independent contractors;
- supervisorial employees;
- workers employed by an employer subject to another federal labor-management statute, such as the **RLA**; and
- workers employed by the federal state or local government.

Concept Summary
NLRA, as Amended by Taft-Hartley

The NLRA addresses the following:

- gives nonsupervisory private-sector employees the right to organize and join a union, to choose their own union representation, and to bargain collectively with their employer over wages, hours, working conditions, and work rules;
- establishes the right to engage in peaceful strikes, picketing, and concerted activities;
- establishes the National Labor Relations Board (the "board" or the "NLRB");
- defines (in §8) certain acts and practices of employers as unfair labor practices;
- empowers the NLRB to conduct a secret-ballot election when a petition is filed requesting one (Any union, worker, or employer can file a petition. Workers or a union may request an election if at least 30 percent of the workers have signed a petition or authorization cards. An employer may voluntarily recognize a union if a majority of workers has executed authorization cards.);
- prohibits employers from punishing employees who exercise their rights to join a union and participate in lawful union activities; and
- provides that all workers in a bargaining unit are entitled to the benefits obtained through collective bargaining, regardless of whether the workers are members of the union. Nonunion workers employed by a unionized company enjoy the same benefits as union members.

The National Labor Relations Act

The **NLRA** radically changed federal policy toward the rights of workers to organize and bargain collectively. The **NLRA** was an important part of President Roosevelt's New Deal legislation. The **NLRA**:

- recognized the right of employees to organize and join a union;
- encouraged **CBAs** (an agreement between the employer and organized workers over wages, hours, rules, and working conditions);
- outlawed company unions;
- identified **unfair labor practices** of both employers and unions (i.e., unlawful practices);
- created the **NLRB**, empowered to supervise union elections, conduct administrative law hearings on **unlawful labor practice charges**, and take appropriate legal action to secure a remedy against such practices;
- established the procedures by which union organization would occur;
- forbade employer interference with respect to organizing, bargaining, or engaging in **concerted activities** by workers (defined by the **NLRB** as any activity of two or more employees who attempt to improve their working conditions, such as wages and benefits);

National Labor Relations Board (NLRB)
An independent U.S. administrative agency that conducts labor union elections and investigates and adjudicates unfair labor practices.

Example: Two or more employees request an employer to improve fringe benefit packages offered to employees. A single worker speaking on behalf of one or more co-workers about protected subjects is also covered. These employees do not have to be members of a union to be protected under the **NLRA**.

- recognized the use of lawful strikes;
- protected union members from discrimination by their unions; and
- made it unlawful for an employer to refuse to bargain in good faith with a union or nonunion employees engaged in concerted action on a lawful topic.

Federal labor laws cover workers in an employer-employee relationship; that is, the employer directs and controls the work and the means by which it is accomplished. They do *not* cover independent contractors, but they *would cover* the employees of an independent contractor. Before the passage of the Immigration Reform and Control Act (IRCA), addressed in a later chapter, undocumented aliens were "employees" under the **NLRA**. However, in enacting the IRCA, Congress ensured that U.S. immigration laws take precedence over the protections offered by the **NLRA**. Compliance with IRCA requires employers to discharge a worker on learning of the worker's undocumented status and, thus, his or her status as unauthorized to work in the United States.

Congress intended **supervisors** to be excluded from the category of covered employees under the federal labor law. The term ***"supervisor"*** means any individual having authority, in the interest of the employer, to hire, transfer, suspend, lay off, recall, promote, discharge, assign, reward, or discipline other employees or who possesses the responsibility for directing them or for adjusting their grievances, which, in effect, means recommending such action. The foregoing activities must involve the exercise of authority, beyond the routine or clerical, requiring the use of independent judgment.[9] Managers and owners of businesses are also excluded from coverage under these federal statutes.

The **NLRA** does have a relationship with the earlier-enacted **RLA**. The courts have held that the **RLA** created a limited exception to the **NLRA** prohibition of federal court interference in transportation disputes. The courts will issue an injunction to preserve the status quo in an interstate transportation dispute that threatens the nation's economic health.[10] Otherwise, the two acts are mutually exclusive in their coverage. When a business is covered by the **RLA**, it is exempt from coverage under the **NLRA**.

The **NLRB** has jurisdiction only with regard to labor disputes that "affect commerce." The enterprise must affect interstate commerce in a manner that is other than purely local in character and that has business of at least minimum sales volumes per year. The Board establishes different annual sales volumes for different industries. The scope of the Commerce Clause is not so broad as to include lay faculty at church-operated institutions; to construe it to include such organizations would result in a conflict with the First Amendment's prohibition against restricting the exercise of religion. Through the 1970 Postal Reorganization Act, the **NLRB**'s jurisdiction was extended to the U.S. Postal Service.

Matters Outside National Labor Relations Board Jurisdiction

The **NLRB** has limited jurisdiction; that is, it has the jurisdiction that Congress has given it or the courts have recognized. The Board does not enforce federal laws within the jurisdiction of other federal agencies. Areas of interest outside the jurisdiction of the **NLRB** include the following.

- Matters under the jurisdiction of the U.S. Department of Labor, including:
  - wages and hours;
  - federal workers' compensation programs;
  - occupational health and safety;
  - Family and Medical Leave Act (FMLA);
  - retirement and other welfare benefit plans covered by the Employee Retirement Income Security Act;
  - Uniformed Service Employment and Reemployment Rights Act;
  - Continuation of Health Benefits Coverage Act; and
  - IRCA.
- Matters within the jurisdiction of the Equal Employment Opportunity Commission, including those relating to:
  - race;
  - color;
  - sex;
  - national origin;
  - religion;
  - age; and
  - disability.

The Federal Labor Relations Authority and the Merit Systems Protections Board have jurisdiction over employees of the federal government. State employee protection agencies similarly exist to protect state workers.

Constitutional Challenges

The substantive and procedural aspects of the **NLRA**, as amended, have been held to be a valid exercise of the constitutional power of Congress to regulate interstate commerce. Immediately following its enactment, unions did not utilize the remedies afforded by the statute because the U.S. Supreme Court had frequently held that Congress lacked the constitutional authority to enact such laws under the Commerce Clause. However, in a series of decisions, the Supreme Court quickly upheld the constitutionality of the **NLRA**.[11] In light of these decisions, industry was compelled to bargain with and respect the rights of organized labor. Subsequent Supreme Court cases have upheld the constitutionality of the statute even though it effectively limits or abridges constitutional rights and protections affecting freedom of speech, the right to trial by jury, the freedom to be free from unreasonable searches and seizures, the freedom of contract, and the right of states to legislate in areas of local concern. These limitations are often found within the terms of an enforceable **CBA**.

The Taft-Hartley Act

The **Taft-Hartley Act** substantially amended the **NLRA**. Passed in 1947, President Truman vetoed it as antagonistic to labor. Congress overrode his veto. In the post–World War II years, Americans were frightened by the "Red scare" of communism and were concerned about the infiltration of labor unions by communists. While the **NLRA** had protected workers' rights to participate in unions, the **Taft-Hartley Act** protected workers' rights *not* to participate in unionization. It comprehensively addressed a number of matters not previously addressed by federal labor policy.

The **Taft-Hartley Act** stated "to bargain collectively is the performance of the mutual obligation of the employer and the representative of the employees to meet at reasonable times, and confer in good faith with respect to wages, hours, and other terms and conditions of employment, or the negotiation of an agreement, or any question arising thereunder, and the execution of a written contract incorporating any agreement reached if requested by either party . . ." Such a contract is known as a **CBA**. This act:

- outlawed "closed shops" (i.e., places in which employees are required to maintain union membership as a condition of employment);
- authorized procedures for the president to delay or avert "national emergency" strikes;
- prohibited supervisory employees from joining a union;
- required the NLRB to sue to enjoin unions engaged in secondary boycotts or jurisdictional strikes;
- required union officials to certify they were not communists;
- rendered illegal union shop agreements contrary to state law;
- changed the administration of the NLRB;
- authorized certain injunctions against unions for specific unfair labor practices;
- recognized a 60-day no-strike and no-lockout period for any party seeking to cancel an existing CBA;
- required unions to file financial reports with the U.S. Department of Labor;
- established the Federal Mediation and Conciliation Service;
- authorized "prehire agreements" in the construction industry (This allows an employer primarily engaged in the construction industry to execute a union-security agreement with a union without the union having been designated as the representative of its employees as otherwise required by the act. The agreement can be made before the employer has hired any employees for a project. The union security provisions of a CBA may become effective for all existing and new employees within seven days. Such provisions can require the employer to notify the union concerning job openings and to provide the union with the opportunity to refer qualified applicants for such jobs based on training or experience, length of service with the employer, the industry, or the geographic area.); and
- stopped the practice of employers' payments to union officials.

Eighty-Day "Cooling-Off" Period

One of the important features of the **Taft-Hartley Act** empowers the president to request that a federal court impose an **80-day "cooling-off" period** blocking strikes or lockouts or threatened strikes or lockouts if, in the opinion of the president, these strikes or lockouts, whether threatened or actual, imperil the "national health or safety." Such strikes are called **national emergency strikes**. Management and labor are given the opportunity to continue their negotiations. The president appoints a fact-finding board to assess the consequences of the strike action and the likelihood that the parties will reach a compromise. If the Board's findings indicate that a compromise will not be reached, the president will order the attorney general to obtain a "cease and desist" injunction from a federal district court. During the first 60 days of the 80-day injunction, while labor is continuing to perform, the **Federal Mediation and Conciliation Services** works at the bargaining table trying to persuade the parties to reach an agreement. After 75 days, the **NLRB** conducts a secret election, giving workers the opportunity to accept management's last offer.

Although the **80-day cooling-off period** may appear to be a panacea for labor-management strife, quite often strikes and job actions continue after the elapse of the **80-day cooling-off period**. The **cooling-off period** does not bar the resumption of labor's response to the impasse, but it may merely postpone job action. If the matter is still not settled, job action by the unions may continue; although Congress could impose a legislative solution to end job-action threats, it has not done so.

Elections and Certification

Recognition of a union to act as a bargaining agent on behalf of employees may be the most fundamental right in these federal laws. The road to an **NLRB** election usually involves employees selecting a bargaining representative through a secret representation election conducted by the **NLRB**. This election occurs only after a petition to conduct the election has been filed with the **NLRB**. The filing of a petition with the **NLRB** is the means by which workers seek union representation or decertification of their current union representation. The most commonly filed petitions involve **representation** and **decertification petitions**. The first is used when employees seek union representation, the latter when employees seek an election to vote an existing union out of the workplace. Any union, employer, or individual may file a petition to obtain an election conducted by the **NLRB**. A petition for **representation** can be filed at any time. However, a **decertification election** involves a series of procedures that define when the petition may be brought. Generally, a **decertification petition** can be brought only during the period 60 to 90 days prior to the expiration of the **CBA**.

An election is indicated after the **NLRB** determines that the business affects interstate commerce and that there is a showing that at least 30 percent of the employees favor a petition for an election. The showing is accomplished through the worker's signature on a union authorization card. The provision for conducting an election is to allow the employer, after being asked to bargain, to test out its doubts as to the union's majority by causing the NLRB to hold a secret election. Note that a union can become the collective bargaining representative of a company's employees without a secret-ballot election if the union presents authorization cards signed by a majority of the employees and the employer or one of its managers reviews them and reaches the conclusion that the union has obtained a majority of votes. For this reason, supervisors and managers should be instructed not to touch, review, discuss, or otherwise be involved with the authorization cards. By avoiding those actions, the union must proceed to petition the **NLRB** for an election. Recognition of a union as the bargaining representative for employees involves three steps:

- determining an appropriate bargaining unit;
- conducting a campaign by both the union and the employer; and
- conducting the election.

The Appropriate Bargaining Unit

An **appropriate bargaining unit** is a group of two or more employees who share a community of interest and may reasonably be grouped together for purposes of collective bargaining. The determination of an appropriate unit for such purposes is, under the act, left to the discretion of the **NLRB**. There are, however, a few limitations on the Board's discretion to approve an **appropriate bargaining unit**. For example, the Board may not approve as appropriate a unit that includes both professional (i.e., licensed) and nonprofessional employees, unless a majority of the professional employees vote to be included in the mixed unit. Another provision of the act prohibits the Board from including plant guards in the same unit with other employees.

Appropriate Bargaining Unit
A group of two or more employees sharing a community of interest who may reasonably be grouped together for purposes of collective bargaining.

Usually those employees who have the same or substantially similar interests concerning wages, hours, and working conditions are grouped together in a **bargaining unit**. In determining whether a proposed unit is appropriate, the following factors are also considered: any history of collective bargaining; the desires of the employees concerned; and the extent to which the employees are organized. A bargaining unit may cover the employees in one plant of an employer or it may cover employees in two or more plants of the same employer. As stated previously, supervisors, managers and noncovered individuals are excluded from a **bargaining unit**.

Campaigning by Both Sides

The **NLRA** guarantees employees the right to engage in union organizing activities, which includes the right to discuss the union among themselves and to organize, solicit for, and distribute propaganda in support of a union. Workers engaged in **protected concerted activity** may convey nonconfidential information obtained in the course of employment. However, companies can restrict access to company information and the public dissemination of their records through carefully drawn confidentiality agreements. Employers may not restrict union-related communication in their workplace unless they can demonstrate that such a restriction is required to maintain discipline or production. If such communication does not interfere with work, the employer may not bar such discussions. Employers must give unions access to company bulletin boards to post union-related notices. Union organizers may not commit a trespass to distribute union literature; thus, if a public parking-lot owner prohibited solicitations on its property, it could restrain the union organizers from soliciting for the union.[12] Employers may bar nonemployee union organizers from company property, provided they have reasonable access to employees outside the workplace.

Protected Concerted Activity
An activity that workers may pursue without fear of retaliation from employers, including the right to self-organize, to form or join a union, or to act together to improve the terms and conditions of employment. These activities are protected with or without union representation of the workers. Protects two or more employees acting together.

Example: Local 919 of the United Food and Commercial Workers Union, AFL-CIO, sought to organize employees at a retail store owned and operated by Lechmere, Inc. The store was located in the Lechmere Shopping Plaza. The union began its campaign to organize the store's 200 employees. After a full-page ad in a local newspaper drew little response, nonemployee union organizers entered Lechmere's parking lot and began placing handbills on the windshields of cars parked in a corner of the lot used mostly by employees. Lechmere's manager immediately confronted the organizers, informed them that Lechmere prohibited solicitation or handbill distribution of any kind on its property, and asked them to leave. They did so, and Lechmere employees removed the handbills. The union organizers renewed this handbilling effort on several subsequent occasions, all with the same response from Lechmere. The union organizers returned daily to a grassy strip next to the entrance to picket Lechmere and recorded license numbers of cars parked in the employee parking area. Obtaining the home addresses of some of the nonsupervisory personnel, the union sent four

> mailings to these employees. Lechmere filed an unfair labor practice charge against the company with the **NLRB** because the nonemployee organizers had been barred from its property. The administrative law judge ruled in the union's favor, which decision was affirmed by the **NLRB**. The federal court of appeals enforced the Board's order, but the Supreme Court reversed. It held that the **NLRA** confers rights only on employees, not on unions or union organizers. Generally, an employer cannot be forced to allow distribution of union campaign literature on its property. Exceptions to this rule apply when there are unique conditions that frustrate the union's access to employees.[13]

Employees may discuss unionization and provide information to co-workers before and after their work shifts or during rest breaks and meal breaks. They are not allowed to engage in these activities when they should be working. The distribution of union campaign materials may occur within a lunchroom, locker room, or parking lot so long as they do not create a safety hazard to employees.

During the union campaign, a targeted company's supervisors and managers should meet with the company's lawyers to review what can be said and done relative to the union campaign. In addition, the company should solicit from these supervisors and managers any information that might have led to the reasons for the unionization effort. They may not discharge or otherwise retaliate against employees who are union organizers. The company may not threaten or make promises to employees to sway the workers. The company should not surveil employees at union organizing meetings or at other union functions. Such surveillance will constitute an **unfair labor practice** in violation of the **NLRA**.

A no-solicitation rule might prevent organizing efforts on the employer's property, however, such a rule should be enforceable.

> ***Example:*** An employer refused to permit the distribution of union literature by non-employee union organizers on company-owned parking lots. Finding that it was unreasonably difficult for the union to reach the employees off company property, the **NLRB** held that the employer had unreasonably impeded the employees' right to self-organization. The employer had not sought to discriminate against the union's efforts to communicate with its workers by mail or telephone or through in-home solicitations. It defended its policy because it had consistently refused access to all kinds of pamphleteering, and it maintained that such distribution of leaflets would litter its property. A federal court of appeals refused to order the employer to give access to the union through nonemployee union organizers on its property.[14]

Organizational or **recognitional picketing** is permitted by a union against the targeted employer for a reasonable period not to exceed 30 days before filing an election petition with the **NLRB**. This type of picketing is not directed against the employer but is aimed at increasing the workers' awareness regarding the organizing effort and at persuading them to join a particular union. However, the law forbids this type of picketing when the employer has lawfully recognized another union and when there has been a valid union recognition election within the previous 12 months.

The length of an election campaign is typically 30 days. Both sides use this period to convince the workers to vote in accordance with their views.

The Election

Representation elections are conducted by the NLRB pursuant to a secret ballot. To be certified as a **bargaining unit**, the labor union must receive a majority of the valid votes.

An employer and a union may agree by consent to the representation election that the **NLRB** oversees. The **NLRB** sets forth the requirements of those who are eligible to vote in the election. These elections normally occur within 30 days after the NLRB directs that they are to be held. The outcome of the election dictates whether the employer must **bargain in good faith** with the union. A validly recognized union is the *exclusive* representative of the employees. The union has this position until the employees choose to decertify the union as their bargaining representative. Unions lose more elections than they win.

The following Supreme Court case addresses the issue of whether an employer unduly interfered with a union election.

CASE 13.1

EMPLOYERS MAY NOT OFFER INDUCEMENTS TO EMPLOYEES TO INTERFERE WITH UNIONIZATION EFFORTS

NLRB V. EXCHANGE PARTS CO.

375 U.S. 405 (1964)

Supreme Court of the United States

Facts. Shortly before a union representation election was scheduled at the Exchange Parts Company, the company offered various economic benefits to its employees. The employees were offered increased vacation and overtime benefits. After the union lost the election, the NLRB found that the benefits had been conferred with the intention of inducing the employees to vote against the union in violation of §8(a)(1) of the NLRA. The company appealed the finding that it had committed an unfair labor practice to the Fifth Circuit Court of Appeals. The court of appeals denied the Board's petition for enforcement of its order. The Supreme Court granted *certiorari*.

Issue. Does the NLRA prohibit an employer from offering benefits to employees to sway the outcome of a union representation election?

Language of the Court. Harlan, J.: **At two meetings on November 4 and 5, 1959, C. V. McDonald, the Vice-President and General Manager of Exchange Parts, announced to the employees that their "floating holiday" in 1959 would fall on December 26 and that there would be an additional "floating holiday" in 1960. On February 25, six days after the Board issued its election order, Exchange Parts held a dinner for employees at which Vice-President McDonald told the employees that they could decide whether the extra day of vacation in**

1960 would be a "floating holiday" or would be taken on their birthdays. The employees voted for the latter. McDonald also referred to the forthcoming representation election as one in which, in the words of the trial examiner, the employees would "determine whether . . . [they] wished to hand over their right to speak and act for themselves." He stated that the union had distorted some of the facts and pointed out the benefits obtained by the employees without a union. He urged all the employees to vote in the election.

The broad purpose of [the act] is to establish "the right of employees to organize for mutual aid without employer interference"(citation omitted). We have no doubt that it prohibits not only intrusive threats and promises but also conduct immediately favorable to employees which is undertaken with the express purpose of impinging upon their freedom of choice for or against unionization and is reasonably calculated to have that effect . . . The danger inherent in well-timed increases in benefits is the suggestion of a fist inside the velvet glove. Employees are not likely to miss the inference that the source of benefits now conferred is also the source from which future benefits must flow and which may dry up if it is not obliged. The danger may be diminished if as in this case, the benefits are conferred permanently and unconditionally. But the absence of conditions or threats pertaining to the particular benefits conferred would be of controlling significance only if it could be presumed that no question of additional benefits or renegotiation of existing benefits would arise in the future; and, of course, no such presumption is tenable.

Decision. Yes. The NLRA prohibits not only intrusive threats and promises, but also immediately favorable conduct by the employer to employees in order to influence a union representation election.

CASE QUESTIONS

Critical Legal Thinking. If the employer offered these benefits but did not threaten reprisal against the employees if they voted for the union, do you think that the Supreme Court made the correct decision? If the decision to offer these benefits was made in response to employee grievances and before the election, is the pertinent issue one of distinguishing between the decision to offer the additional benefits and the timing of their announcement and implementation?

Business Ethics. Was it ethical for the company to offer these inducements to avoid the unionization of its workforce? What are the ethical restraints on management in seeking to persuade employees? Answer the same question as to union organizers.

Contemporary Business. Can you think of any current examples by which management sought to avoid unionization through inducements made to its employees?

Certification

As long as the **NLRB** does not find misconduct in the election process, they will certify the results of the election. A simple majority of votes determines which side wins the election. If the employer wins, it is not required to bargain with the union. If the union wins, the employer must accept the union as the bargaining representative. Either side may protest the conduct of the election. The **NLRB** can either dismiss a charge of misconduct affecting the outcome of the election or certify the election results. It may also order a new election requiring one side or the other to publicly admit to misbehavior during the prior union campaign and election process. The **NLRB** has the power to order the employer to bargain with the union if it has been guilty of gross misconduct during the union process.

> ***Example:*** Following a union organizational campaign, the union obtained authorization cards from a majority of the employees in the bargaining unit. On that basis, the union demanded recognition by the employer. The employer refused and continued a vigorous antiunion campaign that gave rise to numerous unfair labor practice charges. The president of a targeted company repeatedly conveyed that hoodlums ran the union; he stated that the plant would close and eliminate 3,500 jobs and stressed the precarious financial condition of the company. He also emphasized that the age and lack of education of the employees would make it difficult for them to find other employment if the plant closed. The Board found that under the "totality of the circumstances" the company had engaged in an unfair labor practice. The Board also found that the union had a valid authorization card majority, and the company had embarked on a campaign to buy time to dissipate the workers' decision to join the union. The Board set the election aside, entered a cease-and-desist order and ordered the company to bargain on request. The court of appeals affirmed the Board's order. The Supreme Court found that the employer's refusal to bargain was accompanied by independent unfair labor practices that precluded the holding of a fair election. The Court held that an employer could insist on a secret-ballot election unless it engages in contemporaneous unfair labor practices likely to destroy the union's majority and seriously impede the election. It affirmed the Board's order that the employer bargain with the union in good faith.[15]

Prohibited Employer and Union Activities

The **NLRA** forbids employers from interfering with, restraining, or coercing employees in the exercise of their rights to organize, form, join, or assist a labor organization with regard to **collective bargaining** or to engage in or refrain from **protected concerted activities**. Similarly, labor organizations may not restrain or coerce employees in the exercise of these rights.

The **Taft-Hartley Act** declared a number of employer and union practices to constitute **unfair labor practices**. Stated broadly, it is unlawful for an employer to:

- interfere with, restrain, or coerce employees with respect to their right to engage in **protected concerted activity** or union activities;
- control or interfere with the organization or administration of a labor organization;

- discriminate against any employee for engaging in concerted or union activities or refraining from doing so;
- discriminate against any employee who pursues or participates in proceedings before the **NLRB**; and
- refuse to **bargain in good faith** with employee representatives.

Under the act, the following acts by unions became unlawful:

- restraining or coercing employees in the selection of bargaining representatives or in the exercise of their right to refrain from union activities;
- engaging in picket-line misconduct, such as threatening, assaulting, or barring nonstrikers from the employer's premises;
- causing an employer to discriminate against an employee (including discriminating against an employee whose membership in a union has been denied or terminated on some ground other than the employee's failure to pay initiation fees or dues required for membership);
- refusal by the union to bargain in good faith with the employer;
- engaging in **secondary boycotts** (i.e., a boycott by workers who refuse to work for, purchase, or handle products of a business with which the workers have no dispute in an effort to compel one affected business to exert pressure on another business to deal with the union);
- requiring excessive initiation or continuing dues;
- engaging in **featherbedding** (i.e., forcing an employer to hire unnecessary workers);
- **picketing** for union recognition for more than 30 days without petitioning the **NLRB** for an election; and
- entering into a **hot-cargo agreement** with the employer (i.e., a provision in a **CBA** allowing employees to refuse to handle or work on products shipped from a plant subject to a strike or to provide services to an employer listed on a **union unfair practices** list).

Secondary Boycott
An attempt by a union to coerce neutral employers and employees of neutral employers with the object of forcing these neutral employers to cease doing business with an employer that is the target of a union strike or primary boycott.

The procedure for enforcing an **unfair labor practice** begins with the filing of a charge with the **NLRB**. Upon its receipt, an investigation occurs; if the regional office of the Board determines that an **unfair labor practice** has occurred, a complaint is issued. When an employer and a union have an agreed-on grievance arbitration procedure that will resolve the dispute, the Board defers processing the unfair labor practice case and awaits the resolution through the grievance arbitration procedure. If the Board accepts the grievance procedure, the Board may accept the final resolution and defer that decision; if not, the Board may proceed.

An **unfair labor practice** hearing is conducted before an **NLRB** administrative law judge. Following the hearing on evidence submitted, the law judge presents the findings and a recommendation to the Board. All parties to the hearing may appeal the law judge's decision to the full Board. If the Board decides that a violation of the law has occurred, it may issue a cease-and-desist order and order affirmative remedial action. Complaints may only be issued if the unfair labor practice has occurred within six months of the filing of the charge with the Board. If the regional office refuses to issue a complaint in any case, the aggrieved party may appeal the decision to the General Counsel in Washington, D.C.

The Board has jurisdiction to take evidence to decide jurisdictional disputes between or among unions competing to represent employees assigned to perform particular work by an employer. In addition, certain charges are given priority for hearing, including those relating to boycotts, picketing, and work stoppages.

If an employer or a union fails to comply with the **NLRB**'s order, the Board may petition the U.S. court of appeals for a court decree enforcing the order of the Board enjoining the conduct that the Board has found to be an unfair labor practice. Any party to the underlying proceeding may also apply for relief from the appropriate circuit court of appeals. The court of appeals hears a petition concerning the Board's order. It may enforce the order, remand it to the Board for reconsideration, amend it, or deny its enforcement. If the court of appeals issues a judgment enforcing the Board's order, the judgment may be enforced by criminal contempt and/or monetary fines. Appeal to the U.S. Supreme Court is possible when the decision involves a unique application of the law or a conflict arises among the federal circuit courts of appeals on the same significant issue.

Courts will enforce the **NLRB**'s order in a proceeding if the Board's factual findings are supported by substantial evidence and its conclusions have a reasonable basis in law.[16] The courts will defer to the Board's inferences and conclusions drawn from the facts before the Board.

When an employer is signatory to a **CBA**, not every one of its failings is a violation of the labor agreement. The question of whether something is subject to adjustment pursuant to the terms of the **CBA** is determined by reference to the agreement itself, federal common law with respect to the interpretation of such agreements, and other federal laws. For example, pay disputes might be determined under the **CBA** and/or the Fair Labor Standards Act (FLSA). Typically, the pay dispute would be determined by reference to the FLSA because the **CBA** would not control the dispute unless the employer violated the express terms of the **CBA** or repudiated its application to the dispute.

Federal Preemption of State Labor Laws

Congress has the power to legislate and empower federal administrative agencies to regulate in a particular area to the complete exclusion of state or local law. It "preempts" and makes unenforceable state and local laws that occupy the same area as the federal legislation or regulation. When the federal government makes clear in its legislation and rule making that it intends to allow state laws to occupy the same field, the state laws are not invalidated. The federal civil rights law invites such collaboration but that is *not* often the case in the area of federal management-labor law.

> ***Example:*** An employee claims a retaliatory firing because he engaged in union or other protected concerted activity under federal law. Federal law will preempt any lawsuit the employee might bring in a state court. In the typical case, the employee will pursue remedies before the **NLRB**. Unless the Board determines that it is neither a protected activity nor prohibited by federal law, the employee will not pursue a remedy in state court. Jurisdiction does not lie in the state courts, even when that federal agency refuses to act.

The following U.S. Supreme Court case addresses the issue of federal labor-law preemption with respect to state labor laws.

CASE 13.2

NLRB JURISDICTION PREEMPTS STATE JURISDICTION

SAN DIEGO BUILDING TRADES COUNCIL ET AL. V. GARMON ET AL.

359 U.S. 236 (1959)

Supreme Court of the United States

Facts. Two partners in a California lumber business filed a state court action to enjoin two unions from picketing their business. In March of 1953, unions sought from [the employer] an agreement to retain in their employ only those workers who were already members of the unions or who applied for membership within 30 days. The company refused, claiming that none of its employees had shown a desire to join a union, and it could not acknowledge the employees' designation of such an arrangement until one of the unions had been lawfully designated as a collective bargaining agent. The unions began at once to peacefully picket the place of business and to exert pressure on customers and suppliers to persuade them to stop dealing with the company. The employer obtained a state court injunction against the unions. The unions contested this finding, claiming that the only purpose of their activities was to educate the workers and persuade them to become members. Based on its findings, the court enjoined the unions from picketing until one of them had been properly designated as a collective bargaining agent and awarded damages in the amount of $1,000 for losses found to have been sustained. The state supreme court reversed the trial court's injunction against the unions but affirmed the award of damages. At the time the state court lawsuit was filed, the owners also filed a petition before the NLRB, but the NLRB declined jurisdiction.

Issue. If federal preemption prevents a state court from issuing an injunction over protected concerted activity, does the state court have jurisdiction to award damages arising out of peaceful union activity when the NLRB has failed to exercise its jurisdiction?

Language of the Court. Frankfurter, J.: **By the Taft-Hartley Act, Congress did not exhaust the full sweep of legislative power over industrial relations given by the Commerce Clause. Congress formulated a code whereby it outlawed some aspects of labor activities and left others free for the operation of economic forces. As to both categories, the areas that have been pre-empted by federal authority and thereby withdrawn from state power are not susceptible of** delimitation by fixed metes and bounds. Obvious conflict, actual or potential, leads to easy judicial exclusion of state action. . . . [T]he Labor Management Relations Act "leaves much to the states, though Congress has refrained from telling us how much. . . . This penumbral area can be rendered progressively clear only by the course of litigation." (Citation omitted.)

When it is clear or may fairly be assumed that the activities which a State purports to regulate are protected by §7 of the National Labor Relations Act, or constitute an unfair labor practice under §8, due regard for the federal enactment requires that state jurisdiction must yield. To leave the States free to regulate conduct so plainly within the central aim of federal regulation involves too great a danger of conflict between power asserted by Congress and requirements imposed by state law. Nor has it mattered whether the States have acted through laws of broad general application rather than laws specifically directed towards the governance of industrial relations. Regardless of the mode adopted, to allow the States to control conduct which is the subject of national regulation would create potential frustration of national purposes.

It is essential to the administration of the Act that these determinations be left in the first instance to the National Labor Relations Board. What is outside the scope of this Court's authority cannot remain within a State's power and state jurisdiction too must yield to the exclusive primary competence of the Board. (Citations omitted.) When an activity is arguably subject to §7 or §8 of the Act, the States as well as the federal courts must defer to the exclusive competence of the National Labor Relations Board if the danger of state interference with national policy is to be averted.

Since the National Labor Relations Board has not adjudicated the status of the conduct for which the State of California seeks to give a remedy in damages, and since such activity is arguably within the compass of §7 or §8 of the Act, the State's jurisdiction is displaced. Nor is it significant that California asserted its power to give damages rather than to enjoin what the Board may restrain though it could not compensate. Our concern is with delimiting areas of conduct which must be free from state regulation if national policy is to be left unhampered. Such regulation can be as effectively exerted through an award of damages as through some form of preventive relief. The obligation to pay compensation can be, indeed is designed to be, a potent method of governing conduct and controlling policy. Even the States' salutary effort to redress private wrongs or grant compensation for past harm cannot be exerted to regulate activities that are potentially subject to the exclusive federal regulatory scheme.

Decision. The decision of the Supreme Court of California was reversed and the case remanded to the state court for further proceedings.

CASE QUESTIONS

Critical Legal Thinking. Why did Congress leave it to the federal courts to determine the scope and construction of federal labor laws?

Business Ethics. Do you think that it is fair to management for jurisdiction to remain with the NLRB when it has refused to act?

Contemporary Business. With preemption, is there a role for states to play in the labor context? Can you think of any such laws in your state that would affect organized labor? (*Hint*: Consider criminal laws and the rights of agricultural workers.)

How Unions Are Organized

Local unions represent members in a specific geographic area. These local unions are part of a national union, which through affiliation unites all local unions under one union constitution. Local unions are allowed to make decisions for their local members.

National unions unite the many local unions. Some unions have international membership, such as the United Auto Workers union, which has members in Canada.

The senior level of labor-union organization is the federation. It is composed of many national or international unions. The purpose of the federation level is to coordinate the affiliated unions, settle jurisdictional disputes among them, and advance the political interests of union members. The AFL-CIO is an example of such a labor federation.

Overview of the NLRB

The **NLRB** has the following characteristics and duties:

- The **NLRB** is an independent agency of the U.S. government. It has responsibility for conducting elections for union representation and for investigating and remedying unfair labor practices. It is the chief quasi-judicial body under the **NLRA** (i.e., it has powers akin to those of a judge to adjudicate disputes under administrative law);
- The **NLRB** is composed of five members appointed by the president of the United States, with the advice and consent of the Senate, for five years. Terms of board members are staggered.

- The **NLRB** is administered by an executive secretary, who is charged with assigning and monitoring cases.
- The **NLRB** oversees an Information Division, which is responsible for public communications.
- The **NLRB**'s solicitor acts as its chief legal advisor.
- Administrative law judges overseen by the **NLRB** function as triers of fact in unfair labor practice proceedings, render decisions containing findings of fact and conclusions of law, and make a recommendation to the Board for its final decision.
- The **NLRB**'s General Counsel, appointed by the president with the consent of the Senate, exercises general supervision over all attorneys employed by the Board, except for administrative law judges and Board members' assistants and staff.
- Finally, the **NLRB** *does not initiate any case*; it only acts on those cases brought before it. All proceedings originate from filings by the unions, employers, and individuals engaged in interstate commerce.

A current controversy that will be resolved by the Supreme Court deals with the number of board members. Terms of three members expired during the presidency of George W. Bush. President Bush refused to make some nominations, and the Senate Democrats refused to confirm those he did make. Just before the Board lost a quorum, the five members agreed to delegate their authority to a three-person panel, two of whom would remain on the Board. The Board concluded these two members constituted a quorum of the panel and their actions were permitted by the NLRA. Whether the acts of the Board constituted in this fashion are in accordance with law will be decided in the matter of *New Process Steel v. National Labor Relations Board.*[17]

Concept Summary
Bargaining in Good Faith

- Each of the employer and the union representatives must listen to the other side, keep an open mind, and try to reach an agreement on issues.
- A company has the legal right to bargain to an impasse if the negotiation does not result in an agreement on an issue.

The Duty of Good-Faith Bargaining

Under the **NLRA** and the **RLA**, the duty of both the union and the employer to "bargain collectively" is considered a mutual obligation under federal labor law. They have as well a corresponding duty between them to **bargain in good faith**. Only complete refusals to bargain are deemed an **unfair labor practice**. Several court cases have defined **bargaining in good faith** as it is required by the **NLRA**. In the following case the court set forth a test for determining if bad-faith bargaining had occurred.

CASE 13.3

THE TOTALITY OF CIRCUMSTANCES ARE REVIEWED TO DETERMINE BAD-FAITH BARGAINING

CONTINENTAL INSURANCE CO. V. NLRB

495 F.2d 44 (2nd Cir. 1974)

U.S. Court of Appeals for the Second Circuit

Facts. A subsidiary of the Continental Insurance Company petitioned the federal court of appeals to review and set aside an order of the NLRB issued against the company to cease refusing to bargain collectively in good faith and to recognize the Teamsters as the bargaining representative of the employees. It also sought review of the company's practice of making changes in wages and other terms and conditions of employment without giving notice to the union and affording it the opportunity to bargain as to those changes on behalf of the affected employees. The Teamsters were certified as the bargaining representative for claims adjustors and others following an election conducted by the Board. The federal court of appeals had ordered Continental to bargain in good faith with the union six years earlier. On the request of the union, the NLRB ordered Continental to bargain. Continental appealed to have the order of the Board set aside, and the Board filed a cross application for enforcement of its order.

Issue. Given the totality of the circumstances relating to this case, was there substantial evidence in the record as a whole to support the Board's findings?

Language of the Court. Mansfield, C.J.: **The lion's share of the six-year delay arises from the parties' inability to reach agreement, despite some 27 bargaining sessions held. . . . During the course of these negotiations the Union . . . filed charges with the Board alleging that the Company [was] in violation of [the duty to bargain in good faith]. Hearings were held before Administrative Law Judge Herbert Silberman. He found that "the Company conducted its negotiations with no desire or intention of reaching any agreement with the Union," a conclusion based upon a detailed analysis of the evidence, which revealed that the Company had prolonged negotiations unduly by various delaying tactics, including unreasonable fragmentization of bargaining sessions, captious questioning of the Union's proposals, and presentation of Company proposals that were unnecessarily complicated, outside of the scope of mandatory collective bargaining, or patently unfair and unreasonable. He further found that the Company had violated its duty to bargain collectively with the Union by by-passing the Union as the employees' exclusive bargaining agent and dealing directly with the** employees, unilaterally transferring some out of the unit and adjusting the wages of others. The Board adopted his recommended order. The Board's findings must, of course, be upheld if they are supported by substantial evidence on the record as a whole. At the outset we summarize those basic principles by which we are governed in reviewing a charge of bad faith bargaining.

The problem in resolving a charge of bad faith bargaining, is to ascertain the state of mind of the party charge[d], insofar as it bears upon that party's negotiations. Since it would be extraordinary for a party directly to admit a "bad faith" intention, his motive must of necessity be ascertained from circumstantial evidence (citation omitted). Specific conduct, while it may not, standing alone, amount to a per se failure to bargain in good faith, may when considered with all of the other evidence, support an inference of bad faith.

. . . Viewed in its entirety the record reveals that the Company pursued a pattern of tactics designed to delay the negotiations as long as possible, to denigrate and undermine the Union, to make it impossible for the Union to reach a collective bargaining agreement without virtually surrendering its right to represent the employees in disputes over working conditions, and to make it appear to the employees that they would be worse off with Union representation and a collective bargaining agreement than if they had neither. A few examples will suffice.

At the outset of negotiations, which were delayed for more than 1 1/2 years by the Company's pursuit of an appeal from the Board's bargaining unit determinations, the Company refused to bargain jointly for its two units certified by the Board, even though the Company was represented by one spokesman for both units, the Union's proposals for both were virtually identical, and joint negotiations would minimize delay without in any way affecting the Company's right to bargain separately for each unit. Instead the Company insisted upon wasteful, duplicative sessions with respect to each unit, which necessitated repetitious discussion of identical terms and unnecessarily prolonged the bargaining process. From this evidence, the Board was entitled to infer that the Company's objective was to delay and frustrate the bargaining process.

Turning to the content of the bargaining sessions themselves, the Company's proposals and its positions with respect to such basic terms and conditions as Union recognition, vacations, severance pay, wage rates, grievances and arbitration procedure all provide ample evidence of Company insincerity. For instance, in objecting to the Union's proposal for inclusion of the usual provision for recognition of the Union as the sole and exclusive collective bargaining representative for each of the units, the Company made wholly unreasonable demands with respect to matters entirely outside the scope of mandatory collective bargaining under the Act, such as that the Union agree not to organize or represent any other Company employees. When it came to severance pay, it took the position for the first four months of negotiations that it was flatly opposed to severance pay. It then made a proposal which was so inadequate as to be patently disingenuous. Similarly, with respect to vacations the Company's sole representative for some time took the extraordinary position that vacations were not an earned right but were provided to enable

employees to do a better job for the Company. He then proposed stringent eligibility requirements that disregarded existing practices permitting employees to select their vacations on the basis of seniority.

The effect of [another] clause would have been to place the employees in a worse position than if they had no contract at all and to require the Union in effect to waive its right to represent employees with respect to disputes over employment conditions. The Board was fully justified in concluding that the proposal was not made in good faith.

Another example of the Company's bad faith is found in the terms of its wage increase proposals, which were less than the increases given to its employees the previous year and which made no provision for retroactivity. Furthermore, the Company proposed in effect to bargain individually with respect to each separate employee by granting increases in such amounts and at such times as it deemed appropriate for the employee. Hand in hand with these foot-dragging proposals the Company sought to undermine the Union's position as the bargaining representative of the employees by continually refusing the Union's proposal that it put into effect the Company's suggested increases without prejudice to further bargaining on the subject, following which the Company put the increases into effect with an announcement to the employees blaming the Union for the delay.

. . . A unilateral grant of a wage increase constitutes an independent violation of the Act, regardless whether any showing of bad faith is made. (Citation omitted.) The Company's conduct further evidences an intention to by-pass, undermine and discredit the Union as the exclusive bargaining agent in the two units. (Citation omitted.)

Decision. Yes. There is substantial evidence to support the board's findings of unfair labor practices on the part of the Company. The totality of the circumstances is considered in deciding if an unfair labor practice has occurred.

CASE QUESTIONS

Critical Legal Thinking. How would you now describe the duty to bargain in good faith?

Business Ethics. Was the company's behavior ethical? Related to this question is that, under the Canon of Ethics adopted in every state, the company's attorneys are required to advocate the company's positions. Were the positions taken by Continental's attorneys ethically defensible?

Contemporary Business. Was this an example of just "hard ball" negotiating or was it unlawful? Where are the boundaries of such characterizations? Can you think of examples of any companies who have aggressively defended themselves against unionization efforts to this extent? What has been the public relations effect on the company? Has it affected its stock price?

As part of the **good-faith bargaining** process, both the employer and the union must provide relevant information to the other.[18] An employer discloses to the union only such information as is relevant to the negotiation or administration of a **CBA**.[19] To promote the purposes of **Taft-Hartley**, the threshold for what is deemed relevant to the negotiations is low. For example, if an employer wanted union members to contribute more to the health insurance premiums required to be paid, a union could request information regarding the union members' medical claims history, subject to the requirements of maintaining the health information privacy required by the federal law Health Insurance Portability and Accountability Act. However, an employer may withhold trade secret information from the union if the need for confidentiality outweighs the union's need for the information.[20] The **NLRB** and federal courts have broadly defined the scope of the information to be provided by the employer to the union, including costs of subcontracting, fringe-benefit data, and similar costs.

Alter Ego Liability

An alter ego operation is a nonunion business entity established or controlled, directly or indirectly, by the employer of a union business who thus seeks to divert work from the union entity to the nonunion entity. When union labor rates and benefits put employers at a competitive disadvantage, some may try to escape the obligations of its CBA with the union in this manner. Unions are entitled to disclosure from the union and the nonunion employers of information that may reveal the double-breasted operation. This information will include the identity of the officers, directors, shareholders, and customers of both companies; the decision-makers with respect to the control of the labor-relations policies for each company; and any business transactions in common, such as common financing or shared equipment or tools or supervisory, office, or support operations. This is also known as a double-breasted allegation by the union, by which the union seeks to include the supposed nonunion operation within that subject to the CBA.

Lockouts

A lockout occurs when an employer refuses to allow employees to return to work without a signed contract. It may occur for several reasons. Following the expiration of a labor agreement, the employer might choose to keep the employees from working despite labor's interest in continuing to work. The employer might do so because it fears that the union might strike in the future at a more inopportune time for the employer. Any employer might also do so when it senses that only part of a union will vote to strike; in that case, the lockout may put pressure on the union and its membership by reducing the number of members who are able to sustain themselves when not working. In addition, an employer may impose a lockout if the anticipated strike would severely hamper the work of nonstriking workers or if violence or damage to the plant and equipment occurs or is threatened. Temporary replacement workers may be hired by the employer following a lockout. Quite often, lockouts are used when union membership has elected to reject the company's last, best offer at negotiations and offers to return to work under the same conditions of employment as existed under the expired contract. While employers attempt to provoke a strike, unions counter with work slowdowns. Most recent examples have occurred with regard to professional football, basketball, and hockey. Recent sports reporting indicates that the National Football League may be facing another lockout within a few years.

The Rights of Employees Under §7 of Taft-Hartley

The Right to Strike

Section 7 of the Taft-Hartley Act states in part, "Employees shall have the right . . . to engage in other concerted activities for the purpose of collective bargaining or other mutual aid or protection." **Strikes** are included among the **concerted activities** protected for employees by §7. Strikes and the threat of strikes are important tools for organized labor. In a strike, employees withhold their labor. They refuse to return to work until the employer agrees to changes in the terms of the labor-management agreement. Whether a strike is lawful is not easy to determine, and often it must be left to the **NLRB** to decide. The consequences of the determination can be serious for striking employees or their employers, involving issues such as reinstatement of the strikers and their entitlement to back pay.

Types of Strikers

Employees who strike for a lawful object fall into two classes: **"economic strikers"** and **"unfair labor practice strikers."** Both classes continue as employees, but **unfair labor practice strikers** have greater rights of reinstatement to their jobs. Employees who participate in an unlawful strike may be discharged and are not entitled to reinstatement.

If the object of a strike is to obtain from the employer some economic concession such as higher wages, shorter hours, or better working conditions, the striking employees are called **economic strikers**. *They retain their status as employees and cannot be discharged, but their employer can replace them.*[21] If the employer has hired bona fide permanent replacements that are filling the jobs of the economic strikers when the strikers apply unconditionally to go back to work, the strikers are not entitled to reinstatement at that time. However, if the strikers do not obtain regular and substantially equivalent employment, they are entitled to be recalled to jobs for which they are qualified when openings in such jobs occur if they, or their bargaining representative, have made an unconditional request for their reinstatement.

Economic Strikers
Workers who strike an employer to obtain an economic concession from the employer, such as better pay, benefits, or working conditions.

Employees who strike to protest an unfair labor practice committed by their employer are **unfair labor practice strikers**. The employer may neither discharge nor permanently replace them. *When the strike ends, unfair labor practice strikers, absent serious misconduct on their part, are entitled to have their jobs back, even if employees hired to do their work have to be discharged.* If the **NLRB** finds that **economic strikers** or **unfair labor practice strikers** who have made an unconditional request for reinstatement have been unlawfully denied reinstatement by their employer, the **NLRB** may award such strikers back pay starting at the time they should have been reinstated.

The genesis for the **NLRA**'s protection of lawful strikes is in the First Amendment's protections of freedom of speech and association. When a strike is a lawful exercise of those protections, it is, by definition, not an **unfair labor practice** or a threat to the public safety. Private-sector employers may hire "permanent replacements" for striking workers; there is no comparable authority to replace public-sector strikers.

Strikes conducted by employees that are not authorized by the union are known as "wildcat strikes." They are illegal because the employer is required to negotiate with individual workers rather than with the union as the workers' authorized representative.

STRIKES UNLAWFUL BECAUSE OF TIMING: EFFECT OF NO-STRIKE CONTRACT. A strike that violates a **no-strike** provision of a contract is *not protected* by the act, and *the striking employees can be discharged or otherwise disciplined, unless the strike is called to protest certain kinds of unfair labor practices committed by the employer.* Strikes protesting unsafe working conditions have been held not to violate a no-strike provision of a **CBA**.

In its landmark decision in *Boys Market, Inc. v. Retail Clerks Union,*[22] the U.S. Supreme Court held that federal courts could enjoin violations of no-strike clauses in **CBAs** where the underlying grievance leading to the strike was subject to arbitration under that agreement. This decision effectively excluded from the jurisdiction of state courts the ability to issue injunctions in breach of collective bargaining cases. In this decision, the Supreme Court observed, "as labor organizations grew in strength and developed toward maturity, congressional emphasis shifted [by enactment of the Taft-Hartley Act] from protection of the nascent labor movement to the encouragement of collective bargaining and to administrative techniques for the peaceful resolution of industrial disputes."[23]

STRIKES UNLAWFUL BECAUSE OF STRIKERS' MISCONDUCT. Strikers who engage in serious misconduct (such as intimidation of nonstriking employees, blocking persons from entering or leaving the struck employer's premises, coercion, or acts of violence or vandalism) in the course of a strike may lawfully be refused reinstatement. This prohibition applies to *both* **economic strikers** and **unfair labor practice strikers**. The Supreme Court has ruled that this prohibition does not protect a "sit down" strike in which employees simply stay in the plant and refuse to work.

The Right to Picket

Likewise, the right to picket is subject to limitations and qualifications. Picketing is the lawful gathering of persons outside an employer's place of business. It is lawful conduct if it is done by persons in furtherance of a trade dispute and at or near the place of work. It may involve only the peaceful communication of information or the persuasion of another person to abstain from working. While there are many types of picketing, its legality depends on the circumstances. As with the right to strike, picketing can be prohibited because of its object or its timing or due to misconduct on the picket line. Examples of *unlawful* activities relating to picketing include:

- mass picketing in such numbers that nonstriking employees are physically barred from entering the employer's facility;
- threats of force or violence on the picket line; and
- fining or expelling members for crossing an unlawful picket line or one that is in violation of a CBA.

A special problem arises at a shared work site or **"common situs" workplace**. When employees of a primary employer and those of a secondary employer work on the same premises, the usual rules do not apply. For example, when a subcontractor is in dispute with a union, it, as the primary employer, may be engaged with others at a **common work site**. Picketing is permitted as to that subcontractor-employer during work hours but it is forbidden if it is directed at *other* or secondary employers at the worksite. Typically a separate, **marked reserve work gate entrance** is established for the secondary employers' workers to gain access to the site. In this manner, those workers who are not involved in a dispute with that particular subcontractor can freely access the work site.

Lawful Picketing

Right-to-Work Laws
Laws adopted by states to prohibit union–management agreements requiring union membership or payment of union dues as a condition of hire or continued employment.

A union may picket an employer if it wants continued recognition from both the employer and the workers of its standing as the employees' bargaining agent or when union members are seeking a new contract with the employer.

Publicity picketing is intended to inform the public that the employer does not employ union members or have a contract with a labor organization. However, if that picketing has a substantial effect on the employer's business such that it causes "any individual employed by any other person" to refuse to pick up, deliver goods, or perform other services at the employer, the **publicity picketing** is an **unfair labor practice.**[24]

Management Application
States' Right-to-Work Laws

"Open shops" are commonly promoted under state laws referred to as **"right-to-work"** laws. Under the **open shop rule**, employees are free to decide whether to join or pay the equivalent of dues to a union. The employee enjoys protection from the decision to join or not join the union. Among other things, the **Taft-Hartley Act** prohibited the **"closed shop"** in which employees within a unionized place of business are required to maintain membership in a union as a condition of employment. The employees are forced to join the union. The act did permit employers and unions to agree to a **"union shop,"** which requires all new employees to join the union after a minimum period following hiring. Under such rules, employees who fail to pay their continuing union dues must be discharged. Under the **"agency shop" rule**, employees not in the union must pay the equivalent amount of dues to the union as if they *were* members of the union, but they need not actually join the union. An employee who is in this situation is known as a **"free rider."** A **free rider** is one who pays no union dues or agency shop fees, but who enjoys the benefits of union representation in bargaining as if he or she were a union member. The **NLRB** refers to these agreements as **"union-security agreements."** This type of agreement, usually part of a CBA, provides that an employer and a union agree on the extent to which the union may compel employees to join or pay union fees. Stated differently, a **free rider** is a nonunion employee who is bound by the terms of the union contract with the employer. The union has the duty to represent all employees fairly, including those who do not pay dues. Section 14(b) of the **Taft-Hartley Act** provides:

> Nothing in this subchapter shall be construed as authorizing the execution or application of agreements requiring membership in a labor organization as a condition of employment in any State or Territory in which such execution or application is prohibited by State or Territorial law.

Under this section, Congress authorizes individual states to prohibit the **union shop** and the **agency shop** in their jurisdictions. The following states have enacted **right-to-work laws:**

Alabama	Nevada
Arizona	North Carolina
Arkansas	North Dakota
Florida	Oklahoma
Georgia	South Carolina
Idaho	South Dakota
Iowa	Tennessee
Kansas	Texas
Louisiana	Utah
Mississippi	Virginia
Nebraska	Wyoming

Management Application
Company-Sponsored Unions

In its decision in *Electomation, Inc.*, the NLRB considered the use of employment committees in a nonunion workplace. The Board held that the company's Action Committees were established to assist in improving quality-assurance programs. These committees were established as a way to deal with morale problems, and they resulted in a change in the attendance bonus policies. Participation on committees was voluntary, and the committees discussed wages, bonuses, incentive pay, attendance programs, and leave policy. The administrative law judge found that they were unlawful. When it considered the petition on review, the Board stated that an unlawful employee participation plan is a labor organization if employees participate, the organization (i.e., the committee exists) at least in part for the purposes of "dealing with" the employer. These dealings would naturally concern the conditions of work or other issues subject to NLRB jurisdiction over labor organizations. The Board further held that an unlawful group can result even if it does not have any formal trappings of a union. The Board held that it might be a labor organization "even if [it] lacks a formal structure, [has] no elected officers, constitution, or bylaws, does not meet regularly, and does not require payment of initiation fees or dues." The Board held that the Action Committees were labor organizations and that the company's conduct toward them constituted unlawful domination and interference with them.[25]

The Labor-Management Reporting and Disclosure Act (the "Landrum-Griffin Act")

In the period following World War II, many labor organizations grew corrupt and demonstrated undemocratic governing practices. In response to U.S. Senate hearings on the influence of communism and organized crime on the major unions and employers, the **Labor-Management Reporting and Disclosure Act** (the **"Landrum-Griffin Act"**) was enacted in 1959. Senate hearings revealed widespread corruption among union officials, the use of violence, and wrongful diversion of union funds. The act was intended to enhance governmental regulation of internal union matters. Its major provisions made significant amendments to the **NLRA** and **Taft-Hartley Act**. It covers both private-sector workers and unions within the coverage of the **Taft-Hartley Act** and the **RLA**. Unions of government workers are not covered by **Landrum-Griffin**. It does not preempt state laws regulating unions' relationships with their members unless those state laws conflict with the federal laws. The principal provisions of the **Landrum-Griffin** provide for:

- safeguards for protecting union funds and assets; the act requires full disclosure of union accounting and record keeping through periodic reports filed with the U.S. Department of Labor;
- guarantees for union members' freedom of speech and the periodic secret election of union officers (i.e., a "Bill of Rights" for union members);
- exclusion of former communists and convicted felons from membership and from holding union office;
- fiduciary responsibilities for every union officer handling the assets and affairs of the union; and
- authority to states to exercise jurisdiction in labor matters outside the jurisdiction of the **NLRB**.

Example: In 1975, the state of California enacted its own version of the **NLRA** with respect to agricultural employers and their union employees. It was created to ensure peace in the agricultural fields of California, guarantee justice to all agricultural workers, and achieve stability in agricultural labor relations.[26]

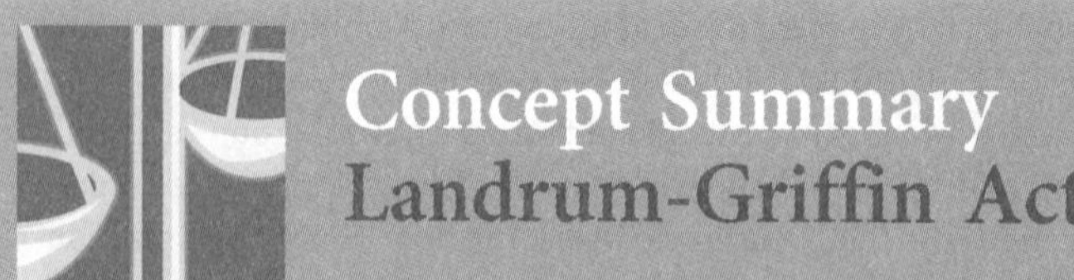

Concept Summary
Landrum-Griffin Act

The Landrum-Griffin Act:

- is administered by the U.S. Department of Labor, not the NLRB;
- requires that unions have constitutions and bylaws;
- requires unions to hold secret-ballot elections for union officers; and
- provides procedures for filing financial reports with the Department of Labor.

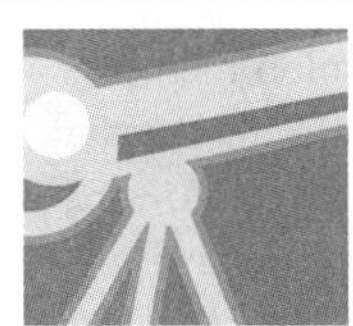

Management Application
Union Membership in the United States

In January 2010, the Bureau of Labor Statistics within the Department of Labor released a data survey showing that, as of the end of 2009, the number of workers belonging to a union had recently dropped to a total of 15.3 million.[27] Union members accounted for 12.3 percent of employed wage and salary workers. In 1983, the first year for which it had comparable data, the Department of Labor reported that union membership was 20.1 percent. These are some highlights from the 2009 study:

- Workers in the public sector (7.9 million, or 37.4 percent) had a union membership rate nearly five times that of private-sector employees, of whom only 7.2 percent were union members.
- Education, training, and library occupations had the highest unionization rates among all occupations, at 38.1 percent, followed closely by protective service occupations at 35.2 percent.
- Private-sector industries with high unionization rates included transportation and utilities (22.2 percent), telecommunications (16.0 percent), and construction (14.5 percent).
- Among demographic groups, the union membership rate was higher for African American workers than for white, Asian, or Hispanic workers.
- The union membership rate was higher for men (13.3 percent) than for women (11.3 percent).
- Black men (15.4 percent) had the highest union membership rate, while Hispanic women had the lowest rate (9.7 percent).
- By age, union membership was highest among workers ages 55 to 64 (16.6 percent) and lowest among those ages 16 to 24 (4.7 percent).
- Union membership provided workers with median weekly earnings of $908, while those not represented by a union had median weekly earnings of $710.
- The largest numbers of union members were shown to live in California (2.5 million) and New York (2.0 million). Nearly half of all union members resided in six states: California, New York, Illinois (1.0 million), Pennsylvania (0.8 million), Michigan, and New Jersey (0.7 million each).

Focus on Ethics
Labor Union Conducts Mock Funeral

Labor unions have the right to strike and to engage in picketing. Sometimes the lawfulness of picketing by labor union members is questioned. Consider the following case. The Sheet Metal Workers' International Association Local 15, AFL-CIO (Union) had a labor dispute with Massey Metals, Inc. and Workers Temporary Staffing, which supplied Massey Metals with nonunion labor employees for various construction projects. The Brandon Regional Medical Center (Hospital) employed Massey Metals as the metal fabricator and installation contractor for a construction project at the hospital.

The striking union members staged a mock funeral procession in front of the hospital. The procession consisted of four union representatives acting as pallbearers and carrying a large coffin back and forth on the sidewalk near the entrance to the hospital. Another union representative, dressed as the "Grim Reaper," accompanied the procession. The funeral procession took place about 100 feet from the hospital. The union broadcasted somber funeral music over loudspeakers mounted on a flatbed trailer that was positioned nearby. Four other union representatives, who did not impede ingress to or egress from the hospital, distributed handbills to persons entering and leaving the hospital that stated, "Going to Brandon Regional Hospital Should Not Be a Grave Decision." The procession lasted approximately two hours and was videotaped.

The regional director of the NLRB immediately filed a petition for a temporary injunction against the union's mock funeral. The NLRB alleged that the union's mock funeral procession at the hospital constituted illegal secondary boycott picketing. The district court agreed and issued an injunction against the union, prohibiting such mock funeral processions at the hospital. The union appealed.

On appeal, the U.S. court of appeals reversed, finding that the mock funeral was not coercive, threatening, restraining, or intimidating, and therefore not illegal secondary picketing or a boycott. The court cited the fact that the funeral took place about 100 feet from the hospital, that the union members did not impede ingress to or egress from the hospital, and that picketers were not confrontational toward hospital patrons. The court of appeals stated:

> *Nor was their "message"—invoking the iconography of the funeral rite and stating, "Going to Brandon Hospital Should Not Be a Grave Decision"—one by which a person of ordinary fortitude would be intimidated. Their message may have been unsettling or even offensive to someone visiting a dying relative, but unsettling and even offensive speech is not without the protection of the First Amendment. The right to free speech may not be curtailed simply because the speaker's message may be offensive to his audience.*

The U.S. court of appeals held that the union's mock funeral procession at the hospital did not constitute an illegal secondary boycott picketing because there was no coercive, threatening, restraining, or intimidating conduct by the union members. The court of appeals remanded the case to the NLRB for proceedings consistent with the court's opinion.[28]

Ethics Questions

1. What was the purpose of the union holding a mock funeral procession at the hospital?
2. Do you think that the mock funeral was offensive to anyone? Explain.
3. Did the union act ethically in this case?

Other Federal Laws

Federal Arbitration Act

The **Federal Arbitration Act (FAA)** does not directly apply to **collective bargaining agreements.** When the **FAA** and the **Taft-Hartley Act** conflict, the remedy should be resolved in favor of the **Taft-Hartley Act**. In one case, a race discrimination plaintiff had not been party to a union agreement, but the employer had requested the union to enroll the plaintiff. A dispute eventually arose as to whether the employee should have been enrolled in the union and whether the union should have sued for unpaid dues. The plaintiff sued under §1981 and Title VII, but the union relied on **§301** of the **Taft-Hartley Act**, which created a federal remedy for breach of a **CBA**. The court of appeals held that the proper approach was to apply the terms of the **FAA** tied into the construction of the **CBA** and not the civil rights statutes.[29]

Labor Arbitration

In enacting the **Taft-Hartley Act**, Congress expressly endorsed and authorized arbitration enforcement actions in place of court actions. While §**301** of the act permits parties to a **CBA** to file suit in federal district court over a **CBA** dispute, federal law provides that the parties may agree on alternative dispute resolution mechanisms to resolve disputes over the interpretation and application of the **CBA**. In its decision in *Textile Workers v. Lincoln Mills*,[30] the Supreme Court declared, "It seems, therefore, clear to us that Congress adopted a policy which placed sanctions behind agreements to arbitrate grievance disputes." As such, there is a strong public policy favoring arbitration, and courts will order the parties to arbitration.

The Supreme Court has issued a number of landmark decisions defining the relationship between an arbitration provision in a **CBA** and the pursuit of statutory discrimination claims in federal court. In *Wright v. Universal Maritime Service Corp.*,[31] the Court held that employees may sue over alleged discrimination under the ADA when the union contract requires all grievances to be resolved through arbitration. In response to such cases, employers often insist on statutory claims being subject to the arbitration provisions of the collective bargaining agreements. This approach is not any different from that taken by employers in the nonunionized workforce context.

The arbitration preemption provision does not extend to all claims that the employee may present. For example, an employee's rights under the FLSA *cannot be waived* by contract or through collective bargaining. In addition, the federal regulations interpreting the FMLA provide that employees "cannot trade off the right to take FMLA leave against some other benefit offered by the employer."[32] Reinstatement to the prior position following the taking of an FMLA leave is controlled by that statute and *not* by the **CBA**. Thus, if an FMLA leave is taken, the employee may not be passed over for promotion or given a lesser promotion because of a provision within the **CBA**.

A **CBA**'s privacy protections may have substantial impact on an employer's right to invade the employee's interests. The conditions of employment are the subject of the labor agreement between the employer and the union. As a member of the union, the employee's privacy rights will be affected by the terms of the labor agreement, as the next case supports. The application of a provision in a CBA to a privacy lawsuit is discussed in the case.

CASE 13.4

A CBA MAY AFFECT PRIVACY RIGHTS RECOGNIZED UNDER STATE LAW

STIKES V. CHEVRON USA, INC.

914 F. 2d 1265 (9th Cir. 1990)

U.S. Court of Appeals for the Ninth Circuit

Facts. David Stikes was a maintenance worker for Chevron, USA. One of the conditions of his employment was governed by a CBA, which recognized Chevron's right to manage, direct, and determine its workforces as well as to demote or discharge any employee for cause. Chevron instituted as part of its safety program a requirement that its employees submit to random searches of their persons and properties. In July of 1987, Chevron's security chief ordered Stikes to submit to a search of his private vehicle that was parked on company property. He refused to submit to the search, and Chevron terminated him. He filed a state court suit alleging that Chevron was liable for infringing his right to privacy in violation of the California Constitution, wrongful discharge in violation of public policy, and other claims. Chevron removed the case to federal court where, upon Chevron's motion, the district court held that his claims for violation of his right to privacy and other claims under California state law were completely preempted by §301 of the LMRA.

Issue. Does an employer have the right to terminate an employee who refuses to permit the search of his vehicle parked on the company parking lot?

Language of the Court. Schroeder, J.: **Section 301 of the [Labor-Management Relations Act] confers jurisdiction in the district courts of the United States over "suits for violation of contracts between an employer and a labor organization representing employees . . ." Its preemptive force is so powerful that it displaces entirely any state cause of action for violation of a collective bargaining agreement. Many suits by employees against employers are not in the form of suits for breach of the collective bargaining agreement, yet may nonetheless implicate provisions of the agreement. This has given rise to some thorny jurisdictional questions.**

During the past decade, the Supreme Court has handed down a number of decisions defining the scope of Section 301's preemptive effect. At least two

principles have emerged. First, Section 301 preempts state law claims which are founded on rights created by a collective bargaining agreement. . . . Second, section 301 preempts state law claims which are "'substantially dependent on analysis of a collective bargaining agreement.'" . . . (Citations omitted.)

In order to determine whether Stikes' state law claim of privacy substantially depends upon an interpretation of the collective bargaining agreement. Two [prior cases] like this case, involve suits by an employee against an employer for violation of privacy interests protected by the California Constitution. In both cases we . . . determined [that a state cause of action for invasion of privacy] was preempted. We reasoned that a drug and alcohol testing program is a working condition "whether or not it is specifically discussed in the [collective bargaining agreement]." We concluded that "drug testing does not implicate the sort of 'nonnegotiable state law rights' that preclude preemption under Section 301." Rather "an employer's decision to institute a drug testing program is a proper subject for collective bargaining."

Stikes' right to privacy claim is inextricably intertwined with the collective bargaining agreement. This is because a violation of California's constitutional right to privacy requires both that an individual have a "personal and objectively reasonable expectation of privacy" and that the expectation "has been infringed by an unreasonable intrusion."

Decision. Yes. The employer has the right to terminate if the employee was subject to a collective bargaining agreement that permitted the search of vehicles on company property. A right created by state law, although nonnegotiable, must be interpreted by a collective bargaining agreement for its application. As such, the terms of the collective bargaining agreement would preempt the employee's right to sue in state court.

CASE QUESTIONS

Critical Legal Thinking. What is the proper role for a union in attempting to find a balance between advancing the interests of the union as a whole and the rights of its individual members?

Business Ethics. The court barred the privacy claim based upon state law. Do you think that this decision is fair in light of the fact that the LMRA was passed in 1947, almost 30 years earlier than the Supreme Court recognized a right to privacy?

Contemporary Business. This chapter has presented some claims that cannot be bargained away and made subject to a resolution in a collective bargaining agreement. Can you think of any others that you would like to see excluded from the coverage of a CBA?

When an employee wishes to sue a union for discrimination under Title VII, the employee's actions are probably best directed to the local union. Suit against the international union is ill advised unless the local union was acting as an agent on behalf of the international union.

Example: Charlotte Laughon worked in the movie and television industry as a set dresser, set decorator, and props assistant. When she moved to the San Francisco Bay area, she made repeated attempts to join a local union that was part of an international union having jurisdiction over such work with production companies. Her suit against her local for sex discrimination and unlawful retaliation was allowed to proceed, but the claim against the international union was not allowed. "The common law agency test applied to internationals is a middle ground between, on the one hand, liability for actions by any person acting in the international's interest and, on the other, liability only when clear proof of the international's actual participation in or authorization or ratification of illegal acts is before the court."[33]

Labor Union Relevancy in the Twenty-First Century

Once a powerful economic and sociopolitical force, unions had a significant impact on American life. Few jobs were performed without a union card. Sixty years ago, 25 percent of all workers were union members. However, their influence and reach in the private sector have waned. Today, only 12 percent of American workers are union members. Unions now face mounting challenges. Globalization and weakening economies have extracted their toll on unions and their members.

Union critics argue that they have been slow to adapt to changing conditions. Historically, they were not open to members of minority communities. Until the 1930s, black workers were excluded from membership in unions or were assigned to segregated locals. The Brotherhood of Sleeping Car Porters was the most powerful of the black unions. Even then, its president, A. Philip Randolph, was for many years the only black member of the AFL-CIO.

For the last several decades, unions have focused their efforts on promoting political causes and not on the complexities of the labor-management relationship. To sustain the union movement, unions must focus their efforts on reaching the unorganized. As even a preliminary study of the political influence of labor organizations reveals, the substantial spending by unions and their political action committees has not led to the enactment of legislation beneficial to the union movement.

The union message has been reshaped and retargeted over the last decade. The message of organized labor in this century has been that unions are the last line of defense for the protection of workers in the workplace. Without active union representation, unions argue, the American workforce risks losing protection for the health and safety of workers and an increased loss of jobs to the overseas facilities of U.S. employers. They urge the great social cost of the elimination of traditional pension plans for workers. Moreover, without representative bargaining, employees face the minimization or elimination of health-care benefits, due to escalating costs. Union leadership argues that employers may pay more than a community's median wage, but if they don't provide adequate health-care benefits they shift health-care expenses for the uninsured and the underinsured to the public at large in the form of emergency-room costs and government medical and prescription plans.

In reversing its historical hostility to minority communities, the international labor organizations support full legalization of all undocumented workers. The unions' traditional viewpoint had been one of hostility on the part of native-born union members toward immigrant workers, whom they feared would displace them in the job market and undercut their hard-won labor standards. Over the last two decades, however, organized labor has embraced immigrant workers. The AFL-CIO and other labor organizations oppose guest-worker programs on the grounds that they lead to exploitation of workers. They argue that no federal program has ever benefited guest workers. Guest workers are admitted to the United States on the condition that they work for a designated employer, which then controls their working conditions and immigration status. The unions argue that such arrangements are contrary to good public policy. Instead, they favor organizing these immigrant workers and improving their working conditions. Union organizers no longer believe it would be too difficult to organize immigrant workers who live in fear of apprehension by immigration authorities. Immigrant workers have proved to be more receptive to union representation than are native-born workers. Unions see the immigrant communities as offering tremendous potential for expanding their organizing efforts.

In 2005, seven unions and six million workers, formerly members of the AFL-CIO, united to build a new international organization known as Change to Win. The unions have a substantial number of immigrant and first-generation American-born workers in their membership. Change to Win focuses on organizing and representing service-sector workers. Recently, like their predecessors of 50 years ago, these service-sector unions have struggled to make their bargaining unit representation relevant in a diversified global marketplace. Responding to modern trends and to tragedies like those at West Virginia's Sago Mine and Upper Big Branch Mine, unions contend they are advancing their workers' interests of job security, a stable U.S. economy, and workplace health and safety.

Management Application
Who Is an Employee?

Town and Country Electric, Inc. was a nonunion electrical contractor wanting to hire several licensed Minnesota electricians for construction work in Minnesota. The company advertised through an employment agency. It refused to interview 10 of 11 union applicants who responded to the advertisement. The International Brotherhood of Electrical Workers union filed a complaint with the NLRB claiming that the employer and the employment agency had refused to interview the applicants because of their union membership. The NLRB deemed the applicants "employees" as the NLRA defined that term. In the Board's view, it mattered (with respect to the meaning of the word "employee") neither that the union members intended to organize the company if they secured employment with Town and Country nor that the union would pay the employees while they organized the employees when hired. The Board held that the company had committed an unfair labor practice. The case was appealed to the U.S. Supreme Court, and it granted *certiorari* to determine whether applicants were entitled to the protection of employees guaranteed under the NLRA. Town and Country argued before the Court that the paid union organizers serve the union's interests and that the applicant-worker was an employee of the union and not of the employer.[34]

What is your advice to the employer? Is the proper role of the NLRB with respect to applicants both a political and a legal question?

Human Resource Form
NLRB Petition

PLEASE REVIEW THE FOLLOWING IMPORTANT INFORMATION BEFORE FILLING OUT A PETITION FORM!

- Please call an Information Officer in the Regional Office nearest you for assistance in filing a petition. The Information Officer will be happy to answer your questions about the petition form or to draft the petition on your behalf.
- Check one of the boxes listed under Question 1 representing the purpose of the petition: RC — a union desires to be certified as the bargaining representative of employees; RM — an employer seeks an election because one or more individuals or unions have sought recognition as the bargaining representative, or based on a reasonable belief supported by objective considerations that the currently recognized union has lost its majority status; RD — employees seek to remove the currently recognized union as the bargaining representative; UD — employees desire an election to restrict the union's right to maintain a union shop clause; UC — a labor organization or an employer seeks clarification of the existing bargaining unit; or AC — a labor organization or an employer seeks an amendment of a certification issued in a prior Board case.
- Under Question 5, please carefully describe the bargaining unit involved in the petition, listing the job classifications included in the unit and the job classifications excluded from the unit.
- After completing the petition form, be sure to sign and date the petition and mail, fax or hand deliver the completed petition form to the appropriate Regional Office.
- The filing of a petition seeking certification or decertification of a union should be accompanied by a sufficient showing of interest to support such a petition — i.e., a showing that 30% or more of the employees in the bargaining unit seek to be represented by the union or seek to decertify the currently recognized union. If the original showing is not sent to the Region with the filing of the petition, a party must deliver the original showing of interest to the Region within **48 hours** after the filing of the petition, but in no event later than the last day on which a petition may be timely filed.
- Be sure to include telephone and fax numbers of the parties since this will be a significant aid to the processing of the petition.
- Be sure to include the name and address of any other labor organization or individuals known to have a representative interest in any of the employees in the unit described in Question 5 of the petition.
- A petition should be filed with the Regional Office where the bargaining unit exists. If the bargaining unit exists in two or more Regions, it can be filed in any of such Regions. An Information Officer will be happy to assist you in locating the appropriate Regional Office in which to file your petition.

INTERNET
FORM NLRB-502
(2-08)

UNITED STATES GOVERNMENT
NATIONAL LABOR RELATIONS BOARD
PETITION

FORM EXEMPT UNDER 44 U.S.C.

DO NOT WRITE IN THIS SPACE	
Case No.	Date Filed

INSTRUCTIONS: Submit an original of this Petition to the NLRB Regional Office in the Region in which the employer concerned is located.

The Petitioner alleges that the following circumstances exist and requests that the NLRB proceed under its proper authority pursuant to Section 9 of the NLRA.

1. PURPOSE OF THIS PETITION (If box RC, RM, or RD is checked and a charge under Section 8(b)(7) of the Act has been filed involving the Employer named herein, the statement following the description of the type of petition shall not be deemed made.) (Check One)

☐ **RC-CERTIFICATION OF REPRESENTATIVE** - A substantial number of employees wish to be represented for purposes of collective bargaining by Petitioner and Petitioner desires to be certified as representative of the employees.

☐ **RM-REPRESENTATION (EMPLOYER PETITION)** - One or more individuals or labor organizations have presented a claim to Petitioner to be recognized as the representative of employees of Petitioner.

☐ **RD-DECERTIFICATION (REMOVAL OF REPRESENTATIVE) - A substantial number of employees assert that the certified or currently recognized bargaining representative is no longer their representative.**

☐ **UD-WITHDRAWAL OF UNION SHOP AUTHORITY (REMOVAL OF OBLIGATION TO PAY DUES)** - Thirty percent (30%) or more of employees in a bargaining unit covered by an agreement between their employer and a labor organization desire that such authority be rescinded.

☐ **UC-UNIT CLARIFICATION**- A labor organization is currently recognized by Employer, but Petitioner seeks clarification of placement of certain employees: (Check one) ☐ In unit not previously certified. ☐ In unit previously certified in Case No.______

☐ **AC-AMENDMENT OF CERTIFICATION**- Petitioner seeks amendment of certification issued in Case No.______
Attach statement describing the specific amendment sought.

2. Name of Employer	Employer Representative to contact	Tel. No.
3. Address(es) of Establishment(s) involved *(Street and number, city, State, ZIP code)*		Fax No.
4a. Type of Establishment (Factory, mine, wholesaler, etc.)	4b. Identify principal product or service	Cell No.
		e-Mail
5. Unit Involved *(In UC petition, describe* **present** *bargaining unit and attach description of proposed clarification.)*		6a. Number of Employees in Unit:
Included		Present
Excluded		Proposed *(By UC/AC)*
		6b. Is this petition supported by 30% or more of the employees in the unit?* ☐ Yes ☐ No *Not applicable in RM, UC, and AC

(If you have checked box RC in 1 above, check and complete EITHER item 7a or 7b, whichever is applicable)

7a. ☐ Request for recognition as Bargaining Representative was made on (Date) ______ and Employer declined recognition on or about (Date) ______ (If no reply received, so state).

7b. ☐ Petitioner is currently recognized as Bargaining Representative and desires certification under the Act.

8. Name of Recognized or Certified Bargaining Agent *(If none, so state.)*		Affiliation	
Address	Tel. No.	Date of Recognition or Certification	
	Cell No.	Fax No.	e-Mail
9. Expiration Date of Current Contract. If any *(Month, Day, Year)*	10. If you have checked box UD in 1 above, show here the date of execution of agreement granting union shop *(Month, Day and Year)*		
11a. Is there now a strike or picketing at the Employer's establishment(s) Involved? Yes ☐ No ☐	11b. If so, approximately how many employees are participating?		

11c. The Employer has been picketed by or on behalf of *(Insert Name)* ______, a labor organization, of *(Insert Address)* ______ Since *(Month, Day, Year)* ______

12. Organizations or individuals other than Petitioner (and other than those named in items 8 and 11c), which have claimed recognition as representatives and other organizations and individuals known to have a representative interest in any employees in unit described in item 5 above. (If none, so state)

Name	Address	Tel. No.	Fax No.
		Cell No.	e-Mail

13. Full name of party filing petition (If labor organization, give full name, including local name and number)

14a. Address *(street and number, city, state, and ZIP code)*	14b. Tel. No. EXT	14c. Fax No.
	14d. Cell No.	14e. e-Mail

15. Full name of national or international labor organization of which Petitioner is an affiliate or constituent *(to be filled in when petition is filed by a labor organization)*

I declare that I have read the above petition and that the statements are true to the best of my knowledge and belief.

Name *(Print)*	Signature	Title *(if any)*
Address *(street and number, city, state, and ZIP code)*	Tel. No.	Fax No.
	Cell No.	eMail

WILLFUL FALSE STATEMENTS ON THIS PETITION CAN BE PUNISHED BY FINE AND IMPRISONMENT (U.S. CODE, TITLE 18, SECTION 1001)

PRIVACY ACT STATEMENT

Solicitation of the information on this form is authorized by the National Labor Relations Act (NLRA), 29 U.S.C. § 151 *et seq.* The principal use of the information is to assist the National Labor Relations Board (NLRB) in processing unfair labor practice and related proceedings or litigation. The routine uses for the information are fully set forth in the Federal Register, 71 Fed. Reg. 74942-43 (Dec. 13, 2006). The NLRB will further explain these uses upon request. Disclosure of this information to the NLRB is voluntary; however, failure to supply the information will cause the NLRB to decline to invoke its processes.

Key Terms and Concepts

- Yellow-dog contracts
- Railway Labor Act
- National Mediation Board
- Labor union
- National Labor Relations Act (NLRA), also known as the Wagner Act
- National Labor Relations Board (NLRB)
- Labor-Management Relations Act (LMRA)
- Taft-Hartley Act
- Collective bargaining agreement (CBA)
- Clayton Antitrust Act
- Norris-La Guardia Act (the Anti-Injunction Act)
- Unfair labor practices
- Concerted activities
- Secondary boycott
- Featherbedding
- Protected concerted activity
- 80-day cooling-off period
- National emergency strikes
- Appropriate bargaining unit
- Strikes
- Economic strikers
- No-strike clauses
- Common situs workplace
- Marked reserve work gate entrance
- Recognitional picketing
- Organizational picketing
- Publicity picketing
- Open shop
- Right to work laws
- Closed shop
- Union shop
- Agency shop
- Free rider
- Landrum-Griffin Act
- Bargaining in good faith
- Alter ego operations
- Federal Arbitration Act (FAA)

Chapter Summary

- The RLA created the National Mediation Board and required the arbitration of labor disputes in the railway and airline industries.

- The Norris-La Guardia Act severely limited federal court jurisdiction to issue injunctions prohibiting protected concerted activities, including the rights to collectively bargain and to protest employers' actions through strikes, picketing, lawful boycott and others.

- The National Labor Relations Act, also known as the Wagner Act or the NLRA, is the basis for private-sector labor law. It created the NLRB, recognized what activities would constitute unfair labor practices, and established procedures for union representation, union elections, and the means to resolve labor grievances.

- The NLRA and the Norris-La Guardia Act are interpreted together to give meaning and effect to each of the laws. The Norris-La Guardia Act prohibits federal courts from enjoining lawful concerted activities, and the NLRA regulates the conduct of management and labor in the context of a labor dispute.

- The NLRB investigates and enforces collective bargaining agreements. It will defer to an arbitration process if arbitration has been agreed upon in the collective bargaining agreement. Decisions of the NLRB may be appealed to a federal court of appeals.

■ In strikes or threatened strikes that would affect interstate commerce and threaten public health and safety, the president may cause the attorney general to seek a court order to impose an 80-day cooling-off period. During this period, labor and management may continue their negotiations while the union workers return to work.

■ Unions may exercise their rights to picket and strike, but they must do so in accordance with the limitations of Taft-Hartley.

■ The LMRA, also known as the Taft-Hartley Act, amended the NLRA. In material part, it outlawed secondary boycotts by labor unions and rearranged the management of the NLRB so the agency could prosecute unfair labor practices.

■ A variety of arrangements between employers and unions relate to the necessity that nonsupervisorial workers join a union after being hired. Many states have enacted right-to-work laws that forbid union shops and, sometimes, agency shops.

■ The Labor-Management Reporting and Disclosure Act, also known as the Landrum-Griffin Act, created the rights and duties of unions toward employees and employers. It requires financial records be maintained and recognizes workers' rights to fair representation.

■ Both employers and unions have a duty to bargain in good faith concerning the mandatory subjects of bargaining: wages, hours, and other terms of employment.

Online Student Support

- Loislaw legal research and writing assignments.
- Loislaw group projects and class presentations.
- Loislaw access, providing online research including up-to-date cases, statutes, rules, and regulations. Primary law for all 50 states and federal jurisdictions. Registration required for access to this resource.
- Practice questions, including sample true/false, multiple choice, and short answer questions to test your understanding of concepts.
- Additional human resource forms.
- Internet exercises.
- Blogs.
- Supplementary statutory and regulatory materials.

Casc Problems

13.1 Before beginning his acting career, Fred Dryer was one of the NFL's outstanding defensive ends when he played football for the Los Angeles Rams. In 1980, Dryer and the Rams entered into an employment contract drafted pursuant to a collective bargaining agreement between the players' union and the NFL management. Alleging that the Rams removed him from the active roster in violation of his contract, Dryer sued in California superior court, and the Rams responded with a petition to compel arbitration. His contract contained a standard provision requiring binding arbitration under the terms of the CBA in the event of a contract dispute. The state court found that the agreement to arbitrate was unenforceable because one of the provisions of the contract allowed grievances involving "the integrity of, or public confidence in, the game of professional football" to be withdrawn from the arbitration process and handled exclusively by the NFL commissioner. It found the possible intervention of the commissioner to invalidate the entire arbitration provision. The trial court did find that the CBA did affect interstate commerce and was subject to §301 of the LMRA, but it determined that the applicable state and federal principles were compatible. How should an appellate court rule when the state trial court's decision was appealed? (*Dryer v. Los Angeles Rams*, 40 Cal.3d 406 (1985))

13.2 A union has requested that an employer with which it has a CBA provide payroll records of all employees, including supervisors. Does the employer have a duty to provide such information to the union? (*Jaggars-Chiles-Stovall, Inc.*, 249 N.L.R.B. 697 (1980))

13.3 Briscoe was a general contractor employing dozens of ironworkers on a project that suffered from numerous production problems. When the entire project was shut down because of poor weather conditions, there was a general layoff. Following the layoff, five black ironworkers filed racial discrimination charges against Briscoe with the Equal Employment Opportunity Commission. After the layoff, each of them requested to be recalled to the project, but Briscoe's job superintendent stated that Briscoe did not intend to hire the men back as long as the discrimination charges were pending. The black ironworkers filed an unfair labor practice suit against the company because it failed to recall them to work. If racial discrimination is not an unfair labor practice under the NLRB, what argument could you make for the five ironworkers that the employer's actions constituted an unfair labor practice? (*Frank Briscoe, Inc. v. N.L.R.B.*, 637 F.2d 946 (3d Cir. 1981))

13.4 A collective bargaining agreement between the Screen Actors Guild and movie producer Lakeside Productions contained a standard "union security clause" which authorizes an agreement . . . to require as a condition of employment membership in the union on or after the 13th day following the beginning of such employment." The union security clause did not explain that the Supreme Court had held that an employee could satisfy the membership condition by paying to the union an amount equal to its initiation fees and dues. The Court has also held that the nonmember may be required to pay only to the extent that such funds are used for collective bargaining, contract administration, and grievance adjustment activities. Naomi Marquez, a part-time actor, requested that the union monies be paid when the production company had paid her. When the union dues had not been paid by the day before her part was to be filmed, the production company hired a different person to fill the part. She sued the company and the union alleging, among other things, that the union had breached the duty of fair representation by negotiating and enforcing an improper union security clause. How should the Supreme Court rule? (*Marquez v. Screen Actors Guild, Inc., et al.*, 525 U.S. 33 (1998))

13.5 The office clerical and technical employees of Buffalo Forge Company went on strike and picketed its plants during negotiations for a CBA. Members of the Steelworkers union who also worked at the plants honored the picket lines and stopped work in support of the sister unions representing the other employees. The company filed suit against the Steelworkers union under §301 of the LMRA, claiming that the work stoppage violated a no-strike clause in the CBA between the company and the Steelworkers union. The company requested the court order the Steelworkers union to arbitrate and enjoin the sympathy strike pending arbitration. The federal district held that the work stoppage was permissive as a sympathy strike and that it could not issue an injunction because the Steelworkers strike was not an "arbitrable grievance" and not within the *Boys Markets v. Retail Clerks* case exception. How should the Supreme Court rule as to the company's request for an injunction against the sympathy strike pending the outcome of the arbitration? (*Buffalo Forge Co. v. U.S. Steelworkers*, 428 U.S. 397 (1976))

End Notes

1. *NLRB v. Rockline Industries, Inc.*, 412 F.3d 962 (8th Cir. 2005).
2. *http://www.nlrb.gov/nlrb/shared_files/brochures/annual%20reports/NLRB2009.pdf.*
3. *Hitchman Coal & Coke Co. v. Mitchell*, 245 U.S. 229 (1917).
4. 29 U.S.C. §164.
5. 45 U.S.C. §160.
6. *Monongahela Power Co. v. Local No. 2332 IBEW, et al.*, 484 F.2d 1209 (4th Cir. 1973).
7. 29 U.S.C. §§104, 107.
8. 29 U.S.C. §152 (3).
9. 29 U.S.C. §152(11).
10. *Chicago & N.W. R.R. v. United Transp. Union*, 402 U.S. 570, 581 (1971).
11. *NLRB v. Jones & Laughlin Steel Corp.*, 301 U.S. 1 (1937); *Myers v. Bethlehem Shipbuilding Corp.*, 303 U.S. 41 (1938) and *Washington, Va. & Maryland Coach Co. v. NLRB*, 301 U.S. 142 (1937).
12. *Waremart Foods v. NLRB*, 354 F.3d 870 (D.C. Cir. 2004).
13. *Lechmere, Inc. v. N.L.R.B.*, 502 U.S. 527 (1992).
14. *Labor Board v. Babcock & Wilcox Co.*, 351 U.S. 105 (1956).
15. *N.L.R.B. v. Gissel Packing Co.*, 395 U.S. 575 (1960).
16. *Bloomington-Normal Seating Co. v. NLRB*, 357 F.3d 692 (7th Cir. 2004).
17. *New Process Steel v. N.L.R.B.*, 564 F.3d 840 (7th Cir. 2009), *cert granted.*
18. *Detroit Edison Co. v. NLRB*, 440 U.S. 301 (1979).
19. *NLRB v. Lumber and Mill Employers Assn.*, 736 F.2d 707 (9th Cir. 1984).
20. *Grinnell Fire Protection v. NLRB*, 272 F.3d 1028 (8th Cir. 2001).
21. *Mackay Radio & Tel. Co. v. N.L.R.B.*, 304 U.S. 333 (1938).
22. 398 U.S. 235 (1970).
23. 398 U.S. at 251.
24. 29. U.S.C. §158 (c).
25. *Electromation, Inc. and Intl Bro. of Teamsters, etc. v. NLRB*, 35 F.3d 1148 (1994).
26. *http://www.alrb.ca.gov/.*
27. U.S. Department of Labor, Bureau of Labor Statistics, News Release, Jan. 22, 2010, *http://www.bls.gov/news.release/union2.nr0.htm.*
28. *Sheet Metal Workers' International Association, Local 15, AFL-CIO v. National Labor Relations Board*, 491 F.3d 429 (D.C. Cir. 2007).
29. *Smart v. IBEW, Local 702*, 315 F.3d 721 (7th Cir. 2002).
30. 363 U.S. 448 (1957).
31. 525 U.S. 70 (1998).
32. 29 C.F.R. §825.220(d).
33. *Laughon v. IATSE*, 248 F.3d 941 (9th Cir. 2001) *citing Carbon Fuel Co. v. UMW*, 444 U.S. 212, 217 (1979).
34. *NLRB v. Town & Country Electric, Inc. et al.*, 516 U.S. 85 (1995).

Chapter 14
Wage and Hour Laws

The people of this country by an overwhelming vote are in favor of having Congress — this Congress — put a floor below which individual wages shall not fall, and a ceiling beyond which the hours of individual labor shall not rise. —Franklin Delano Roosevelt, thirty-second President of the United States, January 1938

Learning Objectives

1. Identify the scope and application of the federal wage laws.
2. Describe what must be included within employee compensation.
3. Recognize what hours count as compensable time.
4. Understand the overtime laws.
5. Explain the overtime exemption laws.
6. Review when an employer must pay a prevailing wage.

Chapter Outline

Chapter Opening scenario

Faustina Alvarez sued Bonifacio Sanchez in New York state court for underpayment and nonpayment of wages under the Federal Labor Standards Act. She claimed that the defendants requested that she travel from Mexico to New York to work in the defendants' home as a maid. She claimed that she worked in the home for more than nine months, during which she received below federal minimum wages and, sometimes, no wages at all. The defendants denied that Alvarez was employed by them and asserted that if the court found that they did employ her, the plaintiff should not recover because, as an illegal alien, she had no right to recover for the work allegedly performed. How should the court rule?[1]

Introduction

Fair Labor Standards Act (FLSA)
1938 Federal law applicable to employees engaged in interstate commerce or employed by an enterprise engaged in interstate commerce. Sets minimum wages and overtime and regulates youth employment.

Both federal and state laws and regulations govern the area of wages and hours of employment. The principal federal statute is the **Fair Labor Standards Act of 1938 (FLSA)**.[2] When enacted, its purpose was to establish **minimum wage** and **overtime** pay requirements and to restrict the use of child labor. Most government employers are now subject to the **FLSA** standards as well. It is the federal law of broadest application governing minimum wage, **overtime** pay, and youth employment. The **FLSA,** while extensive in scope, does not reach all aspects of this area of the law. For example, the **FLSA** does not address all occupations of work, how compensation is to be paid, or how and when benefits such as vacation and sick leave pay are accrued. Employers must be aware that substantial differences exist between federal law and the laws of the states in which their companies operate. Where there is conflict between them, the law that establishes the higher standard applies. The **FLSA** permits states to adopt higher minimum wage and **overtime** rules than those established under the act and preempts state law only when the state law provides a lesser benefit to the employee than federal law provides. For example, an employer will be required to pay **overtime** to the employee under state law when the employee might be exempt from **overtime** pay under the **FLSA**.

> ***Example:*** Most employers must pay **overtime** to an employee under the **FLSA** only if the employee works more than 40 hours in a workweek. An employee who worked 9 hours one day within that 40-hour workweek would not be paid **overtime**. However, many states, including California, require that **overtime** be paid when an employee works more than 40 hours in a workweek or more than 8 hours in one day.

The Wage and Hour Division of the U.S. Department of Labor enforces the **FLSA**. The law provides for both civil and criminal penalties for a violation of the **FLSA**. The law provides that the secretary of labor may bring a lawsuit to recover unpaid **minimum**

wages and **overtime** pay against an offending employer or seek an injunction against prohibited employer acts. In addition, a private right to sue is given to workers for violations of the **FLSA** and for retaliatory discharge or discrimination relating to wage and hour matters. The private lawsuit can intimidate many employers because recently employers have faced staggeringly expensive wage and hour class-action lawsuits. In terms of federal enforcement, the Wage and Hour Division also enforces, among other laws, the Family and Medical Leave Act; the Employee Polygraph Act; the **Davis-Bacon Act**, discussed in this chapter; and the temporary worker provisions of the Immigration and Nationality Act.

The **FLSA** applies to all employers except Indian tribes, which are exempt from its application because the act would conflict with the tribal right of self-governance. The provisions of the **FLSA** are basic rights granted employees and *cannot be waived* by the employee. Additionally, the **FLSA** will govern if a union collective bargaining agreement sets compensation below the federal rules. In cases involving wage claims of union employees, federal law under the Labor Management Relations Act (LMRA), discussed in the chapter on federal labor law, may preempt the dispute.

In addition to the **FLSA**, employers must be aware of **The Equal Pay Act of 1963 (EPA)**, which prohibits sex-based discrimination in pay. The **EPA** amended the **FLSA**. **The Portal-to-Portal Act of 1947** states that time spent traveling to and from the place of employment and in preliminary or concluding activities is not chargeable to the employer. The **Davis-Bacon Act** and the **Walsh-Healey Act** require the minimum labor rates and standards on government contractors or those who are working on federally funded construction projects.

The Fair Labor Standards Act

The most widely applied federal wage-hour legislation is the **FLSA**. It requires payment of a minimum wage and premium pay for overtime hours and restricts child labor. Before an employer can determine its legal obligation to any particular employee, the employer must determine that the employees are subject to the law and, if so, which laws apply. The law appears straightforward, but it has many exceptions and exemptions. The employer must remember that the wage and hour laws establish the legal minimum required to be paid to employees. An employer's failure to apply the law properly can result in fines and exposure to class-action lawsuits. The employer must review each of the following:

- **FLSA** coverage
- Government contracts and relationships requiring payment of prevailing wages
- The relationship with the worker (e.g., volunteer or independent contractor)
- Employer exemptions
- Employee exemptions

Coverage

FLSA has two requirements for its applicability to an employer's compensation system: it applies only within the employer-employee relationship, and the employer's activities must meet an "in commerce" requirement.

In Chapter 1, we reviewed the definition of "employee." The **FLSA** does not apply to actual independent contractor or principal-agency relationships, as those relationships are within the contracting powers of the parties to the agreements covering those relationships.

The **FLSA** is based on the power of Congress to regulate interstate commerce. The **FLSA** provides for two types of coverage: **enterprise coverage** and **individual coverage**. If the employee is entitled to the **FLSA** protections under either **enterprise** or **individual coverage**, then he or she must receive the **FLSA** prescribed **minimum wages, overtime** pay, and **equal pay** between the sexes.

Enterprise Coverage The most common FLSA protection for workers, applicable when the enterprise for which they work has at least two employees engaged in interstate commerce activities or the enterprise generates a total of at least $500,000 per year.

Individual Coverage FLSA coverage as extended to employees engaged in interstate commerce.

Enterprise coverage of the **FLSA** is the most common way in which it protects employees. Workers will be entitled to **FLSA** protection if the enterprise for which they work has at least two employees engaged in interstate commerce activities or the enterprise generates a total of at least $500,000 per year. It extends to employees of not-for-profit and religious entities if the activity of the employed individuals is connected with commercial operations and has a "business purpose." Congress wanted to ensure that certain workers were covered by the **FLSA** even if they work for an entity that might be exempted. It defines the following organizations as having a business purpose and thus as covered by the statute: (a) a hospital; (b) an institution primarily engaged in the care of the sick or the ill; (c) a school for handicapped or gifted children; (d) a preschool, elementary school, or secondary school; or (e) an institution of higher learning. These entities are subject to the **FLSA** even if they are operated by a nonprofit or religious organization (such as a nonprofit Catholic hospital or high school).

FLSA's enterprise coverage allows a family business exemption. It provides that the **FLSA** does not apply if the *only* regular employees are a business's owner or the parent, spouse, child, or other member of the owner's immediate family. Other than this limited situation, generally *all* employees of an employer qualifying as a **covered enterprise** are entitled to **FLSA** protection.

Individual employee coverage of the **FLSA** will be extended to an employee if he or she is engaged in commerce or in the production of goods for commerce among the states or a state outside the place of production. This interstate commerce activity is easily found if the employee uses an instrumentality of interstate commerce to perform their job (e.g., use of a telephone or other communication device connected to the interstate telephone system, transportation, banking, or insurance). Domestic service workers in private households are deemed to meet the **FLSA** coverage requirements.

The term "employee" includes unauthorized workers who are not authorized under law to work in the United States. Despite that status, an unauthorized worker (i.e., an illegal alien worker) can sue under the **FLSA** to recover for unpaid wages and liquidated damages.

CASE 14.1

ILLEGAL ALIEN WORKERS ARE ENTITLED TO FLSA PROTECTION

PATEL V. QUALITY INN SOUTH

846 F.2d 700 (11th Cir. 1988)

U.S. Court of Appeals for the Eleventh Circuit

Facts. In June of 1982, Rajni Patel came to the United States from India on a visitor's visa. After his visa expired, he remained in the United States, and in July 1983, he began work at a Birmingham, Alabama, hotel, the Quality Inn South. He performed a variety of tasks at the hotel including maintenance and janitorial duties until October 1985. In 1986, he sued the motel and its owners for violating the wage and overtime provisions of the FLSA and sought to recover $47,132 in liquidated damages and attorneys' fees. The district court granted the defendants' summary judgment motion on the basis that it could not find any legal authority for upholding a FLSA award to an undocumented worker.

Issue. Are undocumented aliens entitled to the protections of the FLSA?

Language of the Court. Vance, J.: **Congress enacted the FLSA in 1938 to eliminate substandard working conditions. . . . It requires covered employers to pay their employees a statutorily prescribed minimum wage, and prohibits employers from requiring their employees to work more than forty hours per week unless the employees are compensated at one and one half times their regular hourly rate. For violations of its provisions, the FLSA imposes criminal sanctions and allows employees to bring an action to recover any unpaid minimum wages and overtime plus liquidated damages and attorney's fees.**

In the FLSA Congress defined the term "employee" for the purpose of determining who would be covered by the act. It would be difficult to draft a more expansive definition. The term "employee" was defined to include "any individual employed by an employer."

That Congress intended a broad definition of the term "employee" is also apparent from the FLSA's legislative history. One representative described the act as "the most momentous and far-reaching measure that [Congress has] considered for many years." . . . The remarks of then Senator Hugo Black, the FLSA's chief legislative sponsor, are even more instructive. During debate over the act, Senator Black declared that its "definition of employee . . . is the broadest

definition that has ever been included in any one act. . . ." Given the unequivocal language of the FLSA and its legislative history, it is not surprising that the Supreme Court has adopted an expansive definition of the term "employee" in its decisions under the act. Although it has never faced the question of whether undocumented aliens are covered by the FLSA, the Court consistently has refused to exempt from coverage employees not within a specific exemption. Breadth of coverage was vital to [the FLSA's] mission. . . . Where exceptions were made, they were narrow and specific. . . . Such specificity in stating exemptions strengthens the implication that employees not thus exempted remain within the Act.

Decision. Yes. Because Congress did not exclude them from coverage, undocumented workers are entitled to protection under the FLSA.

CASE QUESTIONS

Critical Legal Thinking. Do you agree with the expansive definition of a covered employee with regard to undocumented workers?

Business Ethics. What should be the breadth of protections offered to unauthorized workers? Why should the United States extend such benefits when other countries do not offer them?

Contemporary Business. Discuss whether there is an incongruity in U.S. public policy (i.e., one policy discourages illegal immigration but another allows undocumented aliens to recover in an action under the FLSA).

State and Local Regulations

Employers must always consult state laws and local ordinances in addition to the **FLSA**. They must follow both federal and these other laws so that the employee receives the greatest benefit required among them. For example, state laws often afford greater or additional benefits than those the **FLSA** offers. For example, federal law does not require the employer to extend to the employee:

- vacation, holiday, severance, or sick pay
- meal or rest periods
- premium pay for weekend or holiday work
- discharge notices, reasons for discharge, or the immediate payment of final wages to terminated employees
- the limit of the number of hours to be worked in a day (however, for public safety reasons federal law does have such rules for positions in transportation)
- fringe benefits

A situation involving a person volunteering his or her services may also result in an employment relationship. For example, an employee cannot "volunteer" his or her services to the employer to perform the same type of service performed by an employee.

Of course, individuals may volunteer or donate their services to religious, public service, and nonprofit organizations, without contemplation of pay, and they are not then considered employees of such organizations. Trainees or students may also be employees, depending on the circumstances of their activities for the employer.[3] The following employer attempted to defeat the "economic realities" of the relationship and avoid payment to its workers.

CASE 14.2

COMMERCIAL ACTIVITIES OF A NONPROFIT ENTITY MAKES THE ENTITY SUBJECT TO FLSA

TONY & SUSAN ALAMO FOUNDATION V. SECRETARY OF LABOR

471 U.S. 290 (1985)

Supreme Court of the United States

Facts. The Department of Labor sued the Alamo Foundation and its officers for violations of the minimum wage, overtime, and record-keeping provisions of the FLSA. The foundation derived income from the operation of commercial businesses, staffed largely by the foundation's "associates," most of whom were drug addicts, derelicts, or criminals before their rehabilitation by the foundation. These workers received no cash salaries, but the foundation provided them with food, clothing, shelter, and other benefits. The district court found that the operation was an "enterprise" within the parameters of the FLSA, engaged in commercial activities, and that the "associates" were employees. The Court of Appeals of the Eighth Circuit affirmed the district court's findings. The Supreme Court granted *certiorari.*

Issue. Does commercial activity of nonprofit business compensating workers with noncash benefits constitute activity protected by the FLSA?

Language of the Court. White, J.: **The District Court found that despite the Foundation's incorporation as a nonprofit religious organization, its businesses were "engaged in ordinary commercial activities in competition with other commercial businesses." . . . The District Court further ruled that the associates who worked in these businesses were "employees" of the Alamos and of the Foundation within the meaning of the Act. The associates who had testified at trial had vigorously protested the payment of wages, asserting that they considered themselves volunteers who were working only for religious and evangelical reasons. Nevertheless, the District Court found that the associates** were "entirely dependent upon the Foundation for long periods." Although they did not expect compensation in the form of ordinary wages, the District Court found, they did expect the Foundation to provide them "food, shelter, clothing, transportation and medical benefits." . . . These benefits were simply wages in another form, and under the "economic reality" test of employment, . . . the associates were employees.

The Court has consistently construed the Act "liberally to apply to the furthest reaches consistent with congressional direction," (citation omitted) recognizing that broad coverage is essential to accomplish the goal of outlawing from interstate commerce goods produced under conditions that fall below minimum standards of decency. (Citation omitted.) The statute contains no express or implied exception for commercial activities conducted by religious or other nonprofit organizations, and the agency charged with its enforcement has consistently interpreted the statute to reach such businesses. The Labor Department's regulation defining "business purpose," which is entitled to considerable weight in construing the Act, explicitly states:

> Activities of eleemosynary, religious, or educational organization [sic] may be performed for a business purpose. Thus, where such organizations engage in ordinary commercial activities, such as operating a printing and publishing plant, the business activities will be treated under the Act the same as when they are performed by the ordinary business enterprise. (29 C.F.R. §779.214 (1984).)

The test of employment under the Act is one of "economic reality," . . . and the situation here is a far cry from that in Portland Terminal. Whereas in Portland Terminal, the training course lasted a little over a week, in this case the associates were "entirely dependent upon the Foundation for long periods, in some cases several years." . . . Under the circumstances, the District Court's finding that the associates must have expected to receive in-kind benefits — and expected them in exchange for their services — is certainly not clearly erroneous. Under Portland Terminal, a compensation agreement may be "implied" as well as "express," . . . and the fact that the compensation was received primarily in the form of benefits rather than cash is in this context immaterial. These benefits are, as the District Court stated, wages in another form.

Decision. Yes. The foundation's religious character does not place its commercial activities undertaken with a "common business purpose" beyond the reach of the Fair Labor Standards Act, and its associates are "employees" within the meaning of the act because they work in contemplation of compensation.

CASE QUESTIONS

Critical Legal Thinking. In its decision, the Court noted that the court brief of the "associates" vehemently argued that they did not want to be covered under the act. Do you think that the act should be applied to those who decline its protections?

Business Ethics. Do you think that the foundation's conduct was ethical? Perform a web search to determine what eventually became of Mr. and Mrs. Alamo.

Contemporary Business. How would you define the limitations of religious practice and belief in relation to the requirements of American law?

Regulation of Wages and Hours

The **FLSA**'s wage and hour provisions do not apply to industries as a whole, but rather to the circumstances of each employment situation. Generally, the **FLSA** covers three main areas of federal regulation: the **minimum wage** laws, how hours worked are calculated, and when and to whom **overtime** must be paid. An employer and employee are free to contract for the wages, hours, and benefits to be paid to the employee; however, the terms must minimally comply with the **FLSA**'s wage and hour requirements. Contracts that violate the **FLSA**'s provisions are void as offensive to public policy.

Overtime
Subject to certain industry-specific exemptions, the hourly rate of one and one-half times their normal pay rate due to nonexempt employees for each hour of work beyond 40 in a workweek.

FEDERAL MINIMUM WAGE. Employees covered by the **enterprise** or **individual coverage** under **FLSA** are entitled to be paid at least the federal **minimum wage** as well as one and one-half times their regular rates of pay for all hours worked beyond the 40-hour workweek, unless an exemption applies. **FLSA** also has youth employment provisions regulating the employment of anyone under 18. Under federal law, employees under 20 years of age may be paid an **"opportunity wage."** This wage rate is a subminimum hourly wage rate of at least $4.25 per hour for the first 90 consecutive days of employment. An employer cannot displace other employees to hire a youth at the lesser rate.[4] The **FLSA** also contains record keeping requirements.

Although the **minimum wage** requirement seems simple enough to state, there are a myriad of wage issues that can arise that can lead to violations of the law and lawsuits by the Department of Labor or employees. These include what type of compensation is included in determining whether the **minimum wage** has been paid, what lawful deductions may be made, and issues surrounding tipped employees and defining the hours worked.

Effective July 24, 2009, the **federal minimum wage** is $7.25 per hour. Under federal law, employees under 20 years of age may be paid less per hour. For hourly employees, the hourly rate of pay must be equal to the federal minimum or more per hour. For piece-rate work employees (i.e., employees paid for each unit of production) the average hourly earnings during the workweek must be at least at or above the federal **minimum wage**. Commissions paid to employees must also be equal to or exceed the **minimum wage**.

Under federal law, when an employee in a single workweek performs two different functions at two different rates of pay, his or her regular wage rate is the weighted average of the two hourly rates.[5] Otherwise, the employer and employee may agree that the overtime pay shall be paid either at one and one-half times the regular pay rate or they may agree to an estimated rate to be used for calculating the **overtime** rate.

Remuneration of the **minimum wage** can be in forms other than cash or check. Payments made in the form of goods, services, or other items of value are considered as wage equivalents. Lodging provided to employees may be considered part of the compensation paid to them. When the benefit conferred is to the employer's business interest, no credit is allowed. Examples would include telephones used for business purposes, uniforms required by the law or an employer or the nature of the business, the necessary tools used on the job, and business-related travel expenses.

A salaried employee must receive at least the statutory minimum hourly rate of pay. The regular hourly rate is determined by dividing the employee's total remuneration for the workweek by the total number of hours the employee actually worked during that workweek. Under federal law, the work hours of a salaried employee may fluctuate from week to week, if the amount of salary paid is sufficient to compensate the employee at a rate at least equal to the applicable **minimum wage** rate for all hours worked in every workweek.

> ***Example:*** While the employer is permitted to compensate employees on an hourly, salaried, commission, piecework, or other basis, an employee's regular rate is nevertheless computed as an hourly rate. The hourly rate is determined by dividing the employee's total pay (after statutory exclusions) in a workweek by the total hours actually worked in that week. That result can never be less but can be more than the minimum wage required by the **FLSA**.

Federal law allows employers to credit tips received from customers toward the **minimum wage** rate to be paid the employee (**"tip credit"**). Employees will be deemed "tipped employees" if their occupation is one in which employees customarily and regularly receive more than $30 per month in tips.[6] However, many state laws do not permit the **tip credit** and require the employer to pay the employee the minimum hourly wage rate. The employer may claim a **tip credit** only if:

- the employer informs each tipped employee about the allowance and how it is calculated;
- the employer can document that the employee received at least enough tips to bring the total wage paid to the employees to at least the minimum wage rate; and
- all tips are retained by the employee and are not shared with the employer or other employees, unless through a valid tip-pooling arrangement.

CALCULATION OF HOURS WORKED. All time an employer requests that an employee spend on its business is compensable; this is also referred to as work time not requested but work suffered or permitted.[7] If the employer knows or has reason to believe that an employee is working, the work is compensable. The employer cannot merely have a policy of ordering employees not to work unauthorized overtime. The employer has a duty to see that work is not performed if the employer does not want the work performed. For example, the employer cannot allow employees to work at home for their convenience after hours to catch up on projects and not count the work time as hours worked. The standard used is to determine if the employee would be able to use the time effectively for his or her own purposes or if the employer controls the time spent by the employee. The time is not counted as hours worked if the employee is completely relieved of any duties and the time off is long enough to allow the employee to effectively use the time for his or her own purposes.

Example: Where an employer has no knowledge that an employee was engaging in **overtime** work and the employee fails to notify the employer or deliberately prevents the employer from acquiring knowledge of the **overtime** work, the employer's failure to pay for the **overtime** is not a violation of the law.[8]

If the work is merely incidental and not indispensable to the employee's performance, the employee is not entitled to be paid under the FLSA.

Example: Eric Buzek, a field service technician for Pepsi Bottling Company, was required to submit end-of-the-day reports from home, detailing his use of a company vehicle. He drove from site to site repairing and servicing ice machines, vending machines, and fountain equipment for Pepsi customers. The employee's submission of the reports took a few minutes at the end of each day. The issue was whether transportation of tools and the reports were merely "incidental to" the use of a company vehicle for commuting.[9]

On-call time poses a special problem for employers. Employers often arrange with employees to be **on-call**. If the employee is required to remain on-call on the employer's premises or so close to the premises that the employee cannot use the time effectively for his or her own purposes, the employee is working while on-call. These hours are compensable work hours. **On-call time** is not counted as work hours when the employee is required to carry a pager or cell phone or to leave word with company officials of where the employee may be reached. If an employee who is **on-call** is free to come and go and to engage in personal activities during idle periods, the on-call time is not counted as hours worked and is unpaid, unless and until the employee actually responds to a call back to duty. However, if such calls were so frequent that the employee is not free to use the off-duty time effectively for the employee's own benefit, the intervening periods as well as the time spent in responding to calls would be counted as compensable hours of work. Employers must study each factual case to determine if it is controlling the **on-call time** of an employee.

On-Call Time
Time during which employees are not required to remain on the employer's premises but are required to be available to work and thus cannot use their time for their own purposes.

Meal periods are not hours worked if the employee is relieved of duties to eat a meal. It is not necessary that the employee be free to leave the employer's workplace, but if employees are required to eat at desks or a work position, the time must be paid. Ordinarily, 30 minutes or more is sufficient for a bona fide **meal period**, although shorter periods under special circumstances might be permitted. **Rest periods** of durations of less than 20 minutes are counted as hours worked and are paid to the employee. Interestingly, the **FLSA** does not require an employer to provide employees with rest periods.

Rest Period
A break in the workday, for example, to use restrooms or for coffee. Not required by FLSA, but state laws often require rest periods for nonexempt employees who work a minimum period of time in a workday.

If an employee is on duty for less than 24 hours, **sleeping time** is not compensable. If he or she is on duty for 24 hours or more, then the employer and employee may agree to exclude a sleeping period of not more than 8 hours, provided adequate sleeping facilities are furnished and the employee can usually enjoy a reasonable period of sleep. Otherwise, sleeping time is compensable. If the sleeping period is interrupted by a duty call, then the nonsleep reporting time is compensable. If employees cannot get at least five hours of sleep, then the entire sleep period is compensable.[10]

Management Application
Berkeley's Living Wage Ordinance

The city of Berkeley, California, has adopted an ordinance setting **minimum wages** above what is required by law. Nationwide more than 100 jurisdictions have similar laws, including New York City and Los Angeles. Enacted in 2000, Berkeley's Municipal Code Chapter 13.27 provides that contractors engaging in a specified amount of business in any 12-month period with the City, unless specifically exempted, must comply with the ordinance.

The ordinance requires a mandated minimum compensation to all eligible employees, an hourly wage of not less than $12.11 per hour plus health benefits or $14.12 per hour without health benefits. It also mandates at least 22 days off per year for sick leave, vacation, or personal necessity, 12 of which must be compensated. The wage rates are adjusted annually for inflation.[11]

Exempt Employee
Employees exempt from overtime pay provisions, from both the minimum wage and overtime pay provisions, or from the child labor provisions of the FLSA.

Nonexempt Employee
A worker entitled to the minimum wage and/or overtime pay protections of the FLSA.

OVERTIME COMPENSATION. All employees are entitled to payment of **overtime** unless they are considered an **exempt employee.** All **nonexempt employees** covered by the **FLSA** must be paid **overtime** after 40 hours worked per workweek at a rate of at least one and one-half times the employees' regular hourly (or hourly equivalent) rate of pay. Under the **FLSA**, the workweek is a fixed and regularly period of time: seven 24-hour periods or 168 hours per week. The workweek can commence on any day of the week for the employees, and the employees may have different workweeks within the company.

> ***Example:*** Some employees may work Monday through Friday and have the weekends off, while other employees' workweeks might begin on Friday and end on Tuesday. The workweek schedule remains fixed for each employee so that an employee's eligibility for **overtime** compensation is determined by the workweek and not by an accumulation of hours over multiple workweeks.

The regular rate of pay is determined by dividing the total earnings in the workweek by the total number of hours worked in the workweek. The regular rate of pay may not be less than the applicable **minimum wage.**

The regular rate of pay does not include the following: gifts (such as those in the nature of birthday gifts), payments for hours not worked because of unpaid vacations and holidays, lunch and rest break expense reimbursements, discretionary bonuses, profit sharing, retirement and insurance plans, **overtime** premium payments, and stock options.

For example, Samir regularly works 48 hours in a workweek and receives a regular rate of pay of $9.00 per hour. He works Saturdays, for which he receives an additional

$100 bonus plus **overtime**. For a record day of production during the week, he received a $200 bonus. His pay for the workweek is calculated as follows:

48 hours × $9.00	=	$432.00
Regular Bonus	=	100.00
		$532.00
$532.00/48	=	$11.08 (regular rate of pay)
$11.08 × 0.5	=	5.54 (overtime rate of pay)
$5.54 × 8	=	44.33 (overtime pay due Samir for that workweek)
Total compensation	=	$776.33 ($532.00 + 44.33 + 200.00)

Federal law permits fluctuating workweeks. A salaried employee may have an agreement with the employer that the fixed salary is for all the hours worked for the workweek, regardless of the number. This agreement is permissible under the **FLSA** if the amount to the salary is sufficient to compensate the employee at a rate at least equal to the applicable **minimum wage** rate for all the hours worked in the workweeks. Under this plan, payments for all hours worked in excess of 40 are paid at one and one-half (1.5) times the regular rate of pay for that workweek. Students should be aware that many states prohibit the fluctuating workweek.

All work hours performed by the employee on behalf of the employer are compensable at minimum and premium **overtime** rates, if necessary. As long as an employer enforces its rules that prior authorization must be secured to work **overtime**, the employer should be able to defend itself successfully in unauthorized **overtime** claim proceedings. If it fails to do so, then the employer is liable for the **overtime**.

The Portal-to-Portal Act: When the Work Day Begins

The Portal-to-Portal Act of 1947[12] amended the **FLSA**. The act dictates when **overtime** is earned. This act generally does not require **overtime** to be paid for time the employee spends in:

- traveling to and from the place of employment; and
- preliminary or concluding activities.

Under this act, employers are required to compensate workers for time spent on job-related activities. Workers are not paid for walking on the employer's premises to and from the location of the employee's principal activity area. That means work that starts and ends at the work site is working time, unless otherwise agreed in an employment contract. Nonworking or idle periods while an employee is on duty at work are compensable working periods. For example, if workers were idle while awaiting parts or a delivery, the time is compensable. However, if that idle time is unrelated to their job

Portal-to-Portal Act 1947 Federal law specifying the types of work-related time spent that are compensable. Generally, such time includes all activity of benefit to the employer. Time for travel to and from the workplace is not compensable.

activities, employees would not be compensated for the idle time. This would include the time spent with fellow workers after work to socialize. Time spent going to or from the workplace is not compensable; however, travel during the workday *is* compensable. If travel out of town must occur on the same day as a return to town, then all travel time, excepting mealtime and travel time to and from the residence and the transportation departure point, is compensable.

Under the Department of Labor regulations, **training time** is deemed not compensable if: (1) attendance is outside the employee's regular working hours; (2) the employee does not perform productive work during the program; (3) attendance is voluntary; and (4) the program is not directly related to the employee's job.[13]

> ***Example:*** Police officers are not entitled to **overtime** compensation for time spent working out at a gym to maintain job-required physical fitness. Gym attendance was not required and was not so directly related to the employee's job that the hours spent should be compensated.[14]

The act provides for a two-year statute of limitations for actions under the **FLSA**, the **Walsh-Healy Act**, and the **Davis-Bacon Act**. However, the act provides for a three-year statute of limitations for "willful" violations.

PRELIMINARY AND POST-WORK ACTIVITIES. If employees must wear certain clothes or safety gear to perform their work, they may be entitled to compensation for the time spent in donning or stowing this gear. The time spent must involve preparatory and concluding activities related to **"integral and indispensable"** parts of the **"principal activity"** for which they are hired. That was the issue considered by the Supreme Court in the following case.

CASE 14.3

INTEGRAL AND INDISPENSABLE PRE- AND POST-WORK SHIFT ACTIVITIES ARE COMPENSABLE

IBP, INC. V. ALVAREZ

546 U.S. 21 (2005)

Supreme Court of the United States

Facts. In two consolidated cases, the Court considered the claims of employees at a meat-packing plant in Washington and a poultry plant in Maine. The employees argued that they were entitled to compensation for time spent walking to their work areas after changing into specialized protective clothing. The employers argued that doing so was not part of the employees' principal activity commencement of which would start the compensable workday. The Ninth Circuit Court of Appeals held that the part of the time spent by the Washington state employees was compensable, but the Court of Appeals for the First Circuit concluded that the walking and waiting times were not compensable under the FLSA. The Supreme Court granted *certiorari.*

Issue. Does the FLSA require employers to pay employees for time spent walking to and from stations that distributed employer-required safety equipment?

Language of the Court. Stevens, J.: **In 1955, eight years after the enactment of the Portal-to-Portal Act and the promulgation of these interpretive regulations, we were confronted with the question whether workers in a battery plant had a statutory right to compensation for the "time incident to changing clothes at the beginning of the shift and showering at the end, where they must make extensive use of dangerously caustic and toxic materials, and are compelled by circumstances, including vital considerations of health and hygiene, to change clothes and to shower in facilities which state law requires their employers to provide. . . ." (Citation omitted.) After distinguishing "changing clothes and showering under normal conditions" and stressing the important health and safety risks associated with the production of batteries, . . . the Court endorsed the Court of Appeals' conclusion that these activities were compensable under the FLSA. In reaching this result, we specifically agreed with the Court of Appeals that "the term 'principal activity or activities' in Section 4 [of the Portal-to-Portal Act] embraces all activities which are an 'integral and indispensable part of the principal activities,' and that the activities in question fall within this category." . . . Thus, activities, such as the donning and doffing of specialized protective gear, that are "performed either before or after the regular work shift, on or off the production line," are compensable under the portal-to-portal provisions of the Fair Labor Standards Act if those activities are an integral and indispensable part of the principal activities for which covered workmen are employed and are not specifically excluded.**

More pertinent, we believe, is the portion of §790.7 that characterizes the time that employees must spend waiting to check in or waiting to receive their paychecks as generally a "preliminary" activity covered by the Portal-to-Portal Act. That regulation is fully consistent with the statutory provisions that allow the compensability of such collateral activities to depend on either the agreement of the parties or the custom and practice in the particular industry.

In short, we are not persuaded that such waiting — which in this case is two steps removed from the productive activity on the assembly line — is "integral and indispensable" to a "principal activity" that identifies the time when the continuous workday begins. Accordingly, we hold that §4(a) (2) excludes from the scope of the FLSA the time employees spend waiting to don the first piece of gear that marks the beginning of the continuous workday.

Decision. Yes. Putting on required safety equipment qualified as a "principal [work] activity" under the FLSA. The workday began when the employees started that activity and included any subsequent time. However, any time spent before then was not paid because it is a "preliminary" activity under the Portal-to-Portal Act.

CASE QUESTIONS

Critical Legal Thinking. Would it make a difference if competitors compensated employees for the preparatory and concluding time?

Business Ethics. If the walking time had been lengthy, do you think the Court would have viewed the facts differently? Is it the amount of time or the type of activity that is at issue?

Contemporary Business. What other activities related to the workplace are unpaid?

COMMUTING. Since the Supreme Court rendered its decision in *IBP, Inc. v. Alvarez,* some employers who permit their employees to commute between home and work in an employer-provided vehicle have been the target of suits for compensation. In these cases, the employees allege that they perform "principal" activities at home before or after their commute. Employers do not have to pay employees for time spent commuting in employer-provided vehicles so long as the following occurs:

1. the employer and employee have an agreement regarding the employee's use of the employer's vehicle for commuting;
2. the employee's travel to his or her job site is within his or her normal commuting area; and
3. the activities employees perform before or after their commute are "incidental" to their use of the employee's vehicle for commuting.

If any of the above conditions is *not* met, the employee is entitled to be paid for the time spent commuting to work in the employer's vehicle. These requirements were part of the Employee Commuting Flexibility Act of 1996.[15]

Exemptions from Minimum Wage and Overtime Requirements

The **FLSA** has a number of complex exemptions that eliminate the requirement to pay **overtime** for certain classes of employees. Under federal law, most employees receive **overtime** pay at the rate of one and one-half the employees' regular rate of pay for all hours worked over 40 in a workweek. However, certain employees are exempt from the payment of **overtime**. Exempt employees are employed in a bona fide **executive, administrative**, or **professional** position, or work as a **computer professional** or an

outside salesperson. These positions are commonly referred to as the **"white collar"** exemption.[16] The tests for these white-collar exemptions are discussed in this section. While job duties may vary among workers with these exemptions, a common factor is that the exempt individuals must be paid on a salary basis at not less than $455 per week.[17] The **FLSA** does not define **"executive, administrative, or professional capacity"**; instead, it expressly delegates that task to the secretary of labor who may, "from time to time," alter the definitions.[18]

Those persons who are not exempt employees must be paid **overtime** whether they are salaried or otherwise. Job titles do not determine the person's exempt status.[19] Many employers mistakenly believe that if an employee is paid on a salary basis, the employee is exempt from **overtime**.

> ***Example:*** Salvatore is paid $750.00 per week for a 40-hour workweek. He regularly works 8 hours of additional work time each workweek.

Salary earnings	=	$750.00
Hours worked	=	48.00
Regular rate	=	18.75 per hour
$18.75 × .5	=	9.38 (overtime rate of pay)
Salary	=	$750.00 (weekly salary)
8 × $9.38	=	75.04 (overtime wages due Sal)
Total due	=	$825.04

For an exemption from the obligation to pay **overtime** to apply, employees must meet the specific job duties and salary requirements of the U.S. Department of Labor's regulations.

Executive Exemption FLSA exemption from overtime pay covering employees whose duties and responsibilities involve managing an enterprise, who customarily and regularly direct two or more employees, who have authority to hire and fire or whose recommendations as to staffing are given particular weight, and who customarily and regularly exercise discretionary powers.

EXECUTIVE EXEMPTION. The **executive exemption** for private employers applies if *all* of the following elements are met:

- the employee is salaried at a rate not less than $455 per week, exclusive of board, lodging, or other facilities (or, alternatively, is an employee who owns at least 20 percent equity interest in the business);
- the employee's primary duty is management of the enterprise in which the employee is employed or of a customarily recognized department or subdivision;
- the employee must customarily and regularly direct the work of two or more employees; and
- the employee must have the authority to hire or fire other employees, or be able to recommend as to hiring, firing, advancement, promotion, or any other change of employee status, and the recommendation will be given particular weight.

Various exceptions to the salary calculation address exceptional circumstances.[20]

The Department of Labor's regulations identify **highly compensated employees** performing office or nonmanual work who are paid a total annual compensation of $100,000 or more on a salary or fee basis (which must include at least $455 per week paid on a salary basis) as exempt from **overtime** if they customarily and regularly perform at least one of the exempt duties or responsibilities of an exempt **executive, administrative**, or **professional employee** identified in the tests for exemption.

The Department of Labor construes "customary and regularly" to include work normally and recurrently performed every workweek.

An employee's primary duty is determined by looking at all the facts relating to the employee's job as a whole. Among the factors considered are:

- the relative importance of the exempt duties as compared to the other duties performed by the individual;
- the amount of time spent performing the exempt work (usually 50 percent or more is required);
- the employee's freedom from direct supervision by others; and
- the relationship between the employee's salary and the wages paid to other nonexempt workers for the same kind of nonexempt work.

With regard to the hiring and firing element, the person may be exempt if his or her recommendation as to a candidate or employee is given particular weight, even if it is reviewed by a higher level of management.

One court has observed that it is appropriate to limit the application of the **"executive" exemption** to those workers who actually direct others and to apply the next exemption, administrative, to persons performing a variety of miscellaneous but important tasks within the business. "In other words, the differentiation between a mere clerk and one with actual administrative ability may be said to lie very largely in, (1) the exercise of discretion and independent judgment, and (2) in receipt of a salary that is above that customarily paid to one engaged primarily in mere manual or clerical work."[21]

Administrative Exemption
Under this FLSA exemption, overtime wages need not be paid to a worker who is compensated at a salary basis of not less than $455 per week, whose primary duty is the performance of office or nonmanual work directly related to management or the general business operations of the employer or its customers, and whose work includes exercise of discretion and independent judgment.

ADMINISTRATIVE EXEMPTION. An employee is engaged in an **administrative capacity** when the employee:

- has the primary duty of performing office or nonmanual work directly related to the management or general business operations of the employer or its customers; and
- in the exercise of the primary duty, regularly exercises discretion and independent judgment with respect to matters of significance.

While every job context is different, "the typical example of the production/administrative dichotomy is a factory setting where the 'production' employees work on the line running machines, while the administrative employees work in an office communicating with the customers and doing paperwork." Administrative tasks constitute an employee's primary duty if the tasks represent "the major part, or over 50% of the employee's time."[22]

> ***Example:*** Work planners who spent the majority of their day in an office creating instruction for the maintenance and repair of machinery were denied **overtime** because they were responsible for "planning" and "advising the management" about the best way to operate.

Performing some manual work does not remove an employee from the executive or administrative exemption classification. The law provides that an employee of a retail or service establishment will still be considered employed in a bona fide **executive** or **administrative capacity** if the number of hours in his or her workweek devoted to activities not directly or closely related to the performance of executive or administrative activities is *less than 40 percent of his or her total hours worked in the workweek.*

> ***Example:*** A federal court allowed Starbucks' managers to sue for unpaid overtime under the **FLSA**. They estimated than 10 percent of their time was spent in managerial tasks. They contended they were entitled to overtime pay based on the number of hours they spent performing nonmanagerial tasks.

PROFESSIONAL EXEMPTION. The **professional** exemption applies if the primary duty of the individual is the performance of work requiring knowledge of an advanced type in a field of science or learning that is customarily acquired by a prolonged course of specialized intellectual instruction. Usually this pertains to those individuals who have been issued licenses to practice a profession by a state licensing authority. Commonly exempt professions would include the medical, dental, nursing, legal, teaching, accountancy, pharmacy, and engineering professions, and other similarly licensed persons. Generally, assistants to these persons are not exempt, such as a paralegal working with an attorney. The primary duty may also involve work requiring invention, imagination, originality, or talent in a field recognized as involving artistic or creative endeavors. Those who are recognized within this exempt category would include musicians, writers, actors, painters, and photographers. In determining whether the exemption applies, courts look to the tasks actually performed by the employee and not to the employee's experience in or licensure for some other type of work.[23]

Professional Exemption
An FLSA exemption from overtime pay for workers who are compensated on a salary basis at a rate not less than $455 per week and whose primary work requires advanced knowledge in a field of science or learning mastery of which is acquired through specialized instruction.

The employer asserting an exemption has the burden of proof. Exemptions are strictly interpreted as occurred in the following case.

CASE 14.4

OVERTIME EXEMPTIONS TO FLSA PAY REQUIREMENTS ARE STRICTLY INTERPRETED

COAST VAN LINES, INC. V. ARMSTRONG

167 F.2d 705 (9th Cir. 1948)

U.S. Court of Appeals for the Ninth Circuit

Facts. Coast Van Lines was engaged in the business of packing, crating, storing, and handling goods, particularly household goods and furniture. Over 55 percent of its business was intrastate, and the balance was performed on an interstate basis. The company employed packers, craters, warehousemen, and others, including occasional drivers.

Issue. Does the FLSA apply to a business that, for the most part, sells and services goods in intrastate commerce?

Language of the Court. Orr, J.: **The history of Sec. 13(a)(2) indicates said amendment was intended to exempt employees of the corner grocery, butcher, dry goods and department store. The intention to exclude from the operation of the Fair Labor Standards Act the local retailer is apparent from a consideration of the congressional debates and hearings conducted prior to the passage of the Act. As Mr. Justice Jackson, then Assistant Attorney General, stated during the hearings, the Act was not intended to apply to the retailer, filling station attendant and pants presser. In the early congressional debates and hearings, no reference may be found to "service" establishments as such, but in the Conference Committee Report of June 1938, an exception was extended to "any employee engaged in any retail or service establishment, the greater part of whose selling or servicing is in intrastate commerce." . . . The inclusion of the words "service" and "servicing" resulted obviously from a recognition of the fact that there were many local purveyors of services, as distinguished from goods, whose business was likewise conducted directly with the consuming public, such as the barber shop, beauty parlor and tailor shop. The reasonable conclusion to be drawn from the history is that Congress did not intend to exempt employees of all sellers of services, but only of those establishments whose business was analogous to the local retailer. In short, the word "service" means in effect "retail service" . . .**

Appellant is not a retailer of goods. The question is then narrowed to whether it is a retail service establishment Appellant's business does not come within this definition.

True, a substantial part of appellant's business consists of rendering service to private individuals. The administrator has ruled that the exemption will only apply where at least 75% of the total business is retail. Int. Bulletin 6 of the Wages and Hour Div. of the Department of Labor. . . . In the instant case, approximately 50 per cent of appellant's business is conducted pursuant to the Navy contract. This is non-retail service, not within the exemption.

Decision. Yes. Only services businesses that are analogous to a retailer are exempt from overtime requirements.

CASE QUESTIONS

Critical Legal Thinking. If a bureaucrat within the Department of Labor established the retail service business at 75 percent of the total business, what percentage would you have established? Is it fair that courts be required to follow the rule making pronouncements of federal agencies?

Business Ethics. Is this a fair interpretation of the congressional exemption for "service" businesses? Does this case extend the reach of federal power too far into the lap of local businesses?

Contemporary Business. Can you think of any other industries where the differentiation of intrastate from interstate commerce would be important?

CASE 14.5

EXERCISING PERSONAL DISCRETION AND JUDGMENT INDICATES ADMINISTRATIVE EXEMPTION FROM OVERTIME

CASH V. CYCLE CRAFT COMPANY, INC.

508 F.3d 680 (1st Cir. 2007)

U.S. Court of Appeals for the First Circuit

Facts. In 2003, Cycle Craft Company dba Harley-Davidson/Buell of Boston ("Boston Harley") hired Thomas Cash to create a new customer service position for which he drafted a job description that was adopted. After approximately a year on the job, he was terminated because of an emotional problem he experienced on the job. He sued under the FLSA for the unpaid overtime hours he worked during his tenure at Boston Harley. The employer moved for summary judgment, and Cash appealed the granting of that motion.

Issue. Was a worker who engaged in responding to customer requests and exercised some minor decision-making entitled to overtime wages?

Language of the Court. Oberforfer, J.: . . . **Cash accepted the offer and started working at Boston Harley on April 26, 2004. His duties included working with various Boston Harley departments to make sure that they outfitted and delivered each motorcycle according to the particular purchase order. If ordered parts were not installed, he was to contact the service manager, Michael Sienkiewicz, and tell him what needed to be done. Once problems were resolved, Cash was to tell the finance department that the motorcycle was ready. That department would then set up a time with the customer for delivery or pickup. Cash then tracked the purchased motorcycles; it was his job to stay in touch with the customers and make sure that they were satisfied so that they would provide positive customer-feedback reports. As Cash's job worked out, he did not coordinate motorcycle ordering, delivery, or part installation. Nor did he supervise or manage any employees. However, he attended management**

meetings, except when Buchbaum [the manager of Boston Harley] instructed him not to. At these meetings, Cash reported the status of previously ordered motorcycles and their scheduled time for pickup or delivery. Often, after Cash provided these reports, Buchbaum told him to leave the meeting.

Cash earned $1,153.85 per week (the prorated amount for his $60,000 salary) during his employment. He received this same salary each week regardless of hours worked, except for two pay periods. . . . Cash states that "he was never paid for hours he worked over 40 hours [per week], yet he was routinely required to work overtime as part of his job, as is reflected in his payroll records."

Cash meets the $455-per-week compensation threshold in the regulation: he received $1,153.83 per week, except for the two weeks he received $769.24 and $961.55. . . .

The next questions are whether Cash's "primary duty" at Boston Harley (a) "was the performance of office or non-manual work directly related to management or general business operations of [Boston Harley] or its customers," and (b) "include[d] the exercise of discretion and independent judgment with respect to matters of significance."

In general, "the exercise of discretion and independent judgment," i.e., the exemption's third requirement, "involves the comparison and the evaluation of possible courses of conduct, and acting or making a decision after the various possibilities have been considered." . . . "The term 'matters of significance,'" to which that discretion must apply, "refers to the level of importance or consequence of the work performed."

Cash's employment at Boston Harley meets the "management" and "discretion" requirements of the administrative exemption. First, like the marketing representatives in John Alden, Cash was "engaged in something more than routine selling efforts focused simply on particular sales transactions." Rather, he focused on improving customer service generally, by coordinating with various Boston Harley departments to ensure that customers were satisfied with their purchase and that they would provide Boston Harley with positive feedback reports. . . . Cash exercised discretion in reacting to the unique needs of Boston Harley's customers. Thus, Cash was "not merely [a] 'skilled' worker who operate[d] within a strict set of rules." . . . Moreover, in return for performing his duties, he earned a $60,000 salary, which was greater or equal to that of all the other managers, except for Buchbaum. Cash's attendance at management meetings, albeit in a limited fashion, further supports his status as a manager. In sum, Cash did not simply produce a product; he exercised independent judgment as he engaged in the company's business operations.

Cash meets each of administrative-exemption requirements under the Fair Labor Standards Act; Boston Harley therefore is not liable to pay him overtime wages.

Decision. No. The employee's duties included managerial decision-making and the exercise of discretion. He fit within the administrative overtime exemption.

CASE QUESTIONS

Critical Legal Thinking. What type of decision-making is required to establish the administrative exemption? For example, is an employee who merely applies specific standards or who grades people or objects pursuant to specified standards entitled to overtime pay?

Business Ethics. Do you think this decision is fair to Cash? Did he really exercise the discretion that the regulations intended to address?

Contemporary Business. What other examples can you cite from recent news stories where the courts have had to consider the exercise of discretion with regard to overtime claims?

Focus on Ethics
Is Ethics Training Mandatory?

The 2004 amendments to the Federal Sentencing Guidelines require all employers, both private and public, to adopt and maintain an effective compliance and ethics program. Training on these programs must be provided to all employees within the organization. Organizations must exercise due diligence to prevent and detect criminal conduct and otherwise promote an organizational culture that encourages ethical conduct and compliance with the law. Companies are required to ensure that the compliance and ethics program is followed, including monitoring and auditing to detect criminal conduct. In addition, the company must periodically evaluate the effectiveness of the program. Companies must publicize a system that allows for anonymous or confidential reporting so that employees and others may report or seek guidance regarding potential or actual criminal conduct without fear of retaliation.

Recent amendments to the Federal Acquisition Regulations require most companies doing business with the federal government to adopt a Code of Conduct and educate all employees on its provisions. The Sarbanes-Oxley Act also requires the adoption of an ethics and code of conduct training.

Such ethics programs will assist in the legal compliance with the wage and hour laws and regulations imposed upon employers. Conduct Internet research to find examples involving organizations that could have benefited from mandatory ethics training and avoided wage and hour litigation from their employees and former employees.

COMPUTER-RELATED EXEMPTION. This exemption relates to workers whose primary duty is the application of systems analysis techniques and procedures, including consulting with users to determine hardware, software, or system specifications and the design, development, documentation, analysis, creation, testing, or modification of computer systems or programs or software. In addition, such workers must receive a guaranteed salary of at least $455 per week or an hourly rate of not less than $27.63 per hour. Since job titles vary and responsibilities evolve so quickly within this industry, the name of a position is not determinative for the application of the exemption. The exemption applies only to those occupying highly skilled positions, not to those in training or those who have not attained a high degree of expertise that allows them to work without close supervision. The exemption does not include employees who are routinely engaged in operating computers and related equipment used in computer manufacture, repair, or maintenance.[24]

Outside Salesperson Exemption
Overtime wages need not be paid to a worker whose primary duty is to make sales or obtain orders or contracts and who is customarily and regularly engaged in work away from the employer's place of business.

OUTSIDE SALESPERSON EXEMPTION. This exemption applies to those whose primary duty is making sales or obtaining orders or contracts for services or facilities for compensation paid by customers. In addition, such a person must be *customarily and regularly engaged* away from the employer's place of business in performing such duties. There is no required minimum compensation that the person engaged in this activity must receive. A subset of this sales exemption applies to retail commissioned sales employees of a retail or service establishment who are paid more than half their total earnings on a commission basis. They may be exempt if their total compensation divided by the number of hours worked or regular rate exceeds one and one-half times the **minimum wage**. To be **exempt**, the worker must be one whose primary duty is to make sales or obtain orders or contracts, and the employee must be customarily and regularly engaged in such work *away from* the employer's place of business. Thus, inside telephone sales forces are not exempt from **overtime**. This result follows because managing the hours of such employees would be easy to do, which is not true for workers spending most of their time at customers' places of businesses.

Concept Summary
FLSA Minimum Wage Exemptions

- Executive, administrative, and professional employees, including academic administrative personnel and teachers in schools
- Computer professionals
- Outside salespersons
- Employees of certain retail or service establishments
- Employees of certain seasonal amusement or recreational establishments, camps, and religious or nonprofit educational conference centers, except employees of private entities providing services or facilities in a national park or forest
- Employees engaged in certain occupations such as fishing, agriculture, seamen on other than American vessels, babysitters, and companions for the aged or infirm; employees who deliver newspapers to consumers
- Employees who are exempted by the secretary of labor (subminimum wages for learners, apprentices, messengers, student workers, handicapped workers, and trainees)

Youth Employment

The **FLSA** protects youth from the abusive employment practices of the past. Children under age 14 may not be employed in nonagricultural occupations covered by the **FLSA**. Young people aged 14 and 15 years may be employed outside school hours in a variety of nonmanufacturing and nonhazardous jobs for limited periods of time and under specified conditions. The work that youths perform must occur between 7 a.m. and 7 p.m. with the exception that during the period from June 1 to Labor Day they may work until 9 p.m. When school is in session, these children may work daily for a maximum of 3 hours and weekly for a maximum of 18 hours. When school is not in session these children may work a daily maximum of 8 hours and a weekly maximum of 40 hours. Parents in occupations other than manufacturing and mining may employ their children who are less than 16 years of age. They may not employ them in occupations declared hazardous by the secretary of labor. Young people aged 16 and above are not limited in the times of day they may work. Children may be employed as actors or performers in motion pictures or in theatrical, radio, or television productions and may have newspaper routes.

The rules covering workers 16 and 17 years of age do not limit their number of work hours or their occupations, with the exception of those declared as hazardous by the secretary of labor. Employers must be aware that states often enact laws relating to youth employment that are more restrictive than those permitted by the **FLSA**. In addition, very specific regulations require accurate record keeping of the hours worked by youths during each workweek.

The **FLSA** requires that youths must be paid the **minimum wage** and paid **overtime** after 40 hours of work in a week.

Miscellaneous FLSA Regulations

In addition to accurate record keeping of hours worked by employees, covered employers must post a notice explaining the **FLSA** in a conspicuous place.

There are a number of federal statutory exemptions from *both* **minimum wage** and **overtime** requirements. Some of these include the following:

- employees of defined amusement or recreational establishments, certain seasonal organized camps, and religious or nonprofit educational conference centers;
- certain employees of fishing and marine product packing companies;
- employees exempted by the secretary of labor as learners, apprentices, and handicapped workers;
- employees of certain small local circulation newspapers;
- certain switchboard operators of very small public telephone companies;
- seamen on non-American vessels; and
- casual domestic babysitters or domestic companions for the aged or infirm.[25]

Employers should be aware of their right to employ others for less than **minimum wage** pursuant to employment that occurs under special certificates issued by the secretary of labor. These include employers in retail or service establishments, agriculture, or institutions of higher learning that employ up to six employees who are full-time students at 85 percent of the **minimum wage** for up to 20 hours per week, except during vacation periods. To employ students at this rate, the employer must obtain a certificate from the secretary of labor.[26]

Federal law does not authorize the use of **compensatory time off** in lieu of wages. Thus, an employee may not request time off instead of extra compensation or **overtime** pay. The time off is provided for work in excess of the agreed-on work hours or in excess of the regular work time. Federal law bars the payment of **compensatory time off** for more than 40 hours in a workweek. However, employers can dictate that the worker take one and one-half hours off for each hour worked in excess of 40 within a workweek in the same period in which the **overtime** was incurred. Thus, by compelling fewer hours in the subsequent workweek (but still within the same biweekly pay period) the employer can regulate the earnings to produce the same effect as if the employee had worked only 40 hours each week.

Enforcement

Administration and enforcement of wage claims made under the **FLSA** are within the jurisdiction of the Wage and Hour Division of the Department of Labor. The Department of Labor can sue an employer to recover unpaid **minimum wages** and **overtime** compensation and to seek an injunction to prevent further violations. The Department of Labor may inspect records and employer files, interview witnesses, and enter employers' premises to determine if the employer is complying with the requirements of law. Subpoenas for records in those investigations may be enforced even if the Department of Labor has not yet proved that the employer is even subject to the **FLSA**.[27] In addition, the victimized employees may also file suit for damages and for retaliatory discharge or discrimination.[28]

> ***Example:*** A federal court permitted Silvia Contreras to bring a retaliation claim under the **FLSA** and seek punitive damages against her employer. Her employer reported her to the Immigration and Naturalization Service for deportation because she filed a claim for unpaid wages and overtime.[29]

The employee may also seek **liquidated damages** in an amount equal to the damages, plus attorneys' fees and court costs. A two year statute of limitations applies to the recovery of back pay, but a three year statute will apply in cases of willful employer violations of the **FLSA**. Any person who willfully commits a violation of the **FLSA** is subject to criminal prosecution.

The U.S. Supreme Court has held that an employee may litigate wage claims in two forums if the employee is subject to a grievance procedure under a collective bargaining agreement. If unsuccessful in the grievance proceeding against the employer, the employee may litigate his or her claim in court on the same facts under the **FLSA**. Allowing two remedies results from the fact that **FLSA** claims cannot be waived by contract or through collective bargaining.[30]

Employer Defenses

An employer may rely upon its good-faith conformity to a written regulation, order, ruling, approval, or interpretation of the Department of Labor's Wage and Hour Division or upon any of administrative or enforcement practices with respect to **FLSA** claims. If the agency was mistaken in its interpretation of the law, employers are protected if they followed the Department of Labor's existing, albeit erroneous, position. However, the same defense is unavailable to an employer who is mistaken in its interpretation or application of the law.

Layoffs and Reductions in Force

Two of the most common methods used by employers to determine whose employment will be terminated in the event of a layoff or **reduction in force (RIF)** are seniority and performance. When an employer uses a length of service or seniority system to determine who must be terminated from employment, the employer is well advised to define the procedure very carefully. An employer could measure length of service in a variety of ways, including seniority in the entire company workforce, in a particular location or department, or in a particular job description. Each of these systems has been scrutinized for discrimination by the courts.

Worker Adjustment and Retraining Notification Act

In the 1980s, as U.S. industrial plants began to rapidly close and institute mass layoffs, many employees, their families, and their surrounding communities found themselves unprepared because they received no prior notice. In response, Congress enacted the **Worker Adjustment and Retraining Notification (WARN) Act** in 1989. The act prohibits employers from:

> order[ing] a plant closing or mass layoff until the end of a 60-day period after the employer serves written notice of such an order:
>
> (1) to each representative of the affected employees as of the time of the notice or, if there is no such representative at that time, to each affected employee; and
>
> (2) to the State or entity designated by the State to carry out rapid response activities [the State dislocated worker unit] . . . and the chief elected official of the unit of local government within which such closing or layoff is to occur.[31]

It also applies to a **mass layoff** that will affect 100 or more full-time workers. Under this act, a written notice must be given to employee representatives, such as a union, or to the affected employees if not represented by a union, and to the state unemployment office. The **WARN** Act is construed broadly by the courts to effect its purpose. The Department of Labor issues regulations for the enforcement of the act. The act applies to:

- Employers of more than 100 employees
  - Part-time employees who work less than 20 hours a week or who worked less than 6 of the 12 months preceding the required notice date are excluded from the count.
  - The 100-employee group can be also be counted as at least 100 employees who, taken together, work at least 4,000 hours per week (**overtime** hours are not included in the calculation).

- For-profit and nonprofit employers
- Employers who are ordering a plant closing or mass layoff affecting 50 or more employees
- Plant closings, which means the permanent or temporary shutdown of either:
  - A single site of employment, or
  - One or more facilities or operating units within a single site of employment if the shutdown results in an employment loss at the single site of employment during any 30-day period for 50 or more employees.

The contents of the notice must state the following information:

- the name and address of the employment site where the plant closing or mass layoff will occur and the contact information of the company official to contact for further information;
- a statement as to whether the action will be permanent or temporary;
- a statement of whether the entire plant is to be closed; and
- the job titles, positions, or descriptions of the employees affected and the names of the persons holding the affected jobs.

Employers are expected to include in the notice the best information available to the employer and must be as descriptive and informative as possible. The **WARN** Act notice does not alter any liability the employer may have as a result of a collective bargaining agreement or other contract or statutory liability imposed on the employer.

To be deemed a **mass layoff** under **WARN**, the layoff must meet two conditions. First, it must be an **RIF** that is not the result of a "plant closing." Second, the reduction must result in an "employment loss" at a single site that affects at least 50 full-time employees who comprise at least 33 percent of the full-time work force or at least 500 full-time employees.

Employer Liability

Employers who violate the federal **WARN** Act are liable to each discharged employee affected by a plant closing or a mass layoff for back pay for each day of the violation, at a rate of compensation not less than the higher of the average regular rate received by the employee during the last three years of employment or the final regular rate received by the employee; and all ERISA fringe benefits, including the cost of medical expenses incurred during the loss of job period that would have otherwise been covered under an employer fringe benefit plan. This liability can be substantial to the noncompliant employer.

In addition, the employer can face civil penalties of up to $500 per day for each day of violation. Acting in error but otherwise operating in good faith does not excuse the employer from liability. Employees may sue the employer for violation of the **WARN** Act and recover their attorneys' fees. In addition to the damages to aggrieved employees, the employer must pay a civil penalty to local governmental bodies.[32]

CASE 14.6

NONCONTIGUOUS SITES NOT SHARING STAFF OR OPERATIONAL PURPOSE ARE NOT A SINGLE SITE OF EMPLOYMENT. GENERAL RELEASES MAY WAIVE WARN RIGHTS

WILLIAMS V. PHILLIPS PETROLEUM CO.

23 F.3d 930 (5th Cir. 1994)

U.S. Court of Appeals for the Fifth Circuit

Facts. In 1992 Phillips Petroleum Company and other affiliates reduced its workforce by laying off over 500 employees in Bartlesville, Oklahoma, and provided them with 60 days' advance written notice. The defendant employers also laid off 27 workers at several locations in Houston to whom they did not provide notice. Six of the claimants alleged that the defendants had violated WARN by failing to provide 60 days' notice to them. All of these plaintiffs and the Bartlesville employees executed releases in connection with their terminations in exchange for enhanced layoff benefits.

Issue. Does an employer have a WARN obligation if a "mass layoff" occurs over multiple, noncontiguous employment sites? What are the requirements for a release waiving WARN liability?

Language of the Court. Williams, J.: **Whether multiple work locations constitute a "single site of employment" under WARN is a mixed question of fact and law (citation omitted). Reviewing de novo the issue of whether the Houston and Bartlesville employment locations constitute a "single site of employment," we agree with the district court and hold that the Houston and Bartlesville locations were not a single site of employment.**

The statute does not define a "single site of employment." The rules promulgated by the Secretary of Labor provide that "non-contiguous sites in the same geographic area which do not share the same staff or operational purpose should not be considered a single site." . . . Groups of structures within a campus or industrial park, or separate facilities across the street from one another, may be considered a single site of employment. Two plants on opposite sides of a town do not constitute a single site of employment if they employ different workers.

The Houston and Bartlesville layoffs cannot be aggregated to bootstrap the Houston plaintiffs over the WARN minimum required for a mass layoff. The regulations indicate that two plants across town will rarely be considered a single site for purposes of a mass layoff. It is not plausible, under any reasonable or good-faith reading of the regulations, that the Houston and Bartlesville plants — located in different states and hundreds of miles apart — could be considered a "single site" for purposes of WARN.

Employees were not rotated between the different sites, and the locations did not share staff and equipment. . . . No other "unusual circumstances" have been alleged that would support classifying the two plants as a "single site." . . . As the Bartlesville and Houston sites are distinct, they may not be aggregated in order to meet the minimum employee requirements . . . The Bartlesville layoffs, accordingly, are irrelevant to the issue of whether the Houston employees were entitled to notice under WARN.

No mass layoff occurred at the single sites of employment where the original plaintiffs worked. Five of the plaintiffs worked at HCC's operations in three different locations in and around Houston. HCC laid off twenty-seven employees over a ten-month period. One of the named plaintiffs worked for PGHC in Houston; PGHC laid off eight employees who worked at that site. The layoffs at HCC and PGHC were not mass layoffs as defined by the Act, as the number of employees laid off did not meet the fifty-employee minimum. Thus, the Houston employees were not entitled to WARN notification.

Each original plaintiff signed a release shortly after his or her termination of employment. The releases stated that signing the release was a condition to participation in the company's enhanced supplemental layoff pay plan, advised the employee to consult an attorney, gave ample time to consider the release, and specifically covered all claims relating to the individual's employment or layoff. The Bartlesville plaintiffs signed similar releases.

Williams has provided no credible evidence that the releases were obtained by fraud or duress. There is no genuine issue of material fact that the releases were valid.

Decision. No. A WARN notice was not required where "mass layoffs" did not occur. The releases of the employees' WARN rights were knowingly and voluntarily given.

CASE QUESTIONS

Critical Legal Thinking. What factors would allow considering multiple plant locations to be a "single site"?

Business Ethics. Is it fair to an economically distressed business to construe the notices for such technical compliance?

Contemporary Business. This case establishes the standard for the validity of releases under **WARN**. Do you think the statute should be amended to state specific notifications of rights being waived, as is required under the Older Worker Benefit Protection Act (discussed in the chapter on age discrimination)?

Many owners and advisors of privately held businesses do not recognize the application of the federal **WARN** Act on the sales of their businesses. Typically, such sales are structured as a sale of assets of the business to a buyer. In such a sale, the buyer is not responsible for the liabilities of the seller unless expressly adopted by the buyer. If at the closing of the sale, the seller terminates the employee staff and the buyer then hires some or all of the employees for the buyer's continued operation of the business, a mass layoff under the **WARN** Act has occurred. Such owners are well advised to provide the proper **WARN** notices to avoid liabilities to the discharged employees. Alternatively, the employer may proceed with the sale and the resulting mass layoff by having the employees execute a waiver and release of their **WARN** Act claims. Usually, such releases are given in exchange for a severance payment to the affected employees.

Other Federal Laws

The Davis-Bacon Act and the Walsh-Healey Act

The **Davis-Bacon Act** of 1931 established the requirement of paying prevailing wages on federal or federally assisted construction projects. All contracts over $2,000 must include protections for paying workers not less than the locally prevailing wages and benefits paid on similar private works projects. The act has been amended several times to also provide that contractors cannot lower wages in a local area to achieve a lower bid and that the cost of fringe benefits may be included in the calculation of prevailing wages. In addition, certified payrolls verifying that prevailing wages are being paid must be submitted to the Department of Labor, which is responsible for the act's enforcement.

Passed in 1936 as part of President Roosevelt's New Deal legislation, the **Walsh-Healey Act** protects employees of government contractors whose contracts exceed the sum of $10,000. It requires the payment of **overtime** for hours worked in excess of 8 hours per day or 40 hours per week, sets the **minimum wage** equal to the prevailing wage in the area of employment, and sets standards for child and convict labor as well as job sanitation and safety standards.

Management Application
Walmart's Pay Practices

Prior to 2008, Walmart was defending almost 100 lawsuits in state and federal courts involving alleged violations of wage and hour laws. Several class actions have been certified by the courts and permitted to proceed. The discovery in the cases indicates that the company employed a centralized scheduling system that instructed store managers of the optimal staffing levels to operate their stores. Managers were financially rewarded for maintaining staffing labor below those levels to save costs. Managers were accused of manipulating time-keeping records and of encouraging employees to work off the clock and to work through rest and lunch breaks.

1. If the plaintiffs' claims were proven to the satisfaction of a jury, what financial impact do you think Walmart would incur?
2. At the end of 2008, the general counsel for Walmart stated that the company had decided to settle the majority of these lawsuits. Agreeing that it would pay at least $352 million and possibly far more, Walmart agreed to the largest settlement in U.S. history for lawsuits over wage violations. Prior to his election, President Obama indicated that he would make wage-and-hour enforcement a priority of his administration. Do you think Walmart reached the settlement to avoid becoming a target of federal enforcement efforts?
3. Walmart continues to enjoy sustained growth from its overseas operations. If foreign law did not prevent such alleged conduct by Walmart and if Walmart employed these alleged techniques in its foreign stores, how would you characterize its ethical behavior?

Walmart is vigorously seeking to improve its public image and to overcome its past associations with ethical lapses in its corporate culture. As part of the Walmart Statement of Ethics, the company maintains the following with regard to wage and hour matters:

> *We are committed to complying fully with all applicable laws and regulations dealing with wage-and-hour issues, including off-the-clock work, meal and rest breaks, overtime pay, termination pay, minimum-wage requirements, wages and hours of minors, and other subjects related to wage-and-hour practices. As Walmart associates, we must:*
>
> - *Comply fully with all corporate policies and procedures related to wage-and-hour issues;*
> - *Comply fully with all applicable federal, state, and local laws and regulations pertaining to wage-and-hour issues;*
> - *Report any violations of wage-and-hour laws or policies to management.*
>
> *It is a violation of law and Walmart policy for you to work without compensation or for a supervisor (hourly or salaried) to request that you work without compensation. You should never perform any work for Walmart without compensation.*[33]

Employment Taxes: FICA and FUTA

FICA: Social Security and Medicare Contributions

Both employers and employees must pay the Social Security and Medicare Tax required by the **Federal Insurance Contributions Act (FICA)**. Social Security and Medicare apply the common law tests of the right to control the result and the details by which the result is accomplished.

FUTA: Federal Unemployment Tax

In 1935, Congress enacted the **Federal Unemployment Tax Act (FUTA)**, which imposes a tax on employers to fund state work assistance agencies. The **FUTA** tax is paid by employers and not by employees. The employer contributes to the federal government, and a credit is allowed for the amounts paid by the employer to state unemployment agencies. The state governments administer the unemployment programs in their respective jurisdictions under general guidelines issued by the federal government. Each state establishes eligibility requirements and the duration of benefits. Applicants must be eligible to work and actively seeking employment. Workers who have been terminated by employers for unlawful conduct or who voluntarily quit their positions without just cause are not entitled to unemployment compensation benefits.

For purposes of the federal unemployment tax, the term "employee" is determined by the common law definition of an employee. **FUTA** taxes are imposed on wages, which includes all compensation for employment.

Designation of Relationship Immaterial

If the relationship of employer and employee exists, the designation or description of the relationship by the parties as anything other than that of employer and employee is immaterial. Thus, if such relationship exists, it is of no consequence that the employee is designated as a partner, co-adventurer, agent, independent contractor, or the like.

All Classes Included in Relationship

All classes or grades of employees are included within the relationship of employer and employee. Thus, superintendents, managers, and other supervisory personnel are employees. Generally, an officer of a corporation is an employee of the corporation. However, an officer of a corporation who does not perform any services or performs only minor services and who neither receives, nor is entitled to receive, directly or indirectly, any remuneration, is not considered an employee of the corporation. A director of a corporation in his or her capacity as such is not an employee.

Employment Tax "Safe Harbor" Provision

In response to the Internal Revenue Service (IRS) aggressively seeking to collect employment taxes, Congress passed **§530** of the Revenue Act of 1978. It was intended to restrain the collection of those taxes from employers who classified their workers as independent contractors even though the workers might not fit the criteria of the 20-factor test. The **"safe harbor"** test applies only to employment taxes. The worker may be treated as an employee for all other purposes. A federal district court considered the application of this act in the following case.

CASE 14.7

INDUSTRY CUSTOMS AND PRACTICES AFFECT STATUS IN EMPLOYMENT TAX CASES

CRITICAL CARE REGISTER NURSING, INC. V. U.S.

776 F. Supp. 1025 (E.D. Pa. 1991)

U.S. District Court for the Eastern District of Pennsylvania

Facts. The IRS contended that a nursing business that provided the services of nurses to hospitals had failed to overcome the presumption that the workers were employees and subject to employment taxes. Following a jury trial in favor of the company, the IRS requested the court overturn the decision of the jury. The facts were that the business provided specialized registered nurses to hospitals in need of temporary staffing. The evidence showed that the company did not dictate the work they were to perform and did not furnish uniforms, transportation, fringe benefits, or the like to the nurses. The nurses were free to choose when, where, and how often they would work. The company argued that the nurses were independent contractors.

Issue. What constitutes a reasonable basis under the Internal Revenue Code to classify a worker as an independent contractor?

Language of the Court. Broderick, J.: **Section 530 (a)(1) provides:**

> **Controversies Involving Whether Individuals are Employees for Purposes of Employment Taxes**
>
> **(a) Termination of certain employment tax liability.—**
>
> **(1) In general.—If—**
>
> **(A) for purposes of employment taxes, the taxpayer did not treat an individual as an employee for any period, and**

(B) . . . all Federal tax returns (including information returns) required to be filed by the taxpayer with respect to such individual for such period are filed on a basis consistent with the taxpayer's treatment of such individual as not being an employee. . . .

In addition, Section 530 (a)(2) provides three statutory "safe havens" for the taxpayer. Pertinent to the present case, it states in part:

(2) . . . a taxpayer shall in any case be treated as having a reasonable basis for not treating an individual as an employee . . . if the taxpayer's treatment of such individual for such period was in reasonable reliance on any of the following:

(C) long-standing recognized practice of a significant segment of the industry in which such individual was engaged.

Even the "safe havens" of Section 530 (a)(2), however, are not the exclusive ways of meeting the reasonable basis requirement. . . . A taxpayer who fails to meet any of the three "safe havens" may nevertheless be entitled to relief if the taxpayer can demonstrate, in some other manner, a reasonable basis for not treating the individual as an employee.

Thus, the Congressional mandate is clear that there are several avenues by which a taxpayer may prove, under Section 530, that it had a reasonable basis for not treating a worker as an employee. . . . .

Congress has not defined "reasonable basis" for the purposes of Section 530(a)(1), which is the section of general applicability . . . After analyzing the statute and legislative history, however, this Court has concluded that, for purposes of Section 530 (a)(1), a taxpayer may establish that it had a reasonable basis for not treating its workers as employees by utilizing the traditional common law rules for determining whether workers are employees or independent contractors. However, under the Congressional mandate of Section 530, the taxpayer need only show that, under the common law rules, its treatment of its workers was reasonable. That is, under Section 530, the taxpayer's burden has been lessened and the taxpayer need only show a reasonable basis for not treating its workers as employees under the traditional common law rules.

This Court, in examining the record, finds that there is ample evidence on which the jury could reasonably have found by a preponderance of the evidence that Critical Care had a reasonable basis under Section 530 (a)(1) for not treating its nurses as employees. . . . Evidence was presented from which the jury could conclude that Critical Care neither directed nor controlled, nor had the right to direct and control, the nurses in the performance of their duties at the hospitals. That is, Critical Care did not prescribe, nor did it have the right to prescribe the nurses' duties or the methods and means by which the nurses were to perform those duties at the hospitals. Critical Care gave no instructions to the nurses as to how the nurses were to perform their duties, and provided no training except for a brief orientation that was designed by a particular hospital and given only when a nurse had not previously worked at that hospital. Further, evidence was presented that the nurses performed no services for Critical Care on Critical Care's premises, and that the nurses were free to

choose when and from whom they would accept work, and were permitted to be registered with Critical Care in addition to their regular jobs with hospitals or their registration with other agencies. From these and other factors ample in the record, this Court holds that there was more than sufficient evidence presented at trial from which the jury could conclude that Critical Care satisfied, by a preponderance of the evidence, the dictates of Section 530 (a) (1) as to a reasonable basis for not treating its nurses as employees.

Decision. The court held the employer had a reasonable basis under §530(a)(1) for not treating its nurses as employees. The employer did not direct and control the nurses in the performance of their duties at the hospitals.

CASE QUESTIONS

Critical Legal Thinking. Do you think that Internal Revenue Code §530 helps or hinders a clear interpretation of the law with regard to hiring of workers?

Business Ethics. If you were working for the IRS, how would you define a "reasonable basis" for a company's treatment of a worker as an independent contractor for purposes of employment taxes?

Contemporary Business. Do you recognize that industry practices with regard to how workers are classified greatly influences whether or not a person is classified as an employee?

Penalties for Misclassification

There are substantial penalties for misclassifying a worker as an independent contractor. These include taxes, penalties, and interest. In addition, the "responsible person" within the employer's company is subject to personal liability and criminal penalties. Penalties range from a few percent to as much as 20 percent of compensation paid per misclassified employee. Because the IRS has agreed to share information with many state unemployment insurance agencies, an audit by one agency often leads to an audit by the other. This type of tax must be paid before the validity of the assessment can be contested in court. Employment taxes owed within three years of a bankruptcy filing cannot be discharged.

In addition, the reclassified employee may then seek unpaid **minimum wages** and **overtime** amounts earned plus penalties and attorneys' fees. In addition, the employer may be required to pay benefits under its benefit plans.

Willful violations of the **FLSA** are crimes punishable by fines up to $10,000 and, on a second violation, imprisonment for up to six months.[34]

Management Application
Defining "Seniority"

When an employment decision must be implemented based on the affected employees' seniority, the employer must be cautious to ensure that it has properly defined and implemented a seniority system. Without clear policies and procedures, the employer's decision can be subject to a number of challenges based on interpretation and the employer's prior practices. For example, the employer should determine what the prior employment practices have been with respect to seniority-based decisions. Part of that analysis should be to determine if employees with greater tenure have been allowed to displace or "bump" employees with less employment in the past. Moreover, the employer must verify what effects breaks in service would have on determining seniority status. Such breaks could have been temporary or permanent due to the employee's personal decisions or for legally cognizable ones (such as extended jury service, military service, pregnancy, or leaves under the Family and Medical Leave Act).

If the employer is a party to a collective bargaining agreement with its employees, it should determine the appropriateness of its actions in light of the agreement and if other federal laws apply (including the National Labor Relations Act and the Railway Labor Act). Within the context of downsizing its workforce, the employer must remain in compliance with all applicable equal opportunity laws and regulations on the federal, state, and local levels. Before initiating any layoff actions, the employer is well advised to consult experienced labor counsel to review the proposed terminations.

A layoff should not always be the first choice of an employer faced with a financially motivated RIF. Other alternatives that should be considered include the following: hiring freezes, reductions or freezes in wages, reductions or elimination of fringe benefits (which may include having employees' pay a higher proportion of the cost of benefits), elimination of overtime, reduction in the workweek, or job sharing.

Employment discrimination claims frequently follow layoff actions by the employer. Those who believe that they have been discriminated against based on characteristics protected by law may pursue claims to contest the layoffs on that basis. As was discussed earlier in the text, former employees can base such claims on a "disparate treatment" or "disparate impact" basis of discrimination.

You should be prepared to discuss in class the effect of seniority systems in the workplace. Do seniority rights perpetuate past discriminatory practices? Should we be concerned with apportioning employment opportunities among differing age groups and genders? What effects do seniority systems have on quality of life, wage and hour, and fringe benefit issues?

Human Resource Form
Overtime, Meal, and Rest Periods

Our company's regular workweek is 40 hours. Eligible overtime pay to nonexempt employees will be paid with your regular paycheck. Your supervisor must approve all overtime in advance. You must complete our overtime form each day overtime is worked. For hourly employees and those salaried employees who are assigned to work a fixed number of hours per week, overtime pay will be calculated at one and one-half times your regular rate of pay for actual time worked in excess of 40 hours.

All employees are required to take a meal period whenever working more than five hours in a workday. The unpaid meal period must be taken within the third to fifth hours of the work shift. The meal period is 30 minutes. You are allowed a meal period for each four hours worked beyond your regular quitting time.

The company provides you with rest periods at the rate of 10 minutes rest for every four hours of work. Your rest period must be taken on company premises.

Date: ____________

Key Terms and Concepts

- Fair Labor Standards Act of 1938 (FLSA)
- The Portal-to-Portal Act of 1947
- Enterprise coverage
- Individual coverage
- Minimum wage
- Opportunity wage
- Tip credit
- Work suffered or permitted
- On-call time
- Meal and rest periods
- Sleeping time
- Overtime
- Training time
- Integral and indispensable
- Principal activity
- Executive exemption
- Highly compensated individual
- Administrative exemption
- Professional exemption
- Computer professional exemption
- Outside salesperson exemption
- Youth employment
- Compensatory time off
- Liquidated damages
- WARN Act
- Mass layoff
- Reduction in force (RIF)
- Davis-Bacon Act
- Walsh-Healey Act
- FICA
- FUTA
- Safe-harbor provision

Chapter Summary

- Provisions under the FLSA:
  - The act applies to employees engaged in interstate commerce or employed by an enterprise engaged in commerce or in the production of goods for commerce, unless the employer is exempt from its coverage.
  - The act applies only if an employment relationship actually exists. It does not apply to independent contractors or volunteers.
  - Minimum wage rates are established and overtime pay of an additional 50 percent for all hours over 40 worked within a workweek is required.
  - Restrictions are placed on the employment of minors.
  - Courts use an "economic reality" test to determine if the worker is actually an independent contractor.
  - Many rules define the hours worked in a workweek. Rest periods *are* counted as compensable working time. Bona fide meal periods *are not* counted as compensable working time. Employees thus must be completely free of duties during the meal period. Employees who must eat at their workstations are entitled to compensation for their meal periods. Federal law provides that 30 minutes is a sufficient bona fide meal period. If an employee is on call or on duty, all waiting time *is* compensable.
  - Restrictions are imposed on the employment of children. An absolute prohibition prevents their employment in oppressive conditions or in hazardous occupations.

- Travel to and from work *is not* compensable unless certain exceptions apply.

- The requirement to pay overtime has several exemptions. They include exemptions for executives, administrators, professionals, computer-related professionals, and outside salespersons.

- Under the WARN Act, employers of more than 100 employees must give a detailed written notice to employees no less than 60 days prior to closing a plant or initiating a mass layoff that will affect 100 or more full-time workers. Failure to give such notice exposes the employer to civil penalties and back-pay damages for the affected workers.

- Federal employment tax statutes use different definitions for employment than does the FLSA.

Online Student Support

- Loislaw legal research and writing assignments.
- Loislaw group projects and class presentations.
- Loislaw access, providing online research including up-to-date cases, statutes, rules, and regulations. Primary law for all 50 states and federal jurisdictions. Registration required for access to this resource.
- Practice questions, including sample true/false, multiple choice, and short answer questions to test your understanding of concepts.
- Additional human resource forms.
- Internet exercises.
- Blogs.
- Supplementary statutory and regulatory materials.

Case Problems

14.1 Armour and Company operated a soap factory in Chicago that produces goods for interstate sale. It maintained a private firefighting force to supplement that provided by the city. The plaintiffs were employed as firefighters only and had nothing to do with the production of goods. These men worked in shifts that began at 8:00 a.m.; during the day, they maintained the company's firefighting equipment. At 5:00 p.m., they "punched out" on the time clock. They remained on call in the fire hall located on the company's property until the following morning at 8:00. They went off duty entirely for the next 24 hours and then resumed work. During their on-call time, they were required to stay in the fire hall, respond to any alarms, and make such repairs to the equipment as were required. The company contended that the FLSA did not apply to the firefighters because they were auxiliary employees who were not engaged in commerce or in the production of goods for commerce. It also contended that time spent sleeping, eating, and recreating cannot be counted as working time. How did the Supreme Court rule? (*Armour & Co. v. Wantock et al.*, 323 U.S. 126 (1944))

14.2 A group of state employees provided in-home supportive services to invalids. Due to extreme budget problems, the state ceased payments to the employees because no state budget had been adopted. The employees filed a FLSA suit due to the state's failure to timely pay the employees their minimum wages when due during the budget impasse. The state defended its action, in part, on the theory that a delayed payment is not the same as nonpayment. Is the state an employer for purposes of the FLSA? How should the court rule? Should the state be assessed liquidated damages? (*Caldman v. State of California*, 852 F. Supp. 898 (E.D. Ca. 1994))

14.3 The secretary of labor sued the owners of the Kitty Clover Potato Chip Company seeking an injunction against them restraining them from violating the FLSA. The defendants were engaged in the business of manufacturing and distributing snack foods. The Department of Labor claimed that the company failed to pay overtime. The company and the employees had agreed to a fixed weekly compensation for a workweek of variable and fluctuating hours. How should the court determine the employees' "regular rate of pay"? What weight should be afforded the company's contracts of employment with its employees? Can the company successfully argue that it has been paying overtime at a rate of not less than one and a half times the regular rate of pay, even if that rate is below the prescribed minimum wage? (*Walling v. Lippold*, 72 F.Supp. 339 (D. Neb. 1947))

14.4 Two technicians covered by a collective bargaining agreement brought a class-action suit against their employer to recover overtime pay, as provided in the agreement and required by the FLSA. The employer provides film and projectors for motion pictures shown on commercial airlines. As part of its service, the technicians installed the equipment, threaded the film, and serviced the other equipment. The union contract required the payment of overtime, but the employer argued that the union and a number of employees waived overtime pay to obtain a larger salary through an extended workweek. The employer argued that if the employees had not agreed to waive the overtime pay, the company would have hired additional technicians to avoid paying overtime. How should the court rule? (*Lerwill v. Inflight Motion Pictures, Inc.*, 582 F.2d 507 (9th Cir. 1978))

14.5 ITT-Rayonier, a pulp mill operation in Hoquiam, Washington, operated 24 hours a day, 7 days a week. Rather than establishing a separate maintenance department for night shifts, the employer's regular policy was to telephone its regular daytime mechanics at home after hours to return to the plant to fix the equipment. The calls could occur at any time of night. After formalizing the policy, employees were required to accept a "fair share" of these call-ins. The employees filed suit under the FLSA seeking overtime compensation for the hours they were required to be available for on-call requests. What factors would you think important in deciding whether the on-call time was compensable? How should the court rule? (*Owens v. Local 169, Assn. of W. Pulp & Paper Workers*, 971 F.2d. 347 (9th Cir. 1992))

End Notes

1. *Alvarez v. Sanchez,* 105 A.D. 2d 1114 (1984).
2. 29 U.S.C. §§201-219.
3. 29 U.S.C. 203(d), (e), (g); Fact Sheet No. 013 Employment Relationship Under The Fair Labor Standards Act.
4. 29 U.S.C. §206(g).
5. 29 C.F.R. §778.115.
6. 29 U.S.C. §203(t).
7. 29 U.S.C. §§201-219.
8. *Forrester v. Roth's I.G.A. Foodliner, Inc.*, 646 F.2d 413 (9th Cir. 1981).
9. *Buzek v. Pepsi Bottling Group,* 501 F. Supp. 2d 876 (S.D. Tx 2007).
10. 29 C.F.R. §785.21-.22.
11. BMC Chapter 13.27 [The Supreme Court denied *certiorari* as to a decision of the Ninth Circuit Court of Appeals, which upheld the ordinance in the matter of *RUI One Corp. v. City of Berkeley,* 371 F.3d 1137 (9th Cir. 2004).]
12. 29 U.S.C. 251-262.
13. 29 C.F.R. §785.27.
14. *Dade County v. Alvarez,* 124 F3d 1380 (11th Cir. 1997).
15. Publ L 104-108, 110 Stat 1755, §§2101-03.
16. 29 U.S.C. §213(a)(1).
17. 29 C.F.R. §541.600.
18. See 29 U.S.C. §213(a)(1).
19. 29 C.F.R. §541.2.
20. 29 C.F.R. §541.100 [An employer must also consider the effect of approved leaves of absence under the Family and Medical Leave Act.]
21. *Stanger et al. v. Glenn L. Martin Co.*, 56 F. Supp. 163, 166 (D. Md.1944).
22. *Kennedy, et al. v. Commonwealth Edison Co.*, 410 F.3d 365 (7th Cir. 2005) *citing* 29 C.F.R. §541.103.
23. *Craig v. Far West Engrg. Co.*, 265 F.2d 251 (9th Cir. 1959).
24. 29 C.F.R. §541.401.
25. 29 U.S.C. §213(a)(3)-(15).
26. 29 U.S.C. §214; 29 C.F.R. §§519.1-519.19.
27. *Oklahoma Press Pub. Co. v. Walling,* 327 U.S. 186 (1946).
28. 29 U.S.C. §3312.
29. *Contreras v. Corinthian Vigor Ins. Brokerage, Inc.*, 25 F. Supp. 2d 1053 (N.D. Ca. 1998).
30. *Brooklyn Savings Bank v. O'Neill,* 324 U.S. 697 (1945).
31. 29 U.S.C. §2102.
32. 29 U.S.C. §2104(a)(3).
33. *http://ethics.walmartstores.com/WalMartEthics.pdf.*
34. 29 U.S. §216(a).

Chapter 15
Occupational Safety and Workers' Compensation

Out of this nettle, danger, we pluck this flower, safety. —*Shakespeare,* Henry IV, Part I

Learning Objectives

1. Identify the jurisdiction of OSHA.
2. Distinguish between a general and a specific duty.
3. Understand what employer defenses are available for OSHA violations.
4. Define workers' compensation remedies.
5. Explain when an accident is covered by workers' compensation.
6. Recognize employer defenses to workers' compensation claims.

Chapter Outline

Chapter Opening scenario

Lorene Byrd sued her deceased husband's employer for negligent violations of the Occupational Safety and Health Act. She alleged that her husband died as the result of injuries sustained in an accident arising out of and in the course and scope of his employment. The employer argued that Ms. Byrd did not have the right to state a private cause of action under the act and that her remedy was to pursue a claim under the state workers' compensation law.[1] Who wins?

Introduction

Since the dawn of civilization, employers have recognized liability to their workers for work-related injuries. The ancient Greek, Roman, and Arab civilizations developed codes to protect workers from injury and to compensate those who nonetheless became injured. However, under European feudalism, the worker enjoyed neither special status nor protection from on-the-job injuries. During the eighteenth and nineteenth centuries, social and institutional changes began to transform Europe, and along with the Industrial Revolution they changed the workplace landscape. Profound economic improvements followed the advent of machine-based manufacturing, but modernization was often accompanied by great risk of injury to the factory worker.

During the era of American industrialization, between the Civil War and World War I, dangerous working conditions existed in the nation's workplaces, and many serious accidents occurred. The initial pressure to reform the workplace came from labor groups. The first state legislation was the Massachusetts Factory Act of 1877. Employer response to these legislative changes varied — some embraced the new requirements, while others often tried to deter facility inspections. Upton Sinclair's book, *The Jungle*, aroused great public response in favor of worker protections and inspired many American politicians to consider legislation to that end. Progressive politicians and labor leaders worked with many state legislatures to create laws requiring employers to provide safer working conditions. During this period, individual tragedies made newspaper headlines, while some industries, including the U.S. steel industry, attempted to make worker safety of leading importance in their corporate programs. However, corporate worker safety programs were not widely adopted. It took several tragedies before the necessary workplace reformations took hold. Some industries were responsible for many of the most dangerous occupations and conditions. Among them was the coal mining industry. The deadliest year in that industry occurred in 1907, when 3,242 deaths occurred, including the loss of 362 people in a mine explosion near Monongah, West Virginia.

The Triangle Shirtwaist Company fire of 1911 spurred the era of reform in workers' safety and health. In that tragedy, a fire, fed by the contents of waste containers full at days' end, spread quickly through a factory on the upper floors of a New York City building. Workers could not escape because the exit doors had been locked. Other escape routes were blocked by machinery, the elevator shaft had only a single car, and fire department ladders reached only to the seventh floor. Many workers, most of them women, died in the fire or jumped to their deaths from the ninth and tenth floors. A United Press reporter who witnessed the scene described how he learned "a new sound — a more horrible sound than description can picture. It was the thud of a speeding, living body on a stone sidewalk." Young women, some of them flaming human torches, crashed to the sidewalk. In response, over 100,000 New Yorkers walked in procession up Fifth Avenue to express their grief, while another 400,000 looked on. Following this tragedy, the New York legislature created a Factory Investigating Commission, established to investigate health and safety conditions in the largest cities in the state.[2]

Federal Laws

During the administration of President Franklin D. Roosevelt, worker health and safety law was forever changed. Mr. Roosevelt persuaded Congress to pass major pieces of legislation, including the Fair Labor Standards Act. As one of the first important pieces of worker safety legislation, that act established laws regulating wages and hours worked, working conditions, entitlement to overtime pay, and regulated youth employment. Another law enacted during that period, the Walsh-Healy Act of 1936, established the first national workplace safety standards for businesses contracting with the federal government. Increasing attention continued to be given to worker safety, and in 1970, during the administration of President Nixon, Congress adopted the **Occupational Safety and Health Act (OSH Act)**. This chapter will review the major aspects of the act, its scope and coverage, the standards used to measure employer compliance, and its enforcement procedures.

Each year the **Occupational Safety and Health Administration** (**OSHA**), the federal agency created by the **OSH Act**, collects and reports data on work-related injuries and illnesses from information supplied by employers in specific industries and of specific sizes. The Department of Labor, which enforces federal **OSHA** requirements, reported in 2008 over 3.7 million incidents of nonfatal occupational injuries and illnesses requiring days away from work.[3] These statistics indicate that even in the modern workplace the risk of injury and illness remains.

Workers' Compensation

While he was no friend of the worker, German chancellor Otto Von Bismarck introduced a compulsory state-run accident compensation system in 1884. Workers and employers financed the program. Our modern system of **workers' compensation** laws can trace its origins to that period. Wisconsin in 1911 was the first state to adopt a **workers' compensation** law, but by 1948 every U.S. state had adopted some form of **workers' compensation**. As we will see, **workers' compensation** is a no-fault system of laws and regulations that often provides the only means for an injured worker to recover compensation for medical expenses and lost wages arising from work-related injuries. Primarily governed by state law, the **workers' compensation** system provides compensation to employees for injuries that occur on the job. This second topic within the workplace health and safety regulatory landscape is also a focus of our study in this chapter.

Occupational Safety and Health Act

Prior to the enactment of the **OSH Act**, only a handful of isolated federal laws regulated workplace safety. This act set a national standard for workplace safety. It was designed to protect workers from dangers, but it was not intended to eliminate all dangers from the workplace. The purpose of the act is to "assure so far as possible every working man and woman in the Nation safe and healthful working conditions."[4] The safety legislation of the **OSH Act** is remedial and preventative in nature; courts liberally construe the act and its regulations to afford the broadest possible protection to workers.

The **OSH Act** created **OSHA** as an agency within the U.S. Department of Labor. The act also created the **National Advisory Committee on Occupational Safety and Health (NIOSH). NIOSH** operates an occupational research center that advises and makes recommendations to the secretaries of the Departments of Labor and of Health and Human Services on **OSHA** matters. It is housed within the Centers for Disease Control and Prevention, a part of the Department of Health and Human Services, not the Department of Labor. At the same time, the **Occupational Safety and Health Review Commission (OSHRC)** was created. It is an independent federal agency that decides contests of decisions concerning citations or penalties resulting from **OSHA** violations. The **OSHRC** is the adjudicatory function of the **OSH Act. OSHA** recommends penalties for violations, and **OSHRC** renders decisions involving the disputes between **OSHA** and the employer relating to those penalties. The Supreme Court decided that any conflict arising between **OSHA** and **OSHRC** over which of the two agencies has the right to set a federal safety and health precedent is resolved in favor of the secretary of labor, who administers **OSHA.**[5]

Coverage

OSHA and **OSHA-approved state programs** regulate safety and health conditions in most private workplaces. The **OSH Act** applies to all employment performed in a U.S. workplace if the employer is engaged in a business affecting interstate commerce. That definition is so broad as to cover almost all employers in the U.S. and its territories. Federal employees are covered, and state and local governments are required to adopt standards for their employees that are as effective as the federal standards. Employers covered by the **OSH Act** must comply with the regulations and safety and health standards issued by **OSHA**. The Department of Labor defines a "business" to be any for-profit or nonprofit commercial activity affecting interstate commerce and involving the employment of one or more employees.[6]

The **OSH Act** provides that states and territories can run their own safety and health programs as long as those programs are at least as effective as the federal program. In return, the federal government pays a portion of the cost of the approved state or territory program. Approximately two dozen states operate plans that cover both the private and the public sectors. New Jersey, New York, and the U.S. Virgin Islands operate plans for public employees only; private-sector employment remains under federal **OSHA** jurisdiction. Primarily, **OSHA** handles enforcement and administration of the **OSH Act** in states under federal jurisdiction.

The act *does not cover*:

- the self-employed;
- farms that employ only immediate members of the farmer's family;

- working conditions for which other federal agencies, operating under the authority of other federal laws, regulate worker safety (such as working conditions in mining, nuclear energy and nuclear weapons manufacture, and certain aspects of transportation industries);
- persons who employ others in their own homes to perform domestic services; and
- employees of state and local governments, unless they are a state or territory operating an OSHA-approved state plan.

Federal Preemption

In enacting **OSHA**, Congress intended that employers should be subject only to the federal scheme of workplace safety. State regulation of safety and health issues is preempted if the secretary of labor has not approved the state regulation and a relevant federal standard is in effect. The substance of almost all state **OSHA** regulations mirrors the federal regulations in effect. However, some states have an advanced regulatory scheme that expands the protection afforded workers under state law beyond that offered under the federal law. In those instances in which the secretary has approved the state plan, an employer may find itself subject to complying with both federal and state laws and regulations.

Employee

For **OSHA** purposes, courts use the economic realities test in determining employee status. When a statute such as **OSHA** "contains no other provision that either gives specific guidance to the meaning of the term 'employee' or suggests that the common law definition is inappropriate, we must presume that Congress intended to incorporate traditional principles of agency law."[7]

OSHA's purpose is to prevent work-related injuries, illnesses, and fatalities by issuing and enforcing workplace safety and health rules. Employers are *not* liable under **OSHA** for injuries to independent contractors. However, under the **multiemployer doctrine**, a general contractor might be liable for the injuries to the employees of a subcontractor on a worksite. A subcontractor would be an independent contractor to the general contractor on a construction site. This is a rule that empowers **OSHA** to issue citations to general contractors at construction sites who have the ability to prevent or abate hazardous conditions created by subcontractors through the reasonable exercise of supervisorial authority. It does not matter which entity employed the workers. The theory is that the general contractor could have corrected or prevented the hazard through its authority as the "controlling" contractor on the job site.

Multiemployer Doctrine
An OSHA policy allowing it to issue citations to general contractors at construction sites who have sufficient control over the site to prevent or abate hazardous conditions caused by its subcontractors. Even if a general contractor did not create the hazard, it can be cited because it could have exercised supervisory authority to eliminate it.

> ***Example:*** Summit Contractors was the general contractor for the construction of a college dormitory in Little Rock, Arkansas. Summit had only four employees on the project because it subcontracted the entire project. Summit's project superintendent had observed the masonry contractor's employees working on scaffolding that lacked guardrails. The superintendent instructed the subcontractor to correct the problems; however, when the subcontractor's employees moved the scaffold to another location on the jobsite, they would again work without fall protection and without guardrails. When an **OSHA** compliance officer observed the subcontractor's employees working under such conditions, it issued Summit a citation for a violation based on the multiemployer doctrine (also known as the

controlling employer doctrine). Summit argued that the legislation only applied to "his employees" and did not impose liability upon it for the employees of other on-site contractors. A federal court of appeals reversed an **OSHRC** ruling in favor of Summit and held that both the employing business (the subcontractor) and the controlling employer (the general contractor) are subject to **OSHA** citations to the employer for violations that do not directly affect the employer's own employees. With this decision, the court reinstated a 30-year-old Department of Labor policy allowing **OSHA** to issue citations to general contractors at construction sites when they have the ability to prevent or abate hazardous workplace conditions.[8]

The general contractor, as a controlling employer for **OSHA** purposes, must exercise reasonable care to prevent and detect violations on the project worksite. While the multiemployer citation authority of **OSHA** applies only to the construction industry, employers should be aware of their **OSHA** responsibilities at all **multiemployer** worksites.

Occupational Safety and Health Administration Standards

Specific Duty
An OSHA requirement imposed on an employer relating to a specific safety problem or hazard.

Recognized Hazards
A condition or practice known to be hazardous by the employer's industry in general or by the specific employer.

General Duty
An OSHA requirement that each employer must furnish a place of employment free from recognized hazards that are causing or are likely to cause death or serious physical harm.

The act assigns **OSHA** two basic functions: setting standards and conducting inspections to ensure that employers provide safe and healthful workplaces. These standards require that employers adopt certain practices, means, methods, or processes reasonably necessary and appropriate to protect workers on the job. Employers are required to be familiar with the standards applicable to their worksites and to eliminate hazards.

Employers have both a **general** and a **specific duty** to provide their employees with safe workplaces, free from recognized, serious hazards. The **general duty** standard requires every employer to use reasonable care to protect its own employees from **"recognized hazards"** likely to cause death or serious injury. The rule does not impose strict liability on employers; rather, it compels them to avoid **recognized hazards**. Section 5(a)(1) of the act, commonly referred to as the **general duty** clause, requires "Each employer . . . [to] furnish each of his employees employment and a place of employment which are free from recognized hazards that are causing or are likely to cause death or serious physical harm to his employees: and, shall comply with the [OSHA standards, rules, regulations and orders issued pursuant to the OSH Act]."

The employer's **general duty** is not limited by traditional common law defenses such as those that might be available in state tort actions involving negligence or strict liability claims. Congress intended to require elimination only of preventable hazards, which is an achievable goal. The standard of care for this **general duty** is an objective one. The standard need not be known by the particular employer, but, taking into account the standard of knowledge in the industry, the employer's good faith or lack of knowledge will not act as a defense — i.e., ignorance is no defense for the employer.[9]

The secretary of labor has promulgated occupational safety and health standards, otherwise known as **"general industry standards."** In addition, the secretary has enacted industry-**"specific duty standards"** that, as authorized by the act, are borrowed from previously enacted federal statutes and regulations. These specific standards include those for the construction, maritime, and agricultural industries. While some standards are specific to one category, others, such as the general industry standard, apply across industries. The general industry standards address topics of general application in the workplace. These include such things as walking and working surfaces, exit routes, ventilation, radiation, medical and first aid, and personal safety protection. The general standards apply to any type of employment in any industry, including construction, maritime, and agricultural industries, to the extent that particular standards for those other industries do not apply.

When a specific **OSHA** standard will not protect workers against a particular hazard, the employer must follow the **general duty standard** to protect workers.

> ***Example:*** Historically, the **general duty clause** was preempted whenever a specific standard applied to a hazardous condition. However, a federal court of appeals held that General Dynamics violated the **general duty clause** in connection with the manufacture of M-1 tanks for the Department of Defense even though it had followed a specific standard, finding that if "an employer knows a particular safety standard is inadequate to protect his workers against the specific hazard it is intended to address or that the conditions in his place of employment are such that the safety standard will not adequately deal with the hazards to which his employees are exposed, he has a duty under Section 5(a)(1) to take whatever measures may be required by the Act, over and above those mandated by the safety standard, to safeguard his workers."[10]

A hazard under the act is a physical condition or practice that harms employees. The employees must be those of an employer who is subject to the compliance requirement, subject to the **multiemployer doctrine** in the construction industry. Moreover, the hazard must be **"recognized."** A **recognized hazard** is a condition or practice that is known to be hazardous by the employer's industry in general or by the specific employer.

> ***Example:*** Safety experts familiar with the industry who could recognize the existence and scope of the hazard presented could be used to prosecute or defend an employer in an OSHA-violation proceeding.

The hazard must be one "likely" to cause "death or serious physical harm." **OSHA** does not need to prove the probability of harm; it is required only to establish the existence of a hazard to the degree that few persons would doubt that it should be abated.

The secretary of labor promulgates new **OSHA** regulations. There are three types of standards: interim, permanent, and emergency. The interim standards were in effect for two years following the enactment of the **OSH Act**. They were replaced by the permanent standards that were issued thereafter, through the rule making power of the Department of Labor. Rule making occurs in three basic ways. In the first, national consensus standards are adopted and established as federal standards. **OSHA** promulgates these standards without having to comply with the requirements of the Administrative Procedure Act (APA). Congress enacted the APA to regulate and standardize the manner in which federal agencies adopt, administer, and enforce federal regulations. The APA also sets forth the manner in which federal courts may directly review the decisions of a federal administrative agency. The second procedure for the issuance of standards involves compliance with the APA. The third method involves issuance of temporary emergency standards to avoid potential deaths or injuries that might occur because the usual rule making process takes a long time. Given the gravity of the matters it must address, **OSHA** is empowered to issue, in the first and third cases, standards and regulations without having to comply with the complexity of the APA.

Any **OSHA** standard dealing with toxic materials or harmful physical agents must be considered under two separate aspects: **technological feasibility** and **economic**

feasibility. Before it publishes a rule for adoption, **OSHA** prepares a final economic analysis to accompany the standard. The economic analysis includes a description of affected industries, the benefits attributed to adoption of the rule, the technological feasibility of the rule, the estimated costs of compliance, and a determination of the economic and other impacts on businesses, including small companies, in affected industries. To assess **technological feasibility, OSHA** applies a standard articulated by a federal court of appeals in 1980: "within the limits of the best available evidence . . . OSHA must prove a reasonable possibility that the typical firm will be able to develop and install engineering and work practice controls that can meet [the permissible exposure levels] in most of its operations."[11] When considering **economic feasibility, OSHA** must question whether a standard under consideration would eliminate or alter the competitive structure of an industry.

The types of workplace changes created by OSHA regulations include establishing permissible worker exposure limits to toxic chemicals and dusts; requiring the use of personal protective equipment in the workplace (e.g., respirators); requiring the lockout of energy to power equipment during repairs or maintenance; setting specific standards for worker safety within confined spaces (e.g., workers working inside tanks and manholes); setting trench and excavation practices and shoring standards for workers below ground level; requiring the use of guards on moving equipment parts; establishing process safety management systems for large complex industries, such as the petrochemical industry; adopting standards for blood-borne pathogens; and regulating exposure to asbestos in the workplace.

When a standard is to be issued by an agency, those affected by it may challenge the validity of the standard in a federal court of appeals. In the following case, the Supreme Court considered whether **OSHA** and the secretary of labor were required to consider the costs of the standard relative to the benefits to be achieved.

CASE 15.1

NO COST-BENEFIT ANALYSIS NEEDED BEFORE OSHA ADOPTS A SAFETY AND HEALTH STANDARD

AMERICAN TEXTILE MANUFACTURERS INSTITUTE V. DONOVAN

452 U.S. 490 (1981)

Supreme Court of the United States

Facts. Representatives of the cotton industry challenged the validity of proposed OSHA industry standard known as the "Cotton Dust Standard." The standard was proposed to minimize or eliminate the incidence among cotton mill workers of "brown lung" disease, which is caused by exposure to cotton dust. After many hearings, OSHA established that workers' exposure to such dust should be limited during the workday. The agency chose an implementation strategy for the standard that depended primarily on a mix of engineering controls, such as installation of ventilation systems, and work practice controls, such as special floor-sweeping procedures. It also required that employers provide respirators to employees; monitor their exposure to cotton dust; conduct medical surveillance of all employees; conduct medical examinations, employee education, and training programs; and post warning notices. Based on the evidence in the hearing record, the secretary of labor determined that exposure to cotton dust represented a "significant health hazard to employees" and that these standards would reduce the incidence of brown lung disease. The industry contended in the federal court of appeals that the OSH Act required OSHA to demonstrate that its standard reflected a reasonable relationship between the costs and benefits associated with the standard. The secretary of labor and two labor organizations countered that the "economic feasibility" of OSHA standards was not required. The court of appeals upheld the standard. The Supreme Court granted *certiorari* to decide the question.

Issue. Does the Secretary of Labor in enacting safety and health standards have to determine that the costs of the standard bear a reasonable relationship to the benefits?

Language of the Court. Brennan, J.: **[The cotton industry representatives] interpret [OSH Act] as mandating that OSHA enact the most protective standard possible to eliminate a significant risk of material health impairment, subject to the constraints of economic and technological feasibility. The Court of Appeals held that the Act did not require OSHA to compare costs and benefits.**

The starting point of our analysis is the language of the statute itself. . . . Section 6(b)(5) of the Act . . . provides:

> **The Secretary, in promulgating standards dealing with toxic materials or harmful physical agents under this subsection, shall set the standard which most adequately assures, to the extent feasible, on the basis of the best available evidence, that no employee will suffer material impairment of health or functional capacity even if such employee has regular exposure to the hazard dealt with by such standard for the period of his working life.**

Although their interpretations differ, all parties agree that the phrase "to the extent feasible" contains the critical language in §6(b)(5) for purposes of these cases.

The plain meaning of the word "feasible" supports respondents' interpretation of the statute. According to Webster's Third New International Dictionary of the English Language 831 (1976), "feasible" means "capable of being done, executed, or effected." . . . Any standard based on a balancing of costs and benefits by the Secretary that strikes a different balance than that struck by Congress would be inconsistent with the command set forth in §6(b)(5). Thus, cost-benefit analysis by OSHA is not required by the statute because feasibility analysis is.

Even though the plain language of §6(b)(5) supports this construction, we must still decide whether . . . the general definition of an occupational safety and health standard, either alone or in tandem with §6(b)(5), incorporates a cost-benefit requirement for standards dealing with toxic materials or harmful physical agents. . . . Perhaps most telling is the absence of any indication whatsoever that Congress intended OSHA to conduct its own cost-benefit analysis before promulgating a toxic material or harmful physical agent standard. The legislative history demonstrates conclusively that Congress was fully aware that the Act would impose real and substantial costs of compliance on industry, and believed that such costs were part of the cost of doing business.

Decision. No. Congress defined the basic relationship between costs and benefits by placing the "benefit" of the worker's health above all other considerations except for those making attainment of this "benefit" unachievable.

CASE QUESTIONS

Critical Legal Thinking. If the agency is left to determine industry standards, is it likely that the agency will unrealistically attempt to mandate absolute safety in the workplace?

Business Ethics. Discuss the ethical considerations between the cost of compliance for continuing operations in the United States and sending the work offshore to a country where such compliance is not required.

Contemporary Business. Can you think of any other laws or regulations that impose heavy compliance costs on employers?

Variance

If a particular standard applies to a workplace and the employer needs more time to comply with the standard, or if the employer has different but equivalent safeguards from those required by the standard, the employer may apply to **OSHA** for a temporary or permanent variance.

Congressional Disapproval

Occasionally, Congress will disapprove of regulations issued by administrative agencies. It exercises such power though the **Congressional Review Act of 1996.**[12] In summary, this act establishes special congressional expedited procedures to overturn a broad range of federal agency regulations. Before any rule covered by the act (including those issued under **OSHA**) takes effect, the federal agency that promulgates the rule must submit it to Congress. In an expedited procedure, both houses of Congress may disapprove a rule. Technically, the act permits Congress to enact a "resolution of disapproval," which if passed by both houses and signed by the president, or passed by two-third majorities in both houses to overcome a presidential veto, overturns a federal agency rule or regulation. If a congressional disapproval resolution is enacted, the rule may not take effect and the agency may issue no substantially similar rule without subsequent statutory authorization. Any rule that is disapproved after it has gone into effect is "treated as though [it] had never taken effect." If such a disapproval resolution is made, but is rejected by Congress, the rule takes effect at once.

Example: At the end of the Clinton administration, **OSHA** issued regulations affecting ergonomics in the workplace. This had been a massive Department of Labor effort to regulate workplace injuries linked to repetitive motions. Since most of these types of last-minute regulations cannot be reversed at the agency level when the next administration comes into office, Congress disapproved of the regulation, and President Bush signed the disapproval resolution into law. It was the first such regulatory rejection under the Congressional Review Act.

Employee Protections

OSHA regulations provide employees, their designated representatives, and the agency itself a **right of access** to medical records, including records related to an employee's exposure to toxic substances. In addition, federal regulations required employers to provide employees with **personal safety equipment**, designed for their protection against certain hazards, and to ensure that the employees have been effectively trained on the use of this equipment. In addition, manufacturers and importers of hazardous materials must provide customers with **material safety data sheets**. Employers must use these **material safety data sheets** to train their employees to recognize and avoid the hazards presented by these materials.

Material Safety Data Sheets
Forms provided by manufacturers and importers containing data on the properties of particular materials or substances they sell to U.S. businesses. This information is used by employers to train their employees to recognize and avoid hazards.

Employee Rights

The **OSH Act** grants employees several rights. Among them is the right to file a complaint with **OSHA** regarding safety and health conditions at their workplaces. Such complaints may be filed confidentially. They may also contest the amount of time **OSHA** gives an employer to correct a workplace condition, and they may participate in **OSHA** workplace inspections.

The act protects private-sector employees who exercise these **OSHA-protected rights** against retaliation. Employees have 30 days within the discriminatory reprisal to report it to **OSHA. OSHA** will then investigate, and if retaliation is determined to have occurred, **OSHA** will request the employer to reverse the effects of the retaliation. If necessary, **OSHA** can sue the employer to reverse the retaliatory actions.

Example: Hoy Shoe was a family-owned business that manufactured and distributed sandals. Anita Godsey operated a machine that molded polyurethane into shoes. After a few months at Hoy Shoe, she voiced certain health concerns to her supervisors related to the chemical spray used in the operation of her equipment. Shortly before she was terminated, she filed an informal complaint to the local office of **OSHA**. Following an **OSHA** inspection of the plant, she was terminated for excessive tardiness. She then complained to **OSHA** that her discharge violated the antidiscrimination provision of the **OSH Act**. The agency found that Godsey was the first person to be disciplined under any attendance policy. Recognizing that Congress placed great reliance on employee assistance in enforcing the act, the federal court of appeals found that an employer that retaliates against an employee because of the employer's suspicion or belief that the employee filed an **OSHA** complaint violated the act.[13]

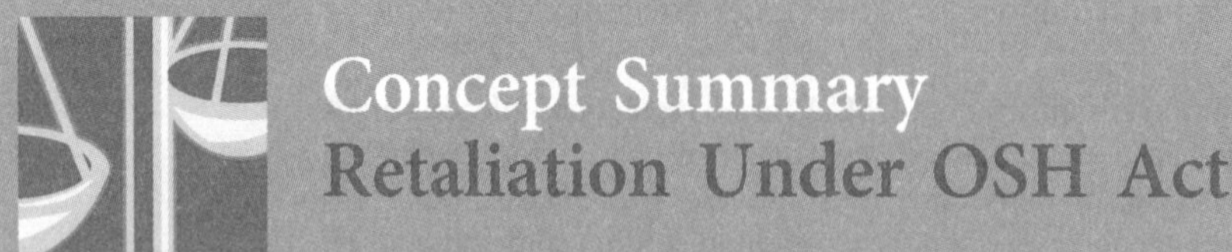

Concept Summary
Retaliation Under OSH Act

Plaintiff charging retaliation for communicating with OSHA must prove:

- a relationship between the protected activity (such as reporting a safety concern to OSHA) and
- a subsequent adverse action against the employee by the employer (i.e., a causal connection between the protected activity and the subsequent discharge) and any reason given by the employer for the adverse action is pretextual (i.e., not the real reason for the adverse action).

No Private Right of Action

OSHA does not provide for a private cause of action for violation of its requirements. The open question among courts is whether an injured worker may use an **OSHA** violation to support a tort theory of recovery. While the secretary of labor has sole jurisdiction to enforce **OSHA**, the statute does not create a private right to sue. For example, an employee cannot recover damages against his or her employer or a third-party equipment manufacturer or supplier for personal injuries suffered because of a violation of the act.

> ***Example:*** Lester Russell sued his employer for injuries suffered during the course of employment. He argued that his injuries were the result of his employer's failure to comply with the provisions of **OSHA**. He claimed that he was injured when a ditch in which he was working collapsed. In applying the express language of the act, the federal court of appeals held that it is clear that nothing in the legislative history or case law exists to support the proposition that **OSHA** created a private civil remedy.[14]

> ***Example:*** Ernest Minichello worked as a tool and die maker for Ford Motor company when he was injured on the job. He suffered a facial laceration and a shoulder separation when working on a piece of equipment. The manufacturer of the equipment asserted as a defense that the equipment did not violate **OSHA** standards. A federal court of appeal held that it was improper to use **OSHA** regulations to establish whether a product was unreasonably dangerous.[15]

A worker does have the right to refuse dangerous work. In the following case, the Supreme Court defined a worker's right to refuse work where an employee has a reasonable apprehension that death or serious injury or illness might occur because of performing the work.

CASE 15.2

EMPLOYEES ARE ENTITLED TO A SELF-HELP REMEDY UNDER OSH ACT

WHIRLPOOL CORP. V. MARSHALL, SECRETARY OF LABOR

445 U.S. 1 (1980)

Supreme Court of the United States

Facts. At the Marion, Ohio, Whirlpool manufacturing plant, two workers were directed by their supervisor to perform their usual maintenance duties of removing objects from a suspended wire mesh guard screen. Previously, serious injuries and a death had resulted from falling through the guard screen. OSHA had conducted an investigation and cited the company over the unsafe walking and working surfaces, but allowed the company additional time to correct the unsafe condition. The men met with the plant's safety director and asked for the name and telephone number of a representative of the local OSHA office. Although the safety director told the men that they "had better stop and think about what [they] were doing," they were given the information and contacted an OSHA official to discuss the situation. The following day, when requested by their supervisor to clean the guard screen, the workers refused to do so, claiming that the screen, on which they sometimes had to step, was unsafe. The supervisor sent the workers to the personnel office, where they were ordered to punch out without working or being paid for the remaining hours of their shift. They were subsequently issued reprimands that were placed in their personnel files. The secretary of labor filed suit claiming the workers were discriminated against in violation of OSHA. The district court found that the employees had justifiably refused to perform the task, but they found the secretary's regulation to be inconsistent with the law as Congress had enacted it. The Court of Appeals for the Sixth Circuit reversed. The Supreme Court granted *certiorari.*

Issue. May an employee lawfully use a self-help remedy to refuse to follow an employer's directive in the workplace?

Language of the Court. Stewart, J.: **The Occupational Safety and Health Act of 1970 (Act) prohibits an employer from discharging or discriminating against any employee who exercises "any right afforded by" the Act. The Secretary of Labor (Secretary) has promulgated a regulation providing that, among the**

rights that the Act so protects, is the right of an employee to choose not to perform his assigned task because of a reasonable apprehension of death or serious injury coupled with a reasonable belief that no less drastic alternative is available. The question presented in the case before us is whether this regulation is consistent with the Act.

To accomplish this basic purpose, the legislation's remedial orientation is prophylactic in nature. (Citation omitted.) The Act does not wait for an employee to die or become injured. It authorizes the promulgation of health and safety standards and the issuance of citations in the hope that these will act to prevent deaths or injuries from ever occurring. It would seem anomalous to construe an Act so directed and constructed as prohibiting an employee, with no other reasonable alternative, the freedom to withdraw from a workplace environment that he reasonably believes is highly dangerous.

Moreover, the Secretary's regulation can be viewed as an appropriate aid to the full effectuation of the Act's "general duty" clause. That clause provides that "[each] employer . . . shall furnish to each of his employees employment and a place of employment which are free from recognized hazards that are causing or are likely to cause death or serious physical harm to his employees." . . . As the legislative history of this provision reflects, it was intended itself to deter the occurrence of occupational deaths and serious injuries by placing on employers a mandatory obligation independent of the specific health and safety standards to be promulgated by the Secretary. Since OSHA inspectors cannot be present around the clock in every workplace, the Secretary's regulation ensures that employees will in all circumstances enjoy the rights afforded them by the "general duty" clause.

The regulation thus on its face appears to further the overriding purpose of the Act, and rationally to complement its remedial scheme. In the absence of some contrary indication in the legislative history, the Secretary's regulation must, therefore, be upheld, particularly when it is remembered that safety legislation is to be liberally construed to effectuate the congressional purpose. (Citation omitted.)

Decision. Yes. The regulation of an employee's right to self-help is constitutional.

CASE QUESTIONS

Critical Legal Thinking. This decision affirms the right of employees to refuse to follow instructions when presented with a risk of serious injury or death. Does this decision promote disputes between the employer and the employee over the employees' subjective appreciation of the risk posed by a job task or site?

Business Ethics. What is the proper balance between promoting worker safety as compared to worker productivity? Did Whirlpool act ethically in this situation?

Contemporary Business. If the statute enacted by Congress did not provide for a "self help" remedy, as was recognized by the Court, what are the reasonable limits to the powers exercised by administrative agencies charged with implementing the provisions of law? Should a greater allowance be made to agency decisions involving health and safety? How about those involving privacy? National security?

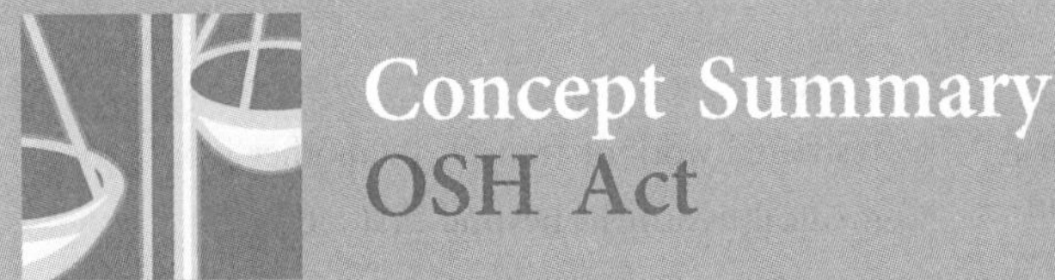

Concept Summary OSH Act

An employer is obligated to:

- observe the general duty standard of providing safe work and working conditions for all employees;
- observe the general industry regulations pertaining to the workplace;
- observe all OSHA specific duty standards and regulations that apply to the specific job and workplace in which its employees are working; and
- maintain and observe all requirements relating to record keeping, reporting, providing notices and posting informational posters.

Regulatory Requirements

OSHA exempts small businesses with ten or fewer employees from its injury and illness reporting requirements. In all other cases, **OSHA** injury and illness records must be kept. All employers covered by the **OSH Act** must report to **OSHA** any workplace incident that results in a fatality or the hospitalization of three or more employees.

For those employers whose business is in an industry classified as low hazard, and in the absence of a federal directive to the business to keep them, a partial industry classification exemption applies. These industries do not need to keep records. These include auto dealerships; clothing and accessory stores; eating and drinking places; most finance, insurance, and real estate industries; personal and business services; medical and dental offices; and legal, educational, and membership organizations. Unless exempt, all employers are required to keep a separate log and summary of injuries and illnesses.

All employers must report any workplace incident to **OSHA** within eight hours after the death of any employee from a work-related incident or the in-patient hospitalization of three or more employees. Employers must orally report the fatality or multiple hospitalizations by telephone or in person to the area **OSHA** office nearest the site of the incident.

All covered employers are required to display conspicuously and to keep displayed the **OSHA**-approved posters, unless the employer's workplace is located in a state that operates an OSHA-approved state plan. Federal agency employers have other posters to display.

All employees, including former employees, have the right to review the OSHA Form 300, Log of Work-Related Illnesses and Injuries. Employers are required to post the Summary of Work-Related Injuries and Illnesses in a visible location so that employees are aware of those that occur in their workplace.

Concept Summary
Record Keeping and OSHA Reporting

OSH Act regulations require employers to maintain a log and summary of all recordable occupational injuries and illnesses and to compile an annual summary. The regulations define a recordable occupation injury or illness as:

- death;
- days away from work;
- restricted work or transfer to another job;
- medical treatment beyond first aid;
- loss of consciousness;
- significant injury or illness diagnosed by a physician or other licensed health care professional.

The log must be maintained on a calendar-year basis, retained for five years, and made available for inspection by an authorized federal representative. Within eight hours after the occurrence of an employment accident fatal to one or more employees or resulting in the hospitalization of three or more employees, the employer of those individuals must report the accident to the local office of **OSHA.**[16]

Focus on Ethics
May Employers Cease Operations to Avoid OSHA Liabilities?

Jacksonville Shipyards, Inc. (JSI) shuttered its operations. Before it closed down, it had been engaged in a ship repair business in Florida. Two JSI employees were killed in a work-related fall at a naval station repair facility. The U.S. Department of Labor issued OSHA citations totaling $692,000, including citations for alleged willful violations leading directly to the deaths. While the case was pending, JSI sold almost all of its assets. Retaining only a small number of administrative employees to wind up the business, JSI then filed a motion with the ALJ to have the case dismissed as moot. The ALJ granted the motion and the Department of Labor appealed.[17]

You have been asked to write the brief in favor of the Department of Labor in seeking to have the citations remain viable and to continue to hold JSI as an employer under OSHA. What are the main arguments in favor of and against a motion to dismiss the case?

Enforcement and Remedies

The secretary of labor has broad enforcement powers and, among the federal administrative agencies, is given the sole responsibility to enforce the law and regulations of **OSHA**. The Department of Labor is authorized to inspect worksites to uncover instances of noncompliance with **OSHA**.

Example: The secretary of labor cited an Ohio railway for a violation of **OSHA**. The company contested the citation arguing that the Federal Railway Administration had jurisdiction, not the secretary. The Supreme Court held that the secretary has unreviewable discretion to determine if a citation should be issued to an employer for unsafe working conditions. The secretary has the discretion not to issue or to withdraw a citation.[18]

Concept Summary OSHA Enforcement

Most of the laws we have studied so far have allowed injured parties to file suit or pursue administrative claims for compensatory damages or to seek injunctive relief against discriminatory practices.

Unlike statutes such as Title VII or the FLSA, OSHA does *not* authorize private-party enforcement. Enforcement lies with the Department of Labor.

OSHA and the MSHA

In addition to the **OSH Act**, the U.S. Department of Labor also administers The Mine Act through which it inspects all surface and underground mines in the United States. Like **OSHA** inspections, the Mining Safety and Health Administration (MSHA) inspectors determine whether a mine is in compliance with the department's health and safety standards or with any citation, order, or decision issued under the Mining Act. They also determine whether an imminent danger exists.

Under the MSHA, the agency investigates mine accidents, complaints of retaliatory discrimination filed by minors, hazardous condition complaints, and knowing or willful (criminal) violations committed by mine operators or their agents. The agency also develops mandatory safety and health standards and assesses penalties for their violation. Due to the extremely hazardous nature of mining, the MSHA may conduct warrantless searches of mining property, assert strict liability on the mining operator, and issue citations for violations of the law, regardless of when they occurred.

Federal inspectors have the authority to issue orders of withdrawal from a mine in situations of imminent danger as well as notices of violation. Miners enjoy the right to request a federal inspection of the mines. Annual inspections and mandatory safety training of miners are required. Each underground coal mine is required to have specific emergency response and rescue plans in effect.

Unlike the immunity from liability for negligent inspections afforded OSHA inspectors, the Supreme Court ruled in 2005 that when the negligence of federal mine inspectors helped cause a mine accident, the inspectors could be sued for damages arising from their negligence. Applying the Federal Tort Claims Act, the Court held that a court must look to the state-law liability of private parties, not to that of state public entities, when determining the government's liability for activities that private persons do not perform, such as the inspection of mines. The Supreme Court held that the United States waived sovereign immunity from such suits. In this case, the plaintiffs alleged that their personal injuries resulted from the inspector's failure to evaluate several complaints concerning safety hazards and to inspect the mine adequately.[19]

Officer and Director Liability for OSHA Violations

The roles of officers and directors in the operation of a small corporate entity may be so pervasive and total that the individual is, in fact, the corporation and an employer under **OSHA**. If an individual is classified as an employer, the individual may also be subject to liability for the **OSHA** violation as an aider and abettor.

Aider and Abettor
A person who assists or helps one or more other persons commit a crime.

Acting as an Employer

Industrial accidents can result in death or devastating injuries. The question of whether a party exercised "substantial supervision" at a place of employment is often determinative of **OSHA** liability, as the next case shows.

CASE 15.3

REASONABLENESS STANDARD USED IN DEFINING PLACE OF EMPLOYMENT

REICH V. SIMPSON, GUMPERTZ & HEGER, INC.

3 F.3d 1 (1st Cir. 1993)

U.S. Court of Appeals for the First Circuit

Facts. Simpson, Gumpertz & Heger, Inc. (SGH) was a structural engineering firm retained to perform certain services for an architectural firm in connection with the construction of a laboratory at Worcester Polytechnic Institute in Worcester, Massachusetts. The building was to consist of five floors of poured concrete placed over a base of steel and temporary metal decking. SGH had the duty to review the general contractor's shop drawings for the metal decking, which would indicate any shoring necessary to support the decking during the pouring of the concrete decks. SGH made various notations regarding the shoring to be used. The drawings did not indicate how much time should elapse between the first and second pours of concrete or how much shoring would be required in certain areas of the job. When the general contractor noticed a section of the metal decking was beginning to sag during the concrete installation, it contacted SGH, which responded that the deflection was "normal." Shortly after that conversation and in an area that was improperly shored and unable to support the weight of both layers of wet concrete, a part of the metal decking collapsed, injuring five workers. SGH had no employees at the worksite. The secretary of labor cited SGH for failure to design the shoring. SGH contested the violation, and the secretary then filed a complaint against SGH before the commission requesting that this action be affirmed. The administrative law judge (ALJ) granted SGH's motion for summary judgment. The secretary appealed.

Issue. What is a place of employment for purposes of OSHA if a company does not regularly place its employees at the site of the injury?

Language of the Court. Stahl, J.: **[S] hortly after the Act became effective, the Secretary summarily adopted a group of federal standards for the construction industry that had previously been promulgated under the Construction Safety Act of 1969. . . .**

The [Construction Safety Act] standards . . . are adopted as occupational safety and health standards under section 6 of Act and shall apply, according to the provisions thereof, to every employment and place of employment of every employee engaged in construction work. Each employer shall protect the employment and places of employment of each of his employees engaged in construction work by complying with the appropriate standards prescribed in this paragraph.

In the proceedings below, the parties characterized the dispositive issue in the case as whether SGH's employees were engaged in "construction work" as defined by the regulation. Relying upon previous Commission precedent, . . . the Commission held that design professionals could only be found liable under Part 1926 to the extent that they exercise "substantial supervision" over the "actual construction." The Commission found that SGH's actions could not, even when viewed in a light most favorable to the Secretary, constitute "substantial supervision." It therefore affirmed the ALJ's decision to grant SGH's motion for summary judgment.

Decision. An employer must have a material presence at the site of the injury to be held liable under OSHA.

CASE QUESTIONS

Critical Legal Thinking. Do you think this is a fair decision? What arguments would you make on behalf of the injured workers that SGH should be held liable for the workers' injuries? Does justice require a broader construction of the term *"place of employment,"* or is this imposing too much liability on third parties?

Business Ethics. Suppose the structural engineer was the most qualified party to recognize safety hazards on the site. In your opinion, would this court's decision seem to be the best ethical outcome? Why or why not?

Contemporary Business. As technological advances allow businesses to become increasingly dispersed, is it appropriate to define narrowly "places of employment"?

Despite widespread public concern over medical malpractice tort liability, it is surprising that public health and safety inspectors are not liable if the inspector fails to discover a hazard and a worker is injured. In the typical lawsuit against a tortfeasor who happens to be a federal employee, the injured party can sue if the government employee is exercising discretionary authority. That is a rare case. The employer is charged with the responsibility of providing a safe workplace. The government inspector is merely exercising a regulatory enforcement role. When inspectors appear on the employer's premises, they do so to police the employer's compliance with the law, not to render services to the employer by assuming some duty of the employer toward its workers. Such was the issue discussed in the following case.

CASE 15.4

OSHA IS IMMUNE FROM SUITS FOR NEGLIGENT INSPECTION OF WORKSITES

IRVING V. UNITED STATES OF AMERICA

162 F.3d 154 (1st Cir. 1998)

U.S. Court of Appeals for the First Circuit

Facts. Gail Merchant Irving suffered horrific injuries in a workplace accident at the Somersworth Shoe Company's manufacturing plant in New Hampshire. When she stooped to retrieve a glove, she dropped her hair and was drawn into a vacuum created by the high-speed rotation of a drive shaft that delivered power to an adjacent machine, incurring grievous injuries. OSHA inspectors had twice inspected the plant but had failed to note the hazard presented by the machine. After the accident, the company was cited for "serious" violations. Irving sued the United States under the Federal Tort Claims Act, claiming that OSHA inspectors negligently performed their duties and had proximately caused her injuries. In an earlier proceeding, Irving's case was allowed to go to trial under New Hampshire state law, and she was awarded $1.0 million in damages. The U.S. government contested the award and appealed to the court of appeals.

Issue. Can OSHA be held liable for the negligent acts of its inspectors whose failures directly contributed to the serious injuries of a worker?

Language of the Court. Selya, C.J.: **The FTCA [Federal Tort Claims Act] is a limited waiver of sovereign immunity. In enacting the statute, Congress prescribed a number of situations in which the waiver would not attach. . . . One such exception is for claims "based upon the exercise or performance or the failure to exercise or perform a discretionary function or duty on the part of a federal agency or an employee of the Government, whether or not the discretion involved be abused." . . .**

In this instance, the plaintiff claims that workplace inspections, negligently performed by OSHA compliance officers, proximately caused her injuries. In analyzing the nature of this conduct, we begin with the language of the OSH Act because "it will most often be true that the general aims and policies of the controlling statute will be evident from its text," . . . and, in turn, these aims and policies will offer valuable insights into the nature of the conduct.

In relevant part, the OSH Act authorizes the Secretary of Labor to "inspect and investigate during regular working hours and at other reasonable times, and within reasonable limits and in a reasonable manner, any such place of employment and all pertinent conditions, structures, machines, apparatus, devices, equipment, and materials therein. . . ." (Citation omitted.) Under this authority, OSHA conducts both programmed general administrative inspections — known in the bureaucratic argot that OSHA so readily attracts as "full-scope" or "wall-to-wall" inspections — and more focused efforts pinpointed to threats of imminent danger. Aside from a reasonableness limitation on the time and manner of inspections, the statute places virtually no constraint on the Secretary's discretion to conduct such inspections in any way that she deems fit. (Citation omitted.)

We are not persuaded by the plaintiff's contention that all inspections ought to be painstakingly comprehensive because individual companies rely on OSHA inspections to improve their health and safety conditions. The OSH Act, in no uncertain terms, places primary responsibility for workplace safety on employers, not on the federal government. (Citations omitted.)

Decision. No. The doctrine of sovereign immunity prevents a plaintiff from suing the government for the negligent acts of its agents.

CASE QUESTIONS

Critical Legal Thinking. If the doctrine of sovereign immunity has been recognized as a legal defense for centuries, why was this case not disposed of much earlier in time?

Business Ethics. The plaintiff suffered horrendous injuries due to the negligence of the OSHA compliance officers. Is this decision fairly decided? If a private inspection firm would have been liable in negligence for Irving's injuries, do you think it is fair for the government to enjoy sovereign immunity from such suits?

Contemporary Business. Would you make any exceptions to the application of the doctrine of sovereign immunity in cases such as these? If so, how would you apply them?

While the injured employee cannot recover damages for a statutory violation of the act, the standard of care established by the relevant regulations will assist the employee in a suit for tort damages as in a case of negligence. In many state jurisdictions, the **OSHA** standard may be introduced at trial to establish the standard of care owed by the defendant to the injured worker. In most states, the injured employee cannot directly sue the employer for damages (except in cases of gross negligence or willful misconduct) and must pursue a **workers' compensation** claim. The **workers' compensation** claim does not bar the employee from suing culpable third parties who may be liable for the injuries. The employee might sue another company on a construction worksite under the **multiemployer doctrine** discussed above.

Violence in the Workplace

OSHA has issued guidelines on violence perpetrated on employees. All employers have a duty to maintain a workplace free from a recognized hazard of violence. Such an act is violence or the threat of violence that can occur at or outside the workplace. **OSHA** estimates that more than two million American workers are victims of workplace violence each year. It has identified workers who are at increased risk. They include those who exchange money with the public; those who deliver passengers, goods, or services; and those who work alone or in small groups during late-night or early-morning hours in high crime areas or in community settings and group homes where they have extensive contact with the public. This includes health-care and social-service workers such as visiting nurses, psychiatric evaluators, and probation officers as well as community workers such as gas and water utility employees, telephone and cable TV installers, postal carriers, retail workers, and taxi drivers. **OSHA** encourages each employer to develop and implement a **Workplace Violence Prevention Plan** in furtherance of the employer's duties under the **general duty clause.**

Workplace Violence Prevention Plan
An OSHA recommendation that employers establish and maintain a program directed at reducing and eliminating work-related assaults, lessening the severity of injuries sustained by employees as a result of such violence, decreasing such threats to worker safety, and reducing the level and nature of threats faced by employees.

Focus on Ethics
Employer Violates Occupational Safety Rules

Employers are required to provide safe working conditions for employees. However, sometimes employers violate occupational safety rules. Consider the following case. Corbesco, Inc. (Corbesco), an industrial roofing and siding installation company, was hired to put metal roofing and siding over the skeletal structure of five aircraft hangars at Chennault Air Base in Louisiana. Corbesco assigned three of its employees to work on the partially completed flat roof of Hangar B, a large single-story building measuring 60 feet high, 374 feet wide, and 574 feet long. Soon after starting work, one of the workers, Roger Matthew, who was on his knees installing insulation on the roof, lost his balance and fell 60 feet to the concrete below, where he was killed.

The next day, an OSHA compliance officer cited Corbesco for failing to install a safety net under the work site. The officer cited an OSHA safety standard that requires that safety nets be provided when workers are more than 25 feet above the ground. Corbesco argued that the flat roof on which the employees were working served as a "temporary floor," and therefore it was not required to install a safety net. An ALJ from the Occupational Safety and Health Review Commission (Commission) held that Corbesco had committed a serious violation of the OSH Act by failing to install a safety net at the work site. Corbesco appealed.

The U.S. Court of Appeals rejected Corbesco's argument. The Court of Appeals held that Corbesco had notice that it was required to install safety nets under its crew while they were working on the edge of a flat roof some 60 feet above a concrete floor. The Court of Appeals stated:

> *Moreover, we do not believe that the Commission has abused its discretion by determining that a flat roof cannot be a temporary floor. The purpose of the safety devices listed in the regulation is to provide fall protection, and a roof cannot provide fall protection if workers must operate along the perimeter.*

The Court of Appeals held that Corbesco had violated OSHA's rules by not providing a safety net below its employees who were working more than 25 feet above the ground.[20]

Ethics Questions

1. Do you think extensive federal occupational safety rules are needed? Note that one or more courts have commented that it is difficult if not impossible for an employer to be aware of all OSHA rules applicable to its business. Should such rules be imposed on employers? Why or why not?
2. How should society manage funding the cost of employing a sufficient number of federal inspectors?
3. Did Corbesco act ethically in arguing that the flat roof created a temporary floor that relieved it from the duty to install a safety net?

OSHA Inspections

The act authorizes **OSHA** to conduct workplace inspections and investigations to determine whether employers are complying with the general duty clause and the standards issued by the agency. The inspections are always conducted without advance notice. **OSHA** may give notice to the employer, but such notice will be normally less than 24 hours in the following situations:

- imminent danger situations
- accident investigations where the employer has notified **OSHA** of a death or catastrophe
- those that must take place after regular business hours or that require special preparation
- where notice is required to ensure that the employer's personnel will be represented
- where the inspection must be delayed for more than five working days when there is good cause
- when the **OSHA** area director determines that advance notice would produce a more thorough or effective inspection

On arrival, the **OSHA** compliance officer presents proper identification to the employer. The Supreme Court has held that a search warrant must be issued before inspection with the exception of three circumstances: (1) the employer consents to the inspection; (2) the site is open to public view; and (3) if an emergency situation exists. Typically, employers will agree to an inspection without the necessity of a warrant. Both the employer and the employees may designate a representative to accompany the inspector during the inspection. The inspector may make written observations, take instrument readings, measure noise levels, take toxic exposure samplings, and inspect records. The inspection officer may stop and question workers, in private, about safety and health conditions and practices in their workplaces. The act protects each employee from discrimination by the employer for exercising safety and health rights. At the conclusion of the inspection, the compliance officer conducts a closing conference with the employer, employees, and/or the employees' representative. During the conference, all unsafe or unhealthful conditions observed and all apparent violations for which a citation may be issued are discussed.

Management Application
OSHA Penalties

There are certain types of violations that may be cited and penalties that may be imposed during an OSHA inspection.

The OSH Act authorizes OSHA to treat certain violations, which have no direct or immediate relationship to safety and health, as *de minimus,* requiring no penalty or abatement. OSHA does not issue citations for *de minimus* violations.

Other Than Serious Violation

A violation that has a direct relationship to job safety and health but probably would not cause death or serious physical harm is an "other than serious violation." The proposed penalty of up to $7,000 for each violation is discretionary. This type of violation is also known as a "nonserious violation."

Serious Violation

A "serious violation" is a hazard with a substantial probability that death or serious physical harm could result and that the employer knew, or should have known, about. A penalty of up to $7,000 for each violation must be proposed.

Willful Violation

A **"willful violation"** is one that the employer intentionally and knowingly commits. The employer either knows that what he or she is doing constitutes a violation or is aware that a condition creates a hazard and has made no reasonable effort to eliminate it. The act provides that an employer who willfully violates the act may be assessed a civil penalty of not more than $70,000 but not less than $5,000 for each violation. Proposed penalties for other-than-serious and serious violations may be adjusted downward depending on the employer's good faith. Proposed penalties for willful violations may be adjusted downward depending on the size of the business. Usually no credit is given for good faith.

If an employer is convicted of the **willful violation** of a standard that has resulted in the death of an employee, the offense is punishable by a court imposed fine or by imprisonment for up to six months, or both. A fine of up to $250,000 for an individual or $500,000 for an organization may be imposed for a criminal conviction.

> ***Example:*** A falling beam killed two construction workers at a Chicago construction site. The accident occurred because the beam was not properly secured. OSHA brought criminal charges against the company, and a jury found the company's actions to be a willful violation. The company was fined $1.0 million dollars and put on five years of probation.[21] Despite the risk of criminal prosecution, very few companies have been prosecuted criminally for OSHA violations.

Repeat Violation

A violation of any standard, regulation, rule, or order where, upon reinspection, a substantially similar violation is found is a "repeat violation." Repeat violations can bring fines of up to $70,000 each. To serve as the basis for a repeat citation, the original citation must be final; a citation under contest may not serve as the basis for a subsequent repeat citation.

Failure to Abate Violation

Failure to correct a prior violation may bring a civil penalty of up to $7,000 for each day the violation continues beyond the prescribed abatement date.

Citation and penalty procedures may differ somewhat in states with their own OSH programs.[22]

Appeals by Employees and Employers

If a complaint from an employee prompted the inspection, the employee or authorized employee representative may request an informal review of any decision not to issue a citation.

Employees may not contest citations, amendments to citations, penalties, or lack of penalties. Within 15 working days of the employer's receipt of the citation, the employer may submit a written objection to OSHA. This objection is known as the Notice of Contest. If the written Notice of Contest has been filed within 15 working days, the OSHA area director forwards the case to the OSHRC. The commission is an independent agency not associated with OSHA or the Department of Labor. The commission assigns the case to an ALJ. The ALJ may disallow the contest if it is found to be legally invalid, or a hearing may be scheduled for a public place near the employer's workplace. The employer and the employees have the right to participate in the hearing; the OSHRC does not require that attorneys represent them.

Once the ALJ has ruled, any party to the case may request a further review by OSHRC. In addition, any of the three OSHRC commissioners may individually move to bring a case before the commission for review. Commission rulings may be appealed to the U.S. Courts of Appeals.

Employer Defenses

There are few available defenses for employers with regard to an **OSHA** violation. Each of the following defenses subjects the employer to a burden of proof to establish the defense with admissible evidence before the trier of fact.

Due Process

The citation must comport with due process requirements. The employer must receive fair notice of the citation and of the particular standard, regulation, rule, or decision which it is charged as having violated.

> ***Example:*** Diamond Roofing Co., Inc. contested a violation because the citation relied on was applicable to floors and not the roofs it constructed. Construing the regulation to give effect to the natural and plain meaning of its words, a federal court of appeals dismissed the citation because a regulation cannot be construed to mean what the agency intended but did not adequately express in its regulation.[23]

Unforeseeable Employee Misconduct

The employer must prove that it established work rules to prevent the violation, communicated them to the employees, monitored the workplace for safety violations, and enforced the rules when violations were discovered.

> ***Example:*** To establish employee misconduct as an affirmative defense, an employer must carry its burden of showing that due to the existence of a thorough and adequate safety program that is communicated and enforced as written, the conduct of its employee(s) in violating that policy was idiosyncratic and unforeseeable.[24]

Greater Hazard Defense

This defense involves a showing that the risk of complying with an **OSHA** standard is greater than the hazards posed by noncompliance. This defense is very narrowly construed by the courts. Besides demonstrating that a greater hazard would result from compliance, the employer must also show that "alternate means of protecting employees are unavailable" and that "a variance . . . would be inappropriate."

> ***Example:*** General Electric objected to a nonserious **OSHA** citation at its Erie, Pennsylvania, plant. GE established that none of the standards on which it was charged was applicable and that compliance with them "would diminish rather than enhance the safety of employees." The argument was rejected by a federal court of appeals in *General Electric Co. v. Secty. of Labor,*[25] wherein the court stated, "General Electric contends that an employer who correctly believes that his working conditions are safer than those prescribed in the standards should not be penalized for bypassing the variance procedures and taking his chances that he will not be cited or that he will prevail in an enforcement proceeding. The flaw in this argument is that some employers will believe incorrectly that their working conditions are safer than those prescribed in the standards. By removing this incentive to seek variances,

the Commission would be allowing an employer to take chances not only with his money, but also with the lives and limbs of his employees. This we cannot do."

Impossibility

The employer must show that compliance with a standard was impossible or unfeasible or that the literal compliance would have made work impossible. In addition, the employer must show that it used alternative means of protection or that alternate means were not available.

Example: The Loomis Cabinet Company lost its appeal of penalties assessed against it. Loomis argued that the nonserious citations were **de minimis** in nature or could not be "justifiably" abated to improve workplace safety. The court of appeals did not buy its argument of **impossibility**. In *Loomis Cabinet Co. v. OSHA Review Comm. et al.*,[26] the court stated, "Nevertheless, this defense should be narrowly construed and the burden lies with the employer to prove **impossibility**. **Impossibility** will not be found if the employer shows merely that compliance would be difficult, inconvenient, or expensive. Loomis failed to sustain its burden because it merely argued that it could better make a determination regarding the 'reasonably necessary or appropriate' safety standards for its workshop than could the government regulators."

Infeasibility

In light of the custom and practice of the industry, an employer can defend non-compliance because it is **infeasible** to comply.

This defense can be asserted only against **OSHA** standards for which **OSHA** is under a requirement to demonstrate feasibility. For example, **OSHA** has a noise and hearing standard. When it cites an employer for violating a workplace safety standard, **OSHA** must determine the economic feasibility of eliminating or abating the risk (e.g., the cost of hearing protection).

To be successful, an employer's **economic infeasibility** argument is proved by showing:

- it is extremely costly for the employer to comply with the standard;
- the employer either used alternate means of protection or that such means were infeasible; and
- the employer cannot absorb the cost and remain in business.

Example: McNulty & Co., Inc. was a precast concrete contractor who assembled precise concrete slabs to create walls, ceilings, and floors. These slabs weigh as much as 40 tons and rise to as high as three stories; cranes are required for their installation. On a project in White Plains, New York, McNulty failed to erect guardrails to protect workers from falling off the edges of recently installed floors. **OSHA** cited McNulty for numerous violations of workplace safety regulations that require construction companies to use guard-rails or safety nets to protect workers from dangerous falls. A federal court of appeals rejected the company's infeasibility defense. It noted that freestanding guardrails were feasible and could have been installed without interfering with the construction activity. McNulty failed to demonstrate the infeasibility of implementing the safety standard at that worksite.[27]

Another aspect of the **feasibility defense** is whether it is **technologically feasible**.

> ***Example:*** A public interest group and a group of unions challenged an **OSHA** standard to regulate the occupational exposure of workers to hexavalent chromium, a toxic substance. It is a by-product of certain welding operations, and is an impurity found in Portland cement, a common building material. In considering the standard, a federal court of appeals observed that
>
> > in adopting a new standard, **OSHA** must establish that workers face a significant risk of harm. **OSHA** considered more than 40 studies of workers [in this case]. . . . Based on this information, **OSHA** concluded that [the chemical] caused "material impairment of health or functional capacity" within the meaning of the **OSH Act**. The court undertook a comprehensive review of the extensive administrative hearing record, the scientific body of evidence and medical research, and the relevant case law and upheld the agency's decision. The court sided with **OSHA** and upheld the proposed **OSHA** standard by finding that the much lower exposure standard advocated by the public interest group would have been technologically unattainable for certain industries and economically unattainable for most businesses.[28]
>
> ***Example:*** Unions petitioned the federal court of appeals to review the secretary of labor's standard for exposure to asbestos dust under **OSHA** in *AFL-CIO v. Hodgson.*[29] They objected to portions of the standards. In denying the unions' petition, the court commented on this defense:
>
> > There can be no question that **OSHA** represents a decision to require safeguards for the health of employees even if such measures substantially increase production costs. This is not, however, the same thing as saying that Congress intended to require immediate implementation of all protective measures technologically achievable without regard for their economic impact. To the contrary, it would comport with common usage to say that a standard that is prohibitively expensive is not "feasible."

In a situation involving a **feasibility defense**, the employer is still obligated to comply to the greatest extent possible, even if it cannot completely comply with the **OSHA** standard. In this case, the employer may not ignore the standard entirely; it must meet the standard to the extent possible.

Other Applicable Standard

Generally, **OSHA** does not have jurisdiction to regulate industries or occupations that are subject to the safety and health requirements of other federal laws. Exempt employers include airlines, operators of atomic energy plants, shipping concerns, businesses involved in the sale and storage of explosives, mining companies (covered under The Mine Act and MSHA), motor carriers, offshore oil platform operators, pipelines owners, and certain railroad operations.

Statute of Limitations

OSHA must issue a citation within six months following the occurrence of any violation. If the violation occurred earlier than that period, the employer may move the ALJ to dismiss the complaint. An exception applies when the employer has deliberately failed to report a fatality as required by law. All criminal prosecutions for **OSHA** violations must be brought within five years of the occurrence.

Workers' Compensation

All states have **workers' compensation** laws that provide for payments to workers for injuries suffered on the job. Most states have enacted laws that provide employees with an **exclusive remedy** to be compensated for work-related injuries or occupational disease. Before the adoption of these statutes, injured workers would have to hire attorneys to sue their claims against employers through lawsuits based on tort law. Often, employers could prevail by asserting that the employee had contributed to the injuries and that the employee's suit was barred because the employee was contributorily negligent or that the negligent acts of others, including fellow employees, were the cause of the injury. The **workers' compensation** laws eliminated much of the injustice injured employees would otherwise encounter.

Workers' Compensation
A no-fault system of laws and regulations that often provides the only means for an injured worker to recover compensation for medical expenses and lost wages arising from work-related injuries.

Theories of Recovery

The injury or illness in question must arise out of the **course and scope of employment**. If the injury occurs during the employee's personal time, the injury is not covered. Liability under a workers' compensation act is not a tort (i.e., wrongful conduct for which a person should pay damages). It is imposed as an incident of the employment relationship, as a cost to be borne by the business enterprise, rather than as an attempt to extend redress for the wrongful act of the employer.[30]

Course and Scope of Employment
A term relating to the time, place, or circumstances under which an injury was sustained during the performance of one's job duties.

A second basis for making a compensable **workers' compensation** claim exists. If the employee can establish that the accidental personal injury **arose out of the employment**, the employee may establish entitlement to benefits. The injuries must have a causal connection with the risks incident to employment. It is generally permissible to show that the employment is a contributory, and not the sole, cause for the injury. This basis is distinct from the ground that the injury occurs during the **course and scope of employment**. In most states, the terms are not synonymous. State courts have taken three approaches to determining if the injuries **"arose out of employment."**

First, the burden is on the injured worker to rule out idiopathic causes for the injuries (i.e., the injuries were from unknown causes). This approach requires the court to consider if the connection to the work is sufficient to be compensable. The burden is on the employee to establish a negative fact (i.e., to rule out nonexplainable causes for his injuries).

> ***Example:*** A worker eliminates idiopathic causes for a fall (i.e., he shows that he did not suffer from a prior disease or injury) that caused him injury that then allows the workers' compensation referee to infer that the fall arose out of employment.

Second, the employee can show a causal connection between the injury and the employment. This can be a difficult level of proof when the injury occurs without a logical explanation. However, in most cases this can be overcome by showing the origin of the accident or injury.

> ***Example:*** A causal connection between the injury and the conditions under which the work is required to be performed is sufficient. A nurse was awarded workers' compensation benefits when she underwent treatment for a preexisting condition of tuberculosis. She developed significant adverse reactions to the drug treatment she received and could

not continue to work. The treatment of her disease was a condition of continued employment.

Third, the worker can apply the **"positional risk doctrine."** Under this doctrine, an injury arises out of the employment if it would not have occurred *but for* the employment, because the claimant would not have been in the position in which it was possible to become injured. This approach lowers the threshold of proof for the employee. It imposes on the employer the burden to show that the injury was caused by the personal activities of the employee. This doctrine is often applied in cases where the injuries arose from workplace risks that are nonthreatening or neutral in nature.

> ***Example:*** A housekeeper twisted her ankle while exiting her car when arriving at work. She proceeded to her job but left work early due to the pain of her sprained ankle. She developed an infection, and her right leg was amputated to prevent the spread of infection. She was initially denied workers' compensation benefits, but the Indiana Supreme Court reversed the denial. It held that her ankle injury was without explanation and was neutral in risk. The cause of the injury was neither personal to the claimant nor distinctly associated with her employment. The injury would not have occurred had the conditions of her employment not placed her in the parking lot where she was injured.[31]

The monies paid for a compensable **workers' compensation** injury is often the sole source of support for disabled workers suffering from the injuries or diseases acquired during the **course and scope of** their **employment**. Under the state laws that establish the compensation systems in each state for injured workers, monies are awarded to injured employees under a strict liability system and fault is not considered in making an award. **Workers' compensation** is administered either through a state agency, as in Nevada, or through insurance companies. Some states allow employers to self-insure the risk if they have adequate financial resources to pay potential claims.

In most states, employers are required to purchase insurance for their workers from approved **workers' compensation** insurance carriers. Texas is unique among the states in not requiring all employers to participate in the **workers' compensation** system. In that state, an employer may opt out of the state **workers' compensation** system and will be liable for damages only in cases of gross negligence that results in an employee's death and only when the injured worker proves that level of negligence in court. Of course, the risk is that the Texas employer opting out is faced with the prospect of unlimited liability for such claims. Some states exempt small employers from the requirement, while others require that all employees, regardless of their number or whether they are full- or part-time workers, be covered by a **workers' compensation** program. The benefits are paid pursuant to a state-issued payment formula.

Finally, some states permit an employee to avoid a workers' compensation proceeding and sue the employer directly for damages when the employer has been convicted of a willful **OSHA** violation. Other states will increase the workers' compensation benefit if the injury was due to a willful **OSHA** violation.

Who Is Covered?

Most employees, but *not* independent contractors, are entitled to **workers' compensation** benefits. Under the laws of most states, the following employees are *not* covered by workers' compensation: the owners of the business, casual laborers (who are usually considered independent contractors), volunteers, and those covered under other special state or federal statutes. Courts will scrutinize the contracts or contentions of parties who assert independent contractor status. Depending on the severity of the injury, the worker and employer may vigorously assert opposing arguments on the nature of their relationship at the time of the injury.

What Is Covered?

Injuries sustained during the **"course and scope of employment"** are covered. The most difficult of factual situations are often those presented to determine whether the injured worker was within the **course and scope of employment.**

Suing the Employer

One of the features of the **workers' compensations** laws throughout the United States is that employers enjoy immunity from lawsuits from injured employees, although there are some exceptions to that rule. When the employer fails to carry **workers' compensation** insurance, the employee may sue the employer. When an *employer commits an intentional act* or is *grossly negligent* with respect to the situation that caused the employee's injury or occupational disease, the *employee can sue the employer* in court. The damages available are those that any litigant could pursue. The worker is not required to pursue the **workers' compensation** remedy.

The **workers' compensation** system provides benefits for physical injuries and illnesses and limited damages in the event of death. Medical expenses are normally entirely compensable, but lost wages are subject to statutory caps. State laws typically provide the following benefits:

- Medical expense coverage for injuries and covered occupational diseases.
- Temporary disability benefits (i.e., lost wages) during the recovery period based on a percentage of the employee's lost wages, subject to monetary caps.
- Permanent disability benefits. Scheduled disabilities are those for the loss of a particular part of the body, such as leg or arm. The amount of compensation is intended to represent the lost wages due to the permanent disability. Unscheduled disabilities are those that are not scheduled but involve a loss of earning capacity following a fact-finding investigation by a vocational resource expert.
- Vocational rehabilitation service payments are paid to retrain the worker for a wage earning position.
- Death benefits are paid to spouses (or domestic partners) and dependents of workers who die because of an on-the-job event. All states have a statutory maximum amount that will be paid.
- Some states permit workers to recover for mental or emotional stress injuries. In addition, some states allow an employee to collect **workers' compensation** benefits for sexual harassment, but by doing so the employee will waive the right to pursue a claim in tort for a hostile work environment involving sexual harassment.

If an employee is injured as the result of an accident or disease contracted during prior periods of employment, liability for the payment of compensation as between the successive employers ordinarily rests on the one in whose service the accident or disease occurred. However, usually, in cases in which service periods with successive employers contributed to the worker's condition, **apportionment of liability** between or among those employers will be required. Some states apply the **"last injurious exposure rule"** to place full liability on the last employer. This rule eliminates the difficulty in apportioning liability in successive employer cases.

Apportionment of Liability
The division of liability among two or more defendants who caused a tortious personal injury or property damage.

If a worker cannot return to work following the disabling event, the employee may qualify for **Social Security disability benefits**. The benefits are available to those who suffer from a severe physical or mental impairment or combination of impairments constituting an injury that prevents the employee from performing any "substantial gainful activity." The disability must have lasted or can be expected to last for at least 12 continuous months.

Federal Workers' Compensation Laws

The U.S. Department of Labor administers several disability compensation programs that provide benefits for workers and their dependents because of work-related injuries or illnesses. These programs include the following:

Federal Employers' Liability and Compensation Act.[32] This Act provides for federal **workers' compensation** benefits for the three million federal civilian and postal workers who work for the federal government domestically and internationally. The Act pays medical, surgical, and hospital services and for supplies needed for treatment of an injury. The workers can receive temporary total disability payments, paid at the rate of two-thirds of the salary if the employee has no dependents and three-quarters of the salary if he or she has dependents. Vocational rehabilitation and training benefits are available to the worker. Additionally, compensation is paid for the permanent effects of an injury or for death.

Federal Employment Liability Act.[33] This statute protects railroad employees who are entitled to benefits when the railroad employer causes the employee's injury or death.

Merchant Marine Act of 1920.[34] Injured seamen may obtain damages from their employers for the negligence of the ship owner, the captain, or other crew members. A person qualifies as a seaman if the worker's duties contribute to the functioning of a vessel. The worker's job does not have to be limited to transportation duties that directly aid the vessel's navigation.

Longshore and Harbor Workers' Compensation Act.[35] This Act provides compensation for disability or death of an employee or for injuries to an employee occurring on navigable waters or adjoining areas of the navigable waters of the United States. Covered employers are private maritime related companies and their employees.

Less-well-known federal laws provide coverage for eligible Department of Energy nuclear workers at atomic energy and weapons plants. In addition, coal mine workers are covered by the Federal Black Lung Program, which provides for compensation to miners totally disabled by disease arising from coal mine employment.

CASE 15.5

UNDOCUMENTED ALIENS MAY RECOVER WORKERS' COMPENSATION BENEFITS

MADERA SUGAR PINE CO. V. INDUSTRIAL ACCIDENT COMMISSION OF CALIFORNIA

262 U.S. 499 (1923)

Supreme Court of the United States

Facts. The Madera Sugar Pine Company in California appealed two cases together to the U.S. Supreme Court involving the employment of two laborers who sustained fatal injuries arising out of and in the course of the scope of their employment. Their partially dependent mother and sisters, being aliens residing in Mexico, sought death benefits under California's workers' compensation law. The Supreme Court of California permitted the awards to stand. The state's workers' compensation commission sought a *writ of certiorari* before the Supreme Court, which it granted.

Issue. Are nonresident alien dependents entitled to death benefits under a state workers' compensation system?

Language of the Court. Sanford, J.: **The argument is, in substance, that while an employer may lawfully be compelled to make compensation to the resident dependents of employees whose death was caused by no legal wrong, on the ground that the State is interested in preventing such dependents from becoming public charges, this justification does extend to the case of foreign dependents, who would not become public charges of the State; and, therefore, that an act requiring compensation to be made to such foreign dependents in the absence of legal wrong, is not a reasonable exercise of the police power of the State.**

Provision is universally made in workmen's compensation acts for compensation not only to disabled employees but also to the dependents of those whose injuries are fatal. And the two kinds of payment are "always regarded as components parts of a single scheme of rights and liabilities" arising out of "the relation of employer and employee . . ." (citation omitted). The object of such acts "is single — to provide for the liability of an employer to make compensation for injuries received by an employee," whether to the employee himself or to those who suffer pecuniary loss by reason of his death. . . .

A strong argument in support of the view that as part of a system of compulsory compensation established by a State to protect employees from loss through industrial accidents, the death benefits may properly be extended to alien dependents, is also found, by analogy, in the reasons stated in various decisions holding that employers' liability acts authorizing recovery for the death of employees caused by negligence, inure to the benefit of alien as well as resident beneficiaries. Thus, as the Federal Employers' Liability Act, in order to protect the life of the employee gives compensation to those who had relation to it, it makes no difference where they may reside; it being "the fact of their relation to the life destroyed that is the circumstance to be considered, whether we consider the injury received by them or the influence of that relation upon the life destroyed." (Citation omitted.) Such employers' liability statutes are designed to benefit all employees (citation omitted). They have the interest of the employees in mind and are primarily for the protection of their lives; the action is given to the beneficiaries on their account and they are not intended to be less protected if their beneficiaries happen to live abroad (citation omitted). "Many of these toilers in mines, on public works, railroads and the numberless fields of manual labor, receive a moderate wage and are compelled to leave in foreign lands those who are dependent upon them and for whose support they patiently work on, indulging the hope that ultimately they may bring to these shores a mother, or wife and children. . . . The statute not only benefits the survivors, but protects the laboring man. . . . The laborer, leaving wife and children behind him and coming here from abroad, has a right to enter into the contract of employment, fully relying upon the statute." (Citation omitted.)

Decision. Yes. The purpose of workers' compensation is to assist the injured worker whether or not the worker is authorized to work in the United States.

CASE QUESTIONS

Critical Legal Thinking. State the reasons why the Court made a sound public policy decision in this case.

Business Ethics. If the Court reached a contrary decision, what would have been the societal consequences?

Contemporary Business. Can you think of any other circumstances whereby unauthorized workers are protected to the same degree as legal workers?

Employer Defenses

Employers and their insurance carriers are not responsible for all injuries. Exceptions to employer responsibility include:

- injuries occurring elsewhere than within the employment relationship or within the course and scope of the employment (i.e., the injury occurred

during personal time or during work time that was not for the benefit of the employer);
- injuries occurring due to the intoxication of the employee (whether from alcohol or an illegal substance);
- injuries caused by the willful intention of the employee to injure or kill him- or herself or another (i.e., a nonaccidental injury);
- injuries arising out of an altercation in which the injured employee was the initial physical aggressor; or
- injuries caused during the commission of a serious crime by the injured employee.

Many jurisdictions recognize that a worker may be denied benefits if, as an applicant, he or she made false representations as to physical condition that the employer relied on and that subsequently had a causal connection to the employee's injury.

Example: Steven Johnson was employed as a senior public defender with the state of Wyoming public defender's office. He left home in Gillette, Wyoming, to travel to the annual public defender seminar in Saratoga, Wyoming. Prior to embarking on his trip, Johnson purchased food, camping supplies, and a case of beer and a fifth of schnapps. Johnson arrived at a campground campsite and telephoned his wife to inform her he had arrived safely. Approximately three hours after making the call to his wife, Johnson's vehicle and body were discovered on a highway a short distance from the entrance of the campsite. An investigation revealed that Johnson's vehicle crossed the highway, and when he overcorrected his steering, the vehicle rolled and ejected him from the vehicle. After Johnson was pronounced dead, the coroner drew a blood sample from his body. Johnson's blood alcohol concentration was determined to be 0.23 percent — well in excess of the legal limit for safe operation of a motor vehicle. The state workers' compensation examiner's decision to deny workers' compensation death benefits to the surviving widow and her two minor children was upheld.[36]

CASE 15.6

HORSEPLAY WORKPLACE INJURIES ARE NOT COMPENSABLE WORKERS' COMPENSATION CLAIMS

BRIAN CLODGO V. INDUSTRY RENTAVISION, INC.

166 VT. 548; 701 A.2d 1044 (Vt. 1997)

Supreme Court of Vermont

Facts. On July 22, 1995, Brian Clodgo was working as manager of Rentavision's store in Brattleboro. During a lull between customers, Clodgo began firing staples with a staple gun at a co-worker who was sitting on a couch watching television. The co-worker first protested, but after Clodgo had fired 20 or 30 staples at him, the co-worker fired three staples back at Clodgo. As Clodgo ducked, the third staple hit him in the eye. Clodgo eventually reported the injury and filed a claim for workers' compensation benefits. Rentavision contested the award, arguing that the claimant was engaged in noncompensable horseplay at the time of the injury. Following a hearing in March 1996, a state workers' compensation commissioner awarded permanent partial disability and vocational rehabilitation benefits, medical expenses, and attorney's fees and costs. This appeal followed to the Vermont Supreme Court.

Issue. Is a claimant entitled to workers' compensation benefits if the injury occurred during the workday while the claimant was engaged in horseplay?

Language of the Court. Gibson, J: **Compensable injuries under Vermont's Workers' Compensation Act are those received "by accident arising out of and in the course of . . . employment." (Citation omitted.) Although only work-related injuries are compensable, we recognize that "even [employees] of mature years [will] indulge in a moment's diversion from work to joke with or play a prank upon a fellow [employee]." (Citation omitted.) For such a horseplay-related injury to be compensated, however, claimant must show that it both (1) arose out of the employment, and (2) occurred in the course of the employment. . . .**

Although the accident here would not have happened but for claimant's participation in the horseplay and therefore was not exclusively linked to his employment, it also was not a purely personal risk that would have occurred regardless of his location and activity on that day. He was injured during work hours with a staple gun provided for use on the job, and thus the findings support a causal connection between claimant's work conditions and the injury adequate to conclude that the accident arose out of his employment.

Nonetheless, claimant must also show that the injury occurred in the course of the employment. An accident occurs in the course of employment when it was within the period of time the employee was on duty at a place where the employee was reasonably expected to be while fulfilling the duties of the employment contract. (Citation omitted.) Thus, while some horseplay among employees during work hours can be expected and is not an automatic bar to compensation, the key inquiry is whether the employee deviated too far from his or her duties. . . .

The facts show that the accident was unrelated to any legitimate use of the staplers at the time, indicating there was no commingling of the horseplay with work duties. The Commissioner focused on the slack time inherent in claimant's job, but this factor alone is not dispositive. Although some horseplay

was reasonably to be expected during idle periods between customers, the obvious dangerousness of shooting staples at fellow employees and the absence of connection between duties as a salesperson and the horseplay events indicate the accident occurred during a substantial deviation from work duties. Therefore, we reverse the Commissioner's award.

Decision. No. If the circumstances giving rise to injuries are not sufficiently connected with the scope of employment, the claimant is not entitled to workers' compensation benefits.

CASE QUESTIONS

Critical Legal Thinking. If you were a state court judge, how would you define the standards for determining if an injury or illness arose out of the course and scope of employment?

Business Ethics. Clodgo was denied benefits because his actions were not part of his duties as a worker at Rentavision. What kinds of job activities can you imagine in which injuries such as the one Clodgo suffered would be compensable?

Contemporary Business. What employer safety training programs can you envision are necessary, if any, with respect to employees such as Clodgo to avoid workers' compensation claims?

Would the injuries have been deemed to be within the course of employment if they had occurred during work-related recreational or "extracurricular" activities (i.e., a company-sponsored sporting event or social gathering) instead of during staple-gun horseplay? Generally, yes, if they occurred on the employer's business premises during normal work breaks or otherwise incident to employment (such as required conditioning to maintain fitness for the employment position) or if the employer derives some direct benefit from the employee's off-hours activity (e.g., Napa Valley wine tasting during company-sponsored client entertainment trips). Foreseeable injuries occurring during personal time during the workday are also covered under **workers' compensation.**

> ***Example:*** Robert Bender worked as a ski-lift operator at Deer Mountain Ski Area near Lead, South Dakota, and was injured while skiing during one of his breaks. He sought compensation for his injuries. Because lift operators work outside on the ski slope, they were not required to "clock out" during their breaks. It was common for lift operators to take ski runs on their breaks. The Supreme Court of South Dakota followed the general rule in such cases and held that since Bender was injured while engaging in recreational or social activities on the employer's premises on a scheduled break, the injury arose out of and in the course of employment as long as the activity was a "regular incident of the employment."[37]

Management Application
Wrongful Termination and Public Policy Violations

Courts will recognize a wrongful termination claim by a former employee that arises from a discharge based on a public policy violation. Reporting an OSHA violation to the proper authorities will give rise to such protections, as will filing a workers' compensation claim. Consider the following case.

Rose Marie Niblo worked for Parr Manufacturing, Inc., a company located in Polk County, Iowa. When she began her employment, she worked with plastisol, a chemical used in the manufacture of fuel filters. Within six months of her employment, she noticed that she was developing a skin condition on her face. She was referred to a dermatologist, who diagnosed her skin condition as work related. Following conversations with her supervisor and the president of the corporation, she was terminated from her employment. She sued Parr Manufacturing, Inc. for retaliatory discharge and for lost wages and emotional distress.

It was undisputed that her employment was at-will and that no term of definite employment existed between Niblo and Parr. Iowa law provided that if on the job injuries were compensable under workers' compensation, then any discharge relating to a workers' actual or potential claim would violate public policy.

Niblo introduced the following facts at the time of trial. She had contacted her supervisor about going to a doctor. The supervisor ignored her first inquiry and responded to her second request by stating that he did not care what she did, but that Parr was not going to pay her to go to a doctor. After Parr went to a dermatologist, Niblo told the Parr president of her visit and of the doctor's opinion that her skin condition was work related. After a follow-up visit with the doctor, Niblo was informed that she had a severe case of chloracne caused by contact with chemicals at work. The president became irate when Niblo told him that she needed goggles, protective cream, and continued treatment. The president told her that he was not going to pay workers' compensation or unemployment benefits and that he did not think her skin problem was his fault or "factory related." He said that he was not going to pay to have her face worked on at all. At the conclusion of this outburst, the president fired Niblo.

At the time of trial, Parr defended its position by arguing that Niblo never said she wanted to or intended to file a workers' compensation claim or that she had done so. Parr claimed that the evidence at trial merely showed that its management and Niblo had a dispute concerning the payment of her doctor bills. Upon appeal to the Iowa Supreme Court, it affirmed the jury verdict including emotional distress damages in a public policy tort workers' compensation retaliation claim.[38]

Discussion Questions

1. Under what circumstances may an employee file a workers' compensation claim?
2. The Iowa court permitted the recovery of an award for emotional distress or mental anguish damages because Niblo had suffered physical injury. If Niblo had not suffered a physical injury related to work, state the reasons for and against the award of emotional distress damages to her.
3. Are the damages for emotional distress better linked to the wrongful discharge claim than to the workers' compensation claim? State your reasons for your conclusion.
4. Should a claimant be allowed to recover emotional distress damages more easily in a wrongful discharge case based on a violation of a public policy than in a workers' compensation setting? Why or why not?

Outcomes

In its August 2007 report, the National Academy of Social Insurance stated that workers' compensation programs in the 50 states, the District of Columbia, and the federal government paid $55.3 billion in benefits in 2005. Of the total, $26.2 billion was for medical care and $29.1 billion was for cash benefits. Social Security and Medicare, in contrast, pay benefits to workers with long-term disabilities from any cause, but only when the disabilities preclude work. Social Security begins after a five-month waiting period, and Medicare begins 29 months after the onset of a medically verified inability to work. In 2005, Social Security paid $85.4 billion in cash benefits to disabled workers and their dependents, while Medicare paid $48.8 billion for health care for disabled persons under age 65.[39]

Human Resource Form
OSHA Form 301

OSHA's Form 301
Injury and Illness Incident Report

Attention: This form contains information relating to employee health and must be used in a manner that protects the confidentiality of employees to the extent possible while the information is being used for occupational safety and health purposes.

U.S. Department of Labor
Occupational Safety and Health Administration

Form approved OMB no. 1218-0176

This *Injury and Illness Incident Report* is one of the first forms you must fill out when a recordable work-related injury or illness has occurred. Together with the *Log of Work-Related Injuries and Illnesses* and the accompanying *Summary*, these forms help the employer and OSHA develop a picture of the extent and severity of work-related incidents.

Within 7 calendar days after you receive information that a recordable work-related injury or illness has occurred, you must fill out this form or an equivalent. Some state workers' compensation, insurance, or other reports may be acceptable substitutes. To be considered an equivalent form, any substitute must contain all the information asked for on this form.

According to Public Law 91-596 and 29 CFR 1904, OSHA's recordkeeping rule, you must keep this form on file for 5 years following the year to which it pertains.

If you need additional copies of this form, you may photocopy and use as many as you need.

Completed by ____

Title ____

Phone (____) ____-____ Date ____/____/____

Information about the employee

1) Full name ____

2) Street ____

City ____ State ____ ZIP ____

3) Date of birth ____/____/____

4) Date hired ____/____/____

5) ☐ Male
☐ Female

Information about the physician or other health care professional

6) Name of physician or other health care professional ____

7) If treatment was given away from the worksite, where was it given?

Facility ____

Street ____

City ____ State ____ ZIP ____

8) Was employee treated in an emergency room?
☐ Yes
☐ No

9) Was employee hospitalized overnight as an in-patient?
☐ Yes
☐ No

Information about the case

10) Case number from the *Log* ____ *(Transfer the case number from the Log after you record the case.)*

11) Date of injury or illness ____/____/____

12) Time employee began work ____ AM / PM

13) Time of event ____ AM / PM ☐ Check if time cannot be determined

14) ***What was the employee doing just before the incident occurred?*** Describe the activity, as well as the tools, equipment, or material the employee was using. Be specific. *Examples:* "climbing a ladder while carrying roofing materials"; "spraying chlorine from hand sprayer"; "daily computer key-entry."

15) ***What happened?*** Tell us how the injury occurred. *Examples:* "When ladder slipped on wet floor, worker fell 20 feet"; "Worker was sprayed with chlorine when gasket broke during replacement"; "Worker developed soreness in wrist over time."

16) ***What was the injury or illness?*** Tell us the part of the body that was affected and how it was affected; be more specific than "hurt," "pain," or sore." *Examples:* "strained back"; "chemical burn, hand"; "carpal tunnel syndrome."

17) ***What object or substance directly harmed the employee?*** *Examples:* "concrete floor"; "chlorine"; "radial arm saw." *If this question does not apply to the incident, leave it blank.*

18) ***If the employee died, when did death occur?*** Date of death ____/____/____

Public reporting burden for this collection of information is estimated to average 22 minutes per response, including time for reviewing instructions, searching existing data sources, gathering and maintaining the data needed, and completing and reviewing the collection of information. Persons are not required to respond to the collection of information unless it displays a current valid OMB control number. If you have any comments about this estimate or any other aspects of this data collection, including suggestions for reducing this burden, contact: US Department of Labor, OSHA Office of Statistical Analysis, Room N-3644, 200 Constitution Avenue, NW, Washington, DC 20210. Do not send the completed forms to this office.

Key Terms and Concepts

- OSH Act
- OSHA
- NIOSH
- OSHRC
- Administrative Procedures Act (APA)
- Multiemployer doctrine
- General duty
- Recognized hazards
- General industry standards
- Specific duty
- Material safety data sheets
- Recognized hazards
- Congressional Review Act
- Variance
- Right of access
- *De minimis* violation
- Nonserious violation
- Serious violation
- Repeat violation
- Serious condition
- Sovereign immunity
- Unforeseeable employee misconduct
- Greater hazard defense
- Impossibility defense
- Economic infeasibility
- Technological infeasibility
- Workplace Violence Prevention Plan
- Workers' compensation
- Exclusive remedy
- Course and scope of employment
- Arose out of employment
- Apportionment of liability
- Positional risk doctrine
- Last injurious exposure rule

Chapter Summary

- The federal OSHA statute, enforced by the U.S. Department of Labor, is a remedial statute intended to protect employees from recognized hazards in the workplace.

- OSHA is intended to police the workplace by imposing compliance standards on employers. It does not establish a remedy for employees.

- Employers are subject to general duty and specific duty standards.

- OSHA standards are to be liberally construed to promote the protection of workers.

- OSHA will issue monetary citations to employers for violations of its regulations.

- Employees may refuse to carry out an employer's directive if doing so would constitute a violation of a general duty standard.

- Sovereign immunity generally protects OSHA and its inspectors from their acts and omissions during workplace inspections.

- Employers have several defenses to a purported OSHA violation, including the greater hazard defense.

- The workers' compensation system, implemented in all states, provides payment of benefits for workers suffering from injuries, illnesses, and covered diseases arising from their employment. If the worker is covered by workers' compensation, the worker is deemed an employee and must pursue the exclusive remedies afforded by the state workers' compensation benefits system. If a worker is not an employee for which workers' compensation benefits would apply, the worker can file a lawsuit to recover damages in tort against the culpable parties.

- Compensable workers' compensation claims are those that occur during the course and scope of employment or arise out of the employment relationship. The term *"in the course and scope"* relates to the time, place, or circumstances in or under which the injury was sustained. The term *"arise out of employment,"* means the claimant is able to establish a causal connection between the injury and the risks incident to employment. The two requirements are distinct and are not synonymous.

Online Student Support

- Loislaw legal research and writing assignments.
- Loislaw group projects and class presentations.
- Loislaw access, providing online research including up-to-date cases, statutes, rules, and regulations. Primary law for all 50 states and federal jurisdictions. Registration required for access to this resource.
- Practice questions, including sample true/false, multiple choice, and short answer questions to test your understanding of concepts.
- Additional human resource forms.
- Internet exercises.
- Blogs.
- Supplementary statutory and regulatory materials.

Case Problems

15.1 An explosion occurred on a barge owned by Mallard Bay Drilling. OSHA cited the company for a number of violations. Mallard Bay challenged OSHA's jurisdiction to issue the citations because it contended that the Coast Guard regulated matters relating to marine safety, including matters such as fire extinguishers, life preservers, engine flame arrestors, engine ventilation, and emergency locating equipment. The Coast Guard determined that the barge was not subject to comprehensive Coast Guard regulation and did not cite the company for violation of any of its regulations. How should the OSHA ALJ rule with regard to Mallard Bay's challenges to OSHA's jurisdiction? (*Chao, Secretary. of Labor v. Mallard Bay Drilling, Inc.*, 534 U.S. 235 (2002))

15.2 Lester Russell was injured while in the course and scope of his employment with the Bartley and Barton Company, allegedly because of the employer's failure to comply with provisions of OSHA. Russell sued his employer for the OSHA violations that precipitated the collapse of the ditch in which he was working. He also sued the consulting engineer who designed the plans and specifications for the project he was working on when he was injured, arguing that the engineer was a joint and concurrent cause of his injuries. How should the court rule on the defendant's motions to dismiss and for summary judgment? (*Russell v. Bartley and Barton et al.*, 494 F.2d 334 (6th Cir. 1974))

15.3 The American Smelting and Refining Co. appealed citations issued by OSHA arising from general duty violations. OSHA charged American Smelting and Refining with exposing its employees to hazardous airborne concentrations of lead. The company argued that no recognized hazard existed because the term *"recognized under the law"* meant it was recognized by human senses without the assistance of any technical instruments. How do you think the court should rule? (*American Smelting and Refining Co. v. OSHA,* 501 F.2d 504 (8th Cir. 1974))

15.4 A widow sued for her deceased husband's conscious suffering and wrongful death attributable to the Silverline Manufacturing Company's negligent sale and defective manufacture of aluminum powder. She also sued the officers and directors of her deceased husband's employer because they failed to secure workers' compensation insurance and deprived her of widow's benefits. After the fire that resulted in the deceased's death, the employer went out of business. Should the court find that a plaintiff could sue for negligence for the employer's failure to secure workers' compensation coverage? Who within a corporation should be personally liable for the corporation's failure to obtain that coverage? (*LaClair v. Silverline Mfg. Co., Inc.*, 379 Mass. 21, 393 N.E.2d 867 (1979))

15.5 Matthew George Smith was a 16-year-old high school student in Dunwoody, Georgia, when he spent his spring vacation working for his father's business, Coastal Tire and Auto Service. He was injured when another car struck the automobile operated by his father. At the time of the accident, he was assisting his father in testing the automobile. He made a claim for workers' compensation benefits that were awarded to him by the South Carolina Workers' Compensation Commission. The workers' compensation insurance carrier for the employer protested the award. The carrier appealed on the ground that Matthew was not a regular employee of the company and as a casual worker was not entitled to coverage. It was stipulated at the hearing that the young Mr. Smith's employment relationship was flexible and that he had no specified days or time when he was required to report for work. How should the court rule on the insurer's contention that he was a noncovered casual employee? (*Smith v. Coastal Tire & Auto Service and Am. Mutual Liab. Ins.*, 263 S.C. 77, 207 S.E.2d 810 (1974))

End Notes

1. *Byrd v. Fieldcrest Mills, Inc.*, 496 F.2d 1323 (4th Cir. 1974).
2. *http://www.dol.gov/oasam/programs/history/mono-regsafepart07.htm.*
3. *http://www.bls.gov/news.release/osh.nr0.htm.*
4. 29 USC §651(b).
5. *Martin v. OSHRC,* 499 U.S. 144 (1991).
6. 29 C.F.R. §652(5).
7. *Nationwide Mutual Ins. Co. v. Darden,* 503 U.S. 318 (1992).
8. 588 F.3d 815 (8th Cir. 2009).
9. *U.S. v. B & L Supply Co.*, 486 F.Supp. 26 (N.D. Tex. 1980).
10. *UAW v. General Dynamics Land Systems Division,* 815 F.2d, 1570 (D.C. Cir.), *cert. denied,* 484 U.S. 976 (1987).
11. *United Steelworkers of America, etc. v. Marshall,* 647 F.2d 1189 (D.C. Cir. 1980).
12. 5 U.S.C. §§801-808.
13. *Reich v. Hoy Shoe, Inc.*, 32 F.3d 361 (8th Cir. 1994).
14. *Russell v. Bartley,* 494 F.2d 334 (6th Cir. 1974).
15. *Minichello v. Industries, Inc.*, 756 F.2d 26 (6th Cir. 1985).
16. 29 C.F.R. §1904.
17. *Reich v. OSHA Review Commission,* 102 F.3d 1200 (11th Cir. 1997).
18. *Cuyahoga Valley RR Co. v. United Trans. Union et al.*, 474 U.S. 3 (1985).
19. *United States v. Olson,* 546 U.S. 43 (2005).
20. *Corbesco, Inc. v. Dole, Secretary of Labor,* 926 F.2d 422 (5th Cir. (1991).
21. *U.S. v. Pitt-Des Moines, Inc.*, 168 F.3d 976 (7th Cir. 1999).
22. Fact Sheet No. OSHA 91-36.
23. *Diamond Roofing Co., Inc. v. OSHA,* 528 F.2d 645 (5th Cir 1976).
24. *Brock v. L. E. Myers Company, High Voltage Division et al.*, 818 F.2d 1270 (6th Cir. 1987).
25. 576 F.2d 558, 561 (3d Cir. 1978).
26. 20 F.3d 938 (9th Cir. 1994).
27. *McNulty & Co., Inc. v. Secretary of Labor,* 283 F.3d 328 (D.C. Cir. 2002).
28. *Public Citizen v. U.S. Dept. of Labor,* 557 F.3d 165 (3d Cir. 2009).

29. 162 U.S. App. D.C. 331 (1974).
30. *Alaska Packers Assn. v. Industrial Accident Commission of California, et al.*, 294 U.S. 532 (1935).
31. *Milledge v. The Oaks, A Living Center,* 784 N.E. 2d 926 (2003).
32. 5 U.S.C. §§8101-8193.
33. 45 U.S.C. §51-60.
34. 46 U.S.C. §688.
35. 33 U.S.C. §§901-950.
36. *Johnson v. State ex rel. Wyoming Workers' Compensation Div.*, 911 P.2d 1054 (Wyo. (1996)).
37. *Bender v. Dakota Resorts Mgmt Group, Inc.*, 700 N.W. 2d 739 (S.D. 2005).
38. *Niblo v. Parr Mfg., Inc.*, 445 N.W. 2D 351 (Iowa 1989).
39. National Academy of Social Insurance, *Highlights: Workers' Compensation: Benefits, Coverage, and Costs, 2005* (August 2007), 1-2.

Chapter 16
Retirement and Employee Benefits

Musicians don't retire; they stop when there's no more music in them. —Louis Armstrong, American jazz trumpeter and singer

Learning Objectives

1. Understand the scope of ERISA regulation of fringe benefits.
2. Understand the difference between pension and welfare benefit plans.
3. Explain the extent of state regulation of welfare benefit plans.
4. Define the characteristics of defined benefit and defined contribution plans.
5. Identify the potential legal exposure of plan fiduciaries to participants.
6. Describe what rights states have in the regulation of employee welfare plans.

Chapter Outline

- Introduction
- Overview: Employee Retirement Income Security Act and Benefit Plans
- Employee Pension Benefit Plans
- Types of Retirement Plans
- Employers' Fiduciary Duties

Case 16.1 Varity Corp. v. Howe

Case 16.2 LaRue v. DeWolff, Boberg & Associates

Case 16.3 Metropolitan Life Insurance Co. v. Glenn

- ERISA's Discrimination Provisions
- Nonqualified Deferred Compensation Plans
- Entitlement to Participation
- Vesting and Enforcement
- Welfare Benefit Plans

Case 16.4 Metropolitan Life Insurance Co. v. Massachusetts

Case 16.5 Rush Prudential HMO, Inc. v. Moran

Case 16.6 Kentucky Association of Health Plans, Inc. v. Miller

- Focus on Ethics: Microsoft Violates Employee Benefit Law
- Consolidated Omnibus Budget Reconciliation Act of 1986
- Health Insurance Portability and Accountability Act
- 2010 Health Care Act
- Dissolution of Marriage
- Management Application: The Importance of Written Documentation
- Human Resource Form: Your Medical Benefits

Chapter Opening scenario

During the 1980s, Salomon Smith Barney (Salomon) entered into a transaction with an **ERISA** pension plan of Ameritech Corporation that was prohibited by **ERISA**; namely, Salomon acted as a broker in executing stock trades at the direction of the plan administrator and, during the same period, Salomon sold commercial properties to an investment manager of the pension plan. The pension plan administrator learned that what had been sold to the pension plan was nearly worthless and had been at the time of the transaction. Salomon was sued for the damages suffered because it had engaged in a practice that was prohibited by **ERISA**. Salomon defended the case because **ERISA** permits suits against fiduciaries who caused the plan to enter into the transaction, but not against the other party to the prohibited transaction. How do you think the Supreme Court decided the case?[1]

Introduction

Employers are required by federal and state laws to make contributions into a limited set of social insurance programs. These programs were enacted to in response to the financial distress precipitated by the stock market crash of October 1929 and the resulting period of economic turmoil known as the Great Depression. These contributions include payments into the federal Social Security program, state unemployment insurance programs, and state mandated workers' compensation systems. These topics, along with benefits arising from federal and state versions of the Family and Medical Leave Act, are presented in other chapters of this text. Other than under these programs, employers are not required to provide any other paid benefits to employees, including vacation and sick leave, health and other fringe benefits, or, as we shall next discuss, **retirement plans**. When a company does offer a pension or other employee benefit plan, federal law does not require any minimum level of benefits.

Competition in the hiring of the best available candidates has compelled employers to offer the best in fringe benefit packages. Candidates will often choose one position over another based on the strength of the benefits packages offered by the employer. Similarly, given the high cost of personally paying for those benefits, employees carefully balance the loss of benefits when considering leaving a position with a generous employee benefit program for one that might offer a higher wage but fewer fringe benefits.

Amid the recent tumult in the stock and financial markets, many in Congress are advocating the complete restructuring of the retirement plan laws of the United States. In particular, Congress is reviewing whether it should amend the provisions of the **401(k)** retirement plan, discussed later in this chapter, and increase the funding of Social Security benefit payments to older and disabled Americans. Whatever the future may bring, business people will need to know well the law applicable to retirement planning for themselves and their employees.

Overview: Employee Retirement Income Security Act and Benefit Plans

In 1974, Congress enacted landmark legislation entitled the **Employee Retirement Income Security Act** of 1974, known as **ERISA**. The law was originally intended to address conflicts arising from employer-paid **retirement plans** known as **defined contribution plans**. In this regard, substantial changes were made to federal labor and tax law provisions administered by the United States Department of Labor and the Department of Treasury's Internal Revenue Service (IRS). Since its enactment, Congress left it to the courts and, in particular, the U.S. Supreme Court to interpret and apply that law and the complex regulations issued by these two federal agencies. This chapter reviews **ERISA** and the significant types of **retirement, deferred compensation**, and **welfare benefit plans** that employers have adopted.

Employee Retirement Income Security Act (ERISA)
Federal law setting minimum standards for protection of private employee benefit plan participants and beneficiaries. Law requires disclosure and reporting of information and sets standards of conduct, duties and obligations for plan fiduciaries, and remedies.

What Is an Employee Benefit Plan?

Within the meaning of **ERISA**, an **employee benefit plan** is one that, under the circumstances, allows a reasonable person to ascertain the intended benefits, identify the source of financing for the benefits, identify the beneficiaries, and identify the procedures for receiving the benefits.[2] **ERISA** covers a plan only if it requires an ongoing practice or scheme to provide benefits to employees.

Two Types of Plans

The law of **ERISA** divides **employee benefit plans** into two types: **pension plans** and **welfare plans. Pension plans** defer salary until retirement, while **welfare plans** are any type of other benefit plan covered by **ERISA** that is not a pension plan. These include plans, funds, and programs that provide medical, surgical, or hospital care; vision or dental benefits; benefits in the event of sickness, accidental disability, unemployment, or death; day care assistance; and educational assistance programs. In the area of pensions and **retirement plans**, the law is largely governed by federal and *not* state law. The stated policy of **ERISA** is, among other things, to protect the interests of participants in **employee benefit plans** and their beneficiaries by requiring the disclosure and reporting of financial and other information to participants and beneficiaries and by establishing standards of conduct, responsibility, and obligation for **fiduciaries** and to provide appropriate remedies.[3] Unlike other federally mandated benefits, such as Social Security, **ERISA** does not require employers to establish **employee benefit plans**. The employer may tailor an employee benefit plan to its needs and those of its employees. As the Supreme Court has stated "[i]n contrast to the obligatory, nationwide Social Security program, [n]othing in **ERISA** requires employers to establish **employee benefit plans**. Nor does **ERISA** mandate what kind of benefits employers must provide if they choose to have such a plan."[4] Unless exempted, **ERISA** regulates all **employee pension benefit plans**. The extent of regulation is complete and covers participation

Pension Plan
Agreement by which salary and other contributions are deferred from taxation until retirement, when they will provide participants with income when they are no longer earning a regular income from employment.

Welfare Plans
ERISA-covered plans that do not involve salary deferral and retirement plans, such as medical, dental, and disability insurance plans.

Fiduciary
A person or business entity who exercises either discretionary authority or control regarding the management of a retirement plan or its assets. The term includes both those who administer a plan and those who provide investment advice to plan administrators.

requirements, vesting, employer- and employee-funding of the plan, and the **fiduciary** responsibilities of the **plan administrators**.

Federal Preemption

To ensure a uniform treatment of benefit plans and sponsors, **ERISA** preempts all state laws that fall within its scope of coverage. The breadth of this preemption includes state laws consistent with **ERISA**'s substantive provisions. **ERISA** preempts all state laws, court decisions, and administrative regulations. All ambiguities in interpreting **ERISA** are to be resolved by referencing federal and not state rules relating to the interpretation of contracts. This **preemption** is broader than any we have studied thus far and has been characterized by one court as complete preemption or the "**super preemption** of ERISA."[5] For example, if an employee wished to make a claim against the plan administrator for a breach of a **fiduciary** duty, that claim would lie exclusively in federal and not in state court. **ERISA** specifically provides that it shall not be construed to conflict with any other federal law, rule, or regulation. Thus, other laws we have studied, including those based on equal opportunity and veteran or other protected status rights may have an impact on the construction and interpretation of such **employee benefit plans**. States have been frustrated by the complete preemption of the federal law in the area of **pension plans**, but as our study of health insurance cases will reveal, they have been able to retain jurisdiction in some important **welfare benefits** arenas such as health insurance.

While **ERISA** is a very complex area of the law, some broad characterizations are helpful. The statute has four elements:

Summary Plan Description
ERISA requirement that employers inform participants in writing about their rights to benefits. The description must be distributed to employees within 90 days of their eligibility for the benefit plan.

- Title I protects employees' rights to their benefits. In this regard, employers must inform participants about their rights in a **summary plan description. Benefit plan administrators** are required to provide periodic, no cost reports to employees and to respond to employee inquiries. The **summary plan description** may take one of two forms. It may take the form of providing a booklet summarizing the plan in its essentials to each employee or of a notice posted on the company's bulletin board containing all the information required by law. The employees must be advised that a copy of the complete plan is available for inspection. The **summary plan description** must be provided to employees within 90 days of their becoming eligible under the benefit plans. **ERISA** requires employers to state in specific detail the terms and conditions of the plan in the written plan documents. Oral representations are insufficient and may not be relied on by a plan participant. Employers act as a **fiduciary** to the participants and to the plan. No more than 10 percent of a plan's assets may be invested in the employer's publicly traded stock.
- Title II of **ERISA** outlines the requirements for a retirement plan to receive tax favored or qualified treatment. These requirements include prohibitions against discriminating against senior managers and highly paid individual employees, and they require that certain pension funding and vesting rules be observed. This title also sets ceilings for the maximum amounts to be paid from defined benefit pension plans and the amount of contributions that can be made into a **defined contribution pension plan**. These types of plans will be discussed in this chapter along with **individual retirement accounts**, which this Title also introduced. Title II also sets limits on the maximum tax deduction that can be taken with

respect to a pension plan contribution and states when a penalty may be assessed for early withdrawals.

- Title III of **ERISA** provides that the federal Departments of Labor and Treasury will coordinate their efforts in enforcing **ERISA** requirements.
- Title IV created the **Pension Benefit Guaranty Corporation (PBGC)**, which provides for federally insured benefits when plans are terminated with insufficient resources to meet future plan obligations to participants.[6] In 1980, Congress enacted the **Multiemployer Pension Plan Amendments Act of 1980**, intended to prevent employers from withdrawing from **multiemployer pension plans** without paying their share of unfunded, vested retirement benefit liabilities. Withdrawal of such firms would threaten the plans' financial solvency. Under this act, a withdrawing employer may pay the amount owed to the fund in a lump sum and escape liability for future contributions.

The **PBGC** is privately funded and does not receive a portion of federal tax revenues. Its funding sources include the insurance premiums paid by sponsors of **defined benefit pension plans** and investment income. The law fixes the maximum pension benefit guaranteed by the **PBGC**. In 2010, for workers retiring at age 65, the sum was about $54,000 per year.[7]

Unlike the protections afforded under a **defined contribution fund**, contributions are always fully funded in a **defined contribution plan**. The **PBGC** does not provide insurance for such plans.

Defined Benefit Pension Plan
A type of retirement plan in which a participant is guaranteed a certain payout or monthly stipend at retirement. Form 5500 is required to be filed annually by the plan administrator. An actuary must determine annual contributions, which are primarily funded by the employer. Generally must be offered to all employees at least 21 years of age who worked at least 1,000 hours in a previous year.

Employee Pension Benefit Plans

Retirement plans may be characterized as either a **defined benefit** or a **defined contribution plan** according to how the benefits are to be determined. In the first type, a plan participant is guaranteed a certain payout or monthly stipend at retirement. This is usually calculated based on the employee's salary and the number of years of participation in the plan. The second type, the **defined contribution plan**, will provide a payout at retirement that will vary among participants based on the amount of money each contributed (or that was contributed by employers on employees' behalf, as through matching programs) and the performance of the investments made with these contributions. A third type of plan, not widely used, is known as a cash balance or hybrid plan because it features parts of both the **defined benefit** and the **contribution plans**. The scope of such a plan is beyond the reach of this text; however, it is a highly complex area of pension law as it involves hypothetical accounts with cash balances. Companies and employees should proceed cautiously with regard to converting a **defined benefit plan** to a hybrid or cash balance plan.

Defined Contribution Plan
A type of retirement plan that provides a payout at retirement that will vary among participants based on the amount of money each contributed (or that was contributed by employers on employees' behalf, as through matching programs) and the performance of the investments made with these contributions.

In a **defined contribution plan**, money or property contributions (such as company stock) are paid into an individual retirement account for each participant. The contributions are invested in the stock market, and the profits or losses resulting from those investments are credited to the participant's account. When the employee retires, the amount in the account is used to provide retirement income, usually through the purchase of an **annuity contract**. An **annuity** is an investment offered by institutions that will pay to the individual annuitant a certain sum each month until death. Some plans are exempt from **ERISA** provisions. They include unfunded plans maintained by an employer for providing deferred compensation to senior managers and highly compensated individuals, individual retirement accounts or annuities, and certain types of employee-funded trusts.

In recent years, virtually all public companies have terminated their **defined benefit plans** in favor of **defined contribution plans**. Current practice is to shift the risk of funding retirement benefits from the employer to the employee. However, as noted at the beginning of this chapter, Congress may strengthen Social Security retirement benefits to reduce the risk posed to employees who have suffered reversals in their retirement funds as a result of the disastrous stock market valuations in their personally directed investment plans.

Types of Retirement Plans

Many types of programs are recognized by the IRS in the regulations it issued under the authority of the Internal Revenue Code (IRC) and the Department of Labor. Among the **defined contribution plans** are the **401(k)**, the **SIMPLE IRA**, and the **Keogh plans**.

401(k) Plan

401(k)
A type of defined contribution retirement plan through which employees may choose to defer a portion of their salary; the funds in this account are invested in a variety of investment opportunities, including stocks, bonds, mutual funds, and other investment vehicles.

This type of plan is the most popular type of retirement plan in current use. A **401(k)** is qualified to operate when it meets the standards set forth in the IRC. When the law went into effect in 1980, company sponsors quickly adopted it so employees would not be taxed on income they chose to receive as deferred compensation. The **401(k)** can take many forms, including employer-sponsored profit sharing and stock bonus plans. In its usual form, the plan allows eligible employees to make pretax elective deferrals of their wages through a payroll deduction. The employee elects to have a portion of his or her wages paid directly to his or her **401(k)** account. The effect is to defer income taxation of those wages until they are withdrawn from the account. Typically, a retired worker is in a lower tax bracket in retirement than during employment and can realize a savings in income taxes for the amounts deferred. In addition, the employer may also contribute on behalf of all participants by matching the contributions made by the plan participants. Various rules apply to nondiscrimination aspects of the plan so that the plan does not favor the highly compensated employee participant. In its most common form as a salary reduction plan, the employee participant selects from a number of investment options, usually mutual funds. These funds invest in a variety of opportunities, including common and preferred stocks, bonds, foreign and domestic bonds, natural resources, and real estate. The employee can generally reallocate money among these investment choices at any time. In a less common form, the employer appoints trustees who decide how the plan's assets will be invested for the entire class of employee participants.

In another type of **401(k) defined contribution plan**, the employer may establish a **profit-sharing plan**, in which the plan specifies, for example, a certain percentage of company profits will be contributed to the plan and distributed among the plan participants. In a final type of **defined contribution plan**, known as a money purchase pension plan, a percentage of the employees' annual salaries are contributed.

Among the benefits of **401(k)** plans is that they are tax-qualified plans covered by **ERISA**, meaning their assets are generally protected from creditors of the account holder. Moreover, when an employee leaves a job, the **401(k)** account is portable and may be taken with the employee and "rolled over" into an IRA. In the event of the employer's bankruptcy, the federal Pension Benefit Guaranty Corporation insures all plans. The amount of protection thus afforded is quite limited, as the protection extends neither to losses in the value of investments selected by participants nor to the value of employer stock in the plan if the employer liquidates.

Account balances must begin to be drawn out beginning April 1 of the calendar year after the attainment of age $70\frac{1}{2}$, unless the participant is still employed at the company sponsoring the **401(k)** plan. A **401(k)** plan is much cheaper for an employer to maintain than a **defined benefit pension plan**. Instead of making required pension contributions, the employer need only pay for plan administration costs if it elects not to match employee contributions to the plan. The employer can elect in one year to match the contribution and in another year not to do so. Plan sponsors want to take advantage of the exemption from the **fiduciary duty** to diversify plan assets to minimize the risk of damage claims from participants arising from poor investment outcomes. Thus, **defined contribution plans** have individual accounts for each participant, and the sponsor avoids the risk of substantial fluctuations in the value in the investment accounts. Similar plans are available for government workers under IRC §457(g) and for those employed by educational institutions under IRC §453.

CONTRIBUTION LIMITS. Given its advantages, Congress did limit the amount to which an employee can defer pretax salaries. In 2010, the limit was $16,500. In years thereafter, the limit may be indexed for inflation, increasing in increments of $500. Employees who have reached the age of at least 50 may make additional "catch up" contributions of up to $5,500 for 2010. After 2010, the catch-up provision will be indexed to inflation. If any employee contributes too much to a plan in a given year, the excess contribution as well as the earnings on that excess will be taxable and cannot remain in the otherwise qualified plan. In addition, the employer contributions cannot exceed their own limits. In 2009, that sum was $49,000.

WITHDRAWAL OF FUNDS. Almost universally, employers impose restrictions on employee withdrawals while the person remains employed by the company and is under the age of $59\frac{1}{2}$. Any withdrawal permitted before that age is subject to an excise tax equal to 10 percent of the amount distributed, including any amounts withdrawn to pay expenses due to a hardship, except for those allowed by the IRC. The amounts withdrawn are subject to ordinary income tax as well as the excise tax of 10 percent. Some limited exceptions include the employee's death, the employee's total and permanent disability, qualified medical expenses exceeding 7.5 percent of the employee's adjusted gross income, and a qualified domestic relations order issued by a court adjudicating a divorce proceeding involving the employee.

SIMPLE IRA

The **SIMPLE IRA** was created so that small businesses could offer an effective, cost-efficient plan to their employees. This type of plan is available to employers with 100 or fewer employees who received at least $5,000 in compensation from the employer for the preceding calendar year. Employees who are eligible to participate in a **SIMPLE IRA** plan may not receive any contributions or benefit accruals under any other retirement plan offered by the employer.

Keogh Plans

Keogh plans include both self-employed persons and their employees. **Keogh plans** are subject to **ERISA** coverage. As with the other plans mentioned, pretax money placed in a **Keogh** grows tax-free until it is withdrawn. Full-time employees must be included in a **Keogh** plan if they have worked for the employer for more than three years. A **Keogh** plan can set eligibility requirements, but as with other plans, it may not discriminate in favor of highly compensated employees. It can have requirements for minimum age (not to exceed 21 years of age), length of service, full-time employment (more than 1,000 hours), and vesting. The disadvantages of the **Keogh** plan include all the costs and complexities associated with **defined contribution plans**, including penalties for early withdrawal and mandatory withdrawals after reaching $70\frac{1}{2}$ years of age, whether or not the participant has retired.

Employee Stock Ownership Plans

An **employee stock ownership plan (ESOP)** is a type of **ERISA** plan designed to invest primarily in the stock of the employer who created it. It is both an employee retirement benefit plan and an opportunity for employees to own the stock of the company. The **ESOP** is a very common form of employee participation in company ownership. The ESOP operates through a trust, established by the employer, that accepts tax deductible contributions from the company to purchase company stock. The contributions made by the company are distributed to individual employee accounts in the trust. The employees receive amounts of stock according to a formula set up by the plan. Employees cash out the shares they own after vesting in the plan or on leaving the company. The employees may also receive their vested portion of these payments upon termination of employment, disability, death, or retirement. There are several tax advantages of establishing an **ESOP**. Although **ESOPs** are exempt from certain **ERISA** requirements, such as asset diversification, the **fiduciary** duties of loyalty and care as well as the prohibition of self-dealing by trustees are in effect. The plan administrators are deemed **fiduciaries**. They can be held liable if they knowingly participate in improper transactions.

Employers' Fiduciary Duties

ERISA defines a **fiduciary** as a person or business entity who (i) exercises either discretionary authority or control regarding the management of the plan or its assets; or (ii) renders investment advice for a fee or other direct or indirect compensation concerning the plan monies or property, or who has authority or responsibility to do so; or (iii) has any discretionary authority or responsibility in the administration of the plan.[8] In applying **ERISA**, courts will cloak persons with the mantle of the **fiduciary** if they were acting as one; the courts liberally apply **fiduciary duties** to effect the protections intended under the law. The **fiduciary** status is imposed on anyone who carries out **fiduciary duties**. Under **ERISA**, "a person is a **fiduciary** with respect to a plan to the extent (i) he exercises any discretionary authority or discretionary control respecting management of such plan or exercises any authority or control respecting management or disposition of its assets, (ii) he renders investment advice for a fee or other compensation, direct or indirect, with respect to any moneys or other property of such plan, or has any authority or responsibility to do so, or (iii) he has any discretionary authority or discretionary responsibility in the administration of such plan."[9]

ERISA requires every **employee benefit plan** to have an **administrator**, and each plan will specifically designate the person or entity that is to serve as an **administrator**. By the very nature of the duties imposed on the **plan administrator**, the administrator is a **fiduciary** for the purposes of ensuring the integrity of a plan. The administrator owes **fiduciary** duties *to the plan and not to the individual beneficiaries*. The law is clear with regard to the **fiduciary** duties imposed on a **plan administrator**:

> A **fiduciary** shall discharge his duties with respect to a plan solely in the interest of the participants and beneficiaries and
>
> for the exclusive purpose of: providing benefits to participants and beneficiaries; and defraying the reasonable expenses of administering the plan;
>
> with the care, skill, prudence, and diligence, under the circumstances then prevailing, that a prudent person acting in like capacity and familiar with such matters would use in the conduct of an enterprise of a like character and like aims;
>
> by diversifying the investments of the plan to minimize the risk of large losses, unless, under the particular circumstances, it is clearly not prudent to do so; and
>
> in accordance with the documents and instruments governing the plan to the extent that those documents and instruments are consistent with the provisions of **ERISA**.

These **fiduciary** duties include loyalty, the prudence a reasonable person would exercise in investing, and diversification of the portfolio while staying in compliance with the plan documents. The Supreme Court has held that a private cause lawsuit may be brought by a **plan beneficiary** against a nonfiduciary who participated in a transaction with the plan that was prohibited by **ERISA**. A provision of **ERISA** authorizes a "participant, beneficiary, or fiduciary" of a plan to bring a civil action to obtain "appropriate equitable relief" to redress violations of **ERISA**.

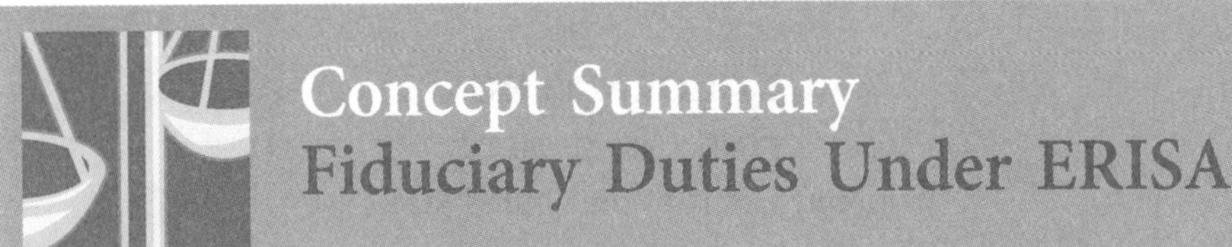

Concept Summary
Fiduciary Duties Under ERISA

A person acting in a fiduciary capacity owes the duties of:

- Ensuring all actions and transactions performed on behalf of the plan are for the exclusive purpose of providing benefits to plan participants and defraying reasonable expenses of administering the plan. The Supreme Court has found fiduciary liability in misstatements about future employer decisions relative to the plan;
- Acting with prudence; the fiduciary must act with the same care, skill, prudence, and diligence with which a prudent person familiar with such matters would act;
- Diversifying plan assets (this rule does not apply to ESOPs); and
- Acting in accordance with plan documents, unless they are inconsistent with ERISA.

Many courts are expanding the definition of *fiduciary* to include the company's board of directors or its compensation committee if the directors have the power to appoint plan fiduciaries. This often occurs in the case of an ESOP and is especially true when the decision-makers of a closely held and related entity serve as ERISA fiduciaries with respect to the appointment and removal of trustees or the plan administrator.

ERISA prohibits fiduciaries from engaging in the following types of transactions:

- Self-dealing: A fiduciary may not use plan assets for personal gain, engage in transactions on behalf of parties whose interests are adverse to the plan, or realize personal gain in connection with any plan transaction.
- Party-in-interest transactions: Subject to certain exceptions, a fiduciary may not provide services to the plan or sell, loan, exchange, or transfer any plan assets.

Fiduciary Breach Liability imposed on a fiduciary who fails to run a plan solely in the interest of participants and beneficiaries and for the exclusive purpose of providing benefits and paying plan expenses. A fiduciary must act prudently, diversify the plan's investments to minimize the risk of large losses, and avoid conflicts of interest.

A plan **fiduciary** is personally liable if the **fiduciary** breaches its prescribed duties. An employer that is also the administrator of its employees' **welfare benefit plan** violates the **fiduciary** obligations if it knowingly and substantially deceives the plan's beneficiaries as to the financial viability of the new plan entity and the future of its benefits. Such was the lesson learned in our next case.

CASE 16.1

EMPLOYERS MAY BE DEEMED ERISA FIDUCIARIES AND SUED FOR MISLEADING EMPLOYEES

VARITY CORP. V. HOWE

516 U.S. 489 (1996)

Supreme Court of the United States

Facts. Charles Howe and other employees formerly worked for Massey-Ferguson, Inc., a farm equipment manufacturer, and a wholly owned subsidiary of Varity Corporation. Howe and the others were participants in a benefit plan subject to the provisions of ERISA. When this division began losing money, Varity transferred the benefit plan assets into a separate subsidiary and persuaded the employees of the failing divisions to change employers and benefit plans. It conveyed the message that the employees' benefits would remain safe when they transferred. In fact, the new corporation was insolvent the day it was created and following its second year of operations it ended up in a bankruptcy-like condition. The employees sued under ERISA claiming that through the deception they had been led to withdraw from their old plan and had forfeited their benefits. The Court of Appeals for the Eighth Circuit affirmed the federal district court's decision that the companies had violated §404 of ERISA, which required the plan's fiduciaries to administer the plan "solely in the interest of the [plan's] participants and beneficiaries" and that §502 gave the plaintiffs a right to "appropriate equitable relief . . . to redress" the harm the deception had caused them. The employer appealed and the Supreme Court granted *certiorari* to resolve differences among the various federal courts of appeals as to the scope of remedies available under that section.

Issue. Did Varity and its subsidiary act as ERISA fiduciaries when they deliberately misled the plan beneficiaries?

Language of the Court. Breyer, J.: **Varity was both an employer and the benefit plan's administrator, as ERISA permits. . . . But, obviously, not all of Varity's business activities involved plan management or administration. Varity argues that when it communicated with its Massey-Ferguson workers about transferring to Massey Combines, it was not administering or managing the plan; rather, it was acting only in its capacity as an employer and not as a plan administrator. The District Court, however, held that when the misrepresentations regarding employee benefits were made, Varity was wearing its "fiduciary," as well as its "employer," hat.**

In arguing about ERISA's remedies for breaches of fiduciary obligation, Varity says that Congress intended ERISA's fiduciary standards to protect only the financial integrity of the plan, not individual beneficiaries. This intent, says Varity, is shown by the fact that Congress did not provide remedies for individuals harmed by such breaches; rather, Congress limited relief to remedies that would benefit only the plan itself. This argument fails, however, because, in our view, Congress did provide remedies for individual beneficiaries harmed by breaches of fiduciary duty, as we shall next discuss. The remaining question before us is whether or not the remedial provision of ERISA that the beneficiaries invoked, authorizes this lawsuit for individual relief. . . . [W]ithin ERISA's "Civil Enforcement" provision (as it stood at the times relevant to this lawsuit):

> **Sec. 502. (a) A civil action may be brought—**
>
> **(1) by a participant or beneficiary— . . .**
>
> **(2) by the Secretary, or by a participant, beneficiary or fiduciary for appropriate relief under section 409 [entitled "Liability for Breach of Fiduciary Duty"];**
>
> **(3) by a participant, beneficiary, or fiduciary (A) to enjoin any act or practice which violates any provision of this title or the terms of the plan, or (B) to obtain other appropriate equitable relief (i) to redress such violations or (ii) to enforce any provisions of this title or the terms of the plan;**

The words of subsection three—"appropriate equitable relief" to "redress" any "act or practice which violates any provision of this title"—are broad enough to cover individual relief for breach of a fiduciary obligation. . . . For these reasons, the judgment of the Court of Appeals is affirmed.

Decision. Yes. Varity was acting as an ERISA "fiduciary" when it misled its employees. The Supreme Court relied on the district court's findings, unchallenged by Varity, that when Varity misrepresented the facts, it was acting in the capacity of a plan fiduciary within the meaning of ERISA. Reasonable employees could have assumed that the company was speaking both as an employer and as plan administrator.

CASE QUESTIONS

Critical Legal Thinking. Does ERISA's general purpose of protecting beneficiary interests favor providing employees with expansive remedies? To what degree will a plan fiduciary's behavior be affected by the prospect of unlimited personal liability for breach of its fiduciary duties? If the risk were that great, who would voluntarily serve as a plan administrator?

Business Ethics. Was it ethical for Varity to rely on a strained and technical interpretation of ERISA to support its actions? To what degree do you think a company should be allowed legally to shed its financial obligations under its ERISA plans?

Contemporary Business. What impact will this decision have on the administration of ERISA plans and the investment choices made available to plan participants?

Following the issuance of the *Varity v. Howe* decision, the federal circuit courts of appeals issued a number of conflicting opinions on its application. They differed on the types of available remedies for **ERISA** claims and whether a single individual participant as opposed to all plan participants had to be injured to sue. The law was unclear whether recovery from a **fiduciary** for breach of **fiduciary duty** would be limited to recovery for the benefit of the plan as a whole and *not* cover an individual participant. These differences were the reason the Court granted *certiorari* in the next case.

CASE 16.2

ERISA PLAN PARTICIPANTS MAY SUE PLAN ADMINISTRATORS FOR BREACH OF FIDUCIARY DUTIES

LARUE V. DEWOLFF, BOBERG & ASSOCIATES

552 U.S. 248 (2008)

United States Supreme Court

Facts. James LaRue's former employer sponsored a 401(k) plan, and individual plan participants made investment decisions. Mr. LaRue was a participant, and he claimed that the plan's fiduciaries failed to follow his instruction to sell securities in his retirement account. This failure to switch to safer investments resulted in a loss of $150,000 in his retirement account. The company plan managers argued that ERISA did not permit an individual retirement account holder to sue a retirement plan to recover for such losses. The court of appeals affirmed the federal district court's dismissal of his lawsuit because §502 of ERISA provided remedies only for entire classes of plan participants and not for an individual participant. The Supreme Court granted *certiorari* to clarify its ruling in a prior decision that denied recovery to an individual participant.

Issue. May an individual plan participant sue ERISA plan administrators for breach of fiduciary duties for failing to follow the participant's investment instructions?

Language of the Court. Stevens, J.: **As the case comes to us we must assume that respondents breached fiduciary obligations defined in §409(a) [which are duties imposed regulating the proper management, administration and investment of plan assets], and that those breaches had an adverse impact on the value of the plan assets in petitioner's individual account. Whether petitioner can prove those allegations and whether respondents may have valid defenses to the claim are matters not before us. Although the record does not reveal the relative size of petitioner's account, the legal issue under §502(a)(2) is the same whether his account includes 1% or 99% of the total assets in the plan. As we explained . . . in Varity Corp. v. Howe . . . §502(a) of ERISA identifies six types of civil actions that may be brought by various parties. The second, which is at issue in this case, authorizes the Secretary of Labor as well as plan participants, beneficiaries, and fiduciaries, to bring actions on behalf of a plan to recover for violations of the obligations defined in §409(a). The principal statutory duties imposed on fiduciaries by that section "relate to the proper management, administration, and investment of fund assets," with an eye toward ensuring that "the benefits authorized by the plan" are ultimately paid to participants and beneficiaries. . . . The misconduct alleged by the petitioner in this case falls squarely within that category.**

We . . . hold that although §502(a)(2) does not provide a remedy for individual injuries distinct from plan injuries, that provision does authorize recovery for fiduciary breaches that impair the value of plan assets in a participant's individual account.

Decision. Yes. ERISA plan fiduciaries are subject to the damage claims of individual participants based on alleged fiduciary breaches in handling an individual participant's account.

CASE QUESTIONS

Critical Legal Thinking. Chief Justice Roberts stated in a concurring opinion that the court's decision might allow some employees to restate a retirement benefits claim as a breach of fiduciary duty to overcome the many obstacles Congress enacted to protect retirement plan administrators. As an employer, would this decision give you any concern? What should be done to minimize such risks to the persons acting as plan administrators?

Business Ethics. ERISA was created under a different retirement and fringe benefit climate than the one existing today. Most of ERISA applied to defined benefit plans and has few to no remedies for today's more popular 401(k) defined contribution plans and fringe benefit plans, such as health insurance. The Court refused to apply a prior case on a contrary ground, as it applied to a defined benefit plan as opposed to the defined contribution plan, as in this case. Why do you think it did so?

Contemporary Business. This case poses the possibility of applying a cause of action to a variety of other types of ERISA claims. What legislative changes would you suggest Congress adopt to balance the interests of plan participants and administrators?

This decision does not address the circumstances, if any, when a plan administrator should override the investment choices of plan participants. Do you think a fiduciary should be able to do so to protect the beneficiary from financial disaster?

Plan beneficiaries can sue the **plan fiduciaries**, such as the trustees of an **ESOP**, for damages. Under **ERISA**, fiduciaries can be held jointly and severally liable for all losses related to their misconduct. When a nonparty to a transaction covered by **ERISA** knowingly participates in a breach by **fiduciaries** to the transaction, even they can be sued for **ERISA** violations as well. As the Supreme Court explained in its 2000 decision in *Harris Trust & Savings Bank v. Salomon Smith Barney*, to state an **ERISA** violation "the plaintiff must allege only that a fiduciary violated . . . [**ERISA**] and the nonfiduciary knowingly participated in the conduct that constituted the violation."[10]

Example: Several current and former employees sued the trustees of the company's **ESOP**. In his capacity as president of Noll Manufacturing Co., Clair Couturier, with the consent of the other ESOP trustees, diverted almost $35 million, or about one-third of the company's assets, to himself. A federal court held that the **ESOP fiduciaries** breached their duties by paying excessive compensation to Couturier. However, the liability did not end at that point. The court also held that Couturier's brother, who served on the Noll board of directors, knowingly participated in the prohibited transactions of his brother. The court also held that if an officer is knowingly involved in a prohibited **ERISA** transaction, the officer might be liable to **plan beneficiaries**, even though the officer was not a plan fiduciary at the time. It also barred officers from having their attorney's fees paid by the **ESOP**.[11]

Example: Founded in 1857, the Tribune Company (Tribune) became a publicly traded company worth billions that owned, among other assets, 10 daily newspapers, 25 television stations, websites, significant real estate holdings, and the Chicago Cubs baseball team. Eventually, the board of directors agreed to an **ESOP** transaction that would take the company private and make the employees owners in December 2007. Sam Zell helped engineer the transaction that left the Chicago Tribune Company **ESOP** with almost $13 billion in debt, even if he was not a **fiduciary** to the **ESOP** at the time. Zell was not a **fiduciary** when he proposed the deal, but he joined the Tribune board of directors after the deal was made but before the merger. The Tribune was forced into bankruptcy following the transaction. Six workers filed suit contending that the buyout deal was imprudent because it resulted in the **ESOP** acquiring too much debt. The plaintiffs argued that the **ESOP** paid too much for its shares of the Tribune Company, that the shares were not marketable, that the Tribune Company paid too much for the shares it bought to take the company private, and that it should not have given Zell the right to voting shares to control the transaction or enter into a voting agreement relating to the shares. A U.S. district court rejected real estate investor Sam Zell's request to dismiss the **ESOP** breach of **fiduciary duty** lawsuit. The court held that the employees' lawsuit stated a claim against Zell "for knowingly participating in a **fiduciary breach**."[12]

CASE 16.3

AN ADMINISTRATOR WHO EXERCISES DISCRETION IN DETERMINING ENTITLEMENT TO BENEFITS AND PAYS BENEFIT PLAN BENEFITS MAY HAVE A CONFLICT OF INTEREST

METROPOLITAN LIFE INSURANCE CO. V. GLENN

554 U.S. __________, 128 S. CT. 2343 (2008)

Supreme Court of the United States

Facts. MetLife was an ERISA plan administrator for the Sears, Roebuck & Company's long-term disability insurance plan. As administrator of the plan, MetLife had the discretionary authority to determine whether an employee's benefits claim was valid. MetLife was then responsible as the insurer of the plan for paying valid claims. MetLife terminated the benefits of Wanda Glenn, a Sears employee. She was granted 24 months of benefits following her diagnosis of a heart disorder. She was encouraged by MetLife to apply for permanent disability benefits under Social Security. When MetLife determined that she was capable of performing sedentary work, it denied her application for benefits. She sought review of the district court ruling that denied her relief. The U.S. Court of Appeals for the Sixth Circuit reversed, finding the fact that MetLife had both determined eligibility for benefits and paid benefits to be a conflict of interest warranting set aside of MetLife's denial of benefits to Glenn. The Supreme Court granted MetLife's petition for *certiorari.*

Issue. Does an ERISA plan administrator have a conflict of interest when it both evaluates and pays claims in making discretionary benefit determinations?

Language of the Court. Breyer, J.: That answer is clear where it is the employer that both funds the plan and evaluates the claims. In such a circumstance, "every dollar provided in benefits is a dollar spent by . . . the employer; and every dollar saved . . . is a dollar in [the employer's] pocket." (Citation omitted.) The employer's fiduciary interest may counsel in favor of granting a borderline claim while its immediate financial interest counsels to the contrary. Thus, the employer has an "interest . . . conflicting with that of the beneficiaries," the type of conflict that judges must take into account when they review the discretionary acts of a trustee of a common-law trust.

[W]hen judges review the lawfulness of benefit denials, they will often take account of several different considerations of which a conflict of interest is one. This kind of review is no stranger to the judicial system. Not only trust law, but also administrative law, can ask judges to determine lawfulness by taking account of several different, often case-specific, factors, reaching a result by weighing all together. . . .

In such instances, any one factor will act as a tiebreaker when the other factors are closely balanced, the degree of closeness necessary depending upon the tiebreaking factor's inherent or case-specific importance. The conflict of interest at issue here, for example, should prove more important (perhaps of great importance) where circumstances suggest a higher likelihood that it affected the benefits decision, including, but not limited to, cases where an insurance company administrator has a history of biased claims administration.

The Court of Appeals' opinion in the present case illustrates the combination-of-factors method of review. The record says little about MetLife's efforts to assure accurate claims assessment. The Court of Appeals gave the conflict weight to some degree; its opinion suggests that, in context, the court would not have found the conflict alone determinative. . . . The court instead focused more heavily on other factors. In particular, the court found questionable the fact that MetLife had encouraged Glenn to argue to the Social Security Administration that she could do no work, received the bulk of the benefits of her success in doing so (the remainder going to the lawyers it recommended), and then ignored the agency's finding in concluding that Glenn could in fact do sedentary work. . . . This course of events was not only an important factor in its own right (because it suggested procedural unreasonableness), but also would have justified the court in giving more weight to the conflict (because MetLife's seemingly inconsistent positions were both financially advantageous).

Decision. Yes. MetLife had a conflict of interest and abused its discretion in denying benefits.

CASE QUESTIONS

Critical Legal Thinking. Do you recognize that the applicability of this decision would also apply to employers who administer their own benefit plans? What risks are posed to plan administrators?

Business Ethics. What advice would you have given to MetLife to avoid the conflict of interest issues that it encountered?

Contemporary Business. How should it have treated the claims department relative to other parts of the company? Can you think of other circumstances whereby a company has liability to others for conflicts of interest within its decision-making processes?

Benefit plan administrators are subject to the inherent conflict of interest caused by a **fiduciary** requirement to keep the plan financially sound while at the same time making benefit claim decisions for plan beneficiaries. This area of benefits law has generated much litigation following the Court's decision in *Glenn*. The reason is that the *Glenn* Court explicitly declined to specify how courts should resolve the conflict. In federal appellate case law subsequent to the *Glenn* decision, the courts have stated that a beneficiary must show that the conflict influenced the denial of the benefit claim. Courts have required claimants show that the administrator's procedures were so flawed that they influenced the administrator's denial of the claim.[13] One court suggested that if a plan reasonably safeguarded participants' interests to overcome the tendency of plan administrators *to favor unconsciously* the financial welfare of the plan and the administrator acted reasonably, then the plan administrator's action should be left undisturbed.

Example: Michael Marrs ceased working for Motorola because of a psychiatric condition and began drawing benefits under the company's disability income plan. Six years later the company amended the plan to place a two-year limit on benefits for disability resulting from "mental, nervous, alcohol, [or] drug-related" conditions, including Marrs's. Previously, Motorola had imposed no time limit on the receipt of such benefits. Marrs sued the company on behalf of himself and others in the same position in a class-action lawsuit. He relied on the Supreme Court decision in Glenn. The court held that "it is thus not the existence of a conflict of interest, which is a given in almost all ERISA cases — but the *gravity* of the conflict, as inferred from the circumstances, that is critical." Marrs lost because the court could find no indication that the plan administrator's conflict of interest in amending the plan caused him to *unconsciously* decide against the applicant and in favor of the plan.[14]

The liability of a **plan administrator** in a **defined benefit plan** is much clearer than in respect to a **defined contribution plan** wherein the participant directs the investment of the funds. Many employees experienced great financial loss when the contributions they made or their matching employers' contributions were the common stock of the company. Following the spectacular failure of so many public companies, employees who did not or could not adequately diversify their **401(k)** stock portfolio beyond ownership of their employer's common stock experienced the loss of their retirement savings. We can expect more legislation in this area requiring diversification of invested assets within **defined contribution plans**.

ERISA's Discrimination Provisions

ERISA prohibits an employer from discharging, suspending, disciplining, or otherwise discriminating "against a participant or beneficiary for exercising any right to which he is entitled under the provisions of an employee benefit plan . . . or for the purpose of interfering with the attainment of any right to which such participant may become entitled under the plan" (29 U.S.C. §1140). Plaintiffs alleging **discrimination** under **ERISA** bear the burden of proving the employer intentionally discriminated against the employee for interfering with benefits.

Plan administrators must be alert to **discrimination claims** with regard to all aspects of the **pension plan**. Sometimes claims may arise even when the administrators' actions are based on sound actuarial decisions. For example, the U.S. Supreme Court held in *City of Los Angeles v. Manhart*[15] that the Los Angeles Department of Water and Power discriminated against female employees by requiring them to contribute a higher percentage of their wages to the pension plan than was required of males. This decision was based on a determination made following a study of mortality tables and its own experience that females lived longer and would be paid retirement benefits for longer periods than would males. The Court noted that not all females would live longer than their male counterparts and that they would be harmed by such a policy by receiving less compensation over time. The Court held that the underlying policy of **ERISA** was to promote fairness to individuals rather than fairness to entire classes of employees, such as females. The *Manhart* holding reflects the influence of equal opportunity laws on the interpretation and application of a pension plan.

Courts carefully parse the facts of alleged **discrimination claims** arising under **ERISA**. As long all participants are affected by any plan conditions or changes, a **discrimination claim** might not be well founded. This will not be true, however, if a condition or change singles out a class of employees. For example, the federal Fifth Circuit Court of Appeals has permitted an employer to respond to an AIDS-afflicted employee's filing of a health insurance benefit claim by reducing the $1 million lifetime maximum payment to $5,000 for the treatment of AIDS. Although the claimant was the only person in the plan with AIDS and the reduction was made immediately following the filing of the claim, the court held that **ERISA** was not violated. The court took note of the fact that the employer could change all employees' level of benefits at any time. This decision in the case of *McGann v. H&H Music Co.*[16] was allowed to stand when the Supreme Court denied *certiorari.*[17] The Supreme Court's position with regard to employer's modifications to welfare benefit plans is that they are legal as long as they do not discriminate against individuals. In contrast to this decision, the Eleventh Court of Appeals found that a real estate company violated **ERISA** when it did not wish to pay for health insurance and a **401(k)** plan for one group of employees but kept such benefits in force for others.[18] Students are cautioned that the *McGann* decision would probably not be decided in the same way today, following the passage of the Americans with Disabilities Act.

Nonqualified Deferred Compensation Plan
A contractual agreement in which an employee or independent contractor agrees to be paid in the future for services currently rendered. Payments usually start at termination of employment, including by retirement, death, or disability.

Nonqualified Deferred Compensation Plans

A **nonqualified deferred compensation plan** is an unfunded contract that involves the employer's promise to employees to pay an amount of money to them in the future. No funds are set aside in trust for these employees' benefit. An employee therefore must rely on the general financial solvency of the company only as of the time of payment. For example, if an employer maintained a salary deferral plan for employees, the payment of that future summay be called into question depending on the future financial success of the enterprise. Sometimes these plans, also known as **"top-hat pension plans,"** are unfunded, executive deferred compensation plans. As an unfunded liability, the plan is exempt from **ERISA**'s coverage.

Top-Hat Pension Plan
A type of unfunded, executive deferred compensation plan that is exempt from most ERISA regulations but subject to annual reporting and disclosure requirements.

Entitlement to Participation

ERISA requires that as a condition of participation, a plan cannot require a period of employment service beyond the date the employee attains 21 years of age or the date the employee completes one "year of service." **ERISA** defines 65 years as the normal retirement age of participants in such a plan but allows **pension plans** to define that age as later than 65 years. A **qualified plan** must meet certain minimum participation rules to ensure the plan does not discriminate in favor of executives or highly compensated individuals. Employers may exclude certain categories of employees from coverage (such as temporary or probationary employees) and need not include those persons who do not meet the common law definition of employee.

Vesting and Enforcement

Generally, a pension plan must include certain minimum **vesting** requirements. Both **defined benefit** and **defined contribution plans** must provide that a participant's right to accrued benefits becomes nonforfeitable at certain rates during the years of continued employment and must contain a provision that a retirement benefit becomes vested on reaching normal retirement age under the plan. **Vesting** gives the employee the absolute right to receive those benefits even if employment is terminated prior to retirement. Usually the employer sets the period for **vesting** of benefits. **Multiemployer pension plans** generally employ **"cliff vesting,"** which provides employees with a nonforfeitable right to the benefits after a fixed number of years of service or accumulation. The law also provides for immediate **vesting** of benefits upon plan termination.

Vesting
The point at which a participant's right to accrued benefits becomes nonforfeitable.

ERISA provides the exclusive remedy for plan participants and beneficiaries seeking redress for their rights under an **ERISA** plan. A plaintiff must allege the fiduciary's conduct interfered with a right the employee has or may acquire. The secretary of labor or private parties may sue in the federal district court in the district in which the plan is administered. In any civil action for enforcement of **ERISA** rights by a party or beneficiary to the plan, the federal court may in its discretion award reasonable attorney's fees and court costs.[19] This is known as the **"fee shifting"** provision and poses risk to those who pursue extended **ERISA** litigation on tenuous grounds while rewarding parties with genuine claims with the ability to recover fees from a well-financed corporate employer in litigation that would have otherwise been too expensive to pursue.

Welfare Benefit Plans

ERISA does not require employers to provide health insurance to their employees or retirees. When offered by an employer, such plans vary in their range of coverage. Typically, they can include health insurance or reimbursement (indemnity), prescription drug coverage, dental insurance, disability insurance, and vision insurance. These benefits are known as **welfare benefit plans**, and through them state courts and legislatures have made inroads into the otherwise preemptive field of benefit plan regulation enjoyed by the federal government. This is particularly so in the area of state regulation of the insurance companies that issue such policies, as the next case reflects.

CASE 16.4

DESPITE FEDERAL PREEMPTION, STATES HAVE A ROLE IN INDIRECT REGULATION OF CARRIERS THAT UNDERWRITE EMPLOYEE BENEFITS

METROPOLITAN LIFE INSURANCE CO. V. MASSACHUSETTS

471 U.S. 724 (1985)

Supreme Court of the United States

Facts. After the enactment of ERISA, the state of Massachusetts enacted a statute requiring that certain minimum mental health care benefits be provided to state residents who were insured under a general health insurance policy or an employee health care plan covering hospital and surgical expenses. Metropolitan Life as the insurer that issued such policies contended before the Supreme Court that such legislation was preempted by ERISA.

Issue. Does ERISA preempt the right of states to require that health insurance policies provide minimum benefits of coverage?

Language of the Court. Blackmun, J.: **General health insurance typically is sold as group insurance to an employer or other group. Group insurance presently is subject to extensive state regulation, including regulation of the carrier, regulation of the sale and advertising of the insurance, and regulation of the content of the contracts. The substantive terms of group health insurance contracts, in particular, also have been extensively regulated by the States. . . . Section 47B was designed to address problems encountered in treating mental illness in Massachusetts. The Commonwealth determined that its working people needed to be protected against the high cost of treatment for such illness. It also believed that, without insurance, mentally ill workers were often institutionalized in large state mental hospitals, and that mandatory insurance would lead to a higher incidence of more effective treatment in private community mental health centers.**

Though §47B is not denominated a benefit plan law, it bears indirectly but substantially on all insured benefit plans, for it requires them to purchase the mental health benefits specified in the statute when they purchase a certain kind of common insurance policy. The Commonwealth does not argue that §47B, as applied to policies purchased by benefit plans, does not relate to those plans, and we agree with the Supreme Judicial Court that the mandated benefit law, as applied, relates to ERISA plans, and thus is covered by ERISA's broad preemption provision set forth in §514(a). Nonetheless, the sphere in which §514(a) operates was explicitly limited by §514(b)(2). The insurance saving clause preserves any state law "which regulates insurance, banking, or securities." The two preemption sections, while clear enough on their faces, perhaps are not a model of legislative drafting, for while the general preemption clause broadly preempts state law, the saving clause appears broadly to preserve the States' lawmaking power over much of the same regulation. While Congress occasionally decides to return to the States what it has previously taken away, it does not normally do both at the same time.

Section 47B obviously regulates the spreading of risk: as we have indicated, it was intended to effectuate the legislative judgment that the risk of mental health care should be shared. . . . It is also evident that mandated benefit laws directly regulate an integral part of the relationship between the insurer and the policyholder by limiting the type of insurance that an insurer may sell to the policyholder. Finally, the third criterion is present here, for mandated benefit statutes impose requirements only on insurers, with the intent of affecting the relationship between the insurer and the policyholder. Section 47B, then, is the very kind of regulation that this Court has identified as a law that relates to the regulation of the business of insurance as defined in the McCarran-Ferguson Act. Congress was concerned [in the McCarran-Ferguson Act] with the type of state regulation that centers around the contract of insurance. . . . The relationship between insurer and insured, the type of policy which could be issued, its reliability, its interpretation, and enforcement — these were the core of the "business of insurance." [T]he focus [of the statutory term] was on the relationship between the insurance company and the policyholder. Statutes aimed at protecting or regulating this relationship, directly or indirectly, are laws regulating the "business of insurance."

Nor is there any contrary case authority suggesting that laws regulating the terms of insurance contracts should not be understood as laws that regulate insurance. In short, the plain language of the saving clause, its relationship to the other ERISA preemption provisions, and the traditional understanding of insurance regulation, all lead us to the conclusion that mandated benefit laws such as §47B are saved from preemption by the operation of the saving clause. Nothing in the legislative history of ERISA suggests a different result. There is no discussion in that history of the relationship between the general preemption clause and the saving clause, and indeed very little discussion of the saving clause at all.

Decision. No. The Massachusetts statute is a law that regulates insurance and is not preempted by ERISA.

CASE QUESTIONS

Critical Legal Thinking. Review the public policy considerations before the Court. ERISA's broad preemption provision states it shall "supersede any and all State laws insofar as they may now or hereafter relate to any employee benefit plan." Do you think the Court reached a strained interpretation that the "insurance savings" clause allows states to regulate insurance companies? Would the "savings clause" stated in ERISA be rendered meaningless if states were preempted from enacting laws that "relate to" ERISA plans?

Business Ethics. Is the effect of this decision to allow states to indirectly regulate ERISA plans in areas as to which they cannot directly regulate? Is this an ethical approach to dealing with the Tenth Amendment and federal question preemption?

Contemporary Business. Comment on the fact that the Court observed ERISA both preempts state law and preserves state power in such areas of preemption. What importance do you believe the Court placed on the fact that states have been regulating the substantive aspects of contracts of insurance for many years before this case was decided?

CASE 16.5

ERISA DOES NOT PREEMPT STATE REGULATION OF HMOS

RUSH PRUDENTIAL HMO, INC. V. MORAN

536 U.S. 355 (2002)

Supreme Court of the United States

Facts. The petitioner Rush Prudential HMO, Inc. was a health maintenance organization (HMO) that contracts to provide medical services for employee welfare benefit plans covered by ERISA. It denied Moran's request to have surgery performed by an unaffiliated specialist on the ground that the procedure was not medically necessary. Ms. Moran made a written demand for an independent medical review of her claim as permitted by an Illinois statute. The HMO refused her demand, and she sued in state court to compel compliance with the Illinois law. The state court ordered the review that found the treatment necessary.

However, Rush denied the claim again. Rush removed the case to federal court as an ERISA covered claim. The federal district court denied the claim as being preempted by ERISA, but the Seventh Circuit Court of Appeals reversed the district court holding that the state law requiring independent medical review of a denied claim was not preempted by ERISA.

Issue. Is an HMO an insurer for purposes of the insurance saving clause of ERISA preemption?

Language of the Court. Souter, J.: **In trying to extrapolate congressional intent in a case like this, when congressional language seems simultaneously to preempt everything and hardly anything, we "have no choice" but to temper the assumption that "the ordinary meaning . . . accurately expresses the legislative purpose," . . . with the qualification that the historic police powers of the States were not [meant] to be superseded by the Federal Act unless that was the clear and manifest purpose of Congress. . . .**

In Metropolitan Life, we said that in deciding whether a law "regulates insurance" under ERISA's saving clause, we start with a "common-sense view of the matter," . . . under which "a law must not just have an impact on the insurance industry, but must be specifically directed toward that industry." . . . We then test the results of the commonsense enquiry by employing the three factors used to point to insurance laws spared from federal preemption under the McCarran-Ferguson Act. . . . Although this is not the place to plot the exact perimeter of the saving clause, it is generally fair to think of the combined "commonsense" and McCarran-Ferguson factors as parsing the "who" and the "what": when insurers are regulated with respect to their insurance practices, the state law survives ERISA.

The commonsense enquiry focuses on "primary elements of an insurance contract [which is] the spreading and underwriting of a policyholder's risk." The Illinois statute addresses these elements by defining "health maintenance organization" by reference to the risk that it bears. (Citation omitted.) (An HMO "provide[s] or arrange[s] for . . . health care plans under a system which causes any part of the risk of health care delivery to be borne by the organization or its providers.")

In sum, prior to ERISA's passage, Congress demonstrated an awareness of HMOs as risk-bearing organizations subject to state insurance regulation, the state Act defines HMOs by reference to risk bearing, HMOs have taken over much business formerly performed by traditional indemnity insurers, and they are almost universally regulated as insurers under state law. . . . Thus, the Illinois HMO Act is a law "directed toward" the insurance industry, and an "insurance regulation" under a "commonsense" view.

Decision. Yes. ERISA does not preempt the Illinois state law as it relates to the regulation of health maintenance organizations.

CASE QUESTIONS

Critical Legal Thinking. In 2002, a federal judge noted, "We have spilled much ink over the last few decades trying to interpret this statute."[20] Courts have struggled with ERISA's relationship with state laws. They have created distinctions between complete preemption of a state statute and preemption only when there is a direct conflict between ERISA and the state statute. What conditions are inhibiting Congress from clarifying the intent and scope of this important statute?

Business Ethics. When construing a federal statute, what is the proper role of the Supreme Court in delineating what is left to state legislation? What *should* a court do in this regard?

Contemporary Business. If you were advising a state legislature on the limits of federal preemption of state legislation in matters relating to health care, how would you define the permissible limits of state legislation?

CASE 16.6

THE SUPREME COURT BROADENS STATE REGULATION OF HEALTH INSURANCE PLANS

KENTUCKY ASSOCIATION OF HEALTH PLANS, INC. V. MILLER

538 U.S. 329 (2003)

Supreme Court of the United States

Facts. In 1994, Kentucky enacted a law stating that HMOs could not discriminate against health-care providers who were willing to meet the requirements for plan participation. This "any willing provider" law meant any health-care provider who met the minimum requirements for the insurer should be compensated for services rendered to an insured under the plan. This law was one of the broadest enacted in the United States requiring carriers to compensate for a full range of health services. A group of Kentucky-based HMOs sued the Kentucky Insurance Commissioner, asserting that the state law was preempted by ERISA. The federal district court granted judgment for the commissioner. On appeal, the Court of Appeals for the Sixth Circuit affirmed the district court's decision and held that the Kentucky statute did regulate insurance "as a matter of common sense." The Supreme Court granted *certiorari* to resolve the preemption question, since there had been divergent holdings among the federal circuits with regard to requiring insurers to compensate "any willing provider" under state legislation.

Issue. Can states prohibit HMOs from limiting their provider networks as an exemption from preemption of ERISA?

Language of the Court. Scalia, J.: **Kentucky law provides that [a] health insurer shall not discriminate against any provider who is located within the geographic coverage area of the health benefit plan and who is willing to meet the terms and conditions for participation established by the health insurer, including the Kentucky state Medicaid program and Medicaid partnerships. Moreover, any "health benefit plan that includes chiropractic benefits shall . . . permit any licensed chiropractor who agrees to abide by the terms, conditions, reimbursement rates, and standards of quality of the health benefit plan to serve as a participating primary chiropractic provider to any person covered by the plan." We granted certiorari to decide whether the Employee Retirement Income Security Act of 1974 (ERISA) pre-empts either, or both, of these "Any Willing Provider" (AWP) statutes.**

Today we make a clean break from the [prior case law interpreting a federal act exempting state regulation of insurance companies] and hold that for a state law to be deemed a "law . . . which regulates insurance" . . . it must satisfy two requirements. First, the state law must be specifically directed toward entities engaged in insurance. . . . Second, the state law must substantially affect the risk pooling arrangement between the insurer and the insured. Kentucky's law satisfies each of these requirements.

Decision. Yes. The statutory prohibition substantially affected the business of the regulation of insurance within a state and was thus not preempted by ERISA. The Court ruled that states can regulate their HMOs and upheld the Kentucky law that requires insurers to reimburse services of any health-care provider who is willing and able to meet established criteria.

CASE QUESTIONS

Critical Legal Thinking. This decision was the Supreme Court's third attempt in four years to clarify ERISA's insurance saving clause. In his opinion, Justice Scalia abandoned the prior use of the McCarren-Ferguson test (i.e., that state regulation of insurance is preempted by federal law) and its focus on whether a practice constitutes the "business of insurance." The Court established a new test requiring that the state law meet two requirements for a practice to constitute regulation of insurance: (i) the law must be directed specifically towards companies engaged in insurance (instead of just relating to the insurance industry in general), and (ii) must substantially affect the risk pooling arrangement between the insurer and the insured. In doing so, the Supreme Court did not deal with the policy arguments of the managed health-care industry that the decision would increase medical costs. Does this decision increase consumer choice in the selection of appropriate health care, or does it adversely affect the quality and cost of health care by increasing administrative costs?

Business Ethics. Some experts have opined that in light of this decision the health insurance industry will lose the ability to control costs by negotiating discounted rates with health-care providers in exchange for higher patient volume. What are your thoughts concerning the effect this decision will have on society's efforts to contain rising health-care costs? Does this decision, for example, increase competition among health-care providers and actually contain costs?

Contemporary Business. If you were a state legislator, what public policy considerations would you think needed to be addressed with respect to compelling health insurance carriers to provide open access to health care providers?

Focus on Ethics
Microsoft Violates Employee Benefit Law

Microsoft Corporation is the world's largest provider of computer operating systems, software programs, and Internet browsers. The company has grown into one of the largest corporations in the United States, making one of its founders, Bill Gates, the richest person in the world.

Microsoft is headquartered in the state of Washington. In addition to having regular employees, Microsoft used the services of other workers, classified as independent contractors (called freelancers) and temporary agency employees (called temps). Most of these special employees worked full-time for Microsoft, doing jobs that were identical to jobs performed by Microsoft's regular employees. Microsoft paid the special employees by check as outside workers.

However, Microsoft was caught nickel-and-diming some of its workers. The situation was brought to light by an IRS investigation. The IRS conducted an employment tax examination and determined that Microsoft had misclassified these special workers as independent contractors and that the workers in these positions had to be reclassified as employees for federal tax purposes.

The IRS investigation was not the end of the story. Microsoft contributed 3 percent of each employee's salary to the stock option plan for its permanent employees. Microsoft, however, had *not* contributed this 3 percent of salary to the stock option plan on behalf of its temporary employees who had been found by the IRS to be permanent employees. Plaintiff Donna Vizcaino and other freelancers sued Microsoft in a class-action lawsuit, alleging that they had been denied employment benefits, especially employee stock options, that were paid to regular employees.

The U.S. Court of Appeals agreed with the plaintiffs, citing the IRC that requires that such stock option plans to be available to all employees. The Court of Appeals stated, "It is our conclusion that Microsoft either exercised, or retained the right to exercise, direction over the services performed.

This control establishes an employer-employee relationship."

Thus, Microsoft's attempt to define certain full-time employees as freelancers and temps was rebuffed by the courts. Microsoft settled the case, paying $97 million to the class of plaintiffs. The court also ordered Microsoft to pay $27 million in fees to the plaintiffs' attorneys.[21]

Ethics Questions

1. Why did Microsoft classify full-time workers as freelancers and temps?
2. Were the stock options in this case a valuable employee benefit?
3. Did Microsoft act ethically in this case?

Consolidated Omnibus Budget Reconciliation Act of 1986

Congress passed the **Consolidated Omnibus Budget Reconciliation Act of 1986 (COBRA)** to address the problem arising when a private-sector employee loses health insurance following termination of employment. **COBRA** allows employees to continue health benefits at their individual expense. The act gives workers and their families who lose their health benefits because of separation from their employment the right to choose to continue the group health benefits provided by the group health plan for a limited period. The triggers can include voluntary or involuntary job loss, reduction in the hours worked, changing jobs, death, and divorce. Qualified individuals may be required to pay the entire premium for coverage, up to 102 percent of the cost of the plan plus 2 percent for administration costs for the employer for a total of 104 percent of the premium. This statute, unlike other statutes such as the Family Medical Leave Act, does not require the employer to pay for the cost of providing continuation coverage.

COBRA
Consolidated Omnibus Budget Reconciliation Act of 1986; a federal law passed to address the problem arising when a private-sector employee loses health insurance following termination of employment. COBRA allows employees to continue health benefits at their individual expense.

COBRA requires that group health plans sponsored by employers with 20 or more full-time equivalent employees in the prior year offer employees and their families the opportunity for a temporary extension of health coverage. This extension is called continuation coverage. The federal act requires that the group health insurance for employers with 20 or more employees on more than 50 percent of its typical business days in the previous calendar year is subject to **COBRA**. Both full-time and part-time employees are counted to determine if a plan is subject to **COBRA** coverage. Each part-time employee counts as a fraction of an employee, with the fraction equal to the number of hours that the part-time employee worked divided by the hours an employee must work to be considered full time.

A qualified beneficiary is generally considered an individual who is either an employee, the spouse of an employee or the employee's dependent child covered by a group health plan on the day before a qualifying event. In specific situations, a retired employee or his or her spouse and/or dependent children may also be considered qualified beneficiaries. In addition, children who are born to or adopted by a covered employee during the **COBRA** coverage period are considered qualified beneficiaries. Agents, independent contractors, and directors who participate in the group health plan may also be qualified beneficiaries.

Qualifying events are those that would cause a covered individual to lose health coverage. The plan must offer the health coverage to all qualifying events for the employee, spouses, and dependent children of an insured. Qualifying events for:

- Employees:
  - Voluntary or involuntary termination of employment for reasons other than gross misconduct
  - Reduction in the number of hours of employment
- Spouses:
  - Voluntary or involuntary termination of the covered employee's employment for reasons other than gross misconduct
  - Reduction in the number of hours worked by the covered employee
  - The covered employee becomes entitled to Medicare
  - Divorce or legal separation from the covered employee
  - Death of the covered employee
- Dependent children:
  - Loss of dependent child status under the plan rules
  - Reduction in the number of hours worked by the covered employee
  - The covered employee becomes entitled to Medicare
  - Divorce or legal separation of the covered employee
  - Death of the covered employee

To become eligible for **COBRA** continuation coverage, the individual must have been enrolled in the employer's health plan when the covered employee was working, and the health plan must continue to be in effect for active employees. **COBRA** continuation coverage is available on the occurrence of a qualifying event that would, except for the **COBRA** continuation coverage, cause an individual to lose his or her health care coverage.

A qualified beneficiary must notify the administrator of the health plan of a qualifying event within 60 days after divorce or legal separation or a child ceases to be covered as a dependent under plan rules. Plan participants and beneficiaries generally must send an election to be covered notice not later than 14 days after the administrator receives notice that a qualifying event has occurred. The individual then has 60 days to decide whether to elect **COBRA** continuation coverage. The person has 45 days after electing coverage to pay the individual premium. A parent or legal guardian may elect on behalf of a minor child. The employer or plan administrator measures the 60-day election period from the later of the coverage loss date or the date the **COBRA** election notice is provided. The election notice must be provided in person or by first-class mail within 14 days after the plan administrator receives notice of a qualifying event.

Disability can extend the minimum 18-month period of continuation coverage for a qualifying event when there has been a termination of employment or reduction of hours. This requires that the Social Security Administration determine that the individual became disabled within the first 60 days of **COBRA** continuation coverage. In addition, the disabled individual must send a timely notice of the disability determination to the plan administrator. If these requirements are met, the entire family qualifies for an additional 11 months of **COBRA** continuation coverage. Plans can charge 150 percent of the premium cost for the extended period of coverage.

A qualified beneficiary can waive **COBRA** coverage during the election period, but may revoke that waiver of coverage before the end of the election period.

The benefits offered to qualified beneficiaries must be identical to those available to the individual before qualifying for continuation coverage. **COBRA** coverage begins on the date that health-care coverage would otherwise have been lost because of the qualifying event. It will end earlier if: the premiums are not paid by or on behalf of the qualifying individual; the employer ceases to maintain any group health plan; after the **COBRA** election, coverage is obtained with another employer's group health plan that does not contain any exclusion or limitation with respect to any preexisting condition of such beneficiary. However, if other group health coverage is obtained prior to the **COBRA** election, the employer may not discontinue COBRA coverage, even if the other coverage continues after the **COBRA** coverage.

COBRA beneficiaries are eligible for group coverage during a maximum of 18 months for qualifying events. A second qualifying event during the initial period of coverage may permit a beneficiary to receive a maximum of 36 months of coverage. Additionally, **COBRA** beneficiaries who are spouses or dependent children can, under certain conditions, extend eligibility from 18 to 36 months.

COBRA does not prohibit plans from offering continuation health coverage that goes beyond the **COBRA** periods. Some plans allow participants and beneficiaries to convert health coverage to an individual policy. If the option is generally available from the plan, then the individual must be allowed to enroll in a conversion health plan within 180 days before **COBRA** coverage ends. The conversion policy may be more expensive than the premium for the group plan and the scope of benefits may be less than that offered by a group plan.

COBRA premiums may be increased if the plan premium costs increase, although they may only be raised every 12 months. The premiums can be paid monthly or at intervals that are more frequent if the plan allows for it. The initial premium must be made within 45 days after the date of the **COBRA** election by the qualified beneficiary. Payment must cover the period of coverage from the date of **COBRA** election retroactive to the date of the loss of coverage due to the qualifying event. Premiums for successive periods of coverage are due on the date stated in the plan with a minimum 30-day grace period for payments. Payment is considered to be made on the date it is sent to the plan. The plan is required to notify a qualified beneficiary that a payment less than the full amount due, but not significantly less, was received and allow the beneficiary a reasonable period, such as up to 30 days, to pay the difference. The plan is not required to send monthly premium notices.

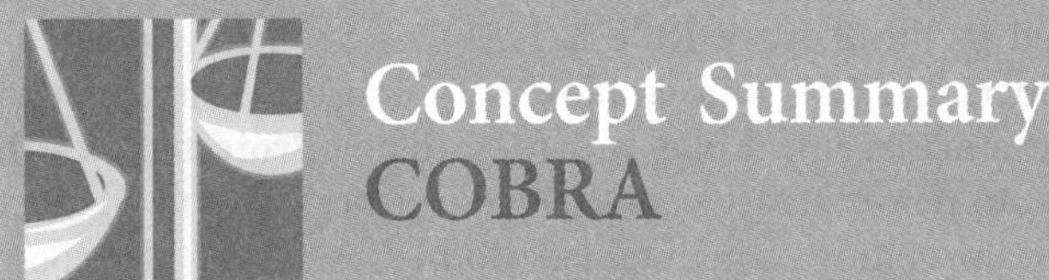

Concept Summary
COBRA

COBRA provides:

- certain former employees, retirees, spouses, former spouses, and dependent children with the right to continue health coverage at group premium rates;
- coverage for employees who work for employers with 20 or more employees;
- availability only when coverage is lost due to certain specific qualifying events;
- coverage identical to that the beneficiary received before qualifying for continuation coverage;
- a limit on the cost to beneficiaries of a premium rate not to exceed 102 percent of the cost to the plan; and
- coverage up to 18 months (and in certain situations for 36 months).

Health Insurance Portability and Accountability Act

HIPAA
Health Insurance Portability and Accountability Act is a federal law that limits the ability of a new employer-sponsored health-care plan to exclude coverage for preexisting conditions; provides opportunities to enroll in a group health plan if health insurance coverage is lost or other covered life events occur; prohibits discrimination against employees and their dependent family members based on preexisting health factors, including medical conditions, claims experience, and genetic information; and guarantees that certain persons will be able to enroll and renew individual health insurance policies. Also provides protections from disclosures of personal health information.

The **Health Insurance Portability and Accountability Act (HIPAA)**, enacted by Congress in 1996, addresses two concerns. The first part of the act protects health insurance coverage for workers and their families on change in or loss of employment. The second part, known as the Administrative Simplification provisions, requires that health-care providers, health insurance plans, and employers follow specific requirements with regard to the security and privacy of health data. **HIPAA** amended **ERISA**.

Title I of **HIPAA** limits restrictions that a health insurance carrier can place on applicants for coverage of preexisting conditions. Group health plans may refuse to provide benefits relating to preexisting conditions for a period of 12 months after enrollment or 18 months in the case of late enrollment. Individuals may reduce this exclusion period if they had health insurance prior to enrollment in the new plan. This title of **HIPAA** allows the exclusion period to be reduced by the amount of time that the employees had "creditable coverage" under another health insurance plan. For example, if a new employee with a prior history of both a preexisting condition and prior health coverage enrolled in a group health plan on July 1, two prior employers had covered the employee in the preceding year for a total of five months of coverage. In this instance, the five months of coverage can be credited against the exclusion period for insuring the preexisting condition. There are also complex requirements relating to the similarity in insurance coverage for the employee to overcome the exclusion period.

Probably the most well-known provision of **HIPAA** is the **Privacy Rule**. This provision has been interpreted to include any part of a patient's medical or payment history. Known as **Protected Health Information**, health-care providers, insurance carriers, and employers must undertake reasonable efforts to ensure that only minimum necessary information relating to the patient is made known to third parties. Those providers, carriers, and employers who possess such information must keep track of the disclosure of such information and must document all privacy policies and procedures. They must designate a privacy official and a contact person responsible for receiving and processing complaints regarding the wrongful disclosure of such information.

Another procedure linked to the **Privacy Rule** is HIPAA's **Security Rule**. The **Security Rule** requires providers, carriers, and employers to adopt a written set of privacy procedures, to provide a management plan to safeguard any **Protected Health Information** in its possession, to report breaches of such confidences, and to conduct detailed security audits of the information so maintained. Both physical and electronic access to such information should be controlled. The federal Department of Health and Human Services has jurisdiction to enforce **HIPAA**. Its regulations provide for the assessment of fines for violations of the law.

2010 Health Care Act

The **Patient Protection and Affordable Care Act, as amended by the Healthcare Education Affordability Reconciliation Act**, signed into law by President Obama in March 2010, expands health insurance coverage to an estimated 32 million uninsured Americans through a combination of cost controls, individual and business subsidies, and mandates. Both employers and employees are affected by the provisions of the act. The following summarizes selected provisions of the act.

Individual Mandate

U.S. citizens and legal residents must have qualifying health coverage or be subject to a tax penalty. Beginning in 2014, those without qualifying health coverage will pay a tax penalty of the greater of (a) $695 per calendar year, up to a maximum of $2,085, per family member; or (b) 2.5 percent of household income over a threshold amount (in 2010, the filing threshold is $9,350 for a single person or a married person filing separately and $18,750 for a married couple filing jointly).

Tax credits ("the premium assistance credit") are extended to low- and middle-income individuals and families. The credit is paid in advance directly to the insurer to subsidize the purchase of certain health insurance plans through a health insurance exchange. The individual then pays the plan to which he or she is enrolled the dollar difference between the credit amount and the total premium charged for the plan. The premium assistance credit will be available for individuals with annual earnings of up to $43,320 and for families with annual earnings of up to $88,200 for a family of four. These credits will be available only if those persons are ineligible for Medicaid, employee-sponsored insurance, or other acceptable health insurance coverage. The amount of this tax credit will be calculated on a sliding-scale basis and will be based on the percentage of income the premium costs represent.

Health Insurance Exchanges

The uninsured and self-employed will be able to purchase insurance through state-based health insurance exchanges using the tax credit subsidies.

Starting in 2014, separate exchanges will be created at which small businesses will be able to purchase coverage.

Illegal immigrants will not be allowed to buy health insurance in the exchanges, even if they pay the premiums.

Employer Mandate

Technically, the act does not establish an employer mandate. Employers with more than 50 employees must provide health insurance or pay a penalty of $2,000 per worker each year if any worker receives federal subsidies to purchase health insurance.

A qualified small employer will be entitled to a tax credit for any employer contributions it provides to purchase health insurance for employees. Such employers will generally be those with no more than 25 full-time equivalent employees and whose employees have an average annual full time-time equivalent wage rate of no more than $50,000.

Paying for the Plan

Medicare payroll taxes will be increased in 2013. Single people earning more than $200,000 and married couples earning more than $250,000 will be taxed at an additional 0.9 percent or 2.35 percent on their wages. Taxpayers who earn these levels through investment income will be taxed at the rate of 3.8 percent.

Beginning in 2018, insurance companies will pay a 40 percent excise tax on so-called "Cadillac" high-end insurance plans with premiums of over $27,500 for families and $10,200 for individuals. Dental and visions plans are exempt and are not counted in the total cost of a family's plan.

An excise tax of 10 percent, to be collected by the service operator, will be assessed for indoor tanning services.

Medicare

For Medicare-covered seniors, the act will eliminate by 2020 the so-called "donut hole" of out-of-pocket costs they now must pay for prescription drugs. In 2010, the "donut hole" gap in out-of-pocket drug expenses was between $2,830 and $4,550 per individual covered by Medicare. In addition, beginning in 2011, during the Medicare prescription drug coverage gap now in effect that requires seniors to pay the entire cost of prescription medications before Medicare pays its share, seniors will instead receive a 50 percent discount on brand-name drugs. This discount does not apply to generic drugs. Until 2020, this provision means that, while in the gap, seniors will only pay 50 percent of the cost of brand-name medications instead of the 100 percent they paid before the act went into effect.

Insurance Reforms

The act specifies that insurance companies can no longer deny children coverage because of a preexisting condition. In addition, insurers must allow dependent children to remain insured on their parent's health-care plans until age 26.

Starting in 2014, insurers cannot deny coverage to anyone with a preexisting condition.

Group health plans may not establish lifetime limits on the dollar value of the essential benefits of any participant. Medical plans are now restricted in their ability to impose annual benefit limitations.

A plan may not rescind or cancel coverage except for fraud or a misrepresentation of a material fact.

Restrictions on Cafeteria Plans

A **cafeteria** or **flexible spending account** (FSA) plan is a type of employee benefit plan, authorized by the IRC, that allows participating employees to be reimbursed for qualifying out-of-pocket health expenses, such as deductibles for medical office visits or other costs that exceed those reimbursed by the employee's medical plan. The cafeteria plan usually operates through a salary reduction agreement, made through a payroll deduction, and allows the employee to pay for qualifying items on a tax-free basis.

After 2013, the amount of contributions to an FSA will be limited to $2,500 per year indexed for inflation. In addition, the cost of over-the-counter medicine (other than insulin or other prescribed medicine) will no longer be reimbursable through the health FSA.

Dissolution of Marriage

When spouses divorce, pension and other welfare benefits may be assigned from one spouse to another. Such benefits are subject to the courts' powers of equitable distribution at the dissolution of the marital estate. These court orders will override the provisions within the **ERISA** law that contain broad antiassignment rules. The 1984 Retirement Equity Act amended **ERISA** to allow **ERISA**-qualified welfare and pension benefits to be assigned pursuant to a **qualified domestic relations order (QDRO)**. The purpose is to recognize a spouse's right to receive benefits payable by a retirement plan because those benefits are considered a community asset. Rights and benefits payable under a **QDRO** are exempt from the preemption from state laws and judgments to which **ERISA** is otherwise entitled. Under **ERISA**, the plan must pay the beneficiary of the state court domestic-relations order if it is deemed to be a qualified order. Until distributed pursuant to the **QDRO, ERISA** plan provisions govern the management of the plan monies.

Qualified Domestic Relations Order (QDRO)
A federal law amended ERISA to allow ERISA-qualified welfare and pension benefits to be divided between divorcing spouses. Court orders are issued by the state domestic relations court and then reviewed by the plan administrator for compliance with ERISA and the terms of the plan.

Management Application
The Importance of Written Documentation

At the time Virgil Hein was hired as a company vice president, he was told the company maintained a salary continuation plan. The subject of vesting was never discussed, and the salary continuation plan was never prepared in the form, including disclosures, required by **ERISA**. The insurance company that provided life insurance policies on all plan participants summarized the salary continuation plan. The salary continuation plan contained no provision regarding vesting of benefits for any employee. The summary provided that if employment were terminated, so would the salary continuation plan. When Hein became president, he attempted to amend the plan to provide for vesting of the salary continuation plan when he learned that the company was being sold.
The company's attorney provided a backdated document showing him fully vested prior to the sale, and the former president of the company signed it for Hein prior to the sale. When Hein was replaced following the sale, he asserted that his benefits were vested, an assertion the new owner denied, claiming the unauthorized backdated document was misleading and untruthful. The new owner contended that Hein could not argue that the company made any representation to Hein, by express promise or otherwise, that Hein would continue to be covered by the salary continuation plan if his employment was terminated.[22] Who has the better ethical position to argue to the trial court?

Discussion Questions

1. Should the salary continuation plan be considered an employee pension benefit plan covered by ERISA?
2. Who should bear the risk of the employer's failure to conform the salary continuation plan to the summary plan description requirements of ERISA?
3. Should something more than just the failure of the employer to comply with its duties under ERISA be necessary to establish a right to alleged benefits (i.e., should the statute be turned into one of strict liability for the employer)?

Human Resource Form
Your Medical Benefits

After 60 days of continuous employment at our company, all regular, full-time employees are covered by our group medical plan. Temporary, introductory, and part-time employees are not eligible for these medical benefits. Eligibility requirements are as set forth in the Summary Plan Description that will be furnished to you as soon as you become eligible. Everything stated in this employment handbook is subject to what is stated in the Summary Plan Description. In the event of a conflict, the terms of the Summary Plan Description control.

You should verify your eligibility for coverage before undergoing any health care–related treatment in order to ensure that you are covered under the group medical policy. To verify your insurance coverage, secure a claim form, or request further information, contact the Human Resources (HR) Department.

You must inform the HR Department of any changes in your address. If you get married, become a registered domestic partner, or divorce, or if the number of your dependents changes, you are urged to immediately contact the HR Department. If you do not, you could jeopardize medical coverage for these persons.

We reserve the right to change, amend, or discontinue the benefits the plan offers at any time. Our right to make these changes can occur at any time and upon reasonable notice to you.

[The above provision is the kind of statement that would be included in an employee handbook. **ERISA** requires that a welfare benefit plan be defined in detail in an understandable Summary Plan Description that sets forth all material terms and conditions of the plan. That document would also describe the participant's **ERISA** rights under the plan. The handbook may not contradict or supersede what is stated in the Summary Plan Description.]

Key Terms and Concepts

- Retirement plans
- ERISA
- Pension plans
- Plan administrator
- Defined contribution plans
- Deferred compensation plans
- Welfare benefit plans
- Fiduciaries
- Fiduciary breach
- Federal preemption
- Super preemption
- Summary plan description
- Defined benefit pension plans
- Individual Retirement Accounts
- Multiemployer Pension Plan Amendments Act of 1980
- Pension Benefit Guaranty Corporation
- Annuity contract
- 401(k) plan
- Profit sharing plan
- SIMPLE IRA plan
- Keogh plans

- Fiduciary duties
- Discrimination claims
- Top-hat pension plans
- Qualified plans
- Nonqualified deferred compensation plans
- Vesting
- Cliff vesting
- COBRA
- HIPAA
- Privacy rule
- QDRO

Chapter Summary

- Fringe benefits are voluntary programs initiated by the employer and are not required by law.

- There are two types of employee benefit plans: pension plans and welfare plans. Pension plans defer salary until retirement, while welfare plans are any other benefit plans. Both types are subject to the federal law known as ERISA.

- Congress has severely limited the rights of states to enact legislation compelling employer-required offerings of fringe benefits. ERISA typically preempts state law and regulation within its subject matter.

- Employers must issue a summary plan description and communicate to employees their rights under the plan.

- Pension plans fall into two categories: defined benefit and defined contribution plans. The Pension Benefit Guaranty Corporation covers defined benefit plans. Among defined contribution plans are the 401(k), SIMPLE IRA, and Keogh plans. Restrictions on contribution limits and withdrawal of funds are established.

- Employers have fiduciary duties under these plans, but plan administrators are not fiduciaries under ERISA unless they exercise fiduciary powers. Fiduciary duties include loyalty, prudence of a reasonable person in investing, and diversification of the portfolio while staying compliant with plan documents.

- ERISA requires that, as a condition of participation, a plan must include all employees who are 21 years of age or older or who have completed one year of employment.

- By timely electing COBRA coverage, a qualified beneficiary may extend health insurance coverage at his or her own expense for a minimum of 18 months following the qualifying event triggering the COBRA election.

- Pension and welfare benefit plan distributions may not be assigned or attached by creditors except pursuant to a qualified domestic relations order issued within a state court divorce proceeding.

- HIPAA limits restrictions health insurance carriers can place on applicants for coverage with preexisting conditions. Group health plans may refuse to provide benefits relating to preexisting conditions for a period of 12 months after enrollment, or 18 months in the case of late enrollment. Individuals may reduce this exclusion period if they had health insurance prior to enrollment in the new plan. HIPAA also requires employers to maintain the privacy of employees' health information.

- A QDRO will allow the allocation of welfare and pension benefits between divorcing couples.

Online Student Support

- Loislaw legal research and writing assignments.
- Loislaw group projects and class presentations.
- Loislaw access, providing online research including up-to-date cases, statutes, rules, and regulations. Primary law for all 50 states and federal jurisdictions. Registration required for access to this resource.
- Practice questions, including sample true/false, multiple choice, and short answer questions to test your understanding of concepts.
- Additional human resource forms.
- Internet exercises.
- Blogs.
- Supplementary statutory and regulatory materials.

Case Problems

16.1 Plaintiffs sued their health maintenance organizations (HMOs) because the HMOs refused to cover certain medical services, in violation of an HMO's duty "to exercise ordinary care" under the Texas Health Care Liability Act, and those refusals "proximately caused" the plaintiffs' injuries. The HMOs had the case removed (i.e., transferred to federal court, maintaining that the claims were completely preempted by §502 of ERISA). If you were a sitting justice when the case reached the Supreme Court, how would you rule on the plaintiffs' contention that Texas state negligence law should allow the case to proceed in state court? (*Aetna Health, Inc. et al. v. Davila, et al.*, 524 U.S. 200 (2004))

16.2 Should a participant in a health-care plan subject to ERISA be able to sue her medical health plan under ERISA for her physician's malpractice? Upon discovering an inflammation in her abdomen, a plaintiff's physician decided that she would have to wait 8 days for an abdominal ultrasound. Before that time elapsed, the plaintiff's appendix burst, causing peritonitis. She sued the doctor and the HMO for malpractice and fraud. Her fraud claim was premised on the HMO's practice of rewarding physician-owners for limiting medical care, which she stated created an inherent breach of an ERISA fiduciary duty to promote the participant's interests. Were the treatment decisions made by the HMO through the physician's fiduciary acts within the meaning of ERISA? (*Pegram v. Herdrich*, 530 U.S. 211 (2000))

16.3 A family had paid for a health insurance plan through a company that ceased to exist without notice or warning. Ed Klosterman began working for the Prairie Maize Company and participated in the company's health benefit plan. The employer and an insurance company, which also acted as the claims administrator for the health plan, funded the plan. After working for the company for a year, Ed lost his job, but he continued his health coverage through a COBRA election. The summary plan document stated that the participant had the right to convert to an individual policy. After Klosterman paid the COBRA premiums and received the claims administrator's confirmation that the health insurance was in place, the Klostermans' son was diagnosed with a chronic disease. The Klostermans learned that Prairie Maize Company had gone out of business and had retroactively cancelled all of its health insurance. The insurance company then refused Klosterman's request to convert to an individual health policy. They filed suit against the insurance company under ERISA for failing to state in the summary plan description that the conversion privilege would not exist if the underlying plan terminated. Who wins? (*Klosterman v. Western General Management, Inc.*, 32 F.3d 1119 (7th Cir. 1994))

16.4 Under ERISA, the Secretary of Labor sued three trustees of the Grumman Corporation for an alleged breach of their fiduciary duties. The complainant alleged that the trustees breached their fiduciary duties by spending pension plan assets for the purchase of the company's stock in an effort to fend off the tender offer made by a competitor. The trustees were also officers and board members of Grumman. The alleged violations of ERISA arise from the difficult task presented to the defendants during the time of the competitor's tender offer of simultaneously serving two masters — Grumman and the pension plan. With such dual loyalties at stake, how should the court rule with regard to the alleged breach of fiduciary duties to protect the participants and beneficiaries? (*Donovan v. Bierwirth et al.*, 538 F. Supp. 463 (E.D.N.Y. 1981))

16.5 The plaintiffs alleged that the fiduciaries of their ERISA plan failed to monitor the plan's investments and provide participants with complete and accurate information with respect to the plan's investment in the employer's stock. The duty to administer the plan was delegated to a committee of persons and not to the employer that established the plan. The plaintiffs alleged that the committee had the specific authority to add and drop investments, which should have included ceasing to invest in the employer's stock during a period of worsening economic outlook for the company. Were any fiduciary duties violated and should the committee members be dismissed from the litigation? (*In re: Williams Companies ERISA Litigation*, 271 F. Supp. 2d 1328 (N.D. Okla. 2003))

End Notes

1. *Harris Trust and Savings Bank v. Salomon Smith Barney, Inc.*, 530 U.S. 238 (2000).
2. *Feifer v. Prudential Ins. Co.*, 306 F. 3d 1202 (2d Cir. 2002).
3. 29 U.S.C. §1001.
4. *Black & Decker Disability Plan v. Nord*, 538 U.S. 822 (2003) (citing *Lockheed Corp. v. Spink*, 517 U.S. 882, 887 (1996)).
5. *Hardy v. Welch*, 135 F. Supp. 2d 1171 (M.D. Ala. 2000).
6. 29 U.S.C. §§1301-1461.
7. *http://www.pbgc.gov/workers-retirees/benefits-information/content/page14090.html.*
8. 29 U.S.C. §1002(21)(A)(i).
9. 29 U.S.C. §1002(21)(A).
10. 530 U.S. 238, 246 (2000).
11. *Johnson v. Couturier*, 572 F.3d 1067 (9th Cir. 2009).
12. *http://legacy.plansponsor.com/uploadfiles/ChiTribESOPsuitruling.pdf.*
13. *Cusson v. Liberty Life Assurance Co. of Boston*, 592 F.3d 215 (1st Cir. 2010).
14. *Marrs v. Motorola*, 577 F.3d 783 (7th Cir. 2009).
15. 435 U.S. 702 (1978).
16. 946 F.2d 401 (5th Cir. 1991).
17. 506 U.S. 981 (1992).
18. *Seaman v. Arvida Realty Sales*, 985 F.2d 543 (11th Cir. 1993), cert. denied, 510 U.S. 916 (1993).
19. 29 U.S.C. §1132(g)(1).
20. *Roark v. Humana Inc.*, 307 F.3d 298 (5th Cir. 2002).
21. *Vizcaino v. United States District Court for the Western District of Washington*, 173 F.3d 713 (9th Cir. 1999), *cert. denied*, 2000 U.S. LEXIS 479.
22. *Hein v. TechAmerica Group, Inc.*, 17 F.3d 1278 (10th Cir. 1994).

Part IV
The Global Employment Environment

Chapter 17
Immigration and Nationality

Everywhere immigrants have enriched and strengthened the fabric of American life.
—John F. Kennedy, thirty-fifth President of the United States

Learning Objectives

1. Distinguish between nationality and citizenship discrimination.
2. State an employer's duties under INA.
3. Identify an employer's obligations under IRCA of 1986.
4. Explain the documents that establish identity for employment.
5. Recognize those documents that may establish work eligibility.
6. Understand the penalties employers face for IRCA violations.
7. Explain the limitations of the E-Verify program.

Chapter Outline

- Introduction
- National Origin and Citizenship Distinctions
- Naturalized Citizens
- Application of the Civil Rights Laws
- Immigration and Nationality Act

Case 17.1 Mathews v. Diaz, et al.

- Management Application: Constitutional Restraints on Alien Employment

Case 17.2 De Canas et al. v. Bica et al.

- Immigration Reform and Control Act of 1986

Case 17.3 Hoffman Plastic Compounds, Inc. v. N.L.R.B.

- Who May Be Employed in the United States?
- Management Application: The 30-60 Day Rule
- Employment Verification

Case 17.4 Mester Manufacturing Co. v. INS

- ICE Investigations
- Employer Sanctions
- Focus on Ethics: Employer Fined for Violating Immigration Laws
- Unfair Employment Practice (INA §274B)
- Other Federal Laws
- Administrative and Judicial Review
- Focus on Ethics: Should Courts Protect All Civil Rights Based on Alienage?
- Human Resource Form: I-9 Form

Chapter Opening scenario

Two legal resident aliens residing in Puerto Rico, Maria C. Flores de Otero, a native of Mexico, and Sergio Perez Nogueiro, a native of Spain, were denied the right to practice civil engineering under a Puerto Rican statute that permitted only U.S. citizens to practice privately as civil engineers. They sued the Puerto Rican engineering licensing board, alleging the statute was unconstitutional because it violated their civil rights.[1] As you read this chapter, consider the following questions:

1. How would the Supreme Court weigh the equal protection arguments raised by the would-be engineers and the territory?
2. Should U.S. citizens be considered more suitable candidates for professional licensure than aliens when the work might involve critical infrastructure projects?
3. Would you want to know the rationale on which the Puerto Rican legislature based its requirement of citizenship?

Introduction

Official efforts of the U.S. government to restrain the influx of authorized aliens who desire to work here have far-reaching implications. One recent study found that each year more than one million skilled immigrant workers, including Indian and Chinese scientists and engineers and their families, compete for more than 100,000 permanent U.S. resident visas, creating a sizeable imbalance between the U.S. workforce and those of other nations. The United States limits the number of employment visas issued to immigrants from any single country. Compounding this problem is the "reverse brain drain" of U.S.-trained, foreign-born scientists and engineers returning to their native countries. They do so to pursue their own entrepreneurial interests and to strengthen the technological, financial, and defense industries of their native states. Limiting the number of skilled workers who may enter the United States to work in areas such as engineering and technology thus harms the country's intellectual capital. The report indicates that unless the immigration of people highly educated in science, technology, math, and engineering-related disciplines increases, the United States risks losing its edge in innovation and the ability to capitalize on it.[2] These issues must be resolved at the federal level. In the meantime, when considering the possibility of hiring an alien, employers must carefully follow all U.S. immigration requirements or risk substantial fines and penalties.

Although it is impossible to establish the exact number of aliens, authorized and not, who are employed in the United States, the Census Bureau reported in March 2007 that the nation's immigrant population reached a record 37.9 million in 2007, nearly one-third of whom are unauthorized aliens.[3] In light of federal preemption over immigration, the authority of the federal government relative to the employment of **aliens** is greater than the authority of state and local governments. Every employer in the United States is required to comply with the **Immigration Reform and Control Act of 1986 (IRCA)**, as amended. Employers are subject to the act even if they are not involved in interstate commerce, nor must they employ a minimum the number of employees to be affected by it. However, the number of employees does make a difference with regard to discrimination claims based on national origin or citizenship status. This chapter will review the standards employed in a post-9/11 United States for the employment of foreign nationals. In this chapter, we will review the laws that regulate the hiring and retention of **authorized aliens**, that is, foreign nationals who may legally work in the United States.

National Origin and Citizenship Distinctions

The distinction between national origin and **citizenship** under Title VII and American immigration law presents unique considerations for business managers, including the following:

- Title VII makes it unlawful to "discriminate against any individual" (42 U.S.C. §2000e-2(a)).
- The **IRCA** compels employers to terminate unauthorized **aliens** upon discovery of their illegal immigration status.

Unauthorized aliens are non–U.S. citizens who enter the United States without permission or whose immigration status does not permit employment in the country. A worker who is not authorized to be in the country can be arrested and deported. An **unauthorized alien** is also known as an **undocumented alien**, that is, one who is neither a lawful permanent resident nor a person authorized for employment by U.S. law. The employer of such a person faces several civil and criminal penalties for hiring and continuing to employ **unauthorized aliens**.

Due to the perceived relationship between two terms, it is important to note that national origin is not the same as **citizenship**. In *Espinoza v. Farah Manufacturing Co.*,[4] the Supreme Court held that the Title VII protection from "national origin" discrimination does not embrace **citizenship**. The Court stated:

> The question posed . . . is not whether **aliens** are protected from illegal discrimination under the Act, but what kinds of discrimination the Act makes illegal. Certainly, it would be unlawful for an employer to discriminate against **aliens** because of race, color, religion, sex, or national origin — for example, by hiring **aliens** of Anglo-Saxon background but refusing to hire those of Mexican or Spanish ancestry. **Aliens** are protected from illegal discrimination under the Act, but nothing in the Act makes it illegal to discriminate because of the lack of citizenship or alienage.[5]

Citizenship
Legal status of a person who has satisfied a nation's legal requirements to be a member of that nation. In exchange for obeying the nation's laws, citizenship allows persons to enjoy all rights and privileges afforded persons with that status.

Alien
A citizen of one country living in a foreign country.

Unauthorized Aliens
Persons who entered the United States without a visa or who overstayed the period permitted by a visa.

Undocumented Aliens
Persons who entered the United States without a visa or who overstayed the period permitted by a visa.

Courts typically apply the more restrictive conditions of **IRCA.** This is due to the federal courts' recognition that certain rights are afforded citizens that are not available to noncitizens.

> ***Example:*** An **undocumented alien** could not pursue a Title VII claim for discrimination because his undocumented status rendered him ineligible for lawful work in the United States.[6]

Not surprisingly, the EEOC took a contrary view until the Supreme Court issued its decision in the *Hoffman Plastics* case discussed later in this chapter.

Historical Overview of Key Federal Immigration Acts

- ***Naturalization Act of 1790.*** The first law granting **citizenship**, this act limited **naturalization** to **aliens** who were "free white persons" of "good moral character" and who had lived in the United States for at least two years. It also established the U.S. **citizenship** of children of **citizens** born abroad without the need for **naturalization**. Until 1790, there were no direct legal restrictions on immigration into the United States.
- ***Naturalization Act of 1795.*** This act repealed the prior one and increased the period of residency to five years and required oath of allegiance to the United States and renunciation of allegiance to the sovereignty of one's place of birth.
- ***Naturalization Act of 1870.*** This act outlawed fraudulent practices and provided for the **naturalization** of residents of "African descent."
- ***The Page Act of 1875.*** The Page Act addressed immigration from China, Japan, or any other Asian country into the United States. It also made unlawful the importation of women for purposes of prostitution or of anyone for coolie labor, and it forbade immigration of convicted felons and "obnoxious" persons.
- ***The Chinese Exclusion Act (1882).*** Passed in xenophobic response to increased Chinese immigration following the California gold rush and the building of the transcontinental railroad, this act aimed to exclude Chinese from immigrating into the country and penalized people of Chinese origin living in the United States who sought to leave and then return. Immigrants of Chinese ancestry were required to register and obtain a certificate of registration. The act was found constitutional by the U.S. Supreme Court in *Chae Chan Ping v. U.S.* (*The Chinese Exclusion Case*), 130 U.S. 581 (1889). It was strengthened in 1885 and 1887 by additional laws that increased the deportation penalties for persons who entered the United States in violation of the contract labor laws.[7] The act was repealed in 1943.
- ***Naturalization Act of 1906.*** This act required **naturalized** citizens to speak English.
- ***Gentlemen's Agreement of 1907.*** Immigration from Japan was restricted under this agreement, but immigration into the territory of Hawaii remained unrestricted, and from Hawaii, Japanese people could migrate to the mainland United States. The Gentlemen's Agreement was intended to address anti-Japanese sentiment in San Francisco.

- ***Immigration Act of 1917.*** This act barred persons from the geographic area from Afghanistan to the Pacific Ocean, with the exception of persons from Japan and the Philippines, from admission into the United States.
- ***Emergency Quota Act (1921).*** This act limited immigration from each foreign nation to 3 percent of that nationality already residing in the United States.
- ***Immigration Act of 1924 (the National Origins Quota Act).*** This act banned all Asians from migration into the United States and nullified the Gentlemen's Agreement of 1907.
- ***Bracero Program (1942).*** The shortage of manual laborers during World War II led the United States to establish a guest worker program with Mexico, which was in effect from 1942 to 1962. Many human rights and financial abuses occurred under this program.
- ***Immigration and Nationality Act of 1952 (INA).*** Under this act, discussed more fully below, racial restrictions were abolished and replaced with a quota and preference system for immigration.
- ***Immigration Act of 1965.*** This legislation eliminated the national origins quota system, created the category of "immediate relatives," removed restrictions relating to persons from Asia, and established an annual quota of 170,000 for immigrants from countries outside the Western Hemisphere, prohibited immigration of more than 20,000 persons from any single foreign state, reformulated the preference systems based on family relationships and skills in allocating immigrant visas, and restricted Western Hemisphere migration based on skills except in the case of shortages of U.S. workers.
- ***Immigration Act of 1990 (IMMACT90).*** IMMACT90 established a lottery program for the assignment of visas, allowed exceptions to English testing procedures, and removed AIDS from the list of illnesses that rendered people ineligible for immigration. Employers were prohibited from demanding more documentation than that required by the **IRCA** to establish **identity and employment verification**. Based on themes of family unity and creation of employment in the United States, a worldwide immigration ceiling was set at 700,000. The "employment creation" category was established by allocating up to 10,000 visas for immigrants who established businesses in the United States with a capital investment of $1.0 million or more or half that much if the business was established in a rural or high unemployment area.
- ***USA Patriot Act** (Pub. L. No. 107-56, 115 Stat. 272).* Among other things, this act required development of a system for verifying the identity of persons applying for a visa or entering the country and required the attorney general to develop biometric technology for use at border stations. It also authorized the detention of persons for seven days before officials decided whether to charge them with violating an immigration statute and permitted indefinite detention after securing a deportation and removal order.
- ***REAL ID Act of 2005.*** This act made broad juridical review and jurisdictional changes in immigration practices. Judicial review of removal orders based on constitutional or question of law claims were transferred from the U.S. district courts to federal appellate courts. *Habeas corpus* petitioning as a means of review for immigration court-based removal orders was eliminated.
- ***Secure Fence Act of 2006.*** This act authorized construction of a border fence along the U.S. border with Mexico to deter illegal immigration and drug trafficking.
- ***Executive Order No. 12989.*** This executive order prohibited, as federal policy, federal contracting with any employer who knowingly hires unauthorized workers in violation of **IRCA**.

Naturalized Citizens

U.S. law does not recognize "classes" of **citizenship**, with perhaps the single exception of who may serve as president. In all other respects, naturalized citizens are on the same plane as native-born **citizens**. A person who was born in another country or otherwise reared as a foreigner but has been granted U.S. citizenship has all the rights and privileges of that status. The process by which a nonnative person obtains citizenship is called **naturalization**.

Naturalization
Process of acquiring citizenship in a country other than that of one's birth.

> ***Example:*** A federal district court held a Georgia state statute requiring its state troopers to be native-born **citizens** and not **naturalized citizens** was unconstitutional as a violation of **equal protection**.[8]

Application of the Civil Rights Laws

Under the Civil Rights Act of 1866 (42 U.S.C. §1981), all persons within the United States have the same rights to make and enforce contracts, sue, be parties to a lawsuit, give evidence, and otherwise share the full and equal benefit of all laws enjoyed by white citizens. This statute has been construed as prohibiting governmental discrimination against **aliens** as to certain rights and liberties. In 1948, the Supreme Court struck down a California statute barring issuance of commercial fishing licenses to persons "ineligible to citizenship." The Court found no correlation between **citizenship** and a state interest in protecting the fish swimming in coastal waters. The Civil Rights Act of 1991 extended the provisions of §1981 to private as well as governmental discrimination.

Students should recall the discussion of the Civil Rights Act of 1871 from an earlier chapter. That statute provides that:

> [A]ny person who, under color of any statute, ordinance, regulation, custom, or usage of any state, territory, or the District of Columbia, subjects, or causes to be subjected, any person within the jurisdiction of the United States to the deprivation of any rights, privileges, or immunities secured by the Constitution and laws, is liable to the party injured, in an action at law, suit in equity, or other proceeding for redress.[9]

Courts have interpreted the words "any person" as used in the statute to mean that the statute applies to **citizens** and noncitizens alike. Thus, all persons are protected under §1981.

Immigration and Nationality Act

The **McCarran-Walter Act**, commonly known as the **Immigration and Nationality Act of 1952 (INA)**, is the principal federal act governing immigration and the right to work in the United States. The **INA** was designed to promote a uniform immigration and nationalization policy. Federal courts have required that states adopt a uniform federal definition in determining rights under state laws and regulations. **INA** restricted immigration into the United States, retaining a **quota system** as well as a prior policy of restricting immigration from certain countries. The **INA** defines three types of immigrants: the first two, those with special skills or those who are relatives of U.S. **citizens**, were exempt from quotas and could be admitted without restrictions; the third, limited category was of immigrants from areas of the globe from which immigration was limited when the annual quota was 270,000 persons (this held until the act was amended in 1990).

Courts rarely intrude on the right of Congress to legislate in the area of immigration law, provided the laws so enacted have a **rational basis** under the **Equal Protection Clause** of the Fourteenth Amendment. When courts are confronted with a contest between the congressional interest in regulating **aliens** within the United States and an infringement of an individual's constitutional rights, they generally favor congressional interests and provide limited judicial review of **alien** claims.

The **Board of Immigration Appeals (BIA)** issues appellate administrative decisions arising from the orders of administrative law judges. The decisions are binding on all offices and immigration judges unless modified or overruled by the U.S. Department of Justice or a federal court. The **BIA** is part of the administrative law function of the executive branch of the federal government; it is not a federal court, but its decisions may be reviewed by a federal court.

Undocumented aliens are those persons who are illegally present in the United States. Courts view skeptically their challenges to federal immigration laws and regulations based on violations of due process or equal protection. As an example, the Supreme Court held in *Woodby v. INS*[10] that the due process clause requires that an **alien** receive a notice of a deportation hearing and a fair hearing thereafter at which the **Immigration and Naturalization Service (INS)** must prove by "clear, unequivocal, and convincing evidence" that the **alien** is subject to deportation. For those employed by federal, state, or local governments or agencies, the U.S. Constitution may provide protections not afforded under private employment. The Supreme Court has recognized that the responsibility of regulating the relationship between **aliens** and the United States is within the authority of the executive and legislative branches. In the following case, the Court distinguished rights afforded the **citizen** and the **alien**. Thus, what might be an illegal employment action against a citizen might be permissible if practiced against an **alien**. The appellees were two of more than 440,000 Cuban refugees who were admitted to the U.S. who sought Medicare benefits.

CASE 17.1

DISCRIMINATION BETWEEN BENEFITS AFFORDED CITIZENS AND NONCITIZENS IS PERMITTED

MATHEWS V. DIAZ, ET AL.

426 U.S. 67 (1976)

Supreme Court of the United States

Facts. A class action was filed in the U.S. District Court for the Southern District of Florida challenging the constitutionality of the provisions of the Social

Security Act granting eligibility for the Medicare supplemental medical insurance program to resident citizens who are 65 years or older but which deny eligibility to aliens and others unless they have been admitted for permanent residence and have resided in the United States for at least five years. The district court entered judgment for the plaintiffs holding that the residency requirement violated the due process clause of the Fifth Amendment. A direct appeal to the Supreme Court was taken.

Issue. By denying Security Benefits to resident aliens who have not met a residency requirement, has Congress denied them liberty or property without due process of law?

Language of the Court. Stevens, J.: . . . **There are literally millions of aliens within the jurisdiction of the United States. The Fifth Amendment, as well as the Fourteenth Amendment, protects every one of these persons from deprivation of life, liberty, or property without due process of law (citations omitted). . . . Even one whose presence in this country is unlawful, involuntary, or transitory is entitled to that constitutional protection.**

The fact that all persons, aliens and citizens alike, are protected by the Due Process Clause does not lead to the further conclusion that all aliens are entitled to enjoy all the advantages of citizenship or, indeed, to the conclusion that all aliens must be placed in a single homogeneous legal classification. For a host of constitutional and statutory provisions rest on the premise that a legitimate distinction between citizens and aliens may justify attributes and benefits for one class not accorded to the other; and the class of aliens is itself a heterogeneous multitude of persons with a wide-ranging variety of ties to this country.

In the exercise of its broad power over naturalization and immigration, Congress regularly makes rules that would be unacceptable if applied to citizens. The exclusion of aliens and the reservation of the power to deport have no permissible counterpart in the Federal Government's power to regulate the conduct of its own citizenry. The fact that an Act of Congress treats aliens differently from citizens does not in itself imply that such disparate treatment is "invidious."

Any rule of constitutional law that would inhibit the flexibility of the political branches of government to respond to changing world conditions should be adopted only with the greatest caution. The reasons that preclude judicial review of political questions also dictate a narrow standard of review of decisions made by the Congress or the President in the area of immigration and naturalization.

We may assume that the five-year line drawn by Congress is longer than necessary to protect the fiscal integrity of the program. We may also assume

that unnecessary hardship is incurred by persons just short of qualifying. But it remains true that some line is essential, that any line must produce some harsh and apparently arbitrary consequences, and, of greatest importance, that those who qualify under the test Congress has chosen may reasonably be presumed to have a greater affinity with the United States than those who do not. In short, citizens and those who are most like citizens qualify. Those who are less like citizens do not.

In this case, since appellees have not identified a principled basis for prescribing a different standard than the one selected by Congress, they have, in effect, merely invited us to substitute our judgment for that of Congress in deciding which aliens shall be eligible to participate in the supplementary insurance program on the same conditions as citizens. We decline the invitation.

Decision. No. Congress had no duty to provide all aliens with benefits afforded to citizens.

CASE QUESTIONS

Critical Legal Thinking. How does the Court distinguish between those rights that should be extended to undocumented aliens and those which should not be extended to them?

Business Ethics. Do you think the Court struck the right balance of competing interests in making its decision? If you do not believe that the decision is fair, how would you frame the issue before the Court?

Contemporary Business. What sorts of life activities or workplace benefits do you think a modern Supreme Court should recognize as protected under the Equal Protection Clause or the Due Process Clause?

Management Application
Constitutional Restraints on Alien Employment

[N]or shall any person . . . be deprived of life, liberty, or property, without due process of law. . . .

— U.S. Constitution, Amendment V

Section 1. All persons born or **naturalized** in the United States, and subject to the jurisdiction thereof, are citizens of the United States and of the State wherein they reside. No State shall make or enforce any law which shall abridge the privileges or immunities of citizens of the United States; nor shall any State deprive any person of

> life, liberty, or property, without due process of law; nor deny to any person within its jurisdiction the equal protection of the laws.
> — U.S. Constitution, Amendment XIV

The Supreme Court analyzes the **Equal Protection Clause** of the Fourteenth Amendment three different ways, depending on the issue before it, using three tests:

- **Strict scrutiny test.** Any government activity or regulation that classifies persons based on a *suspect class* (i.e., race) is reviewed for lawfulness using a **strict scrutiny test**. This means that the government must have a **compelling governmental interest** for treating persons differently because of their race for such unequal treatment to be lawful. Under this standard, many governmental classifications of persons based on race are found to be unconstitutional.
- **Intermediate scrutiny test.** The lawfulness of government classifications based on *protected classes* other than race (such as sex or age) is examined using an **intermediate scrutiny test**. This standard requires that the classification be substantially related to advancing a legitimate government purpose or objective.
- **Rational basis test.** The lawfulness of all government classifications that do not involve suspect or protected classes is reviewed under a **rational basis test**. Under this test, the courts will uphold a government regulation as long as there is a justifiable reason for the law. This standard permits much of government business regulation.

Can you think of any industries or jobs for which U.S. citizenship is a prerequisite to employment? Why should courts uphold this requirement for employment in those particular industries or jobs? Which equal protection test would be used by the court in deciding the constitutionality of the requirement?

In *Yick Wo v. Hopkins*,[11] the Supreme Court held that **aliens** are protected under **Equal Protection** from governmental discrimination. In that case, the Court struck down an ordinance that was administered to exclude **aliens** from pursuing the lawful occupation of laundry worker. The Court found unconstitutional a San Francisco ordinance regulating public laundries that was enforced primarily against Chinese-Americans. With the application of the **strict scrutiny** standard in later cases, few offending state actions were upheld as constitutional. Another interesting note from this case is that it is the first in which the Court recognized protection from **citizenship discrimination**. Later cases reaffirmed this view. State laws that discriminate because of alienage will generally be upheld only if they promote a **compelling state interest** by the least restrictive means available. The Court has recognized exceptions to this **strict scrutiny** standard, however, including the two explored in the following sections.

Political Function or Public Interest Exception

This exception applies to laws that exclude **aliens** from positions intimately related to the process of democratic self-government. For example, **aliens** may be prohibited from certain occupations (such as public school teaching and law enforcement) or from receiving publicly funded contracts. Such laws are considered necessary to protect special interests of the state or its **citizens**.

> ***Example:*** States can enforce state laws that may bar **aliens** from teaching in public schools because teachers have direct, day-to-day contact with students, exercise unsupervised discretion over them, act as role models, and influence their students' understanding of government and the political process.[12] However, duties such as those required of a notary

> public, even though notaries may be designated by a state as a public officer, do not extend to the heart of representative government. As such, requiring **citizenship** for a position such as a notary public would fail to demonstrate a compelling state interest, and the law may be denied enforcement because of its **equal protection** violation.[13]

The Supreme Court has observed that "the Court's decisions have established that classifications based on **alienage**, like those based on **nationality** or race are inherently suspect and subject to close judicial scrutiny." **Aliens** as a class are a prime example of a "discrete and insular" minority for whom such heightened judicial solicitude is appropriate. Accordingly, "the power of a state to apply its laws exclusively to its **alien** inhabitants as a class is confined within narrow limits."[14] Such language informs us that the Court will strictly review job rights that are conditioned upon citizenship.

Basic Right to Work

Aliens who have been lawfully admitted to work in the United States cannot be denied the basic right to work in lawful employment. State laws that inhibit such rights violate the **Equal Protection Clause,** unless the legislation is required to protect the special interests of the state. If the work is necessary to protect the public welfare, exclusion of **aliens** from employment or an occupation is within the police power of the state.[15] While **immigration** is within the purview of the federal authorities, in the following case the Supreme Court considered whether states can enact laws affecting **alien** employment.

CASE 17.2

STATES MAY LEGISLATE IN MATTERS AFFECTING ALIENS UNLESS CONGRESS HAS MADE IT CLEAR THAT FEDERAL LAW WILL PREEMPT SUCH STATE LAWS

DE CANAS ET AL. V. BICA ET AL.

424 U.S. 351 (1976)

Supreme Court of the United States

Facts. Immigrant farm workers sued a group of farm labor contractors in a California state court alleging that the contractors had refused them continued employment because of a surplus of labor. This surplus resulted from the defendant's violation of a statute that provided that no employer shall knowingly employ an alien who is not entitled to lawful residence in the country if such employment would have an adverse effect on lawful resident workers. The state courts dismissed the case holding that the statute was unconstitutional as improperly legislating within the reach of the INA (the predecessor to the IRCA). The Supreme Court granted *certiorari.*

Issue. May a state enact a law that prohibits an employer from hiring unauthorized aliens if such employment would have an adverse effect on resident workers?

Language of the Court. Brennan, J.: **California Labor Code Ann. §2805(a) provides that "[N]o employer shall knowingly employ an alien who is not entitled to lawful residence in the United States if such employment would have an adverse effect on lawful resident workers." The question presented in this case is whether §2805(a) is unconstitutional either because it is an attempt to regulate immigration and naturalization or because it is pre-empted under the Supremacy Clause, [and] by the Immigration and Nationality Act.**

The Superior Court, in an unreported opinion, dismissed the complaint, holding "that Labor Code 2805 is unconstitutional . . . [because] [i]t encroaches upon, and interferes with, a comprehensive regulatory scheme enacted by Congress in the exercise of its exclusive power over immigration. . . ." . . . The California Court of Appeal . . . held that §2805(a) is an attempt to regulate the conditions for admission of foreign nationals, and therefore unconstitutional because, "in the area of immigration and naturalization, congressional power is exclusive." . . . The Court of Appeal further indicated that state regulatory power over this subject matter was foreclosed when Congress, "as an incident of national sovereignty," enacted the INA as a comprehensive scheme governing all aspects of immigration and naturalization, including the employment of aliens, and "specifically and intentionally declined to add sanctions on employers to its control mechanism." The Supreme Court of California denied review. We granted certiorari. . . . We reverse.

Power to regulate immigration is unquestionably exclusively a federal power. (Citations omitted.) But the Court has never held that every state enactment which in any way deals with aliens is a regulation of immigration and thus per se pre-empted by this constitutional power, whether latent or exercised. For example, Takahashi v. Fish & Game Comm'n, (citation omitted), and Graham v. Richardson, (citation omitted), cited a line of cases that upheld certain discriminatory state treatment of aliens lawfully within the United States. Although the "doctrinal foundations" of the cited cases, which generally arose under the Equal Protection Clause, . . . they remain authority that, standing alone, the fact that aliens are the subject of a state statute does not render it a regulation of immigration, which is essentially a determination of who should or should not be admitted into the country, and the conditions under which a legal entrant may remain. . . . In this case, California has sought to strengthen its economy by adopting federal standards in imposing criminal sanctions against state employers who knowingly employ aliens who have no federal right to employment within the country; even if such local regulation has some purely speculative and indirect impact on immigration, it does not thereby become a constitutionally proscribed regulation of immigration that Congress itself would be

powerless to authorize or approve. Thus, absent congressional action, §2805 would not be an invalid state incursion on federal power.

"[F]ederal regulation . . . should not be deemed pre-emptive of state regulatory power in the absence of persuasive reasons — either that the nature of the regulated subject matter permits no other conclusion, or that the Congress has unmistakably so ordained." In this case, we cannot conclude that pre-emption is required either because "the nature of the . . . subject matter [regulation of employment of illegal aliens] permits no other conclusion," or because "Congress has unmistakably so ordained" that result.

States possess broad authority under their police powers to regulate the employment relationship to protect workers within the State. Child labor laws, minimum and other wage laws, laws affecting occupational health and safety, and workmen's compensation laws are only a few examples. California's attempt in §2805(a) to prohibit the knowing employment by California employers of persons not entitled to lawful residence in the United States, let alone to work here, is certainly within the mainstream of such police power regulation. Employment of illegal aliens in times of high unemployment deprives citizens and legally admitted aliens of jobs; acceptance by illegal aliens of jobs on substandard terms as to wages and working conditions can seriously depress wage scales and working conditions of citizens and legally admitted aliens; and employment of illegal aliens under such conditions can diminish the effectiveness of labor unions. These local problems are particularly acute in California in light of the significant influx into that State of illegal aliens from neighboring Mexico. In attempting to protect California's fiscal interests and lawfully resident labor force from the deleterious effects on its economy resulting from the employment of illegal aliens, §2805(a) focuses directly upon these essentially local problems and is tailored to combat effectively the perceived evils.

Decision. Yes. The state statute is constitutional and is not preempted by federal law.

CASE QUESTIONS

Critical Legal Thinking. What is your understanding of the scope of federal preemption and the right of states to exercise their police powers to regulate matters that are of special interest to states?

Business Ethics. What is the scope of the role that states should play with regard to the employment of unauthorized workers? In recessionary times, how popular would the Court's philosophy be with unemployed U.S. citizens? Would these citizens actually undertake the work performed by the unauthorized workers?

Contemporary Business. Can you identify other areas of the employment of unauthorized aliens that should be reserved to state legislation?

Following the decision in the *De Canas v. Bica* case, a federal court denied a Canadian lawyer the right to sue under **NAFTA** (the North American Free Trade Agreement, which we study in the last chapter) to challenge a Louisiana state court rule requiring that every applicant for the state bar be a **citizen** or a permanent resident **alien.**[16]

In applying the **INA**, the Supreme Court held in *Sure-Tan, Inc. v. NLRB*[17] that an employer had committed an unfair labor practice against undocumented **alien** employees who were members of the unionized workforce of the employer; however, the employees would not be eligible for back pay for any time when they were not lawfully entitled to be present, and thus employed, in the United States. At the time of the Court's decision, the act stated it was lawful to hire an undocumented **alien** and for an undocumented worker to accept employment from a U.S. employer. Public outrage followed the *Sure-Tan* decision, and Congress amended the **INA** by enacting the **Immigration Reform and Control Act of 1986 (IRCA)**.

Immigration Reform and Control Act of 1986

In 1986, Congress enacted legislation to control illegal immigration by sanctioning those who employed them in the United States. The **IRCA** attempts to control this immigration by prohibiting the knowing employment of illegal **aliens** by requiring employers to verify the eligibility for employment of prospective workers.[18] The **IRCA** was amended by the **Illegal Immigration Reform and Immigrant Responsibility Act of 1996 (IIRIRA)**, which clarified the acceptable documentation to be submitted to an employer in relation to the employment eligibility form **(Form I-9)**, discussed below, providing employers with the possibility of a **good-faith defense** for technical paperwork violations.

As amended and as it pertains to employment law, this federal act covers three subjects:

1. Requirements for employment verification and prohibition of discrimination based on citizenship status. Concerning employer compliance, it also sets forth penalties for document abuse;
2. Legalization of certain **alien** classifications; and
3. Agricultural worker reforms.

Immigration Reform and Control Act of 1986 (IRCA)
A federal law prohibiting discrimination against applicants and employees based on their citizenship or national origin. IRCA makes it illegal to knowingly hire or recruit unauthorized aliens and requires employers to verify workers' identity and employment eligibility to work in the United States.

IRCA included guidelines for identifying employers subject to its requirements.

1. The requirements relating to identity verification and employment authorization apply to *all* U.S. employers regardless of size.
2. The **IRCA**'s **antidiscrimination** provisions apply only to those employers with four or more workers, *but* they do not apply to employers who are already subject to Title VII, which is triggered for companies engaged in interstate commerce with 15 or more employees.

The act is meant to ensure that employers do not knowingly employ unauthorized workers. Structurally, it assists immigration policy enforcement by imposing stiffer penalties on employers that hire such aliens. Provisions of the act increased criminal penalties for those who fraudulently use government-issued documents, such as birth certificates, passports, drivers' licenses, and Social Security cards.

Employment Recruitment and Retention

The act makes it unlawful for employers, or those who recruit or refer potential workers to employers for a fee, to knowingly hire, recruit, or refer unauthorized **aliens** for employment in the United States.[19] It also makes it unlawful for an employer to continue to employ an **alien** knowing that he or she is, or has become, an unauthorized **alien** with respect to such employment.[20]

Employment Verification

IRCA requires employers to examine specified documents of new employees to make sure the employees are authorized to work in the United States.[21] This examination occurs *after* the employee's acceptance of an offer of employment conditioned upon his or her eligibility to be employed in the United States.

It also requires employers to complete **Form I-9** for each employee. This form is the employer's verification that, under penalty of perjury, all its employees are U.S. **citizens** or **aliens** authorized to work in the United States. In addition, the hired individuals must attest to their own eligibility.[22]

Finally, **IRCA** requires employers to keep records for each employee showing his or her eligibility to work in the United States.[23]

Employer Penalties and Antidiscrimination

The act is violated if the employer has knowledge of an employee's unauthorized work status or if the employer deliberately fails to investigate suspicious circumstances.

An employer's **"pattern or practice"** of immigration employment violations may lead to criminal penalties against it. A failure to adhere to the employment verification system, referred to as a **"paperwork violation,"** will result in only a civil money penalty of a lesser amount than would an employment violation.[24]

Employers who employ more than three employees are prohibited from discriminating against any individual (other than an unauthorized **alien**) with respect to the hiring, recruitment, or referral for a fee of the individual or the discharging of any individual because of the individual's national origin or citizenship status.[25] This provision does not apply to those employers who are subject to Title VII.

Federal Enforcement

The duty to investigate violations of **IRCA** has been assigned to the U.S. Citizenship and Immigration Services (USCIS) (formerly the INS). It imposes monetary and criminal penalties on employers for violations and noncompliance.[26]

Persons charged with an **IRCA** violation are entitled to notice and to an evidentiary hearing conducted by an **administrative law judge (ALJ)** in accordance with the federal Administrative Procedures Act.[27] The **ALJ** may require offending employers to pay civil money penalties and may issue **cease-and-desist orders** requiring future compliance with the statute.[28] The government must show by a preponderance of the evidence that the employer knowingly employed an unauthorized **alien**.

The **ALJ** order becomes a final agency order within 30 days after its issuance if the agency does not modify or vacate it. A party adversely affected by a final order may petition in the federal court of appeals for review within 45 days after the order becomes final. A reviewing court must defer to the agency's reasonable construction of the **IRCA** and may only overturn agency findings of fact that are unsupported by substantial evidence.

Preemption

The Supreme Court has held that **aliens** may be barred from holding "important non-elective executive, legislative, and judicial position."[29] In addition, the act provides for express preemption of state and local law, with an exception as they relate to licensure. According to the act, "provisions of this section preempt any State or local law imposing civil or criminal sanctions (other than through licensing and similar laws) upon those who employ, recruit, or refer for a fee for employment, unauthorized **aliens**." The limited exception in the statute relates only to state or local laws that suspend, revoke, or refrain from renewing licenses that would have been issued to entities, but for their violation of the act. Because of this language in the statute, Congress clearly intended to prevent state and local laws and regulations from imposing civil or criminal sanctions on employers.

Other employment law issues arise with regard to implied preemption. Under this concept, congressional intent to preempt may be inferred from circumstances. Courts have wrestled with questions in which the circumstances are governed by federal immigration laws or might be considered as falling within a state or local agency's lawful rights to regulate employment. The answer in a particular case will revolve around how the court chooses to define the application of the act.

In addition, courts have found that an individual's wrongful termination claims are preempted by **IRCA** when compliance with **IRCA** is the basis for the termination. Nevertheless, a wrongful termination claim may be filed when the employer fires an employee when the employee had the opportunity to change his or her visa status or otherwise to become a legal resident eligible for continued employment.

> ***Example:*** A federal circuit court of appeals held that **IRCA** did not preempt a state labor law that forbade employers from firing an employee without good cause. The court found that an individual who was promoted to manager of Fendi's Beverly Hills store and who received positive performance reviews could have been suspended or placed on leave without pay for a reasonable period while he obtained the work authorization to which he was entitled.[30]

Form I-9
A federal form required to be completed and retained by all U.S. employers for each person hired. The form must be completed by citizens and noncitizens. Employers must examine all employees' employment eligibility and identity documents.

Form I-9 establishes that the employer has properly verified its employees' identities and employment authorization. Section 1 is to be completed by new employees at the time of hire. The employer must complete section 2 within three business days after the employee commences work. In addition, the employer must attest under penalty of perjury that it has examined the documents presented by the employee and that they appear to be genuine and related to the employee and that to the best of the employer's knowledge the person is authorized to work in the United States.

CASE 17.3

UNDOCUMENTED WORKERS ARE NOT ENTITLED TO BACK PAY

HOFFMAN PLASTIC COMPOUNDS, INC. V. N.L.R.B.

535 U.S. 137 (2002)

Supreme Court of the United States

Facts. Jose Castro submitted a false birth certificate to support his application for employment with Hoffman Plastic Compounds, Inc., a nonunion employer. Several months after he was hired, he engaged in activities supportive of union organizing at Hoffman. He was terminated in 1992. The National Labor Relations Board (NLRB) found that Hoffman Plastic Compounds, Inc. had unlawfully fired Castro in violation of the National Labor Relations Act and awarded him back pay. Hoffman appealed to the District of Columbia Circuit Court of Appeals and was denied. The Supreme Court granted *certiorari.*

Issue. Is the NLRB authorized to award back pay for violations of the National Labor Relations Act to an undocumented immigrant who was unlawfully terminated from his employment?

Language of the Court. Rehnquist, C.J.: **In 1986, two years after Sure-Tan, Congress enacted IRCA, a comprehensive scheme prohibiting the employment of illegal aliens in the United States. As we have previously noted, IRCA "forcefully" made combating the employment of illegal aliens central to "the policy of immigration law." (Citation omitted.) It did so by establishing an extensive "employment verification system designed to deny employment to aliens who (a) are not lawfully present in the United States, or (b) are not lawfully authorized to work in the United States. . . . This verification system is critical to the IRCA regime. To enforce it, IRCA mandates that employers verify the identity and eligibility of all new hires by examining specified documents before they begin work. If an alien applicant is unable to present the required documentation, the unauthorized alien cannot be hired.**

Similarly, if an employer unknowingly hires an unauthorized alien, or if the alien becomes unauthorized while employed, the employer is compelled to discharge the worker upon discovery of the worker's undocumented status. Employers who violate IRCA are punished by civil fines, and may be subject to criminal prosecution. IRCA also makes it a crime for an unauthorized alien

to subvert the employer verification system by tendering fraudulent documents. It thus prohibits aliens from using or attempting to use "any forged, counterfeit, altered, or falsely made document" or "any document lawfully issued to or with respect to a person other than the possessor" for purposes of obtaining employment in the United States. Aliens who use or attempt to use such documents are subject to fines and criminal prosecution. There is no dispute that Castro's use of false documents to obtain employment with Hoffman violated these provisions.

Under the IRCA regime, it is impossible for an undocumented alien to obtain employment in the United States without some party directly contravening explicit congressional policies. Either the undocumented alien tenders fraudulent identification, which subverts the cornerstone of IRCA's enforcement mechanism, or the employer knowingly hires the undocumented alien in direct contradiction of its IRCA obligations. The Board asks that we overlook this fact and allow it to award back pay to an illegal alien for years of work not performed, for wages that could not lawfully have been earned, and for a job obtained in the first instance by a criminal fraud. We find, however, that awarding back pay to illegal aliens runs counter to policies underlying IRCA, policies the Board has no authority to enforce or administer. Therefore, as we have consistently held in like circumstances, the award lies beyond the bounds of the Board's remedial discretion.

We therefore conclude that allowing the Board to award back pay to illegal aliens would unduly trench upon explicit statutory prohibitions critical to federal immigration policy, as expressed in IRCA. It would encourage the successful evasion of apprehension by immigration authorities, condone prior violations of the immigration laws, and encourage future violations. However broad the Board's discretion to fashion remedies when dealing only with the NLRA, it is not so unbounded as to authorize this sort of an award.

Decision. No. The award of back pay by the NLRB would violate IRCA's prohibition on the employment of undocumented aliens.

CASE QUESTIONS

Critical Legal Thinking. Is the Court's decision based on the narrowness of the definition of "employee" or can the Court's decision be applied to a broader context than that presented in this case?

Business Ethics. Does this decision foreclose states from enforcing their own minimum wage and hour laws on behalf of undocumented workers?

Contemporary Business. The dissent argued that the Court's decision "undermines the public policies that underlie the Nation's labor laws." Do you think that this decision has the effect of compelling illegal laborers to remain in an underground economy, fearful of reporting substandard, illegal working conditions to avoid deportation?

Following the *Hoffman* decision, a number of federal and state courts wrestled with its application to contexts not involving back-pay awards under the NLRA. The courts have been creative in their efforts to avoid **preemption** of state wage, hour, unemployment, and safety laws and regulations with respect to the undocumented worker. While the courts and administrative agencies construe the *Hoffman* case, there appears to be a developing bright line in its interpretation. Courts and agencies note that *Hoffman* addressed the award of back pay for work not actually performed and judgments and awards for uncompensated work previously performed.

State administrative agencies are confronting novel questions in light of the ruling in *Hoffman*. For example, should undocumented workers be included within the coverage of a state workers' compensation system? The Supreme Court left open to further congressional action the enactment of laws that would address the following questions.

- If an illegal **alien**'s status is discovered, is he or she entitled to continued workers' compensation benefits?
- Is the employer compelled to rehire or offer modified work for the undocumented **alien** following rehabilitation?
- Should wage scales be adjusted for the country of origin in lieu of applying state and federal wage standards?
- What is the cost of the burden imposed on employers for controlling illegal immigration as compelled by the **IRCA**?

Concept Summary
IRCA

IRCA provisions relating to the verification of identity and employment authorization of new employees apply to every U.S. employer, both public and private, and all persons or entities recruiting or referring individuals for a fee.

Federal law specifies that is unlawful for a person or entity to:

- Hire, recruit, or refer for a fee for employment in the United States an **alien**, knowing that person is unauthorized to work in the United States;
- Hire an individual for employment in the United States without complying with the employment verification requirements of federal law; and
- Continue to employ the **alien** in the United States on learning that the **alien** is or has become unauthorized to work in the country. The employer must terminate the **alien** within a reasonable time after learning of that status.[31]

IRCA's antidiscrimination provisions apply only to employers that employ more than three persons. They do not apply to employers who have 15 or more employees and are already subject to Title VII.

Who May Be Employed in the United States?

Authorized Workers

The Supreme Court in the *Hoffman Plastics* case provided the following definition: "[f]or an **alien** to be 'authorized' to work in the United States, he or she must possess 'a valid social security account number card' . . . or 'other documentation evidencing authorization of employment in the United States which the Attorney General finds, by regulation, to be acceptable for purposes of this section.' "[32]

A partial listing of the classes of **aliens** authorized to be employed in the United States (on issuance of an employment authorization document from the federal government) include the following:

- lawful permanent resident **aliens**, their parents, and dependents;
- lawful temporary residents, lawful refugees, and asylees; and
- **aliens** admitted as a nonimmigrant spouse or child of such **alien.**[33]

In the United States, an asylee is a person seeking asylum. Temporary visitors to the United States and others transiting through the country are ineligible for any employment while they are here.

If an **alien**'s application for employment authorization is denied, the applicant is notified in writing, which will include the basis for the decision; however, no appeal lies from the denial of the application.[34]

U.S. Employment of Foreign Nationals

Foreign nationals must possess permanent resident status (i.e., have a "green card") or a visa that permits them to work in the United States and its territories. The USCIS issues numerous types of visas. The visas most often used in the employment context are the following:

- **E-1 or E-2:** These visas are for treaty traders or investors, to whom some of the traditional nonimmigrant visa rules do not apply. **E-visas** allow a person to remain in the United States indefinitely under a reciprocal treaty of commerce and navigation between the United States and the country of nationality. The trader must be engaged in "substantial trade" between the United States and his or her home country. The treaty investor, an **E-2** visa holder, must be developing or directing an enterprise in which he or she has invested a substantial amount of capital.
- **H-1:** These visas are for persons of distinguished merit or skill and are rarely granted.
- **H-2:** Temporary workers, including agricultural workers, are issued H-2 visas.
- **L-1:** L-1 visas are issue to temporary high-level employees in intracompany transfers from a foreign subsidiary to a U.S. operation (limited to seven years of employment for executives and senior managers and five years for those with "specialized knowledge"). Like the **H-1B**, the **L-1** visa does not preclude the visa holder from seeking lawful permanent status while resident in the United States.

Managers are defined as persons who manage a function or oversee a component of a company, establish the goals and policies of an organization or a major part or function of an organization, exercise wide latitude of discretionary decision-making, and receive only general supervision or direction from higher-level executives.[35]

- **F-1/J-1:** These visas are for students entering limited employment for training purposes. Overseas applicants to U.S. schools apply directly to U.S. consulates abroad by presenting a Form I-20 from the school they wish to attend. **F-1** students are authorized to attend school and to work in limited circumstances, including on-campus employment and practical skills training.
- **H-1B:** Persons in "specialty occupations" requiring a bachelor's degree or higher (limited to six years of employment) may be accorded an H-1B visa. The visa is reserved for those in positions requiring both theoretical and practical application of highly specialized knowledge. The spouse and children of a person in **H-1B** status may apply to reside in the United States during the same period. Unlike other classifications of nonimmigrant visa applicants, the **H-1B** applicant does not have to prove a negative, namely, that they do not intend to immigrate to the United States. An **H-1B** applicant can intend to work in the country temporarily in H-1B status and to immigrate permanently at a later point in time.[36] The law requires employers to pay **H-1B** employees at least the prevailing wage in the area where the work will be performed or the actual wage paid other employees with the same job description and qualifications, whichever wage rate is higher. This requirement protects American workers from an influx of foreign workers seeking to work for lower wages. These classifications are granted on the basis that these persons are priority workers entitled to special preferences.
- **EB-5:** The attorney general can issue an investment-based immigration visa for those immigrants who seek to enter the United States to engage in a new commercial business and who have $1.0 million or more in capital to invest, subject to adjustment. This classification is targeted for commercial businesses in specific employment areas.[37]
- **H-1C:** These visas are provided for professional nurses working in health-care areas experiencing professional shortages. The nurse visa applicant can only be sponsored by hospitals qualified by the **USCIS** under the foreign **H-1C** foreign registered nurse work visa program.
- **TN:** Chapter 16 of NAFTA and of the NAFTA Implementation Act added a new **"NAFTA professional"** classification. Under these provisions, the **TN visa** may be issued to nationals of Canadian or Mexican nationals, and to the **alien**'s spouse and children, intending to engage in business activities at the professional level. If the applicant is a professional, the visa is similar to the **H-1B**, but without limitation on the length of stay in the United States.

Mexicans are treated differently from Canadians under the **TN visa** program. The Canadian need only show that he or she is a "professional" coming to work in his or her field, based on a job offer, and may request admission at the border. The Mexican applicant must present the application before a U.S. Consul. For Mexican visa applicants, various additional forms of identification are required, and the applicant must be fingerprinted before the **TN visa** will be issued.

Numerical Limitations

Except for an emergency, there are a limited number of **aliens** who may be admitted in any fiscal year. In the case of refugees and asylees, the president fixes the annual limitation but retains flexibility to admit additional persons during emergencies, after appropriate consultation with the Senate.[38] Any **alien** who has been admitted to the United States as a refugee and has not been granted permanent resident status, has been physically present in the country for at least one year, has not had his or her admission terminated by the attorney general, or has not acquired permanent resident status must return to his or her country of origin or apply for immigration status.

Exclusive of the emergency classification, **aliens** who are admitted for employment purposes have a numerical ceiling. The worldwide level of employment-based immigration into the United States for a fiscal year is equal to 140,000 plus certain specific statutory adjustments.[39]

Management Application
The 30-60 Day Rule

To qualify for a nonimmigrant visa, an applicant must overcome the presumption that all persons entering the United States, even on nonimmigrant visas, intend to immigrate and remain in the country permanently. The **30-60 day rule** was developed by the Department of State to help consular officers determine if someone has committed **visa fraud**. Anyone who applies for nonimmigrant status (such as a visitor's visa) and then within 30 days of admission to the United States submits a second application requesting a change of status in their nonimmigrant visa application, will be denied the status change under **"the 30-60 day rule."** If the application is filed after 60 days, there is no presumption of fraud. In the view of the federal government, a violation of this rule creates the presumption that the nonimmigrant entered in the United States under false pretenses.

Employment Verification

USCIS has designated the following documents as acceptable for establishing both **identity and employment authorization**:

- United States passport (unexpired or expired);
- Alien Registration Receipt Card or Permanent Resident Card (also known as a "green card");
- An unexpired foreign passport that contains a temporary I-551 stamp;
- An unexpired Employment Authorization Document issued by the USCIS or its predecessor agency, the INS, that contains a photograph;

- In the case of a nonimmigrant **alien** authorized to work for a specific employer incident to status, an unexpired foreign passport with an Arrival-Departure Record (Form I-94) bearing the same name as the individual and containing an endorsement of the **alien**'s nonimmigrant status that has not yet expired and does not conflict with any restrictions identified on Form I-94; and
- Any other document designated by the attorney general, if the document (1) contains a photograph of the individual and sufficient identifying information, (2) is evidence of employment authorization, and (3) contains security features that make it resistant to tampering, counterfeiting, and fraudulent use.

If the employee presents a document from the above list of documents, no other documentation is necessary to establish the right to work. If applicants cannot produce one of the above-listed documents, then one document must be presented to establish identity and a second one to establish authorization to work in the U.S.

To establish identity only, one of the following documents may be used:

- A state-issued driver's license or state-issued identification card containing a photograph (if the document does not contain a photograph, identifying information such as name, address, date of birth, sex, height, and color of eyes should be included);
- School identification card with a photograph;
- Voter's registration card;
- United States military card or draft record;
- Identification card issued by federal, state, or local government agencies (if the document does not contain a photograph, identifying information such as name, address, date of birth, sex, height, and color of eyes should be included);
- Military dependent's identification card;
- Native American tribal documents;
- United States Coast Guard Merchant Mariner Card; or
- Canadian driver's license.

Individuals under age 18 who are unable to produce one of the above documents may establish identity by presenting:

- School record or report card;
- Clinic, doctor, or hospital record; or
- Day-care or nursery school record.

Persons under age 18 who cannot produce a document from either list above may be exempted from producing any identity document under the following conditions:

- The minor's parent or legal guardian:
    - Completes section 1 of **Form I-9** ("Employee Information and Verification");
    - In the space designated for the minor's signature, writes "minor under age 18"; and
    - Completes on **Form I-9** the "Preparer/Translator Certification"; and
- The employer, recruiter, or referrer writes in the space for documents examined, "minor under age 18."

People with disabilities who are unable to produce one of the identity documents and who are being employed by a nonprofit organization or association or as part of a rehabilitation program, may follow the procedures for minors, substituting the term "special placement" for "minor under age 18" where appropriate.[40]

The following documents have been designated as acceptable **to establish employment authorization only**:

- Social Security card other than one that states on its face that it is not valid for employment purposes;
- Unexpired employment authorization document issued by the USCIS or its predecessor agency, the INS;
- Native American tribal document;
- United States Citizen Identification Card (Form I-197);
- Identification Card for Use of Resident Citizens in the United States (Form I-179);
- An original or certified copy of a birth certificate issued by a state, county, municipal authority, or outlying possession of the United States bearing an official seal;
- Certification of Report of Birth (Form DS-1350, issued by the Department of State); or
- Certification of Birth Abroad (Form FS-545, issued by a Foreign Service post).[41]

An employer should never demand more documentation than **IRCA** requires from an applicant or a new employee. If more documentation is requested, an adverse employment decision should not be based on the failure to provide the requested information.

Beyond the point of employment eligibility, **IRCA** requires employers to maintain the verification information for three years following the execution of the **Form I-9** or a period of one year following employment termination, whichever is later.[42]

Employer's Duty to Examine Documents

INA §247B
Subject to exceptions required by law, employers with four or more employees may not discriminate or retaliate against any individual (other than an unauthorized alien) with respect to hiring, recruitment, or discharge because of the person's national origin or status as an authorized alien. The section also applies to an employer's refusal to accept permissible documents presented by an employee to comply with Form I-9 requirements.

Employers are allowed to use the information provided by the new employee only for purposes of complying with the **IRCA**'s requirements. An employer may copy the applicant's documentation for purposes of requirement verification. The **IRCA** applies a **"good-faith standard"** with respect to the examination, review, and retention of the documents. If the documents presented appear to be genuine and to relate to the applicant, the employer has met its burden of complying with the law. Under **INA §274B**, employers may not specify which document(s) the person must present. Employers may not require additional documentation if those presented by the new employee appear to conform to the law. To do so would lead to a potential claim for discrimination under either **IRCA** or Title VII.

Employers are required to retain the **Form I-9** along with records showing that they have examined the identity and employment authorization documents. They must make these records available for inspection upon reasonable notice by the **Bureau of Immigration and Customs Enforcement (ICE)**, a unit of USCIS. **ICE** may exercise subpoena powers to enforce the inspection and compliance requirements. The employer-retained forms may be maintained in electronic form pursuant to a 2005 change in the law. If an employee is terminated and later rehired, the employer may require the employee to execute a new **I-9** form or to review the previously completed form, if available.

The act makes it unlawful to "continue to employ the **alien** . . . knowing the **alien** is (or has become) an unauthorized **alien** with respect to such employment." Absent the element of knowledge, the employer will not violate the law. Under the act's regulations, "[t]he term knowing includes having actual or constructive knowledge. Constructive knowledge is knowledge that may fairly be inferred through notice of certain facts and circumstances that would lead a person, through the exercise of reasonable care, to know about a certain condition" (*pending regulations* 8 C.F.R. part 274a).

The determination of what constitutes a reasonable time for the employer to terminate such an employee is a factual one. Courts will review the certainty of the information that establishes the unauthorized status. In the following case, the court considered the constitutionality of the **IRCA** as well as the reasonableness of the time the employer took to take action against the employee.

CASE 17.4

"KNOWING" EMPLOYMENT OF UNAUTHORIZED ALIENS INCLUDES CONSTRUCTIVE KNOWLEDGE

MESTER MANUFACTURING CO. V. INS

879 F.2d 561 (9th Cir. 1989)

U.S. Court of Appeals for the Ninth Circuit

Facts. Mester Manufacturing Co. manufactures furniture at an El Cajon, California, facility and employed an average of 70 people on the premises. In July 1987, an INS Border Patrol agent made an educational visit to Mester and left the employer a copy of written information on complying with IRCA. In August 1987, following an inspection of I-9 forms, Mester's president received specific information that several employees were likely to be unauthorized. The president made no further inquiry of the INS and failed to take appropriate corrective action. The aliens turned out to be unauthorized. Mester was cited for violating the law by, among other things, not terminating one employee until two weeks had elapsed from the date the president learned the employee was unauthorized. Mester protested the citations before an ALJ and lost. It then petitioned the Ninth Circuit Court of Appeals for a review of an order of an administrative law judge penalizing Mester for violating the IRCA.

Issue. Was an employer required to terminate an unauthorized employee as soon as it became aware of the unauthorized status, or should the company have been allowed a reasonable period of time in which to allow the employee to wind up his employment?

Language of the Court. Beezer, J.: This is the first circuit court review of employer sanctions under IRCA. IRCA is a major change in immigration law. IRCA puts part of the burden of compliance upon employers. . . . It is unlawful for an employer knowingly to hire an alien who is unauthorized to be employed in the United States, or to continue to employ an alien in the knowledge that his employment is unauthorized. . . . The statute sets up an employment verification system under which an employer must execute a verification form ("I-9") attesting, under penalty of perjury, that it has verified that each employee (whether a U.S. citizen or an alien) is not an unauthorized alien by examining the requisite document, or documents, showing identity and employment authorization. . . . The individual hired must also attest to his own eligibility.

The knowledge element was satisfied; Mester had constructive knowledge, even if no Mester employee had actual specific knowledge of the employee's unauthorized status.

Counsel for the INS recognized that employer sanctions for the five-minute violation would likely be unreasonable, but maintained that 21 or 30 days continued employment would not be reasonable, especially in light of the allegedly transient and casual nature of much border employment. It appears that the INS wishes to proceed on an entirely ad hoc basis that will undoubtedly force this court to sketch out some standard of reasonableness in future litigation. Legislative or regulatory action that would set forth some reasonable time frame for termination acceptable to employers and the INS would seem appropriate. Absent any such guidance, however, or any independent reason to apply a different construction of the statute than that of the ALJ, we defer to the ALJ's conclusion, based on the relevant facts, that a two-week delay in firing Castel-Garcia amounted to an IRCA violation.

In this case, the ALJ considered the steps taken, or not taken, by Mester to confirm the information provided by the INS on September 3 before terminating employees. It is apparent that an inquiry into a reasonable time frame for termination will include consideration, in certain cases, of factors other than the number of days alone — such as the certainty of the information providing the knowledge of unauthorized status, and steps taken by the employer to confirm it. In none of the situations at issue here do we conclude that the ALJ finding of an IRCA violation was an unreasonable application of the statute, based on our consideration of all the relevant facts.

Decision. Yes. The employer must timely investigate and discharge from employment an unauthorized alien.

CASE QUESTIONS

Critical Legal Thinking. The court of appeals determined that the statute did not have a bright line test for when termination of an unauthorized alien should occur. What facts and circumstances do you believe are relevant in determining whether a violation of the act has occurred?

Business Ethics. Where should the ethical line be drawn for defining employers' duties when receiving knowledge of unauthorized status investigating that information, and terminating unauthorized employees?

Contemporary Business. Can you think of circumstances under which the federal government may enter an employer's premises to conduct audits of records?

The **IIRIRA** allows an employer a **good-faith compliance defense** when the employer is found to have made technical or procedural errors in preparing or completing the **I-9** form. However, the **good-faith defense** is not available to an employer who failed to complete a **Form I-9** for an **unauthorized alien employee.**[43] An unintentional oversight to prepare and retain the **Form I-9** will not excuse the violation, but it will be a factor in determining the penalty assessed under the law. The **IIRIRA** requires that if the employer made a **good-faith** attempt to comply, the government must explain the problem to the employer and allow the employer at least 10 business days to correct it. However, if the employer is engaged in a **pattern or practice** of **IRCA** violations, this defense is not available.

> ***Example:*** A supermarket failed to prepare a **Form I-9** for individual employees. The company then attempted to correct all of the violations referred to in the INS (now **ICE**) citation, and, in fact, mistakenly believed that it had done so. However, due to a clerical oversight, 135 record-keeping errors remained uncorrected, including 132 instances in which a **Form I-9** had not been prepared. Upon reinspection, the government issued a citation seeking substantial penalties. While holding it proper to impose a fine for the 135 violations, the administrative law judge considered the substantial "**good faith**" of the employer throughout the investigation. Upon appeal to the federal court of appeals, the court held that while it was an unintentional oversight on the part of the supermarket's management employees that the **Form I-9s** were not prepared or corrected, that action does not excuse the violation but does serve to mitigate the penalty.[44]

E-Verify Program

In 2009, the Obama administration issued an executive order requiring federal contractors and subcontractors to verify employee eligibility to work in the United States. The federal government will award contracts only to those firms that enroll in the **E-Verify system.** This online program uses federal databases to confirm if a worker is authorized to work in the country. It has been reported that the program will cover approximately 169,000 federal contractors and subcontractors who employ approximately 3.8 million workers. In addition, all financial institutions that received federal stimulus monies are subject to the rule. This approach replaces a prior federal initiative, known as the "no match" rule, that permitted the Social Security Administration to verify the correctness of Social Security numbers for every worker. However, this program was never implemented because a federal district judge issued an injunction against its enforcement.

Under the **E-Verify program**, a federal contractor or subcontractor has 30 days to enroll in the program. Contractors use a secure website to check the legal status of workers involved in a government project. Only those existing employees assigned to work on the federal project and all new hires are subject to the program. Once the

E-Verify
An Internet-based system operated by the U.S. Citizenship and Immigration Services that allows an employer, using information reported on an employee's I-9, to determine the employee's eligibility to work in the United States. Participation is required for federal contractors and subcontractors.

contractor completes the project it may withdraw from participation in the **E-Verify program.** While the system verifies documentation, it does not verify identities. As a result, an unauthorized worker who uses the identity of another person who is authorized to work in the United States would be difficult to detect.

ICE Investigations

ICE may conduct investigations for suspected violations of the immigration laws and may directly request that employers produce employees' status confirmation documents. When agents of **ICE** seek to search, detain, or arrest suspected undocumented **aliens** in an employer's workplace, they need either the employer's consent or a search warrant based upon probable cause.

> ***Example:*** In one federal case, the court considered the following facts: "Plaintiffs allege that the Immigration and Naturalization Service (INS) has engaged in a **pattern and practice** of carrying out workplace raids in violation of the Fourth Amendment. The INS and Border Patrol agents arrive at workplaces in such a manner so as to provoke exigent circumstances to justify a warrantless entry. Otherwise, the agents enter with constitutionally deficient warrants, or without warrants and without consent. Consent, when requested, is coerced or involuntary. Once inside, the agents target employees of Hispanic appearance for questioning and detention, whether or not the agents have reasonable, articulable suspicion of illegal **alien** status. Workers are forcibly detained and arrested without probable cause." As a result, the federal court permitted Hispanic farmers to pursue a discrimination case because of the INS **pattern and practice** of carrying out workplace raids in violation of the Fourth Amendment.[45]

Federal law authorizes **ICE** agents to make arrests of **undocumented workers** at an employer's premises without an arrest warrant if the **ICE** enforcement agent has reasonable cause to believe that the **alien** so arrested is likely to escape before a warrant can be obtained for his or her arrest.

The second type of investigation arises from reports received by complaining parties. **ICE** may issue administrative subpoenas to compel employer compliance with the regulations. **ICE** can then issue and serve on the employer either a warning notice or a notice of intent to fine. The notice of intent to fine will result in an administrative hearing at which the employer may be represented by legal counsel.

Employer Sanctions

ICE may conduct its own investigation or **ICE** may do so in response to any person or entity filing a complaint alleging an unlawful hiring of an **alien**. After investigating the employer's compliance, **ICE** may issue and serve a notice of intent to fine or a warning notice. The applicable sanctions are as follows:

- Employers who fail properly to complete, retain, or present **I-9** forms for inspection are subject to a civil penalty for violations ranging from $110 to

$1,200 per employee. Factors considered in setting the fine include the size of the employer's business, the employer's good faith, the severity of the violation, and the employer's history of compliance with the law. In addition, the attorney general may sue in district court seeking injunctive relief (i.e., compelling the employer to cease violating the law).[46]

- For unlawfully hiring an alien, an employer can face fines ranging from $275 to $2,200 for each unauthorized worker; from $2,200 to $5,500 for each unauthorized employee if the employer has previously been in violation; and $3,300 to $11,000 for each unauthorized individual if the employer was subject to more than one cease-and-desist order.[47]
- Employers convicted of a **pattern or practice** of knowingly hiring unauthorized aliens or continuing to employ aliens knowing they are or have become unauthorized to work in the United States may be fined up to $3,000 for each unauthorized employee and/or six months of imprisonment.[48]

Focus on Ethics
Employer Fined for Violating Immigration Laws

Immigration laws apply to employers and restrict their ability to hire undocumented aliens as workers. Employers can be fined by the United States government if they are caught violating this law. Consider the following case.

Furr's/Bishop's Cafeteria, L.P. (Furr's) owns and operates more than 500 cafeterias and restaurants located throughout the midwestern United States. Furr's divides its cafeterias into regions. Regional directors have the authority to terminate nonmanagement employees at cafeterias located in their regions. The general manager of each cafeteria is responsible for hiring between 40 and 80 employees for the day-to-day operation of the cafeteria. The federal government investigated and found that, in violation of federal immigration laws, Furr's had hired undocumented aliens in two of its cafeterias located in different regions. The federal immigration service found that the two violations made Furr's a two-time offender and ordered Furr's to pay two fines to the government as a repeat offender with violations at two different cafeterias in two different regions.

Furr's challenged the fines, arguing that it should not be found to be a repeat offender since the two violations occurred at different cafeterias and not at the same location. The U.S. Court of Appeals affirmed the finding that Furr's is a repeat offender and upheld the imposition of two fines.[49]

Ethics Questions

1. Can any ethical arguments be made that hiring undocumented aliens as employees was appropriate even though it violated U.S. law? Is it ethical to violate the immigration laws purposefully?
2. Provide the ethical argument for Furr's position that it was not a repeat offender.
3. Do you think many employers in the United States employ undocumented workers? What are the policy and ethical arguments for and against why employers are subject to sanctions?

Unfair Employment Practice (INA §274B)

It is an **unfair immigration-related employment** practice for an employer to discriminate against any individual other than an unauthorized alien as defined in **IRCA (INA §274B(a))**. Employers with four or more employees are prohibited from discriminating based on **citizenship** status and/or national origin. Such claims arise when an adverse employment decision is based on an individual's real or perceived citizenship or immigration status. Employers with far more employees are prohibited from committing what is commonly referred to as **"document abuse."** This occurs when an employer requests an applicant or employee to produce a specific document or different documents than are required to establish employment eligibility or rejects valid documents that reasonably appear genuine on their face. **IRCA**'s antidiscrimination provisions prohibit small employers (i.e., those with four to fourteen employees) from committing national origin discrimination. Title VII of the Civil Rights Act already covers larger employers.

IRCA prohibits employers from refusing to hire noncitizens with work permits or those noncitizens whose appearance or speech characterizes them as nonnative-born persons. This protection extends to current employees as well. It is unlawful for an employer to discriminate against any individual because of the individual's national origin or citizenship status (with the exception of an unauthorized worker). **IRCA** protects the **"protected individual"** with regard to **citizenship status,** including:

- A **citizen** or a national of the United States; or
- An **alien** who is:
  - Lawfully admitted for permanent residence in the United States
  - Lawfully admitted for temporary residence in the United States
  - Admitted as a refugee
  - Granted asylum

Even though the antidiscrimination provisions exist, they apply only to employers with four or more employees, they are subject to three exceptions:

1. The employee must be a **citizen** or a **protected individual** at the time of the discrimination.
2. The **IRCA** permits employers to favor citizenship between two equally qualified employees: "Notwithstanding any other provision of this section, it is not an unfair immigration-related employment practice for a person or other entity to prefer to hire, recruit, or refer an individual who is a **citizen** or national of the United States over another individual who is an **alien** if the two individuals are equally qualified."
3. The **"public function"** exception: an employer may make hiring decisions based on citizenship status if required to do so by law, regulation, or executive order and may discriminate against noncitizens if required by law. For example, an **alien** engineer from south Asia might be ineligible for hiring by a U.S. defense industry company if the company is required by a federal contract to have only **citizens** with proper security clearances in its employ.[50]

If an employer has practiced discrimination in violation of the **IRCA**, an **ALJ** for the **USCIS** may order any of the following:

- The employer must hire the subject individual with or without back pay.
- The employer must pay a fine of between:
  - $250 and $2,000 for each subject employees;
  - $2,000 to $5,000 for each employee if a prior order has been rendered against the employer;
  - $3,000 to $10,000 for each individual discriminated against if the employer has a series of orders; or
  - $110 to $1,100 for each individual from whom the employer requested more or different documents than those required to establish employment verification or refused to accept those that on their face appear to be genuine.
- If the employer acted in **good faith**, the penalty will be excused if the violations are deemed minor. The employer can exercise this **"good-faith compliance defense"** if the employer voluntarily corrects the failure within 10 business days after the violation notice date. These are deemed **"paperwork violations."**

Paperwork Violation
An employer's violation of IRCA requirements to complete, correct, or supplement Form I-9 for each of its employees. Violations can occur following the employer's failure to reverify employees' continuing employment authorization when an expiration date on the employees' visa forms has passed.

Since the **IRCA** sanctions employers who knowingly hire **unauthorized aliens** into their workforces, the possibility that employers would refuse to hire anyone who looked or sounded "foreign" persuaded Congress to enact **INA §274B**. This section provides that it is an **immigration-related unfair employment practice** for an employer to discriminate:

- because of the person's national origin, or
- in the case of a protected individual (i.e., a U.S. citizen or national), because of **citizenship status**.

Section 274B does not apply to employers with three or fewer employees or to employers covered by Title VII. A protected individual can only bring **citizenship discrimination** lawsuits.

Pattern or Practice Violations of IRCA

While it is not certain how many violations constitute a **pattern or practice**, the conservative view is that more than two violations would qualify for such a classification. An employer charged with a **pattern or practice violation** should immediately retain a white-collar criminal defense attorney because a person or entity so charged faces a fine of no more than $3,000 for each unauthorized **alien** and/or imprisonment for not more than 6 months for the entire **pattern or practice**.

Document Fraud: INA §274C

Persons who knowingly use fraudulent identification documents may be fined and imprisoned for up to five years.[51] The prohibition extends to those who create, use, possess, or otherwise prepare an application based on them. Civil penalties for such violations range from:

- $275 to $2,200 for each document used, accepted, or created, and

- $2,200 to $5,500 for each document that is the subject of a violation where the person or the entity using, accepting, or creating the document was previously subject to a cease-and-desist order.

Enforcement

Individuals may make a claim for discrimination under **IRCA** for **"immigration-related unfair employment practices."** The intent of the law is to protect against discrimination in the implementation of the employer-sanction provisions of **IRCA**. The claim is filed with the Office of Special Counsel within the U.S. Department of Justice or with the EEOC for national origin discrimination. However, the claimant *cannot* prosecute claims concurrently with both agencies.[52] The victim must file the charge with the special counsel within 180 days of the alleged unfair immigration-related employment practice. The special counsel must investigate the charge within 120 days of receipt of the complaint and may propound civil litigation discovery procedures during its investigation. The special counsel determines whether there is "reasonable cause" to believe that a violation of **IRCA** has occurred and whether a complaint will be brought before an administrative law judge. If a determination is made to the contrary, the complainant may file an administrative law complaint with the Department of Justice within 90 days. Following the claimant's filing, the Justice Department can elect to intervene (i.e., join the proceeding). If, by a preponderance of evidence it is found that discrimination has taken place, the administrative law judge may order hiring or reinstatement, back pay, injunctive relief, attorney's fees, supervision of the employer for up to three years, and a civil penalty. Appeals are taken to the U.S. court of appeals in the circuit where the alleged violation took place or where the employer resides or conducts business. If the Special Counsel has not filed a complaint within 120 days of receipt of a charge, the claimant may file a private action before an administrative law judge. The private action may only be based on a charge that alleges "knowing and intentional discriminatory activity or a pattern or practice of discriminatory activity."

Other Federal Laws

- ***Homeland Security Act of 2002.*** This Act abolished the Immigration and Naturalization Service, and its functions were transferred to the **Department of Homeland Security (DHS)**. The Undersecretary for Border and Transportation Security has the duty to execute immigration enforcement. Under the act, **DHS** has established a voluntary program for employers. Under the **E-Verify** program, employers may check employment eligibility verification and enroll in the Social Security Number Verification Service. The Internet-based system is available throughout the United States and is without charge to employers.
- ***Immigration Marriage Fraud Amendments of 1986.*** Under a series of laws, Congress increased the criminal penalties and immigration status consequences for those who engage in the fraud of attempting to obtain citizenship by marrying an American **citizen**.

- ***North American Free Trade Act (NAFTA).*** Under Chapter 16 of NAFTA, Canadian or Mexican citizens, along with their spouses and children, may enter the United States as a **"NAFTA professional."** The nonimmigrant **alien** is allowed to reside in the United States and to obtain employment under an authorized visa. Quotas are established for those from Mexico.
- ***Immigration and Nationality Technical Corrections Act of 1994.*** This Act provided clarifications to the law, including eligibility requirements for citizenship.
- ***The Immigration Act of 1990.*** Under this act, immigration for family unity was fostered, with employment categories and quotas restructured to facilitate immigration of spouses and children of permanent residents and of certain professional and skilled workers.
- ***The Illegal Immigration Reform and Immigrant Responsibility Act of 1996.*** This act excluded certain **aliens** from the family unity program of the 1990 act and thus barred them from employment in the United States.
- ***Personal Responsibility and Work Opportunity Reconciliation Act of 1996.*** This act restricted welfare and public benefits for aliens. In its statement of findings, Congress stated that the availability of such benefits should not act as an incentive to immigrate to the United States. The intent of the legislation was to encourage self-reliance and the pursuit of employment opportunities among those immigrating to America.

Administrative and Judicial Review

Historically, when an employee's employment status was challenged, the employer usually terminated the employment based on immigration status. In addition, immigration status decisions issued by the federal immigration administrative law agencies were rarely subject to judicial review. Further, the actions of the agency charged with enforcement, now known as **ICE**, were rarely reviewed by the federal courts.

Under current law, there are five federal agencies involved in Immigration-related issues: the **Departments of Homeland Security (DHS)**, Justice, State, Labor, and Health and Human Services. Before the governmental reorganization creating the **DHS**, all the adjudicatory and enforcement functions relating to employment-related immigration rights were within the Justice Department. Most applications and petitions for employment-related immigration benefits are submitted to the **DHS** for review. If the applicant wishes to appeal, he or she must do so before the Administrative Appeals Office of the **DHS**. Appeals are then taken to the **BIA**. The **BIA** grants further appeals only on certification to the attorney general or the **DHS** secretary.[53]

In an effort to severely limit judicial review, Congress enacted two laws in 1996, the **Antiterrorism and Effective Death Penalty Act of 1996** and the **IIRIRA**. Together these laws had the effect of removing a federal court's direct appellate jurisdiction over final orders of deportation and removal (thus affecting persons found not eligible to work in the United States). Thereafter, in 2005, Congress amended the statute pursuant to the **REAL ID Act** to allow petitions for review to federal courts of appeals upon very limited grounds. The act also prohibited the district courts from deciding *habeas corpus* petitions for review of final deportation orders. In enacting the **REAL ID Act**, Congress sought to insulate from reversal most decisions relating to immigration and employment. The statute provides that the administrative findings of fact before the immigration judge, if appealed to the Board of Immigration Appeals, may only be reversed if a "reasonable adjudicator would be compelled to conclude" otherwise than in the original determination.[54]

Focus on Ethics
Should Courts Protect All Civil Rights Based on Alienage?

Linden Anderson was a citizen of Jamaica who immigrated to the United States in 1968. He began working for a local of the Carpenters Union. Anderson was elected to the position of the business representative of the local union, but the Carpenter's constitution provided: "No member shall be eligible to be an officer or business representative, delegate or committee member unless such member is a citizen of the U.S. or Canada, and the member, to be eligible to serve in any such capacity, must be a citizen of the country in which the Local Union is located." Upon learning of his noncitizenship, an officer caused Anderson to be removed. Anderson sued under §1981 for discrimination based on his alienage. In weighing whether the statute should be extended to prohibit alienage discrimination, what factors do you think the court should take into account?[55] Read the provisions of §1981 stated above and recall from that in *Espinoza v. Farah Mfg. Co.*, 414 U.S. 86 (1973), the Supreme Court concluded that Title VII does not bar discrimination based solely on alienage.

After reaching your conclusion, note that in response to the *Espinoza* decision, Congress amended the INA (pursuant to INA §274 B) to create an office of "Special Counsel for Immigration-Related Unfair Employment Practices" in the Department of Justice. This office is to investigate and pursue charges of discrimination based on "national origin" or "citizenship status." However, this law protects only U.S. nationals and those who intend to become citizens (i.e., a lawful permanent resident alien, a newly legalized alien, or a refugee or an asylee who demonstrates intent to become a citizen). Nonimmigrants (even those authorized to work in the United States) are not protected by the amendment.

Human Resource Form: Form I-9

OMB No. 1615-0047; Expires 08/31/12

Department of Homeland Security
U.S. Citizenship and Immigration Services

Form I-9, Employment Eligibility Verification

Read instructions carefully before completing this form. The instructions must be available during completion of this form.

ANTI-DISCRIMINATION NOTICE: It is illegal to discriminate against work-authorized individuals. Employers CANNOT specify which document(s) they will accept from an employee. The refusal to hire an individual because the documents have a future expiration date may also constitute illegal discrimination.

Section 1. Employee Information and Verification *(To be completed and signed by employee at the time employment begins.)*

Print Name: Last	First	Middle Initial	Maiden Name
Address *(Street Name and Number)*		Apt. #	Date of Birth *(month/day/year)*
City	State	Zip Code	Social Security #

I am aware that federal law provides for imprisonment and/or fines for false statements or use of false documents in connection with the completion of this form.

I attest, under penalty of perjury, that I am (check one of the following):

- ☐ A citizen of the United States
- ☐ A noncitizen national of the United States (see instructions)
- ☐ A lawful permanent resident (Alien #) ______
- ☐ An alien authorized to work (Alien # or Admission #) ______
  until (expiration date, if applicable - *month/day/year*)

Employee's Signature | Date *(month/day/year)*

Preparer and/or Translator Certification *(To be completed and signed if Section 1 is prepared by a person other than the employee.) I attest, under penalty of perjury, that I have assisted in the completion of this form and that to the best of my knowledge the information is true and correct.*

Preparer's/Translator's Signature	Print Name
Address *(Street Name and Number, City, State, Zip Code)*	Date *(month/day/year)*

Section 2. Employer Review and Verification *(To be completed and signed by employer. Examine one document from List A OR examine one document from List B and one from List C, as listed on the reverse of this form, and record the title, number, and expiration date, if any, of the document(s).)*

	List A	OR	List B	AND	List C
Document title:					
Issuing authority:					
Document #:					
Expiration Date *(if any)*:					
Document #:					
Expiration Date *(if any)*:					

CERTIFICATION: I attest, under penalty of perjury, that I have examined the document(s) presented by the above-named employee, that the above-listed document(s) appear to be genuine and to relate to the employee named, that the employee began employment on *(month/day/year)* ______ **and that to the best of my knowledge the employee is authorized to work in the United States. (State employment agencies may omit the date the employee began employment.)**

Signature of Employer or Authorized Representative	Print Name	Title
Business or Organization Name and Address *(Street Name and Number, City, State, Zip Code)*		Date *(month/day/year)*

Section 3. Updating and Reverification *(To be completed and signed by employer.)*

A. New Name *(if applicable)*	B. Date of Rehire *(month/day/year) (if applicable)*

C. If employee's previous grant of work authorization has expired, provide the information below for the document that establishes current employment authorization.

Document Title: ______ Document #: ______ Expiration Date *(if any)*: ______

I attest, under penalty of perjury, that to the best of my knowledge, this employee is authorized to work in the United States, and if the employee presented document(s), the document(s) I have examined appear to be genuine and to relate to the individual.

Signature of Employer or Authorized Representative	Date *(month/day/year)*

Form I-9 (Rev. 08/07/09) Y Page 4

LISTS OF ACCEPTABLE DOCUMENTS

All documents must be unexpired

LIST A **Documents that Establish Both Identity and Employment Authorization**	**OR**	**LIST B** **Documents that Establish Identity**	**AND**	**LIST C** **Documents that Establish Employment Authorization**
1. U.S. Passport or U.S. Passport Card		**1.** Driver's license or ID card issued by a State or outlying possession of the United States provided it contains a photograph or information such as name, date of birth, gender, height, eye color, and address		**1.** Social Security Account Number card other than one that specifies on the face that the issuance of the card does not authorize employment in the United States
2. Permanent Resident Card or Alien Registration Receipt Card (Form I-551)		**2.** ID card issued by federal, state or local government agencies or entities, provided it contains a photograph or information such as name, date of birth, gender, height, eye color, and address		**2.** Certification of Birth Abroad issued by the Department of State (Form FS-545)
3. Foreign passport that contains a temporary I-551 stamp or temporary I-551 printed notation on a machine-readable immigrant visa		**3.** School ID card with a photograph		**3.** Certification of Report of Birth issued by the Department of State (Form DS-1350)
4. Employment Authorization Document that contains a photograph (Form I-766)		**4.** Voter's registration card		**4.** Original or certified copy of birth certificate issued by a State, county, municipal authority, or territory of the United States bearing an official seal
5. In the case of a nonimmigrant alien authorized to work for a specific employer incident to status, a foreign passport with Form I-94 or Form I-94A bearing the same name as the passport and containing an endorsement of the alien's nonimmigrant status, as long as the period of endorsement has not yet expired and the proposed employment is not in conflict with any restrictions or limitations identified on the form		**5.** U.S. Military card or draft record		**5.** Native American tribal document
6. Passport from the Federated States of Micronesia (FSM) or the Republic of the Marshall Islands (RMI) with Form I-94 or Form I-94A indicating nonimmigrant admission under the Compact of Free Association Between the United States and the FSM or RMI		**6.** Military dependent's ID card		**6.** U.S. Citizen ID Card (Form I-197)
		7. U.S. Coast Guard Merchant Mariner Card		**7.** Identification Card for Use of Resident Citizen in the United States (Form I-179)
		8. Native American tribal document		**8.** Employment authorization document issued by the Department of Homeland Security
		9. Driver's license issued by a Canadian government authority		
		For persons under age 18 who are unable to present a document listed above:		
		10. School record or report card		
		11. Clinic, doctor, or hospital record		
		12. Day-care or nursery school record		

Illustrations of many of these documents appear in Part 8 of the Handbook for Employers (M-274)

Form I-9 (Rev. 08/07/09) Y Page 5

Key Terms and Concepts

- Immigration Reform Control Act (IRCA)
- Citizenship
- Unauthorized alien
- Naturalization
- Immigration and Nationality Act (INA)
- Board of Immigration Appeals (BIA)
- Quota system
- Rational basis
- Intermediate scrutiny
- Strict scrutiny
- Form I-9
- Pattern or practice
- Paperwork violation
- Administrative law judge (ALJ)
- Cease-and-desist order
- The 30-60 day rule
- NAFTA professional
- Identity and employment authorization
- Bureau of Immigration and Customs Enforcement (ICE)
- Good-faith compliance defense
- E-Verify program
- INA §247B
- Citizenship discrimination
- Immigration-related unfair employment practices
- Constructive knowledge
- Antiterrorism and Effective Death Penalty Act of 1996
- REAL ID Act
- Department of Homeland Security (DHS)
- Immigration Reform and Immigrant Responsibility Act (IIRIRA)

Chapter Summary

- National origin is not the same as citizenship.

- States and local governments may enact laws and regulations that govern or affect the employment relationships of aliens unless there is clear intent within federal law that such laws and regulations are preempted. Typically, these laws and regulations will be upheld if there is a compelling state interest in the subject matter of the legislation and if government intrudes on the interest by the least restrictive means available.

- An "unauthorized alien" in the United States is an alien who is not a lawful permanent resident or an alien authorized by ICE for employment.

- IRCA makes it unlawful for employers and paid recruiters knowingly to hire, recruit, or refer unauthorized aliens for employment in the United States.

- IRCA makes it an unfair immigration-related employment practice for employers with more than three employees to discriminate based on national origin or citizenship status. The IRCA does not apply to discrimination because of national origin if the discrimination is covered under Title VII (i.e., employers with 15 or more employees).

- The IRCA represents Congress's efforts to respond to the need for immigration enforcement reform. Congress found the most effective method for controlling immigration to be through employer sanctions. By establishing an "employment verification" system intended to deny employment to aliens who are not lawfully present in the

United States or who are not authorized to work in the United States, Congress intended the first defense to unlawful immigration to rest with employers. Employer action is used to deter unlawful employment relationships, and employers are required, under threat of civil and criminal sanctions, to assure their employees comply with U.S. law.

- Three types of conduct are made specifically illegal by IRCA: (1) hiring, recruiting, or referring for a fee an alien knowing that he or she is unauthorized to work in the United States; (2) continuing to employ an alien knowing that he or she has become unauthorized to work in the country; and (3) hiring any person (citizen or alien) without following the record-keeping requirements of IRCA. Employers must examine documents with respect to the worker's identity and authorization to work in the United States prior to hiring. Employers must request only certain types of documents and must maintain copies of them for verification by ICE inspectors.

- IRCA imposes monetary and criminal penalties on employers for violations of IRCA and for non-compliance with its requirements. If an employer complies with the employment verification and record-keeping requirements, it may assert an affirmative defense of good-faith compliance if charged with violations of the law.

- With respect to employers with four or more employees, IRCA prohibits discrimination because of the individual's national origin or citizenship status.

Online Student Support

- Loislaw legal research and writing assignments.
- Loislaw group projects and class presentations.
- Loislaw access, providing online research including up-to-date cases, statutes, rules, and regulations. Primary law for all 50 states and federal jurisdictions. Registration required for access to this resource.
- Practice questions, including sample true/false, multiple choice, and short answer questions to test your understanding of concepts.
- Additional human resource forms.
- Internet exercises.
- Blogs.
- Supplementary statutory and regulatory materials.

Case Problems

17.1 Four federally registered resident aliens were discharged from civil service positions with the city of New York. The city had enacted an ordinance prohibiting employment of aliens in competitive classified civil service positions. The tasks of persons in such competitive classifications ranged from the menial to policy making. The city defended its action, in part, based on its legitimate state interest to confine the use of public resources to those having the privileges of citizenship. How should the U.S. Supreme Court rule? (*Sugarman v. Dougall et al.*, 413 U.S. 634 (1973))

17.2 An organization of forty-one Roman Catholic orders and six individual nuns filed suit to enjoin the INS (now ICE) from enforcing employer sanctions under IRCA. They alleged their Church imposed on them a religious duty to offer employment to people in need, without regard to residence, nationality, or immigration status. Such enforcement would violate their rights of free exercise under the First Amendment. How should the court rule and why? (*Intercommunity Center for Justice and Peace v. I.N.S.*, 910 F.2d 42 (2d Cir. 1990))

17.3 A class-action lawsuit was filed to seek an order declaring that individual aliens were denied due process with regard to a policy of **INS** to initiate deportation proceedings against anyone whose work authorizations or "green cards" were lost or confiscated. Processing of replacement green cards often took longer than the period required to deport the subject individuals. What order should the court issue? (*Etuk, et al. v. Slattery, et al.*, 936 F.2d 1433 (2d Cir. 1991))

17.4 The Perkins Restaurant and Bakery operated two restaurants in Minnesota in which Maria Torres worked as a cook. She alleged that one of her managers began to sexually harass her, including unwelcome interactions outside the workplace. Torres refused the supervisor's alleged sexual advances, and the supervisor began to treat her differently than other cooks and threatened to report her to immigration authorities. Her hours were reduced. She was given more responsibilities after complaining about her harassment and was eventually told she could not continue to work without a valid work authorization documentation. As an undocumented alien, she lacked standing to sue under the federal civil rights laws. The employer argued that under the *Hoffman Plastic Compounds* case discussed in this chapter, Torres lacked standing to pursue her claims. Does the EEOC have jurisdiction to pursue a sexual harassment and retaliatory discharge claim on behalf of Torres? (*EEOC v. The Restaurant Company*, 490 F. Supp. 2d 1039 (D. Minn. 2007))

17.5 An illegal alien worked for a construction subcontractor on a construction project for a Walmart store in Manchester, New Hampshire. He was seriously injured during the course and scope of his employment. He sued the general contractor for lost earnings incurred while recuperating from his work-related injuries. Should he be entitled to make such a claim? Should the lost wages be limited to the amount of earnings that he could anticipate receiving in his country of full citizenship, Brazil? As a defense to the wage loss claim, should the general contractor be entitled to introduce testimony as to the plaintiff's immigration status and his lack of legal entitlement to work in the United States? (*Rosa v. Partners in Progress, Inc.*, 152 N.H. 6, 686 A. 2d 994 (2005))

End Notes

1. *Examining Bd. of Engineers, Architects and Surveyors v. Flores de Otero*, 426 U.S. 572 (1976).
2. *http://www.kauffman.org/research-and-policy/reverse-brain-drain.aspx.*
3. *http://www.census.gov/population/www/documentation/twps0061/twps0061.html.*
4. 414 U.S. 86 (1973).
5. 414 U.S. at 95.
6. *Egbuna v. Time Life Libraries, Inc.*, 153 F.184, 186-188 (4th Cir. 1998) *cert. denied* 525 U.S. 1142 (1999).
7. Act of Feb. 26, 1885, 23 Stat. 332; Act of Feb. 23, 1887, 24 Stat. 414.
8. *Fernandez v. Georgia*, 716 F. Supp. 1475, 1477 (M.D. Ga. 1989).
9. 42 U.S.C. §1983.
10. 385 U.S. 276 (1966).
11. 118 U.S. 356 (1886).
12. *Ambach v. Norwick*, 441 U.S. 68 (1979).
13. *Bernal v. Fainter*, 467 U.S. 216 (1984).
14. *Graham v. Richardson*, 403 U.S. 365 (1971).
15. *Crane v. People of the State of N.Y.*, 239 U.S. 195 (1915).
16. *Leclerc v. Webb*, 270 F.Supp. 2d 779 (E.D. La. 2003).
17. 467 U.S. 883 (1984).
18. 8 U.S.C. §1324a.
19. 8 U.S.C. §1324a(a)(1).
20. 8 U.S.C. §1324a(a)(2).
21. 8 U.S.C. §1324a(b).
22. 8 U.S.C. §1324a(b)(2); 8 C.F.R. §274a.2(a).
23. 8 U.S.C. §1324a(b)(3); 8 C.F.R. §274a.2(a)
24. 8 U.S.C. §1324a(e)(5).
25. 8 U.S.C. §1324b(a).
26. 8 U.S.C. §1324a(e)(4), (f).
27. 8 U.S.C. §1324a(e)(3).
28. 8 U.S.C. §1324a(e)(4).
29. *Sugarman v. Dougall*, 413 U.S. 634 (1973).
30. *Incalza v. Fendi North America*, 479 F.3d 1005 (9th Cir. 2007).
31. 8 U.S.C. §1346.

32. 535 U.S. 137, n.3 (2002).
33. 8 U.S.C. §1157 *et seq.*
34. 8 C.F.R. §214.2(a)(8).
35. 8 U.S.C. §§1101(a)(44)(A) and (B).
36. 8 C.F.R. §214.2(h)(16).
37. 8 U.S.C. §1153(b)(5)(B)(ii).
38. 8 U.S. §1157 (a)(2).
39. 8 U.S.C. 1157(d).
40. 8 U.S.C. §1324a(b)(1)(D); 8 C.F.R. §274a.2(b)(1)(v)(B).
41. 8 U.S.C. §1324a(b)(1)(C); 8 C.F.R. §274a.2(b)(1)(v)(C).
42. 8 C.F.R. §274a.2(c).
43. *Maka v. U.S.I.N.S.*, 904 F.2d 1351 (9th Cir. 1990), *amended on other grnds*, 932 F.2d 1352 (9th Cir. 1991).
44. *Big Bear Super Market No. 3 v. I.N.S.*, 913 F. 2d 754 (9th Cir. 1990).
45. *Pearl Meadows Mushroom Farm, Inc. v. Alan Nelson*, 743 F. Supp. 432, 435 (N.D. Ca. 1989).
46. 8 C.F.R. §274a.10 (b)(2).
47. 8 C.F.R. §274a.10(b)(1)(C).
48. INA §274A(f).
49. *Furr's/Bishop's Cafeterias, L.P. v. U.S. Immigration and Nationalization Service*, 976 F.2d 1366 (10th Cir. 1992).
50. 8 U.S.C. §1324b(a)(2)(A).
51. 8 U.S.C. §1324c(e).
52. 8 U.S.C. §1324b(b)(2).
53. 8 C.F.R. §2.1.
54. 8 U.S.C. §1252(b)(4).
55. *Anderson v. Conboy*, 156 F.3d 167 (2d Cir. 1998).

Chapter 18
Employment Law for the Global Employer

International law, or the law that governs between nations, has at times, been like the common law within states, a twilight existence during which it is hardly distinguishable for morality or justice, till at length the imprimatur of a court attests its jural quality. —Justice Benjamin Cardozo, U.S. Supreme Court Associate Justice

Learning Objectives

1. Explain the domestic and foreign application of U.S. discrimination laws.
2. Identify how foreign employers are subject to U.S. employment laws.
3. Describe European Union efforts to protect workers.
4. Distinguish between U.S. and EU protected classes of workers.
5. Recognize what comparable worth means under EU law.
6. Differentiate between U.S., Canadian, and Mexican laws with regard to worker terminations.

Chapter Outline

- Introduction
- Foreign Employers Operating in the United States

Case 18.1 Sumitomo Shoji America, Inc. v Avagliano et al.
Case 18.2 MacNamara v. Korean Air Lines

- Focus on Ethics: Treaty Permits Discrimination Based on Citizenship
- Extraterritorial Application of U.S. Employment Laws

Case 18.3 Morelli v. Cedel
Case 18.4 Kang v. U. Lim America, Inc.

- Management Application: FCN Treaties and U.S. Whistleblower Laws
- Employment Law in the European Union

Case 18.5 Defrenne v. SA Belge de Navigation Aerienne (SABENA)
Case 18.6 B.N.O. Walrave and L.J.N. Koch v. Association Union cycliste internationale, et al.

- Focus on Ethics: Outsourcing
- Management Application: NAFTA
- Employment Law of Canada and Mexico
- International Labor Organization

Chapter Opening scenario

Isaac is an African-American U.S. citizen working in Africa for a U.S. employer as a customer service manager. Isaac alleges race discrimination after he was transferred to a less desirable and less public position. The new position involved a loss of pay and lack of upward career mobility opportunities. The employer admitted that it transferred Isaac because its predominantly white customers did not want to deal directly with nonwhites. Would the U.S. employer be able to assert that acceding to the customer preference was lawful because the activity occurred outside the United States?[1]

Introduction

Companies of all sizes engage in international trade. No longer is international trade restricted to large multinational corporations. U.S. businesses must comply with domestic and foreign employment laws, U.S. government policies and treaties, and the terms of the international contractual arrangements they negotiate. Efforts to standardize the employment process in an international context can be extremely complex. Some areas of law are similar across borders. For example, basic contract law regulating the sale of goods and services is similar across many jurisdictions. It is often subject to a common treaty among nations, such as the Convention for the International Sale of Goods. However, unlike contracts involving the sale of goods, labor and employment issues vary greatly between nations. More specifically, employment laws and regulations overseas are very different from those in the United States.

The United States primarily utilizes "at-will" employment agreements. This allows employers to hire and fire employees with no notice and little regulation. Although this may seem like an unfair practice, consider that the U.S. workforce is also one of the most nimble and adaptive in the world. The fairness of equal opportunity under the law has promoted self-initiative and organizational strength. Many other countries, such as Canada, have either abandoned this principle or adopted others. Some countries even require government permission to fire an employee. In this chapter, we shall survey the employment and labor issues frequently encountered by an employer with global operations and survey the labor and employment laws of selected countries.

Friendship, Commerce, and Navigation Treaty (FCN)
Among other provisions, this type of treaty between the United States and a foreign nation often provides that companies of both countries can discriminatorily select executive employees to work in the host country without regard to national origin considerations.

Foreign Employers Operating in the United States

A foreign employer operating in the United States can invoke a **Friendship, Commerce, and Navigation (FCN) treaty** to justify employing its own nationals. An **FCN** is a treaty between nations that provides protection to foreign nationals doing business in a host country. Each treaty is unique in its provisions; however, all typically state that each country will permit the establishment of foreign branches of subsidiary corporations. In addition, the treaty will provide for the unrestricted exchange of capital and technology from the foreign country to the host country, freedom of travel, and other recognition of other trade protections. The treaty between the United States and Japan, like many other **FCN** treaties, contains a provision that allows nationals and companies of either party-country to hire executive personnel "of their choice" within the territory of the host country. Japanese businesses with operations in the United States have asserted the absolute right to favor Japanese executives over American executives in employment decisions. This was the issue addressed in the following case.

CASE 18.1

U.S. SUBSIDIARIES OF FOREIGN CORPORATIONS ARE SUBJECT TO U.S. DISCRIMINATION LAWS

SUMITOMO SHOJI AMERICA, INC. V. AVAGLIANO ET AL.

457 U.S. 176 (1982)

Supreme Court of the United States

Facts. Past and present female secretarial employees of Sumitomo were U.S. citizens. Sumitomo Shoji America, Inc. was a New York corporation and a wholly owned subsidiary of a Japanese general trading company. Following timely complaints with the Equal Employment Opportunity Commission (EEOC), the plaintiffs received "right to sue" letters from the EEOC. The employees brought a class action in federal district court against Sumitomo claiming that its practice of hiring only male Japanese citizens to fill executive, managerial, and sales positions violated Title VII of the Civil Rights Act of 1964. Sumitomo moved to dismiss the complaint because a treaty between the United States and Japan exempted it from Title VII. The district court refused to dismiss the case. The Second Circuit Court of Appeals reversed in part, but the Supreme Court granted *certiorari.*

Issue. Are U.S. subsidiaries of foreign corporations subject to U.S. discrimination laws?

Language of the Court. Burger, C.J.: **Contrary to the view of the Court of Appeals and the claims of Sumitomo, adherence to the language of the Treaty would not "overlook the purpose of the Treaty." . . . The Friendship, Commerce and Navigation Treaty between Japan and the United States is but one of a** series of similar commercial agreements negotiated after World War II. The primary purpose of the corporation provisions of the Treaties was to give corporations of each signatory legal status in the territory of the other party, and to allow them to conduct business in the other country on a comparable basis with domestic firms. Although the United States negotiated commercial treaties as early as 1778, and thereafter throughout the 19th century and early 20th century, these early commercial treaties were primarily concerned with the trade and shipping rights of individuals. Until the 20th century, international commerce was much more an individual than a corporate affair.

As corporate involvement in international trade expanded in this century, old commercial treaties became outmoded. Because "[corporations] can have no legal existence out of the boundaries of the sovereignty by which [they are] created," (citation omitted), it became necessary to negotiate new treaties granting corporations legal status and the right to function abroad. A series of Treaties negotiated before World War II gave corporations legal status and access to foreign courts, but it was not until the postwar Friendship, Commerce and Navigation Treaties that United States corporations gained the right to conduct business in other countries. The purpose of the Treaties was not to give foreign corporations greater rights than domestic companies, but instead to assure them the right to conduct business on an equal basis without suffering discrimination based on their alienage.

The Treaties accomplished their purpose by granting foreign corporations "national treatment" in most respects and by allowing foreign individuals and companies to form locally incorporated subsidiaries. These local subsidiaries are considered for purposes of the Treaty to be companies of the country in which they are incorporated; they are entitled to the rights, and subject to the responsibilities of other domestic corporations. By treating these subsidiaries as domestic companies, the purpose of the Treaty provisions — to assure that corporations of one Treaty party have the right to conduct business within the territory of the other party without suffering discrimination as an alien entity — is fully met.

Nor can we agree with the Court of Appeals view that literal interpretation of the Treaty would create a "crazy-quilt pattern" in which the rights of branches of Japanese companies operating directly in the United States would be greatly superior to the right of locally incorporated subsidiaries of Japanese companies. The Court of Appeals maintained that if such subsidiaries were not considered companies of Japan under the Treaty, they, unlike branch offices of Japanese corporations, would be denied access to the legal system, would be left unprotected against unlawful entry and molestation, and would be unable to dispose of property, obtain patents, engage in importation and exportation, or make payments, remittances, and transfers of funds. That this is not the case is obvious; the subsidiaries, as companies of the United States, would enjoy all of those rights and more.

We are persuaded, as both signatories agree, that under the literal language of . . . the Treaty, Sumitomo is a company of the United States; we discern no

reason to depart from the plain meaning of the Treaty language. Accordingly, we hold that Sumitomo is not a company of Japan and is thus not covered by . . . the Treaty.

Decision. Yes. The U.S. subsidiary was not exempted from the application of U.S. law under the language of the FCN treaty between the United States and Japan.

CASE QUESTIONS

Critical Legal Thinking. The treaty between the United States and Japan allowed "[n]ationals and companies" of Japan to hire specified employees of their choice. This provision would seemingly exempt them from the application of Title VII. The subsidiary could invoke the Japanese FCN Treaty as a complete defense. Why do you think that the Supreme Court interpreted the treaty so that a foreign company does not have an unrestricted license to violate American employment laws? Would it have made a difference in this case if the Japanese subsidiary was incorporated in Japan and doing business in the United States as an alien corporation?

Business Ethics. Defend your opinion on whether you think it is ethical for foreign employers to hire only their nationals for managerial positions.

Contemporary Business. Can you think of any situations wherein it would be unfair to apply a FCN treaty?

Following the Supreme Court's decision in *Sumitomo,* the American employees felt vindicated. Since the American-incorporated subsidiary of the Japanese trading company could not defend the employment discrimination suit based on the **FCN** treaty, employment litigation against such businesses would have a better chance of prevailing. Unfortunately, that victory might have been short-lived. In *Fortino v. Quasar Co.,*[2] the Seventh Circuit Court of Appeals created a loophole in the *Sumitomo* general rule. In *Fortino,* the court concluded that an American subsidiary of a Japanese corporation could assert the **FCN** treaty rights where the Japanese parent company, and not the American subsidiary, was responsible for the discrimination. In *Fortino,* the appellate court acknowledged that the American employees had been treated unfairly and that the treatment afforded the Japanese nationals was favoritism. However, the court held the **FCN** treaty controlled if where it conflicted with the terms of Title VII.

Many Japanese companies argue that as Japan is a country with a homogeneous population, its population shows a high correlation between citizenship and national origin; almost all of citizens of Japan were born there. There is a corresponding need for executives of Japanese companies to understand Japanese culture and business management practices. A preference for Japanese citizens would exclude individuals not only based on national origin, but also on race, color, and gender as well. Even if the courts could legitimately distinguish discrimination based on citizenship from discrimination based on national origin, the other three grounds for discrimination would still be available to plaintiffs. Such an approach conflicts directly with Title VII's recognition of equal employment opportunity for all persons. Nevertheless, Title VII cannot take back from the Japanese with one hand what the **FCN** treaty had given them with the other.

While the terms of each treaty are unique and reference to each one must be made in analyzing whether a claim will survive a defendant's motion to dismiss, many contain the language at issue in the following case, *MacNamara v. Korean Air Lines.* In this decision, a conflict arose between the provisions of Title VII and the **FCN** treaty between the United States and Korea that allowed Korean firms to exercise a hiring preference for Korean nationals for executive, managerial, and technical positions.

CASE 18.2

DISPARATE TREATMENT BUT NOT DISPARATE IMPACT DISCRIMINATION MAY APPLY TO SOME FOREIGN EMPLOYERS OPERATING IN THE UNITED STATES

MACNAMARA V. KOREAN AIR LINES

863 F.2d 1135 (3d Cir. 1988)

U.S. Court of Appeals for the Third Circuit

Facts. Thomas MacNamara, an American citizen, was fifty-seven years old when he was dismissed as district sales manager for a mid-Atlantic territory for Korean Airlines (KAL). A Korean citizen replaced him. He exhausted his administrative remedies and sued the airline on the basis that his firing violated Title VII, the Age Discrimination in Employment Act (ADEA), and the Employee Retirement Income Safety Act (ERISA). He specifically complained that the airline had discriminated against him because of race, national origin, age, and citizenship. The district court granted the airline's motion to dismiss, and MacNamara appealed the order of dismissal to the Court of Appeals for the Third Circuit.

Issues. Can an international treaty permit discrimination based on citizenship, but not because of race, age, or national origin? Is a foreign employer subject to disparate impact claims because of its selection of its citizens for executive positions at U.S. locations?

Language of the Court. Stapleton, J.: **The Korean FCN Treaty is one of a series of Friendship, Commerce and Navigation Treaties the United States signed with various countries after World War II. Although initially negotiated primarily for the purpose of encouraging American investment abroad, the**

Treaties secured reciprocal rights and thus granted protection to foreign businesses operating in the United States. . . . The specific provision of the Korean FCN Treaty relied upon by KAL in this case provides as follows:

> Nationals and companies of either Party shall be permitted to engage, within the territories of the other Party, accountants and other technical experts, executive personnel, attorneys, agents and other specialists of their choice. Moreover, such nationals and companies shall be permitted to engage accountants and other technical experts regardless of the extent to which they may have qualified for the practice of a profession within the territories of such other Party, for the particular purpose of making examinations, audits and technical investigations for, and rendering reports to, such nationals and companies in connection with the planning and operation of their enterprises, and enterprises in which they have a financial interest, within such territories.

8 U.S.T. at 2223. KAL argued to the district court that the "of their choice" language in the first sentence of [the above] Article . . . gave it the right to employ executives of its own choosing, unhampered by domestic anti-discrimination employment statutes.

In response to KAL's motion, MacNamara, joined by the United States as amicus, claimed that Article secured to a foreign business only the right to select managerial and technical personnel on the basis of citizenship and did not provide a broad exemption from laws such as Title VII and the ADEA which prohibit employment decisions on the basis of race, national original, or age.

We believe it was these considerations that prompted the Supreme Court's observation in Sumitomo that the purpose of the Treaty was not to give foreign corporations greater rights than domestic corporations but rather to free them from "discrimination based on their alienage." . . . This observation is consistent with MacNamara's position, but not with that of KAL. If [this] Article is read as protecting a foreign corporation's right to employ its own citizens, it is thereby guaranteed the same access to its own citizens as domestic employers have to theirs. If it is interpreted to confer an immunity from Title VII and the ADEA in connection with personnel decisions involving citizens of the foreign company's country, it would give to foreign businesses a right not possessed by domestic employers.

Having concluded that KAL cannot purposefully discriminate on the basis of age, race, or national origin, we now turn to the most difficult aspect of this case. To this point, we have confined our analysis to liability for intentional discrimination.

As we have noted, MacNamara complains because KAL has replaced all its "American" sales managers with "Koreans." This, together with counsel's comments at oral argument, suggests that he is challenging the practice of favoring Korean nationals on the ground that it has the effect of discriminating against others on grounds of race or national origin. See, e.g., Espinoza v. Farah

Manufacturing Co. (citation omitted). In establishing this kind of disparate impact liability, parties generally rely exclusively on statistical evidence of disproportionate effect.

The fact that empirical evidence can satisfy the substantive standard of liability would pose a substantial problem in disparate impact litigation for corporations hailing from countries, including perhaps Korea, whose populations are largely homogeneous. Because a company's requirement that its employees be citizens of the homogeneous country from which it hails means that almost all of its employees will be of the same national origin and race, the statistical disparity between otherwise qualified non-citizens of a particular race and national origin, and citizens of the foreign country's race and national origin is likely to be substantial. As a result, a foreign business from a country with a homogeneous population, by merely exercising its protected Treaty right to prefer its own citizens for management positions, could be held in violation of Title VII. Thus, unlike a disparate treatment case where liability cannot be imposed without an affirmative finding that the employer was not simply exercising its Article VIII(1) right, a disparate impact case can result in liability where the employer did nothing more than exercise that right.

For this reason, we conclude that disparate impact liability under Title VII and the ADEA for a foreign employer based on its practice of engaging its own nationals as managers cannot be reconciled with [the above] Article. Accordingly, we hold that such liability may not be imposed.

Decision. Yes, a treaty may authorize companies of two nations to hire executives "of their choice" within the territory of the other. That authorization does not exempt the foreign company from claims of intentional discrimination because of race, age, or national origin. The foreign employer is not subject to disparate impact claims.

CASE QUESTIONS

Critical Legal Thinking. Because of this decision, treaties can exempt employers from discrimination claims based on citizenship — a form of disparate treatment discrimination. However, the decision makes other disparate treatment discrimination claims such as race, age, or national origin unlawful. Do you agree with the court's analysis that a foreign employer should be exempt from disparate impact claims?

Business Ethics. Does this case recognize that U.S. foreign policy interests sometimes outweigh the interests of individuals? Is this a fair result?

Contemporary Business. Are there other ways in which a company's proprietary information could be better protected or national interests could be advanced?

The *MacNamara* court concluded that the treaty simply barred the use of citizenship as a criterion for employment. With that conclusion, the court found no direct conflict with Title VII, which does *not* prohibit the use of citizenship as a criterion for employment.

Concept Summary
EEO Responsibilities of Multinational Employers

- Multinational employers that operate in the United States or its territories (American Samoa, Guam, the Commonwealth of the Northern Mariana Islands, Puerto Rico, and the U.S. Virgin Islands) are subject to the EEO laws to the same extent as are U.S. employers, unless a treaty that limits the application of the U.S. discrimination laws covers the employer.
- Companies based in the United States that employ U.S. citizens outside the country or its territories are subject to Title VII, the ADEA, and the Americans with Disabilities Act (ADA) with respect to those employers. The EEO laws do not apply to non-U.S. citizens outside the United States or its territories.
- An employer will be considered a U.S. employer if it is incorporated or based in the United States or if it has sufficient connection with the United States. Relevant connection factors include the location of the primary place of business activities, the nationality of dominant shareholders and those controlling the enterprise, and the nationality and location of management.
- Title VII, the ADEA, and the ADA cover employers operating outside the United States only if a U.S. employer controls them. Relevant factors determining such control are whether the operations are interrelated, whether there is common management, whether there is centralized control of labor relations, and whether there is common ownership or financial control.
- U.S. employers are not required to comply with U.S. antidiscrimination laws if adherence to them would violate a law of the country in which the workplace is located.

Focus on Ethics
Treaty Permits Discrimination Based on Citizenship

Can a foreign company doing business in the United States only employ citizens of its own country to work in the United States? It can if the United States has a treaty with that foreign country that allows it. One such treaty is the Treaty of Friendship, Commerce, and Navigation between the United States and Japan (Treaty). The United States has similar treaties with Israel and South Korea.

The treaty with Japan provides that a Japanese company operating in the United States can employ executives who are Japanese citizens, to the exclusion of American executives, if the company is at least half owned by Japanese nationals and has substantial trade or investment relations with Japan. This protection also extends to Japanese companies with U.S. subsidiary corporations that are at least half owned by Japanese nationals.

The treaty is sometimes invoked as a defense to a claim of discrimination alleged to violate Title VII of the Civil Rights Act of 1964. Consider the following case. Quasar Company is a subsidiary of Matsushita Electric Industrial, a Japanese corporation. In the United States, Quasar markets products made in Japan by Matsushita.

U.S. citizens John Fortino, Carl Meyers, and F. William Schultz were employed as executives by Quasar in the United States. When Quasar experienced financial difficulties, it terminated the employment of these three executives but did not terminate executives who were Japanese citizens.

Fortino, Meyers, and Schultz sued Quasar in U.S. district court alleging that the company violated Title VII by engaging in national origin discrimination. The U.S. district court agreed and held that Quasar had violated Title VII by giving preferential treatment to Japanese executives over American executives. Quasar appealed.

The U.S. court of appeals reversed the trial court and held that the Treaty allowed Quasar, as a subsidiary of a Japanese corporation, to discriminate lawfully in favor of Japanese citizens over American citizens when it terminated executive employees of the corporation. The court of appeals stated:

> *If this conclusion seems callous toward the Americans who lost their jobs at Quasar, we remind [them] that the rights granted by the Treaty are reciprocal. There are Americans employed abroad by foreign subsidiaries of U.S. companies who, but for the Treaty, would lose their jobs to foreign nationals. Indeed, the treaty provisions were inserted at the insistence of the United States. Japan was opposed to it.*[3]

National origin discrimination would result if a foreign corporation doing business in the United States is not subject to treaty protection and it unlawfully favors its nationals over American executives. For example, if a Mexican corporation conducting business in the United States discriminates in favor of Mexican nationals and against U.S. nationals in its hiring of executives to work in the United States, this would probably constitute national origin discrimination.

Ethics Questions

1. What is national origin discrimination in the context of international employment?
2. What purpose does the FCN treaty serve in this case?
3. Is it ethical for companies to discriminate in favor of its nationals over the nationals of the host country?

Extraterritorial Application of U.S. Employment Laws

Title VII and the ADA

American companies doing business within the United States are subject to the employment laws we have studied in earlier chapters. Title VII does not explicitly state whether it applies to employers overseas. The Supreme Court considered the question in *EEOC v. Arabian American Oil Company.*[4] In that case, Ali Bourassa, a U.S. citizen, was working for ARAMCO, a Delaware corporation, at the company's Saudi Arabian facility. Following his discharge, he sued ARAMCO for race, religious, and national origin discrimination in violation of Title VII. The Supreme Court held that Title VII would not extend to such overseas employment. The Court held that under international law there is a presumption against the extraterritoriality of the U.S. laws unless Congress has expressed an explicit intent to the contrary. The decision allowed U.S. employers to ignore U.S. employment law with regard to their overseas employees. In response to the decision, Congress amended Title VII and the Americans with Disabilities Act by the **Civil Rights Act of 1991**.

The **Civil Right Act of 1991** expanded the definition of an employee under Title VII and the Americans with Disabilities Act to include U.S. citizens working in a foreign country for an employer otherwise covered by the respective statute. As a result, overseas employees of U.S. firms are subject to this statute, unless their application would violate the law of the foreign country in which the employee is stationed. This defense is known as the **foreign laws defense**.

In contrast, Title VII and the ADA both contain exclusions to their application to foreign employers' foreign operations. These employment discrimination statutes recognize the well-established **principle of sovereignty**, which holds that no nation has the right to impose its labor standards on another country. For example, a Frenchman working in the Paris office of a French company would not be subject to U.S. discrimination laws, even if the company maintained offices in the United States that operated according to American labor and employment laws. This concept is related to another legal principle known as the **act of state doctrine**, which originated from a Supreme Court case entitled *Underhill v. Hernandez.*[5] In that decision, the Court held that federal courts do not have jurisdiction over acts undertaken by a sovereign nation within its own territory.

In a 1984 revision to the Age Discrimination in Employment Act of 1967, the ADEA was limited so that an employee at a workplace in a foreign country is not protected under the ADEA if the employer is a foreign business not controlled by an American employer. The EEOC regulations provide some guidance on whether the foreign employers are controlled by an American company. These regulations are discussed below. In the following case, the Second Circuit Court of Appeals considered whether that legislative history indicated that Congress intended to restrict the application of the ADEA with respect to the American-based operations of foreign employers.

Extraterritorial Application
As established by diplomatic agreement, the status of being either subject to or exempt from the jurisdiction of local or national law. Often affects employment in foreign countries by giving alien persons immunity from local laws.

Foreign Laws Defense
Proof offered by a U.S. employer that compliance with a U.S. employment law, such as the ADEA, would cause the employer to violate the laws of the foreign country in which it is doing business and in which the violation of U.S. law occurred.

Principle of Sovereignty
The legal principle that a nation may lawfully control activities only within its territory and that it does not have authority within the domain of another nation.

Act of State Doctrine
The legal principle holding that a nation is sovereign within its own territory and that courts of other nations have no jurisdiction to question its actions taken within its own borders.

CASE 18.3

TITLE VII APPLIES TO FOREIGN CORPORATIONS TO THE EXTENT THEY DISCRIMINATE AGAINST U.S.-BASED EMPLOYEES

MORELLI V. CEDEL

141 F.3d 39 (2d Cir. 1998)

U.S. Court of Appeals for the Second Circuit

Facts. Ida Morelli sued her employer under the Age Discrimination in Employment Act of 1967 (ADEA), ERISA, and a New York state civil rights statute.

The federal district court dismissed the complaint on the basis that the defendant employer, a Luxembourg bank, was not subject to the ADEA. Morelli appealed to the Second Circuit Court of Appeals.

Issues. Are U.S.-based employees of foreign corporations protected under the Age Discrimination in Employment Act of 1967? If so, are the foreign corporation's foreign employees counted in determining whether the corporation has enough employees to be subject to the ADEA?

Language of the Court. Cudahy, J.: **It is undisputed that Cedel is a foreign employer with fewer than 20 employees in its sole U.S. branch. The 1984 revision to the definition of "employee" in [the act] was intended "to assure that the provisions of the ADEA would be applicable to any citizen of the United States who is employed by an American employer in a workplace outside the United States." . . . The other 1984 amendments . . . conform the ADEA's reach to "the well-established principle of sovereignty, that no nation has the right to impose its labor standards on another country." . . . Thus, the ADEA merely limits the scope of the amended definition of employee, so that an employee at a workplace in a foreign country is not protected under the ADEA if the employer is a foreign person not controlled by an American employer. (Citation omitted.) There is no evidence in the legislative history that these amendments were intended to restrict the application of the ADEA with respect to the domestic operations of foreign employers.**

It is not apparent why the domestic operations of foreign companies should be subject to Title VII and the ADA, but not to the ADEA.

Because "the Age Discrimination Act is remedial and humanitarian legislation," it should be "construed liberally to achieve its purpose of protecting older employees from discrimination." (Citation omitted.) The exemption of the domestic operations of foreign employers from the ADEA would only undermine the purpose of the ADEA to "promote employment of older persons based on their ability rather than age." . . . International comity does not require such an exemption; the 1984 amendments anticipate that American corporations operating abroad will be subject to foreign labor laws and Congress presumably contemplated that the operations of foreign corporations here will be subject to U.S. labor laws.

We therefore agree with the E.E.O.C., the agency charged with the enforcement of the ADEA . . . the law generally applies "to foreign firms operating on U.S. soil." . . . For the reasons we have discussed, we are confident that Congress has never clearly expressed a contrary intent.

Are employees based abroad counted in determining whether a U.S.-based branch of a foreign employer is subject to the ADEA? Cedel will still not be subject to the ADEA by virtue of its U.S. operations unless Cedel is an "employer" under the ADEA. A business must have at least twenty "employees"

to be an "employer." . . . Cedel maintains that, in the case of foreign employers, only domestic employees should be counted. Cedel contends that because it has fewer than 20 employees in the United States, it is the equivalent of a small U.S. employer. . . . This is implausible with respect to compliance and litigation costs; their impact on Cedel is better gauged by its worldwide employment. Cedel would not appear to be any more a boutique operation in the United States than would a business with ten employees each in offices in, say, Alaska and Florida, which would be subject to the ADEA. Further, a U.S. corporation with many foreign employees but fewer than 20 domestic ones would certainly be subject to the ADEA.

Decision. Yes. The ADEA generally applies to foreign firms operating on U.S. soil. Employees of a common employer are counted for the threshold application of U.S. discrimination laws, even though they are permanently employed outside of the United States.

CASE QUESTIONS

Critical Legal Thinking. Does it make a difference if a foreign employer does not have a U.S. office? Would American civil rights laws apply to such an employer?

Business Ethics. Does it seem fair to you that the 20-employee threshold for ADEA application can be met on a worldwide basis?

Contemporary Business. If this decision were applied to most multinational corporations operating in the United States, what advice would you give to their senior managers to avoid its application to their companies?

The EEOC has issued guidance to employers with overseas workforces. In *Enforcement Guidance on Application of Title VII and the Americans with Disabilities Act to Conduct Overseas and to Foreign Employers Discriminating in the United States,*[6] the EEOC issued its interpretations as to the reach of these laws. In determining the nationality of an employer, the EEOC will consider the nationality of the principal of the business, the dominant shareholders' nationalities or status, and the nationalities and locations of company officers and directors. In assessing whether an American employer controls a foreign corporation, the factors considered include:

- the interrelationship of operations (including the commonality of contacts and communications between the entities);
- common management structure;
- centralized control of labor relations; and
- common ownership or financial control between the entities.

The following case considers these factors in the context of outrageous employer behavior involving a company with operations in southern California and Mexico.

CASE 18.4

AN INTEGRATED ENTERPRISE MAY SUBJECT THE EMPLOYER TO TITLE VII COVERAGE

KANG V. U. LIM AMERICA, INC.

296 F.3d 810 (9th Cir. 2002)

U.S. Court of Appeals for the Ninth Circuit

Facts. Soo Cheol Kang was a U.S. citizen of Korean national origin. In 1994, he began working for a California corporation known as U. Lim America, Inc. All of U. Lim America's employees were of Korean heritage. Yoon was Kang's supervisor, and he subjected Kang and other Korean workers to oral and physical abuse and discriminatorily long work hours. The abuse consisted, among other things, of Yoon's screaming at Kang for up to three hours a day and calling him "stupid," "cripple," "jerk," "son of a bitch," and "asshole." The physical abuse consisted of striking Kang in the head with a metal ruler on approximately 20 occasions, kicking him in the shins, pulling his ears, throwing metal ashtrays, calculators, water bottles, and files at him, and forcing him to do "jumping jacks." Kang was terminated after cutting back on the required overtime to spend time with his pregnant wife. Yoon also abused other Korean workers verbally with epithets such as "son of a bitch" and "son of a vagina" (which the district court noted was a particularly offensive epithet in the Korean language) and physically by hitting them.

U. Lim America had six or fewer employees located in the United States. However, the U.S.-based company owned and operated U. Lim de Mexico, an electronics manufacturing company organized under the laws of Mexico and operating in Tijuana, Mexico. All of U. Lim America's employees worked at the Tijuana factory. U. Lim de Mexico employed between 50 and 150 workers — all citizens of Mexico. Kang sued in California state court against U. Lim America and Yoon for national origin discrimination and harassment in violation of Title VII and the California civil rights statute. The defendants removed the case to federal court. The district court granted summary judgment to U. Lim America and Yoon. Kang appealed to the Ninth Circuit Court of Appeals.

Issue. May a court consider a U.S. business location to be sufficiently integrated with a foreign employer so as to subject the employer to Title VII?

Language of the Court. Browning, J.: This circuit applies a four-part test to determine whether two entities are an integrated enterprise for purposes of Title VII coverage. . . . The four factors are: (1) interrelation of operations, (2) common management, (3) centralized control of labor relations, and (4) common ownership or financial control.

The first factor, interrelation of operations, weighs in favor of finding the two companies to be an integrated enterprise. U. Lim America and U. Lim de Mexico shared a facility in Mexico; neither had a facility in the United States. All of U. Lim America's employees worked in the Tijuana factory, commuting across the border each day. U. Lim America kept U. Lim de Mexico's accounts, issued its paychecks, and paid its bills. (Citation omitted) (examining such factors as whether the companies operated at separate locations, filed separate tax returns, held separate director and shareholder meetings, conducted separate banking, purchased goods separately, entered into lease agreements separately, and were separately managed).

The second factor, common management, also favors finding the two companies to be integrated for Title VII purposes. Yoon was the Vice-President of U. Lim America and President of U. Lim de Mexico. U. Lim de Mexico supervisors reported directly to U. Lim America's managers. (Citation omitted) (finding common management where the two companies had a "common management structure" and the President of the subsidiary operated out of the parent's office).

The third factor, centralized control of labor relations, is the "most critical." U. Lim America had the authority to hire and fire U. Lim de Mexico employees. The Mexican supervisors reported to U. Lim America management. U. Lim America had essentially complete control over U. Lim de Mexico's labor relations.

The fourth factor also weighs in favor of finding the two companies to be an integrated enterprise. U. Lim America and U. Lim de Mexico were owned and controlled by the same person, Yoon's father Ki Hwa Yoon. Furthermore, U. Lim de Mexico essentially made no profit and transferred all its funds to U. Lim America. . . .

U. Lim America argued that the definition of employee in Title VII prohibits counting foreign employees of U.S. controlled corporations for purposes of Title VII coverage. [In] Morelli v. Cedel, the court explained that Congress amended the ADEA to specify that the term employee included U.S. citizens working for U.S. companies outside the U.S., not to exclude counting foreign employees. . . .

. . . Since we broadly interpret ambiguous language in civil rights statutes to effectuate the remedial purpose of the legislation, we hold that Title VII's definition of "employee" does not prohibit counting the foreign employees of U.S.-controlled corporations for determining coverage.

The fact that some of the employees of the integrated enterprise are not themselves covered by federal antidiscrimination law does not preclude counting them as employees for the purposes of determining Title VII coverage. . . . "The nose count of employees relates to the scale of the employer rather than to the extent of protection." . . . U. Lim America combined with its large Mexican operation is not a small business of the type Congress intended to protect with the minimum employee limitation.

Decision. Yes. Courts use a practical integrated business enterprise test to determine if Title VII applies.

CASE QUESTIONS

Critical Legal Thinking. If Kang was terminated for his failure to work the required overtime, was he discriminated against because he was Korean or for his failure to work the required overtime?

Business Ethics. Given the history of the harassment and abuse, is there any ethical basis to assert that Title VII did not apply? Is it fair to subject U. Lim America, with no more than five employees in the U.S. at a time, to Title VII when the alleged discriminatory conduct occurred in Mexico?

Contemporary Business. Can you think of any other instances where courts have applied U.S. law to wrongful conduct occurring overseas?

Management Application
FCN Treaties and U.S. Whistleblower Laws

U.S. laws often protect whistleblowers. That term describes a person who publicly raises a concern about wrongdoing occurring in a private or public organization. The misconduct must involve a matter of an important public law or a threat to a public interest, such as fraud, health and safety violations, and integrity among public officials and in public contracts. At the same time, U.S. treaties with foreign nations often exempt foreign-owned companies operating in the United States from the application of certain U.S. laws that would otherwise affect the operation of those companies. Consider the following case.

JAL is a Japanese commercial air carrier based in Tokyo, Japan. HACS was a Hawaiian corporation with it principal place of business in Honolulu. HACS provided contract flight crews to JAL. Martin Ventress, a flight engineer, and Jack Crawford, a commercial pilot, were employed by HACS to work on JAL flights. In their California federal lawsuit against JAL and HACS, they alleged that JAL required a seriously ill pilot to fly in June 2001. That action violated American and Japanese aviation laws as well as JAL's operations manual. Crawford expressed his concern to a JAL official in Honolulu. Following that report he experienced harassment from his superiors, including repeated performance checks, questions, and homework assignments. Within six months, HACS informed Crawford that his assignment to JAL was cancelled because of unsatisfactory performance. During the same month, Ventress submitted reports on the June incidents to JAL, HACS, and aviation regulators. Thereafter, Ventress claimed, he was repeatedly harassed by JAL employees, including a demand that he undergo psychiatric evaluations. Ventress was not allowed to fly after filing his reports. Crawford and Ventress sought recovery for violation of California's whistleblower statute, wrongful termination in violation of public policy protecting whistleblowers, and emotional distress.

The California whistleblower law stated: "An employer may not retaliate against an employee for disclosing information to a government or law enforcement agency, where the employee has reasonable cause to believe that the information discloses a violation of state or federal statute, or a violation or noncompliance with a state or federal regulation."

After the case was transferred from California federal court to Hawaii, the Hawaii district court granted judgment for JAL on the ground that the 1953 Friendship, Commerce, and Navigation Treaty between the U.S. and Japan preempted all of the plaintiffs' claims.

The Ninth Circuit Court of Appeals reversed the district court decision. The court noted, "Given the purpose and history of the FCN treaties, our sister circuits have consistently held that foreign employers do not enjoy immunity from domestic employment laws that do not interfere with the employers' ability to hire their fellow citizens." The Court held that JAL would be liable for the charge that it violated the California whistleblower protection law.[8]

Discussion Questions

1. Why would the district court conclude that JAL had a treaty right to ignore domestic employment law, including personnel decisions that involved only non-Japanese citizens?
2. Would the district court's construction lead to absurd results, such as exempting foreign employers from American collective bargaining laws?
3. To what degree is the enforcement of the California whistleblower law a burden on international trade? Why should JAL be exempt from its application?

Employment Law in the European Union (EU)

As of 2010, the following countries are members of the EU: Austria, Belgium, Bulgaria, Cyprus, the Czech Republic, Denmark, Estonia, Finland, France, Germany, Greece, Hungary, Ireland, Italy, Latvia, Lithuania, Luxembourg, Malta, the Netherlands, Poland, Portugal, Romania, Slovakia, Slovenia, Spain, Sweden, and the United Kingdom. Each is known as a member state of the European Union or European Community.

The law of the EU Community operates alongside the laws of the member states. In some cases, the EU preempts the national law of a member state. The concept of supremacy or preemption occurs in many areas affecting employment law. The member states agree to a common set of laws that are applied throughout the EU membership nations. The European Commission that acts as the executive branch to the Council of the European Union and the European Parliament initially proposes new laws such as those discussed in the following section. By treaty, the commission, the council, and the parliament issue laws that are binding on the member states. Employment law within the community is derived from the Treaty of Rome adopted in 1957. All laws must reference the specific treaty that is the source for the authority of the legislation. The European Court of Justice principally enforces EU law. The Maastricht Treaty on European Union introduced the idea of European citizenship across the membership states of the EU. The treaty has been officially renamed the European Community (EC) Treaty. As a result, workers in the EU who are citizens of a member nation have the benefits of a federal employment law system similar to that of the United States.

Directives under EC Article 39

Directive
A legislative act of the EU that requires member states to achieve a particular result without dictating the means to be used in achieving it.

EU **directives** define goals to be achieved while allowing member states to determine how they will adapt their national laws to meet those goals. EU law and member nations' national employment laws overlap in the execution of **directives**, meaning the European Union lacks a comprehensive employment law system similar to that of the United States. American companies operating in the EU should consider several **directives** to be of particular interest. They arise from **Article 39 EC**, which provides for the **free movement of workers**, the self-employed, and their families.

> **Article 39**
>
> *1. Freedom of movement for workers shall be secured within the Community.*
>
> *2. Such freedom of movement shall entail the abolition of any discrimination based on nationality between workers of the Member States as regards employment, remuneration and other conditions of work and employment.*
>
> *3. It shall entail the right, subject to limitations justified on grounds of public policy, public security or public health:*
>
> *(a) to accept offers of employment actually made;*
>
> *(b) to move freely within the territory of Member States for this purpose;*
>
> *(c) to stay in a Member State for the purpose of employment in accordance with the provisions governing the employment of nationals of that State laid down by law, regulation or administrative action;*
>
> *(d) to remain in the territory of a Member State after having been employed in that State, subject to conditions which shall be embodied in implementing regulations to be drawn up by the Commission.*
>
> *4. The provisions of this article shall not apply to employment in the public service.*

European Court of Justice (ECJ)
The highest judicial body in the European Union.

The **European Court of Justice (ECJ)** has interpreted this **Article 39** to prohibit direct and indirect discrimination and any conduct that impedes the **free movement of workers**. The **ECJ** applies this doctrine to extraterritorial applications as well. The one exception to this right relates to public-sector employment, in which a person filling a position with a governmental agency of a particular member nation, including positions in the judiciary, law enforcement, and the armed forces, may be required to be a citizen of that nation state.

The **freedom of movement for workers** established by **Article 39** authorizes all citizens and legally resident aliens of the member states to seek employment on the same basis as nationals of the EU state in which the employment is located. This article also allows EU workers to bring their families with them. Unlike the United States, with its social welfare programs such as Social Security and Medicare, the European Union offers no overarching welfare system. Consequently, the EU law provides for equal treatment of claims made against a specific country's system affording fringe benefits such as health care, retirement, and workers' compensation. EU workers and their families are permitted to reside in another member nation for a six-month period while searching for work.

Article 141: Equal Pay for Equal Work

Under the European Union Treaty, **Article 141** provides, in part:

1. Each Member State shall ensure that the principle of equal pay for male and female workers for equal work or work of equal value is applied.

2. For the purpose of this article, "pay" means the ordinary basic or minimum wage or salary and any other consideration, whether in cash or in kind, which the worker receives directly or indirectly, in respect of his employment, from his employer.

Equal pay without discrimination based on sex means:

(a) that pay for the same work at piece rates shall be calculated on the basis of the same unit of measurement;

(b) that pay for work at time rates shall be the same for the same job.

3. The Council, acting in accordance with the procedure referred to in Article 251, and after consulting the Economic and Social Committee, shall adopt measures to ensure the application of the principle of equal opportunities and equal treatment of men and women in matters of employment and occupation, including the principle of equal pay for equal work or work of equal value.

4. With a view to ensuring full equality in practice between men and women in working life, the principle of equal treatment shall not prevent any Member State from maintaining or adopting measures providing for specific advantages in order to make it easier for the underrepresented sex to pursue a vocational activity or to prevent or compensate for disadvantages in professional careers.

Article 141
With Article 12, this EC Treaty provision prohibits discrimination between men and women, though only as far as equal pay is concerned.

Many court cases extend this principle to sexual equality. This article was the first of the EC's efforts to establish equal pay for equal work for men and women. It was part of the original treaty, the Treaty of Rome, which established the EU. The principle was adopted because French law already required it and if it were not made part of the EU law France would be at a competitive disadvantage to the other member states. This principle was extended to apply to sex discrimination in the following case, *Defrenne v. SABENA*. This case serves as strong precedent in the EU for the principle of **"comparable worth."** Article 119, which has now been incorporated into Article 141, is discussed.

Comparable Worth
A concept from Article 141 of the EC Treaty providing that women should receive equal pay for equal work or work of comparable value.

CASE 18.5

ALL EC WORKERS AND NATIONAL COURTS MAY RELY ON PAY EQUALITY

DEFRENNE V. SA BELGE DE NAVIGATION AERIENNE (SABENA)

Case 43/75 (1976) ECR 455

European Court of Justice

Facts. Article 119 of the EC Treaty required member states to ensure and maintain the principle that men and women should receive equal pay for equal work. Ms. Gabrielle Defrenne worked as a flight attendant for SABENA, a Belgian government owned and operated airline. Her contract of employment stated that she would have to retire at the age of 40, and she was terminated when she reached that age. She sued in a Belgian court because she had suffered employment sex discrimination under Article 119. She claimed that she had been paid less during her employment than her male counterparts and that her retirement benefits would accordingly be less. During the course of proceedings, SABENA admitted it paid females less than males for the same duties, but argued that Article 119 did not apply. It argued that it was inherently too complex a requirement and that more detailed national legislation on the meaning and application of equal pay for equal work was required before the article could be enforced. The action was originally dismissed by the Belgian court. It was appealed to an intermediate court that, in turn, requested the European Court of Justice to rule on certain issues pertaining to Defrenne's claims.

Issue. May EU citizens sue for employers' violations of equal pay for equal work regulations?

Language of the Court. **The very wording of Article 119 shows that it imposes on states a duty to bring about a specific result to be mandatorily achieved within a fixed period. To accept a contrary view would be to risk raising the violation of the right to the status of a principle of interpretation, a position the adoption of which would not be consistent with the task assigned to the court by Article 164 of the Treaty.**

In its reference to "member states," Article 119 is alluding to those states in the exercise of all those of their functions which may usefully contribute to the implementation of the principle of equal pay. Thus, contrary to the statements

made in the course of the proceeding this provision is far from merely referring the matter to the powers of the national legislative authorities.

Therefore, the reference to "member states" . . . cannot be interpreted as excluding the intervention of the courts in direct application of the treaty. Furthermore, it is not possible to sustain any objection that the application by national courts of the principle of equal pay would amount to modifying independent agreements concluded privately or in the sphere of industrial relations such as individual contracts and collective labour agreements.

In fact, since Article 119 is mandatory in nature, the prohibition on discrimination between men and women applies not only to the action of public authorities, but also extends to all agreements which are intended to regulate paid labour collectively, as well as to contracts between individuals.

Decision. Yes. The ECJ held that the equal pay for equal work provisions of Article 119 are binding on member states and private employers. Individuals may rely on some of the treaty articles to enforce labor and employment rights in the national courts of member states.

CASE QUESTIONS

Critical Legal Thinking. Under this decision, the EU embraced the rule of comparable worth that has been rejected by U.S. courts. Can you identify the U.S. law adopted in 1963 that applies to claims by one gender against an employer because the employer has not paid equal wages due to sex discrimination?

Business Ethics. The problem with the concept of comparable worth is in determining whether two job functions are comparable. For example, should file clerks performing manual labor within a company be paid the same as the laborers working in the company's grounds and landscaping department?

Contemporary Business. The Court held that the EC had not guaranteed equality between men and women in working conditions other than remuneration. This holding would permit discrimination between the sexes as it may relate to nonpay disputes. Will the EC adopt a legal framework as broad as American nondiscrimination law?

In light of the *Defrenne* decision, employers must determine the value of the work performed in all positions in the company's workforce. In response to determining comparable worth, EU employers have begun to analyze the activity content of each job function. Points and grades are awarded in each category of work relative to the overall value of the job to be performed. Each member state has approached the process differently. Council Directive 75/117 implements this article and makes equal pay applicable to jobs of equal value to the employer. This directive requires that employers establish nondiscriminatory job classifications to measure the **comparable worth** of one job with another one.

The **equal pay for equal work** requirement of Directive 75/117 has been extended to **equal treatment** of workers. Similar to the American prohibition of discrimination relating to "terms and conditions" of employment, the directive prohibits discrimination based on the sex, family, or marital status of employed and self-employed workers. The equal treatment principal has three exceptions for which member states may provide in their national laws:

- if gender is a determining factor in the ability to perform the work and the provision protects women;
- if the occupational activity involved is appropriate for workers of one sex only; or
- if the law promotes equal opportunity for males and females.

Related to the foregoing antidiscrimination laws are two other EU directives. Directive 2000/43 provides for **equal treatment** regardless of race or national origin. Directive 2000/78 prohibits employment discrimination based on religious belief, disability, age, or sexual orientation.

Other EU directives of interest to the global employer include the following:

- **Directive 91/533: Employee protections.** The law of the EU specifies information that employers must provide to their employees. This information includes the following:
  - ☐ The job description
  - ☐ The term of employment
  - ☐ Periods of paid leave (including vacations and pregnancy leaves)
  - ☐ The terms of compensation
- Related **Directive 96/71** requires employers transferring workers to another member state to adhere to host country rules on minimum pay and benefits, work periods, paid leaves, and health and safety rules.
- Fringe benefits (and the employer's contribution to them) are also covered under **Directive 91/533.**
- Under related **Directive 96/34**, each worker is granted unpaid parental leave rights for up to three months. Employees with one or more years' tenure have a vested right to be reinstated in their original or a similarly situated position following their return from such leave.
- Description and applicability of any collective bargaining agreements also appear under **Directive 91/533.**
- **Directive 98/59: Mass Lay-off Protections.** Similar to the WARN Act we studied in Chapter 10, **Directive 98/59** provides that employers with 20 or more workers must give 30 days' prior written notice with "all relevant information" to the employees or their representatives (i.e., union representatives). For employers with workforces of fewer than 100 workers, this notice is triggered upon the layoff of 10 or more employees. For workforces of 100 to 300 employees, the notice is triggered when 10 percent or more of the employees are to be laid off. The procedure requires consultations between the employer and the affected employees. These meetings must also involve

local governmental authorities. Some countries, such as Germany, have notification requirements that are more stringent.

- **Directive 77/187 (2001/23): Employee Rights Following Business Transfers.** This directive requires issuance of prior written notice of qualified transfers with an explanation of the repercussions for the workers following the business transfer. The transfer is the continuance of a business following the sale, merger, or acquisition of stock or assets. All employees of the target company retain their existing compensation and other terms and conditions of employment following the transfer. All collective bargaining agreements are preserved and binding on the purchaser. The law provides that employers may not dismiss any employee except for economic, technical, or organizational reasons following the transfer. This philosophy is completely contrary to the model employed in the United States following a business acquisition, in which the new employer is likely to move to reduce costs, consolidate operations, and maximize worker productivity by eliminating duplicative or unnecessary job functions.
- **Directive 80/987: Protection from Insolvent Employers.** Member states must guarantee certain employee unpaid wage claims when an insolvent employer ceases operations.

Nationality Discrimination and Article 39

In the following **ECJ** case, the Court considered whether **Article 39** would apply to employment discrimination caused not by a member state but rather by a private organization.

Article 39
Article of the EC Treaty providing that EU citizens may move freely among the EC member nations while looking for employment. After working in a member nation, they may continue to reside in that country. Migrant workers enjoy equal treatment with nationals with regard to access to employment, working conditions, and all other benefits.

CASE 18.6

EU LAW PROHIBITS DISCRIMINATION BASED ON NATIONALITY

B.N.O. WALRAVE AND L.J.N. KOCH V. ASSOCIATION UNION CYCLISTE INTERNATIONALE, ET AL.

Case 36-74, 1974 E.C.R. 1405

European Court of Justice

Facts. Two Dutch bicyclists, Walgrave and Koch, sued a senior official of a private bicycling organization to overturn one of its rules. The rule prohibited these two Dutchmen from acting as pacemakers on French roads for cyclists of non-Dutch nationalities. The Dutchmen wanted to work for non-Dutch teams. They challenged the rule based on nationality discrimination, the free movement of workers, and the presumption of the free movement of the self-employed.

Issue. Can individual citizens of the EU sue a private organization for denial of EU-protected rights?

Language of the Court. **Prohibition of such discrimination does not only apply to the action of public authorities but extends likewise to rules of any other nature aimed at regulating in a collective manner gainful employment and the provision of services.**

The abolition as between Member States of obstacles to freedom of movement for persons and to freedom to provide services, which are fundamental objectives of the Community . . . , would be compromised if the abolition of barriers of national origin could be neutralised by obstacles resulting from the exercise of their legal autonomy by associations or organizations which do not come under public law.

Since, moreover, working conditions in the various Member States are governed by means of provisions laid down in law or regulations and sometimes by agreements and other acts concluded by private persons, to limit the prohibitions in question to acts of a public authority would risk creating inequality in their application.

Decision. Yes. The ECJ held that the directives applied equally to discrimination against EU citizens by both private organizations and member states.

CASE QUESTIONS

Critical Legal Thinking. Why do you think the ECJ applied Articles prohibiting discrimination by member states to actions involving private parties? If it had not applied them to private parties would this have effectively permitted nationality-based discrimination in employment?

Business Ethics. The Court also allowed discrimination with respect to the selection of members of national cycling teams, which it viewed as "having nothing to do with economic activity." Do you agree with that exception to EU discrimination law?

Contemporary Business. Does the vagueness of EU law lie in its attempt to satisfy many constituencies?

European Convention on Human Rights in the European Union

Adopted by the Council of Europe in 1950 to protect human rights and fundamental freedoms, members of the European Union subscribe to the **European Convention on Human Rights** that provides in part for the following:

> **Article 8 — Right to respect for private and family life**
>
> *Everyone has the right to respect for his private and family life, his home and his correspondence. There shall be no interference by a public authority with the exercise of this right except such as is in accordance with the law and is necessary in a democratic society in the interests of national security, public safety or the economic well-being of the country, for the prevention of disorder or crime, for the protection of health or morals, or for the protection of the rights and freedoms of others. The Convention established the European Court of Human Rights before which any person who contends their rights have been violated under the convention by a European state may file suit and seek damages. Both that court and national European courts have defined correspondence as including all forms of communication including telephones and e-mail. Interception of private correspondence is permitted in cases of suspected criminal activity.*

Because of this article, any person (not necessarily a citizen of the EU) residing in an EU country enjoys privacy protections more extensive than those enjoyed by U.S. citizens.

Enforcement

When a member state fails to enforce a directive within its borders, or does so inadequately or incorrectly, the commission may sue the member state to compel compliance in the European Court of Justice. The commission has the power to fine the member state that refuses to comply with a resulting judgment. The national laws of member states must conform to EU directives.

Focus on Ethics
Outsourcing

Many U.S. companies outsource the manufacture of products that they later import and sell to consumers in the United States. Why do U.S. companies outsource much of their manufacturing? The obvious answer is cost. It is much cheaper to have clothing, shoes, and other items manufactured in countries that have cheaper labor. However, why is this labor cheaper? Much of the reason is because many of these foreign countries do not provide the safety and other protections afforded to workers in the United States.

Consider these facts. If goods are manufactured in the United States, the manufacturer must obey occupational safety laws and provide safe working conditions to its workers. In addition, the employer must pay overtime wages when they are due. Additional burdens include the payment of workers' compensation insurance and payroll taxes. Often, the employer must pay expensive health-care benefits to attract the best workers. The employer must lawfully respond to all employment, labor, and retirement benefit laws under federal, state, and local laws and regulations.

Therefore, it makes monetary sense for U.S. companies to avoid the costs of such protections and programs by having by their goods produced in countries that do not afford such protections. Is this "outsourcing" ethical if a U.S. company has knowledge of the poor working conditions in these other countries? Consider the case of Nike. Nike produces shoes, apparel, and sports gear to sell in the United States and worldwide. The majority of Nike's shoes are produced by subcontractors located in some of the poorest countries of the world.

Nike faced a public relations and ethical nightmare when it was accused of selling shoes made by forced and child labor in Vietnam, where workers labored under horrid conditions. In Vietnam, where 12 percent of Nike's shoes were manufactured, subcontractors worked employees six days per week and paid them as little as $40 per month in wages. These workers, who were mostly women in their 20s, worked under terrible conditions. They were subject to working in hot and noisy workplaces, exposed to toxic chemicals and fumes, and mistreated by managers. Workers were hit for not working fast enough or for talking, were made to run in stifling heat or to lick the factory floor if they did not do what the managers told them, and were subject to sexual harassment.

These conditions were brought to light by humanitarian organizations. After first vehemently denying the allegations, Nike backed down and agreed to improve the working conditions at its subcontractors' factories in Vietnam.

Nike agreed to undertake the following steps:

1. It required that many subcontractor managers be fired because of their abusive conduct.
2. It reduced the toxic petroleum-based compounds used in making Nike shoes.
3. It banned subcontractors from paying below Vietnam's minimum wage of $45 per month.
4. It installed Nike managers in subcontractor plants to monitor working conditions.
5. It opened the subcontractor's manufacturing plants to outside inspectors.

Nike states that it has taken the necessary steps to prohibit and prevent abuses by its subcontractors throughout the world. Meanwhile, professional athletes endorsing Nike products often make more money for their endorsements than the total earned by all the overseas workers who manufactured the products. In the year 2008, it was reported by marketing industry experts that Nike had spent $260 million in advertising endorsements.

Ethics Questions

1. Why do U.S. companies outsource the production of clothing, shoes, and other items to poorer foreign countries?
2. Do you think Nike was aware of its subcontractors' working conditions before the humanitarian organizations exposed them?
3. Is outsourcing ethical? Why or why not?

Management Application NAFTA

The U.S. Senate ratified the **North American Free Trade Agreement** (NAFTA) in 1993. Its purpose was to create a free trade zone among Canada, the United States, and Mexico that would be able to meet the competition expected from the European Union. Its central undertaking is to eliminate the vast majority of tariffs on products traded among these nations. The terms of the agreement called for these tariffs to be phased out gradually. A significant side agreement of the treaty is **The North American Agreement on Labor Cooperation,** briefly discussed here. The immigration aspects of NAFTA were reviewed in the chapter above on immigration and nationality.

It is difficult to measure NAFTA's effect on the U.S. labor market. Using data gathered before the current period of economic turmoil, the U.S. Trade Representative, an office within the executive branch of the U.S. government, reported that:

- U.S. employment rose from 110.8 million people in 1993 to 137.6 million in 2007, an increase of 24 percent.
- The average unemployment rate was 5.1 percent in the period between 1994 and 2007, compared to 7.1 percent during the period 1980 to 1993.

In addition, it claimed that the U.S. manufacturing base was not harmed. It concluded:

- U.S. manufacturing output rose by 58 percent between 1993 and 2006, as compared to 42 percent between 1980 and 1993.
- Manufacturing exports in 2007 reached an all time high with a value of $982 billion.

It also reported that NAFTA did not suppress U.S. wages. In this regard, it stated:

- U.S. business sector real hourly compensation rose by 1.5 percent each year between 1993 and 2007, for a total of 23.6 percent over the full period.
- From 1979 to 1993, the annual rate of real hourly compensation rose by 0.7 percent each year, or 11 percent over the full 14-year period.[9]

Many economists agree with this data, but they also note the painful consequences of the globalization of American manufacturing and distribution, which has been advanced by the terms of the treaty. The AFL-CIO and many other labor organizations have steadfastly opposed NAFTA. It has taken the position that NAFTA did not create thousands of promised good jobs — the jobs it did create were less stable, with lower wages, and fewer benefits. The union claims that the treaty's failure to create decent jobs has forced many workers, especially those in Mexico, to search for employment in other countries. Furthermore, it urges that the industrial base of each country has not increased. Finally, it reaches a contrary conclusion regarding the impact on the labor market. It claims that job losses have been realized in the United States and Canada and that the wages, benefits, and rights of Mexican workers have been suppressed because of the operation of maquiladora plants, which make products to be sold in the other two countries.[10]

Discussion Questions

1. What is your opinion on the relative benefit of the NAFTA treaty with regard to U.S. employment and trade?
2. Identify who is helped by NAFTA and who is harmed by it.
3. Should the United States renegotiate the treaty? Why have succeeding White House administrations refrained from doing so?

Employment Laws of Canada and Mexico

Canada

In Canada, unless federal law applies, provincial and territorial law determines employment issues in Canada. If federal law regulates an industry, federal law will control employment and labor law relations for employees in that industry throughout Canada.

If not governed by federal law, a company must comply with provincial and territorial law. Provincial laws cover such matters as the following:

- Minimum wages
- Hours of work
- Overtime
- Maternity and parental leave
- Termination of employment

EMPLOYEE TERMINATION. While American law endorses the concept of "at-will" employment, Canadian law does not. If there is no cause for termination, all Canadian employees are entitled to receive "reasonable" notice of termination prior to discharge or a payment in place of that notice. Thus, under the normal situation, the employer and employee agree in advance to the amount of notice or payment to be made in the event of an employer directed "no cause" termination. What constitutes a reasonable notice period for a no-cause discharge is a subjective matter. Courts look at all the factors involved in the particular dismissal. These factors range from the qualifications and experience of the individual employee, the employee's ability to obtain other work, and the circumstances of the hiring and termination. The higher the degree of compensation, the longer the notice period the courts will require. Court-ordered payments by the employer range from a matter of weeks of salary to two years of salary.

Such laws do not cover termination for cause. Union workforces are covered by the terms and conditions of their collective bargaining agreements. Wrongful employment termination lawsuits may be filed when there is no reasonable grounds for the termination or the employer has not given the requisite prior notice to the worker. Punitive damages for a humiliating or abusive termination may be awarded in addition to a compensatory damage award for lost wages and benefits. Employers must be honest and forthright with their employees at the time of the exit interview.

> ***Example:*** When a 14-year employee was summarily dismissed without cause, he filed suit against his employer. When he joined the company following a 25-year term with a competitor, he had been assured that as long as he reasonably performed his work he would be able to continue working until his retirement. In response to his lawsuit for a bad-faith discharge, the company asserted that the worker had been fired for cause, which was untrue. It abandoned this position only when the trial commenced. The worker suffered psychiatric injuries and due to his age of nearly 60 years, it was unlikely he would secure alternate employment. The court awarded additional emotional distress damages for the manner in which the company handled the termination.[11]

During the term of employment, the employer may not substantially change the duties and responsibilities of an employee unilaterally and without prior notice. Similar to the American concept of "constructive discharge," a worker may sue for damages if the changes are material, not accepted by the employee or the employer lacks a legitimate business reason for their implementation. Similar to the U.S. WARN Act, Canadian law requires group termination notices to be given prior to mass terminations or layoffs. Provincial laws vary in their requirements and range from two to four months' notice.

Noncompetition clauses in employment agreements are permitted if they are reasonable in scope and duration, usually to a maximum of two years. In Quebec, a covenant not to compete cannot be enforced by an employer if the employer cancelled the employment agreement with the employee unless the termination occurred for cause or the employer has a good-faith reason for doing so. In other provinces, a covenant not to compete will be enforced in only limited circumstances. Courts will review whether a reasonable covenant-not-to-compete agreement is narrowly written. It will construe the agreement in a fashion that protects the employer's legitimate business interests. The employee must possess information that would impede the employer's business if used by the former employee.

LABOR UNIONS. Union laws are similar in approach and application to U.S. law. Strikes and lockouts may not occur during the term of a collective bargaining agreement. Union certification, recognition, and good-faith bargaining requirements are similar to those under U.S. law. Provincial and federal level labor relations boards administer the provincial and federal aspects of Canadian labor law.

EMPLOYEE PRIVACY RIGHTS. Another law affecting the employment of persons in Canada is the **Personal Information Protection and Electronic Documents Act**. The act is a series of directives that limit trade with nations not providing privacy protection equivalent to the European Union standards. The law gives individuals the right to be apprised of why and how an organization is collecting, using, or disclosing personal information. It restricts the disclosure of information to the scope of the consent given by the individual to the collecting and disseminating organization. It is intended to restrict the disclosure of personal "information about an identifiable individual." This restriction includes such things as race, color, ethnic origin, gender, marital status, religion, medical records, criminal history, employment or financial history, and identifiers such as blood type. If unauthorized disclosure does occur, an affected individual can file a complaint with the Privacy Commissioner of Canada who, although lacking enforcement powers, will issue an investigatory report. After receiving the report, the individual can sue in the Federal Court of Canada for damages and an order seeking compliance from the offending company. This law restricts an employer's ability to collect and disseminate employee information.

Mexico

The **Mexican Federal Labor Law (FLL)** governs virtually all management-labor relationships in Mexico. The federal Social Security Law governs those provisions not covered by the **FLL**. Not only legal duties but also social rights and duties are recognized in the **FLL**. The employment relationship in Mexico is based on the Mexican Constitution. The provisions and directives of the **FLL** are mandatory and may not be bargained away.

Mexican Federal Labor Law (FLL)
One of two national laws governing labor issues in Mexico. The other is the federal Social Security Law.

A summary of the **FLL** is as follows:

- All employment contracts must be in writing through either a collective bargaining agreement or an individual contract with the employee. The law is very specific with regard to the information that must be included in the contracts. Such information includes the age, sex, marital status, and nationality of the worker.

- The employment contract must state whether the job is for a definite or an indefinite term. A contract for a fixed period will be considered as extended beyond its term if circumstances require the worker's continued employment to complete the assigned tasks.
- The Mexican worker is entitled to a 6-day, 48-hour workweek. Overtime is paid at the rate of twice the base wage rate and three times that rate for overtime hours in excess of nine hours per workweek.
- Minimum wages are based on the economic zones in which the business operates. Union wage agreements may require compensation in excess of the mandated federal minimum wages. Quite often, compensation paid to skilled workers and managers may rival that paid in the United States.
- Mexican law mandates that certain minimum benefits be afforded each employee. Among them are the following:
  - **Christmas bonus.** For those in the employer's employ for more than a year, 15 days' salary must be paid before December 20 each year; employees with less longevity receive a prorated bonus.
  - **Vacation pay.** Vacation time accrues at the rate of 6 days for the first year, 8 days for the second, and 12 days of the fourth year of service. Thereafter, vacation accrues at the rate of two additional days for every additional five years of service. Employees on vacation receive their normal wage plus a vacation bonus of 225 percent.
  - **Sunday bonus pay.** If a normal work schedule requires work on a Sunday, the the employee earns a premium of 25 percent for that day.
  - **Regular time off.** Workers are entitled to one day off for every six days worked. If the worker works on a scheduled day off, a two-day regular pay bonus is given in addition to regular compensation.
  - **Holidays.** There are a minimum of seven federal paid holidays.
- In addition to compensation and benefits paid to its employees, the employer of Mexican workers must pay into various social security, housing fund, disability, retirement, death insurance, and workers' compensation programs managed by the federal government.
- A unique aspect of employment in Mexico is the employer's duty to share 10 percent of the employer's gross profits with its workers. This amount is apportioned among the workers based on the salary earned and number of days worked each year. Every employee except the company's director general, who functions like the chief executive officer in a U.S. company, is entitled to the profit-sharing bonus each year.
- Other voluntary benefits may be bestowed by employers on their workers.

EMPLOYEE TERMINATION. Employers may not terminate employees without just cause. Dismissal for reasons other than those listed below permits the worker to file suit for reinstatement or indemnification. Mexican law affords the worker the presumptions that he or she was an employee and was dismissed without cause. If the employee prevails in a lawsuit, the worker is entitled to reinstatement plus all back wages. If the employee does not prevail, he or she is entitled to three months' salary, all back wages, and all fringe benefits not received while the matter was in dispute.

The **FLL** provides that an employee may be terminated only upon the following events:

- Mutual consent
- Death of the worker
- Completion of the task for which the employee was hired or the expiration of the fixed term of employment
- Worker disability sufficient to prevent the worker from performing the assigned work
- Circumstances beyond the control of either party
- The insolvency of the firm or cost-prohibitive labor arrangements
- The firm's bankruptcy
- When the installation of new machinery eliminates the need for a worker's position

Unless the employment is terminated by mutual consent or for cause, the employer must pay severance pay. Termination for cause is defined in the **FLL** as including acts of dishonesty and wrongful disclosure of the employer's trade secrets. When dismissal is for cause, the employer must state the grounds in a written notice served upon the employee. If that does not occur, the dismissal is deemed without cause.

The **FLL** recognizes the concepts of constructive discharge and the employee's right to resign at any time. Mexican law grants workers with years of service longevity severance premiums tied to the number of years worked. The law provides for specific severance payouts to employees depending on the reason for the termination. For example, if an employee is terminated because his or her work is now being performed by new machinery, the employee can receive many months of severance pay.

LABOR UNIONS. Mexican law warmly embraces labor unions and collective bargaining. Two or more workers may affiliate for the purposes of unionizing. Company unions represent the workers of a single company, and workers who work for two or more companies within the same industry form industrial unions. Industrial unions work hard to establish long-lasting relationships with local, provincial, and federal governments. Most of the industrial unions are also highly professional and interested in ensuring labor peace. Except for managers and those with a position of confidence (such as supervisors and administrative staff), all workers are entitled to join a union. The federal Arbitration and Conciliation Board serves a role analogous to that performed by the National Labor Relations Board in the United States. In the event of a conflict between unions, the board administers a voting procedure to determine which union will represent the workers.

Federal district and territorial employment legislation and local ordinances are also binding on employers. In addition to the **FLL**, employers must be aware of the laws to which they may be subject on the national, state, and local level, as they are required to do in the United States.

Every unionized employer maintains a Commission on Labor Disputes to resolve disputes between the worker and the employer. An equal number of appointees representing management and workers staff the commission. The Trade Union Committee handles instances when the commission fails to achieve an agreement or the employee wishes to appeal the decision reached. The employee may appeal from that body to a People's Court. Management's right of appeal is limited to legal issues. The People's Court has jurisdiction to issue equitable remedies such as reinstatement and back pay to an amount equal to three months' compensation.

International Labor Organization

The International Labor Organization of the United Nations (ILO) deals with labor issues. This agency maintains offices in Geneva, Switzerland, and is administered by a governing body of 28 governmental representatives, 14 employer representatives, and 14 employee trade union representatives. Its purpose is to establish labor standards to be adopted by individual nations or groups of nations through conventions. The topics addressed by the ILO include child labor, working conditions in hazardous industries, and health and safety issues. The ILO formulates labor policies for adoption by individual nations and by international regions. Ratification of a convention is voluntary, and many nations selectively adopt provisions of the ILO standards. American labor unions, such as the AFL-CIO, maintain relationships with international labor organizations such as the ILO.

Key Terms and Concepts

- Friendship, Commerce, and Navigation Treaty
- Foreign laws defense
- Principle of sovereignty
- Act of state doctrine
- European Court of Justice (ECJ)
- Article 39: free movement of workers and families
- Article 141: equal pay for equal work
- Comparable worth
- Directive 75/117: jobs of equal value and pay
- Directive 2000/43: equal treatment regardless of race or national origin
- Directive 96/71: host country laws apply to transferred employees
- Directive 96/34: parental leave rights
- Directive 98/59: protections from mass layoffs
- Directive 77/187: postacquisition employee rights
- Directive 80/987: state payment of wages following insolvency
- Extraterritorial application
- EU Convention on Human Rights
- Personal Information Protection and Electronic Documents Act
- Mexican Federal Labor Law (FLL)

Chapter Summary

- An FCN treaty is made between the United States and another country and affords protections to workers in companies of the two signatory countries. Such treaties offer certain protections to companies from the party-country operating in the United States and to American companies employing U.S. citizens overseas.

■ U.S. subsidiaries of foreign corporations operating in the United States are subject to U.S. employment and discrimination laws. However, a foreign employer's Title VII discrimination based on national origin is permitted if it occurs in the context of exercising treaty rights. FCN treaties do not prohibit disparate impact discrimination. An FCN treaty permits companies of the two signatory nations to hire senior managers of their own choosing, including those of their home country, even if the result is a discriminatory practice.

■ The Civil Rights Act of 1991 compels a U.S. employer operating overseas to comply with U.S. discrimination laws with regard to U.S. citizens and authorized aliens. However, employers are not required to do so if such compliance would violate the laws of the foreign host country.

■ Foreign employers operating overseas are not subject to U.S. discrimination law due to the principle of sovereignty. Under the act of state doctrine, American courts do not have jurisdiction over disputes involving the official acts of foreign governments.

■ The ADEA has been amended to broaden the definition of "employee." The act provides that it includes any individual who is a citizen of the United States employed by an employer in a workplace in a foreign country. The foreign firm must be controlled by an American business. If it is not so controlled, then that U.S. citizen working in a foreign country is not protected by the ADEA.

■ Foreign corporations operating in the U.S. may not discriminate against U.S. employees if they have the requisite number of foreign and domestic employees to trigger coverage under U.S. discrimination laws. The EEOC has issued guidelines that assist in determining whether a foreign corporation is sufficiently controlled by a U.S. firm to extend coverage of U.S. discrimination law to the foreign corporation.

■ The European Union has a variety of employment-related laws, including regulations on the freedom of movement of workers throughout the Union; the payment of equal pay for equal work (which is construed as work of comparable worth); prohibiting discrimination in compensation based on gender for jobs involving comparable worth; equal treatment of workers regardless of their race or national origin; specific disclosures of information relating a job that must be provided to an employee upon hiring; parental leave rights; protections from mass layoffs; and worker protections following a transfer of business ownership. EU requirements apply to all employees, even if based in a non-EU country, if the employment relationship was created within the EU.

■ Directives under EC Article 39 provide for the free movement of workers. An EU national is a citizen from one of the member states of the EU. For an EU national to live indefinitely in a member state other than that in which he or she is a citizen, a permit is necessary. The permit applicant would need to show that he or she had lived and worked there for a five-year period. This procedure guarantees the right of all citizens and legally resident aliens in EU member states to seek employment on the same basis as nationals of the member state in which the employment is located. Certain limitations apply with respect to nationals from Romania and Bulgaria.

■ Article 141 of the EU Treaty provides for equal pay for equal work. Unlike U.S. law, the EU law has adopted the principle of comparative worth with regard to gender pay differentials.

■ The laws of many important U.S. trading partners provide both complementary and distinctly different requirements for U.S. employers with foreign operations. Under Canadian law, for example, federal employment law applies but provincial law must be reviewed to ensure compliance with wage and hour regulations and rights relating to termination. Canadian workers enjoy a widely defined privacy law that prohibits disclosure of personal information.

■ Mexico has stringent requirements for companies that hire directly. As a result, most foreign companies doing business in Mexico use labor brokers to secure the workforce needed. Labor unions work cooperatively with large employer groups and governmental agencies to ensure labor peace.

Online Student Support

- Loislaw legal research and writing assignments.
- Loislaw group projects and class presentations.
- Loislaw access, providing online research including up-to-date cases, statutes, rules, and regulations. Primary law for all 50 states and federal jurisdictions. Registration required for access to this resource.
- Practice questions, including sample true/false, multiple choice, and short answer questions to test your understanding of concepts.
- Additional human resource forms.
- Internet exercises.
- Blogs.
- Supplementary statutory and regulatory materials.

Case Problems

18.1 The concept of comparable worth has been adopted in the EU but it remains a subject of substantial controversy in the United States. American courts have even disagreed on how to define the term. The U.S. Supreme Court considered the issue of comparable worth in a 1981 decision.[12] The Supreme Court held that female employees could sue for sex-based wage discrimination under Title VII without having to satisfy the equal work standard of the Equal Pay Act. However, in order to prevail, the employee must prove that differences in wages are the result of intentional (i.e., disparate treatment) discrimination. Recent court decisions applying the Supreme Court decision reject the comparable worth theory in the absence of proof of intentional discrimination. They have adopted the argument that employers would be liable for pay disparities for which they have not made independent business judgments. Compare the holding in *American Nurses' Ass'n. v. State of Illinois,* 606 F. Supp. 1313 (N.D. Ill. 1985) with Article 141 of the European Community, discussed in this chapter. Discuss the merits of both approaches to compensating workers.

18.2 Mr. Angonese was an Italian national whose native language was German and who studied in Austria. After completing his studies, he applied to take part in a competition for a post with a private banking business in Bolzano, Italy. The bank required that applicants have a certificate of bilingualism in Italian and German. The certificate was to be issued by the public authorities in Bolzano. The local authorities made it difficult for Angonese to secure the certificate in time to take the bank's qualifying examination. Mr. Angonese claims that that the bank's requirement penalized job candidates who were not residents of Bolzano. He argued in his lawsuit against the bank that the certificate requirement was contrary to Article 39 (then known as Article 48) of the EC Treaty. Should the court rule that Article 39 applies to private employers and strike down the requirement as intruding on the principle of free movement of workers? (*Case C-281/98 Angonese v. Cassa di Riparmio di Bolzano SpA* (2000), ECR 1-4139)

18.3 Lisa Grant was employed by South-West Trains Ltd., a railway company. Her contract of employment stated that she and her "spouse and dependants" could be granted certain travel concessions, at the employer's discretion. She applied for travel concessions for her female partner with whom she declared she had had a "meaningful relationship" for more than two years. SWT refused the application, stating that the nonmarried concession only applied to partners of the opposite sex. Grant argued that the refusal constituted discrimination based on sex, as her predecessor, a man who had declared a "meaningful relationship" with a woman for more than two years, had enjoyed the benefit now refused to her. Grant contended that Article 141 (then called Article 119) on nondiscrimination created an obligation to treat homosexual partners the same as married partners. She argued that SWT's refusal constituted discrimination based on sexual orientation, which is included in the concept of "discrimination based on sex." How should the European Court of Justice rule on her case? (*Grant v. South-West Trains Ltd.* (1998), C-249/96)

18.4 Rudy Grzelczyk was a French national who began a course of university studies in physical education at a private university located in Belgium. He applied for social security benefits from Belgium to allow him to continue his university studies. The issue presented to the court is whether students who are citizens of the European Union when they move to another member state to study in the host country lose the right to apply for educational benefits afforded to citizens of the host member state. Do the nondiscrimination provisions relating to free movement of EU citizens apply in this situation? (*Grzelczyk v. Centre Public d'Aide Sociale d'Ottignies-Louvain-la-Neuve* (2001), ECR 1-6193)

18.5 W.G. Bennett sued his employer, Total Minatome Corporation (TMC), for employment discrimination in violation of Title VII, the ADEA and 42 U.S.C. §1981. TMC was a wholly owned subsidiary of TOTAL, a Paris-based French corporation. After Bennett had been promoted within TMC, a corporate restructuring took place. TMC dismissed all managers over the age of 50 and reassigned Bennett to a position of lesser authority. French nationals then held all key TMC managerial positions. In his lawsuit, Bennett claimed that his transfer was a demotion and that TMC continued to discriminate against him because of his age, national origin, and race. Can Bennett assert a discrimination claim based on the fact that he was "not of French ancestry"? Is Bennett's claim barred by a FCN treaty executed between France and the United States similar to the FCN treaties studied in this chapter? (*Bennett v. Total Minatome Corporation,* 138 F.3d 1053 (5th Cir. 1998))

End Notes

1. *http://www.eeoc.gov/facts/multi-employees.html.*
2. *Fortino v. Quasar,* 950 F.2d 389, 392-93 (7th Cir. 1991).
3. *Fortino v. Quasar, supra.*
4. 499 U.S. 244 (1991).
5. 168 U.S. 250 (1897).
6. 42 U.S.C. §§12101-12214.
7. See *http://www.unodc.org/unodc/en/treaties/CAC/index.html.*
8. *Ventress v. Japan Airlines,* 486 F.3d 1111 (9th Cir. 2007).
9. *http://www.ustr.gov/sites/default/files/uploads/factsheets/2008/asset_upload_file71_14540.pdf.*
10. *http://blog.aflcio.org/2009/08/14/nafta-has-failed-new-development-plan-needed.*
11. *Wallace v. United Grain Growers Ltd.* (1997) 3 S.C.R. 701.
12. *County of Washington v. Gunther,* 452 U.S. 161 (1981).

Glossary

20-factor test guidelines formerly used by the I.R.S. to determine if a worker is an employee or independent contractor. Factors are still considered but are afforded less weight by I.R.S. auditors than they were in the past.

30-60 day rule a rule under which U.S. consular officials presume an individual has committed immigration visa fraud and deny all future visa applications from him or her. It applies when an alien who has declared or stated in a visa application that its purpose is tourism or a family visit, but then more than 30 days but less than 60 days after entry into the country seeks unauthorized employment or a status adjustment to permanent resident.

80-day cooling-off period a Taft-Hartley Act provision that empowers the president to request a federal court to enjoin an actual or threatened strike or lockout to allow management and labor additional time to resolve their differences.

401(k) a type of defined contribution retirement plan through which employees may choose to defer a portion of their salary; the funds in this account are invested in a variety of investment opportunities, including stocks, bonds, mutual funds, and other investment vehicles.

706 Agency agencies created strictly for employment discrimination claims and that deal directly with the EEOC.

act of state doctrine the legal principle holding that a nation is sovereign within its own territory and that courts of other nations have no jurisdiction to question its actions taken within its own borders.

ADA see **Americans with Disabilities Act Amendments Act of 2008 (ADAAA).**

ADEA see **Age Discrimination in Employment Act** of 1967.

administrative exemption under this FLSA exemption, overtime wages need not be paid to a worker who is compensated at a salary basis of not less than $455 per week, whose primary duty is the performance of office or nonmanual work directly related to management or the general business operations of the employer or its customers, and whose work includes exercise of discretion and independent judgment.

administrative law judge (ALJ) judges appointed pursuant to Article I of the Constitution who adjudicate disputes arising from federal administrative agency actions. ALJs conduct hearings like court judges (but without juries), hear testimony, consider evidence and legal arguments, and render decisions based on the record before them.

adverse impact a facially neutral employment practice that adversely impacts a protected class without justification or business necessity.

affirmative action public policies that take into account an individual's protected characteristic in employment, public contracting, and other public programs.

after-acquired evidence evidence provided by an employer *after* terminating or taking other adverse employment action against an employee used as evidence to justify the employer's decision and possibly reduce its back-pay liability.

age as a BFOQ an employer may enforce age limits where age is a BFOQ reasonably necessary to the normal operation of the particular business, such as hiring young actors to play young characters or imposing retirement on pilots for medical fitness reasons.

age discrimination employment discrimination against persons age 40 or older. The act does not protect workers under the age of 40, although some states have laws that protect younger workers from age discrimination.

Age Discrimination in Employment Act (ADEA) a federal act applying to employers with 20 or more workers that are engaged in interstate commerce. Prohibits employment discrimination against persons aged 40 and older.

age harassment offensive remarks, behaviors, and conduct with reference to a person's age; requires frequent or severe conduct creating a hostile or offensive work environment.

agency shop place of employment in which a union represents the interests of all employees, regardless of union membership, and requires that nonmembers pay union dues or fees.

aider and abettor a person who assists or helps one or more other persons commit a crime.

alien a citizen of one country living in a foreign country.

alter ego operation circumstance in which a union employer controls, directly or indirectly, a nonunion employer to which work is diverted by the union employer to avoid the costs of a unionized workforce.

alternative dispute resolution a nonjudicial process that seeks to resolve disputes between parties, including through mediation and arbitration.

Americans with Disabilities Act Amendments Act of 2008 (ADAAA) a federal law intended to overturn a series of Supreme Court decisions that interpreted the ADA so narrowly as to make it difficult to prove an impairment was a covered disability.

Americans with Disabilities Act of 1990 (ADA) a federal law making it illegal to discriminate against a qualified person with a disability in private-sector and state and local government employment and outlawing retaliation in response to discrimination claims. Employers must reasonably accommodate known physical or mental limitations of an otherwise qualified disabled individual, unless doing so would impose undue hardship on the employer's business. Prohibits private entities providing public accommodations from denying goods, services, and programs to persons with a disability. Requires that new construction and modifications be accessible to persons with a disability.

annuity an investment contract by which a person pays a life insurance company in exchanged for the tax-deferred growth of the investment, which is distributed back to the owner. Annuity contracts provide for a guaranteed distribution of income until the death of the individual annuitant.

Antiterrorism and Effective Death Penalty Act of 1996 (AEDPA) Congressional act limiting the power of federal judges to grant habeas corpus petitions arising from state and federal criminal convictions unless the state court's decision is contrary to established federal law or unreasonable in light of the evidence.

appearance-based discrimination image-based discrimination relating to preferences or rules regulating an employee's personal appearance.

apportionment of liability the division of liability among two or more defendants who caused a tortious personal injury or property damage.

appropriate bargaining unit a group of two or more employees sharing a community of interest who may reasonably be grouped together for purposes of collective bargaining.

arbitration a legal proceeding in which disputes are resolved by a neutral third party appointed by the parties to make a binding and final determination.

arose out of employment obligation or liability arising from exposure or risks from the employment relationship.

Article 39 article of the EC Treaty providing that EU citizens may move freely among the EC member nations while looking for employment. After working in a member nation, they may continue to reside in that country. Migrant workers enjoy equal treatment with nationals with regard to access to employment, working conditions, and all other benefits.

Article 141 along with Article 12, this EC Treaty provision prohibits discrimination between men and women, though only as far as equal pay is concerned.

associational protections Title VII protection from discrimination due to individual association with a protected individual, such as a person who was dating a person of a different race or ethnicity.

at-will employment employment that is terminable by either party without liability to the other; the general condition of employment, with some exceptions.

back pay the sum of money that a person should have received but was not paid.

bargaining in good faith requirement that the employer and the employees' designated representative meet at reasonable times and willingly negotiate with respect to wages, hours, benefits, and other conditions of employment to execute an agreement incorporating any agreement reached. It does not require agreement or the making of a concession.

behavioral control one of three categories used by the I.R.S. to determine employee status. Reviews the circumstantial ability of the principal to direct and control how work is performed by the worker.

Board of Immigration Appeals (BIA) highest administrative body for interpreting and applying U.S. immigration laws. The board does not conduct courtroom proceedings; it decides appeals by conducting a "paper review" of cases. Has nationwide jurisdiction to hear decisions rendered by immigration judges and by district directors of the Department of Homeland Security. Its decisions are binding on all DHS officers and immigration judges, unless modified or overruled by the attorney general or a federal court.

bona fide executive mandatory retirement of an executive at age 65 if the person is in a high policy-making position and entitled to a pension above a stipulated minimum yearly amount.

bona fide occupational qualification (BFOQ) a necessary quality or attribute that employers may consider in the selection, retention, promotion, and termination of employees.

burden of proof the requirement that a plaintiff must convince a judge or jury that the plaintiff is entitled to the relief sought.

business necessity criteria that bear a substantial relationship to the job requirements.

caregivers federal EEO statutes do not prohibit discrimination based solely on parental or other caregiver status. If discrimination is based on a related characteristic, such as sex or race, protection may be afforded the employee.

cause of action a legally recognized claim based on a set of facts that gives a person the right to petition a court or arbitrator for damages or relief against another person.

cease-and-desist order a court or governmental agency order to stop or prohibit further unlawful activity or action.

circumstantial evidence admissible evidence that proves facts from which a reasonable inference or presumption can be made.

citizenship legal status of a person who has satisfied a nation's legal requirements to be a member of that nation. In exchange for obeying the nation's laws, citizenship allows persons to enjoy all rights and privileges afforded persons with that status.

citizenship discrimination with certain exceptions relating to defense and national security, U.S. employment laws prohibit employers from discriminating against applicants or employees on the basis of citizenship whether they citizens, permanent residents, or aliens authorized to work in the United States.

Civil War Amendments the Thirteenth, Fourteenth, and Fifteenth Amendments to the Constitution.

Clayton Antitrust Act a federal law enacted in 1914 that recognized unions could lawfully organize but did not bar continued use of injunctions against union strikes and boycotts.

cliff vesting the right of a participating employee to receive the benefits from a plan that will take effect at a specified time rather than in increasing amounts over an extended period. It provides employees with a nonforfeitable right to the benefits after a fixed number of years of service or accumulation.

closed shop a place of employment at which an employer is bound by a collective bargaining agreement to hire and employ only union members.

collective bargaining agreement (CBA) a negotiated agreement between a labor union and an employer.

color lightness or darkness of skin pigmentation.

color discrimination discrimination based on skin color, complexion, shade, or tone. May occur between persons of different races or between persons of the same race or ethnicity.

Commerce Clause Article I, Section 8 of the Constitution, granting Congress wide power to regulated commerce between and among states, foreign nations, and Native American tribes.

common law nonstatutory theories developed by courts covering legal relief for one person against another.

common-law test a test to determine employment status that focuses on the hiring principal's right to control the manner and means by which the worker pursues the work result to be accomplished.

common situs workplace job site location at which union picketing is banned during an economic strike. Striking union workers cannot interfere with other trades at a common work site, such as a construction site, when these other trades are employed by businesses not employing the striking workers.

comparable worth a concept from Article 141 of the EC Treaty providing that women should receive equal pay for equal work or work of comparable value.

comparative qualifications comparison of the particular skills, education, experience, or abilities possessed by qualified applicants or employees.

compelling governmental interest part of a strict scrutiny review by courts used when considering an issue concerning equal protection. Requires an asserted government interest so necessary or crucial as to justify intrusion into personal rights.

compensatory damages damages awarded to replace the actual loss or harm suffered, such as for personal property loss or pain and suffering.

compensatory time off (CTO) paid time off from a job that is earned and accrued by the employee instead of a cash payment for working overtime.

computer professional exemption FLSA exemption from overtime pay covering qualified workers paid at least $455 per week or an hourly rate not less than $27.63 per hour.

confidential information nonpublic information, data, compilations, techniques, know-how, algorithms, software, and formulas as well as research and planning not generally known to the public, of economic benefit to the holder, and subject to reasonable efforts to maintain its secrecy.

confidentiality agreement an agreement by which one person promises to maintain the confidentiality of nonpublic, confidential, information provided to the person by another, such as an employer.

Congressional Review Act of 1996 a federal law establishing special congressional procedures for disapproving a broad range of regulatory rules issued by federal agencies.

Consolidated Omnibus Budget Reconciliation Act of 1986 (COBRA) a federal law passed to address the problem arising when a private-sector employee loses health insurance following termination of employment. COBRA allows employees to continue health benefits at their individual expense.

constructive discharge workplace conditions so intolerable, extraordinary, and egregious that any reasonable person would be led to quit the employment.

constructive knowledge knowledge of a condition or fact imputed to another person, such as an employer, because the knowledge should have been acquired through ordinary care and diligence.

construct studies tests that measure job applicants' characteristics considered to be important to the performance of a particular job.

content validation measures of how well a job applicant scores in performing tasks required for the job.

course and scope of employment a term relating to the time, place, or circumstances under which an injury was sustained during the performance of one's job duties.

covenant not to compete a written contract executed by an employee with an employer in which the employee agrees that for a certain number of years the employee will not compete with the employer within a geographic area or as to particular customers.

CRA of 1964 Civil Rights Act; a federal law protecting individuals against outlawed unequal application of voter registration requirements, racial segregation in public schools, and discrimination in employment or facilities serving the general public based on race, color, religion, sex, and national origin. Amendments have extended coverage to pregnancy discrimination.

CRA of 1991 Civil Rights Act; a federal law permitting the right to jury trial and expanding available remedies in employment discrimination cases.

criminal background check pre- and post-employment screening and verification of criminal records through checks by employers and others.

criterion-related testing an evaluative approach that substantiates the validity of a test by comparing the test outcomes with measures of job performance.

Davis-Bacon Act a federal law establishing minimum labor rates and standards for government contractors or those working on federally funded construction projects.

defamation a factually false statement communicated to a third person regarding a person or business that causes injury to reputation or character. May expose the target to public hatred, contempt, or ridicule. The communication may be made orally, in writing, or through images.

deferred compensation plan a program in which a portion of an employee's wages is paid at a future date and not when that income is actually earned. Examples include pensions, retirement plans, and stock options. Plans usually include deferral of income taxes.

defined benefit pension plan a type of retirement plan in which a participant is guaranteed a certain payout or monthly stipend at retirement. A Form 5500 is required to be filed annually by the plan administrator. An actuary must determine annual contributions, which are primarily funded by the employer. Generally must be offered to all employees at least 21 years of age who worked at least 1,000 hours in a previous year.

defined contribution plan a type of retirement plan that provides a payout at retirement that will vary among participants based on the amount of money each contributed (or that was contributed by employers on employees' behalf, as through matching programs) and the performance of the investments made with these contributions.

***de minimus* cost for accommodation** the insubstantial expense to an employer to provide a religious accommodation to an applicant or employee.

***de minimis* violation** minor, trifling violation of the law or regulation.

Department of Homeland Security (DHS) formed in 2003, this federal executive branch agency consolidated a number of U.S. executive agencies. It has responsibility for, among other things, enforcing U.S. immigration laws.

direct evidence proof that establishes a fact by itself, without the need to infer the fact, such as an admission by wrongdoer.

directive a legislative act of the EU that requires member states to achieve a particular result without dictating the means to be used in achieving it.

disability a recognized physical or mental impairment that substantially limits the individual in the performance of one or more major life activities.

disability discrimination the less favorable treatment by a covered employer or entity of an applicant or employee because the person has a history of a disability or is believed to have a physical or mental impairment expected to last six months or longer.

disability harassment unwelcome behavior toward a person with a disability or perceived disability, including frequent or severe behavior that creates a hostile or offensive work environment or results in an adverse employment action.

discriminatory intent proof of discriminatory motive for adverse employment action.

disparate impact discrimination that occurs when a facially neutral selection standard disqualifies particular races or groups at a significantly higher rate than it does other races or groups and that is not justified by a business necessity.

disparate treatment discrimination that occurs when some individuals are intentionally treated less favorably than are others because of race, color, sex, religion, national origin, age, or disability.

drug testing employer-required testing of a worker's urine, blood, or hair samples to determine if the worker is under the influence of alcohol or an illegal drug. Can occur pre-employment; randomly on a "neutral-selection" basis; for cause, following an accident that led to a fatality, serious injury, or significant property damage; for verification of success in a rehabilitation program; and in safety-sensitive positions.

Due Process Clause a fundamental right and constitutional guarantee that all legal proceedings will be held on prior notice and will provide a fair opportunity for the party to rebut the charges confronting him or her. Guaranteed under the Fifth and Fourteenth Amendments.

economic-realities test a test to determine a worker's status in which the worker's activities are viewed in the actual employment circumstances, even though the worker may be considered an independent contractor by the employer.

economic strikers workers who strike an employer to obtain an economic concession from the employer, such as better pay, benefits, or working conditions.

economic unfeasibility a court defense in which the employer must prove that in light of the custom and practice of its industry it is economically unfeasible for it to comply with the safety standards.

EEO1 report required filing with the EEOC by employers with 100 or more employees and by federal government contractors and first-tier subcontractors with 50 or more employees and a contract of $50,000 or more. Identifies employees by job category and ethnicity, race, and gender.

elements of the relationship tangible aspects of a principal-worker relationship, including existence of a written contract describing the relationship the parties intended and/or the extension of fringe benefits to the worker.

emotional distress damages damages for intentional and unreasonable infliction of mental or emotional harm resulting in foreseeable physical injury to another.

employee person who acts under a contract in the service of another, the employer, who can control and direct the means and methods of how the work is to be performed.

Employee Polygraph Protection Act of 1998 (EPPA) a federal law generally preventing employers from requiring applicants or employees to take lie detector tests.

Employee Retirement Income Security Act (ERISA) federal law setting minimum standards for protection of private employee benefit plan participants and beneficiaries. Law requires disclosure and reporting of information and sets standards of conduct, duties and obligations for plan fiduciaries, and remedies.

employment discrimination an employer's illegal distinction between two individuals relative to a term or condition of employment because they belong to different groups.

enterprise coverage the most common FLSA protection for workers, applicable when the enterprise for which they work has at least two employees engaged in interstate commerce activities or the enterprise generates a total of at least $500,000 per year.

Equal Pay Act of 1963 (EPA) a federal law amending the Fair Labor Standards Act, which provides employees are to be paid the same compensation regardless of gender for substantially equal work requiring equal skill, effort, and responsibility and performed under similar working conditions.

Equal Protection Clause part of the Fourteenth Amendment that affords persons equal protection of the law from state action, including public contracting.

equitable orders court orders not providing nonmonetary relief, such as reinstatement or an injunction.

essential functions of a job the functions that an individual must be able to perform unaided or with the assistance of a reasonable accommodation; this determination is made based on the functions to be performed, the skills required to perform them, and the time necessary for and criticality of the tasks.

European Court of Justice (ECJ) the highest judicial body in the European Union.

e-Verify an Internet-based system operated by the U.S. Citizenship and Immigration Services that allows an employer, using information reported on an employee's I-9, to determine the employee's eligibility to work in the United States. Participation is required for federal contractors and subcontractors.

exclusive remedy unless an employer intentionally injures an employee or is grossly negligent, the employee's legal relief is limited by statute or regulation to the benefits payable under workers' compensation.

executive exemption FLSA exemption from overtime pay covering employees whose duties and responsibilities involve managing an enterprise, who customarily and regularly direct two or more employees, who have authority to hire and fire or whose recommendations as to staffing are given particular weight, and who customarily and regularly exercise discretionary powers.

executive order directives by the chief executive to executive branch departments to promote, prohibit, or inhibit conduct relating to the executive's policy decisions.

Executive Order 11246 an order issued by President Lyndon Johnson prohibiting every federal contractor and subcontractor from discriminating based on race, color, religion, sex, or national origin.

Executive Order 13087 an order issued by President Clinton in 1998 prohibiting discrimination based on sexual orientation in federal civilian employment. Certain positions and executive agencies are exempt from its coverage.

exempt employee employees exempt from overtime pay provisions, from both the minimum wage and overtime pay provisions, or from the child labor provisions of the FLSA.

express and implied employment contracts binding promises from an employer that arise in the employment context from oral or written statements made directly to an applicant or employee or impliedly through employee handbooks or manuals.

extraterritorial application as established by diplomatic agreement, the status of being either subject to or exempt from the jurisdiction of local or national law. Often affects employment in foreign countries by giving alien persons immunity from local laws.

facially neutral law, practice, or conduct neutral in appearance but applied in a prejudicial manner or with a prejudicial result.

Fair Credit Reporting Act a federal law regulating entities that collect and disseminate credit and background investigative reports, including those of job applicants and employees.

Fair Labor Standards Act (FLSA) 1938 federal law applicable to employees engaged in interstate commerce or employed by an enterprise engaged in interstate commerce. Sets minimum wages and overtime and regulates youth employment.

false arrest condition in which a person, based on employer allegations, is held in custody by law enforcement without probable cause.

False Claims Act a federal law enacted during the Civil War to allow criminal prosecution of persons engaged in defrauding the federal government.

false imprisonment direct restraint of a person for an appreciable period against his or her will.

Family Medical Leave Act (FMLA) a 1993 federal act requiring covered employers to provide eligible employees with job protections for unpaid leave due to serious health conditions affecting the employee or a family member or to care for a new child.

family responsibility discrimination disparate treatment against employees based on their responsibilities to care for family members, such as children or aging parents. Not prohibited under Title VII.

featherbedding a practice of requiring more workers to be hired than are necessary to perform a specific task; also indicates work processes that are intentionally inefficient and time consuming.

Federal Arbitration Act (FAA) a 1925 federal law upholding arbitration agreements as valid, irrevocable, and enforceable contracts, unless an exception applies.

Federal Insurance Contributions Act (FICA) a federal law requiring employers to withhold a portion of employee wages and forward them to the government trust fund that provides retirement and Medicare benefits. More commonly known as Social Security.

Federal Unemployment Tax Act (FUTA) a federal law requiring employers to pay a tax to fund unemployment benefits and state work assistance programs. Most employers pay both a federal and a state unemployment tax.

fiduciary a person or business entity who exercises either discretionary authority or control regarding the management of a retirement plan or its assets. The term includes both those who administer a plan and those who provide investment advice to plan administrators.

fiduciary breach liability imposed on a fiduciary who fails to run a plan solely in the interest of participants and beneficiaries and for the exclusive purpose of providing benefits and paying plan expenses. A fiduciary must act prudently, diversify the plan's investments to minimize the risk of large losses, and avoid conflicts of interest.

Fifteenth Amendment Constitutional amendment prohibiting state and federal governments from using a citizen's race or color as a voting qualification.

financial control monetary aspects of a principal-worker relationship, including the degree to which the principal funds the work performed by the worker. Courts review to what extent the principal reimburses the worker's expenses, the investment of money in the business by the worker, the extent to which services are offered to third parties, and the distinct business aspects pursued by the worker independent of those of the principal.

foreign laws defense proof offered by a U.S. employer that compliance with a U.S. employment law, such as the ADEA, would cause the employer to violate the laws of the foreign country in which it is doing business and in which the violation of U.S. law occurred.

form I-9 a federal form required to be completed and retained by all U.S. employers for each person hired. The form must be completed by citizens and noncitizens. Employers must examine all employees' employment eligibility and identity documents.

four-fifths rule an EEOC guideline that holds that a selection rate for any race, sex, or ethnic group that is less than four-fifths the selection rate of the most frequently selected group will generally be regarded as evidence of adverse impact.

Fourteenth Amendment Constitutional amendment providing a broad definition of citizenship, applying the Bill of Rights to the states, and compelling recognition of substantive and procedural due process and equal protection under the law for all persons.

Fourth Amendment relative to employment, this amendment protects a person's "reasonable expectation of privacy," including the right to be free from unreasonable searches and seizures by the government.

fraud misrepresenting a material fact on which a person reasonably relies to their detriment and as a result they suffered damages.

free rider an employee who is not a union member but is bound by and benefits from the terms of the union contract with the employer.

Friendship, Commerce, and Navigation Treaty (FCN) among other provisions, this type of treaty between the United States and a foreign nation often provides that companies of both countries can discriminatorily select executive employees to work in the host country without regard to national origin considerations.

front pay damages awarded for lost earnings during the period between judgment and reinstatement or, if reinstatement does not occur, payment in place of reinstatement.

fundamental rights court recognition of individual freedoms so essential to liberty that government may not intrude on them.

gender characteristics distinguishing males and females, including social roles and behaviors.

gender discrimination the unfair treatment in employment of a person because of his or her gender.

gender stereotyping requiring or expecting a person to act, behave, or dress a certain way based on his or her gender.

general duty an OSHA requirement that each employer must furnish a place of employment free from recognized hazards that are causing or are likely to cause death or serious physical harm.

Genetic Information Nondiscrimination Act of 2008 (GINA) a federal law making it illegal for health insurers to deny an individual coverage or to charge him or her a higher rate or premium based solely on the individual's genetic predisposition to develop a disease in the future.

glass ceiling a perceived barrier preventing certain classes of individuals from climbing the highest rungs of corporate leadership.

Glass Ceiling Commission a 21-member bipartisan commission assembled by President George H. Bush the main purpose of which was to investigate the artificial barrier to advancement and promotions faced by women and minorities employment.

good-faith compliance defense employer's defense to immigration law violations if a Form I-9 was completed correctly for each new hire and the employer does not have actual or constructive knowledge of the worker's ineligibility to work in the United States. Designed to avoid hardship for employers that did all that could reasonably be expected to determine its workers' status.

greater hazard defense a rarely available defense under OSHA by which an employer must show, among other things, that there are no alternative means of employee protection.

harassment persistent and unwanted behavior in the workplace with regard to any protected class. Many forms include bullying, stalking, abusive comments, actions or gestures, or hazing.

Health Insurance Portability and Accountability Act (HIPPA) a federal law that limits the ability of a new employer-sponsored health-care plan to exclude coverage for preexisting conditions; provides opportunities to enroll in a group health plan if health insurance coverage is lost or other covered life events occur; prohibits discrimination against employees and their dependent family members based on preexisting health factors, including medical conditions, claims experience, and genetic information; and guarantees that certain persons will be able to enroll and renew individual health insurance policies. Also provides protections from disclosures of personal health information.

highly compensated exemption overtime exemption covering employees earning more than $110,000, which includes at least $455 per week on a salary basis; whose primary duty includes performing office or nonmanual work; and who customarily and regularly performs at least one of the exempt duties or responsibilities of an exempt executive, administrative, or professional employee.

hostile work environment workplace activity that is offensive, intimidating, or oppressive. Usually involves pattern of exposure that is intentional, severe, or pervasive; affects the individual with regard to the terms, conditions, or privileges of employment; and constitutes conduct that would offend a reasonable person. Management must have either known about the conduct, or should have known, and did nothing to stop it.

identity and employment authorization requirement imposed on all U.S. employers to verify that every employee hired is authorized to work in the United States. Along with completion of the Form I-9, employees must provide acceptable documentation to establish proof of citizenship or eligibility to work in the United States.

idiopathic injury one that has an unexplained origin or cause.

Illegal Immigration Reform and Immigrant Responsibility Act of 1996 (IIRIRA) a federal law requiring that unless pardoned a person must remain outside the United States for three years if they have been in the United States for 180 days but less than 365 days. If the person has been unlawfully in the United States for 365 days or more, he or she must remain outside the country for ten years, unless pardoned. If the person returns to the United States without the pardon, the person cannot apply for a waiver for a period of ten years. The act requires the U.S. government to collect records of arrival and departure for every alien entering the United States and allows for identification of non-immigrants who remain beyond the period authorized for their stay.

Immigration and Customs Enforcement (ICE) a federal investigation and enforcement agency within Department of Homeland Security that enforces federal statutes relating to national security and public safety, including immigration enforcement, visa fraud, and counterterrorism.

Immigration and Nationality Act of 1952 (INA) a federal law that sets forth the conditions for the temporary and permanent employment of aliens in the U.S. and addresses employment eligibility and employment verification.

Immigration Reform and Control Act of 1986 (IRCA) a federal law prohibiting discrimination against applicants and employees based on their citizenship or national origin. IRCA makes it illegal to knowingly hire or recruit unauthorized aliens and requiring employers to verify workers' identity and employment eligibility to work in the United States.

immutable characteristics unalterable physical traits, including skin color, hair texture, or certain facial features associated with persons of a particular race, color, sex, or national origin, even though not all members of that group necessarily share the trait.

impairment a condition that substantially limits a person in the performance of one or more life activities as compared to an average person in the general population. The determination is made without regard to the use of mitigating measures, such as medication. If the person's condition would qualify without such aids, the person has a protected disability. Impairments do not include conditions requiring eyeglasses and contact lenses.

implied contractual liability liability arising from promises made indirectly, such as relying on statements made in an employee handbook, on which an employee relied to his or her detriment.

implied covenant of good faith and fair dealing a "catch-all" basis on which to award damages to a discharged employee because the firing occurred without good cause under the circumstances. A small number of states allow this exception to the at-will doctrine.

impossibility defense employer defense to OSHA charges by which an employer must show that compliance with the cited standard was functionally impossible or would prevent the performance of work and that alternative methods of protects were in use or available.

INA §247B Immigration and Nationality Act; under this section and subject to exceptions required by law, employers with four or more employees may not discriminate or retaliate against any individual (other than an unauthorized alien) with respect to hiring, recruitment, or discharge because of the person's national origin or status as an authorized alien. The section also applies to an employer's refusal to accept permissible documents presented by an employee to comply with Form I-9 requirements.

independent contractor a nonemployee worker who exercises independent judgment in the means and methods of performing work for and under contract with a principal.

individual coverage FLSA coverage as extended to employees engaged in interstate commerce.

Individual Retirement Account (IRA) a type of self-directed retirement account that defers income taxation on earnings until withdrawals are taken. Contributions to this account are usually tax-deductible.

inevitable disclosure of trade secrets under this theory, employers rely on the assumption that a court will act to protect their trade secrets.

injunctive relief court-ordered action or prohibition against action granted at a party's request.

integration clause language inserted into a written contract between parties that is intended by them to be the final expression of their agreement, indicating that any term not stated will not be considered part of the agreement.

intentional infliction of emotional distress viewed by a reasonable person the intentional, extreme, and outrageous conduct of another person that is certain or substantially certain to cause emotional distress to the victim. Can occur without physical injury or contact between the parties.

interference with contractual relations conduct involving actions that intentionally and without excuse interfere with the contractual benefits of another person.

intermediate scrutiny the lawfulness of government classifications based on protected classes other than race (such as sex or age) is examined using an intermediate scrutiny test. This standard requires that the classification be substantially related to advancing a legitimate government purpose or objective.

Internet applicant rule a requirement that federal contractors who accept employment applications submitted electronically retain records on any applicant meeting these four criteria: the applicant expresses interest in a position through the Internet; the contractor considers the person for employment; the person appears to be qualified for the position; and the individual does not withdraw from consideration for employment.

interstate commerce activity involving commercial trade, business, movement of goods or money, or transportation both directly and indirectly affecting activities within two or more state jurisdictions.

Interstate Commerce Clause see **Commerce Clause.**

invasion of privacy claim tortious conduct involving unconsented public disclosure of private facts about a person that may be true but are embarrassing.

job related the specific skills, education, and training needed to perform a task.

joint-employment liability liability shared by a leasing employer and client company concerning compliance with federal and state wage and hour laws.

jury trials legal proceeding in which a group of community persons makes a decision or makes findings of fact that are applied by a judge.

Keogh plan a type of retirement plan, extended to both self-employed persons and their employees, in which pretax money is placed into a Keogh account where it grows tax-free until it is withdrawn.

Labor-Management Relations Act (LMRA) also known as the Taft-Hartley Act; a federal law addressing unfair labor practices on the part of unions.

labor union organization or association of individuals formed for the purpose of negotiating with employers on behalf of employees with regard to rates of pay, wages, hours of employment, or other conditions of employment.

laches unreasonable, inexcusable, and prejudicial delay in prosecuting a claim that results in harm to the other party.

Landrum-Griffin Act 1959 federal law regulating internal affairs of unions and union officers' relationships with employers.

last injurious exposure rule state workers' compensation rule that shifts to the most recent employer the entire responsibility for payments and care due to injured, sick, or diseased workers.

law mandates that govern the social and economic order among individuals and the individual's relationship to society.

leased employee a type of contingent worker lent to an employer by a third-party business. The third-party business is primarily responsible for the worker's legal compliance.

least discriminatory approach Alternative method of testing applicants or promotion candidates that both follows EEOC testing requirements and is the least discriminatory selection method available.

legitimate business reason business justification for treating one or more applicants or employees differently than others.

libel defamation arising from a written or permanent form of publication.

Lilly Ledbetter Fair Pay Act of 2009 a federal law allowing a pay discrimination charge to reset the 180-day statute of limitations with each discriminatory paycheck.

liquidated damages a fixed amount of damages, usually twice the amount of unpaid back pay due a claimant.

Longshore and Harbor Workers' Compensation Act a federal law that provides compensation for disability or death of an employee for injuries occurring on navigable waters or in adjoining areas.

major life activity an expansive definition used in disability cases for the variety of tasks important in most people's daily lives, such as eating, walking, or reading.

managerial employee person who formulates and applies corporate polices to subordinate workers.

mass layoff a reduction in force that affects 100 or more full-time workers. Generally covered by WARN Act.

material safety data sheets (MSDS) forms provided by manufacturers and importers containing data on the properties of particular materials or substances they sell to U.S. businesses. This information is used by employers to train their employees to recognize and avoid hazards.

meal periods a break in the workday for a meal; not required to be given under the FLSA, but some states have laws and regulations requiring them.

mediation a nonjudicial process in which the participants, with the help of neutral person, attempt to reach an agreement to resolve their dispute.

Merchant Marine Act of 1920 a federal law that allows injured seamen to recover damages from their employers for the negligence of the ship owner, the captain, or other crew members.

Mexican Federal Labor Law (FLL) one of two national laws governing labor issues in Mexico. The other is the federal Social Security Law.

minimum wage the minimum amount of money per hour set by federal or state statute due to a worker. State or local wage laws requiring higher wage rates than that required by federal law prevail.

ministerial exemption an exemption that prevents the application to clergy members of Title VII, including the provisions relating to race, sex, national origin, and religion.

misappropriation of a trade secret unauthorized disclosure or use of another's trade secrets, acquired by improper means from a third party, by a person who reasonably should have known that the information was a trade secret.

misrepresentation intentional misstatement or omission of material fact on which another reasonably relies to their detriment.

mitigation legal principle requiring a plaintiff after suffering any injury or breach of contract to undertake all reasonable actions necessary to reduce the potential damages plaintiff may suffer because of the harm or breach suffered.

mixed-motive evidence an employer's evidence showing that the same adverse decision would have been made against an employee even in the absence of the impermissible motivating factor.

motivating factor evidence that demonstrates a Title VII violation has occurred when an employer exercises improper intent or pursues a practice involving a protected characteristic, even though other factors were present for the employment action. Sometimes also called "mixed motive."

multiemployer doctrine an OSHA policy allowing it to issue citations to general contractors at construction sites who have sufficient control over the site to prevent or abate hazardous conditions caused by its subcontractors. Even if a general contractor did not create the hazard, it can be cited because it could have exercised supervisory authority to eliminate it.

Multiemployer Pension Plan Amendments Act of 1980 a federal act preventing employers from withdrawing from multiemployer pension plans without paying their share of the unfunded, vested retirement benefit liabilities.

narrowly tailored plans racial classifications by federal, state, or local government measured by strict-scrutiny review and which advance a compelling government interest. Governmental plan must be justified and not unduly trammel interests of majority.

National Advisory Committee on Occupational Safety and Health (NIOSH) an occupational research center that advises and makes recommendations to the Secretary of Labor and the Secretary of Health and Human Services on OSHA matters.

national emergency strikes strikes occurring within an industry considered to be essential to the nation, such as those involving public health and safety.

National Labor Relations Act (NLRA) also known as the Wagner Act; the 1935 federal law recognizing and protecting the rights of workers to organize and collectively bargain with employers. Requires employers to bargain with the exclusive representative of the workers.

National Labor Relations Board (NLRB) an independent U.S. administrative agency that conducts labor union elections and investigates and adjudicates unfair labor practices.

National Mediation Board the federal agency that facilitates the resolution of labor-management disputes in the transportation industry.

national origin country or place from which an individual or at least some of his or her ancestors originated.

national origin discrimination actions which treat applicants or employees unfavorably because they are from a particular country or part of the world, exhibit a certain ethnicity or accent, or appear to be of certain ethnicity even if they are not.

national origin harassment treating applicants or employees unfavorably due to their national origin (or presumed national origin); may involve responses to the individual's ethnicity, accent, or appearance or other perceptions held by others toward the individual.

Native American preference exemption provision of Title VII permitting preferential treatment by a business with regard to Native Americans living on or near a reservation.

naturalization process of acquiring citizenship in a country other than that of one's birth.

negligent evaluation a basis on which some courts have allowed employees to sue an employer for its failure to provide the employees notice of performance deficiencies before taking adverse action against them.

negligent hiring legal theory under which an employer may be held responsible for injuries caused by a worker because the employer failed to use due care in inquiring into the employee's background and fitness for the position, such as failing to verify prior employment history that would have shown the employee's inability to control use of alcohol.

negligent termination allegation that the employer in making its decision to terminate an employee failed to use due care in its procedures, such as by negligently administering tests.

nepotism the practice of bestowing favored treatment on one's relatives, especially in the areas of hiring and promotion.

noncapability an employer may lawfully use an employee's nonfitness for continued employment, advancement, or training to defend an age discrimination claim.

non-competition contract an agreement between an employer and employee by which the employee agrees he or she will not, during or after employment, compete directly or indirectly against the employer in the same business.

nonexempt employee a worker entitled to the minimum wage and/or overtime pay protections of the FLSA.

nonqualified deferred compensation plan a contractual agreement in which an employee or independent contractor agrees to be paid in the future for services currently rendered. Payments usually start at termination of employment, including by retirement, death, or disability.

nonserious (or other-than-serious) violation an OSHA violation that has a direct relationship to job safety and health but is unlikely to cause death or serious injury.

nonstatutory theories legal theories of relief recognized by courts as arising out of common law and not statutory or regulatory authority.

Norris-LaGuardia Act also known as the Anti-Injunction Act; this 1932 federal act barred courts from issuing injunctions against union strike activities, unless such strikes might result in dangerous or coercive conditions. Act made yellow-dog contracts illegal.

no-strike clauses provisions of a collective bargaining agreement by which unions agree not to strike during the term of the agreement provided the employer abides by the terms of the labor agreement.

Occupational Safety and Health Act (OSHA) legislation that set a national standard for workplace safety. Designed to protect workers from danger but not intended to eliminate all dangers from the workplace.

Occupational Safety and Health Review Commission (OSHRC) independent federal agency that performs the adjudicatory function of OSHA. OSHA recommends penalties to OSHRC for violations and OSHRC determines and assesses the employer penalties.

Older Worker's Benefit Protection Act of 1990 (OWBPA) a federal law that amended the ADEA to prohibit employers from denying benefits to older employees. Waivers of age discrimination claims must be knowing or voluntary.

on-call time time during which employees are not required to remain on the employer's premises but are required to be available to work and thus cannot use their time for their own purposes.

open shop a place of employment in which employees are not required to join or support a union.

opportunity wage subminimum hourly wage of at least $4.25 per hour allowable for the first 90 consecutive days of employment.

ordinance law enacted by a local jurisdiction such as a county, borough, or municipality.

outside salesperson exemption overtime wages need not be paid to a worker whose primary duty is to make sales or obtain orders or contracts and who is customarily and regularly engaged in work away from the employer's place of business.

outsourcing work performed for a business by an outside company that manages the entire project or contract for the business. The outsourcing company can be located on or outside the business's premises. It hires workers and supervises them independently of the business that contracted it. Outsource companies are usually not considered a joint employer with the outsourcing business.

overtime subject to certain industry-specific exemptions, the hourly rate of one and one-half times their normal pay rate due to nonexempt employees for each hour of work beyond 40 in a workweek.

paperwork violation employer's violation of IRCA requirements to complete, correct, or supplement Form I-9 for each of its employees. Violations can occur following the employer's failure to reverify employees' continuing employment authorization after the date on the employees' visa forms has passed.

pattern and practice case plaintiff's use of both statistical and anecdotal evidence of discriminatory treatment to prove *prima facie* case.

Pension Benefit Guaranty Corporation (PBGC) a federal corporation established by ERISA to provide for federally insured benefits when plans are terminated with insufficient resources to meet future plan obligations to participants.

pension plan agreement by which salary and other contributions are deferred from taxation until retirement, when they will provide participants with income when they are no longer earning a regular income from employment.

personal appearance discrimination unfavorable treatment due to a person's outward appearance, regardless of sex but with regard to bodily condition or characteristics, manner or style of dress, or manner or style of personal grooming, including hair style and facial hair. Not protected under federal law, but subject to a few state laws (relative to height and weight) and municipal ordinances.

personal safety equipment equipment designed to protect employees against certain hazards.

physical or mental impairment any disorder, condition, disfigurement, or anatomical loss that affects a major body system or mental or psychological state. The ADAAA requires expansive interpretation and application of the term in favor of individuals.

plan administrator a fiduciary for the purposes of ensuring the integrity of a plan governed by ERISA.

police power inherent power of government to make and enforce laws.

Portal-to-Portal Act 1947 federal law specifying the types of work-related time spent that are compensable. Generally, such time includes all activity of benefit to the employer. Time for travel to and from the workplace is not compensable.

positional risk doctrine workers' compensation rule that injuries will be found to have arisen out of employment if they would not have occurred but for the fact that the condition and obligations of employment placed the claimant in the position of being injured.

pre-employment testing testing that occurs after an offer of employment has been made and on the results of which actual hiring depends.

preemption legal doctrine by which the laws of a higher authority displace the application of laws issued by a lower jurisdiction when the lower jurisdiction's laws conflict with those of the higher jurisdiction.

Pregnancy Discrimination Act (PDA) a federal act passed in 1978, amending Title VII, prohibiting employment discrimination on the basis of pregnancy, childbirth, or related medical conditions.

preponderance of evidence plaintiff's evidence establishing that the claim is more likely to be true than not.

pretext an excuse created to conceal the true facts.

prima facie legal principle holding that a plaintiff who proves certain facts by a preponderance of evidence is entitled to damages or other relief.

principal activity majority or most important duty that the employee performs.

principle of sovereignty the legal principle that a nation may lawfully control activities only within its territory and that it does not have authority within the domain of another nation.

privacy the desire or right to be left alone or the right to restrict public access to personal information, history, and affairs.

privacy rule provision within HIPAA that requires employers and health-care providers to ensure that all parts of employees' or patients' medical or payment history is kept confidential.

professional employer organization (PEO) a third-party provider of services to employers. The PEO becomes the employer of record for tax and insurance purposes of the employees who are directed in their daily activities by the principal. PEOs benefit employers by aggregating the number of workers under contract to secure lower workers' compensation and health insurance premiums and to facilitate administrative matters.

professional exemption a FLSA exemption from overtime pay for workers who are compensated on a salary basis at a rate not less than $455 per week and whose primary work requires advanced knowledge in a field of science or learning mastery of which is acquired through specialized instruction.

profit-sharing plan any employer with one or more employees can establish a plan under which the employer makes annual, discretionary contributions for employees. Subject to maximum annual contributions. Generally must be offered to all employees at least 21 years of age who worked at least 1,000 hours in the previous year.

protectable trade secret information, including a formula, pattern, compilation, program device, method or technique, or process from which a company derives independent economic value.

protected class a group of persons sharing common characteristics who have historically suffered discrimination or the effects of discrimination.

protected concerted activity an activity that workers may pursue without fear of retaliation from employers, including the right to self-organize, to form or join a union, or to act together to improve the terms and conditions of employment. These activities are protected with or without union representation of the workers. Protects two or more employees acting together.

public accommodations public and private commercial establishments having a connection to interstate commerce and that own, lease or lease to, or operate to serve the interests of the public.

publicity picketing union picketing of an employer to inform members of the public that the employer does not employ union members or have a union contract or about other matters of concern to union members.

public policy decisions, regulatory acts, and enforcement policies of a governmental body regarding particular issues that influence its administration and operations.

punitive damages damages beyond those necessary to compensate for losses suffered awarded an injured party for intentional or egregious conduct with the intention of punishing the wrongdoer or setting an example.

qualified domestic relations order (QDRO) a federal law amended ERISA to allow ERISA-qualified welfare and pension benefits to be divided between divorcing spouses. Court orders are issued by the state domestic relations court and then reviewed by the plan administrator for compliance with ERISA and the terms of the plan.

qualified individual with a disability a person with a disability who meets the specified level of skills, experience, education, or other requirements for a position and who can perform the essential functions of the job.

qualified plans under ERISA, a plan that permits the deposit of pretax wages and deferral of tax payments on the deposit. Money accumulating from the investment of deposited wages grows tax free.

***quid pro quo* sexual harassment** unlawful conduct in which the harasser uses submission to or rejection of sexual requests as a basis for employment decisions, such as hiring, firing, compensation, and promotions. The Latin phrase translates as "this for that."

quota system numeric limitation on number of persons based on national origin allowed to immigrate to the United States, beginning in 1921 and ending in 1965. Replaced by an immigration policy putting all persons seeking to immigrate to the United States on equal footing.

race a term not defined in Title VII, but usually interpreted, in the context of discrimination, in terms of ancestry or the physical or cultural characteristics associated with a certain race.

race-norming employment practice of adjusting scores on a standardized test by using different curves for different racial groups.

racial discrimination unequal treatment in the workplace based on the race or perceived racial characteristics of a person.

racial harassment unwelcome conduct that unreasonably interferes with an individual's work performance or creates an intimidating, hostile, or offensive work environment.

Railway Labor Act the 1926 federal act requiring that transportation industry employers bargain collectively and not discriminate against unions.

rational basis The lawfulness of all government classifications that do not involve suspect or protected classes is reviewed under a rational basis test. Under this test, the courts will uphold a government regulation as long as there is a justifiable reason for the law. This standard permits much of government business regulation.

REAL ID Act of 2005 a federal law establishing minimum standards for state-issued drivers' licenses and other identification cards.

reasonable accommodation, disability a modification or adjustment to a job or work environment enabling a qualified applicant or employee with a recognized disability to pursue employment or perform the essential job functions. The three categories of reasonable accommodation are changes in the conditions or format of the job application process; changes to the work environment or the manner of performing the work; and changes that enable an employee with a disability to enjoy equal benefits and privileges of employment (such as access to training).

reasonable accommodation, religion an employer must make reasonable adjustments to the work environment to permit an applicant or employee to practice his or her religious beliefs.

Reasonable Factor Other than Age (RFOA) a principle holding that employers may take an adverse action against an applicant or employee over age 40 if the supporting rationale is reasonable and other than the person's age.

reasonable victim a standard used to determine whether specific conduct would be considered sexual harassment to the reasonable person.

recognitional picketing permitted union picketed against a targeted employer for up to 30 days before a NLRB union representation election.

recognized hazards a condition or practice known to be hazardous by the employer's industry in general or by the specific employer.

record of such impairment having a history of a disability or perceived disability.

reduction in force (RIF) an employer has the right to reduce its workforce in a nondiscriminatory manner and to select employees for retention retain who have the requisite skills, experience, and training.

regarded as having such impairment — with regard to substantially limited impairment an applicant or employee is subject to an action prohibited by the ADA (e.g., the failure to hire or a termination) because of a nontransitory and nonminor impairment.

Rehabilitation Act of 1973 a federal law prohibiting discrimination on the basis of disability in federal employment, in the employment practices of federal contractors, or in programs operated by federal agencies or receiving federal funding and requiring affirmative action to prevent or reverse such discrimination.

reinstatement the act of restoring or promoting an individual to a position to which they would have been assigned but for a wrongful employment action.

religion sincerely held religious, ethical, or moral beliefs as to what is right and wrong; need not include a belief in a supreme being.

religious discrimination an employer's failure to ensure that the conditions of employment allow for an applicant's or worker's sincerely held religious beliefs and practices, unless doing so creates undue hardship.

religious practice or observance beliefs, prayers, worship, and outwardly expressed rituals and ceremonies of a religious nature.

repeat violation a violation of any standard, regulation, rule, or order when, on re-inspection, a substantially similar violation is found.

respondeat superior the legal doctrine imposing liability on an employer for the acts and omissions of an employee.

Restatement a treatise by legal scholars addressing uncertainties as to the state of the law and indicating the common trend in understanding or the legal interpretation of an issue.

Restatement (Second) of Agency legal doctrine used to classify employment status of worker. Focuses on the worker's skill, sources of business, ownership and use of tools, longevity of relationship, discretion exercised by the worker, and matters within each party's control.

rest period a break in the workday, for example, to use restrooms or for coffee. Not required by FLSA, but state laws often require rest periods for nonexempt employees who work a minimum period of time in a workday.

retaliation adverse action taken against an applicant or employee by an employer because the person alleged, participated in, or pursued a claim of employment discrimination or other violation of the law.

retention the continued employment or hiring relationship between a principal and another person.

reverse discrimination discrimination practiced against those in the majority in favor of members of a minority or historically disadvantaged group.

reverse gender discrimination discrimination alleged because of affirmative action programs that attempt to eliminate past effects of employment gender discrimination.

right of access OHSA requirement that employers permit employees and their representatives and OHSA itself the right to review the medical records of employees, including those related to employees' exposure to toxic substances.

right-to-sue letter EEOC or 706 agency authorization that permits an applicant or employee to file a private lawsuit against an employer in federal court.

right-to-work laws laws adopted by states to prohibit union-management agreements requiring union membership or payment of union dues as a condition of hire or continued employment.

safe harbor provision within the federal tax code that the principal may treat a worker as an independent contractor if the employer has declared with the I.R.S. that the worker is an independent contractor, has consistently treated all contract workers in the same fashion, and has a reasonable basis for treating the worker as an independent contractor.

Sarbanes-Oxley Act (SOX) legislation enacted by Congress in 2002 to encourage corporate fraud reporting following in the wake of the Enron, WorldCom, and other corporate scandals of that time.

secondary boycotts an attempt by a union to coerce neutral employers and employees of neutral employers with the object of forcing these neutral employers to cease doing business with an employer that is the target of a union strike or primary boycott.

Section 703(h) Title VII provision permitting different standards of compensation, or different terms, conditions, or privileges of employment due to a bona fide seniority or merit system or a system that measures earnings by differences in quantity or quality of production.

Section 1981 a federal law protecting individuals from intentional racial or national origin discrimination in employment and housing.

Section 1983 a federal law that protects person from violations of their constitutional rights by persons acting under state or federal authority.

Section 1985 a federal law protecting individuals from racial and gender-based discrimination in employment and from interference with contractual, property, and other rights. Often involves conspiracies to harm or injure others based on race or gender.

self-compelled publication tortious conduct committed by a former employer giving false and defamatory grounds for an employee's discharge, which the former employee then feels compelled to disclose to prospective employers.

serious condition (OSHA) a situation posing a substantial probability that death or serious harm could result.

serious health condition (FMLA) an illness, injury, impairment, or physical or mental condition requiring hospitalization or continuing treatment by a health-care provider.

serious violation an OSHA violation arising from circumstances presenting a substantial probability that death or serious physical harm could result and the employer knew, or should have known, of the hazard.

severe and pervasive characteristic of a hostile work environment in which employees are subject to a pattern of exposure to unwanted, prohibited conduct. Requires fact-based inquiry without a universal definition for all workplaces.

sex distinctive traits of individuals characterizing them as either male or female. The traits are not necessarily related to behavior or sexual orientation.

sex discrimination unfavorable workplace treatment of a person because of that person's sex. Includes sexual harassment and retaliation.

sex-plus discrimination employer policies or practices by which the employer treats employees unfairly on the basis of gender plus another characteristic, such as marital status, race, or age.

sexual/gender identity a person's various individual attributes, as they are understood to be masculine and/or feminine.

sexual favoritism Title VII does not prohibit isolated instances of preferential treatment based on consensual romantic relationships. If an employee is coerced into sexual conduct, however, the situation can become quid pro quo harassment or constitute a sexually hostile work environment.

sexual harassment unwelcome sexual conduct that is a term or condition of employment; may include intimidation, bullying, or coercion of a sexual nature.

sexual identity discrimination wrongful treatment of a worker based on the person's self-identification with a gender, whether it is the same as or opposite to the person's birth gender.

sexual orientation an adult's choice of sexual partner according to gender.

shared-employee doctrine principle that applies when a worker is employed by two or more employers having the right to control the activities of the shared employee. In such cases, all employers are liable for the acts and omissions of their common worker.

Simple 401(k) Salary reduction plan that may be set up by any employer with 100 or fewer employees that does not currently maintain another retirement plan. No annual filing required from the employer. Employer's contributions can be adjusted, but employer must make contributions or contribute 2 percent of each employee's compensation. Subject to maximum annual contributions. Contributions are immediately vested.

sincerely held a fact-specific finding determination as to an employee's fidelity to religious beliefs and practices.

slander defamation arising from oral utterance.

sleeping time under Department of Labor regulations, an employee required to be on duty for less than 24 consecutive hours is entitled to count all on-duty hours as compensable, even if the employee is permitted to sleep or engage in personal activities when not busy. If the employee is required to be on duty for 24 or more consecutive hours, the employer and employee may agree to exclude from compensable hours sleeping periods of not more than eight hours, if certain conditions are met.

Social Security disability benefits benefits payable by the Social Security Administration because a person suffers from a severe physical or mental impairment or combination of impairments constituting an injury that prevents the employee from performing any "substantial gainful activity."

sovereign immunity legal doctrine prohibiting or exempting claims or lawsuits against a government without its consent.

specific duty an OSHA requirement imposed on an employer relating to a specific safety problem or hazard.

stare decisis legal principal that requires a court to apply prior appellate case holdings as precedent binding on the court once certain facts have been established.

state action action by or on behalf of a governmental body that violates the civil rights or legal interests of a person.

statistical proof assumption that something is probably true.

statute a law enacted by federal or state legislatures.

statute of limitations maximum legal period during which a legal proceeding may be initiated, measured from date of occurrence of the event giving rise to the right to pursue the legal claim.

statutory employee class of worker who is protected and characterized as an employee, such as corporate officers and outside sales persons. Can include ex-employees of an employer.

statutory nonemployee an I.R.S.-defined category for a worker who is not treated as an employee for federal tax purposes. Includes direct sellers of services and licensed real estate agents.

strict scrutiny most stringent standard of judicial review of equal protection issues. Any government activity or regulation that classifies persons based on a suspect class (i.e., race) is reviewed for lawfulness using a strict scrutiny test. Approach must be justified by compelling governmental interest, narrowly tailored, and involve the least restrictive means to achieve that result.

strike work stoppage by workers who refuse to continue work until their demands are met by management.

substantial gainful activity work activity measured by gross earnings per month.

substantially limits a major life activity a factual finding regarding an impairment's nature and severity, duration or expectation of duration, and permanence or long-term impact or expected impact on a person.

summary judgment motion court determination made without a trial as to the merits of a case or specific claims based on parties' declarations of the facts made under oath.

summary plan description ERISA requirement that employers inform participants in writing about their rights to benefits. The description must be distributed to employees within 90 days of their eligibility for the benefit plan.

super preemption circumstance in which Congress has so completely preempted a particular area of the law that even if a claim is characterized by the plaintiff as involving state law claims, it is deemed essentially a federal claim and must be removed (i.e., transferred) from state court to federal district court. Removal to federal court is required when a state law claim is preempted by ERISA and falls within its coverage.

supervisor person with immediate or successively higher authority over one or more other employees.

Taft-Hartley Act see **Labor Management Relations Act.**

Tenth Amendment reserves to state and local governments those powers not granted to the federal government in the Constitution.

terminations violating strong public policies termination of employment that contravenes an important public policy, such as termination because an employee seeks to serve jury duty.

Thirteenth Amendment abolished slavery and involuntary servitude, except as a punishment for a criminal conviction.

tip credit under FLSA, employees' tips earned may be credited toward the employer's obligation to pay the minimum wage to them. Often prohibited under state law.

Title VI of the CRA of 1964 section of the Civil Rights Act prohibiting discrimination by federal, state, or local governmental agencies receiving federal funding.

Title VII section of the Civil Rights Act of 1964 that pertains to discrimination in employment on the basis of race, color, national origin, sex, and religion. This federal law prohibits most workplace discrimination and harassment. It covers employers, state and local governments, and educational institutions with 15 or more employees. Later amendments have been enacted to protect against discrimination because of pregnancy, sex stereotyping, and sexual harassment of employees.

tolling legal doctrine allows an employer to suspend accrual of front- and back-pay liability by extending an unconditional job offer identical or substantially equivalent to that originally denied.

top-hat pension plan a type of unfunded, executive deferred compensation plan that is exempt from most ERISA regulations but subject to annual reporting and disclosure requirements.

tort a civil wrong, whether intentional or accidental, for which a claim for damages may be brought.

training time participation time spent during training programs need not be counted as compensable working time if four criteria are met: (a) attendance is outside of the regular working hours; (b) attendance is voluntary; (c) the activity is not directly related to the employee's job; and (d) the employee does not perform any productive work during such attendance. Otherwise it is compensable.

transgendered individual a person who identifies with and adopts the gender identity of a member of the opposite biological sex.

triable issue of fact a fact of such importance that it must affect the outcome of a case under the law applicable to that case.

unauthorized aliens or undocumented aliens persons who entered the United States without a visa or who overstayed the period permitted by a visa.

undue hardship, disability the determination that accommodation of a person's disability would be too difficult or too expensive to provide, in light of the employer's size, financial resources, and the needs of the business. An employer may not refuse an accommodation simply on the basis of cost. An employer need not provide the exact accommodation desired by the disabled individual, but may choose among satisfactory alternates.

undue hardship, religion circumstance excusing an employer from accommodating an employee's religious practices if doing so involves more than ordinary administrative costs, diminished efficiency of other workers, infringement on other employees' rights, impairment of workplace safety, or increased work responsibilities for others.

unfair labor practice conduct and practices by either employers or unions determined under the NLRA or by the NLRB to be unlawful.

unforeseeable employee misconduct OSHA defense by which the employer shows that it established a work rule to prevent the subject behavior, adequately communicated the rule to employees, took steps to discover noncompliance, and enforced safety rules when violations were discovered.

Uniformed Services Employment and Reemployment Rights Act (USERRA) a 1994 federal law applicable to U.S. employers, requiring them to reemploy returning service members in the jobs they would have attained had they not been on active duty, including the same seniority, status, pay, and benefits.

union shop place of employment requiring workers to join a particular union and pay dues within a specified period after beginning work.

variance an employer request to OSHA for more time to comply with a safety standard.

vesting the point at which a participant's right to accrued benefits becomes nonforfeitable.

vicarious tort liability imposition of derivative liability on an employer for an employee's actions.

Vietnam Era Veterans Readjustment Assistance Act (VEVRAA) a federal law requiring employers with federal contracts or subcontractor of $25,000 or more to provide equal opportunity and affirmative action for Vietnam-era veterans, disabled veterans, and veterans who served on active duty during a war or an authorized campaign.

voluntary affirmative action plan adopted without the compulsion of a court order, a plan providing for employment preferences based on racial, ethnic, or gender criteria. Does not require evidence of employer's prior discriminatory acts.

wage discrimination unfair treatment in compensating a worker based on the person's gender.

Wagner Act see **National Labor Relations Act.**

Walsh-Healey Act a federal law that requires payment of the prevailing minimum wage and overtime, restricts youth employment, and promotes safe working conditions applicable to employers with a contract for more than $10,000 with a federal agency for the manufacture or furnishing of materials, supplies, or articles.

welfare plans ERISA-covered plans that do not involve salary deferral and retirement plans, such as medical, dental, and disability insurance plans.

whistleblower an employee who reports the wrongdoings of employers to authorities.

whistleblowing statutes statutes that prevent employers from discharging, disciplining, or retaliating against employees for reporting the employer's wrongful actions, such as discriminatory conduct.

willful violation OSHA violation occurring when the employer knows either that what employees are doing constitutes a violation or is aware that a condition creates a safety hazard and has made no reasonable effort to eliminate it.

Worker Adjustment and Retraining Notification Act (WARN) a federal law that prohibits employers from ordering a plant closing or mass layoff until 60 days after the employer has served written notice of such an order. Violations require employers to pay back pay and benefits for that period, attorneys' fees, and civil penalties to local agencies.

workers' compensation a no-fault system of laws and regulations that often provides the only means for an injured worker to recover compensation for medical expenses and lost wages arising from work-related injuries.

workplace violence prevention plan an OSHA recommendation that employers establish and maintain a program directed at reducing and eliminating work-related assaults, lessening the severity of injuries sustained by employees as a result of such violence, decreasing such threats to worker safety, and reducing the level and nature of threats faced by employees.

workweek seven consecutive 24-hour periods.

wrongful discharge termination of employment that involves an exception to the freedom of an employer to terminate an employee at will.

yellow-dog contract an agreement between an employer and a potential employee that, as a condition of being hired or of continuing employment, the employee will not join a labor union.

youth employment area of FLSA supervision, in which it limits the types of jobs and number of hours various categories of minors may work.

Table of Cases

[References are to page numbers.]

Index